The Cambridge Handbook of the Global Work–Family Interface

The Cambridge Handbook of the Global Work–Family Interface is a response to growing interest in understanding how people manage their work and family lives across the globe. Given global and regional differences in cultural values, economies, and policies and practices, research on work–family management is not always easily transportable to different contexts. Researchers have begun to acknowledge this, conducting research in various national settings, but the literature lacks a comprehensive source that aims to synthesize the state of knowledge, theoretical progression, and identification of the most compelling future research ideas within the field. *The Cambridge Handbook of the Global Work–Family Interface* aims to fill this gap by providing a single source where readers can find not only information about the general state of global work–family research, but also comprehensive reviews of region-specific research. It will be of value to researchers, graduate students, and practitioners of applied and organizational psychology, management, and family studies.

KRISTEN M. SHOCKLEY is Assistant Professor of Psychology at the University of Georgia. She is passionate about studying how employees can have a meaningful work and family life. Her research appears in several top journals and books.

WINNY SHEN is Assistant Professor of Psychology at the University of Waterloo, Ontario. Her research examines how workers from diverse backgrounds and organizations can lead healthy, happy, and productive lives. Her work has been published in leading journals.

RYAN C. JOHNSON is Assistant Professor of Psychology at Ohio University in Athens, OH. His research explores the intersection of work and health, aiming to improve lives and build more effective organizations. His work has been published in leading journals and books.

The Cambridge Handbook of the Global Work–Family Interface

Edited by

Kristen M. Shockley
University of Georgia

Winny Shen
University of Waterloo

Ryan C. Johnson
Ohio University

CAMBRIDGE
UNIVERSITY PRESS

CAMBRIDGE
UNIVERSITY PRESS

University Printing House, Cambridge CB2 8BS, United Kingdom

One Liberty Plaza, 20th Floor, New York, NY 10006, USA

477 Williamstown Road, Port Melbourne, VIC 3207, Australia

314–321, 3rd Floor, Plot 3, Splendor Forum, Jasola District Centre, New Delhi – 110025, India

79 Anson Road, #06–04/06, Singapore 079906

Cambridge University Press is part of the University of Cambridge.

It furthers the University's mission by disseminating knowledge in the pursuit of education, learning, and research at the highest international levels of excellence.

www.cambridge.org
Information on this title: www.cambridge.org/9781108415972
DOI: 10.1017/9781108235556

© Cambridge University Press 2018

First published 2018

Printed in the United Kingdom by Clays, St Ives, plc

A catalogue record for this publication is available from the British Library.

Library of Congress Cataloging-in-Publication Data
Names: Shockley, Kristen M., editor. | Shen, Winny, editor. | Johnson, Ryan C., 1984– editor.
Title: The Cambridge handbook of the global work–family interface / edited by Kristen M. Shockley, University of Georgia, Winny Shen, University of Waterloo, Ryan C. Johnson, Ohio University.
Description: Cambridge, United Kingdom ; New York, NY : Cambridge University Press, 2018. | Includes index.
Identifiers: LCCN 2017043881 | ISBN 9781108415972
Subjects: LCSH: Work and family – Cross-cultural studies.
Classification: LCC HD4904.25 .C356 2018 | DDC 306.3/6–dc23
LC record available at https://lccn.loc.gov/2017043881

ISBN 978-1-108-41597-2 Hardback
ISBN 978-1-108-40126-5 Paperback

Contents

Figures

Tables

Contributors

TAMMY D. ALLEN, Department of Psychology, University of South Florida, United States

E. ANNE BARDOEL, Department of Management and Marketing, Swinburne University of Technology, Australia

ALZBETA BARTOVA, Department of Public Administration and Sociology, Erasmus University Rotterdam, The Netherlands

KELLY A. BASILE, Department of Business and Economics, Emmanuel College, United States

T. ALEXANDRA BEAUREGARD, Department of Management, Leadership and Organisations, Middlesex University, United Kingdom

SCOTT BEHSON, Department of Management and Silberman Global Faculty Fellow, Fairleigh Dickinson University, United States

ANDREW BIGA, Human Resources, GoHealth Urgent Care, United States

PAULA BROUGH, School of Applied Psychology, Griffith University, Australia

CARRIE A. BULGER, Department of Psychology, Quinnipiac University, United States

FIORELLA L. CARLOS CHAVEZ, Department of Family & Child Sciences, Florida State University, United States

EUNAE CHO, Psychology, School of Social Sciences, Nanyang Technological University, Singapore

YEEUN CHOI, Department of Psychology, Yonsei University, South Korea

AARON COHEN, Department of Public Administration, School of Political Science, University of Haifa, Israel

LYN CRAIG, School of Social and Political Sciences, University of Melbourne, Australia

MIHAELA DIMITROVA, Department of Global Business and Trade, Vienna University of Economics and Business, Austria

NICOLE DODD, Department of Industrial Psychology (Military), University of Stellenbosch, South Africa

SONER DUMANI, American Institutes for Research, United States

LILLIAN T. EBY, Department of Psychology, University of Georgia, United States

HILAL E. ERKOVAN, Department of Psychology, Baruch College and Graduate Center, City University of New York, United States

HELENA FALKENBERG, Department of Psychology, Stockholm University, Sweden

SARAH FLOOD, Minnesota Population Center, University of Minnesota, United States

ANNIE FOUCREAULT, Department of Psychology, Université du Québec A Montréal Canada

KIMBERLY A. FRENCH, Department of Psychology, University of South Florida, United States

JOAN GARCÍA ROMÁN, Minnesota Population Center, University of Minnesota, United States and Centre d'Estudis Demogràfics, Autonomous University of Barcelona, Spain

ANNE H. GAUTHIER, Faculty of Behavioural and Social Sciences, University of Groningen and Netherlands Interdisciplinary Demographic Institute, The Netherlands

EMILY GILREATH, Department of Psychology, University of Georgia, United States

NEENA GOPALAN, School of Business, University of Redlands, United States

JOSEPH G. GRZYWACZ, Department of Family & Child Sciences, Florida State University, United States

JARROD HAAR, Faculty of Business, Auckland University of Technology, New Zealand

RUTH HABGOOD, Social Policy Research Centre, UNSW, Sydney, Australia

LESLIE B. HAMMER, Psychology Department, Portland State University and Oregon Institute of Occupational Health Sciences, Oregon Health & Science University, United States

E. JEFFREY HILL, Brigham Young University, United States

MARK E. HOFFMAN, Department of Engineering, Quinnipiac University, United States

ERIN KRAMER HOLMES, School of Family Life, Brigham Young University, United States

SATORIS S. HOWES, College of Business, Oregon State University, United States

REMUS ILIES, Department of Management & Organisation, National University of Singapore, Singapore

RYAN C. JOHNSON, Department of Psychology, Ohio University, United States

MICHAEL K. JUDIESCH, Department of Management and Marketing, Manhattan College, United States

LEILA KARIMI, School of Psychology and Public Health, La Trobe University, Australia

KAITLIN M. KIBURZ, SPX FLOW, Inc., United States

KAREN KORABIK, Department of Psychology, University of Guelph, Canada

ELLEN ERNST KOSSEK, Krannert School of Management & Susan Bulkeley Butler Center for Leadership Excellence, Purdue University, United States

BORA LEE, Department of Education, Korea University, Korea

CONSTANZE LEINEWEBER, Stress Research Institute, Stockholm University, Sweden

PEDRO I. LEIVA, Facultdad de Economia y Negocios, Universidad de Chile, Chile

SUZAN LEWIS, Department of Management and Organisations, Middlesex University, United Kingdom

XINXIN LI, Department of Management & Organisation, National University of Singapore, Singapore

BETH A. LIVINGSTON, Department of Management and Organizations, Tippie College of Business, University of Iowa, United States

VIVIAN MIU-CHI LUN, Department of Applied Psychology, Lingnan University, Hong Kong, SAR

KAREN S. LYNESS, Department of Psychology, Baruch College and The Graduate Center, City University of New York, United States

HECTOR MADRID, Escuela de Administracion, Pontificia Universidad Catolica de Chile, Chile

VALERIE MARTINEZ, Department of Psychology, University of Georgia, United States

ALINE D. MASUDA, Department of Strategy Leadership and People, EADA Business School, Spain

CYNTHIA K. MAUPIN, Department of Psychology, University of Georgia, United States

JEREMIAH T. MCMILLAN, Department of Psychology, University of Georgia, United States

JUSTIN VAN DER MERWE, Centre for Military Studies, University of Stellenbosch, South Africa

ZITHA MOKOMANE, Department of Sociology, University of Pretoria, South Africa

HEATHER N. ODLE-DUSSEAU, Department of Management, Gettysburg College, United States

ARIANE OLLIER-MALATERRE, Organisation and Human Resources Department, School of Management (École des sciences de la gestion), Université du Québec A Montréal, Canada

RACHEL OMANSKY, Department of Psychology, Baruch College and Graduate Center, City University of New York, United States

MATTHEW M. PISZCZEK, Mike Ilitch School of Business, Wayne State University, United States

ANGELA K. PRATT, Kellogg North America, United States

JIRI RADA, School of Psychology and Public Health, La Trobe University, Australia

TRICIA VAN RHIJN, Department of Family Relations and Applied Nutrition, University of Guelph, Canada

NATHAN L. ROBBINS, School of Family Life, Brigham Young University, United States

JUAN I. SANCHEZ, Department of Management, Florida International University, United States

COMILA SHAHANI-DENNING, Department of Psychology, Hofstra University, United States

WINNY SHEN, Department of Psychology, University of Waterloo, Canada

KRISTEN M. SHOCKLEY, Department of Psychology, University of Georgia, United States

AARTI SHYAMSUNDER, Psymantics Consulting, India

PAUL E. SPECTOR, Department of Psychology, University of South Florida, United States

ELIZABETH SVOBODA, Educational Psychology, University of Nebraska–Lincoln, United States

SARA TEMENT, Department of Psychology, Faculty of Arts, University of Maribor, Slovenia

CYNTHIA A. THOMPSON, Zicklin School of Business, Baruch College, City University of New York, United States

REBECCA J. THOMPSON, Division of Applied Behavioral Sciences, University of Baltimore, United States

ALEXANDRA M. TUMMINIA, Department of Psychology, Baruch College and Graduate Center, City University of New York, United States

OLIVIA VANDE GRIEK, Department of Psychology, University of Georgia, United States

SARAH L. WALLACE, Department of Psychology, Kalamazoo College, United States

MINA WESTMAN, Faculty of Management, Tel Aviv University, Israel

LOREY A. WHEELER, Nebraska Center for Research on Children, Youth, Families and Schools, University of Nebraska–Lincoln, United States

SOWAN WONG, Independent Researcher, Hong Kong, SAR

PETER P. YU, Department of Psychology, Baruch College and Graduate Center, City University of New York, United States

PART I

Overview

1 Introduction

Kristen M. Shockley, Winny Shen, and Ryan C. Johnson

Over the past three decades, academic, organizational, and popular press interest in understanding the intersection of employees' work and family lives has mushroomed (Allen, 2012). Early research in the area was mostly conducted in the United States, but more recently there has been an increase in studies conducted in other countries and research including samples from multiple cultural contexts. Additionally, the backgrounds of researchers themselves are becoming more international. At the most recent meeting of the Work Family Researchers Network in Washington, DC (2016), the program included scholars from over forty countries. Given that work and family dynamics are entrenched in larger societal contexts, such as gender role norms, national policies, economic stability, and cultural values, this expansion is merited. Further, understanding societal or cultural variations of work–family interactions has important implications for human resource practices in this era of increasing globalization.

Despite a growing literature on cross-cultural work–family research, there have been few attempts in the literature to integrate findings. Specifically, the expansion of this research has not been particularly programmatic in nature. This stems from the cross-disciplinary and often interdisciplinary nature of work (e.g., psychology, business, family studies, sociology, political science, and economics) as well as the fact that some studies involve basic replication in another cultural context, others address unique questions in new contexts, and yet others make explicit comparisons based on measured cultural values or presence of social policies or structures. Such progression has resulted in a somewhat disjointed literature, making a complete understanding of the state of knowledge, theoretical progression, and identification of the most compelling future research ideas in cross-cultural work–family research challenging (Shockley, Douek, Smith, Yu, Dumani, & French, 2017). The major previous effort to provide a reference for international work–family research was published by Steven Poelmans' (2005) edited volume entitled *Work and Family: An International Research Perspective*. This book provided a valuable overview of international work–family research published prior to the mid-2000s, but considering the large amount of research that has been conducted since that time, an updated volume is merited. This research growth and expansion has also allowed for novel insights and new chapter content to emerge.

With this in mind, the goal of the present volume is to provide a single source where readers can find in-depth reviews of extant research in particular regions as well as comparative cross-cultural work, insight regarding best practices from a methodological standpoint, and ideas about how a global lens is useful for understanding organizational, familial, and individual implications of work–family dynamics. We aim to achieve these goals through forty-one chapters divided into nine parts: (i) Overview, (ii) Assessing Cultural and Structural Differences, (iii) Methodological Considerations, (iv) Review of Research in Regions across the Globe, (v) Cultures within Cultures, (vi) Organizational Perspectives, (vii) Family Perspectives, (viii) Individual Perspectives, and (ix) Conclusion. The chapters are written by many leading scholars and researchers in the field as well as practitioners concerned with applied global work–family issues in organizations. In total, the *Handbook* authors represent seventeen unique country affiliations from all continents except Antarctica, contributing to a truly international perspective. We briefly review the content of each of section below.

Overview

The Overview part includes the present chapter (Chapter 1) followed by a chapter summarizing the extant work–family cross-cultural research by Shockley, French, and Yu (Chapter 2). Shockley et al.'s chapter is important in that it provides both a narrative review of the literature as well as a comprehensive summary table including every cross-cultural study (i.e., a study that included at least two different cultures) that includes a work–family construct, information about the countries included, the focus of the study's research questions, and a succinct summary of findings. This is important in providing future researchers with a comprehensive review for easy reference as well as a way to identify gaps in the extant cross-cultural work–family literature.

Assessing Cultural and Structural Differences

The question of how to best operationalize and understand cultural differences is one that has plagued researchers for decades (Nardon & Steers, 2009). Indeed the definition of culture in and of itself has been a topic of debate. In fact, as far back as 1952, Kroeber and Kluckhohn compiled a list of 164 unique definitions of culture. The goal of this section is to provide background to various conceptualizations of culture that have particular relevance to work–family issues, namely the work of Project GLOBE and their nine cultural value dimensions (Olliere-Malatere and Foucreault; Chapter 3) and Schwartz's cultural values framework (Masuda; Chapter 4). Because structural issues, defined as the constraints and opportunities produced by legal, economic, and social structures, are also highly relevant to the way people manage work and family, we also include two chapters devoted to these topics. Piszczek (Chapter 5) discusses social policies and economic concerns, while Gauthier and Bartova (Chapter 6) focus specifically on policies regarding parental leave.

Methodological Considerations

The trustworthiness and usefulness of any stream of research is contingent upon its methodological rigor; to this end, Part III is focused on methodological considerations in global work and family research. The six chapters within this section approach methodology from a number of different angles. The section opens with a review of methods used in global work and family research by Yu (Chapter 7). He discusses both the state of methodology in this literature, important considerations for future researchers, and a useful table detailing information about large, multi-country archival datasets. The next three chapters focus on specific types of methodologies, including meta-analysis (Dumani, French, and Allen; Chapter 8), qualitative research (Wong and Lun; Chapter 9), and archival time use data (Román and Flood; Chapter 10). The authors of each chapter are experienced researchers in applying that particular methodology, often in a cross-cultural or comparative context. As such, they offer tried and true advice involving best practices, summaries of other global work–family research that uses the methodology, and identify future opportunities they see for applying these methodologies to further advance cross-cultural work–family research. Lastly, the section closes with two chapters from authors involved in large, multi-country collaborative projects. Korabik and van Rhijn (Chapter 11) discuss best practices in scale translation and testing for measurement equivalence, drawing from their experiences with Project 3535. Spector and Sanchez (Chapter 12) provide an overview of conducting and successfully managing collaboration in a large scale cross-cultural project, including the best practices and particular challenges, highlighting their experiences with CISMS.

Review of Research in Regions across the Globe

Whereas Chapter 2 (Shockley, French, and Yu) provides a broad overview of all cross-cultural work and family research, chapters in this section of the volume provide more in-depth reviews of research that has been conducted in particular regions of the globe. Given that work–family research has historically been North America-centric, the strong influence of this region can be found in the comparative work that is reviewed, which tends to use this region (particularly American-based findings) as the referent. Each chapter covers not only comparative cross-cultural work but also studies that are based solely on samples from countries in that region, some of which may not be easily accessible to work–family researchers around the world due to language or other barriers (e.g., lack of subscription access to local journals). Additionally, each chapter touches on the unique characteristics of the region that are relevant to the work–family interface as well as recommendations for future research. In total, this section includes nine chapters, covering Western/ Southern Europe (Tumminia and Omansky; Chapter 13), Central/Eastern Europe (Tement; Chapter 14), Nordic regions (Leineweber and Falkenberg; Chapter 15), Latin America (Leiva, Madrid, and Howes; Chapter 16), Africa (Mokomane; Chapter 17), the Middle East and North Africa (McMillan, Karimi, and Rada;

Chapter 18), South East Asia (Shahani-Denning and Shyamsunder; Chapter 19), Confucian Asia (Cho and Choi; Chapter 20), and Australia and New Zealand (Bardoel and Haar; Chapter 21).

Cultures within Cultures

Typically when we think of cross-cultural research, we consider a nation as the delineating boundary. However, there are several circumstances where distinct cultures exist within nations as a function of a country's history or by virtue of immigration or expatriation. This section includes three chapters that focus on case studies of cultures within cultures from a national standpoint, including the case of the United States (Eby, Vande Griek, Maupin, Allen, Gilreath, and Martinez; Chapter 22), Israel (Cohen; Chapter 23), and South Africa (Dodd and van der Merwe; Chapter 24). These chapters provide a rare glimpse into important work–family factors that differentiate subcultures in a single nation. Given the relative dearth of comparative research *within* national cultures, the authors also provide many ideas for future research. The last two chapters in this section include an assessment of work–family concerns of immigrants (Grzywacz, Gopalan, Carlos Chavez; Chapter 25), as well as a specific case of immigration–expatriation (Dimitrova; Chapter 26). Both chapters offer informative theoretical models to both provide a holistic sense of the theoretical state of the literature and guide future work.

Organizational Perspectives

Organizations are affected by the work–family and broader work–life concerns of their employees and thus often have a vested interest in supporting their employees to more effectively manage the work–family interface. The first chapter in this section reviews cross-cultural research on careers, highlighting how country-level variation in cultural values and national structures can affect the work–life interface and workers' career outcomes, particularly those of women and parents (Lyness, Judiesch, and Erkovan; Chapter 27). In the next chapter, we turn to an applied perspective on organizational issues as Pratt, Kiburz, and Wallace (Chapter 28) describe the challenges that multinational companies often face in managing their workers' work–life concerns globally. They provide examples of programs and policies that have been enacted (and in some cases, discarded) before turning to an in-depth case study of one company, Kellogg's, approach to work–life management. Finally, the last set of chapters focuses on common work–family organizational policies and initiatives, highlighting cross-cultural research and yet unanswered questions on workplace flexibility (Thompson and Kossek; Chapter 29), organizational work–family culture (Beauregard, Basile, and Thompson; Chapter 30), and family-supportive supervision (Kossek, Odle-Dusseau, and Hammer; Chapter 31).

Family Perspectives

The work–family interface lies at the intersection of two domains: work and family. This section takes a cross-cultural and global perspective on the importance of and considerations within the family domain that may affect workers' experiences and behaviors in managing their dual responsibilities, as well as the impact work may have on others in the family sphere. The first two chapters in this section focus on gender-related roles; Livingston (Chapter 32) takes a multi-level perspective regarding issues of gender and gender norms and their impact on the work–family interface across cultures, and Behson, Kramer Holmes, Hill, and Robbins (Chapter 33) focus specifically on international and cross-cultural research on fatherhood. The next three chapters concentrate on dyadic interdependencies between partners. Brough and Westman (Chapter 34) review research on dual-earner couples, exploring the unique challenges and opportunities these couples may face across cultural contexts. Craig and Habgood (Chapter 35) focus more specifically on how partners divide paid and unpaid labor across the globe. Li and Ilies (Chapter 36) focus specifically on emotional reactions to the work–family interface, which can often crossover between partners, and demonstrate similarities and differences cross-culturally. Finally, the last chapter in this section by Wheeler, Lee, and Svoboda (Chapter 37) takes a cross-cultural perspective and reviews how parents' work, family, and work–family demands and experiences affect children's well-being.

Individual Perspectives

Although individuals' experiences of the work–family interface take place within specific, cultural/national, organizational, and familial contexts, the individual continues to play a key role in shaping their own experiences. In this final section of the volume, we explore critical issues related to the individual perspective from a cross-cultural lens. First, Bulger and Hoffman (Chapter 38) review cross-cultural research on individuals' preferences and practices with regard to segmenting or integrating their work and family roles. Second, Lewis and Beauregard (Chapter 39) describe research and introduce new ideas regarding workers' search for and sense of meaning with regard to the construct of work–life balance and how this sense-making process is shaped by the broader national or cultural context. Finally, Allen, Cho, Shockley, and Biga (Chapter 40) introduce the concept of personal responsibility for work–life balance and provides some evidence for how this construct differs across cultural contexts.

Conclusion

We aim for this volume to serve many audiences: researchers already conducting this important work, those who wish to dip their toes into the cross-cultural work–family waters, practitioners and organizational/national policy decision makers, and interested individuals hoping to better understand this aspect of our world. It is our hope that this *Handbook* impacts the field of cross-cultural work–family by focusing what we know while broadening our scope of inquiry. In doing so, we hope the book inspires new research and application, and, quite simply, sparks responses to the many calls for future research and policy work herein.

References

Allen, T. D. (2012). The work–family interface. In S. W. J. Kozlowski (Ed). *The Oxford Handbook of Organizational Psychology* (pp. 1163–1198). New York, NY: Oxford University Press.

Kroeber, A.L. & Kluckhohn, C. (1952). *Culture: A Critical Review of Concepts and Definitions*. Cambridge, MA: Peabody Museum.

Nardon L., & Steers R. M. (2009). The culture theory jungle: Divergence and convergence in models of national culture. In R.S. Bhagat & R. M. Steers (Eds.), *Cambridge Handbook of Culture, Organizations, and Work* (pp. 3–22). Cambridge, UK: Cambridge University Press.

Poelmans, S. A. Y. (2005). *Work and Family: An International Research Perspective*. Mahwah, NJ. Lawrence Erlbaum and Associates.

Shockley, K.M., Douek, J., Smith, C.R., Yu, P.P., Dumani, S., & French, K.A. (2017). Cross-cultural work and family research: A review of the literature. *Journal of Vocational Behavior*. 101, 1–120.

2 A Comprehensive Review and Synthesis of the Cross-Cultural Work–Family Literature

Kristen M. Shockley, Kimberly A. French, and Peter P. Yu

Research devoted to understanding the intersection of employees work and family lives is now abundant (Allen, 2012). Seminal research conducted on the topic (e.g., Greenhaus & Beutell, 1985; Kanter, 1977) was focused on Western contexts, and often the United States in particular. As the field grew, however, researchers began to question whether findings from Western settings would generalize to other contexts, spurring a body of work conducted in other regions of the globe as well as cross-cultural comparative work (Casper, Allen, & Poelmans, 2014). Likely owing to the interdisciplinary nature of work–family (WF) studies and the complexity of cross-cultural research, this literature has not developed in a particularly programmatic manner. That is, studies have examined a host of different research questions in different cultural contexts using different types of samples, making it difficult to have a clear sense of the state of research to date and to identify opportunities for integration and yet unanswered questions for the future.

The purpose of this chapter is to help researchers in this regard by providing a comprehensive review of all known published cross-cultural studies to date that quantitatively assessed a variable that involves the intersection of the work and family domains (e.g., WF conflict, enrichment, spillover). We define "cross-cultural" as any study that includes at least two distinct cultural groups, typically defined by national boundaries, and that includes some type of comparison between samples (i.e., studies that included people from multiple countries but grouped them together for analyses were not included). Previous summaries of cross-cultural research do exist (Aycan, 2008; Ollier-Malaterre, 2016; Poelmans, O'Driscoll, & Beham, 2005; Shaffer, Joplin, & Hsu, 2011), but ours is unique in two ways. First, it is fully comprehensive of the literature to date whereas past narrative reviews tend to just focus on common themes and do not cover all extant studies. Second, we provide a summary table of all of these studies that can serve as an easy reference point for researchers who wish to understand the research focus of various cross-cultural studies, the regions studied, and the cross-cultural findings. We hope that providing a common ground and synthesis will not only give researchers a sense of what has been studied in the field but can also provide insight to build future theory based on the pattern of findings. The latter goal seems particularly critical given that a recent theoretical review of the cross-cultural WF literature (Shockley, Douek, Smith, Yu, Dumani, & French, 2017) found that researchers have used various, and often conflicting, theories in building their hypotheses.

Method

Relevant articles for the current review were drawn from a larger cross-cultural work–family review project. Two methods were used to search for relevant articles. First, we identified English-language articles published before 2017 via database searches (i.e., PsycINFO, Web of Science) using the search terms "work–family," "work–life," and "work-nonwork" along with "cultur*," "cross-cultur*," and "nation*." Next, we searched references sections of cross-cultural and region-specific WF chapters and articles (i.e., Aycan, 2008; Bardoel, De Cieri, & Santos, 2008; Ollier-Malaterre, 2016; Poelmans, O'Driscoll, & Beham, 2005; Shaffer, Joplin, & Hsu, 2011) to locate previously unidentified cross-cultural WF studies.

To be included in the current review, studies must have (1) included at least two samples from distinct countries or cultural groups within a given country and (2) quantitatively assessed a construct that involved the WF interface (i.e., WF conflict, enrichment, facilitation, fit, positive spillover, negative spillover, pressure, balance). Thus, we focused the scope of our review by excluding topics that are within the realm of WF, but do not specifically assess the work–family interface (e.g., national fertility, workplace flexibility, or percentage of women in the labor force). We also excluded studies that collected data from multiple cultures or countries but collapsed across cultures for analyses involving WF interface constructs (i.e., Begall & Mills, 2011; Bull & Mittelmark, 2008, 2009; Christaens & Bracke, 2014; Day & Chamberlain, 2006; Erickson, Martinengo, & Hill, 2010; Grzywacz et al., 2007; Grzywacz, Quandt, Arcury, & Marin, 2005; Hill, Erickson, Fellows, Martinengo, & Allen, 2014; Hsu, Chen, Wang, & Lin, 2010; Romeo, Berger, Yepes-Baldó, & Ramos, 2014; Shukri, Jones, & Conner, 2016; Wang, Lawler, & Shi, 2010). Finally, we excluded expatriate studies (Kempen, Pangert, Hattrup, Mueller, & Joens, 2015; Shaffer, Harrison, Gilley, & Luk, 2001; Shih, Chiang, & Hsu, 2010; Takeuchi, Yun, & Tesluk, 2002) and studies that presented redundant analysis and data (e.g., Timms, Brough, Siu, O'Driscoll, & Kalliath, 2015 is redundant with Brough et al., 2014; Spector et al., 2005 is redundant with Spector et al., 2004). The search yielded a total of seventy-four eligible published articles (fifty-eight independent datasets). The studies came from a variety of disciplines including psychology, sociology, family studies, human resources, public health, and medicine.

Each eligible primary study was coded by one of six trained coders and reviewed by the first author. Each coder recorded the information listed in

Table 2.1, including the focus of the study (i.e., mean differences in a WF construct, an imputed or measured cultural value tested as a predictor of a WF construct, country/cultural value tested as a moderator of the relationship between an antecedent and a WF construct, country/cultural value tested as a moderator of the relationship between a WF construct and an outcome, or a large model tested in multiple countries), the countries included in the study, and a summary of the findings relevant to cultural differences. We also noted when a study came from a larger dataset.

Results

Table 2.1 provides a summary of the coded information and research findings from each individual study. In total, 51% of the studies focused on mean differences, 12% imputed or measured cultural values as a predictor of a WF construct, 39% tested country or cultural values as a moderator of the relationship between an antecedent and a WF construct, 24% tested country or cultural values as a moderator of the relationship between a WF construct and an outcome, and 15% tested a model across various cultural/country contexts. Note that these percentages do not add up to 100% because some studies conducted multiple types of analyses and addressed multiple questions. 38% of studies included a comparison between two countries/cultures, whereas the remaining 62% included three or more countries.

Below, we also synthesize the findings and focus of these studies in a narrative review. We first review the mean differences in WF interface constructs, followed by results that speak to country/culture as a moderator for the relationship between the WF interface and its antecedents (i.e., work-related, family-related, and gender) and outcomes (i.e., work-related, family-related, and well-being), and finally national-level constructs as predictors of the WF interface.

Summary of Findings

Mean differences in WF conflict. Numerous studies provided comparative information about the prevalence of WF conflict across cultures.[1] In many cases, significance testing was not reported (i.e., Brough et al., 2014; Cousins & Tang, 2004; Gallie & Russell, 2009; Kasearu, 2009; Kucharova, 2009; Ng & Feldman, 2014; Oishi, Chan, Wang, & Kim, 2014; Rantanen, Kinnunen, Mauno, & Tement, 2013; Sanseau & Smith, 2012; Simon, Kummerling, Hasslehorn, 2004; Strandh & Nordenmark, 2006; Van der Lippe, Jager, & Kops, 2006; Weckstrom, 2011; Wharton & Blair-Loy, 2006; Yang, Chen, Choi, & Zhou, 2000), making it difficult to draw conclusions.

In cases where significant differences were reported, synthesizing results is challenging, given the large inconsistencies. For example, among the six studies that included comparisons of an Anglo country to a Confucian Asian country, three

---

[1] Note that throughout the review we use the term WF conflict/enrichment to refer to overall or non-directional conflict and the terms work-to-family and family-to-work conflict to refer to directional conflict or enrichment.

Table 2.1 *Summary of cross-cultural WF studies*

Study	Imputed/Measured Cultural Value as Predictor	Country/Cultural Value as Moderator of Antecedent	Country/Cultural Value as Moderator of Outcome	Large Model Tested in Multiple Countries	Countries Examined
Abendroth & den Dulk (2011) EU Quality of Work and Life in a Changing Europe	Mean Differences: Work–life balance satisfaction				Bulgaria, Finland, Germany, Hungary, Netherlands, Portugal, Sweden, UK
	Summary of Cultural Differences Found: Comparisons were only made with Sweden as the referent. Finland and Bulgaria have higher WLB satisfaction than Sweden. Germany has significantly lower WLB satisfaction than Sweden.				
Agarwala, Arizkuren-Eleta, Castillo, Muniz-Ferrer, & Gartzia (2014)	Work-to-family conflict, Family-to-work conflict, Work–life conflict	Relationships between managerial support and work–life conflict by country	Relationships between work–life conflict and affective commitment by country		India, Peru, Spain
	Summary of Cultural Differences Found: No mean differences in work-to-family conflict; family-to-work conflict and work–life conflict were higher in India than in Peru or Spain. Work–life conflict were negatively related to affective commitment in all countries. Managerial support and work–life conflict negatively related only in Spain and Peru and not India.				

Study	Relationship		Countries
Allen et al. (2014) CISMS 2	Relationship between duration of government-provided paid leave and work-to-family conflict/family-to-work conflict		Australia, Canada, Finland Greece, Japan Netherlands, New Zealand, Slovenia South Korea, Spain UK, US

Summary of Cultural Differences Found: Small but significant effects were observed. Longer paid parental leave was associated with less time-based work-to-family conflict. Longer sick leave was associated with less time-based family-to-work conflict, less strain-based work-to-family conflict, and less strain-based family-to-work conflict. Longer annual leave was associated with more time-based work-to-family conflict. There were also some moderating effects of family-supportive organization perceptions and family supportive-supervision such that the relationship between leave and WF conflict was more negative when support was high and in some cases the relationship was actually positive when support was low.

| Anderson, Coffey, Liu, & Zhao (2008) | Relationships between flexibility, dependent care supports, manager support, perceptions of negative career consequences and work-to-family conflict by country | Relationships between work-to-family conflict/ family-to-work conflict and job satisfaction, turnover intentions, absenteeism, and job stress by country | China, US (US sample is from previous research) |

Summary of Cultural Differences Found: The following associations were found in the US but not in China – relationship between managerial support and work-to-family conflict, relationship between work-to-family conflict and job satisfaction and turnover intentions, and relationship between family-to-work conflict and absenteeism.

Table 2.1 (*cont.*)

Study	Mean Differences	Imputed/Measured Cultural Value as Predictor	Country/Cultural Value as Moderator of Antecedent	Country/Cultural Value as Moderator of Outcome	Large Model Tested in Multiple Countries	Countries Examined
Annink, den Dulk, & Steijn (2016) 2010 ESS		Relationship between state support (parental leave and public childcare) and WF conflict				Belgium, Bulgaria, Czech Republic, Denmark, Estonia, Finland, France, Germany, Hungary, Netherlands, Norway, Poland, Portugal, Slovenia, Spain, Sweden, UK

Summary of Cultural Differences Found: None; no significant association between parental leave or public childcare and WF conflict.

Study	Mean Differences	Imputed/Measured Cultural Value as Predictor	Country/Cultural Value as Moderator of Antecedent	Country/Cultural Value as Moderator of Outcome	Large Model Tested in Multiple Countries	Countries Examined
Aryee, Fields, & Luk (1999)					Compared a model linking job (family) involvement to work-to-family conflict (family-to-work conflict) to job, family, and life satisfaction in HK to a similar model tested by Frone et al. (1992) with US sample	Hong Kong, US

Summary of Cultural Differences Found: Path from work-to-family conflict to family-to-work conflict is larger than the path from family-to-work conflict to work-to-family conflict in Hong Kong; no differences in path size in the US. Family involvement relates to family-to-work conflict in the US but not Hong Kong; Job satisfaction and family satisfaction co-vary in the US but not in Hong Kong.

Study	Variables	Hypotheses/Description	Countries
Barnes-Farrell et al. (2008) SWAT-Healthcare		Nation as a moderator between shiftwork characteristics and work-to-family conflict	Australia, Brazil, Croatia, US

Summary of Cultural Differences Found: None observed; no evidence of significant moderating effect.

Study	Variables	Hypotheses/Description	Countries
Beham, Drobnic, & Prag (2014)	Work-to-family conflict, Satisfaction with WF balance	Relationship between professional status and work-to-family conflict/satisfaction with WF balance by country	Germany, Netherlands, Portugal, Sweden, UK

Summary of Cultural Differences Found: Mean comparisons with significance testing were only conducted in comparison to the UK. Satisfaction with WLB was higher in Sweden, the Netherlands, and Germany than in the UK. No differences between Portugal and the UK. Work-to-family conflict was lower in Sweden and the Netherlands than in the UK. No differences between Germany and the UK or Portugal and the UK. The association between professional status and work-to-family conflict is smaller in the Netherlands, Germany, and Portugal than the UK and Sweden. There were no country differences in these analyses with satisfaction with WF balance.

Study	Variables	Hypotheses/Description	Countries
Billing, Bhagat, Babakus, Krishnan, et al. (2014a)	Country as a moderator of the interactive relationship between WF conflict and decision latitude on psychological strain.	Test a model linking WF conflict to psychological strain and in turn to job satisfaction, organizational commitment, and turnover intentions	Canada, India, Indonesia, US, South Korea

Summary of Cultural Differences Found: The path model fit well for all 5 countries, although there were some differences in strengths of paths (the path from psychological strain to turnover intentions was stronger in India than in Indonesia and Canada). Decision latitude only moderates the relationship between WF conflict and psychological strain in the US and Canada; no evidence of moderation in India, Indonesia, or South Korea.

Table 2.1 (cont.)

Study	Mean Differences	Imputed/Measured Cultural Value as Predictor	Country/Cultural Value as Moderator of Antecedent	Country/Cultural Value as Moderator of Outcome	Large Model Tested in Multiple Countries	Countries Examined
Billing, Bhagat, Babakus, Srivastava, Shin & Brew (2014b)		Individually measured vertical and horizontal individualism and collectivism as predictors of WF conflict	Country as a moderator of relationships between individually measured vertical and horizontal individualism and collectivism	Individually measured individualism/ collectivism as a moderator of the relationship between WF conflict and turnover intentions		Australia, Japan South Korea, US

Summary of Cultural Differences Found: Vertical individualism positively related to WF conflict except for in South Korea. Horizontal individualism is not related to WF conflict in any country. Vertical collectivism is only related (negatively) with WF conflict in the US. Horizontal collectivism is negatively related to WF conflict in all countries but Japan. The strength of association between vertical individualism and WF conflict is higher in the US than in Japan and South Korea. No other moderator effects of country were significant. WF conflict positively related to turnover intentions in the US, Australia, and South Korea, but not Japan.

Study	Mean Differences	Imputed/Measured Cultural Value as Predictor	Country/Cultural Value as Moderator of Antecedent	Country/Cultural Value as Moderator of Outcome	Large Model Tested in Multiple Countries	Countries Examined
Brough et al. (2014)	Work–life balance				Tested a model with job demands as a predictor of work–life balance, which in turn predicts family and job satisfaction which in turn predict psychological strain and turnover intentions	Australia, New Zealand

Summary of Cultural Differences Found: Significance of mean differences not reported, so impossible to ascertain. Path coefficients in model were generally similar across the two countries; no formal tests of significance were conducted.

Study	Outcomes	Variables / Model	Sample
Cinamon (2009)	Work-to-family conflict, Family-to-work conflict	Relationship between spouse values, work values, work commitment, colleague, and spouse support and work-to-family conflict/ family-to-work conflict by cultural group	Arab Israelis, Jewish Israelis

Summary of Cultural Differences Found: Work-to-family conflict higher in Jewish Israel than in Arab Israel; no significant differences in family-to-work conflict. Spouse values related to work-to-family conflict only for Arab Israelis; work values, work commitment, colleague and spouse support predictors of family-to-work conflict only for Jewish Israelis.

Study	Outcomes	Variables / Model	Sample
Cousins & Tang (2004)	WF conflict	Relationship between working hours and WF conflict by country	Netherlands, Sweden, UK

Summary of Cultural Differences Found: Impossible to determine, as the authors did not provide significance testing, only descriptive statistics.

Study	Outcomes	Variables / Model	Sample
Drobnic & Guillen Rodriguez (2011) 2003 European Quality of Life Survey and 2004 ESS	Work-to-family conflict, Satisfaction with work–life balance	Regression model of several job characteristics and work conditions (work hours, commute, job stress, time pressure, health risk, job insecurity, job control, career prospects, pay) and family	Germany, Spain

Table 2.1 (cont.)

Study	Mean Differences	Imputed/Measured Cultural Value as Predictor	Country/Cultural Value as Moderator of Antecedent	Country/Cultural Value as Moderator of Outcome	Large Model Tested in Multiple Countries	Countries Examined
			demographics (partner, partner employment status, age of child) predicting work-to-family conflict and satisfaction with work–life balance in two separate samples (both with Spanish and German participants).			

Summary of Cultural Differences Found: Germans report significantly less work-to-family conflict in one sample but not in other. No significant differences in satisfaction with work–life balance by country. Some job characteristic predictors vary across cultures, though there is no discernable pattern.

Study	Mean Differences	Imputed/Measured Cultural Value as Predictor	Country/Cultural Value as Moderator of Antecedent	Country/Cultural Value as Moderator of Outcome	Large Model Tested in Multiple Countries	Countries Examined
Estryn-Behar et al. (2007) NEXT research project				Relationship between WF conflict and nurses' intention to turnover by country		Belgium, Finland, France, Germany, Italy, Norway, Poland Netherlands, Slovakia

Summary of Cultural Differences Found: Impossible to ascertain, as the authors did not provide significance testing, only descriptive statistics.

| Gallie & Russell (2009) 2004 ESS | WF conflict | The effect of controlling for various work and family predictors (child age, housework hours, partner employment, income, partner's housework, job type, work hours, task discretion, schedule flexibility, job pressure, health/safety risk, job security, partner's work hours) on country level coefficients predicting WF conflict by gender. | Denmark, France, Germany, Netherlands, Norway, Sweden, UK |

Summary of Cultural Differences Found: the Netherlands, Norway, and Sweden have lower WF conflict than the UK, although it is unclear if these differences are significant. When family characteristics are controlled, female employees in the Netherlands and Norway have significantly lower WF conflict than women in the UK. When controlling for work conditions, WF conflict for Swedish women becomes significantly lower than for UK women. For men, controlling for family characteristics makes little difference to the country coefficients. However, when work characteristics are introduced the differences between the Nordic countries and the UK are reduced substantially.

| Galovan, Fackrell, Buswell, Jones, Hill, & | | Tested a model involving the relationship between work hours, satisfaction with | Singapore, US |

Table 2.1 (cont.)

Study	Mean Differences	Imputed/Measured Cultural Value as Predictor	Country/Cultural Value as Moderator of Antecedent	Country/Cultural Value as Moderator of Outcome	Large Model Tested in Multiple Countries	Countries Examined
Carroll (2010) 2006 Singapore National Study of Work–Life Harmony and 2008 US NSCW					earnings and schedule flexibility and work-to-family conflict/family-to-work conflict; relationship between work-to-family conflict/family-to-work conflict and depression/marital satisfaction/job satisfaction.	

Summary of Cultural Differences Found: Work hours and schedule flexibility are more strongly related to family-to-work conflict in Singapore than in the US. Family income is more strongly related to work-to-family conflict in Singapore. Earnings satisfaction and schedule flexibility are more strongly related to work-to-family conflict in the US. Relationship between work-to-family conflict and depression is stronger in the US. Relationship between family-to-work conflict and depression is stronger is Singapore. Relationship between work-to-family conflict and job satisfaction is stronger in the US. Relationship between family-to-work conflict and job satisfaction is negative in Singapore and positive in the US. Work-to-family conflict is not related to marital satisfaction in either sample. Family-to-work conflict is more strongly related to marital satisfaction in the US.

Study	Mean Differences	Imputed/Measured Cultural Value as Predictor	Country/Cultural Value as Moderator of Antecedent	Country/Cultural Value as Moderator of Outcome	Large Model Tested in Multiple Countries	Countries Examined
Gaspar (2013) 2002 ISSP	WF conflict		Relationship between sex, age, children, income, household hours, work hours, education and WF conflict by country			Spain, UK

Summary of Cultural Differences Found: Spanish women experience higher levels of WF conflict than GB women, both which are higher than men in either country. Gender, age, children, hours per week in domestic labor, hours per week in paid labor are significantly related to WF conflict in Spain; only hours per week in domestic labor, hours per week in paid labor, and educational level are significant predictors of WF conflict in GB.

| Haar, Russo, Sune, & Ollier-Malaterre (2014) | Country-level individualism and gender egalitarianism as moderators in the relationship between work–life balance and job satisfaction/ life satisfaction/ anxiety/ depression | China, France, Italy, Malaysia, New Zealand – Maori, New Zealand – European, Spain |

Summary of Cultural Differences Found: Individualism moderates the relationship between work–life balance and job and life satisfaction, such that the relationships are stronger in more individualistic countries. Gender egalitarianism moderates the relationship between work–life balance and job and life satisfaction and anxiety, such that that relationships were stronger in countries with higher gender egalitarianism.

| Halbesleben, Wheeler, & Rossi (2012) | Tested a model of work-linked relationship status (working in same organization or occupation as spouse) to instrumental spouse support and WF conflict, which in turn was linked to emotional exhaustion. | Brazil, US |

Table 2.1 (cont.)

Study	Mean Differences	Imputed/Measured Cultural Value as Predictor	Country/Cultural Value as Moderator of Antecedent	Country/Cultural Value as Moderator of Outcome	Large Model Tested in Multiple Countries	Countries Examined
Hassan, Dollard, & Winefield (2010)	Work-to-family conflict, Family-to-work conflict	Summary of Cultural Differences Found: None observed, as path coefficients and model fit were similar for both countries.				Australia, Canada, Finland, Malaysia, New Zealand, US
	Summary of Cultural Differences Found: Compared sample they collected in Malaysia to data from 15 previously published studies in Anglo/Finish cultures. Family-to-work conflict is higher in Malaysia than all other samples. Work-to-family conflict is lower in Malaysia than in most of the other samples (11 of 15), but is significantly higher than 4 samples (although we note that the significant testing in this study is suspect given their stated lack of information about standard deviations from other samples).					
Hill, Hawkins, Martinson, & Ferris (2003) 2001 IBM Global Work and Life Issues Survey	Work-to-family conflict, Family-to-work conflict, WF fit					Australia, Asia, Canada, Europe (Eastern), Europe (Western), Latin America, New Zealand, Scandinavia, US
	Summary of Cultural Differences Found: Detailed data is not provided; the authors only summarize finding. They note that work-to-family conflict was highest in Asia and lowest in Scandinavia. Family-to-work conflict was highest in Asia and lowest in Eastern Europe. WF fit was greatest in Scandinavia.					

Hill, Yang, Hawkins, & Ferris (2004) 2001 IBM Global Work and Life Issues Survey	Tested a model of job characteristics (responsibility, workload, travel) predicting work-to-family conflict; job flexibility predicting work-to-family conflict, family-to-work conflict, and WF fit; family characteristics (responsibility for kids, elders, and marital status) predicting family-to-work conflict, and WF fit predicting job satisfaction.	Argentina, Australia, Austria, Belgium, Bolivia, Brazil, Canada, Chile, China, Colombia, Czech Republic, Denmark, Ecuador, Finland, France, Germany, Hong Kong, Hungary, India, Indonesia, Ireland, Israel, Italy, Japan, Malaysia, Mexico, Netherlands, New Zealand, Norway, Paraguay, Peru, Philippines, Poland, Russia, Singapore, Slovakia, South Africa, South Korea, Spain, Sweden, Switzerland, Taiwan, Thailand, UK, Uruguay, US, Venezuela

Summary of Cultural Differences Found: Tested whether the model was invariant across four country clusters (East, West-Developing, West-Affluent, US). Model was invariant, suggesting negligible differences, though there was some variation in the size of paths across the country clusters. Most noticeably, the relationship between responsibility for children and family-to-work conflict was weakest in the East cluster and the relationship between job flexibility and WF fit was weakest in the US.

Table 2.1 (*cont.*)

Study	Mean Differences	Imputed/Measured Cultural Value as Predictor	Country/Cultural Value as Moderator of Antecedent	Country/Cultural Value as Moderator of Outcome	Large Model Tested in Multiple Countries	Countries Examined
Janssen, Peeters, de Jonge, Houkes, & Tummers (2004)					Tested a model linking psychological job demands, emotional demands, support, and job control as predictors of work-to-family conflict, which was linked to outcomes of emotional exhaustion and job satisfaction.	Netherlands, US
Summary of Cultural Differences Found: The model was not invariant across samples and had to be modified separately to achieve adequate fit. Main differences were in a non-significant path from work-to-family conflict to job satisfaction in the US which was positive in the Netherlands sample; non-significant paths from support and emotional demands to work-to-family conflict in the US which were significant in the Netherlands.						
Jin, Ford, & Chen (2013)	Work-to-family conflict, Family-to-work conflict, Work-to-family enrichment, Family-to-work enrichment		Relationships between work and family support and work-to-family conflict/WFE by culture.	Relationships between work-to-family conflict/WFE and job and family satisfaction by culture.		China, North America
Summary of Cultural Differences Found: No differences in mean levels work-to-family conflict or work-to-family enrichment; China had significantly higher family-to-work conflict and family-to-work enrichment. Several differences in size of path coefficients for the cultures. Most are stronger in North America than in China.						

Study	Variable	Countries
Kasearu (2009) 2004 ESS	Work-to-family conflict	Estonia, Germany, Slovenia, Sweden, UK

Summary of Cultural Differences Found: Significance testing was not conducted, but trend is such that work-to-family conflict is highest in UK and Germany and lowest in Slovenia.

Study	Variable	Countries
Kucharová (2009) Generations and Gender Survey	WF balance Differences in strengths of predictors (age, education, gender, work hours, occupation, number and age of children, job satisfaction, income sufficiency, division of labor) of WF conflict among only women in the samples.	Bulgaria, Czech Republic, France, Georgia

Summary of Cultural Differences Found: The authors report that there are significant differences in WFB overall, but the nature of significant differences is not listed. Some differences in strength of predictors of WF conflict across cultures. Notably, age is a stronger predictor in France than elsewhere, and work hours and occupation are strongest in Georgia.

Study	Variable	Countries
Laaksonen, Lallukka, et al. (2010) Helsinki Health Study and Whitehall II Study	Relationship between physical health and work-to-family conflict/ family-to-work conflict by country	Finland, Great Britain

Summary of Cultural Differences Found: Impossible to ascertain, as significance values are not listed.

Table 2.1 (*cont.*)

Study	Mean Differences	Imputed/Measured Cultural Value as Predictor	Country/Cultural Value as Moderator of Antecedent	Country/Cultural Value as Moderator of Outcome	Large Model Tested in Multiple Countries	Countries Examined
Laaksonen, Martikainen, et al. (2009) Helsinki Health Study and Whitehall II Study			Relationship between mental health and work-to-family conflict/ family-to-work conflict by country			Finland, Great Britain
Summary of Cultural Differences Found: Impossible to ascertain, as significance values are not listed.						
Lallukka, Rahkonen, Lahelma, & Arber (2010) Helsinki Health Study, Whitehall II Study, Japanese Civil Servants Study				Relationship between work-to-family conflict and smoking, heaving drinking, physical inactivity, and unhealthy food habits based by gender and country		Finland, Great Britain, Japan
Summary of Cultural Differences Found: Relationships vary by country, gender, and dependent variable with no discernable pattern.						

Citation	Constructs	Role of Culture	Model / Findings	Countries
Lapierre et al. (2008) CISMS 2			Tested a model linking family-supportive organization perceptions to work-to-family conflict and family-to-work conflict which in turn were linked to job and family satisfaction and then to life satisfaction.	Australia, Canada, Finland, New Zealand, US

Summary of Cultural Differences Found: None, as the model was invariant across cultures.

Citation	Constructs	Role of Culture		Countries
Law (2011)	Work-to-family conflict, Family-to-work conflict			China, Hong Kong

Summary of Cultural Differences Found: Work-to-family conflict higher in Hong Kong; no differences in family-to-work conflict.

Citation	Constructs	Role of Culture		Countries
Lu et al. (2010)	WF conflict	Country as moderator of the relationship between supervisor support and WF conflict	Country as a moderator of the relationships between WF conflict and work/family satisfaction	Taiwan, UK

Summary of Cultural Differences Found: No significant mean differences in WF conflict. Country was a significant moderator such that the WF conflict and work/family satisfaction relationships were stronger in the UK but supervisor support-WF conflict relationship was stronger in Taiwan.

Table 2.1 (cont.)

Study	Mean Differences	Imputed/Measured Cultural Value as Predictor	Country/Cultural Value as Moderator of Antecedent	Country/Cultural Value as Moderator of Outcome	Large Model Tested in Multiple Countries	Countries Examined
Lu, Gilmour, Kao, & Huang (2006)	Work-to-family conflict, Family-to-work conflict		Relationships between work and family demands and work-to-family conflict/family-to-work conflict by country			Great Britain, Taiwan

Summary of Cultural Differences Found: Work-to-family conflict and family-to-work conflict are higher in Taiwan than Great Britain. Workload was a stronger predictor of work-to-family conflict for Great Britain than Taiwan. Household chores were a stronger predictor of family-to-work conflict for Great Britain than Taiwan.

Study	Mean Differences	Imputed/Measured Cultural Value as Predictor	Country/Cultural Value as Moderator of Antecedent	Country/Cultural Value as Moderator of Outcome	Large Model Tested in Multiple Countries	Countries Examined
Lunau, Bambra, Eikemo, van der Wel, & Dragano (2014) 2010 EWCS		Relationship between welfare state regime type and work–life balance				Austria, Belgium, Bulgaria, Croatia, Czech Republic, Denmark, Estonia, Finland, France, Germany, Greece, Hungary, Ireland, Italy, Latvia, Lithuania, Luxembourg, Netherlands, Norway, Poland, Portugal, Romania, Slovakia, Slovenia, Spain, Sweden, UK

Study	Variables	Summary of Cultural Differences Found	Countries
Lyness, Gornick, Stone, & Grotto (2012) 1997 ISSP	Macro-level country characteristics (GDP per capita, social expenditure, women's labor force participation rate, service sector unemployment, union coverage, weekly hours policy and paid leave policy) as predictors of worker control over work schedule and work hours which are tested as predictors of strain-based work-to-family conflict	Impossible to ascertain, as significance tests were not conducted. Trends suggest that the smallest proportion of people report poor work–life balance in Scandinavian regimes and the largest proportion is in Southern European and Former Soviet Union regimes.	Bulgaria, Canada, Czech Republic, Denmark, France, Hungary, Italy, Japan, New Zealand, Norway, Poland, Portugal, Russia, Slovenia, Spain, Sweden, UK, US

Summary of Cultural Differences Found: GDP per capita, social expenditures, union coverage, and paid leave policy relate to worker control over schedule. GDP per capita, women's labor force participation rate, service sector unemployment, and paid leave policy relate to working excess hours. GDP per capita, social expenditure, women's labor force participation rate, and paid leave policies relate to working deficient (fewer than desired) hours. Excess hours and deficient hours predict work-to-family conflict.

Table 2.1 (*cont.*)

Study	Mean Differences	Imputed/Measured Cultural Value as Predictor	Country/Cultural Value as Moderator of Antecedent	Country/Cultural Value as Moderator of Outcome	Large Model Tested in Multiple Countries	Countries Examined
Lyness & Judiesch (2014) – Center for Creative Leadership dataset			Societal gender egalitarianism as a moderator of the relationship between gender and work–life balance (self and supervisor rated)			Argentina, Australia, Brazil, Canada, China, Denmark, Egypt, Finland, France, Germany, Greece, Hong Kong, India, Indonesia, Ireland, Italy, Japan, Malaysia, Mexico, Netherlands, New Zealand, Philippines, Poland, Portugal, Russia, Singapore, South Korea, South Africa, Spain, Sweden, Switzerland, Thailand, Turkey, UK, US, Venezuela

Summary of Cultural Differences Found: Gender egalitarianism as measured by the World Values Survey patriarchy values for a given country and by the UN Gender Equality Index for a given country (but not when imputed as GLOBE GE values or practices) moderated the relationship between gender and both self- and supervisor-reports of work–life balance such that gender differences were smaller in more egalitarian countries.

Study	Description	Outcome	Countries
Lyness & Kropf (2005) Catalyst & The Conference Board Study	Tested national gender equality as a predictor of organizational WF culture and flexible work arrangement availability, which is tested as a predictor of WF balance for managers working in their host country and as expatriates.		Austria, Belgium, Czech, Denmark, Finland, France, Germany, Greece, Hungary, Ireland, Italy, Luxembourg, Netherlands, Norway, Poland, Portugal, Spain, Sweden, Switzerland, UK

Summary of Cultural Differences Found: National gender equality positively relates to organizational work–family culture, which positively relates to WF balance for managers working in their org's headquarter country. For managers working outside of the org's headquarter company, the headquarter country gender egalitarian positively relates to flexible work arrangements which positively relates to WF balance. Host country gender egalitarian also positively relates to organizational WF culture and WF balance.

Study	Description	Countries
Lyonette, Crompton, & Wall (2007) 2002 ISSP	WF conflict	Great Britain, Portugal

Summary of Cultural Differences Found: Women in Portugal overall report higher WF conflict than women in Great Britain, but this varies by full-time and professional status.

Study	Description	Countries
Malinen & Johnston (2011)	WF conflict	Australia, Canada, Denmark, Finland, India, Israel, Japan, Netherlands, New Zealand (immigrants from the US), New

Table 2.1 (cont.)

Study	Mean Differences	Imputed/Measured Cultural Value as Predictor	Country/Cultural Value as Moderator of Antecedent	Country/Cultural Value as Moderator of Outcome	Large Model Tested in Multiple Countries	Countries Examined
						Zealand (natives), Philippines, Portugal, South Korea
Summary of Cultural Differences Found: No differences in WF conflict between New Zealand natives and immigrants.						
Masuda et al. (2012) CISMS 2	Work-to-family conflict					Argentina, Australia, Bolivia, Canada, Chile, China, Hong Kong, Japan, New Zealand, Peru, Puerto Rico, South Korea, Taiwan, UK, US
Summary of Cultural Differences Found: Anglo and Latino cluster report significantly higher time-based work-to-family conflict than Confucian Asian cluster. Strain-based work-to-family conflict is highest in Anglo, then Latino, and lowest in Confucian Asian.						
Mortazavi, Pedhiwala, Shafiro, & Hammer (2009)	Work-to-family conflict, Family-to-work conflict		Relationship between work and family hours and work-to-family conflict/family-to-work conflict			Iran, Ukraine, US
Summary of Cultural Differences Found: No significant mean differences in work-to-family conflict or family-to-work conflict across countries, but some differences by gender. Iranian men reported more family-to-work conflict than Ukraine men, followed by US men. Work hours only predicted work-to-family conflict for women in Iran.						

Netemeyer, Brashear-Alejandro, & Boles (2004)	Tested a path model linking work-to-family conflict, family-to-work conflict, role conflict, and role ambiguity to job stress and job performance, which in turn were linked to job satisfaction and ultimately turnover intentions.	Puerto Rico, Romania, US

Summary of Cultural Differences Found: The model was not invariant. Two of the 12 paths differed across countries. Work-to-family conflict to job stress was strongest in Romania, then Puerto Rico, then US and role conflict to job satisfaction was strongest in the US, then Puerto Rico, then Romania.

Ng & Feldman (2012)	Relationship between changes in organizational and community embeddedness and changes in work-to-family conflict and family-to-work conflict. Interaction between individual-level individualistic values and embeddedness in predicting work-to-family conflict/ family-to-work conflict.	China, US

Table 2.1 (*cont.*)

Study	Mean Differences	Imputed/Measured Cultural Value as Predictor	Country/Cultural Value as Moderator of Antecedent	Country/Cultural Value as Moderator of Outcome	Large Model Tested in Multiple Countries	Countries Examined
		Summary of Cultural Differences Found: Changes in organizational embeddedness significant predictor of changes in work-to-family conflict in China but not the US. Significant interaction between individualistic values and changes in organizational embeddedness on work-to-family conflict in China but not the US. Significant interaction between individualistic values and changes in community embeddedness on family-to-work conflict in the US but not China.				
Ng & Feldman (2014)			Country as a moderator of the mediated relationships between organizational embeddedness, work-to-family conflict and negative mood/chronic insomnia and the mediated relationships between community embeddedness, family-to-work conflict and negative mood/chronic insomnia			Singapore, US

Summary of Cultural Differences Found: Country did not moderate the relationship between organizational embeddedness and work-to-family conflict. Country did moderate the relationship between community embeddedness and family-to-work conflict such that it was stronger in the US than in Singapore.

Notten, Grunow, & Verbakel (2016) 2010 ESS	Relationship between state support (parental leave and public childcare) and parent's WF conflict, controlling for country welfare regime	State support (parental leave and childcare) as moderators of the relationship between educational status and parent's WF conflict by gender	Belgium, Bulgaria, Czech Republic, Denmark, Finland, France, Germany, Greece, Hungary, Ireland, Netherlands, Norway, Poland, Portugal, Slovakia, Slovenia, Spain, Sweden, UK

Summary of Cultural Differences Found: Policies supporting child care negatively related to work-to-family conflict and family-to-work conflict. No association between parental leave and work-to-family conflict or family-to-work conflict. For men, the relationship between childcare policies and work-to-family conflict is moderated by educational level, such that for policies are most beneficial (result in lowest conflict) for men with lower education levels. There is no moderating effect for women or for leave policies. For men, the relationship between leave and childcare policies and family-to-work conflict is moderated by educational level, such that for policies are most beneficial (result in lowest conflict) for men with lower education levels. There is no moderation effect for women.

O'Brien, Del Pino, Yoo, Cinamon, & Han (2014)	Work-to-family conflict, Work-to-family enrichment	Tested a model liking WF conflict and WFE to spousal support and employer support and in turn to depression in mothers.	Israel, South Korea, US

Summary of Cultural Differences Found: No differences in mean levels of work-to-family conflict across cultures. US and Israeli mothers reported higher work-to-family enrichment than South Korean mothers. The model generally fit all cultures, although spousal support was only a mediator between work-to-family enrichment and depression for South Korean and US women.

Table 2.1 (cont.)

Study	Mean Differences	Imputed/Measured Cultural Value as Predictor	Country/Cultural Value as Moderator of Antecedent	Country/Cultural Value as Moderator of Outcome	Large Model Tested in Multiple Countries	Countries Examined
Oishi, Chan, Wang, & Kim (2015) Standard Questionnaire on Social Quality	Work-to-family conflict, Family-to-work conflict		Relationships between part-time work, involuntary status of part-time work, children, living with frail elderly person, gender role beliefs, and gender and work-to-family conflict/family-to-work conflict by country			Hong Kong, Japan, South Korea, Taiwan

Summary of Cultural Differences Found: Impossible to ascertain for mean differences as significance testing was not done. Being a part-time worker was only a significant negative predictor of work-to-family conflict in South Korea. Having children was not a significant predictor of work-to-family conflict or family-to-work conflict in any country. Living with a frail elderly person was a significant positive predictor of work-to-family conflict and family-to-work conflict in Japan and South Korea but not in other countries. Gender interacted with gender role beliefs to predict work-to-family conflict in South Korea.

Study	Mean Differences	Imputed/Measured Cultural Value as Predictor	Country/Cultural Value as Moderator of Antecedent	Country/Cultural Value as Moderator of Outcome	Large Model Tested in Multiple Countries	Countries Examined
Ollier-Malaterre, Sarkisian, Stawiski, & Hannum				Welfare state regime as a moderator of the relationship between work–life balance and job		Austria, Australia Belgium, Canada, Cyprus, Denmark, Finland, France, Germany, Greece,

		Iceland, Ireland, Italy, Luxembourg, Malta, New Zealand, Netherlands, Portugal, Spain, Switzerland, UK, US
(2013) Center for Creative Leadership dataset	performance. Relationship between work–life balance and performance as a leader is stronger for women than for men across welfare state regimes.	

Summary of Cultural Differences Found: Work–life balance is positively associated with performance only in the liberal and Mediterranean welfare regime clusters and not in the social democratic and conservative. No gender differences in the association between work–life balance and performance across welfare regimes.

Öun (2012) 2002 ISSP	WF conflict	Denmark, Finland, Norway, Sweden

Summary of Cultural Differences Found: Compared to Sweden as the referent, those in Denmark and Finland report less WF conflict. There are no significant differences between Norway and Sweden.

Pal & Saksvik (2006)	WF conflict Relationships between gender, age, education, work hours, job demands, job control, social support, and flexible working hours, and WF conflict by country	India, Norway

Summary of Cultural Differences Found: Indians reported higher levels of WF conflict than Norwegians. Formal education, work hours, job demands significant predictors of WF conflict in Norway and not India. Job control, social support, and flexibility significant predictors in India but not Norway.

Table 2.1 (cont.)

Study	Mean Differences	Imputed/Measured Cultural Value as Predictor	Country/Cultural Value as Moderator of Antecedent	Country/Cultural Value as Moderator of Outcome	Large Model Tested in Multiple Countries	Countries Examined
Pal & Saksvik (2008)				Relationships between work-to-family conflict and family-to-work conflict and job stress by country and by occupation		India, Norway

Summary of Cultural Differences Found: Work-to-family conflict is only a significant predictor of job stress in Norwegian nurses; family-to-work conflict is only a significant predictor of job stress in Indian nurses. Neither work-to-family conflict nor family-to-work conflict predicts job stress in Norwegian or Indian doctors, although the sample size is quite small.

Study	Mean Differences	Imputed/Measured Cultural Value as Predictor	Country/Cultural Value as Moderator of Antecedent	Country/Cultural Value as Moderator of Outcome	Large Model Tested in Multiple Countries	Countries Examined
Posthuma, Joplin, & Maertz (2005)				Relationship between work-to-family conflict and turnover intention by country		Mexico, US

Summary of Cultural Differences Found: None observed

Study	Mean Differences	Imputed/Measured Cultural Value as Predictor	Country/Cultural Value as Moderator of Antecedent	Country/Cultural Value as Moderator of Outcome	Large Model Tested in Multiple Countries	Countries Examined
Rantanen, Kinnunen, Mauno, & Tement (2013)			Used cluster analyses to place people into groups based on their patterns of WF conflict and WF enrichment.			Finland, Slovakia

Examined demographic correlations of belonging to particular cluster and whether clusters differed by country.

Summary of Cultural Differences Found: In all four countries, the same three profiles emerged. Some variation in demographic correlates (age, relationship status, number of dependents) across cultures within each profile.

Belgium, Denmark, Finland, France, Germany, Netherlands, Norway, Sweden, UK, US

Ruppanner (2013)

National policies (family leave, school scheduling, work scheduling, early childhood education and care) as a moderator between the relationship of having a young child and work-to-family conflict and family-to-work conflict by gender.

Summary of Cultural Differences Found: For men, significant interaction between having a child under 6 and family leave policies on family-to-work conflict and no significant interactions for work-to-family conflict. For women, significant interaction between having a child under 6 and family leave on family-to-work conflict and significant interactions of having a child under 6 and family leave and school scheduling on work-to-family conflict.

Table 2.1 (cont.)

Study	Mean Differences	Imputed/Measured Cultural Value as Predictor	Country/Cultural Value as Moderator of Antecedent	Country/Cultural Value as Moderator of Outcome	Large Model Tested in Multiple Countries	Countries Examined
Ruppanner & Huffman (2014) 2005 ISSP			Societal gender empowerment as a moderator of the relationships between gender, parental status and family-to-work conflict/work-to-family conflict.			Australia, Bulgaria, Canada, Cyprus, Czech Republic, Denmark, Dominican Republic, Finland, Flanders, France, Germany, Great Britain, Hungary, Ireland, Israel, Japan, Latvia, Mexico, New Zealand, Norway, Philippines, Portugal, Russia, Slovenia, South Africa, South Korea, Spain, Sweden, Switzerland, Taiwan, US

Summary of Cultural Differences Found: As gender empowerment increases, fathers, likelihood of experiencing family-to-work conflict increases whereas it remains relatively stable for mothers and childless men, and for women without children, the odds decrease. There are no interactive effects of gender x parental status x gender empowerment on work-to-family conflict.

Study	Construct	Finding	Countries
Sanseau & Smith (2012) European Working Conditions Survey 1990 – 2005	Work–life integration		France, US

Summary of Cultural Differences Found: Impossible to ascertain, as significance values are not listed.

Study	Construct	Finding	Countries
Schieman & Young (2015) 2011 Canadian Work, Stress, and Health Study and 2002 NSCW	Income, education, and supervisor status as predictors of WF multitasking across countries.		Canada, US

Summary of Cultural Differences Found: The authors do not conduct explicit statistical tests of differences, but note that findings are generally consistent with one exception – the fact that Americans with less than a high school education report more frequent multitasking deviates from the Canadian pattern.

Study	Construct	Finding	Countries
Simon, Kümmerling & Hasslehorn (2004)	Work-to-family conflict, Family-to-work conflict	Relationship between WF conflict and turnover intentions by country	Belgium, Finland, France, Germany, Italy, Netherlands, Poland, Slovakia

Summary of Cultural Differences Found: Impossible to ascertain as significance values are not listed. Trends were such that work-to-family conflict was highest in Italy and lowest in the Netherlands. Family-to-work conflict was highest in Belgium and lowest in Germany and Finland. The association between WF conflict and turnover intentions was weakest in Slovakia.

Table 2.1 (*cont.*)

Study	Mean Differences	Imputed/Measured Cultural Value as Predictor	Country/Cultural Value as Moderator of Antecedent	Country/Cultural Value as Moderator of Outcome	Large Model Tested in Multiple Countries	Countries Examined
Smyrnios, Romano, Tanewski, Karofsky, Millen & Yilmaz (2003)					Tested a model linking business dissatisfaction, interrole conflict, after hours work to work-to-interpersonal conflict and work-to-family conflict which was then related to family cohesion and ultimately anxiety.	Australia, US
	Summary of Cultural Differences Found: None, as the model was invariant across countries.					
Spector et al. (2004) CISMS 1	WF pressure		Region as a moderator between working hours and WF pressure			Argentina, Australia, Brazil, Canada, China, Colombia, Ecuador, Hong Kong, Mexico, New Zealand, Peru, Taiwan, UK, Uruguay, US
	Summary of Cultural Differences Found: WF pressure was significantly higher in Asia, followed by Latin America, and lowest in Anglo regions. The relationship between working hours and WF pressure is stronger in Anglo regions than in Asia or Latin America.					

Spector et al. (2007) CISMS 2	Work-to-family conflict	Region as a moderator between working hours/ workload and work-to-family conflict	Region as a moderator between work-to-family conflict and job satisfaction/turnover intentions	Argentina, Australia, Bolivia, Bulgaria, Canada, China, Hong Kong, Japan, New Zealand, Peru, Poland, Puerto Rico, Romania, Slovenia, South Korea, Taiwan, UK, Ukraine, US

Summary of Cultural Differences Found: Time-based work-to-family conflict significantly higher in Anglo clusters than in Asian. No differences with East Europe or Latin America. The significant moderating effects were as follows: The relationship between work hours and time-based work-to-family conflict is stronger in Anglo clusters compared to Asian clusters. The relationship between strain-based work-to-family conflict and job satisfaction and turnover intentions were stronger in the Anglo region than in the other three clusters. The relationship between time-based work-to-family conflict and job satisfaction was stronger for the Anglo cluster versus the East European cluster.

Steiber (2009) 2004 ESS		National context (GDP per capita, unemployment rate, public childcare, emancipation pressure) as predictor of strain- and time-based work-to-family conflict	Austria, Belgium, Czech Republic, Denmark, Estonia, Finland, France, Germany, Greece, Hungary, Iceland, Ireland, Italy, Luxembourg, Netherlands, Norway, Poland, Portugal, Slovakia, Slovenia, Spain, Sweden, Switzerland, Turkey, UK

Table 2.1 (*cont.*)

Study	Mean Differences	Imputed/Measured Cultural Value as Predictor	Country/Cultural Value as Moderator of Antecedent	Country/Cultural Value as Moderator of Outcome	Large Model Tested in Multiple Countries	Countries Examined
	Summary of Cultural Differences Found: GDP and unemployment rate positively relate to strain- and time-based work-to-family conflict.					
Strandh & Nordenmark (2006) 2001 Household Work and Flexibility Project	Work-to-family conflict		Relationships between gender and work hours and work-to-family conflict by country			Czech Republic, Hungary, Netherlands, Sweden, UK
	Summary of Cultural Differences Found: Only overall levels of significance are indicated (i.e., no post hoc tests to describe nature of differences), but the trend appears that work-to-family conflict is higher in Sweden than in the other nations. Gender (being female) is related to work-to-family conflict only in Sweden, the Netherlands, and the UK. Work hours are related to work-to-family conflict in all countries.					
Syed, Arain, Schalk, & Freese (2015)			Country as a moderator of the relationship between family/work overload and work-to-family conflict	Country as a moderator of the relationship between work-to-family conflict and work–family balance psychological contract breach		Netherlands, Pakistan

Summary of Cultural Differences Found: The relationship between work overload and work-to-family conflict was stronger in the Netherlands than in Pakistan The relationship between family overload and work-to-family conflict was stronger in Pakistan than in the Netherlands. Country did not moderate the relationship between work-to-family conflict and psychological contract breach regarding work–family balance obligations.

Author	Outcome	Relationships	Countries
Van der Lippe, Jager, & Kops (2006)	Work-to-family conflict	Relationships between work hours, overtime, managerial and professional status, higher grade, spouse employment, spouse's paid hours, responsibility for household tasks, children, education, and age and work-to-family conflict by country and gender.	Bulgaria, Czech Republic, Hungary, Netherlands, Romania, Slovenia, Sweden, UK

Summary of Cultural Differences Found: Only overall levels of significance are indicated (i.e., no post hoc tests to describe nature of differences), but the trend appears that UK and Swedish men and UK and Slovenian and Swedish women experience the highest work-to-family conflict. Different predictors emerge across the different countries and genders with no discernable pattern.

Author	Relationships	Countries
Wang, Lawler, & Shi (2011)	Relationships between perceived availability of child-care and flexibility organizational policies and WF conflict by country.	China, India, Kenya, Thailand

Table 2.1 (*cont.*)

Study	Mean Differences	Imputed/Measured Cultural Value as Predictor	Country/Cultural Value as Moderator of Antecedent	Country/Cultural Value as Moderator of Outcome	Large Model Tested in Multiple Countries	Countries Examined
Summary of Cultural Differences Found: Perceived availability of childcare policy was only related to WF conflict in Kenya and perceived availability of flexibility policy was not related to WF conflict in any country, though there are some nuanced findings in based on the importance of the policy to the individual across countries.						
Wang, Lawler, Walumbwa, & Shi (2004)				Country as moderator of the relationships between work-to-family conflict/ family-to-work conflict and job withdrawal intentions. Individually measured idiocentrism and allocentrism as moderators of the association between work-to-family conflict/family-to-work conflict and job withdrawal intentions		China, US

Summary of Cultural Differences Found: Work-to-family conflict and job withdrawal intentions were related in the US but not China. No country moderating effects observed with family-to-work conflict and withdrawal intentions. Individually measured idiocentrism moderated the relationship between work-to-family conflict/family-to-work conflict and job withdrawal intentions. No moderating effects of allocentrism.

Study	Construct	Countries
Weckstrom (2011) 2004 ESS	WF conflict	Austria, Belgium, Denmark, Finland, France, Germany, Greece, Netherlands, Portugal, Spain, Sweden, UK

Summary of Cultural Differences Found: Impossible to ascertain, as significance testing was not reported.

Study	Construct	Countries
Wharton & Blair-Loy (2006)	Work-to-family conflict	England, Hong Kong, US

Summary of Cultural Differences Found: Only overall levels of significance are indicated (i.e., no post hoc tests to describe nature of differences), but the trend appears that work-to-family conflict is highest in Hong Kong and lowest in the US.

Study	Construct	Countries
Wierda-Boer, Gerris, Vermulst, Malinen, & Anderson (2009) Family Life and Professional Work: Conflict and Synergy	Work-to-family conflict, Family-to-work conflict	Finland, Germany, Netherlands

Summary of Cultural Differences Found: Impossible to ascertain, as significance testing between countries was not reported.

Table 2.1 (*cont.*)

Study	Mean Differences	Imputed/Measured Cultural Value as Predictor	Country/Cultural Value as Moderator of Antecedent	Country/Cultural Value as Moderator of Outcome	Large Model Tested in Multiple Countries	Countries Examined
Yang (2005)	Work-to-family conflict, Family-to-work conflict			Relationships between work-to-family conflict/ family-to-work conflict and personal well-being, job satisfaction, work role effectiveness, stress-related disorders, turnover intentions, absenteeism		China, US

Summary of Cultural Differences Found: Work-to-family conflict is higher in China than in the US; no differences in family-to-work conflict. The relationships between work-to-family conflict/family-to-work conflict and work role effectiveness and turnover intentions are stronger in the US than China. Relationship between family-to-work conflict and absenteeism is stronger in the US than China. Family-to-work conflict is more strongly associated with stress-related disorders in the US than China; no differences for work-to-family conflict and stress-related disorders.

Yang, Chen, Choi, & Zou (2000) – Study 2			Country as a moderator of the relationships between work and family demands and WF conflict.			China, US

Summary of Cultural Differences Found Family demands are a stronger predictor of WF conflict in the US than China. Work demands are a stronger predictor of WF conflict in China than the US.

Yeh (2015) 2005 ISSP	WF conflict	Japan, Taiwan, South Korea

Summary of Cultural Differences Found: There is a significant difference in WF conflict across the three countries. Post hoc tests are not conducted to isolate the differences but it appears that Japan and S. Korea have significantly higher WF conflict than Taiwan.

Note. CISMS = Collaborative International Study of Managerial Stress. ESS = European Social Survey. SWAT = Survey of Work and Time. NEXT = Nurses' Early Exit Study. NSCW = National Study of the Changing Workforce. ISSP = International Social Survey Programme. EWCS = European Working Conditions Survey.

found that work-to-family conflict was lower in Asia (i.e., Hassan, Dollard, & Winefield, 2010; Masuda et al., 2012; Spector et al., 2007, though note that the latter two studies are based on the same dataset), two reported no differences (i.e., O'Brien, Del Pino, Yoo, Cinamon, & Han, 2014; Jin, Ford, & Chen, 2013), and one found that family-to-work conflict was higher in Asian countries (i.e., Lu, Gilmour, Kao, & Huang, 2006). One study investigated WF pressure, a construct that conceptually overlaps with WF conflict. Findings suggest pressure was significantly higher in Asian countries than in Latin America, which was in turn significantly higher than in Anglo countries (Spector et al., 2004).

There are fewer studies in other regions. Cinamon (2009) found that work-to-family conflict was higher among Jewish Israelis than among Arab Israelis. Drobnic and Guillén Rodríguez (2011) included two separate samples comparing Germany and Spain in their study; work-to-family conflict was higher in Germany in one sample, but not in the other sample. One study comparing within Asian regions also found differences, such that Hong Kong has significantly higher work-to-family conflict than Taiwan (Law, 2011). Mortazavi et al. (2009) reported no overall differences in work-to-family conflict across the United Kingdom, Ukraine, and Iran. Similarly, Agarwala, Arizkuren-Eleta, Castillo, Muniz-Ferrer, and Gartzia (2014) found no differences in work-to-family conflict among India, Peru, and Spain.

Results with other constructs, namely non-directional WF conflict, family-to-work conflict, WF balance, and WF enrichment, are similarly difficult to synthesize. Two studies found that women in Great Britain reported less WF conflict than their female counterparts in two Latin European countries — Portugal (Lyonette, Crompton, & Wall, 2007) and Spain (Gaspar, 2013). In a study of Nordic countries, Öun (2012) found that WF conflict was lower in Denmark and Finland than in Sweden or Norway. Pal and Saksvik (2006) report higher WF conflict among Indian versus Norwegian employees, and Malinen and Johnston (2011) reported no differences when comparing native New Zealanders with immigrants in New Zealand who came from the United States. Comparing within Asian countries, Yeh (2015) found Japan and South Korea have significantly higher WF conflict compared to Taiwan.

Most studies that included family-to-work conflict compared Anglo to Confucian Asian countries. These results are consistent, with three studies finding greater conflict in Asian countries compared to Anglo countries (Hassan et al., 2010; Jin et al., 2013; Lu et al., 2006). Other comparisons across countries are less conclusive. Law (2011) found no differences in family-to-work conflict when comparing Hong Kong and Taiwan. Moratzavi et al. (2009) also report no differences across the United Kingdom, Ukraine, and Iran. Finally, Agarwala et al.'s (2014) results showed family-to-work conflict was higher in India compared to Peru or Spain.

Two studies each have examined work–life balance and work–family enrichment mean differences. Drobnic and Guillén Rodríguez (2011) found no differences in balance across Spanish and German workers. Abendroth and den Dulk (2011) compared work–life balance satisfaction in Sweden to seven other European countries. They found that people in Finland and Bulgaria have higher work–life balance satisfaction than Swedes, while Germans had significantly lower work–life balance satisfaction than Swedes. The two studies examining WF enrichment found relatively consistent Asian-Anglo differences. O'Brien et al. (2014) found greater reported work-to-family enrichment in South Korea compared to the United States, and Jin et al. (2013) found greater reported family-to-work enrichment in China compared to North America.

Given the diversity of findings, comparison of mean differences across cultures is a research question that seems particularly amenable to quantitative review through meta-analysis. One such meta-analysis examined cross-national differences in work-to-family and family-to-work conflict across several cultural and economic values (Allen, French, Dumani, & Shockley, 2015). Consistent with our qualitative review, few mean differences were significant. Gender gap (i.e., the extent of gender inequality in a nation) and individualism-collectivism predicted mean differences, with higher rates of family-to-work conflict in countries that have a wide gender gap or are more collectivistic (particularly among Asian countries).

Work-related predictors of WF conflict. The most commonly studied predictor of WF conflict is work hours. Three studies compared the relationship between work hours and negative WF outcomes in Confucian Asian countries versus Anglo cultures. Spector et al. (2007) found that the correlation between work hours and time-based work-to-family conflict was stronger in Anglo regions than in Asian regions and found no evidence for a moderating effect of culture with strain-based work-to-family conflict. Spector et al. (2004) found a similar trend with WF pressure, such that the relationship between work hours and pressure was stronger in Anglo regions than in Confucian Asian (and Latin America). Galovan et al. (2010), on the other hand, did not find evidence for relationships of different strengths for Singaporean and American workers in their model linking work hours to work-to-family conflict. They did find a difference with family-to-work conflict, but in the opposite pattern of the Spector et al. findings, such that the association was stronger in the Singaporean than in the American sample.

In all three studies, the authors relied on individualism-collectivism as the reason behind why cultural differences were expected, citing that the collectivistic view of work as a means to support and honor family alters (i.e., reduces) the perception of work demands as creating conflict. This lack of observed differences with Singapore versus a composite of Asian regions could relate to other unaccounted for cultural differences. For example, Singapore is higher in future orientation and lower in humane orientation than many other Confucian Asian cultures (Ashkanasy, Gupta, Mayfield, Trevor-Roberts, 2004; Kabasakal & Bodur, 2004). In line with this speculation, Oishi et al.'s (2015) comparison across four Asian countries showed part-time work was related to less work-to-family conflict compared to full-time work in South Korea, but not in Taiwan, Hong Kong, or Japan.

Additionally, there is some evidence that the relationship between work hours and WF conflict may be weaker in Eastern European countries than in other regions; Van der Lippe et al. (2006) found that work hours were predictive of work-to-family conflict in the Netherlands, the United Kingdom, and Sweden for both men and women, but was not a significant predictor in Slovenia, Hungary or Romania (along with women in the Czech Republic and men in Bulgaria). Mortazavi et al. (2009) found that work hours were not related to work-to-family conflict in the Ukraine (or the United States), but there was a significant association for Iranian women (but not men). These findings may also be accounted for by collectivism, as Eastern Europe scores similarly on in-group collectivism as Asian cultures (House et al., 2004). Lastly, other studies found little or no evidence for differences in work hours-WF conflict relationships by culture, including Stradh and Nordemnark (2006) (comparing the United Kingdom, Sweden, Czech Republic, and the Netherlands), Kucharova (2009) (comparing Czech Republic, France, Bulgaria, and Georgia), Gaspar (2013) (comparing Spain and Great Britain), and Pal and Saksvik (2006) (comparing Norway and India).

Beyond work hours, several studies examined other job demands as predictors of WF conflict. With regard to Confucian Asian and Anglo comparisons, two studies found that job demands were a stronger predictor of work-to-family conflict in Anglo cultures than in Asian cultures (work role overload in North America and China, Jin, Ford, & Chen, 2013; workload in Great Britain and Taiwan, Lu et al., 2006). However, Yang et al. (2000) found the opposite pattern — that work demands were more strongly related to WF conflict in China versus the United States — based on a non-directional measure of conflict. Syed, Arain, Schalk, and Freese (2015) also found cross-national differences such that the relationship between work overload and work-to-family conflict was stronger in the Netherlands than in Pakistan. On the other hand, several studies find little evidence for cross-national differences in the job demands and WF conflict relationship. Regarding Asian-Anglo comparisons, Aryee, Fields, and Luk (1999) note that the association between job conflict and job involvement with work-to-family conflict is similar in their Hong Kong sample as an American sample published in Frone, Russell, and Cooper (1992). Similarly, Hill, Yang, Hawkins, and Ferris (2004) compared Asian countries (by combining Confucian and Southern Asia) with Western-developing, Western-affluent and US clusters and found path coefficients similar in magnitude between workload and work-to-family conflict across the country clusters. Schieman and Young (2015) also found no differences among American versus Canadian employees in the strength of the relationship between various job demands and WF multitasking at home (i.e., performing both work and family responsibilities simultaneously). Three additional studies found little differences in the relationships between job demands and WF constructs across countries when comparing Norway and India (Pal & Saksvik, 2006), Germany and Spain (Drobnic & Guillen Rodriguez, 2011), and New Zealand and Australia (Brough et al., 2014).

In terms of work-related support variables, schedule flexibility and social support have been the most commonly studied. Galoven et al. (2010) found that schedule flexibility was negatively related to work-to-family conflict and unrelated to family-to-work conflict in the United States, but was positively related to both types of conflict in Singapore. Pal and Saksvik (2006) found that flexibility in working hours was negatively related to non-directional WF conflict in India, but was not associated with conflict in Norway. In a model comparison involving Eastern, Western-Developing, Western-Affluent, and US clusters, Hill et al. (2004) found that the path from job flexibility to WF fit was weaker in the United States than the other country clusters. In a comparison of Kenya, Thailand, China, and India, Wang, Lawler, and Shi (2011) found that the availability of schedule flexibility did not relate to non-directional WF conflict in any of the countries, although it did interact with ratings of policy importance, such that schedule availability was a significant negative predictor when considered highly important to the individual in China, Kenya, and Thailand (but not India).

In terms of support, some differences across regions have been noted, although patterns of these findings are not clear as there is little consistency in the constructs and regions compared. Specifically, Cinamon (2009) found that colleague support was a significant negative predictor of family-to-work conflict for Jewish Israelis, but not for Arab Israelis. Janssen, Peeters, de Jonge, Houkes, and Tummers (2004) found that workplace social support from colleagues and supervisors was significantly related to work-to-nonwork conflict in their Dutch sample, but not in the American sample. Anderson, Coffey, Liu, and Zhao (2008) found a relationship between managerial support and work-to-family conflict in the United States, but not in China. Agarwala et al. (2014) also found differential relationships, such that managerial support was significantly related to work–life conflict in Spain and Peru, but not in India. WF support was not associated with work-to-family conflict among either Chinese or North American employees, but showed differential relationships to WF enrichment, such that the relationship was stronger in North America than China (Jin et al., 2013).

Another handful of studies do not find substantial cross-national differences. In a study comparing Taiwanese and British employees, supervisor support was similarly and negatively related to WF conflict in both samples (Lu et al., 2010). With regard to WF balance, Lyness and Kropf (2005) found that WF organizational culture significantly predicted WF balance for employees working in the country their organization's headquarters are located in. This relationship was not tested across cultures, but national gender equality of the country significantly predicted a more supportive WF organizational culture. In a model testing family-supportive organizational perception as a predictor of time-, behavior- and strain-based work-to-family and family-to-work conflict, Lapierre et al. (2008) found that the model was invariant across the United States, Canada, Australia, New Zealand, and Finland. Similarly, O'Brien et al. (2014) found a model linking employer support to work-to-family conflict and work-to-family enrichment fit across Israeli, South Korean, and American samples.

Family-related predictors. Commonly studied family-related predictors of WF constructs include family demands and support. Beginning with family demands, the presence of children is commonly studied as a predictor of WF conflict. Results suggest that there is considerable variation in whether an association exists between these two variables across cultures. Across the studies, presence of children was related to WF conflict among employees in Spain, women in France, women in the Netherlands, and men in Sweden, but no significant relationships were found among women in Georgia or employees in the United Kingdom, Slovenia, Hungary,

Romania, Taiwan, Hong Kong, Japan, or South Korea (Gaspar, 2013; Lu et al., 2006; Kuchařová, 2009; Van der Lippe et al., 2006). Studies were contradictory in findings from the Czech Republic and Bulgaria, with some studies finding non-significant relationships and others citing a positive one (Kuchařová, 2009; Van der Lippe et al., 2006). With regard to more nuanced comparisons, Lu et al. (2006) found that the age of employees' youngest children predicted both work-to-family and family-to-work conflict in both countries (Taiwan and the United Kingdom). Hill et al. (2004) compared the strengths of relationships between responsibility for children in relation to family-to-work conflict and the trend was such that the effect was weaker in Eastern countries, particularly in comparison to Western-Affluent countries and the United States. Öun (2012) calculated probabilities of experiencing WF conflict across four Nordic countries (i.e., Norway, Denmark, Sweden, Finland) and found that men and women with children generally experience more WF conflict than those without, the exception being Danish women where the trend was in the opposite direction.

Another common family demand studied in relation to WF conflict across cultures is time spent in household labor. Studies generally find a positive association with WF conflict regardless of cultural context (Czech Republic, France, Bulgaria, and Georgia, Kucharova, 2009; Spain and Great Britain, Gasper, 2013; Taiwan and Great Britain, but only for work-to-family conflict for Taiwan, Lu et al., 2006). Exceptions include one study that found no association between household labor hours and work-to-family or family-to-work conflict in the United States, Ukraine, or Iran (Mortazavi et al., 2009) and another study that found the association was only present among women in the Czech Republic, Slovenia, and Romania, but not in men in these countries or men or women in the Netherlands, the United Kingdom, Sweden, Hungary, or Bulgaria (Van der Lippe et al., 2006).

A few studies have examined family-related support, and there are noticeable differences across cultures. Cinamon (2009) found that spousal support was related to family-to-work conflict for Jewish Israelis, but not Arab Israelis. Halbesleben, Wheeler, and Rossi (2012) tested a link between instrumental spousal social support and time-, behavior-, and strain-based work-to-family conflict in the United States and Brazil. Although the authors did not provide significance tests of path differences, the path from instrumental spouse support to behavior-based conflict appeared to be substantially larger in the United States than Brazil (−.28 versus −.14). Jin et al. (2013) found that family support was a stronger predictor of family-to-work conflict in China than in North America, but the opposite pattern was true for family-to-work enrichment. Finally, O'Brien et al. (2014) showed that a model linking spousal support with work-to-family conflict and work-to-family enrichment yielded good model fit across samples from Israel, South Korea, and the United States.

Demographic predictors. The only demographic variable that has been considered with any consistency was gender. Although gender is often included in WF studies, it is important to note that explicit comparisons about the differential effect of gender on WF constructs are less common. Moreover, most studies that include such a comparison do so in the context of regression, where the interpretation involves the effect of gender on WF constructs when controlling for other variables (which differ across studies, making comparisons more difficult). The following studies employed such a methodology, unless otherwise noted. No gender differences in WF conflict were observed in studies conducted in Great Britain (Gaspar, 2013), Czech Republic, France, and Georgia (Kucharavo, 2009), and Norway and India (Pal & Saksvik, 2006). Alternatively, several studies found that women reported greater WF conflict than men, including women in Spain (Gaspar, 2013), Bulgaria (Kucharova, 2009), Norway, Denmark, Sweden, and Finland (Öun, 2012), and the United States, England, and Hong Kong (Wharton & Blair-Loy, 2006). One study examined cross-national relationships between gender and WF balance (Lyness & Judeisch, 2014). Results suggest women have less WF balance (based on both self- and supervisor reports) compared to men in lower (vs. higher) gender egalitarian countries.

In a study that reported gender results without other variables in the regression equation, no gender differences in WF conflict were observed in Great Britain, but women reported more conflict than men in Portugal (Lyonette et al., 2007). A second study that did not employ control variables found gender differences varied depending on the direction of conflict (Ruppanner & Huffman, 2014). Specifically, men reported greater work-to-family conflict than women in five countries (Cyprus, France, the United Kingdom, Norway, and the United States), whereas women reported greater work-to-family conflict than men in two countries (Australia and Japan). On the other hand, women reported greater family-to-work conflict than men in six countries (France, Japan, New Zealand, Russia, South Korea, and the United States), whereas men reported greater family-to-work conflict than women in only two countries (Cyprus and Sweden). No gender differences were found in the remaining twenty countries examined (Belgium, Bulgaria, Canada, Czech Republic, Denmark, Dominican Republic, Finland, Germany, Hungary, Ireland, Israel, Latvia, Mexico, Philippines, Portugal, Slovenia, South Africa, Spain, Switzerland, and Taiwan).

Interestingly, one study reported results regarding gender and WF conflict both with and without control variables. When work hours were not controlled for, WF conflict was only higher for women in Sweden; no gender differences were observed in the Netherlands, the United Kingdom, Czech Republic, or Hungary. Once work hours were controlled for, differences were apparent in Sweden, the Netherlands, and the United Kingdom, such that women experienced greater conflict than men. This generally speaks to the idea of including controls in cross-cultural research, particularly if the samples across countries are not matched, in which case it is difficult to ascertain the source of observed differences (Lytle, Brett, Barsness, Tinsley, & Janssens, 1995). As working hours and job types not only vary within country by gender, but also across countries (e.g., the gender gap in work hours is much larger in the Netherlands than in Hungary, OECD, 2013), this is one particularly salient example where the use of statistical controls to equate samples is imperative.

Work-related outcomes. The most commonly studied work-related outcome variables are turnover intentions and job satisfaction. Studies relating work-to-family conflict to turnover intentions in Confucian Asian and Anglo countries are generally consistent. That is, Yang et al. (2000), Wang et al. (2004), Spector et al. (2007), and Anderson et al. (2009) all found that the associations between these variables were stronger in Anglo countries than in Asian countries. Yang et al. (2000). and Wang et al. (2004) also tested the link between family-to-work conflict and turnover intentions and did not find a moderating effect of country. Another study involving WF conflict and turnover intentions was conducted comparing the United States and Mexico and reported no differences across the two countries in the magnitude of the effect (Posthuma, Joplin, & Maertz, 2005). Additionally, three studies (Brough et al., 2014; Estryn-Behar et al., 2007; Simon et al., 2004) included these variables in their cross-national analyses, but statistical significance information was not included, making it difficult to draw conclusions.

Research with job satisfaction in Anglo vs. Confucian Asian comparisons mimics the turnover intention results. Several researchers cite a stronger negative relationship between work-to-family conflict and job satisfaction in Anglo compared to Confucian Asian cultures (Anderson et al., 2009; Galovan et al., 2010; Lu et al., 2010; Spector et al., 2007). However, Jin et al. (2013) found no evidence for country moderating this relationship, though their comparison involved North American countries and incorporated a non-Anglo country (Mexico). This could account for the lack of results. Differences seem to be less clear in other regional comparisons as Lapierre et al.'s (2008) model linking work-to-family and family-to-work conflict to job satisfaction was invariant across countries (New Zealand, the United States, Canada, Australia, and Finland), as was Hill et al.'s (2004) model of WF fit and job satisfaction involving many countries grouped into four regions. Additionally, Janssen et al. (2004) found that work-to-family conflict was positively related to job satisfaction in a Dutch sample, but was unrelated in an American sample. A similarly odd pattern (i.e., positive association) was found with family-to-work conflict and job satisfaction in the United States, whereas the correlation was negative in Singapore (Galovan et al., 2010). One study investigated cross-national differences between work–life balance and job satisfaction (Haar, Russo, Sune, & Ollier-Malaterre, 2014). Results showed a stronger positive association between work–life balance and job satisfaction in collectivist cultures and countries (Malaysia, China, and the native Maori in New Zealand) compared to more individualistic ones (non-Maori New Zealand, Spain, France, and Italy).

Four studies investigated cross-national context as a moderator for the relationship between a WF interface variable and performance-related outcomes. Both Anderson et al. (2009) and Yang (2005) found evidence that suggests family-to-work conflict is more strongly associated with absenteeism in the United States compared to China. Similarly, Yang (2005) found work-to-family conflict was more strongly associated with role effectiveness in the United States compared to China. Ollier-Malaterre, Sarkisian, Stawiski, and Hannum (2013) found work–life balance was positively associated with job performance in liberal (e.g., Canada, New Zealand) and Mediterranean (e.g., Greece, Portugal) welfare regime clusters, but not in social democratic (e.g., Denmark, Sweden) and conservative (e.g., France, Germany) clusters. Finally, Netemeyer, Brashear-Alejandro, and Boles (2004) found that the relationship between family-to-conflict and job performance was invariant across the United States, Romania, and Puerto Rico.

Family-related outcomes. Considerably less research has been conducted with family-related outcomes and little evidence for country differences have been found. In the same model described above, Lapierre et al. (2008) included a link from work-to-family and family-to-work conflict to family satisfaction and found that it was invariant across the five countries. Smyrnios et al. (2003) also found that a model including a link from work-to-family conflict to family cohesion was invariant across Australian and American samples. Using a variable that was a combination of WF conflict and enrichment, Wiese and Salmela-Aro (2008) reported similarly sized correlations with partner satisfaction and with partnership engagement in Finland and Germany. The sole case of a differential pattern of effects was observed by Lu et al. (2010), as the relationship between work-to-family conflict and family satisfaction was stronger in the United Kingdom than in Taiwan.

Well-being outcomes. Relatively little research has examined cross-national differences in the relationship between the WF interface and well-being outcomes, and consistent with previous sections, most studies focus on comparing Anglo/individualistic (e.g., the United States, New Zealand, Spain, France, Italy) with Confucian Asian/collectivistic countries and cultures (e.g., Singapore, China, Malaysia, the native Maori in New Zealand). This research generally concludes that psychological well-being constructs, such as life satisfaction, anxiety, depression, stress, and stress-related disorders, are more strongly associated with work-to-family conflict (Anderson et al., 2008; Galovan et al., 2010), family-to-work conflict (Yang, 2005), and WF balance (Haar et al., 2014) in Anglo/individualistic countries and cultures compared to Asian/collectivistic ones. As exceptions, Yang (2005) found no China–United States differences in the relationship between work-to-family conflict and stress-related disorders, and both Anderson et al. (2008) and Galovan et al. (2010) found stronger relationships between family-to-work conflict and stress and depression in China and Singapore, respectively, compared to the United States.

Comparisons across other regions are relatively more diverse. Netemeyer et al. (2004) found the strongest relationship between work-to-family conflict and job stress in Romania, followed by Puerto Rico and then the United States. Pal and Saksvik's (2008) study of nurses and doctors found that work-to-family conflict was related to job stress in Norwegian nurses, but not Indian nurses, whereas family-to-work conflict was related to job stress in Indian nurses, but not Norwegian nurses. Neither work-to-family nor family-to-work conflict predicted job stress in Norwegian or Indian doctors. Finally, Lalluka, Rahkonen, Lahelma, and Arber (2010) found no consistent patterns when comparing a model of work-to-family conflict and health behaviors (i.e., smoking, alcohol consumption, physical activity, and unhealthy eating) across Great Britain, Japan, and Finland.

Culture as a predictor. A few studies incorporated macro-level variables as predictors of WF constructs. In these cases, many countries were included in the analyses, allowing adequate variation. Most commonly, researchers have positioned national leave and childcare policies as national-level resources that should theoretically reduce work–family conflict. Studies typically find non-significant relationships between work-to-family and family-to-work conflict and both parental leave and the availability and use of public childcare (Allen et al., 2014; Annink, den Dulk, & Stein, 2016; Notten, Grunow, & Verbakel, 2016; Steiber, 2009). Allen et al. (2014) also investigated the amount of paid sick leave and annual leave in relation to conflict. They found that greater sick leave availability was most consistently related to lower work-to-family and family-to-work conflict. In contrast, annual leave was associated with *greater* time-based work-to-family conflict. The latter finding is consistent with work by Lyness, Gornick, Stone, and Grotto (2012) who found paid leave is positively associated with working excess hours and job control, which are in turn associated with increased WF conflict across twenty-one countries. Some research suggests a more nuanced view of gender and family roles is needed in order to see the benefits of these national policies. For example, Notten et al. (2016) found an interaction that suggests that policies may be beneficial for men with lower education levels, and Steiber (2009) found public childcare was weakly associated with only time-based conflict in women.

Two studies have examined gender norms and economic prosperity in relation to WF conflict. Ruppaner and Huffman (2014) examined national-level gender empowerment as a predictor of work-to-family and family-to-work conflict. Gender empowerment was operationalized using the percentage of parliamentary seats held by women, the rate of family to male employment for those fifteen years and older, and the ratio of female to male earned income. They found that gender empowerment positively related to both directions of conflict for men, although the direct relationship between gender empowerment and work-to-family conflict was no longer significant when controls were entered into the equation. Similarly, Steiber's (2009) study of twenty-eight countries showed a weak positive association between emancipation pressure (i.e., pressure for men to take equal responsibility for children as women) and strain-based work-to-family conflict in men, but not women. Steiber (2009) also examined gross domestic product (GDP) per capita and unemployment rate, finding that both positively related to both time- and strain-based work-to-family conflict for both men and women. Lyness et al. (2012) also found evidence to suggest GDP per capita is indirectly associated with greater WF conflict via greater excessive work hours. Meta-analytic evidence, however, shows no relationships between GDP and unemployment and both directions of WF conflict (Allen et al., 2015).

Finally, two studies investigated welfare regime as a possible predictor of WF interface variables. Notten et al. (2016) compared liberal (i.e., Ireland, the Netherlands), conservative (i.e., Spain, France), post-communist (i.e., Hungary, Poland), and social democratic (i.e., Finland, Sweden) welfare regimes in multiple regression models predicting work-to-family and family-to-work conflict. Their results indicate men in conservative regime countries reported greater work-to-family conflict than men in liberal regime countries; no differences were found for women or for family-to-work conflict across regimes. Lunau, Bambra, Eikemo, van der Wel, and Dragano (2014) investigated welfare state regime type as a predictor of work–life balance. Although no significance tests were conducted, trends seem to indicate that Scandinavian regimes have the smallest proportion of people with poor work–life balance and Southern European and former Soviet Union regimes have the largest proportion of people with poor work–life balance.

Conclusions and Future Research Recommendations

Our review highlights the many ways in which researchers have empirically examined the WF interface across countries. Due to the high prevalence of Asian–Anglo comparisons, the firmest conclusions can be drawn regarding these two regions. In terms of mean differences, findings generally indicate that employees from Confucian Asian countries (e.g., China, Hong Kong, Taiwan) report more family-to-work conflict and work-to-family enrichment compared to those in Anglo countries (e.g., Australia, the United Kingdom, the United States). Findings for work-to-family conflict are less conclusive, but the available studies suggest that the opposite pattern may exist, such that employees in Anglo countries experience greater work-to-family conflict compared to those in Confucian Asian countries. These overall results align with those from a recent meta-analysis of cross-national differences in both directions of WF conflict (Allen et al., 2015), which suggests that in-group collectivism may be driving these mean differences. When examining country as a moderator, associations between the WF interface and correlates tend to be stronger in Anglo countries compared to Asian countries. Again, these differences appear to be attributable to in-group collectivism, as similar patterns are observed when comparing Eastern European countries to Anglo countries.

Gender differences appear to vary quite a bit across countries, with no clear patterns. These inconsistent results mimic a recent meta-analysis, which found little evidence for gender differences in WF conflict generally or when examining culture values as a moderator (Shockley, Shen, Denunzio, Arvan, & Knudsen, in press). These inconsistent findings may be attributable to sampling procedures. That is, because many studies in our review used convenience samples, it could create an "apples and oranges" comparison in the sense that the samples in different countries could be quite different on influential individual-level characteristics such as occupation or age (Spector, Liu, & Sanchez, 2015). This ultimately makes it difficult to disentangle cultural effects from sample effects. The use of matched samples in future research would help to overcome this issue.

Given the diverse findings reviewed and the small effect sizes found when using national-level predictors of the WF interface, we conclude that macro-level effects on individual-reported WF experiences are quite distal and small in magnitude. Nearly all studies that investigated national leave or childcare policies as a predictor of work–family interface variables found null results. Thus, these policies likely have minimal direct impact on individuals' reported WF experiences. In contrast, both gender norms and GDP tended to have consistent relationships with WF conflict, although effect sizes were small. Specifically, men in countries that have high gender egalitarian norms report more WF conflict than those in countries with lower gender egalitarian norms. This finding may be due to the fact that men and women have more equitable distribution of labor in high gender egalitarian countries, such as Denmark, compared to lower gender egalitarian countries, such as Australia and the United States (Craig & Mullan, 2010). Another consistent finding is that GDP relates positively to conflict, which may be a result of the different work situations (e.g., more pressure and longer hours) and cultural contexts (e.g., high achievement pressure; McClelland, 1961) typically seen in high GDP countries. Exploration of potential mediators, such as time allocation and perceptions of demands and support, is needed to better understand how macro-level factors relate to individual WF experiences. Furthermore, these findings reinforce the need to examine WF interface variables in low income countries and regions, as the majority of studies that examine GDP do so in countries with mid to high GDP.

Correlates in the family domain appear to be relatively consistently related to the WF interface across countries when compared to work domain correlates, with the exception of child care responsibilities. These consistencies may indicate that the family domain is universally valued across cultures and that the perceived value and role of work is relatively more variable across countries. Accordingly, some have suggested that Anglo-Asian differences emerge due to differing perspectives on the role of work as part of the family (Aryee et al., 1999). Others have suggested cross-national differences can be attributed to differences in the extent to which cultures view work roles as integrated with family roles (Allen, 2013). Cross-national research that compares work and family role centrality, role contrast, and role integration across countries is needed to empirically test these ideas.

Several findings reviewed in this chapter found no or inconclusive evidence for cross-national differences. One reason for these null results may be the countries chosen for comparison. Given that the effects associated with country characteristics are small, perhaps large national differences are needed to find significant results. This would explain why few differences were found when comparing countries within the same region along with countries that are similar in terms of cultural or economic characteristics. We encourage future cross-national researchers to purposefully choose countries that differ greatly in terms of the theoretical national-level difference of interest (Spector et al., 2015). This purposive sampling strategy would also help to widen the scope of cross-national comparisons to include currently underrepresented countries that are more extreme in terms of their economic or cultural characteristics, such as those in African, Arabic, Oceanic, or South Asian countries.

Overall, we urge researchers to exercise greater rigor in their cross-national research. A large number of studies could not be synthesized simply due to a lack of significance testing information, an issue that is easily resolved by reporting means, standard deviations, and zero-order correlations by sample. We also encourage researchers to present comparisons both with and without control variables in order to better assess the effect that their inclusion have on cross-national comparisons and allow cleaner comparisons across studies. Finally, we note that measurement invariance testing was relatively rare. Measurement invariance allows researchers to determine the extent that constructs have a shared meaning and are measured in the same way across groups (Vandenberg & Lance, 2000). Given that work and family are conceptually different across cultures and countries (e.g., Aryee et al., 1999; Grzywacz et al., 2007), we strongly encourage researchers to test measurement invariance when comparing cultures to ensure measurements of WF interface variables are equivalent.

In conclusion, there has been a substantial amount of research conducted around the world focused on understanding employees' work–family experiences. Our narrative review of the literature revealed that there is a great deal of inconsistencies in findings across studies, which makes it difficult to draw firm conclusions about the nature of cross-cultural differences. Nonetheless, our review also revealed some interesting insights, particularly that cross-cultural differences seem to relatively consistently emerge along the individualism-collectivism dimension. We hope that future researchers will use our review as a guide to highlight areas in need of future research, both as a way to reconcile inconsistent past research and to explore under-studied regions and topics.

References

Studies included in the review are indicated with *.

*Abendroth, A.-K., & den Dulk, L. (2011). Support for the work–life balance in Europe: The impact of state, workplace and family support on work–life balance satisfaction. *Work, Employment & Society, 25,* 234–256. doi:10.1177/0950017011398892

*Agarwala, T., Arizkuren-Eleta, A., Del Castillo, E., Muñiz-Ferrer, M., & Gartzia, L. (2014). Influence of managerial support on work–life conflict and organizational commitment: an international comparison for India, Peru and Spain. *The International Journal of Human Resource Management, 25,* 1460–1483. doi:10.1080/09585192.2013.870315

Allen, T. D. (2012). The work–family interface. In S. W. J. Kozlowski (Ed). *The Oxford Handbook of Organizational Psychology* (pp. 1163–1198). New York: Oxford University Press. doi:10.1093/oxfordhb/9780199928286.013.0034

(2013). Some future directions for work–family research in a global world. In S. A. Y., Poelmans, J. H. Greenhaus, & M. L. H. Maestro (Eds.), *Expanding the Boundaries of Work-Family Research: A Vision For The future* (pp. 333–347). Basingstoke, UK: Palgrave. doi:10.1057/9781137006004_15

Allen, T. D., French, K. A., Dumani, S., & Shockley, K. M. (2015). Meta-analysis of work–family conflict mean differences: Does national context matter? *Journal of Vocational Behavior, 90,* 90–100. doi:10.1016/j.jvb.2015.07.006

*Allen, T. D., Lapierre, L. M., Spector, P. E., Poelmans, S. A. Y., O'Driscoll, M., Sanchez, J. I., ... Woo, J.-M. (2014). The link between national paid leave policy and work–family conflict among married working parents: National policy and work–family conflict. *Applied Psychology, 63,* 5–28. doi:10.1111/apps.12004

*Anderson, S. E., Coffey, B. S., Zhao, S., Liu, Y., & Zhang, J. (2008). Perspectives on work–family issues in China: The voices of young urban professionals. *Community, Work & Family, 12,* 197–212. doi:10.1080/13668800902778967

*Annink, A., den Dulk, L., & Steijn, B. (2016). Work–family conflict among employees and the self-employed across Europe. *Social Indicators Research, 126,* 571–593.

*Aryee, S., Fields, D., & Luk, V. (1999). A cross-cultural test of a model of the work–family interface. *Journal of Management, 25,* 491–511.

Ashkanasy, N., Gupta, V., Mayfield, M., & Trevor-Roberts, E. (2004). Future orientation. In R. House, P. Hanges, M. Javidan, P. Dorfman, & W. Gupta (Eds.), *Culture, Leadership, and Organizations: The GLOBE Study of 62 Societies* (pp. 282–342). Thousand Oaks, CA: Sage.

Aycan, Z. (2008). Cross-cultural perspectives to work–family conflict. In K. Korabik & D. Lero (Eds.), *Handbook of work–Family Conflict* (pp. 359–371). London: Cambridge University Press.

Bardoel, E. A., De Cieri, H., & Santos, C. (2008). A review of work–life research in Australia and New Zealand. *Asia Pacific Journal of Human Resources, 46,* 316–333. doi:10.1177/1038411108095762

*Barnes-Farrell, J. L., Davies-Schrils, K., McGonagle, A., Walsh, B., Milia, L. D., Fischer, F. M., . . . Tepas, D. (2008). What aspects of shiftwork influence off-shift well-being of healthcare workers? *Applied Ergonomics, 39,* 589–596.

Begall, K., & Mills, M. (2011). The impact of subjective work control, job strain and work–family conflict on fertility intentions: A European comparison. *European Journal of Population, 27,* 433–456. doi:10.1007/s10680-011-9244-z

*Beham, B., Drobnič, S., & Präg, P. (2014). The work–family interface of service sector workers: A comparison of work resources and professional status across five European countries. *Applied Psychology, 63,* 29–61. doi:10.1111/apps.12012

*Billing, T. K., Bhagat, R. S., Babakus, E., Krishnan, B., Ford, D. L., Srivastava, B. N., . . . Nasurdin, A. M. (2014a). Work–family conflict and organisationally valued outcomes: The moderating role of decision latitude in five national contexts. *Applied Psychology, 63,* 62–95.

*Billing, T. K., Bhagat, R., Babakus, E., Srivastava, B., Shin, M., & Brew, F. (2014b). Work–family conflict in four national contexts: A closer look at the role of individualism-collectivism. *International Journal of Cross Cultural Management, 14,* 139–159.

*Brough, P., Timms, C., O'Driscoll, M. P., Kalliath, T., Siu, O.-L., Sit, C., & Lo, D. (2014). Work–life balance: A longitudinal evaluation of a new measure across Australia and New Zealand workers. *The International Journal of Human Resource Management, 25,* 2724–2744. doi:10.1080/09585192.2014.899262

Bull, T., & Mittelmark, M. B. (2008). Subjective well-being among employed lone mothers in Europe: The effects of level of work/family conflict and self-enhancement versus self-transcendence value orientation. *International Journal of Mental Health Promotion, 10,* 26–33. doi:10.1080/14623730.2008.9721766

(2009). Work life and mental wellbeing of single and non-single working mothers in Scandinavia. *Scandinavian Journal of Social Medicine, 37,* 562–568. doi:10.1177/1403494809340494

Casper, W. J., Allen, T. D., & Poelmans, S. A. (2014). International perspectives on work and family: An introduction to the special section. *Applied Psychology, 63,* 1–4. doi:10.1111/apps.12020

Christiaens, W., & Bracke, P. (2014). Work–family conflict, health services and medication use among dual-income couples in Europe. *Sociology of Health & Illness, 36,* 319–337. doi:10.1111/1467-9566.12049

*Cinamon, R. G. (2009). Role Salience, social support, and work–family conflict among Jewish and Arab Female teachers in Israel. *Journal of Career Development, 36,* 139–158.

*Cousins, C. R., & Tang, N. (2004). Working time and work and family conflict in the Netherlands, Sweden and the UK. *Work, Employment & Society, 18,* 531–549.

Craig, L., & Mullan, K. (2010). Parenthood, gender and work-family time in the United States, Australia, Italy, France, and Denmark. *Journal of Marriage and Family, 72,* 1344–1361. doi:10.1111/j.1741-3737.2010.00769.x

Day, A. L., & Chamberlain, T. C. (2006). Committing to your work, spouse, and children: Implications for work–family conflict. *Journal of Vocational Behavior, 68,* 116–130. doi:10.1016/j.jvb.2005.01.001

*Drobnic, S., & Guillén Rodríguez, A. M. (2011). Tensions Between Work and Home: Job Quality and Working Conditions in the Institutional Contexts of Germany and Spain. *Social Politics: International Studies in Gender, State & Society, 18,* 232–268.

Erickson, J. J., Martinengo, G., & Hill, E. J. (2010). Putting work and family experiences in context: Differences by family life stage. *Human Relations, 63,* 955–979. doi:10.1177/0018726709353138

*Estryn-Behar, M., Van der Heijden, B.I.J.M., Oginska, H., Camerino, D., Le Nézet, O., Conway, P. M., & the NEXT Study Group (2007). The impact of social work environment, teamwork characteristics, burnout, and personal factors upon intent. *Medical Care, 45,* 939–950.

Frone, M. R., Russell, M., & Cooper, M. L. (1992). Antecedents and outcomes of work–family conflict: testing a model of the work–family interface. *Journal of Applied Psychology, 77,* 65–78. doi:10.1037/0021-9010.77.1.65

*Gallie, D., & Russell, H. (2009). Work–family conflict and working conditions in Western Europe. *Social Indicators Research, 93,* 445–467. doi:10.1007/s11205-008-9435-0.

*Galovan, A. M., Fackrell, T., Buswell, L., Jones, B. L., Hill, E. J., & Carroll, S. J. (2010). The work–family interface in the United States and Singapore: Conflict across cultures. *Journal of Family Psychology, 24,* 646–656. doi:10.1037/a0020832

*Gaspar, M. O. (2013). The modernisation process through the perceptions of work–family in Spain and Great Britain. *European Societies, 15,* 707–728.

Greenhaus, J. H., & Beutell, N. J. (1985). Sources of conflict between work and family roles. *Academy of Management Review, 10,* 76–88.

Grzywacz, J. G., Arcury, T. A., Marín, A., Carrillo, L., Burke, B., Coates, M. L., & Quandt, S. A. (2007). Work–family conflict: Experiences and health implications among immigrant Latinos. *Journal of Applied Psychology, 92,* 1119–1130. doi:10.1037/0021-9010.92.4.1119

Grzywacz, J. G., Quandt, S. A., Arcury, T. A., & Marín, A. (2005). The work–family challenge and mental health: Experiences of Mexican immigrants. *Community, Work and Family, 8,* 271–279. doi:10.1080/13668800500142236

*Haar, J. M., Russo, M., Suñe, A., & Ollier-Malaterre, A. (2014). Outcomes of work–life balance on job satisfaction, life satisfaction and mental health: A study across seven cultures. *Journal of Vocational Behavior, 85,* 361–373. doi:10.1016/j.jvb.2014.08.010

*Halbesleben, J. R. B., Wheeler, A. R., & Rossi, A. M. (2012). The costs and benefits of working with one's spouse: A two-sample examination of spousal support, work–family conflict, and emotional exhaustion in work-linked relationships. *Journal of Organizational Behavior, 33,* 597–615. doi:10.1002/job.771

*Hassan, Z., Dollard, M. F., & Winefield, A. H. (2010). Work-family conflict in East vs Western countries. *Cross Cultural Management: An International Journal, 17,* 30–49. doi:10.1108/13527601011016899

Hill, E. J., Erickson, J. J., Fellows, K. J., Martinengo, G., & Allen, S. M. (2014). Work and family over the life course: Do older workers differ? *Journal of Family and Economic Issues, 35,* 1–13. doi:10.1007/s10834-012-9346-8

*Hill, E. J., Hawkins, A. J., Martinson, V., & Ferris, M. (2003). Studying "working fathers": Comparing fathers' and mothers' work–family conflict, fit, and adaptive strategies in a global high-tech company. *Fathering, 1,* 239–261.

*Hill, J. E., Yang, C., Hawkins, A. J., & Ferris, M. (2004). A cross-cultural test of the work–family interface in 48 countries. *Journal of Marriage and Family, 66,* 1300–1316.

House, R. J., Hanges, P. J., Javidan, M., Dorfman, P., & Gupta, V. (2004). *Culture, Leadership and Organizations: The GLOBE Study of 62 societies.* Thousand Oaks, CA: Sage.

Hsu, B. F., Chen, W. Y., Wang, M. L., & Lin, Y. Y. (2010). Explaining supervisory support to work–family conflict: The perspectives of guanxi, LMX, and emotional intelligence. *Journal of Technology Management in China, 5,* 40–54. doi:10.1108/17468771011032787

*Janssen, P. P. M., Peeters, M. C. W., Jonge, J. de, Houkes, I., & Tummers, G. E. R. (2004). Specific relationships between job demands, job resources and psychological outcomes and the mediating role of negative work–home interference. *Journal of Vocational Behavior, 65,* 411–429. doi:10.1016/j.jvb.2003.09.004

*Jin, J. F., Ford, M. T., & Chen, C. C. (2013). Asymmetric differences in work–family spillover in North America and China: Results from two heterogeneous samples. *Journal of Business Ethics, 113,* 1–14. doi:10.1007/s10551-012-1289-3

Kabasakal, H., & Bodur, M. (2004). Humane orientation in societies, organizations, and leader attributes. In R. House, P. Hanges, M. Javidan, P. Dorfman, & V. Gupta (Eds.), *Culture, Leadership, and Organizations: The GLOBE Study of 62 Societies* (pp. 564–601). Thousand Oaks, CA: Sage.

Kanter, R. M. (1977). Work and family in the United States: A critical review and agenda for research and policy. *Social Science Frontiers.* Russell Sage Foundation.

*Kasearu, K. (2009). The effect of union type on work–life conflict in five European countries. *Social Indicators Research, 93,* 549–567. doi:10.1007/s11205-008-9432-3

Kempen, R., Pangert, B., Hattrup, K., Mueller, K., & Joens, I. (2015). Beyond conflict: The role of life-domain enrichment for expatriates. *The International Journal of Human Resource Management, 26,* 1–22. doi:10.1080/09585192.2014.919954

*Kuchařová, V. (2009). Work–life balance: Societal and private influences. *Sociologický časopis/Czech Sociological Review,* (06), 1283–1310.

*Laaksonen, E., Lallukka, T., Lahelma, E., Ferrie, J. E., Rahkonen, O., Head, J., … Martikainen, P. (2011). Economic difficulties and physical functioning in Finnish and British employees: Contribution of social and behavioural factors. *European Journal of Public Health, 21,* 456–462. doi:10.1093/eurpub/ckq089

*Laaksonen, E., Martikainen, P., Lallukka, T., Lahelma, E., Ferrie, J., Rahkonen, O., … Head, J. (2009). Economic difficulties and common mental disorders among Finnish and British white-collar employees: The contribution of social and behavioural factors. *Journal of Epidemiology and Community Health, 63,* 439–446. doi:10.1136/jech.2008.077198

* Lalluka, T., Rahkonen, O., Lahelma, E., & Arber, S. (2010). Sleep complaints in middle-aged women and men: The contribution of working conditions and work-family conflicts. *Journal of Sleep Research, 19,* 466–477.

*Lapierre, L. M., Spector, P. E., Allen, T. D., Poelmans, S., Cooper, C. L., O'Driscoll, M. P., ... Kinnunen, U. (2008). Family-supportive organization perceptions, multiple dimensions of work–family conflict, and employee satisfaction: A test of model across five samples. *Journal of Vocational Behavior*, *73*, 92–106. doi:10.1016/j.jvb.2008.02.001

*Law, L. K. (2011). The impact of work–family conflict on Chinese employees. *Marriage & Family Review*, *47*, 590–604. doi:10.1080/01494929.2011.625104

*Lu, L., Cooper, C. L., Kao, S.-F., Chang, T.-T., Allen, T. D., Lapierre, L. M., ... Spector, P. E. (2010). Cross-cultural differences on work-to-family conflict and role satisfaction: A Taiwanese-British comparison. *Human Resource Management*, *49*, 67–85.

Lu, L., Gilmour, R., Kao, S. F., & Huang, M. T. (2006). A cross-cultural study of work/family demands, work/family conflict and wellbeing: The Taiwanese vs British. *Career Development International*, *11*, 9–27. doi:10.1108/13620430610642354

*Lunau, T., Bambra, C., Eikemo, T. A., van der Wel, K. A., & Dragano, N. (2014). A balancing act? Work–life balance, health and well-being in European welfare states. *The European Journal of Public Health*, *24*, 422–427. doi:10.1093/eurpub/cku010

*Lyness, K. S., Gornick, J. C., Stone, P., & Grotto, A. R. (2012). It's all about control: Worker control over schedule and hours in cross-national context. *American Sociological Review*, *77*, 1023–1049. doi:10.1177/0003122412465331

*Lyness, K. S., & Judiesch, M. K. (2014). Gender egalitarianism and work–life balance for managers: Multisource perspectives in 36 countries. *Applied Psychology*, *63*, 96–129.

*Lyness, K. S., & Kropf, M.B. (2005). The relationships of national gender equality and organizational support with work–family balance: A study of European managers. *Human Relations*, *58*, 33–60. doi:10.1177/0018726705050934

*Lyonette, C., Crompton, R., Wall, K. (2007). Gender, occupational class and work–life conflict: A comparison of Britain and Portugal. *Community, Work & Family,10*, 283–308.

Lytle, A. L., Brett, J. M., Barsness, Z. I., Tinsley, C. H., & Janssens, M. (1995). A paradigm for confirmatory cross-cultural research in organizational-behavior. *Research in Organizational Behavior*, *17*, 167–214.

*Malinen, S., & Johnston, L. (2011). Seeking a better work–life balance: Expectations and perceptions of work-related practices and attitudes of recent immigrants to New Zealand. *Asian & Pacific Migration Journal*, *20*, 233–252.

*Masuda, A. D., Poelmans, S. A. Y., Allen, T. D., Spector, P. E., Lapierre, L. M., Cooper, C. L., ... Moreno-Velazquez, I. (2012). Flexible work arrangements availability and their relationship with work-to-family conflict, job satisfaction, and turnover intentions: A comparison of three country clusters: Work-to-family conflict across countries. *Applied Psychology: An International Review*, *61*, 1–29.

McClelland, D. C. (1961). *The Achievement Society*. Princeton, NJ: Von Nostrand.

*Mortazavi, S., Pedhiwala, N., Shafiro, M., & Hammer, L. (2009). Work–family conflict related to culture and gender. *Community, Work & Family*, *12*, 251–273.

*Netemeyer, R. G., Brashear-Alejandro, T., & Boles, J. S. (2004). A cross-national model of job-related outcomes of work role and family role variables: A retail sales context. *Journal of the Academy of Marketing Sciences*, *32*, 49–60.

*Ng, T., & Feldman, D. C. (2012). The Effects of Organizational and Community Embeddedness on Work-to-Family and Family-to-Work Conflict. *Journal of Applied Psychology*, *97*, 1233–1251.

(2014). Embeddedness and well-being in the United States and Singapore: The mediating effects of work-to-family and family-to-work conflict. *Journal of Occupational Health Psychology*, *19*, 360–375. doi:10.1037/a0036922

*Notten, N., Grunow, D., & Verbakel, E. (2016). Social policies and families in stress: Gender and educational differences in work–family conflict from a European perspective. *Social Indicators Research.* Advance online publication. doi:10.1007/s11205-016-1344-z

*O'Brien, K. M., Ganginis Del Pino, H. V., Yoo, S.-K., Cinamon, R. G., & Han, Y.-J. (2014). Work, family, support, and depression: Employed mothers in Israel, Korea, and the United States. *Journal of Counseling Psychology, 61,* 461–472. doi:10.1037/a0036339

OECD (2013). *Usual working hours per week by gender.* Retrieved from www.oecd.org/els/family/LMF2_1_Usual_working_hours_by_gender_July2013.pdf

*Oishi, A. S., Chan, R. K. H., Wang, L. L.-R., & Kim, J.-H. (2015). Do part-time jobs mitigate workers' work–family conflict and enhance wellbeing? New evidence from four East-Asian societies. *Social Indicators Research, 121,* 5–25. doi:10.1007/s11205-014-0624-8

Ollier-Malaterre, A. (2016). Cross-national work–life research: Cultural and structural impacts for individuals and organizations. *Journal of Management, 43,* 111–136. doi:10.1177/0149206316655873

*Ollier-Malaterre, A., Sarkisian, N., Stawiski, S., & Hannum, K. M. (2013). Work–life balance and performance across countries: Cultural and institutional approaches. In D. A. Major & R. Burke (Eds.), *Handbook of Work–Life Integration Among Professionals: Challenges and Opportunities* (pp. 357–380). Northampton, MA US: Edward Elgar Publishing.

*Öun, I. (2012). Work–family conflict in the Nordic countries: A comparative analysis. *Journal of Comparative Family Studies,* 165–184.

*Pal, S., & Saksvik, P. O. (2006). A comparative study of Work and Family Conflict in Norwegian and Indian Hospitals. *Nordic Psychology, 58,* 298.

(2008). Work–family conflict and psychosocial work environment stressors as predictors of job stress in a cross-cultural study. *International Journal of Stress Management, 15,* 22–42.

Poelmans, S.A.Y., O'Driscoll, M., & Beham, B. (2005). An overview of international research on the work–family interface. In S.A.Y. Poelmans (Ed.), *Work and Family: An International Research Perspective* (pp. 3–37). Mahwah, NJ: Lawrence Erlbaum Associates.

*Posthuma, R. A., Joplin, J. R. W., & Maertz, C. P. (2005). Comparing the validity of turnover predictors in the United States and Mexico. *International Journal of Cross Cultural Management, 5,* 165–180.

*Rantanen, J., Kinnunen, U., Mauno, S., & Tement, S. (2013). Patterns of conflict and enrichment in work–family balance: a three-dimensional typology. *Work & Stress, 27,* 141–163.

Romeo, M., Berger, R., Yepes-Baldó, M., & Ramos, B. (2014). Adaptation and validation of the Spanish Version of the "Survey Work-Home Interaction–NijmeGen" (SWING) to Spanish speaking countries. *Annals of Psychology, 30,* 287–293. doi:10.6018/analesps.30.1.148291

*Ruppanner, L. (2013). Conflict between work and family: An investigation of four policy measures. *Social Indicators Research, 110,* 327–347.

*Ruppanner, L., & Huffman, M. L. (2014). Blurred boundaries: Gender and work–family interference in cross-national context. *Work and Occupations, 41,* 210–236.

*Sanseau, P., & Smith, M. (2012). Regulatory change and work–life integration in France and the UK. *Personnel Review, 41,* 470–486.

*Schieman, S., & Young, M. (2015). Who engages in work–family multitasking? A study of Canadian and American workers. *Social Indicators Research, 120*, 741–767.

Shaffer, M. A., Harrison, D. A., Gilley, K. M., & Luk, D. M. (2001). Struggling for balance amid turbulence on international assignments: Work–family conflict, support and commitment. *Journal of Management, 27*, 99–121. doi:10.1177/014920630102700106

Shaffer, M. A., Joplin, J. R., & Hsu, Y. S. (2011). Expanding the boundaries of work–family research: A review and agenda for future research. *International Journal of Cross Cultural Management, 11*, 221–268. doi:10.1177/1470595811398800

Shih, H. A., Chiang, Y. H., & Hsu, C. C. (2010). High involvement work system, work–family conflict, and expatriate performance–examining Taiwanese expatriates in China. *The International Journal of Human Resource Management, 21*, 2013–2030. doi:10.1080/09585192.2010.505101

Shockley, K.M., Douek, J., Smith, C.R., Yu, P.P., Dumani, S., & French, K.A. (in press) Cross-cultural work and family research: A review of the literature. *Journal of Vocational Behavior.*

Shockley, K.M., Shen, W., Denunzio, M.M., Arvan, M.L., & Knudsen, E.A. (in press). Disentangling the relationship between gender and work-family conflict: An integration of theoretical perspectives using meta-analytic methods. *Journal of Applied Psychology.*

Shukri, M., Jones, F., & Conner, M. (2016). Work factors, work–family conflict, the theory of planned behaviour and healthy intentions: A cross-cultural study. *Stress and Health, 32*, 559–568. doi:10.1002/smi.2662

*Simon, M., Kümmerling, A., & Hasselhorn, H.-M. (2004). Work-home conflict in the European nursing profession. *International Journal of Occupational and Environmental Health, 10*, 384–391. doi:10.1179/oeh.2004.10.4.384

*Smyrnios, K. X., Romano, C. A., Tanewski, G. A., Karofsky, P. I., Millen, R., & Yilmaz, M. R. (2003). Work–family conflict: A study of American and Australian family businesses. *Family Business Review, 16*, 35–51. doi:10.1111/j.1741-6248.2003.00035.x

Spector, P. E., Allen, T. D., Poelmans, S. A., Cooper, C. L., Bernin, P., Hart, P., ... & Yu, S. (2005). An international comparative study of work/family stress and occupational strain. In S. A. Y. Poelmans (Ed.), *Work and Family: An International Research Perspective* (pp. 71–84). Mahwah, NJ: Lawrence Erlbaum.

*Spector, P. E., Allen, T. D., Poelmans, S. A., Lapierre, L. M., Cooper, C. L., O'Driscoll, M., ... Widerszal-Bazyl, M. (2007). Cross-national differences in relationships of work demands, job satisfaction, and turnover intentions with work–family conflict. *Personnel Psychology, 60*, 805–835.

*Spector, P. E., Cooper, C. L., Poelmans, S., Allen, T. D., O'Driscoll, M., Sanchez, J. I., ... Yu, S. (2004). A cross-national comparative study of work–family stressors, working hours, and well-being: China and Latin American versus the Anglo world. *Personnel Psychology, 57*, 119–142.

Spector, P.E., Liu, C., & Sanchez, J.I. (2015). Methodological and substantive issues in conducting multinational and cross-cultural research. *Annual Review of Organizational Psychology and Organizational Behavior, 2*, 101–31.

*Steiber, N. (2009). Reported levels of time-based and strain-based conflict between work and family roles in Europe: A multilevel approach. *Social Indicators Research, 93*, 469–488. doi:10.1007/s11205-008-9436-z

*Strandh, M., & Nordenmark, M. (2006). The interference of paid work with household demands in different social policy contexts: Perceived work-household conflict in

Sweden, the UK, the Netherlands, Hungary, and the Czech Republic. *British Journal of Sociology, 57*, 597–617.

*Syed, S., Arain, G. A., Schalk, R., & Freese, C. (2015). Balancing work and family obligations in Pakistan and the Netherlands: A Comparative Study. *Global Business and Organizational Excellence, 34*, 39–52. doi:10.1002/joe.21625

Takeuchi, R., Yun, S., & Tesluk, P. E. (2002). An examination of crossover and spillover effects of spousal and expatriate cross-cultural adjustment on expatriate outcomes. *Journal of Applied Psychology, 87*, 655–666. doi:10.1037/0021–9010.87.4.655

Timms, C., Brough, P., Siu, O. L., O'Driscoll, M., & Kalliath, T. (2015). Cross-cultural impact of work–life balance on health and work outcomes. In L. Lu & C. L. Cooper (Eds.), *Handbook of Research on work–Life Balance in Asia*, 295–314.

*Van der Lippe, T., Jager, A., & Kops, Y. (2006). Combination pressure: The paid work–family balance of men and women in European countries. *Acta Sociologica, 49*, 303–319.

Vandenberg, R. J., & Lance, C. E. (2000). A review and synthesis of the measurement invariance literature: Suggestions, practices, and recommendations for organizational research. *Organizational Research Methods, 3*, 4–70. doi:10.1177/109442810031002

*Wang, P., Lawler, J. J., & Shi, K. (2011). Implementing family-friendly employment practices in baking industry: Evidences from some African and Asian countries. *Journal of Occupational and Organizational Psychology, 84*, 493–517.

(2010). Work–family conflict, self-efficacy, job satisfaction, and gender: Evidences from Asia. *Journal of Leadership & Organizational Studies, 17*, 298–308. doi:10.1177/1548051810368546

*Wang, P., Lawler, J. J., Walumbwa, F. O., & Shi, K. (2004). Work–family conflict and job withdrawal intentions: The moderating effect of cultural differences. *International Journal of Stress Management, 4*, 392–412.

*Weckstrom, S. (2011). Working mothers in Finland: A cross-country comparison of work to family interference, work characteristics and satisfaction with life. *Finnish Yearbook of Population Research, 46*, 71–94.

*Wharton, A. S., & Blair-Loy, M. (2006). Long work hours and family life: A cross-national study of employees' concerns. *Journal of Family Issues, 27*, 415–436.

*Wierda-Boer, H. H., Gerris, J., Vermulst, A., Malinen, K., & Anderson, K. (2009). Combination strategies and work–family interface among dual-earner couples in Finland, Germany, and the Netherlands. *Community, Work, & Family, 12*, 233–249.

Wiese, B.S., & Salmela-Aro, K. (2008). Goal conflict and facilitation as predictors of work–family satisfaction and engagement. *Journal of Vocational Behavior, 73*, 490–497.

*Yang, N. (2005). Individualism-collectivism and work–family interfaces: A Sino-U.S. comparison. In S. A. Y. Poelmans (Ed.), *Work and Family: An International Research Perspective* (pp. 287–318). Mahwah, NJ: Lawrence Erlbaum Associates.

*Yang, N., Chen, C. C., Choi, J., & Zou, Y. (2000). Sources of work–family conflict: A Sino-U.S. Comparison of the effects of work and family demands. *Academy of Management Journal, 43*, 113–123. doi:10.2307/1556390

*Yeh, H.-J. (2015). Job demands, job resources, and job satisfaction in East Asia. *Social Indicators Research, 121*, 47–60. doi:10.1007/s11205-014-0631-9

3 GLOBE's Cultural Dimensions: Implications for Global Work–Family Research

Ariane Ollier-Malaterre and Annie Foucreault

The Global Leadership and Organizational Behavior Effectiveness (GLOBE) project was initiated in 1991 by Robert J. House. Among the existing frameworks that capture culture at the country level, GLOBE stands out as a very rigorous and coordinated effort to improve on prior research. On the one hand, GLOBE builds on prior research, including the seminal work of de Tocqueville (1946) and Mead (1967), and the later work of Hofstede, Inglehart, Schwartz, and Triandis (Hofstede, 1980; Inglehart, 1997; Schwartz, 1994; Triandis, 1989). On the other hand, no other project has been so encompassing in terms of including local scholars into the design and the implementation of the study, uniting a team of 170 "country co-investigators" and fourteen coordinators and research associates across sixty-two countries.

The GLOBE project identified nine cultural dimensions. Despite its great potential, this framework is still largely untapped in work–life research. In this chapter, we begin by presenting GLOBE's framework: we introduce the nine cultural dimensions, the country clusters, and propose a brief critique of the framework's strengths and weaknesses. A second section reviews work–life research that draws on GLOBE's dimensions, whether at the theoretical or the empirical level. Lastly, we outline the main gaps in current work–life research using GLOBE and sketch out an agenda for research.

GLOBE's Cultural Dimensions and Country Clusters

The main objective of GLOBE was to capture cross-national similarities and/or differences in norms, values, beliefs, and practices (House, Hanges, Javidan, Dorfman, & Gupta, 2004). The research team conceptualized culture as a multi-layer concept characterized by values and assumptions at the base and by practices and artifacts at the surface. Thus, the project aimed to capture both practices ("as is") and societal values ("should be"; Yeganeh, Su, & Sauers, 2009).

Data Collection

GLOBE collected data from 17,300 middle managers in 951 organizations in the food processing, financial services, and telecommunication services industries over the period of 1995–1999. This careful sampling has ensured stronger generalizability across industry sectors and respondent gender than Hofstede's otherwise popular work (Hofstede, 1980), as Hofstede had designed the IBM surveys as head of the Personnel Research Department and collected data from IBM male managers only (Moulettes, 2007). In addition, GLOBE relied on a team of 170 scholars around the world (House et al., 1999; Terlutter, Diehl, & Mueller, 2006), thereby offering a less ethnocentric perspective than Geert Hofstede who, despite all his travels, was embedded in a single cultural context.

Respondents were asked to describe beliefs and norms within their organization and within the society they lived in. Most of the questionnaire was written as sets of four questions having similar structures across two levels of analysis (societal and organizational) and across the two cultural manifestations (values = "should be" and practices = "as is"), using seven-point Likert response scales. The full questionnaires in several languages can be accessed at: www.uvic.ca/gustavson/globe/research/instru ments/index.php. The questionnaires at the organizational level are labeled Alpha (www.uvic.ca/gustavson/globe/assets/docs/GLOBE-Phase-2-Alpha-Questionnaire-2006.pdf) and the questionnaires at the societal level are labeled Beta (www.uvic.ca /gustavson/globe/assets/docs/GLOBE-Phase-2-Beta-Questionnaire-2006.pdf).

The Nine Cultural Dimensions

Nine cultural dimensions were identified by the GLOBE project (House, Javidan, & Dorfman, 2001). Each dimension is defined below, with sample items for values ("should be") and practices ("as is"). Responses are set on a Likert scale with the specific content of the scale points indicted. In Table 3.1, we present the three main countries that scored the lowest and the highest for each value and practice. The country scores for these dimensions are also available on the GLOBE website: http://globeproject.com/study_2004_2007#data.

(1) **Power distance** is the extent to which individuals in a society agree about an unequal division of power, that is, a stratification of power such that power is concentrated at higher levels of an organization or government. A sample item for the value of power distance is: "When in disagreement with adults, young people should defer to elders: strongly disagree – strongly agree." A sample item for the practice of power distance is: "In this society, followers are expected to: obey their leader without questions – question their leaders when in disagreements."

(2) **Uncertainty avoidance** is the degree to which people try to avoid future unpredictability by relying on social norms, rituals, and bureaucratic practices. A sample item for the value of uncertainty avoidance is: "I believe that a person who leads a structured life that has few unexpected events: has a lot to be thankful for – is missing a lot of excitement." A sample item for the practice of uncertainty avoidance is: "This society has rules or laws to cover: almost all situations – very few situations."

(3) **Institutional collectivism** is the degree to which individuals in a society receive encouragements and rewards for the collective distribution of resources and

Table 3.1 *Countries that scored the lowest and the highest on each GLOBE cultural dimension*

Cultural Dimensions	Values		Practices	
	Lowest	Highest	Lowest	Highest
Power distance	Colombia	Czech Republic	Czech Republic	Morocco
	Finland	South Africa	Denmark	Nigeria
	Spain	New Zealand	South Africa	El Salvador
Uncertainty avoidance	Switzerland	Thailand	Russia	Switzerland
	Netherlands	Nigeria	Hungary	Sweden
	Germany (West)	Albania	Guatemala	Singapore
Institutional collectivism	Georgia	El Salvador	Greece	Sweden
	Czech Republic	Brazil	Hungary	South Korea
	Russia	Iran	Germany (East)	Japan
In-group collectivism	Czech Republic	El Salvador	Czech Republic	Philippines
	Switzerland	Colombia	Denmark	Georgia
	South Africa	New Zealand	Sweden	Iran
Gender egalitarianism	Egypt	England	South Korea	Hungary
	Qatar	Sweden	Kuwait	Russia
	Kuwait	Ireland	Egypt	Poland
Future orientation	Czech Republic	Thailand	Russia	Singapore
	Denmark	Namibia	Argentina	Switzerland
	China	Zimbabwe	Poland	South Africa
Assertiveness	Turkey	Japan	Sweden	Albania
	Austria	China	New Zealand	Nigeria
	Russia	Philippines	French Switzerland	Hungary
Humane orientation	Czech Republic	Nigeria	Germany (West)	Zambia
	New Zealand	Finland	Spain	Philippines
	Costa Rica	Singapore	Greece	Ireland
Performance orientation	Czech Republic	El Salvador	Greece	Switzerland
	South Africa	Zimbabwe	Venezuela	Singapore
	Japan	Colombia	Russia	Albania

Note. The information presented in this table is derived from the database of GLOBE's (2004) phase 2 aggregated societal level data for society culture scales.

collective action. A sample item for the value of institutional collectivism is: "I believe that in general, leaders should encourage group loyalty even if individual goals suffer: strongly disagree – strongly agree." A sample item for the practice of institutional collectivism is: "In this society, being accepted by the other members of a group is very important: strongly disagree – strongly agree."

(4) **In-group collectivism** is the degree to which people in a society are prone to demonstrate their loyalty, their pride and their cohesiveness to others and in particular their families and organizations. A sample item for the value of

in-group collectivism is: "In this society, children should take pride in the individual accomplishments of their parents: strongly disagree – strongly agree." A sample item for the practice of in-group collectivism is: "In this society, aging parents generally live at home with their children: strongly disagree – strongly agree."

(5) **Gender egalitarianism** is the extent to which a society reduces gender role differences and discrimination and promotes gender equality. A sample item for the value of gender egalitarianism is: "I believe that this society would be more effectively managed if there were: many more women in positions of authority than there are now – about the same number of women in positions of authority as there are now – many less women in positions of authority than there are now." A sample item for the practice of gender egalitarianism is: "In this society, boys are encouraged more than girls to attain a higher education."

(6) **Humane orientation** is the extent to which fairness, altruism, caring, friendliness, and generosity are encouraged and rewarded in a society. A sample item for the value of humane orientation is: "In this society, people should be encouraged to be: very tolerant of mistakes – not at all tolerant of mistakes." A sample item for the practice of humane orientation is: "In this society, people are generally: very sensitive toward others – not at all sensitive toward others."

(7) **Performance orientation** is the degree to which performance improvement and excellence are rewarded in a society. A sample item for the value of performance orientation is: "I believe that people should set challenging goals for themselves: strongly disagree – strongly agree." A sample item for the practice of performance orientation is: "In this society, major rewards are based on: only performance effectiveness – performance effectiveness and other factors – only factors other than performance (for example, seniority or political connections)."

(8) **Assertiveness** is the extent to which individuals are assertive, confrontational and aggressive when interacting with others. A sample item for the value of assertiveness is: "In this society, people should be encouraged to be: dominant – non-dominant." A sample item for the practice of assertiveness is: "In this society, people are generally: assertive – nonassertive."

(9) **Future orientation** is the degree to which a society values future-oriented behaviors such as planning, investing in the future, and delaying individual or collective gratification. A sample item for the value of future orientation is: "I believe that people who are successful should: plan ahead – take life events as they occur." A sample item for the practice of future orientation is: "In this society, social gatherings are: planned well in advance (2 weeks or more in advance) – spontaneous (planned less than an hour in advance)."

Country Clusters

Beyond the nine cultural dimensions, GLOBE also provided a set of ten country clusters, illustrated in Figure 3.1 (House et al., 2004). The purpose of these clusters is to represent overall cultural similarity and differences across countries. Cultural similarity is greatest among societies that constitute a cluster and the location of

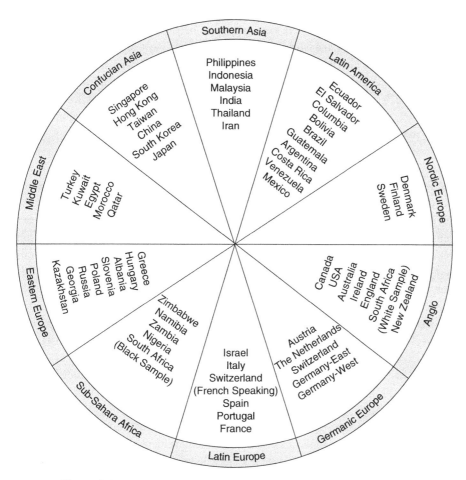

Figure 3.1 *GLOBE's country clusters.*
Source: Adapted from House, R.J., Hanges, P.K., Javidan, M., Dorfman, P.W., & Gupta, V. (2004). *Culture, Leadership, and Organizations: The GLOBE Study of 62 Societies.* Copyright @ 2004, Sage Publications, Inc. Reprinted with permission.

clusters on Figure 3.1 indicates how similar different clusters are to each other. For instance, respondents from the ten countries comprising the Latin American cluster, including Argentina, Brazil and Mexico, answered the questions in ways that present similarities. These countries are also more different than the Sub-Sahara Africa culture, positioned diagonally from the Latin American cluster on the figure, than from the Southern Asia or Nordic European clusters which are adjacent.

Strengths and Weaknesses of the GLOBE Framework

Many strengths of the GLOBE project have been recognized by scholars. These include the following: (1) diverse (quantitative and qualitative) methodologies were employed to increase the richness of the framework, (2) the measures used to develop the nine dimensions have been proven to be reliable and valid, and (3) more than 170 scholars around the world have worked on this project, allowing for a reduction of the ethnocentric bias that was present in Hofstede's work (House et al., 1999).

In spite of all these strengths, however, it is extremely challenging to measure culture at such a global scale, and the GLOBE project, like all the other research that has attempted to do so, has been criticized. First, the data were collected only from middle managers; although this helps to ensure comparability across countries, it also reduces the representativeness of the sample (Hofstede, 2006). Second, the measures present some challenges. In particular, some of the items used to capture the dimensions seem to have a narrow scope – for instance, two items of the gender egalitarianism practice scales pertain to education and two pertain to athletic programs and to being "physical" – the meaning of the latter may be unclear. Items' heterogeneity (Maseland & Van Hoorn, 2009) is also a challenge, as the responses scales vary within some of the dimensions. Third, some of the dimensions (e.g., performance orientation) have been considered not broad enough to be regarded as pure cultural values; it has been argued that instead they should be seen as organizational values (Yeganeh et al., 2009). Perhaps the most perplexing for scholars using the country scores or collecting data using the scales is the fact that the values and practices scores are generally negatively correlated. This means that for the same dimension (e.g., power distance), a given country can score high on the "should be" items and low on the "as is" items. Thus, the research findings are not easily interpreted (Maseland & Van Hoorn, 2009). Maseland and Van Hoorn (2009) explained these negative correlations between practices and values with the principle of diminishing marginal utility. They supposed that if an objective such as gender equality is satiated (i.e., high scores on the practice dimension), the value people attached to the achievement of this objective falls. By opposition, when individuals are far from achieving an objective (i.e., low scores on the practice dimension), this objective is generally valued highly. Scholars thus need to be clear on their theoretical reasoning (is it values or practices or both that should be considered) and on their measures (i.e., values or practices scores/scales) so that knowledge on the interpretation of these negative correlations can accumulate.

Review of Cross-National Work–life Research Drawing on GLOBE's Dimensions

In this section, we review theoretical arguments as well as empirical research linking work–life constructs at the individual or organizational level to each of GLOBE's nine dimensions. Table 3.2 illustrates the studies that are reviewed as well as the work–life constructs that they examine.

Power Distance

Only one known study in the work–life literature has empirically examined power distance, building on Ashforth, Kreiner, and Fugate's (2000) ideas about integration

Table 3.2 *Empirical studies on the impact of GLOBE's cultural dimensions on the work–life interface*

Cultural Dimensions	Work–Life Constructs	Studies
Power distance	Work–family conflict	Ollo-López and Goñi-Legaz (2015)
Uncertainty avoidance	Work–family conflict Work–life balance (well-being)	Ollo-López & Goñi-Legaz (2015) Lucia-Casademunt et al. (2015)
Institutional collectivism	Work–family conflict Work–family enrichment	Allen et al. (2015); Beham et al. (2014)
In-group collectivism	Work–family conflict	Allen et al. (2015); Masuda et al. (2012); Ollo-López & Goñi-Legaz (2015); Spector et al. (2004, 2007); Yang et al. (2000)
	Work–life balance Flexible work arrangements	Haar et al. (2014) Masuda et al. (2012)
Gender egalitarianism	Work–family conflict	Allen et al. (2015); Lyness & Judiesch (2014); Ollo-López & Goñi-Legaz (2015)
	Work–life balance Work–family enrichment	Lyness & Judiesch (2014) Beham et al. (2017)
Humane orientation	Work–family conflict Work–family enrichment	Ollo-López & Goñi-Legaz (2015) Beham et al. (2014)

and segmentation of life roles. Ollo-López and Goñi-Legaz (2015) hypothesized that individuals in high (versus low) power distance societies would experience lower work–family conflict because they would be more likely to segment roles, reducing the opportunity for conflict. Cultures high in power distance are characterized by stricter social order, respect for tradition and limited upward social mobility and, as stated by Ollier-Malaterre (2015), the more differences in status and power there are in a culture, the more individuals are likely to segment their life roles. Others have argued that work–family conflict is higher in lower power distance societies because the greater empowerment and responsibility of employees in low power distance cultures may create higher job demands and internalized work pressures, which relate positively to work–family conflict (Billing et al., 2013; Ollier-Malaterre, 2015). However, Ollo-López and Goñi-Legaz (2015) tested this main effect based on data from the Second European Quality of Life Survey collected from 5,959 employees in 17 countries in 2008 and found no significant relationship between practices ("as is") scores of power distance and work–family conflict (aggregate measure of work-to-family and family-to-work conflict).

Moreover, two additional hypotheses have been put forth but remain untested. First, Ollier-Malaterre (2015) suggested that individuals in low (versus high) power distance societies should experience greater work–family enrichment. She posited that, as individuals in these societies have more autonomy in achieving their tasks, their jobs are usually more empowering and rewarding. In turn, rewarding jobs may promote resource gains at work, such as positive emotions, that could spill over into the personal life domain and benefit employees' family role (Ollier-Malaterre, 2015). The second hypothesis pertains to segmentation/integration of life roles. Similar to what Ollo-López and Goñi-Legaz (2015) suggested but based on different rationale, it has been argued that individuals in low (versus high) power distance societies should integrate their work and life roles more because low power distance societies may be conducive of greater informality and more holistic reasoning (Ashforth et al., 2000; Ollier-Malaterre, 2015).

Uncertainty Avoidance

Ollo-López and Goñi-Legaz (2015) also hypothesized that high uncertainty avoidance would be associated with lower work–family conflict, reasoning that high uncertainty avoidance leads to the development of transition rituals and more rigid boundaries, to lesser permeability and flexibility of roles, and therefore to behaviors geared toward greater segmentation (Ashforth et al., 2000; Ollier-Malaterre, 2015). Indeed, high uncertainty avoidance practices scores ("as is") were significantly associated with lower work–family conflict across the seventeen European countries in the sample (Ollo-López & Goñi-Legaz, 2015). However, the specific hypothesis that boundary management behaviors mediate this relationship (Ollier-Malaterre, 2015), because individuals in low (versus high) uncertainty avoidance societies may integrate their work and life roles more, has not been tested yet.

GLOBE's uncertainty avoidance dimension has also been tested in relation to the effectiveness of organizational work–family practices in tourism firms, which offer 24/7 services and therefore place high demands on their employees. Based on data from the 2010 European Working Conditions Survey, and using uncertainty avoidance values scores as the moderator, work–family practices (i.e., flexibility in the scheduling of work and fit between work hours and family/social commitments outside of work) were found to be positively associated with employees' well-being in high uncertainty avoidance but not in low uncertainty avoidance cultures (Lucia-Casademunt, García-Cabrera, & Cuéllar-Molina, 2015).

Institutional Collectivism

Only one known primary study has drawn on GLOBE's institutional collectivism dimension. Beham et al. (2014) found that in seven European countries, among a sample of 2,687 service workers who were cohabiting or married with at least one child in the household, developmental work–family enrichment (i.e., the degree to which investment in one role allows for a transfer of skills and knowledge in another role; Carlson, Kacmar, Wayne, & Grzywacz, 2006) was associated positively with institutional collectivism practices ("as is") and negatively with institutional collectivism values ("should be"). These authors suggested that in societies high in institutional collectivism practices, which have a collective interest and maintain group loyalty, the integration of family and paid employment is generally supported by the state. In these countries, the actions undertaken by the state can thus offer opportunities for work–family enrichment. However, as the GLOBE project reports a negative relationship between institutional collectivism practices and values, individuals in countries scoring high on institutional collectivism values may lack the institutional practices that facilitate work–life integration. These findings thus illustrate the complexity of interpreting empirical findings when the values and practices scores are negatively correlated.

In-group Collectivism

It has been hypothesized that members of in-group collectivistic (versus individualistic) cultures should experience: (1) less work–family conflict, because they receive more social support from their extended family (e.g., for childcare or meal preparation), (2) greater work–family enrichment, because involvement in work is perceived as a way of supporting one's family (Ollier-Malaterre, 2015; Powell, Francesco, & Ling, 2009), and (3) greater integration of their work and life roles, because identities tend to be based on group memberships and they might thus be more likely to view their different roles as integrated than individuals in individualistic cultures (Ashforth et al., 2000).

To date, only the hypothesis regarding work–family conflict has been tested. In a meta-analysis that involved aggregating information from many primary studies of work–family conflict conducted across the globe, Allen et al. (2015) found that individuals from individualistic (versus collectivistic) countries reported less family-to-work conflict, but there were no significant differences regarding work-to-family conflict. They also noted that it is important to disentangle culture from ethnicity, as collectivism may have different origins and implications across ethnicities. They found that individuals in Asian cultures, where collectivism stems from Confucianism and implies a range of duties toward elders, reported greater family-to-work conflict than individuals in Latin/Hispanic collectivistic cultures, where family may be a greater source of support (Allen et al., 2015).

Other studies examined in-group collectivism as a moderator between work–life constructs and antecedents or outcomes. Spector and colleagues (2004, 2007) used several measures of individualism-collectivism, including GLOBE's in-group collectivism practices ("as is"). In two exemplar studies of fifteen and twenty countries that collected data through a network of local scholars, the Collaborative International Study of Managerial Stress (CISMS) and CISMS 2, the relationship between work demands and strain-based work-to-family conflict was found to be more negative in individualistic (versus collectivistic) countries (Spector et al., 2007; Spector et al., 2004). They argued that individuals in the Anglo cluster of countries (i.e., individualistic cultures) likely view working long hours as detracting from their families, which may provoke feelings of guilt and an increased perception of work-to-family conflict. By contrast, individuals in China and Latin American (i.e., collectivistic cultures and also developing economies) are more likely to perceive long working hours as necessary to provide for the family and open up new opportunities for children (Spector et al., 2004; Yang, Chen, Choi, & Zou, 2000). Another study also examined in-group collectivism practices ("as is") with regard to the outcomes of work–life balance across seven cultures and found that high levels of work–life balance were more positively associated with job and life satisfaction for individuals in individualistic (versus collectivistic) cultures (Haar, Russo, Sune, & Ollier-Malaterre, 2014).

Lastly, Masuda and colleagues (2012), using the CISMS country clusters, found that part-time, flextime, and telecommuting work were more prevalent in individualistic (versus collectivistic) cultures, perhaps because these practices reflect the individualistic values of autonomy and transactional employment relationships (Masuda et al., 2012). In addition, they found cultural differences in the outcomes of these practices: flextime had very favorable outcomes for Anglo managers, part-time work had favorable outcomes in terms of strain-based work–family conflict for Latin American but not Asian managers, and telecommuting had negative outcomes in terms of strain-based work–family conflict for Asian managers (Masuda et al., 2012).

To summarize previous studies on in-group collectivism, it has been hypothesized that individuals will experience more work–life enrichment and integration in collectivistic (versus individualistic) cultures (Ashforth et al., 2000; Ollier-Malaterre, 2015; Powell et al., 2009). However, to date, this has not been verified and only the influence of in-group collectivism on work–family conflict and work–family balance has been empirically tested. Results indicate that individuals from individualistic (versus collectivistic) countries report less family-to-work conflict, but the findings regarding work-to-family conflict are less clear and may be driven by ethnicity more than by national culture (Allen et al., 2015). In addition, individuals in individualistic cultures benefit from more formal work–family organizational initiatives (e.g., flextime; Masuda et al., 2012), and report higher levels of job and life satisfaction when they are satisfied with their level of balance between their work and family roles (Lyness & Judiesch, 2014).

Gender Egalitarianism

Powell et al. (2009) hypothesized that work-to-family and family-to work conflict are more gender-dependent in low egalitarian (versus high egalitarian) cultures. This proposition is based on the argument that traditional gender roles are emphasized more in low gender egalitarian (versus high egalitarian) cultures. According to Greenhaus and Parasuraman (1987), when individuals invest their resources in one role, they have more difficulty responding to another role's demands. It is thus expected that due to the greater investment of men at work and of women at home in low egalitarian (versus high egalitarian) cultures, women will perceive higher levels of family-to-work conflict and lower levels of work-to-family conflict than men. Empirically, results have been mixed. In a 36-country study, Lyness and Judiesch (2014) found that women reported higher work–family conflict in countries where achieved gender equality was low. In this study, gender equality was evaluated with the Gender Inequality Index (GII; United Nations Development Programme, 2010), a composite of objective measures of gender inequalities (e.g., women's representation in the labor force). However, in another study conducted by Ollo-López and Goñi-Legaz (2015), GLOBE's gender egalitarianism practices did not predict work–family conflict for men nor for women.

With regard to other constructs, Lyness and Judiesch (2014) also examined work–life balance for men and women. Although GLOBE's gender egalitarianism practices and values scores were not associated with self-rated work–life balance for men or women, other measures of gender egalitarianism were predictive of employees' work–life balance. These other measures were the GII (United Nations Development Programme, 2010) and a measure of patriarchal values of the World Values Survey (WVS; World Values Survey Association, 2009). However, Lyness and Judiesch (2014) also reported that supervisors rated women's work–life balance lower than men's in countries with low gender egalitarianism values ("should be"), but not in countries with high gender egalitarianism values. This indicates that individuals in a position of power (i.e., supervisors) rely more on gender role stereotypes than on individuating information in their evaluations. The same effect was not seen with gender egalitarian practices, perhaps because they had little variance across the thirty-six countries (Lyness & Judiesch, 2014). Regarding work–family enrichment, gender differences in work–family enrichment have been found to be greater in countries with higher gender egalitarianism practices in a sample of eight European countries, contrary to Powell et al.'s (2009) hypothesis. This finding could be explained by the greater prevalence of part-time work in the gender egalitarian countries of the sample, enabling women to experience greater enrichment than men (Beham et al., 2017).

Humane Orientation

Few empirical studies have included GLOBE's humane orientation dimension. It has been hypothesized that individuals in low (versus high) humane-oriented cultures should experience greater work-to-family conflict because they receive less social support in these cultures, but that they should experience less family-to-work conflict (Powell et al., 2009) because family may be of less importance and thus create fewer demands (Hassan, Dollard, & Winefield, 2010). Partially in line with Powell et al.'s (2009) predictions, Ollo-López and Goñi-Legaz (2015) found that men, but not women, report lower work–family conflict (using a combined measure of work-to-family and family-to-work conflict) in high humane orientation practices countries.

Powell et al. (2009) hypothesized that individuals may experience greater work–family enrichment in high humane-oriented cultures as individuals express more social support in these cultures and that the support received in one role (e.g., organizational support such as parental leave) may increase positive interactions between domains. Supporting this hypothesis, Beham et al. (2014) found a direct positive association between humane orientation practices and the specific dimension of developmental work–family enrichment. However, these authors also examined the influence of culture on the relationship between work resources and work–family enrichment and found a moderating effect in the opposite direction than the one posited by Powell et al. (2009), such that job variety (a resource) was more strongly associated with work–family enrichment in low (versus high) humane-oriented cultures. In cultures where humane orientation is high, individuals may have similar chances to transfer their work-related resources (e.g., job variety) in a work–family enrichment process, while in low humane-oriented cultures, only individuals having a high level of job variety may be able to do so in an efficient way.

Another hypothesis regarding role segmentation is that individuals in low (versus high) humane-oriented cultures may segment their work and life roles more because they may perceive themselves as more self-sufficient than those in high humane-oriented cultures that value concern for others and care (Ollier-Malaterre, 2015). This hypothesis remains empirically untested.

Performance Orientation

Theoretically, GLOBE's performance orientation dimension should be related to work–life balance, although this relationship has not been tested yet. It has been argued, specifically, that individuals may experience greater work–life balance in low performance orientation cultures because these cultures tend to value quality of life and relationships and emphasize who you are more than what you do, whereas high performance orientation cultures are competitive, value materialism, and emphasize what you do more than who you are (Ollier-Malaterre, Sarkisian, Stawiski, & Hannum, 2013). In fact, in societies that are high in performance orientation and in which objective performance is valued more than interpersonal relationships, balancing work and life demands may be less realistic and reachable than in societies that are low in performance orientation and in which the emphasis lies more on interpersonal loyalty and quality of life (Ollier-Malaterre et al., 2013).

Assertiveness

Although it has not been discussed in the literature, we posit that assertiveness could have implications for the work–life interface, but the nature of these relationships remains unclear. On the one hand, individuals in assertive cultures may be more able to request and secure social support or to access organizational work–life practices than individuals in less assertive cultures. On the other hand, it is also possible that social support is greater in less assertive cultures that are less confrontational, and that demands are greater at work and in the family domains in more aggressive cultures. None of this has, to our knowledge, been tested so far.

Future Orientation

Likewise, there has been little attention paid to future orientation in work–life studies. This may be important because it is possible that experiences of work–life conflict and of work–life enrichment have different time horizons. Consider for instance typical occurrences of work–life conflict, such as being late to pick up a child at daycare, or worrying that one may lose one's job if a dependent falls sick again: these experiences tend to occur on a recurring and short-term basis. By contrast, becoming aware of the acquisition or refinement of skills, knowledge, and perspectives at work that helps one to be a better family member, or vice versa (Carlson et al., 2006), requires time and a retrospective or prospective reflection on the benefits of being involved in multiple life roles. Likewise, building up and becoming aware of the psychosocial resources that are accumulated through involvement in multiple life roles, such as a sense of security, confidence, accomplishment, or self-fulfillment (Carlson et al., 2006), likely happens over the course of several years. Therefore, we argue that being oriented toward a longer time horizon may help individuals to focus less on the daily hurdles of juggling work and life, which are typically experienced as work–life conflict, and more on the benefits of being engaged in several life roles, which contribute to perceptions of work–life enrichment and possibly work–life balance as well.

It is also likely that managers in longer-term oriented cultures are more sensitive to sustainability issues and, therefore, more likely to see the long-term value of giving their employees access to flexible working arrangements and schedule controls so that they are able to strive for work–life balance and avoid burnout.

Agenda for Future Research

Although GLOBE appears to be one of the most rigorous and accessible cultural frameworks for cross-national work–life research, this review points out that very little cross-national research draws on GLOBE so far. In addition, most studies build on in-group collectivism and on gender egalitarianism, which are also the most studied dimensions in other work–life studies that have relied on other cultural frameworks (Ollier-Malaterre & Foucreault, 2017). Another important gap regards the constructs that are examined: most research focuses on work–family conflict, whereas there is little research on work–life enrichment and balance, virtually none on boundary management or other important work–life constructs such as cross-over between partners or between supervisors and employees, or work and family identity salience (Ollier-Malaterre, 2015). Likewise, there is very little research on the influence of GLOBE's cultural dimensions (or any other dimensions from commonly used cultural frameworks in cross-national work–life research) on employer provision of work–life practices and on employees' use of work–life practices (Ollier-Malaterre, 2017).

More specifically regarding GLOBE, we call for research that includes both practices ("as is ") and values ("should be") measures and clearly states hypotheses and findings regarding these two measures which are theoretically distinct. Great confusion arises from the fact that most studies use either one or the other, and often do not specify which one they used. Therefore, a theory-driven systematic examination of the relationship between practices and values measures and work–life constructs would be very valuable. In addition, in the spirit of advancing knowledge and publishing both significant and non-significant findings, studies that use both values and practices scores should report both sets of findings.

In addition, we call for more studies that include not only GLOBE's dimensions but also compare them with other measures. For instance, the CISMS studies classified countries in individualistic or collectivistic countries based on GLOBE as well as the work of Geert Hofstede and of Harry Triandis (Masuda et al., 2012; Spector et al., 2007). Likewise, Lyness and Judiesch (2013) included four measures of gender egalitarianism, including GLOBE's practice and values measures, the United Nations Gender Inequality Index, and a measure of patriarchal values from the World Values Survey. This enabled them to paint a very comprehensive picture of the impact of gender egalitarianism and of achieved gender equality on self-reported and supervisor-reported work–life balance.

Going even one step further, cross-national work–life research should ideally strive to include *culture*, that is GLOBE's and other cultural measures, as well as *structure* that is the legal, economic, and social factors that impact the work–life interface, such as labor laws regulating working times, the unemployment rate, and family structures (for a review, see Ollier-Malaterre & Foucreault, 2017). This calls for interdisciplinary research teams and either large samples providing enough variation to conduct multi-level analyses or smaller samples taking a qualitative and systemic approach. In both cases, relying on local teams of scholars to gain emic insights into cultural specificities (Gudykunst, 1997) has proven to increase the relevance of the research design, data collection, and data analysis.

Therefore, what is needed now in cross-national work–life research is a more systematic examination of (1) a broader range of cultural dimensions among the nine that GLOBE includes, (2) a broader range of work–life constructs, going beyond the current focus on work–life conflict, and (3) a theory-driven systematic examination of main, moderating, and mediating effects of culture on the work–life interface which considers the relationship between practices and values as well as the interaction between both cultural and structural dimensions.

Conclusion

GLOBE is a major cultural framework that offers largely untapped potential at the theoretical and empirical levels for cross-national work–life research. We hope that this chapter will foster renewed interest for GLOBE's cultural dimensions, including their relation to other cultural frameworks and to structural factors at the country-level, in the burgeoning field of cross-national work–life research.

References

Allen, T. D., French, K. A., Dumani, S., & Shockley, K. M. 2015. Meta-analysis of work–family conflict mean differences: Does national context matter? *Journal of Vocational Behavior*, 90: 90–100.

Ashforth, B. E., Kreiner, G. E., & Fugate, M. 2000. All in a day's work: Boundaries and micro role transitions. *Academy of Management Review*, 25: 472–491.

Beham, B., Drobnič, S., Präg, P., Lewis, S., & Baierl, A. 2014. *Work-to-family enrichment across national cultures: A study among employees from seven European countries.* Paper presented at the 2014 Work and Family Researchers Network Conference, New York.

Beham, B., Drobnič, S., Präg, P., Baierl, A., & Lewis, S. 2017. Work-to-family enrichment and gender inequalities in eight European countries. *The International Journal of Human Resource Management*, 1–22. doi:10.1080/09585192.2017.1355837

Billing, T. K., Bhagat, R., Babakus, E., Srivastava, B. N., Shin, M., & Brew, F. 2013. Work–family conflict in four national contexts: A closer look at the role of individualism-collectivism. *International Journal of Cross Cultural Management*, 14: 139–159.

Carlson, D. S., Kacmar, K. M., Wayne, J. H., & Grzywacz, J. G. 2006. Measuring the positive side of the work–family interface: Development and validation of a work–family enrichment scale. *Journal of Vocational Behavior*, 68: 131–164.

de Tocqueville, A. 1946. *Democracy in America.* New York: Knopf (First US edition 1840).

GLOBE. 2004. Phase 2 aggregated societal level data for society culture scales: May 17, 2004. Retrieved from: http://globe.bus.sfu.ca/study_2004_2007#data.

Greenhaus, J. H., & Parasuraman, S. 1987. A work-nonwork interactive perspective of stress and its consequences. In J. M. Ivancevich & D. C. Ganster (Eds.), *Job stress: From theory to suggestion.* 37–60. New York, NY: Haworth.

Gudykunst, W. B. 1997. Cultural variability in communication. *Communication Research*, 24(4): 327–348.

Haar, J., Russo, M., Sune, A., & Ollier-Malaterre, A. 2014. Outcomes of work–life balance on job satisfaction, life satisfaction and mental health: A study across seven cultures. *Journal of Vocational Behavior*, 85(3): 361–373.

Hassan, Z., Dollard, M. F., & Winefield, A. H. 2010. Work–family conflict in East vs. Western countries. *Cross Cultural Management: An International Journal*, 17(1): 30–49.

Hofstede, G. 1980. *Culture's Consequences: International Differences in Work-Related Values.* Beverly Hills, CA: Sage Publications.

Hofstede, G. 2006. What did GLOBE really measure? Researchers' minds versus respondents' minds. *Journal of International Business Studies*, 37(6): 882–896.

House, R., Javidan, M., & Dorfman, P. 2001. Project GLOBE: an introduction. *Applied Psychology*, 50(4): 489–505.

House, R. J., Hanges, P. J., Javidan, M., Dorfman, P. W., & Gupta, V. 2004. *Culture, leadership, and organizations: The GLOBE study of 62 societies.* Thousand Oaks, CA: Sage Publications.

House, R. J., Hanges, P. J., Ruiz-Quintanilla, S. A., Dorfman, P. W., Javidan, M., Dickson, M., & Gupta, V. 1999. Cultural influences on leadership and organizations: Project GLOBE. *Advances in Global Leadership*, 1: 171–233.

House, R., Javidan, M., & Dorfman, P. 2001. Project GLOBE: an introduction. *Applied Psychology*, 50(4): 489–505.

Inglehart, R. 1997. *Modernization and Post-Modernization: Cultural, Economic, and Political Change in 43 Societies.* Princeton, N.J.: Princeton University Press.

Lucia-Casademunt, A. M., García-Cabrera, A. M., & Cuéllar-Molina, D. G. 2015. National culture, work–life balance and employee well-being in European tourism firms: The moderating effect of uncertainty avoidance values. *Tourism & Management Studies*, 11(1): 62–69.

Lyness, K. S., & Judiesch, M. K. 2014. Gender egalitarianism and work–life balance for managers: Multisource perspectives in 36 countries. *Applied Psychology*, 63: 96–129.

Maseland, R., & Van Hoorn, A. 2009. Explaining the negative correlation between values and practices: A note on the Hofstede–GLOBE debate. *Journal of International Business Studies*, 40(3): 527–532.

Masuda, A. D., Poelmans, S. A. Y., Allen, T. D., Spector, P. E., Lapierre, L. M., Cooper, C. L., Abarca, N., Brough, P., Ferreiro, P., Fraile, G., Lu, L., Lu, C.-Q., Siu, O. L., O'Driscoll, M. P., Simoni, A. S., Shima, S., & Moreno-Velazquez, I. 2012. Flexible work arrangements availability and their relationship with work-to-family conflict, job satisfaction, and turnover intentions: a comparison of three country clusters. *Applied Psychology*, 61(1): 1–29.

Mead, M. 1967. *Cooperation and competition among primitive people*. Boston: Beacon.

Moulettes, A. 2007. The silencing of women in Hofstede's cultural consequences: A postcolonial reading. Paper presented at the EURAM conference, Paris.

Ollier-Malaterre, A. 2015. Cross-national work–life research: A review at the individual level. In T. D. Allen & L. E. Eby (Eds.), *Oxford Handbook of Work and Family* (pp. 315–330). Oxford, UK: Oxford University Press.

Ollier-Malaterre, A. 2017. National context and employer-driven work–life policies. In R. Burke & L. Calvano (Eds.), *The Sandwich Generation: Caring for Oneself and Others at Home and at Work*. 177–195. Cheltenham, UK: Edward Elgar Publishing.

Ollier-Malaterre, A., & Foucreault, A. 2017. Cross-national work–life research: Cultural and structural impacts for individuals and organizations. *Journal of Management*, 43(1): 111–136.

Ollier-Malaterre, A., Sarkisian, N., Stawiski, S., & Hannum, K. M. 2013. Work–life balance and performance across countries: cultural and institutional approaches. In Debra A. Major & R. J. Burke (Eds.), *Handbook of Work–life Integration Among Professionals: Challenges and Opportunities* (pp. 357–380). Cheltenham, UK: Edward Elgar Publishing.

Ollo-López, A., & Goñi-Legaz, S. 2015. Differences in work–family conflict: Which individual and national factors explain them? *The International Journal of Human Resource Management*: 1–27.

Powell, G. N., Francesco, A. M., & Ling, Y. 2009. Towards culture-sensitive theories of the work–family interface. *Journal of Organizational Behavior*, 30: 597–616.

United Nations Development Programme. 2010. *Human Development Report 2010: The Real Wealth of Nations: Pathways to Human Development*. New York: United Nations Development Programme.

Schwartz, S. H. 1994. Beyond individualism/collectivism: new cultural dimensions of values. In U. Kim, H. C. Triandis, Ç. Kâğitçibaşi, S.-C. Choi, & G. Yoon (Eds.), *Individualism and Collectivism: Theory, Methods, and Applications* (Vol. 18, pp. 85–119). Thousand Oaks, CA: Sage.

Spector, P. E., Allen, T. D., Poelmans, S. A. Y., Lapierre, L. M., Cooper, C. L., O'Driscoll, M., Sanchez, J. I., Abarca, N., Alexandrova, M., Beham, B., Brough, P., Ferreiro, P., Fraile, G., Lu, C. Q., & Lu, L. e. A. 2007. Cross-national differences in relationships of work demands, job satisfaction and turnover intentions with work–family conflict. *Personnel Psychology*, 60: 805–835.

Spector, P. E., Cooper, C. L., Poelmans, S. A. Y., Allen, T. D., O'Driscoll, M. P., Sanchez, J. I., Siu, O. L., Dewe, P., Hart, P., Lu, L., Renault de Moraes, L. F., Ostrognay, G. M., Sparks, K., Wong, P., & Yu, S. 2004. A cross-national comparative study of work–family stressors, working hours and well-being: China and Latin America versus the Anglo world. *Personnel Psychology*, 57(1): 119–142.

Terlutter, R., Diehl, S., & Mueller, B. 2006. The GLOBE study—applicability of a new typology of cultural dimensions for cross-cultural marketing and advertising research. In Diehl, S. & Terlutter, R. (Eds.), *International Advertising and Communication: Current Insights and Empirical Findings* (pp. 420–438). Wiesbaden: Gabler Edition Wissenschaft.

Triandis, H. C. 1989. The self and social behavior in differing cultural contexts. *Psychological Review*, 96: 506–520.

World Values Survey Association. 2009. World Values Survey 1981–2008 Official Aggregate v.20090901. Retrieved from: www.worldvaluessurvey.org/wvs.jsp

Yang, N., Chen, C. C., Choi, J., & Zou, Y. 2000. Sources of work–family conflict: A Sino-U.S. comparison of the effects of work and family demands. *Academy of Management Journal*, 43: 113–123.

Yeganeh, H., Su, Z., & Sauers, D. 2009. The applicability of widely employed frameworks in cross-cultural management research. *Journal of Academic Research in Economics* (1): 1–24.

PART II

Assessing Cultural and Structural Differences

4 Schwartz Cultural Values: Implications for Global Work–Family Research

Aline D. Masuda

Scholars often acknowledge the important role that culture plays in people's work–family experiences (Haar, Suñe, & Ollier-Malaterre; 2014; Lyness & Kropf, 2005; Powell, Francesco, & Ling, 2009; Spector et al., 2004, 2007). For example, Powell et al. (2009) called for the development and testing of culturally sensitive theories of the work–family interface, noting that the state of the empirical literature at that time was a bit sparse. Since then, more studies have emerged examining the role of the national context, particularly cultural dimensions, on work–family outcomes (see Lyness & Judiesch, 2014; Masuda et al., 2012; Ollier-Malaterre & Foucreault, 2016; Ollier-Malaterre, 2016; Ollo-Lópeza & Goñi-Legaza, 2015). In fact, in 2013, the *European Management Journal* published a special issue consisting of theoretical and empirical papers that explored the role of national context in the work–life interface (see Ollier-Malaterre et al., 2013).

Despite the increasing number of studies on the topic, the majority of studies relating culture and the work family interface have focused on the cultural dimensions drawn from Hofstede's (1980) theory of cultural values and the cultural dimensions defined by researchers from the Global Leadership and Organizational Behavior Effectiveness (GLOBE) project lead by Robert J. House (e.g., Spector et al., 2004, 2007; Masuda et al., 2012; Ollier-Malaterre, 2016; Lyness & Kroft, 2005; Lyness & Judiesch, 2014; Harr, Suñe, & Ollier-Malaterre. 2014). While these theoretical frameworks have been useful to move cross-cultural work–family research forward, I argue that value orientations, which have not been a major focus of previous work and are not isomorphic with Hofstede and House et al.'s conceptualizations, also seem highly relevant.

According to Schwartz (2006), "Value emphases express shared conceptions of what is good and desirable in the culture" (p. 139). Cultural values shape goals at the individual levels and goals, practices, and norms at the group, organizational, and the national level (Schwartz, 2006). Given the importance of cultural values in predicting behaviors and attitudes, cultural value orientations can be useful in explaining individuals' experiences related to the work–family interface.

In this chapter I encourage work–family scholars to examine Schwartz's cultural value orientations when studying the work–family interface. In doing so, I first describe Schwartz's (2006) cultural dimensions in contrast with others in the cross-cultural literature (e.g., Hofstede, 1980; House et al., 2004; Inglehart, 1997). Second, I describe the research on work–family conflict (WFC) and work–family enrichment (WFE), two important constructs that capture the positive and negative side of the work–family interface. Last, based on the work–family research reviewed, and Powell, Francesco, and Ling's (2009) culture-sensitive theory of work–family interface, I propose a research agenda to test the role of each cultural value orientation and how they interact to predict WFC and WFE.

Schwartz's Theory of Cultural Value Orientations

Theory Development

Schwartz's theory of cultural value orientations was developed based on a priori theorizing. Specifically, Schwartz (2006) explains that cultural value orientations emerge as societies face three basic questions in regulating human activity: (1) How should people derive meaning in life? (2) How should people avoid the deterioration of the social fabric? and, (3) To what degree should people modify or adapt to the natural world to fit their needs?

Schwartz operationalizes cultural value orientations by capturing basic individual human values that are relevant across all life situations. Currently, there are two scales that measure Schwartz values. A longer version of the scale, Schwartz Value Survey (SVS: Schwartz, 1992), includes forty-five items. In this version, a list of abstract items (e.g., social justice, creativity, pleasure, and ambition) is presented along with the definition of each item. Respondents are asked to rate how important these values are as guiding principles in their lives using a Likert response scale (−1 = values opposite to the respondents' principles, 0 = not at all important, to 6 = very important). A shorter version of the questionnaire, the Portrait Values Questionnaire (PVQ: Schwartz et al., 2001), includes twenty-one items. This questionnaire provides a portrait of a person and respondents need to assess how similar they are to each portrait. For instance, "Thinking up new ideas and being creative is important to her. She likes to do things in her own original way." Respondents are asked to answer "How much like you is this person?" answered on a scale from 1 = not at all like me and 6 = very much like me.

Schwartz (2006) tested the empirical structure of the cultural values using two separate datasets. The first data set was used to validate the longer version of the questionnaire and was based on samples of school teachers and college students from sixty-seven countries (Schwartz, 1994; Fontaine, Poortinga, Delbeke, & Schwartz, 2008). The second dataset was used to validate the shorter version of the questionnaire and was based on a sample of twenty countries from the European Social Survey. To validate his theory, Schwartz (2006) first captured the responses for each item at the individual level and then computed mean ratings for each of the items at the country level. Schwartz then conducted multidimensional scaling analyses using the country level scores for each item. The obtained correlation plots of the responses for each item averaged by country empirically supported the presence of seven spaces representing each cultural value orientation (Schwartz, 2006). Based on Schwartz's (2006) theory, to test the effects of cultural value orientations on other variables, researchers compute mean ratings for each item at the country-level, and then average the items that fall into the respective cultural value domain. A single score that represents the polarity of the cultural values is then computed. Specifically, researchers subtract the mean country score of each cultural value orientation from its opposite. For example, the mean country score of autonomy is subtracted from the mean country score of embeddedness, the mean country score of harmony is subtracted from the mean country score of mastery, and the mean country score of egalitarianism is subtracted from the mean country score of hierarchy (see Vauclair & Fischer, 2011, for an example of how values are used to predict attitudes).

Previous research has demonstrated the cultural equivalence of forty-five items from the original SVS scale (Fontaine et al., 2008). Further, multi-group confirmatory factor analyses of PVQ21 items support the near equivalence of meaning of the individual values across European Social Survey countries (Bilsky, Janik, & Schwartz, 2011; Schwartz & Rubel, 2005). Hence, both instruments provide cross-cultural comparable data.

The Seven Cultural Value Orientations

Schwartz's (2006) theory of cultural values identifies seven cultural value orientations, defined below:

(1) **Affective autonomy** describes a society where most people find meaning in life by fulfilling hedonistic and stimulation values such as variety, excitement, and pleasure.
(2) **Intellectually autonomy** describes a society where most people find meaning in life by pursuing self-direction values such as intellectual freedom, curiosity, and broadening of one's mind.
(3) **Embeddedness** describes a society where people find meaning in life by complying with traditions and fulfilling values such as conformity, family, national security, and social order.
(4) **Mastery** describes a society where people believe they should try to change the natural world to accomplish their goals. Most people in this society place importance on achievement values such as ambition, competence, influence, and success.
(5) **Harmony** describes a society where most people believe that they should adapt to nature. In this society individuals place importance on values such as world of peace, unit with nature, and protecting the environment.
(6) **Egalitarianism** describes a society that avoids deterioration of social fabric by sharing values such as collaboration and caring for the welfare of others. Most people in this society share universalistic and benevolent values such as social justice, equality for all, and helping others.
(7) **Hierarchy** describes a society where most people avoid the deterioration of social fabric by relying on ascribed social roles to maintain social behavior. In this society people share values such as wealth and power.

The cultural value orientations described above form three bipolar cultural dimensions that represent different resolutions to each of the three fundamental problems that face all countries or cultures: (1) autonomy (affective and intellectual versus embeddedness, (2) hierarchy versus egalitarianism, and (3) mastery versus harmony. These three bipolar dimensions form a circular structure of values. In this structure compatible values are closer to each other (e.g., autonomy, harmony, and egalitarianism) while incompatible values are opposite to each other (see Figure 4.1).

Specifically, the opposite pole of each value orientation shows different solutions for the same problem in society. For this reason, these values are in tension with each other. For example, seeking excitement as a guiding principle for life fulfillment (i.e., high affective autonomy) is incompatible with seeking security (i.e., high embeddedness). This is because autonomy values lead to different behaviors and norms to define life fulfillment that are in contrast with embedded values. For instance, autonomy values could lead to the acceptable social norm of seeking jobs that are novel and stimulating instead of seeking jobs simply to ensure financial security.

Further, while values opposite to each other represent incompatibility, values that are proximal to each other in Figure 4.1 indicate the sharing of some common

Figure 4.1 *Cultural dimensions: prototypical structure from Schwartz (2006).* Reprinted with permission from author: Schwartz, S.H. (2006). A theory of cultural value orientations: Explication and applications. *Comparative Sociology,* 5, 137–182

assumptions. For example, hierarchy and embeddedness values are next to each other in the circular structure because they share the assumption that individuals are part of a group with obligations. Autonomy and mastery also share the assumptions that individuals are free to make changes in society. However, in mastery societies the changes are related to wealth and gaining competencies. Mastery is also correlated with hierarchy because being competitive implies getting ahead and, thus, promoting unequal distribution of power.

Using this circular structure, we can characterize and compare countries (see the cultural map provided by Schwartz, 2006). For example, Americans are relatively higher in affective autonomy, but lower in hierarchy compared with Indians who are also lower in affective autonomy, and higher in hierarchy. Both cultures however are high in mastery value orientations.

Comparing Schwartz Cultural Values, the GLOBE Project, Hofstede, and Inglehart

Schwartz (2006) explains that the cultural value orientations overlap with cultural dimensions defined by other researchers (e.g., Hofstede, 1980; House et al., 2004; Inglehart, 1997). For example, embeddedness values, which "emphasizes maintaining the status quo, propriety, and restraint of actions or inclinations that might disrupt the solidary group or the traditional order in which people are embedded" (Smith et al., 2002, p. 193), overlap with Hofstede's concept of collectivism and House et al.'s concept of in-group collectivism. Specifically, similar to collectivism, embeddedness value orientation also emphasizes the importance of individual's social ties over the individual's own interests and goals. In fact, empirical research has shown a correlation of .64 between collectivism and embeddedness (Smith et al., 2002). Although these constructs are related, Schwartz (2006) explains that embeddedness is broader than collectivism because it also encompasses conservatism values, such as social order, national security, and the importance of following traditions and customs.

Egalitarianism, which is defined as "the belief that all people are of equal worth and should be treated equally in society" (Schwartz, 2001, p. 65), is another cultural value that overlaps the cultural dimension of gender egalitarianism described in the GLOBE Project as "the degree to which a collective minimizes gender inequality" (House et al., 2004, p. 30). Specifically, both constructs pertain to individuals being treated equally in society. However, egalitarian value orientation is broader than gender egalitarianism because it does not focus only on gender equality, but it also captures the degree to which people are willing to cooperate by choice to care for the well-being of others. Specifically, egalitarianism is based on the assumption that all people should have their basic human rights fulfilled and should cooperate for the good of others. Individuals in this society primarily value equality, social justice, responsibility, and solidarity. For example, while individuals in gender egalitarian countries believe that men and women should equally contribute to care taking responsibilities, individuals in societies high in egalitarian value orientation share the belief that all citizens regardless of their socioeconomical background should have the right to have the ability to care for children, give them basic education, and basic health care.

Schwartz cultural values orientation can also be contrasted with Inglehart's cultural dimensions of traditional versus secular-rational. The traditional/secular-rational dimension in Inglehart's model contrasts societies that place importance on religion, nationalism, and family (i.e., traditional societies) with societies that deemphasize such values (i.e., secular-rational societies) (Inglehart & Baker, 2000). This dimension overlaps conceptually with that of embeddedness versus autonomy. Both dimensions describe the degree to which individuals in societies belief that they are submerged in a group with mutual obligations and where respecting traditions are important. According to Schwartz (2006), the main distinction between these two dimensions is the traditional dimension emphasizes religion more than the embeddedness dimension. Taken together, because there are unique aspects to the cultural values proposed by Schwartz, I believe that studying these variables could contribute to the small base of knowledge on cultural values that has relied primarily on those from other frameworks.

Linking Schwartz's Cultural Values to the Work–Family Interface

Two constructs have dominated the empirical research in the work–family interface. Work–family conflict (WFC) describes the negative side of the work–family interface and is defined as "a form of inter-role conflict in which the role pressures from the work and family domains are mutually incompatible in some respect" (Greenhaus & Beutell, 1985, p. 77). WFC is regarded as bidirectional, such that work can interfere with family and family can interfere with work (Frone et al., 1992). Role theory is frequently used to explain the causes of WFC (Greenhaus & Beutell, 1985). One of the assumptions of role theory is that people have a finite amount of energy and time (Marks, 1977). Hence, demand pressures from participating in work and family roles impedes the fulfillment of responsibilities of both roles involved (Katz & Kahn, 1978).

A large body of literature has accumulated examining predictors of WFC, which include work and family demands and resources (e.g., Michel et al., 2011). One area of particular interest to cultural differences is social support. Research evidence shows that perceptions of support directly and negatively relate to WFC (see Kossek, Pichler, Bodner, & Hammer, 2012). Further, social support has been suggested to indirectly predict WFC by helping individuals reduce work and family demands (Greenhaus & Parasuraman, 1994). Social support can come in many forms, including tangible or emotional support from family member, coworkers, or supervisors at the individual level, formal family-supportive policies at the organizational level, or and government policies at the country level (Butts, Casper, & Yang, 2013; Greenhaus & Parasuraman, 1994; Lewis, 2009).

Another important construct of the work–family interface is work–family enrichment (WFE). WFE concerns the positive side of the work–family interface and describes "the extent to which experiences in one role improves the quality of life in the other role" (Greenhaus & Powell, 2006, p. 73). WFE, like WFC, is also regarded as bidirectional in nature, such that work enriches family (work-to-family enrichment) and vice versa. Greenhaus and Powell's (2006) WFE theory describes several resources (e.g., skills and perspectives, psychological and physical resources, social-capital resources, flexibility, and material resources) that may be acquired in one role to improve performance in the other role. This transfer can occur through two mechanisms, the direct enhancement of performance or via improved affect.

To date, there are no known studies linking Schwartz's (2006) cultural values orientation to WFC or WFE. Powell et al. (2009), in a theoretical paper, describe how certain cultural values (i.e., collectivism, specificity/diffusion, gender egalitarianism, and humane orientation) could indirectly predict WFC by influencing social support and work–family demands. They further note that cultural values could also play a role in WFE. Specifically, the relationships between resources generated in role A (work or family) with performance in role B (work or family) along instrumental and affective paths are moderated by collectivism, specificity/diffusion, and humane orientation values. Further, they argue that gender differences in work family enrichment are moderated by gender egalitarianism such that these differences are stronger in low gender egalitarian countries. In a similar vein, I expect that cultural value orientations could also influence both WFC and WFE. Below, I expand on these ideas.

Embeddedness versus autonomy. Embeddedness and autonomy cultural value orientations could indirectly relate to WFC for several reasons. First, individuals in embedded oriented societies may experience more social support compared with those in autonomous societies thus alleviating work and family demands and consequently WFC. In fact, there has been empirical research showing that countries in Asian region, which are higher in embeddedness compared with Anglo region, experience more coworker support compared with countries in the Anglo and Western European region (Glazer, 2006). Glazer (2006) uses Schwartz cultural values to explain that "it appears logical, then, that the more one feels embedded within his or her work group, the greater he or she will perceive instrumental support from co-workers" (p. 618).

Further, individuals in embedded oriented societies may experience more social support from family members not only because they have larger families for which they can rely on for caretaking responsibilities (Schwartz, 2006), but also because individuals in embeddedness oriented societies are more likely to feel a sense of obligation towards family (Schwartz, 2006). For example, embeddedness is positively associated with the belief that one must respect parents irrespective of their qualities and that divorce is never justified (Schwartz, 2006). In this sense, individuals in embedded oriented societies may feel obliged to care for elder family, children, and even more extended family members.

Thus, although it is possible that individuals in high embedded oriented societies experience less WFC by having more social support from family members and coworkers, it is also possible that they may experience higher WFC by reporting higher family involvement and family demands compared with individuals high in autonomous value orientation societies. Specifically, the sense of obligation for caring for their family coupled with the higher household sizes could lead to higher family involvement and higher family demands. This is consistent with research showing that people with more children living at home experience higher family demands and WFC (Byron, 2005; Kinnunen & Mauno, 1998; Michel, Kotrba, Mitchelson, Clark, & Baltes, 2011). Hence, although the embeddedness norms of solidarity to the group coupled with the size of family households may lead to higher social support, these values can influence norms that impose more demands as individuals in these societies may feel more involved and obliged to care for their extended family members. Research is needed to test the veracity of these ideas as well as disentangle which force is stronger, or if they ultimately have a canceling out effect on WFC experiences.

Proposition 1a: *People in societies higher in embeddedness versus autonomy experience less WFC than those in societies lower in embeddedness versus autonomy through an increase in social support received.*

Proposition 1b: *People in societies higher in embeddedness versus autonomy experience more WFC than those in societies low in embeddedness versus autonomy through an increase in family demands.*

Embeddedness and autonomy could also play an integral role in predicting WFE. Specifically, individuals in high embeddedness-oriented compared with affective and intellectual autonomous oriented cultures could be more likely to experience enrichment via the instrumental path because they experience a higher sense of obligation to care for family members (Schwartz, 2006). By feeling obligated to care for family members, resources acquired from work are more likely to be used to care for family responsibilities in embedded oriented societies. For example, while in high embedded oriented societies a person with a stable job may feel obliged to help family members such as a nephew by paying his college tuition; in high intellectual autonomous societies the person may not feel the pressure to pay for their own child's college tuition let alone the college tuition of a nephew.

Proposition 2: *People in societies higher in embeddedness versus autonomy will experience more WFE than people in societies high in autonomy versus embeddedness.*

Mastery orientation versus harmony. Previous scholars have encouraged the exploration of mastery versus harmony cultural value orientation as a possible predictor of WFC (Powell et al., 2009; Ollier-Malaterre & Foucreault, 2016). Smith et al. (2002) stated that individuals in mastery oriented societies are likely to focus on achievement by being more assertive. Hence, in high mastery societies, success at work is very important, and individuals in these societies may be more involved at work. Because individuals in high mastery oriented societies experience normative pressures to be more successful at work, they may experience more pressure to work longer hours, and consequently experience greater work demands and WFC. On the other hand, because individuals in harmony-oriented societies do not place much importance on achievement, they may be less involved at work, experience less pressure to work longer hours and thus experience lower WFC.

This same logic could also carry over to WFE. That is, because individuals in mastery oriented cultures value achievement, competence, and success at work, they may also experience more resource gain related to knowledge, skill development, and financial resources. By experiencing more resource gain, they may be more likely to transfer these resources from work to the family domain. In short, because this cultural value orientation captures values that are linked to work (e.g., ambition, development), it could be very useful to study its effects on both WFE and WFC.

Proposition 3: *People in societies higher in mastery versus harmony orientation will experience more WFC than people in societies high in harmony versus mastery orientation.*

Proposition 4: *People in societies higher in mastery versus harmony orientation will experience more WFE than people in societies high in harmony versus mastery orientation*

Egalitarianism versus hierarchy. There is reason to suspect that egalitarian values could be associated with WFC through social support. Egalitarianism societies typically have formal and informal institutions that support equality and fairness. Specifically, research has shown that egalitarianism is associated positively with democracy, non-corruption, and with the proportion of GDP per capita spent on social security, health, unemployment and sickness benefits, and other welfare investments (Schwartz, 2006; Siegel, Licht, & Schwartz, 2011). Hence, individuals in egalitarianism societies may experience lower WFC because they experience more support from society in the forms of the adoption of more government policies that care for the welfare of its citizens.

Further, egalitarianism values such caring for the welfare of others and equality, could be translated to fair practices at home such as equal share of both family and work responsibilities by partners, or fair practices in the workplace such as higher adoption of part-time or flexitime by both care takers. Hence, it is possible that individuals in countries high in egalitarianism versus hierarchy may receive more social support necessary to cope with work and family demands and thus experience lower WFC compared with individuals in hierarchical cultural value orientations.

Individuals in countries higher in hierarchy cultural values orientation could also experience more WFC because individual in these societies, by definition, share values such as seeking power and wealth. Hence, individuals in these societies may experience high job involvement and feel pressured to earn high incomes and positions of high status in the organizational hierarchy. As such, individuals in cultures with hierarchical cultural value orientation may experience more work demands which could lead to higher WFC. Further, since these individuals by definition put less emphasis on values such as collaborating for the good of others, individuals in these societies may also receive lower support from government at the country level, and from coworkers and family members at the group level.

Proposition 5: *People in societies higher in egalitarianism versus hierarchy orientation will experience less WFC than people in societies high in hierarchy versus egalitarianism orientation.*

It might also be worthy to study the effects of egalitarianism versus hierarchical values orientation on WFE since this cultural value orientation may influence work demands and social support. For example, if individuals in egalitarian societies are more likely to experience social support, then they may be more likely to transfer this resource to other domains. As such, studying the role of this cultural value orientation on WFE would be fruitful.

Proposition 6: *People in societies higher in egalitarianism versus hierarchy orientation will experience more WFE than people in societies high in hierarchy versus egalitarianism orientation*

Interactive effects of cultural values. Although cultural value orientations are posited to predict WFC individually, scholars have acknowledged that it could be useful to examine the interactive effects of cultural dimensions on the work–family interface (Ollier-Malaterre & Foucreault, 2016). Below I suggest some ideas along these lines specific to Schwartz's value framework.

In order to understand how values interact to predict work–family outcomes, we can work inductively, drawing from previous empirical studies of countries that experience lower and highest level of WFC. For example, based on a sample of thirty-one European countries, Ollo-Lópeza and Goñi-Legaza, (2015) found that individuals in Scandinavian countries experience lower WFC compared with individuals in eastern European and Mediterranean countries. Similarly, Crompton and Lyonette (2006) found that WFC was lower in Finland and Norway compared with France, Portugal, and Britain. Scandinavian countries are relatively high on autonomy, egalitarianism, and harmony compared with other European countries. Thus, it may be that the profile of these three variables relates to the most benefits in terms of reduced WFC.

To explicitly test these interaction effects, researchers could use methods such as applied polynomial regression, together with the response surface method (Edwards & Parry, 1993; Edwards, 1994) and the moderated polynomial regression (Edwards, personal website: http://public.kenan-flagler.unc.edu/faculty/edwardsj/resources.htm) to test the effects of multiple value orientations and their possible interaction on both WFC as well as enrichment. This would allow the (1) detection of more precise patterns of interaction among the value orientations and the resulting relationship between specific configurations and outcomes, (2) investigate possible curvilinear relationships, and (3) obtain a more detailed picture of the joint effect of multiple value orientations beyond only testing interaction effects (Kutner, Nachtsheim, Neter, & Li, 2005). Specifically, by examining the shape of the surface with the help of testing the slope and curvature of special lines of interests on the surface (Edwards & Parry, 1993), and by comparing the level of each cultural value orientation at different corners of the response surfaces, we are able to discover the optimal levels and combination of autonomy, egalitarianism, and harmony values to predict lower levels of WFC and enrichment in a more comprehensive and specific way.

By posing these research questions and testing them, we could find that it is undesirable to have extreme levels of certain cultural values. For example, it could be undesirable to have extreme levels of embedded cultural value orientations since individuals in embedded oriented cultures could experience higher social support but, simultaneously, could also experience higher family involvement and family demand. On the other hand, the more emphasis a country places on egalitarianism and harmony orientation the better to predict lower conflict. Since the research in this area is non-existent, I encourage simply testing exploratory research questions to accumulate empirical knowledge that ultimately could help scholars to inductively build a theory of cultural values on work family conflict and enrichment inductively.

Conclusion

The purpose of this chapter was to encourage work–family scholars to use cultural value orientations when studying the work–family interface. Schwartz´s (2006) theory of cultural value orientations was reviewed and used to propose the testing of research questions linking values with WFE and WFC. Lastly, I proposed the examination of cultural value orientations profiles as predictor of WFE and conflict. I hope this chapter will encourage work–family scholars to move beyond other cultural dimensions to include cultural values configurations on the work–family interface and thus move cross-cultural work–family research and theory forward.

References

Bilsky, W., Janik, M.J., & Schwartz, S.H., (2011). The structural organization of human values-evidence from three rounds of the European social survey (ESS). *Journal of Cross Cultural Psychology, 42*, (*5*), 759–776. doi:10.1177/0022022110362757

Butts, M.M. Casper, W.J., & Yang, T.S. (2013). How important are work–family support policies? A meta-analytic investigation of their effects on employee outcomes. *Journal of Applied Psychology, 98*, (1), 1–25. doi: 10.1037/a0030389

Byron, K. (2005). A meta-analytic review of work–family conflict and its antecedents. *Journal of Vocational Behavior, 67*, (2), 169–198.

Crompton, R., & Lyonette, C. (2006). Work–life 'balance' in Europe. *Acta Sociologica, 49*, (4), 379–393. doi: 10.1177/0001699306071680

Edwards, J. R. (1994). The study of congruence in organizational behavior research: Critique and a proposed alternative. *Organizational Behavior and Human Decision Processes, 58*, (*1*) 51–100.

Edwards, J. R., & Parry, M. E. (1993). On the use of polynomial regression equations as an alternative to difference scores in organizational research. *Academy of Management Journal, 36*(6), 1577–1613.

Fontaine, J. R., Poortinga, Y. H., Delbeke, L., & Schwartz, S. H. (2008). Structural equivalence of the values domain across cultures: Distinguishing sampling fluctuations from meaningful variation. *Journal of Cross-Cultural Psychology, 39*(4), 345–365.

Frone, M. R., Russell, M. D., & Cooper, M. L. (1992). Antecedents and outcomes of work–family conflict: Testing a model of the work–family interface. *Journal of Applied Psychology, 77*, (1), 65–78.

Glazer, S. (2006). Social support across cultures. *International Journal of Intercultural Relations, 30*, (5), 605–622.

Greenhaus, J. H., & Beutell, N. J. (1985). Sources of conflict between work and family roles. *Academy of Management Review, 10*, (1), 76–88.

Greenhaus, J. H., & Parasuraman, S. (1994). Work–family conflict, social support, and well-being. In M. J. Davidson & R. J. Burke (Eds.), *Women in management: Current research issues* (pp. 213–229). London: Paul Chapman.

Greenhaus, J.H., & Powell, G.N. (2006). When work and family are allies: A theory of work–family enrichment. *Academy of Management Review, 31*, (1), 72–92.

Haar J.M., Russo, M. Suñe A., & Ollier-Malaterre A. (2014). Outcomes of work–life balance on job satisfaction, life satisfaction and mental health: A study across seven cultures. *Journal of Vocational Behavior, 85*, (3), 361–373.

Hofstede, G. (1980). *Culture's Consequences: International Differences in Work-Related Values*. Beverly Hills CA: Sage

House, R. J., Gupta, V., Hanges, P. J., Javidan, M., & Dofman, P. W. (2004). *Culture, Leadership and Organizations: The GLOBE Study Of 62 Societies*. Thousand Oaks, CA: Sage.

Inglehart, R. (1997). *Modernization and Postmodernization: Cultural, Economic and Political Change in 43 Societies*. Princeton, NJ: Princeton University Press.

Inglehart, R., & Bakker, W.E. (2000). Modernization, cultural change, and the persistence of traditional values. *American Sociological Review, 65*, (1), 19–51.

Katz, D., & R. L. Kahn. (1978). *The Social Psychology of Organizations* (2nd ed). New York: Wiley.

Kinnunen, U., & Mauno, S. (1998). Antecedents and outcomes of work–family conflict among employed women and men in Finland. *Human Relations, 51*, (2), 157–177.

Kossek, E.E., Pichler, S., Bodner, T., & Hammer, L. (2012). Workplace Social Support and work–family conflict: A meta-analysis clarifying the influence of general and work–family-specific supervisor and organizational support. *Personnel Psychology, 64*, 289–313. 10.1111/j.1744–6570.2011.01211.x

Kutner, M. H., Nachtsheim, C. J., Neter, J., & Li, W. (2005). *Applied Linear Statistical Models* (5th ed). New York: McGraw-Hill.

Lewis, J., (2009). *Work–family Balance, Gender and Policy* (1st ed). Cheltenham, UK: Edward Elgar Publishing.

Lyness, K. S., & Judiesch, M. K. (2014). Gender egalitarianism and work–life balance for managers: Multisource perspectives in 36 countries. *Applied Psychology, 63*, 96–129.

Lyness, K.S., & Kropf, M.B. (2005). The relationships of national gender equality and organizational support with work–family balance: A study of European managers. *Human Relations, 58*, (1), 33–60. doi: 10.1177/0018726705050934.

Marks, S. R. (1977). Multiple roles and role strain: Some notes on human energy, time and commitment. *American Sociological Review. 41*, 921–936.

Masuda, A.D., Poelmans, S., Allen, T. D., Spector, P. E., Lapierre, L. M., Cooper, C. L., Brough, P., Ferrero, P., Fraile, G., Lu, L., Lu, C., Siu, O., O'Driscoll, M. P., Simoni, A., Shima, S., & Moreno-Velazquez, I. (2012). Flexible working arrangements availability and their relationship with work-to-family conflict, job satisfaction, and turnover intentions: A comparison of three country clusters. *Applied Psychology: An International Review, 61*, (1), 1–29. doi: 10.1111/j.1464-0597.2011.00453.x

Michel, J.S., Kotrba, L.M., Mitchelson, J.K., Clark, M.A., & Baltes, B.B. (2011). Antecedents of work–family conflict: A meta-analytic review. *Journal of Organizational Behavior, 32*, (5), 689–725. doi: 10.1002/job.695

Ollier-Malaterre, A. (2016). Cross-national work–life research: A review at the individual level. In T.D. Allen & L.T. Eby (Eds.), *The Oxford Handbook of Work And Family*, Oxford Library of Psychology.

Ollier-Malaterre, A., & Foucreault, A. (2016). Cross-National Work–life Research: Cultural and Structural Impacts for Individuals and Organizations. *Journal of Management, 43*, 1–26. doi: 10.1177/0149206316655873

Ollier-Malaterre, A., Valcour, M., Den Dulk, L., & Kossek, E.E. (2013). Theorizing national context to develop comparative work–life research: A review and research agenda. *European Management Journal, 31*, (5), 433–447.

Ollo-Lópeza, A., & Goñi-Legaza, S. (2015). Differences in work–family conflict: which individual and national factors explain them? *The International Journal of Human Resources Management, 1–26. doi:* 10.1080/09585192.2015.1118141

Powell, G.N., Francesco, A.M., & Ling, Y. (2009). Toward culture-sensitive theories of the work–family interface. *Journal of Organizational Behavior, 30*, (5), 597–616. doi: 10.1002/job.568.

Schwartz, S.H. (1992). Universals in the content and structure of values: Theory and empirical tests in 20 countries. In M. Zanna (Ed.), *Advances in Experimental Social Psychology* (Vol. 25, pp. 1–65). New York: Academic Press.

(1994). Are there universal aspects in the content and structure of values? *Journal of Social Issues, 50*, (4), 19–45. doi: 10.1111/j.1540-4560.1994.tb01196.x

Schwartz, S.H. (2001). Egalitarianism. In: Lipset, S. (Ed.), *Political Philosophy: Theories, Thinkers and Concepts* (pp. 64–71). Washington, DC: Congressional Quarterly Inc.

(2006). A theory of cultural value orientations: Explication and applications. *Comparative Sociology, 5*, (2), 137–182. doi: 10.1163/156913306778667357

Schwartz, S. H., Melech, G., Lehmann, A., Burgess, S., & Harris, M. (2001). Extending the cross-cultural validity of the theory of basic human values with a different method of measurement. *Journal of Cross Cultural Psychology, 32*, (5), 519–542. DOI: 10.1177/0022022101032005001

Schwartz, S.H., & Rubel, T. (2005). Sex differences in value priorities: Cross-cultural and multimethod studies. *Journal of Personality and Social Psychology, 89*, (6), 1010–1028. DOI: 10.1037/0022-3514.89.6.1010

Siegel, J. I., Licht, A. N., & Schwartz, S. H. (2011). Egalitarianism and international investment. *Journal of Financial Economics*, 102(3), 621–642.

Smith, P.B., Peterson, M.F., & Schwartz, S.H. (2002). Cultural values, sources of guidance, and their relevance to managerial behavior: A 47-Nation Study. *Journal of Cross Cultural Psychology, 33*, (2), 188–208.

Spector, P. E., Allen, T. D., Poelmans, S. A. Y., Lapierre, L. M., Cooper, C. L., O'Driscoll, M., et al. (2007). Cross-national differences in relationships of work demands, job satisfaction, and turnover intentions with work–family conflict. *Personnel Psychology, 60*, (4), 805–835. doi: 10.1111/j.1744-6570.2007.00092.x

Spector, P. E., Cooper, C. L., Poelmans, S. A., Allen, T. D., O'Driscoll, M., Sanchez, J. I., et al. (2004). A cross-national comparative study of work–family stressors, working hours, and well-being: China and Latin America versus the Anglo world. *Personnel Psychology*, *57*, (1), 119–142. doi: 10.1111/j.1744-6570.2004.tb02486.x

Vauclair, C. M., & Fischer, R. (2011). Do cultural values predict individuals' moral attitudes? A cross-cultural multilevel approach. *European Journal of Social Psychology*, 41 (5), 645–657.

5 Relationships between Social Policy, Economic Characteristics, and the Work–Family Interface

Matthew M. Piszczek

Introduction

As the work–family interface is often navigated through the more proximal level of the workplace, much work–family research focuses on organizational policies and practices. However, work–family support can also be provided directly through government, family, or community. Moreover, organizations operate in the context of a broader socioeconomic climate and organizational policies and practices are created and enacted in consideration of market forces (Abendroth & den Dulk, 2011). Many socioeconomic country-level factors thus may affect the ways in which individuals form and manage work and family roles (den Dulk, Groeneveld, Ollier-Malaterre, & Valcour, 2013), either directly or through organizations.

Social policy and economic characteristics are two such factors. They create opportunities and constraints for individuals to enact their work and family roles in particular ways by opening, closing, incentivizing, or deincentivizing pathways to various forms of physical and temporal work flexibility. Some of these pathways are affected explicitly, such as in the form of federal laws that grant employees the right to parental leave, while other pathways are affected less directly, such as through social policy that makes it easier for mothers to return to the workplace. These broad factors shape the work–family experience of individual employees and create broader patterns in the work–family interface in a given country context.

Organizations are also critical actors in the shaping of the work–family experience of employees through their work–family policies and practices, which are usually meant to help individuals better manage their often conflicting life roles (Kossek & Michel, 2011) by increasing control over their work–family role boundaries (Kossek, Lautsch, & Eaton, 2006). These policies and practices must be consistent with governmental policies, and frequently organizations and their management are gateway entities through which an individual can access their legal rights. Thus, organizations frequently act as a filter of these broader institutional forces on individual work–family role boundaries, and it is difficult to discuss the role of institutional forces without consideration of their impact on organizations.

Although much research has been dedicated to understanding the effectiveness of organizational work–family policies for organizations and their employees, only recently has focus shifted to understanding the influence of the contexts in which these policies are designed and enacted. In recognition of the importance of these relationships, a growing body of research is now examining the impact of country-level contextual differences on the organizational adoption of work–family policies and their effectiveness at both individual and organizational levels (e.g., Ollier-Malaterre & Foucreault, 2016; Piszczek & Berg, 2014). Organizations must craft their work–family policies in the presence of socioeconomic institutions which may affect the ways that human resource managers perceive, offer, and enact them. Similarly, these same institutions affect the way that employees can use and benefit from work–family policies.

Two primary perspectives for examining contextual effects on the work–family interface are the cultural and structural perspectives (Ollier-Malaterre & Foucreault, 2016). Culture includes collective societal beliefs, values, and norms while structure can be defined as "legal, economic, and social structures producing rules that organize and constrain human interaction" (Ollier-Malaterre & Foucreault, 2016, p. 5). International work–family research has largely focused on cultural rather than structural factors (Ollier-Malaterre, 2014). The goal of this chapter is to provide an overview of and recommendations for research on structural context. Specifically, the chapter reviews social policy, economic characteristics, and their interactions as they relate to the work–family interface with special attention to their interpretation and enactment through organizations.

Social Policy

Social policy broadly describes a government's actions related to the welfare of its citizens. Most directly relevant, it includes laws that govern the type and form of family-related policies and practices workplaces must offer (or must refrain from enacting). Social policy outside workplace regulations may also prioritize or otherwise address particular perceived societal needs. This chapter thus broadly divides social policies into two categories: regulative institutions and social institutions.

Regulative institutions may directly grant benefits to employees or restrict employers from making certain demands of employees. These include laws that guarantee employees maternity or paternity leave, require organizations to provide employees occasional leave from work, and limit employee working hours. These regulative institutions may also incentivize or deincentivize particular behaviors. For example, following the financial crisis France offered partial retirement benefits to older workers (Berg, Bosch, & Charest, 2014). In the United States, organizations are deincentivized from requiring long work hours by overtime provisions which make such requirements more expensive. In terms of structural work–family forces, regulative institutions have received a relatively high amount of attention in work–family research.

Social institutions may promote or deter certain patterns in work–family role management. These institutions include laws and norms that affect country-level patterns in, for example, gender roles, family forms, or retirement behaviors and are generally broader than regulative institutions. These social institutions do not directly grant employees rights or opportunities through employers, but have an indirect effect on the management of the work–family interface by incentivizing or deincentivizing particular work–family role management behaviors, adjusting the organization of work, or affecting employee voice and equity in the employment relationship. Thus, rather than providing benefits to enact existing work–family role structures, they shape work–family role structures themselves. Though there is extensive research on these social institutions, these studies are not always framed around the work–family interface and thus form a less cohesive body of work–family literature. For example, though retirement is arguably one of the biggest work–family role transitions one can make in his or her lifetime, retirement is not typically framed as a work–family issue. Additionally, though social institutions are a structural force, they are arguably more richly intertwined with culture than regulative institutions and thus difficult to understand outside of a cultural context. Despite this, however, both forms of social policy similarly create opportunities and restrictions for managing the work–family interface.

Regulative Institutions

Regulative institutions are laws or other regulations that may directly affect the work–family interface by legally mandating rights and responsibilities to employers and employees. First, they may restrict organizations from requiring particular work demands that interfere with family role functioning, such as long work hours or working while sick. Second, regulative institutions compel organizations to offer specific policies or practices to their employees through legislative mandate (Piszczek & Berg, 2014). Typical benefits mandated by regulative institutions in some countries include vacation, maternity leave, or medical leave. These institutions, often through organizations, create opportunities for employees to manage their work–family role boundaries in ways consistent with their own personal preferences or more generally with greater flexibility.

These institutions vary in key ways (Piszczek & Berg, 2014). Some countries' regulations compel organizations to offer more generous versions of benefits than others (e.g., Australia's maternity leave is paid while in the United States maternity leave is not paid). Others may offer unique policies not offered at all by others (e.g., the right to request a flexible work schedule in the United Kingdom that is absent in the United States). Coverage, too, varies by country in the form of eligibility requirements. Some policies may have relatively strict requirements compared to others. For example, family and medical leave in the United States is unavailable to many newly hired and part-time workers who fail to meet eligibility thresholds regarding minimum hours worked as outlined in the Family Medical and Leave Act.

A recent review finds that research has not supported a direct relationship between regulative institutions and individual work–family role management outcomes generally for most types of policy benefits (Ollier-Malaterre, 2014). This may be in part due to the Anglo-centric conceptualization of the work–family interface popular in research (Lewis, Gambles, & Rapoport, 2007), suggesting effects of policies are too contextually dependent to be able to generalize. Standards for work–family role management may vary across contexts, making popular measures and conceptualizations of work–family constructs difficult to apply. In other words, similar policies may have vastly different meanings to employees from one country to another. Another possible reason for this is that regulative institutions are not aligned with the needs of the public (Yerkes, Standing, Wattis, & Wain, 2010). If policy benefits are not meeting the needs of the public receiving them, then one would expect no change in work–family outcomes. Finally, this disconnect may also be due to the role of organizations in enacting regulative institutions, which varies significantly across countries as a function of public perception of the organization as a legitimate provider of work–family benefits (Ollier-Malaterre, 2009; Wood & de Menezes, 2007).

As mentioned above, regulative institutions are created directly by the government and thus their benefits for employees can be attributed to government. But in most cases, organizations are responsible for managing these benefits. This raises a number of questions and an additional layer of complexity in understanding how and why organizations offer work–family policies. One issue at the organization level that has received research attention is how organizations interpret, enact, and respond to government mandates to offer particular policies. For example, many employees legally eligible for unpaid work leave under the Family and Medical Leave Act in the US report being unable to afford to take it or, despite protections from retaliation, fear the undesirable effects the leave may have on their careers (Jorgensen & Appelbaum, 2014). Pay, ease of use, and policy awareness are factors under organizational control that may create variation within a single regulative context, diminishing the variation in individual outcomes attributable to regulative institutions.

A related issue of interest at a more macro theoretical level is the relationship between work–family regulative institutions and non-mandatory organizational work–family policy offerings. One study by den Dulk and colleagues (2013) highlights two opposing perspectives of this relationship based on previous research. The first argues that regulative institutions increase organizational work–family policy proliferation because they coerce organizations into offering more and more generous work–family practices in order to remain legally compliant (Piszczek & Berg, 2014) and, in the face of normative pressure to be family-friendly, socially legitimate (Wood & de Menezes, 2007). For example, organizations may adopt additional, non-mandatory work–family policies as a result of perceived pressure from more generous regulative institutional mandates (Poelmans & Sahibzada, 2004). The second perspective argues that regulative institutions create a substitution effect; organizations may decide not to offer additional benefits if they perceive that those offered through government mandate are enough. According to this perspective, when regulative institutions are weak, organizations will be more likely to adopt work–family policies because regulative institutions will be insufficient to meet public demand, creating an economic opportunity for employers to attract and retain talented or otherwise in-demand workers. Other studies suggest it is a combination of these pressures – both institutional and economic – that lead to policy adoption by organizations. For example, Ollier-Malaterre (2009) identified several contributing factors including the legal framework and the social nature of work and non-work roles, which suggest that non-mandatory policies may be adopted by organizations both because they create economic or competitive advantages and because the organization is seen as an important actor in helping employees maintain manageable work–family roles.

The work–family literature on this subject also suggests that the baseline benefits granted to employees by regulative institutions is important in determining the strategic value of work–family offerings for organizations. Piszczek and Berg (2014) developed a theoretical model of the role of regulative institutions in organizational adoption of work–family human resource practices. They argue that in country or regional contexts offering more generous work–family mandates, it is more difficult and less cost-effective for organizations to go beyond the baseline with additional or more generous work–family policies. The ability of the organization to offer unique work–family solutions to employees is limited when social policy can provide a substitute mechanism for organizational policy. Thus in countries with weaker social work–family policy, such as the United States (Sweet, Pitt-Catsouphes, Besen, & Golden, 2014), there may be greater room for organizations to offer strategically valuable work–family practices.

Despite growing attention to the importance of contextual influences on the work–family interface, the potential effects of regulative institutions on organizations and individuals remains largely ignored in most work–family studies. Additionally, the sheer variety, range, and breadth in regulative work–family institutions has prevented the development of a systematic framework of regulative institutions to allow for an empirical comparison (Ollier-Malaterre & Foucreault, 2016). Further complicating this research is the confounding of other country-level factors with regulative institutions such as culture and economic characteristics. As a result, much of our understanding of regulative institutions is piecemeal, coming from smaller comparisons and the few single-country studies that focus on contextual differences.

One potentially fruitful avenue for research is comparative studies of region-level (as opposed to country-level) variation in regulative institutions. Lower-level comparisons may help parse out the effects of legal policy independent from culture. For example, a useful study would be one which compares the effects of paid sick leave in a city where it is legally mandated at the city-level compared to a nearby, culturally and economically similar city where it is not legally mandated. This has been done with other laws which vary substantially within-country such as protections from employment discrimination based on sexual orientation (Barron & Hebl, 2013). Although such a study would not capture all the complexities of international differences, by designing out large cultural and socioeconomic differences one might observe across countries, the results would help clearly determine effects of regulative institutions. This may inform expectations for international comparative research. Another potentially more challenging option is the use of comparative data with rich cultural and economic controls. The GLOBE study (House, Hanges, Javidan, Dorfman, & Gupta, 2004) includes a number of broad country-level cultural dimensions that have been used as broad proxies for culture in international work–family research (e.g., Kassinis & Stavrou, 2013). The cultural dimensions used in

GLOBE may make useful albeit broad cultural controls for better understanding the effects of regulative institutions.

Social Institutions

In addition to regulative institutions, a number of other social institutions may be important factors in individual navigation of the work–family interface. As mentioned above, these institutions indirectly shape the work–family interface. Rather than directly providing benefits through workplaces, these institutions incentivize or deincentivize work–family structures either financially or through the establishment of social norms.

A key social institution is family policy, which may include public childcare options such as subsidized private care, public daycares, or the public education system. Strong public childcare options can provide a source of work–family support that allows for greater female labor force participation. Instead of taking on the traditional childcare role, the government partially takes on this role, freeing up traditional caretakers to use that time instead for the work role. Like regulative institutions, social institutions like family policy vary by country. For example, countries vary in the extent, type, and coverage of public childcare options offered to citizens. Childcare options may be limited to school and thus school-aged children or, such as in the case of Germany, they may be available to younger children as well.

Relatedly, family policy may reaffirm pressure for individuals to manage their work–family roles in certain ways. For example, the controversial German *Betruengsgeld* benefit enacted in 2012 provided an allowance from the federal government for families of children aged two to three who kept the children out of public daycare. Critics claimed that this policy could have the effect of pushing new mothers out of the labor market by incentivizing extension of maternity leave and increasing social pressure on women to maintain the traditional role of caretaker. The policy was ruled unconstitutional by Germany's high court in 2015. Even tax systems may incentivize particular family structures (Ollier-Malaterre, 2014). In the United States, married couples generally receive more favorable tax rates than single or co-habitating individuals.

Retirement policy is also important to management of the work–family interface. Retirement is a major work–life event as it usually marks a macro-level transition out of the work role. It is increasingly more important to understand the motivations behind retirement decisions and their effects on organizations and economies as the global workforce is rapidly aging and the number of retirements is expected to similarly rise (Berg, Hamman, Piszczek, & Ruhm, 2015). Retirement policy at the country level shapes how and when individuals make the retirement transition and the options available to organizations to help manage it.

In the face of global workforce aging, most Organization for Economic Cooperation and Development (OECD) countries have undergone policy reform regarding retirement in order to extend working lives (OECD, 2015), which is thought to ease the financial burden of an older population on public pension systems (Greller, 2012; Maestas & Zissimopoulos, 2010). Some have simply extended the age at which state pensions can be claimed. Others have introduced more complicated forms of retirement transition. For example, for several years Germany subsidized partial retirement to allow older workers to work part-time in hopes they would choose to remain in the workforce longer at reduced hours as opposed to an abrupt retirement. Results are mixed with regard to the success of partial retirement initiatives in various countries. Studies have found that they extend working lives in Germany (Berg et al., 2015) and Sweden (Wadensjö, 2006), while another suggests they instead replace full-time employment in Austria (Graf, Hofer, & Winter-Ebmer, 2011).

If these policies do in fact successfully extend working lives, then organizations and employees will be challenged with the management of work–family roles in even later stages of life. There is some evidence that preferences for work–family flexibility changes over the life-span and that older workers typically have less access to flexibility (Pitt-Catsouphes, Matz-Costa, & Besen, 2009), but research has not yet discovered how or why these preferences change. Country context likely further complicates these changes and will affect the success of retirement policy initiatives. For example, many Germans were able to use the state-sponsored partial retirement initiative in a "block model." Rather than working 50 % time during the next, for example, four years, an employee could declare a retirement date four years out and work 100 % time for the first two years and zero hours for the final two years. The use of this model arguably grew out of a combination of part-time work norms in Germany and the broad language in the partial retirement law. Thus, although it is clear that retirement policy will shape the macro transition from work to non-work and the proportion of older workers in the labor market, much work remains to be done in understanding these relationships and how they vary from context to context.

Economic Characteristics

The form and status of a country's economy and its key industrial sectors are also important contextual factors for managing the work–family interface. However, most work–family theory is based on the assumption of a relatively developed economy rather than less-developed, more heavily regulated economies. As yet, while there are many localized studies of the work–family interface in regional journals, little is known about how macro-economic indicators are systematically related to the work–family interface of individuals (Ollier-Malaterre, 2014). Some better understood economic characteristics are welfare and working time regimes and industrial relations systems. These factors are closely related to social policy, and both reciprocally influence one another.

Welfare regimes are a commonly discussed economic characteristic and frequently used as a framework for examining country-level differences in work–family research (e.g., Abendroth & den Dulk, 2011; Beham, Drobnič, & Präg, 2014; Chung & Tijdens, 2012; den Dulk, Peters, Poutsma, & Ligthart, 2010; Ollier-Malaterre, 2009; Poelmans & Sahibzada, 2004; Tomlinson, 2007). Welfare regimes describe the extent to which countries grant social rights to citizens (Ollier-Malaterre & Foucreault, 2016). Although there has been considerable discussion around and expansion of the welfare regime typology (e.g., Leon, 2005), the framework most commonly used was created by Esping-Anderson (1990, 1999) and describes three main types. In liberal welfare states (e.g., the United States), social benefits are largely granted by market forces rather than by government. In conservatist welfare states (e.g., France), the government provides social insurance. In social-democratic welfare states (e.g., Scandinavian countries), the government provides high levels of benefits which largely eliminates the involvement of market forces from their provision. In the context of the work–family interface, welfare regimes are generally used to explain the source of individual's work–family benefits: either from the free market (i.e., organizations) or from the government (i.e., regulative and social institutions). In more market-driven regimes, employers are thought to be legitimate sources of work–family benefits while in less market-driven regimes, the opposite is true (Ollier-Malaterre, 2009). Thus welfare regimes are often argued to predict organizational work–family policy offerings with work–family policy being organization-driven in more liberal regimes.

However, although the welfare regime framework describes a country's regulative institutions well, empirical evidence suggests it is less consistently predictive of organizational work–family policy offerings. A study by den Dulk and colleagues (2010) found that state support for childcare was negatively related to organizational involvement in childcare, but generally positively related in liberal welfare regimes (albeit with higher levels of organization-level variation). Another study found that organizations in liberal welfare regimes were more likely to offer work–family practices, but that cultural norms of gender equality were also an important factor (Beham et al., 2014). This research suggests that welfare regimes are a useful framework but should be examined in concert with other lower-level factors, as they cannot capture within-regime variation in organizational work–family offerings common in some types of welfare regimes. Researchers should take extra care when using a welfare regime framework to describe policy offerings in more market-driven regimes.

Another key economic characteristic in a country is its industrial relations system (Ollier-Malaterre, 2009; Parboteeah & Cullen, 2003). Industrial relations systems are closely tied to social institutions, such as labor unions and the related process of collective bargaining, through which some employees establish terms and conditions of employment with employers. The strength and structure of labor unions vary significantly across countries due to regulative institutions, public perception, and employee-employer power structures. Many countries have social institutions that similarly collectivize labor but operate in addition to or instead of labor unions. Germany, for example, has labor unions as well as works councils and a system of codetermination which give additional voice to workers (Huebler & Jirjahn, 2003). Many European countries have relatively centralized collective bargaining structures, with framework agreements negotiated at the industry-level between unions and employer associations. For example, a 1987 metalworking industry agreement from Denmark set a 37-hour standard work week, eventually spreading to other industries (Bishop, 2004). Framework agreements may also operate at the international level, such as between the Latin-American Coordination of Banana Workers Unions and the multinational enterprise Chiquita (Riisgaard, 2005).

Generally, research shows that stronger labor institutions are associated with more desirable work–family outcomes for employees. Unions can have a positive effect on access to work–family practices when wages are less of a focus in collective bargaining (Berg, Kossek, Misra, & Belman, 2014). Union coverage is also positively related to employee schedule control (Lyness, Gornick, Stone, & Grotto, 2012) and union and management strategies are related to employee control over working time (Berg, Appelbaum, Bailey, & Kalleberg, 2003). Labor institutions can also contribute to collective agreements that result in more negotiated working time configurations as opposed to mandated or employer-guided unilateral working time configurations (Berg, Bosch, et al., 2014). Union strength has also been linked to other constructs related to work–family role management such as work centrality (Parboteeah & Cullen, 2003).

However, the extent to which unions and other labor institutions play a role in organizational work–family policy also varies across countries. Recently, researchers have expanded the equality bargaining framework, originally aimed at understanding gender-based equity in collective bargaining processes and outcomes (Williamson & Baird, 2014), to apply to work–family outcomes. This research has found that country-level contextual factors such as public policy support and bargaining centralization affect the ability of labor unions to bargain for work–family practices (Berg, Kossek, Baird, & Block, 2013; Berg & Piszczek, 2014). However, some research also suggests that union centralization and alternative forms of employee representation such as works councils can complicate and deter the adoption of work–family practices (Ollier-Malaterre, 2009). The industrial distribution of union power may also affect their role in negotiating work–family benefits as traditionally male-dominated unions may have a harder time investing bargaining capital in work–family practices if they are viewed by the unions as women's issues rather than family issues (Berg & Piszczek, 2014).

There are a number of other country-level economic factors that affect the work–family interface. Labor market characteristics such as diffusion of work–family benefits, slack (i.e., number of workers relative to jobs), and gender composition may create patterns of work–family practice adoption within organizations (Poelmans & Sahibzada, 2004). Empirical results relating labor market characteristics to organizational policy adoption are mixed. For example, in a study of nineteen European countries, den Dulk and colleagues (2013) found that low male country-level unemployment rates did not predict the number of work–family provisions offered by organizations, but an organization's proportion of female workers was positively related to number of work–family provisions offered.

At the meso level, industry structures affect the nature of work and may create opportunities or restrictions for managing working time in particular ways (Sweet et al., 2014). Because of this, a country's industrial profile may broadly shape the work–family needs of its citizens. For example, when a country's economy is rooted in knowledge-based work, the typical employee may be able to manage work–family roles more flexibly. On the other hand, an economy with a bigger manufacturing sector may have more employees who must be physically present at the workplace, potentially at undesirable times such as nights and weekends. These factors may affect the pressure and rationale behind the adoption of work–family policies (or lack thereof) for both organizations and governments (Poelmans & Sahibzada, 2004). In some countries, industry associations may also be heavily involved in the negotiation of working time standards (Berg, Bosch, et al., 2014). This may introduce additional variation in the importance of a country's industrial profile in determining organizational and governmental work–family policies.

Discussion

An important first point of discussion is that it is difficult to ignore the impact of culture when discussing country-level differences in the work–family interface. Cultural factors have dominated cross-national work–family research and are deeply interwoven with structural factors (Ollier-Malaterre, 2014). Perhaps a key link between cultural and structural influences on the work–family interface is that social policy is often based on the needs of both employees and the economy. For example, a country in economic turmoil cannot likely afford to offer generous social benefits like public childcare or subsidized early retirement. Additionally, the needs of the people generally inform the social policy in a country; laws are not solely top-down forces but rather are informed by people and organizations. In democratic countries these needs can be voiced by the employees themselves; in other contexts, these needs may be observed and acted on by policymakers. When regulative institutions are reflective of cultural norms or expectations, they may also function to further cement those norms in that cultural context.

Social movements are one way that culture can affect structure in the work–family context and are a promising framework for understanding how national culture and structure interact. Social movements are collective actions driven by shared group identity, often targeting the change or adoption of particular social policy. Social movements are important in the context of international work–family structures because they represent a bottom-up process for community-driven policy change that may counter the homogenizing effects of globalization (Marquis & Battilana, 2009). For example, the United States is currently host to social movements related to work–family policy for paid sick leave, paid maternity leave, income equality, and guaranteed income.

In addition to pressuring policymakers, cultural forces like social movements can also affect work–family policy adoption at the organization level (Beham et al., 2014; Masuda et al., 2012). The target of such pressure may be a function of public perceptions of governmental and organizational legitimacy in managing family role demands, which can in turn be explained by welfare regimes (Ollier-Malaterre, 2009). Though researchers have long recognized the link between social movements and work–family issues in a society (e.g., Lewis & Cooper, 1996), there remains little theory or empirical research about work–family social movements. An exception is research suggesting unions may play an active role in social movements in order to effect change in social policy related to work–family roles and gender (e.g., Berg & Piszczek, 2014; Briskin, 2006; Gerstel & Clawson, 2000). Still, social movements remain an interesting framework for understanding drivers of socio-regulative institutional change and cultural and structural interaction.

A second issue of discussion is an overall lack of systematic theory of country-level influences on the work–family interface. Due to the complexity of socio-political systems, theoretical frameworks that adequately capture the relationships between these various institutional forces remain elusive. Indeed, even the broad framework used in this chapter dividing structural forces into social policy and economic characteristics is tenuous given the powerful interactions between the two (Ollier-Malaterre, 2014).

Theoretical work has helped fill in some of the gaps in our understanding. One broad but useful framework for understanding the combined effects of institutional forces are working time regimes. Working time regimes are the national "set of legal, voluntary and customary regulations which influence working-time practice" (Rubery, Smith, & Fagan, 1998, p. 72). Working time regimes relate to expectations and needs surrounding standard and non-standard work hours in an economy and thus affect the work–family interface through creation of norms surrounding working time. For example, the standard work week in economically developed countries is traditionally thirty-five to forty-four hours per week, with an additional overtime premium of 25–50% of normal hourly wages (Berg, Bosch, & Charest, 2014). Working time regimes also affect the promulgation and negotiation of part-time and undesirable work hours (Rubery et al., 1998), which also affect the work–family interface for individual employees. For example, Wielers and Raven (2013) argue that the explosive growth of part-time work among women in the Netherlands has corresponded with a decrease in adherence to work obligation norms (i.e., work centrality) and traditional gender norms.

Berg and colleagues (2014) provide a useful framework for analyzing working time regimes by providing three ideal types of country-level working time configurations that highlight relationships between social and economic institutions and the work–family interface. These working time configurations may help explain the relative importance of different institutional forces in a given context. They argue that working time configurations can be classified into ideal types of unilateral, negotiated, or mandated (though notably most countries do not perfectly align with one of these three ideal types). Under unilateral configurations, employers control working time. Under negotiated configurations, employers and employees together agree upon working time. Under mandated configurations, the state establishes working time, generally through regulation. Another study finds similar patterns in working time regimes. Chung and Tijdens (2012) used factor analysis to show that countries can largely be classified as either flexible for employers or for employees, but that some working time practices (e.g., part-time work, phased retirement, and flexible work hours) were equally present in both types of regimes.

Considering how work hours are determined provides valuable insights into the relative importance of particular institutions. For example, regulative institutions are likely of relatively little concern under more unilateral configurations while they are likely very important to the work–family interface under a mandated configuration. Industrial relations systems are likely more important determinants of the nature of the work–family interface under negotiated configurations.

A third point of discussion is that country-level institutions are not the highest theoretical level of analysis for understanding the work–family interface. In some cases, a country's social policy and economic characteristics may be influenced by involvement in international organizations such as the European Union (EU). Such organizations may influence social policy at the country-level role through prioritization of social issues. EU policy directives are legislated goals that EU members must achieve, but through a path determined by each individual country. These directives include minimum standards for parental leave and part-time work (Kossek, Lewis, & Hammer, 2010). This creates a baseline for country regulative institutions and social policy but still allows for country-level variation. For example, an EU policy directive currently requires the offering of four months of parental leave but individual countries can decide whether it should be paid or unpaid (Russell, O'Connell, & McGinnity, 2009). The EU may also make non-binding recommendations related to other social institutions. For example, the EU sets a target for 90 % of children between age three and school-age and 33 % of children two and under to have formal childcare arrangements (European Commission, 2013).

Conclusion

Although the body of research on structural influences on the work–family interface has grown rapidly in recent years, there remain many unanswered questions and challenges. Though researchers have provided a handful of multilevel theoretical frameworks relating structural components to organizational and individual outcomes, these frameworks remain broad and largely empirically untested. Recent reviews have begun to organize and make sense of these frameworks, but more research is needed to understand the more nuanced relationships proposed within them. For example, a question of particular importance is how organizational leaders make sense of structural characteristics to determine work–family policy offerings. Several theoretical frameworks suggest that regulative institutions create pressure on organizations to adopt them (Piszczek & Berg, 2014; Poelmans & Sahibzada, 2004), but there is little research to empirically explain why some organizations respond to these pressures differently than others.

Additionally, structural focus has largely been on regulative institutions and welfare regimes with less attention on other social policy and economic characteristics. For example, industrial relations systems have not typically been a structural focus of work–family research. In some contexts this system may play a major part in negotiating work–family policies and practices and thus warrants consideration in international and comparative work–family research. Similarly, social movements are also poorly understood in the organizational work–family literature despite having potentially large effects on socio-regulative institutional structures. Similarly, social movements play an important role in contributing to work–family structures but little is known about how they affect organizational adoption of work–family policies or employee needs and preferences for work–family role management. Cross-disciplinary research that examines culture and structure simultaneously may help organizational scholars better understand the formation and effects of social movements. Such research is needed to help predict the economic and societal effects of such social movements and corresponding structural changes. Overall, international work–family research must broaden beyond regulative institutions, not only because the impact of other structural factors is poorly understood, but also because the impact of regulative institutions themselves must be contextualized within additional structural (and cultural) factors.

This review highlights the importance of contextualization of work–family research as well as the need to study the work–family interface in new contexts. Though there is a large and growing body of international and comparative work–family research, much of the broader work–family literature omits contextual information about culture and structure that could be useful for developing stronger theories about macro-level influences on the work–family interface and designing more interesting comparative studies. As work–family researchers become more aware of structural and cultural influences that may affect work–family policy adoption and effectiveness within their study's samples, it is critical that these influences are discussed in each study. Even in research from the United States, scholars should be aware of and discuss the institutional forces that may affect their results and their generalization to other contexts. Over time, this discussion can contribute to a body of work–family research that acknowledges the rich and complex cultural, legal, and economic forces that shape the work–family experiences of employees and organizations across the world.

References

Abendroth, A. K., & den Dulk, L. (2011). Support for the work–life balance in Europe: The impact of state, workplace and family support on work–life balance satisfaction. *Work, Employment & Society, 25*(2), 234–256. http://doi.org/10.1177/0950017011398892

Barron, L. G., & Hebl, M. (2013). The force of law: The effects of sexual orientation anti-discrimination legislation on interpersonal discrimination in employment. *Psychology, Public Policy, and Law, 19*(2), 191–205. http://doi.org/10.1037/a0028350

Beham, B., Drobnič, S., & Präg, P. (2014). The work–family interface of service sector workers: A comparison of work resources and professional status across five European countries. *Applied Psychology, 63*(1), 29–61. http://doi.org/10.1111/apps.12012

Berg, P., Appelbaum, E., Bailey, T., & Kalleberg, A. (2003). Contesting time: International comparisons of employee control of working time. *Industrial & Labor Relations Review, 57*(3), 331–349. Retrieved from http://heinonlinebackup.com/hol-cgi-bin/get_pdf.cgi?handle=hein.journals/ialrr57&section=26

Berg, P., Bosch, G., & Charest, J. (2014). Working–time configurations: A framework for analyzing diversity across countries. *Industrial & Labor Relations Review, 67*, 805–837. http://doi.org/10.1177/0019793914537452

Berg, P. B., Hamman, M. K., Piszczek, M. M., & Ruhm, C. K. (2015). *Can Policy Facilitate Partial Retirement? Evidence from Germany* (IZA Discussion Paper Series No. 9266). Bonn, Germany.

Berg, P., Kossek, E. E., Baird, M., & Block, R. N. (2013). Collective bargaining and public policy: Pathways to work–family policy Adoption in Australia and the United States. *European Management Journal, 31*(5), 495–504.

Berg, P., Kossek, E. E., Misra, K., & Belman, D. (2014). Work–life flexibility policies: Do unions affect employee access and use? *Industrial & Labor Relations Review, 67*(1), 111–137. Retrieved from https://litigation-essentials. lexisnexis.com/webcd/app?action=DocumentDisplay&crawlid=1&doctype= cite&docid=67+Ind.+%2526+Lab.+Rel.+Rev.+111&srctype=smi&srcid= 3B15&key=1fb78c4a8895062c484fece912256721

Berg, P., & Piszczek, M. M. (2014). The limits of equality bargaining in the USA. *Journal of Industrial Relations, 56*(2), 170–189. http://doi.org/10.1177/0022185613517469

Bishop, K. (2004). Working time patterns in the UK, France, Denmark, and Sweden. *Labor Market Trends*, (March), 113–122.

Briskin, L. (2006). *Equity Bargaining/Bargaining Equity.* Toronto: Centre for Research on Work and Society. York University. Retrieved from www.yorku.ca/lbriskin/pdf/ bargainingpaperFINAL3secure.pdf

Chung, H., & Tijdens, K. (2012). Working time flexibility components and working time regimes in Europe: using company-level data across 21 countries. *The International Journal of Human Resource Management, 24*(December 2014), 1–17. http://doi.org/10.1080/09585192.2012.712544

Den Dulk, L., Groeneveld, S., Ollier-Malaterre, A., & Valcour, M. (2013). National context in work–life research: A multi-level cross-national analysis of the adoption of work-place work–life arrangements in Europe. *European Management Journal, 31*(5), 478–494. http://doi.org/10.1016/j.emj.2013.04.010

Den Dulk, L., Peters, P., Poutsma, E., & Ligthart, P. E. M. (2010). The extended business case for childcare and leave arrangements in Western and Eastern Europe. *Baltic Journal of Management, 5*(2), 156–184. http://doi.org/10.1108/17465261011045106

Esping-Andersen, G. (1990). *The Three Worlds of Welfare Capitalism.* Wiley. Retrieved from http://books.google.com/books?hl=en&lr=&id=KHdnAgAAQBAJ&pgis=1

Esping-Andersen, G. (1999). *Social Foundations of Postindustrial Economies.* Chicago, IL: Oxford University Press.

European Commission. (2013). *Barcelona Objectives: The development of childcare facilities for young children in Europe with a view to sustainable and inclusive growth.* Retrieved from http://ec.europa.eu/justice/gender-equality/files/documents/ 130531_barcelona_en.pdf

Gerstel, N., & Clawson, D. (2000). Unions responses to family concerns. In *Work and Family: Expanding the Horizons* (Vol. 48, p. 277). San Francisco, CA. http://doi.org/ 10.1525/sp.2001.48.2.277

Graf, N., Hofer, H., & Winter-Ebmer, R. (2011). Labor supply effects of a subsidized old-age part-time scheme in Austria. *Zeitschrift Für ArbeitsmarktForschung* (March 2013), 1–13. http://doi.org/10.1007/s12651-011-0072-8

Greller, M. (2012). Workforce planning with an aging workforce. In J. W. Hedge & W. C. Borman (Eds.), *The Oxford Handbook of Work and Aging* (pp. 365–379). New York, NY: Oxford University Press.

House, R. J., Hanges, P. J., Javidan, M., Dorfman, P. W., & Gupta, V. (2004). *Culture, Leadership, and Organizations: The GLOBE Study of 62 Societies.* Thousand Oaks, CA: SAGE Publications.

Huebler, O., & Jirjahn, U. (2003). Works councils and collective bargaining in Germany: The impact on productivity and wages. *Scottish Journal of Political Economy, 50*(4).

Jorgensen, B. H., & Appelbaum, E. (2014). *Documenting the Need for a National Paid Family and Medical Leave Program: Evidence from the 2012 FMLA Survey.* Center for Economic Policy and Research, Washington, DC.

Kassinis, G. I., & Stavrou, E. T. (2013). Non-standard work arrangements and national context. *European Management Journal, 31*(5), 464–477. http://doi.org/10.1016/j.emj.2013.04.005

Kossek, E. E., Lautsch, B. A., & Eaton, S. C. (2006). Telecommuting, control, and boundary management: Correlates of policy use and practice, job control, and work–family effectiveness. *Journal of Vocational Behavior, 68*(2), 347–367. http://doi.org/10.1016/j.jvb.2005.07.002

Kossek, E. E., Lewis, S., & Hammer, L. B. (2010). Work–life initiatives and organizational change: Overcoming mixed messages to move from the margin to the mainstream. *Human Relations, 63*(1), 3–19. http://doi.org/10.1177/0018726709352385

Kossek, E. E., & Michel, J. S. (2011). Flexible Work Schedules. In S. Zedeck (Ed.), *APA Handbook of Industrial and Organizational Psychology Volume 1* 535–572. Washington, DC: American Psychological Association.

Leon, M. (2005). Welfare State regimes and the social organization of labour: Childcare arrangements and the work/family balance dilemma. *Sociological Review, 53* (SUPPL. 2), 204–218. http://doi.org/10.1111/j.1467-954X.2005.00581.x

Lewis, S., & Cooper, C. C. L. (1996). Balancing the work/home interface: A European perspective. *Human Resource Management Review, 5*(4), 289–305. http://doi.org/10.1016/1053-4822(95)90011-X

Lewis, S., Gambles, R., & Rapoport, R. (2007). The constraints of a "work – life balance" approach: An international perspective. *The International Journal of Human Resource Management, 18*(3), 360–373. http://doi.org/10.1080/09585190601165577

Lyness, K. S., Gornick, J. C., Stone, P., & Grotto, a. R. (2012). It's all about control: Worker control over schedule and hours in cross-national context. *American Sociological Review, 77*(6), 1023–1049. http://doi.org/10.1177/0003122412465331

Maestas, N., & Zissimopoulos, J. (2010). How longer work lives ease the crunch of population aging. *Journal of Economic Perspectives, 24*(1), 139–160. http://doi.org/10.1257/jep.24.1.139

Marquis, C., & Battilana, J. (2009). Acting globally but thinking locally? The enduring influence of local communities on organizations. *Research in Organizational Behavior, 29*, 283–302. http://doi.org/10.1016/j.riob.2009.06.001

Masuda, A. D., Poelmans, S. A. Y., Allen, T. D., Spector, P. E., Lapierre, L. M., Cooper, C. L., . . . Moreno-Velazquez, I. (2012). Flexible work arrangements availability and their relationship with work-to-family conflict, job satisfaction, and turnover intentions: A comparison of three country clusters. *Applied Psychology, 61*(1), 1–29. http://doi.org/10.1111/j.1464-0597.2011.00453.x

OECD. (2015). *Pensions at a Glance 2013: OECD and G20 Indicators*. Paris: OECD Publishing. Retrieved from http://dx.doi.org/10.1787/pension_glance-2013-en

Ollier-Malaterre, A. (2009). Organizational work–life initiatives: Context matters. *Community, Work & Family, 12*(2), 159–178. http://doi.org/10.1080/136688009 02778942

(2014). Cross-national work–family research: A review at the individual level. In T. D. Allen & L. T. Eby (Eds.), *Oxford Handbook of Work and Family* (pp. 1–38). Oxford: Oxford University Press.

Ollier-Malaterre, A., & Foucreault, A. (2016). Cross-national work–life research: Cultural and structural impacts for individuals and organizations. *Journal of Management, XX*(X), 1–26. http://doi.org/10.1177/0149206316655873

Parboteeah, K. P., & Cullen, J. B. (2003). Social institutions and work centrality: explorations beyond national culture. *Organization Science, 14*(2), 137–148. http://doi.org/10.1287/orsc.14.2.137.14989

Piszczek, M. M., & Berg, P. (2014). Expanding the boundaries of boundary theory: Regulative institutions and work–family role management. *Human Relations, 67*(12), 1491–1512. http://doi.org/10.1177/0018726714524241

Pitt-Catsouphes, M., Matz-costa, C., & Besen, E. (2009). Workplace flexibility: Findings from the Age & Generations Study. The Sloan Center on Aging & Work. Boston, MA.

Poelmans, S., & Sahibzada, K. (2004). A multi-level model for studying the context and impact of work–family policies and culture in organizations. *Human Resource Management Review, 14*(4), 409–431. http://doi.org/10.1016/j.hrmr.2004.10.003

Riisgaard, L. (2005). International framework agreements: a new model for securing workers rights? *Industrial Relations, 44*(4), 707–737.

Rubery, J., Smith, M., & Fagan, C. (1998). National working-time regimes and equal opportunities. *Feminist Economics, 4*(1), 71–101. Retrieved from www.annualre views.org/doi/abs/10.1146/annurev.physchem.57.032905.104601

Russell, H., O'Connell, P. J., & McGinnity, F. (2009). The impact of flexible working arrangements on work–life conflict and work pressure in Ireland. *Gender, Work and Organization, 16*(1), 73–97. http://doi.org/10.1111/j.1468-0432.2008 .00431.x

Sweet, S., Pitt-Catsouphes, M., Besen, E., & Golden, L. (2014). Explaining organizational variation in flexible work arrangements: why the pattern and scale of availability matter. *Community, Work & Family, 17*(2), 115–141. http://doi.org/10.1080/13668803.2014.887553

Tomlinson, J. (2007). Employment regulation, welfare and gender regimes: a comparative analysis of women's working-time patterns and work–life balance in the UK and the US. *The International Journal of Human Resource Management, 18*(February 2014), 401–415. http://doi.org/10.1080/09585190601167466

Wadensjö, S. (2006). *Part-time pensions and part-time work in Sweden. IZA Discussion Paper Series, No. 2273*. Institute of Labor Economics, Nuremberg, Germany.

Wielers, R., & Raven, D. (2013). Part-time work and work norms in the Netherlands. *European Sociological Review, 29*(1), 105–113. http://doi.org/10.1093/esr/jcr043

Williamson, S., & Baird, M. (2014). Gender equality bargaining: Developing theory and practice. *Journal of Industrial Relations, 56*(2), 155–169. http://doi.org/10.1177/0022185613517468

Wood, S. J., & de Menezes, L. M. (2007). Family-friendly management, organizational performance and social legitimacy. *The International Journal of Human Resource Management*, *21*(10), 1–42. http://doi.org/10.1080/09585192.2010.500484

Yerkes, M., Standing, K., Wattis, L., & Wain, S. (2010). The disconnection between policy practices and women's lived experiences: combining work and life in the UK and the Netherlands. *Community, Work & Family*, *13*(4), 411–427. http://doi.org/10.1080/13668801003619407

6 The Impact of Leave Policies on Employment, Fertility, Gender Equality, and Health

Anne H. Gauthier and Alzbeta Bartova

Leave policies is an umbrella term which encompasses several types of governmental support associated with childbirth and that allow parents to temporarily interrupt their economic activity in order to be at home with their children. These different types include maternity, paternity, parental and homecare/childcare leave (see their definitions below). The origins of such policies date back more than 100 years and were introduced to protect the health of mothers and infants (Gauthier & Koops, forthcoming). Today leave policies pursue broader aims related to gender equality and work–family reconciliation (Haas, 2003). In a few countries, leave policies also pursue a pronatalist objective (i.e., to increase the country's fertility level) but this is rather exceptional (Spiess & Wrohlich, 2008). Instead, it is generally recognized that by helping women and men combine work and family responsibilities, leave policies may also help parents in deciding to have children even though raising fertility may not be the intention of the leave policies (Duvander et al., 2016).

In this chapter, we review the literature on the impact of such leave policies on the work–family interface by focusing on four domains: employment, fertility, the gender division of unpaid work, and health. These four domains are intrinsically related but are rarely reviewed together and are instead the subject of distinct bodies of literature. Moreover, the inclusion of the health domain in our review taps into a relatively new body of literature and suggests important spillovers from the health domain onto both the work and family spheres.

Our review takes a global approach in that we did not restrict ourselves to specific countries or specific regions of the world. It remains that the literature on the impact of leave policies tends to be dominated by European and North American studies. We start the review by defining the different types of leave policies covered in this chapter and introducing some key terms. We then proceed by reviewing the empirical evidence and methodological developments regarding each of the four domains. In each sub-section of our chapter, we also examine whether the impacts of the policies were found to be the same across different segments of the population or whether there were instead significant differences. We conclude the chapter by reflecting on the broader policy implications of the findings, especially in connection with their objectives of gender equality and work–family reconciliation.

Overview of the Different Types of Leave Policies

There are four main types of leave policies that are associated with child-birth – maternity, paternity, parental, and homecare leave. Maternity leave is generally defined as a job-protective leave for female employees with the aim to protect the health of the mother and her child shortly before and after birth (Landau & Beigbeder, 2008; OECD, 2007). Such leave is usually job-protected in that the mother can return to her previous job at the end of her leave. The duration of the leave varies across countries but is generally around four to six months, while its wage-replacement rate is often equal to 100 %. The counterpart for men is paternity leave, which is usually of very short duration (i.e., a few days), is reserved for fathers after the birth of their child, and is usually job-protected (OECD, 2007). In some countries, such a right is not restricted to working fathers and is instead available to all fathers (Moss, 2009; Rostgaard, 2009; Salmi & Lami-Taskula, 2009).

In most countries, maternity and paternity leave can be followed by additional leave. The OECD distinguishes between two types of such leave – parental and homecare leave. The former is a job-protected leave aimed at employed parents, whilst homecare leave is a form of leave available to parents regardless of their economic status (OECD, 2007). In the latter case, the policy thus covers both employed and non-employed parents who are provided with the same financial support. In both cases, the leave can be of a considerable duration (one year or more) and may be paid or unpaid (with large variations in its wage-replacement rate across countries). Moreover, as its name implies, parental leave is not restricted to mothers but can usually be shared between parents. In some countries parents are free to decide how to share the leave between them (e.g., Germany) while in others a portion of the leave is reserved for each parent and is non-transferable. For example, in Norway, the individual right to parental leave for fathers (the "daddy quota") is strictly reserved for the father and cannot be transferred to the mother if he decides not to use it.

The take-up rate of parental and homecare leave varies highly across countries and is usually quite low in the case of fathers. In particular, fathers' use of leave entitlement is believed to be dependent primarily on whether their entitlements are transferable or non-transferable. For example, in countries where fathers are entitled to non-transferable leave, the leave take-up amongst fathers reaches about 90% (e.g., Spain: 80%, Denmark: 89%, Sweden: 90%, Iceland: 91%; Carmen Castro-García & Maria Pazos-Moran, 2016). However, when fathers are presented with leave entitlements that can be fully transferred to the mother, their take-up declines below 10% in most countries (an exception is Denmark: 24%, Iceland: 19.7%, and Sweden: 18%).

Leave Arrangements and Labor Force Participation

Leave arrangements are considered an important lever to promote gender equality in employment especially as a way of encouraging the return to work of mothers after childbirth, and in turn, as a way of reducing the motherhood pay penalty[1] (Budig, Misra, & Boeckmann, 2016). In general, the literature has concluded that job-protected paid leave arrangements of a medium duration have a positive impact on female labor force participation (Hegewisch & Gornick, 2011). For example, a recent cross-national analysis based on data from the European Community Household Panel revealed that job-protected leave of at least one year increased the likelihood of return to work after childbirth (Pronzato, 2009). Moreover, the literature has consistently shown that a high level of wage replacement is a key factor in the take-up rate of such leaves and in the return to work after childbirth. In contrast when the leave is unpaid or when the level of wage replacement is low, the take-up rate of leave is generally low (Hegewisch & Gornick, 2011). The United States provide a good "natural" experiment since – in the absence of a country-wide maternity leave for all female employees – only a fraction of mothers are entitled to paid leave.[2] Studies have demonstrated that American mothers with access to paid leave have a higher return to work after childbirth than their counterparts without access to such a leave (Berger & Waldfogel 2004). However, findings also suggest that financial constraints may actually speed up the return to work after childbirth when mothers are entitled to a leave with a low level of wage replacement (Baxter, 2008; Whitehouse, Hosking, & Baird, 2008; Ziefle & Gangl, 2014).

When it comes to the duration of leave, findings are rather mixed. For example, while some studies suggest that women with access to a leave of a long duration are less likely to return to work at the end of their leave, as compared to women with access to a shorter leave (Jaumotte, 2003; Lalive & Zweimüller, 2009), other studies instead conclude that this is not the case (Ruhm, 1998).[3] Moreover, there is no unanimity in the literature as to the optimal duration of different types of leave. For instance, while Akgunduz and Plantenga (2013) recently suggested that leaves between 20 and 30 weeks would maximize female labor force participation, Thévenon and Solaz (2013) instead concluded that paid leaves up to two years had no negative influence on female employment rates or the gender ratio of employment. Findings from the literature are more consistent when it comes to the negative effects of leaves of long duration on other dimensions of female employment. More specifically, studies agree that longer leave arrangements are associated with a long-term pay penalty (Datta Gupta, Smith, & Verner, 2008), a lower likelihood of upward occupational mobility once back on the labor market (Evertsson & Duvander, 2010), and a higher degree of gender job segregation (Akgunduz & Plantenga, 2013).

In the literature on the impact of leave policies on labor force participation, one dimension that has started to receive more attention is the possible differential impact of leave arrangements for different subgroups of the population, especially in terms of socioeconomic status (SES). There are several reasons why such

---

[1] The term "motherhood pay penalty" refers to the long-term shortfall in earnings for women who withdrew from the labor market for periods of time to take care of their children at home.

[2] The federal unpaid maternity leave in the United States applies only to women with larger employers (fifty of more employees). However, some states and some employers do offer paid maternity leave.

[3] One possible explanation is that women postpone their return to work in order to have another child. See the section on fertility for more details.

a differential impact can be expected. On the one hand, women of higher SES or higher level of education may have a longer history of employment prior to childbirth and may therefore be more likely to be eligible for leave arrangements than women of lower SES. Women with a higher level of education may also be more likely to have access to employer-provided leave, which may offer even better terms (duration and wage replacement) than those that are nationally mandated or may be in a better position to actually negotiate such better terms with their employer. On the other hand, women of higher SES are also likely to have higher pay and may therefore be less willing to forego income, especially when the leave comes with a low-level of wage replacement. Women of higher SES may also have a higher level of labor force attachment and may therefore be unwilling to withdraw from the labor market for longer periods of time. In practice, what we know is that take-up rates of extended leaves tend to be higher among women with lower levels of education. In turn, these women tend also to have lower rates of return to work after childbirth (Hegewisch & Gornick, 2011).

One area where contemporary literature on leave arrangements has shown particular promise is in the use of sophisticated methodological design to allow for a better measurement of the impact of policies and their variations across subpopulations. For example, the use of quasi- or natural-experiments has gained considerable popularity in order to better isolate the impact of leave arrangements from other possible confounding factors (Ang, 2015; Asai, 2015; Bergemann & Riphahn, 2015; Geyer, Haan, & Wrohlich, 2015) and to reveal the differential impact of leave arrangements on different subgroups in the population. Moreover, there has been a call for more nuanced analyses including a better discerning of the impact of different components of the leave arrangements (e.g., duration, pay) on female employment and a broadening of the analyses to other employment outcomes (e.g., occupational segregation, job-related training and wages) (Dearing, 2015). Finally, there is the unresolved issue of the role of contextual factors in moderating the impact of leave arrangements. For example, a specific leave arrangement may have a different impact depending on the gender norms in place in one country (Cascio, Haider, & Nielsen, 2015). Such contextual factors may matter in explaining the observed mixed findings regarding the impact of policies across and within countries.

Leave Arrangements and Fertility

Fertility in developed countries has been steadily declining over several decades and all OECD countries – with an exception of Israel, Mexico and Turkey – currently face unprecedented fertility rates below population replacement levels (in the developed world that corresponds to 2.1 children per woman) (OECD, 2016). The literature on employment and fertility behavior is densely interwoven with a belief that policies which enable a better combination of employment and care responsibilities can help prevent further decline in fertility or may even reverse the trend (Adsera, 2011; Esping-Andersen & Billari, 2015; Gauthier, 2007; Hilgeman &

Butts, 2009; Sleebos, 2003). Amongst the policies that facilitate work–family balance are, for instance, flexible employment, subsidies for childcare providers and provisions of leave policies for parents. Some studies find a positive association between the combination of such policies and fertility (Bonoli, 2008; Luci-Greulich & Thévenon, 2013) but others do not (Harknett, Billari, & Medalia, 2014; Lee & Lee, 2014).

Leave policies often have complex designs characterized by strict eligibility criteria that does not only determine the access to the policy but also the extent of financial compensation and in some cases the leave duration. Research investigating the association between leave policies and fertility rarely covers all these eligibility characteristics. A handful of studies compare the differences in the likelihood of birth between eligible and non-eligible women. For instance, Cannonier (2014) compares the timing of first and second birth amongst American women who could have benefited from the introduction of the Family and Medical Leave Act in 1993 and those women who would not be entitled to the support from this policy. His findings reveal that after the introduction of this policy, eligible women had their first child up to one year earlier than their non-eligible counterparts. Cordula Zabel (2009) conducted a similar analysis using British data. She found some evidence that women who fulfilled the eligibility conditions for maternity leave following its introduction in 1976 had a higher transition rate to first birth than women who would not be able to draw on this policy. Evidence based on eligibility criteria also come from countries having in place a so-called "speed premium," an option that allows mothers of at least one child to renew their leave entitlements if they give birth to an additional child within a certain time frame (Andersson, Hoem, & Duvander, 2006). Empirical evidence, suggests that this is the case for example, in Sweden (Hoem, 1993) and Austria (Lalive & Zweimüller, 2009; Šťastná & Sobotka, 2009).

Research that investigates the effect of leave duration on fertility behavior has so far led to inconclusive results. In Norway and Austria, where the leave for new parents exceeds one year, mothers who use their leave entitlements for an extended period of time have a smaller probability of having a second child compared to mothers who opt for a shorter leave (Duvander, Lappegård, & Andersson, 2010; Lalive & Zweimüller, 2009). However, it is important to note that neither of the studies was conducted on a sample of women at the end of their reproductive period (generally at the age of forty-five, but forty is sometimes used as a benchmark). It means that although the results revealed differences in the propensity to second births amongst mothers depending on the duration of leave, we do not know whether the women who opted for a longer leave with their first child eventually managed to have second child but later than women who opted for a shorter leave. In other words, we cannot be sure whether the effect of leave is affecting only the timing of the second births or whether it also has an impact on the total number of children a woman has during her life course. Moreover, the findings are not unanimous across countries. In Sweden, for example, the relationship between leave duration and second births appears to be curvilinear such that mothers who are using moderately long leave have a higher likelihood of having a second child compared to mothers who choose a short or very long leave (Duvander et al., 2010; Duvander & Andersson, 2006).

Recent analysis of maternity and parental leave policies in Europe suggests that the effect of the leave duration on fertility outcomes may be dependent on their financial compensation (Bartova, 2016). A study by Matysiak and Szalma (2014) that compared parental leave benefits in Hungary and Poland found that generous universal benefits are positively associated with second births compared to poorly compensated and means-tested benefits, which are reserved only for parents with low income. In contrast, more recent research conducted in Germany revealed that parental leave benefits that reflect pre-birth earnings lead to greater postponement of second births amongst mothers with low-income (Cygan-Rehm, 2016). These findings suggest that the characteristics of home-care leave may produce a difference in fertility responses amongst women with different positions in the labor market. Nonetheless, little research has been conducted to uncover the socio economic differences in leave uptake and its effects on fertility behavior.

Some studies do not distinguish between leave duration and financial benefits and instead combine the two measures. This is the case of studies that observed the contextual effects of the leave policies on fertility behavior and used macro-level indicators. Harknett, Billari, and Medalia (2014) calculated the so-called full-rate equivalent which shows how long a leave would be if it was compensated at 100% of pre-birth earnings. They applied this indicator to comparative data covering twenty European countries. However, contrary to other studies, their results show that there is no association between their indicator of childcare leave and the propensity of either first or second birth. Baizán, Arpino, and Delclos (2016) used the same indicator of leave policies and observed their effect on completed fertility (i.e., the number of children women had at the end of their reproductive period) amongst women from sixteen European countries and also did not find any association between the leave indicators and fertility. Luci-Greulich and Thévenon (2013) also conducted a comparative analysis amongst European countries using macro-level policy indicators. They chose a slightly different approach using total fertility rates and included only the leave duration that is accompanied with financial compensation and decided not to include leave that is unpaid. However, their approach also found no significant effect of the child-related leave on fertility. Recent analysis of maternity and parental leave policies in Europe suggests that the effect of financial compensation on first and second births decreases with the leave duration (Bartova, 2016). Overall, this literature thus suggests complex relationships between various dimensions of the leave policies (e.g., duration, wage-replacement, eligibility) and fertility. These relationships may also vary at the individual-level depending on women's characteristic (e.g., labor market history) and at the macro-level depending on the national and institutional context.

In recent years, the attention has turned also to fathers and their use of paternity and parental leave entitlements in an attempt at estimating the extent to which it also influences fertility decisions. The scope of the research is, however, limited because fathers still do not have a right to paternity leave and do not have an individual right to parental leave in all developed countries, meaning that the law does not determine a share of leave that would be available solely to fathers. Consequently, the research focuses only on those countries that ensure such a right to fathers and also have a greater number of fathers who use these entitlements. Consequently, the knowledge we have so far on this issue comes mostly from the Nordic countries. For instance, researchers in Iceland observed that introducing the opportunity of parental leave for fathers, which not only provides them with the right to the leave but also compensates them for a large share of their earnings, was associated with an increase in fertility rates (Gíslason, 2007). Research conducted using Swedish and Norwegian data provides some evidence that fathers who use at least some parental leave with their first and second child have a higher propensity to have both a second and third child (Duvander et al., 2010). Moreover, the same study found that, with the exception of very long leave, there is a positive association between the duration of leave used by fathers and the propensity to have a second and third child. In an earlier study, Oláh (2003) found a positive association between leave uptake amongst fathers and the probability of second birth in Sweden.

In all of these studies, a major limitation of the data come from incomplete information on the take-up rate of the leave schemes. Currently, the most comprehensive information about leave uptake is available in Nordic countries, which may explain the large share of research into leave policies that comes from these countries. More recently new research emerged from Germany (Cygan-Rehm, 2013; Tamm, 2013) which introduced a substantial reform into their parental leave scheme in 2007 that was inspired by the Nordic parental leave schemes. Although such case studies are very valuable and informative, it is not clear whether such leave designs are transferable to other countries and whether such transformation of leave policies could yield similar fertility outcomes in different cultural and political context. Some answers could be provided through comparative analyses that would take into consideration the variation in the maternity, paternity and parental leave designs whilst also acknowledging the cultural and socio economic differences in which these policies exist (Bartova & Emery, 2016).

Leave Arrangements and Gender Equality at Home

The transition to parenthood can considerably alter the division of paid and unpaid work between partners. Upon becoming mothers, women tend to shorten their time in paid work in order to invest more time in child care, whilst men tend to adjust their time schedules only marginally (Argyrous, Craig, & Rahman, 2016; Craig & Mullan, 2010; Frenette, 2010). Some authors argue that the traditional division of labor between partners is particularly persistent in countries with rigid family policies and low support for gender equality (Geist & Cohen, 2011; Neilson & Stanfors, 2014). Amongst policy measures that are targeted at families, the leave policies are the most obvious measures that could facilitate parents' division of childcare responsibilities following birth (Schober, 2014).

The character of the rights to parental leave (transferable or non-transferable to the mother) and the amount of financial support are particularly important for fathers to share the leave with the mothers. Fathers are most likely to use their entitlement to leave if they are provided with a non-transferable right to leave and when the financial compensation for their time invested in child care is very close to the earnings they forego (Castro-García & Pazos-Moran, 2015; Kaufman, Lyonette, & Crompton, 2010; Kotsadam & Finseraas, 2011; Schober, 2014). In turn, when fathers are entitled to unpaid or poorly paid leave or their entitlements are not specifically addressed to them through paternity leave or a "daddy quota," the uptake of leave by fathers tends to be very low (Han & Waldfogel, 2003). The opportunities for fathers to provide child care to a similar degree as mothers are therefore likely to be limited in countries that do not provide paternity leave and base the parental leave solely, or its significant part, on an individual transferable right. The literature shows that when presented with a choice over the allocation of parental leave time between mothers and fathers, mothers often take the entire or vast share of this parental leave (Castro-García & Pazos-Moran, 2015).

The difficulties with the individual transferable right to parental leave do not lie only in the transferability between parents but also in their association with flat-rate benefits (i.e., benefits expressed in terms of an absolute value instead as a proportion of earnings). This is particularly true of low financial benefits. The combination of an individual transferable right to leave and low benefit level can act as a strong disincentive for fathers to use their entitlements. This is because men are still more likely to have higher earnings than their female partners and opting for a leave would, therefore, represent a sizeable reduction in family income. Recent research also suggests that fathers may prefer part-time or flexible leave arrangements over full-time leave (Brandth & Kvande, 2016). The flexibility in the use of leave is another characteristic of these policies that may facilitate the higher use of leave entitlements amongst fathers but these characteristics have been often overlooked in the literature.

The characteristics of the policies that have the potential to encourage fathers to participate in child care from birth can have important implications for the subsequent gender division of childcare tasks. There is, for example, some evidence that fathers who act upon their right to take time off work to provide care for their children are more likely to provide care even after their leave entitlements expire as compared to fathers who did not take any leave (Bünning, 2015; Pragg & Knoester, 2015; Schober & Zoch, 2015). However, it is yet not entirely clear whether such an outcome could be a result of a selection effect where those fathers who use their leave entitlements are also those who would be more engaged in child care regardless of their rights to leave. The effect of the leave uptake amongst fathers and their subsequent participation in child care and housework also seems to be dependent on how long a leave they take. In this case, the findings suggest that if fathers take short leave the effect on their involvement is smaller than amongst fathers who use a longer period of leave (Almqvist & Duvander, 2014; Romero-Balsas, 2015).

Apart from the character of the leave policies, individual characteristics of fathers and their partners matter in fathers' motivation to use childcare leave. Fathers are more likely to use their entitlements if they have higher earnings, are employed on permanent working contacts, are employed in the public sector, in a female-dominated workplace or a larger size company (Bygren & Duvander, 2006; Escot, Fernández-Cornejo, & Poza, 2013; Geisler & Kreyenfeld, 2011; Lappegård, 2012; Rønsen & Sundström, 2002; Whitehouse, Diamond, & Baird, 2007). Fathers may also be more inclined to use childcare leave if they have male colleagues who have done so in the past (Bygren & Duvander, 2006). If their partner is in full-time employment, has comparable earnings, or works in a male-dominated workplace, fathers are also more inclined to use their leave entitlements (Almqvist, 2008; Escot et al., 2013; Lappegård, 2012; Lundquist, Misra, & O'Meara, 2012; Naz, 2010). It is important to mention that lack of paternity or parental leave for fathers does not necessarily mean that men do not take any time off in order to provide care. This is especially the case in the time immediately following the birth when fathers without a right to paternity leave or with an entitlement to unpaid paternity leave seek alternative arrangements such as a use of their annual vacation time (Kaufman et al., 2010; Whitehouse et al., 2007).

Paternal child care and uptake of parental leave amongst fathers is an expanding research area. The research points to the important role of parental leave targeted at fathers. Yet, it is still not entirely clear how big a role the leave policies actually play in the gender division of unpaid work. The existing research does not provide a satisfying answer to the question of whether the leave policies for fathers support the underlying tendencies towards engaged fatherhood or whether they actually encourage greater involvement in child care amongst fathers who would not otherwise be inclined to do so. The strategies fathers adopt in countries with a lack of support for paternal child care in order to provide child care or to help their female partner has also not been sufficiently investigated so far. Moreover, we have little knowledge about the potential strain new fathers may experience when taking leave and/or increasing their involvement in child care, about the consequences for their psychological and physical health, and how these may in turn affect maternal labor market outcomes, fertility behavior, health or relationship stability.

Leave Arrangements and Health

In contrast to the previous domains, there has been much less research on the possible impact of leave arrangements on the health domain. Yet, the health domain is likely a crucial element linking policies and employment as well as policies and fertility. For without good health and a satisfying sense of work–family balance, parents may be less likely to maintain a continuous employment trajectory and/or to consider having another child. Moreover, and as discussed below, the impact of leave arrangements is not restricted to parental health but also extends to child health.

Maternal and Paternal Health

The literature on the impact of leave arrangements on maternal health has mostly focused on the impact of the duration of leave as opposed to other dimensions.

In particular, the literature has revealed the negative impact of leave of short durations on a wide range of health indicators including depression and overall health status (Burtle & Bezruchka, 2016; Chatterji & Markowitz, 2012; Dagher, McGovern, & Dowd, 2014). Several of these studies, however, are based on American data where the absence of a nation-wide paid maternity leave scheme frames the question of the impact of leave in a very specific context. In other countries, the evidence regarding the impact of leave arrangements on maternal health is rather mixed. For example, in their systematic review of seven studies from different countries, Aitken et al. (2015) found evidence of a positive impact of leave arrangements on a wide-range of health indicators in four studies (based on Australian, American, and Lebanese data) but not in the other three (based on Canadian, Norwegian, and Swedish data). The key difference appears however not to be related to the countries themselves but rather to the methodology used in these studies. While a positive impact of leave arrangements on maternal health was found in studies based on individual-level experience of leave arrangement, no impact was found in studies based on country-level policy variations. Commenting on the methodological limitations of these studies, including confounding bias and the possibility of reverse causation, the authors concluded that "longitudinal studies are needed to further clarify the effects of paid maternity leave on the health of mothers in paid employment" (p. 40).

Some recent studies have also examined the very long-term impact of leave arrangements on health. The idea here stems from the cumulative inequality (or cumulative disadvantage) theory which posits that positive or detrimental health experiences that occurred early in life can have long-term consequences (Ferraro & Shippee, 2009). Evidence from women aged fifty years old and older from eight countries in the Survey of Health, Ageing and Retirement in Europe confirms the positive impact of maternity leave on mental health at older ages. More specifically, the extension of maternity leave from a limited coverage to a more comprehensive one was found to reduce depression scores later in life (Avendano, Berkman, Brugiavini, & Pasini, 2014). Similarly, a Swedish study found a positive impact of having taken paternity leave on health, specifically a decreased risk of mortality at older ages (Månsdotter, Lindholm, & Winkvist, 2007). This is a relatively new body of literature and it remains somewhat unclear the extent to which these long-term effects may be explained by self-selection into maternity or paternity leave or by other confounding factors.

Child Health

The study of the impact of leave arrangements on child health forms a relatively recent body of literature but one that has grown rapidly. It follows three main research designs: studies using aggregate data and that employ a time-series cross-national pooled approach, studies based on individual-level data and which compare the health of children whose mothers have returned rapidly (or not) to the labor market after childbirth or have (or have not) taken maternity leave, and finally designs centered around the introduction of a major policy reform. Overall the literature has concluded that there is a positive impact of job-protected paid maternity and parental leave on a wide range of child health indicators. Studies have found such leave arrangements to be associated with reduced infant mortality, reduced incidence of low birth weight, reduced incidence of premature birth, increased immunization rates, and increased duration and initiation of breastfeeding (Khanam, Nghiem, & Connelly, 2016; Shim, 2013; Tanaka, 2005). The suggested mechanism is that by being granted some time off from work, mothers can devote more time to their own health and that of their children, can better attend to their children's needs, and generally can improve their own well-being and that of their children in a way that results in better health outcomes. However, these studies have found evidence of such a positive impact only in the case of job-protected paid maternity and parental leave. Other leaves (including unpaid leave and non-job protected leave) do not appear to have the same beneficial impact on child health.

Other Child Outcomes

Finally, some recent studies have attempted to measure the possible long-term impact of leave arrangements on children's academic performance. Studies from Germany (Dustmann & Schönberg, 2012), Austria (Danzer & Lavy, 2013), and Denmark (Rasmussen, 2010) found no evidence of a positive impact of parental leave on children's educational outcome. However, there is some evidence of a differential impact by socioeconomic status through which children with higher SES benefit positively from parental leave in Austria (Danzer & Lavy, 2013) and Sweden (Liu & Skans, 2010). The reverse was however found in Norway where an expansion of parental leave appears to have improved mainly the educational outcome of children of mothers with low SES (Carneiro, Løken, & Salvanes, 2015). This longer-term impact of leave arrangements is one area that warrants further investigation.

Conclusion

The arguments for job-protected leave with high income replacement are numerous. As reviewed above, such leaves are generally associated with higher female labor force participation, higher employment continuity, greater gender pay equality, greater gender equality in unpaid work, better parental and child health, and higher fertility. Although leave policies are generally associated with positive outcomes, especially when they are paired with generous financial compensation, the findings are inconclusive regarding leave duration with respect to both maternal employment and fertility outcomes. Furthermore, the sheer eligibility for such leave arrangements is an issue that has often been overlooked in the literature. In particular, in several countries, parents on short-term contracts, working part-time, or being self-employed are not eligible to leave arrangements (see Koslowski, Blum, & Moss, 2016). The eligibility rules in terms of a minimum duration of employment prior to pregnancy may further restrict the proportion of women entitled to leave arrangements, especially in the context of increasing temporary work. Moreover, the obligation of employers to honor leave arrangements may even result in job discrimination against young women of childbearing ages. In theory, such job discrimination is not allowed by law in several countries but may be happening under other pretenses. Empirical evidence appears to be lacking on this topic.

The impact of leave arrangements on the work–family interface constitutes a rapidly growing body of literature utilizing increasingly sophisticated longitudinal designs or semi-experimental designs to better isolate the impact of policies and understand population heterogeneity. In particular, the differential impact of leave arrangements on parents of different SES constitutes a very important topic with large policy implications (Keck & Saraceno, 2013). It remains that our knowledge of the impact of leave arrangements is incomplete, especially when it comes to non-Western countries and/or less developed countries (see Hajizadech, Heymann, Strumpf, Harper, & Nandi, 2015). The discrepancies in the findings of studies that were conducted on an individual versus country-level have not been resolved and introduce additional questions as to what extent and for whom the leave policies actually matter in the work–family interface. Such outcomes call for a more thorough understanding of the individual-level processes and their implications for the aggregated outcomes. Moreover, a father's perspective continues to be lacking in numerous studies and in the design of work–family reconciliation policies (Bunning & Pollmann-Schult, 2016; O'Brien, 2013).

Despite the often inconclusive findings in virtually all domains of life covered in this chapter, the research shows that leave policies are not a marginal part of the work–family interface but instead play an important role in this context. They have the potential to include mothers in the labor market as well as to strengthen their position there. What is more, they are also capable of encouraging fathers in taking larger share in the childrearing role, which in turn can cement the positive effect on female employment and consequently also on women's and child's health. The research also suggests that the character of the leave policies matter and that the boundary between the positive and negative implications for people's lives can be very narrow. It is therefore important not to evaluate the leave policies only in terms of their presence or absence in various cultural contexts but also take into consideration the eligibility conditions, duration, financial compensation, and flexibility, which all contribute to the final outcomes.

References

Adsera, A. (2011). Where Are the Babies? Labor Market Conditions and Fertility in Europe. *European Journal of Population*, *27*(1), 1–32.

Aitken, Z., Garrett, C. C., Hewitt, B., Keogh, L., Hocking, J. S., & Kavanagh, A. M. (2015). The maternal health outcomes of paid maternity leave: A systematic review. *Social Science & Medicine*, *130*, 32–41.

Akgunduz, Y. E., & Plantenga, J. (2013). Labour market effects of parental leave in Europe. *Cambridge Journal of Economics*, *37*(4), 845–862.

Almqvist, A.-L. (2008). Why Most Swedish Fathers and Few French Fathers Use Paid Parental Leave: An Exploratory Qualitative Study of Parents. *Fathering*, *6*(2), 192–200.

Almqvist, A.-L., & Duvander, A.-Z. (2014). Changes in gender equality? Swedish fathers' parental leave, division of childcare and housework. *Journal of Family Studies*, *20*(1), 19–27.

Andersson, G., Hoem, J. M., & Duvander, A.-Z. (2006). Social differentials in speed-premium effects in childbearing in Sweden. *Demographic Research*, *14*, 51–70.

Ang, X. L. (2015). The Effects of Cash Transfer Fertility Incentives and Parental Leave Benefits on Fertility and Labor Supply: Evidence from Two Natural Experiments. *Journal of Family and Economic Issues*, *36*(2), 263–288.

Argyrous, G., Craig, L., & Rahman, S. (2016). The Effect of a First Born Child on Work and Childcare Time Allocation: Pre-post Analysis of Australian Couples. *Social Indicators Research*.

Asai, Y. (2015). Parental leave reforms and the employment of new mothers: quasi-experimental evidence from Japan. *Labour Economics*, *36*, 72–83.

Avendano, M., Berkman, L., Brugiavini, A., & Pasini, G. (2014). The Long-Run Effect of Maternity Leave Benefits on Mental Health: Evidence from European Countries. *Social Science & Medicine* 132 (2015): 45–53.

Baizan, P., Arpino, B., & Delclòs, C. E. (2016). The Effect of Gender Policies on Fertility: The Moderating Role of Education and Normative Context. *European Journal of Population*, *32*(1), 1–30. http://doi.org/10.1007/s10680-015-9356-y

Bartova, A. (2016). *"Genderising" Aspects of Birth-Related Leave Policies and Fertility Behaviour in Europe: Understanding Policy from an Individual's Perspective* (PhD Thesis). Edinburgh: University of Edinburgh.

Bartova, A., & Emery, T. (2016). Measuring Policy Entitlements at the Micro-Level: Maternity & Parental Leave in Europe. *Community, Work & Family*.

Baxter, J. (2008). Is money the main reason mothers return to work after childbearing? *Journal of Population Research*, *25*(2), 141–160.

Bergemann, A., & Riphahn, R. T. (2015). Maternal Employment Effects of Paid Parental Leave. Bonn. Retrieved from http://ftp.iza.org/dp9073.pdf

Berger, L., & Waldfogel, J. (2004). Maternity leave and the employment of new mothers in the United States. *Journal of Population Economics*. 17: 331. doi:10.1007/s00148-003-0159-9

Bonoli, G. (2008). The impact of social policy on fertility: evidence from Switzerland. *Journal of European Social Policy*, *18*(1), 64–77.

Brandth, B., & Kvande, E. (2016). Fathers and flexible parental leave. *Work, Employment & Society*, *30*(2), 275–290.

Budig, M. J., Misra, J., & Boeckmann, I. (2016). Work–family policy trade-offs for mothers? Unpacking the cross-national variation in motherhood earnings penalties. *Work and Occupations*, *43*(2), 119–177.

Bünning, M. (2015). What Happens after the "Daddy Months"? Fathers' Involvement in Paid Work, Childcare, and Housework after Taking Parental Leave in Germany. *European Sociological Review*, *31*(6), 738–748.

Bunning, M., & Pollmann-Schult, M. (2016). Family policies and fathers' working hours: cross-national differences in the paternal labour supply. *Work, Employment & Society*, *30*(2), 256–274.

Burtle, A., & Bezruchka, S. (2016). Population health and paid parental leave: what the United States can learn from two decades of research. *Healthcare*, *4*(30).

Bygren, M., & Duvander, A.-Z. (2006). Parents' Workplace Situation and Fathers' Parental Leave Use. *Journal of Marriage and Family*, *68*(2), 363–372.

Cannonier, C. (2014). Does the Family and Medical Leave Act (FMLA) Increase Fertility Behavior? *Journal of Labor Research*, *35*(2), 105–132.

Carneiro, P., Løken, K. V., & Salvanes, K. G. (2015). A Flying Start? Maternity Leave Benefits and Long-Run Outcomes of Children. *Journal of Political Economy*, *123*(2), 365–412.

Cascio, E. U., Haider, S. J., & Nielsen, H. S. (2015). The effectiveness of policies that promote labor force participation of women with children: a collection of national studies. *Labour Economics*, *36*, 64–71.

Castro-García, C., & Pazos-Moran, M. (2015). Parental Leave Policy and Gender Equality in Europe. *Feminist Economics*, *5701*(April), 1–23. http://doi.org/10.1080/13545701 .2015.1082033

(2016). Parental Leave Policy and Gender Equality in Europe. *Feminist Economics*, *22*(3), 51–73.

Chatterji, P., & Markowitz, S. (2012). Family Leave After Childbirth and the Mental Health of New Mothers. *Journal of Mental Health Policy and Economics*, *15*, 61–76.

Craig, L., & Mullan, K. (2010). Parenthood, Gender and Work–family Time in the United States, Australia, Italy, France, and Denmark. *Journal of Marriage and Family*, *72*(5), 1344–1361.

Cygan-Rehm, K. (2013). *Parental leave benefit and differential fertility responses : Evidence from a German reform*. BGPE Discussion Paper, No. 142. Retrieved from www.lsw .wiso.uni-erlangen.de/BGPE/texte/DP/142_Cyganrehm.pdf

(2016). Parental leave benefit and differential fertility responses: evidence from a German reform. *Journal of Population Economics*, *29*, 73–103.

Dagher, R. K., McGovern, P. M., & Dowd, B. E. (2014). Maternity leave duration and postpartum mental and physical health: Implications for leave policies. *Journal of Health Politics, Policy and Law*, *39*(2), 369–416.

Danzer, N., & Lavy, V. (2013). *Parental Leave and Children's Schooling Outcomes: Quasi-Experimental Evidence from a Large Parental Leave Reform (No. w19452)*. Working paper. Published by the National Bureau of Economic Research.

Datta Gupta, N., Smith, N., & Verner, M. (2008). PERSPECTIVE ARTICLE: The impact of Nordic countries' family friendly policies on employment, wages, and children. *Review of Economics of the Household*, *6*(1), 65–89.

Dearing, H. (2015). Does parental leave influence the gender division of labour? Recent empirical findings from Europe. *Vienna University of Economics and Business, Institute for Social Policy Working Paper*.

Dustmann, C., & Schönberg, U. (2012). Expansions in maternity leave coverage and children's long-term outcomes. *American Economic Journal: Applied Economics*, *4*(3), 190–224.

Duvander, A., & Andersson, G. (2006). Gender Equality and Fertility in Sweden: A Study on the Impact of the Father's Uptake of Parental Leave on Continued Childbearing. *Marriage & Family Review*, *39*(1–2), 37–41.

Duvander, A.-Z., Lappegård, T., & Andersson, G. (2010). Family policy and fertility: fathers' and mothers' use of parental leave and continued childbearing in Norway and Sweden. *Journal of European Social Policy*, *20*(1), 45–57.

Duvander, Lappegård T., Andersen, S. N., Garðarsdóttir, Ó., Neyer, G., & Viklund, I. (2016). Gender Equal Family Policy and Continued Childbearing in Iceland, Norway and

Sweden, 1–30. Retrieved from http://www.su.se/polopoly_fs/1.299123
.1474874646!/menu/standard/file/WP_2016_01.pdf

Escot, L., Fernández-Cornejo, J. A., & Poza, C. (2013). Fathers' use of childbirth leave in
Spain. The effects of the 13-day paternity leave. *Population Research and Policy
Review, 33*(3), 419–453.

Esping-Andersen, G., & Billari, F. C. (2015). Re-theorizing family demographics. *Population
and Development Review, 41*(1), 1–31.

Evertsson, M., & Duvander, A.-Z. (2010). Parental leave - possibility or trap? Does family
leave length effect Swedish women's labour market opportunities? *European
Sociological Review, 27*(4), 435–450.

Ferraro, K. F., & Shippee, T. P. (2009). Aging and cumulative inequality: How does inequality
get under the skin? *The Gerontologist, 49*(3), 333–343.

Frenette, M. (2010). How does the stork delegate work? Childbearing and the gender division
of paid and unpaid labour. *Journal of Population Economics, 24*(3), 895–910.

Gauthier, A. H. (2007). The impact of family policies on fertility in industrialized countries:
a review of the literature. *Population Research and Policy Review, 26*(3), 323–346.

Gauthier, A. H., & Koops, J. (forthcoming). The history of family policy research.
In T. Rostgaard (Ed.), *Handbook of Child and Family Policy.*

Geisler, E., & Kreyenfeld, M. (2011). Against all odds: Fathers' use of parental leave in
Germany. *Journal of European Social Policy, 21*(1), 88–99.

Geist, C., & Cohen, P. N. (2011). Headed Toward Equality? Housework Change in
Comparative Perspective. *Journal of Marriage and Family, 73*(4), 832–844.

Geyer, J., Haan, P., & Wrohlich, K. (2015). The effects of family policy on maternal labor
supply: combining evidence from a structural model and a quasi-experimental
approach. *Labour Economics, 36,* 84–98.

Gíslason, I. (2007). *Parental Leave in Iceland: Bringing the Fathers in. Report. Reykjavik,
Ministry of Social Affairs and Centre for Gender Equality.* Centre for Gender
Equality, Akureyri.

Haas, L. (2003). Parental leave and gender equality: Lessons from the European Union.
Review of Policy Research, 20(1), 89–114.

Hajizadech, M., Heymann, J., Strumpf, E., Harper, S., & Nandi, A. (2015). Paid maternity
leave and childhood vaccination update: longitudinal evidence from 20 low- and
middle-income countries. *Social Science & Medicine, 140,* 104–117.

Han, W.-J., & Waldfogel, J. (2003). Parental leave: The impact of recent legislation on
parents' leave taking. *Demography, 40*(1), 191–200.

Harknett, K., Billari, F. C., & Medalia, C. (2014). Do family support environments influence
fertility? Evidence from 20 European countries. *European Journal of Population,
30*(1), 1–33.

Hegewisch, A., & Gornick, J. C. (2011). The impact of work–family policies on women's
employment: a review of research from OECD countries. *Community, Work &
Family, 14*(2), 119–138.

Hilgeman, C., & Butts, C. T. (2009). Women's employment and fertility: A welfare regime
paradox. *Social Science Research, 38*(1), 103–117.

Hoem, J. (1993). Public policy as the fuel of fertility: Effects of a policy reform on the pace of
childbearing in Sweden in the 1980s. *Acta Sociologica, 36,* 19–31.

Jaumotte, F. (2003). Labour force participation of women: Empirical evidence on the role of
policy and other determinants in OECD countries. *OECD Economic Studies,* (37).

Joesch, J. M. (1997). Paid leave and the timing of women's employment before and after birth. *Journal of Marriage and Family, 59*, 1008–1021.

Kaufman, G., Lyonette, C., & Crompton, R. (2010). Post-birth employment leave among fathers in Britain and the United States. *Fathering, 8*(3), 321–340. http://doi.org/10.3149/fth.0803.321

Keck, W., & Saraceno, C. (2013). The impact of different social-policy frameworks on social inequalities among women in the European Union: The labour-market participation of mothers. *Social Politics, 20*(3), 297–328.

Khanam, R., Nghiem, S., & Connelly, L. (2016). The effects of parental leave on child health and postnatal care: evidence from Australia. *Economic Analysis and Policy*, (49), 17–29.

Koslowski, A., Blum, S., & Moss, P. (2016). *12th International Review of Leave Policies and Related Research 2016*. Retrieved from www.leavenetwork.org/lp_and_r_reports/

Kotsadam, A., & Finseraas, H. (2011). The state intervenes in the battle of the sexes: Causal effects of paternity leave. *Social Science Research, 40*(6), 1611–1622.

Lalive, R., & Zweimüller, J. (2009). How does parental leave affect fertility and return to work? Evidence from two natural experiments. *The Quarterly Journal of Economics, 124*(3), 1363–1402.

Landau, E. C., & Beigbeder, Y. (2008). *From ILO Standards to EU Law; The Case of Equality between Men and Women at Work*. Martinus Nijhoff Publishers.

Lappegård, T. (2012). Couples' parental leave practices: The role of the workplace situation. *Journal of Family and Economic Issues, 33*(3), 298–305.

Lee, G. H. Y., & Lee, S. P. (2014). Childcare availability, fertility and female labor force participation in Japan. *Journal of the Japanese and International Economies, 32*, 71–85. http://doi.org/10.1016/j.jjie.2014.01.002

Liu, Q., & Skans, O. N. (2010). The Duration of Paid Parental Leave and Children's Scholastic Performance. *The B.E. Journal of Economic Analysis & Policy, 10*(1), 1–35.

Luci-Greulich, A., & Thévenon, O. (2013). The impact of family policies on fertility trends in developed countries. *European Journal of Population, 29*(4), 387–416.

Lundquist, J. H., Misra, J., & O'Meara, K. (2012). Parental leave usage by fathers and mothers at an American university. *Fathering, 10*(3), 337–363.

Månsdotter, A., Lindholm, L., & Winkvist, A. (2007). Paternity leave in Sweden—Costs, savings and health gains. *Health Policy, 82* (1), 102–115.

Matysiak, A., & Szalma, I. (2014). Effects of parental leave policies on second birth risks and women's employment entry. *Population (English Edition), 69*(4), 599–636.

Moss, P. (2009). *International Review of Leave Policies and Related Research* (Employment). BIS: Department for Business Innovation & Skills.

Naz, G. (2010). Usage of parental leave by fathers in Norway. *International Journal of Sociology and Social Policy, 30*(5/6), 313–325.

Neilson, J., & Stanfors, M. (2014). It's about time! Gender, parenthood, and household divisions of labor under different welfare regimes. *Journal of Family Issues, 35*(8), 1066–1088.

O'Brien, M. (2013). Fitting fathers into work–family policies: international challenges in turbulent times. *International Journal of Sociology and Social Policy, 33*(9), 542–564.

OECD. (2007). *Babies and Bosses – Reconciling Work and Family Life. Family Life*. OECD Publishing.

OECD. (2016). Fertility Rates (indicator). doi: 10.1787/8272fb01-en (Accessed on 10 November 2017)

Oláh, L. S. (2003). Gendering fertility: Second births in Sweden and Hungary. *Population Research and Policy Review, 22*, 171–200.

Pragg, B., & Knoester, C. (2015). Parental Leave Use Among Disadvantaged Fathers. *Journal of Family Issues*, 1–29.

Pronzato, C. D. (2009). Return to work after childbirth: does parental leave matter in Europe? *Review of Economics of the Household, 7*(4), 341–360.

Rasmussen, A. W. (2010). Increasing the length of parents' birth-related leave: The effect on children's long-term educational outcomes. *Labour Economics, 17*(1), 91–100.

Romero-Balsas, P. (2015). Consequences paternity leave on allocation of childcare and domestic tasks. *Revista Española de Investigaciones Sociológicas, 149*, 87–108.

Rønsen, M., & Sundström, M. (2002). Family Policy and after-birth employment among new mothers – a comparison of Finland, Norway and Sweden. *European Journal of Population, 18*, 121–152.

Rostgaard, T. (2009). Denmark. In P. Moss (Ed.), *International Review of Leave Policies and Related Research* (Employment, pp. 149–156). BIS: Department for Business Innovation & Skills.

Ruhm, C. J. (1998). The economic consequences of parental leave mandates: Lessons from Europe. *The Quarterly Journal of Economics, 113*(February), 285–317.

Salmi, M., & Lami-Taskula, J. (2009). Finland. In P. Moss (Ed.), *International Review of Leave Policies and Related Research* (Employment, pp. 163–178). BIS: Department for Business Innovation & Skills.

Schober, P. S. (2014). Parental leave and domestic work of mothers and fathers: A longitudinal study of two reforms in west Germany. *Journal of Social Policy, 43*(2), 351–372.

Schober, P. S., & Zoch, G. (2015). Change in the gender division of domestic work after mummy or daddy took leave: An examination of alternative explanations. *SOEP Papers on Multidisciplinary Panel Data Research, 803–2015.*

Shim, J. Y. (2013). *Family Leave Policy and Child Health: Evidence from 19 OECD Countries from 1969–2010.* Columbia University.

Sleebos, J. E. (2003). Low fertility rates in OECD countries: Facts and policy responses. *OECD Social, Employment and Migration Working Papers, 15.*

Spiess, C. K., & Wrohlich, K. (2008). The parental leave benefit reform in Germany: costs and labour market outcomes of moving towards the Nordic model. *Population Research and Policy Review, 27*(5), 575–591.

Šťastná, A., & Sobotka, T. (2009). *Changing Parental Leave and Shifts in Second and Third-Birth Rates in Austria.* Vienna: Vienna Institute of Demography Working Papers 7/2009.

Tamm, M. (2013). The impact of a large parental leave benefit reform on the timing of birth around the day of implementation. *Oxford Bulletin of Economics and Statistics, 75*(4), 585–601. http://doi.org/10.1111/j.1468-0084.2012.00707.x

Tanaka, S. (2005). Parental leave and child health across countries. *The Economic Journal, 115*(501), F7–F28.

Thévenon, O., & Solaz, A. (2013). Parental Leave and Labour Market Outcomes: Lessons from 40 Years of Policies in OECD Countries. *INED, Documents de Travail 199.* Retrieved from http://ideas.repec.org/p/idg/wpaper/199.html

Whitehouse, G., Diamond, C., & Baird, M. (2007). Fathers' use of leave in Australia. *Community, Work & Family, 10*(4), 387–407.

Whitehouse, G., Hosking, A., & Baird, M. (2008). Returning too soon? Australian mothers' satisfaction with maternity leave duration. *Asia Pacific Journal of Human Resources*, *46*(3), 288–302.

Zabel, C. (2009). Eligibility for maternity leave and first birth timing in Great Britain. *Population Research and Policy Review*, *28*(3), 251–270.

Ziefle, A., & Gangl, M. (2014). Do women respond to changes in family policy? A quasi-experimental study of the duration of mothers' employment interruptions in Germany. *European Sociological Review*, *30*(5), 562–581.

PART III

Methodological Considerations

7 Review of Methods Used in Global Work and Family Research

Peter P. Yu

Interest in work–family (WF) research continues to increase in popularity world-wide, encouraging advances in WF researchers' methods and practices. Generally, WF research involves many different methodological considerations that have been previously reviewed (cf. Casper, De Hauw, & Wayne, 2013; Casper, Eby, Bordeaux, Lockwood, & Lambert, 2007; Lapierre & McMullan, 2016); however, the fact that WF research is increasingly being conducted in the global context introduces additional methodological complexities that warrant discussion. Therefore, the purpose of this chapter is to provide an overview of several key research considerations specific to global WF research (i.e., WF research conducted in countries and regions beyond the United States or comparative studies that include multiple countries or regions). First, I discuss how global WF research examining single- and multiple-country contexts has been conducted to date. This is followed by descriptions of sampling techniques and types of participants typically involved in such research as well as the various research designs commonly used. Last, brief summaries of various data collection methods relevant to global WF research are presented.

Country Considerations

The number of different countries that have been examined within the WF literature is quite large. However, important distinctions must be made between WF studies conducted in single (i.e., all participants are from one country or cultural region) versus multiple country (i.e., participants are from two or more countries or cultural regions) contexts.

Single-Country Studies

WF studies most commonly examine participants within a single national context. Such research has typically been conducted within industrialized Anglophone contexts similar to the United States, such as the United Kingdom and Australia. Beyond these contexts, WF research conducted within single countries is prolific across the European continent (e.g., the Netherlands, Spain, Finland) and East Asia (e.g., China, Japan, and South Korea). Less commonly, WF research has occurred in South and Southeast Asia (e.g., India, Pakistan, Malaysia), the Middle East (e.g., Lebanon,

Iran, Israel), and Latin America (e.g., Brazil, Mexico, Dominican Republic). Almost no research has been conducted in Africa, with a few studies conducted in Nigeria and Kenya serving as the main exceptions. These single-country studies are necessary to build basic foundational understanding of how WF constructs and processes operate in places with different cultural, political, and economic contexts than the oft studied Anglophone countries. However, it is difficult to compare findings across studies as researchers often employ different sampling strategies and measures. Furthermore, results may not be generalizable over time if the country in question has undergone significant political, economic, legislative, or social changes that can impact individuals' employment and family roles.

Multiple-Country Studies

WF researchers have also included participants from different countries within a single study, usually for cross-national and cross-cultural comparative purposes. The number of different countries included depends largely on the type of data collected; studies that collect primary data typically do so using two or three different countries, whereas archival data from large-scale surveys are typically used when examining a larger number of countries.

Multiple-country WF studies are beneficial because they allow for direct comparison of how WF constructs operate in different cultural, economic, political, and religious contexts. Comparisons between Anglophone and East Asian countries is common (see Shockley, Douek, Smith, Yu, Dumani, & French, 2017, for a review). The theoretical basis for such comparisons often lies in collectivism-individualism (i.e., the degree that cultures value collective distribution of resources, collective action, and cohesiveness with one's organization and family; House, Hanges, Javidan, Dorfman, & Gupta, 2004). Researchers often use country affiliation to infer participants' cultural values given that Anglo countries are designated as highly individualistic and East Asian countries are collectivistic in nature (House et al., 2004; Matsumoto & Yoo, 2006). Furthermore, the impetus behind these cultural comparisons is that the cultural value of interest (e.g., collectivism) impacts the way work and family interest and/or patterns of correlates with work–family constructs. For example, researchers often explain weaker relationships between WF conflict and individual well-being among East Asian versus Western samples by arguing that individuals from East Asian cultures may perceive work success as being more integral for meeting family responsibilities and therefore do not view conflict as detrimental in the same was that those in individualistic countries such as the United States do (Aryee, Fields, & Luk, 1999). Additionally, other cross-cultural WF researchers chose the specific countries based on the fact that there is a dearth of research conducted in those areas. For example, Wang, Lawler, and Shi (2011) surveyed participants from China, Thailand, Kenya, and India to examine how family-friendly organizational policies relate to WF conflict for both the overall combined sample and across countries. Lastly, multiple-country WF research has also been conducted in countries that have similar cultural values and share geographic boundaries. Such studies are important because they examine whether these cultural and geographic similarities translate into similarities in WF constructs and processes. For example, Öun's (2012) study of four Scandinavian countries found significantly lower levels of WF conflict in participants from Finland compared to those from Denmark, Norway, or Sweden (among which there were no significant differences). This study highlights the importance of considering national context in WF research even when such contexts are traditionally viewed as being culturally similar; as globalization increases across time, meaningful changes in what a country's culture constitutes is likely to occur (Matsumoto & Yoo, 2006).

At an even higher level of analysis, multiple-study WF research also compares different groups of countries. This involves sorting countries into categories based on meaningful country-level characteristics. This approach was used in Spector et al.'s (2004) study of three country clusters that combined countries into Anglophone, Latin American, and East Asian clusters for analysis. Such studies allow for a more macro-level perspective on how WF constructs operate across a truly globalized context, providing insight as to whether and how WF processes can even be aggregated across many different country contexts.

Important differences exist regarding how WF researchers account for participants from different countries in multiple-country studies. Some studies account for country membership by conducting separate analyses by country (e.g., Lallukka et al., 2010) or examining country membership as a moderating variable (e.g., Barnes-Farrell et al., 2008). However, other studies simply conduct analyses on the entire multiple-country sample without such considerations, effectively treating them as a single sample (e.g., Hill, Erickson, Fellows, Martinegro, & Allen, 2014). Combining samples via this method is problematic because it does not allow for the comparison of results across samples and thus contributes very little in understanding WF on a global scale. Researchers are thus urged to somehow account for differences among participants in terms of country affiliation. Researchers should also consider controlling for relevant country-level variables which may account for why country differences are observed in multiple-country WF research; doing so would provide greater support that observed effects are due to cross-*cultural* factors rather than other factors. For example, economic, legal, and technological differences across countries (e.g., prevalence of part-time labor, mandated parental leave laws, availability of infrastructure to support telecommuting) represent credible bases for differences in how effectively individuals manage work and family (Joplin, Francesco, Schaffer, & Lau, 2003).

Participant and Sampling Considerations

Consideration of participant demographics and sampling methods within global WF studies is critical given the extreme diversity of individuals around the world. This is especially important for WF research given that individuals' work and family backgrounds undoubtedly play an important role in forming hypotheses, interpreting results, and determining if results can be compared across studies and contexts. Specifically, meaningful comparisons across countries within a single study are difficult when the samples are critically different (e.g., comparing physicians to front line hotel workers). These sample differences (versus country or cultural differences) may be what is actually driving any observed differences (Spector, Liu, & Sanchez, 2015). The next section outlines several specific participant and sampling characteristics that researchers should keep in mind when conducting and interpreting global WF research.

Diversity within specific countries. Potential confounding factors may exist within WF studies conducted in countries that are extremely diverse or that include participants who are not "the norm" for a particular country. These characteristics have typically corresponded to within-country differences in region, race, and religion. For example, WF research conducted in India typically identifies participants as being from a specific region, such as the Northern (Larson, Verma, & Dworkin, 2001), Western (Baral & Bhargava, 2011), or Southern (Namasivayam & Zhao, 2007) regions. These regional distinctions are important given India's large population size, widely-varying physical terrain, and deep political history that all contributed to major regional differences in what exactly constitutes the Indian culture and identity (cf. Mohammada, 2007). Concerning race, WF studies conducted in New Zealand typically involve White participants consistent with its position in the Anglo country sphere (e.g., O'Driscoll et al., 2003). However, Haar, Roche, and Taylor's (2012) study in New Zealand examined the relationship between conflict and turnover intentions among the indigenous Maori people. This distinction is important given the major socioeconomic and cultural differences between the Anglo and Maori people within New Zealand, which likely corresponds to differences in how they manage work and family responsibilities. Religious distinctions have also been made in single-country WF research. For example, Sharabi (2010) used religion to differentiate between Jewish and Muslim Israelis and found that Jewish Israelis valued work less and family more than Muslim Israelis.

These examples above all highlight the importance of clearly describing relevant participant characteristics and highlighting how well they represent the broader population within a country. If authors do not clearly report such distinctions, then readers and subsequent researchers may erroneously conflate findings based on unique sub-populations with findings from other studies conducted in that country.

Expatriate and immigrant samples. The studies reviewed thus far assume that participants are native to the countries they are surveyed in. However, WF researchers have also examined individuals residing in countries other than their native ones (e.g., Van der Zee, Ali, & Salomé, 2005), allowing for better understanding of how WF processes operate among individuals who are adjusting from one national context to another (Caligiuri, Hyland, & Joshi, 1998). Such research is relatively uncommon and mostly concerns expatriates (i.e., those living and working in countries they are not natively from). For example, Shih, Chiang, and Hsu (2010) examined the relationships between WF conflict and job performance and job satisfaction among Taiwanese expatriates in China. On a larger scale, Shaffer, Harrison, Gilley, and Luk (2001) surveyed expatriates in forty-six different countries to examine how WF conflict related to their thoughts of withdrawing from their expatriate assignments.

WF research has also been conducted on immigrants, allowing for further exploration of how WF processes operate within those in unfamiliar national and cultural contexts (e.g., Grzywacz et al., 2007; Malinen & Johnston, 2011). Although comparable to expatriates in that they both live and work in non-native countries, immigrants face additional difficulties that have implications for WF processes. For example, immigrants may experience ambivalence and stress over the fact that they are helping provide financially for their families back home by virtue of having to live apart from them in a foreign country (Grzywacz, Quandt, Arcury, & Martin, 2005). Also, whereas expatriates begin their assignments with the knowledge that living abroad is temporary, there is a greater sense of permanence for immigrants regarding their life in a new culture. This has implications for acculturation and adjustment that may serve as more of a stressor for immigrants and impact their ability to effectively manage work and family in a new cultural context. Additionally, expatriates are often supported financially (and generously) by their organizations, whereas this is often not the case for immigrants. Furthermore, immigrants' children will likely grow up internalizing their parents' culture in addition to the culture of their current country; these differences between immigrant parents' and their children's cultures may introduce additional parenting struggles and thus higher family demands.

Global WF Research Designs

Cross-sectional studies. Cross-sectional designs are extremely common in the global WF literature, involving both single and multiple countries. Studies with this design are severely limited in their ability to draw causal inferences from their data (Casper et al., 2007). However, cross-sectional approaches may represent the only realistic means of conducting WF research in certain country or participant contexts that make it difficult to use more complicated designs. For example, it may only be feasible to collect data from refugees or immigrants at one point in time if they face job and life changes which make them difficult to reach again in the future.

Longitudinal studies. A much smaller portion of the global WF literature employs longitudinal designs, and such studies are typically conducted within single countries. The benefits of longitudinal over cross-sectional studies mostly involve their ability to track the development of variables over time, allowing for examination of dynamic processes that would not be detectable at a single point in time (e.g., how WF conflict changes over time in relation to changes in work hours). Longitudinal studies are inherently time-consuming and require a certain degree of confidence from researchers that participant attrition will be manageable. Thus, conducting longitudinal research in industrialized countries with professional employees may simply be less risky, and thus more appealing, to global WF researchers. This is problematic because the choice in using longitudinal approaches may introduce biases in terms of which countries and participants are ultimately examined. Indeed, existing longitudinal studies have mostly been conducted with white-collar employees in European countries, such as Finland (Mauno, 2010), the Netherlands (Andres, Moelker, & Soeters, 2012), and Norway (Innstand, Langballe, Espnes, Falkum, & Aasland, 2008). Longitudinal WF research in countries beyond Europe has been conducted in Canada (Bouchard & Poier, 2011; Leiter & Durup, 1996), China (Lu, 2011), and Israel (Westman, Etzion, & Gattenio, 2008). This lack of diversity in regional representation limits the extent to which longitudinal findings can be compared across country contexts, and conducting such studies in underrepresented countries and participants represents an important avenue for future research.

Experimental and quasi-experimental studies. Experiments that focus on WF issues are rare in the literature, and no true experimental study exists examining WF constructs in a global context. Similarly, quasi-experiments are also rare in the global WF literature. One exception is Wilson, Polzer-Debruyne, Chen, and Fernandes (2007) who examined the extent that WF conflict differed among factory workers in New Zealand who underwent different forms of training. The lack of experimental and quasi-experimental designs in the global WF context is not surprising, considering that WF constructs are not amenable to manipulation. Indeed, this trend mimics the broader WF literature (Casper et al., 2007). However, manipulations of the salience of cultural concepts provides an interesting avenue for future cross-cultural WF research. For example, researchers could expose participants from the same country to different conditions that prime a cultural value to be more or less salient (e.g., collectivism in East Asian countries) and then have them report on WF experiences. If making collectivism more salient significantly impacts reports of means levels of WF conflict, this would shed some insight into the causal relationships of these variables.

Meta-analyses. Meta-analyses combine the results from multiple studies to calculate effect sizes that are more precise and generalizable to a larger population than any single study alone. Meta-analyses also allow for examination of whether methodological differences (e.g., the country a study was conducted in, the occupational class of participants) serve as meaningful determinants of different results across studies. Whereas meta-analyses that examine WF issues are abundant in the literature (e.g., Amstad, Meier, Fasel, Elfering, & Semmer, 2011; Byron, 2005; Ford, Heinen, & Langkamer, 2007), only one published WF meta-analysis currently exists that explicitly considers national context. Allen, French, Dumani, and Shockley (2015) examined whether mean levels of work-to-family and family-to-work conflict differed based on the countries that such studies were conducted in by imputing country-level variables (e.g., gross domestic product, unemployment rate, gender gap, OECD work–life balance scores, collectivism-individualism, gender egalitarianism values). Their results suggested that mean levels of work-to-family and family-to-work conflict did not differ among countries based on country-level unemployment rate, gross domestic product, gender egalitarianism, or work–family balance rankings from the OECD. They did, however, find that people in studies conducted in individualistic countries reported significantly less family-to-work-conflict (but not work-to-family conflict) than those conducted in collectivistic countries. This same pattern of results was observed for studies conducted in the United States versus outside the United States and also studies conducted in countries with a higher versus lower gender economic gap.

A second meta-analysis which was presented at the Work–family Researchers Network conference (Shockley, Shen, DeNunzio, Arvan, & Knudsen, 2014) focused on gender and WF conflict and tested national indicators of gender egalitarianism (defined in four ways; Project GLOBE values and practices ratings, World Economic Forum's Global Gender GAP Index, and the United Nations' Development Programme's Gender Inequality Index) as a moderator of the gender-WFC relationship. There was no evidence for a significant moderating effect for any of the indicators or for either direction of WF conflict. Further review and recommendations for meta-analyses are provided in Chapter 10 of this handbook (Dumani, French, & Allen).

Data Collection Methods

Primary survey data. Global WF researchers have typically taken one of two approaches to using surveys in their research: using previously created surveys or creating new items for a specific study. When utilizing pre existing scales, important determinations should be made concerning measurement equivalence – the extent to which a certain procedure or scale maintains its construct validity when adapted or used in different cultural or participant contexts (cf. Riordan & Vandenberg, 1994). Because the majority of commonly used scales in global WF research were initially validated in Western countries and contain items written in English (e.g., Carlson, Kacmar, & Williams, 2000; Netemeyer, Boles, & McMurrian, 1996), they may not assess WF constructs in the same ways across different countries, participants, or translations. This can impact the extent to which people in different contexts are interpreting and conceptualizing the content of survey items in the same ways (Milfont & Fischer, 2010). Chapter 8 of this handbook (Korabik & van Rhijn) contains a deeper discussion of translation and measurement equivalence issues.

Archival survey data. The use of archival data in global WF research is also common, especially in cross-national studies where a large number of countries are being sampled from such as Spector et al.'s (2004) twenty-country comparison of WF conflict using data from the Collaborative International Study of Managerial Stress. Other researchers have used archival data from other large-scale datasets, such as the European Social Survey (e.g., Gallie & Russell, 2009; Kasearu, 2009) and the International Social Survey Programme (e.g., Öun, 2012). An overview of global WF archival datasets is provided in Table 7.1. Clear benefits of utilizing these datasets stems from the large sample sizes and variety of countries surveyed, allowing researchers to conduct secondary research on these datasets without having

Table 7.1 *Overview of Global WF archival datasets*

Dataset Name	Years Included	Design	Countries Included	Relevant WF Variables	Publicly Available?
Collaborative International Study of Managerial Stress (CISMS) – Phase 1	1997–2000	Cross-sectional	Argentina, Australia, Belgium, Brazil, Bulgaria, Canada, China, Colombia, Ecuador, Estonia, France, Germany, Hong Kong, India, Israel, Japan, Mexico, New Zealand, Peru, Poland, Portugal, Romania, Slovenia, South Africa, Spain, Sweden, Taiwan, Ukraine, Uruguay, United Kingdom, United States	Pressure	No
Collaborative International Study of Managerial Stress (CISMS) – Phase 2	2003–2005	Cross-sectional	Argentina, Australia, Bolivia, Bulgaria, Canada, Chile, China, Estonia, Finland, Greece, Hong Kong, Japan, Netherlands, New Zealand, Peru, Poland, Puerto Rico, Romania, Slovenia, South Korea, Spain, Taiwan, Turkey, Ukraine, United Kingdom, United States	W-F & F-W Conflict (behavior, strain, time), Family-supportive org. perceptions, Family-supportive org. policies (availability), Family-supportive supervision	No
European Quality of Life Survey (EQLS)	2003, 2007, 2012, 2016 (ongoing)	Cross-sectional	All European Union countries at time of survey	Balance (time), W-F, & F-W Conflict (strain, time)	Yes (www.eurofound .europa.eu/surveys/eur opean-quality-of-life-surveys)

Survey	Years	Design	Countries	Constructs	Available
European Social Survey (ESS)	2004, 2010 (ongoing)	Cross-sectional	All European Union countries at time of survey	W-F & F-W Conflict (strain, time), Satisfaction with time balance	Yes (www.europeansocialsurvey.org/)
European Working Conditions Survey (EWCS)	2005, 2010, 2015 (ongoing)	Cross-sectional	All European Union countries at time of survey	Balance (time), W-F Conflict (time), Flexibility (schedule)	Yes (www.eurofound.europa.eu/surveys/european-working-conditions-surveys)
EU-Households, Work, and Flexibility	2000–2003	Cross-sectional	Bulgaria, Czech Republic, Hungary, Netherlands, Romania, Slovenia, Sweden, United Kingdom	W-F & F-W Conflict, Flexibility (place, schedule)	Yes (www.abdn.ac.uk/socsci/research/new-europe-centre/work-care-projects/households-work-and-flexibility-project-320.php)
EU-Project FamWork	2003–2005	Cross-sectional	Austria, Belgium, Finland, Italy, Germany, Portugal, Netherlands, Switzerland	W-F & F-W Conflict (time), Family-supportive org. culture, Flexibility (schedule)	Yes (www.improving-ser.jrc.it/default/)
Generations and Gender Survey (GGS)	Varies by country (ongoing)	Longitudinal	Australia, Austria, Belgium, Bulgaria, Czech Republic, Estonia, France, Georgia, Germany, Hungary, Italy, Japan, Lithuania, Netherlands, Norway, Poland, Romania, Russia, Sweden	W-F & F-W Conflict (strain, time), Flexibility (schedule)	Yes (www.ggp-i.org)
International Social Survey Programme (ISSP)	2002, 2005, 2012, 2015 (ongoing)	Cross-sectional	Argentina, Australia, Austria, Belgium, Bulgaria, Canada, Chile, China, Croatia, Cyprus, Czech	W-F & F-W Conflict, Flexibility (schedule)	Yes (www.issp.org)

Table 7.1 (*cont.*)

Dataset Name	Years Included	Design	Countries Included	Relevant WF Variables	Publicly Available?
			Republic, Denmark, Dominican Republic, Finland, France, Germany, Iceland, India, Ireland, Israel, Japan, Latvia, Lithuania, Mexico, Netherlands, New Zealand, Norway, Philippines, Poland, Portugal, Russia, Slovakia, Slovenia, South Africa, South Korea, Spain, Sweden, Switzerland, Taiwan, Turkey, United States, United Kingdom, Venezuela		
Project 3535	2003	Longitudinal	Australia, Canada, China, India, Indonesia, Israel, Spain, Taiwan, Turkey, United States	W-F & F-W Conflict (strain, time), W-F & F-W Enrichment, Family-supportive org. policies (availability, use)	No

Note. W-F = work-to-family. F-W = family-to-work.

to expend time or money conducting the research themselves. However, a drawback to using these datasets concerns the lack of flexibility in which variables are included. In other words, the research questions that can be informed by these datasets are limited to those involving the variables that are included.

Qualitative methods. Qualitative global WF studies also exist and are extremely helpful in gaining a rich understanding of the particular cultures and backgrounds of the countries and participants included. Such research can involve structured or semi-structured personal interviews (e.g., Ng, Fosh, & Naylor, 2002) and ethnographic techniques (Poster & Prasad, 2005). The benefits of qualitative data in global WF research was highlighted in Grzywacz et al.'s (2007) study of immigrant Latinos residing in the United States. Although participants reported low mean levels of WF conflict, examination of the interview responses indicated that they actually did experience high degrees of strain-based conflict. It is unclear why this conflict was then not captured in the survey data, which included both time-based and strain-based WF conflict items. This example illustrates how qualitative data can provide insights above and beyond survey data in terms of providing greater detail and flexibility in what participants can report. More information regarding qualitative research can be found in Chapter 9 of this handbook (Wong & Lun).

Conclusion

This chapter reviewed several key methodological considerations specific to WF research conducted in a global context. Because of the wide range of countries, participants, designs, and data collection methods that such studies can include, continued work is vital in understanding how variations in these methodological considerations affect the results and interpretation of global WF research. Of utmost importance for future researchers is the need to determine the extent that cultural values are consistent among individuals from the same country (Spector et al., 2015); this is especially important for research conducted in countries that have large populations and established ethnic diversity (e.g., China, India) that may require additional considerations, such as regional location within a country or specific demographic subgroups. Furthermore, the increase in globalization and technological advancements in recent history brings into question the relevance of traditional assumptions regarding different countries that are often incorporated into hypothesis development in cross-cultural research. Despite arguments that culture is largely stable and resistant to change (Hofstede, 2001), subsequent research is needed to determine if this truly is the case today given increased migration and cross-cultural communication. In addition to these issues and those presented in this chapter, various unknown methodological issues may emerge in the future alongside advances in global WF theory. Consideration of methodology thus constitutes an important area of focus for the entire global WF research community.

References

Allen, T. D., French, K. A., Dumani, S., & Shockley, K. M. (2015). Meta-analysis of work–family conflict mean differences: Does national context matter? *Journal of Vocational Behavior*, *90*, 90–100.

Amstad, F. T., Meier, L. L., Fasel, U., Elfering, A., & Semmer, N. K. (2011). A meta-analysis of work–family conflict and various outcomes with a special emphasis on cross-domain versus matching-domain relations. *Journal of Occupational Health Psychology*, *16*, 151–169.

Andres, M., Moelker, R., & Soeters, J. (2012). A longitudinal study of partners of deployed personnel from the Netherlands' armed forces. *Military Psychology*, *24*, 270.

Aryee, S., Fields, D., & Luk, V. (1999). A cross-cultural test of a model of the work–family interface. *Journal of Management*, *25*, 491–511.

Baral, R., & Bhargava, S. (2011). Predictors of work-family enrichment: Moderating effect of core self-evaluations. *Journal of Indian Business Research*, *3*, 220–243.

Barnes-Farrell, J. L., Davies-Schrils, K., McGonagle, A., Walsh, B., Di Milia, L., Fischer, F. M., . . . & Tepas, D. (2008). What aspects of shiftwork influence off-shift well-being of healthcare workers? *Applied Ergonomics*, *39*, 589–596.

Bouchard, G., & Poirier, L. (2011). Neuroticism and well-being among employed new parents: The role of the work–family conflict. *Personality and Individual Differences*, *50*, 657–661.

Byron, K. (2005). A meta-analytic review of work–family conflict and its antecedents. *Journal of Vocational Behavior*, *67*, 169–198.

Caligiuri, P. M., Hyland, M. M., Joshi, A., & Bross, A. S. (1998). Testing a theoretical model for examining the relationship between family adjustment and expatriates' work adjustment. *Journal of Applied Psychology*, *83*, 598–614.

Carlson, D. S., Kacmar, K. M., & Williams, L. J. (2000). Construction and initial validation of a multidimensional measure of work–family conflict. *Journal of Vocational Behavior*, *56*, 249–276.

Casper, W. J., Eby, L. T., Bordeaux, C., Lockwood, A., & Lambert, D. (2007). A review of research methods in IO/OB work–family research. *Journal of Applied Psychology*, *92*, 28–43.

Casper, W. J., De Hauw, S., & Wayne, J. H. (2013). Concepts and measures in the work–family interface: Implications for work–family integration. In D. A. Major & R. J. Burke (Eds.), *Handbook of Work–Life Integration Among Professionals: Challenges and Opportunities* (pp. 35–57). Cheltenham: Edward Elgar Publishing.

Ford, M. T., Heinen, B. A., & Langkamer, K. L. (2007). Work and family satisfaction and conflict: a meta-analysis of cross-domain relations. *Journal of Applied Psychology*, *92*, 57–80.

Gallie, D., & Russell, H. (2009). Work–family conflict and working conditions in Western Europe. *Social Indicators Research*, *93*, 445–467.

Grzywacz, J. G., Quandt, S. A., Arcury, T. A., & Marín, A. (2005). The work–family challenge and mental health: Experiences of Mexican immigrants. *Community, Work and Family*, *8*, 271–279.

Grzywacz, J. G., Arcury, T. A., Marín, A., Carrillo, L., Burke, B., Coates, M. L., & Quandt, S. A. (2007). Work–family conflict: Experiences and health implications among immigrant Latinos. *Journal of Applied Psychology*, *92*, 1119–1130.

Haar, J. M., Roche, M., & Taylor, D. (2012). Work–family conflict and turnover intentions of indigenous employees: The importance of the whanau/family for Maori. *The International Journal of Human Resource Management, 23*, 2546–2560.

Hill, E. J., Erickson, J. J., Fellows, K. J., Martinengo, G., & Allen, S. M. (2014). Work and family over the life course: Do older workers differ? *Journal of Family and Economic Issues, 35*, 1–13.

Hofstede, G. (2001). *Culture's Consequences: Comparing Values, Behaviors, Institutions, and Organizations Across Nations*. London, UK: Sage Publications, Inc.

House, R.J., Hanges, P.J., Javidan, M., Dorfman, P.W., & Gupta, V. (2004). *Culture, Leadership, and Organizations: The GLOBE Study of 62 Societies*. Thousand Oaks, CA: Sage Publications.

Innstrand, S. I., Langballe, E. M., Espnes, G. A., Falkum, E., & Aasland, O. G. (2008). Positive and negative work–family interaction and burnout: A longitudinal study of reciprocal relations. *Work & Stress, 22*, 1–15.

Joplin, J. R., Shaffer, M. A., Francesco, A. M., & Lau, T. (2003). The macro-environment and work–family conflict development of a cross cultural comparative framework. *International Journal of Cross Cultural Management, 3*, 305–328.

Kasearu, K. (2009). The effect of union type on work–life conflict in five European countries. *Social Indicators Research, 93*, 549–567.

Lallukka, T., Chandola, T., Roos, E., Cable, N., Sekine, M., Kagamimori, S., … & Lahelma, E. (2010). Work–family conflicts and health behaviors among British, Finnish, and Japanese employees. *International Journal of Behavioral Medicine, 17*, 134–142.

Lapierre, L. M., & McMullan, A. D. (2016). A review of methodological and measurement approaches to the study of work and family. In T. D. Allen & L. T. Eby (Eds.), *The Oxford Handbook of Work And Family* (pp. 36–52). Oxford: Oxford University Press.

Larson, R., Verma, S., & Dworkin, J. (2001). Men's work and family lives in India: The daily organization of time and emotion. *Journal of Family Psychology, 15*, 206–224.

Leiter, M. P., & Durup, M. J. (1996). Work, home, and in-between: A longitudinal study of spillover. *The Journal of Applied Behavioral Science, 32*, 29–47.

Lu, L. (2011). A Chinese longitudinal study on work/family enrichment. *Career Development International, 16*, 385–400.

Malinen, S., & Johnston, L. (2011). Seeking a better work–life balance: Expectations and perceptions of work-related practices and attitudes of recent immigrants to New Zealand. *Asian and Pacific Migration Journal, 20*, 233–252.

Masuda, T., & Nisbett, R. E. (2001). Attending holistically versus analytically: comparing the context sensitivity of Japanese and Americans. *Journal of Personality and Social Psychology, 81*, 922–934.

Matsumoto, D., & Yoo, S. H. (2006). Toward a new generation of cross-cultural research. *Perspectives on Psychological Science, 1*, 234–250.

Mauno, S. (2010). Effects of work–family culture on employee well-being: Exploring moderator effects in a longitudinal sample. *European Journal of Work and Organizational Psychology, 19*, 675–695.

Milfont, T. L., & Fischer, R. (2010). Testing measurement invariance across groups: Applications in cross-cultural research. *International Journal of Psychological Research, 3*, 111–130.

Mohammada, M. (2007). *The Foundations of the Composite Culture in India*. Delhi: Aakar Books.

Namasivayam, K., & Zhao, X. (2007). An investigation of the moderating effects of organizational commitment on the relationships between work–family conflict and job satisfaction among hospitality employees in India. *Tourism Management, 28*, 1212–1223.

Netemeyer, R. G., Boles, J. S., & McMurrian, R. (1996). Development and validation of work–family conflict and family–work conflict scales. *Journal of Applied Psychology, 81*, 400–410.

Ng, C. W., Fosh, P., & Naylor, D. (2002). Work–family conflict for employees in an East Asian airline: impact on career and relationship to gender. *Economic and Industrial Democracy, 23*, 67–105.

O'Driscoll, M. P., Poelmans, S., Spector, P. E., Kalliath, T., Allen, T. D., Cooper, C. L., & Sanchez, J. I. (2003). Family-responsive interventions, perceived organizational and supervisor support, work–family conflict, and psychological strain. *International Journal of Stress Management, 10*, 326–344.

Öun, I. (2012). Work–family conflict in the Nordic countries: A comparative analysis. *Journal of Comparative Family Studies*, 165–184.

Poster, W. R., & Prasad, S. (2005). Work–family relations in transnational perspective: A view from high-tech firms in India and the United States. *Social Problems, 52*, 122–146.

Riordan, C. M., & Vandenberg, R. J. (1994). A central question in cross-cultural research: Do employees of different cultures interpret work-related measures in an equivalent manner? *Journal of Management, 20*, 643–671.

Shaffer, M. A., Harrison, D. A., Gilley, K. M., & Luk, D. M. (2001). Struggling for balance amid turbulence on international assignments: Work–family conflict, support and commitment. *Journal of Management, 27*, 99–121.

Sharabi, M. (2010). Ethnicity, ethnic conflict and work values: the case of Jews and Arabs in Israel. *Journal of Peace, Conflict and Development, 15*, 60–73.

Shih, H. A., Chiang, Y. H., & Hsu, C. C. (2010). High involvement work system, work–family conflict, and expatriate performance–examining Taiwanese expatriates in China. *The International Journal of Human Resource Management, 21*, 2013–2030.

Shockley, K.M., Douek, J., Smith, C.R., Yu, P.P., Dumani, S., & French, K.A. (2017). Cross-cultural work and family research: A review of the literature. *Journal of Vocational Behavior. 101*, 1–20.

Shockley, K.M., Shen, W., Denunzio, M., Arvan, M., & Knudsen, E. (2014). Clarifying gender and work–family conflict: A meta-analytic approach. In M.J. Mills (Chair) *Work–life Interface Meets Employee Gender: Challenge and Opportunity*. Symposium presented at the Work Family Researchers Network conference. New York, NY.

Spector, P. E., Cooper, C. L., Poelmans, S., Allen, T. D., O'Driscoll, M., Sanchez, J. I., . . . & Lu, L. (2004). A cross-national comparative study of work-family stressors, working hours, and well-being: China and Latin America versus the Anglo world. *Personnel Psychology, 57*, 119–142.

Spector, P. E., Liu, C., & Sanchez, J. I. (2015). Methodological and substantive issues in conducting multinational and cross-cultural research. *Annual Review of Organizational Psychology and Organizational Behavior, 2*, 101–131.

Van der Zee, K. I., Ali, A. J., & Salomé, E. (2005). Role interference and subjective well-being among expatriate families. *European Journal of Work and Organizational Psychology, 14*(3), 239–262.

Wang, P., Lawler, J. J., & Shi, K. (2011). Implementing family-friendly employment practices in banking industry: Evidences from some African and Asian countries. *Journal of Occupational and Organizational Psychology, 84,* 493–517.

Westman, M., Etzion, D., & Gattenio, E. (2008). International business travels and the work-family interface: A longitudinal study. *Journal of Occupational and Organizational Psychology, 81,* 459–480.

Wilson, M. G., Polzer-Debruyne, A., Chen, S., & Fernandes, S. (2007). Shift work interventions for reduced work–family conflict. *Employee Relations, 29,* 162–177.

8 Meta-Analysis as a Tool to Synthesize Global Work–Family Research Findings

Soner Dumani, Kimberly A. French, and Tammy D. Allen

Research examining the interplay between work and family roles has flourished over the past few decades (Allen, 2012; Eby, Casper, Lockwood, Bordeaux, & Brinley, 2005). What started as an area that predominantly relied on North American samples has increasingly adopted a cross-cultural perspective to understand the prevalence of work–family experiences and the generalizability of findings across different cultural contexts (Allen, 2012). Given the challenges with obtaining representative samples in certain cultures and conducting cross-cultural research (Beins, 2011), the progress of the cross-cultural work–family literature has been slow but steady (Casper, Allen, & Poelmans, 2014). One way to critically examine how individuals from different cultural contexts experience work and family domains is to conduct meta-analytic studies.

Modern meta-analysis began to take shape in the 1970s and Glass coined the term in 1976 (Shadish, 2015). Historically, mathematical ways of dealing quantitatively with varying observations dates back to the seventeenth century and these quantitative approaches mostly helped determine the value of possible gambles in games of chance (O'Rourke, 2007). Mathematicians and astronomers began summarizing results from different studies in the eighteenth and nineteenth centuries, and in the twentieth century statisticians began combining results from different clinical trials. Today meta-analysis refers to a systematic set of methods for searching for and coding comparable studies, the statistical synthesis of the resulting data, and the interpretation and presentation of the results (Schmidt, 2015).

Meta-analysis helps the researcher make sense of the existing literature, aiding in the accumulation and organization of scientific knowledge on a topic. It offers advantages over narrative reviews. Narrative reviews can be inefficient to extract and report information, especially when a body of literature is large or conflicting. Moreover, narrative reviews are considered to be more subjective and thus vulnerable to bias. While narrative reviews tend to focus on statistical significance versus nonsignificance, meta-analysis permits the computation of the strength/magnitude and the variability of the effect size between two variables, across all studies (Glass, 2015).

Many meta-analytic studies are de facto *international* by including all relevant publications (De Leeuw & Hox, 2003). However, in addition to the inclusion of studies from different countries and cultures, explicit hypothesizing and testing for cross-cultural variation are essential for a meta-analysis that aims to extend our understanding of global work and family phenomena. In this respect, a meta-analysis researcher adopting a cross-cultural lens may follow two approaches. First, he or she may explicitly focus on the mean levels of constructs of interest in certain cultural contexts. Second, he or she may examine the relationships involving the constructs of interest across certain cultural contexts (i.e., assess culture as a moderator). These two approaches of using meta-analysis to understand the global work–family interface are similar to what we typically observe in primary cross-cultural work–family studies (see Shockley, Douek, Smith, Yu, Dumani, & French, 2017).

The first approach examines the direct role of culture by typically comparing mean levels or prevalence rates. These comparisons may be made across countries or based on countries clustered according to cultural values (e.g., collectivism) and/or regions (e.g., Latin America). For example, in a primary study, Allen, Shockley, and Biga (2010) reported mean differences in work–life effectiveness (i.e., the absence of work-to-family conflict) across countries clustered into high, medium, and low bands with regard to the cultural values of gender egalitarianism, collectivism, humane orientation, and performance orientation. The second approach examines the moderating role of culture. In this case, the researcher investigates whether relationships, such as that between work demands and work-family conflict (WFC), vary across cultural context. For example, in a primary study, Lallukka, Chandola, Roos, Cable, Sekine, Kagamimori et al. (2010) investigated if relationships between bidirectional WFC and health behaviors differed across samples of British, Finnish, and Japanese employees. Again, countries or country clusters may be used for such comparisons.

The purpose of this chapter is to provide an in-depth overview of adopting a meta-analytical approach to understand the work–family interface from a cross-cultural perspective. Through this chapter, we hope to convey to readers: (1) the potential research questions a meta-analysis on global work and family issues can answer compared to individual studies, (2) effective strategies for conducting a meta-analysis, and (3) the importance of meta-analysis for global work and family research. We aim to achieve these objectives by providing a succinct and comprehensive summary of existing meta-analytical studies on work and family research, and identifying future research directions. In order to encourage readers to use meta-analysis to address the gaps in the literature, we also present an overview of how to conduct a comprehensive meta-analysis with an emphasis on specific lessons we have learned from conducting our own cross-cultural meta-analytic studies (Allen, French, Dumani, & Shockley, 2015; French, Dumani, Allen, & Shockley, 2015).

Throughout the chapter, we use the terms "culture" and "country" interchangeably to encompass both cultural context and country characteristics. Culture and country do not always reference the same underlying mechanism due to imposed national boundaries, political differences within a country, and existence of subcultures (Schaffer & Riordan, 2003). However, country is typically used as a proxy for culture in cross-cultural research and especially in work–family research, culture is not assessed at the individual level. This precludes fine-grained distinctions between "culture" and "country" (Allen, French, Dumani, & Shockley, 2015).

Meta-Analysis in Work and Family Research

The popularity of meta-analysis in the field of I-O psychology is unprecedented (DeGeest & Schmidt, 2011). Accordingly, the number of meta-analytic studies in work and family research has also been on the rise. Given that national context is typically regarded as the "elephant in the room" for work and family research (Ollier-Malaterre, Valcour, Den Dulk, & Kossek, 2013) and most of the primary studies on work–family research originate from North America (Powell, Francesco, & Ling, 2009), it is not surprising that the majority of work–family meta-analyses do not empirically investigate culture. Table 8.1 provides a brief description of the extant meta-analytic studies published in the organizational work and family literature. We identified twenty-three meta-analyses and examined them in terms of their objective, their coding scheme (whether or not country/nationality of sample is coded), and their acknowledgement of potential cultural differences in findings either as part of moderator analyses and/or the discussion of findings.

Several observations can be made about the progression of meta-analytic studies in work and family research across time. First, the construct of WFC has been studied more extensively than alternative inter-role constructs, such as work–family enrichment (WFE) or work–family balance. Earlier meta-analyses focused primarily on identifying the most consistent predictors and outcomes of WFC (e.g., Allen, Herst, Bruck, & Sutton, 2000; Kossek & Ozeki, 1998). In recent years, the complexity of meta-analytic research questions paralleled the increase in primary studies on the topic. The focus shifted towards testing cross-domain models of work-to-family conflict (WIF) and family-to-work conflict (FIW) (e.g., Ford, Heinen, & Langkamer, 2007), comparing alternative models of WFC (Michel et al., 2009), examining relationships specifically based on different theoretical perspectives such as cross-domain versus matching domain hypotheses (Amstad, Meier, Fasel, Elfering, & Semmer, 2011), and using path models to determine the temporal directionality of the WFC and strain relationship (Nohe, Meier, Sonntag, & Michel, 2015). The nomological network of WFC and WFE has also expanded over time. Recent meta-analyses explored the relationships between WFC and personality variables (Allen, Johnson, Saboe, Cho, Dumani, & Evans, 2012), flexible work arrangements (Allen, Johnson, Kiburz, & Shockley, 2013), work–family policies (Butts, Casper, & Yang, 2013), and leadership interactions (Litano, Major, Landers, Streets, & Bass, 2016).

Although the complexity of research questions posed by meta-analyses in the work and family research domain has increased, several major limitations exist given the limited number of primary studies on specific relationships. For example, job attitudes (e.g., job satisfaction, organizational commitment, turnover intentions) and health-related outcomes (e.g., psychological strain) related to WFC are often studied, yet evidence for performance (e.g., organizational citizenship, family performance) and career success correlates are limited. For example, Allen and colleagues (2000) identified only two independent samples reporting relationships between WIF and career satisfaction, and a decade later Amstad and colleagues (2011) reported only

Table 8.1 *Work–family meta-analyses*

Reference	Study Objective	Coded for Country Sample	Moderators Examined	National Culture as a Moderator?	Acknowledgment of Potential Cultural Differences
Kossek & Ozeki, 1998	Examine the relationship between WIF/FIW and job satisfaction and life satisfaction	No	Gender, marital status, dual-earner status, specific measurement of study variables	No	None
Kossek & Ozeki, 1999	Examine relationship between WIF/FIW and six work outcomes	No	None	No	None
Allen et al., 2000	Examine the relationship between WIF and work-related, nonwork-related, and stress-related outcomes	Yes	No explicit moderators	No	The significant relationship between WIF and job satisfaction for studies conducted outside of the US is mentioned
Byron, 2005	Examine the relationship between individual, work-related, and nonwork related- antecedents of WFC, WIF, and FIW	No	Gender, parenting status, measurement of antecedents	No	None
Mesmer-Magnus & Viswesvaran, 2005	Investigate the convergence of WIF and FIW measures and determine their potential incremental	No	None	No	None

Table 8.1 (cont.)

Reference	Study Objective	Coded for Country Sample	Moderators Examined	National Culture as a Moderator?	Acknowledgment of Potential Cultural Differences
	prediction over outcome variables				
Mesmer-Magnus & Viswesvaran, 2006	Examine the relationship between different facets of family-friendly work environments and WIF, FIW	No	None	No	None
Ford et al., 2007	Test two cross-domain path models 1) work domain antecedents-WIF-family satisfaction and 2) family domain antecedents-FIW-job satisfaction	Only North American samples included	Gender, time spent at work, family characteristics (marital status, parental status), dual-earner status,	No	The authors discussed culture as a potential moderator due to the potential differences in the meaning of work and family and cognitive attributional judgments, and intracultural differences in work and family values.
Michel & Hargis, 2008	Compare indirect effect work–family conflict models and direct effect segmentation models in explaining job and family satisfaction	No	None	No	None

Michel et al., 2009	Use meta-analytic path analyses to examine theoretical work–family models and an integrative model	No	None	No	None
Hoobler et al., 2010	Examine the relationships among WIF, FIW, work performance, objective (e.g., salary) and subjective (e.g., career satisfaction) career outcomes	No	Age	No	None
McNall et al., 2010	Examine the relationships between WFE, FWE, and work-related, nonwork-related, and health-related outcomes	No	Gender, construct labeling of positive spillover (e.g., enrichment, spillover, facilitation, enhancement)	No	None
Michel, Kotrba, et al., 2010	Test three competing models of antecedents of WIF and FIW	No	None	No	None
Michel, Mitchelson, et al., 2010	Examine different categories of antecedents (e.g., role stressors, social support, work/family characteristics, personality) of WIF and FIW	No	Marital status, parental status, gender	No	None
Amstad et al., 2011	Examine the work-related, family-related, and domain-	Yes	Time spent at work, parental status	No but explicitly stated that the origin	No but economic changes in non-US

Table 8.1 (cont.)

Reference	Study Objective	Coded for Country Sample	Moderators Examined	National Culture as a Moderator?	Acknowledgment of Potential Cultural Differences
	unspecific outcomes associated with WIF and FIW from both cross-domain and matching domain perspectives			of sample was not included as a moderator due to almost all studies being from the US	countries were mentioned in the discussion
Kossek et al., 2011	Examine the relationship between different types of perceived work social support and WIF	No	None	No	Yes, the potential impact of cultural contexts on the type and source of social support is mentioned in the discussion
Michel et al., 2011	Examine the unique and combined effects of five-factor personality model on WIF, FIW, WFE, and FWE.	No	None	No	None
Shockley & Singla, 2011	Incorporate domain specificity and source attribution perspectives to understand the relationships between WIF, FIW, WFE, FWE, job satisfaction, and family satisfaction.	Yes	Gender	No	None

Allen et al., 2012	Examine the relationships between dispositional variables and WIF, FIW	No	Gender, parental status, marital status	None
Allen et al., 2013	Examine the relationship between flexible work arrangements and WIF, FIW	No	Gender, marital status, parental status, work hours	None
Butts et al., 2013	Test several models linking work–family support policy availability and use to family-supportive perceptions, WIF, and work attitudes	Yes (US vs. Non-US)	Number of work-support policies, gender, marital status, dependent care status	No	None
Allen et al., 2015	Investigate country-level cultural, institutional, and economic factors to understand mean differences in WIF and FIW	Yes	N/A	N/A	Yes
Nohe et al., 2015	Use path analyses to determine the directionality of the relationship between WIF/FIW and work-related strain	Yes	Gender, time lag between the measurement waves, study type (published vs. unpublished), model type (cross-lagged vs. common factor)	No	None
Litano et al., 2016	Examine the relationships between leader-member exchange, and WIF, FIW, WFE, and FWE	Yes	Cultural context, job autonomy, leader-member exchange measurement, study type	Yes (individualism-collectivism and power distance)	Yes

It is important to note that the information displayed in Table 8.1 is based on what the authors explicitly reported in their published work. It might be the case that some authors in fact coded for country as part of their sample characteristics but failed to suggest so in their articles. In this case, this information was still presented as "country of sample is not coded."

four correlations for the same relationship. The limited number of correlations or effect sizes makes it impossible to study moderators, including those moderators related to culture. Even when a larger number of primary studies exists for a given relationship (e.g., WIF with job satisfaction or turnover intentions), the moderators examined by researchers tend to be restricted to those variables typically used as controls in primary studies such as demographic variables (e.g., gender, marital status, parental status) and work/family characteristics (e.g., work hours, dependent care status). Only a handful of meta-analyses looked at potential moderating roles of operational definitions of measures, time lag between measures, and study type (published vs. unpublished studies).

Current meta-analyses in work and family research are empirically inconclusive about the extent to which observed relationships can be generalized cross-culturally. Among twenty-three meta-analyses identified in Table 8.1, only eight explicitly indicated that country/nationality of primary samples was part of the structured coding procedure. However, in five out of these eight studies, authors were unable to conduct further analyses using country due to the limited number of non-US samples. For example, in Byron's (2005) meta-analysis, country of origin was not used as a moderator because most of the included studies were conducted in the United States and Canada.

Cross-cultural differences are also largely ignored conceptually in the development and discussion of the majority of published meta-analyses. Only six of the meta-analyses mentioned potential cross-cultural differences in their interpretation of study findings and study limitations. For example, Kossek and colleagues (2011) examined the relationship between different types of perceived support at work and WIF. The authors did not explicitly mention country as one of their coding criteria but in the discussion section, argued that cultural context matters in these relationships because culture directly impacts both types and sources of support at work. Ford and colleagues (2007) only included studies that were conducted in North America in their meta-analysis but highlighted the potential role of cultural context in the meaning of work and family and cognitive attributional judgments as theoretical implications. Allen et al. (2000) coded for country in their meta-analysis, and tested the relationship between WIF and job satisfaction for studies conducted outside of the United States (the relationship remained significant). We applaud these authors for advancing cross-cultural thinking despite limited empirical data from non-US countries. As we wait for more primary studies outside of the United States to accumulate, we strongly believe that acknowledging cross-cultural differences and providing rationale for potential differences across tested relationships are important for both theory development and practical implications.

Currently, two meta-analyses in work and family research incorporate cultural variables. Allen and colleagues (2015) investigated the relative cross-cultural mean difference in levels of both WIF and FIW. The authors focused on the cultural dimensions of gender egalitarianism and individualism/collectivism to define cultural context. They also examined other national-level contextual variables including institutional (i.e., Organization for Economic Co-operation and

Development work–family balance rankings and US/non-US distinction as a proxy for national work–family policies), and national economic (i.e., gross domestic product, unemployment rate, and gender gap index score) factors. The authors identified eighteen studies with fifty-three independent samples assessing WIF and/or FIW across two or more countries. No significant differences in WIF or FIW were found for high versus low gender egalitarian cultures. In addition, there were no significant mean level differences in WIF for collectivistic versus individualistic cultures. However, individualistic cultures reported less FIW than collectivistic cultures. This difference was driven by Asian collectivistic societies, which reported greater FIW relative to Anglo societies. The same finding emerged when US samples were compared to non-US samples. The authors also found that higher gender gap countries reported greater FIW than lower gender gap countries.

The findings of Allen and colleagues (2015) meta-analysis are important in that they bring to light three key issues. First, understudied macro-level factors such as cultural context appear to have more critical implications for FIW than WIF. The authors attribute this finding to the stronger association between work-related factors and WIF relative to non-work related factors identified in previous meta-analyses. Second, those implications may differ based on specific countries within the same cultural dimension (e.g., Asian versus Latin American cultures although both are collectivistic). Lastly, assumptions, such as the United States experiencing more WFC due to lack of national work–family policies, might not be supported by the empirical literature.

In another recent meta-analysis, Litano and colleagues (2016) tested whether the cultural dimensions of individualism/collectivism and power distance moderated the negative relationship between leader-member exchange (i.e., the quality of the reciprocal relationship between a supervisor and a subordinate) and WIF. Culture was not examined as a moderator for FIW, WFE, or FWE due to limited country variation across samples. In line with the Allen et al.'s (2015) findings, the authors did not find support for collectivism/individualism as a moderator of the relationship between leader-member exchange and WIF. However, a stronger negative relationship between leader-member exchange and WIF was observed for low power distance cultures compared to high power distance cultures. This finding demonstrates that the intensity to which quality work relationships reduce WFC may depend on specific cultural context. Given that current theories in work and family research, such as the Job Demands-Resources model, are used to explain the negative relationship between high quality relationships and WIF, incorporating culture-specific variables to explain both the boundary conditions of such relationships and the mediating mechanisms becomes important to extend the applications of our theoretical models cross-culturally.

As evident in the aforementioned meta-analyses, there is a need for a conceptually and methodologically sophisticated understanding of the cross-cultural work–family interface. The following section outlines suggestions to help interested readers conduct their own cross-cultural meta-analysis in order to contribute to this aim.

Conducting a Comprehensive Cross-Cultural Meta-Analysis

Conducting a thorough and rigorous meta-analysis takes ample time, effort, and thought. Several books (e.g., Borenstein, Hedges, Higgins, & Rothstein, 2009; Schmidt & Hunter, 2014) as well as several published articles (e.g., Aguinis, Pierce, Bosco, Dalton, & Dalton, 2011; Aytug, Rothstein, Zhou, & Kern, 2012) are available to provide guidelines and best practices for conducting a comprehensive and rigorous meta-analysis. For the purposes of this chapter, we highlight best practices for meta-analyses with a cross-cultural focus during each phase of the study.

Clarifying the objective. The objective of any meta-analytic study is important, as it determines what information the author will collect, from where, and how it will be analyzed. For cross-cultural meta-analysis, there are two important points to clarify within the objective. First, is the focus on examining mean differences across countries/cultures, or instead, examining country/culture as a moderator? If the meta-analysis focuses on mean differences, the authors may convert means to a scale that reflects the percentage of the total maximum scale in order to compare means across diverse rating scales (see Meyer, Stanley, Jackson, McInnis, Maltin, & Sheppard, 2012). This approach allows for the inclusion of many studies. However, researchers must be careful to ensure rating scales are conceptually equivalent in order to warrant mean comparisons. For example, Meyer and colleagues (2012) used this approach, but only focused on one popular, validated measure of commitment. If researchers wish to include diverse scales (as is common in work–family meta-analyses), we recommend only including studies that report means for multiple countries using the same items (see for example Allen et al., 2015). While this latter approach limits the size of the meta-analytic comparisons, it helps to ensure conceptual clarity that might be muddled by comparing diverse scales. These means are then used to compute a standardized difference score within each study, and the standardized scores from each study would then be meta-analytically combined (e.g., Allen et al., 2015). If the meta-analysis focuses on country or culture as a moderator, single country studies can be included by treating country as a categorical or continuous between-study moderator (e.g., Litano et al., 2016).

The second question to address is whether the study will use reported cultural values or imputed cultural values. Given that only a limited number of work–family studies collect self-reported cultural values (Shockley et al., 2017), the pool of eligible studies using self-reported cultural values would likely be too small for meta-analytic methods. Fortunately, several large cross-cultural studies and databases exist that provide cultural values for specific countries. These values may be imputed into the meta-analysis to allow for cross-cultural comparisons. For example, in our work, we have imputed cultural values from the GLOBE study and economic values from the World Economic Forum. The GLOBE study provides numeric values representing several cultural dimensions for sixty-two different societies (House et al., 2004). Similarly, the World Economic Forum provides country-specific economic information, such as unemployment rate and GDP, for most countries around the world. We imputed values into our meta-analysis by matching the country associated with a sample to its corresponding cultural information in the cross-cultural study or database (Allen et al., 2015; French et al., 2015).

If imputed values are used, consideration should be given to the potential frameworks that could be used and the coding that will be necessary for each. The choice of framework should be appropriate for the study purpose, and ideally should be constructed based on up-to-date, empirically validated information. For example, we used the House et al.'s (2004) GLOBE study because it reflects the most recently developed set of cultural values, and it contains dimensions commonly used in previous WFC research (e.g., Spector et al., 2007). However, using the GLOBE study meant we could only include data based on countries that were included in the sixty-two GLOBE societies, and some countries needed to be coded for more specific "societies" within a country (e.g., Germanic vs. French Switzerland). Other frameworks, such as Hofstede (1980) and Triandis (1989), have also been used to explain cross-cultural differences in the work–life interface (Ollier-Malaterre & Foucreault, 2016).

Locating sources. In order to capture all relevant primary studies, meta-analytic searches should be conducted across multiple databases (e.g., PsychINFO, ABI/INFORM Global, Google Scholar, JSTOR). For cross-cultural meta-analysis, country or a country characteristic (e.g., culture, policies) is likely included as a second-level substantive variable. That is, studies are nested within countries. It is therefore ideal to have a great deal of variation in both the number of countries and studies within country, so that the meta-analysis has sufficient power to detect country-level effects. Doing a thorough literature search ensures such variability. One way to ensure sufficient variation is by combining traditional search terms (e.g., work–family) with country names (see for example Shockley et al., 2017). This strategy might also be useful for targeting research within a particular country or region of interest. Expanding the search to include dissertations, conference submissions, and specific journals that publish cross-cultural work is also important to ensure representativeness. For example, in addition to the traditional database searches, Amstad et al. (2011) examined two leading European journals in the field of work and organizational psychology to specifically include studies conducted outside of North America. Inter-library loan services are helpful during this process, as many potentially relevant articles will be located overseas, in book chapters, or in dissertation records that may be inaccessible through local library resources. In the event that one cannot locate a full-text or need additional information, such as a correlation table or measure items, authors may be contacted directly. As a final data collection step, unpublished data can be collected by using relevant listserv announcements or by directly reaching out to authors who regularly study your work–family phenomenon of interest.

We recommend that researchers closely document their search process in order to maintain methodological clarity and rigor. For example, in our work we have created a spreadsheet to indicate which studies were screened (authors, title, outlet, type of study), where the studies were identified, and whether or not the study was included.

If a study was excluded, we also indicated why the study was excluded. This information can be used to create a PRISMA flow chart that depicts the screening and exclusion process step-by-step (see Figure 8.1; Moher, Liberati, Tetzlaff, & Altman, 2009). We have found such charts are increasingly expected by editors and journals that publish high-quality meta-analyses.

Coding. In coding data for cross-cultural meta-analysis, at a minimum it is essential to code the country in which the data was collected, basic sample description, and data collection year, in addition to basic information needed for analysis (e.g., sample size, effect size). For many cultural/country frameworks, this information will be important for mapping the study onto imputed values. Most studies report the country associated with data collection. When this information is not reported, the researcher may choose to use unambiguous author affiliation as a substitute (e.g., all authors are from the United States). If the country is not clear based on author affiliation, primary study authors can be contacted to clarify the country in which data were collected. The description of the sample can also help identify ambiguous samples. For example, data from crowdsourcing websites, such as Mechanical Turk, can come

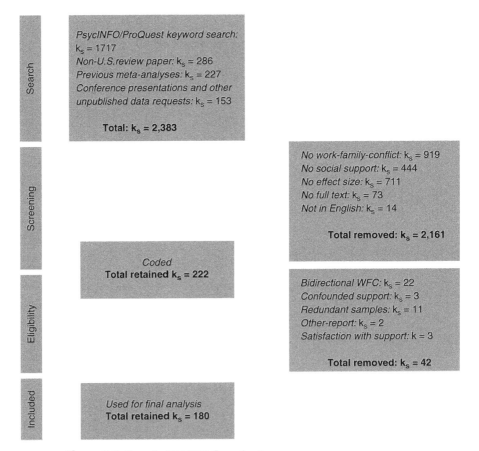

Figure 8.1 *Sample PRISMA flow chart.*

from multiple countries. In such cases, contacting the authors would help to clarify the extent to which the data may or may not be multi-national, and the authors may be able to provide separate effect sizes for single nation subsamples within their data set. If sample information is not verified, researchers should report how often author affiliation is used as a proxy to maintain transparency in methodology.

Data collection year is often omitted from the final manuscript of primary studies. In the event that the date of data collection cannot be determined, a consistent estimate can be used. This estimate might be data-driven, such as the mean or median length of time between data collection and publication for the studies that have year of data collection reported in the extant database. It might also be an a priori rule. For example, the publication date minus two years to account for time for analysis, write-up, and revisions is an option (see for example French et al., 2015).

A clear codebook is essential for identifying relevant and irrelevant information and taking into account possible country differences. A meta-analysis codebook outlines the variables that will be collected, how they will be recorded (e.g., mean income or median income), and any decision rules that are to be used during the coding process. For example, a researcher might be interested in recording average income of each sample. However, currency and the value of that currency differs across countries, making raw values not directly comparable. Before coding, the researcher should think carefully about such culturally invariant raw values and identify a coding scheme that allows for comparable codes. In this case, coding both raw values (income as reported in the study), and then rescaled values (e.g., average income in US dollars) to ensure income is both recorded and recomputed accurately, is recommended. This level of detail also extends to conceptual scales. Construct labels do not always match construct operationalizations, or how the variable is actually measured. For example, we found study authors use different variable labels for the construct of WFC, and constructs that are labeled WFC are in fact at times alternative inter-role constructs, such as work–family balance or work–life conflict. Per our codebook, we only included measures in which 75% of the items were in line with our definition of WFC to ensure our operationalization of WFC were conceptually and operationally clear and aligned with one another. Thinking in advance about what the common construct labeling issues are within your area of meta-analytic focus, and having a way to identify such discrepancies as part of the coding process, can help ensure the same constructs are being recorded across all studies. In most instances, coding both the label used for a construct in the study (e.g., WFC) and the recoded variable based on consistent operationalizations or measurement (e.g., work–family balance) is warranted.

Typically, cross-cultural studies and databases that provide cultural values provide a value for each country. To make imputing simple, effect sizes should be separated by country. In the event that an effect size is confounded with multiple countries and cannot be separated (e.g., 65% of the sample is from Japan and 35% of the sample is from China), a cultural value can be imputed that is weighted to reflect the proportion of the sample from each country.

As a final note, meta-analysis coding can be a draining process. Mistakes are likely to occur for even the most conscientious coder armed with a clear codebook.

This is especially true for complex cross-cultural meta-analyses, which are often large in scale and include a diverse range of operationalizations and methodological approaches. Therefore, it is important that data be coded by multiple coders to ensure any errors are detected and corrected. In addition, double coding ensures any judgment calls that must be made are consistent across multiple independent coders.

Analyzing and interpreting results. Cross-cultural studies often include more than two countries that can be compared. Before meta-analyzing the data, it is important to aggregate effect sizes as necessary to avoid over-counting samples or countries. For example, Spector and colleagues (2007) collected data on WFC and correlates across 36 countries. For our analyses comparing mean WFC in US versus non-US countries (Allen et al., 2015), we first computed thirty-five mean difference effect sizes, one for each mean difference in WFC between the United States and the thirty-five non-US countries. Because each effect size is dependent (all use the same US comparison sample), we then aggregated these effect sizes into one summary effect size using formulas that accounted for dependencies (Borenstein et al., 2009). As a second example, some studies in our meta-analysis on WFC and support reported correlations between three facets of WFC (time, strain, and behavior-based conflict) and one measure of social support (French et al., 2015). In this case, the relationships between each facet of WFC and social support are dependent, as they are computed using the same sample. We combined the three effect sizes using formulas that account for dependencies (Borenstein et al., 2009; Schmidt & Hunter, 2014) to form one composite effect size, representing the overall relationship between WFC and support for that sample. The cultural framework will largely determine when and how samples must be aggregated to avoid over-counting samples. It is critical that authors review effect sizes to ensure no one sample is double-counted. This is especially the case in cross-cultural meta-analysis, where double-counting a particular country may have substantial impact on the results. A full discussion of dependent effect size aggregation is beyond the scope of the current chapter; we direct the interested meta-analyzer to textbook resources for a full discussion of the use and implementation of aggregation formulas (e.g., Borenstein et al., 2009; Schmidt & Hunter, 2014).

Meta-analyses are computed using either fixed- or random-effects models (Borenstein et al., 2009). The fixed-effects model assumes there is a single true population mean effect size and that consequently any deviation from this effect size represents random error. In contrast, the random-effects model assumes there are multiple true population effect sizes, which form a distribution of population effect sizes. When conducting cross-cultural meta-analyses within the work–family field, random-effects model is almost certainly the correct analytic choice. Indeed, the notion of cross-cultural effect size differences itself implies that there is a population of true effect sizes, rather than a single true effect size across all studies.

Regarding the presentation of results, beginning with the most simple and then moving to more complicated analyses can help readers follow and interpret the findings. Starting with random-effects models for the proposed relationships across all samples can be a good strategy to estimate average effects for the sample of studies. Next, incorporate country or cultural dimension as a categorical or continuous moderator of the effect size of interest. To isolate effects for each potential moderator, we also recommend estimating each moderator one at a time. For this approach, cultural values should be chosen carefully, as testing several cultural moderators on the same relationship may inflate family-wise alpha rate, increasing the chances of finding a significant moderation when it in fact does not exist in the population (i.e., Type I error). If there are several comparisons made and Type I error inflation is a concern, the researcher might consider an alpha correction.

When interpreting results, three pieces of information are important: the mean effect size, the confidence interval associated with the mean effect size, and the credibility interval associated with the mean effect size. In random effect models, the mean effect size represents the average of the distribution of true population effect sizes, providing an estimate of the overall strength/magnitude and direction of a relationship (Aguinis et al., 2011). The confidence interval provides information about the precision of the estimated mean true effect size. A small confidence interval indicates the mean effect size is precisely estimated, while a larger confidence interval indicates the mean effect size may not be accurate. Typically, effects are interpreted as significantly different from zero when the confidence interval does not include zero. The credibility interval indicates the range of true effect sizes that could be found in the population. Thus, a small credibility interval represents a homogeneous true effect size distribution, while a large one indicates there is a wide range of true effect sizes.

In general, cross-cultural differences are distal in nature. Many country-level attributes (e.g., economic prosperity, culture, policy) influence individual experiences through more proximal individually enacted norms and values (e.g., work and family labor hours, work and family centrality). Because country-level attributes are distal, cross-cultural differences in effect sizes are often small and difficult to statistically detect (e.g., French et al., 2015; Litano et al., 2016). Within-country variation may also contribute to wide credibility intervals, indicating more moderators could be examined. These issues underscore the importance of a thorough literature search with sufficient within and between-country studies in order to estimate effects as accurately as possible.

Lessons Learned and Next Steps

We have encountered many challenges conducting and publishing cross-cultural meta-analytic work. We use this section to share a few essential lessons that are particularly pertinent to the aspiring cross-cultural researcher interested in using meta-analytic methods. Specifically, we discuss the importance of casting a wide search net, inclusion of non-English studies, and measurement invariance.

First, it is important to know a meta-analysis is only as good as the included primary studies. Therefore, the quality of meta-analysis depends largely on the selection of primary studies, operationalization of the main variables, coding plan, and the thoroughness of the methodology. For example, if a meta-analysis includes only published studies, the magnitude of observed correlations may be overestimated due to what is known as the file drawer problem. The file drawer problem refers to the fact that unpublished studies are more likely to include nonsignificant effects than are published studies (e.g., Aguinis et al., 2011). Further, inclusion of unpublished manuscripts is expected for publication in rigorous journal outlets. Exclusion of such studies will need to be justified and, at the very least, explicitly stated as a limitation. As we mentioned in the previous section, we believe adopting multiple strategies to locate primary studies is important and whenever possible, conference submissions, dissertations, unpublished papers, and raw data sets should be screened for inclusion.

Second, all of the work–family meta-analyses listed in Table 8.1 limit primary studies to those written in the English language. Excluding non-English studies is a particularly critical issue when the meta-analysis aims to look at cross-cultural variations. When non-English studies are excluded, the researcher might directly restrict country-level variance and study representativeness. At the same time, including such studies without excellent translation is likely to introduce confounds, such as incorrectly interpreted variables or results. We recommend researchers who are willing to conduct cross-cultural meta-analysis be cognizant of this issue and explicitly mention the inclusion/exclusion of such studies in their manuscripts. Specifically, providing information on the number of studies written in a language other than English, the original language in which they are written, and the reasoning behind their inclusion/exclusion can be helpful. For example, if there are few non-English studies compared to the total number of studies and no new countries would be introduced by including non-English studies, then exclusion of non-English sources might be an acceptable strategy. Working with colleagues who are native or fluent non-English speakers is also an excellent strategy for accessing information in non-English sources.

Third, a truly cross-cultural meta-analysis relies on the assumption that the data are comparable across studies so that effect sizes can be combined (De Leeuw & Hox, 2003). This assumption often suggests that variables of interest are perceived and understood the same way across participants from different countries. However, studies comparing multiple countries sporadically conduct explicit tests of measurement invariance. There is some evidence that the construct of WFC might not mean the same thing for individuals from different cultures. For example, Yang, Chen, Choi, and Zou (2000) found that factor loadings of items on family demand, work demand, and WFC scales were not comparable between participants from the United Sates and China. Therefore, we recommend researchers report which measures display measurement invariance across which countries, as this information has implications for the strength of conclusions drawn from the meta-analysis (Allen et al., 2015). For primary cross-cultural studies, multiple-group confirmatory factor analysis and between groups structural equation modeling can be used to explicitly test for measurement equivalence (Schaffer & Riordan, 2003: see also Chapter 11 of this Handbook, Korabik, & Rhijn).

Future Directions in Cross-Cultural Work–Family Meta-Analysis

Moving forward, there are many potential ways meta-analysis can illuminate cross-cultural work–family relationships. First, meta-analyses have been conducted almost exclusively using correlational methods, collapsing across different types of designs (see Nohe et al., 2015 for an exception). However, we know WFC is dynamic, changing daily (e.g., Shockley & Allen, 2013), across time (e.g., Matthews, Winkel, & Wayne, 2014), and across life stages (e.g., Allen & Finkelstein, 2014). Given cross-cultural differences in the perception of time (e.g., future orientation; House et al., 2004), there may be interesting cultural differences in the timing of WFC episodes, or the relationship between change in WFC and change in correlates over time. Experimental and quasi-experimental studies are also not accounted for in existing work–family meta-analyses. Although existing experimental studies in work–family research are scarce, a meta-analysis that replicates experimental findings across different countries or cultures would be valuable for establishing theoretical and empirical boundary conditions for existing findings.

Second, the existing cross-cultural work uses culture as a theoretical framework for explaining findings, and meta-analytic work directly imputes cultural values associated with a given country (e.g., Shockley et al., 2017; Allen et al., 2015). However, research has shown this approach ignores the substantial cultural variability within a given country and may create problems especially when different regions or subcultures within the same country have different cultural values (Taras, Kirkman, & Steel, 2010). For example, two states of Brazil, São Paulo and Rio Grande do Sul, have been shown to have distinct characteristics in terms of time orientation and attachment to money and possessions (Lenartowicz, Johnson, & White, 2003). These distinct factors may lead to differences in how work and family roles are experienced between these two subcultures. Again, applying a blanket cultural framework by country ignores these potentially important differences. Future cross-cultural meta-analyses might explore subcultures more thoroughly by either meta-analyzing self-reported cultural values, or meta-analyzing subregions or societies. In addition to potential within-country variations, culture also changes over time (Olivas-Lujan, Harzing, & McCoy, 2004) and imputation of cultural values should reflect the timeframe within which participant data are collected. We hope to see more primary cross-cultural studies that assess culture at the individual level by asking participants to report on their own values and/or *perceptions* of the culture.

Third, there is a need to use additional cultural dimensions to understand the work–life interface. Ollier-Malaterre and Foucreault (2017) offer an excellent source on extant typologies and dimensions of culture used in work–life research. In addition to their suggestions, we believe that understudied dimensions such as performance orientation and assertiveness (GLOBE; House et al., 2004), inner versus outer direction (the extent to which individuals in a certain culture seek to control their environment versus choose to live in harmony with their environment), and specificity versus diffusion (Trompeenars, 1993) may have critical implications for understanding work–family experiences. For example, performance orientation, the extent to which cultures value competition and materialism over quality of life and relationships, may further influence work and family roles. Individuals from high performance orientation cultures might experience more WIF and less work–family balance compared to those from low performance orientation cultures. Similarly, the specificity/diffusion dimension, which reflects the extent to which cultures treat private and work life domains separate (specific) or interdependent (diffuse), can be expected to have direct impact on individuals' segmentation and integration preferences.

Fourth, we have a limited understanding of the positive side of the work–family interface. Only three of our reviewed meta-analyses focused on WFE or positive spillover, and no meta-analyses have been conducted on work–family balance. Both WFE and work–family balance are relatively under-studied in comparison to WFC. For example, in cultures where individuals have more autonomy in their work and they feel more empowered (e.g., low power distance cultures versus high power distance cultures), positive effects of WFE are likely to be observed. Cultures that rely on rigid gender-based roles and value earnings and recognitions over job security and freedom might also pose further challenges for work–family balance. Consequently, we call for additional primary cross-cultural research on these constructs so meta-analytic methods may eventually be applied.

Lastly, we propose expanding the scope of work–family meta-analyses beyond interrole phenomena, such as conflict, enrichment, and balance. For example, there is a healthy, interdisciplinary body of research on parent working conditions and child outcomes (Cho & Ciancetta, 2016). A cross-cultural meta-analysis that examines cultural similarities and differences on the relationship between parent working demands and child well-being has implications for not only work–family research, but also for policy makers and organizational decision makers across the globe. Time allocation across work and family domains could also be examined meta-analytically. Currently, primary studies show interesting differences in time allocation between work and family by country (e.g., Craig & Mullan, 2010), and that time allocation matters for well-being (Dahm, Glomb, Manchester, & Leroy, 2015). Future meta-analytic work could focus on cross-cultural differences in time allocation, as well as culture as a moderator for the relationship between time allocation and domain outcomes (e.g., job satisfaction, family satisfaction). Additionally, as primary studies with cross-cultural comparisons increase, we believe that a multilevel approach to meta-analysis (e.g., Van Den Noortgate, & Onghena, 2003) that allows testing interactions between country-level variables (e.g., culture) and individual-level variables (e.g., segmentation/integration preferences, perceived organizational work–family culture) will also contribute significantly to our understanding of global work–family phenomena.

Concluding Thoughts

Meta-analytic approaches offer a comprehensive look at work–family phenomena, and their flexibility in terms of design affords opportunities for multinational research that would be difficult, if not impossible, to examine with primary studies alone. However, meta-analysis is not free of challenges, and conducting a theoretically informative and rigorous meta-analytic study takes time and careful thinking. Our chapter outlined existing meta-analyses, suggestions, lessons learned, and future directions for those aspiring to inform cross-cultural work–family study using meta-analysis. We hope this chapter stimulates research along this vein and provides future meta-analysts with valuable guidance.

References

Aguinis, H., Pierce, C. A., Bosco, F. A., Dalton, D. R., & Dalton, C. M. (2011). Debunking myths and urban legends about meta-analysis. *Organizational Research Methods*, *14*, 306–331.

Allen, T. D. (2012). The work–family interface. In S. W. J. Kozlowski (Ed). *The Oxford Handbook of Organizational Psychology* (pp. 1163–1198). New York: Oxford University Press.

Allen, T. D., & Finkelstein, L. M. (2014). Work–family conflict among members of full-time dual-earner couples: An examination of family life stage, gender, and age. *Journal of Occupational Health Psychology*, *19*, 376–384.

Allen, T. D., French, K. A., Dumani, S., & Shockley, K. M. (2015). Meta-analysis of work–family conflict mean differences: Does national context matter?. *Journal of Vocational Behavior*, *90*, 90–100.

Allen, T. D., Herst, D. E., Bruck, C. S., & Sutton, M. (2000). Consequences associated with work-to-family conflict: A review and agenda for future research. *Journal of Occupational Health Psychology*, *5*, 278.

Allen, T. D., Johnson, R. C., Kiburz, K. M., & Shockley, K. M. (2013). Work–family conflict and flexible work arrangements: Deconstructing flexibility. *Personnel Psychology*, *66*, 345–376.

Allen, T. D., Johnson, R. C., Saboe, K. N., Cho, E., Dumani, S., & Evans, S. (2012). Dispositional variables and work–family conflict: A meta-analysis. *Journal of Vocational Behavior*, *80*, 17–26.

Allen, T. D., Shockley, K. M., & Biga, A. (2010). Work and family in a global context. In K. Lundby (Ed). *Going Global: Practical Applications and Recommendations for HR and OD Professionals in the Global Workplace* (pp. 377–401). San Francisco, CA: Jossey-Bass.

Amstad, F. T., Meier, L. L., Fasel, U., Elfering, A., & Semmer, N. K. (2011). A meta-analysis of work–family conflict and various outcomes with a special emphasis on cross-domain versus matching-domain relations. *Journal of Occupational Health Psychology*, *16*, 151–169.

Aytug, Z. G., Rothstein, H. R., Zhou, W., & Kern, M. C. (2012). Revealed or concealed? Transparency of procedures, decisions, and judgment calls in meta-analyses. *Organizational Research Methods*, *15*, 103–133.

Beins, B. C. (2011). Methodological and conceptual issues in cross-cultural research. In K. D. Keith (Ed.), *Cross-Cultural Psychology* (37–55). West Sussex: Wiley-Blackwell.

Borenstein, M., Hedges, L. V., Higgins, J. P. T., & Rothstein, H. R. (2009). *Introduction to Meta-Analysis*. United Kingdom: John Wiley & Sons, Ltd.

Butts, M. M., Casper, W. J., & Yang, T. S. (2013). How important are work–family support policies? A meta-analytic investigation of their effects on employee outcomes. *Journal of Applied Psychology, 98,* 1–25.

Byron, K. (2005). A meta-analytic review of work–family conflict and its antecedents. *Journal of Vocational Behavior, 67,* 169–198.

Casper, W. J., Allen, T. D., & Poelmans, S. A. (2014). International perspectives on work and family: An introduction to the special section. *Applied Psychology, 63*(1), 1–4.

Cho, E., & Ciancetta, L. (2016). Child outcomes associated with parent work–family experiences. In T.D. Allen & L. T. Eby (Eds.), *The Oxford Handbook of Work And Family* (pp. 151–164). New York: Oxford University Press.

Craig, L., & Mullan, K. (2010). Parenthood, gender and work-family time in the United States, Australia, Italy, France, and Denmark. *Journal of Marriage and Family, 72,* 1344–1361.

Dahm, P. C., Glomb, T. M., Manchester, C. F., & Leroy, S. (2015). Work–family conflict and self-discrepant time allocation at work. *Journal of Applied Psychology, 100,* 767–792.

DeGeest, D. S., & Schmidt, F. L. (2011). The impact of research synthesis methods on industrial–organizational psychology: The road from pessimism to optimism about cumulative knowledge. *Research synthesis methods, 1*(3-4), 185–197.

De Leeuw, E. S., & Hox, J. J. (2003). The use of meta-analysis in cross-national studies. In J. A. Harkness, F. J. R., van de Vijver, & P. P. Mohler (Eds). *Cross-Cultural Survey Methods* (pp. 329–345). New York: Wiley.

Eby, L. T., Casper, W. J., Lockwood, A., Bordeaux, C., & Brinley, A. (2005). Work and family research in IO/OB: Content analysis and review of the literature (1980–2002). *Journal of Vocational Behavior, 66*(1), 124–197.

Ford, M. T., Heinen, B. A., & Langkamer, K. L. (2007). Work and family satisfaction and conflict: A meta-analysis of cross-domain relations. *Journal of Applied Psychology, 92,* 57–80.

French, K. A., Dumani, S., Allen, T. D., & Shockley, K. M. (2015). *A Meta-Analysis of Support Across Cultures.* Poster presentation for the 2015 Annual Conference of the Society of Industrial and Organizational Psychology, Philadelphia, PA.

Glass, G. V. (2015). Meta-analysis at middle age: A personal history. *Research Synthesis Methods, 6,* 221–231.

Hofstede, G. (1980). Culture and organizations. *International Studies of Management & Organization, 10,* 15–41.

Hoobler, J. M., Hu, J., & Wilson, M. (2010). Do workers who experience conflict between the work and family domains hit a "glass ceiling?": A meta-analytic examination. *Journal of Vocational Behavior, 77,* 481–494.

House, R. J., Hanges, P. J., Javidan, M., Dorfman, P. W., & Gupta, V. (Eds.). (2004). *Culture, Leadership, and Organizations: The GLOBE Study of 62 Societies.* Sage publications.

Kossek, E., & Ozeki, C. (1998). Work–family conflict, policies, and the job–life satisfaction relationship: A review and directions for organizational behavior–human resources research. *Journal of Applied Psychology, 83,* 139–149.

(1999). Bridging the work–family policy and productivity gap: a literature review. *Community, Work, & Family, 2,* 7–32.

Kossek, E. E., Pichler, S., Bodner, T., & Hammer, L. B. (2011). Workplace social support and work–family conflict: A meta-analysis clarifying the influence of general and work–family-specific supervisor and organizational support. *Personnel Psychology, 64,* 289–313.

Lallukka, T., Chandola, T., Roos, E., Cable, N., Sekine, M., Kagamimori, S., Tatsuse, T., Marmot, M., & Lahelma, E. (2010). Work–family conflicts and health behaviors among British, Finnish, and Japanese employees. *International Journal of Behavioral Medicine*, *17*, 134–142.

Lenartowicz, T., Johnson, J. P., & White, C. T. (2003). The neglect of intracountry cultural variation in international management research. *Journal of Business Research*, *56*(12), 999–1008.

Litano, M. L., Major, D. A., Landers, R. N., Streets, V. N., & Bass, B. I. (2016). A meta-analytic investigation of the relationship between leader-member exchange and work–family experiences. *The Leadership Quarterly*. Advance online publication. doi: 10.1016/j.leaqua.2016.06.003

Matthews, R. A., Winkel, D. E., & Wayne, J. H. (2014). A longitudinal examination of role overload and work–family conflict: The mediating role of interdomain transitions. *Journal of Organizational Behavior*, *35*, 72–91.

McNall, L. A., Nicklin, J. M., & Masuda, A. D. (2010). A meta-analytic review of the consequences associated with work–family enrichment. *Journal of Business and Psychology*, *25*, 381–396.

Mesmer-Magnus, J. R., & Viswesvaran, C. (2005). Convergence between measures of work-to-family and family-to-work conflict: A meta-analytic examination. *Journal of Vocational Behavior*, *67*, 215–232.

Mesmer-Magnus, J. R., & Viswesvaran, C. (2006). How family-friendly work environments affect work/family conflict: A meta-analytic examination. *Journal of Labor Research*, *27*, 555–574.

Meyer, J. P., Stanley, D. J., Jackson, T. A., McInnis, K. J., Maltin, E. R., & Sheppard, L. (2012). Affective, normative, and continuance commitment levels across cultures: A meta-analysis. *Journal of Vocational Behavior*, *80*, 225–245.

Michel, J. S., Clark, M. A., & Jaramillo, D. (2011). The role of the Five Factor Model of personality in the perceptions of negative and positive forms of work–nonwork spillover: A meta-analytic review. *Journal of Vocational Behavior*, *79*, 191–203.

Michel, J. S., & Hargis, M. B. (2008). Linking mechanisms of work–family conflict and segmentation. *Journal of Vocational Behavior*, *73*, 509–522.

Michel, J. S., Kotrba, L. M., Mitchelson, J. K., Clark, M. A., & Baltes, B. B. (2010). Antecedents of work–family conflict: A meta-analytic review. *Journal of Organizational Behavior*, *32*, 689–725.

Michel, J. S., Mitchelson, J. K., Kotrba, L. M., LeBreton, J. M., & Baltes, B. B. (2009). A comparative test of work–family conflict models and critical examination of work–family linkages. *Journal of Vocational Behavior*, *74*, 199–218.

Michel, J. S., Mitchelson, J. K., Pichler, S., & Cullen, K. L. (2010). Clarifying relationships among work and family social support, stressors, and work–family conflict. *Journal of Vocational Behavior*, *76*, 91–104.

Moher, D., Liberati, A., Tetzlaff, J., & Altman, D. G. (2009). Preferred reporting items for systematic reviews and meta-analyses: The PRISMA statement. *Annals of Internal Medicine*, *151*, 264–269.

Nohe, C., Meier, L. L., Sonntag, K., & Michel, A. (2015). The chicken or the egg? A meta-analysis of panel studies of the relationship between work–family conflict and strain. *Journal of Applied Psychology*, *100*, 522–536.

O'Rourke, K. (2007). An historical perspective on meta-analysis: Dealing quantitatively with varying study results. *Journal of the Royal Society of Medicine*, 100, 579–582.

Olivas-Luján, M. R., Harzing, A. W., & McCoy, S. (2004). September 11, 2001: Two quasi-experiments on the influence of threats on cultural values and cosmopolitanism. *International Journal of Cross Cultural Management, 4,* 211–228.

Ollier-Malaterre, A., & Foucreault, A. (2016). Cross-national work–life research: Cultural and structural impacts for individuals and organizations. *Journal of Management, 43*(1), 111–136.

Ollier-Malaterre, A., Valcour, M., Den Dulk, L., & Kossek, E. E. (2013). Theorizing national context to develop comparative work–life research: A review and research agenda. *European Management Journal, 31,* 433–447.

Powell, G. N., Francesco, A. M., & Ling, Y. (2009). Toward culture-sensitive theories of the work–family interface. *Journal of Organizational Behavior, 30,* 597–616.

Shadish, W. R. (2015). Introduction to the special issue on the origins of modern meta-analysis. Research Synthes

Schaffer, B. S., & Riordan, C. M. (2003). A review of cross-cultural methodologies for organizational research: A best-practices approach. *Organizational Research Methods, 6,* 169–215.

Schmidt, F. L. (2015). History and development of the Schmidt-Hunter meta-analysis methods. *Research Synthesis Methods, 6,* 232–239.

Schmidt, F. L., & Hunter, J. E. (2014). *Methods of Meta-Analysis: Correcting Error and Bias In Research Findings.* Sage publications.

Shockley, K. M., & Allen, T. D. (2013). Episodic work–family conflict, cardiovascular indicators, and social support: An experience sampling approach. *Journal of Occupational Health Psychology, 18,* 262–275.

Shockley, K.M., Douek, J., Smith, C.R., Yu, P.P., Dumani, S., & French, K.A. (2017). Cross-cultural work and family research: A review of the literature. *Journal of Vocational Behavior. 101,* 1–20.

Shockley, K. M., & Singla, N. (2011). Reconsidering work–family interactions and satisfaction: A meta-analysis. *Journal of Management, 37,* 861–886.

Spector, P. E., Allen, T. D., Poelmans, S. A., Lapierre, L. M., Cooper, C. L., Michael, O. D., . . . & Brough, P. (2007). Cross-national differences in relationships of work demands, job satisfaction, and turnover intentions with work–family conflict. *Personnel Psychology, 60,* 805–835.

Taras, V., Kirkman, B. L., & Steel, P. (2010). Examining the impact of culture's consequences: A three-decade, multilevel, meta-analytic review of Hofstede's cultural value dimensions. *Journal of Applied Psychology, 95,* 405–439.

Triandis, H. C. (1989). The self and social behavior in differing cultural contexts. *Psychological Review, 96,* 506–520.

Trompenaars, F. (1993). Riding the Waves of Culture: Understanding Diversity in International Business. *Irwin, Chicago.*

Van Den Noortgate, W., & Onghena, P. (2003). Multilevel meta-analysis: A comparison with traditional meta-analytical procedures. *Educational and Psychological Measurement, 63*(5), 765–790.

Yang, N., Chen, C. C., Choi, J., & Zou, Y. (2000). Sources of work-family conflict: a Sino-US comparison of the effects of work and family demands. *Academy of Management Journal, 43,* 113–123.

9 Conducting Qualitative Work–Family Research across Cultures

Sowan Wong and Vivian Miu-Chi Lun

Managing both work and family roles has increasingly become an issue, if not a challenge, faced by individuals around the globe in the last few decades. At the same time, interest in studying issues which stem from the work–family interface has also increased (Poelmans, Greenhaus, & Maestro, 2013). Amongst the burgeoning research on the work–family interface, attempts have been made to investigate and compare the various phenomena in the work–family interface across cultures with quantitative studies being the dominant approach (see for example the meta-analysis by Allen, French, Dumani, & Shockley, 2015). However, when investigating the work–family interface across cultures, it is important to also take into account the different meanings that constructs may have in different cultural contexts, which may affect the understanding and interpretations of the findings from quantitative studies (Ollier-Malaterre & Foucreault, 2017).

Qualitative research is a valuable tool in discovering the local meanings and individual experiences of the work–family interface in different cultures. The goal of qualitative research is to help investigators understand and clarify specific phenomena of interest from a particular social-cultural context (Seale, Gobo, Gubrium, & Silverman, 2004). Qualitative research is especially appropriate for exploring relatively under-investigated or highly complex phenomena, as well as understanding contradictions and discrepancies found in existing studies (Goldberg & Allen, 2015). This is achieved by collecting data via the narratives of local respondents, then analyzing and interpreting those textual data, with an emphasis on the perceptions and interpretations from the respondents' perspectives.

The unique contribution of cross-cultural, qualitative research in the work–family interface is twofold. First, as an end, cross-cultural, qualitative research can be adopted to explore concepts or phenomena in the work–family interface across different cultures, and be used to compare the similarities and/or differences of those experiences and perceptions across different cultural groups. This is following the derived etic approach of cross-cultural research (Smith, Fischer, Vignoles, & Bond, 2013), in which comparisons on the culturally universal (etic) elements of the phenomenon of interest may be achieved through integrating various culturally specific (emic) studies conducted in the cultures involved (e.g., Shordike et al., 2010).

Second, as a means, the findings from qualitative research can also be used to lay the foundation for quantitative studies by establishing functional equivalence of concepts across different cultures, as well as highlighting the unique (non-equivalent) components of various concepts in different cultural contexts. Functional equivalence concerns whether a certain psychological construct can be said to exist across cultures, and extensive qualitative work such as interviews or focus groups is essential to establish in-depth understanding about each cultural context of interest before one can make informed judgement as to whether quantitative comparison on the construct is meaningful (Smith et al., 2013). Alternatively, cross-cultural, qualitative research may also be used to complement quantitative research by clarifying unexpected quantitative results and findings, through interviews and/or focus groups with local respondents.

Review of Existing Cross-Cultural Qualitative Research

Work–family global qualitative studies can be divided into two groups, those that focus on a single culture – and cross-cultural comparisons which include multiple countries or cultures. Most of these studies fall in the former category and are mono-cultural. Several researchers have focused on gaining a general understanding of the work–family experiences of female IT professionals in India (Valk & Srinivasan, 2011), airline employees in Hong Kong (Ng, Fosh, & Naylor, 2002), life insurance agents in Singapore (Chan, 2002), young Chinese urban professionals (Coffey, Anderson, Zhao, Liu, Zhang, 2009), Russian cosmonauts (Johnson, Asmaro, Suedfeld, & Gushin, 2012), entrepreneurs in New Zealand (Kirkwood & Tootell, 2008), Austrian managers (Kasper, Meyer & Schmidt, 2005), and business travelers in the United Kingdom (Nicholas & McDowall, 2012). Somech and Drach-Sahavy (2007) conducted novel research on work–family coping strategies using an Israeli sample; Burgess, Henderson, and Strachan (2007) interviewed HR professionals about the informal family-friendly practices that their companies offered in Australia; and Ba' (2011) explored integration and segmentation behaviors in a dual-earner UK sample.

Although some findings throughout these studies are unique to their cultural or occupational context, many find similar themes to those noted in Beigi and Shirmohammadi's (2017) review of the qualitative work–family literature: parenthood, gender differences, family-friendly policies and non-traditional work arrangements, and coping strategies. One interesting finding comes from Grzywacz et al. (2007) who conducted both qualitative and quantitative research. They examined the experiences of work–family conflict among Latino immigrant workers in the United States poultry processing industry. The qualitative interviews suggested that the workers, particularly the women, experienced a great deal of work–family conflict, largely due to the physically demanding nature of the job. However, the study also included a quantitative portion, and the male and female workers reported low mean scores on the typical quantitative work–family conflict measures. This is one example of where important findings may have been masked if the question was only examined quantitatively and speaks to the need for future research to understand how the meaning of work–family conflict itself may vary across cultures. Grzywacz, Gopalan, and Carlos Chavez speculate on this further in Chapter 25 of this handbook.

There are fewer qualitative studies that involve an explicit cross-cultural agenda; we review each below. Using focus groups along with archival data from five cultures (China, Hong Kong, Singapore, Mexico, and the United States), Joplin, Francesco, Shaffer, and Lau (2003) explored the influences of macro-cultural level factors on the work–family interface. Their findings suggested that higher rates of economic, social, technological and legal changes in the macro environment would lead to higher level of work–family conflict. Using semi-structured interviews, Wong and Goodwin (2009) explored the impact of work on family in Hong Kong, China, and the United Kingdom. They found that about half of the respondents from each culture did not experience work interference with family; however, the protective factors mentioned varied across the three cultures. For instance, more Hong Kong-Chinese reported that having a manageable workload helped prevent work from interfering into the family; while more participants from the United Kingdom mentioned that having non-standard work helped prevent work-to-family conflict.

The remaining studies compare two cultures. Using focus groups from Hong Kong and Singapore, Thein, Austen, Currie, and Lewin (2010) explored the concepts of work–family balance with professional women in these two cultures. They found that most respondents from both cultures did not perceive much work–family conflict, and this phenomenon was partly attributed to the specific economic conditions in both cultures. With the high cost of living in both cultures, it is a normative expectation that females engage in full-time job to help meet the financial and material needs of their families. In sum, these studies yield important insights to the influence of culture on the work–family interface and laid the foundation for further research on relevant constructs. Peus and Traut-Mattausch (2008) interviewed female managers in the United States and Germany. They noted that German women were more skeptical about combining work and family and, despite more generous state-sponsored work–life policies, felt that such policies were detrimental in that they create discrimination in hiring women. Poster and Prassad (2005) studied work–family relations in high-tech firms in India and the United states. They noted that work–family experiences vary in each country largely based on the varying social contracts between workers and the states and the tendency for people to either segment or integrate work and family lives. Lastly, Brough, O'Driscoll, and Briggs (2009) focused on the impact of parental leave on work–family balance in an Australian and New Zealand sample. Most of their cultural differences are centered on the fact that significantly more New Zealand versus Australian parents have access to parental leave.

Best Practices for Conducting Cross-cultural, Qualitative Work–Family Research

Although guidelines and signposts for conducting qualitative research have been widely published (e.g., Goldberg & Allen, 2015), this section aims to highlight several specific issues to be considered when conducting cross-cultural, qualitative research specifically with a focus on the work–family interface.

Defining culture and the specific research question. Various attempts have been made to define culture; common to these definitions are the emphases on shared meaning about things (e.g., Rohner, 1984) or way of life (Berry, Poortinga, Segall, & Dasen, 1992) of a group of people, and that this shared meaning or way of life is transmitted within the group. These emphases suggest that cultures are differentiable from one another according to the views and understandings *shared* by members within any group. In other words, the concept of culture can be applied to many groups that extend beyond nations, such as those that share common ethnicities, languages, sexual orientations, or religions (Frisby, 1998; Matsumoto & Juang, 2017). Although most cross-cultural research has been focused on nations (Smith et al., 2013), it is possible to conduct cross-cultural research based on different groups, such as comparison across states or provinces within a nation, depending on the theoretical assumptions the researchers hold about the culture of these groups (see for example Chapter 22 in this handbook; Eby, Vande Griek, Maupin, Allen, Gilreath, & Martinez).

Having decided upon the specific cultures of interest, researchers can then determine which factors associated with these cultures are likely to impact work–family outcomes, and design research questions and interview protocol around these ideas. For instance, the meaning of family may differ across cultures; people in individualistic cultures may interpret the term family to mean only the nuclear family, whereas people in more collectivistic cultures may refer to broader kinship relations and extended family (Georgas, 2006). One consequence of different conceptions of family is that the scope of familial responsibilities may also vary across cultures, which in turn leads to different perceptions about what constitute work–family conflicts in individualistic versus collectivistic cultural contexts. Taking care of aging parents may then be more positively evaluated and be construed as a part of core familial duties in collectivistic cultures (Löckenhoff, Lee, Buckner, Moreira, Martinez, & Sun, 2015).

Designing the research. When conducting cross-cultural, qualitative research, compared to conducting a mono-cultural study, various additional issues need to be considered to ensure the validity and reliability of the data, such as equivalence of interview or focus group questions in each culture studied, culturally appropriate data collection methods, and transcription-translation-interpretation of data. A detailed set of general guidelines for conducting qualitative and quantitative cross-cultural studies has been laid out by Smith et al. (2013). Many of the suggestions center around how to ensure that the design of research materials (e.g., interview protocols) and the data-collection procedures (e.g., instructions given by interviewers) are equivalent in each cultural setting, so that the results obtained from each culture are subjected to minimal influence of extraneous variables. As such, a cross-cultural, collaborative research team with researchers from each culture participating in the research project provides valuable resources and manpower to cater to the various needs that arise in such research (Mitteness & Barker, 2004).

After designing the core set of questions and subsequent probes for the data collection, these questions need to be translated to the local language of each culture studied. Specifically, two common approaches have been used in cross-cultural research to ensure linguistic equivalence of instruments before and after translation: back translation (Brislin, Lonner, & Thorndike, 1973) and the committee approach. The former involves translation of materials from what are typically written in English into a target language, and another bilingual translator will then back-translate this language-version into English. An independent native user of English will then compare the original English version with the back-translated English version to look for any inconsistency between the two versions and improve the translation accordingly. The back-translation method is cost-effective and easy to implement, but sometimes may result in problems such as awkward phrases adopted by an individual translator. This shortfall may be addressed by the committee approach, where a group of bilinguals work together to translate and discuss the appropriateness of the translation. A combination of the back-translation and committee approach may also be adopted to take advantages of both approaches (see Smith et al., 2013). See Chapter 11 of this handbook for additional discussion of translation processes (Korabik & Rhijn).

Sampling. The target population is an important consideration in qualitative research. In work–family studies, researchers must decide, for example, whether to include individuals who are working part-time, work from home, or are shift-workers, in addition to those who work in full-time employment. In addition, researchers also have to decide whether to include individuals who are cohabitating, or those who are in single-parent or step families. The decision-making process will depend on the theoretical assumptions, and the specific cultural backgrounds of the cultural groups studied. The inclusion criteria of perspective respondents can then be clearly defined.

The issue of sample size has been a long-contended issue in qualitative research. Although the sample size for qualitative research is generally smaller than that required for quantitative research, the breadth and scope of the topic of investigation, as well as the heterogeneity of the population should be considered when deciding on the sample size (Baker & Edwards, 2012). The attainment of saturation (Glaser & Strauss, 1967), which occurs when no new insight can be obtained by inclusion of new data, is sometimes regarded as a criterion for determining sample size. It is usually applied when a grounded-theory approach is adopted, with data generated from a few in-depth interviews (Goldberg & Allen, 2015; Nelson, 2017). Other guidelines have also been stipulated in the literature, suggesting a sample sizes that range from six to fifty for qualitative interviews (Baker & Edwards, 2012). The analytical technique used is also a factor to be considered when deciding on sample size, as different sampling procedures require different amounts of data. When a quantitative component is included, sample size calculation can be conducted to ensure that there is enough power in identifying the prevalence of themes (Fugard & Potts, 2015), or enough statistical power in the quantitative analyses, such as Chi-square or logistic regression analysis.

Data collection. Qualitative interviews and focus groups are two common data collection methods used in qualitative research. Both methods are compatible with a phenomenological, interpretative approach, which emphasizes the understanding of social phenomenon from individuals' own perspectives (Kvale, 1996). With qualitative interviews, researchers can explore "how and why people behave, think and make meaning as they do" (Ambert, Adler, Adler, & Detzner, 1995, p. 880). With focus groups, face-to-face interactions amongst representative groups of individuals, along with a moderator, can generate new thinking and in-depth discussion of a topic of interest (Krueger & Casey, 2000). The data generated via focus group discussions may be more useful in gauging whether a statement has broad consensus or is just the idiosyncratic view of one individual.

The decision on which data collection method to adopt in a qualitative study also depends on issues of privacy and sensitivity of topics. For instance, in Wong and Goodwin's (2009) study, their aim was to investigate individuals' personal experiences of how their work influenced their marriages. The topic was deemed rather personal and sensitive, and one that individuals might not feel comfortable discussing with a group of strangers in a focus group; therefore, qualitative interviews were adopted as the data collection method. In contrast, Thein et al.'s (2010) study focused on professional women's perceptions of work–life balance and how various support structures were useful to their management of work–life balance. Interactions among participants were helpful in eliciting ideas about issues related to the broader socioeconomic context (e.g., government support to women), which may not have been brought up if only individual interviews were utilized.

When qualitative interviews are adopted as the method of data collection for the study, the method in which the interviews should be conducted is another important consideration (e.g., face-to-face or phone interviews). The choice of the mode of interview is dependent in part on the theoretical approach and the research question of the study; however, if the non-verbal, visual cues afforded only by face-to-face interviews are not the focus of the study, there may not be a significant difference between the quality of face-to-face and that of phone interview (Novick, 2008; Sturges & Hanrahan, 2004). Additionally, specific cultural issues may need to be taken into consideration. For instance, in places where most people live in cramped living conditions, and value privacy of their homes more, such as in Hong Kong and urban China (Wong, 2003), phone interviews may allow for a relatively high degree of privacy to the respondents as the interviewers do not need to 'intrude' into their homes. In addition, safety issues of the interviews may also need to be considered as a certain degree of risk may be involved when the interviewers need to conduct field visits for the interviews, depending on the neighborhoods or locations that the respondents live or work. When the perceived risk is high, phone interview may be a better option. While it may be easier for the interviewer to ensure the privacy of the respondents by physically checking the suitability of the location where the interviews take place, the same can be achieved in phone interviews by checking with the respondents before the start of the interview that they are talking on the phone in private, without the presence of others.

Another advantage of using a cross-cultural research team is that local researchers are available for the data collection (e.g., conducting the qualitative interviews or focus group discussions in each locality). Sharing a common cultural background with the respondents may help the researcher establish rapport with the respondents, as well as cater to their cultural and linguistic backgrounds, such as the probing for interpretations of local slang and jargon, or interpreting non-verbal cues in high-context cultures (Hall & Hall, 2000). As the quality of the data from qualitative interviews or focus groups depends a great deal on the quality of the interviewers or moderators, all the interviewers or moderators should be well-trained and familiarized with the standardized protocol established for the study, and discuss the process and issues with the research team before the start of the data collection.

Data analysis. Common qualitative data analytical approaches adopted in work–family research include content analysis, thematic analysis, and template analysis. These approaches can help researchers establish meaning directly from the data (Mojtaba, Turnnen, & Bondas, 2013). Content analysis is a systematic coding and categorizing approach, which classifies and quantifies large amount of textual data, with the use of pre determined categories to count the frequencies of each code in a reliable manner (Green, 2004; Mojtaba et al., 2013). This approach is used to elucidate the phenomenon of interest by identifying the prevalence of various themes identified among the respondents and can be used in conjunction with quantitative statistical analysis to compare the frequencies of responses. For example, in Johnson and colleagues' (2012) study with retired Russian cosmonauts, the relative frequencies of different types of work–family conflicts and interactions experienced in their pre-career, during career, and post-career period were compared, based on the data analyzed with a content analysis approach. However, the use of a pre determined, fixed, coding scheme in content analysis may not be suitable in picking up unique, emic components when conducting cross-cultural, qualitative studies.

On the other hand, thematic analysis can be used to identify and analyze patterns in qualitative data. With this approach, researchers become familiarized with the data, collate and code quotes from the data, search for themes amongst the codes, review the themes, then define and name the themes (Braun & Clarke, 2006). Thus, the aim of this approach is more focused on the identification of common themes versus the specific frequencies of occurrences (Braun & Clarke, 2006). For instance, in Nicholas and McDowall's (2012) study, thematic analysis was used to analyze the data collected via semi-structured interviews with business travelers from the United Kingdom. The authors identified four main themes of achieving work–family balance across their group of respondents, such as accepting their lifestyle choice and role and through negotiation. The findings were then interpreted within the framework of work–family border theory. In their cross-cultural study with female professionals from Hong Kong and Singapore, Thein and colleagues (2010) analyze their data collected from focus groups conducted in Hong Kong and Singapore with a grounded-theory approach. Fourteen categories were identified and linked to their model of work–family balance.

Similar to thematic analysis, template analysis also allows more flexibility in producing an interpretation of the qualitative data. With template analysis, themes in the initial template can be defined a priori (King, 1998) based on previous research and theorizing about the phenomena of interest. However, the themes in the initial template are then modified or discarded, and new themes are included during close readings of all the qualitative data until a final template is constructed, which is then used for coding of all the data. In the final template, themes or codes are organized hierarchically (King, 1998), with those related to each other clustered together under higher-order codes. Higher-level codes represent broad themes and lower-level codes represent more focused themes or themes of finer distinctions. Template analysis also allows researchers to quantify and analyze the qualitative data statistically by counting frequencies of each theme. This technique was used in Wong and Goodwin's (2009) three-culture study to analyze the data collected from semi-structured interviews in each location. In this study, an initial template was defined a priori based on previous research and theorizing regarding work–family conflict (Greenhaus & Beutell, 1985) and used as a basis for the subsequent analysis. The production of the final template and the actual analysis, however, were not constrained by the initial template, but allowed emic elements to emerge from the data from the different cultures involved. Both culturally universal and culturally specific themes or codes regarding work–family interactions were identified in the study; for instance, across the three cultures studied, separation between work and family was mentioned as a protective factor against work–family conflict; however, more respondents from the United Kingdom mentioned part-time employment and more respondents from Hong Kong mentioned having reasonable work hours as buffers to work–family conflict, which were specific factors afforded by the respective cultural contexts.

Once the initial coding is conducted, typically by the principal investigator, a portion of the data can be subjected to multiple coding by having different researchers code the data independently. This can help ensure the rigor and reliability of the coding procedure (Armstrong, Gosling, Weinman, & Marteau, 1997; Barbour, 2001). However, in cross-cultural studies, the focus is not only on ensuring a high degree of concordance amongst the coders, but also to explore and investigate the content of disagreement in the coding to uncover any cultural-specific meaning of the topic of interest (Barbour, 2001). From the discussion of the discrepancies of the coding results, insights and new understanding can be obtained. In Wong and Goodwin's study (2009), reliability of the coding was established by having approximately one-third of the transcripts from each culture coded independently by a researcher who was native from the respective culture. Each set of coding was then compared with the coding conducted by the chief investigator based on the same set of transcripts. Discrepancies found were discussed and negotiated, and inter-rater reliability was calculated in terms of inter-rater agreement. Inter-rater agreement (Miles & Huberman, 1994) was used in the study because the unit of analysis was the thematic unit, and the transcript of each respondent could be coded into multiple themes.

In most cross-cultural studies, the qualitative data from different cultures studied are transcribed verbatim and then translated into English for subsequent analyses. However, having the coding conducted based on the transcripts written in the original language can help preserve the original meanings of the qualitative data.

For example, in Wong and Goodwin's (2009) three-cultural study, the data from the qualitative interviews were transcribed verbatim in the original language, and the subsequent analyses were conducted based on these transcripts. This approach was possible because the principal investigator and other researchers in the study were bilingual, and spoke the local languages of the cultures studied. This analytical method helped preserve the original meaning of the data gathered from different cultural contexts and afforded emic elements to emerge from the data.

Recommendations for Future Qualitative Cross-Cultural Work–Family Research

Although cross-cultural, qualitative work–family research is relatively rare, it has great potential to contribute to work–family theory and practice. It provides a tool to investigate and understand the similarities and differences in the perceptions and experiences of the work–family interface across diverse cultural contexts. This understanding of the culturally similar versus culturally specific elements of the different components of work–family relations can help in the development and refinement of culturally sensitive models of the work–family interface, which can then be further validated using quantitative data with larger samples. With this mixed-method approach, the results of the qualitative work can help establish equivalence of constructs across the cultures studied, and refine items to be used in quantitative surveys. This is critical to help ensure the validity of measures adopted in large-scale cross-cultural research, which are often quite costly. Moreover, this also helps lay the groundwork for subsequent unpackaging studies (Smith et al., 2013) which aim to explain the observed cultural differences in the work–family interface with relevant individual-level variables across cultures.

Another advantage of qualitative research is that it can be used to investigate and provide explanations to unexpected findings that are observed in cross-cultural, quantitative studies. Thus, in this type of mixed-method approach, the qualitative study supplements the findings in quantitative study. For instance, in Allen and colleagues' (2015) meta-analysis, no significant difference was found in the levels of work-to-family conflict between individuals from individualistic and collectivistic cultures, while individuals from cultures higher in individualism reported lower levels of family-to-work conflict than their counterparts in cultures higher in collectivism. These findings were inconsistent with their hypotheses that individuals from more collectivistic cultures should report less work-to-family and family-to-work conflicts than their counterparts from less collectivistic cultures. A cross-cultural, qualitative study involving individuals from cultures on the individualism-collectivism continuum may help further investigate these unexpected results.

Similarly, Lu, Huang, and Bond (2016) quantitatively examined how cultural values influence work centrality. It was found that perceived independence at work predicted work centrality only for males, but not for females; it is not clear which cultural variable would be useful to account for such difference. Lu et al. (2016)

conjectured that the difference could be explained by differences in gender role socialization, but they also acknowledged that "in the work–life balance literature, although the role of gender has been stressed, when gender similarity arises or gender difference emerges is still not clearly understood" (p. 290). While gender role socialization offers a possible explanation, it is important to note that gender role ideology differs across cultures and changes as societies undergo change (Gibbons, Hamby, & Dennis, 1997). In this case, a qualitative study could assess this conjecture by examining how perceived relative importance and independence of work differ across genders in different cultural contexts.

Given the relative dearth of cross-cultural work–family research, there are many qualitative research opportunities moving forward. One of the possibilities is to examine the meaning of work–family balance across cultures. Cultural values and beliefs influence individuals' perception of work and family, and the perception of work–family conflict may vary in different cultural contexts (Grzwaycz et al., 2007). Along the same line, the meaning and experience of work–family balance may also vary across cultures. For instance, in cultures where egalitarian gender roles are more emphasized, marital partnership or equality may be perceived as an integral strategy in striving for work–family balance (Zimmerman, Haddock, Current, & Ziemba, 2003). A related issue concerning spousal and family support may also be of interest. Spousal support can have various benefits to marital relationship (Cutrona, 1996), such as the prevention of emotional withdrawal in times of stress. However, differential emphasis on egalitarianism in different cultures may influence the types of spousal and family support that are valued in the work–family interface, and these specific types of support (e.g. sharing of housework, childcare, sharing of emotions, respect and value work–life goals of both partners) may be difficult to uncover without qualitative work. Another interesting topic in work–family research across cultures is the concept of work–family boundaries (Ashforth, Kreiner, & Fugate, 2000), specifically, how individuals negotiate the physical and psychological boundaries between work and family domains. Segmentation and integration of work and family roles have been suggested as two possible strategies in managing the work–family interface (Rothbard, Phillips, & Dumas, 2005). Although Ashforth et al. (2000) proposed that there may be cultural differences in segmentation-integration practices, this has only been empirically studied in one study comparing American and Indian workers in high tech firms, finding greater integration in the United States and more segmentation in India (Poster & Prassad, 2005). Given that previous qualitative work has found that people differ in their boundary management strategies based on other contextual factors such as employment condition and identity (Ba', 2011), it seems a worthwhile area of future investigation into additional cultural and employment contexts.

From a practical point of view, empirical cross-cultural, qualitative research not only can elucidate our understanding about the cultural influences on work–family interface, as well as the local meanings and experiences of work and family in different cultural contexts, it can also provide insights to policy-makers and multinational companies in devising culturally sensitive and appropriate work–family policies and interventions (e.g., De Cieri & Bardoel, 2009). For instance, it is suggested that the concept of work–family balance has long been a less recognized issue in Chinese societies, given the high importance placed on work (Lewis, Gambles, & Rapoport, 2007); such that in order to make flexible work–family arrangements effective, the mindset of local managers has to be trained and attuned accordingly (De Cieri & Bardoel, 2009).

References

Allen, T. D., French, K. A., Dumani, S., & Shockley, K. M. (2015). Meta-analysis of work–family conflict mean differences: Does national context matter? *Journal of Vocational Behaviour, 90*, 90–100.

Ambert, A. M., Adler, P. A., Adler, P., & Detzner, D. F. (1995). Understanding and evaluating qualitative research. *Journal of Marriage and Family, 57*, 879–893.

Armstrong, D., Gosling, A., Weinman, J., & Marteau, T. (1997). The place of inter-rater reliability in qualitative research: An empirical study. *Sociology, 31*, 597–606.

Ashforth, B. E., Kreiner, G. E., & Fugate, M. (2000). All in a day's work: Boundaries and micro role transitions. *Academy of Management Review, 25*, 472–491.

Ba', S. (2011). Symbolic boundaries: Integration and separation of work and family life. *Community, Work & Family, 14*, 317–334.

Baker, S. E., & Edwards, R. (2012). How many qualitative interviews is enough? Expert voices and early career reflections on sampling and cases in qualitative research. National Centre for Research Methods Review Paper. National Centre for Research Methods, Southampton, the U.K. Retrieved from http://eprints.ncrm.ac.uk/2273/

Barbour, R. S. (2001). Checklists for improving rigour in qualitative research: A case of the tail wagging the dog? *British Medical Journal, 322*, 1115–1117.

Beigi, M., & Shirmohammadi, M. (2017). Qualitative research on work–family in the management field: a review. *Applied Psychology: An International Review*, doi:10.1111/apps.12093

Berry, J. W., Poortinga, Y. H., Segall, M. H., & Dasen, P. R. (1992). *Cross-Cultural Psychology: Research and Applications*. Cambridge: Cambridge University Press.

Braun, V., & Clarke, V. (2006). Using thematic analysis in psychology. *Qualitative Research in Psychology, 3*, 77–101.

Brislin, R. W., Lonner, W., & Thorndike, R. M. (1973). *Cross-Cultural Research Methods*. New York, NY: John Wiley & Sons.

Brough, P., O'Driscoll, M.P., Biggs, A. (2009). Parental leave and work–family balance among employed parents following childbirth: An exploratory investigation in Australia and New Zealand. *New Zealand Journal of Social Sciences Online, 4*, 71–87.

Burgess, J., Henderson, L., & Strachan, G. (2007). 'I just juggle': Work and family balance in Australian organisations. *Hecate, 33*(1), 94.

Chan, K. B. (2002). Coping with work stress, work satisfaction, and social support: An interpretive study of life insurance agents. *Asian Journal of Social Science, 30*(3), 657.

Coffey, B. S., Anderson, S. E., Shuming, Z., Yongqiang, L., & Jiyuan, Z. (2009). Perspectives on work–family issues in China: the voices of young urban professionals. *Community, Work & Family, 12*(2), 197–212. doi:10.1080/13668800902778967

Cutrona, C. E. (1996). Social support as a determinant of marital quality: The interplay of negative and supportive behaviours. In G. R. Pierce, B. R. Sarason, & I. G. Sarason (Eds.), *Handbook of Social Support And The Family* (pp. 173–194). New York: Plenum.

De Cieri, H., & Bardoel, E. A. (2009). What does "work–life management" mean in China and Southeast Asia for MNCs? *Community, Work & Family, 12*, 179–196.

Frisby, C. L. (1998). Culture and cultural differences. In J. H. Sandoval, C. L. Frisby, K. F. Geisinger, J. D. Scheuneman, & J. R. Grenier (Eds.), *Test Interpretation and Diversity: Achieving Equity in Assessment* (pp. 51–73). Washington, DC: American Psychological Association.

Fugard, A. J. B., & Potts, H. W. W. (2015). Supporting thinking on sample sizes for thematic analysis: A quantitative tool. *International Journal of Social Research Methodology, 18*, 669–684.

Georgas, J. (2006). Families and family change. In J. Georgas, J. W., Berry, F. J. R. van de Vijver, Ç. Kagitçibasi, & Y. H. Poortinga, (Eds.), *Families Across Cultures: A 30-Nation Psychological Study* (pp. 3–50). Cambridge, UK: Cambridge University Press.

Gibbons, J. L., Hamby, B. A., & Dennis, W. D. (1997). Researching gender role ideologies internationally and cross-culturally. *Psychology of Women Quarterly, 21*, 151–170.

Glaser, B. G., & Strauss, A. L. (1967). *The Discovery of Grounded Theory: Strategies For Qualitative Research*. London, U.K.: Aldine Transaction.

Goldberg, A. E., & Allen, K. R. (2015). Communicating qualitative research: Some practical guideposts for scholars. *Journal of Marriage and Family, 77*, 3–22.

Green, B. (2004). Personal construct psychology and content analysis. *Personal Construct Theory and Practice, 1*, 82–91.

Greenhaus, J. H., & Beutell, N. J. (1985). Sources of conflict between work and family roles. *Academy of Management Review, 10*, 76–88.

Grzywacz, J. G., Arcury, T. A., Marín, A., Carrillo, L., Burke, B., Coates, M. L., & Quandt, S. A. (2007). Work–family conflict: Experiences and health implications among immigrant Latinos. *Journal of Applied Psychology, 92*, 1119–1130.

Hall, E. T., & Hall, M. R. (2000). Key concepts: Underlying structures of culture. In H. W. Lane, J. J. DiStefano, & M. L. Maznevski (Eds.), *International Management Behavior: Test, Readings, and Cases* (pp. 199–206). Cambridge, MA: Blackwell Publishers.

Johnson, P. J., Asmaro, D., Suedfeld, P., & Gushin, V. (2012). Thematic content analysis of work–family interactions: Retired cosmonauts' reflections. *Acta Astronautica, 81*, 306–317.

Joplin, J. R. W., Francesco, A. M., Shaffer, M. A., & Lau, T. (2003). The macro-environment and work–family conflict: Development of a cross-cultural comparative framework. *International Journal of Cross-Cultural Management, 3*, 305–328.

Kasper, H., Meyer, M., & Schmidt, A. (2005). Managers dealing with work-family-conflict: an explorative analysis. *Journal of Managerial Psychology, (20)* 5, 440–461.

King, N. (1998). Template analysis. In G. Symon & C. Cassell (Eds.), *Qualitative Methods and Analysis in Organizational Research* (pp. 118–134). London, UK: Sage.

Kirkwood, J., & Tootell, B. (2008). Is entrepreneurship the answer to achieving work–family balance? *Journal of Management & Organization, 14(3)*, 285–302.

Krueger, R. A., & Casey, M. A. (2000). *Focus groups: A Practical Guide for Applied Research* (3rd ed). Thousand Oaks, CA: Sage.

Kvale, S. (1996). *InterViews: An introduction to qualitative research interviewing.* Thousand Oaks, CA: Sage Publications.

Lewis, S., Gambles, R., & Rapoport, R. (2007). The constraints of a 'work–life balance' approach: An international perspective. *International Journal of Human Resource Management, 18,* 360–373.

Löckenhoff, C. E., Lee, D. S., Buckner, K. M. L., Moreira, R. O., Martinez, S. J., & Sun, M. Q. (2015). Cross-Cultural Differences in Attitudes About Aging: Moving Beyond the East-West Dichotomy. In S.-T., Cheng, I. Chi, H. H. Fung, L. W. Li, & J. Woo (Eds.), *Successful Aging: Asian Perspectives* (pp. 321–337). Dordrecht, the Netherlands: Springer.

Lu, Q., Huang, X., & Bond, M. H. (2016). Culture and the working life: Predicting the relative centrality of work across life domains for employed persons. *Journal of Cross-Cultural Psychology, 47,* 277–293.

Matsumoto, D., & Juang, L. (2017). *Culture and Psychology* (6th ed). Boston, MA: Cengage Learning.

Miles, M., & Huberman, A. (1994). *Qualitative Data Analysis: An Expanded Sourcebook.* London, U.K.: Sage Publications.

Mitteness, L., & Barker, J. (2004). Collaborative and team research. In C. Seale, G. Gobo, J. F. Gubrium, & D. Silverman (Eds.), *Qualitative Research Practice.* London, the U.K.: Sage.

Mojtaba, V., Turnnen, H., & Bondas, T. (2013). Content analysis and thematic analysis: Implications for conducting a qualitative descriptive study. *Nursing and Health Sciences, 15,* 398–405.

Nelson, J. (2017). Using conceptual depth criteria: Addressing the challenge of reaching saturation in qualitative research. *Qualitative Research, 17* (5), 554–570.

Ng, C. W., Fosh, P., & Naylor, D. (2002). Work–family conflict for employees in an East Asian airline: Impact on career and relationship to gender. *Economic & Industrial Democracy, 23*(1), 67–15.

Nicholas, H., & McDowall, A. (2012). When work keeps us apart: A thematic analysis of the experience of business travellers. *Community, Work & Family, 15,* 335–355.

Novick, G. (2008). Is there a bias against telephone interviews in qualitative research? *Research in Nursing and Health, 31,* 391–398.

Ollier-Malaterre, A., & Foucreault, A. (2017). Cross-national work–life research: Cultural and structural impacts for individuals and organizations. *Journal of Management, 43,* 111–136.

Peus, C., & Traut-Mattausch, E. (2008). Manager and mommy? A cross-cultural comparison. *Journal of Managerial Psychology, 23*(5), 558–575.

Poelmans, S. A. Y., Greenhaus, J. H., & Maestro, M. L. H. (2013). *Expanding the Boundaries Of work–Family Research: A Vision for The Future.* Basingstoke, UK: Palgrave.

Poster, W. R., & Prasad, S. (2005). Work–family relations in transnational perspective: a view from high-tech firms in India and the United States. *Social Problems, 52*(1), 122–146.

Rohner, R. P. (1984). Toward a conception of culture for cross-cultural psychology. *Journal of Cross-Cultural Psychology, 15*(2), 111–138.

Rothbard, N. P., Phillips, K. W., & Dumas, T. L. (2005). Managing multiple roles: Work–family policies and individuals' desire for segmentation. *Organizational Science, 16,* 243–258.

Seale, C., Gobo, G., Gubrium, J. F., & Silverman, D. (Eds.). (2004). *Qualitative Research Practice.* London, UK: Sage.

Shordike, A., Hocking, C., Pierce, D., Wright-St. Clair, V., Vitayakorn, S., Rattakorn, P., & Bunrayong, W. (2010). Respecting regional culture in an international multi-sight study: A derived etic method. *Qualitative Research, 10*, 333–335.

Smith, P. B., Fischer, F., Vignoles, V. L., & Bond, M. H. (2013). *Understanding Social Psychology across Cultures: Engaging with Others in a Changing World* (2nd ed). Thousand Oaks, CA: Sage.

Somech, A., & Drach-Zahavy, A. (2007). Strategies for coping with work–family conflict: The distinctive relationships of gender role ideology. *Journal of Occupational Health Psychology, 12*(1), 1–19. doi:10.1037/1076-8998.12.1.1

Sturges, J. E., & Hanrahan, K. J. (2004). Comparing telephone and face-to-face qualitative interviewing: A research note. *Qualitative Research, 4*, 107–118.

Thein, H. H., Austen, S., Currie, J., & Lewin, E. (2010). The impact of cultural context on the perception of work/family balance by professional women in Singapore and Hong Kong. *International Journal of Cross-Cultural Management, 10*, 303–320.

Valk, R., & Srinivasan, V. (2011). Work–family balance of Indian women software professionals: A qualitative study. *IIMB Management Review, 23*, 39–50.

Wong, O. M. H. (2003). Postponement or abandonment of marriage? Evidence from Hong Kong. *Journal of Comparative Family Studies, 34*, 531–554.

Wong, S., & Goodwin, R. (2009). The impact of work on marriage in three cultures: A qualitative study. *Community, Work & Family, 12*, 213–232.

Zimmerman, T. S., Haddock, S. A., Current, L. R., & Ziemba, S. (2003). Intimate partnership: Foundation to the successful balance of family and work. *American Journal of Family Therapy, 31*, 107–124.

10 Leveraging Archival Data in Global Work–Family Research: The Case of Time Use Data

Joan García Román and Sarah Flood

Time use studies analyze how individuals allocate their time. Data on time use allow researchers to document and understand human behavior and population lifestyles and to implement policies for development and planning policies (Harvey & Pentland, 1999). Time is a scarce resource that each person uses differently, and through the study of time we can analyze whether these differences are voluntary or forced and predict change in future population behavior (Durán, 2010). Time use data have been widely used to analyze changes over time and differences between cultures. For example, Bianchi et al. (2006) used time use data for the United States from 1965 forward to analyze the time allocation patterns of changing American families. They found that decreases in housework and increases in multitasking help explain how mothers' time with children has remained steady despite increases in paid work. Gershuny (2000) found convergence in time use patterns both across time and across countries with different social and cultural backgrounds.

In this chapter we introduce time use data as a resource for studying work and family. While we broadly introduce different types of time use data, our primary focus is on time diary data. We review the historical relevance of time use studies, and we describe data collection methods. We discuss challenges for comparing time diary data across time and space. Finally, we include a case study illustrating how time diary data may be used to compare family time in the United States and Spain.

The Historical Relevance of Time Use Survey Methodology

Time diary techniques were used as early as the turn of the twentieth century in Russia and London (Pember-Reeves, 1913; Bevans, 1913), with the earliest time diaries collected in the United States and the Soviet Union in the 1920s (Strumilin, 1925; Szalai, 1966; Kneeland, 1929). In the first known time diary study (Szalai,

This study was supported by the Minnesota Population Center at the University of Minnesota (HD041023) and the Data Extract Builder of the American Time Use Survey (University of Maryland, HD053654), both funded through grants from the Eunice Kennedy Shriver National Institute for Child Health and Human Development (NICHD). It was also supported by the CERCA Programme / Generalitat de Catalunya and Juan de la Cierva-incorporación Post-doctoral Fellowship (IJCI-2015–23382).

1984), Bevans (1913) examined the non-work time of employed men from New York City and surrounding New York state areas. In an effort to understand and alleviate poverty, Pember-Reeves (1913) used time diaries to document the experiences of working-class women in London in 1909–1913. In the early 1920s in the Soviet Union, Strumilin undertook a study of industrial workers for the purposes of economic planning (Zuzanek, 1980; Szalai, 1984). These early studies laid the foundation for future time diary data collection.

The first large-scale time diary studies in the United States were funded by the 1925 Purnell Act, which required federal funding for agricultural research, and were fielded by the United States Department of Agriculture. These studies focused on the time use efficiency of farm and town homemakers (Gershuny & Harms, 2016). Using these data, Kneeland (1929) argued that women's unpaid domestic work should be considered part of the national economy (Gershuny & Harms, 2016). During the Great Depression, Russian exile Pitirim Sorokin, in collaboration with Clarence Berger (Sorokin & Berger, 1939), conducted a large-scale study of young adults in the Boston area of the United States who were unemployed or underemployed, including individual episodes recording what people were doing and who they were with (Michelson, 2015).

The collection and analysis of time diary became more widespread in the 1960s (Andorka, 1987). In the mid-1960s Szalai began a foundational study (Andorka, 1987) sampling the population of twelve countries (Bulgaria, Czechoslovakia, German Democratic Republic, Hungary, Poland, Soviet Union, Yugoslavia, France, Belgium, German Federal Republic, Peru, and the United States) in a time diary survey that recorded what individuals were doing, when they did the activities, where they were, and who they were with. Since Szalai's early work in the area, hundreds of surveys have been fielded in over 100 countries around the world (Fisher, 2015).

Methods of Collecting Time Use Data

Information on time use is mainly collected via stylized questions or through time diaries. Stylized questions elicit information about the frequency and time spent performing a series of pre established activities (e.g., paid work, housework, childcare, eldercare). By contrast, the time diary is a record of the sequence and duration of activities carried out by an individual over a specified period of time, typically twenty-four hours (Converse, 1968). The time diary format allows researchers to know what individuals do at all times of the day as opposed to just how much time is spent in pre established activities, from which the *timing and sequencing* throughout the day is missing. Additional information is often collected in time diaries about with whom activities are performed (e.g., with partner, with children or with friends), where activities take place (e.g., at home or at work), and even how respondents feel during activities (e.g., happy or stressed), providing contextual information for analyzing the use of time at the intersection of the moment of the day and space (Durán & Rogero, 2009).

Diaries of activities provide unique opportunities to learn about daily life and how it has changed over time and how it varies across cultures. Despite their complexity, time diary data allow for much more flexibility than other types of time use data and allow researchers to approach the data from many different perspectives. They allow researchers to examine how daily life is structured and provide the basis for contrasting theories about the nature of social change in modern societies (Robinson, 1999). Time diary data also provide an opportunity for researchers to investigate the sequence and order of activities, tapping into issues of fragmentation and quality of time (Bianchi et al., 2006).

Diaries are considered the most valid and reliable data source for the study of time use (Gershuny & Sullivan, 1998; Gershuny, 2000; Marini & Shelton, 1993; Durán & Rogero-García, 2009; Robinson, 1999; Bonke, 2005), and are becoming the standard method for collecting information on the organization of daily life and time spent on market work, non-market work, and leisure (Sevilla, 2014). For example, the use of diaries avoids the difficulty of estimating the time spent on a particular activity and the over- or under-reporting of activities due to social desirability bias, that is overestimating the time spent in socially desirable activities (e.g., reading a book to children) or underestimating less socially acceptable activities (e.g., watching TV) (Press & Townsley, 1998; Juster et al., 2003; Hofferth, 2006). Research comparing time diary and stylized estimates (i.e., questions that ask respondents to estimate how much time they spend in certain activities) of time devoted to work activity (Juster & Stafford, 1991; Robinson & Bostrom, 1994) show that stylized estimates may overstate time spent in paid work (but see Frazis & Stewart, 2004). Such comparisons have also been made for household tasks (Bianchi et al., 2000; Presser & Robinson, 2000), religious activity (Presser and Stinson, 1998), and reading to children (Hofferth, 1999), all of which provide evidence suggesting that stylized estimates are more likely to overstate activity participation compared to time diary estimates. Moreover, diaries distinguish between main and secondary activities and capture the relative importance of one activity versus another for the respondent (Durán & Rogero, 2009). Finally, the sum of all activities collected by means of a diary is twenty-four hours (1,440 minutes), while stylized questions sometimes exceed this amount (Juster et al., 2003).

Data Collection by Time Diaries

Time diaries spanning a 24-hour period generally take one of three forms; the choice depends on the research objectives and resources available. In the open diary format, respondents provide the sequence of activities and the start and end time of each. There is no specific interval of time for which respondents must report what they are doing, so that the burden on the respondents is lower than for other methods. Diaries with fixed intervals require that the respondents report the activity performed for a specified time interval (EUROSTAT recommends every ten minutes). Larger time intervals mean less work for the respondent, but some detail, especially for shorter activities, is lost (Gershuny, 2000). Finally, using simplified diaries, activities are pre defined (i.e., participants select from a list of activities) and the respondent must indicate times of day when they performed such activities.

In addition to collecting information about primary activities, time diary data collections often include additional contextual information. The most common types of contextual information include whether respondents are doing a simultaneous activity and what the activity is, with whom they carry out the activity, and where it is done. How respondents feel during an activity and whether they are using electronic devices are also sometimes, though less commonly, collected.

Time use surveys also differ in the number of members per household who participate in the survey. Some surveys include all household members, others sample those individuals in a certain age range, while others sample only one member of the household. In each case, the surveys generally collect sociodemographic information of other household members and general characteristics of the household. Gathering time use information about multiple individuals per household allows researchers to analyze how tasks and roles are divided within the household.

Another difference across time use surveys is the number of diaries completed by each respondent. Respondents may fill only one 24-hour diary, two diaries (usually one on a week day and one on a weekend), or a diary for each day of the week. The availability of more than one diary per respondent allows researchers to compare time allocation under different circumstances, for example, when respondents work or when they do not. Although the information collected in time diaries generally covers only a single day, or in some cases up to a week, the number of respondents who complete diaries is usually large enough to ensure the representativeness of both weekdays and weekends and different demographics (Durán & Rogero, 2009). Moreover, the collection of data across individuals is usually spread over a full a year, capturing the periodicity of certain activities as well as allowing for investigation of seasonal and, potentially, weather effects on time allocation.

The information in the diary may be reported in a respondent's own words or chosen from a predefined list of activities. The data are more valuable when respondents provide information about the activity in an open-ended format, but it also requires subsequent coding; this is not an issue if activities are predefined. Furthermore, when there is no predefined list of activities, the information is less biased since no research objectives are shown (Durán & Rogero, 2009). Own words reports are simpler to code now than they were previously given the development of harmonized lists of activities and the classification of activities in coding schemes with different levels of detail. Szalai's early studies (1966) have been the basis on which activity codes have been modified and adapted. The International Classification of Activities for Time Use Statistics (ICATUS) is another commonly used activity list that has different levels of detail where the most detailed activities together aggregate into a smaller number of second-level activities and the second-level activities aggregate into still a smaller number of first-level activities. An example of first-level detail is: *Providing unpaid domestic services for own final use within household* is classified in category 06. This category is divided in the following divisions: *Working time in providing unpaid domestic services for own final use* (061), *Travel related to provision of unpaid domestic services* (062), and *Unpaid domestic services not specified* (069). Category 061, for example, is then divided in the following groups: *Unpaid domestic services* (0611), *Shopping* (0612). *Unpaid domestic services* is further split into *Food management* (06111), *Cleaning and upkeep of dwelling and surroundings* (06112), *Do it yourself decoration, maintenance and small repairs* (06113), *Care of textiles and footwear* (06114), *Household management* (06115), and *Pet care* (06116). A nested classification allows for easy context-specific modification to include activities that are common in different contexts. For example, a new activity with code 0613 can be created in the third level if it is relevant in the data collection. A detailed list of the ICATUS can we found in the Statistical Division of United Nations (http://unstats.un.org/UNSD/cr/registry/regcst.asp?Cl=231&Lg=1).

Another source of variation in data collection is whether the information is self-reported or collected by an interviewer. When an interviewer collects the data via direct observation, respondents do not have the opportunity to define the activities they are doing. On the other hand, the behavior of the respondent may be affected by the observer (Durán & Rogero, 2009; Robinson, 1999). Time diaries completed by respondents themselves may be filled in throughout the day or completed retrospectively. With retrospective diaries, respondents may have problems remembering some activities, while throughout the day diaries are more burdensome for the respondent, which may produce a higher rate of non-response (Marini & Shelton, 1993).

Time Diary Data Challenges

The main problem with time diary data collection is the relatively high cost, which increases as more details about time use are collected (Marini & Shelton, 1993). Other major problems with collecting time diaries include the burden on the respondent and high rates of non-response. Bonke (2005) estimates a response rate of 49% for surveys collecting information by means of diaries and a response rate of 66% when information is obtained through stylized questions. These problems may lead to concerns about the data because people who are invited to participate but do not respond tend to be busier (Gershuny, 2000), though other evidence highlights weak integration in one's community as being more problematic for non-response than busyness (Abraham, Maitland, & Bianchi, 2006). The implications of research on non-response suggest that specific types of activities, such as volunteering, may be overestimated because people who volunteer are more likely to participate in surveys (Abraham, Maitland, & Bianchi, 2006). Nevertheless, technological advances and the development of apps for data collection have reduced the cost and burden associated with collecting time diary data.

Collecting information about a single day allows one to extrapolate information about the daily dynamics of households, but it is more difficult to know the weekly, monthly, and yearly dynamics (Durán & Rogero, 2009), and there is also a risk that the day is atypical (Robinson, 1999; Marini & Shelton, 1993). This concern is largely addressed with a good sample design that yields representativeness for every day of the week, especially in terms of working days, weekends, and holidays (Marini & Shelton, 1993). At the population level, typical and atypical days should together constitute a reliable picture about daily time use. Furthermore, in some cases, respondents may indicate if the day of interview was typical or atypical (e.g., holiday, illness), allowing researchers to decide how to handle different types of days.

Open-ended responses in time diary data do mean that coding activities requires careful consideration. For example, should "read the Bible" be coded as a reading activity or a religious activity (Chenu & Lesnard, 2006)? The open-endedness of time diary data also means that the most sensitive activities (e.g., sexual and other biological activities) and illegal activities (e.g., drug use) tend to be excluded from the diaries because individuals do not report them (Robinson, 1999). There may also be significant variation in the quantity of content in respondents' diaries, with some respondents detailing many activities and others reporting fewer (Robinson, 1999). Some authors consider secondary activities underreported because of the fatigue or lack of awareness of the respondent (Durán, 2010). Time use questionnaires are long and require a higher level of commitment by the respondent to complete the 24 hour diary compared to other surveys. Respondents may complete the main parts of the questionnaire, but skip some parts that they consider less relevant. Researchers argue that multitasking may be underreported because respondents are less apt to report a secondary activity.

Existence of Time Use Data Globally

The large number of countries that conduct time use surveys signifies their importance for scientific research and policy making. Most of the surveys have been fielded by country-specific National Statistical Institutes due to the complexity and cost of fielding the surveys; there are, however, some surveys conducted by other institutions and organizations. Since 1960, 107 countries have conducted time use studies at a national level or for a large geographical area. In eighty-two of those countries, data are collected based on a diary of activities.

The number and periodicity of surveys for each country varies greatly. Figure 10.1 shows which countries have time use surveys and how many. In general, time use studies are more frequent in developed countries; few developing countries have engaged in time use studies, and most of these are not based on diaries of activities. For countries with a long tradition of time use studies, like the United States, the United Kingdom, the Netherlands, and South Korea, there is a long series of periodically collected time diary data. In other countries, time use studies are more recent and the availability of data is limited, but the expectation for most is that the surveys will be repeated in the near future.

In the United States, although an official national survey was not conducted until 2003 when the American Time Use Survey (ATUS) was initiated, time diary data

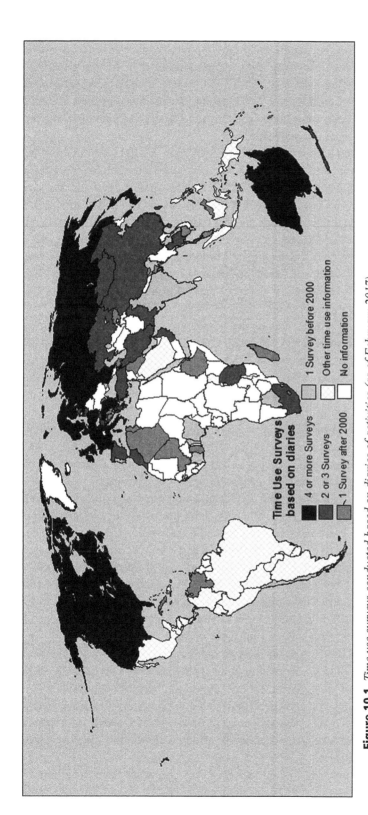

Figure 10.1 *Time use surveys conducted based on diaries of activities (as of February 2017).*
Source: www.timeuse.org, http://unstats.un.org/unsd/gender/timeuse/, Charmes (2015). For Argentina, Brazil, and Mexico there are surveys based on diaries for specific regions or cities. Other time use information mainly refers to surveys based on stylized questions, but there are also some surveys based on small qualitative samples.

collection was conducted from the 1960s onwards by the Institute of Social Research at the University of Michigan and the Survey Research Center at the University of Maryland, yielding time-use diary data spanning more than fifty years. This is similar in Canada, where the availability of time use studies goes back to the 1960s. In the case of Canada, a subset of the individuals interviewed in the 1970s were also interviewed ten years later, providing longitudinal information about time use, which is rare in time use studies.

Several European countries also have long data series that date back to the 1960s. The most important round of surveys, however, took place around 2000, when fifteen countries carried out a time use survey following the guidelines of the Statistical Agency of the European Commission (EUROSTAT). A second round of surveys took place around 2010, and the plan is to conduct more surveys in the future, although there is not an established periodicity. Among the countries with the longest series of time diary data are the United Kingdom, where time use surveys are available every decade since the mid-1960s, and the Netherlands, where time diary surveys have been carried out every five years since 1975. French data are also available since the 1970s, but surveys based on diaries are more limited in other Mediterranean countries such as Spain, Greece, and Portugal. Among the Nordic countries, Denmark has collected time use diary data since 1964, Norway since 1971, and Finland since 1979. In Sweden the fielding of time-use surveys began in 1982.

Eastern European countries have a long tradition of collecting time use data. Data from this region is rich and spans decades in some countries, notably Bulgaria, Hungary, and Poland. Hungarian data was first collected in 1965 during Szalai's project, with other surveys have been fielded periodically ever since. In Russia, the collection of time use information goes back to the 1920s; different surveys since then have gathered information, but access to these surveys is complicated. For other Eastern European countries the information is mainly available for more recent decades.

The series of data is also growing for Japan, where time use studies have been done every five years since 1996, although there are older surveys since 1940. In South Korea, the main national broadcaster (KBS) and KOSTAT also conduct time use surveys every five years, with the KBS and KOSTAT surveys two to three years apart. KBS started collecting time use data in the 1980s; the first KOSTAT survey took place in 1999. China, Indonesia, Mongolia, Thailand, and other East and South-East Asian countries have one-off-large scale national time use surveys, with the possibility of collecting future surveys. Moving South, in Australia, time use studies have taken place periodically since the 1970s.

In Latin America, time use surveys based on diaries of activities are uncommon and information on time use is mainly collected by means of stylized questions, sometimes as a part of more general surveys. However, there are some studies based on diaries of activities for specific regions such as Buenos Aires in Argentina, Mexico City in Mexico, and Neuma Aguiar in Brazil. The exception for a national level survey in Latin America is Venezuela, which carried out a time use survey based on diaries in 2011.

Time use studies are also limited in Africa. Few countries have done time use surveys, and they have generally been infrequent. South Africa and Tanzania are the only African countries to have a time series of time diary data available. Surveys were conducted in 2000 and 2010 and 2006 and 2014, respectively. Ghana (2009), Ethiopia (2013), Morocco and Algeria (2012) are some of the countries that have done a time use study based on dairies recently.

Challenges Comparing Time Use Data Worldwide

Despite their prevalence, access to time-use data, comparability across time and place, and complexity of the data are important barriers to conducting time-use research. Some countries, such as Spain and the United States, provide free access to all datasets. This is not the case everywhere, however, and in many cases it is necessary to apply in order to use the data. Moreover, in some countries the access is limited only to researchers in the country, necessitating multi-national collaborations to explore any cross-cultural research questions.

Further, although core methodological similarities exist across time and countries, there are some key differences with significant implications for how the data can be used. For example, variable coding differs among surveys, especially regarding activities, but also regarding background and contextual information of the activities such as location or who is present during the activity. To solve this issue, several efforts have been made to "harmonize" original surveys to get data that are comparable across time and place. Data resulting from the harmonization processes have consistent codes across time and countries. US data from 1965 forward have been harmonized and disseminated by the Centre for Time Use Research (CTUR) as the American Heritage Time Use Study (AHTUS). Similarly, researchers at CTUR have also harmonized data from different countries and created the Multinational Time Use Study (MTUS), which provides time use surveys from more than 60 datasets from 25 countries since the 1960s. The most basic information from the European surveys conducted in the 2000 and 2010 rounds is also available in the Harmonized European Time Use Survey (HETUS) by means of pre defined tables.

The complexity of the data also presents a barrier to their use. To facilitate access to and research using time use data, the IPUMS Time Use project (www.ipums.org/timeuse.html), a collaboration of the Minnesota Population Center at the University of Minnesota, the Maryland Population Research Center at the University of Maryland, and the Centre for Time Use Research at the University of Oxford, provides free individual-level time use data for research purposes. Currently, this project provides access to data from the American Time Use Survey (www.atusdata.org), the AHTUS (www.ahtusdata.org), and the MTUS (www.mtusdata.org). Data are delivered by a web-based data extraction system that makes it easy to create datasets containing diaries of activities for each respondent, aggregated measures of time use from the diary, and personal and household characteristics. Data are free and provided in an easy-to-access format ready for use with the main statistical packages, making them more accessible to a broader audience.

Case Study: Paid Work and Family Time in the United States and Spain

We now turn to a research example utilizing time-use data to explore patterns in paid work and family time in the United States and Spain. Differences in social, cultural, and policy contexts that may contribute to cross-national differences in work and family time will be discussed, in addition to methodological variations in survey design. We also address some data comparability issues between surveys that need to be taken into account.

Data

The American Time Use Survey (ATUS) is the only publicly available annual time diary survey. It began in 2003, and is conducted by the United States Census Bureau and funded by the United States Bureau of Labor Statistics. The sample is comprised of a subset of households that previously participated in the Current Population Survey (CPS). The CPS is a monthly household survey of the civilian, non-institutionalized population. One member per household aged fifteen years or older is selected to complete the time diary by telephone. Respondents report all their activities for one day from 4:00 a.m. to 4:00 a.m., including when the activity starts and ends, if they are providing childcare as a secondary activity, where the activity takes place, and the co-presence of household members and non-members during the activity. For household members present during the activity, additional information, like age and relationship to the respondent, is collected as part of a household roster. For non-household members, relationship of the individual to the respondent is collected as a part of the time diary. In addition to the main questionnaire, different modules have been included periodically to obtain information about topics such as well-being, employee leave, eating, and health. The study discussed here uses the 2010 data, which consists of 13,260 diaries.

The Spanish Time Use Survey (STUS) is conducted by the National Statistical Institute (INE) following the time diary guidelines from EUROSTAT. According to the guidelines, all household members aged ten and older must complete a time diary and report all their activities spanning twenty-four hours. The survey doesn't have a defined periodicity; so far the INE has carried out two surveys in 2002–2003 and 2009–2010. The information is collected via a self-report diary instrument where each person reports their activities in 10-minute intervals from 6:00 a.m. to 6:00 a.m. The diary collects information about the main activity, when it starts and ends, whether respondents are doing a secondary activity, and the presence during the activity of a partner, father or mother, children of the household under ten years old, other members of the household, and known non-household members. What we report here is based on the 2009–2010 survey containing 19,295 diaries from 9,541 households.

Although both surveys cover a twenty-four hours diary, the starting and ending points are different. The population from which the samples are drawn are also slightly different with information for children aged between ten and fourteen years only available for Spain. For Spain, time use information is available for all household members while for the United States only one member filled a diary. Additional relevant differences in methodology are described where applicable in the examples below.

Paid Work in the United States and Spain

For our analysis of paid work in the United States and Spain, we limit our sample to respondents between fifteen and sixty-four years old whose diary represents a weekday. Figure 10.2 is a tempogram showing the proportion of respondents doing paid work throughout the diary day. The solid lines correspond to all respondents (8,063 respondents for the United States [gray] and 11,540 for Spain [black]), while the dotted lines represent the respondents who reported at least one minute of paid work in the diary (4,132 in the United States [gray] and 5,228 respondents in Spain [black]).

The figure shows that the work day begins and finishes earlier in the United States than in Spain. For those who worked on the diary day, 50% were working at 8:00 a.m. in the United States. Prior to noon, the percentage of people working is always

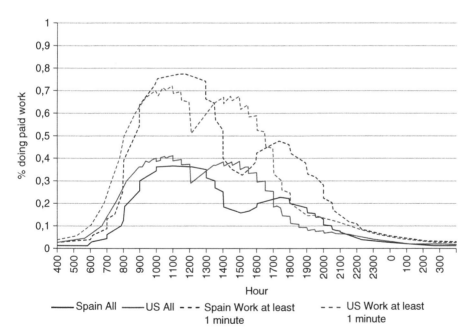

Figure 10.2 *Proportion of population engaging in paid work during a day.*
Sources: American Time Use Survey 2010 and Encuesta de Empleo del Tiempo 2009–2010.
Note: Work at least 1 minute indicates that the sample was restricted to only people who reporting working at all that day.

10 points lower in Spain than in the United States. In Spain, a rate of 50% working is not recorded until forty minutes after the same rate is reached in the United States. In the evening, only 20% of workers in the United States are working at 6:00 p.m., while more than twice the percentage of Spanish workers are still working. The figure also shows different timing and duration for the main breaks in the work schedule. In Spain, the decrease in the proportion of people doing paid work is observed around 2:00 p.m. The break also lasts longer in Spain than in the United States and is more common, representing a relatively constant percentage until 4:00 p.m., when the proportion of people working increases again, though not to pre-break levels.

Lines for overall populations (continuous lines) also show the different unemployment rate in both countries. In Spain, the unemployment rate is much higher than in the United States, and, as a consequence, the proportion of people who don't work any minutes during the twenty-four hour diary is also higher. In this sense, the proportion of the population doing paid work is higher in the United States during almost the entire day, except a short period at noon and between 5:00 p.m. and 9:00 p.m., when the proportion is slightly larger in Spain. This second period is a consequence of the Spanish labor market that is characterized by work schedules that often involve very long breaks and late finishes (Gracia & Kalmijn, 2016).

Family Time in the United States and Spain

Utilizing these same datasets, García Román, Flood, and Genadek (2017) examine time with a spouse in the United States, Spain, and France. Here, we expand to examine family time, defined as time spent with a partner and/or children, using the information about the co-presence of others during the activity from the time diary. In general, that type of information is not collected for personal care, sleeping activities, or paid work, so we exclude these activities from consideration for our family time measure. Co-presence refers to the presence of others during the activity and does not necessarily translate into interaction between the respondent and the individuals they report being with at the time. For example, respondents and others could be in the same room but doing different activities. Information on co-presence is also reported in different ways in the two surveys. In the ATUS, respondents list the people who are with them during activities, while in the STUS respondents have to check which relatives or non-relatives are present in their paper diary. Another issue to consider is the measurement of co-presence in the two surveys. In the ATUS, the presence of others means that another person is in the same room as the respondent. In Spain, the condition of being in the same room is not explicit, thus there may be differences in reports of co-presence between the two samples. To correct for this difference between the ATUS and other surveys for time with children, Mullan and Craig (2009) propose that researchers consider children as co-present when respondents have a child under their responsibility during the activity (secondary childcare in the ATUS) or when a child is present in the ATUS.

More importantly, in the STUS the presence of children ten and older is captured in the "other household members" category, which means that we cannot distinguish children ten and older from other household members such as siblings or other relatives. For that reason, our analysis is limited to families of adult couples between the ages of twenty and sixty-five with children under ten years old. The final sample contains 1,614 cases for the United States and 1,840 cases for Spain.

Based on these cases, we compute time spent in the following activities: personal care and sleeping, paid work, family time (activities with spouse and children), time with children (activities with children but not partner), time with partner (activities with partner but not children), and time without family (activities neither with partner nor children). Figure 10.3 shows the average minutes per day spent in each type of activity described. The total time for each country sums to 1,440 minutes (or twenty-four hours).

Time spent in personal care (such as sleeping and grooming) and paid work is similar in both countries. The average time spent in personal care is around nine hours while time spent in paid work is around four hours and ten minutes. More differences are observed in the measures of time with a partner and children. The main differences are in time spent with children. In Spain, family time (time with a partner and children together) is more common, and parents spend more than four hours together as a family. In the United States, 37 fewer minutes are spent with family. On the other hand, parents in the United States

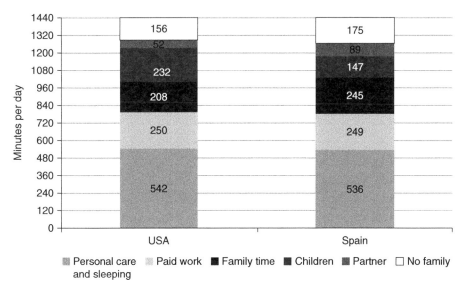

Figure 10.3 *Average minutes per day spent in personal care and sleeping, paid work, and activities with spouse and children.*
Sources: 2010 American Time Use Survey and Encuesta de Empleo del Tiempo 2009–2010.

spend more time alone with children compared to parents in Spain. In the United States, 24 more minutes are spent alone with children per day compared to family time, while in Spain the reverse is true, with much more time being spent as a family (98 more minutes) compared to time alone with children. The sums of the two measures of time with children (family time and time with only children) yield a gap of 48 minutes, with parents in the United States spending 48 more minutes with their children.

Differences between the United States and Spain in time with a partner and not with children are also significant. Spanish parents spend 37 more minutes alone together than US parents. Combining time with a partner only and time as a family, we find that Spanish couples spend almost one hour and 15 minutes more together than parents in the United States.

Figure 10.4 illustrates the timing of the different types of activities analyzed. Percentages represent the activity carried out, and for the activities for which we have information, with whom it is done.

Similar to Figure 10.3, time with a partner and children over the course of the day reflects the daily schedule in each country. In the United States, the percentages are quite constant between 8:00 a.m. and 5:00 p.m. with a little bit more than 10% of respondents reporting being with a partner and children and 20% alone with children. After 6:00 p.m. there is a peak in family time, which largely corresponds with dinner time. Time with a partner and children hits a maximum of 45% around 7:00 p.m. The highest proportion of time alone with children occurs slightly earlier, between 5:00 p.m. and 5:30 p.m. The highest proportion of time alone with a partner is observed at 9:30 p.m., when almost 23% of parents report being with their partner without children present.

In the case of Spain, the graph shows two family time peaks, which correspond with main meal times: one for lunch and another for dinner. Meals are more frequently shared with family in Spain, and Spaniards spend more time in this activity. Compared to Spain, time for lunch is less evident in the United States, and the graph only shows a slight decrease of time in paid work. One third of parents are with a partner and children between 2:00 p.m. and 2:30 p.m. The peak for dinner is observed later in Spain than in the United States: at 9:00 p.m., with 50% of respondents reporting being with spouse and children. The highest proportion of time alone with a partner is also observed later in Spain, around 10:30 p.m.

Our results show that time with a partner is much higher in Spain than in the United States. Spanish couples spend more time alone together than couples in the United States, and Spanish couples spend more time with a partner and children than couples in the United States. Paid work constraints explain a small part of the differences in couples' shared time that we observe between countries. Other differences appear to be rooted more in norms about family life and the cultural rhythms of daily life, such as the importance of meals and how non-work time is allocated.

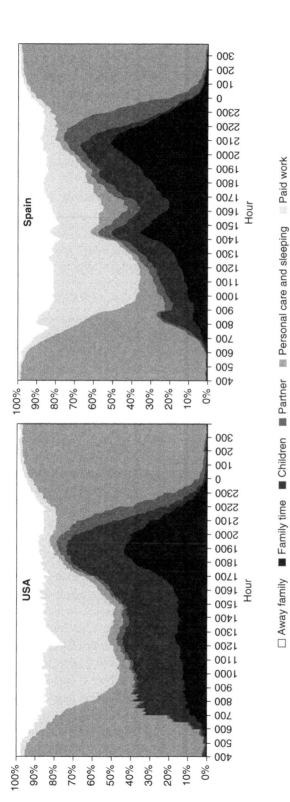

Figure 10.4 *Percentage of time in personal care and sleeping, paid work and with family during a day.*
Sources: American Time Use Survey 2010 and Encuesta de Empleo del Tiempo 2009–2010.

Conclusion

In this chapter, we described time use surveys as a data source to study global work and family issues. We discussed their main advantages and disadvantages, arguing that time use surveys based on diaries are the most reliable way to collect time use data. We also detailed the existence and accessibility of time use surveys as not homogenous over the world, however, their incidence is increasing and more countries are gathering diary data. Finally, we compared paid work and couples' shared time in the United States and Spain to illustrate how the data might be used to study work and family.

In our case study, we highlight some comparability issues that need to be addressed for analyses across countries. Time use studies are not limited to the activities carried out; they also provide access to additional information such as the co-presence of others or the place where the activity is done. The collection of information for all household members provides additional value because it allows for investigation of relative time use, for example, between the respondent and a partner, children, or other people in the household. Similarly, when multiple days are collected per respondent, researchers have opportunities to compare time use across days to better understand weekend/weekday differences in time use or differences across days when people work or not.

Time diary data provide many opportunities for research at the intersection of work and family, especially cross-culturally. Given space constraints, we describe only a few of the numerous examples of research that could leverage the rich time diary data available to the scholarly community. Countries like Spain, France, Austria, and the UK have datasets that contain multiple respondents per household, which can facilitate estimating household-level division of labor and improve our understanding of the ways in which couples combine paid work, unpaid housework, and childcare. Data from the Netherlands and the UK, which include multiple time diaries per person, can help illuminate variability in caregiving across days of the week, a key issue in determining burden for caregivers, and how caregivers combine care work and paid work, which is especially relevant given population aging. The availability of data from Eastern Europe, Asia, South Africa, and Latin America allow researchers to conduct comparative studies of the gender revolution in time use.

Time diary data also have many important policy applications. Time diary data allow for a more complete understanding of economic activity through the inclusion of nonmarket work, such as housework, unpaid care work, and volunteer work (National Research Council, 2000). The availability of such data allow for cross-time and cross-country comparisons of productive activities (e.g., Gershuny & Harms, 2016; Bridgman et al., 2012). Related, there is considerable interest in how different tax and employment policies (e.g. tax credits, family leave policies, unemployment benefits) influence individual and household decision making regarding paid work and unpaid care work (National Research Council, 2000). Time diary data are also extremely useful in examining the relationship between time use and the receipt of Supplemental Nutrition Assistance Program (SNAP) benefits in the United States (e.g., Rose, 2007; Davis & You, 2011) as well as knowledge regarding the use of and need for public infrastructure for the purposes of leisure and transportation (National Research Council, 2000).

Data comparability and complexity of the surveys are barriers to working with time use surveys across countries. However, initiatives at the Centre for Time Use Research at the University of Oxford in collaboration with the University of Minnesota and the University of Maryland have partially addressed these issues by providing easier access to the datasets and making them easier to manage.

References

Abraham, K.G., Maitland, A., & Bianchi, S.M. (2006). Nonresponse in the American Time Use Survey: Who is missing from the data and how much does it matter? *Public Opinion Quarterly* 70(5): 676–703.

Andorka, R. (1987). Time budgets and their uses. *Annual Review of Sociology* 13:149–164.

Bevans, G. E. (1913). *How Workingmen Spend Their Spare Time*. New York: Columbia University Press.

Bianchi, S. M., Milkie, M.A., Sayer, L.C., & Robinson, J.P. (2000). Is Anyone Doing the Housework? Trends in the Gender Division of Household Labor. *Social Forces*, 79 (September), 191–228.

Bianchi, S.M., Robinson, J.P., & Milkie, M.A. (2006). *Changing the Rhythms of American Family Life*. New York: Russell Sage Foundation.

Bonke, J. (2005). Paid Work and unpaid work: diary information versus questionnaire information. *Social Indicators Research* 70:349–368.

Bridgman, B, Dugan, A., Lal, M., Osborne, M., & Villones, S. (2012). Accounting for Household Production in the National Accounts, 1965–2010. *Survey of Current Business* 92(5):23–36.

Charmes, J. (2015). *Time Use Across the World: Findings of a World Compilation of Time Use Surveys*. 2015 UNDP Human Development Report Office.

Chenu, A., & Lesnard, L. (2006). Time use surveys: a review of their Aims, methods and results. *European Journal of Sociology*, vol. 3(47), pp. 335–359.

Converse, P.E. (1968). Time budgets. In David Sills (Ed.), *International Encyclopedia of the Social Sciences*. New York: Macmillan, pp. 42–47.

Davis, G.C., & You, W. (2011). Not enough money or not enough time to satisfy the Thrifty Food Plan? A cost difference approach for estimating a money-time threshold. *Food Policy* 36(2):101–107.

Durán, M.A. (2010). *Tiempo de vida y tiempo de trabajo*. Conferencias Magistrales: Fundación BBVA: Bilbao.

Durán, M. Á. & Rogero-García, J. (2009). *La investigación sobre el uso del tiempo*. Cuadernos Metodológicos, Vol. 44. Madrid: CIS, p. 214.

Fisher, K. (2015). *Metadata of Time Use Studies*. Last updated 31 December 2014. Centre for Time Use Research, University of Oxford, United Kingdom. www.timeuse.org/information/studies/

Frazis, H., & Stewart, J. (2004). What Can Time Diary Data Tell Us About Hours of Work? *Monthly Labor Review*, 127(December), 3–9.

García Román, J., Flood, S., & Genadek, K. (2017). Parents' time with a partner in cross-national context: A comparison of the US, Spain, and France. *Demographic Research*, 36 (4): 111–144.

Gershuny, J. (2000). *Changing Times: Work and Leisure In Post-Industrial Society.* Oxford: Oxford University Press.

Gershuny, J., & Harms, T. (2016). Housework Now Takes Much Less Time: 85 Years of us Rural Women's Time Use. *Social Forces* 1–22.

Gershuny, J., & Sullivan, O. (1998). The sociological uses of time-use diary analysis."*European Sociological Review* 14(1):69–85.

Gracia, P., & Kalmijn, M. (2016). Parents' family time and work schedules: The splitshift schedule in Spain. *Journal of Marriage and Family* 78(2): 401–415. doi:10.1111/jomf.12270.

Harvey, A. S., & Pentland, W. E. (1999). Time use research, in Pentland, W. E. et al. (Eds.), *Time Use Research in The Social Sciences*, New York: Kluwer Academic Publishers Group. p. 3–18.

Hofferth, S.L. (1999). Family Reading to Young Children: Social Desirability and Cultural Biases in Reporting. Paper prepared for the Workshop on Measurement of and Research on Time Use, Committee on National Statistics, National Research Council, Washington, DC, May 27–28.

Hofferth, S. L. (2006). Response bias in a popular indicator of reading to children. *Sociological Methodology*, 36: 301–315.

Juster, F.T., & Stafford, F.P. (1991). The Allocation of Time: Empirical Findings, Behavioral Models, and Problems of Measurement. *Journal of Economic Literature*, 29 (June), 471–522.

Juster, F. T., Ono, H., & Stafford, F. P. (2003). An assessment of alternative measures of time use. *Sociological Methodology*, 33: 19–54.

Kneeland, H. (1929). Woman's economic contribution in the home. In *Special issue: Women in the Modern World. Annals of the American Academy of Political and Social Science*143:33–40.

Marini, M.M., & Shelton, B.A. (1993). Measuring household work: recent experience in the United States. *Social Science Research*, 22: 369–382.

Michelson, W.H. (2015). *Time use: Expanding Explanation in the Social Sciences.* New York, Routledge.

National Research Council. (2000). *Time-Use Measurement and Research: Report of a Workshop.* Washington, DC: The National Academies Press.

Mullan, K., & Craig, L. (2009). Harmonising extended measures of parental childcare in the time-diary surveys of four countries – proximity versus responsibility. *Electronic International journal of Time Use Research*, 6 (1): 48–72.

Pember-Reeves, M. (1913). *Round about a pound a week.* London: G. Bell and Sons, Ltd.

Press, J.E., & Townsley, E. (1998). Wives' and husband's housework reporting. Gender, class, and social desirability. *Gender and Society*, 12: 188–218

Presser, S., Robinson, J. (2000). Estimating Daily Activity Times: Comparing Three Approaches in Relation to Time Diaries.Paper presented at the annual meeting of the American Association for Public Opinion Research. Portland, Oregon.

Presser, S., & Stinson, L. (1998). Data Collection Mode and Social Desirability Bias in Surveys: Social Desirability, Memory Failure and Source Monitoring. *American Sociological Review*, 63(1), 137–145.

Robinson, J.P. (1985). "The validity and reliability of diaries versus alterative time use measures." In Juster, F.T. & Stafford, F.P. (Eds.), *Time, Goods and Well-Being*. Ann Arbor: University Press of Michigan. pp. 33–62.

Robinson, J. P. (1999). The time diary method. Structure and uses. In Pentland, W. E. *et al.* (Eds.), *Time Use Research in the Social Sciences*, New York: Kluwer Academic Publishers. pp. 47–89.

Robinson, J., & Bostrom, A. (1994). The Overestimated Workweek? What Time Diary Measures Suggest. *Monthly Labor Review*, 117 (August), 11–23.

Rose, D. (2007). Food Stamps, the Thrifty Food Plan, and Meal Preparation: The Importance of the Time Dimension for US Nutrition Policy. *Journal of Nutrition Education and Behavior* 39(4):226–232.

Sevilla, A. (2014). On the importance of time diary data and introduction to a special issue on time use research. *Review of Economics of the Household*, 12, 1–6.

Sorokin, P.A., & Berger, C.Q. (1939). *Time-budgets of human behaviors*. Harvard Sociological Studies 2. Cambridge, MA: Harvard Univ. Press.

Strumilin, S.G. (1961). Problemy socializma I kommunizma v SSSR. Moscow: Ekonomizdat.

Strumilin, S.G. (1925). Time-budgets of Russian workers in 1923–1924. Planovoe khozyaistvo, 7.

Szalai, A. (1966). The Multinational Comparative Time Budget Research Project A Venture In International Research Cooperation. *American Behavioral Scientist* 10 (4): 1–31.

Szalai, A. (1984). The concept of time budget research. In Harvey, A. (Ed.), *Time budget research: An ISSC workbook in comparative analysis*. New York: Campus. 17–35.

Zuzanek, J. (1980). Work and leisure in the Soviet Union. A time-budget analysis. New York: Holt Saunders Ltd. P. 430.

11 Best Practices in Scale Translation and Establishing Measurement Equivalence

Karen Korabik and Tricia van Rhijn

Studies carried out in English-speaking countries have long dominated the literature on the work–family (WF) interface (Powell, Francesco, & Ling, 2009). Recently, however, due to forces like increasing globalization and immigration (Schmitt & Kuljanin, 2008), there has been an explosion of WF research from different parts of the world, including many cross-national comparisons. Accordingly, researchers must now pay more attention to the role of language and culture in influencing how people conceptualize and communicate concepts and ideas (Cheung, Leung, & Au, 2006).

The Shapir–Whorf hypothesis postulates that the structure of a language shapes the thought processes of those who speak it. In this way, language can influence how individuals view their work and family roles and how they experience the WF interface. Similarly, cultural values have been shown to affect the legal, economic, and social structures that pertain to work and family (e.g., employment and family legislation, government policies regarding WF reconciliation) in different national contexts (Bagger & Love, 2010; Ollier-Malaterre & Foucreault, 2016). Cross-national research has indicated that there is much diversity in work and family dynamics in different parts of the world (Korabik, Aycan, & Ayman, 2017). It is highly likely, therefore, that those from diverse cultural, ethnic, and linguistic backgrounds will have differing perspectives that might affect their understanding and interpretation of the WF interface and the questions on surveys pertaining to it (Davidov, Meuleman, Cieciuch, Schmidt, & Billiet, 2014; Trimble, 2007).

These different perspectives necessitate careful attention to issues related to scale translation and measurement equivalence/invariance (ME/I) in order to assure the validity of results when making cross-cultural comparisons from survey data. Proper scale translation is necessary to assure that versions of a survey in different languages are linguistically and semantically equivalent. However, because it does not provide any statistical evidence about whether the different versions have comparable psychometric properties, scale translation alone is not sufficient to establish cross-cultural validity (Epstein, Santo, & Guillemin, 2015). ME/I analysis is needed to assure that results obtained in different national contexts are due to actual cultural differences instead of due to measurement and scaling artifacts. The purpose of this chapter is to discuss best practices in scale translation and ME/I. Throughout the chapter we draw upon examples from Phase Three of Project 3535, a multinational research project on the WF interface, to illustrate our points.

Scale Translation

Assuring that a measure constructed in one culture can be validly used in another culture is a very complicated process. The first issue that must be addressed is whether translation is even necessary and, if so, into how many different languages and/or dialects given that many countries are multicultural and multilingual. Moreover, the degree of fluency with a language may vary widely from person to person within a country. Some individuals may not speak the principal language at all, whereas others may be fluent in more than one language (Davidov et al., 2014). It may be tempting to forego translation when respondents understand the language in which the survey was originally constructed in addition to their native language. However, the gains made in terms of equivalent wording may be outweighed by the fact that respondents may be less familiar with and less able to express themselves articulately in their non-native language (Schaffer & Riordan, 2003).

Forward Translation

Early work in the field of scale translation concentrated on establishing linguistic equivalence (Trimble, 2007). This involved forward translation, or the translation of a measure from a source language into a target language, usually by a single translator. This method has been shown to produce unreliable results, because the results are very dependent on the individual who does the translation and are frequently not able to be replicated by other translators (Hambleton & Patsula, 1998).

Additionally, a focus on simple linguistic accuracy can be problematic. It ignores the fact that languages have many idioms and colloquialisms (e.g., glass ceiling) that are nonsensical if translated verbatim. Words or items can also mean very different things or have no equivalent meaning in different cultural contexts (Epstein et al., 2015). For example, the word family may invoke different meanings to those in a nuclear versus extended family living situations. Further, certain constructs (e.g., "guanxi" in China) may not even be meaningful in another culture. Therefore, the cultural relevance of all concepts should be assessed prior to undertaking a study or constructing a survey (Hambleton & Patsula, 1998). For these reasons, many scholars recommend moving beyond an emphasis on linguistic equivalence to a more comprehensive process, scale adaptation, that also includes assuring semantic, conceptual, content, and measurement equivalence (Epstein et al., 2015; Hambleton & Patsula, 1998). We will now turn to the extra steps necessary to achieve these goals.

Back Translation

Due to the problems inherent in the use of forward translation alone, it has been recommended that it be supplemented by back translation. In the typical forward–back translation procedure, a bilingual person translates the survey questions from the source language to the target language and a second bilingual person independently translates them back to the original language. The differences between the original source language version and the back-translated target language version are then reconciled (Davidov et al., 2014). Most often, those responsible for the translation-back translation are also those responsible for doing the reconciliation.

In its most comprehensive form, reconciliation would include an examination of: (1) semantic equivalence (is there correspondence in the meaning of the words?), (2) idiomatic equivalence (have idioms and colloquialisms been dealt with properly?), (3) experiential equivalence (is the situation depicted similarly?), and (4) conceptual equivalence (is the overall meaning the same?) (Hambleton & Patsula, 1998). Based on the results, discrepancies would be identified and improvements (e.g., rewording or eliminating problematic items) made. This may result in an iterative process that consists of additional rounds of translation, back translation, and reconciliation. Epstein et al.'s (2015) review of the methodological strategies used for cross-cultural adaptation of scales indicated that, although back translation was the most commonly used procedure in the literature, there was a lack of standardization in how it was applied. For example, there was considerable variation in the number of translators and back translators used, their characteristics and training, the number of rounds of translation-back translation undertaken, who was involved in the reconciliation process, the procedures that were used to identify and resolve discrepancies, and to what extent all of the necessary steps were followed (Epstein et al., 2015).

In terms of best practices, however, there is general agreement that translators should be bicultural (i.e., have an in-depth familiarity with both cultures) as well as fluently bilingual (Epstein et al., 2015; Hambleton & Patsula, 1998). This is because someone can be proficient in a language without ever having spent time in a culture where it is spoken. In addition, translators should be knowledgeable about the topic and content area of the survey (Epstein et al., 2015), have some background in test construction and item writing (Hambleton & Patsula, 1998), and be familiar with the research setting and context (Schaffer & Riordan, 2003). Since it may be difficult to find all of these qualities in two individuals, it is recommended that the translation-back translation-reconciliation process be carried out by a team of multinational experts (Davidov et al., 2014; Hambleton & Patsula, 1998). This also has the advantage of allowing discussions among those with diverse perspectives to take place.

Pilot Testing

An accurate back translation is insufficient in and of itself and, in most cases, does not assure that all semantic and conceptual inconsistencies have been dealt with, nor does it guarantee the validity of a survey (Hambleton & Patsula, 1998). Because of this, as a best practice a survey also needs be pilot tested (Davidov et al., 2014; Epstein et al., 2015; Hambleton & Patsula, 1998; Schaffer & Riordan, 2003). Pilot testing is important because it can identify issues that might affect the reliability and validity of the translated survey, such as problems with item clarity, ambiguity, phrasing, and completeness of concept coverage (Schaffer & Riordan, 2003; van de Vijver & Leung, 1997). Pilot studies are also useful for making sure that culturally unique (i.e., emic) items or constructs are not overlooked (Schaffer & Riordan, 2003).

Ideally, at least two rounds of pilot testing should take place. In the first, the content of the post-reconciliation prototype survey is reviewed by a few individuals similar to those in the target population using either focus groups or cognitive debriefing (Epstein et al., 2015). In contrast to focus groups, which are a group interviewing technique, cognitive debriefing consists of conducting in-depth one-on-one semi-structured interviews. Based on the results of the first pilot test, the prototype survey may need to undergo another round of revision. Following this, a second pilot test would take place where a small sample of those from the target population would complete the revised version of the translated prototype survey. Preliminary psychometric tests, which might include examining internal consistency reliability, test-retest reliability (stability), homogeneity of variance, construct validity (convergent and/or discriminant), and criterion-related validity (concurrent and/or predictive), would then be conducted on the results.

Scale Translation in Project 3535

Project 3535 is a multinational study of the WF interface (Korabik et al., 2017). It consisted of three phases, involving the collection of social policy, focus group, and survey data, respectively. The participants for the Phase Three survey were 2,830 organizationally employed, married/cohabiting parents from ten countries: Australia, Canada, China, India, Indonesia, Israel, Spain, Taiwan, Turkey, and the United States. The average number of participants per country was 283 (range 150–561). Sampling was drawn from individuals in the dominant subculture with the exceptions of Israel, where both Jewish and Arabic participants were sampled, and Canada, where both Anglophones and Francophones were sampled. A standardized sampling framework designed to recruit a large, heterogeneous sample with representation by both men and women, and managers and non-managers was utilized. This resulted in a sample composed of 45% men and 40% managers.

The Project 3535 survey consisted of an English version that was used in Australia, Canada (Anglophone subsample), and the United States. The English version was translated into seven other languages (i.e., Chinese, French Canadian, Hebrew, Hindi, Bahasa Indonesian, Spanish, and Turkish) for use in the remaining countries. The survey included a wide range of measures including those assessing core WF interface constructs (i.e., WF conflict, positive spillover, and guilt) and their antecedents and consequences in the work and family domains. Measures of cultural values and moderating and mediating variables were also included.

Project 3535 embodied several of the best practices recommended for translation and adaptation of surveys across cultures (Korabik et al., 2017). These included: (1) the use of expert bilingual *and* bicultural indigenous translators, (2) forward and back translation, (3) multiple rounds of review and reconciliation by a multinational team, (4) multiple rounds of pilot testing, and (5) extensive documentation of the procedures followed (Ekrut et al., 1999; Hambleton & Patsula, 1998; Schaffer & Riordan, 2003). Because most of the measures included in the survey had originally been developed and validated in English in the United States, members of our team of fourteen indigenous researchers reviewed whether they could be meaningfully used in each culture, as well as whether any items needed to be added to them for content validity. For example, we chose to use items from three different existing measures of gender-role attitudes to assure that we had a full range of coverage of the types of attitudes that would characterize societies with very traditional as well as those with very egalitarian views about women's roles. In addition, focus groups were conducted to identify emic issues and additional items and constructs (e.g., work–family guilt) were incorporated based on the results. The first pilot test was conducted using cognitive debriefing after which the prototype survey was revised and pilot tested again with a larger sample size.

What makes Project 3535 unique, however, is that it also exemplified best practices in terms of the team processes that were adopted (Aycan, 2017; see also Chapter 9 of this handbook, Spector & Sanchez). Many cross-cultural researchers have noted shortcomings in the typical translation/scale adaptation process as described above (see Ekrut et al., 1999). They point out that multinational research teams are usually controlled by a few individuals from developed (usually Western) countries, with those from other cultures acting primarily as data collectors (Aycan, 2017). This results in a predominance of Western ideas, methods, and measures that can result in problems with validity by producing translations that are culturally irrelevant and insensitive (Ekrut et al., 1999). Disciplinary bias is another problem that may arise when forming a team. This is a particular issue in the WF field where often researchers who have been trained in industrial-organizational psychology or business management have limited understanding of family science (Jaskiewicz, Combs, Shanine, & Kacmar, 2017) and vice versa. Project 3535 instituted several processes to guard against these problems. Our team was composed of researchers deliberately chosen to represent a wide variety of disciplines (e.g., cross-cultural and industrial-organizational psychology, management, family science, health). During all stages of the project, the team members functioned as full and equal partners. The team worked together to collaboratively develop a culturally sensitive research plan (Powell et al., 2009) and everyone was involved in all aspects of the research process, including deciding on the research questions and constructs, developing the survey items, and delineating implementation procedures (Aycan, 2017). At each stage, the team members discussed the results and offered suggestions for improvements. This, along with consensus-based decision making, guarded against any one cultural or disciplinary view being predominant (Aycan, 2017).

In summary, it is worth expending the time and effort necessary to assure linguistic, semantic, and conceptual equivalence during the survey translation/adaptation phase. As well, it is essential to formulate a culturally sensitive research plan (Powell et al., 2009) and ensure team dynamics that will facilitate its implementation (Aycan, 2017). This emphasis on early prevention will decrease the likelihood of discovering after data have been collected that one's measures are not comparable across cultures and that few options remain as to what can be done about it (Davidov et al., 2014). In addition, before finalizing the items or measures that will be included on a survey, it is advisable to check the statistical requirements for carrying out ME/I analyses. For example, a ME/I done using a CFA approach usually requires a minimum of three items per scale/subscale with items measured at the ordinal, interval, or ratio level. After the data have been collected using a cross-cultural survey, it becomes necessary to assess ME/I before making cross-cultural comparisons. We turn now to describing this process.

Measurement Equivalence/Invariance

Measurement equivalence/invariance (ME/I) refers to the comparability of measures across different groups or time periods (Davidov et al., 2014; Vandenberg & Morelli, 2016). According to Vandenberg and Lance (2000), "if one set of measures means one thing to one group and something different to another group, a group mean comparison may be tantamount to comparing apples and spark plugs" (p. 9). Thus, ME/I aims to assess whether those who differ in some way (e.g., demographics, personality, or culture) are using the same conceptual framework and ascribing the same meaning when responding to survey items (Cheung & Rensvold, 2002; Milfont & Fischer, 2010; Vandenberg, 2002). A measure is said to be invariant if the relationship between a latent variable and an observed variable is equivalent across different groups. For example, ME/I for gender would exist if there was a correspondence between men's and women's scores on the latent construct being assessed and their observed or "true" scores at the item and/or subscale level (Raju, Laffitte, & Byrne, 2002; Schmitt & Kuljanin, 2008).

ME/I can be applied to the investigation of any between-group differences that characterize one's sample. For example, ME/I analyses conducted on different modes of survey administration have found invariance in multinational samples, permitting data from paper-and-pencil and web-based surveys to be aggregated for purposes of analysis (Cole, Bedeian, & Feild, 2006; De Beuckelaer & Lievens, 2009). Groups may differ on a wide variety of characteristics (e.g., gender, age, race/ethnicity), however, so one must examine only those deemed most relevant to one's research purpose as looking at too many becomes unwieldy. In this chapter we will confine ourselves to discussing ME/I for culture and gender as these are the most relevant to cross-cultural WF research.

ME/I is particularly important for cross-cultural research because, if a measure is not operating similarly across groups, comparisons between cultures may be meaningless. In the absence of ME/I, the interpretation of between-group differences is fraught with ambiguity because one cannot definitively tell if those differences are due to actual differences on the construct of interest or, rather, to scaling artifacts or psychometric differences in how people respond to survey items (Byrne & Stewart, 2006; G. W. Cheung & Rensvold, 2002; Davidov, Dulmer, Schluter, Schmidt, & Meuleman, 2012; Schmitt & Kuljanin, 2008). For example, those in one culture may be more predisposed to respond to survey items using certain response sets (e.g., leniency) or response styles (e.g., social desirability) than those in another culture (Byrne & Watkins, 2003). Because of this, ME/I is a prerequisite for carrying out cross-national comparisons (Milfont & Fischer, 2010; Oreg et al., 2008); yet, despite this recognition, few cross-cultural studies have incorporated ME/I analyses (Davidov et al., 2014).

Methods for Establishing Measurement Equivalence/Invariance

The two approaches most often used to establish ME/I are confirmatory factor analysis (CFA) and item response theory (IRT) (Meade & Lautenschlager, 2004; Raju et al., 2002; Schaffer & Riordan, 2003; Tay, Meade, & Cao, 2015). The CFA approach is based on multigroup structural equation modelling (SEM), whereas IRT is based on a differential item functioning (DIF) approach. Each of these methods provides different ME/I information and each gives only an incomplete picture (Meade & Lautenschlager, 2004). CFA is linear, whereas IRT is not, allowing it to be used with nominal and dichotomously scored variables (Meade & Lautenschlager, 2004; Raju et al., 2002; Tay et al., 2015). CFA consists of a series of sequential tests that allow one to specify the type of invariance that exists. By contrast, IRT estimates item parameters simultaneously, focuses solely on item equivalence, and does not allow one to test the invariance of uniqueness terms and factor covariances (Vandenberg & Morelli, 2016). Because CFA provides information about the relationships among latent factors, it is preferable when one's purpose is to examine the equivalence of a multifactorial structure. By contrast, IRT may be a better choice for those focused on whether the responses to items on a specific scale are equivalent (Meade & Lautenschlager, 2004). Meade and Lautenschlager (2004) suggest that whenever possible it is best to conduct multiple ME/I tests using both IRT and CFA methods.

In the cross-cultural literature, CFA analyses are much more commonly used than those based on IRT. This may be because researchers are generally more familiar with CFA methodology, and it is less cumbersome and more user-friendly (Tay et al., 2015). In addition, IRT analyses generally require larger sample sizes and more items per scale and can be unmanageable when comparing several groups (Meade & Lautenschlager, 2004; Tay et al., 2015). By contrast, CFA can easily handle multiple latent constructs and multiple groups (Raju et al., 2002). The remainder of this chapter focuses on CFA, and uses Project 3535 as a working example to illustrate application of CFA for ME/I purposes. We refer the reader to Tay et al. (2015) for details about the IRT approach.

The CFA Approach to Establishing ME/I

Multiple group CFA using SEM is the most frequently used method for testing ME/I across culturally diverse groups (Davidoff et al., 2014). It consists of a series of sequential hierarchically ordered, multigroup model tests beginning with a baseline model and adding increasingly restrictive nested constraints (Kline, 2011; Steenkamp & Baumgartner, 1998). Prior to testing for ME/I, the measurement model should be tested individually for each group (e.g., culture) separately using CFA procedures (Byrne & Stewart, 2006) to ensure adequate fit based on typical goodness-of-fit indices (see discussion below). If the model fit is not adequate for each group, exploratory work may be required before moving on to testing for ME/I. This exploratory work might involve dropping items from the latent indicators or correlating error covariances for items that are closely related to one another (based on a strong theoretical rationale) (see Byrne, 2001, pp. 91–93, for a discussion of exploratory CFA work). The resulting group-specific baseline model should be determined based on considerations of parsimony and conceptual meaning (Byrne, 2012). Once established, this baseline model is utilized for multigroup ME/I testing.

Many different types of ME/I tests can be carried out. Vandenberg and Morelli (2016) state that the minimal requirements are a test for configural invariance (equivalence of factor structure) followed by a test for metric or weak invariance (equivalence of factor loadings). The number and type of other tests that are performed will depend upon their relevance to the purpose at hand (Schmitt & Kuljanin, 2008; Vandenberg & Morelli, 2016). We discuss three tests here as these are sufficient for addressing most substantive research questions (Byrne & Stewart, 2006). In addition to configural invariance and metric or weak invariance we also include an example pertaining to a test of scalar or strong invariance (equivalence of intercepts) (Byrne, 2012; Kline, 2011; Vandenberg & Lance, 2000). Stricter forms of ME/I can also be established, including residual invariance (equivalence of measurement error), but these are often difficult to achieve and rarely necessary (Schmitt & Kuljanin, 2008). At each level of ME/I testing not only must the model being tested fit the data well, but its fit must not be significantly worse than that of the preceding model.

Configural invariance. Establishing configural invariance means that those from different groups conceptualize a construct in the same way and utilize the same conceptual framework when responding to a measure (Milfont & Fischer, 2010). For configural invariance to be supported, the same items must load on the same latent variables across groups (Davidov et al., 2014). The data from each group (e.g., country) must have the same factor structure, with the same number of factors, same pattern of factor loadings, and same items associated with each factor (Milfont & Fischer, 2010; Schmitt & Kuljanin, 2008).

In testing the configural model, all model parameters are allowed to freely estimate. In other words, configural invariance tests an unconstrained factor structure to determine whether the same factor pattern is valid in all groups. In this way, the configural model is a multigroup representation of the baseline model that allows invariance tests to be conducted concurrently across several groups, and provides fit values against which subsequent invariance models can be compared (Byrne & Stewart, 2006).

Byrne and Watkins (2003) point out that, despite what many researchers think, finding configural invariance alone does not allow one to conclude that cross-cultural ME/I exists. For example, configural invariance does not guarantee that respondents from different cultures are using the same measurement scale in the same way (Steenkamp & Baumgartner, 1998). However, establishing configural invariance is necessary before one can proceed with more stringent tests assessing further aspects of ME/I, as these are nested within the configural model.

Metric invariance. Once configural invariance is established, the next step is to constrain the factor loadings across the groups to test for metric invariance. Metric invariance indicates that the magnitude of all factor loadings (or weights) is equivalent across groups. This means that those items are perceived and interpreted in the same way across groups (Milfont & Fischer, 2010). Metric invariance holds if goodness-of-fit is adequate and the fit of the constrained metric model is not significantly worse than that of the configural model. Establishing metric equivalence allows the comparison of difference scores (i.e., mean-corrected scores like unstandardized regression coefficients and covariances) across cultures (Davidov et al., 2014). It is necessary, therefore, to establish metric equivalence before the data from different countries can be combined for analyses using correlation-based statistics (e.g., in SEM models).

Scalar invariance. The next step is to establish scalar invariance by additionally constraining the intercepts to be equal across groups (Byrne & Stewart, 2006). Examination of this level of invariance is necessary only for those interested in comparing mean group differences (Schmitt & Kuljanin, 2008; Vandenberg & Lance, 2000). In other words, before conclusions about cross-cultural differences in observed (latent) group means can be drawn, cross-cultural equivalence in intercepts (scalar invariance) must first be established (Steenkamp & Baumgartner, 1998). Despite this, scalar invariance is seldom achieved (Davidov et al., 2012).

Scalar or intercept invariance implies that measurement scales have the same operational definition across groups (i.e., have the same intervals or units of measurement and origins or zero points) (Byrne & Stewart, 2006; Cheung & Rensvold, 2002). Failure to find scalar invariance may indicate that those from different groups are using a scale in different ways. For example, it may reflect the presence of systematic response biases (like leniency) or response threshold differences between groups.

Goodness-of-fit and comparative fit. To determine whether invariance exists, one must examine the goodness-of-fit statistics for the relevant model (i.e., configural, metric, or scalar, respectively). A number of fit statistics, all indicating how well a proposed model fits the data, are usually reviewed including the chi-square, comparative fit index (CFI), goodness-of-fit index (GFI), and Tucker-Lewis Index (TLI). The chi-square should ideally be nonsignificant, but is very often significant with large sample sizes such as those found in most cross-cultural research, often making it not the best indicator of model fit. Although there are no hard and fast rules, it is suggested that the CFI, GFI and TLI should be >.9 (with values closer to .99 being better). The root mean square error of approximation (RMSEA) should ideally be <.05; however, values up to .08 are acceptable (Kline, 2011).

In addition, when moving from configural to metric or from metric to scalar invariance, the fit of the subsequent model must not be significantly worse than that of the preceding model. Traditionally, this has been assessed by the Likelihood Ratio Test (the differences in $\chi 2$ between the two nested models) (Vandenberg & Lance, 2000). Thus, one would calculate the difference in chi-square ($\Delta\chi^2$) between the fit of the configural and metric models and if it is minimal, there would be evidence of metric invariance. Similarly, one would calculate the $\Delta\chi^2$ between the fit of the metric and scalar models and if it is minimal, there would be evidence of scalar invariance.

Researchers have demonstrated, however, that $\Delta\chi^2$ is dependent on sample size in the same way that the chi-square fit statistic is (Cheung & Rensvold, 2002). As noted above, cross-cultural research deals with very large sample sizes, so the $\Delta\chi^2$ statistic is nearly always significant in cross-cultural studies, making it an unrealistic criterion for establishing ME/I (Byrne & Stewart, 2006). Because of this challenge, alternatives have been proposed. One of the most accepted is the ΔCFI where a value of $\leq.01$ indicates that invariance exists, a value $\geq.02$ indicates a lack of invariance, and values between .01 and .02 are indicative of some differences (Cheung & Rensvold, 2002; Oreg et al., 2008). Cheung and Rensvold (2002) also suggest using other criteria, including ΔGamma hat $<.-001$ and ΔMcDonald's Noncentrality Index $<-.02$.

Partial invariance. As noted above, ME/I needs to be established at each stage (i.e., configural, metric, and scalar) before one can move to the next stage. What happens when the ME/I of a particular model cannot be demonstrated? For example, when testing for configural invariance, the baseline models may not be completely identical across groups. The best-fitting model for one group may include an error covariance or a cross-loading not present in another group (Byrne & Stewart, 2006). In such cases one can investigate whether partial ME/I exists by relaxing some constraints (Steenkamp & Baumgartner, 1998); to determine which constraints, the focus should be on determining the particular indicator(s) responsible for the noninvariance (Cheung & Rensvold, 2002). Vandenberg and Lance (2000) propose that this be done only when strong theoretical justification exists for doing so and when it is confined to a minority of the indicators so as to limit its impact. Thus, depending on the level at which the noninvariance was found, one can relax some invariant error covariances, factor loadings, or intercepts, respectively in an attempt to attain partial invariance.

Strategies for dealing with nonequivalence. A number of strategies have been suggested for dealing with situations in which there is a failure to obtain even partial ME/I. One of these is to drop noninvariant items; however, one must make sure the meaning of the concept has not changed as a result (Davidov et al., 2014). Another stringent approach is to only compare the subset (or subsets) of countries, identified through cluster analysis, in which ME/I holds. This may, however, severely reduce the number of groups included in the study (Davidov et al., 2014) – a problem for researchers interested in comparing an already small number of cultures/countries. A third strategy is to identify items that function differently because of their relationships with certain individual difference variables (e.g., age) and to control this variance by regressing these items on those individual difference variables (Davidov et al., 2014).

Programs to Run Measurement Invariance Tests

While there are many statistical programs that can be utilized for ME/I (any programs that can run multigroup CFA), AMOS and Mplus are two commonly used programs. AMOS (Analysis of Moment Structures; Arbuckle, 2014) is a user-friendly SPSS add-on program allowing users to draw graphical models and attach and run SEM analyses. Due to its graphical nature, AMOS can lack the ability to be flexible as the user has limited control over the analyses (since they are integrated within the graphical configuration). Moreover, when using a data set with missing data, modification indices cannot be generated in AMOS. Mplus (Muthén & Muthén, 1998–2011) is a syntax-based program and has greater flexibility than AMOS in that it is able to run mixed models (using both categorical and continuous data), it deals well with missing data and will still generate modification indices, and it allows for Maximum Likelihood Robust (MLR) estimation, a method of estimation that deals well with data that is not normally distributed.

Examples of ME/I Testing from Project 3535

We present two examples of ME/I tests using the data from Project 3535, one relating to cultural invariance the other relating to gender invariance. First, we present configural and metric ME/I analyses across all ten countries (Australia, Canada, China, India, Indonesia, Israel, Spain, Taiwan, Turkey, and the United States) for three WF interface constructs (i.e., WF conflict, positive spillover, and guilt). Then, we provide an example of scalar and partial invariance for gender using the work interference with family subscale of the WF conflict measure with data only from Canada and the United States.

Measures. WF conflict was assessed with Carlson, Kacmar, and Williams' (2000) measure (see Korabik et al., 2017, for detailed descriptions of all measures). Four subscales were used from this measure: time- and strain-based work interference with family conflict (WIF) and time- and strain-based family interference with work conflict (FIW). The measure was modeled with the WIF and FIW subfactors each having time- and strain-based subcomponents (see Figures 11.1 and 11.2, respectively).WF positive spillover was assessed with Grzywacz and Mark's (2000) scale which was modeled as having two three-item subfactors: work-to-family and family-to-work spillover (see Figure 11.3). WF guilt was assessed with a seven item WF guilt scale and was modeled as having two subfactors: work interference with family and family interference with work guilt (see Figure 11.4). Preliminary model testing confirmed that the hypothesized factor structures portrayed in Figures 11.1–11.4 were a good fit to the data from each separate country.

Analytic strategy. Each of the measurement models was tested for invariance across the respective groups (ten countries; two genders). The multigroup CFAs were conducted using MLR with Mplus (Version 6.11; Muthén & Muthén, 1998–2011). To assess the fit of the individual models, multiple goodness-of-fit indices were reviewed, including the $\chi 2$, RMSEA, and CFI. Because the ME/I analysis for culture was more complex due to the large sample size and the inclusion of data from ten countries, the ΔCFI was used to compare the fit of the different models to one another. By contrast, for the ME/I analysis for gender, the differences between the different models were assessed using the Sartorra-Bentler Scaled Chi-Square difference test ($\Delta SB\chi^2$).

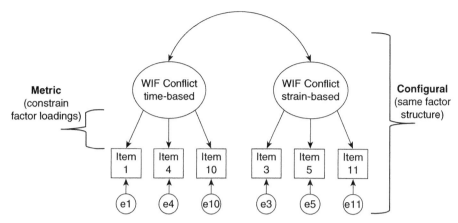

Figure 11.1 *Factor structure of work interference with family conflict.*

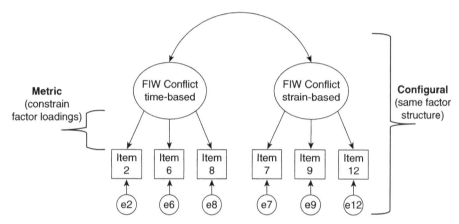

Figure 11.2 *Factor structure of family interference with work conflict.*

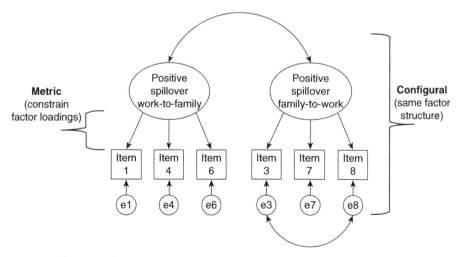

Figure 11.3 *Factor structure of positive spillover.*

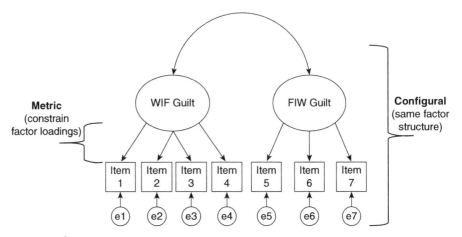

Figure 11.4 *Factor structure of work–family guilt.*

Results for cultural invariance of work–family interface measures. As can be seen from Table 11.1, the CFI values were ≥.96 and the RMSEAs were ≤.03 for all configural models. This indicated that the factor structures illustrated in Figures 1–4 were equivalent across all ten countries in that the number of factors and the items associated with each factor were the same. From this we can conclude that those in each of our ten countries are using the same conceptual framework when responding to the three measures and that the constructs measured have equivalent meaning across cultures.

Moreover, not only were CFI values ≥.95 and RMSEAs ≤.03 for all metric models, but all ΔCFIs were ≤.01. This indicated that the factor weights and loadings for all the paths indicated in Figures 11.1–11.4 were equivalent across all ten countries and that the scale items were perceived and interpreted in the same way in each country. Because cross-cultural ME/I was established at the metric level for all three WF interface measures, the combined data from the ten countries could be used for purposes of correlation-based analyses (e.g., to test SEM models) with these measures. Because the primary purpose of Project 3535 was to test cross-cultural hypotheses using SEM and hierarchical linear modeling, configural, and metric level invariance were sufficient for our purposes and scalar level invariance tests were not carried out on most constructs. However, researchers who are interested in determining whether between-group mean differences exist will need to also examine scalar level invariance. We now present an example of this which also illustrates the issue of partial invariance.

Results for gender invariance of WIF conflict. This analysis was done only for the WIF subscale of the WF conflict measure. The configural CFI and RMSEA values were excellent and the χ^2 for the model was not significant demonstrating fit of the model (see Table 11.2). This confirmed that the factor structure was the same for both genders with items 1, 4, and 10 loading on time-based WIF conflict and items 3, 5, and 11 loading on strain-based WIF conflict (see Figure 11.1). From this we can conclude that the meaning of WIF conflict is the same for men and women (i.e., that

Table 11.1 *Measurement invariance tests for culture of WF interface measures*

Models	χ^2 (df)	RMSEA	CFI	Model Comparison	Δ CFI
WIF Conflict					
1. Configural	335.8 (80)	.03	.96		
2. Metric	424.8 (116)	.03	.96	2 vs. 1	.007
FIW Conflict					
1. Configural	296.3 (80)	.03	.97		
2. Metric	414.3 (116)	.03	.96	2 vs. 1	.01
Positive Spillover					
1. Configural	142.8 (70)	.02	.98		
2. Metric	211.6 (106)	.02	.97	2 vs. 1	.01
WF Guilt					
1. Configural	474.3 (130)	.03	.96		
2. Metric	623.1 (175)	.03	.95	2 vs. 1	.01

Table 11.2 *Measurement invariance tests for gender for work interference with family conflict*

Models	χ^2 (df)	RMSEA	CFI	Model Comparison	Δ SBχ^2 (df)
1. Configural	25.88 (14)	.06	.99		
2. Metric	31.19 (18)	.06	.99	2 vs. 1	−4.72 (4)
3. Scalar	46.33 (22)	.07	.98	3 vs. 2	−16.40 (4)*
4. Partial Scalar	34.09 (21)	.05	.99	4 vs. 2	−2.59 (3)

* p <.05, ** p <.01

men and women were using the same cognitive frame of reference; Vandenberg & Morelli, 2016). When constraints were added to the factor loadings to test for metric invariance, the CFI and RMSEA fit indices remained excellent and the Δ SBχ^2 was not significant. Therefore, as Table 11.2 illustrates, metric level ME/I for gender was established for WIF conflict. This means that the factor weights and loadings were the same for both genders and that men and women interpreted each of the subscale items in the same way.

Next, constraints were added to the item intercepts to test for scalar invariance; however, scalar invariance was not demonstrated (as per the significant Δ SBχ^2) for the measure. Yet, due to indications from modification indices that the difference was related to a single item intercept, the freeing up of that particular intercept allowed for partial scalar invariance to be demonstrated. This provided good evidence for the equality of factor loadings and the majority of item intercepts for these measurement models across gender (Byrne, 2012). The item that was not invariant (and freed up for the analysis) was: "I have to miss family activities due to the amount of time

I must spend on work responsibilities." The item remained in the analysis with the constraint for that item released, which allowed the item to freely estimate in the analysis. Once the constraint for that item was released, the change in model fit from the metric model to this partial scalar model was no longer significant and retained excellent RMSEA and CFI values.

Based on the above analysis, the partial scalar invariance of the WIF subscale was established for gender. This means that men and women responded to the WIF subscale in an equivalent way and that the units of measurement, scale intervals, and origins or zero points were the same for both genders. This result allows one to conclude that men and women had similar response styles (e.g., response biases or thresholds). It demonstrates that "individuals who have the same score on the latent construct would obtain the same score on the observed variable regardless of their group membership" (Milfont & Fischer, 2010, p. 115), and, therefore, that latent mean comparisons could be made for men and women for this construct.

Conclusion

When translating WF measures for use across cultures, there should be an emphasis on conceptual, in addition to linguistic and semantic, equivalence. Thus, best practices in this area involve the use of a consensus-based, concept-driven approach by a team of indigenous researchers who together formulate and implement a culturally sensitive research plan. Further, forward and back translation should be carried out by fluently bilingual and bicultural translators who are knowledgeable about the subject matter and research context and have experience with survey construction. In addition, a committee composed of multinational content experts should oversee the reconciliation process. Following this there should be multiple rounds of pilot testing that involve both focus groups and cognitive debriefing. Throughout, there should be a focus on whether concepts are meaningful in different cultural contexts and whether any emic issues have been overlooked. Finally, the requirements necessary for conducting ME/I analyses should be understood before choosing items or measures to be included on a survey.

In terms of best practices for ME/I, it is essential to first understand that configural invariance is a necessary, but not a sufficient prerequisite for establishing ME/I across cultures. Secondly, deciding which of the many available ME/I tests should be carried out should be determined by one's purpose. If one wishes to examine interrelationships among constructs cross-nationally, configural and metric level equivalence will be sufficient. However, if one wishes to compare group means cross-nationally, configural, metric, and scalar invariance are necessary. As a best practice one should examine multiple goodness-of-fit indicators (including the χ^2, CFI, GFI, TLI, and RMSEA) to assess model fit at each level. We suggest that for cross-cultural WF research, when moving from one level of ME/I to the next (e.g., from configural to metric or metric to scalar), the ΔCFI should be used as the criterion, particularly when sample sizes are large. If full invariance is not found, when appropriate, researchers should attempt to establish partial invariance using the methods we have described above.

Establishing ME/I for cross-cultural work is neither quick nor easy. It is complicated and takes skill and effort. Nevertheless, establishing ME/I is a necessary foundation to support the validity of any cross-cultural comparisons.

References

Arbuckle, J. L. (2014). *Amos* (Version 23.0). Chicago, IL: IBM SPSS.

Aycan, Z. (2017). Introducing Project 3535: Lessons learned from a multicultural collaborative research on the work-family interface. In K. Korabik, Z. Aycan, & R. Ayman (Eds.), *The Work-Family Interface in Global Context* (pp 3–17). New York, NY: Routledge.

Bagger, J., & Love, J. (2010). Methodological considerations in conducting cross-national work-family survey research. In S. Sweet & J. Casey (Eds.), *Work and Family Encyclopedia*. Chestnut Hill, MA: Sloan Work and Family Research Network.

Byrne, B. M. (2001). *Structural Equation Modeling with AMOS: Basic Concepts, Applications, and Programming*. Mahwah, NJ: Lawrence Erlbaum Associates.

(2012). *Structural Equation Modeling with Mplus: Basic Concepts, Applications, and Programming*. New York, NY: Routledge.

Byrne, B. M., & Stewart, S. M. (2006). The MACS approach to testing for multigroup invariance of a second-order structure: A walk through the process. *Structural Equation Modeling, 13*(2), 287–321.

Byrne, B. M., & Watkins, D. (2003). The issue of measurement invariance revisited. *Journal of Cross-Cultural Psychology, 34*(2), 155–175. doi:10.1177/0022022102250225

Carlson, D. S., Kacmar, K. M., & Williams, L. J. (2000). Construction and validation of a multidimensional measure of work-family conflict. *Journal of Vocational Behavior, 56*, 249–276. doi:10.1006/jvbe.1999.1713

Cheung, G. W., & Rensvold, R. B. (2002). Evaluating goodness-of-fit indexes for testing measurement invariance. *Structural Equation Modeling, 9*(2), 233–255.

Cheung, M. W. L., Leung, K., & Au, K. (2006). Evaluating multilevel models in cross-cultural research. *Journal of Cross-Cultural Psychology, 37*(5), 522–541.

Cole, M. S., Bedeian, A. G., & Feild, H. S. (2006). The measurement equivalence of web-based and paper-and-pencil measures of transformational leadership: A multinational test. *Organizational Research Methods, 9*(3), 339–368.

Davidov, E., Dulmer, H., Schluter, E., Schmidt, P., & Meuleman, B. (2012). Using a multilevel structural equation modeling approach to explain cross-cultural measurement noninvariance. *Journal of Cross-Cultural Psychology, 43*(4), 558–575. doi:10.1177/0022022112438397

Davidov, E., Meuleman, B., Cieciuch, J., Schmidt, P., & Billiet, J. (2014). Measurement equivalence in cross-national research. *Annual Review of Sociology, 40*, 55–75. doi:10.1146/annurev-soc-071913-043137

De Beuckelaer, A., & Lievens, F. (2009). Measurement equivalence of paper-and-pencil and internet organisational surveys: A large scale examination in 16 countries. *Applied Psychology: An International Review, 58*(2), 336–361. doi:10.1111/j.1464-0597.2008.00350.x

Ekrut, S., Alarcon, O., Coll, C. G., Tropp, L. R., & Garcia, H. A. V. (1999). The dual-focus approach to creating bilingual measures. *Journal of Cross-Cultural Psychology, 30* (2), 206–218.

Epstein, J., Santo, R. M., & Guillemin, F. (2015). A review of guidelines for cross-cultural adaptation of questionnaires could not bring out a consensus. *Journal of Clinical Epidemiology, 68*(435–441).

Grzywacz, J. G., & Marks, N. F. (2000). Reconceptualizing the work-family interface: An ecological perspective on the correlates of positive and negative spillover between work and family. *Journal of Occupational Health Psychology, 5*(1), 111–126. doi:10.1037//1076-8998.5.1.111

Hambleton, R. K., & Patsula, L. (1998). Adapting tests for use in multiple languages and cultures. *Social Indicators Research, 45*(153–171).

Jaskiewicz, P., Combs, J.G., Shanine, K.K., & Kacmar, K.M. (2017). Introducing the family: A review of family science with implications for management research. *Academy of Management Annuals, 11 (1)*, 309–341; doi: https://doi.org/10.5465/annals.2014 .0053.

Kline, R. B. (2011). *Principles and practice of structural equation modeling* (3rd ed). New York, NY: Guilford.

Korabik, K., Aycan, Z., & Ayman, R. (2017). *The work–family interface in global context*: Routledge.

Meade, A. W., & Lautenschlager, G. J. (2004). A comparison of item response theory and confirmatory factor analytic methodologies for establishing measurement equivalence/invariance. *Organizational Research Methods, 7*(4), 361–388. doi:10.1177/1094428104268027

Milfont, T. L., & Fischer, R. (2010). Testing measurement invariance across groups: Applications in cross-cultural research. *International Journal of Psychological Research, 3*(1), 2011–2084.

Muthén, L. K., & Muthén, B. O. (1998–2011). *Mplus users guide. Sixth Edition*. Los Angeles, CA: Muthén & Muthén.

Ollier-Malaterre, A., & Foucreault, A. (2016). Cross-national work-life research: Cultural and structural impacts for individuals and organizations. *Journal of Management*, 1–26. doi:10.1177/0149206316655873

Oreg, S., Bayazit, M., Vakola, M., Arciniega, L., Armenakis, A., Barkauskiene, R.,... van Dam, K. (2008). Dispositional resistance to change: Measurement equivalence and the link to personal values across 17 nations. *Journal of Applied Psychology, 93*(4), 935–944. doi:10.1037/0021-9010.93.4.935

Powell, G. N., Francesco, A. M., & Ling, A. Y. (2009). Toward culture-sensitive theories of the work-family interface. *Journal of Organizational Behavior, 30*, 597–616. doi:10.1002/job.568

Raju, N. S., Laffitte, L. J., & Byrne, B. M. (2002). Measurement equivalence: A comparison of methods based on confirmatory factor analysis and item response theory. *Journal of Applied Psychology, 87*(3), 517–529. doi:10.1037//0021-9010.87.3.517

Schaffer, B. S., & Riordan, C. M. (2003). A review of cross-cultural methodologies for organizational research: A best-practices approach. *Organizational Research Methods, 6*(2), 169–215. doi:10.1177/1094428103251542

Schmitt, N., & Kuljanin, G. (2008). Measurement invariance: Review of practice and implications. *Human Resource Management, 18*, 210–222. doi:10.1016/j. hrmr.2008.03.003

Steenkamp, J.-B. E. M., & Baumgartner, H. (1998). Assessing measurement invariance in cross-national consumer research. *The Journal of Consumer Research*, *25*(1), 78–90.

Tay, L., Meade, A.W., & Cao, M. (2015). An overview and practical guide to IRT measurement equivalence analysis. *Organizational Research Methods*, *18*, 3–46.

Trimble, J. E. (2007). Cultural measurement equivalence. In C. S. Clauss-Ehlers (Ed.), *Encyclopedia of Cross-Cultural School Psychology*. New York, NY: Springer.

van de Vijver, F. J. R., & Leung, K. (1997). *Methods and Data Analysis for Cross-Cultural Research*. Thousand Oaks, CA: Sage.

Vandenberg, R., J. (2002). Toward a further understanding of and improvement in measurement invariance methods and procedures. *Organizational Research Methods*, *5*(2), 139–158.

Vandenberg, R., J., & Lance, C. E. (2000). A review and synthesis of the measurement invariance literature: Suggestions, practices, and recommendations for organizational research. *Organizational Research Methods*, *3*(1), 4–70. doi:10.1177/109442810031002

Vandenberg, R.J., & Morelli, N.A. (2016). A contemporary update for testing for measurement equivalence and invariance. In J.P. Meyer (Ed.), *Handbook of Employee Commitment* (pp. 449–461). Cheltenham, UK: Edward Elgar Publishing Ltd.

12 Getting the Global Band Together: Best Practices in Organizing and Managing International Research Teams

Paul E. Spector and Juan I. Sanchez

A by-product of the globalization of the world economy has been a rapid increase in research aimed at understanding the role of cultural and national factors on not only work, but also the work-nonwork interface. Conducting research across national boundaries, however, brings with it a unique set of challenges from initial design to interpretation of data and publication of results. There is a rich literature on methodologies for conducting global workplace research that covers the technical intricacies of isolating effects of culture and nationality while controlling for other third-variable confounds (for an overview, see Spector, Liu, & Sanchez, 2015; van de Vijver & Leung, 1997). This chapter will focus, not on such methodological and statistical concerns, but on the often overlooked strategies for organizing and managing research teams engaged in global studies. This "best practice" guide will cover issues that can arise in conducting research across national boundaries that can involve teams of researchers whose efforts need to be coordinated and standardized.

In this chapter we will focus on nine issues that must be carefully considered in the design, implementation, and overall management of a global study. These include:

1. Scope of the study
2. Assembling the team
3. Agreements over data use and publication
4. Study design and management approach
5. Base language for the study
6. Coordinating data collection
7. Data handling
8. Political and societal issues
9. Publication

As a unifying example, we will discuss our experiences with the two-phase Collaborative International Study of Managerial Stress (CISMS). The CISMS project was chosen, not only because we are part of the core team, but because it was focused on work-nonwork issues, and it illustrates all of the issues we will discuss. It should be kept in mind, however, that CISMS is but one model for a successful (in producing multiple papers in rigorously peer-reviewed journals) global collaboration, and there certainly are others that have been just as successful, if not more so.

The CISMS collaboration began in the early 1990s as a study of stress in managers, including work-nonwork issues. Each of the two phases involved approximately 7,000 managers from more than twenty-four countries. Between the two phases there were forty-six researchers involved in CISMS, not counting those who later came on board after data were collected to assist (or take the lead) in publication (e.g., Yang et al., 2012). Phase I was focused on stress in general (including the work-nonwork interface), whereas Phase II was a follow-up that focused primarily but not exclusively on the work-nonwork interface, attempting to shed further light on and explain the Phase 1 results. In addition, there were a number of small scale spin-off projects that derived from CISMS involving small numbers of the CISMS researcher community.

Scope of the Study

The first issue to be confronted with a global study is the purpose and scope of a project. As with any investigation, one must specify research goals, that is, what are the underlying questions to be addressed, and hypotheses (if applicable). However, particularly with large scale projects involving multiple countries, making adjustments in methodology and instrumentation as a project progresses can be a lot more complicated than with the usual single-country study. For instance, the possibility of gaining access to a sample at more than one point in time to collect a new wave of data decreases when samples come from multiple countries. Similarly, adding new instruments and regaining access to the same or a new sample might differentially alter the time span of the study from country to country, as it might delay data completion in certain countries. Therefore, researchers might end up with incomplete datasets where some scales were administered in some countries but not in others, or time lags might vary across countries, thereby provoking potential confounds. Thus it is important to carefully plan a study so that changes are minimized once it begins.

Another issue that one confronts is the scope of the project, that is, how many national samples will be involved? This is a vital question when the purpose of a study is to explore differences across a cultural variable, such as values. It is difficult to draw conclusions about why country differences might have occurred when one has only two (or a small number) of countries to compare. Studies that address cultural differences at the country or sample level are best considered from a multi-level perspective. Isolating the cultural variable from a host of national differences potentially confounded with culture requires having multiple country samples that vary reliably on that cultural variable. That is, to have sufficient power to detect differences and avoid confounding of country with the cultural variable requires not only a sufficient number of samples, but the sampling strategy should include multiple samples that run the gamut of low, high, and intermediate values on the cultural variable of interest. In CISMS Phase II for example, we wanted to isolate the cultural value of individualism-collectivism to determine its impact on work–family conflict (Spector et al., 2007). A country selection strategy was chosen that allowed a comparison of individualistic with collectivistic samples by choosing five countries from each of four regions that prior research found differed on this variable: Anglo, Asia, East Europe, and Latin America (for discussion of using external data on values, see Taras, Kirkman, & Steel, 2010).

Assembling the Team

Collecting data from multiple countries is best done with the coordinated efforts of an international team of research partners. Although it might be possible to collect data from a variety of countries remotely through electronic media, such methods are quite limited in providing reasonable research controls over sampling and methods. In addition, countries vary in idiosyncratic factors that make their citizens differentially inclined to participate in a research study. In collectivistic countries, for instance, potential respondents might be reluctant to participate in a study that does not have the endorsement of a trustworthy source close to them or their ingroup. Our approach in CISMS mirrored that of other multinational studies (e.g., Peterson, Smith, Akande, Ayestaran, et al., 1995) in assembling an international team of research partners who were willing and able to contribute to the study. In both phases there was a central team who designed and planned the study and recruited the partners who were responsible for survey translation and back-translation, data collection, and providing a clean dataset to the central team for analysis. Partners varied in their involvement in dissemination of results, including contributing to write-ups, and even writing papers. Some of the partners were seasoned researchers with established research records, whereas others had limited research experience prior to their involvement in CISMS. These variations in research expertise turned into developmental opportunities for the more junior researchers. For instance, drafts of manuscripts were circulated among all participants who were given a chance to offer comments and edits on them. They had a chance to participate in and witness how responses addressing the reviewers' concerns in journal submissions were crafted. Even for researchers who did not participate much in the writing of manuscripts, witnessing the process from beginning to end (i.e., several rounds of revise-and-resubmit) was undoubtedly a learning experience.

Our experience is that there are many researchers around the world eager to collaborate on multinational projects. They can be recruited through personal contacts and networking, either by targeting specific individuals, or by putting out open calls for research partners on appropriate listservs or via social media. Before recruitment of collaborators begins, the roles of the team members should be carefully specified so that individuals will know from the outset the rules for their participation. For instance, are they being offered payment for collecting data that the central team will own, or are they being offered a larger role in the research team? Do members "own" the data that they collect and can proceed to write a separate article or do they need to give other team members a chance to participate in the writing? There also needs to be clear policies and procedures for governing the study, which brings us to the issue of data agreements.

Agreements over Data Use and Publication

There are perhaps no aspects of a multinational study that have more potential for conflict than ownership and use of data. Although the central team might have designed the study and study protocols, the country partner who collected a sample of data might have ownership rights to those data. Agreements over how those data will be used and disseminated at conferences and in print form should be developed at the onset of the study. In this way expectations are clarified early, and the rules governing participation in the study are well known to all team members, so that each is treated fairly.

There are different models that can be used that inform the kinds of agreements that might be reached. At one extreme is the possibility of paying individuals to collect data, with the agreement that they will have no ownership rights. In such cases the individual country partners would have no substantive contribution, and would merely enact the data collection protocols provided. At the other extreme is a true partnership, where partners become full members of the research team who have the ability to influence the design and execution of the project, as well as dissemination of results.

Perhaps the most controversial issue of data agreements concerns authorship in potential publications resulting from the study. For example, how does one earn the right to serve as a lead author, and who is to be a coauthor, and in what order? In CISMS each individual partner owned the dataset he or she collected, and thus deserved co-authorship in each article in which that dataset was used. For each paper, one individual member of the team would take the lead and be first author to pursue a specific research question(s) that he or she championed. The remaining co-authors followed in order according to contribution to that paper, followed in order by contribution to the main project design (generally the central team), and lastly followed by those who made smaller contributions related to instrumentation (e.g., producing measurement-equivalent back-translated scales) and data collection. When people were approximately equal in contribution, they were listed alphabetically. Different team members took the lead on individual papers that involved most or all countries and that focused on the lead author's own research idea. A few of the country partners published papers using solely their own country dataset, or a small number of country datasets. Adherence to just a few basic principles regulating order of authorship helped CISMS avoid conflicts over data ownership and publication.

Study Design and Management Approach

International studies vary in their underlying management model, particularly in their degree of centralization. CISMS is an example of a centralized model with a central team that designed the study and recruited country partners, or what

Sanchez and Spector (2012) termed the "NATO model." An alternative involves recruiting an international team that designs and carries out the study, more like a cooperative. Sanchez and Spector termed this approach the "UN model," suggesting a relative lack of hierarchy. Whereas the UN model can work well with small numbers of countries and partners, as the project grows in size and scope, the advantages of having a centralized group to design the study and plan how it will be conducted becomes apparent.

The UN approach has the advantage of maximizing diversity of inputs, and can best incorporate country-specific perspectives. In a sense it has the potential to maximize the emic-ness of a study, that is, the extent to which investigation of country-specific or culture-specific characteristics is built into the study. This is because each country partner would be free to make inputs and to design the study in a way that best reflects local issues. This sort of project lends itself well to a mixed-methods approach, combining qualitative and quantitative aspects. An initial qualitative component can be helpful in isolating the most relevant variables, with a following quantitative component to explore relationships and test hypotheses (Niblo & Jackson, 2004). Although this could be done with a NATO approach, the UN approach maximizes the country-specific aspect of the study, as all partners can have equal input into the questions asked in the qualitative portion, and the variables chosen for the quantitative portion of the project. For example, Yang et al. (2012) found that the relationship between the number of work hours and perceived work overload was stronger for individuals in individualistic than collectivistic countries. They speculated that the coping mechanisms employed in individualistic cultures might be less effective to cope with long work hours than those employed in collectivistic cultures. It follows that coping with work–family conflict might take different forms in different cultures as traditional gender roles might often dictate who takes over certain home chores and family obligations. Armed with these insights plus additional ones gained through qualitative studies, researchers might develop emic measures of work–family coping mechanisms fit to the realities of collectivistic cultures.

A UN approach that does not allow for any centralized control can result in a study in which country datasets are not comparable, perhaps with different questions/items that reflect local usages and customs that are quite difficult to translate, or with somewhat different procedures for sampling or data collection. The NATO approach is perhaps preferred when the purpose is to investigate general principles, requiring the control of third variables, that is, biases and confounds that might arise if insufficient research controls are in place. These threats to the validity of the design are likely to happen in a more loosely organized UN study in which a central person or team is not "in charge" of the study. Such a person can help coordinate data collection efforts, and would serve as a resource to all partners concerning how and when data should be collected. Of course, excessive centralization and standardization can backfire when standardized measures and methods do not work equivalently in all samples. For example, the core CISMS team realized early on that the measure of values we chose (Hofstede, 1994) did not have acceptable internal consistency reliability and comparable factor structure in some countries.

For many projects, a hybrid approach might be preferred in which there is a central team that plans the study, but input is solicited from all research partners. An iterative procedure could be used where the central team produces an initial draft document that states the purpose of the study, outlines a proposed study design, and lists potential measures. Feedback from all research partners would be solicited and then incorporated into the document, with each draft circulated to everyone for input. The iterative process would continue until all issues were resolved through discussion, and no new issues were raised. Once finalized, this document serves as the study's "constitution," which can be used to explain the research goals. If needed, this document can be later employed to recruit additional collaborators across nations. All these collaborators are treated as research partners and are free to add additional measures as they see fit, they are also expected to administer the scales adopted by the core central team. Of course, one must be careful that additions do not make the questionnaire too long and unwieldy, thus adversely affecting data quality.

Base Language for the Study

A multi-country study is most effectively conducted if the project is managed using a common language. For CISMS the base language for communication was English, with all documents and emails written in English. Since English is the most universal language for publishing organizational and work-nonwork research, it was not difficult to recruit research partners who were sufficiently fluent in English to communicate with the central team.

For CISMS, English was also the base language for questionnaire development, containing a mixture of existing scales and new items. The English version of the questionnaire was provided to country partners who handled the translation and back-translation (for discussion of back-translation procedures see Spector et al., 2015). Of course, it is possible to assemble a questionnaire that consists of scales that were developed in a variety of languages, for example, English and Spanish. It would be most manageable in such cases to produce a single-language version of all scales (e.g., translate the English scales into Spanish) so that translations of the completed questionnaire would involve one source language. Large-scale cross-national studies are still an emerging area, and further research is needed on whether variations in the base language produce conflicting results. The Sapir–Whorf or Whorfian hypothesis (Werner & Campbell, 1970) suggests a strong bond between language and cognition, and therefore, the choice of a specific base language should be carefully considered. For example Sanchez, Alonso, and Spector (2000) found signs of measurement non-equivalence among back-translated measures administered twice to the same bilingual participants, as well as evidence suggesting that altering the order of language across the two administrations changed the results. Together, these results hint that the meaning of certain constructs might be intrinsically bound to the choice of language, and that even back-translations might not always produce measurement equivalence.

Coordinating Data Collection

Whether the project is designed centrally via a NATO approach or designed by the broader group of partners via a UN approach, someone needs to coordinate and manage the data collection across countries. With both phases of CISMS, a member of the central team was identified as a point of contact with the research partners. This person kept in contact with all partners, answering their questions, noting problems that occurred including the necessity to deviate from the study protocol, and collecting datasets. The contact person maintained contact beyond data collection, asking for answers to questions as they arose during the data analysis and write-up stages of the project. Having a single point of contact helped avoid confusion as the partners had one person with whom to communicate, and there were not conflicting messages flowing among partners. The partners were certainly free to communicate with one another, and some did, but having the main messages centralized assured that the central team could be kept apprised of study progress over the several years it took for data collection to be completed for each phase. Obviously, we make no claims of our approach being either the only or best one. A potentially fruitful alternative approach may be to outsource the data collection to a third party, such as a consulting company with an international presence. However, releasing control of data collection to a third party, or any other approach that involves delegating or cascading down the data collection to unaccountable parties, elevates the risk of ending up with poor quality data furnished simply to obtain a short-term financial gain.

Data Handling

The management and analysis of data from a multi-country study can be a challenging endeavor, especially when there are more than a few samples. Data management efforts begin with the design of an investigation, and procedures for how data are to be collected and handled should be incorporated into the initial study plan. This is the case whether data are qualitative or quantitative, even though the analysis process might be quite different. In order to conduct cross-country or cross-cultural comparative analyses, data must be compiled into a uniform format that allows for analysis. Variation in mode of survey administration (paper-and-pencil versus web-based) across countries creates a potentially critical confound that should be avoided if possible. However, differences in economic development and technology infrastructure may make web-based surveys difficult in some locations. An even more complicated confound would be created if the same procedure (e.g., web-based survey) is followed in every country, because it might result in a biased sample whereby participants from emerging economies might represent, not average workers, but privileged individuals with prompt access to the internet. Enforcing web-based surveys as the sole method of data collection might also result in other types of sampling biases such as an over-representation of white collar employees with direct access to computers at work.

Planning data collection and handling. Whether the study adopts a NATO, UN, or hybrid approach, standardization will be required so that data can be directly compared. With qualitative studies, this means that comparable questions should be used across countries, and with quantitative studies, measurement-equivalent instruments should be employed. A limitation to conducting research across countries where people speak different languages is that measurement-equivalent translations are often challenging to produce. This can introduce noise and potential confounds into an investigation as there can be variation in exact meaning of items and questions. Nevertheless, to the greatest extent possible, equivalence should be the goal, so carefully developed back-translations (Brislin, 1986) are in order. Back-translation requires that a party translates the scale to the target language first so that an independent party translates it back to the source language. Then the two versions of the same language are compared to detect linguistic problems in the translation. Even though back-translations do not necessarily guarantee measurement equivalence, they are an essential step towards it.

For quantitative studies, statistical methods have been developed to test that measurement equivalence/invariance (ME/I) has been achieved (Spector et al., 2015; Vandenberg & Lance, 2000). Most of these methods are based either on item response theory (IRT) or structural equation modeling (SEM) approaches. IRT methods show that item response distributions are similar across country samples, whereas SEM methods show equivalence of inter-item factor structure. The testing of ME/I with one or both methods has become standard practice in studies where samples are drawn from different countries. See Chapter 8 of this handbook (Korabik & Rhijn) for a detailed discussed of translation and ME/I issues.

Another aspect of data planning concerns avoiding confounding country with sample characteristics by choosing samples that are as similar as possible. One would not, for example, choose physicians for one country sample and plumbers for another, as it would not be possible to disentangle differences due to country from those due to occupation. In addition to controlling for occupation, one should control for industry sector, employing organization characteristics (e.g., sector and size), and demographic variables.

Collecting and cleaning datasets. To facilitate data processing all country partners should send datasets to a central data custodian who has the responsibility of cleaning and combining the datasets in preparation for analysis. With CISMS one person was point-of-contact and another person was data custodian who cleaned the data and handled preliminary analyses. Having a single person handled all data sets ensures a homogeneous treatment of, for instance, missing values and random response patterns. It is perhaps easiest if each country partner provides a spreadsheet with the item names in the first row, as well as a copy of the survey as used in that country. Whoever is processing the data at this stage should obviously inspect each dataset for uniformity. Our experience with CISMS is that often, country partners would make small modifications to the original survey. In some cases scales were omitted, whereas in others some additional questions or scales were added. Thus the order of items and even scales might not always be the same, and this could readily be seen in the spreadsheet.

Another variation from the original was in the coding of some items, particularly demographics. Some partners coded gender, for example, as 1 = male and 2 = female, but others did the reverse, and some used 0 and 1 rather than 1 and 2. Often questions arose that required back-and-forth discussion with partners to clarify what things might have been changed. Still another issue is whether researchers in each country followed the same procedure to treat missing values and to declare that an incomplete survey lacks sufficient answers and should be excluded from the study. Some partners left missing items blank, whereas others inserted a 9 for each digit with missing data, that is, 9 for a one-digit number and 99 for a two-digit number.

All of the deviations from standard procedures should be documented so that they can be incorporated into the data analysis stage. Deviations can be handled by changing values in the dataset. For example, if the coding of gender is to be standardized to 1 = male and 2 = female, samples where the coding was reversed could be manually changed. If there are few items that need changing, this might be a reasonable approach. However, if there are many deviations, an easier and less error prone approach would be to automate recoding by programming rules into the data analysis software. For CISMS we used SAS which is a fully functioning program language that easily allowed for such recoding.

Data analysis. Only after cleaning and testing for data integrity (e.g., checking that values for all variables are within possible range) has been done, should the analysis of data proceed. With multi-country studies, programming the combining and scoring of data can be extensive. For example, the CISMS scoring and analysis program is more than 1,000 lines of SAS code. That is because each country dataset needed recoding for standardization, the individual datasets were merged into a single master dataset, and scoring of instruments was completed. At this stage each case in the dataset represented a person, identified by country. Analyses were then conducted on the master dataset, both within country and between country. Output datasets were created as needed when analyses were conducted using software other than SAS. One member of the central team conducted the initial analyses with SAS and provided text-format datasets to other partners who wished to conduct further analyses for papers they took the lead to write. An added advantage of a centralized approach to data analysis is that a complete copy of the raw data is always available from the data custodian of the central team. The existence of this raw dataset allows researchers to go back to the data that were originally gathered in each country, rather than data that have been transformed and recoded in ways that can make it difficult to reconstruct how the data were processed.

Political and Societal Issues

When conducting research across countries, there is potential for political and societal issues to arise. Societal issues can result when potentially sensitive areas of inquiry are addressed, for example, a work–family study might include same-sex couples. Asking questions about such arrangements might not be considered accep-table in some traditional and non-secular societies, and thus there might be concerns raised by partners about the appropriateness of certain areas of inquiry. As another example, conventions regarding gender roles might limit access to females in certain cultures, or they may result in a preponderance of participants from certain age ranges. Furthermore, offering rewards for study participation may provoke conflicts of interest in participants when such rewards are not proportional to the effort demanded of the study for the particular location.

Political issues can also be problematic, and are particularly likely when research partners are in countries that are engaged in political disputes. The CISMS project encountered two such issues. The first had to do with terminology and how we identified countries. In an initial draft of the first CISMS paper, China and Taiwan were referred to as separate countries. The Chinese partner objected, suggesting that China and Taiwan were both part of the same country and should be noted as such. The compromise that solved the issue was to use the term "nations/provinces" (Spector, Cooper, Sparks, et al., 2001) or "geopolitical entities" (Spector et al., 2002).

The second political issue was more complicated, as it involved an underlying conflict between two of the countries in which the partners lived. In Phase 1 of CISMS, two of the country partners were from countries in the midst of a political conflict. When one of the partners realized that another partner was from a "forbidden" country, she withdrew from the study. It was not that the researcher had an objection to collaborating with a colleague from the other country. Rather she was concerned that she would get into political trouble in her own country if officials found out she was working with someone from the other country, even though the contact was indirect and through the central team. That this is not so farfetched is illustrated by American history during the McCarthy era of the 1950s cold war when even a hint of collaboration with communist countries could result in being black-listed (losing one's job) and worse.

Dealing with political issues and cultural differences can require sensitivity and a willingness to compromise. It is best handled with open communication, and by everyone being kept informed about the project, including who is involved, what is being studied, and how data are to be collected. Even with the best pre planning, unforeseen issues can arise both in conducting the study and in the broader societies where partners live.

Publication

One of the main drivers that leads international researchers to participate in multi-country studies is the possibility of attaining one or more refereed publications. Given the importance of publication in well-cited outlets, there is significant potential for conflict. Issues can arise about who takes the lead and writes papers, author order, the content of papers, the framing and interpretation of results, and the outlets for publication. For this reason, it is vitally important that publication agreements be stated in writing at the beginning of a project to minimize misunderstandings at the publication phase. Earlier we gave an overview of the CISMS agreement about data use and publication.

Both CISMS phases were large-scale studies that collected more data than could be reasonably included in a single research report, so each phase resulted in a series of conference papers and journal articles. Some were preplanned and involved testing hypotheses that each phase was designed to address, but others evolved in a more exploratory way. For example, Phase 1 was intended to test the impact of cultural values on stressors and strains, but during early data analysis it became apparent that there were psychometric weaknesses with the values scale chosen, so it was decided to write a paper about that issue (Spector, Cooper, Sparks, et al., 2001). Some papers involved all countries (Yang et al., 2012), whereas others involved only a subset (Allen et al., 2014). A few of the country partners wrote papers from only their own dataset, and some partners pooled their own datasets to write papers about a single region or simply a smaller set of countries. Table 12.1 contains a sampling of peer-reviewed CISMS papers showing for each the countries involved and the purpose. We firmly believe that giving researchers this type of freedom to toss ideas around and to test them in the manner that they deemed most appropriate using parts or all of the data was key to the success of the project, as everyone was challenged to be creative and to test his or her own ideas while being part of a large research team.

Related to the previous point, our approach made the establishment of solid trust bonds among participating researchers possible, and that resulted in long-term research relationships. After the success of Phase I, many of the same individuals continued in Phase II, as well as participated in smaller spin-off projects (e.g., Spector, Sanchez, Siu, Salgado, & Ma, 2004).

Although most of the CISMS researchers had a background in organizational psychology or organizational behavior, several had other backgrounds (e.g., medicine). Although this did not become an issue for CISMS, it is possible that researchers from different disciplines would have difficulty agreeing on outlets for publication, given that academic rewards are often tied to within-discipline recognition, which can result in different preferences for where papers are published. The potential outlets for publication should be part of the early negotiation as multi-country teams are assembled so later conflicts and misunderstandings about publication outlet can be avoided.

Conclusions

Conducting research studies across multiple countries is a challenging, but rewarding endeavor. Given the involvement of many individuals who are geographically dispersed, there are many challenges including communication, coordination, and cooperation. The almost universal availability of the internet is perhaps the most important tool for carrying out such collaborations, as communication is quick and efficient. Email is the major tool for sharing documents and information, but face-to-face electronic communication is possible in many places via video chat. Storing data in a central cloud-based repository is certainly feasible, but one should be cautious about unrestricted access and potential data theft. Given the rules of participation in CISMS, for instance, country partners were promised authorship in

Table 12.1 *CISMS publications*

Reference	Journal	Phase	Countries/Regions	Purpose
Miller et al. (2000)	Stress Medicine	I	South Africa, Taiwan, UK, US	Examined gender and culture differences in work stress.
Spector, Cooper, Sparks, et al. (2001)	Applied Psychology: An International Review	I	Belgium, Brazil, Bulgaria, Canada, China (PR), Estonia, France, Germany, Hong Kong, India, Israel, Japan, New Zealand, Poland, Romania, Slovenia, South Africa, Spain, Sweden, Taiwan, UK, Ukraine, US	Explored psychometric properties of Hofstede's VSM 94.
Spector, Cooper, Sanchez, et al. (2001)	Journal of Organizational Behavior	I	Australia, Belgium, Brazil, Bulgaria, Canada, China (PR), Estonia, France, Germany, Hong Kong, India, Israel, Japan, New Zealand, Poland, Romania, Slovenia, South Africa, Spain, Sweden, Taiwan, UK, Ukraine, US	Country-level study of link between individualism-collectivism, locus of control, and well-being at work.
Spector et al. (2002)	Academy of Management Journal	I	Australia, Belgium, Brazil, Bulgaria, Canada, China (PR), Estonia, France, Germany, Hong Kong, India, Israel, Japan, New Zealand, Poland, Romania, Slovenia, South Africa, Spain, Sweden, Taiwan, UK, Ukraine, US	Individual-level study of link between locus of control and well-being at work.
Bernin et al. (2003)	International Journal of Stress Management	I	Bulgaria, India, Sweden, UK, US	Studied gender differences in stress coping strategies.
Spector, Cooper, et al. (2004)	Personnel Psychology	I	Regions: Anglo (Australia, Canada, New Zealand, UK, US), China (Hong Kong, PR, Taiwan), Latin (Argentina, Brazil, Colombia, Ecuador, Mexico, Peru, Uruguay)	Tested hypotheses about regional differences in responses to working hours and work–family stressors.

Table 12.1 (*cont.*)

Reference	Journal	Phase	Countries/Regions	Purpose
Spector et al. (2007)	Personnel Psychology	II	Regions: Anglo (Australia, Canada, New Zealand, UK, US), Asia (China (PR), Hong Kong, Japan, Korea, Taiwan), East Europe (Bulgaria, Poland, Romania, Slovenia, Ukraine), Latin America (Argentina, Bolivia, Chile, Peru, Puerto Rico)	Tested hypotheses about cultural differences in responses to work–family conflict.
Lapierre et al. (2008)	Journal of Vocational Behavior	II	Australia, Canada, Finland, New Zealand, US	Tested a model linking perceptions of family supportive work environment to work–family conflict, family, job, and life satisfaction.
Lu et al. (2009)	International Journal of Stress Management	II	Taiwan, UK	Two country comparison of work resources, work family conflict, and well-being.
Masuda et al. (2012)	Applied Psychology: An International Review	II	Regions: Anglo (Australia, Canada, New Zealand, UK, US), Asia (China (PR), Hong Kong, Japan, Korea, Taiwan) Latin America (Argentina, Bolivia, Chile, Peru, Puerto Rico)	Investigated regional differences in the relationship of flexible work arrangements to work family conflict and well-being.
Yang et al. (2012)	Journal of International Business Studies	II	Argentina, Australia, Bolivia, Bulgaria, Canada, Chile, China (PR), Estonia, Finland, Germany, Greece, Hong Kong, Japan, Korea, Netherlands, New Zealand, Peru, Poland, Puerto Rico, Romania, Spain, Taiwan, Turkey, UK Ukraine, US	Multi-level study of individualism-collectivism as a moderator of the work demand-strain relationship.
Allen et al. (2014)	Applied Psychology: An International Review	II	Australia, Canada, Finland, Greece, Japan, Korea, Netherlands, New Zealand, Slovenia, Spain, UK, US	Investigated national paid leave policies and work–family conflict in working parents.

any manuscript that included their country's data and therefore, data leakages would threaten fulfillment of that promise.

Table 12.2 provides a summary of what might be considered best practices in carrying out a multi-country study. It is organized around the nine issues covered in the chapter. A core theme running through these best practices concerns clear communication among all members of the research team, and the need to put all agreements and procedures in writing. Doing so will reduce the potential for conflicts and disagreements.

Table 12.2 *Best practices for carrying out multi-country studies*

Issue	Best Practices
Scope of the study	Specify the purpose including hypotheses and research questions
	Choose countries based on purpose
Assembling the team	Use personal contacts to identify team members
	Be sure team has expertise in all areas needed
Agreements over data use and publication	Have written agreements that include data ownership/use and publication
	Each team member's responsibility should be clearly stated
Study design and management approach	Choose management model that best suits purpose. NATO when strict protocol needs following; UN when country-specific input is vital
Base language for the study	Choose a base language for team communication, likely English
	Team members chosen must be able to communicate in base language
	Choose base language for instrument development
Coordinating data collection	One person should serve as liaison with country partners
	Individuals should have responsibility for coordinating/ managing various functions such as gathering data sets and data processing
Data handling	One person collects data sets from partners
	Check for variation in instruments, questionnaires, and research materials
	Document rules for standardizing data
	Run checks for data errors
	Pick statistical package/language for main data processing and scoring
Political and societal issues	Be alert for cultural misunderstandings and political issues that might arise
	Be flexible in dealing with potential conflicts and issues
Publication	Publication products and outlets should be part of the initial written plan for the project
	Have written agreements that covers what papers will be written, who will take the lead, and author order

Multi-country studies require a significant effort over a considerable length of time that can stretch into several years. It is important to carefully plan such studies, assemble a good team able and willing to carry out the project, and to methodically process the complex data that are collected. Given the effort and time required, it makes sense to use these projects to collect an extensive dataset that can serve as an archival resource to answer new questions as they arise for years to come. Large-scale studies involving more than a few countries are not very common, so they are potentially important contributions to the literature. We hope that this chapter is of assistance to researchers who are considering conducting such studies in the work-nonwork and other domains.

References

Allen, T. D., Lapierre, L. M., Spector, P. E., Poelmans, S. A., O'Driscoll, M., Sanchez, J. I., . . . Woo, J.-M. (2014). The link between national paid leave policy and work–family conflict among married working parents. *Applied Psychology: An International Review*, *63*(1), 5–28. doi:http://dx.doi.org/10.1111/apps.12004

Bernin, P., Theorell, T., Cooper, C. L., Sparks, K., Spector, P. E., Radhakrishnan, P., & Russinova, V. (2003). Coping strategies among Swedish female and male managers in an international context. *International Journal of Stress Management*, *10*(4), 376–391. doi:http://dx.doi.org/10.1037/1072-5245.10.4.376

Brislin, R. W. (1986). The wording and translation of research instruments. In W. J. Lonner & J. W. Berry (Eds.), *Field Methods in Cross-Cultural Research* (pp. 137–164). Thousand Oaks, CA: Sage.

Hofstede, G. (1994). *Values Survey Module 1994 Manual*. Maastricht, The Netherlands: University of Limburg.

Lapierre, L. M., Spector, P. E., Allen, T. D., Poelmans, S., Cooper, C. L., O'Driscoll, M. P.,. . . Kinnunen, U. (2008). Family-supportive organization perceptions, multiple dimensions of work–family conflict, and employee satisfaction: A test of model across five samples. *Journal of Vocational Behavior*, *73*(1), 92–106. doi:http://dx.doi.org/10.1016/j.jvb.2008.02.001

Lu, L., Kao, S.-F., Cooper, C. L., Allen, T. D., Lapierre, L. M., O'Driscoll, M.,. . . Spector, P. E. (2009). Work resources, work-to-family conflict, and its consequences: A Taiwanese-British cross-cultural comparison. *International Journal of Stress Management*, *16*(1), 25–44. doi:http://dx.doi.org/10.1037/a0013988

Masuda, A. D., Poelmans, S. A., Allen, T. D., Spector, P. E., Lapierre, L. M., Cooper, C. L.,. . . Moreno-Velazquez, I. (2012). Flexible work arrangements availability and their relationship with work-to-family conflict, job satisfaction, and turnover intentions: A comparison of three country clusters. *Applied Psychology: An International Review*, *61*(1), 1–29. doi:http://dx.doi.org/10.1111/j.1464-0597.2011.00453.x

Miller, K., Greyling, M., Cooper, C., Lu, L., Sparks, K., & Spector, P. E. (2000). Occupational stress and gender: A cross-cultural study. *Stress Medicine*, *16*(5), 271–278. doi:http://dx.doi.org/10.1002/1099-1700%28200010%2916:5%3C271::AID-SMI862%3E3.0.CO;2-G

Niblo, D. M., & Jackson, M. S. (2004). Model for combining the qualitative emic approach with the quantitative derived etic approach. *Australian Psychologist*, *39*(2), 127–133. doi:http://dx.doi.org/10.1080/00050060410001701843

Peterson, M. F., Smith, P. B., Akande, A., Ayestaran, S., et al. (1995). Role conflict, ambiguity, and overload: A 21-nation study. *Academy of Management Journal*, *38*(2), 429–452.

Sanchez, J. I., Alonso, A., & Spector, P. E. (2000). *Linguistic Effects on Translated Organizational Measures: A Study of Bilinguals*. Paper presented at the Academy of Management, Toronto, August.

Sanchez, J. I., & Spector, P. E. (2012). Administrative, measurement, and sampling issues in large-scale cross-national research: UN or NATO approach? [References] *Conducting Multinational Research: Applying Organizational Psychology in The Workplace* (pp. 123–147). Washington, DC: American Psychological Association.

Spector, P. E., Allen, T. D., Poelmans, S. A., Lapierre, L. M., Cooper, C. L., O'Driscoll, M.,. . . Widerszal-Bazyl, M. (2007). Cross-national differences in relationships of work demands, job satisfaction, and turnover intentions with work–family conflict. *Personnel Psychology*, *60*(4), 805–835. doi:http://dx.doi.org/10.1111/j.1744-6570.2007.00092.x

Spector, P. E., Cooper, C. L., Poelmans, S., Allen, T. D., O'Driscoll, M., Sanchez, J. I.,. . . Yu, S. (2004). A cross-national comparative study of work–family stressors, working hours, and well-being: China and Latin America versus the Anglo world. *Personnel Psychology*, *57*(1), 119–142. doi:http://dx.doi.org/10.1111/j.1744-6570.2004.tb02486.x

Spector, P. E., Cooper, C. L., Sanchez, J. I., O'Driscoll, M., Sparks, K., Bernin, P.,. . . Yu, S. (2001). Do national levels of individualism and internal locus of control relate to well-being: An ecological level international study. *Journal of Organizational Behavior*, *22*(8), 815–832. doi:http://dx.doi.org/10.1002/job.118

(2002). Locus of control and well-being at work: How generalizable are Western findings? *Academy of Management Journal*, *45*(2), 453–466. doi:http://dx.doi.org/10.2307/3069359

Spector, P. E., Cooper, C. L., Sparks, K., Bernin, P., Buessing, A., Dewe, P.,. . . Yu, S. (2001). An international study of the psychometric properties of the Hofstede Values Survey Module 1994: A comparison of individual and country/province level results. *Applied Psychology: An International Review*, *50*(2), 269–281. doi:http://dx.doi.org/10.1111/1464-0597.00058

Spector, P. E., Liu, C., & Sanchez, J. I. (2015). Methodological and substantive issues in conducting multinational and cross-cultural research. *Annual Review of Organizational Psychology and Organizational Behavior*, *2*(1), null. doi: doi:10.1146/annurev-orgpsych-032414-111310

Spector, P. E., Sanchez, J. I., Siu, O. L., Salgado, J., & Ma, J. (2004). Eastern versus Western control beliefs at work: An investigation of secondary control, socioinstrumental control, and work locus of control in China and the US. *Applied Psychology: An International Review*, *53*(1), 38–60. doi:http://dx.doi.org/10.1111/j.1464-0597.2004.00160.x

Taras, V., Kirkman, B. L., & Steel, P. (2010). Examining the impact of Culture's consequences: A three-decade, multilevel, meta-analytic review of Hofstede's cultural value dimensions. *Journal of Applied Psychology*, *95*(3), 405–439. doi:http://dx.doi.org/10.1037/a0018938

van de Vijver, F. J. R., & Leung, K. (1997). *Methods and Data Analysis for Cross-Cultural research*. Thousand Oaks, CA: Sage Publications, Inc.

Vandenberg, R. J., & Lance, C. E. (2000). A Review and Synthesis of the Measurement Invariance Literature: Suggestions, Practices, and Recommendations for Organizational Research. *Organizational Research Methods*, *3*(1), 4–70. doi:10.1177/109442810031002

Werner, O., & Campbell, D. (1970). Translating, working through interpreters, and the problem of decentering. In R. Carroll & R. Cohen (Eds.), *A Handbook of Methods in Cultural Anthropology* (pp. 398–420). New York: Natural History Press.

Yang, L.-Q., Spector, P. E., Sanchez, J. I., Allen, T. D., Poelmans, S., Cooper, C. L.,. . . Woo, J.-m. (2012). Individualism-collectivism as a moderator of the work demands-strains relationship: A cross-level and cross-national examination. *Journal of International Business Studies*, *43*(4), 424–443. doi:http://dx.doi.org/10.1057/jibs.2011.58

PART IV

Review of Research in Regions across the Globe

13 A Review of Work–Family Research in Western and Southern Europe

Alexandra M. Tumminia and Rachel Omansky

Changes in workforce demographics have led to an increasing focus on the work–family interface. For example, women's labor force participation has increased throughout Europe over the past five decades (Eurostat, 2016), and the European Union (EU) has set a target goal of 75% employment among working-age adults (both men and women) by 2020 (European Commission, 2010). Given the contemporary relevance of work–family issues and the substantial variation across countries and regions in government, legal, and organizational factors, it is important to understand how work–family dynamics play out within specific regions. This chapter focuses on work–family issues specifically in Western and Southern Europe. Although there are geographic and geopolitical differences in how people define regions of Europe, based on classifications by the United Nations (UN) and America's Central Intelligence Agency (CIA), we define Western Europe as encompassing Austria, Belgium, France, Germany, Liechtenstein, Luxembourg, Monaco, the Netherlands, Switzerland, and the United Kingdom. Further, although the UN offers a maximal list of Southern European countries, we choose to define Southern Europe minimally, as comprised of Greece, Portugal, Spain, Italy, and Cyprus. In the following sections, we review the socioeconomic context of the area, where evolving demographic trends are being met with public policy in an attempt to facilitate work–family management. Next, we provide an overview of the relatively brief work–family research history in Western and Southern Europe, a body of literature that has expanded over the past two decades. Then, we review the extant literature addressing work–family issues in countries within these regions to highlight regional trends and findings. Finally, we propose recommendations for future research to advance our understanding of work–family issues in Western and Southern Europe.

Socioeconomic Context

The need to reconcile work and home demands has become progressively more salient due to de-industrialization, modernization, and subsequent changes in the nature of work. At the end of the twentieth century, the changing nature of work from physically demanding industrial jobs to service-oriented work created opportunities for women to engage in paid employment (Crompton & Lyonette, 2006). Gender differences in labor force participation have greatly diminished across

Europe (Oláh, 2015), and the resulting participation of both genders in paid work introduces new challenges at both the individual and societal level. Across Europe, de-industrialization has been met with declining fertility rates since the 1970s (Myrskylä, Kohler, & Billari, 2009), with rates in Western Europe hovering below the necessary level for population replacement, and rates in Southern Europe remaining well below replacement level (Oláh, 2015). As fertility rates and women's employment rate serve as indicators of the effectiveness of work–family supports, low birth rates reported in these regions may be indicative of women's inability to manage work and family in a satisfactory manner (Kuchařová, 2009).

The role of the European Union (EU). Declining fertility rates are only one of the notable societal consequences posited to follow from struggles with work–family management. Other consequences include gender inequality, suboptimal productivity, and population aging (Drobnič & Guillén Rodríguez, 2011). As such, policy makers have prioritized the facilitation of work–family management throughout the EU, of which many Western and Southern European countries are member states. In the early 1900s, the EU began introducing directives aimed at facilitating work–life management by providing paid maternal leave, including the Pregnant Workers Directive (CEC, 1992), which ensures fourteen weeks of maternity leave for working mothers. Since then, the EU has implemented the Working Time Directive to limit the number of hours an employee can spend working per day and per week (EU, 2003), and the Parental Leave Directive, which provides three months of maternal and paternal leave for births or adoptions (CEC, 1996). More recently, the European Commission (2015, 2016) has launched consultations with organizations across Europe to understand better the factors facilitating and hindering work–family management.

Although EU-level policies attempt to promote work–family management, the relationship between the enactment of these policies and the public's experience of work–family issues can be complex. One issue is that these policies often inadvertently promote traditional gender roles, with their basis in normative assumptions about the appropriate duties for men and women (Kuchařová, 2009; Lewis, 2001). These policies can impact cultural norms about the ideal way to reconcile work and non-work demands, subsequently impeding working parents' choices in regards to reconciliation efforts (Hobson, 2011; Lewis, 2001). Many family friendly policies were developed to facilitate women's participation in paid work in a manner similar to men. As such, women are more likely than men to be targeted as beneficiaries of these policies, further reinforcing gendered divisions of paid and unpaid labor (Aybars, 2007). Policies intended to increase employment opportunities for women, such as state-funded childcare and work hour limits, do little to change societal norms about the division of unpaid labor (Ciccia & Bleijenbergh, 2014). As a result, many of these policies may inadvertently be perpetuating the gendered division of labor.

Additional issues with EU-level policies are that they may not invariably reduce work-family tension, and may have differential impacts on employees depending on the cultural and political characteristics of a given country (Haas, 2003; Haas, Hwang, & Russell, 2000). For example, while the French government provides high levels of support for reconciling work and family, French working mothers reported higher levels of work–family conflict than mothers in Western European countries with lesser state-provided supports, such as Great Britain or Italy (Gallie & Russell, 2009). Thus, more state provisions may not equate to reduced work–family issues. Further, although the majority of working parents across surveyed countries in Western (i.e., Austria, Belgium, France, Germany, Great Britain, Ireland, the Netherlands) and Southern (i.e., Greece, Portugal, Spain) Europe report the desire to reduce their working hours, the preferred amount of working hours varies widely across countries (Lewis, Campbell, & Huerta, 2008). This country-based variation suggests that EU-level provisions – like those limiting working hours – may not facilitate work–family management equally for employees across member states.

To supplement blanket policies enacted by the EU, organizations may implement their own practices to reduce work–family issues in ways that meet their employees' needs. However, organization-based work–family initiatives remain marginalized, with most organizations merely complying with governmentally set minimum standards (Kossek, Lewis, & Hammer, 2010). The adequacy of existing legislation, such as that implemented by the EU, was frequently cited by organizations as a reason for a lack of supplementary work–family policies (BMFSF, 2010). Yet, a study showing that work characteristics play a larger role in work-home tension than home characteristics (Drobnič & Guillén Rodríguez, 2011) highlights the importance of organizational determinants of work–family issues and the organization's responsibility to facilitate work–family management.

Institutional context. Determining which policies and practices will best promote work–family management can be challenging. There is considerable variation in the prevalence of work–family constructs as well as predictors of these constructs across countries (Dragano, Siegrist, & Wahrendorf, 2011; Niedhammer, Sultan-Taïeb, Chastang, Vermeylen, Parent-Thirion, 2012). To understand these variations across countries in Western and Southern Europe, one must understand the institutional context within which countries develop cultural norms and preferences impacting employee perceptions of work–family constructs. Two popular typologies used to classify countries based on institutional context are Esping-Anderesen's (1990, 1999) and Ferrera's (1996) welfare state typologies. Countries in Western Europe are often classified as one of two types of welfare state – liberal (also referred to as Anglo-Saxon) or conservative (also referred to as continental, corporatist, or Bismarckian). Countries belonging to the liberal regime – including England, Scotland, Wales, and Ireland – maintain that the state should have limited involvement in its citizens' private lives. These countries provide little state support, leaving families to develop their own practices for reconciling paid and unpaid work (Lunau, Bambra, Eikemo, van der Wel, & Dragano, 2014). One way in which parents make their own arrangements in liberal welfare states is by coordinating schedules. For example, British mothers reported the highest levels of part-time work among working mothers across Europe (Crompton & Lyonette, 2006). European women in liberal welfare states reported more favorable work–life balance than women in conservative welfare states and those in Southern Europe, a finding potentially fueled by the availability of part-time work (Lunau et al., 2014). However, although parents in liberal welfare states like Britain often split unpaid labor in a more egalitarian way, long work hours and little state support are thought to be two primary obstacles to work–family management (Crompton & Lyonette, 2006).

Policies implemented in conservative countries – including France, Germany, Switzerland, Austria, Belgium, Luxembourg, and the Netherlands – are often rooted in the values espoused by the Catholic Church and are intended to maintain existing societal patterns, promoting the traditional family and division of domestic labor. Despite many of these countries providing high levels of public support for families, the structure of benefits and taxes further promotes the male breadwinner model (Harknett et al., 2014). For example, although French women benefit indirectly from state-provided supports, these supports are intended to be pro-birth and are not connected to a pro-equality agenda (Jenson, 1989; Crompton & Lyonette, 2006). Consequently, despite extensive state-provided support, entrenched traditional views on the division of domestic labor leave women in France experiencing more work–family conflict than women in other European countries (Crompton & Lyonette, 2006).

In Southern Europe, the majority of countries – including Italy, Greece, Portugal, Spain, Cyprus, and Malta – are classified as familistic (also called Mediterranean) welfare states. Countries in the familistic welfare state regime believe in the centrality of family. The heavy emphasis on family discourages policy makers from implementing family-friendly policies, with family members typically providing care in lieu of state-provided aid. In these countries, women are viewed as caretakers and are often responsible for caring for dependent family members (Drobnič & Guillén Rodríguez, 2011). Employees in Portugal reported more traditional views on division of domestic labor than employees in countries in Western Europe (Crompton & Lyonette, 2006), reflecting deeply entrenched ideas about the women's role. Minimal public provision is coupled with little opportunity to utilize part-time work to reconcile work and non-work demands (Lunau et al., 2014), making familistic welfare states inhospitable to women's employment (Crompton & Lyonette, 2006), such that fewer mothers reported working in Spain and Italy compared to mothers in non-familistic countries (e.g., Finland and the UK, Drobnič & Guillén Rodríguez, 2011). Southern European employees also report less favorable work–life balance than employees in Western Europe (Lunau et al., 2014). These findings reflect the severity of work–family reconciliation issues in Southern Europe, especially for women and mothers.

Cultural values. The differing policies enacted across the region's distinct welfare states reflect its diverse cultural values. Differences in values and practices among societies have been defined by the cultural dimensions established in the GLOBE program of research (House, Hanges, Javidan, Dorfman, Gupta, 2004). Societal clustering based on these dimensions suggests that up to four cultural clusters exist in the region: Anglo (e.g., England, Ireland), Germanic Europe (e.g., Austria, Germany, the Netherlands), Latin Europe (e.g., France, Portugal, Spain, Italy), and Eastern Europe (e.g., Greece).

Anglo countries are often competitive and results-oriented, with little formal intrusion in terms of rules (Gupta, Hanges, & Dorfman, 2002). In these countries, a strong performance-orientation, little uncertainty avoidance, and an emphasis on merit-based rewards fosters competition. High gender egalitarianism and low institutional collectivism align with the institutional context of these countries, where governments do little to intervene in familial affairs. While countries in the Germanic Europe cluster are also described as competitive (i.e., assertive, individualistic, and results-oriented), they differ from Anglo countries in that countries in the Germanic European cluster tend to value future-orientation and practice uncertainty avoidance (Szabo, Brodbeck, Den Hartog, Reber, Weibler, & Wunderer, 2002). Germanic European countries also tend to be lower in gender egalitarianism, aligning with the policies enacted in these countries that support the traditional family.

In contrast to the aforementioned clusters, countries in the Latin European cluster value both in-group and institutional collectivism and only put moderate emphasis on performance. Practices in these countries are defined by high power distance and low gender egalitarianism, reflecting the presence of Catholicism in the region (Jesuino, 2002). Jesuino (2002) notes that Italy, Portugal, and Spain form a sub-cluster separate from France, which may echo the differences in welfare state regimes (i.e., France being a conservative country and the others being familistic countries). While Greece shares this familistic welfare state, it has been included in the Eastern Europe cluster based on cultural values; a cluster defined by group support and gender equality. However, Greece's reigning values seem to depart from the values of the other countries in this cluster. In fact, some interpretations of the values defining this cluster seem to adequately explain findings only when excluding Greece (Bakacsi, Sándor, András, & Viktor, 2002).

Overview of Work–Family Research in Western and Southern Europe

Key researchers and contributions. With the widespread decline of the male breadwinner model across Europe, work–family issues became a prominent focus for both policy makers and researchers in the 1990s. EU initiatives attracted scholarly attention, with resultant research focusing on the relationship between these policies and work-related outcomes. Specifically, a body of work developed examining how the enactment of policies developed to aid work–family reconciliation impacts parental employment (e.g., Bruning & Plantenga, 1999). Gornick, Meyers, and Ross (1997, 1998) investigated international differences in policy and the impact of these differences on maternal employment in both Western and Southern Europe as well as North America and Australia. In the early 2000s, motivated by women's increasing participation in paid labor and the changing nature of work (Geurts, Rutte, & Peeters, 1999), research programs in the Netherlands began investigating antecedents and consequences of incompatible work and non-work demands. This early research led by scholars from the Netherlands (e.g., Bakker & Geurts, 2004; Demerouti, Bakker, Nachreiner, & Schaufeli, 2001; Geurts, Taris, Kompier, Dikkers, Van Hooff, &

Kinnunen, 2005; Schaufeli, Leiter, Maslach, & Jackson, 1996) established models and measures that have influenced work–family research for over a decade.

Alongside others, Netherlands-based researchers continue to advance work–family scholarship today. More recently, researchers from the Netherlands have collaborated with Spanish scholars to further develop work–family research in Southern Europe (e.g., Del Líbano, Llorens, Salanova, & Schaufeli, 2012; Moreno-Jiménez, Mayo, Sanz-Vergel, Guerts, Rodríguez-Muñoz, & Garrosa, 2009). In Belgium, faculty from Ghent University are examining the relationship between work–family conflict and absenteeism (Clays, Kittel, Godin, De Bacquer, & De Backer, 2009), introducing new concepts like specific stress associated with the role of combining work and non-work demands (Vercruyssen & Van de Putte, 2013), conducting longitudinal studies on work-home incompatibility (Wille, De Fruyt, & Fey, 2013), and considering the role of work–family conflict in non-response bias (Vercruyssen, Roose, & Van de Putte, 2011). Beham, Drobnič, and Präg (2011, 2012, 2014) have explored employee satisfaction with work–family balance and tested models of both work-home interference and work-home enrichment within Germany and across Western Europe. The aforementioned works are only a few examples of the continually evolving research programs addressing work–family issues in Western and Southern Europe.

Many substantive theoretical and methodological contributions originate from the area, particularly from the Netherlands. One such theoretical contribution is the job demands–resources (JD–R) model of burnout (Demerouti et al., 2001), which posits that job characteristics can be categorized as either demands (i.e., job aspects requiring physical or mental effort) or resources (i.e., job aspects that facilitate work goals, reduce physical/psychological costs of work, or promote personal growth). The model suggests that (1) high job demands lead to exhaustion, (2) a lack of job-related resources leads to withdrawal, and (3) the presence of these two unfavorable outcomes is an indication of burnout. Today, the JD-R model is a widely accepted and utilized framework for understanding job stress, often used to explore the relationship between job demands, job resources, and work–family constructs (e.g., Bakker, ten Brummelhuis, Prins, & van der Heijden, 2011; Beham & Drobnič, 2010) and continually being refined (Schaufeli & Bakker, 2004; Demerouti & Bakker, 2011; Schaufeli & Taris, 2014).

Authors involved in developing the JD–R model explored additional models related to the relationship between work and non-work demands, proposing a dual-process model of work-home interference (Bakker & Geurts, 2004). Bakker and Geurts built upon the demands and resources aspects of the JD–R to propose that increased job demands lead to exhaustion, which leads to negative work-home interference. The presence of job resources, on the other hand, leads to increased motivation, resulting in a positive impact of work on home behavior. This dual-process model incorporated the Dutch developed effort–recovery (E–R) model (Meijman & Mulder, 1998), suggesting a lack of recovery is the mechanism underlying the demands-exhaustion relationship. The continual development and integration of theories developed in the area demonstrates a dedication to improving understanding of evolving issues regarding work–family management.

The Netherlands also contributed a measure of both the direction and quality of work-home interaction known as the Survey Work-home Interaction – NijmeGen (SWING; Geurts et al., 2005). Prior to the SWING, most research focused on the detrimental impact of work demands on non-work domains. However, Geurts and colleagues (2005) were interested in developing a measure to assess the potential energizing effects that work could have on non-work aspects of life and vice versa. Recognizing the potentially beneficial and detrimental impact of work-home interaction, as well as the bidirectional nature of this interaction, the SWING measures positive and negative work-home interference as well as positive and negative home-work interference. The SWING has been used by work–family researchers to study the different directions and quality of work-home interactions across Europe (e.g., Bekker, Willemse, & de Goeij, 2010; Gracia, Silla, Pieró, Ferreira, 2007; Hetty van Emmerik & Peeters, 2009).

Conceptualizing work–home interactions. The SWING measure defines work–home interaction as the influence (negative or positive) of load reactions in one domain on behavior in another domain (work or non-work). As such, the four subscales of the SWING measure the negative impact of work on behavior at home, the negative impact of home on behavior at work, the positive impact of work on home behavior, and the positive impact of home on work behavior. Items are worded to conceptualize "home" as a broad, non-work domain with no explicit connection to partnerships or children, making the measure appropriate for assessment of work–home interaction regardless of marital or parental status (Geurts et al., 2005).

Although the SWING is a frequently used measure of work–home interaction in the region, Netemeyer, Boles, and McMurrian's (1996) American scales of work–family conflict and family–work conflict are often utilized by Western and Southern European researchers as well (e.g., Andres, Moelker, & Soeters, 2012; Camerino, Sandri, Sartori, Conway, Campanini, & Costa, 2010; Hornung, Glaser, Rousseau, Angerer, & Weigl, 2011). However, the use of items measuring "family" as opposed to a broader conceptualization of the non-work domain prompts questions about the generalizability of findings yielded by these measures because the scales may fail to pick up load reactions related to non-work domains that employees do not perceive as family (e.g., friends, partners).

The distinct differences between the conceptualization of non-work domains in Geurts and colleagues' (2005) SWING measures and Netemeyer et al.'s (1996) two scales introduce a question of construct equivalence in work–family research. Additionally, many of the comparative studies conducted in Europe utilize large, cross-national, archival data sets such as the International Social Survey Programme (ISSP), the European Quality of Life Survey (EQLS), and the European Social Survey (ESS). In many of these studies, researchers construct alternative indices of work–family from various survey items, which further calls into question construct equivalence. For example, Crompton and Lyonette (2006) utilized data collected via the ISSP (2002), where four items are used to construct a "work–life conflict" scale. These items address different directions of the work–home interaction (e.g., two items address home–work interference, two items address work–home interference), and have different emphases on the non-work domain (e.g., two items address home, two items address family). Drobnič and Guillén Rodríguez (2011) use a two-item measure derived from the EQLS and a four-item measure from the ESS2 (2004), both of which address only work–home interference. These examples illustrate a lack of construct equivalence, prompting concern over whether studies using data collected via the ISSP can be directly compared to those using data collected via the EQLS or the ESS, and what the indices derived from these surveys truly represent.

Methodological trends. Several methodological trends became apparent when reviewing research conducted in these regions. One such trend is the use of samples from a single country to examine work–family issues within a given country. Although many researchers discuss the generalizability of their findings to studies conducted with samples from other countries or cultures, the majority of studies do not actually empirically compare samples from different populations (e.g., Calvo-Salguero, Martínez-de-Lecea, & del Carmen Aguilar-Luzón, 2012; Cortese et al., 2010). Furthermore, although cross-national comparative research is limited (McGinnity & Calvert, 2009), those studies that do compare across countries often use data collected via the aforementioned international surveys.

Supported by the EU, the European Commission developed several programs of research intended to address socio economic issues directly and indirectly related to work–family issues in Europe. The Fifth Framework Programme (FPS, 1998–2002) supported the Households, Work, and Flexibility Project aimed at examining the impact of evolving forms of flexibility on the reconciliation of work and family life. Research produced within this project includes studies on the influence of working hours on work–family conflict (Cousins & Tang, 2004), work–home conflict perceptions (Strandh & Nordenmark, 2006), and gender differences in conflict experiences (Van der Lippe, Jager, & Kops, 2006). A subsequent research program, the Sixth Framework Programme (FP6; 2002–2006) supported the Economic Change, Quality of Life, and Social Cohesion (EQUALSOC) Network of Excellence. Associated research investigated the impact of working conditions and household characteristics on work–family conflict (Gallie & Russell, 2009), the relationship between time- and strain-based conflict on work and family demands (Steiber, 2009), the influence of different kinds of support on satisfaction with work–life balance (Abendroth & Den Dulk, 2011), and the relationship between social class and work–family conflict across Europe (McGinnity & Calvert, 2009).

Although these surveys facilitate international comparison across and beyond Western and Southern Europe, they are somewhat limited by their cross-sectional nature. Reflecting a trend in the broader work–family literature, researchers in these countries tend to utilize survey-based, cross-sectional designs with self-report response formats. A notable exception is a study by Falco and colleagues (2012), who used both self and observer (i.e., spouse) responses to assess work–family conflict. In more recent work, researchers have begun to address the limitations of cross-sectional research by employing more complex designs, such as longitudinal and daily diary methodologies (see Andres et al., 2012; Derks & Bakker, 2014; Derks, Duin, Tims, & Bakker, 2015; Wille et al., 2013). This recent work features methodological advancements that can provide valuable insight into work–family issues and work–family processes, particularly as they unfold over time.

Research Findings in Western and Southern Europe

As detailed above, the evolution of the work environment and the social, political, and legal changes that accompanied this evolution spurred a great deal of research in Western and Eastern Europe. In the following sections, we review extant research from several countries in this area and highlight research trends and notable findings.

Southern Europe. In Cyprus, the majority of work–family research has focused on both directions of conflict (i.e., work–family and family–work) in relation to work outcomes and attitudes (Karatepe & Kilic, 2007, 2009; Karatepe & Uludag, 2008), finding that work–family conflict negatively relates to job satisfaction (Karatepe & Kilic, 2007; Karatepe & Uludag, 2007) and job performance (Karatepe & Kilic, 2009), and positively relates to turnover intentions (Karatepe & Kilic, 2007). Researchers have also explored demographic (e.g., gender, education, marital status, tenure, number of children, and age) factors in relation to conflict, but have found mixed results (e.g., Karatepe & Uludag, 2007; Karatepe & Kilic, 2007). However, research suggests supervisor support is a useful resource for combating work–family conflict (Karatepe & Kilic, 2007). As published research in Cyprus has focused entirely on the hotel industry, future research should examine employees in other occupations to determine whether these findings generalize to other industries.

In Greece, researchers have largely focused on organizational and individual antecedents of employee perceptions of and reactions to work–family conflict. This focus is potentially fueled by the disconnect between the changing nature of the Greek work environment and the lack of family-friendly policies and attitudes at both the organizational and national levels, which is reflective of prevailing traditional views toward women. Glaveli, Karassavidou, and Zafiropoulos (2013) found that family-supportive organizational culture and family-supportive management were negatively related to work–family conflict perceptions and family supportive management was positively related to job satisfaction. Further, quantitative job demands (i.e., work overload and work pressure) and emotional demands were positively linked to emotional exhaustion and emotional demands were positively linked to depersonalization directly and indirectly through work–family conflict perceptions (Montgomery et al., 2006).

Traditional conceptions of gender roles also pervade Italian society, and Italy has been slow to adopt and implement work–family reconciliation policies consistent with the EU's gender equality directives (Donà, 2012). Research in Italy has examined stereotypically female occupations, such as teachers (Guglielmi, Panara, & Simbula, 2012; Simbula, 2010) and healthcare employees (Camerino et al., 2010; Cortese et al., 2010; Russo & Buonocore, 2012). Researchers have also linked work–family conflict to job satisfaction (Buonocore & Russo, 2013; Cortese et al., 2010), mental fatigue (Guglielmi et al., 2012), emotional exhaustion (Camerino et al., 2010; Simbula, 2010), as well as sleep and presenteeism (Camerino et al., 2010). Additionally, researchers have explored resources leading to work–family enrichment, such as various types of support (i.e., supervisor support, Molino, Ghislieri, & Cortese, 2013; co worker support, Molino et al., 2013; Simbula, 2010; and family support, Ghislieri, Martini, Gatti, & Colombo, 2011) and opportunities for professional development (Molino et al., 2013). These trends suggest that work–family research is driven by the need to help employees find ways to compensate for the lack of institutional support.

As compared to work–family research in the aforementioned countries, research in Spain has examined more complex relationships and a wider variety of outcomes, antecedents, and moderators. For example, the two types of conflict (i.e., work–family, family–work) have been found to differentially predict life satisfaction (Moreno-Jiménez et al., 2009), psychological strain (Moreno-Jiménez et al., 2009; Sanz-Vergel, Demerouti, Mayo, & Moreno-Jiménez, 2010), organizational citizenship behaviors (Beham, 2011), and job satisfaction (Calvo-Salguero, Martínez-de-Lecea, & Carrasco-Gonzalez, 2011). Researchers have also examined a variety of individual and organizational antecedents to work–family variables, such as neuroticism, work and non-work support (Blanch & Aluja, 2009), work self-efficacy and workaholism (Del Líbano et al., 2012), and day-specific recovery (Sanz-Vergel, Demerouti, Moreno-Jiménez, & Mayo, 2010). Additionally, employee perceptions of culture regarding flexible work arrangements and coworker use of these arrangements relates to employees' use of these arrangements (de Sivatte & Guadamillas, 2013), suggesting merely offering family-friendly policies without making other organizational cultural adjustments may not be adequate.

The examination of gender as a moderator has provided a richer understanding of the complex nature of work–family interactions for Spanish employees. Notable findings include that women experience family-to-work conflict more than men (Calvo-Salguero et al., 2012; Sánchez-Cabezudo & López Peláez, 2014), whereas men experience more work-to-family conflict than women (Calvo-Salguero et al., 2012; Sánchez-Cabezudo & López Peláez, 2014). This is potentially due to the amount of time individuals of each gender spend in the work versus the family domain. Further, family-to-work conflict is more strongly negatively related to organizational citizenship behaviors for tasks and for individuals for women than men (Beham, 2011). These findings highlight the trouble employees currently face in reconciling work and home demands, which may in part be due to Spanish governmental and organizational hesitance to adopt, implement, and promote work–family policies to help modern families cope with competing demands.

Western Europe. In Belgium, researchers have produced interesting and timely work on the nuances of work–family conflict. Van Veldhoven and Beijer (2012) found that single fathers experienced the most work–family conflict, the link between workload and work–family conflict is higher for dual-earner fathers than for dual-earner mothers, and work–family conflict was more strongly related to health complaints for dual-earner mothers than dual-earner fathers. These findings suggest that work–family issues are relevant to and problematic for men and non-traditional families. Vercruyssen, Roose, and Van de Putte (2011) found evidence that those suffering the most from work–family issues tend to choose not to participate in work–family research, which may skew the results of this research and the subsequent inferences drawn from it.

In Germany, researchers have largely focused on examining individual and organizational level demands and resources that contribute to work–family conflict and enrichment, as well as subgroup differences in conflict perceptions. Findings from these studies suggest that a variety of demands relate to work-home interference, including perceived organizational time expectations (Beham & Drobnič, 2010), psychological job demands, job insecurity (Beham & Drobnič, 2010; Beham et al., 2011), time pressure, cognitive and emotional irritation (Höge, 2009), and hours worked (Steinmetz, Frese, & Schmidt, 2008). Research suggests that work–family conflict is higher for hospital physicians compared to the general German population (Fuß, Nubling, Hasselhorn, Schwappach, & Rieger, 2008). Additionally, supervisors, women (Beham et al., 2011), and depressed individuals (Steinmetz et al., 2008), report experiencing more work–family conflict than men, employees without supervisory responsibilities, and individuals who are not depressed. A number of work and non-work resources have been found to be helpful in combating work–family conflict (e.g., job variety, supervisor support, coworker support, Beham & Drobnič, 2010; Beham et al., 2011; use of flexible work arrangements Beham et al., 2011; Hornung & Glaser, 2009). Further, job variety, use of flexible work arrangements, and work support are associated with higher work-home enrichment (Beham et al., 2011), which suggests that organizational resources play a critical role in facilitating work–family management.

Research in the United Kingdom has focused primarily on individual difference predictors of work–family issues and differential outcomes of work–family issues for these various subgroups. Personality variables (e.g., neuroticism, Hughes & Parkes, 2007; Noor, 2003; extraversion, Noor, 2003; trait emotional intelligence, Biggart, Corr, O'Brien, & Cooper, 2010), gender (Noor, 2003, 2004; Swanson & Power, 1999), marital status, and education (Noor, 2003) differentially predicted work–family conflict. Consistent with research from Germany and Cyprus, research in the United Kingdom also suggests that individuals in certain fields, such as health care (e.g. Swanson & Powers, 1999) and service occupations (e.g., Kinman, 2009), experience high levels of work-home conflict. Additionally, work–family conflict has been linked to several negative outcomes, such as job dissatisfaction (Noor, 2003; Farquharson, Allan, Johnston, Choudhary, & Jones, 2012), intention to leave and sickness absence (Farquharson et al., 2012), and distress symptoms (Hughes & Parkes, 2007; Noor, 2003, 2004).

Future Research Directions

The evolving body of research associated with work–family issues in Western and Southern Europe has contributed significantly to the broader body of literature addressing work–family issues. However, our review also highlights several areas ripe for future research. In this section, we elaborate on several potential future directions, including the examination of the importance of culture in explaining variation in work–family management across the region, and the consideration of new theories that address the effects of more macro-level factors on work–family issues. Given an influx in immigration in the area leading to a changing demographic landscape, examining the role of cultural values in on work–family management is of great contemporary relevance.

To better understand variation in work–family management across countries in the region, it is important to address the lack of consideration of cultural difference across the area. Studies comparing across multiple countries typically use widely available data sets (e.g., ISSP, ESS), which do not explicitly address cultural factors. One exception is Spector and colleagues' (2007) study, which showed that work demands differentially predicted work-to-family conflict for individualistic versus collectivistic country clusters, with this relationship being stronger for the individualistic clusters. Additionally, GLOBE country clusters moderated the relationships between work-to-family conflict and job satisfaction and turnover intentions. These results highlight the importance of examining potential sources of differences in work–family management at multiple levels of analysis. Though individual characteristics are frequently examined in an attempt to explain variation in work–family management, there is a dearth of research examining macro-level factors that can influence these issues, such as inter-organizational, inter-national, or inter-regional differences. Examining such factors may improve our understanding of when, where, and why work–family management varies.

Although work–family issues have been treated as universal across the region's countries, future research might employ the societal approach (Maurice, Seller, & Silvestre, 1986) to examine how differences in cultural values may influence a seemingly "universal" phenomenon. This approach involves demonstrating that regional or country-level differences in a construct of interest exist after accounting for factors known to impact that construct (see Gallie, 2003). For example, Crompton and Lyonette (2006) used this approach to demonstrate that when accounting for sex, age, social class, working hours, and having a child in one's household, having a more traditional division of domestic labor was related to increased work–life conflict *only* in France (as opposed to Britain, Finland, Norway, and Portugal). The results suggest that the traditional division of domestic labor itself does not lead to work–life conflict; it is the combination of this gendered division of household labor and other societal factors (in the case of France, valuing gender egalitarianism) that leads to conflict. Therefore, research demonstrating societal effects suggest that cultural values may influence quality of life and the experience of work–family conflict. Continued consideration of cultural values in work–family issues in these regions is critical for understanding international variation in work–family management that cannot be otherwise explained by policies and work conditions. Future research might attempt to identify the numerous values that indirectly impact the reconciliation of work and non-work demands, how these values are differentially endorsed, and variations in the centrality of these values across countries.

Finally, researchers should consider alternative theoretical models, such as those addressing cultural values and institutional context, to supplement the models currently used to understand the experience of work–family issues in the region. Although resource-demands models, like the JD-R model, provide a framework for understanding the direction and quality of work-home interactions, they do not explain why specific job characteristics are perceived by the employee as stressors or resources (Drobnič & Guillén Rodríguez, 2011). Hobson and Fahlén (2009a, 2009b) have applied Sen's (1992, 2006) capabilities framework to work–family balance, suggesting that balancing work and non-work demands is a form of functioning attained via an individual's capability set (i.e., the resources an individual has to facilitate work–family balance), and that the capability sets that lead to successful work–family balance may vary across contexts. Perspectives like the capabilities framework may help explain variations in work–family balance across countries and welfare state regimes.

Conclusion

The aim of this chapter was to summarize the findings of work–family research in Western and Southern Europe while considering socioeconomic trends and institutional contexts in the region. Although women's participation in the workforce advances their equality in paid work, the absence of effective policies and resources at the societal and organizational levels coupled with the fact that women remain chiefly responsible for unpaid labor in the region remain obstacles for effective work–family management. While a dual-earner/dual-carer model – where paid and unpaid work are divided equally among men and women – is the somewhat utopian ideal for equality among partners, welfare states and the policies they enact often continue to promote the male breadwinner model (Ciccia & Bleijenbergh, 2014). From this social context emerges a variety of multi-faceted concerns about work–family issues in the area – to what extent do cultural, institutional, and individual factors impact the experience of work–family conflict? Determining whether these or other factors are responsible for the cross-national variation in employees' experiences of work–family issues and management is a critical next step toward reducing work–family tension.

References

Abendroth, A. K., & Den Dulk, L. (2011). Support for the work–life balance in Europe: The impact of state, workplace and family support on work–life balance satisfaction. *Work, Employment & Society, 25*, 234–256.

Andres, M., Moelker, R., & Soeters, J. (2012). The work–family interface and turnover intentions over the course of project-oriented assignments abroad. *International Journal of Project Management, 30*, 752–759.

Aybars, A. I. (2007). Work–life balance in the EU and leave arrangements across welfare regimes. *Industrial Relations Journal, 38*, 569–590.

Bakacsi, G., Sandor, T., Andras, K., & Viktor, I. (2002). Eastern European cluster: Tradition and transition. *Journal of World Business, 37*, 69–80.

Bakker, A. B., & Geurts, S. A. (2004). Toward a dual-process model of work-home interference. *Work and Occupations, 31*, 345–366.

Bakker A. B., ten Brummelhuis, L. L., Prins J. T., & van der Heijden F. M. M. A. (2011). Applying the job demands–resources model to the work–home interface: A study among medical residents and their partners. *Journal of Vocational Behavior, 79*, 170–180.

Beham, B. (2011). Work–family conflict and organizational citizenship behaviour: Empirical evidence from Spanish employees. *Community, Work, & Family, 14*, 63–80.

Beham, B., & Drobnič, S. (2010). Satisfaction with work–family balance among German office workers. *Journal of Managerial Psychology, 25*, 669–689.

Beham, B., & Drobnič, S. (2011). Job demands and work-home interference: Empirical evidence from service sector employees in eight European Countries. In *Work–life Balance in Europe* (pp. 95–119). UK: Palgrave Macmillan.

Beham, B., Drobnič, S., & Präg, P. (2011). Work demands and resources and the work–family interface: Testing a salience model on German service sector employees. *Journal of Vocational Behavior, 78*, 110–122.

Beham, B., Präg, P., & Drobnič, S. (2012). Who's got the balance? A study of satisfaction with the work–family balance among part-time service sector employees in five western European countries. *The International Journal of Human Resource Management, 23*, 3725–3741.

Beham, B., Drobnič, S., & Präg, P. (2014). The work–family interface of service sector workers: A comparison of work resources and professional status across five European countries. *Applied Psychology, 63*, 29–61.

Bekker, M. H., Willemse, J. J., & De Goeij, J. W. (2010). The role of individual differences in particular autonomy-connectedness in women's and men's work–family balance. *Women & Health, 50*, 241–261.

Biggart, L., Corr, P., O'Brien, M., & Cooper, N. (2010). Trait emotional intelligence and work–family conflict in fathers. *Personality and Individual Differences, 48*, 911–916.

Blanch, A., & Aluja, A. (2009). Work, family and personality: A study of work–family conflict. *Personality and Individual Differences, 46*, 520–524.

Bruning, G., & Plantenga, J. (1999). Parental leave and equal opportunities: *experiences in eight European countries*. *Journal of European Social Policy, 9*, 195–209.

Buonocore, F., & Russo, M. (2013). Reducing the effects of work–family conflict on job satisfaction: The kind of commitment matters. *Human Resource Management Journal, 23*, 91–108.

Calvo-Salguero, A., Martínez-de-Lecea, J. M. S., & del Carmen Aguilar-Luzón, M. (2012). Gender and work–family conflict: Testing the rational model and the gender role expectations model in the Spanish cultural context. *International Journal of Psychology, 47*, 118–132.

Calvo-Salguero, A., Martínez-de-Lecea, J. M. S., & Carrasco-González, A. M. (2011). Work–Family and Family–Work Conflict: Does Intrinsic–Extrinsic Satisfaction Mediate the Prediction of General Job Satisfaction? *The Journal of Psychology, 145*, 435–461.

Camerino, D., Sandri, M., Sartori, S., Conway, P.M., Campanini, P., & Costa, G. (2010). Shiftwork, work–family conflict among Italian nurses, and prevention efficacy. *Chronobiology International, 27*, 1105–1123. doi: 10.3109/07420528.2010.490072

Ciccia, R., & Bleijenbergh, I. (2014). After the male breadwinner model? Childcare services and the division of labor in European countries. *Social Politics: International Studies in Gender, State & Society, 21*, 50–79.

Clays, E., Kittel, F., Godin, I., De Bacquer, D., & De Backer, G. (2009). Measures of work–family conflict predict sickness absence from work. *Journal of Occupational and Environmental Medicine, 51*, 879–886.

Cortese, C.G., Colombo, L., & Ghislieri, C. (2010). Determinants of nurses' job satisfaction: The role of work–family conflict, job demand, emotional charge, and social support. *Journal of Nursing Management, 18*, 35–43.

Crompton, R., & Lyonette, C. (2006). Work–life 'balance' in Europe. *Acta Sociologica, 49*, 379–393.

Council of the Europeans Communities (1992). Council Directive 92/85/EEC of 19 October 1992 concerning the implementation of measures to encourage improvements in the safety and health of pregnant workers, women workers who have recently given birth and women who are breastfeeding.

Council of the European Communities (1996). Council Directive 96/34/EC of 3 June 1996 on the framework agreement on parental leave concluded by UNICE, CEEP and the ETUC.

Cousins, C. R., & Tang, N. (2004). Working time and work and family conflict in the Netherlands, Sweden and the UK. *Work, Employment & Society, 18*, 531–549.

Del Líbano, M., Llorens, S., Salanova, M., & Schaufeli, W.B. (2012). About the dark and bright sides of self-efficacy: Workaholism and work engagement. *The Spanish Journal of Psychology, 15*, 688–701.

Demerouti, E., & Bakker, A. B. (2011). The job demands-resources model: Challenges for future research. *SA Journal of Industrial Psychology, 37*(**2**), 1–9.

Demerouti, E., Bakker, A. B., Nachreiner, F., & Schaufeli, W. B. (2001). The job demands-resources model of burnout. *Journal of Applied Psychology, 86*, 499–512.

De Sivatte, I., & Guadamillas, F. (2013). Antecedents and outcomes of implementing flexibility policies in organizations. *The International Journal of Human Resource Management, 24*, 1327–1345.

Derks, D., & Bakker, A. B. (2014). Smartphone use, work–home interference, and burnout: A diary study on the role of recovery. *Applied Psychology, 63*, 411–440.

Derks, D., Duin, D., Tims, M., & Bakker, A. B. (2015). Smartphone use and work–home interference: The moderating role of social norms and employee work engagement. *Journal of Occupational and Organizational Psychology, 88*, 155–177.

Donà, A. (2012). Using the EU to Promote Gender Equality Policy in a Traditional Context: Reconciliation of Work and Family Life in Italy. In M. Forest & E. Lombardo (Eds.), *The Europeanization of Gender Equality Policies: A Discursive Sociological Approach* (pp. 99–120). New York: Palgrave Macmillan.

Dragano, N., Siegrist, J., & Wahrendorf, M. (2011). Welfare regimes, labour policies and unhealthy psychosocial working conditions: a comparative study with 9917 older employees from 12 European countries. *Journal of Epidemiology and Community Health, 65*, 793–799.

Drobnič, S., & Guillén Rodríguez, A. M. (2011). Tensions between work and home: job quality and working conditions in the institutional contexts of Germany and Spain. *Social Politics: International Studies in Gender, State & Society, 18*, 232–268.

Esping-Andersen, G. (1999). *Social Foundations of Postindustrial Economies*. New York: Oxford University Press.

(1990). The three political economies of the welfare state. *International Journal of Sociology, 20*, 92–123.

European Commission (2010). *Europe 2020, A European strategy for smart, sustainable and inclusive growth*. Brussels: European Commission.

European Commission (2015). *First phase consultation of social partners under article 154 TFEU on possible action addressing the challenges of work–life balance faced by working parents and caregivers*. European Commission, Brussels.

European Commission (2016). *Second-stage consultation of the social partners at European level under Article 154 TFEU on possible action addressing the challenges of work–life balance faced by working parents and caregivers*. European Commission, Brussels.

European Union, European Parliament (2003). *Directive 2003/88/EC of the European Parliament and of the Council of 4 November 2003 concerning certain aspects of the organization of working time*.

Eurostat (2012). Employment Rate, By Sex, http://epp.eurostat.ec.europa.eu/portal/page/portal/eurostat/home/. Last accessed September 2016.

Eurostat (2016). *Online statistics*. Available at: http://ec.europa.eu/eurostat/web/lfs/data/database. Last accessed September 2016.

Falco, A. Kravina, L., Girardi, D, Dal Corso, L., Di Sipio, A., & De Carlo, N. A. (2012). The convergence between self and observer ratings of workaholism: A comparison between couples. *Testing, Psychometrics, Methodology in Applied Psychology, 19*, 311–24.

Farquharson, B., Allan, J., Johnston, D., Johnston, M., Choudhary, C., & Jones, M. (2012). Stress amongst nurses working in a healthcare telephone-advice service: Relationship with job satisfaction, intention to leave, sickness absence, and performance. *Journal of Advanced Nursing, 68*, 1624–1635.

Federal Ministry for Family Affairs, Senior Citizens, Women, and Youth—BMFSFJ (2010). *European company survey on reconciliation of work and family life*. Retrieved from: www.bmfsfj.de/BMFSFJ/Service/volltextsuche,did=165112.html

Ferrera, M. (1996). The 'Southern model' of welfare in social Europe. *Journal of European Social Policy, 6*, 17–37.

Fuß, I., Nübling, M., Hasselhorn, H. M., Schwappach, D., & Rieger, M. A. (2008). Working conditions and work–family conflict in German hospital physicians: Psychosocial and organisational predictors and consequences. *BMC Public Health, 8*, 353–369.

Gallie, D. (2003). The quality of working life: is Scandinavia different? *European Sociological Review, 19*(**1**), 61–79.

Gallie, D., & Russell, H. (2009). Work–family conflict and working conditions in Western Europe. *Social Indicators Research, 93*, 445–467.

Geurts, S., Rutte, C., & Peeters, M. (1999). Antecedents and consequences of work–home interference among medical residents. *Social Science & Medicine, 48*, 1135–1148.

Geurts, S. A., Taris, T. W., Kompier, M. A., Dikkers, J. S., Van Hooff, M. L., & Kinnunen, U. M. (2005). Work-home interaction from a work psychological perspective: Development and validation of a new questionnaire, the SWING. *Work & Stress, 19*, 319–339.

Ghislieri, C., Martini, M., Gatti, P., & Colombo, L. (2011). The 'bright side' of the work–family interface: a brief work–family enrichment scale in a sample of health professionals. *TPM–Testing, Psychometrics, Methodology in Applied Psychology, 18*(4), 211–230.

Glaveli, N., Karassavidou, E., & Zafiropoulos, K. (2013). Relationships among three facets of family supportive work environments, work–family conflict and job satisfaction: A research in Greece. *The International Journal of Human Resource Management, 24*, 3757–3771.

Gornick, J. C., Meyers, M. K., & Ross, K. E. (1997). Supporting the employment of mothers: Policy variation across fourteen welfare states. *Journal of European social policy, 7*, 45–70.

Gornick, J. C., Meyers, M. K., & Ross, K. E. (1998). Public policies and the employment of mothers: A cross-national study. *Social Science Quarterly*, 35–54.

Gracia, F. J., Silla, I., Silla, J. M. P., & Ferreira, L. F. (2007). The state of the psychological contract and its relation to employees' psychological health. *Psychology in Spain, 11*, 33–41.

Guglielmi, D., Panari, C., & Simbula, S. (2012). The determinants of teachers' well-being: The mediating role of mental fatigue. *European Journal of Mental Health, 7*, 204–220.

Gupta, V., Hanges, P. J., & Dorfman, P. (2002). Cultural clusters: Methodology and findings. *Journal of World Business, 37*, 11–15.

Harknett, K., Billari, F. C., & Medalia, C. (2014). Do family support environments influence fertility? Evidence from 20 European countries. *European Journal of Population, 30*, 1–33.

Haas, L. (2003). Parental leave and gender equality: Lessons from the European Union. *Review of Policy Research, 20*, 89–114.

Haas, L. L., Hwang, P., & Russell, G. (2000). Organizational change and gender equity. *International Perspectives on Fathers and Mothers at the Workplace*. Thousand Oaks, CA: Sage.

Hetty van Emmerik, I. J., & Peeters, M. C. (2009). Crossover specificity of team-level work–family conflict to individual-level work–family conflict. *Journal of Managerial Psychology, 24*, 254–268.

Hobson, B. (2011). The agency gap in work–life balance: Applying Sen's capabilities framework within European contexts. *Social Politics: International Studies in Gender, State & Society, 18*, 147–167.

Hobson, B., & Fahlén, S. (2009a). Competing scenarios for European fathers: Applying Sen's capabilities and agency framework to work–family balance. *The Annals of the American Academy of Political and Social Science, 624*, 214–233.

(2009b). Applying Sens Capabilities Framework to Work Family Balance within a European Context: Theoretical and Empirical Challenges. *REC-WP Working Papers on the Reconciliation of Work and Welfare in Europe, 03–2009* 6–47.

Höge, T. (2009). When work strain transcends psychological boundaries: An inquiry into the relationship between time pressure, irritation, work–family conflict and psychosomatic complaints. *Stress and Health, 25*, 41–51.

Hornung, S., & Glaser, J. (2009). Home-based telecommuting and quality of life: Further evidence on an employee-oriented human resource practice. *Psychological reports, 104*, 395–402.

Hornung, S., Glaser, J., Rouseau, D. M., Angerer, P., & Weigl, M. (2011). Employee-oriented leadership and quality of working life: mediating roles of idiosyncratic deals. *Psychological reports, 108*, 59–74.

House, R. J., Hanges, P. J., Javidan, M., Dorfman, P. W., & Gupta, V. (2004). *Culture, leadership, and organizations: The GLOBE study of 62 societies*. Thousand Oaks, CA: Sage.

Hughes, E. L., & Parkes, K. R. (2007). Work hours and well-being: The roles of work-time control and work–family interference. *Work & Stress, 21,* 264–278.

Jenson, J. (1989). Paradigms and political discourse: Protective legislation in France and the United States before 1914. *Canadian Journal of Political Science, 22,* 235–258.

Jesuino, J. C. (2002). Latin Europe cluster: From south to north. *Journal of World Business, 37,* 81–89.

Karatepe, O.M., & Kilic, H. (2007). Relationships of supervisor support and conflicts in the work–family interface with the selected job outcomes of frontline employees. *Tourism Management, 28,* 238–252.

 (2009). The effects of two directions of conflict and facilitation on frontline employees' job outcomes. *The Service Industries Journal, 29,* 977–993.

Karatepe, O.M., & Uludag, O. (2007). Conflict, exhaustion, and motivation: A study of frontline employees in Northern Cyprus hotels. *Hospitality Management, 26,* 645–665.

 (2008). Affectivity, conflicts in the work–family interface, and hotel employee outcomes. *International Journal of Hospitality Management, 27*(**1**), 30–41.

Kinman, G (2009). Emotional labour and strain in "front-line" service employees: Does mode of delivery matter? *Journal of Managerial Psychology, 24,* 118–135.

Kossek, E., Lewis, S., & Hammer, L. (2010). Work family initiatives and organizational change: mixed messages in moving from the margins to the mainstream. *Human Relations, 61*(**3**), 3–19.

Kuchařová, V. (2009). Work–life balance: Societal and private influences. *Sociologický Časopis/Czech Sociological Review, 45,* 1283–1310.

Lewis, J. (2001). The decline of the male breadwinner model: implications for work and care. *Social Politics: International Studies in Gender, State & Society, 8,* 152–169.

Lewis, J., Campbell, M., & Huerta, C. (2008). Patterns of paid and unpaid work in Western Europe: gender, commodification, preferences and the implications for policy. *Journal of European Social Policy, 18*(**1**), 21–37.

Lunau, T., Bambra, C., Eikemo, T. A., van der Wel, K. A., & Dragano, N. (2014). A balancing act? Work–life balance, health and well-being in European welfare states. *European Journal of Public Health, 24,* 422–427. doi:10.1093/eurpub/cku010

Maurice, M., Sellier, F., & Silvestre, J. J. (1986). *The Social Foundations of Industrial Power: A Comparison of France and Germany.* Cambridge, MA: MIT Press.

McGinnity, F., & Calvert, E. (2009). Work–life conflict and social inequality in Western Europe. *Social Indicators Research, 93*(3), 489–508.

Meijman, T. F., & Mulder, G. (1998). Psychological aspects of workload. *Handbook of Work and Organizational Psychology. Volume 2.*

Molino, M., Ghislieri, C., & Cortese, C.G. (2013). When work enriches family-life: The mediational role of professional development opportunities. *Journal of Workplace Learning, 25,* 98–113.

Montgomery, A. J., Panagopolou, E., & Benos, A. (2006). Work–family interference as a mediator between job demands and job burnout among doctors. *Stress and Health, 22,* 203–212.

Moreno-Jiménez, B., Mayo, M., Sanz-Vergel, A.I., Geurts, S., Rodríguez-Muñoz, A., & Garrosa, E. (2009). Effects of work–family conflict on employees' well-being: The moderating role of recovery strategies. *Journal of Occupational Health Psychology, 14,* 427–440.

Myrskylä, M., Kohler, H. P., & Billari, F. C. (2009). Advances in development reverse fertility declines. *Nature, 460*, 741–743.

Netemeyer, R. G., Boles, J. S., & McMurrian, R. (1996). Development and validation of work–family conflict and family–work conflict scales. *Journal of Applied Psychology, 81*, 400–410.

Niedhammer, I., Sultan-Taïeb, H., Chastang, J. F., Vermeylen, G., & Parent-Thirion, A. (2012). Exposure to psychosocial work factors in 31 European countries. *Occupational Medicine, 62*, 196–202.

Noor, N. M. (2003). Work-and family-related variables, work–family conflict and women's well-being: Some observations. *Community, Work & Family, 6*, 297–319.

Noor, N. M. (2004). Work–family conflict, work-and family-role salience, and women's well-being. *The Journal of Social Psychology, 144*, 389–406.

Oláh, L. S. (2015). Changing families in the European Union: Trends and policy implications. *Families and Societies: Working Paper Series, 44*, 2–54.

Russo, M., & Buonocore, F. (2012). The relationship between work–family enrichment and nurse turnover. *Journal of Managerial Psychology, 27*, 216–236.

Sánchez-Cabezudo, S., & López Peláez, A. (2014). Social work with middle-class Spanish families: The challenge of the work–family conflict. *International Journal of Social Welfare, 23*, 100–111.

Sanz-Vergel, A. I., Demerouti, E., Moreno-Jiménez, B., & Mayo, M. (2010). Work–family balance and energy: A day-level study on recovery conditions. *Journal of Vocational Behavior, 76*, 118–130.

Schaufeli, W. B., & Bakker, A. B. (2004). Job demands, job resources, and their relationship with burnout and engagement: A multi-sample study. *Journal of Organizational Behavior, 25*, 293–315.

Schaufeli, W. B., Leiter, M. P., Maslach, C., & Jackson, S. E. (1996). Maslach Burnout Inventory—General Survey. In C. Maslach, S. E. Jackson, & M. P. Leiter (Eds.), *Maslach Burnout Inventory—Test manual* (3rd ed, pp. 22–26). Palo Alto, CA: Consulting Psychologists Press.

Schaufeli, W. B., & Taris, T. W. (2014). A critical review of the Job Demands-Resources Model: Implications for improving work and health. In G.F. Bauer & O. Hämming (Eds.), *Bridging Occupational, Organizational and Public Health* (pp. 43–68). The Netherlands: Springer.

Sen, A. (1992). *Inequality reexamined*. Oxford: Oxford University Press.
    Conceptualizing and measuring poverty. *Poverty and Inequality, 30*–46.

Simbula, S. (2010). Daily fluctuations in teachers' well-being: A diary study using the job demands-resources model. *Anxiety, Stress, & Coping, 23*, 563–584.

Spector, P. E., Allen, T. D., Poelmans, S. A., Lapierre, L. M., Cooper, C. L., Michael, O. D., . . . & Brough, P. (2007). Cross-national differences in relationships of work demands, job satisfaction, and turnover intentions with work–family conflict. *Personnel Psychology, 60*, 805–835.

Steiber, N. (2009). Reported levels of time-based and strain-based conflict between work and family roles in Europe: A multilevel approach. *Social Indicators Research, 93*, 469–488.

Steinmetz, H., Frese, M., & Schmidt, P. (2008). A longitudinal panel study on antecedents and outcomes of work–home interference. *Journal of Vocational Behavior, 73*, 231–241.

Strandh, M., & Nordenmark, M. (2006). The interference of paid work with household demands in different social policy contexts: perceived work–household conflict in

Sweden, the UK, the Netherlands, Hungary, and the Czech Republic. *The British Journal of Sociology, 57*, 597–617.

Swanson, V., & Power, K. G. (1999). Stress, satisfaction and role conflict in dual-doctor partnerships. *Community, Work & Family, 2*, 67–88.

Szabo, E., Brodbeck, F. C., Den Hartog, D. N., Reber, G., Weibler, J., & Wunderer, R. (2002). The Germanic Europe cluster: Where employees have a voice. *Journal of World Business, 37*, 55–68.

Van der Lippe, T., Jager, A., & Kops, Y. (2006). Combination pressure the paid work–family balance of men and women in European countries. *Acta Sociologica, 49*, 303–319.

Van Veldhoven, M. J., & Beijer, S. E. (2012). Workload, Work-to-Family Conflict, and Health: Gender Differences and the Influence of Private Life Context. *Journal of Social Issues, 68*, 665–683.

Vercruyssen, A., Roose, H., & Van de Putte, B. (2011). Underestimating busyness: Indications of nonresponse bias due to work–family conflict and time pressure. *Social Science Research, 40*, 1691–1701.

Vercruyssen, A., & Van de Putte, B. (2013). Work–family conflict and stress: indications of the distinctiveness of role combination stress for Belgian working mothers. *Community, Work & Family, 16*, 351–371.

Wille, B., De Fruyt, F., & Feys, M. (2013). Big five traits and intrinsic success in the new career era: A 15-year longitudinal study on employability and work–family conflict. *Applied Psychology: An International Review, 61*, 124–156.

14 A Review of Work–Family Research in Central and Eastern Europe

Sara Tement

Reconciling work and family is a goal shared by many people across many countries, yet the understanding of how this goal can be reached may differ and is often uniquely shaped by factors that lie beyond the individual. Arguably, countries in Central and Eastern Europe (CEE) experienced similar historical transitions, adopted comparable policies, and formed collective identities, which laid the groundwork for common threats and opportunities in managing the work–family interface (Trefalt, Drnovšek, Svetina-Nabergoj, & Adlešič, 2013). The CEE region encompasses countries which are geographically located in central and central-eastern Europe and experienced major changes in their socio economic systems in terms of moving beyond state-socialist systems to a free-market economy (e.g., Kuitto, 2016). Although the delineation is often not clear, the literature predominantly views Estonia, Lithuania, and Latvia (i.e., Baltic countries), Slovenia and Croatia (i.e., countries of former Yugoslavia), Poland, Czech Republic, Slovakia, and Hungary (sometimes referred to as Visegrad Group, an economic and political alliance), and Bulgaria and Romania, which are full members of the European Union (EU), as most representative for "countries in transition" in CEE.

Recent work–family literature has, in fact, acknowledged that a specific national context reflected in a number of institutional and cultural factors has the potential to determine individual experiences of the intersection between work and family (Ollier-Malaterre, 2016; Powell, Francesco, & Ling, 2009; Trefalt et al., 2013). Institutional factors include public policies and national legislation that provide structure to nations and their economies, organizations, and families and thus regulate individual action and place constraints upon it (Ollier-Malaterre & Foucreault, in press). Examples of these factors are paid sick leave, parental leave, and national labor laws or employment relationship acts. However, they also encompass informal rules and regulations. Ollier-Malaterre and Foucreault (2017), for instance, discuss social and economic structures, such as extent of gender equality or the state of the economy within this context. Cultural factors, on the other hand, are solely informal values, assumptions, and beliefs that are shared between individuals, are transmitted over generations, and exist within a specific institutional context (Ollier-Malaterre & Foucreault 2017; Schooler, 1996).

The author would like to thank Rudi Klanjšek for his constructive comments on an earlier version of the chapter.

Cultural factors can be understood by gaining insight into how individuals with a common historical background view and approach societal problems (Hofstede, 2005).

The specific challenges of combining work and family in the CEE region have not received much attention in the past literature (Mihelič, 2014a; Trefalt et al., 2013). The present chapter strives to address this by providing a review of work–family reconciliation in CEE countries, including a description of the national context, specific research challenges, and main findings. The chapter opens with a brief description of similarities and differences between CEE countries in terms of historical developments, national policies, as well as cultural factors shaping the work and family context. However, a thorough review of policies, standards of living, working conditions, and family structures is beyond the scope of this chapter and can be found in statistical yearbooks (e.g., Eurofound, 2014) and other publications (Schulze & Gergoric, 2015). The chapter further emphasizes theoretical and measurement issues in work–family research in this region. Next, key empirical findings are discussed, including the identification of both unique aspects of the studies and aspects which frequently emerge in work–family research from other regions. The last part of the chapter highlights main gaps in work–family research within CEE countries and discusses implications for future research in the region and across other countries.

The Work Context in Central and Eastern Europe

Countries within the CEE region show several cultural, political, and economic differences, yet all share the background of a system which was aimed at erasing inequalities and providing social justice. Throughout the region in the pre-transition period after World War II, the government secured full-time employment for workers and guaranteed universal health care, free education at all levels, and subsidized housing (Berend, 2009). On the downside, CEE countries had mostly one-party, non-parliamentary (hence non-democratic) regimes (Flere & Klanjšek, 2014; Schwartz & Bardi, 1997). Their economies were hampered by numerous inefficiencies, including bureaucratization, institutional unresponsiveness, and low productivity. Due to a non-competitive market and lack of foreign investments that both stifled innovations, the dominant industries mostly relied on outdated technology. In the late 1980s and early 1990s, several CEE countries started their independence and transition processes (e.g., dissolution of the Soviet Union, breakup of Yugoslavia) which brought political (e.g., countries moved toward a democratic system), economic (e.g., privatization, liberalization, exposure to international competition), and social changes (e.g., increased unemployment, inequality, and poverty) (Berend, 2009; Kuitto, 2016). This included significant changes in labor markets. For example, unemployment rates between 1990 to 2000 increased from virtually zero to double-digit numbers, with most dramatic increases in Slovakia (18.8% in 2000), Lithuania (16.4% in 2000), Bulgaria (16.4% in 2000), and Poland (16.1% in 2000) (Berend, 2009; Eurostat, 2012).

After a period of recovery, the economic crises of 2008 again obstructed employment possibilities in the CEE region (Eurofound, 2013), further influencing employees' perceptions and attitudes. For instance, employees increasingly have high job insecurity perceptions. For example, in Slovenia and Latvia the percentage of those who reported fearing that they may lose their job in the near future, increased from 8.8% to 33.7%, and from 13.0% to 25.4% from 2007 to 2012, respectively (Eurofound, 2013). Another indication of demanding work conditions can be found in the latest European Working Conditions Survey (Holman, 2013). Namely, data suggest that CEE countries exhibit a higher proportion of high-strain jobs compared to other country clusters (i.e., those with a social democratic welfare regime, including the Nordic countries; those with a continental/conservative welfare regime, such as Austria or Germany; those with a liberal welfare regime such as the United Kingdom; those with a Southern European/Mediterranean regime, such as Italy or Spain). Moreover, jobs in CEE countries lag behind in terms of pay with lowest mean gross annual earnings compared to other EU countries, with the biggest gaps in Romania and Bulgaria (Eurostat, 2012). The region is also characterized by very low shares of part-time employment (Eurostat, 2012), presumably due to economic strain, policy drawbacks, and limited recognition of the business case among employers (den Dulk, Peters, Poutsma, & Ligthart, 2010; Kanjuo Mrčela & Černigoj Sadar, 2011).

In the face of the economic transitions and downturns in CEE countries, some of the previously highly developed social polices gradually started to dissolve (den Dulk et al., 2010). In the past three decades, CEE countries have developed a new welfare model grounded in their socialist roots and influenced by policy imitation and several austerity measures (Kuitto, 2016). Several authors have argued that the institutional context of CEE countries is "hybrid" between the three traditional welfare regime contexts (i.e., liberal, continental/conservative, and social democratic) (Esping-Andersen, 1990). According to Esping-Andersen (1990), the institutional context of countries can be defined by determining the sources of support or welfare (i.e., state, market, family). In liberal welfare states (e.g., the United Kingdom, the United States), support for employees is contingent on market forces and its ability to provide social benefits and services. State-provided benefits are modest and intended for those who are unable support themselves. In conservative states (e.g., Germany, Austria) welfare is grounded on contributions collected from employers and employees. Traditionally, policies in such states were aimed at strengthening the family as a main source of support (e.g., benefits for single-earner families, generous part-time employment opportunities for women). The social democratic welfare state model found in Nordic countries is universalistic and most generous in state-provided support for unemployment, sickness leave, and health care. Welfare is granted independently of labor market participation, whereas policies and benefits do not increase dependence on family support (e.g., through high quality public childcare). Mimicking the continental/conservative model, welfare benefits (e.g., sickness insurance) in CEE countries are based on moderate to relatively strong contributions from employees and employers (Kuitto, 2016). However, several countries such as Slovenia, Czech Republic, Latvia, and Estonia exhibit universalistic elements (e.g., income replacement benefits in case of unemployment) and are thus more aligned with the social democratic welfare state model. It also appears that there is no general agreement in policies between specific CEE countries (e.g., Kuitto, 2016).

Hofstede's cultural comparison studies (2005) and related findings from the GLOBE project (House, Hanges, Javidan, Dorfman & Gupta, 2004) may yield some insight into how the cultural context shapes work attitudes and job strains in CEE countries. In general, CEE countries have been identified as high power distance countries, meaning they exhibit high acceptance of hierarchical order, authority, and high dependence of subordinates on supervisors (Hofstede, 2005). Most of the CEE countries are also considered collectivistic (e.g., Berend, 2009). The large cross-cultural GLOBE dataset confirmed these propositions by showing that several CEE countries exhibit high institutional collectivism (e.g., practices which support collective action and collective distribution of resources), as well as in-group collectivism (i.e., individual expressions of pride and loyalty to families and organizations) (Bakacsi, Sándor, András, & Viktor, 2002). Another important cultural influence may derive from higher levels of uncertainty avoidance in CEE, which refers to low resilience to ambiguous situations and high need for laws, rules, and regulations (Hofstede, 2005). When comparing values (i.e., desired state of affairs) and practices (i.e., actual states of affairs) reflected in the GLOBE survey, the desire for reducing uncertainty is more pronounced than the actual laws and regulations in these countries (Bakacsi et al., 2002).

In addition, CEE countries exhibit low to moderate performance orientation characterized by a lower sense of urgency, placing loyalty, belongingness, and harmony above competitiveness, as well as an avoidant attitude toward feedback at work. A recent report based on the European Values Survey may challenge these findings at a first glance, as "work centrality is substantially more dominant in Eastern Europe" (World Bank, 2016, p. 33). Yet, this importance of work in life may actually be extrinsically motivated due to economic strains in several CEE countries. It should be noted that cultural characteristics also vary significantly between countries, and the information stated above is simply overall trends. Altogether, CEE countries experienced a common past, which dramatically influenced the work context, yet developed in different directions and nowadays face specific challenges when "catching up" with Western countries (Berend, 2009).

The Family Context in Central and Eastern Europe

Family life in CEE countries was also very much under the influence of the state-socialist history and political, economic, and social transitions. The past regime between World War II and late 1980s/early 1990s, for instance, aimed at diminishing inequalities also within the families. The male-breadwinner model was not characteristic for the CEE region, as full-time employment was a given fact and female labor force participation was systematically encouraged. However, traditional labor division was encouraged by state-sponsored benefits intended exclusively for mothers (e.g., parental leave) (Pascall & Kwak, 2005). Nowadays, the CEE region also has several positive and negative outliers with respect to gender equality.

In recent years, several countries have experienced relatively high gaps between male and female employment (e.g., Czech Republic, Romania, Slovakia), smaller differences are present only in the Baltic countries and Slovenia (Eurostat, 2015). Slovenia, for instance, is among the few countries where female labor participation increases after parenthood and even after having two or more children (e.g., Michoń, 2015). Moreover, in Slovenia and Poland, the gender pay gap is very small, even compared with the EU average (2.3% and 4.5%, respectively, compared with the average of 16.1%; Eurostat, 2015). On the other hand, Estonia exhibits one of the highest gender pay gaps (27.3%).

In terms of family structure, pre-transition CEE countries were characterized by high rates of marriages, relatively young age at first marriage, and childbearing exclusively within marriage. After the 1990s, fertility rates have declined notably and family formation has been delayed (Thornton & Philipov, 2009). Moreover, the general aging of the population has affected several CEE countries (Botev, 2012). For instance, Slovenia and the Baltic states accounted for some of the highest increases in the shares of people aged 65 years or over between 1990 and 2010 in the EU (5.9% in Slovenia, 5.6% in Latvia, 5.5% in Estonia, and 5.3% in Lithuania; Eurostat, 2012). Given the trends of delayed childbearing and aging population, many working-age individuals may be "sandwiched" between child and elder care responsibilities (Neal & Hammer, 2007).

During the state-socialist period between the late 1940s and early 1990s, family formation was very much encouraged and facilitated by many policies, such as cash childcare allowances and paid parental leave (e.g., Ferrarini & Sjöberg, 2010). Higher fertility rates in the pre-transition period can be also traced back to higher job security, low-cost housing, free education, and free health care. In the 1990s, several cuts were made in the overall generous family policies (Abendroth & den Dulk, 2011; Ferrarini & Sjöberg, 2010). For instance, in some countries, childcare allowances are now provided only for low-income families and for those with disabilities. Nevertheless, paid maternity, parental, and, in some cases, paternity leave remain among the pillars of social policy in CEE countries. In fact, CEE countries have a higher average length of maternity leave (approximately 27 weeks) than other EU countries (20.4 weeks) (Schulze & Gergoric, 2015). In several countries, the compensation rate during maternity leave is provided for the whole period and equals the income earned prior to childbirth (Lithuania, Estonia, Croatia, and Slovenia). Paternity leave is present to a lesser extent. The Czech Republic and Slovakia do not provide any paternity leave, whereas Slovenia provides one of the longest paid paternity leaves, which is also fully compensated. Parental leave varies substantially, but in most countries can be taken by both parents. Due to high state involvement in providing family-friendly policies, employer involvement in terms of flexible work arrangements and benefits is lower (den Dulk et al., 2010). For this reason, some managers in CEE countries may even hold negative attitudes toward organizational benefits (e.g., den Dulk et al., 2011).

Additionally, CEE families exhibit several distinct features in terms of cultural contexts. Despite the historical trends and generous policies fostering equality, the underlying reasons behind engagement of women in paid work may be economic necessity rather than egalitarian attitudes and values (Schwartz & Bardi, 1997). In general, the GLOBE project findings point to rather moderate gender egalitarian practices and values, which are reflected in average occupational gender segregation and involvement of women in decision-making roles (Bakacsi et al., 2002). A recent analysis of World Values Survey data (i.e., survey reflecting attitudes and values in forty-seven countries since 1981) in Poland and the Baltic states, for instance, has found that women's life satisfaction is still closely linked to childbearing, and the fear of negative consequences for children's well-being when mothers are employed has increased (Michoń, 2010). The prevailing attitude in some countries (e.g., Hungary) favors child care provision by the mother rather than in organized child care facilities (e.g., Michoń, 2015). Positive attitudes toward child care provision within the family may also be reflected in the high involvement of grandparents in raising children (Botev, 2012), another characteristic of CEE countries. In general, the CEE countries that are more economically developed, that exhibit higher education levels of women, and that place less importance on religious institutions, are more supportive of dual-earner families and gender equality (Voicu, 2010).

Theoretical Issues in Work and Family Research in Central and Eastern Europe

Institutional and cultural characteristics have been found to determine work–family reconciliation at least to a certain extent (e.g., Allen, French, Dumani & Shockley, 2015; Allen et al., 2014). Interestingly, work–family research in the CEE region makes little reference to the specifics of the national context in theoretical conceptions and empirical studies. In general, samples from CEE countries have been examined as a part of cross-national comparison studies or in separate studies. Only a few studies published rather recently in international peer-reviewed journals are based solely on samples from CEE countries. Most of them focus on work–family conflict (WFC), work–family enrichment (WFE), or examine both concepts simultaneously. Many theoretical perspectives that have been used in work–family research developed in the West have been carried over to the CEE context. Examples include role theory (e.g., Greenhaus & Beutell, 1985), the conservation of resources theory (Hobfoll, 1989), job-demands resources model (Bakker & Demerouti, 2007), and identity theory (Stryker & Burke, 2000).

On the other hand, the CEE region has been increasingly covered in cross-national comparisons which rely on theoretical frameworks elucidating the impact of institutional and cultural factors. Studies have either focused on cross-national differences in institutional factors (e.g., 'family-friendly' policies, availability of part-time work; Strandh & Nordenmark, 2006), cultural factors (e.g., culture dimensions of the GLOBE model, Ollo-López & Goñi-Legaz, 2017), or considered both influences simultaneously (e.g., gender egalitarianism, 'family-friendly' policies, van der Lippe, Jager, & Kops, 2006). In some cases, researchers have used differences between countries as proxies for differences in policy contexts or welfare systems (e.g., Strandh & Nordenmark, 2006). Others have directly focused on social policies, such as paid sick leave, parental leave, or annual vacation leave, and collapsed data across a wide range of countries (e.g., Allen et al., 2014). This dichotomy aligns with what Powell et al. (2009) termed culture-as-referent versus culture-as-dimension studies. Culture-as referent studies derive hypotheses from potential cultural attributes of specific countries, but use country itself as the grouping variable, whereas culture-as-dimension studies explicitly measure or impute cultural dimensions. A combined approach has also been utilized, where country differences were hypothesized based on distinct cultural values, but inferences about cultural values driving those differences were verified using the results of the GLOBE project (Ollo-López & Goñi-Legaz, 2017; Spector et al., 2007). In terms of specific cultural dimensions, gender egalitarianism, individualism/collectivism, power distance, uncertainty avoidance, and humane orientation (i.e., high importance of values such as fairness, friendliness, and altruism; House et al., 2004) have all been implicated, yet the precise role of these dimensions when predicting WFC is not straightforward (Ollo-López & Goñi-Legaz, 2017).

Generally, studies in the CEE countries have relied on theoretical models which are not unique to the region. Recently, Trefalt et al. (2013) proposed a theoretical framework which may be specifically utilized in the context of CEE countries. The authors argue that transition countries are specifically faced with structural misalignment (i.e., lack of fit between higher level structures, such a legislation, and lower level structures, such as organizations and families), social, economic, and temporal comparisons (i.e., comparing one's status pre- and post-transition and with the status of past generations), as well as choice overload (i.e., burden by the sudden occurrence of a multitude of choices). It is further proposed that sudden changes prevented a gradual alignment of higher and lower level structures (e.g., working schedules have changed, yet child care facilities have not adapted their opening hours), which in turn may be associated with higher levels of WFC and lower levels of WFE compared to traditional capitalist countries. Trefalt et al. (2013) also propose that changes are accompanied by reflections on whether one is better or worse off in comparison with a previous point in time and with older family members. As countries in transition experience a decline in social security, they may experience worse outcomes due to comparison processes. On the other hand, as transition to a free-market economy brings about better incomes and more challenging jobs, positive outcomes for the intersection of work and family may be expected as well. Additionally, the authors pointed out that in past state-socialist systems, choices in terms of products, services, and life paths were notably restricted. The sudden multitude of choices after transition is further hypothesized to have negative effects on work–family reconciliation.

Methodological Issues in Work and Family Research in Central and Eastern Europe

Past studies involving the CEE region are either based on large international databases, focus on the comparison of a few different countries, or include CEE samples only. To date, the CEE region has been represented in the Collaborative

International Study of Managerial Stress (CISMS, e.g., Spector et al., 2007), European Quality of Life Survey (EQLS, e.g., Ollo-López & Goñi-Legaz, 2017), European Social Survey (ESS, e.g., Steiber, 2009), ISSP – International Social Survey Programme (ISSP, e.g., Stier, Lewin-Epstein, & Braun, 2012), and the Household, Work and Flexibility survey (HWF survey, e.g., van der Lippe et al., 2006).

Cross-national comparison studies as well as studies based on a single country sample generally follow the established approaches in construct measurement such as the use of validated WFC scales by Carlson, Kacmar, and Williams (2000) or Netemeyer, Boles, and McMurrian (1996). Most work–family research in the region has also recognized the bi-directional nature of WFC (i.e., work-to-family and family-to-work; Mihelič, 2014a, 2014b; Spector et al., 2007; Tement & Korunka, 2015). However, only a few studies examined WFC dimensions separately (time, strain, behavior; Spector et al., 2007; Tement & Korunka, 2013). Moreover, ways by which work and family may benefit the other domains has to date received attention only in single-sample studies (i.e., work-to-family and family-to-work enrichment; Mihelič, 2014a, 2014b; Tement & Korunka, 2013, 2015). It is also important to note that the domain of reference has mostly been the family and rarely other activities outside work (for an exception, see Šverko, Arambašić, & Galešić, 2002).

In cross-national comparison studies, information about questionnaire development, reliability, validity, and measurement equivalence across countries is not provided in every study. However, most of these studies followed strict guidelines of questionnaire development and validation. The European Social Survey, for instance, employed a methodology involving stages of translation, review, adjudication, pretesting, and documentation which correspond to best practice recommendations (Schaffer & Riordan, 2003). In general, studies within the CEE region report psychometric properties of the translated questionnaires mostly by using reliability and (confirmatory) factor analyses (e.g., Mihelič, 2014a, 2014b; Tement & Korunka, 2013).

Some studies based on only one sample from a CEE country focused on heterogeneous datasets, yet other studies examine specific occupational groups, such as managers (Mihelič, 2014b), nurses (Rantanen, Kinnunen, Mauno & Tement, 2013), employees in the hospitality industry (Karatepe & Karadas, 2014), and retail salespeople (Netemeyer, Brashear-Alejandro, & Boles, 2004). These studies predominantly relied on convenience sampling and the snowball method of data collection. Of the studies reviewed for this chapter, none used a daily diary design, only one used a longitudinal design (two weeks in-between three measurement waves, Karatepe & Karadas, 2014), and only one study was identified that used a dyadic study design (dual-earner couples, Obradović & Čudina-Obradović, 2009).

Generally, studies from CEE countries strongly draw from established work–family research in terms of content, but they seem to pay less attention to advancements in terms methodological approaches (e.g., Lapierre & McMullan, 2016). Presumably, specific expectations regarding social factors may discourage researchers from this region to use probability sampling and advanced research methods. As distrust in organizations, institutions, and politics is particularly high in CEE countries (e.g., Eurostat, 2015), researchers may fear low study motivation and low response rates. In less populous countries, such as Slovenia (total population: 2.06 m) and the Baltic countries (total population – Estonia: 1.31 m; Latvia: 1.99 m; Lithuania: 2.92 m; Eurostat, 2016), researchers may additionally be concerned about "over-surveying", which may not only contribute to low study motivation but may also threaten the validity of the results.

Key Findings in Work and Family Research in Central and Eastern Europe

Cross-National Work–Family Research

Several cross-national research projects have focused on WFC. Using data from the HWF study, van der Lippe and colleagues (2006) tested the impact of the national context and individual-level factors such as work hours or age of children on WFC. The study found that CEE countries (i.e., Czech Republic, Romania, Bulgaria, and Hungary) experienced less WFC than western countries such as the Netherlands, the United Kingdom, and Sweden, possibly due to a more traditional division of labor in CEE countries. Slovenia, however, represented an outlier, as women especially reported higher WFC. Utilizing the HWF dataset, Strandh and Nordenmark (2006) further explored which factors are likely to account for the cross-national differences in WFC. Three conclusions about CEE countries can be drawn from their findings. First, women from the Czech Republic and Hungary experience less WFC than women from Sweden, whereas they did not differ from women in the Netherlands or the United Kingdom. Second, differences between men from CEE and other European countries were less pronounced, as only men from Hungary experienced lower WFC than Swedish men. Third, women's WFC in CEE countries was found to be lower compared to other countries even after accounting for differences in household composition (i.e., working partner), work hours, and occupational status. However, other research based on large datasets has not replicated these findings. Specifically, based on data from EQLS, Ollo-López and Goñi-Legaz (2017) found that CEE and Mediterranean countries (e.g., Greece, Portugal, Spain) tended to exhibit higher levels of WFC compared to Scandinavian countries. The robustness of cross-national differences in WFC is further called into question based on analyses of the ESS data, in which country differences explained only a small amount of variation in WFC (Steiber, 2009). A variety of factors may explain these inconsistencies in cross-national differences (e.g., gender composition, inclusion of countries in specific datasets, the way WFC is measured). It is also important to keep in mind that there is rather large variation in WFC experiences within various CEE countries, as suggested by the findings from the ISSP (Stier et al., 2012).

Moving beyond mean-level differences in WFC, cross-national research projects have focused also on the question of whether institutional and cultural factors moderate the link between work or family characteristics and WFC. In the CISMS, Spector et al. (2007) grouped CEE countries along with Asia and Latin America to a collectivist cluster and compared them with an Anglo country cluster when predicting time- and strain-based WFC from workload. The relation between workload and WFC was found to be stronger for Anglo countries compared to all three groups of collectivistic countries, thus confirming that assumption that in collectivistic countries additional work investment may not disturb family life, but is rather perceived as a contribution to it. Spector et al. (2007) also tested the association between WFC and work attitudes (i.e., turnover intentions, job satisfaction), and found a null effect in CEE and other collectivistic countries, but a significant, negative association for Anglo countries. A possible explanation for such findings is the consideration of interests of coworkers, supervisors, and organizations above self-interest in collectivistic countries, resulting in weaker reactions to WFC.

However, these findings have not been extensively replicated in other research. Hill, Yang, Hawkins, and Ferris (2004), for instance, tested a model linking various work and family demands to forms of WFC and organizational consequences. The model was invariant across several country clusters, one of which was titled "West-developing" and included several CEE countries. Moreover, Netemeyer et al. (2004) examined the links between work-to-family and family-to-work conflict and various organizational outcomes (i.e., stress, performance, job satisfaction, and turnover intention) across employees in the United States, Puerto Rico, and Romania. None of the links between both aspects of WFC and organizational outcomes was notably different across countries. However, work-to-family conflict was more strongly related to job stress in Romania than in the other two countries. Support for similarities between countries was also found in the study by Rantanen and colleagues (2013). The authors used a person-oriented approach to test for the emergence of different clusters of work–family reconciliation in Slovenia (nurses) and several Finnish samples (nurses, social care workers, service sector employees). The different clusters, which were characterized by combinations of high versus low levels of WFC and WFE, were robust across both nations and occupations. Several differences in psychological well-being between the clusters were found. For instance, those in the cluster characterized by low WFC and high WFE exhibited higher life satisfaction and vigor at work compared to the high WFC and high WFE cluster. These differences were again cross-nationally invariant. In another comparison to the Nordic context, a qualitative study found differences in strategies of dealing with WFC among parents from Sweden and Slovenia, despite similar family policies in the two countries (Grönlund & Javornik, 2014). In sum, these mixed findings prevent strong conclusions about the CEE region in comparison to other countries.

CEE-Based Work–Family Research

Single-sample studies from CEE countries have tended to focus on correlates of WF constructs. In a study of Slovenian employees, Tement and Korunka (2013) found that job demands such as workload, were linked to higher WFC and lower WFE. The study also offered a more nuanced view on different forms of work-to-family conflict (i.e., time, strain, behavior) and enrichment (i.e., affect, capital, development), with comparable results across the dimensions. Job resources were found to diminish WFC and to foster WFE. Interestingly, the links from autonomy and coworker support to WFC were not consistently negative, which contradicts meta-analytic findings (Michel, Kotrba, Mitchelson, Clark, & Baltes, 2011), and potentially highlights a culture-specific view of these job resources. Speculatively, this may be because in higher power distance countries (like Slovenia), greater autonomy at work may be seen as unfavorable, as it places greater responsibility in employees' rather than in the manager's or employer's hands. In another study among Slovenian managers, Mihelič (2014b) found that job commitment predicted both time and strain-based WFC, which is in line with previous findings (Michel et al., 2011). Generally, WFC and WFE were predicted by a series of general work characteristics, such as work hours (Tement & Korunka, 2013).

Compared to work characteristics, antecedents in the family domain are less frequently examined in CEE countries. Parental status has been found to predict higher WFC (Obradović & Čudina-Obradović, 2009; Tement & Korunka, 2013), but also higher WFE in a Slovenian sample (Tement & Korunka, 2013). Parents who simultaneously cared for an elderly family member experienced higher WFC (Tement & Korunka, 2015). Moreover, child and elder care responsibilities moderated the link between job characteristics and WFC as well as WFE. Among others, the relation between workload and WFC was more pronounced for employed parents and those "sandwiched" between child and elder care. As different caregiving responsibilities have not received much attention within the work–family field, future studies in other countries are needed to elucidate whether this result can be generalized or is country-specific. In another study in Slovenia, greater marital commitment unexpectedly did not predict family-to-work conflict (Mihelič, 2014b). This finding can be traced back to high work centrality in Slovenia, where work is often valued over family life. As a consequence, family schedules need to comply with work schedules. However, a recent meta-analysis found that the link between marital commitment and family-to-work conflict is generally not pronounced (Michel et al., 2011). Thus, any conclusion about potential country specifics in terms of values and practices may be premature.

Work–family research within the CEE region has also acknowledged the role of personality in WFC and WFE. In a Romanian sample, Karatepe and Karadas (2014) found that psychological capital, encompassing self-efficacy, optimism, resilience, and hope, negatively predicted work-to-family as well as family-to-work conflict. Further drawing from personality perspectives, another study found that positive affectivity was linked to higher WFE, whereas negative affectivity was positively linked to WFC (Tement & Korunka, 2013). These two affective traits are also found to moderate the link between job characteristics and WFC/WFE. More specifically, negative affectivity was found to strengthen the positive relation between workload and WFC and weaken the negative relation between supervisor support and WFE. Positive affectivity, in contrast, buffered potential negative effects of variety on WFC and further intensified positive effect of autonomy on WFE. Given that personality reflects relatively uniform and universal patterns of thinking, feeling, and behaving with biological underpinnings, it is not surprising that results from CEE countries are the same as in other samples (Allen et al., 2012; Michel et al., 2011).

Studies in CEE countries have also found that WFC is associated with certain costs. Adam, Gyorffy, and Susanszky (2008) found positive associations between WFC and burnout among physicians from Hungary. Šverko and colleagues (2002) found that both work-to-family and family-to-work conflict predict lower well-being among Croatian employees with a higher level of education. More precisely, family-to-work conflict was associated with well-being to a smaller extent. Similar results were found in a study among hotel employees from Romania (Karatepe, 2013). These findings and the specific patterns are in line with meta-analyses on consequences of WFC (Allen, Herst, Bruck, & Sutton, 2000; Amstad, Meier, Fasel, Elfering, & Semmer, 2011) and are thus not unique for the CEE region. Further supporting the matching domain perspective (Amstad et al., 2011; Shockley & Singla, 2011), Mihelič (2014a) found that work-to-family conflict and enrichment are more strongly related to job satisfaction than conflict and enrichment stemming from the other direction (i.e., family-to-work).

Another study focused on well-being outcomes from a cross-domain rather than a matching-domain perspective (Mihelič, 2014b). Time-based work-to-family conflict predicted lower marital satisfaction, whereas time-based family-to-work conflict was linked to lower career satisfaction. Unexpectedly, strain-based family-to-work conflict was positively related to career satisfaction. This finding stands out and may reflect a specific notion of success at work in CEE countries. Handling stressful family issues at work may not be seen as disturbing, but instead may project an image of success and sacrifice for work, and thus foster career advancements. Challenging these findings, two studies found that family-to-work conflict was a stronger predictor of turnover intentions than work-to-family conflict (Karatepe & Karadas, 2014; Mihelič, 2014a). Outcomes of WFC have also been studied from a crossover perspective. A study of Croatian dual-earner couples found a bi-directional (from wives to husbands and vice versa) crossover effect (i.e., interpersonal dyadic transmission of experiences) of WFC on marriage quality, which again is in line with previous studies in the dyadic context (Westman, 2005). To summarize, work-to-family and family-to-work conflict have been associated with a range of negative outcomes which do not appear to be unique for the region. There is, however, some evidence that employees in CEE countries are more likely disturbed by family intrusions in the work domain than vice versa. Further supporting this argument, one cross-national comparison study found that getting a job which allows family time is not as valued in CEE countries as it is in the United States (Olson et al., 2006).

The Future of Work and Family Research in Central and Eastern Europe

Work–family research in the CEE region is still in its infancy. The present review suggests that research in the CEE region has an overemphasis on WFC, mimicking the broader work–family literature (Eby, Casper, Lockwood, Bordeaux, & Brinley, 2005). Additionally, studies exploring the interplay between institutional, cultural, and individual factors when predicting consequences of WFC and WFE are limited. Interestingly, work–family research in the CEE region also makes little reference to the specifics of the national context in theoretical conceptions and empirical studies. Based on the review, three possible additions to the literature could be identified. First, future research should closely examine antecedents of WFE and boundary management, as they are becoming increasingly important constructs in work–family literature. Second, more research is needed on a full range of outcomes of work–family reconciliation with the focus on how the national context shapes these interrelations. Third, scholars should further explore the specifics of the CEE region, which can, in turn, expand established theoretical perspectives.

As previously noted, WFE represents a distinct aspect of the work–family interface (Carlson, Kacmar, Wayne, & Grzywacz, 2006). Following the distinction between hygiene (i.e., factors which need to be maintained to prevent dissatisfaction) and motivation factors (i.e., factor which are needed to promote growth and motivation) (Herzberg, Mausner, & Snyderman, 1959), it may be assumed that some institutional factors are indispensable for preventing WFC, while others may contribute to WFE. The above proposition also opens the possibility for further cross-national research, as countries largely differ in the foundations of support (i.e., state, market or family) and additional support systems. Both the absence of WFC and the presence of WFE are crucial in order to secure a happy, healthy, and productive workforce, and thus need to be considered when mapping cross-national similarities and differences. As WFC and WFE may be experienced simultaneously (e.g., Rantanen et al., 2013), future work should be directed at further exploring whether different profiles of positive and negative work–family experiences differ based institutional and cultural influences.

Moreover, notably absent from the literature is research on work–family boundary management. As work is often placed above family life in CEE countries, work intrusions in the family domain and the motivation behind them should deserve closer attention. Arguably, in CEE countries such a behavior may be motivated by economic needs or job insecurity perceptions (e.g., World Bank, 2016). Previous research found that work-related activities during off-job time which are extrinsically motivated are associated with more negative consequences in terms of well-being than are intrinsically motivated work-related off-job activities (ten Brummelhuis & Trougakos, 2014). As high work intrusions in the family life may be extrinsically motivated in CEE countries, it may be assumed that employees in these countries may face more negative consequences compared to other countries where high work investment may be intrinsically motivated to a greater extent. This reasoning also opens up a more general discussion on the motivational underpinnings and consequences of boundary management, which should be explored in future studies.

As dual-earner couples have always been the norm in CEE countries, both men and women have repeatedly experienced tensions between work and family at least to a certain extent. Surprisingly, the literature in this region still focuses more closely on why WFC occurs rather than on its relationship with outcomes. A thorough examination of outcomes related to work performance and health has not been adequately covered in CEE research. A greater focus on these outcomes opens the possibility of relying on data other than self-reports, such as manager-rated job performance or objective physical health measures, which have been used in previous work–family studies in other national contexts (Lapierre & McMullan, 2016). Different institutional and cultural factors are also likely to determine the relations between different aspects of the work–family interface (i.e., WFC, WFE) and their outcomes (Spector et al., 2007). For instance, the possibility of care arrangements within the extended family, which are common in the CEE region, are likely to dampen the positive link between WFC and psychological strain (Grönlund & Javornik, 2014). This specific characteristic of the CEE region may again point to an important implication for work–family research outside the region. Drawing on the notion of homeostasis in the stress literature (Hobfoll, 1989), a person may strive to minimize the tension between work and family by all possible means of support and may choose from either state-level support, organizational-level support, or from support within the family. If one form of support is not available, presumably other forms will be utilized. As the mobilization of different systems of support and compensation of a potential breakdown in one system by another may take place on episodic or day-to-day basis or also across a longer period of time, this reasoning can also be incorporated in more advanced research designs (longitudinal or daily-diary research). For instance, on days when a care arrangement within the family is not available, an employee may experience greater WFC and greater negative consequences. Arguably, these assumptions have neither been tested nor acknowledged when explaining the role of the national context.

Recently, specific characteristics of the CEE region have been considered in a new theoretical framework (Trefalt et al., 2013). However, no study to date explicitly tested the proposed mechanisms. In addition, research should pay attention to unique tensions between institutional and cultural factors in CEE countries, which may become visible in individuals' behaviors related to work and family (e.g., Hofstede, 2005; Schooler, 1996). Unfairness perceptions due to provision of family-friendly workplace policies for parents (Parker & Allen, 2001), for instance, may escalate to a greater extent in CEE countries because of deeply rooted ideas of equal opportunities for everyone. Consequently, employees and employers may accept organizational benefits with reservations. Another overlooked theoretical issue when focusing on cultural factors affecting the work–family interface is the strength of norms. Cultural tightness and looseness reflect tolerance to deviant behavior, as well as the clarity and number of social norms within different life contexts (Gelfand et al., 2011). It may be argued that transition countries are "loose" cultures in terms of weak norms and a high tolerance for deviant behavior, as cultural, political, and economic stabilizations are still taking place. The few available studies, in fact, support these claims (Gelfand et al., 2011; Mandel & Realo, 2015). It may be of particular importance to study this relatively new notion or dimension of culture in CEE as well as other countries, as it may interact with other cultural and institutional characteristics. For instance, there is sometimes a fine line between use and abuse of work–family benefits in organizations (Kirby & Krone, 2002), which is more likely to be crossed in loose cultures where the collective pressure against such behavior is not as strong.

To conclude, CEE research has the potential to evolve in many fruitful directions. However, researchers may have to overcome several barriers to be able to align their research with that of other countries. Although CEE countries can hardly be considered as a uniform cluster and have developed in different directions in the past decades, research focusing on this region may have implications for the work–family literature in general. In this vein, Hagestad and Herlofson (2007) pointed out that CEE countries may "constitute compelling 'laboratories' for studying the complex interplay of culture, demographic structures and social policy" (p. 353).

References

Abendroth, A.-K., & den Dulk, L. (2011). Support for the work–life balance in Europe: The impact of state, workplace and family support on work–life balance satisfaction. *Work, Employment & Society, 25*, 234–256.

Adam, S., Gyorffy, Z., & Susanszky, E. (2008). Physician burnout in Hungary—A potential role for work–family conflict. *Journal of Health Psychology, 13*, 847–856.

Allen, T. D., French, K. A., Dumani, S., & Shockley, K. M. (2015). Meta-analysis of work–family conflict mean differences: Does national context matter? *Journal of Vocational Behavior, 90*, 90–100.

Allen, T. D., Herst, D. E. L., Bruck, C. S., & Sutton, M. (2000). Consequences associated with work-to-family conflict: A review and agenda for future research. *Journal of Occupational Health Psychology, 5*, 278–308.

Allen, T. D., Johnson, R. C., Saboe, K. N., Cho, E., Dumani, S., & Evans, S. (2012). Dispositional variables and work–family conflict: A meta-analysis. *Journal of Vocational Behavior, 80*, 17–26.

Allen, T. D., Lapierre, L., Spector, P. E., Poelmans, S. A. Y., O'Driscoll, M., Sanchez, J. I., Woo, J.-M. (2014). The link between national paid leave policy and work–family conflict among married working parents. *Applied Psychology: International Review, 63*, 5–28.

Amstad, F. T., Meier, L. L., Fasel, U., Elfering, A., & Semmer, N. K. (2011). A meta-analysis of work–family conflict and various outcomes with a special emphasis on cross-domain versus matching-domain relations. *Journal of Occupational Health Psychology, 16*, 151–169.

Bakacsi, G., Sándor, T., András, K., & Viktor, I. (2002). Eastern European cluster: Tradition and transition. *Journal of World Business, 37*, 69–80.

Bakker, A. B., & Demerouti, E. (2007). The job demands–resources model: State of the art. *Journal of Managerial Psychology, 22*, 309–328.

Berend, T. I. (2009). *From the Soviet bloc to the European Union: The economic and social transformation of Central and Eastern Europe since 1973*. Cambridge, UK: Cambridge University Press.

Botev, N. (2012). Population ageing in Central and Eastern Europe and its demographic and social context. *European Journal of Ageing*, *9*, 69–79.

Carlson, D. S., Kacmar, K. M., Wayne, J. H., & Grzywacz, J. G. (2006).Measuring the positive side of work–family interface: Development and validation of work–family enrichment scale. *Journal of Vocational Behavior*, *68*, 131–164.

Carlson, D. S., Kacmar, K. M., & Williams, L. J. (2000). Construction and initial validation of a multidimensional measure of work–family conflict. *Journal of Vocational Behavior*, *56*, 249–276.

den Dulk, L., Peters, P., Poutsma, E., & Ligthart, P. E. (2010). The extended business case for childcare and leave arrangements in Western and Eastern Europe. *Baltic Journal of Management*, *5*, 156–184.

den Dulk, L., Peper, A., Sadar, N. Č, Lewis, S., Smithson, J., & van Doorne-Huiskes, J. (2011). Work family and managerial attitudes and practices in the European work-place: Comparing Dutch, British and Slovenian financial sector managers. *Social Politics*, *18*, 300–329.

Eby, L. T., Casper, W. J., Lockwood, A., Bordeaux, C., & Brinley, A. (2005). Work and family research in IO/OB: Content analysis and review of the literature (1980–2002). *Journal of Vocational Behavior*, *66*, 124–197.

Esping-Andersen, G. (1990). *The three worlds of welfare capitalism*. Princeton, NJ: Princeton University Press.

Eurofound. (2013). *Impact of the crisis on working conditions in Europe*. Retrieved from: http://www.eurofound.europa.eu/observatories/eurwork/comparative-information/impact-of-the-crisis-on-working-conditions-in-europe

Eurofound. (2014). *Third European quality of life survey – Quality of life in Europe: Families in the economic crisis*. Luxembourg: Publications Office of the European Union.

Eurostat. (2012). *Europe in figures – Eurostat yearbook 2012*. Luxembourg: Publications Office of the European Union.

Eurostat. (2015). *Quality of life – facts and views*. Luxembourg: Publications Office of the European Union.

Eurostat. (2016). *Population on 1 January*. Retrieved from http://ec.europa.eu/eurostat/tgm/table.do?tab=table&plugin=1&language=en&pcode=tps00001

Ferrarini, T., & Sjöberg, O. (2010). Social policy and health: Transition countries in a comparative perspective. *International Journal of Social Welfare*, *19*, S60–S88.

Flere, S., & Klanjšek, R. (2014). Was Tito's Yugoslavia totalitarian? *Communist and Post-Communist Studies*, *47*, 231–245.

Gelfand, M. J., Raver, J. L., Nishii, L., Leslie, L. M., Lun, J., Lim, B. C., Yamaguchi, S. (2011). Differences between tight and loose cultures: A 33-nation study. *Science*, *332*, 1100–1104.

Greenhaus, J. H., & Beutell, N. J. (1985). Sources of conflict between work and family roles. *Academy of Management Review*, *10*, 76–88.

Grönlund, A., & Javornik, J. (2014). Great expectations: Dual-earner policies and the management of work–family conflict: The examples of Sweden and Slovenia. *Families, Relationships and Societies*, *3*, 147–161.

Hagestad, G. O., & Herlofson, K. (2007). *Micro and macro perspectives on intergenerational relations and transfers in Europe*. Retrieved from United Nations Department of

Economic and Social Affairs website www.un.org/en/development/desa/population/publications/ageing/age-structure.shtml

Herzberg, F., Mausner, B., & Snyderman, B. (1959). *The motivation to work*. New York, NJ: Wiley.

Hill, E. J., Yang, C., Hawkins, A. J., & Ferris, M. (2004). A cross-cultural test of the work–family interface in 48 countries. *Journal of Marriage and Family, 66,* 1300–1316.

Hobfoll, S. E. (1989). Conservation of resources: A new attempt at conceptualizing stress. *American Psychologist, 44,* 513–524.

Hofstede, G. (2005). *Cultures and organizations: Software of the mind*. London, UK: McGraw-Hill.

House, R. J., Hanges, P. J., Javidan, M., Dorfman, P. W., & Gupta, V. (2004). *Culture, leadership, and organizations: The GLOBE study of 62 societies*. Thousand Oaks, CA: Sage.

Holman, D. (2013). Job types and job quality in Europe. *Human Relations, 66,* 475–502.

Kanjuo Mrčela, A., & Černigoj Sadar, N. (2011). Social policies related to parenthood and capabilities of Slovenian parents. *Social Politics, 18,* 199–231.

Karatepe, O. M. (2013). The effects of work overload and work–family conflict on job embeddedness and job performance: The mediation of emotional exhaustion. *International Journal of Contemporary Hospitality Management, 25,* 614–634.

Karatepe, O. M., & Karadas, G. (2014). The effect of psychological capital on conflicts in the work–family interface, turnover and absence intentions. *International Journal of Hospitality Management, 43,* 132–143.

Kirby, E. L., & Krone, K. (2002). "The policy exists but you can't really use it": Communication and the structuration of work–family policies. *Journal of Applied Communication Research, 30,* 50–77.

Kuitto, K. (2016). *Post-Communist Welfare States in European Context: Patterns of Welfare Policies in Central and Eastern Europe*. Cheltenham, UK: Edward Elgar Publishing.

Lapierre, L. M., & McMullan, A. D. (2016). A review of methodological and measurement approaches to the study of work and family. In T. D. Allen & L. E. Eby (Eds.), *The Oxford Handbook of Work and Family* (pp. 36–50). New York, NJ: Oxford University Press.

Mandel, A., & Realo, A. (2015). Across-time change and variation in cultural tightness–looseness. *PLoS ONE, 10,* e0145213.

Michel, J. S., Kotrba, L. M., Mitchelson, J. K., Clark, M. A., & Baltes, B. B. (2011). Antecedents of work–family conflict: A meta-analytic review. *Journal of Organizational Behavior, 32,* 689–725.

Michoń, P. (2010). "Stay at home dear" – mothers, labour markets and state policy in Poland and Baltic States. In C. Klenner & S. Leiber (Eds.), *Welfare states and gender inequality in Central and Eastern Europe* (pp. 151–180). Brussels, Belgium: ETUI.

Michoń, P. (2015). Waiting for the incentives to work: Comparative analysis of the parental leave policies in the Visegrad countries. *Community, Work & Family, 18,* 182–197.

Mihelič, K. K. (2014a). Work–family interface, job satisfaction and turnover intention: A CEE transition country perspective. *Baltic Journal of Management, 9,* 446–466.

Mihelič, K. K. (2014b). Commitment to life roles and work–family conflict among managers in a post-socialist country. *Career Development International, 19,* 204–221.

Neal, M. B., & Hammer, L. B. (2007). *Working Couples Caring for children and Aging Parents: Effects on Work and Well-Being.* Mahwah, NJ: Lawrence Erlbaum Associates Publishers.

Netemeyer, R. G., Boles, J. S., & McMurrian, R. (1996). Development and validation of work–family conflict and family–work conflict scales. *Journal of Applied Psychology, 81*, 400–410.

Netemeyer, R. G., Brashear-Alejandro, T., & Boles, J. S. (2004). A cross-national model of job-related outcomes of work role and family role variables: A retail sales context. *Journal of the Academy of Marketing Science, 32*, 49–60.

Obradović, J., & Čudina-Obradović, V. (2009). Work-related stressors of work–family conflict and stress crossover on marriage quality. *Društvena istraživanja [Journal for Generic Social Issues], 3*, 437–460.

Ollier-Malaterre, A. (2016). Cross-national work–life research: A review at the individual level. In T. D. Allen & L. E. Eby (Eds.), *The Oxford Handbook of Work and Family* (pp. 315–332). New York, NJ: Oxford University Press.

Ollier-Malaterre, A., & Foucreault, A. (2017). Cross-national work–life research: Cultural and structural impacts for individuals and organizations. *Journal of Management, 41*, 111–136.

Ollo-López, A., & Goñi-Legaz, S. (2017). Differences in work–family conflict: Which individual and national factors explain them? *The International Journal of Human Resource Management, 28*, 499–525.

Olson, J. E., Frieze, I. H., Wall, S., Zdaniuk, B., Telpuchovskaya, N., Ferligoj, A., Rus Makovec, M. (2006). Economic influences on ideals about future jobs in young adults in formerly socialist countries and the United States. *Cross-Cultural Research, 40*, 352–376.

Parker, L., & Allen, T. D. (2001). Work/family benefits: Variables related to employees' fairness perceptions. *Journal of Vocational Behavior, 58*, 453–468.

Pascall, G., & Kwak, A. (2005). *Gender regimes in transition in Central and Eastern Europe.* Bristol, UK: Policy Press.

Powell, G. N., Francesco, A. M., & Ling, Y. (2009). Towards culture- sensitive theories of the work- family interface. *Journal of Organizational Behavior, 30*, 597–616.

Rantanen, J., Kinnunen, U., Mauno, S., & Tement, S. (2013). Patterns of conflict and enrichment in work–family balance: A three-dimensional typology. *Work & Stress, 27*, 141–163.

Schaffer, B. S., & Riordan, C. M. (2003). A review of cross-cultural methodologies for organizational research: A best-practices approach. *Organizational Research Methods, 6*, 169–215.

Schooler, C. (1996). Cultural and social-structural explanations of cross-national psychological differences. *Annual Review of Sociology, 22*, 323–349.

Schulze, E., & Gergoric, M. (2015). *Maternity, paternity and parental leave: Data related to duration and compensation rates in the European Union.* Brussels, Belgium: European Parliament.

Schwartz, S. H., & Bardi, A. (1997). Influences of adaptation to communist rule on value priorities in Eastern Europe. *Political Psychology, 18*, 385–410.

Shockley, K. M., & Singla, N. (2011). Reconsidering work–family interactions and satisfaction: A meta-analysis. *Journal of Management, 37*, 861–886.

Spector, P. E., Allen, T. D., Poelmans, S., Lapierre, L. M., Cooper, C. L., Widerszal-Bazyl, M. (2007). Cross-national differences in relationships of work demands, job satisfaction and turnover intentions with work–family conflict. *Personnel Psychology, 60*, 805–835.

Steiber, N. (2009). Reported levels of time-based and strain-based conflict between work and family roles in Europe: A multilevel approach. *Social Indicators Research, 93*, 469–488.

Stier, H., Lewin-Epstein, N., & Braun, M. (2012). Work–family conflict in comparative perspective: The role of social policies. *Research in Social Stratification and Mobility, 30*, 265–279.

Strandh, M., & Nordenmark, M. (2006). The interference of paid work with household demands in different social policy contexts: Perceived work–household conflict in Sweden, the UK, the Netherlands, Hungary, and the Czech Republic. *British Journal of Sociology, 57*, 597–617.

Stryker, S., & Burke, P. J. (2000). The past, present, and future of an identity theory. *Social Psychology Quarterly, 63*, 284–297.

Šverko, B., Arambašić, L., & Galešić, M. (2002). Work–life balance among Croatian employees: Role time commitment, work-home interference and well-being. *Social Science Information, 41*, 281–301.

Tement, S., & Korunka, C. (2013). Does trait affectivity predict work-to-family conflict and enrichment beyond job characteristics? *Journal of Psychology: Interdisciplinary and Applied, 147*, 197–216.

Tement, S., & Korunka, C. (2015). The moderating impact of types of caregiving on job demands, resources and their relation to work-to-family conflict and enrichment. *Journal of Family Issues, 36*, 31–55.

ten Brummelhuis, L. L., & Trougakos, J. P. (2014). The motivating potential of intrinsically versus extrinsically motivated off- job activities. *Journal of Occupational and Organizational Psychology, 87*, 177–199.

Thornton, A., & Philipov, D. (2009). Sweeping changes in marriage, cohabitation and child-bearing in Central and Eastern Europe: New insights from the developmental idealism framework. *European Journal of Population, 25*, 123–156.

Trefalt, Š., Drnovšek, M., Svetina-Nabergoj, A., & Adlešič, R.V. (2013). Work–life experiences in rapidly changing national contexts: Structural misalignment, comparisons and choice overload as explanatory mechanisms. *European Management Journal, 31*, 448–463.

Voicu, M. (2010). The effect of democratization and support for democracy on gender attitudes in 19 European societies. In L. Hallman & M. Voicu (Eds.), *Mapping value orientations in Central and Eastern Europe* (pp. 239–260). Leiden, The Netherlands: Brill.

van der Lippe, T., Jager, A., & Kops, Y. (2006). Combination pressure: The paid work–family balance of men and women in European countries. *Acta Sociologica, 49*, 303–319.

Westman, M. (2005). Cross-cultural differences in crossover research. In S. A. Y. Poelmans (Ed.), *Work and family: An international research perspective* (pp. 241–260). Mahwah, NJ: Lawrence Erlbaum Associates Publishers.

World Bank. (2016). *Work values in Western and Eastern Europe.* Retrieved from http://documents.worldbank.org/curated/en/365971468185035876/Work-values-in-Western-and-Eastern-europe

15 A Review of Work–Family Research in the Nordic Region

Constanze Leineweber and Helena Falkenberg

A fundamental issue concerning work and family is the extent that women and men work and take care of children. The Nordic countries (i.e., Sweden, Denmark, Norway, Finland, and Iceland for the purposes of this review) are characterized by a "dual-worker model" in which a majority of both women and men participate in paid work, but are also, to some extent, characterized by a "dual-carer model" in which both women and men actively take part in the upbringing of their children (Edlund & Öun, 2016). The Nordic countries have a history of family policies being directed toward both mothers and fathers, and state provisions for dual-earner family support and childcare were developed in a political context with women's equality in mind (Ellingsaeter & Leira, 2006). Still, the challenge of combining work and family domains is under continual debate and development in the Nordic countries. In the next sections, we will briefly describe the general trends of women's participation in the labor market in relation to the development of the welfare system. This historical development is crucial for the understanding of how women and men combine work and family in the Nordic countries today.

Women's Participation in the Labor Market and the Welfare State

Historical Trends and Current Statistics

Near the end of the 1960s there was a simultaneous demand for labor from Nordic industries and an emergent women's movement that saw women's participation in the labor market as a mean to increase gender equality (Boye & Nermo, 2014). These simultaneous interests led to a marked increase in the number of women participating in the labor force. Finland was first in this development followed by Sweden, Denmark, and Norway. By the mid-1970s, almost half of all mothers of preschool children in these Nordic countries were participating in the labor market, although many worked part-time (Leira, 2006). This was a time of political reforms that extended publicly funded services, such as daycare for children, care for the elderly, and healthcare. The increase in welfare services also meant increased demand for labor in the public sector, a workforce which was largely composed of women. Consequently, these jobs in the welfare sector were constructed in a way that was conducive to managing work and family, meaning many part-time jobs (Gonäs,

Johansson, & Svärd, 1997). As men were still seen as the primary breadwinner, salaries in these jobs were generally low.

This historical development is still present in the statistics today. All of the Nordic countries are characterized by a high employment rate among women (above 70% in all Nordic countries, Nordic Council of Ministers, 2014) accompanied by a marked gender segregation between sectors and occupations. Of those working in the public sector (which is responsible for childcare, eldercare, healthcare, and education), 74% are women (Nordic Council of Ministers, 2014). There is also a gender gap in part-time work with a higher proportion of women working part-time compared to men in all the Nordic countries. However, the rate of part-time work among women differs somewhat between countries. Although about 30% or more of the women in Sweden, Norway, Denmark, and Iceland work part-time, only about 19% work part-time in Finland (Nordic Council of Ministers, 2014). At the same time, the rate of employed mothers with young children is considerably higher in Sweden, Norway, and Denmark (above 70%) than in Finland (59%) (Ellingsaeter & Leira, 2006; Rostgaard, 2014). The rate of men working part-time is below 15% in all Nordic countries, with the lowest rate in Finland (below 10%). It is worth noting that part-time work in the Nordic countries often means relatively long hours. That is, for example, the mean work hours for women in Sweden is 30 hours per week (compared to men's 37 hours per week) (Statistics Sweden, 2014), and within Europe, the weekly duration of part-time work for women is the longest in Sweden (Eurostat, 2009). Additionally, even if gender differences in the division of household labor are smaller in all Nordic countries compared with other regions, women are still doing a bigger part of the unpaid work than men (Duran, 2015).

Child Care and Parental Leave

A prerequisite for the high employment rate among women in the Nordic countries is the rather well-developed childcare service that is largely financed by public means. Between 92% and 97% of all children between the ages of 3 and 5 use childcare services in the Nordic countries, and many children enter childcare around age one. The exception is Finland, where "only" around 74% of children between ages of 3 and 5 are in daycare (Nordic Council of Ministers, 2014). All the Nordic countries are similar in the sense that they have statutory parental leave (with some level of paid benefit) of about a year or longer that can be shared between the parents (Rostgaard, 2014). Finland stands out from the other Nordic countries since a higher proportion of women receive cash benefits for child home care (cash-for-care benefit) (Ellingsaeter & Leira, 2006).

Policies encouraging fathers' participation in caring for children differ between the Nordic countries. Compared to Denmark and Finland, in Norway, Sweden, and, more recently, Iceland, there has been greater emphasis on policies encouraging fathers' participation in caring for children (Öun, 2012). In Norway, Sweden, and Iceland, some amount of time of the parental leave is reserved for just one of the parents. This so-called "father's quota" was introduced in Norway and Sweden in the 1990s and then in Iceland in 2000 as a means to increase father's parental leave use (see Rostgaard, 2014 for a review of the family policies in the Nordic countries). After the introduction of parental leave, fathers in Iceland increased their use of such leave considerably and the gap in use of parental leave between mothers and fathers is now lowest in Iceland, where fathers use 29% of all parental leave days available to mothers and fathers. In Norway and Sweden fathers use more than 20% of the parental leave days, while in Finland and Denmark fathers use about 10% of the days of parental leave (Nordic Council of Ministers, 2014).

Changes in the Public Sector

With the economic recession in the late 1980s and early 1990s, the costs and quality of services in the public sector in the Nordic countries was increasingly criticized and solutions from the private sector were introduced into the public sector (so-called "new public management"). The increased influence of market forces was argued to lead to more competition, more cost-efficiency, higher quality of the services in the public sector, and more freedom of choice for the citizens (Ellingsaeter & Leira, 2006; Falkenberg, 2010). Consequently, the public sector in the Nordic countries underwent large-scale changes, including downsizing with staff-reductions and privatizations.

One result of these changes was an increase in working demands in many of the public sector jobs primarily occupied by women (Johansson, 2002). In fact, the least favorable psychosocial working conditions (e.g., low control, high demands, and low social support) are now found in the female-dominated public sector (Lidwall, Bill, Palmer, & Bohlin Olsson, 2014). The aforementioned structural changes might have been especially detrimental because of the nature of the work in the public sector with many occupations which are, to a relatively high degree, characterized by the need to respond and adapt to other humans' needs. Demands from humans are often more difficult to control, postpone, or dismiss than demands from objects (Sverke, Falkenberg, Kecklund, Magnusson Hanson, & Lindfors, 2016), which can make the planning of work more difficult in these occupations. Work in the public sector, especially in health care, is also relatively highly regulated in terms of time and space (Allvin, Mellner, Movitz, & Aronsson, 2013), and employees often have little control over their work hours and time off (Albrecht, Kecklund, Tucker, & Leineweber, 2016). Taken together, these factors suggest that the working conditions in the female-dominated public sector no longer seem to facilitate combining work and family.

Key Academic Findings

In this section we describe some of the work–family research that has been conducted in the Nordic countries. Although work–family research is relatively nascent in the Nordic countries, the literature is rather extensive and we only touch upon some key findings while trying to give a broad picture of what has been studied to date. First, we concentrate on research that has investigated the potential work and family have to enhance and enrich each other (i.e., work–family enrichment) and the importance of organizational culture. After that, we review research investigating possible health outcomes of work–family conflict.

Work–Family Enrichment

Only in the recent years did researchers start to increasingly examine the beneficial effects of dual roles. Although focus on positive work–family interactions lags behind research on the negative side (i.e., work–family conflict), there is a considerable amount of research conducted in Nordic countries on the topic. Specifically, several researchers have examined work–family enrichment, which occurs when experiences in one role enhances the quality of life in the other role (Greenhaus & Powell, 2006), in relation to outcomes. The trend is that enrichment plays a beneficial role. In a Finnish cross-sectional study, Kinnunen et al. (2006) found that positive work-to-family spillover was negatively related to job exhaustion. Another Finnish study based on a longitudinal sample (Hakanen, Peeters, & Perhoniemi, 2011) found that work-to-family enrichment positively related to work engagement and that family-to-work enrichment positively related to home resources and marital satisfaction. Another study investigated the moderating effect of type of work contract (i.e., temporary or permanent) on the relationship between work–family enrichment and job exhaustion as well as turnover intentions (Mauno et al., 2015). There was a moderating effect of type of work contract such that work–family enrichment had a lagged effect on reduced job exhaustion in temporary but not permanent employees. Facilitation between work and family has also been shown to relate to lower levels of emotional exhaustion and disengagement from work two years later in a Norwegian study (Innstrand, Melbye Langballe, Espnes, Falkum, & Gjerløw Aasland, 2008). The same study also found support for reverse relations, showing that higher levels of emotional exhaustion and disengagement from work at Time 1 were related to lower levels of facilitation between work and family at Time 2.

Organizational Culture

In the Nordic countries many work–family arrangements are legally mandated at a national level and, as such, their uptake might not be as dependent on the prevailing organizational work–family culture as in many other countries (Mauno, Kinnunen, & Piitulainen, 2005). For example, the Swedish Discrimination Act (2008) bans unfavorable treatment in connection with parental leave, such as employment/ dismissal, promotion, training for promotion, vocational training on-the-job, salary, or other terms of employment. Nonetheless, organizational culture may still play an important role and has been the focus of research in several Nordic studies.

One Finnish study investigated lagged associations between family-friendly organizational culture (operationalized as both managerial work–family support and work– family barriers) and work–family conflict. The authors found that managerial work–family support showed a significant and negative lagged relationship with work–family conflict two years later, but work–family barriers were not significantly related to work–family conflict (Mauno, 2010). Another study based on knowledge workers in Denmark found that a family-friendly culture was negatively associated with work–family conflict one year later (Albertsen, Persson, Garde, & Rugulies, 2010). Interestingly, this study also revealed an interaction between family-friendly culture and degree of influence a person has to make decisions concerning their work. Among those working in a family-friendly culture, those who could influence their own work experienced less work–family conflict compared to those with less influence. In contrast, among those working in less family-friendly organizational cultures, greater possibilities to make decisions concerning their own work (i.e., greater influence) was actually associated with a higher levels of work–family conflict. A study from Sweden showed the importance of a family-friendly organizational culture and work group norms for father's use of parental leave. The study found that the company's commitment to caring values and work group norms that facilitated fathers' time off to care for children predicted both whether fathers took leave or not and the number of days of parental leave that they used. Additionally, work groups norms that emphasized long working hours and visual time at work predicted fewer days of parental leave taken among fathers (Haas, Allard, & Hwang, 2002).

Health Outcomes

Health outcomes have been the focus of a fair amount of work–family research globally. Like most work–family research (Casper, Eby, Bordeaux, Lockwood, & Lambert, 2007), much of this literature is cross-sectional, which makes cause and effect indistinguishable. However, the number of longitudinal studies, which allow for stronger inferences about causality, have increased during the past years in the Nordic context. In our review of health outcomes below, we focus mostly on long-itudinal work.

Sickness Absence

In the Nordic countries (with the exception of Finland), women more often take sickness absence than men (Nordic Social Statistical Committee, 2015). In Sweden women account for 63% of all sickness days (Försäkringskassan, 2013). Similar numbers are reported from Denmark and Norway with women accounting for 61% (Eurofound, 2010) and 76% (Statistics Norway, 2016) of all sickness absence, respectively. In terms of women with children, findings are a bit more nuanced. Some of studies have found that women with children are less prone to (short-term) sickness absence than other groups (Björklund, 1991; Bratberg, Dahl, & Erling, 2002; Vogel, Kindlund, & Diderichsen, 1992), while other studies report either no relationship (Abrahamsen, 1991) or even a positive relationship between mother-hood and sickness absence (Hansen, 1996).

Some studies found even more complex results based on additional factors. For example, mothers of young children take fewer short-term but more long-term sickness absences (Björklund, 1991; Blank & Diderichsen, 1995). One prospective study based on a Swedish sample of female municipality workers found that having children was not a risk factor for repeated sick leave spells or long-term sickness absence for married/cohabiting women, but a relationship was found among single women with children (Voss et al., 2008). A study using data from twins in Sweden compared women who gave birth during a certain time-period (different time-periods were analyzed) with their twin-sisters who did not give birth. The result showed no major differences in the uptake of sick-leave for women who gave birth compared to women who did not give birth. However, women who gave birth had higher levels of sick leave the year before the birth of their child (Alexanderson et al., 2013). Lastly, results presented in a report from the Swedish Social Insurance Agency (Försäkringskassan, 2013) suggest that the risk for sickness absence increases in cases where women are responsible for a disproportionate amount of child care tasks while also having occupations of similar responsibility as their male spouses. Speculatively, the double-burden from home and paid work might be a reason for greater sickness absence. Taken together, there seems to be little evidence that having children in and of itself has any strong impact on sickness absence for women, but there are likely important moderators of the relationship (Mastekaasa, 2000).

Although the Nordic countries dominate the empirical research investigating the relationship between family responsibilities and sickness absence (and absence more generally), few studies have invested the relationship between a direct measure of work–family conflict and sickness absence. Instead work–family conflict is measured via different proxies (e.g., having children living at home). An exception to this is a Finnish study where the authors found that severe negative work–family spillover was associated with a higher rate of sickness absence (Väänänen et al., 2005). However, a Swedish study found work–family conflict to be only weakly associated with long-term sickness absence (Lidwall, Marklund, & Voss, 2010).

Mental Health

Although a number of studies have investigated the relationship between work–family conflict and mental health over time, they have produced divergent results, making it difficult to draw firm conclusions. For example, Kinnunen et al. (2004) found that among employed women with a partner and/or children, a high level of work–family conflict at Time 1 predicted psychological symptoms one year later, but psychological strain at Time 1 did not predict later work–family conflict (i.e., no reverse relation was found). For men, however, the relationship was the opposite; psychological distress at Time 1 predicted work family conflict one year later, but no relationship in the other direction was found. In terms of depression, one study investigated the relationship between work–home interference and depression, measured as both major depression and prescription of anti-depressants over a time-period of two years, based on a large Swedish sample. Results from this study indicated a positive link between work–home interference and subsequent major depression among women and work–home interference and prescription use of anti-depressants among men (Hanson, Leineweber, Chungkham, & Westerlund, 2014).

Additionally, this study found reverse relationships from major depression to subsequent high work–home interference among both women and men.

Other mental health outcomes, such as emotional exhaustion, have also been examined. A Finnish study did not find any long-term association between work–life balance and job exhaustion (Rantanen, Kinnunen, Feldt, & Pulkkinen, 2008), whereas a Swedish study reported increased odds for emotional exhaustion for women and men who reported high levels of work–family conflict two years earlier (Leineweber, Baltzer, Magnusson Hanson, & Westerlund, 2013). Yet another study found that baseline emotional exhaustion was associated with work–family conflict two years later (Richter, Schraml, & Leineweber, 2015), but work–family conflict at baseline did not predict later emotional exhaustion. Another study by Innstrand et al. (2008) found that work–family conflict was positively related to emotional exhaustion and disengagement from work two years later. Support for reverse relations, that higher levels of emotional exhaustion and disengagement from work at Time 1 were related to higher levels of work–family conflict at Time 2, were also found.

Sleep

A number of studies, mainly Finnish, investigated the association between work–family conflict and sleep problems using cross-sectional designs (Lallukka, Chandola, et al., 2010; Lallukka, Rahkonen, Lahelma, & Arber, 2010; Nylen, Melin, & Laflamme, 2007). These studies found that both work-to-family and family-to-work conflict were negatively related to sleep quality (Nylen et al., 2007), even when controlling for working conditions and health behaviors (Lallukka, Rahkonen, et al., 2010). In a study with a sophisticated design based on prescribed drugs registry data, Lallukka and colleagues (2013) found a clear association between family-to-work conflict and subsequent prescribed sleep medication, and a somewhat weaker association between work-to-family conflict and subsequent prescribed sleep medication among women, but no such associations were found among men. Another Finnish study found that work–family conflict was related to self-reported sleep problems one year later (Mäkelä, Bergbom, Tanskanen, & Kinnunen, 2014).

Health Behaviors

There is a relative scarcity of studies linking work–family conflict and actual health behaviors in Nordic countries. This may be attributable partly to the fact that measuring health behaviors is challenging and results might be biased due to social desirability and recall errors. However, there are some studies, mainly from Finland, which focus on the association between work-to-family and family-to-work conflict and various behavioral health outcomes. In a Finnish study, work-to-family conflict was associated with a lower likelihood of getting the recommended amount of physical activity (Roos, Sarlio-Lähteenkorva, Lallukka, & Lahelma, 2007) and a higher likelihood of problem drinking (Roos, Lahelma, & Rahkonen, 2006) among both women and men. Similarly, women and men experiencing family-to-work conflict were found to have a lower likelihood to report following nationally recommended food habits (Roos et al., 2007). Yet, these studies suggest some gender differences, too. Only among women, work-to-family conflict was associated with heavy drinking (Roos et al., 2006) and unhealthy food habits (Lallukka, Chandola, et al., 2010; Roos et al., 2007), though this association was no longer significant after controlling for work-related factors in Roos et al. (2007). Only among men, higher levels of work-to-family conflict were associated with smoking (Lallukka, Chandola, et al., 2010). All the aforementioned findings are based on cross-sectional studies. To the best of our knowledge, there is only one study in the Nordic region examining the association between work–family conflict and health behavior over time. This Swedish study reports a positive association between work–family conflict and problem drinking two years later among men, but not among women (Leineweber, Baltzer, Magnusson Hanson, & Westerlund, 2013).

Comparative Findings

The Nordic countries are often considered to be frontrunners with regard to gender equality, and it has been suggested that women and men in Nordic countries should experience less conflict and more balance between work and family demands than elsewhere. Indeed, a cluster analysis conducted by Öun (2012) revealed that most women and men (61%) in the Nordic region (inclusive of Denmark, Sweden, Norway, and Finland) fit best in a cluster labeled "work and family balance," while about one third (36%) fit into a cluster indicating "occupational work overload" (i.e., experiencing work spilling into family life). Only around 3% fell into a cluster labeled "dual work overload," indicating high levels of both work-to-family and family-to-work conflict. Moreover, this study also reported some differences between the Nordic countries. Women in Finland reported significantly less work–family conflict than women in Denmark, Sweden, and Norway. Öun (2012) explained this finding as due to women having to make a more distinct choice between work and family in Finland, as there are fewer possibilities for part-time work on the one hand, but cash-for-care benefits are available on the other hand.

However, when comparing the Nordic countries to other country clusters, results are not clear. In contrast to what might be expected, several studies found that parents in Nordic countries report higher levels of work–family conflict than those in other European countries (Boye, 2011; Strandh & Nordenmark, 2006; van der Lippe, Jager, & Kops, 2006). For example, one study comparing single and cohabiting mothers in Southern Europe (Greek, Spain, and Portugal) to those living in the Nordic countries (Denmark, Norway, and Sweden) found that coupled mothers living in the Nordic countries experienced more work–family conflict than those in Southern Europe. At the same time, mothers in the Nordic countries (both single and coupled) were more satisfied with life, experienced their job as more enriching, and reported less financial problems than mothers from South European countries (Bull, 2009). This finding is in line with the idea of the beneficial effect of dual roles. Differences in experienced work–family conflict are possibly due to the relatively longer working hours and the higher proportion of women and mothers in paid work in Nordic countries. Indeed, this hypothesis is partly supported in a study comparing work-household conflict in five European countries (Strandh & Nordenmark, 2006). In this study, the relatively higher levels in work-household conflict reported by women in Sweden compared to women in the United Kingdom and the Netherlands were explained by a higher education level and longer working hours among women in Sweden (i.e., when education and working hours were accounted for statistically, the differences disappeared).

However, the difference between Sweden and Hungary/the Czech Republic could not be explained by those variables (i.e., education and work hours). The relatively higher levels of work–home conflict in Sweden in comparison to the Eastern European countries might instead be explained by the gender culture hypothesis (van der Lippe et al., 2006). This hypothesis states that as combining work and family life is an issue in the Nordic countries, feeling stressed and hurried has become part of the culture. It has also been suggested that the generous social provisions to support work–life balance in the Nordic countries put social demand on women (and men) to "perform well in all spheres of life" (i.e., they must be a good employee, a good parent, and a good partner) (Guest, 2002). This in turn generates feelings of incompetence and conflict. In a similar vein, Elvin-Nowak (1999) suggested that mothers were exposed to two conflicting norm systems, the norm of equality between women and men (sharing equally on work and parenting) and the norm of the "good mother" – that children's access to the mother is of special importance for the development of the child. This data was gathered some time ago and as social norms develop, it is hard to say to what extent these two norms systems still collide and to what extent they also affect fathers.

In contrast to the previously mentioned studies, other studies found less work–family conflict in the Nordic countries in comparison to others. One study investigated the relationship between work–family and family-work conflict and family-friendly policies in 10 countries and found that fathers and mothers in countries with more expansive family leave (i.e., Nordic countries) reported less family-work conflict (Ruppanner, 2013). Another study found that publically available childcare facilities alleviated the adverse effect of children on work–family conflict for mothers (Crompton & Lyonette, 2006). Also, in the OECD better life index, the Nordic countries are among those with best work–life balance. Taken together the results indicate that national policies and institutional arrangements make a difference and enhance gender equality as well as work–life balance for women and men (Stier, Lewin-Epstein, & Braun, 2012). Still, the presence of a family-friendly policies is not a guarantee for a better compatibility of paid and unpaid work, as organizational and national culture also play a critical role.

Future Research Directions

As noted previously, most of the research in the Nordic countries has concentrated on the negative effects of combining work and family. Although there is an increasing interest regarding possible positive work–family effects, much remains to be done. Further research about longitudinal relationships between antecedents of work–family enrichment and its effects on health and well-being as well as work-related outcomes is warranted.

As we discussed in the Comparative Findings section, it remains unclear how well people in the Nordic countries perform in terms of work–family management given the mixed research findings. One important aspect in better understanding these conflicting findings might be found in the individual expectations that people hold about being able to balance work and family demands. Both women and men have often place high expectations on themselves regarding success in working life and in terms of being an engaged and attentive parent. This together with highly individualized societies where everyone is responsible for her/himself might be one underlying reason for the still relatively high number of women and men experiencing work family conflict in the Nordic countries. The importance of expectations is worthy of future investigation.

In regard to the negative effects of work–family conflict on health, the health registries available in the Nordic countries provide a unique and still underutilized methodological contribution. Those registries cover a diversity of health outcomes (e.g., dates of sickness absence and hospitalization with medical diagnosis, cause of death, and prescribed drugs) and cover the entire population. Those data can be linked to questionnaire data on, for example, work–family conflict by the unique personal identification number given to every resident. Until recently, few studies have used the unique information available from registries to link work-family conflict to objective measures of health outcomes and further research is warranted.

Modern working life is rapidly changing, as is family life, and the proportion of home-based teleworkers (measured as the percentage of total labor force that telecommutes) among European countries is highest in the Nordic Countries (i.e., Finland, Sweden, and Denmark) (Rapp & Jackson, 2013). The introduction of new technologies and telework increases flexibility in working life, but also allow for constant availability. Possible drawbacks, such as an increased risk of employees being constantly involved in work – even during their free time – may impair both family life and recovery (Demerouti, Derks, ten Brummelhuis, & Bakker, 2014) and are worthy of further investigation. Additionally, certain groups might be affected differently by the introduction of new technologies and the accompanying flexibility. For example, some research suggested that women benefit more from increased control over their working time than men, but it has also been proposed that work-time flexibility may have adverse consequences for women's work–home balance, as women may end up engaging in more non-work responsibilities (Hammer, Neal, Newsom, Brockwood, & Colton, 2005). Future research might shed light about the positive and negative sides of increased telework and the resulting flexibility on work time and place given the high prevalence of flexibility use in Nordic countries.

As described previously, the labor market is strongly gender segregated in the Nordic countries with women overrepresented in the public sector and men overrepresented in the private sector. How work is organized in these sectors influence the ability to combine work and family not only for the individual, but also for their spouse, as family members work and family behaviors are interdependent upon each other's' working conditions. More research is needed regarding which factors hinder or facilitate the successful combination of work and home demands at the couple level, and the Nordic setting seems apt for such research given the high degree of participation in the labor market among both women and men and the high prevalence of gender occupational segregation.

Conclusion

The Nordic countries have long been focused on developing and sustaining dual-earner/dual-carer societies and, as such, experience high gender equality comparatively across the globe (World Economic Forum, 2014). Even so, the gender differences in caring are still large in the Nordic countries and the labor market is highly gender segregated. On the one hand, when both women and men are fully engaged in work and care, the risk of work–family conflict may be increased. On the other hand, the positive aspect of being deeply involved in these two valued spheres of life might counterbalance some of the potential negative consequences. Taken together, there is a large amount of work–family research in the Nordic region, especially regarding possible health consequences following work–family conflict. Still, further research making use of more advanced study designs and registry data is warranted.

References

Abrahamsen, B. (1991). Pleiearbeid og helse. Daglige belastninger, slitasjelidelser og syke-fravaer blant hjelpepleiere (Nursing and health. Daily work load, musculoskeletal health problems and sickness absence among state enrolled nurses). *ISF-Report 91/6*. Oslo: Institute for Social Research.

Albertsen, K., Persson, R., Garde, A. H., & Rugulies, R. (2010). Psychosocial determinants of work-to-family conflict among knowledge workers with boundaryless work. *Applied Psychology: Health and Well Being*, *2*(2), 160–181.

Albrecht, S. C., Kecklund, G., Tucker, P., & Leineweber, C. (2016). Investigating the factorial structure and availability of work time control in a representative sample of the Swedish working population. *Scandinavian Journal of Public Health*, *44*(3), 320–328.

Alexanderson, K., Björkenstam, A., Kjeldgård, L., Narusyte, J., Ropponen, A., & Svedberg, P. (2013). *Barnafödande, sjuklighet och sjukfrånvaro: En studie av tvillingsystrar [Childbirth, illness and sickness absence: A study of twin sisters]*. Retrieved from Karolinska Institutet: http://ki.se/sites/default/files/rapporten_barnafodande.pdf

Allvin, M., Mellner, C., Movitz, F., & Aronsson, G. (2013). The diffusion of flexibility: Estimating the incidence of low-regulated working conditions. *Nordic Journal of Working Life Studies*, *3*(3), 99–116.

Björklund, A. (1991). Vem får sjukpenning? En empirisk analys av sjukfrånvarons bestämningsfaktorer (Who receives sickness benefits? An empirical analysis of the determinants of sickness absence). *Arbetskraft, arbetsmarknad och produktivitet, Extrarapport no 4*, 285–299.

Blank, N., & Diderichsen, F. (1995). Short-term and long-term sick-leave in Sweden: relationships with social circumstances, working conditions and gender. *Scandinavian Journal of Social Medicine, 23*(4), 265–272.

Boye, K. (2011). Work and well-being in a comparative perspective – the role of family policy. *European Sociological Review, 72*(1), 16–30.

Boye, K., & Nermo, M. (2014). *Lönsamt arbete: Familjeansvarets fördelning och konsekvenser [Gainful employment: Family responsibility and it's distribution and consequenses]*. Forskningsrapport till Delegationen för jämställdhet i arbetslivet [Research report for the Delegation for equality at work]: Statens offentliga utredningar [Governmental report].

Bratberg, E., Dahl, S.-Å., & Erling, R. A. (2002). "The double burden": do combinations of career and family obligations increase sickness absence among women? *European Sociological Review, 18*(2), 233–249.

Bull, T. (2009). Work life and mental well-being: single and coupled employed mothers in Southern Europe and Scandinavia. *Global Health Promotion, 16*(3), 6–16. doi:10.1177/1757975909339674

Casper, W. J., Eby, L. T., Bordeaux, C., Lockwood, A., & Lambert, D. (2007). A review of research method in IO/OB work–family research. *Journal of Applied Psychology, 92*, 28–43.

Crompton, R., & Lyonette, C. (2006). Work–life 'balance' in Europe. *Acta Sociologica, 49*(4), 379–393.

Demerouti, E., Derks, D., ten Brummelhuis, L. L., & Bakker, A. B. (2014). New ways of working: Impact on working conditions, work–family balance, and well-being. In C. Korunka & P. Hoonakker (Eds.), *The impact of ICT on quality of life*. Dordrecht: Springer Science & Business Media.

Duran, M.-A. (2015). The Contribution of Unpaid Work to Global Wellbeing: Exploration of Well-Being of Nations and Continents. In W. Glatzer, L. Camfield, V. Møller, & M. Rojas (Eds.), *Global Handbook of Quality of Life* (pp. 381–411). New York: Springer.

Edlund, J., & Öun, I. (2016). Who should work and who should care? Attitudes towards the desirable division of labour between mothers and fathers in five European countries. *Acta Sociologica, 59*(2), 151–169.

Ellingsaeter, A.L., & Leira, A. (2006). *Politicising Parenthood in Scandinavia*. Bristol: Polity Press.

Elvin-Nowak, Y. (1999). *Accompanied by guilt: Modern motherhood the Swedish way*. (Doctoral dissertation), Stockholm University Stockholm.

Eurofound. (2010). *Absence from work – Denmark*. Retrieved from http://www.eurofound.europa.eu/print/observatories/eurwork/comparative-information/national-contributions/denmark/absence-from-work-denmark

Eurostat. (2009). Reconciliation between work, private and family life in the European Union. *Statistical book*.

Falkenberg, H. (2010). *How privatization and corporatization affect healthcare employees' work climate, work attitudes and ill-health: Implications of social status*. (Doctoral dissertation), Stockholm University, Stockholm, Sweden.

Försäkringskassan. (2013). *Kvinnors sjukfrånvaro. [Sickness absence among women]*. Stockholm: Socialdepartementet.

Gonäs, L., Johansson, S., & Svärd, I. (1997). *Lokala utfall av den offentliga sektorns omvandling [Local outcomes of public sector transformation]. In Rapport till*

Utredningen om fördelning av ekonomisk makt och ekonomiska resurser mellan kvinnor och män [Report to the commission on the distribution of economic power and economic resources between women and men]. Statens offentliga utredningar [Governmental report]

Greenhaus, J. H., & Powell, G. N. (2006). When work and family are allies: A theory of work–family enrichment. *Academy of Management Review*, *31*(1), 72–92. doi:10.5465/amr.2006.19379625

Guest, D. E. (2002). Work–life balance within a European perspective: issues arising in the symposium discussion. *Social Science Information*, *41*(2), 319–322.

Haas, L., Allard, K., & Hwang, P. (2002). The impact of organizational culture on men's use of parental leave in Sweden. *Community, Work & Family*, *5*(3), 319–342.

Hakanen, J. J., Peeters, M. C. W., & Perhoniemi, R. (2011). Enrichment processes and gain spirals at work and at home: A 3-year cross-lagged panel study. *Journal of Occupational and Organizational Psychology*, *84*(1), 8–30.

Hammer, L. B., Neal, M. B., Newsom, J. T., Brockwood, K. J., & Colton, C. L. (2005). A longitudinal study of the effects of dual-earner couples' utilization of family-friendly workplace supports on work and family outcomes. *Journal of Applied Psychology*, *90*(4), 799–810. doi:10.1037/0021-9010.90.4.799

Hansen, H. T. (1996). *Trygd: en midlertidig bro, eller en vei ut av arbeidsmarkedet (Social insurance: a temporary bridge, or a road out of the labour market)?* (Doctoral thesis), University of Bergen, Norway, Bergen.

Hanson, L. L., Leineweber, C., Chungkham, H. S., & Westerlund, H. (2014). Work–home interference and its prospective relation to major depression and treatment with antidepressants. *Scandinavian Journal of Work, Environment and Health*, *40*(1), 66–73. doi:10.5271/sjweh.3378

Innstrand, S. T., Melbye Langballe, E., Espnes, G. A., Falkum, E., & Gjerløw Aasland, O. (2008). Postive and negative work–family interaction and burnout: A longitudinal study of reciprocal relations. *Work & Stress*, *22*(1), 1–15.

Johansson, G. (2002). Work–life balance: the case of Sweden in the 1990s. *Social Science Information*, *41*(2), 303–317. doi:10.1177/0539018402041002007

Kinnunen, U., Feldt, T., Geurts, S. A. E., & Pulkkinen, L. (2006). Types of work–family interface: Well-being correlates of negative and positive spillover between work and family. *Scandinavian Journal of Psychology*, *47*(2), 149–162. doi:10.1111/j.1467-9450.2006.00502.x

Kinnunen, U., Geurts, S. A. E., & Mauno, S. (2004). Work-to-family conflict and its relation-ship with satisfaction and well-being: a one-year longitudinal study on gender differences. *Work & Stress*, *18*(1), 1–22.

Lallukka, T., Arber, S., Laaksonen, M., Lahelma, E., Partonen, T., & Rahkonen, O. (2013). Work–family conflicts and subsequent sleep medication among women and men. A longitudinal registry linkage study. *Social Science and Medicine*, *79*, 66–75.

Lallukka, T., Chandola, T., Roos, E., Cable, N., Sekine, M., Kagamimori, S., Tatsue, T., Marmot, M., Lahelma, E. (2010). Work–family conflicts and health behaviors among British, Finnish, and Japanese employees. *International Journal of Behavioural Medicine*, *17*, 134–142.

Lallukka, T., Rahkonen, O., Lahelma, E., & Arber, S. (2010). Sleep complaints in middle-aged women and men: the contribution of working conditions and work–family conflicts. *Journal of Sleep Research*, *19*(3), 466–477. doi:10.1111/j.1365-2869.2010.00821.x

Leineweber, C., Baltzer, M., Magnusson Hanson, L. L., & Westerlund, H. (2013). Work–family conflict and health in Swedish working women and men: a 2-year prospective analysis (the SLOSH study). *European Journal of Public Health*, *23*(4), 710–716. doi:10.1093/eurpub/cks064

Leira, A. (2006). Parenthood change and policy reform in Scandinavia, 1970s-2000s. In A. L. Ellingsaeter & A. Leira (Eds.), *Politics Parenthood in Scandinavia: Gender relations in welfare states* (pp. 27–51). Bristol: The University Press.

Lidwall, U., Bill, S., Palmer, E., & Bohlin Olsson, C. (2014). Sjukfrånvaro i psykiska diagnoser. [*Sickness absence due to mental diagnoses*]. *Vol. 4. Socialförsäkringsrapport (Social Insurance Report)*. Stockholm: Försäkringskassan.

Lidwall, U., Marklund, S., & Voss, M. (2010). Work–family interference and long-term sickness absence: a longitudinal cohort study. *European Journal of Public Health*, *20*(6), 676–681.

Mastekaasa, A. (2000). Parenthood, gender and sickness absence. *Social Science and Medicine*, *50*, 1827–1842.

Mauno, S. (2010). Effects of work–family culture on employee well-being: Exploring moderator effects in a longitudinal sample. *European Journal of Work and Organizational Psychology*, *19*(6), 675–195.

Mauno, S., De Cuyper, N., Kinnunen, U., Ruokolainen, M., Rantanen, J., & Mäkikangas, A. (2015). The prospective effects of work–family conflict and enrichment on job exhaustion and turnover intentions: comparing long-term temporary vs. permanent workers across three waves. *Work & Stress*, *29*(1), 75–94.

Mauno, S., Kinnunen, U., & Piitulainen, S. (2005). Work–family culture in four organisations in Finland: Examining antecedents and outcomes. *Community, Work & Family*, *8*(2), 115–140.

Mäkelä, L., Bergbom, B., Tanskanen, J., & Kinnunen, U. (2014). The relationship between international business travel and sleep problems via work–family conflict. *Career Development International*, *19*(7), 794–812. doi:10.1108/CDI-04-2014-0048

Nordic Council of Ministers. (2014). *Nordic Statistical Yearbook*. Retrieved from Copenhagen: http://norden.diva-portal.org/smash/get/diva2:763002/FULLTEXT07.pdf

Nordic Social Statistical Committee. (2015). *Sickness absence in the Nordic countries*. Retrieved from Copenhagen: http://norden.diva-portal.org/smash/get/diva2:811504/FULLTEXT06.pdf

Nylen, L., Melin, B., & Laflamme, L. (2007). Interference between work and outside-work demands relative to health: unwinding possibilities among full-time and part-time employees. *International Journal of Behavioural Medicine*, *14*(4), 229–236.

Öun, I. (2012). Work–family conflict in the Nordic countries: A comparative analysis. *Journal of Comparative Family Studies*, *43*(2), 165–184.

Rantanen, J., Kinnunen, U., Feldt, T., & Pulkkinen, L. (2008). Work–family conflict and psychological well-being: Stability and cross-lagged relations within one- and six-year follow-up. *Journal of Vocational Behavior*, *73*, 37–51.

Rapp, B., & Jackson, P. (2013). *Organisation and Work Beyond 2000*. Heidelberg: Springer Verlag.

Richter, A., Schraml, K., & Leineweber, C. (2015). Work–family conflict, emotional exhaustion and performance-based self-esteem: reciprocal relationships. *International Archives of Occupational and Environmental Health*, *88*(1), 103–112. doi:10.1007/s00420-014-0941-x

Roos, E., Lahelma, E., & Rahkonen, O. (2006). Work–family conflicts and drinking behaviours among employed women and men. *Drug and Alcohol Dependence, 83*, 49–56.

Roos, E., Sarlio-Lähteenkorva, S., Lallukka, T., & Lahelma, E. (2007). Associations of work–family conflicts with food habits and physical activity. *Public Health Nutrition, 10*(3), 222–229. doi:10.1017/S1368980007248487

Rostgaard, T. (2014). *Family Policies in Scandinavia*. Retrieved from Aalborg University, Denmark: http://vbn.aau.dk/da/publications/family-policies-in-scandinavia (471991a9-8288-4610-a50a-cd45fdb50290).html

Ruppanner, L. (2013). Conflict between work and family: An investigation of four policy measures. *Social Indicators Research, 110*, 327–347.

Statistics Norway. (2016). Sickness absence, Q2 2016. Retrieved from www.ssb.no/en/sykefratot/

Statistics Sweden. (2014). *På tal om kvinnor och män – Lathund om jämställdhet 2014 [Women and men in Sweden 2014 – Facts and figures]*. Retrieved from Örebro: www.scb.se/statistik/_publikationer/le0201_2013b14_br_x10br1401.pdf

Stier, H., Lewin-Epstein, N., & Braun, M. (2012). Work–family conflict in comparative perspective: The role of social policies. *Research in Social Stratification and Mobility, 30*(3), 255–279.

Strandh, M., & Nordenmark, M. (2006). The interference of paid work with household demands in different social policy contexts: perceived work-household conflict in Sweden, the UK, the Netherlands, Hungary, and the Czech Republic. *The British Journal of Sociology, 57*(4), 597–617.

Sverke, M., Falkenberg, H., Kecklund, G., Magnusson Hanson, L., & Lindfors, P. (2016). *Women and men and their working conditions: The importance of organizational and psychosocial factors for work-related and health-related outcomes*. Report 2016: 2 Eng. Stockholm: Swedish Work Environment Authority. Retrieved from: https://www.av.se/en/work-environment-work-and-inspections/knowledge-compilations/women-and-men-and-their-working-conditions/

Van der Lippe, T., Jager, A., & Kops, Y. (2006). Combination pressure: The paid work–family balance of men and women in European countries. *Acta Sociologica, 49*(3), 303–319. doi:10.1177/0001699306067711

Vogel, J., Kindlund, H., & Diderichsen, F. (1992). *Arbetsförhållanden, ohälsa och sjukfrånvaro 1975–1989*. Stockholm: Statistics Sweden.

World Economic Forum. (2014). *The global gender gap report 2014*. Cologny/Geneve.

Voss, M., Josephson, M., Stark, S., Vaez, M., Alexanderson, K., Alfredsson, L., & Vingard, E. (2008). The influence of household work and of having children on sickness absence among publicly employed women in Sweden. *Scandinavian Journal of Public Health, 36*(6), 564–572.

Väänänen, A., Kevin, M. V., Ala-Mursula, L., Pentti, J., Kivimäki, M., & Vahtera, J. (2005). The double burden of and the negative spillover between paid and domestic work: Associations with health among men and women. *Women and Health, 40*(3), 1–18. doi:10.1300/J013c40n03_01

16 A Review of Work–Family Research in Latin America

Pedro I. Leiva, Hector Madrid, and Satoris S. Howes

Latin America is a region marked by a diverse mix of sophisticated cultures and progressive social change. It is also an area with high levels of economic, social, political, and territorial inequality (Riffo, 2011). Similarly, the area is well-known for its machismo, or strong sense of masculine pride and assumption of male superiority (Faur, 2006; Puyana Villamizar, 2012). These issues make research on work–family dynamics both interesting and essential. They also make such research difficult and somewhat nuanced from other parts of the globe. In this chapter, we explore the unique aspects of Latin America on matters related to the interplay of work and family issues. Specifically, we examine the region's economic growth and social development policies and how they impact families and the quality of life therein. Further, we highlight some of the key findings from work–family research conducted in this region, and how they relate to findings conducted elsewhere. In our examination, we touch on some of the underlying assumptions that seem to appear in work–family research emerging from Latin America, as well as unique challenges to conducting research in this region.

Defining the Region

It is important to identify what countries comprise Latin America. For the purposes of this chapter, we are limiting our investigation to those regions of the American continent that, because of language, religion, colonization, as well as international affairs history, share some social and sociopolitical similarities (Quijada, 1998). In particular, we define Latin America as comprising select countries from North America (i.e., Mexico), Central America (i.e., Guatemala, Honduras, El Salvador, Nicaragua, Costa Rica, and Panama), and South America (i.e., Venezuela, Colombia, Ecuador, Peru, Bolivia, Brazil, Uruguay Paraguay, Argentina, and Chile).

We note the exclusion of Belize, an English-speaking country from Central America, French Guyana, and Suriname in South America, as well as the Caribbean islands as part of Latin America. The reasons for these exclusions lie in the fact that they have some distinct cultural aspects from the aforementioned countries (Quijada, 1998). A detailed explanation of such differences beyond the scope of this chapter. Rather than elucidate them, we simply focus our investigation on the countries that fall within our defined region, and invite readers to interpret and reflect on our findings accordingly.

Latin American Context

In order to fully understand the driving force behind the types of work–family research being conducted and the findings that may be unique to Latin America, it is important to understand the general context of the region. In terms of issues that have clear relevance to work–family dynamics, we focus our discussion on (a) historical events that have led to economic turmoil and work insecurity, (b) the machismo mindset, gender roles, and gender inequality that exists within the population, (c) the degree of collectivism and focus on the family that are traditional hallmarks of the region, and (d) the contemporary challenges to traditional views that are occurring in Latin America. Each of these issues, both separately and in combination with one another, contributes to the need for work–family research in the area and serves as an explanation for differences that emerge in comparative studies of the region with others.

Economic Turmoil, Inequity, and Work Insecurity

First, it is important to note the economic turmoil the region has faced and the impact on work insecurity that continues to exist. In Latin America, the globalization of the economies was accompanied by the implementation of economic adjustment policies and the neo-liberal economic model (Ramos, 1997). Although free markets and global free trade are certainly not new concepts, the move toward a more capitalistic approach has had unfortunate consequences for workers in the region. In particular, the move toward neoliberalism has resulted in a reduction of the welfare state, along with improvements to the macro economy, lessened social protection, a liberalization of labor regulations, and incentivized economic activity. These changes have introduced precarious, poorly paid, insecure, and unprotected work (Faur, 2006). Taken together, these issues have clear relevance for work–family issues, as the work side of the equation is clearly impacted.

In addition to economic turmoil and work insecurity, there is a large degree of economic inequality that exists within Latin America. As a stark example, despite most South American countries reducing their poverty level during the first eight years of this century, the Gini coefficient, which measures the disparity of income, has increased and remains the highest compared to other world regions (Ortiz & Cummins, 2011; Riffo, 2011). Similarly, although the proportion of households below poverty level decreased from 41% to 35% between 1990 and 1999, the overall population in poverty has increased as the population has grown and a greater number of children are living in low income households (Arriagada, 2001). Moreover, because of the strong concentration of economic activity in a few places in each country, as well as concentration of the population in specific geographic areas, economic growth and social change are stronger in some areas than others. As a result, the inequality is not only economic, but also social, political, and territorial (Riffo, 2011). Thus, there remains widespread disproportionate economic hardship within Latin America, potentially having a great impact on both current and future generations.

Machismo, Gender Roles, and Gender Inequality

The machismo mindset of much of Latin America and the accompanying gender roles that exist in these societies also has direct relevance for work–family scholarship. The strong sense of masculine pride, a key characteristic of machismo cultures, has resulted in social regulation of women and power asymmetry between men and women. As Jelín (2007) describes, the origin of this machismo culture comes from Spanish and Portuguese colonization, where social regulation was based on Catholic canonical principles. Although civil law gradually incorporated some secular principles, much of Latin America remained largely patriarchal for quite some time, such that men held the right to decide on the life and death of their relatives and women were expected to be obedient to their father first, and their husband later, as a public policy imperative. According to law, women were not citizens, had no full legal competence, were dependent, in need of protection, and unable to conduct public activities themselves. Also, the power asymmetry served as one of the foundations of violence toward women in different social contexts, resulting in high incidence rates of domestic violence in Latin America (Arriagada, 2007b; Bárcena & Prado, 2010). Although not this extreme in all parts of Latin America today, the current distribution of resources, power, and time in much of Latin America continue to give women unequal participation in the labor market, political realm, and public life compared to their male counterparts (Arriagada, 2002).

Along with the machismo culture is a strong set of beliefs about how men and women should present themselves and for what roles they should be responsible. For example, a number of qualitative studies have shown that whereas work and paternity are seen as mandatory for men within Latin America, maternity, caregiving, and household duties are seen as mandatory for women (Faur, 2006; Olavarría, 2002; Puyana Villamizar, 2012). Thus, when women in Latin America engage in paid work, they not only challenge the traditional view that women are solely responsible for household and caregiving responsibilities, but they likewise challenge their gender identities. In other words, by working, women are creating a situation in which men may need to assist with household duties, and as such they are challenging men's experience of masculinity, as well as their own experience of femininity (Olavarría, 2002).

Along these lines, strong traditional assumptions remain about the responsibilities of Latin American men and women in domestic and paid labor. Along the second half of the twentieth century, particularly with the growth of capitalism at the end of the century, women entered into the labor market in large numbers (Puyana Villamizar, 2012). However, the influx of women into the labor market has not necessarily resulted in more egalitarian views toward household responsibilities, as women, despite sharing the role of provider, still take on the bulk of caregiving responsibilities (Faur, 2006; Puyana Villamizar, 2012).

Indeed, a great deal of inequity exists between the sexes in Latin America, both in terms of how men and women are treated within the workplace as well as how they divide household duties. For example, the reduction of the welfare state and the resulting precarious work described above has not only differentially impacted the poorest of the population, but also has taken a greater toll on women, thereby exacerbating not only economic inequity but social inequity as well (Faur, 2006; Hopenhayn, 2007). Within Latin America, initial job opportunities for women were somewhat limited and often included informal, non-regulated jobs they could perform from home. However, at the end of the 1990s due to family financial requirements and work regulation liberalization, women began working in part-time jobs outside of the home (Schkolnik, 2004). Unfortunately, the insecure, lower-paying, and unprotected nature of the part-time jobs that women had access to had the unfortunate result of increasing gender inequity, particularly in low-income families. By the beginning of the twenty-first century, although women had higher educational attainment and had increased their participation in regulated full-time jobs, they still held non-regulated and precarious jobs to a greater proportion than did men (Abramo & Valenzuela, 2005; De Oliveira & Ariza, 2000; Faur, 2006; Hopenahyn, 2007; Schkolnik, 2004).

In addition, gender inequality appears to exist at home, with household duties still unequally distributed despite women being more active participants in the workplace, creating a hardship for women with regard to work–family management. Research in this region suggests that Latin American men are uncomfortable taking over household tasks; therefore, they react by increasing their participation in paternity-related responsibilities (e.g., taking children to school, helping them with homework, playing with them, taking them to bed), while leaving household tasks to women (Burín, 2004; Cosse, 2009; Wainerman, 2000). These nonpaid "jobs" at home may explain why Latin American women report working, in total, more hours compared to their male counterparts with similar paid jobs. Moreover, the lack of help from their male counterparts may be creating even more work for women, as there is evidence that women heading a single-parent family spend less time in domestic duties than when they live with a partner (Arriagada, 2009; Bárcena & Prado, 2010; Díaz & Medel, 2002; Milosavljevic & Tacla, 2007; Mires & Toro, 2010; OIT, 2009).

Women in Latin America experience a double burden because of the addition of duties from work on top of the ones from the family (Arriagada, 2005; Hopenhayn, 2007; Pautassi, Faur, & Gherardi, 2005; Reinecke, 2011; Schkolnik, 2004). According to Pomar and Martinez (2007), some Latin American women have opted to eliminate the burden by either quitting their work or choosing not to raise children. They found that those who have opted to work and have children experience the stress of working along with feelings of guilt caused by leaving their gender role aside. Finally, they found that only a few, usually young women, are able to manage work and family by developing more egalitarian relationships with their partners. Surprisingly, however, even though people in Latin America reported working more hours than did individuals from Anglo, Asian, and East European countries, the relationship between work demands and work interference with family was stronger for the sample of Anglo countries than for Latin American country samples (Spector et al., 2007). Also, in-depth interviews in several studies reveal women are not acutely aware of the double burden they experience when they become mothers, neither realizing their feelings of guilt because they are not taking care of their household and caring duties, nor keenly identifying the difficulties they face along their careers and the segregation of which they are object (Avendaño & Román, 2011; Burín, 2008; Heller, 2013).

Finally, research suggests that Latin American women face different sources of discrimination than do the men in the region. The unemployment rate for women is higher than it is for men, and women are discriminated against when searching for jobs because men are prioritized in the hiring process (ECLAC, 2015; Todaro, Mauro, & Yáñez, 2000). In other words, it is harder for women to get a job than it is for men to secure similar employment. In addition, women's salaries are lower than those of men in the same positions (De Oliveira & Ariza, 2000; Heller, 2013; Orlando & Zúñiga, 2000). The differential job opportunities, as well as career discontinuities related to childbearing, have a negative impact on women's career development opportunities, segregating them to lower-status jobs that are seen as stereotypically female as well as to lower-level positions within organization (Acevedo, 2012; Cerrutti, 2000; De Oliveira & Ariza, 2000; Heller, 2013; Mires, 2003; Orlando & Zúñiga, 2000). While many of these issues are not unique to Latin America, with women worldwide often facing discrimination and pay inequity, these issues are particularly salient within Latin America given the strong gender roles and gender identities that exist in the region.

Collectivism and Family Focus

A third contextual issue relevant to work–family scholarship is the degree of collectivism and focus on the family that is seen in Latin America. Most people from Latin American countries are collectivistic (Hofstede, Hofstede, & Minkov, 2010), meaning they develop their unique identities based on their group. For Latin Americans, family in particular plays a central role as a source of identity because of the strong family values that exist, as well as the intensity of the sense of belonging (Carteret, 2012). As a result, the conflict between work and family domains may be viewed differently for Latin American individuals compared to individuals from areas in which family is of lesser importance. For example, results of comparative studies (described later in this chapter) indicate that individuals in Latin America report less work–family conflict despite reporting that they work more hours than individuals from other areas (Spector et al., 2004). One explanation that has been suggested for this is because one's work is instrumental for financial resources, which are necessary to family survival. Thus, work is not seen as conflicting with one's family.

Another area of particular relevance for work–family research, especially with regard to differences from other regions, is the nature of family itself. In Latin America, the family is not limited to parents, children, and spouses, but rather includes members from one's extended family (e.g., grandparents, aunts, uncles, and cousins). Furthermore, family may also include individuals not biologically related to an individual, such as those who have gained the trust of family members, but remain outside of the formal definition of family (Carteret, 2012).

This collectivism and family focus may also interact with the findings regarding gender inequality discussed in the previous section. That is, while women worldwide face similar experiences, an additional barrier that women in Latin America face is the strong focus on collectivism and importance of family to one's identity. This heightened importance of the family combined with the crux of the family responsibilities falling on them leads to an extreme feeling of guilt because they feel they are (or are seen as) abandoning their family responsibilities, even when they plan and make sure the family demands are satisfied (Burín, 2008; Díaz & Medel, 2002; Heller, 2013; Morais, Nogueira, Menezes, Luiz, & Palmeira, 2012; Pomar & Martínez, 2007; Reinecke & Valenzuela, 2000).

Challenges to Traditional Views

Paradoxically, another factor of relevance to work–family issues within Latin America is the ever-changing landscape. Although the region has traditionally been one of collectivism, machismo, and the other points noted above, the contemporary landscape is one that has begun challenging those issues on multiple levels, creating a fertile landscape for continued work–family research. One clear example of a challenge to traditional views involves the changing structure of the family. Since 1990, there has been a reduction of the standard nuclear two-parent families, with a rise in single-parent families, especially with women as head of the household, and an increase in non-family households, particularly single/one-person situations (Arriagada, 2007b; Cerrutti & Binstock, 2009; Hopenhayn, 2007; OIT, 2009). Even in the "standard" nuclear families, however, there have been changes that has impacted work–family issues. For example, among nuclear families, one of the most important changes is the increase in the number of families in which both parents work (Arriagada, 2007b, Faur, 2006). Also, there has been an increase in the number of extended and blended families (Cerrutti & Binstock, 2009; Hopenhayn, 2007). In addition, in the past decade, migration, as a familiar economic strategy, has fragmented families and created more long-distance or transnational families (Arriagada, 2009).

Challenges to gender roles are also emerging with greater force. For example, as women have entered the workforce in greater numbers, scholars have examined their views of work and their meaning of work. Findings reveal that the meaning of work for Latin American women is diverse and different compared to the meaning of work for their male counterparts. Whereas men perceive their job as mandatory and necessary for providing for their families, women perceive their job less instrumentally and more linked to intrinsic motivations (Ochoa, 2012). According to Pomar and Martinez (2007), for women of a high socioeconomic status, work is seen as allowing them to reach a professional self-realization. For middle-class women, work is seen as increasing their self-realization because the income can support them to improve their family and children's well-being. Finally, for women in low-income households, work is viewed as providing a feeling of independence from their husbands and the pride to stand on one's own. Along these lines, Latin American women identify household and caregiving jobs as being reflective of inactivity and confinement, while working in a paid job reinforces their individuality (López et al., 2011).

These findings suggest that women's views of gender roles may be changing, though men's views may not be (or at least not at the same rate as women's, as evidenced by the earlier findings regarding inequity with regard to domestic duties). One possible impetus for a change in gender roles and gender inequality across sexes lies in the distribution of power that exists with various types of couples. According to Burín (2007), traditional couples are those in which the man holds the economic/ rational power and the woman holds the affective power. In such couples, no change in gender roles is possible because the woman's femininity as well as the man's masculinity are challenged when the woman holds a paying job. Conversely, innovative couples are egalitarian, whereby both the man and the woman share the economic/rational as well as the affective power. In innovative couples, gender roles are equal because the man and the woman can undertake paid work as well as household and care duties without challenging their gender identities. Since innovative couples reach gender role equality, they are in a better position to manage the work–family interface. Finally, transitional couples are those in which the man keeps the economic/rational power and the woman maintains the affective power, showing characteristics of the traditional couple, but when family needs necessitate an additional income, usually because the man is unemployed, gender roles become flexible, and while the woman takes over the provider role, the man takes over household and care duties. Even though transitional couples share qualities of innovative couples, men and women in these couples experience feelings of guilt because they do not take on their "mandatory" roles. Although it is unclear whether some types of couples are more prevalent than others – or will become more prevalent over time – the point is clear: as family structures and couple dynamics change, the traditional views of men and women are likely to change as well and could have direct implications for work–family matters.

For example, because the traditional assumption of the Latin American family pattern maintains that there is a male provider and a female caregiver, the design and implementation of public policies fail to account for these different familial arrangements and leave a disproportionate amount of household as well as child and elder care duties to women (Arriagada, 2007a, 2009; Schkolnik, 2004). According to Arriagada (2001, 2007b), the diverse social institutions responsible for the design and implementation of family public policies perform scattered interventions and uncoordinated programs in health, education, social security, poverty reduction, and eradication of violence among many other objectives, instead of designing and implementing explicit policies to protect families. Even the labor regulations, instead of facilitating the conciliation between work and family, make conflicting contributions to work–family balance in Latin America (Marco, 2010), giving men no obligation to engage in caregiving duties (Marco, 2011). Since conciliation practices are arranged for women, the conciliation of the family and work duties is reinforced institutionally as a female subject (Castro, 2008; Díaz & Medel, 2002; Faur, 2006). In this scenario, the costs of the weakness of current solutions to reconcile work and family in Latin America still remain on women (Anderson, 2011).

Work–Family Research in Latin America

Work–family research in Latin America has been conducted by a variety of scholars. Some notable studies have been conducted by the United Nations Regional Commissions in Latin America, the Economic Commission for Latin America, and the Caribbean (ECLAC) and the International Labour Organizational (ILO).These studies have primarily focused on the economic and social context of the work–family interface, the influx of women in the labor market, and the economic and social effects as well as the inequalities in the distribution of jobs and the required changes, particularly in terms of public policies and labor laws, to improve work–family balance. Most of these studies used data gathered by the national statistic units of each country and merged by the United Nations Commissions Statistic Units.

Other noteworthy Latin American studies have not been conducted from state-sponsored datasets and have tended to focus on understanding antecedents and consequences of the work–family interface to improve people's quality of life and organizational outcomes. Many of these studies are quantitative and have built on previously identified constructs and previously developed models, usually from other regions. The researchers of these studies usually use surveys, translated and adapted from research in other regions, and sometimes validated in previous local studies. Much of this research is published only in Spanish- or Portuguese-speaking journals with low visibility, and much of the results are only reported in graduate theses or presented at conferences. However, the increasing use of measures with reported empirical evidence of validity and reliability, as well as the high scientific interest on cultural comparisons, should increase the visibility of this research performed in Latin America.

Research in this area has largely mirrored research conducted in other regions. Namely, there has been a focus on antecedents and consequences of work–family conflict and facilitation as well as on strategies to cope with work–family conflict. In addition, comparative studies have examined how work–family issues in Latin America compare to other regions of the globe. We detail some of the findings from these studies below.

Antecedents and Consequences of Work–Family Conflict and Facilitation

Like research in other parts of the world, understanding the antecedents and consequences of work–family conflict has been an area of concern within Latin America as well. In line with the evidence gathered in other regions, in Latin America the antecedents to work–family conflict include work overload (Álvarez & Gómez, 2011; Patlán, 2013), time spent at work (Álvarez & Gómez, 2011; Feldman & Saputi, 2007; Mires & Toro, 2010), and the quality of one's relationships at work (Da Silva Maia, Mata de lima Alloufa, & Medeiros de Arújo, 2016). In addition, job stability and resources along with role conflict and role ambiguity are other antecedents, which may be particularly relevant in Latin America because of the regional expansion of the liberalization of the labor regulations (Álvarez & Gómez, 2011;

Correa & Ferreira, 2011; Feldman & Saputi, 2007). That is, the instability and inequality described earlier could influence these particular antecedents to a greater extent within Latin America, and are therefore worthy of continued study and comparative work.

The effect of the work schedules in specific populations has received considerable attention in research conducted in Latin America. Among female nurses working rotating schedules in Chile, for example, for those nurses with children under twelve years old, only those that lived with a romantic partner had significantly lower psychological health (Avendaño & Román, 2011). Other research has shown that, among male mining workers in Chile, the level of work–family conflict is significantly higher for those who work away from home for some days at the mining site and then go back home for some days, in comparison with those who work in regular shifts and go home daily (Baez & Galdames, 2005). Furthermore, women's job satisfaction seems to depend on whether they hold a full- or part-time job and whether they are mothers. When women have no children, they are more satisfied when holding full-time jobs, but when they have infants they are more satisfied with part-time work (Jiménez, González, & Reyes, 2015).

Effects of work–family conflict in Latin America mirror those in other parts of the world. For example, consequences include changes in mood and physical tiredness (Álvarez & Gómez, 2011; Feldman & Saputi, 2007), lower physical and psychological health (Barros & Barros, 2008), depression and anxiety (Feldman, Vivas, Lugli, Zaragoza, & Gómez, 2008; Grzywacz, Quandt, Arcury, & Marin, 2005), and physical exhaustion and fatigue (Grzywacz et al., 2007). Moreover, feelings of guilt related to one's work–family situations and lack of time at home are related to depression and anxiety (Feldman, 2013). Research in Latin America has also shown that work–family conflict is negatively related to life satisfaction and job satisfaction, motivation, productivity, and concentration, and positively related to work stress (Alvial Salgado, 2012; Barros & Barros, 2008; Da Silva Maia, et al., 2016; Paschoal & Tamayo, 2005; Sá de Souza, 2007).

All of the previously cited research has focused on the negative effects of combining work and family, but there is some research that suggests positive effects, particularly for women. When women working in paid jobs have social support at work and report work–family enrichment, they show higher wellness and self-esteem as well as lower depression and anxiety compared to women who do not work (Feldman et al., 2008; Gómez, Pérez, Feldman, Bajes, & Vivas, 2000). Generally speaking, and not surprisingly, support seems to play an important role in managing work and family. Studies have found that instrumental and emotional support from the spouse or other family members helps women to deal with household and childcare duties (Álvarez & Gómez; 2011; Alivial Salgado, 2012; Barros & Barros, 2008; Feldman, 2013; Jiménez & Fuentes, 2011; Jiménez, Mendiburo, & Olmedo, 2011). Support from community and religious groups also interacts with job and family demands, acting as a buffer and decreasing the negative effect of demands on women's health (Feldman & Saputi, 2007). Another source of support comes in the form of paid services. Availability of reliable domestic workers to take over household duties as well as access to reliable child care reduces work–family conflict among women (Barros & Barros, 2008; Jiménez, & Fuentes, 2011). Support from the family domain also has effects on the work domain, with research showing that support from the spouse helps women to cope with job demands (Pereira, Almeida, Santos, & Cezar-Vaz, 2011).

Coping with Work–Family Conflict

Strategies for dealing with work–family issues has also been an area of interest that has drawn attention from work–family scholars dealing with Latin American populations. Researchers have found that Latin American women implement numerous strategies to manage work–family conflict, many of which mirror those that women outside of Latin America would engage in. For example, individuals talk with their partners about their jobs, family, and future plans (Gonzalez Alfita, 2010; Pereira et al., 2011). Similarly, women increase their satisfaction at work by looking for and viewing work as a means of stability, personal success, or career development (Idrovo & Leyva, 2014). Finally, a coping strategy implemented by women in Latin America, and in line with those recommended for individuals in non-Latin American cultures, is to not bring work home when possible (da Silva Maia et al., 2016).

Unfortunately, some researchers have found coping strategies utilized by Latin American women that may inadvertently contribute to the continued problems that the region has faced in terms of gender inequality. For example, in line with gender role differences yet counter to the changes in family structures, Álvarez and Gómez (2011) found that Latin American women tend to quit their jobs to prioritize family, at least until children start school. In addition, women have opted to reduce work–family conflict by choosing to reduce the number of children they plan to have. On the other hand, researchers have found that some women buck the system, so to speak, and challenge the machismo ideals by reducing the time they dedicate at home and transferring their family duties to their husbands (Almeida Silva, 2006). Still others seem to divide the line, and rather than foster current views or challenge them, they simply implement alternatives. For example, rather than pushing for gender egalitarianism in terms of domestic duties, Morais et al. (2012) confirmed that women with enough resources outsource domestic tasks.

In terms of organizational strategies, a few case studies are illuminating. For example, in Colombia, small and middle-sized companies have sought to increase work–family balance by involving family members in the organization's activities, providing support to families when they are facing crises, offering professional advice to employees (e.g., accounting and legal advice unrelated to work), allowing more flexible work schedules, and giving employees a number of free days to attend to family duties (Flórez, 2014). In Mexico, programs exist but may be influenced to some extent by the gender of the owner, as suggested by research that found that small companies in the trade and services sector led by women implemented egalitarian and flexible work arrangement policies that favor work–family balance, while companies led by men did not (Arredondo, Velásquez, & De La Garza, 2013).

As has been found in other regions, organizational support is also critical in Latin America. For example, studies have found that perceptions of organizational support as well as family-supportive supervisor behaviors, positively related to employees' satisfaction with work–family balance in Chile and Colombia (Idrovo & Bosch, 2014). Similarly, perceptions of supervisor support increased affective commitment and buffered the effects of family interference with work on continuance commitment among Brazilians (Casper, Harris, Taylor-Bianco & Wayne, 2011). In Chile, social support from colleagues helps workers cope with work–family conflict (Jiménez & Fuentes, 2011), and family-friendly organizational culture positively relates to employees' organizational commitment (Jiménez, Acevedo, Salgado, & Moyano, 2009).

Comparative Findings

A large-scale study that was conducted across four Latin American countries with different political and social contexts (i.e., Chile, El Salvador, Mexico, and Peru), in addition to Spain, used the IESE (Instituto de Estudios Superiores de la Empresa – i.e., Enterprise Higher Studies Institute) Family-Responsible Employer Index. The index is based on employees' reports and assesses the degree to which organizations implement family-friendly policies and practices, and the employees' career development does not depend on quitting family responsibilities (Bosch, 2014; Hendricks, Leon, & Chinchilla, 2006). According to data gathered in 2012, 63% of people in Latin America work in company environments that are considered difficult for work–family management, compared to 54% worldwide (Bosch, 2013).

Analyzing the IBM 2001 Global Work and Life Issues Survey, which included a total of forty-eight countries, Hill, Yang, Hawkins, and Ferris (2004) found cross-cultural validity for the effect of job and family responsibilities on work–family conflict, work–family fit, and job satisfaction. The tested model was valid among the four culturally similar countries clusters only with few differences on the magnitude of the relationships among some clusters. Agarwala, Arizkuren-Eleta, Castillo, Muniz-Ferrer, and Gartzia (2014) also found cross-cultural validity on the relationship between work–life balance and affective commitment as well as the effect of managerial support on work–life balance among Spanish, Peruvians, and Indians. Halbesleben, Wheeler, and Rossi (2012), studied couples that work together in the same organization. They found higher levels of spousal support for these couples, which led to lower levels of emotional exhaustion and lower levels of time-based and behavioral-based work–family conflict, but higher levels of strained-based work–family conflict than couples working in different companies. These results did not differ between individuals from the United States and Brazil.

According to the Collaborative International Study of Managerial Stress (CISMS) reported by Spector et al. (2004), work–family stress had negative effects on intentions to quit, job satisfaction, and mental and physical well-being for the samples from Latin American, Chinese, and Anglo countries. However, even though the sample of Latin American countries reported working more hours and having more children than the samples from Chinese countries and Anglo counties, the Latin American and Chinese samples did not show a significant relationship between working hours and work–family stress while those from Anglo countries did. Additionally, the number of children at home did not show a significant relationship on family-work stress among the sample from Latin American countries, while there was a positive relationship among Anglo countries and a negative relationship among Chinese countries. The collectivistic nature of the Latin American and Chinese cultures is one explanation given to explain the significant effect of the workload on work–family stress. Although people from collectivistic cultures would assess work demands as an opportunity to support the family, people from individualistic cultures would experience the stress of not being able to fulfill both domains demands.

The CISMS 2 results reported by Spector et al. (2007), conducted on four regional samples of countries, revealed that individuals from the Latin American countries showed the highest number of working hours and number of children at home compared to the other countries. This study gives additional support to the differential effect of the work demands on the interference of the work on family life. This time, also controlling for domestic help, the relationship between work demands and work interference with family was stronger for the sample of Anglo countries than for the three other samples with countries from Latin America, Asia, and East Europe. The stronger relationship between work demands and work interference with family might be explained because Latin America, Asia and East Europe are more collectivistic than are Anglo countries.

Masuda et al.'s (2012) findings, also based on CISMIS 2 data, shed additional light on the impact of culture on the relationship between flexible work arrangements (i.e., flextime, compressed workweek, telecommuting, and part-time work) and strain and time-based work–family conflict among managers. First, managers in Anglo countries were more likely to work in companies offering flexible work arrangements than people in Asian and Latin American countries. Second, the authors found that among Latin Americans the only type of flexible work arrangements that was negatively related to strain-based work–family conflict was part-time employment. For Anglo countries, flextime was negatively related to strain- as well as time-based work–family conflict, while for Asians flextime was only related to strain-based work–family conflict, but teleworking was positively related to strain-based work–family conflict.

From a macro-level societal analysis, according to Lyness and Judiesch (2014), gender differences in the experience of work–family balance are larger in lower gender egalitarian societies (such as those in Latin America). Furthermore, in societies where people believe that biological sex should determine the social roles, women experience higher work–family conflict than do men. These results are consistent with research in the Latin American region that has shown that women are in charge of domestic duties and receive little support from their male partners (Lyness & Judiesch, 2014). Moreover, according to Ruppanner and Huffman (2014), the experience of work–family conflict is lower in societies in which women are part of the institutions making decisions about work and family policies. Latin America is a region with one of the lowest levels of participation by women among public companies, and especially for private companies (Ruppanner & Huffman, 2014). Therefore, the experience of work–family conflict should be higher than in countries where women have higher level of empowerment.

Summary of Research Findings

The work–family interface has become a topic of interest not only for organizational research in Latin America, but for Latin American economic growth, social development, and gender inequality researchers. Research on the economic growth and social development in this region has focused on the effect of the implementation of the neo-liberal economic model in the influx of women into the labor market as well as the social inequities associated with them. The results of this research highlights the importance of a co-responsibility approach among families, employers, and the state in order to meet the challenges associated with work–family management.

Quantitative research from Latin America has largely replicated the results obtained from other regions, supporting the transcultural validity of the models imported to be tested in Latin America. Findings generally suggest that organizations should create family-friendly organizational cultures, design and implement family-supportive policies and practice, and increase social support from the supervisors and coworkers. Qualitative research findings have provided evidence that the collectivistic nature of the Latin American culture may be driving differential findings for the region. That is, similar to findings from individuals across the globe, the experience of the work–family interface seems to be driven by the number of roles a person holds and the interdependence among them. More importantly for individuals in Latin America, though, is the centrality of each role embraced in groups from different domains, particularly the family. Therefore, the work–family interface in Latin America should to be analyzed from a multiple role perspective.

Suggestions for Future Research

We offer several areas in which scholars interested in work–family dynamics within Latin America might best focus their efforts. First, researchers would be well-advised to better consider the social and economic inequalities that exist in the region when formulating their research questions. Research models must consider the heterogeneity resulting from the economic and social inequalities among territories, families, social classes, and working conditions. These variables may influence the models that have been created based on research in other regions. Testing work–family frameworks without considering the unique characteristics of the Latin American population may result in a misrepresentation of findings and potentially hide the effects of the economic and social inequalities that exist in the region.

Second, another issue that work–family scholars should consider is the lack of awareness that individuals have about gender inequalities and the double jeopardy effect that women experience, which comes from the strong division of labor present in Latin America. Because of this lack of awareness, self-reports might not adequately capture the actual effect of work and family duties on individual, organizational, and social outcomes. Indeed, it may be necessary to use objective measures of work and family demands, such as hours spent on various activities (e.g., work, household tasks, childcare duties, eldercare responsibilities), the number of tasks or duties for which a person is responsible, or the actual number and types of support that an individual utilizes.

A third consideration for research in this region is the strength of individuals' gender identities and the machismo culture in Latin America. In Latin America, cultural norms may elicit more guilt from women for working (compared to men within Latin America and compared to women in other regions). Similarly, men may experience stronger negative reactions to women working as they see it as a threat to masculinity and power. We anticipate that work–family conflict is higher when gender identity is stronger because men and women in such situations are resistant to change their relationship to a more egalitarian one that would facilitate the management of work–family conflict as a couple. Research on this is strongly encouraged.

We also urge researchers in Latin America to take a roles perspective when conducting their work. Depending on how egalitarian the relationship is within a couple, women and men may differentially embrace the various roles of worker, spouse, parent, childcare provider, eldercare provider, and even coworker and relative. The number of roles, their centrality, and how important the work or the family domain is for a person may result in very different experiences of the work–family interface and yield differential effects on individuals' quality of life and associated organizational outcomes. Scholars would do well to consider the various roles and their importance to individuals when conducting work–family research.

Finally, work–family researchers in Latin America should strive to test more complex models to more fully explain the work–family interface, incorporating the culturally driven constructs that influence the experience of work–family conflict. These more complex models require building clear, culturally driven constructs, as well as incorporating valid and reliable measures. Some of the constructs suggested within this chapter include social inequity, gender identity, and relationship style (e.g., egalitarian vs. traditional, and role centrality). Worthy of note is that the complexity of the suggested models will require larger samples with the variability required to test the specific effects of these variables.

Conclusion

In this chapter, we identified the ways in which the Latin American context has implications for work–family research. We identified several aspects of Latin America that have helped inform scholarship in the area, including economic turmoil and insecurity, gender roles and inequality, collectivism and the importance of family, and challenges to traditional views. We then described some of the findings from the extant research, both as standalone studies and as comparative works. We hope this chapter provides a better understanding of the dynamics that exist within Latin America and the influences that each has on the work and the family lives of the individuals within the region. The opportunities for future research are great, and the need continues to swell. Through continued research in the area, improvements can be made for individuals, organizations, and Latin America as a whole.

References

Abramo, L., & Valenzuela, M. E. (2005). Balance del progreso laboral de las mujeres en América Latina. *Revista Internacional del Trabajo*, *124*(4), 399–430.

Acevedo, D. (2012). Desigualdades de género en el trabajo. Evolución y tendencias en la sociedad venezolana. Producción y reproducción. *Revista Venezolana de Estudios de la mujer*, *10*(*24*), 161–188.

Agarwala, T., Arizkuren-Eleta, A., Del Castillo, E., Muniz-Ferrer, M., & Gartzia, L. (2014). Influence of managerial support on work–life conflict and organizational commitment: an international comparison for India, Peru and Spain. *The International Journal of Human Resource Management*, *25*(10), 1460–1483.

Almeida Silva, J. V. (2006). A relação trabalho e família de mulheres empreendedoras. *Perspectivas Contemporâneas*, *1*(1). Taken from: http://revista.grupointegrado.br/revista/index.php/perspectivascontemporaneas/article/view/355/163

Álvarez, A., & Gómez, I. (2011). Conflicto trabajo-familia, en mujeres profesionales que trabajan en la modalidad de empleo. *Pensamiento psicológico*, *9*(16), 89–106.

Alvial Salgado, W. (2012). *Conflicto trabajo–familia y su relación con el apoyo social, la satisfacción vital y laboral en mujeres trabajadoras de hospitales urbanos y rurales de la Provincia del Biobío*. Tesis Doctoral, Universidad de Concepción. Facultad de Ciencias Sociales. Departamento de Psicología. Concepción, Chile.

Anderson, J. (2011). *Responsabilidades por compartir: la conciliación trabajo-familia en Perú*. Santiago de Chile: OIT, Organización Internacional del Trabajo.

Arredondo, F., Velásquez, L., & De La Garza, J. (2013). Políticas de diversidad y flexibilidad laboral en el marco de la responsabilidad social empresarial. Un análisis desde la perspectiva de género. *Estudios Gerenciales*, *29*(127), 161–166.

Arriagada, I. (2001). *Familias latinoamericanas. Diagnóstico y políticas públicas en los inicios del nuevo siglo. Serie Políticas sociales, N° 57*. Santiago de Chile, Comisión Económica para América Latina y el Caribe (CEPAL).

Arriagada, I. (2002). Cambios y desigualdad en las familias latinoamericanas, *Revista de la CEPAL*, *77*, 143–161.

Arriagada, I. (2005). Los límites del uso del tiempo: dificultades para las políticas de conciliación familia y trabajo. En I. Arriagada (Ed.), *Políticas hacia las familias, protección e inclusión sociales, Serie de Seminarios y Conferencias No. 46.*, (pp. 131–148). Santiago de Chile: CEPAL–UNFPA.

(2007a). Familias latinoamericanas: cambiantes, diversas y desiguales. *Papeles de población*, *13*(53), 9–22.

(2007b). Transformaciones familiares y políticas de bienestar en América Latina. En: I. Arriagada (Coord.) *Familia y políticas públicas en América Latina: una historia de desencuentros* (pp. 125–152). Santiago de Chile: Naciones Unidas.

(2009). La diversidad y desigualdad de las familias latinoamericanas. *Revista latinoamericana de estudios de familia, 1*, 9–21.

Avendaño, C., & Román, J. A. (2011). Efectos de los roles múltiples en el bienestar psicológico en enfermeras chilenas. *Psykhe, 11*(2), 2–27.

Baez, X., & Galdames, C. (2005). Conflicto de Rol Familia–Trabajo desde la Perspectiva de los Tipos de Jornada de Trabajo. *Revista de Psicología, 14*(1), 113–123.

Bárcena, A., & Prado, A. (2010). *La hora de la igualdad. Brechas por cerrar, caminos por abrir.* Santiago, Chile: Cepal.

Barros, E., & Barros, M. C. (2008). Conflicto entre trabajo y familia: efectos sobre la salud y resultados laborales en mujeres. *Estudios de Administración, 15*(2), 1–45.

Bosch, M. J. (2013). Conciliar trabajo y familia en Chile. Revista de Egresados ESE. Taken from www.ese.cl/wp-content/blogs.dir/1/files_mf/14350726622013art%C3%ADculoMJBosch.pdf

Bosch, M. J. (2014). El desarrollo de la reciprocidad: El impacto de las culturas con responsabilidad familiar corporativa. *Revista de Egresados ESE.* Taken fromwww.ese.cl/wp-content/blogs.dir/1/files_mf/14350728492014art%C3%ADculoMJBosch.pdf

Burín, M. (2004). Género femenino, familia y carrera laboral: conflictos vigentes. *Subjetividad y procesos cognitivos, 5*, 48–77.

(2007). Trabajo y parejas: impacto del desempleo y de la globalización en las relaciones entre los géneros. Reflexiones sobre masculinidades y empleo. En Jiménez Guzmán, L. y Tena, O. (comp.): *Reflexiones sobre masculinidades y empleo* (pp. 59–80). México: CRIM-UNAM.

(2008). Las "fronteras de cristal" en la carrera laboral de las mujeres. Género, subjetividad y globalización. *Anuario de psicología/The UB Journal of Psychology, 39*(1), 75–86.

Carteret, M. (2012). Dimensions of culture: Cross-culture communications for healthcare professionals. Smashwords Edition.

Casper, W. J., Harris, C., Taylor-Bianco, A., & Wayne, J. H. (2011). Work–family conflict, perceived supervisor support and organizational commitment among Brazilian professionals. *Journal of Vocational Behavior, 79*(3), 640–652.

Castro, V. (2008). *Estrategias de conciliación entre la vida familiar y el trabajo remunerado en el contexto de la flexibilidad laboral.* Tesis para optar el grado de Magister en Estudios de Género, Universidad Nacional de Colombia. Colombia.

Cerrutti, M. (2000). Economic reform, structural adjustment and female labor force participation in Buenos Aires, Argentina. *World Development, 28*(5), 879–891.

Cerrutti, M., & Binstock, G. (2009). *Familias latinoamericanas en transformación: desafíos y demandas para la acción pública. Serie políticas sociales, N° 147*, Santiago de Chile, Comisión Económica para América Latina y el Caribe (CEPAL).

ECLAC. (2015). Statistical Yearbook of Latin America and the Caribbean (LC/G.2656-P). Santiago, Chile: Economic Commission for Latin America and the Caribbean.

Correa, A. P., & Ferreira, M. C. (2011). The impact of environmental stressors and types of work contract on occupational stress. *The Spanish journal of psychology, 14*(1), 251–262.

Cosse, I. (2009). La emergencia de un nuevo modelo de paternidad en Argentina (1950–1975). *Estudios Demográficos y Urbanos,71*, 429–462

Da Silva Maia, K. L., Mata de lima Alloufa, J., & Medeiros de Arújo, R. (2016). Conflito trabalho-familia: A Interacão de papeis na visao de secretaruis executivo. Desenvolve *Revista de Gestão do Unilasalle, 5*(1), p–33.

De Oliveira, O., & Ariza, M. (2000). Género, trabajo y exclusión social en México. *Estudios Demográficos y Urbanos, 15*(1), 11–33.

Díaz, X., & Medel, J. (2002). Familia y trabajo: Distribución del tiempo y relaciones de género. In A. Bell, J. Olavarría, & C. Céspedes (Eds.), *Trabajo y familia, conciliación? seminario-taller, estrategias de conciliación, familia y trabajo con perspectiva de género* (pp.33–54). Santiago, Chile: SERNAM / FLACSO-Chile / CEM.

Faur, E. (2006). Género y conciliación familia-trabajo. Legislación laboral y subjetividades masculinas en América latina. In L. Mora, M. J. Moreno, & T. Rohrer (coords.), *Cohesión social, políticas conciliatorias y presupuesto público: Una mirada desde el género* (pp.129–155). México: UNPFA/GTZ.

Feldman, L. (2013). Estrés, satisfacciones y salud en mujeres trabajadoras con roles múltiples: Un estudio cualitativo. *Mundo Nuevo, 13*, 91–116.

Feldman, L., & Saputi, D. (2007). Roles múltiples, cualidad del rol, apoyo social y salud en mujeres trabajadoras. *Revista Venezolana de Estudios de la Mujer, 12*(29), 91–116.

Feldman, L., Vivas, E., Lugli, Z., Zaragoza, J., & Gómez, V. (2008). Relaciones trabajo-familia y salud en mujeres trabajadoras. *Salud pública de México, 50*(6), 482–489.

Flórez, A. (2014). *La responsabilidad social empresarial en las pymes de Colombia. Tesis para optar al grado de Especialización en Marketing, Universidad EAN*. Bogotá: Colombia.

Gómez, V., Pérez, L., Feldman, L., Bajes, N., & Vivas, E. (2000). Riesgos de salud en mujeres con múltiples roles. *Revista de Estudios Sociales, 6*, 27–38.

González Alfita, E. (2010). Comunicación interpersonal en matrimonios de doble ingreso: retos y estrategias de las mujeres mexicanas para comunicarse con su pareja. *Fonseca, Journal of Communication, 1*, 70–80.

Grzywacz, J. G., Arcury, T. A., Marín, A., Carrillo, L., Burke, B., Coates, M. L., & Quandt, S. A. (2007). Work–family conflict: Experiences and health implications among immigrant Latinos. *Journal of Applied Psychology, 92*(4), 1119–1130.

Gryzywacsz, J. G., Quandt, S. A., Arcury, T. A., & Marin, A. (2005). The work–family challenge and mental health. *Community, Work and Family,* 8(3), 271–279.

Halbesleben, J. R., Wheeler, A. R., & Rossi, A. M. (2012). The costs and benefits of working with one's spouse: A two-sample examination of spousal support, work–family conflict, and emotional exhaustion in work-linked relationships. *Journal of Organizational Behavior, 33*(5), 597–615.

Heller, L. (2013). Mujeres en la cumbre corporativa, el caso de la Argentina. *Revista del Centro de Estudios de Sociología del Trabajo, 3*, 68–96.

Hendricks, A.M., León, C., & Chinchilla, N. (2006). *Estado de las políticas de conciliación en Hispanoamérica*. Universidad de Navarra, Centro Internacional Trabajo y Familia, España.

Hofstede, G., Hofstede, G., & Minkov, M. (2010). *Cultures and organizations: Software of the mind. 3rd Edition*. London, England: McGraw-Hill.

Hopenhayn, M. (2007). Cambios en el paradigma del trabajo remunerado e impactos en la familia. En: I. Arriagada (Coord.) *Familia y Políticas Públicas en América Latina: Una Historia de Desencuentros* (pp. 63–76). Santiago de Chile: Naciones Unidas.

Idrovo, S., & Bosch, M. J. (2014), April. *Comparing the Work–family Interface in Chile and Colombia*. Paper presented at BALAS 2014: Business Association of Latin American Studies Conference, Port of Spain: Trinidad and Tobago.

Idrovo, S., & Leyva, P. (2014). Éxito y satisfacción laboral y personal: Cómo lo perciben mujeres que trabajan en Bogotá. *Pensamiento & Gestión, 36*, 155–183.

Hill, J. E., Yang, C., Hawkins, A. J., & Ferris, M. (2004). A cross-cultural test of the work-family interface in 48 countries. *Journal of Marriage and Family, 66*(5), 1300–1316.

Jelín, E. (2007). Las familias latinoamericanas en el marco de las transformaciones globales. En: I. Arriagada (Coord.) *Familia y Políticas Públicas en América Latina: Una Historia de Desencuentros* (pp. 93–124). Santiago de Chile: Naciones Unidas.

Jiménez, A., & Fuentes, C. E. (2011). Equilibrio trabajo-familia y autoeficacia parental en mujeres profesionales con y sin cargos de dirección en organismos públicos. *Revista Venezolana de Estudios de la Mujer, 17*(38), 207–224.

Jiménez, A., Acevedo, D., Salgado, A. L., & Moyano, E. (2009). Cultura trabajo-familia y compromiso organizacional en empresa de servicios. *Psicología em estudo, 14*(4), 729–738.

Jiménez, A., González, C. G., & Reyes, D., (2015). Satisfacción familiar y laboral de mujeres con distintas jornadas laborales en una empresa chilena de servicios financieros. *Acta Colombiana de Psicología, 12*(1), 77–83.

Jiménez, A., Mendiburo, N., & Olmedo, P. (2011). Satisfacción familiar, apoyo familiar y conflicto trabajo-familia en una muestra de trabajadores chilenos. *Avances en Psicología Latinoamericana, 29*(2), 317–329.

López, E., Ponce, M., Findling, L., Lehner, P., Venturiello, M. P., Mario, S., & Champalbert, L. (2011). Mujeres en tensión: la difícil tarea de conciliar familia y trabajo. *Población de Buenos Aires, 8*(13), 7–25.

Lyness, K. S., & Judiesch, M. K. (2014). Gender egalitarianism and work–life balance for managers: Multisource perspectives in 36 countries. *Applied Psychology, 63*(1), 96–129.

Marco, F (2010), July. *El uso del tiempo y las posibilidades de armonizar empleo y familia en las legislaciones laborales*. Ponencia presentada en XI Conferencia Regional sobre la Mujer de América Latina y El Caribe. Paper presented at the Regional Conference of Latin American and the Caribbean's Women., CEPAL, Brasilia, Brasil.

Marco, F. (2011). Cómo deben ser las familias según la ley de Argentina y Chile. Iberoamericana. *Nordic Journal of Latin American and Caribbean Studies 41*(1–2), 75–96.

Masuda, A. D., Poelmans, S. A., Allen, T. D., Spector, P. E., Lapierre, L. M., Cooper, C. L., . . . & Lu, L. (2012). Flexible work arrangements availability and their relationship with work-to-family conflict, job satisfaction, and turnover intentions: A comparison of three country clusters. *Applied Psychology, 61*(1), 1–29.

Milosavljevic, V., & Tacla, O. (2007). *Incorporando un módulo de uso del tiempo a las encuestas de hogares: restricciones y potencialidades. Serie Mujer y Desarrollo 83*. Santiago, Chile: CEPAL, Unidad Mujer y Desarrollo.

Mires, L. (2003). Situación Laboral de la Mujer en Paraguay. In M. E. Valenzuela (Ed.), Mujeres, *Pobreza y Mercado de Trabajo: Argentina y Paraguay. Proyecto: Género, Pobreza y Empleo en América Latina* (pp. 105–138). Santiago, Chile: OIT.

Mires, L., & Toro, E. (2010). *Encuesta exploratoria sobre el uso del tiempo en el Gran Santiago: Análisis y Perspectivas* (Informe Final). Santiago, Chile: OPS.

Morais M., Nogueira N., Menezes, R., Luiz, G., & Palmeira, P. (2012). Administrando trabalho e família: um estudo de Caso sobre mulheres profissionais com alto nível de instrução. *Oikos: Revista Brasileira de Economia Doméstica, 23*(1), 170–200.

Ochoa, P. (2012). Significado del trabajo en mineros venezolanos, ¿reflejo del empleo en vías de extinción? . . . *Revista Gaceta laboral*, 18(1) 35–56.

OIT (2009). *Trabajo y Familia: Hacia Nuevas Formas de Conciliación con Corresponsabilidad Social*. Santiago, Chile: OIT-PNUD.

Olavarría, J. (2002). Hombres: identidades, relaciones de género y conflictos entre trabajo y familia. In J. Olavarría, & C. Céspedes, *Trabajo y familia, conciliación? Seminario-Taller, Estrategias de Conciliación, Familia y Trabajo con Perspectiva de Género* (pp. 53–76). Santiago, Chile: SERNAM / FLACSO-Chile / CEM.

Olavarría, J. (2002). Los estudios sobre masculinidades en América Latina. Un punto de vista. *Anuario social y político de América Latina y el Caribe, 6*, 91–98.

Orlando, M. B., & Zúñiga, G. (2000), March. *Situación de la Mujer en el Mercado Laboral en Venezuela: Análisis de la Participación Femenina y de la Brecha de Ingresos por Género*. Paper presented at XXII Congreso de la Asociación de Estudios Latinoamericanos, Miami, USA.

Ortiz, I., & Cummins, M. (2011). *Global Inequality: Beyond the Bottom Billion – A Rapid Review of Income Distribution in 141 Countries*. New York: United Nations Children's Fund (UNICEF).

Paschoal, T., & Tamayo, A. (2005). Impacto dos valores laborais e da interferência família-trabalho no estresse ocupacional. *Psicologia: Teoria e Pesquisa, 21*(2), 173–180.

Patlán, J. (2013). Efecto del burnout y la sobrecarga en la calidad de vida en el trabajo. *Estudios Gerenciales, 29*(129), 445–455.

Pautassi, L., Faur, E., & Gherardi, N. (2005). Legislación laboral y género en América Latina, Avances y omisiones. In I. Arriagada (Ed.), *Políticas Hacia las Familias, Protección e Inclusión Sociales, Serie de Seminarios y Conferencias No. 46*., (pp. 111–129). Santiago de Chile: CEPAL–UNFPA.

Pereira, L., Almeida, M., Santos, M., & Cezar-Vaz, M. (2011). Reciprocal influence between professional activity and family life: perceptions of fathers/mothers. *Acta Paulista de Enfermagem, 24*(3), 373–380.

Pomar, S., & Martínez, G. (2007). Resignificación identitaria, trabajo y familia: una disyuntiva para la mujer. *Administración y Organizaciones, 9*(18), 95–109.

Puyana Villamizar, Y. (2012). Las políticas de familia en Colombia: entre la orientación asistencial y la democrática. *Revista Latinoamericana de Estudios de Familia, 4*, 210–226.

Quijada, M. (1998). Sobre el origen y difusión del nombre" América Latina"(o una variación heterodoxa en torno al tema de la construcción social de la verdad). *Revista de Indias, 58*(214), 595–616.

Ramos, J. (1997). Un balance de las reformas estructurales neoliberales. *Revista de la CEPAL, 62*, 15–38.

Reinecke, G. (2011). Trabajo Decente y Política Activa de Generación de Empleo. In: Ministerio de Hacienda de Paraguay, *Construyendo la Agenda de Mediano y Largo Plazo del Paraguay en su Bicentenario* (pp. 45–56). Asunción, Paraguay: Autor.

Reinecke, G., & Valenzuela, M. E. (2000). La calidad de empleo: Un enfoque de género. In M. E. Valenzuela & G. Reinecke (Eds.), *¿Más y mejores empleos para las mujeres? La Experiencia de los Países del Mercosur y Chile* (pp. 29–58), Santiago, Chile: OIT.

Riffo, L. (2011). *Desigualdades económicas regionales en América Latina y el Caribe.* Documento presentado en la Reunión de expertos sobre población, territorio y desarrollo sostenible, Santiago de Chile, 16, y 17.

Ruppanner, L., & Huffman, M. L. (2014). Blurred boundaries: Gender and work–family interference in cross-national context. *Work and Occupations, 41*(2), 210–236.

Sá de Souza, E. (2007). *Um estudo sobre a repercussão do conflito trabalho-família e família-trabalho na satisfação no trabalho e na família e sua consequência na satisfação do hóspede: o caso da rede hoteleira de Porto de Galinhas.* Dissertação de Mestrado não publicada. Mestrado em Administração–Centro de Pesquisa e Pós–Graduação em Administração. Faculdade de Boa Viagem. Recife.

Schkolnik, M. (2004). Tensión entre familia y trabajo. En: I. Arriagaday V. Aranda (comps). *Cambio de las Familias en el Marco de las Transformaciones Globales: Necesidad de Políticas Públicas Eficaces. Serie de Seminarios y Conferencias No. 46*, (pp. 97–118). Santiago, Chile: CEPAL-UNFPA.

Spector, P. E., Cooper, C. L., Poelmans, S., Allen, T. D., O'Driscoll, M., Sanchez, J. I., . . . Lu. L. (2004). A cross-national comparative study of work–family stressors, working hours, and well-being: China and Latin America versus the Anglo world. *Personnel Psychology, 57*, 119–142.

Spector, P. E., Allen, T. D., Poelmans, S. A. Y., LaPierre, L. M., Cooper, C. L., O'Driscoll, M., . . WiderszalBazyl, M. (2007). Cross-national differences in relationships of work demands, job satisfaction, and turnover intentions with work–family conflict. *Personnel Psychology, 60*, 805–835.

Todaro, R., Mauro, A., & Yáñez, S. (2000). Chile: La calidad del empleo.Un análisis de género. In M. E. Valenzuela & G. Reinecke (Eds.), *¿Más y mejores empleos para las mujeres? La Experiencia de los Países del Mercosur y Chile* (pp. 193–267). Santiago, Chile: OIT.

Wainerman, C. (2000). División del trabajo en familias de dos proveedores. Relato desde ambos géneros y dos generaciones. *Estudios Demográficos y Urbanos, 15*, 149–184.

17 A Review of Work–Family Research in Africa

Zitha Mokomane

With the globalization of the world economy, Africa, like most regions, is undergoing an array of socioeconomic and demographic trends that makes the integration of work and family life challenging. As Chinchilla et al. (2010) assert, jobs have become "more complex, demanding, and globalized than ever before, requiring long hours, increased availability, and effort" (p. 7). At the same time, family structures are changing; in Africa, the traditional caregiving role of the extended family is increasingly weakening. Despite African workers with care responsibilities facing similar challenges to their counterparts in other parts of the world, the intersection of work and family as a policy and academic issue in Africa has been left largely unexplored, and research on the subject can be described as emerging.

The aim of this chapter is to give an overview of this emerging research, with particular focus on the sub-Saharan African region. The chapter begins by giving a context of the region in terms of the current socioeconomic and demographic transformations that have implications for work–family management. This is followed by a brief history of major work–family research initiatives in the region. The findings of key African work–family studies conducted in the recent past are then presented before the chapter concludes with a discussion of future research ideas.

Context

Given historical, social, and cultural fluidity and diversity, caution should be exercised in making generalizations or assumptions that family systems in developing societies such as Africa are the same across ethnic, religious, national, regional or linguistic groupings (Joseph, 1994). What is undisputed, however, is that the family lays at the core of society in traditional Africa. For example, it has been argued that "each person in African traditional life lives in or as a part of the family" (Mbiti, 1975, p. 175) and that "the family community was the fundamental element of the African, the basic sphere of action, through which he became integrated with the larger, human community . . . he always acted from within the sphere of the family" (Kisembo et al. 1998, p. 202). Historically, as the unit of production, consumption, reproduction, and accumulation, the traditional African extended family – which was comprised of generations of close relatives living at home and away and within which cooperation, reciprocation, and an intense sense of solidary (Bigombe & Khadiagala, 2003; Ntozi & Zirimenya, 1999; Mokomane, 2013) – provided for the socioeconomic, emotional, psychological, and caregiving needs of family members through specific and well-defined gender and generational roles.

From a work–family interface perspective, the division of labor that was brought about by these roles lessened the work burden of individuals by spreading it across family members. Overall, with African societies being largely patriarchal, men were traditionally seen as the heads and breadwinners of their families and were responsible for the economic well-being of the family. Women, on the other hand, were responsible for the execution of domestic tasks, the provision of care for all family members (particularly children, the aged, the infirm, and the disabled), and for overall household management. Children contributed to the family by running age-appropriate errands and doing household and farm work, while grandparents were important providers of child care and socialization (Ntozi & Zirimenya, 1999; Mokomane, 2013). Other extended family members also had specific roles to play in ensuring the sustenance of the family. For example, female members of the family such as sisters, sisters-in-law, aunts, mothers, mothers–in-law were traditionally expected to offer their assistance in caring for newly born babies and nursing mothers. This, among other things, lessened the new mother's emotional and physical burden, which typically characterizes this early period of childrearing (Mokomane, 2011; Wusu & Isiugo-Abanihe, 2006).

Although the extended family in Africa has, to a large extent, maintained its place as the source of socio economic support and security for its members (Ntozi & Zirimenya, 1999), the multifaceted and ongoing social, economic, and demographic transformations in contemporary Africa have led to notable changes in the structure and function of extended families. This has had important implications for the work burden of family members. Key among these changes include increasing female labor force participation, changes in nuptiality patterns, increased migration, and high prevalence of HIV/AIDS. Unlike in the past when wage employment was the domain of men and women's roles revolved around the performance of domestic duties and agricultural work, one of the most striking labor market trends of recent times has been the growing proportion of African women in the labor force. Specifically, female labor force participation rates in the region increased over the last two decades from 59% in 1990 to 64% in 2014 (World Bank, 2016).

It is noteworthy, however, that the majority (74%) of these women work in the informal sector, such as in subsistence farming, crafts making, small scale manufacturing (e.g., bread-making, tailoring, food catering), informal services (e.g., gardening and domestic work), and informal trade (e.g., tuckshops). This sector is characterized by low-productivity, low and highly volatile earnings, and inadequate social protection coverage (ISSA, 2013; ILO, 2016). It has been found that family responsibilities both steered many African women toward informal employment and constrained their income earning activities as informal economy workers. Overall, although the flexible work hours that are typical of informal sector employment enhance the fulfillment of household and childcare responsibilities, family responsibilities often limit the types of activities and amount of time women can spend on their paid activities, thus aggravating women's poverty levels and other vulnerabilities that come with being informal sector workers (Cassirer & Addati, 2007).

Family structure and composition in traditional Africa hinged, to a large extent, on early dominant models of marriage which stressed several key components that included, *inter alia,* early marriage, especially for women, and almost universal marriage for both sexes (van de Walle, 1993). Since the 1970s, however, a large part of the continent began to experience significant transformations in nuptiality patterns, reflected mainly in the increase in age at first marriage, overall decline in marriage prevalence, and increased marital dissolution through divorce and separation (van de Walle, 1993; Hertrich, 2002). As a result of these nuptiality patterns, female-headed households have become a common phenomenon in contemporary sub-Saharan Africa with recent figures showing that these type of households account for more than 20% of all households in many countries in the region (Mokomane, 2013). These female-headed households are typically smaller than those headed by males, with an average of 3.9 and 5.1 members, respectively (Milazzo & van de Walle, 2015). Female heads of households in Africa are twenty-seven times more likely to live in households in which they are the only adult living with one or more children and, often, with older persons (Milazzo & van de Walle, 2015; Statistics South Africa, 2010). Among other things, these demographics suggest that female heads in the region have higher dependency ratios and care burdens than their male counterparts.

In the past, the caregiving responsibilities of female heads of households could have been addressed, to large extent, by the traditional kinship mode of residential settlement which availed family support for care roles and domestic tasks. While still existent, this type of support is becoming less available due to increased migration which has, among others things, led to the physical separation of family members and the reduced household sizes discussed above (Mokomane, 2013). In a different vein and similar to what Sorj (2004) found in Brazil, the availability of grandparents to allocate a good part of their time to helping their adult children in housework and child care seems to be creating a new generation of grandmothers that is very different from previous generations. This new generation is better educated, more socialized in the world of work, and more active in terms of social life.

Against the background of reduced kin support and assistance for child care, the provision of public childcare services has been identified as the most effective policy option for enhancing work–family balance and increasing women's access to employment in developing countries (Alfers, 2015; Esplen, 2009). However, with few affordable, organized, and comprehensive public childcare services in many African countries, a common strategy for working mothers is to acquire the services of domestic workers or "house helps" (Mapedzahama, 2014; Muasya, 2014). Although this is an important coping mechanism, available evidence suggests that from a child development and health perspective, it is not necessarily ideal. For example, an overwhelming majority of household helpers have no training, whatsoever, in childcare and often do not have any previous relationship with the child's family. In essence, therefore, many working mothers trust and put the care, health and, literally, the life of their minor children in the hands of complete strangers. As Muasya (2014) noted in Kenya, often when the employment relationship between the working mother and the helper sours it is common for the latter to harm the child or collude with criminals to rob the employers of valuable belongings. Additionally, as Reddock and Bobb-Smith (2008) noted in Trinidad and Tobago, household helpers are often mothers themselves with their own work–life challenges.

The HIV and AIDS epidemic has also puts great strain on the care-related activities of families in many parts of Africa. According to UNAIDS figures, 25.8 million people living with HIV are in sub-Saharan Africa, accounting for 70% of the global total (UNAIDS, 2015). Thus, as the primary caregivers for sick family members, working women in many African countries have the extra burden of providing care and support for family and household members with HIV and AIDS. For example, in a study of extended family caring for children orphaned by AIDS in Botswana, Heymann et al. (2007) found that nearly half (47%) of orphan caregivers said that their work sometimes got in the way of their meeting children's needs compared to less than one-third (30%) of those not caring for orphans. Furthermore, orphan caregivers were more likely to state that working overtime, irregular hours, or being far from their family caused difficulty meeting their caregiving responsibilities at home. Among those reporting difficulties, 67% reported being unable to find reliable childcare and 24% reported being unable to help children with school work while working overtime. HIV/AIDS-related care work has also been found to reduce working women's time to do other potentially life-enhancing activities, such as engaging in income generation and skills building projects or further education (ILO, 2004) and to attend to other social relationships. For example, Heymann and colleagues noted that in Botswana, caring for children orphaned by AIDS impacted the time caregivers could care for other family members, including their parents and in-laws: such caregivers spent 34.7 hours per month caring for parents and in-laws compared with 43.7 hours for those without orphan care-giving responsibilities (Heymann et al., 2007).

History of the Study of Work–Family in This Region

The foregoing transformations suggest that support mechanisms that were traditionally offered by the extended family for domestic tasks and caregiving responsibilities in Africa are being stretched and in some cases have been exhausted. The consequence is that families are finding it increasingly difficult to continue caring for their young, old, sick, and disabled members, to reconcile work and family responsibilities, and to maintain intergenerational bonds that sustained them in the past. Taken together, these factors have contributed to the emergence of work–family management as an issue of grave concern at multiple levels – for individuals, societies, organizations, and governments (Dancaster & Baird, 2008). Despite this, work–family issues have not been given high priority in academic circles in the region; political, economic, and labor market issues seem to be deemed more important topics of academic debate and research than the family in general and work–family interface in particular (Mokomane, 2014b; Ziehl, 2003). Indeed, there are essentially only two main institutions in the whole of Africa that have a focused interest in work–family research: *the Nigerian-based Institute for Work and Family Integration* (IWFI) and the Kenyan-based Center for Research on Organizations, Work, and Family (CROWF).

IWFI is a policy research, advocacy, and training center for the *integration* of work and *family* with the stated aim of "highlighting the impact of demographic shifts and rapidly changing technology on the family and the need for corporations to create enabling policies for work and family balance, resulting in Better Family, Better Business, Better Society." The institute has close collaboration with the Lagos Business School, where one of Africa's most prolific scholars on the subject, Chantal Ipie (who is also the chair of IWFI's Board of Trustees), is based. To date the institute has hosted three conferences (2014, 2015, and 2016) and has an active events program (see www.iwfionline.org/category/programmes).

CROWF is a research institution within the Strathmore Business School in Nairobi, Kenya. Established in 2002, the vision of CROWF is to assist companies to manage people and their organizations through sound and well researched corporate policies. One way it does this is through the delivery of a course on work–life balance in the different management programs at the Strathmore Business School. Over the past ten years, the Center hosted a series of annual colloquia on work and family for researchers coming mainly from West, East, and Central Africa. However, the frequency of these colloquia have, over the year, declined due to funding constraints. Current work–family activities of the Center include conducting, in collaboration with the Families & Work Institute in Boston, the annual Employer and Employees General Survey in Kenya. The Center is also one of the only two institutions (the other being the Lagos Business school) that have to date implemented the International Family-Responsible Employer Index (IFREI) in Africa. IFREI is a diagnostic instrument aimed at analyzing the level of implementation of flexibility and work–family reconciliation policies in companies, their effect on the employees, and on the organizations themselves. Spearheaded by the Spain-based International Center for Work and Life at the IESE Business School, IFREI has been implemented globally since 1999 and, as of February 2014, a total of 16,000 people from twenty-one countries on five continents had participated in this cross-cultural international study.

Key Academic Findings

Although IWFI and CROWF are certainly laudable initiatives, their impacts are to a large extent "localized." IWFI's work, for example, is not well-known outside of Nigeria. Similarly, the outputs of CROWF's colloquia were poorly disseminated to the African work–family community. These initiatives have, therefore, had little impact on the continental work–family discourse. This, and the overall paucity of research, means that there is "a disparate and fractured understanding of the dynamic interplay between work and family for those who live and work in [African countries]" (Shaffer et al., 2011, p. 221). One of the first systematic efforts to bridge this research gap was an edited volume entitled *Work–family interface in sub-Saharan Africa: Challenges and responses* (Mokomane, 2014a). With contributions from Botswana, Ghana, Kenya, Nigeria, South Africa, Zambia, and Zimbabwe, the book highlighted "various aspects or work–family interface in sub-Saharan Africa, including the antecedents and consequences of work–family conflict; its impact on workers and their families; workers' current coping strategies and the limitations, and plausible future support and coping strategies" (Mokomane, 2014b, p. 11).

The overall picture that emerged from the book was that not only is work–family research in Africa still rudimentary, but it also relies largely on a "predominant western permeation of conceptualizations, methods and operationalizations," which implies that the results are likely to be inappropriate and not contexualized for African cultures (Shaffer et al., 2011, p. 252). This was particularly evident in a chapter by Mokomane and Chilwane (2014) who conducted a broad review of African work–family literature using "work–life," "work–life balance," "work–family," and "work–family conflict" as keywords to search the following databases: African Journals Online, EBSCOhost, ISI Web of Science, Proquest, SABINET, and the Sloan Work and Family Research Network. Studies. Their criteria for the search were that the study was published between January 2000 and mid-August 2011; published in a peer-reviewed journal; and based on research conducted in an English-speaking sub-Saharan African country. This search retrieved 303 articles, and after eliminating those that did not clearly address the nexus between work–family or work–life issues, only forty-four articles were reviewed. Notwithstanding its limitations (for example, the exclusion of non-English speaking African countries) the review provided cursory insight and a portrait of work–family research in sub-Saharan Africa in terms of the following:

Geographical focus: Much of the work–family research in the region emanates from South Africa and Nigeria, which is hardly surprising given that these are the two major economies in the region, with relatively higher proportion of workers in wage employment.

Content focus: A recent overview of the focus of work–family literature in the United States found that between 2000 and 2010 much of the scholarship focused on the key topics of gender, time, and the division of labor with a notable expansion of the field to consider the work–family issues of low-income populations and greater focus on men and fathers (Bianchi & Milkie, 2010). In a review of work–family and work–life research in Australia and New Zealand, Bardoel et al. (2008) noted that, the top three researched topics between 2004 and 2007 were *organizations* (i.e., policies, programs, strategies and support provided by organizations to alleviate employees' work–life or work–family conflict and to promote work–life and work–family balance); *work* (i.e., working hours and the incidence of alternative work arrangements such as part-time, temporary and causal work as well as flexible work arrangements); and *occupations/industries* (i.e., specific occupations and industries). Mokomane and Chilwane's review revealed that in sub-Saharan Africa much of the literature related to occupations or industries and gender, with the rest spread across different themes as shown in Table 17.1.

Table 17.1 *Focus work–family research, sub-Saharan Africa, 2000–mid-2011*

Occupations/industries	**12**
Women in Academia	4
Breweries	1
Customer care	1
Management	1
Mining	1
Mixed industries (police service, earthmoving equipment, mining, nursing)	1
Nursing	1
Police service	1
Private organizations	1
Gender	**10**
Gender differences	2
Married women and work–family conflict	2
Women's work–life conflict and coping strategies	2
Women's work and breastfeeding	4
Organization	**5**
Family friendly workplaces	2
Organizational support	3
Families	**4**
Children home alone unsupervised	1
Dual-earner families	2
Working caregivers	1
Government	**4**
Breastfeeding policy	1
Parental leave policies	1
Work–life legislation	2
Health	**1**
Employees' health	1
Work	**1**
Teleworking	1
Additional themes	**8**
Employees' Health	1
Measurement	2
Tele-working	1
Time use	2
Work–family conflict and voluntary turnover	2

Source: Mokomane, Z., & Chilwane, D. (2014). A review of work–family research in sub-Saharan Africa. In Z. Mokomane (Ed.), *Work–family Interface in sub-Saharan Africa: Challenges and Responses*. New York: Springer Publishing.

Conceptualization and measurement: Mokomane and Chilwane's (2014) review also found that five of the 44 sub-Saharan African articles were conceptual in nature and explored government policy and legislation. The majority (i.e., the other thirty-nine articles) were empirical, exclusively cross-sectional in design, and largely applied quantitative methodology using primary data from surveys. Relatively few articles were based on studies that used qualitative data and secondary data analysis.

Publication and dissemination of research outputs: In line with the geographic focus of the research discussed earlier, most of the publications appeared in local South African journals, specifically the *South African Journal of Economic and Management Sciences Labour, the South African Journal of Industrial Psychology* as well as the Nigerian journal, *IFE PsychologIA*. Table 17.2 shows the full list of other journals that published the African research. It is noteworthy that only two of the journals (i.e., *Community Work & Family* and *Personnel Psychology*) appear in the list of core academic journals that have been shown to demonstrate a commitment to work–family issues, and through which authors are likely to reach both researchers and policy-makers in the field, thus "proving useful to researchers and [facilitating] further development of the field of work/family research" (Drago & Kashian, 2003, p. 510). This therefore suggests that not only is work–family research in Africa limited, but the little that takes place does not reach the "right people." This may partly explain why workplaces and conditions in the regions continue to be structured around an assumption that all workers have a source of unpaid labor to care for their families or that workers are somehow managing to reconcile their work and family responsibilities.

The limited dissemination of African work–family research is also evident in other fora. For example, at the 2010 inaugural conference of the *Work and Family Researchers Network* in 2010, only six out of more than 200 papers presented were based on studies conducted in African countries. In the same vein, at the 2012 conference, only thirteen out of more than 200 papers on Africa were presented. At the 2016 conference, only ten out of more than 400 papers and two posters out of more than sixty were presented on African countries (Mokomane et al., 2017).

Future Research Ideas

Against the background of the key findings of their literature review, Mokomane and Chilwane (2014) concluded that work–family issues in sub-Saharan Africa require further and broader consideration and that it is "imperative for governments in the sub-region to elevate the issues surrounding work–family interface in their policy agendas" (p. 202). To ensure this, a call was made to ensure that African research on the subject is easily accessible to other work–family researchers and policymakers and to facilitate the development of a work–family research community in the continent and the participation of sub-Saharan African researchers in the global work–family research community (Mokomane & Chilwane, 2014). In response to this call, I convened – with seed funding from the South African National Research Foundation (NRF) – an inaugural workshop aimed at establishing a network of African work–family researchers. The workshop took place at the University of Pretoria in South Africa in September 2015 and was attended by academics and policymakers based in South Africa, the United

Table 17.2 *Journals of publications for sub-Saharan African research on work–family, 2000–mid-2011*

Journals	Number of Articles
*Acta Academia**	1
*Acta Criminologica**	1
*African Journal for the Psychological Study of Social issues**	1
*African Journal of Business Management**	1
*Agenda**	1
*Child Abuse and Neglect***	1
*Community Work & Family***	2
*Eastern Africa Social Science Research Review**	1
*Economic Development and Cultural Change***	1
*European Journal of Scientific Research***	1
*Gender and Behaviour**	2
*Gender in Management***	1
*Health Care for Women International***	2
*IFE PsychologIA**	3
*International Business Research***	1
*International Journal of Human Sciences***	1
*International Journal of Occupational Safety and Ergonomics***	1
*Journal of Comparative Family Studies***	2
*Journal of Diversity Management***	1
*Journal of Human Ecology***	1
*Journal of Social Development in Africa**	1
*Personnel Psychology***	1
*Population Studies***	1
*Social Indicators Research***	1
*South African Journal of Human Resources Management**	2
*South African Journal of Labour Relations**	1
*South African Journal of Industrial Psychology**	4
*South African Journal of Psychology**	1
*The International Business and Economics Research Journal***	1
*The South African Journal of Economic and Management Sciences**	5

Source: Mokomane, Z., & Chilwane, D. (2014). A review of work–family research in sub-Saharan Africa. In Z. Mokomane (Ed.), *Work–family Interface in sub-Saharan Africa: Challenges and Responses*. New York: Springer Publishing.
Notes: * Africa-focus ** International focus

Kingdom, Australia, Kenya, and Nigeria. Consistent with the argument advanced by Njuguna and Itegi (2013), a session dedicated to discussing challenges of undertaking work–family research in Africa identified the limited funding for institutions of higher education and research in Africa and the resultant financial constraints as a key challenge. These challenges not only play a major role in the paucity of work–family research, but they also affect the integrity and quality of activities and outputs on the subject. The paucity and/or incompleteness of appropriate data was identified as another impediment to rigorous and comparative work–family research in Africa.

It was thus agreed that one of the key medium- to long-term aims of the African Research Network on Work and Family (ARNWF) is the development of joint funding proposals for collaborative research projects both within and across countries by members. Among other things, it is envisaged that with some research funding, the answering some of the most urgent and pertinent questions that remain around the subject will become feasible. Mokomane et al. (2017) provide a detailed account of this proposed research agenda which includes calls to explore: the care needs of older people; the extent to which HIV and AIDS continues to contribute to the crisis of care in Africa; the work–family needs and challenges of workers in the informal sector; and the role of employers in the provision of work–family balance arrangements. Additionally, a systematic literature review is being conducted to rigorously assess the state of African work–family research, to identify gaps, and to complement or refocus the proposed research agenda. It is envisaged that the review will be published in a high impact journal for the network of African stakeholders and the global work–family community.

Beyond these efforts, the inaugural ARNWF workshop proposed a few other issues that are worthy of study and further exploration using quantitative and qualitative techniques in a complementarily rather than in a mutually exclusive manner, as is currently the case in African studies on the subject. First, it was agreed that there is a need to conceptualize the meaning of family in Africa. Although the changes taking place within the African family structure are well-documented, the specific dimension of this transformation is not clearly understood. To provide the context within which the challenges of work–family reconciliation can be evaluated, there is a need to first document the systems of family and family traditions in the various countries and societies in the region. This will include assessing the types and patterns of families, their cultural and legal contexts, as well as the trends and factors affecting family development. For example, how do family rituals and routines interact with workplace demands? The composition of families (such as size, headship, organization), as well as the role, socio economic, and demographic characteristics of family members (for example, age, sex, marital status, employment, number, and age of children) are also worthy of study against the background of previous studies that have shown that these variables can have important implications for work–family conflict (see, for example, Blin, 2008).

A second issue is additional examination of the extent and dimensions of work–family conflict in Africa. There is currently little evidence regarding what determines care burdens and work–family conflict in developing countries, or on whether workers of diverse social and cultural backgrounds are affected differently by their care burden (Blin, 2008). In-depth qualitative studies should be used to explore how family and work circumstances influence African workers' work burdens, the types and sources of work–family conflicts experienced by different types of workers, and their capacity to cope with conflict. Specific questions include: Which sources have the most influence on the different types of work–family conflict? Which of types of work–family conflict has the most influence on the well-being of workers and their families? How do workers define and perceive their work burden, and how do the definitions and perceptions differ between different types of workers? What choices and alternatives did the workers have regarding entry into the labor market? Do workers with caring responsibilities feel that these responsibilities have been affected by their entry into the labor force? If so, how?

Another issue is the exploration of the work–family challenges and needs of fathers. Although the tendency for domestic tasks and responsibilities to become the prerogative of women in families still pervades many societies, there is increased willingness and appreciation among some men towards the sharing domestic responsibilities (Reddock & Bobb-Smith, 2008; ILO, 2004). There is, therefore, a need to address the gap in work–family research in which working men and fathers are underrepresented. The following questions are particularly worth addressing in Africa: How do working men and fathers compare with their female counterparts on key measures of work and family characteristics and work–family conflict? What work–family adaptive strategies do working men currently use, and how do these compare with those of working women? What are the work and family characteristics that significantly predict work–family conflict and balance for working men? How do measures of work–family conflict and responsibility for childcare differ among working fathers and working mothers?

To the extent that national culture can influence the kinds of policies adopted by governments and organizations (Epie et al., 2010) the role of labor legislation and collective labor agreements is an area relevant to Africa and worthy of additional research attention. Prevalent African cultures and social norms such as familism (which prioritizes family welfare over the individual's) and patriarchy and its defined gender roles, for example, require African scholars to study the extent to which available mechanisms and provisions made by the public and private sectors actually facilitate the reconciliation of work–family responsibilities in the region.

Support can also occur at the national level, and different countries have various mechanisms available to facilitate the reconciliation between work and family responsibilities. These can range from the services of domestic workers or house helps to formal labor market policies and programs such as parental leave, flexible working arrangements, childcare facilities (Sorj, 2004). What is the range of formal and informal support mechanisms that are available for workers in the different African countries? What gaps exist between the needs for work–family reconciliation and the existing support measures? It would also be important to examine the views of employers (in both the private and public sectors) and trade unions on the broad issue of work–family.

Lastly, it will be worthwhile to explore the extent to which undeveloped infrastructure in most of Africa – for example, bad roads and the resultant chaotic traffic, poor public transport systems, unreliable electricity supplies, and chronic water shortages (Epie et al., 2010) – is exacerbating work–family conflict for workers in the region. Mechanisms to improve or effectively use the available infrastructure with the view of enhancing work–family management through, for example, telecommuting are also worthy of study.

References

Alfers, L. (2015). *WIEGO child care initiative literature review*. London: WIEGO.

Bardoel, E.A., De Cieri, H., & Santos, C. (2008). A review of work–life research in Australia and New Zealand. *Asia Pacific Journal of Human Resources*, Vol 46 (3): 316–33.

Bianchi, S.M. & Milkie, M.A. (2010). Work and family research in the first decade of the 21st century. *Journal of Marriage and the family*, Vol. 72:705–725.

Bigombe, B. & Khadiagala, G.M. (2003). Major trends affecting families in sub-Saharan Africa. In *Major Trends Affecting Families*. (pp. 1–33). New York: United Nations.

Blin, M. (2008). Export-oriented policies, women's work burden and human development in Mauritius. *Journal of Southern African Studies*, Vol. 34(2), 239–253.

Cassirer, N. & Addati, L. (2007). *Expanding Women's Employment Opportunities: Informal Economy Workers and the Need for Childcare*. Geneva: International Labour Organisation, Conditions of Work and Employment programme.

Chinchilla, N., Las Heras, A. & Torres, E. (2010). Work–family balance: A global challenge. In N. Chinchilla, A. Las Heras, & A.D. Masuda (Eds.), *Balancing Work and Family: A practical Guide to Help Organizations Meet the Global Workforce Challenge*. (pp.7–22) Amherst, MA: HRD Press, Inc.

Dancaster, L. & M. Baird. (2008). Work and Care: A Critical Examination of South African Labour Law. *Industrial Law Journal*, Vol. 29: 22–42.

Drago, R. & R. Kashian (2003). Mapping the Terrain of Work/Family Journals. *Journal of Family Issues*, Vol. 24 (4):488–512.

Esplen, E. (2009). *Gender and Care: Overview Report*. Bridge Cutting Edge Pack. Brighton: Institute of Development Studies.

Epie, C., Mwangi, M.J.C., & Masuda, A.D. (2010). Work–family conflict in sub-Saharan Africa. In N. Chinchilla, A. Las Heras, & A.D. Masuda (Eds.), *Balancing Work and Family: A Practical Guide to Help Organizations Meet the Global Workforce Challenge*. (pp. 101–118). Amherst, MA: HRD Press, Inc.

Hertrich, V. (2002). *Nuptiality and gender relationships in Africa: An overview of first marriage trends over the past 50 years*. Paper presented at the annual meeting of the Population Association of America, Atlanta, Georgia (2002).

Heymann, J. Earle, A., Rajaraman, D., Miller, C. & Bogen, K. (2007). Extended family careering for children orphaned by AIDS: balancing essential work and caregiving in a high prevalence nation, *AIDS Care*, Vol.19 (3): 337–345.

ILO. (2004). *Work and family responsibilities: What are the problems?* (Information Sheet No. WF-1). Geneva, International Labour Organisation.

ILO. (2016). *Women at Work: Trends 2016. Geneva*: International Labour Organisation.

ISSA. (2013). Executive summary. *Labour Market Megatrends And Social Security*. Geneva: international Social Security Association. pp 1–2.

Joseph, S. (1994: 194). *Gender and Family in the Arab World*. MERIP

Kisembo B., Magesa L. & Shorter A. (1998). *African Christian Marriage*. Nairobi: Paulines Publications

Mapedzahama, V. (2014). Work and family in a cross-cultural context: A comparative review of work–family experiences of working mothers in Australia and Zimbabwe, In Z. Mokomane (Ed.), *Work–Family Interface in Sub-Saharan Africa: Challenges and Responses* (pp. 37–53). New York: Springer Publishing.

Mbiti, J. (1975). *Introduction to African Religion*. Nairobi: East African Educational Publishers, Ltd.

Milazzo, A. & van de Walle, D. (2015). *Women Left Behind? Poverty and Headship in Africa.* World Bank Group Policy Research Working Paper 7331. http://documents.world bank.org/curated/en/277221468189851163/pdf/WPS7331.pdf

Mokomane, Z. (2011). *Anti-poverty policies focusing on families: Regional overview, Africa.* Paper presented at the United Nations Expert Group Meeting on Assessing Family Policies: Confronting Family Poverty and Social Exclusion & Ensuring Work–family Balance, 1–3 June 2011, New York.

Mokomane, Z. (2013). Social Protection as a Mechanism for Family Protection in sub-Saharan Africa. *International Journal of Social Welfare*, Vol. 22(3): 248–259

Mokomane, Z. (2014a). (Ed.), *Work–Family Interface in Sub-Saharan Africa: Challenges and Responses.* New York: Springer Publishing.

Mokomane, Z. (2014b). Introduction. In Z. Mokomane (Ed.), *Work–Family Interface in Sub-Saharan Africa: Challenges and Responses* (pp. 3–16). New York: Springer Publishing.

Mokomane, Z. & Chilwane, D. (2014). A review of work–family research in sub-Saharan Africa. In Z. Mokomane (Ed.), *Work–family Interface in Sub-Saharan Africa: Challenges and Responses.* New York: Springer Publishing.

Mokomane, Z., van der Merwe, S., Seedat Khan, M., Jaga, A. & Dancaster, L. (2017). Developing an African Research Network on Work Family Interface. *Community, Work and Family.* Vol. 20(3): 366–376.

Muasya, G. (2014). The role of house helps in work–family balance of women employed in the formal sector in Kenya. In Z. Mokomane (Ed.), *Work–family Interface in Sub-Saharan Africa: Challenges and Responses* (pp. 149–160). New York: Springer Publishing

Njuguna, F. & Itegi, F. (2013). Research institutions of higher education in Africa: Challenges and prospects. *European Scientific Journal.* Special edition Vol. 1:352–361.

Ntozi, J., & Zirimenya, S. (1999). Changes in household composition and family structure during the AIDS epidemic in Uganda. In I. Oruboloye, J. Caldwell, & J. Ntozi (Eds.), *The continuing HIV/AIDS epidemic in Africa: Responses and Coping Strategies* (pp. 193–209). Canberra: Health Transition Centre, Australian National University Shaffer, M.A.,

Reddock, C., & Bobb-Smith, Y. (2008). *Reconciling Work and Family: Issues and Policies in Trinidad and Tobago* Geneva, International Labour Organisation, 2008).

Shaffer, M.A., Joplin, J.R. & Hsu, Y. et al. (2011). Expanding the boundaries of work—family research: A review and agenda for future research. *International Journal of Cross Cultural Management*, Vol. 11(2):221–268.

Sorj, B. (2004). *Reconciling Work and Family: Issues and Policies in Brazil.* Geneva: International Labour Organisation.

Statistics South Africa (2010). *Social Profile of South Africa, 2002–2009.* Pretoria: Statistics South Africa.

UNAIDS (2015). *Fact sheet: 2014 statistics.* Available at www.unaids.org

Van de Walle, E. (1993). "Recent trends in marriage ages." In K.A. Foote, K.H. Hill, & L.G. Martin (Eds.), *Demographic Change in Sub-Saharan Africa* (Washington, DC: National Academy Press.

World Bank. (2016). *Labor force participation rate, female (% of female population ages 15+) (modeled ILO estimate).* Available at http://data.worldbank.org/indicator/SL.TLF .CACT.FE.ZS

Wusu, O., & Isiugo-Abanihe, U. (2006). Interconnection among changing family structure, childbearing, and fertility behavior among the Ogo, Southern Western Nigeria: A qualitative study. *Demographic Research, 14*(Article 8): 139–156.

Ziehl, S. (2003). Forging the Links: Globalisation and Family Patterns. *South African Review of Sociology*, Vol. 34(2):320–337.

18 A Review of Work–Family Research in the Middle East

Jeremiah T. McMillan, Leila Karimi, and Jiri Rada

Most research on the work–family (WF) interface has been conducted in Western societies; only a small proportion of studies have been carried out in Middle Eastern countries. This is a significant gap in the literature, considering that the Middle East represents a unique region of the world in terms of factors that might influence WF dynamics, including economic status, the influence of Islamic traditions, and the status of women in society (Metcalfe, 2008). The goal of this review is to explore existing empirical evidence on WF constructs in the Middle East. We start by defining this region and describing its socioeconomic and cultural characteristics. After reviewing the extant research on WF predictors, outcomes, and moderators for this region, we examine the small body of cross-cultural research comparing this region to others. We conclude by providing suggestions for future research.

The Middle Eastern Context

Defining the Middle East. Prior to delving into the overall cultural dimensions of this region, it is important to make explicit the specific countries from which this review pulls. Delineating the precise boundaries of the Middle East is not straightforward. For instance, Turkey is often considered to be straddling the border between Europe and Asia. Additionally, some conceptualizations include parts of North Africa with the Middle East, owing to similar historical and religious traditions, whereas others do not. Several conceptualizations include countries to the east of Iran, such as Tajikistan and Pakistan, whereas others consider these to be more appropriately clustered into their own category or clustered with Southeast Asia. Drawing from consensus among a number of past sources (House, Hanges, Javidan, Dorfman, & Gupta, 2004; Omran & Roudi, 1993; Ronen & Shenkar, 1985), for the present discussion we conceptualize the Middle East as consisting of the following countries: Bahrain, Egypt, Iran, Iraq, Israel, Jordan, Kuwait, Lebanon, Oman, Palestine, Qatar, Saudi Arabia, Syria, Turkey, United Arab Emirates (UAE), and Yemen.

Economic and sociopolitical context. For purposes of economic classification, Middle Eastern countries can largely be divided into those on the Persian Gulf that are oil-producing (i.e., Bahrain, Kuwait, Oman, Qatar, Saudi Arabia, and UAE) and all other countries. Although the economy is on the rise, most Middle Eastern countries possess relatively low per capita gross national incomes around USD 5,000–15,000 (United

337

Nations Development Programme, 2010). Thus, poverty remains an issue for many countries, with Iraq and Yemen demonstrating significantly higher poverty levels than the rest of the region. Oil-producing Persian Gulf countries are an exception, with Qatar boasting a nearly USD 80,000 per capita gross national income. Even within wealthy nations of this region, however, large income inequalities exist. Additionally, the unemployment rate in the Middle East has remained relatively stable since 1999, hovering right above 9%, which is higher than all other world regions except North Africa (United Nations Development Programme, 2010). In total, these statistics demonstrate that the region is economically diverse, both within and between countries.

The region as a whole is marked by political and economic change as it grapples with globalization, leading to the juxtaposition of Westernized business practices with traditional belief systems (Metcalfe, 2008; Sidani & Thornberry, 2009). Numerous Middle Eastern countries have struggled to identify skilled labor to compete with the global economy, holding on to vestiges of the bazaar system of trade (Sharda & Miller, 2001). Nonetheless, change is occurring at different rates throughout the region, and countries such as Turkey represent the opportunity to identify the changing nature of the WF interface as the region shifts to a more Westernized culture (Ergeneli, Ilsev, & Karapınar, 2010).

Government types across countries in the Middle East are a combination of democracies, monarchies, and theocracies (Mortazavi, Pedhiwala, Shafiro, & Hammer, 2009). Governmental policies have important implications for the WF interface. Regarding worker protections, no Middle Eastern country guarantees equal pay for equal work by gender, although all guarantee from fourteen to thirty days of paid leave annually and all guarantee at least some paid maternal leave, with Iran being the most generous at six months. Four countries offer a few weeks of paid paternal leave, and all but three countries guarantee breastfeeding breaks at work for new mothers (World Policy Analysis Center, 2017). In total, these policies are on par with many Westernized countries (and superior to the United States in multiple respects).

Despite what is transpiring at the governmental level, many Middle Eastern countries lag behind leading Western organizations in terms of supportive WF practices (Forster, Al Ali Ebrahim, & Ibrahim, 2013). In fact, legal mandates protecting employee rights are not always strictly enforced (Aycan, 2001). This is potentially problematic because, as countries such as Turkey and the UAE become more Westernized, extended kin networks are progressively replaced by the nuclear family. As a result, employees may become significantly more reliant on organizational and legal policies to assist with work–family conflict (WFC; Forster et al., 2013).

Cultural values. Although individual countries within the region may display significant differences across various cultural dimensions, the GLOBE project (House et al., 2004) and other research has identified the following cultural hallmarks within Middle Eastern countries: a culture of honor (Glick, Sakallı-Uğurlu, Akbaş, Orta, & Ceylan, 2015), low gender egalitarianism, high in-group collectivism and focus on family, and high power distance (Aycan & Eskin, 2005).

Many Middle Eastern societies espouse a "culture of honor," which emphasizes the need to maintain a family's honor within society (Nisbett & Cohen, 1996). Whereas men maintain honor by actively commanding respect and dignity, women maintain honor by avoiding bringing shame upon the family (Glick et al., 2015; Vandello & Cohen, 2003). In Middle Eastern cultures, women largely accomplish this goal by maintaining their modesty. In turn, men are compelled to maintain the family's honor by harshly punishing a wife's intentional or unintentional shaming of the family (Vandello & Cohen, 2003). The notable lack of legal protections for female victims of domestic violence serves as a societal marker of this belief system (Metcalfe, 2008).

Intricately related to the culture of honor is gender egalitarianism, which encompasses a society's norms regarding the allocation of roles based upon biological sex. Countries espousing low gender egalitarianism value discrete role behavior for men and women (House et al., 2004). Historical (mis)interpretations of Islamic teachings in the region have led to low gender egalitarianism, valuing the role of men as leaders of society and women in family supportive roles (Syed, 2008). Although it is important to note that Islam has many forms, the associated patriarchal beliefs often extend into the culture and practices of many organizations (Aycan, 2001). Indeed, Islam-based Shar'ia law indirectly promotes sex discrimination in the workplace rather than forbidding it. For instance, offices may physically segregate male and female workers or may limit the positions or specific tasks in which women are allowed to participate (Metcalfe, 2008). Gender egalitarianism norms also have critical implications for the amount of support organizations provide for work–life balance and the subsequent work–life balance actually experienced by employees (Lyness & Kropf, 2005). Thus, both a culture of honor and low gender egalitarianism may signal challenges for women who violate traditional gender norms by working outside the home.

In-group collectivism signifies the degree to which individuals view themselves as highly interdependent rather than independent of the social groups to which they belong (House et al., 2004). Middle Eastern societies generally exhibit high in-group collectivism, and this manifests as loyalty both to families and to work groups (Sidani & Thornberry, 2009). In Iran, as with other Middle Eastern countries, an individual's identity is largely tied to the extended family. The typical Middle Eastern employee also places a high value on relationships at work and exhibits strong loyalty to other members of the work group (Sidani & Thornberry, 2009). The impact of in-group collectivism on WFC specifically has been tested via meta-analysis (Allen, French, Dumani, & Shockley, 2015); people residing in countries high in in-group collectivism experience greater conflict in the family-to-work direction, but there are no significant differences in the work-to-family direction.

Power distance is a cultural value surrounding the perceived legitimacy and desirability of power and status differentiation among members of society (House et al., 2004). Middle Eastern children are socialized to value conformity and obedience to authority from a young age. In particular, the role of the father as leader is emphasized. These attitudes extend first from the family to educational settings and eventually to the workplace (Sidani & Thornberry, 2009). Combined with high uncertainty avoidance (Hofstede, 1984), high power distance beliefs suggest that a leader will and should wield a great deal of power and should make important decisions for their subordinates. This, in turn, might have important implications for the degree to which workers take initiative in managing their own WF conflict and/or balance.

In sum, the cultural values generally espoused by Middle Easterners may have important implications not only for the frequency of conflict between work and family but also for the qualitative "lived" experience of managing the WF interface. Women may face particular challenges, a point discussed further in the following section.

Women in the workforce. In most Middle Eastern countries, there is a sharp gender divide in workforce participation. Across all countries in the region, women constitute approximately 21% of the workforce, which is roughly half the global average. More specifically, women constitute less than 20% of the workforce in Bahrain, Iran, Iraq, Jordan, Oman, Palestine, Qatar, Saudi Arabia, Syria, and UAE; they constitute between 20% and 40% of the workforce in Egypt, Kuwait, Lebanon, Turkey, and Yemen; and they constitute 46.8% of the workforce in Israel (World Bank, 2014). Female participation in the workforce is positively correlated with a country's general economic success. Although the relationship between economic success and women's participation in the workforce is likely bidirectional and complex, recently scholars have noted the importance of empowering women for increasing the economic performance of Middle Eastern countries (Torabi & Abbasi-Shavazi, 2015).

As is true across the globe, women earn less than men, although the Middle East appears to fare especially poorly. Israel is ranked 65th in the world in income equality, with a female to male earnings ratio of .70, representing the highest ratio in the Middle East. Kuwait is the next highest in equality for the region, representing 113th in the world with a ratio of .65. Yemen fares lowest in the world (i.e., 142nd) with a ratio of .51, with the rankings of all other Middle Eastern countries falling between Yemen and Kuwait (World Economic Forum, 2014).

Aside from earnings levels, occupational sex segregation is very common in Middle Eastern countries. Indeed, women are typically found in traditionally "feminine" sectors such as service, healthcare, and education. In addition, women are severely underrepresented in upper management and executive positions (Metcalfe, 2008). It is important to note that despite historical trends in the region women are making strides in some areas. Today, there are a significant number of Turkish women in professional positions, including pharmacy, medicine, dentistry, law, and academia (Aycan & Eskin, 2005). And in the UAE, initial qualitative research suggests that female entrepreneurs derive a great deal of satisfaction and meaningfulness from their work, despite the ongoing struggle against traditional gender norms (Itani, Sidani, & Baalbaki, 2011).

Countries with large Muslim populations subscribe to gender complementarian values that men are predominantly responsible for earning a living and women are predominantly responsible for tending to household duties, such as caring for children and other dependent household members, preparing meals, and doing other housework (Groth & Sousa-Poza, 2012). As such, employed women bear significant pressure from both home and work responsibilities. These pressures may be substantial considering that families in Middle Eastern cultures are relatively large, with an average fertility rate of 2.9 births per woman (United Nations, 2015). Despite a recent shift in values within a subset of Middle Eastern countries, it appears that experiences of men and women in the workplace may be quite different.

Review of Work–Family Research in the Middle East

Next, we review empirical findings on WF constructs in the Middle East. Note that essentially all research has maintained a focus on work–family conflict (WFC) as the construct of interest (cf. Forster et al., 2013; Karimi & Nouri, 2009); hence, this review reflects this trend. Where appropriate, we specify the directionality of WFC under study: work interfering with family (WIF) and family interfering with work (FIW). As with other regions, the WF literature in the Middle East yields a variety of contradictory findings (Burke & El-Kot, 2010). As will be seen, this makes drawing firm conclusions about this construct and region a challenge.

Predictors of WFC. Empirically examined predictors of WFC in the Middle East can be separated into organizational characteristics, individual differences, and family characteristics. Regarding organizational characteristics, work overload is associated with increased WFC in Turkish frontline hotel employees (Karatepe, Sokmen, Yavas, & Babakus, 2010), nurses (Yildirim & Aycan, 2008), and physicians (Tayfur & Arslan, 2013). In addition to quantity of work, intensity of the work role (i.e., role overload, role ambiguity) is associated with WFC among Egyptian managers (Burke & El-Kot, 2010), Iranian employees (Karimi & Nouri, 2009), and Turkish employees (Koyuncu, Burke, & Fiksenbaum, 2009). Regarding protective factors, perceived organizational support is negatively associated with WFC (Ibrahim & Al Marri, 2015), although this relationship may be stronger for men than for women (Aycan & Eskin, 2005). Supervisor support is also negatively associated with WFC across different nationalities and occupations (Karatepe & Uludag, 2008b; Karimi & Nouri, 2009), although its role may be stronger in reducing FIW than WIF (Farhadi, Sharifian, Feili, & Shokrpour, 2013).

Examining personality and behavioral correlates, positive affectivity is negatively associated with both WIF and FIW in Turkish frontline hotel employees, whereas negative affectivity is positively associated with WIF but unrelated to FIW (Karatepe & Uludag, 2008a). Both need for achievement and workaholism behaviors are positively related to WIF in Egyptian managers (Burke & El-Kot, 2010), but need for achievement has been found to be significantly associated with less WFC in Turkish employees (Koyuncu et al., 2009). The reason for this discrepancy is unclear. Finally, psychological detachment is negatively associated with WFC among Egyptian managers (Burke & El-Kot, 2010).

Men and women experience comparable levels of WFC in Egyptian managerial roles (Burke & El-Kot, 2010). However, in a study of Iranian nurses, male employees experienced higher levels of FIW than did female employees (Farhadi et al., 2013).

In a study of Jordanian frontline hotel workers, female employees experienced higher levels of FIW than did male employees (Karatepe & Baddar, 2006). And in a study of accountants in the UAE, female employees experienced higher levels of WIF and FIW than male employees (Ibrahim & Al Marri, 2015). These data would seem to suggest that there remain unidentified moderators of gender differences in WFC. More concrete is the relationship between age and WFC. Age has been found to be negatively associated with WFC for male Iranian professionals (Karimi & Nouri, 2009) and for Iranian nurses (Farhadi et al., 2013).

Minimal research has examined predictors of WFC on the family side. However, spousal support appears to be negatively associated with WFC. One study on a sample of Turkish white-collar mothers and fathers found that spousal support – both emotional and instrumental – was negatively associated with FIW, but this relationship was stronger for women than men (Aycan & Eskin, 2005). These results may be partially understood by considering that individuals may experience particularly high reductions in stress when receiving support from the domain in which they are traditionally expected to perform (i.e., in the home for women and in the workplace for men).

Outcomes of WFC. Outcomes of WFC in the Middle East can be generally categorized into work outcomes and family outcomes. Although doing so risks creating an artificial dichotomy, this structure is used to guide the present discussion.

Work.

WFC is negatively associated with job satisfaction for Turkish academic professionals (Ergeneli et al., 2010), Turkish managers (Koyuncu et al., 2009), Turkish female public sector workers (Koyuncu, Burke, & Wolpin, 2012), Turkish nurses (Yildirim & Aycan, 2008), and Egyptian managers across numerous industries (Burke & El-Kot, 2010). Additionally, WFC is negatively associated with career satisfaction (Koyuncu et al., 2009; Koyuncu et al., 2012). Examining directionality, FIW is negatively associated with career satisfaction in Turkish hotel workers, whereas, surprisingly, WIF is positively associated with career satisfaction (Karatepe & Uludag, 2008b). Owing to the cross-sectional nature of this study, it is not possible to determine causal relationships. It is possible that work engagement may lead to both WIF and satisfaction, thus rendering their relationship spurious.

Regarding job performance, WIF is positively associated with job performance whereas FIW is negatively associated with job performance in Turkish frontline hotel employees (Yavas, Babakus, & Karatepe, 2008). These results suggest that, although FIW may interfere with one's ability to perform job duties, WIF may signal that the work domain is prioritized.

WFC is associated with turnover intentions in Jordanian and Turkish frontline hotel employees (Karatepe & Baddar, 2006; Yavas et al., 2008) and Turkish female public sector workers (Koyuncu et al., 2012). Additional evidence suggests that the relationship between FIW and turnover intentions appears to be stronger than the relationship between WIF and turnover intentions (Karatepe & Uludag, 2008a). Few studies have separately examined strain-based, time-based, and behavior-based WFC, as described by Greenhaus and Beutell (1985). However, by doing so, one study discovered that strain-based WFC – compared to time-based and behavior-based – is particularly important in predicting turnover intentions in Turkish managers (Koyuncu et al., 2009).

WFC is associated with a variety of strain reactions including psychological and physical exhaustion in a wide range of populations, including Turkish IT professionals (Calisir, Gumussoy, & Iskin, 2011), Turkish female public sector workers (Koyuncu et al., 2012), Turkish hotel employees (Yavas et al., 2008), and Iranian nurses (Farhadi et al., 2013). Furthermore, strain-based WIF specifically is associated with work stress and psychosomatic complaints in Egyptian (Burke & El-Kot, 2010) and Turkish managers (Koyuncu et al., 2009). In one sample of Iranian employees, strain-based WIF was also associated with anxiety and depression in one's job role (Karimi, Karimi, & Nouri, 2011). Extending discussion to both sides of WFC, FIW is associated with strain reactions at work for Iranian nurses (Farhadi et al., 2013). Contrarily, in a study of Jordanian frontline hotel employees, WIF impacted job stress but FIW did not (Karatepe & Baddar, 2006). Finally, strain- and time-based WFC, but not behavior-based, are associated with job stress in Turkish employees, leading to higher levels of exhaustion (Koyuncu et al., 2009). Extending logically from the work overload-WFC relationship and the WFC-exhaustion relationships, WFC has been found to fully mediate the effect of work overload on both exhaustion and disengagement (Karatepe et al., 2010). Thus, it appears that WFC plays a critical role in explaining the impact of work characteristics on negative physical and psychological health outcomes.

Family.

Models of domain specificity suggest that WIF will lead to negative outcomes in the family domain, and FIW will lead to negative outcomes in the work domain (Frone, Russell, & Cooper, 1992). Contrarily, source attribution theory suggests that when WIF occurs, the source of conflict (i.e., work) will be blamed and thus negative outcomes will occur in the work domain; the opposite will happen when FIW occurs (Kinnunen, Feldt, Geurts, & Pulkkinen, 2006). The impact of WFC on family outcomes in the Middle East ultimately lends support to both of these theoretical frameworks.

Providing support for domain specificity, WIF is associated with poor psychological well-being, reduction in satisfaction with one's performance as a parent, and reduction in marital satisfaction for both working mothers and fathers in Turkey (Aycan & Eskin, 2005). Furthermore, WIF is more strongly associated with these outcomes than FIW, despite the fact that FIW is still a significant predictor for working mothers (Aycan & Eskin, 2005). Similarly, WIF is negatively associated with life satisfaction for Egyptian managers (Burke & El-Kot, 2010) and Turkish nurses (Yildirim & Aycan, 2008). Detracting from the domain specificity perspective, however, is the finding that WIF is not associated with family satisfaction and is actually positively associated with life satisfaction in some samples (Karatepe & Uludag, 2008b). Regarding support for source attribution theory, Karatepe and Uludag (2008b) discovered in a sample of Turkish hotel workers that FIW was negatively associated with family and life satisfaction. In a similar sample, FIW was negatively related to marital satisfaction whereas WIF was unrelated (Karatepe &

Uludag, 2008a). A similar pattern has been found for family satisfaction such that FIW is negatively associated whereas WIF is unrelated (Karatepe & Baddar, 2006).

Despite sporadic findings that WFC (i.e., both WIF and FIW) is unrelated to family satisfaction (Farhadi et al., 2013) and life satisfaction (Karatepe & Baddar, 2006), the majority of evidence suggests that there exist significant relationships, especially when WFC is strain-based (Koyuncu et al., 2009) and when female workers are examined (Aycan & Eskin, 2005). Although the domain specificity and source attribution perspectives are not mutually exclusive, more research is warranted to explicitly elucidate the impact of substantive sample differences and methodological artefacts on the contradictory findings above.

Moderators of WFC-outcome relationships. In addition to directly predicting WFC, individual differences may also be a crucial factor in moderating the impact of WFC on outcomes of interest. Although there is scant research on such moderators, two that have been examined previously are personality and gender.

Positive affectivity has been found to mitigate the relationship between WFC and disengagement, but not WFC and exhaustion (Karatepe et al., 2010). Thus, in addition to reducing the overall experience of WFC, positive affectivity may serve as a protective buffer to limit withdrawal behaviors that harm the organization, but it does not necessarily serve to weaken the harmful effect on the individual. In a related vein, Ergeneli and colleagues (2010) examined *stress-predisposing interpretative habits*, which consist of focusing on the negative aspects of events, not recognizing one's own skills, and performing in one's roles out of obligation instead of desire. Lower levels of these habits was associated with an amelioration of the impact of WFC on job dissatisfaction in one Turkish sample (Ergeneli et al., 2010).

Gender also plays an important role, such that the negative association between WFC and job satisfaction is weaker for men than women (Ergeneli et al., 2010). The same pattern of results occurs for the WFC-job performance relationship and the WFC-turnover intention relationship, particularly when examining FIW as the predictor (Yavas et al., 2008). Overall, that men are not as distressed or impeded in their job roles by WFC as women suggests that, although gender roles may be shifting toward equality in Turkey, women still find themselves in a double-bind. That is, they are responsible for both performance in the work and the family role and less able to cope with failing to meet demands, whereas men experience less extreme shifts in job attitudes despite experiencing conflict (Ergeneli et al., 2010).

Cross-Regional Comparisons

Prior to considering substantive differences between the Middle East and other regions, it is essential to establish that the same construct is tapped when examining WFC cross-culturally (Vandenberg & Lance, 2000). Measurement invariance of WFC across Western and Middle Eastern cultures has been largely supported. For example, a six-dimensional model of WFC has been previously developed and widely used within American samples by crossing three types of conflict (i.e., time, strain, and behavior) with two directions (i.e., WIF and FIW; Carlson, Kacmar, & Williams, 2000). This factor structure is valid within Iranian (Karimi et al., 2011), Turkish (Koyuncu et al., 2009), and Egyptian (Burke & El-Kot, 2010) samples. Additionally, FIW and WIF are positively related, with the correlation ranging from $r = .51$ to .74 (Koyuncu et al., 2012; Mortazavi et al., 2009), which is generally in accordance with previous studies (Shockley, in press).

Empirical findings represented in our review above have largely replicated results in the United States and other Western nations. On the predictor side, for instance, previous meta-analytic evidence across cultures supports a contributing role of work overload and negativity affectivity on WFC and an inhibitory role of perceived organizational, supervisor, and spousal support (Michel, Kotrba, Mitchelson, Clark, & Baltes, 2011). Regarding outcomes, findings that WFC is associated with lower work satisfaction, greater turnover intentions, lower psychological well-being, and lower family satisfaction have all been found in Western samples (Eby, Casper, Lockwood, Bordeaux, & Brinley, 2005). Additionally, research in the Middle East provides support for the asymmetric boundary permeability theory (Pleck, 1977): men and women allow work to interfere with family more than they allow family to interfere with work (Aycan & Eskin, 2005; Karimi, 2008b), which is similar to findings in Western cultures (e.g., Burke & Greenglass, 1999; Kinnunen & Mauno, 1998).

However, several findings illustrate differences between the Middle East and other regions. Overall, there is evidence suggesting that Turkish and Egyptian workers experience higher levels of WFC than do American workers (Burke & El-Kot, 2010). Additionally, these mean differences extend to each of three forms of WFC, including time-, strain-, and behavior-based (Koyuncu et al., 2009). These findings may be partially due to low gender equality of these countries (Lyness & Kropf, 2005) or lack of organizational support for work–family issues (Mortazavi et al., 2009). Yet country is a multiply confounded construct (Koyuncu et al., 2012). Therefore, the degree to which other factors may be driving these differences remains unclear. It is also important to note that not all research has uncovered a difference in WFC between the Middle East and the United States (e.g., Mortazavi et al., 2009). Further, cultural differences in WFC may be moderated by gender, as evidence suggests that Turkish male and female employees do not show as large of a difference in WFC as do American male and female employees (Koyuncu et al., 2009).

Future Research Directions

The study of the WF interface in the Middle East is still in its infancy, and the majority of research has transpired only within the last decade. Thus, there are many possible directions for future research. In this final section, we provide recommendations for researchers in the region going forward, noting similarities among existing studies where appropriate and k contributions.

1. Engage in additional cross-regional and cross-cultural research. The fact that many variable correlations in this region are similar to research from other regions does not negate the possibility that significant cultural differences exist. What is lacking is research that explicitly models country or culture as a moderator. Such research would allow researchers to identify the degree to which this region's high levels of in-group collectivism and power distance and low levels of gender egalitarianism have an impact on WFC and associated outcomes. Meta-analytic evidence by Allen et al. (2015) serves as a notable exception, as this study examined the association between in-group collectivism and WFC.

2. Examine a greater diversity of samples. Most research has focused on a limited number of white-collar occupations, such as accounting (Ibrahim & Al Marri, 2015), banking (Aycan & Eskin, 2005), medicine (Benligiray & Sönmez, 2012; Tayfur & Arslan, 2013), and information technology (Calisir et al., 2011), although a subset of studies have considered blue-collar occupations, frontline hotel workers in particular (e.g., Karatepe et al., 2010; Karatepe & Uludag, 2008a, 2008b). Additionally, much research has focused on Turkish citizens, particularly those in urban areas (Aycan & Eskin, 2005; Benligiray & Sönmez, 2012; Calisir et al., 2011; Ergeneli et al., 2010; Karatepe et al., 2010; Karatepe & Uludag, 2008a, 2008b; Koyuncu et al., 2009; Koyuncu et al., 2012; Tayfur & Arslan, 2013; Yavas et al., 2008; Yildirim & Aycan, 2008). Because Turkey serves as a "bridge" between Eastern and Western cultures, it is possible that the large amount of research done in this country is not truly representative of the region as a whole, particularly as this country has demonstrated a steady increase in gender egalitarianism (Aycan & Eskin, 2005). Another country boasting a disproportionate share of research in the region is Iran (Farhadi et al., 2013; Karimi, 2008a; Karimi, 2008b; Karimi et al., 2011; Karimi & Nouri, 2009). To the authors' knowledge, there has been no published WF research consisting of participants from eight out of sixteen of the countries in this region (i.e., Bahrain, Iraq, Kuwait, Oman, Qatar, Saudi Arabia, Syria, and Yemen). To the extent that these countries differ culturally from countries previously examined, valuable theoretical contributions could be gleaned by examining drivers of differences in WF constructs and WF constructs-correlate relationships across countries both within and between regions.

3. Leverage additional methodologies. There exists a great opportunity to utilize advanced methodological and statistical techniques to further research on WF constructs in the Middle East. For instance, all presently examined studies utilized a cross-sectional, self-report only design (e.g., Burke & El-Kot, 2010; Forster et al., 2013; Karimi et al., 2011; Koyuncu et al., 2009; Koyuncu et al., 2012; Yavas et al., 2008). Longitudinal research would allow for removal of methodological artefacts and provide for a more sophisticated understanding of the impact of temporal dynamics on variables of interest. Additionally, using a dyadic level of analysis provides for examining the interaction of spousal attitudes. Such an approach might be beneficial for understanding how husbands' attitudes regarding traditional gender roles interact with wives' decisions to work outside the home, for instance. With the exception of one study (Karatepe et al., 2010), studies in this region have examined direct effects only, not testing for mediation. Additionally, much work has been the replication of variable relationships in slightly different samples (e.g., Burke & El-Kot, 2010; Koyuncu et al., 2009). These points are raised here not to disparage the pioneering work of researchers in the region, but rather to highlight the many opportunities for adding significant contributions to the burgeoning literature.

4. Test interventions. Although numerous researchers have noted the need for Middle Eastern organizations to engage in interventions to improve the WF interface (Koyuncu et al., 2009; Koyuncu et al., 2012; Yavas et al., 2008), no known study has identified the efficacy of such a program for this region. Thus, there exists a gap in elucidating which interventions are effective for reducing WFC and how these interventions may differ from successful programs in Western cultures. Although some strategies may be universally successful, Middle Eastern employees are especially high on power distance (House et al., 2004). Therefore, organizational policies that directly reduce WFC though job design may be more useful than policies emphasizing that employees initiate action on their own. Furthermore, the high in-group collectivism of the region suggests that interventions emphasizing balance as a means to better group and societal outcomes, as opposed to better individual outcomes, may experience a higher success rate. Ultimately these remain empirical questions to be tested.

5. Accentuate the positive. As noted by Karatepe and Uludag (2008a), virtually no research has examined the positive interface between work and family in this region (e.g., work–family enhancement, facilitation, or positive spillover). An initial research aim might be to establish the measurement invariance of these constructs in the Middle East compared with other regions. Due to Middle Eastern cultural values emphasizing a strong work ethic, the integral connection between work and life, and perception of work as a means for social connection (Ali & Al-Owaihan, 2008), it would be interesting to establish if positive spillover occurs differently for individuals in the Middle East compared with countries in which work is viewed more instrumentally. As another substantive research area, to the degree that Middle Eastern countries progress toward greater gender egalitarianism, understanding the psychological benefits of work roles to women in these countries represents an area of potentially fruitful research.

6. Focus on the family domain. Compared with other regions, very little research in the Middle East has identified family domain antecedents of WFC (cf. Aycan & Eskin, 2005). Rather, family characteristics such as marital status and number of children have been utilized primarily as inclusionary criteria for study (Forster et al., 2013; Karatepe & Baddar, 2006) or as control variables (Ibrahim & Al Marri, 2015; Yavas et al., 2008). This seems an especially significant gap. Considering the central role that family plays in this region (Sharda & Miller, 2001), family may represent a strong resource upon which to draw or may represent a stressful obligation, particularly for women held to traditional gender role norms. Thus, future research should examine family values as an antecedent of family-to-work outcomes and as a moderator of work-to-family outcomes.

Conclusion

Research on the WF interface in the Middle East is still in early development. Evidence suggests that this region shares many of the same antecedents and consequences of WFC with other regions in the world. However, the unique religious traditions, economic status, and cultural values of the region hold promise for exciting future research.

References

Ali, A. J., & Al-Owaihan, A. (2008). Islamic work ethic: A critical review. *Cross Cultural Management: An International Journal, 15*(1), 5–19.

Allen, T.D., French, K. A., Dumani, S., & Shockley, K.M. (2015). Meta-analysis of work–family conflict mean differences. Does national context matter? *Journal of Vocational Behavior, 90,* 90–100.

Aycan, Z. (2001). Human resource management in Turkey - Current issues and future challenges. *International Journal of Manpower, 22*(3), 252–260.

Aycan, Z., & Eskin, M. (2005). Relative contributions of childcare, spousal support, and organizational support in reducing work–family conflict for men and women: The case of Turkey. *Sex Roles, 53*(7–8), 453–471.

Benligiray, S., & Sönmez, H. (2012). Analysis of organizational commitment and work–family conflict in view of doctors and nurses. *The International Journal of Human Resource Management, 23*(18), 3890–3905.

Burke, R. J., & El-Kot, G. (2010). Correlates of work-family conflicts among managers in Egypt. *International Journal of Islamic and Middle Eastern Finance and Management, 3*(2), 113–131.

Burke, R. J., & Greenglass, E. R. (1999). Work–family conflict, spouse support, and nursing staff well-being during organizational restructuring. *Journal of Occupational Health Psychology, 4*(4), 327–336.

Calisir, F., Gumussoy, C. A., & Iskin, I. (2011). Factors affecting intention to quit among IT professionals in Turkey. *Personnel Review, 40*(4), 514–533.

Carlson, D. S., Kacmar, K. M., & Williams, L. J. (2000). Construction and initial validation of a multidimensional measure of work–family conflict. *Journal of Vocational Behavior, 56*(2), 249–276.

Eby, L. T., Casper, W. J., Lockwood, A., Bordeaux, C., & Brinley, A. (2005). Work and family research in IO/OB: Content analysis and review of the literature (1980–2002). *Journal of Vocational Behavior, 66*(1), 124–197.

Ergeneli, A., Ilsev, A., & Karapınar, P. B. (2010). Work–family conflict and job satisfaction relationship: The roles of gender and interpretive habits. *Gender, Work & Organization, 17*(6), 679–695.

Farhadi, P., Sharifian, R., Feili, A., & Shokrpour, N. (2013). The effects of supervisors' supportive role, job stress, and work–family conflicts on the nurses' attitudes. *The Health Care Manager, 32*(2), 107–122.

Forster, N., Al Ali Ebrahim, A., & Ibrahim, N. A. (2013). An exploratory study of work–life balance and work–family conflicts in the United Arab Emirates. *Skyline Business Journal, 9*(1), 34–42.

Frone, M. R., Russell, M., & Cooper, M. L. (1992). Antecedents and outcomes of work–family conflict: Testing a model of the work–family interface. *Journal of Applied Psychology, 77*(1), 65–78.

Glick, P., Sakallı-Uğurlu, N., Akbaş, G., Orta, İ. M., & Ceylan, S. (2015). Why do women endorse honor beliefs? Ambivalent sexism and religiosity as predictors. *Sex Roles, 75*(11–12), 543–554.

Greenhaus, J. H., & Beutell, N. J. (1985). Sources of conflict between work and family roles. *Academy of Management Review, 10*(1), 76–88.

Groth, H., & Sousa-Poza, A. (2012). *Population dynamics in Muslim countries: Assembling the jigsaw.* Heidelberg: Springer.

Hofstede, G. (1984). *Culture's consequences: International differences in work-related values.* London: Sage Publications Inc.

House, R. J., Hanges, P. J., Javidan, M., Dorfman, P. W., & Gupta, V. (2004). *Culture, leadership, and organizations: The GLOBE study of 62 societies.* Thousand Oaks: Sage Publications.

Ibrahim, M. E., & Al Marri, A. (2015). Role of gender and organizational support in work–family conflict for accountants in UAE. *International Journal of Commerce and Management, 25*(2), 157–172.

Itani, H., Sidani, Y. M., & Baalbaki, I. (2011). United Arab Emirates female entrepreneurs: motivations and frustrations. *Equality, Diversity and Inclusion: An International Journal, 30*(5), 409–424.

Karatepe, O. M., & Baddar, L. (2006). An empirical study of the selected consequences of frontline employees' work–family conflict and family–work conflict. *Tourism Management, 27*(5), 1017–1028.

Karatepe, O. M., Sokmen, A., Yavas, U., & Babakus, E. (2010). Work–family conflict and burnout in frontline service jobs: Direct, mediating and moderating effects. *E & M Ekonomie a Management, 13*(4), 61–73.

Karatepe, O. M., & Uludag, O. (2008a). Affectivity, conflicts in the work–family interface, and hotel employee outcomes. *International Journal of Hospitality Management, 27*(1), 30–41.

Karatepe, O. M., & Uludag, O. (2008b). Supervisor support, work–family conflict, and satisfaction outcomes: An empirical study in the hotel industry. *Journal of Human Resources in Hospitality & Tourism, 7*(2), 115–134.

Karimi, L. (2008a). Do female and male employees in Iran experience similar work–family interference, job, and life satisfaction? *Journal of Family Issues, 30*(1), 124–142.

(2008b). A study of a multidimensional model of work–family conflict among Iranian employees. *Community, Work & Family, 11*(3), 283–295.

Karimi, L., Karimi, H., & Nouri, A. (2011). Predicting employees' well-being using work–family conflict and job strain models. *Stress and Health, 27*(2), 111–122.

Karimi, L., & Nouri, A. (2009). Do work demands and resources predict work-to-family conflict and facilitation? A study of Iranian male employees. *Journal of Family and Economic Issues, 30*(2), 193–202.

Kinnunen, U., Feldt, T., Geurts, S., & Pulkkinen, L. (2006). Types of work–family interface: Well-being correlates of negative and positive spillover between work and family. *Scandinavian Journal of Psychology, 47*, 149–162.

Kinnunen, U., & Mauno, S. (1998). Antecedents and outcomes of work–family conflict among employed women and men in Finland. *Human Relations, 51*(2), 157–177.

Koyuncu, M., Burke, R. J., & Fiksenbaum, L. (2009). Work–family conflict among Turkish managers: Potential antecedents and consequences. *İş Güç: Endüstri İlişkileri ve İnsan Kaynakları Dergisi. Journal of Industrial Relations and Human Resources, 11* (i), 1–16.

Koyuncu, M., Burke, R. J., & Wolpin, J. (2012). Work-family conflict, satisfactions and psychological well-being among women managers and professionals in Turkey. *Gender in Management: An International Journal, 27*(3), 202–213.

Lyness, K. S., & Kropf, M. B. (2005). The relationships of national gender equality and organizational support with work–family balance: A study of European managers. *Human Relations, 58*(1), 33–60.

Metcalfe, B. D. (2008). Women, management and globalization in the Middle East. *Journal of Business Ethics, 83*(1), 85–100.

Michel, J. S., Kotrba, L. M., Mitchelson, J. K., Clark, M. A., & Baltes, B. B. (2011). Antecedents of work–family conflict: A meta-analytic review. *Journal of Organizational Behavior, 32*(5), 689–725.

Mortazavi, S., Pedhiwala, N., Shafiro, M., & Hammer, L. (2009). Work–family conflict related to culture and gender. *Community, Work & Family, 12*(2), 251–273.

Nisbett, R. E., & Cohen, D. (1996). *Culture of honor: The psychology of violence in the South.* Boulder, CO: Westview Press.

Omran, A. R., & Roudi, F. (1993). The Middle East population puzzle. *Population Bulletin, 48*(1), 1–40.

Pleck, J. H. (1977). The work–family role system. *Social Problems, 24*, 417–427.

Ronen, S., & Shenkar, O. (1985). Clustering countries on attitudinal dimensions: A review and synthesis. *The Academy of Management Review, 10*(3), 435–454.

Sharda, B. D., & Miller, G. A. (2001). Culture and organizational structure in the Middle East: A comparative analysis of Iran, Jordan and USA. *International Review of Sociology, 11*(3), 309–324.

Shockley, K. M. (in press). Managing the work–family interface. In N. Anderson, D. S. Ones, H. K. Sinangil, & C. Viswesvaran (Eds.), *The SAGE handbook of industrial, work, & organizational psychology* (2nd ed). London: SAGE Publications Ltd.

Sidani, Y. M., & Thornberry, J. (2009). The current Arab work ethic: Antecedents, implications, and potential remedies. *Journal of Business Ethics, 91*(1), 35–49.

Syed, J. (2008). A context-specific perspective of equal employment opportunity in Islamic societies. *Asia Pacific Journal of Management, 25*(1), 135–151.

Tayfur, O., & Arslan, M. (2013). The role of lack of reciprocity, supervisory support, workload and work–family conflict on exhaustion: Evidence from physicians. *Psychology, Health & Medicine, 18*(5), 564–575.

Torabi, F., & Abbasi-Shavazi, M. J. (2015). Women's human capital and economic growth in the Middle East and North Africa. *Journal of International Women's Studies, 16*(3), 237–261.

United Nations. (2015). World fertility patterns 2015. Retrieved from www.un.org/en/ development/desa/population/publications/pdf/fertility/world-fertility-patterns -2015.pdf

United Nations Development Programme. (2010). *Human development report 2010.* New York: United Nations Development Programme.

Vandello, J. A., & Cohen, D. (2003). Male honor and female fidelity: Implicit cultural scripts that perpetuate domestic violence. *Journal of Personality and Social Psychology, 84*(5), 997–1010.

Vandenberg, R. J., & Lance, C. E. (2000). A review and synthesis of the measurement invariance literature: Suggestions, practices, and recommendations for organizational research. *Organizational Research Methods*, *3*(1), 4.

World Bank. (2014). Labor and social protection indicators. Retrieved from www.databank.worldbank.org/data/reports.aspx?source=world-development-indicators

World Economic Forum. (2014). *The global gender gap report 2014*. Geneva, Switzerland: World Economic Forum.

World Policy Analysis Center. (2017). Adult labor and working conditions. Retrieved from www.worldpolicycenter.org/topics/adult-labor-and-working-conditions/

Yavas, U., Babakus, E., & Karatepe, O. M. (2008). Attitudinal and behavioral consequences of work-family conflict and family-work conflict. *International Journal of Service Industry Management*, *19*(1), 7–31.

Yildirim, D., & Aycan, Z. (2008). Nurses' work demands and work–family conflict: A questionnaire survey. *International Journal of Nursing Studies*, *45*(9), 1366–1378.

19 A Review of Work–Family Research in South East Asia

Comila Shahani-Denning and Aarti Shyamsunder

Over the last couple of decades, the importance of studying work–family issues outside of the United States or other Western countries has been emphasized by a number of researchers in the field (e.g., Bardoel & De Cieri, 2006; Gambles, Lewis, & Rapoport, 2006; Poelmans, Chinchilla, & Cardona, 2003; Shaffer, Joplin, & Hsu, 2011). Most of the studies to date on work–family issues have been conducted in Western countries that do not share many cultural characteristics and industrial structures with countries in other regions, with Asian countries being particularly distinct (Spector et al., 2004). Thus, the extent to which the majority of the work–family literature generalizes to other cultures remains largely unknown and is an area ripe for additional research.

The goal of this chapter is to review the extant literature on work–family issues in one particular region: South East Asia. In doing so, we first lay out three critical stipulations: (1) For the purposes of this book, we consider South East Asia to comprise the following countries: Bangladesh, Bhutan, India, Indonesia, Malaysia, Maldives, Myanmar, Nepal, Philippines, Sri Lanka, Thailand, and Timor-Leste; (2) "South East Asia" is therefore, a heterogeneous, diverse and complex region, which makes it difficult to capture an overall assessment of work–family issues that is fully representative of the whole region. Nonetheless, there are certain important ways in which the region as a whole differs from the Western world (which has been the focus of most existing work–family research), and as such, it warrants further investigation; (3) Work–family issues are intricately connected to issues of gender equality – especially in developing countries, which show larger gender gaps in education, workforce participation, health, and politics (see the World Economic Forum's Global Gender Gap Index, 2016). As such, much of the discussion in this chapter will focus on gender gaps and opportunities to close them.

Labor Market and Contextual Aspects Influencing Work–Family Issues in South East Asia

Historical, political, economic, social, and cultural aspects of countries and regions influence assumptions regarding division of labor and role expectations at work and within the family (Komarraju, 2006). Therefore, it is important to consider these contextual factors when trying to understand work–family issues in a particular region. Although there are quite a few cultural and institutional factors of relevance

Table 19.1 *Regulatory and legal labor force considerations impacting work–family issues in South East Asia*

	Female versus Male Labor Force Participation[1]	Legally Mandated Paid Maternity Leave (in days)[2]	Legally Mandated Paid Paternity Leave (in days)[2]	Do Women Face Significant Barriers to Equal Employment?[2]	Childcare Subsidized or Publicly Provided?[2]
Bangladesh	60% (F); 87% (M)	112	N/A[4]	No	No
Bhutan	69% (F); 80% (M)	56	5	No	No
India	29% (F); 83% (M)	84	N/A	No	No
Indonesia	54% (F); 86% (M)	90	2	Yes	No
Malaysia	47% (F); 79% (M)	60	N/A	Yes	No
Maldives	58% (F); 80% (M)	60	3	Yes	No
Myanmar[3]	79% (F)	98	15	No	No
Nepal	83% (F); 89% (M)	52	N/A	Yes	No
Philippines	53% (F); 81% (M)	60	7	Yes	Yes
Sri Lanka	39% (F); 81% (M)	84	N/A	No	No
Thailand	71% (F); 86% (M)	90	N/A	No	Yes
Timor-Leste[3]	25% (F)	84	5	Yes	Yes

[1] Source: World Economic Forum (2016). *The Global Gender Gap Report.* www.weforum.org.
[2] Source: World Bank Group. (2015). Women, Business and the Law 2016: Getting to Equal. Washington, DC: World Bank.
[3] Country is not included in the Global Gender Gap report, and as such, male labor force participation data are not readily available.
[4] N/A implies "Not Applicable" – in these cases, there is no provision explicitly spelled out by law regarding parental leave.

(see Brough, Driscoll, & Kalliath, 2005; Hegewisch & Gornick, 2011), we choose to focus on a few key factors and highlight the differences between countries in the South East Asian region based on them. We chose to focus on labor force composition, government mandated access to parental leave and childcare, and access to different kinds of work for women and men, because these factors seemed to have the most potential impact on work–family issues. Table 19.1 helps illustrate some of the major ways in which these countries approach work–life issues in terms of the labor force considerations described below.

The first key factor relates to *labor force composition*. An Asian Development Bank (2015) report states that women in Asia as a whole are on average 70% less likely than men to be in the labor force, with the country-to-country percentage varying from 3% to 80%. This gap persists in spite of economic growth, decreasing fertility rates, and increasing education. Reviewing the 2016 Gender Gap Report of the World Economic Forum (a report that includes 144 economies and ranks country gender gaps based on economic participation and opportunity, educational attainment, political empowerment, and health and survival), it is clear that there is a very pronounced disparity between South East Asia and the other regions of the world.

A second critical regulatory consideration related to work–life issues is paid and unpaid leave, specifically, *access to parental leave*. The ability to take paid and unpaid family leave enables employees to better meet their work and family responsibilities (Baird & Whitehouse, 2012). When there is mandated access to parental leave, most countries in South East Asia provide this leave to mothers more so than to fathers, as illustrated in Table 1. Yet, research suggests that in places where new fathers take parental leave, mothers are more likely to return to the labor market, female employment is higher, and the earnings gap between men and women is smaller (Women, Business and the Law, 2015). Thus, whether and how much parental leave is provided by law can be an important consideration impacting work–family issues in the country or region in question.

A third area of interest is the *nature of work and access to it*, including length of working hours and whether women and men are permitted to work in the same jobs. Most research suggests a direct relationship between work–family conflict and long working hours or pressure to work long hours (e.g., Michel et al., 2011). Most countries in South East Asia's standard work week is between forty and forty-eight hours (with most falling closer to forty-eight). Additionally, there are prevailing restrictions on women's work, including what hours (e.g., night) they cannot work, work deemed hazardous or arduous for women but not men (e.g., mining), and specific tasks (e.g., heavy lifting) or workplaces (e.g., factories) women are not allowed to work in. These are all captured under the broad heading of "Do women face significant barriers to equal employment?" in Table 19.1.

A fourth regulatory consideration is *access to childcare*. Just like with paid parental leave, having access to high quality childcare is considered essential for parents' participation in the workforce. As Bianchi and Milkie (2010) note: "childcare … forms the nucleus of what much 'work–family' conflict is about—how to care for children adequately when parents need or want to work outside the home." (p. 710). Not only does providing help with or access to quality childcare outside the home enable primary caregivers (mostly women) to more quickly return to the workforce, but it also could encourage a more equitable distribution of domestic responsibilities between women and men (Asian Development Bank, 2015), thus further easing potential conflict arising from competing work and family priorities. For example, In India because of the heavy burden of domestic labor, many women (about 45%) leave the workforce mid-career (compared with the overall Asian average of 28%; McKinsey Report). This is the "leaky pipeline" in India that many have described (e.g., Jhangiani, 2016), where organizations lose many talented employees due to work–family conflict and lack of support in a male-oriented workplace.

Although there is variability across countries within the regions, there are some shared characteristics of South East Asian countries worth noting. First, people in South East Asian countries tend to share certain cultural values. The GLOBE project, a study of thousands of managers in sixty-two countries aimed at understanding variation in cultural values (see Chapter 3 in this Handbook (Olliere-Malaterre & Foucreault) for additional details) provides important insight about cultural values that are common to many countries in South East Asia (although note that the GLOBE project uses Southern Asia as the regional classification and not South

East Asia, which includes India, Indonesia, Iran, Malaysia, Philippines, and Thailand, but there is sufficient overlap for us to consider its conclusions here). South East Asian countries in general score highly on the cultural values of in-group collectivism (i.e., the degree to which individuals express pride, loyalty, and cohesiveness in their families), power distance (i.e., degree that cultures expect power to be unequally distributed), and humane orientation (i.e., degree that cultures value and reward helping others) (House, Hanges, Javidan, Dorfman, & Gupta, 2004). Researchers have suggested that all of these values have potential implications for work–family relations. Specifically, numerous researchers have proposed that work–family conflict may be construed differently in collectivistic versus individualistic cultures, as collectivists tend to consider work as a means to enhancing family (e.g., Galovan, Fackrell, Buswell, Jones, Hill, & Carroll, 2010; Hassan, Dollard, & Winefield, 2010; Yang, 2005). Power distance and humane orientation have been considered less often in the context of global work–family relations, but Powell, Francesco, and Ling (2009) included humane orientation in their theoretical model of the impact of culture on work–family conflict, arguing that people in cultures high in humane orientation tend to receive high levels of social support, which should lead to lower levels of work–family conflict compared to those in low humane-oriented cultures.

Additionally, although South East Asia does not stand out as particularly low on gender egalitarianism, defined as the degree that cultures minimize gender inequality, based on GLOBE project data, other metrics suggest that gender roles are quite distinct in this region. Specifically, according to the Global Gender Gap Index (2016), which uses the gap between men and women on several variables such as economic participation and opportunity, health and survival, and political empowerment, to create an overall index of equality, "Asia and the Pacific" is the region with the second lowest levels of gender equality, being surpassed only by the "Middle East and North Africa." The index does not separately report on South East Asia as a region, but we conducted our own calculations based on values reported for individual countries, which included the Philippines, Sri Lanka, Bangladesh, India, Indonesia, Malaysia, the Maldives, Nepal, Thailand, and Timore-Leste. The average gender gap of only these countries is almost identical to that of the broader region.

Beyond cultural values, economic considerations of the South East Asian region are important. Since many countries in South East Asia are considered "developing" countries with weaker economies, work is critical for family survival – and as such, family members may be more accepting of work being conducted in the home environment or otherwise interfering with family life, which would impact mean levels of reported work–family conflict.

There are also major differences between these countries to keep in mind when examining the research. For example, Thailand has had a long history of military rule, but was never colonized by European powers. On the other hand, India is one of the largest democracies whose society bears the remnants of the British Colonial Rule while still retaining its regional social, political, cultural, and economic diversity in that there is no single prevailing commonwealth identity (Banerji & Yik, 2012). The Philippines, on the other hand, is a South East Asian country with a history of colonization most recently by the United States (Rothausen, Gonzalez, & Griffin, 2009). This has resulted in the Philippines having a large English-speaking population that espouses many Western values.

Research on Work–Family Issues in South East Asia: Themes and Challenges

Research on work–life issues in South East Asia is relatively recent and has not appeared much in rigorous, peer-reviewed journals. A vast majority of the research focuses on work–family issues rather than work–life issues, with an emphasis on the participation of women in the workforce and the burdens of managing childcare along with a career. India, Malaysia, and Sri Lanka have received the most research attention; we were unable to find any work–family research focused on the Maldives, Nepal, or Timor-Leste, while the other countries were featured in some, limited research. For example, the Philippines was represented in the IBM Global work and life issues survey, but data was not presented for individual countries (Erickson, Martinengo, & Hill, 2010; Yang & Hawkins, 2004).

Much of the empirical literature focused on South East Asian has relied on collectivism as an explanation for expected cultural differences in comparative studies. As noted previously, different ways of thinking about work and family as separate versus integrated can impact how frequently work–family conflict is experienced. A few studies have examined this idea, although results are a bit mixed. Pal and Saksvik (2006) found that Indians had higher work–family conflict than Norwegians. Agarwala, Arizkuren-Eleta, Del Castillo, Muñiz-Ferrer, and Gartzia (2014) measured work-to-family conflict, family-to-work conflict, and work–life conflict in India, Peru, and Spain. They cite no differences in work-to-family conflict, but family-to-work conflict and work–life conflict was higher in India than in Peru or Spain. Taken together, there is somewhat of a trend of greater work–family conflict in South East Asian countries compared those in other areas of the world. Interestingly, this is counter to what many researchers have proposed, arguing that because collectivism leads people to view work and family as more integrated, people in collectivistic countries are less likely to view work and family as in conflict compared to those in individualistic countries. Thus, it may be other cultural variables along with collectivism that produce these effects.

Collectivism has also been theorized to impact the strength of association of work variables with work–family conflict. In an empirical test of this idea using samples from fifteen countries, Spector et al. (2004) found that working hours have a stronger relationship with work–family conflict in individualistic countries compared to collectivistic countries. Thus, in South East Asia, work may not be perceived as an individual milestone of success, but as a way to improve family welfare, and working long hours may be seen as helping the family rather than as an interference (Annavarjula & Das, 2013; De Cieri & Bardoel, 2009). On the other hand, the same behaviors in individualistic cultures may be viewed as self-centered (Yang, Chen, Choi, & Zou, 2000).

Relatedly, Aycan (2008) posits that Asian cultures perceive work and family as compatible but different facets of life and, therefore, when work–family conflict occurs it is simply something that needs to be managed and potentially even learn and grow from. In contrast, Western, individualistic cultures view work–family conflict as problematic and damaging. Several studies support this idea, either directly or indirectly. Aryee, Srinivas, and Tan (2005) found that in India, the more an employee was involved in his/her job, the less family-to-work conflict the person experienced. Although this may seem counterintuitive within an individualistic society, it is more easily understood in collectivistic societies, such as India, because job involvement is considered critical to ensure the material well-being of the family. However, it important to note that other studies conducted in South East Asia have found that work demands contribute to work–family conflict, and are more predictive of conflict than are family demands (e.g., Fang, Nastiti, & Chen, 2011 in a sample of Indonesian lecturers).

Other research on predictors of work–family constructs focuses on support and individual differences. In a study examining work–life balance in mostly male Indian bank managers located in Madhya Pradesh, a central Indian state, Jain and Jain (2015) found moderate levels of work–life balance among this sample and that supportive HR policies, supervisor and organizational support, teamwork, trust, and openness in communication related positively to work–life balance. In terms of personality, Kappagoda (2014) examined emotional intelligence as a predictor of work–family conflict among school teachers in North-Central Sri Lanka. He found that teachers with high emotional intelligence reported less work-to-family and family-to-work conflict. Noor (2006), in a sample of Malaysian employees, highlighted the importance of locus of control and suggested further investigation of personality variables in understanding the experience of work–family conflict. Lastly, Bhargava and Baral (2009) focused on core self-evaluations, a stable individual difference composed of locus of control, neuroticism, generalized self-efficacy, and self-esteem, which encompasses individuals' evaluations about themselves, their control, and their abilities (Judge, Locke & Durham, 1997). Bhargava and Baral (2009) found a positive relationship between core self-evaluations and work–family effectiveness in a sample of Indian manufacturing and IT managers.

Other studies have examined work–family constructs in relation to outcomes, rather than focusing on antecedents. In a series of studies comparing Indian and Norwegian medical professionals, Pal and Saksvik (2006, 2008) found differential predictors of job stress according to country and occupation. For Norwegian nurses, work–family conflict, job demands, and lack of flexibility were predictors of job stress, but for Indian nurses, family-to-work conflict and social support were predictors of job stress. None of the variables were predictors of job stress among Norwegian doctors, whereas job control predicted job stress for Indian doctors. Findings were explained in terms of national and cultural differences that may impact gender and family policies. The authors discussed cultural differences in the perceptions of demands and social support in these two cultures with the Nordic culture having an employment culture that encourages mothers to work by providing child-care and other family friendly policies. Such support is missing in many Indian organizations.

Other research on work–family conflict and outcomes was conducted only in South East Asia with no explicit comparison to other cultures. Mimicking that which has been found in meta-analytic summaries of the literature in general (e.g., Amstad et al., 2011), Srivasta and Srivasta (2012) found that both work-to-family conflict and family-to-work conflict negatively related to job performance, mental health, and marital satisfaction for a sample of IT professionals. Namasivayan and Zhao (2007) found that family-to-work conflict, but not work-to-family conflict, predicted job satisfaction in a sample of Indian hospitality workers, which aligns with the domain specificity perspective (i.e., satisfaction in the interfered with domain is affected more so than satisfaction in the interfering domain; Frone, Russell, & Cooper, 1992), although this pattern is contrary to what has been found in meta-analytic research (Shockley & Singla, 2011). Although most of the studies examining outcomes typically demonstrate similar trends to that found in Western cultures, Pal and Saksvik (2006, 2008) did find differences when comparing Indian and Norwegian health professionals. More research is needed that specifically compares South East Asia countries to their Western counterparts.

There is also evidence of differences in identity in South East Asian cultures compared to other cultures. Annavarjula and Das (2013) compared American and Indian middle managers and found that American workers placed more emphasis on their family identity whereas Indian workers placed more emphasis on work identity. Although this may seem contradictory to ideas previously discussed (i.e., that family is highly important in collectivistic societies), it can be explained by the fact that because work is considered critical to ensure the material well-being of the family in these cultures (Aryee, Srinivas, & Tan, 2005), they may identify strongly with their work identity. Relatedly, Pawitra (as cited in Fang, Nastiti, & Chen, 2011) suggested that in the Indonesian context, working is an important way to facilitate the communalism inherent in that culture; fulfilling one's work responsibility helps maintain in-group cohesion, which is critical for people who live with collectivistic values. In a developing economy like Indonesia, Indonesians spend more time and energy working as working will allow them to sustain the well-being of the next generation. Said otherwise, workers in collective societies like India, Malaysia, and Indonesia are expected to have high work identity because work is seen as a means to a collective good. Lastly, there is some evidence that these values are changing with generations, at least in India. Singh (2013) found that employees from pre-liberalization India (ages 47–58) saw work as a duty performed for family, but for post-liberalization Indians (ages 24–34), work was seen as a challenge, an opportunity for advancing one's career, and as a means to earn money for leisure.

Additionally, several researchers have made use of qualitative approaches to try to more fully understand the meaning attached to work, family, and work–family conflict in South East Asian contexts. One example is a study conducted in India based on semi-structured interviews with twenty-one dual-earner couples (Kalliath et al., 2011). All of the couples in the study reported experiencing work–family conflict, especially time- and strain-based forms. Time-based conflict was reflected by comments on the hours spent, the need to take work home, and lack of time to spend with their children. Strain-based conflicts were reflected in comments on how the competing demands of work and family roles caused mental stress. Men reported more work-to-family conflict and women reported more family-to-work conflict. Coping strategies included a belief in God, having positive attitudes towards life, getting strength from helping others, and support from family and colleagues. More men reported obtaining support from a spouse than did women. Another example of a qualitative study using in-depth qualitative, semi-structured interviews and observations with mothers was conducted by Kodagoda (2010) who studied a small, purposive sample of five female bank managers and their partners in Sri Lanka. They also interviewed two top level banking sector managers. High levels of work–family stress was reported when there were children in the household, particularly younger children. Both mothers and husbands perceived mothers as being the primary caregivers, and mothers experienced more stress than their husbands. Spousal and family support were also reported as important in reducing work stress, and the need for organizations and society to provide family friendly policies was emphasized. These findings are not substantially different from those found in Western-based work–family research, but help support the idea that there may be some similarities across regions in work–family concerns.

Gender plays an important role in work–family relations in South East Asia, as it does in many cultural contexts. In terms of specific gender-related work–family research in the region, some results have been surprising in light of the fact that there is still a great deal of gender inequity in many South East Asian countries, with women still taking on the bulk of family labor (e.g., Rajadhyaksha, 2012). Specifically, given women's additional family demands, one might expect that work–life balance would be more difficult for women (Noor, 2002a). However, a study of Indian bank managers found that about 67.7% of the women reported that they were able to balance their work and life in contrast to 50.7% of the men (Kakkar & Bhandari, 2016). Because the sample was all people in the same occupation, differences in job characteristics are an unlikely explanation; women did report slightly higher levels of family support than men, which could be a contributing factor. Other research supports this idea regarding support. Noor (1999) suggests that Malay women might be protected from work–family conflict because of the large amount of kinship and religious support that they often receive, although this trend did not hold for urban women who may be more likely to live in isolated nuclear families (Din & Noor, 2009). Additionally, Noor (2002b) found that spousal support moderated the relationship between the number of hours worked and job autonomy and work–family conflict in that Malaysian women with high spousal support experienced less work–family conflict even when working long hours and the lowest level of conflict was reported when spousal support was high and job autonomy was high.

Much of the extant research has taken a conflict perspective, with little attention to positive experiences, such as work–family facilitation or enrichment. Two exceptions to this include Bhargava and Baral (2009) and Pattusamy and Jacob (2015). Bhargava and Baral (2009) studied job characteristics (i.e., autonomy, skill variety, task identity, task significance, feedback from job, feedback from others and dealing with others) and work–life balance programs as predictors of work–family enrichment in a sample of Indian managers. There was evidence for gender effects, such that the relationship between work–life balance programs (e.g., flexible working hours, flexibility in start and end times) and work–family enrichment was stronger for women than men, whereas the relationship between job characteristics and work–family enrichment was stronger for men than women. Women also reported higher mean levels of family-to-work enrichment than men. Pattusamy and Jacob (2015) examined teaching faculty in the United States and India. Both work–family conflict and work–family facilitation predicted job and family satisfaction. Job and family satisfaction in turn predicted work–family balance, which predicted life satisfaction. Despite the relationships differing in magnitude between the two samples to some extent, the proposed theoretical model was similarly predictive for both samples. In general, we argue that more research is needed examining the positive effects of the relationship between work and life.

To summarize, the existing research has focused on work–family conflict rather than work–life conflict and has largely focused on conflict rather than facilitation. Much of the emphasis has been on examining gender differences in the experience of work and family. South East Asia represents a wide range of countries and the research has been uneven across the countries with a great deal of research conducted in India and little research in other countries. A consistent theme in the research reviewed above suggests that the experience of work–family conflict is influenced largely by the central role of work in one's role in the family and society in South East Asian countries, and that even beyond individual differences, external factors (such as family support and organizational support such as work–life balance programs) are quite relevant in South East Asian countries when it comes to mitigating the experience of work–family conflict.

Country Level Initiatives with Potential to Facilitate Work–Family Management

Although research specific to the South East Asia region is somewhat sparse and lacking in systematic focus, there are emergent ideas of how societies as a whole can enact change to better integrate work and life priorities for their workforces. The following section touches upon efforts undertaken by countries in the region to enhance work–life effectiveness.

As illustrated in Table 19.1, there are great disparities between countries in South East Asia in terms of four critical regulatory considerations – women's workforce participation, parental leave provisions by law, equal access to work for all, and publicly available childcare support. In terms of women's workforce participation, a 2015 Asian Development Bank report "Women in the workforce: An unmet potential in Asia and the Pacific" outlined three critical factors determining women's labor force participation: (1) The education and health gap between women and men. (2) Time allocation differences: On average, women spend twice as much time as men on household work, and four times as much on childcare, thus contributing less to the labor market and GDP. Women also have less discretionary time, face more short-term disruptions (such as family member ill health), and suffer negative consequences of societal gender role expectations regarding earning-versus-housework. (3) The nuanced weighing of opportunity costs and social costs against potential wages and available opportunities for work.

Paralleling some of these observations, the report outlined the following major policy options and initiatives to increase female labor force participation: (1) Competition through greater international trade and openness, (2) Skills and vocational training, (3) Employment quotas for women, (4) Information on available employment resources and job matching, (5) Enhancing transport/mobility options, ensuring safety and security for women, at the workplace and on the commute to work, (6) Parental leave, childcare, and flexible work arrangement (FWA) options. We highlight two of these in particular: employment quotas and providing parental leave, childcare, and FWAs. This recommendation is based on the idea that employment quotas may be necessary and effective, especially in countries where low female workforce participation is perpetuated by social norms or discrimination.

Many South East Asian countries (e.g., India, Thailand, Indonesia, and Timor-Leste) have altered their constitutions or party laws to adopt some form of gender quotas in politics. Employment quota policies, if tied to governmental policies regarding loans and multilateral assistance, might increase the pool of available jobs while also raising aspirations among women and girls. Currently an experiment is underway in India, which mandated at least one member of the boards of publicly listed companies to be a woman. Moreover, there seems to be increasing support for quotas, with 55% of businesses in South East Asia supporting the idea (Grant Thornton, 2014).

With regard to parental leave, childcare, and FWAs, the role of the government in regulating this cannot be overlooked. Constraints on women's time are reduced and children's health outcomes are improved, when female employees are provided childcare, maternity leave, and FWAs (e.g., Abu-Ghaida & Klasen, 2004; Heymann, Raub, & Earle, 2011), and these aspects are indirectly improved when incentives are created for men to commit to share domestic responsibilities (Bettio & Villa, 1996). Moreover, women seem to stay longer in the workforce and within specific jobs when parental leave is mandatory (Kim, Lee, & Shin, 2015). Thus, these policies can benefit not only women, but also families and society at large.

India has also made some progress with extending mandatory maternity leave from twelve to twenty-six weeks (over six months) and mandating that organizations with more than fifty female employees must provide a crèche or daycare facilities for children. Sri Lanka offers maternity leave and other forms of paid leave (Kodagoda, 2010). Similarly, Bangladesh has also implemented a six-month maternity leave policy although there is inconsistency in its usage and few provisions for childcare (Akter, 2016). In Malaysia, organizations are likely to implement family-friendly policies mostly comprising of paid time off, medical coverage, and some childcare facilities (Noor, 2006).

The World Bank's *Women, Business and Law* report notes that 155 of the 173 countries in their report have at least one law impeding women's economic opportunities. Moreover, in 100 economies, women face gender-based job restrictions. An example of these restrictions is the Factories Act in India, which prohibits women from working the night shift, thus impacting the representation of women in the manufacturing sector, perpetuating a vicious cycle of lack of access and development. Until such restrictions are lifted, or at least questioned in light of present day realities, individuals and organizations will continue to face barriers while trying to impact work–life integration and better, fairer workforce representation.

Best Practices for Work–Family Management in South East Asia

Research summary. Although work–life balance policies and practices have become increasingly common over the last decade or so, especially in industries with a large influence of multinational companies headquartered outside of South East Asia, they still seem to be viewed by organizational stakeholders as somewhat unnecessary in this region. For a long time, in Asia, FWAs were generally not widely used and relatively few studies on the practice had been carried out (Chow & Chew, 2006). Wang, Lawler, and Shi (2011) argue for the importance of work–life balance related practices in countries with a more collective orientation as employees may expect their employers to take care of them in return for loyalty. They found that in India and Thailand, perceived importance of work–life balance practices moderated the relationship between work flexibility and organizational commitment as well as work flexibility and work–family conflict. Work flexibility was positively related to organizational commitment and negatively related to work–family conflict among people who viewed this policy as important. There was a similar moderating effect for childcare policies in Thailand with childcare benefits being positively related to organizational commitment and negatively related to work–family conflict, and the relationship was stronger among people who viewed childcare as important. In contrast, in India, childcare-related policies were not related to organizational commitment or work–family conflict. In fact, among those who perceived this policy as less important, childcare policies predicted lower organizational commitment and higher perceived work–family conflict. Although there are some work–life balance policies and FWAs being increasingly offered in India (Rathore & Sachitanand, 2007), there also tends to be a view that work–life balance is "a luxury that India cannot afford to focus on until after it has caught up with or exceeded the West in terms of economic development and competitiveness" (Gambles et al., 2006, p. 15).

Organizational case studies. Below we describe five organizations (Hindustan Unilever, Dow Corning, Godrej, Shell, and Proctor & Gamble) with operations in South East Asia that have made an effort to facilitate work–family management for employees and have focused on creating inclusive workplaces.

Hindustan Unilever, a well-respected consumer goods organization that employs around 18,000 people in India, has a strong "agile" work culture where employees can work from anywhere, anyhow, anytime (Catalyst, 2013). The Agile Working program started in 2009 and evolved from a simple flexibility program into a pioneering career work model, with the goal of creating job structures that promote overall culture change with respect to work–family issues. Each employee identifies what they consider essential or non-negotiable in their lives – this may be family, health, career, societal contribution, or other aspects of life – and the organization works with these life needs by allowing flexible timing, flexible office locations to work from, career breaks ranging from six months to five years, and a second careers program (i.e., a career transition program for women who have taken a long career break and wish to reenter the workforce) (Karwa, 2015).

A few years ago, Dow Corning (a multinational organization that supplies silicones and silicones solutions, products, technology and services) noticed that its Asian employees were less interested in traditional FWAs like compressed work weeks. Instead, they were keen on minimizing frequent late-night conference calls (for instance, with their Western colleagues in the United States or in European time zones) – a common occurrence in multinational companies with operations in South East Asia. Responding to this work–life need, the organization rolled out teleconference guidelines requiring employees in Asia, Australia/New Zealand, South America, Europe, and the United States regularly rotate time zones for conference calls.

An Indian conglomerate, Godrej (a large conglomerate that includes chemicals manufacturers, household and consumer products manufacturers, real estate, and metal works), has a number of initiatives to break out of the traditional face-time expectations of working long hours in the office. Godrej's policies are meant to cater to employees of three different generations – Baby Boomers, Gen X, and Gen Y. The policy offers flexible hours and telecommuting, but also supports employees who want to contribute to society by teaching or using their skills for a social cause. They stay away from a one-size-fits-all policy, focusing more on goal-setting and performance measurement than on regulating work hours. They have unlimited sick leave and focus on building a culture of trust where employees can bring their whole selves to work and integrate work and life needs.

Royal Dutch Shell instituted a policy around FWAs over ten years ago, including in its Malaysia operations (Anell & Hartmann, 2007). Shell Malaysia's FWAs at the time (2007) included some typical elements such as telecommuting, flextime, and part-time options as well as sabbaticals and the option to work beyond retirement age. In addition, generous leave policies include such provisions as "half pay leave to care for family members and extend maternity leave" and the possibility of availing of full paid leave for a variety of reasons. Most interestingly, Shell Malaysia had developed a charter, providing each employee and their team a framework to develop their own working norms. For instance: "Staff should enter into a dialogue with their supervisor about how a good balance between working requirements and personal needs can be met"; "Meetings and workshops should be scheduled, where possible, to avoid travel on weekends and holidays"; "An adequate work/rest balance should be maintained during and following business trips or periods of high workload."

Procter & Gamble (P&G) won the Catalyst Award recently for its programmatic efforts to create an inclusive workplace, which included its focus on work–family management (Catalyst, 2015). P&G globally provides location and time flexibility and a variety of leave and reduced-hour arrangements, in order to build a culture where women and men can manage their responsibilities at and outside of work. P&G's Hyderabad (India) plant is the first one of its kind to boast 30% women in its workforce. One of the ways it achieved this unprecedented high proportion in India's manufacturing sector is by working with the local state government to seek an exception to the Factories Act which prohibits women working the night shift. Along with removing this restriction, P&G also ensured an inclusive environment where everyone felt safe and empowered to contribute their best and navigate their work–life boundaries effectively.

Future Research

Research on work–family issues in this region is relatively nascent and, for the most part, less rigorous by academic standards. Some of the countries in South East Asia (e.g., Maldives, Nepal, or Timor-Leste) have not been studied in published academic research to our knowledge. It would be very useful if research was conducted in these regions, particularly as part of large comparative studies, which often focus on European countries or China to the neglect of South East Asia (see Chapter 2 of this Handbook (Shockley, French, & Yu) for an overview of global work–family research). Such studies would not only add to our existing knowledge about the region, but would also allow for explicit comparisons between regions, which can be difficult when studies use different survey questions, methodologies, and samples. In addition to simply conducting more research in South East Asia, we also propose some specific avenues for future research.

Given ideas in existing theoretical work about how work is seen as a means to provide for the family in more collectivistic cultures, the very notion of work–family conflict needs to be reexamined. Said otherwise, do people in South East Asia view work–family conflict (or other work–family constructs such as balance or facilitation) in the same way as those in individualistic cultures where the common measurement instruments (e.g., Carlson, Kacmar, & Williams, 2000; Netemeyer, Boles, & McMurrian, 1996) were developed? Measurement equivalence studies as well as additional qualitative research would help address this question.

Related to this is the need to further understand work–family boundary research with an emphasis on how South East Asian countries' cultures impact these ideas. A key idea in work–family boundary management is integration/segmentation, terms used to describe the ways in which people prefer to manage their home and work domains (Kreiner, 2006; Nippert-Eng, 1996). Segmentation/integration exists on a continuum, whereas some people prefer to keep work and family totally separate (e.g., will physically separate work and family and minimize inter-role transitions) while others prefer to keep them integrated (e.g., will work at home and answer personal calls during work time). Studies on such boundary dynamics have mostly focused on Western contexts, but Ashforth et al. (2000) suggested that the culture in which an individual is embedded likely affects these processes. Specifically, it is likely that individuals from collectivistic, feminine, low uncertainty-avoidance, and/or low power-distance cultures would be more likely to integrate than segment roles. Additionally, Powell et al. (2009) suggested that people in cultures high on diffusion and collectivism (versus specificity and individualism, respectively) are more likely to integrate (versus segment) their work and home roles in order to maintain those role boundaries that are compatible with their cultures. Diffusion versus specificity focusses on the level of wholeness a culture uses to define a construct. People from a diffuse culture prefer to focus on wholeness or integration of different aspects of one's life.

The impact of region/culture on segmentation/integration has only been tested in one study to our knowledge (Ollo-López & Goñi-Legaz, 2015) within a European context; thus, information about segmentation/integration in South East Asian societies remains largely untested. Allen, Cho, and Meier (2014) suggests that it may make sense to consider the integration/segmentation dimension as a separate value altogether, at the cultural level, distinct from existing values. Integration/ segmentation values within a culture may also have implications for the efficacy of organizational support. In cultures where people prefer to keep work and non-work separated, organizational support may be interpreted as infringing on this separation and create additional stress. Further research on segmentation/integration preferences and how those fit with organizational policies would be useful to help shape work design and organizational supports in a way that maximizes work–family management in various regions of the world, including South East Asia.

In South East Asia specifically, given the importance of the family in people's lives, we also recommend that future research focuses more on the family side as a means to enhance work–family outcomes. This suggestion is grounded in the fact that participants in many of the studies reviewed report using informal social support to deal with work–family conflict (e.g., Kalliath et al., 2011; Noor, 1999, 2002b). As a starting place, Erickson et al. (2010) discuss how the workplace can better offer support for employees in different family life stages. Support helpful for a family with infants may be different than support needed for a family with elderly parents to care for. This may be particularly relevant in South East Asia, where there are often expectations to care for aging parents – South East Asia's elderly population is projected to increase by 430% between 2000 and 2050 (Retherford, Westley, Choe, Brown, Mason, & Mishra, 2002).

Conclusion

We have outlined and focused on what is known along with identifying missing gaps in the literature on work–family topics within the region of South East Asia. We would like to take this opportunity to emphasize that we are encouraged by the continued and growing attention to these topics in this region. As work–life balance continues to grow in importance, we anticipate further refinement both in the measurement tools as well the understanding of the complexity of these relationships in South East Asia. Ultimately, we hope that researchers and practitioners will be able to assist workers in South East Asia to meet their work, family, and life needs and goals.

References

Abu-Ghaida, D., & S. Klasen. (2004). The economic and human development costs of missing the millennium development goal on gender equity. *IZA Discussion paper No.1031.*

Agarwala, T., Arizkuren-Eleta, A., Del Castillo M., Muñiz Ferrer, M., & Gartzia, L. (2014). Influence of Managerial Support on Work–life Conflict and Organizational Commitment: An International Comparison for India, Peru and Spain. *The International Journal of Human Resource Management, 25(10),* 1460–1483, DOI: 10.1080/09585192.2013.870315.

Akter, K. (2016). Work–life balance strategies and consequences: A few aspects. *ASA University Review, 10(1),* 35–52.

Allen, T. D., Cho, E., & Meier, L. L. (2014). Work–family boundary dynamics. *Annual Review of Organizational Psychology and Organizational Behavior, 1,* 99–121.

Amstad, F.T, Laurenz, M. L., Fasel, U., Elfering, A., & Summer N. K. (2011). A meta-analysis of work–family conflict and various outcomes with a special emphasis on cross-domain versus matching-domain relations. *Journal of Occupational Healthy Psychology, 16(2),* pp. 151–169.

Annavarjula, M., & Das, D. (2013). Towards a fine balance: Cross Cultural comparison of work–family identities. *Journal of Asia-Pacific Business, 14(1),* 40–57.

Anell, K., & Hartmann, D. (2007). Flexible work arrangements in Asia: What companies are doing, why they are doing it and what lies ahead. Boston College Global Workforce Roundtable Report. Boston College Center for Work & Family: Boston.

Aryee, S., Srinivas, E. S., & Tan, H. H. (2005). Rhythms of life: Antecedents and outcomes of work–family balance in employed parents. *Journal of Applied Psychology, 90(1),* 132–146.

Ashforth, B. E., Kreiner, G. E., & Fugate, M. (2000). All in a day's work: Boundaries and micro role transitions. *Academy of Management Review, 25,* 472–491.

Asian Development Bank. (2015). *Women in the Workforce: An Unmet Potential in Asia and the Pacific.* Mandaluyong City, Philippines: Asian Development Bank.

Aycan, Z. (2008). Cross-cultural perspectives to work–family conflict. In K. Korabik & D. Lero (Eds.), *Handbook of Work–family conflict* (pp. 359–371). London: Cambridge University Press.

Baird, M., & Whitehouse, G. (2012). Paid parental leave: First birthday policy review. *Australian Bulletin of Labour, 38(3),* 184–198.

Banerji, A., & Yik, A. (2012). Diversity & inclusion in Asia Country View—India. *Community Business Limited.*

Baral, R., & Bhargava, S. (2009). Work–family enrichment as a mediator between organizational interventions for work–life balance and job outcomes. *Journal of Managerial Psychology, 25(3),* 274–300.

Bardoel, A., & De Cieri, H. (2006). Developing a work–life strategy in a multinational enterprise, A Sloan work and family encyclopedia entry: http://wfnetwork.bc.edu/encyclopedia_entry.php?id=3814&area=All

Bettio, F., & P. Villa. (1996). Trends and prospects for women's employment in the 90s: Italy. *Report for EC Network on the Situation of Women in the Labor Market.* Manchester, UK.

Bhargava, S., & Baral, R. (2009). Antecedents and consequences of work–family enrichment among Indian managers. *Psychological Studies, (54),* 213–225.

Bianchi, S.M., & Milkie, M.A. (2010). Work and family research in the first decade of the 21st century. *Journal of Marriage and Family, 72*, 705–725.

Brough. P, O'Driscoll, M. P., & Kalliath, T.J. (2005). The ability of 'family friendly' organizational resources to predict work–family conflict and job and family satisfaction, *Stress and Health, (21)*, 223–234.

Carlson, D.S., Kacmar, K.M., & Williams, L.J. (2000). Construction and initial validation of multidimensional measure of work–family conflict. *Journal of Vocational Behavior, 56(2)*, 249–276.

Catalyst (2013). Unilever—Global Reach With Local Roots: Creating a Gender-Balanced Workforce in Different Cultural Contexts. New York: Catalyst.

Catalyst (2015). Procter & Gamble—Everyone Valued, Everyone Included, Everyone Performing at Their Peak™. New York: Catalyst.

Chow, I. H., & Chew, I. K. (2006). The effect of alternative work schedules on employee Performance. *International Journal of Employment Studies, 14 (1)*, 105–130.

De Cieri, H., & Bardoel, E. A. (2009). What does 'work–life management' mean in China and Southeast Asia for MNCs? *Community, Work & Family, 12(2)*, 179–196. doi:10.1080/13668800902778959

Din, M., & Noor, N. (2009). Prevalence and factors associated with depressive symptoms in Malay women. *Women and Health, 49*, 1–19.

Erickson, J. J., Martinengo, G., & Hill, J. (2010). Putting work and family experiences in context: Differences by family life stage. *Human Relations, 63(7)*, 955–979

Fang, M., Nastiti, T., & Chen, C. V. (2011). The tug of work and family: a study of the sources of the work–family conflict among Indonesian lecturers. *International Journal of Management & Enterprise Development, 11(2/3/4)*, 127–141.

Frone, M. R., Russell, M., & Cooper, M. L. 1992. Antecedents and outcomes of work–family conflict: Testing a model of the work–family interface. *Journal of Applied Psychology, 77*: 65–78.

Galovan, A. M., Fackrell, T., Buswell, L., Jones, B. L., Hill, E. J., & Carroll, S. J. (2010). The work–family interface in the United States and Singapore: Conflict across cultures. *Journal of Family Psychology, 24*(5), 646–656. http://doi.org/10.1037/a0020832

Gambles, R., Lewis, S., & Rapoport, R. (2006). The Myth of Work–life Balance. The Challenge of Our Time for Men, Women and Societies. John Wiley & Sons. Ltd.

Gender Promotion program of the International Labour Organization (www.ilo.org/actrav/areas)

GLOBE. (2016). Retrieved January 01, 2017, from http://globeproject.com/results/clusters/southern-asia?menu=cluster

Grant Thornton. (2014). *Women in Business: From classroom to boardroom*. Grant Thornton International Business Report 2014.

Hassan, Z., Dollard, M. F., & Winefield, A. H. (2010). Work-family conflict in East vs Western countries. *Cross Cultural Management: An International Journal, 17*(1), 30–49.

Hegewisch, A., & Gornick, J. (2011). The impact of work–family policies on women's employment: a review of research from OECD countries. *Community, Work & Family, 14 (2)*, 1, 119–138.

Heymann, J., Raub, A., & Earle, A. (2011). Creating and using new data sources to analyze the relationship between social policy and global health: The case of maternal leave. *Public Health Reports, 126*(Suppl 3), 127–134.

House, R.J., Hanges, P.J., Javidan, M., Dorfman, P.W., & Gupta, V. (2004). *Culture, Leadership, and Organizations: The GLOBE Study of 62 Societies*. Thousand Oaks: Sage Publications.

Jain, R., & Jain, S. (2015). Work–life balance among bank mangers: An empirical study of Indian banks. *Abhigyan, 32*(4), 15–26.

Jhangiani, N. (2016). Why we need to develop women leaders of the future. *Livemint*, 9 March 2016.

Judge, T. A., Locke, E. A., & Durham, C. C. (1997). The dispositional causes of job satisfaction: A core evaluations approach. *Research in Organizational Behavior, 19*: 151–188.

Kakkar, J., & Bhandari, A. (2016). A study on work–life balance in the Indian service sector from a gender perspective. *IUP Journal of Organizational Behavior, 15(1)*, 19–36.

Kalliath, P., Kalliath, T., & Singh, V. (2011). When work intersects family: A qualitative exploration of the experiences of dual earner couples in India. *South Asian Journal of Management, 18(1)*, 37–59.

Kappagoda, U. S. (2014). Emotional intelligence as a predictor of work–family conflict among school teachers in North Central Province in Sri Lanka. *IUP Journal of Organizational Behavior, 13(3)*, 53–68.

Karwa, M. (2015). How do Indian employees find their work–life balance? *DNA*. 29 November, 2015.

Kim, J., Lee, J. & K. Shin. (2015). *A Model of Gender Inequality and Economic Growth*. ADB Draft Working Paper.

Kodagoda, T. (2010). Work–family stress of women managers: Experience from banking sector in Sri Lanka. *International Journal of Management & Enterprise Development, 9(2)*, 201–211.

Komarraju, M. (2006). Work–family conflict and sources of support amongst Malaysian dual-career university employees. *Asian Academy of Management, 11*, 83–96.

Kreiner, G. E. (2006). Consequences of work-home segmentation or integration: A person-environment fit perspective. *Journal of Organizational Behavior, 27*, 485–507.

McKinsey and Company (2012). *Women Matter: An Asian Perspective. Harnessing female talent to raise corporate performance*, www.mckinsey.com, last accessed 31 August 2016.

Michel, J.S., Kotrba, L.M., Mitchelson, J.K., Clark, M.A., & Baltes, B.B. (2011). Antecedents of work–family conflict: A meta-analytic review. *Journal of Organizational Behavior, 32(5)*, 689–725.

Namasivayam, K., & Zhao, X. (2007). An investigation of the moderating effects of organizational commitment on the relationships between work–family conflict and job satisfaction among hospitality employees in India. *Tourism Management, (28)*, 1212–1223.

Netermeyer, R., Boles, J., & McMurrian, R. (1996). Development and validation of work–family conflict and family-work conflict scales. *Journal of Applied Psychology, 81(4)*, 400–410.

Nippert-Eng, C. (1996). *Home and Work: Negotiating Boundaries Through Everyday Life*. Chicago: University of Chicago Press.

Noor, N. (1999). Roles and women's well-being: Some preliminary findings from Malaysia. *Sex Roles, 41*, 123–145.

(2002a). Work–family conflict, locus of control, and women's well-being: Tests of alternative pathways. *The Journal of Social Psychology, 12(5)*, 645–662.

(2002b). The moderating effect of spouse support on the relationship between work variables and women's work–family conflict. *Psychologia, 45*, 12–23

(2006). Locus of control, supportive workplace policies and work–family conflict. *Psychologia*, 48–60.

Noor, N., & Zainuddin, M. (2011). Emotional labor and burnout among female teachers: Work–family conflict as mediator. *Asian Journal of Social Psychology.*

Ollo-Lopez, A., & Goni-Legaz, S. (2015). Differences in work–family conflict: which individual and national factors explain them? *The International Journal of Human Resource Management*, 1–27.

Pal, S., & Saksvik, P. (2006). A comparative study of work and family conflict in Norwegian and Indian hospitals. *Nordic Psychology, 58(4)*, 298–314.

(2008). Work–family conflict and psychosocial work environment stressors as predictors of job stress in a cross-cultural study. *International Journal of Stress Management, 15(1)*, 22–42.

Pattusamy, M., & Jacob, J. (2015). A test of Greenhouse and Allen (2011) model on work–family balance. *Current Psychology: A Journal For Diverse Perspectives On Diverse Psychological Issues*, doi:10.1007/s12144-015-9400-4

Poelmans, S.A.Y., & Chinchilla, N., & Cardona, P. (2003). Family-friendly HRM policies and the employment relationship, *International Journal of Manpower, 24*, 128–147.

Powell, G.N, Francesco, A.M., & Ling, Y. (2009). Toward culture-sensitive theories of the work–family interface. *Journal of Organizational Behaviour (30)*, 597–616.

Rajadhyaksha, U. (2012), Work–life balance in South East Asia: the Indian experience, *South Asian Journal of Global Business Research, 1, (1)*, 108–127.

Rathore and Sachitanand, (2007). Winning Them Over: It's an Equal World. *Business Today.* June 17.

Rothausen, J. T., Gonzalez, A. J., & Griffin, A. (2009). Are all the parts there everywhere? Facet job satisfaction in the United States and the Phillipines. *Asia Pacific Journal of Management, 26*, 681–700.

Retherford, R. D., Westley, S. B., Minja, C. K., Brown, T., Mason, A., & Mishra, V. K. (2002). *The Future of Population in Asia*. Honolulu, HI: East-West Center. doi: http://hdl.handle.net/10125/3403.

Shaffer, M. A., Joplin, J., Hsu, Y.S. (2011). Expanding the boundaries of work–family research: A review and agenda for future research. *International Journal of Cross Cultural Management, 11(2)*, 221–268.

Shockley, K.M., & Singla, N. (2011). Reconsidering work–family interactions and satisfaction: A meta-analysis. *Journal of Management, 37*, 861–886.

Singh, V. (2013). Exploring the concept of work across generations. *Journal of Intergenerational Relationships, 11*(3), 272–285. doi:10.1080/15350770.2013.810498

Spector, P. E., Cooper, C. L., Poelman, S., Allen, T., O'Driscoll, M., Sanchez, J, Lu, L. (2004). A cross-national comparative study of work–family stressors, working hours and well-being: China and Latin America versus the Anglo world. *Personnel Psychology, 57*, 119–212.

Srivastava, U., & Srivastava, S. (2012). Outcomes of work–family conflict among Indian information technology (IT) professionals. *Social Science International, 28(1)*, 137–158.

The Council for Gender Equality. Specialist Committee on the Declining Birthrate and Gender-Equal Participation. International Comparison of the Social Environment regarding the Declining Birth Rates and Gender-Equality. Summary Report. www .gender.go.jp/english_contents/basic_data/resarches/pdf/english-1.pdf

Wang, P., Lawler, J., & Shi, K. (2011) Implementing family-friendly employment practices in banking industry: Evidences from some African and Asian countries. *Journal of Occupational Psychology, 84*, 493–517.

World Bank Group. (2015). Women, Business and the Law 2016: Getting to Equal. Washington, DC: World Bank.

World Economic Forum (2016). *The Global Gender Gap Report*. http://reports.weforum.org/ global-gender-gap-report-2016/. Last accessed 6 January 2017.

Yang, N. (2005). Individualism-collectivism and work–family interface: A Sino-US comparison. In S. A. Y. Poelmans (Ed.), *Work and Family: An International Research Perspective* (pp. 287–319). London: Lawrence Erlbaum.

Yang, N., C. C. Chen, J. Choi, & Y. M. Zou. (2000). Sources of Work–Family Conflict: A Sino-US Comparison of the Effects of Work and Family Demands. *Academy of Management Journal, 43 (1)*, 113–123.

Yang, N., & Hawkins, A. (2004). A Cross-Cultural Test of the Work–family Interface in 48 Countries. *Journal of Marriage and Family, 66*, 1300–1316.

20 A Review of Work–Family Research in Confucian Asia

Eunae Cho and YeEun Choi

The objective of this chapter is to review work–family research conducted in Confucian Asia. Confucianism is a school of philosophy that is based on the ideas of Confucius, an ancient Chinese social philosopher. Confucianism has had profound impact on the culture in East and Southeast Asian societies (Neville, 2000). As a code of conduct, Confucian values have shaped various aspects of individual and social lives of people in the region. In this chapter, Confucian Asia refers to China, Hong Kong, Japan, Singapore, South Korea, and Taiwan.

We begin by highlighting some aspects of Confucianism that are deemed important for the work–family interface. First, Confucianism emphasizes five principal relationships that define the role and proper social position for each individual; fulfilling the responsibilities and duties for one's position is important to achieve social hierarchy and maintain harmony (Confucius, 1983). Of relevance, the husband and wife are prescribed to have separate functions in a family, such that the husband is primarily responsible for financial support whereas the wife is responsible for tending the home and children. Second, Confucianism views a family, rather than an individual, as the fundamental unit of society; family is an interdependent unit, in which members are highly involved with each other's life. The centrality of the family role makes fulfilling family responsibility at the center of everyone's social as well as economic roles. As a means to financially support family, work is often viewed as more important than leisure and as instrumental to family welfare (Redding, 1990). Lastly, Confucianism values diligence, persistence, and loyalty (Chan, 1996). The work ethic imbued with Confucianism is manifested in expectations for long work hours (Kang & Matusik, 2014) and performance evaluation practices that emphasize face-time (Won, 2005).

Other characteristics of the Confucian Asian countries that are relevant to the study of work and family deserve mentioning. First, previous research on cultural values has described these countries as highly collectivistic (Hofstede, 2001); group interests tend to supersede individual interests and interdependent self-construal is prevalent in Confucian Asian societies (Markus & Kitayama, 1991). Also, with the exception of Singapore, these countries rank relatively low on gender egalitarianism, the degree to which individuals' biological sex determines their social roles (Emrich, Denmark, & Den Hartog, 2004; Hausmann, Tyson, & Zahidi, 2012). Second, the countries in this region experienced economic growth in past decades (Bloom & Finlay, 2009), which accompanied a rise in the number of women in the workforce and dual-earner couples (Jaumotte, 2004). Together with the rapidly aging population that increases the eldercare needs (Chan, 2005), these changes have incited public and scholarly interest in work–family issues in the region. Finally, the governments of Confucian Asian countries have progressively introduced national initiatives to facilitate work–family reconciliation (e.g., legislation on labor conditions, leave policies, reward scheme for family-friendly organizations), although the type of policies and the degree of support available vary across the specific countries (Cho & Koh, 2015; Iwao, 2010).

In the following sections, we provide a critical synthesis of previous work–family research conducted in Confucian Asia. We first provide an overview of the development and methodology of work–family research in this region. Next, we review the key findings and compare them to the findings in the general work–family literature. We then discuss limitations of the extant literature and conclude with directions for future research.

Study of Work–Family in Confucian Asia

Development of Work–Family Research in Confucian Asia

Work–family research in Confucian Asia started in the 1990s. However, there were only a handful of studies published during this time. Studies at this nascent stage share several characteristics. First, the studies exclusively focused on work–family conflict (WFC; e.g., Matsui, Ohsawa, & Onglatco, 1995). Second, all the studies utilized cross-sectional designs and examined WFC in a single country. Lastly, cultural characteristics of Confucian Asia were not reflected in the hypotheses development, and no study included an explicit measure of cultural values or characteristics. This makes it difficult to attribute any observed discrepancies to cultural characteristics of the region because they could be from alternative sources, such as sampling error, differences in measures used, or other unmeasured variables. One exception is a study by Aryee, Fields, and Luk (1999a) that examined the cross-cultural generalizability of a model of WFC developed in the United States (Frone, Russell, & Cooper, 1992) using a sample of employees from Hong Kong; they hypothesized and found that the relative impact of work-to-family conflict versus family-to-work conflict on employee well-being differed across the two cultures. All in all, the theoretical contribution of the work–family research in the 1990s was somewhat limited. Although the studies documented evidence of WFC in Confucian Asia, they were essentially replications of existing work in the general work–family literature.

The work–family literature in Confucian Asia grew threefold in the 2000s. Some meaningful developments are worth mentioning. First, the positive side of work–family interface started gaining attention (e.g., Lu, Siu, Spector, & Shi, 2009). Second, comparative research that examined different antecedents of WFC in the Western and Confucian Asian countries was published (e.g., Yang, Chen, Choi, & Zou, 2000). Also, several multi-national studies (e.g., Hill, Yang, Hawkins, & Ferris, 2004; Spector et al., 2004, 2007) that explored potential differences in the work–family interface in Confucian Asia versus other cultural clusters appeared. Third, a unique theoretical model that takes into account a cultural characteristic of Confucian Asia (i.e., the specificity-diffusion dimension of culture; Hampden-Turner & Trompenaars, 2000) was tested, demonstrating that within- as well as cross-domain variables may play an important role in WFC in Confucian Asia where the boundaries between work and family domains are often blurred (Luk & Shaffer, 2005).

In the 2010s, the work–family literature in Confucian Asia started to blossom. First, the number of studies examining positive work–family experiences steadily increased, and a novel theoretical model that includes both WFC and work–family enrichment (WFE) was proposed and tested (Chen & Powell, 2012). Second, the scope of the literature expanded with a number of studies on crossover that examined the process through which employees' work experiences affect their family members (e.g., Liu & Cheung, 2015; Song, Foo, Uy, & Sun, 2011). Third, studies in the 2010s are marked by their advanced methodology. More studies utilized longitudinal designs (e.g., Ng & Feldman, 2012), experience sampling methods (e.g., Wang, Liu, Zhan, & Shih, 2010), and multi-source data (e.g., Lau, 2010).

In summary, the study of work and family in Confucian Asia has continued to evolve. Specifically, the literature moved from the replication of existing studies to the examination of the unique conceptual and theoretical issues in the region. Given the trends in the region that more employees are engaged in a dual-earner lifestyle, have caregiving responsibilities, and pursue balance between life domains, the work–family literature in Confucian Asia is likely to flourish in coming decades.

Methodology of Work–Family Research in Confucian Asia

The work–family literature in Confucian Asia is similar to the general work–family literature in methodology (see Casper, Eby, Bordeaux, Lockwood, & Lambert, 2007 for a review). First, most studies to date used cross-sectional designs in field settings, and no known study has used an experimental or quasi-experimental design. Also, the majority of studies relied on single-source data collected from surveys, although an increasing number of studies on crossover between spouses gathered multi-source data. Lastly, the type of families and employees studied were rather homogeneous, and work–family experiences among non-traditional families (e.g., homosexual couples, single parents) were neglected. It is also interesting to note that despite the importance placed on the strong ties with extended family in Confucian Asia, the role of extended families in the nexus of work and family has rarely been studied.

Most work–family research in Confucian Asia used previously validated measures. Scales for the key constructs have been made available in local languages (Chinese, Japanese, and Korean), either by the back-translation method (Brislin, 1970) or local development. For the negative interface, two measures of WFC (Carlson, Kacmar, & Williams, 2000; Netemeyer, Boles, & McMurrian, 1996) have been frequently used (e.g., Aryee, Luk, Leung, & Lo, 1999b; Fu & Shaffer,

2001; Lim, Morris, & McMillan, 2011). For the positive interface, measures of WFE (Carlson, Kacmar, Wayne, & Grzywacz, 2006) and positive work–family spillover (Grzywacz & Marks, 2000) have been used (e.g., Jin, Ford, & Chen, 2013; Lim, Choi, & Song, 2012; Siu et al., 2010).

Despite the critical importance of establishing measurement equivalence in cross-cultural research (van de Vijver & Leung, 1997), limited evidence is available regarding measurement equivalence of key work–family constructs in Confucian Asia. A small number of multi-country studies have been conducted, most of which examined WFC (e.g., Spector et al., 2007; Yang et al., 2000). Furthermore, not all multi-country studies tested measurement invariance. Available evidence (e.g., Ng & Feldman, 2012; Wang, Lawler, Walumbwa, & Shi, 2004) provides full support for the two-factor structure of WFC (i.e., work-to-family and family-to-work) in Confucian Asia (i.e., configural invariance) and partial support for the equivalent strength of item-construct relationships (i.e., factorial invariance) as well as the equivalent intercept of each item (i.e., scalar invariance). For more information on issues of measurement invariance across cultures, please refer to Chapter 8 of this Handbook (Korabik & Rhijn).

Key Findings

In this section, we first summarize academic findings reported in the work–family literature based on samples drawn from Confucian Asia. Then, we discuss the work–family literature in Confucian Asia in relation to the general work–family literature. Finally, we review findings from multi-country studies.

Summary of Findings in Confucian Asia

Several themes emerged from the review of the work–family literature in Confucian Asia. First, work is a source of demands as well as resources. A number of studies underscored that various aspects of work (e.g., role stressors, incivility, unsupportive organizational culture) are a chief contributor to WFC (Aryee et al., 1999b; Kato & Yamazaki, 2009; Lim & Lee, 2011). Work has also been shown to provide important resources (e.g., supervisor support, perceived organizational support) that can reduce WFC, alleviate the impact of the work demands on WFC, and facilitate WFE (Foley, Hang-Yue, & Lui, 2005; Lu et al., 2009). Similarly, family is a source of demands as well as resources for the work–family interface. In parallel with research on the work domain, studies identified various demands (e.g., number of children, family time commitment) and resources (e.g., spouse support, elderly parents' help) residing in the family domain that influence positive and negative work–family experiences (Aryee et al., 1999b; Lu et al., 2009; Luk & Shaffer, 2005).

In terms of consequences, work–family experiences have been associated with a variety of factors in the domains of work, family, and health. On the one hand, WFC has been associated with suboptimal work (e.g., job dissatisfaction, poor job performance; Lu, Wang, Siu, Lu, & Du, 2015), family (e.g., low family satisfaction; Aryee et al., 1999a), and health-related outcomes (e.g., alcohol use; Wang et al., 2010). On the other hand, positive work–family experiences tend to be associated with enhanced outcomes (Lu et al., 2009). The crossover literature indicated that employees' work–family experiences also affect their spouses (Liu & Cheung, 2015; Song et al., 2011) and children (Lau, 2010).

Finally, the abovementioned relations among antecedents, work–family experiences, and outcomes were qualified by individual, organizational, and family factors. For example, studies have found that the positive relationship between work demands and work-to-family conflict was mitigated by perceived organizational support, domestic support, and family-friendly policies (Foley et al., 2005; Luk & Shaffer, 2005). In terms of individual difference variables, the relationship between WFC and outcomes were weaker among individuals who score higher on proactive personality (Lau, Wong, & Chow, 2013), but stronger among employees with higher Chinese work values (i.e., eight work-related values that are rooted in Confucianism, such as collectivism and hard work; Lu, Chang, Kao, & Cooper, 2015).

Comparisons to the Broader Work–Family Literature

Work–family studies in Confucian Asia have provided evidence for the generalizability of fundamental theoretical frameworks in the work–family literature. First, the four-fold conceptualization of work–family interface, conflict and facilitation in two directions (i.e., work-to-family and family-to-work; Frone, 2003), was empirically supported in Confucian Asia (Lu et al., 2009). Second, research on antecedents of WFC provided support for the domain specificity model, which posits that predictors of conflict reside in the originating domain whereas consequences of conflict are in the receiving domain (Frone et al., 1992). That is, most studies examined and demonstrated work-related and family-related factors as antecedent of work-to-family conflict and family-to-work conflict, respectively (e.g., Fu & Shaffer, 2001), although few studies showed the effect of cross-domain antecedents on WFC (e.g., Luk et al., 2005; Foley et al., 2005). Concerning outcomes of WFC, some studies (e.g., Zhao & Namasivayam, 2012) supported the source attribution model, which argues that conflict influences affective outcomes in the originating domain via the cognitive appraisal process (e.g., work-to-family conflict impacts work satisfaction; Shockley & Singla, 2011), but the results were more consistent for the domain specificity model (e.g., Aryee et al., 1999a, 1999b). Notably, two recent studies that explicitly tested the appropriateness of the two models (domain specificity and source attribution) in Confucian Asia (Li, Lu, & Zhang, 2013; Zhang, Griffeth, & Fried, 2012) favored the domain specificity model. The source attribution model was deemed less applicable in Confucian Asia due to the prevailing view of work as a critical tool for family welfare, which likely prevents workers from attributing work-to-family conflict to work.

Key antecedents and outcomes of WFC in the broader work–family literature were also examined in Confucian Asia. Overall, results about the antecedents of WFC (e.g., Aryee et al., 1999b; Foley et al., 2005; Kato & Yamazaki, 2009; Luk & Shaffer,

2005) were similar to findings from the general work–family literature as reported in meta-analyses (Byron, 2005; Michel, Young, Mitchelson, Clark, & Baltes, 2011). In contrast, the relationships between WFC and outcomes were less consistent in Confucian Asia than has been found in broad meta-analyses (e.g., Amstad, Meier, Fasel, Elfering, & Semmer, 2011). For instance, some studies reported a null relationship (Aryee & Luk, 1996; Aryee et al., 1999b) or even a positive relationship (Lu et al., 2009) between WFC and affective outcomes (e.g., job satisfaction, family satisfaction, organizational commitment), which contradicts the typical negative relationships cited in prior meta-analyses.

Next, findings from the crossover literature were in line with results reported in the general work–family literature. Most studies examined crossover among dual-earner couples and showed that experiences of one partner (e.g., WFC, WFE, emotional exhaustion) affected another partner's outcomes (e.g., psychological strain, WFC, life satisfaction; Liu et al., 2015; Shimazu et al., 2013; Zhang et al., 2013). Several studies (Song et al., 2011; Shimazu et al., 2013) reported evidence for the three mechanisms of crossover (Westman, 2001): the direct crossover that refers to the transfer of affective experiences between individuals via empathic process and emotion contagion, the indirect crossover that refers to the transmission of experiences via interpersonal exchanges between individuals, and the common stressors mechanism that occurs when characteristics in a shared environment synchronize affective experiences of individuals. Some studies found moderators of the crossover mechanisms (e.g., empathy, family identity salience; Liu et al., 2015; Lu, Lu, Du, & Brough, 2016). Results on the role of gender were mixed, such that some studies found gender asymmetry in the crossover effect (e.g., Shimazu et al., 2013; Zhang et al., 2013), while others did not (e.g., Lu et al., 2016).

Finally, findings from a few studies on the positive work–family interface were comparable to those reported in the general work–family studies. First, the prevalence of family-to-work enrichment was higher than work-to-family enrichment (Lu et al., 2015; Lu et al., 2009; Siu et al., 2010). Second, resources in work and family (e.g., family-friendly organizational policies, social support; Lu et al., 2009; Siu et al., 2010) promoted WFE. Third, WFE was associated with favorable outcomes (*cf.* McNall, Nicklin, & Masuda, 2010), such as job performance and life satisfaction (Lu et al., 2009; Lu et al., 2015).

Findings from Multi-Country Studies

The majority of multi-country studies to date have contrasted collectivistic Confucian Asian countries with individualistic Anglo countries (e.g., Australia, Canada, New Zealand, the United Kingdom, the United States), with particular focus on WFC. Culture as a predictor of mean levels of WFC as well as culture as a moderator of the relationships between antecedents and WFC and WFC and outcomes has been the topic of interest in this literature. In Confucian Asia, work is perceived as a critical tool that serves the family (Redding, 1990) and the boundaries between the two domains tend to be blurred (Luk & Shaffer, 2005). On the contrary, work is viewed as independent of and competing against family in the individualistic societies. Also, individuals in collectivistic Confucian Asia tend to have a close network of extended family in which they can seek support from (Hofstede, 2001). Due to these fundamental differences across the two cultures, lower prevalence of WFC and weaker relations among antecedents and WFC as well as WFC and outcomes are typically hypothesized in collectivistic Confucian Asia compared to individualistic Anglo countries.

Studies have reported mixed evidence regarding mean differences in WFC across cultures. For the work-to-family direction, some studies found no significant differences (e.g., Jin et al., 2013), while others found small effect sizes indicating a higher prevalence in the individualistic Anglo countries than the collectivistic Confucian Asian countries (e.g., Spector et al., 2007) or vice versa (e.g., Yang, 2005). Similarly for family-to-work conflict, Jin et al. (2013) observed a greater frequency in China than in the United States, whereas Yang (2005) did not find a significant difference between the same two countries. A recent meta-analytic investigation of mean differences in WFC demonstrated that the level of family-to-work conflict was greater among individuals from the collectivistic Asian countries than among those from the individualistic countries, whereas the degree of work-to-family conflict did not differ across the two cultures (Allen, French, Dumani, & Shockley, 2015).

Next, several studies indicated that relationships among demands (e.g., work hours) and WFC are weaker in Confucian Asian countries than in Anglo countries (Jin et al., 2013; Spector et al., 2004, 2007; Yang, 2005; but see Hill et al., 2004 and Yang et al., 2000 for exceptions to this pattern). Fewer studies examined whether the strength of relationships between resources and WFC differed across the cultures, and the results are mixed (Jin et al., 2013; Lu et al., 2010). Interestingly, research on flexible work arrangements suggests that the availability of flexible work arrangements has negative associations with WFC in the United States, but have null or positive associations with WFC in Confucian Asia (Galovan et al., 2010; Masuda et al., 2012). The negative consequences of WFC in terms of domain satisfaction, withdrawal (e.g., absenteeism, turnover intention), and health outcomes (e.g., depression) appeared to be universal, but studies demonstrated a stronger impact of work-to-family conflict in Anglo countries than in Confucian Asian countries (e.g., Galovan et al., 2010; Lu et al., 2010; Spector et al., 2007; Yang, 2005).

Limitation and Future Research Ideas

In this section, we discuss limitations of the current work–family literature in Confucian Asia and highlight fruitful avenues for future research. Commonly criticized limitations of the general work–family literature was also found in the work–family literature in Confucian Asia. Studies of WFC have been dominant, despite the growing body of research on the positive work–family interface. Work–family researchers have paid more attention to factors in the workplace, with less focus on factors in the family domain. Methodologically, most previous research relied on cross-sectional designs, which limits our ability to draw causal conclusion. Data were collected from a single-source, typically in convenience samples.

Some limitations concern the transfer of theories and measurements developed in the general work–family literature to Confucian Asia. Most studies used measures developed in English for the non-English speaking local population, but many of them did not provide information regarding the translation process and evidence of measurement equivalence. This is a critical limitation in that equivalent measurements for key constructs are essential for meaningful cross-cultural comparison of work–family experiences. Next, most studies utilized existing theoretical frameworks developed from a Western perspective, while unique characteristics of Confucian Asia were not taken into consideration in the theory development and study design. A small number of studies based their argument on a cultural value of 'individualism-collectivism' in explaining work–family experiences in Confucian Asia (e.g., Jin et al., 2013; Spector et al., 2007), but other characteristics that are potentially important for the nexus of work and family (e.g., gender equality, power distance, strong familial ties) have rarely been studied.

Previous work–family research tended to overlook the uniqueness of each country in Confucian Asia while emphasizing their similarities. Although countries in Confucian Asia share many similarities, notable differences exist across the countries that are relevant to work–family experiences. For example, paid domestic help is much more common in Hong Kong and Singapore than in Korea (Tsujimoto, 2014). As the work–family literature in Confucian Asia becomes more mature, researchers may want to delve into these differences across the countries in the region to better understand diverse work–family experiences within Confucian Asia.

There are several promising avenues for future work–family research in Confucian Asia. The first is to explore the unique characteristics of the workplace and aspects of family relationships in Confucian Asia. In the work domain, values that employees in Confucian Asia adhere to might be worth further investigation. Confucian work values refer to work-specific values that are tied to Confucianism and include authoritarianism, endurance, hardworking, collectivism, credentialism, functionalism, interpersonal connections, and long-term orientation (Huang, Eveleth, & Huo, 2000). Although benefits of Confucian work values for various organizational outcomes such as organizational commitment, job performance, and transformational leadership have been recognized (Chao, 1990; Lin, Ho, & Lin, 2013; Siu, 2003), scholars have only recently begun to examine the role of Confucian work values in the work–family interface (e.g., Lu, Xu, & Caughlin, 2015; Wong & O'Driscoll, 2016). Given that Confucian work values are still prevalent in modern organizations in Confucian Asia (Chao, 1990; Lu, Kao, Siu, & Lu, 2011), more research is warranted to understand the role these values play in employees' work–family experiences.

In the family domain, individuals in Confucian Asia tend to have high expectations for family obligations and responsibility to care for elderly family members because they perceive themselves as an interdependent part of a family unit (Zhan & Montgomery, 2003). Parents are emotionally involved with their children, such that they take pride in their children's success or blame themselves for their children's failure (Park & Chesla, 2007). Although these strong familial ties can be a source of

demands as well as support for employees, how they shape the work–family interface among individuals in Confucian Asia is not well understood. Relatedly, as it is
not uncommon for employees in Confucian Asia to seek help from their extended
family members, especially from their elderly parents, to take care of their family
demands, implications of such practices warrant greater research. Expanding prior
research reporting that employees who live with extended family members experienced less family-to-work conflict (Lu et al., 2009), future research may inquire into
the impact on well-being of elderly parents or children.

Next, future research might want to explore the work–family interface among
employees in family businesses. Because most companies are family businesses in
East Asia (Ahlstrom, Young, Chan, & Bruton, 2004) and family business exemplifies
a case in which work and family are extremely integrated, this could provide an
interesting context to investigate work–family experiences in Confucian Asia.
Previous research found that the impact of family-to-work conflict on job satisfaction
was weaker among family business owners' than owners of non-family business due
to support from family members and coping strategies (Kwan, Lau, & Au, 2012).
Aspects of family business that are conducive to positive and negative work–family
experiences, conditions in which the family business creates more demands than
resources (or vice versa), and strategies that people who work in family businesses
employ to manage boundaries between work and family are topics worthy of future
research.

Finally, Confucian Asia consists of societies that are rapidly changing. Several
changes are deemed particularly relevant for future work–family research. The first
concerns the changing perspectives toward gender roles. With the cultural change to
embrace gender equality (Inglehart & Norris, 2003), younger generations worldwide
are known to be more gender egalitarian, and those in Confucian Asia are no
exception. However, due to the close familial ties and interdependencies among
family members, more traditional gender ideologies held by older generations may
still influence younger workers' work–family experiences. Generational differences
in the endorsement of prevailing gender role ideologies, its impact on younger
workers' work–family experiences, and how individuals reconcile these potential
discrepancies deserve further attention.

Second, individualism is becoming popular in Confucian Asia, especially among
the younger generations (Wang et al., 2004). Accordingly, proposed cultural differences between Western and Confucian Asian countries (e.g., individualism-
collectivism) may be less salient in the current and future workforce. With this in
mind, perhaps assessing cultural values at the individual-level may provide us with
insights into the role of this value in work–family experiences. Previous research
showed that individualism-collectivism at the individual-level (i.e., idiocentrism-
allocentrism) moderates the relation between work–family conflict and turnover
intention, such that the link was stronger among individuals scoring high on idiocentrism (Wang et al., 2004), which resembles findings at the national-level.

Lastly, career attitudes and family structures are diversifying in Confucian Asia.
Younger generations are proactive in making career-related changes (e.g., seeking
a new employer), value a balance between their work and non-work lives, and

capitalize on entrepreneurial opportunities (Wong, 2007; Yi, Ribbens, & Morgan, 2010). Many young people choose to live alone, to not have children (Jones, 2007), and to live apart from their extended family for various reasons (e.g., a better job, better education for children; Goulbourne, Reynolds, Solomos, & Zontini, 2010). As the diversity in the work and family domain becomes the new normal, further research is needed to better understand work–family experiences among individuals who make these "atypical" choices.

Conclusion

In this chapter we reviewed work–family research in Confucian Asia. The study of work and family in Confucian Asia has continued to grow at an exponential rate, moving from the replication of existing work–family studies to the examination of the unique conceptual and theoretical issues in the region. Our review revealed that the work–family literature in Confucian Asia is similar to the general work–family literature in terms of research questions and methodology. Theoretical frameworks and measurements for key constructs developed in the general work–family literature appeared applicable in this region. Intriguing differences have been detected in the relationships among antecedents, work–family experiences, and outcomes, but more research is needed to illuminate underlying mechanisms.

References

Ahlstrom, D., Young, M. N., Chan, E. S., & Bruton, G. D. (2004). Facing constraints to growth? Overseas Chinese entrepreneurs and traditional business practices in East Asia. *Asia Pacific Journal of Management, 21*, 263–285.

Allen, T. D., French, K. A., Dumani, S., & Shockley, K. M. (2015). Meta-analysis of work–family conflict mean differences: Does national context matter? *Journal of Vocational Behavior, 90*, 90–100.

Amstad, F. T., Meier, L. L., Fasel, U., Elfering, A., & Semmer, N. K. (2011). A meta-analysis of work–family conflict and various outcomes with a special emphasis on cross-domain versus matching-domain relations. *Journal of Occupational Health Psychology, 16*, 151–169.

Aryee, S., & Luk, V. (1996). Work and nonwork influences on the career satisfaction of dual-earner couples. *Journal of vocational Behavior, 49*(1), 38–52.

Aryee, S., Fields, D., & Luk, V. (1999a). A cross-cultural test of a model of the work–family interface. *Journal of Management, 25*, 491–511.

Aryee, S., Luk, V., Leung, A., & Lo, S. (1999b). Role stressors, interrole conflict, and well-being: The moderating influence of spousal support and coping behaviors among employed parents in Hong Kong. *Journal of Vocational Behavior, 54*, 259–278.

Bloom, D. E., & Finlay, J. E. (2009). Demographic change and economic growth in Asia. *Asian Economic Policy Review, 4*, 45–64.

Brislin, R. W. (1970). Back-translation for cross-cultural research. *Journal of Cross-Cultural Psychology, 1*, 185–216.

Byron, K. (2005). A meta-analytic review of work–family conflict and its antecedents. *Journal of Vocational Behavior, 67*, 169–198.

Carlson, D. S., Kacmar, K. M., Wayne, J. H., & Grzywacz, J. G. (2006). Measuring the positive side of the work–family interface: Development and validation of a work–family enrichment scale. *Journal of Vocational Behavior, 68*, 131–164.

Carlson, D. S., Kacmar, K. M., & Williams, L. J. (2000). Construction and initial validation of a multidimensional measure of work–family conflict. *Journal of Vocational Behavior, 56*, 249–276.

Casper, W. J., Eby, L. T., Bordeaux, C., Lockwood, A., & Lambert, D. (2007). A review of research method in IO/OB work–family research. *Journal of Applied Psychology, 92*, 28–43.

Chan, A. (1996). Confucianism and development in East Asia. *Journal of Contemporary Asia, 26*, 28–45.

Chan, A. (2005). Aging in Southeast and East Asia: Issues and policy directions. *Journal of Cross-Cultural Gerontology, 20*, 269–284.

Chao, Y. T. (1990). Culture and work organizations: The Chinese case. *International Journal of Psychology, 25*, 583–592.

Chen, Z., & Powell, G. N. (2012). No pain, no gain? A resource-based model of work-to-family enrichment and conflict. *Journal of Vocational Behavior, 81*, 89–98.

Cho, E., & Koh, C-W. (2015). Governmental interventions and social re-engineering to facilitate work–life balance: Singapore and South Korea. In L. Lu & C. L. Cooper (Eds.), *Handbook of research on work–life balance in Asia* (pp. 271–294). Northampton, MA: Edward Elgar.

Confucius. (1983). *The sayings of Confucius*. Torrance, CA: Heian International, Inc.

Emrich, C. G., Denmark, F. L., & Den Hartog, D. N. (2004). Cross-cultural differences in gender egalitarianism: Implications for societies, organizations, and leaders. In R. J. House, P. J. Hanges, M. Javidan, P. W. Dorfman, & V. Gupta (Eds.), *Culture, leadership, and organizations: The GLOBE study of 62 societies* (pp. 343–394). Thousand Oaks, CA: Sage Publications.

Foley, S., Hang-Yue, N., & Lui, S. (2005). The effects of work stressors, perceived organizational support, and gender on work–family conflict in Hong Kong. *Asia Pacific Journal of Management, 22*, 237–256.

Frone, M. R. (2003). Work–family balance. In J. C. Quick & L. E. Tetrick (Eds.), *Handbook of occupational health psychology* (pp. 143–162). Washington, DC: American Psychological Association.

Frone, M. R., Russell, M., & Cooper, M. L. (1992). Antecedents and outcomes of work–family conflict: Testing a model of the work–family interface. *Journal of Applied Psychology, 77*, 65–78.

Fu, C. K., & Shaffer, M. A. (2001). The tug of work and family: Direct and indirect domain-specific determinants of work–family conflict. *Personnel Review, 30*, 502–522.

Galovan, A. M., Fackrell, T., Buswell, L., Jones, B. L., Hill, E. J., & Carroll, S. J. (2010). The work–family interface in the United States and Singapore: Conflict across cultures. *Journal of Family Psychology, 24*, 646–656.

Goulbourne, H., Reynolds, T., Solomos, J., & Zontini, E. (2010). *Transnational families: Ethnicities, identities and social capital*. London: Routledge.

Grzywacz, J. G., & Marks, N. F. (2000). Reconceptualizing the work–family interface: An ecological perspective on the correlates of positive and negative spillover between work and family. *Journal of Occupational Health Psychology, 5*, 111–126.

Hampden-Turner, C. M., & Trompenaars, F. (2000). *Building cross-cultural competence: How to create wealth from conflicting values*. New Haven: Yale University Press.

Hausmann, R., Tyson, L. D., & Zahidi, S. (2012). *The global gender gap report*. Geneva, Switzerland: World Economic Forum.

Hill, J. E., Yang, C., Hawkins, A. J., & Ferris, M. (2004). A cross-cultural test of the work–family interface in 48 countries. *Journal of Marriage and Family, 66,* 1300–1316.

Hofstede, G. (2001). *Culture's consequences: Comparing values, behaviors, institutions and organizations across nations* (2nd ed). Thousand Oaks, CA: Sage.

Huang, H. J., Eveleth, D. M., & Huo, Y. P. (2000). A Chinese work-related value system. In C. M. Lau, K. S. Law, D. K. Tse, & C. S. Wong (Eds.), *Asian management matters: Regional relevance and global impact* (pp. 33–46). London, UK: Imperial College Press.

Inglehart, R., & Norris, P. (2003). *Rising tide: Gender equality and cultural change around the world*. Cambridge University Press.

Iwao, S. (2010). Government policies supporting workplace flexibility: The state of play in Japan. In K. Christensen & B. Schneider (Eds.), *Workplace flexibility: Realigning 20th- century jobs for a 21st-century workforce* (pp. 317–335). Ithaca, NY: Cornell University Press.

Jaumotte, F. (2004). Labour force participation of women. *OECD Economic Studies, 37,* 51–108.

Jin, J. F., Ford, M. T., & Chen, C. C. (2013). Asymmetric differences in work–family spillover in North America and China: Results from two heterogeneous samples. *Journal of Business Ethics, 113,* 1–14.

Jones, G. W. (2007). Delayed marriage and very low fertility in Pacific Asia. *Population and Development Review, 33,* 453–478.

Kang, J. H., & Matusik, J. (2014, January). The Impact of Confucianism towards Working Overtime in Asian Workplaces. *In Academy of Management Proceedings* (Vol. 2014, No. 1, p. 13048). Academy of Management.

Kato, M., & Yamazaki, Y. (2009). An examination of factors related to work-to-family conflict among employed men and women in Japan. *Journal of Occupational Health, 51,* 303–313.

Kwan, H. K., Lau, V. P., & Au, K. (2012). Effects of family-to-work conflict on business owners: The role of family business. *Family Business Review, 25,* 178–190.

Lau, Y. K. (2010). The impact of fathers' work and family conflicts on children's self-esteem: The Hong Kong case. *Social Indicators Research, 95,* 363–376.

Lau, V. P., Wong, Y. E., & Chow, C. W. C. (2013). Turning the tables: Mitigating effects of proactive personality on the relationships between work-to-family conflict and work-and nonwork-related outcomes. *Career Development International, 18,* 503–520.

Li, C., Lu, J., & Zhang, Y. (2013). Cross-domain effects of work–family conflict on organizational commitment and performance. *Social Behavior and Personality: An International Journal, 41,* 1641–1653.

Lim, D. H., Choi, M., & Song, J. H. (2012). Work–family enrichment in Korea: Construct validation and status. *Leadership & Organization Development Journal, 33,* 282–299.

Lim, S., & Lee, A. (2011). Work and nonwork outcomes of workplace incivility: Does family support help?. *Journal of Occupational Health Psychology,* 16(1), 95–111.

Lim, D. H., Morris, M. L., & McMillan, H. S. (2011). Construct validation of the translated version of the work–family conflict scale for use in Korea. *Human Resource Development Quarterly, 22*, 519–543.

Lin, L. H., Ho, Y. L., & Lin, W. H. E. (2013). Confucian and Taoist work values: An exploratory study of the Chinese transformational leadership behavior. *Journal of Business Ethics, 113*, 91–103.

Liu, H., & Cheung, F. M. (2015). The moderating role of empathy in the work–family crossover process between Chinese dual-earner couples. *Journal of Career Assessment, 23*, 442–458.

Lu, C. Q., Xu, X. M., & Caughlin, D. E. (2015). Work-home interference and employees' well-being and performance: The moderating role of Chinese work value. In L. Lu & C. L. Cooper (Eds.), *Handbook of research on work–life balance in Asia* (pp. 116–136). London, UK: Edward Elgar Publishing.

Lu, L., Cooper, C. L., Kao, S. F., Chang, T. T., Allen, T. D., Lapierre, L. M., ... & Spector, P. E. (2010). Cross-cultural differences on work-to-family conflict and role satisfaction: A Taiwanese-British comparison. *Human Resource Management, 49*, 67–85.

Lu, L., Chang, T. T., Kao, S. F., & Cooper, C. L. (2015). Testing an integrated model of the work–family interface in Chinese employees: A longitudinal study. *Asian Journal of Social Psychology, 18*, 12–21.

Lu, C. Q., Lu, J. J., Du, D. Y., & Brough, P. (2016). Crossover effects of work–family conflict among Chinese couples. *Journal of Managerial Psychology, 31*, 235–250.

Lu, C. Q., Wang, B., Siu, O. L., Lu, L., & Du, D. Y. (2015). Work-home interference and work values in Greater China. *Journal of Managerial Psychology, 30*, 801–814.

Lu, J. F., Siu, O. L., Spector, P. E., & Shi, K. (2009). Antecedents and outcomes of a fourfold taxonomy of work–family balance in Chinese employed parents. *Journal of Occupational Health Psychology, 14*, 182–192.

Luk, D. M., & Shaffer, M. A. (2005). Work and family domain stressors and support: Within- and cross-domain influences on work–family conflict. *Journal of Occupational and Organizational Psychology, 78*, 489–508.

Markus, H. R., & Kitayama, S. (1991). Culture and the self: Implications for cognition, emotion, and motivation. *Psychological Review, 98*, 224–253.

Masuda, A. D., Poelmans, S. A., Allen, T. D., Spector, P. E., Lapierre, L. M., Cooper, C. L., ... & Lu, L. (2012). Flexible work arrangements availability and their relationship with work-to-family conflict, job satisfaction, and turnover intentions: A comparison of three country clusters. *Applied Psychology: An International review, 61*, 1–29.

Matsui, T., Ohsawa, T., & Onglatco, M. L. (1995). Work–family conflict and the stress-buffering effects of husband support and coping behavior among Japanese married working women. *Journal of Vocational Behavior, 47*, 178–192.

McNall, L. A., Nicklin, J. M., & Masuda, A. D. (2010). A meta-analytic review of the consequences associated with work–family enrichment. *Journal of Business and Psychology, 25*, 381–396.

Michel, J. S., Young, L. M., Mitchelson, J. K., Clark, M. A., & Baltes, B. B. (2011). Antecedents of work–family conflict: A meta-analytical review. *Journal of Organizational Behavior, 32*, 689–725.

Netemeyer, R. G., Boles, J. S., & McMurrian, R. (1996). Development and validation of work–family conflict and family–work conflict scales. *Journal of Applied Psychology, 81*, 400–410.

Neville, R. C. (2000). *Boston Confucianism: Portable tradition in the late-modern world*. Albany, NY.: State University of New York Press.

Ng, T., & Feldman, D. C. (2012). The effects of organizational and community embeddedness on work-to-family and family-to-work conflict. *Journal of Applied Psychology, 97*, 1233–1251.

Park, M., & Chesla, C. (2007). Revisiting Confucianism as a conceptual framework for Asian family study. *Journal of Family Nursing, 13*, 293–311.

Redding, G. (1990). *The spirit of Chinese capitalism*. New York: de Gruyter.

Shimazu, A., Kubota, K., Bakker, A., Demerouti, E., Shimada, K., & Kawakami, N. (2013). Work-to-family conflict and family-to-work conflict among Japanese dual-earner couples with preschool children: A spillover-crossover perspective. *Journal of Occupational Health, 55*(4), 234–243.

Shockley, K. M., & Singla, N. (2011). Reconsidering work–family interactions and satisfaction: A meta-analysis. *Journal of Management, 37*, 861–886.

Siu, O. L. (2003). Job stress and job performance among employees in Hong Kong: The role of Chinese work values and organizational commitment. *International Journal of Psychology, 38*, 337–347.

Siu, O. L., Lu, J. F., Brough, P., Lu, C. Q., Bakker, A. B., Kalliath, T., . . . & Sit, C. (2010). Role resources and work–family enrichment: The role of work engagement. *Journal of Vocational Behavior, 77*, 470–480.

Song, Z., Foo, M. D., Uy, M. A., & Sun, S. (2011). Unraveling the daily stress crossover between unemployed individuals and their employed spouses. *Journal of Applied Psychology, 96*, 151–168.

Spector, P. E., Cooper, C. L., Poelmans, S., Allen, T. D., O'Driscoll, M., Sanchez, J. I., . . . Yu, S. (2004). A cross-national comparative study of work–family stressors, working hours, and well-being: China and Latin American versus the Anglo world. *Personnel Psychology, 57*, 119–142.

Spector, P. E., Allen, T. D., Poelmans, S. A., Lapierre, L. M., Cooper, C. L., O'Driscoll, M., . . . Brough, P. (2007). Cross-national differences in relationships of work demands, job satisfaction, and turnover intentions with work–family conflict. *Personnel Psychology, 60*, 805–835.

Tsujimoto, T. (2014). Fulfilling the self and transnational intimacy through emotional labor: The experiences of migrant Filipino domestic workers in South Korea. In J. Yang (Ed.), *The political economy of affect and emotion in East Asia* (pp. 154–173). London: Routledge.

Van de Vijver, F. J. R., & Leung, K. (1997). *Methods and data analysis for cross-cultural research*. Newbury Park, CA: Sage.

Wang, P., Lawler, J. J., Walumbwa, F. O., & Shi, K. (2004). Work–family conflict and job withdrawal intentions: The moderating effect of cultural differences. *International Journal of Stress Management, 11*(4), 392–412.

Wang, M., Liu, S., Zhan, Y., & Shi, J. (2010). Daily work–family conflict and alcohol use: Testing the cross-level moderation effects of peer drinking norms and social support. *Journal of Applied Psychology, 95*, 377–386.

Westman, M. (2001). Stress and strain crossover. *Human Relations, 54*, 717–751.

Won, S. Y. (2005). Play the men's game? Accommodating work and family in the workplace. *Asian Journal of Women's Studies, 11*, 7–35.

Wong, A. L. Y. (2007). Making career choice: A study of Chinese managers. *Human Relations, 60*, 1211–1233.

Wong, K. C. K., & O'Driscoll, M. P. (2016, September 29). Work antecedents, Confucian work values, and work-to-family interference in Hong Kong: A longitudinal study. *International Journal of Stress Management*. Advance online publication. http://dx.doi.org/10.1037/str0000049

Yang, N. (2005). Individualism-collectivism and work–family interfaces: A Sino-US comparison. In S. A. Poelmans (Ed.), *Work and family: An international research perspective* (pp. 287–318). Mahwah, NJ: Erlbaum.

Yang, N., Chen, C. C., Choi, J., & Zou, Y. (2000). Sources of work–family conflict: A Sino-U.S. comparison of the effects of work and family demands. *Academy of Management Journal, 43*, 113–123.

Yi, X., Ribbens, B., & Morgan, C. N. (2010). Generational differences in China: Career implications. *Career Development International, 15*, 601–620.

Zhan, H. J., & Montgomery, R. J. V. (2003). Gender and elder care in China: The influence of filial piety and structural constraints. *Gender & Society, 17*, 209–229.

Zhang, M., Griffeth, R. W., & Fried, D. D. (2012). Work–family conflict and individual consequences. *Journal of Managerial Psychology, 27*, 696–713.

Zhao, X. R., & Namasivayam, K. (2012). The relationship of chronic regulatory focus to work–family conflict and job satisfaction. *International Journal of Hospitality Management, 31*, 458–467.

21 A Review of Work–Family Research in Australia and New Zealand

E. Anne Bardoel and Jarrod Haar

Research on the work–family interface has expanded rapidly in the past few decades, and research on the topic specifically conducted in Australia and New Zealand is no exception to this. The focus of this chapter is to review research within these regions. To the best of our knowledge, there are no prior reviews of research on work and family in this region. The articles nearest to the present work include a review of work–life articles published between 2004 and 2007 by Bardoel, De Cieri, and Santos (2008), and a policy research agenda article on Australia by Drago, Pirretti, and Scutella (2007), but neither article claims to provide a comprehensive review.

This review begins with a section on the historical context for both the study of work and family research and the relevant public policy developments, noting these are firmly anchored in concerns with gender equity in both nations. The second substantive section provides a historical picture of turning points in work and family research, including the development of relevant national surveys and governmental research supports, a brief look at the disciplinary breadth of relevant scholars, and discusses McDonald's (2000) theory linking work and family policies to fertility, the Australian government's household panel data effort (the Household, Income and Labour Dynamics in Australia or HILDA survey), and other novel research contributions from the region. The third section provides a cross-national understanding of how work and family research is performed in the region, the extent to which work and family behavioral models apply to Australia and New Zealand, and summarizes the results of cross-national (and cross-cultural) studies including either Australia or New Zealand. The fourth section covers the limitations of existing research, particularly in terms of gender, race, and ethnicity. The conclusion provides a summary and suggestions for future research.

Note also that in the Bardoel, De Cieri, and Santos's (2008) review of the Australian and New Zealand work–life literature, they found 77% of the articles concerned Australia, 21% were on New Zealand, and 2% on both countries, which is roughly as expected from population differences. We find roughly similar coverage differences in the material below.

General Context

In terms of Hofstede's dimensions of national culture, both Australia and New Zealand have similar profiles (Hofstede, 2001, 2010). They are both low on power distance, indicating managers and employees expect to be consulted and information to be shared frequently. Australia is one of the highest ranking countries on the individualism dimension, and New Zealand's score is also relatively high, which translates into societies that are loose-knit and the general expectation is that people look after themselves and their immediate families. The study by Lu et al. (2006) found that people from individualistic cultures tend to perceive work and family demands as competing for limited personal resources, such as time and energy, and are thus highly likely to experience work–family conflict. Both societies are considered "masculine" societies where conflicts are resolved at the individual level and the goal is to win. New Zealand and Australia also score high on the indulgence dimension and overall exhibit a willingness to realize their impulses and desires regarding enjoying life and having fun (Hofstede, 2001, 2010).

Perhaps the single most important key to understanding research and policy around the work–family interface in Australia or New Zealand is understanding gender inequality issues that are unique to this cultural context (Pocock, 2003). Although gender inequality is hardly unique to these two nations, it is crucial for understanding the historical development of labor market and social welfare policies, the division of labor in the home and workplace, and the framing of relevant policy debates.

Part of the reason gender inequality is taken seriously in both nations is that New Zealand and Australia have long established histories of support of women's rights. New Zealand was the first country to grant women the right to vote in 1893, and in 1902, Australia was the first country to give women both the right to vote in federal elections and also the right to be elected to parliament on a national basis (Australian Government, 2015). However, a woman was not actually elected to federal parliamentary positions until 1943 in Australia (Australian Government, 2011). In New Zealand, women could first stand for parliament in 1919, with the first woman holding national office in 1933 (Ministry for Culture and Heritage, 2014). New Zealand gave women the vote nine years earlier than Australia and New Zealand voted women into parliament twenty-four years earlier than Australia.

As is true elsewhere, interest in the work–family interface in Australia was driven in part by increases in women's labor force participation. In Australia, the rate of labor force participation rose steadily from 43.4% in 1978 to 59.3% in 2016 (ABS, 2016). In New Zealand, women's participation rate rose from 54.6% in 1986 to 64.4% in 2016 (Statistics New Zealand, 2016). Increases in the labor force participation rates of mothers had an even greater impact, and partnered mothers' rates in New Zealand rose from 61.7% in 1994 to 69.6% in 2014 (Flynn and Harris, 2015). In Australia, labor force participation for mothers with a youngest child two years of age climbed from 43% in 1991 to 56% by 2011 (Baxter, 2013).

Gender inequality in work hours, often to accommodate mothers' care for children, is very pronounced among couple families with children. In Australia, the percentage of couples with dependent children with both parents working full-time declined slightly, from 21.4% in 1991 to 21.0% in 2011, while couples with the father employed full-time and the mother employed part-time expanded from 27.0% to 34.0% over the same period (Baxter, 2013). In total, 62% of coupled, employed mothers are part-time workers in Australia. Part-time employment among mothers is less prevalent in New Zealand, with more than half of employed coupled or single mothers working full-time, even with a youngest child aged 0–4 years (Flynn & Harris, 2015). However, a solid majority of part-time employees in both nations are women, who comprised 70.4% of part-timers by 2013 in New Zealand (Statistics New Zealand, 2015) and 68.0% in Australia (ABS, 2016).

Both Australia and New Zealand historically had wages, benefits, and working conditions set through complex arbitration or "awards" systems involving trade unions and employers or employer organizations. Under those systems, many part-time employees were also "casual employees" (Campbell & Brosnan, 2005). As the words suggest, casual employees have few rights (although this is changing) and generally do not accrue any leave entitlements and are entitled to a higher rate of pay to compensate for this difference. "Casual loadings" are approximately 20–25% of pay and are in lieu of vacation, sick days, and retirement benefits (ibid.). This extra pay (or loading) made casual and part-time work attractive to many women, and particularly mothers. However, "casual" jobs are usually temporary, have irregular hours, and are not guaranteed to be ongoing (ACTU, 2017). As Campbell and Brosnan (2005) explain, since the New Zealand labor market was decentralized in 1991 under the *Employment Contracts Act*, casual employment has expanded minimally there, while it grew to encompass over a quarter of Australian employees by 2002. However, within New Zealand, that legislation saw the undermining of the "casual loading" or extra pay, which is far more uncommon now in New Zealand.

An additional reason for part-time employment being relatively more common among Australian mothers than New Zealand mothers lies in differences in the health care insurance systems. Single-payer health care has existed in Australia since 1975 (Biggs, 2004), while New Zealand had a system of public subsidies to health providers, with deregulation in the 1990s increasingly tying access to health care to ability to pay (Barnett & Barnett, 2004). The latter system provides a greater incentive to work full-time. Indeed, within New Zealand, using private health insurance is in the minority, at 31.8% (Health Funds Association, 2010), and is most likely tied to those in full-time employment and not part-time employment, due to the associated costs.

Although the effective promotion of part-time work among Australian mothers might be seen as ameliorating conflicts between work and family, that is not accurate. On the one hand, part-time employment may support high levels of inequality in the division of household labor, with Baxter (2001) finding that Australian married mothers typically perform around two-thirds of all childcare and housework. The division of household labor is similar in New Zealand, with women performing more than twice as much work as men in terms of cleaning/laundry and food preparation, and women under the age of forty-five spending around twice as much time on childcare (Statistics New Zealand, 2001).

Although part-time employment might sometimes be chosen freely, it seems likely that many young Australian women view it as a constrained choice. Although there are different labor market choices available and women might choose to work part-time, for many Australian women with family responsibilities, the only option is to work-part-time because they cannot access sufficient parental leave, flexibility in work hours, and because of the cost and/or difficulty of accessing childcare (Pocock, 2003). In New Zealand, the government recently started collecting data on "under-employment," which is defined as working fewer hours than desired and able to work (Statistics New Zealand, 2013). The government notes that ILO data found New Zealand ranked twenty-first (around 4% under-employment) and Australia twenty-sixth (8% under-employment). The United States ranked tenth with well under 2% under-employment. It also noted that within New Zealand, women make up twice the part-time workforce, but were twice as likely as men to report under-employment. This likely reflects either that women are not able to find a job that allows them to also fulfill household responsibilities, so they work part-time, or women would prefer not to work, perhaps in order to care for children, but must work for financial reasons, and thus engage in part-time labor.

More generally, difficulties women faced in balancing employment and child-rearing may have resulted in low fertility. For New Zealand, fertility fell from the necessary replacement rate of 2.1 in 1993, but only to 2.0, and it hovered between 1.9 and 2.0 until 2007, when it rose to 2.2 for several years, before falling back to the prior pattern in 2013–2015 (Statistics New Zealand, n.d.). In Australia, fertility fell below the replacement level of 2.1 in 1977, was stable at 1.8 or 1.9 from 1978 to 2006, before rising to 2.0 from 2007 to 2010, and falling back to 1.9 in 2011 through 2013 (ABS, 2013).

Various government policies to promote the integration of work and family have been considered over the years. In Australia, unpaid, job-protected leave for new biological mothers was provided through the arbitration system in 1979, expanded to include adoptive mothers in 1985, extended to fathers in 1990, and extended to casual employees in 2001 (Goward et al., 2005). The gendered focus of initial parental leave provisions was echoed in the Sex Discrimination Act of 1984, which explicitly prohibited discrimination based on pregnancy or potential pregnancy, and was interpreted as protecting only employees with caregiving responsibilities who were also women (Sex Discrimination Act 1984). Conservative governments (under the Liberal Party of Australia) responded to the pressure to provide policies facilitating balance by (1) including provisions to enhance flexible work arrangements in the Workplace Relations Act of 1996, and (2) in 2004 introducing a "baby bonus," which provided payments to new mothers regardless of employment status (Risse, 2010). After the Australian Labor Party returned to power, the legal right to request flexibility for caregivers was included in the Fair Work Act of 2009, and a paid parental leave scheme for was introduced in 2011 (ABS, 2011). The parental leave provisions were limited to "primary carers," so effectively excluded most men, although a two-week "use it or lose it" provision for fathers was added in 2013 (Buckmaster, n.d.). The Workplace Gender Equality Act 2012 (Act) replaced the Equal Opportunity for Women in the Workplace Act 1999. The legislation aims to improve and promote equality for both women and men in the workplace and includes a specific aim to "promote, amongst employers, the elimination of discrimination on the basis of gender in relation to employment matters (including in relation to family and caring responsibilities)" (Workplace Gender Equity Agency (WGEA), n.d.).

Within New Zealand, the major legislative additions promoting parenting were the Taxation (Parental Tax Credit) Act 1999, which was then expanded into the Parental Leave and Employment Protection (Paid Parental Leave) Amendment Act 2002, which at the time provided a maximum pay rate of $325/week for twelve weeks. Haar and Spell (2003) found media attention on work and family issues, which steadily increased from 1985 to 1998, may have played a role in passage of the legislation. New Zealand has subsequently raised the threshold and benefits on paid parental leave, with current leave being up to eighteen weeks and paying a maximum of almost $530/week (Ministry of Business, Innovations & Employment, 2016). The new legislation has also been extended to include workers on non-standard working arrangements, and New Zealand still offers up to fifty-two weeks of unpaid parental leave. In summary, in 1998 only the United States, Australia, and New Zealand were countries without paid parental leave legislation in the developed world. In 1999, New Zealand and then in 2011, Australia left the list, with only the United States remaining.

Turning Points in the History of Work–Family Research in Australia and New Zealand

The same focus on gender inequality that pushed much public policy development similarly affected two tracks of work–family research in Australia which emerged by the end of the 1990s. First, a focus on gender inequality in the division of household and paid labor yielded an early interest in measuring and valuing time devoted to family care and housework (Ironmonger, 1989; Russell, James, & Watson, 1988). Ultimately, that interest led to the development and subsequent analysis of national time use surveys in 1992, 1997, and 2006 (e.g., Bittman, 1999; Craig & Bittman, 2008; Craig, Mullan, & Blaxland, 2010), although the survey for 2013 was cancelled (Sawer, Bittman, & Smith, 2013). Second, increasing public discussion of work–family balance and the flexible work arrangements provisions of the Workplace Relations Act of 1996 led other researchers to focus on workplace policies and organizational behavior (e.g., Bardoel, Moss, Smyrnios, & Tharenou, 1999; Russell & Bourke, 1999). This also spurred the inclusion and subsequent analysis of work–family policy items in the government-sponsored Australian Workplace Industrial Relations Survey (AWIRS) of 1995 (e.g., Gray & Tudball, 2003). Additionally, the Australian Work and Life Index (AWALI), first administered in 2007, is a national survey of work–life outcomes of working Australians undertaken by the Centre for Work and Life (Skinner & Pocock, 2014). AWALI was repeated annually until 2010 and then biennially in 2012 and 2014 and has served as an important dataset to examine factors related to work–life conflict and associated social, community, and health outcomes.

Most of the New Zealand research on work–life issues focuses on alternative work arrangements with far less research on wellness, care-giving support, and crisis assistance (Morrison & Thurnell, 2012). Government organizations – the New Zealand Department of Labour, New Zealand Business Council for Sustainable Development, and Diversity Works NZ – have all conducted significant research studies on alternative work arrangements. In New Zealand, practical government support came in two forms. First, public sector employees tended to be underpaid historically, which led the government to promote flexible work arrangements for those employees (Haar, 2008). Second, through the Equal Employment Opportunities Trust, which later became Diversity Works NZ, the government pressed work–life balance policies and practices as one component of a gender equity strategy (see www.diversityworksnz.org.nz).

Research in work–life in Australia and New Zealand has some of the same characteristics of work–life research elsewhere in the developed world. Nonetheless, it has its own flavor. Australia can arguably claim a major theoretical contribution and major contributions in terms of empirical resources, along with several minor but nonetheless unique contributions from both Australia and New Zealand. Among the major contributions is Peter McDonald's (2000) theory linking work–family policies and fertility. As he explains, the theory argues:

> . . . if women are provided with opportunities nearly equal to those of men in education and market employment, but these opportunities are severely curtailed by having children, then, on average, women will restrict the number of children that they have to an extent which leaves fertility at a precariously low, long-term level. (p. 1)

McDonald has since applied and developed the theory both in general and nation-specific contexts (McDonald, 2006, 2009, 2013; McDonald & Moyle, 2010). The theory has influenced both fertility scholars and the understanding of work–family policies around the world (e.g., Gornick & Meyers, 2003) and has resulted in over 700 citations at the writing of this chapter.

The Australian government was a major driver of work–family research in that nation, as indicated by government funding for time use surveys and its inclusion of relevant items in the 1995 AWIRS. Those efforts culminated in a major empirical resource produced in Australia: the Household, Income and Labour Dynamics in Australia (HILDA) survey (Wooden, Freidin, & Watson, 2002). First administered in 2001, the HILDA is an annual, nationally representative, panel survey of households designed to capture income dynamics, labor market dynamics, and family dynamics, making it relevant to the study of work–family issues.

Due in part to the leadership of Mark Wooden at the University of Melbourne, the HILDA data were explicitly designed to promote research on the work–family interface. The data provide longitudinal evidence on perceived work–life balance (Craig & Sawrikar, 2008), as well as validated measures of happiness, job and life satisfaction, physical and mental health, and disabilities (Siahpush, Spittal, & Singh, 2008). It is one of the few large, panel surveys to include dynamic information on usual and preferred work hours (Drago, Wooden, & Black, 2009a), and these have been utilized to understand work–family conflict (Reynolds & Aletraris, 2007) and how usual and preferred work hours are altered by changing family circumstances

(Drago, Wooden, & Black, 2009b). The data also allow the linking of work–family conflict not only with work and family circumstances, but also with community resources (Skinner & Ichii, 2015). Given the close connection between motherhood and part-time employment in Australia, the HILDA has been invaluable in terms of understanding how childcare costs influence mother choices of part-time employment (Rammohan & Whelan, 2007), whether women (Cai, Law & Bathgate, 2014) or single mothers (Fok, Jeon & Wilkins, 2013) become trapped in part-time employment, linkages between happiness and women's and men's part-time employment (Booth & Van Ours, 2009), and levels of work–family conflict associated with part- or full-time employment for mothers (Hosking & Western, 2008). McDonald's theory of fertility and work–family policies has been tested in articles on the effects of the baby bonus on fertility intentions (Risse, 2010) and on fertility rates (Drago et al., 2011), and the effects of childcare subsidies on the labor supply (Guest & Parr, 2013). In response to the introduction of paid maternity leave in 2011, the HILDA data were tested for any long-term adverse wage effects on women who use maternity leave (Baker, 2011). The survey of work–family research in Australia and New Zealand, covering 2004 through 2007, revealed that only six of sixty-three empirical studies utilized longitudinal data (Bardoel, De Cieri, & Santos, 2008); a more recent replication of that survey would probably tilt more heavily towards longitudinal data because of the HILDA survey.

Other contributions include the simultaneous exploration of work–life balance both cross-nationally and cross-culturally (i.e., within nations) in New Zealand (Haar et al., 2014), discussed further below. Theoretically, the possibility of using role balance as a theoretical approach to understand work–life balance was developed in New Zealand (Haar, 2013), and the potential utilization of the construct of employee resilience theory to understand HRM and work–life balance originated in Australia (Bardoel et al., 2014).

Cross-National Perspective on Work–Family Research in Australia and New Zealand

Work–family research in Australia and New Zealand is heavily influenced by research in the United Kingdom and particularly the United States, perhaps in part because of pressures on researchers in Australia and New Zealand to publish in journals based in the United Kingdom and the United States and the prevalence of research produced in those nations. That linkage shows up both in cross-national and national research.

Research in the late 1990s suggested that, relative to corporations in the United States, Australian corporations were less likely to provide work–family policies, including flexible working time, paid paternity leave, on-site or near-site childcare, nursing rooms, employee assistance programs, or child or elder care resource and referral services, but more likely to offer part-time employment (Russell & Bowman, 2000). American corporations were even more likely to take a strategic approach to work–life than Australian corporations (ibid., p. 34). More broadly, Drago, Pirretti, and Scutella (2007) concluded that governmental financial supports for families were more generous in Australia than in the United States, that work–family corporate policies are more common in the United States, and that Australia exhibits higher rates of part-time work for mothers in tandem with a more unequal division of labor in the home. Craig and Mullan (2010) in a study of parenting and paid and unpaid work across Australia, Denmark, France, Italy, and the United States, confirm that the adverse impact of motherhood on the household division of labor is more severe in Australia than in the United States, which they trace in part to high rates of part-time employment among Australian mothers. Of equal importance, they attribute greater equality in Denmark, France, and Italy to the greater availability and use of formal childcare, which reduces demands on fathers and especially mothers.

More directly, some research asks whether behavioral models that fit the United States or the United Kingdom also fit the Australian and New Zealand populations. Using a mixture of scales developed in the United States (e.g., Frone, Russell, & Cooper, 1992) and some developed by the Australian Institute of Family Studies, Smyrnios et al. (2003) found behavioral similarities between Australian and American small business owners for a strain-based model of work–family conflict. Using instruments developed in the United States, Bardoel, Drago, Cooper, and Colbeck (2009) found that academics engaged in behaviors to avoid biases against caregiving, such as minimizing or hiding family commitments; in both nations, women were more likely to engage in the behavior, with the Australian women slightly more likely to do so, which they attribute to cultural differences. In a relatively large study, Lapierre et al. (2008) used instruments developed in the United States to measure time-, strain-, and behavior-based family interference with work and work interference with family, family-supportive organization perceptions, as well as job, family, and life satisfaction, with samples of managers in Australia, Canada, Finland, New Zealand, and the United States. They found relatively standard results (e.g., family-supportive organization perceptions reduced all forms of interference), and with no significant differences across the five samples, suggesting similar circumstances engender similar responses, albeit this study only includes nations typically classified as individualistic.

Other studies address cultural divergence across individualistic and collectivist cultures. Billing et al. (2013) studied levels of work–family conflict for a sample of managers in Australia, Japan, South Korea, and the United States, positing that individuals in the United States tend to be vertical individualists, striving to succeed to demonstrate their superiority, while those in Australia tend to be horizontal individualists, who perceive that they are not superior to others, with the remaining countries tending towards collectivism. They found that vertical individualism is related to work–family conflict in all four nations, while horizontal individualism is not, suggesting an important cultural difference between Australia and the United States. Relatedly, Haar et al. (2014) found the relationship between work–life balance and job and life satisfaction was positive for Chinese, French, Italian, New Zealand European, New Zealand Māori, and Spanish samples, but was moderated by levels of individualism/collectivism and gender egalitarian attitudes. Most broadly, Spector and colleagues (2004, 2007) treated Australia, Canada, England, New

Zealand, and the United States as a single country group, compared to China and Latin American nations (with the latter treated as a single group), and found work hours most strongly related to perceived work–family stressors in the Anglo (individualistic) nations. In their 2007 work, Spector et al. found that working hours were related to work–family conflict. However, they found moderating effects, such that this relationship was exacerbated for Anglo countries (including the United States, the United Kingdom, Australia, and New Zealand) compared to Asian countries. The inference is that, in Asian countries, employees who work more hours have less work–family conflict because there is a cultural norm (around collectivism) where working hard is a benefit for the family unit, and thus less likely to lead to conflict.

A notable effort to simultaneously promote cross-national research and practice while recognizing cultural differences is found in Bardoel and De Cieri's (2014) effort to develop a framework for cross-nationally applicable work–life instruments. Cast at the level of the corporation, the framework calls for standardized measures of the effects of work–life initiatives on both financial and social or moral outcomes, with other measures capturing the extent to which those initiatives respond to local culture and patterns of diversity.

In terms of measures used per se, these are typically drawn from studies conducted in the United States (e.g., Carlson, Kacmar & Williams, 2000; Carlson et al., 2006). The HILDA data include the SF-36 instrument to measure mental and physical health (Ware, Snow, Kosinski, & Gandek, 2000) and the Kessler-10 measure of psychological distress (Kessler et al., 2002), and both were developed in the United States. Further, several Australian studies apply US-derived models to Australian data under the implicit assumption that results found in one nation will also hold in the other (e.g., Thanacoody, Bartram & Casimir, 2009). Perhaps more common are applications of Unites States-derived models in relatively novel ways, such as time- and strain-based interference from or to work and family affecting work–family balance, but with an application to different sectors and types of employees within Australian higher education (Pillay, Kluvers, Abhayawansa & Vranic, 2013) or the Australian construction industry (Lingard & Francis, 2004, 2006, 2007).

These effects are similar in studies that include New Zealand data (e.g., Haar, 2013; Haar et al., 2014). While New Zealand has an indigenous population larger than Australia, with Māori making up approximately 14% of the population and 12% of the workforce (Haar & Brougham, 2013), studies exploring work–life balance, – which included samples from New Zealand Europeans and separately New Zealand Māori (Haar et al., 2014), used the same constructs – work–family conflict (Carlson et al., 2000) and work–family enrichment (Carlson et al., 2006) – that were previously used on American samples. Haar and colleagues' (2014) study also included a measure of work–life balance established in New Zealand (Haar, 2013) that had not been tested on an indigenous population before. Haar, Roche, and Taylor's (2012) study found effects which differed from much of the Western-literature (e.g., family-to-work conflict dimension was more strongly related to turnover intentions than was the work-to-family conflict dimension), highlighting potential issues with these Western constructs in different populations. However, that is somewhat countered by the work–life balance study conducted by Haar et al.

(2014), which found metric measurement invariance across all samples including New Zealand European and New Zealand Māori – including for the constructs of work–family conflict and work–life balance – indicating empirical support for the generalizability of these constructs.

Some research findings are relatively unique to the region. For example, Haar et al. (2014) found work–life balance was positively related to job satisfaction and life satisfaction, and negatively related to anxiety and depression across the whole sample (seven populations from six countries). However, when these effects were broken down into specific countries, they found that work–life balance accounts for much greater variance for some outcomes (e.g., job satisfaction) in some countries (New Zealand Europeans, Italy, Malaysia, and China) than others (France and New Zealand Māori). In New Zealand, the differences in variance explained were 13% for New Zealand Māori, but 42% for New Zealand Europeans. Thus, it was significant predictor for both groups of employees, but clearly a much more powerful predictor for one group than another. There is a tendency among work–life researchers to make broad assumptions about the influence of constructs such as work–family conflict and work–life balance whereas in reality the effects for individual populations may diverge substantially. When considered in relation to the above findings, there is a strong case to conduct further testing within large population groups and include, for example, indigenous populations (e.g., Pacific Peoples in New Zealand) who are often neglected by researchers.

In light of the passage of the Australian right-to-request flexibility legislation in 2009, researchers asked whether requests for flexibility improved work–life balance. The AWALI data from 2009 to 2014 found that most requests were from women, and especially mothers of young children; most requests were approved and work–life outcomes were significantly improved among those whose requests were approved (Skinner & Pocock, 2011, 2014). On a different note, self-employment is sometimes considered a route for women, particularly mothers, to achieve work–life balance (Boden Jr., 1999), but Australian studies find that many of the self-employed work involuntary long hours (Drago, Wooden, & Black, 2009a), and that self-employment does not facilitate work–life balance for mothers (Pocock, Skinner, & Williams, 2007). Together, these unique findings regarding the sources of work–life balance, effects of mother self-employment, and effects of right-to-request flexibility legislation suggest further research on the topics elsewhere in the world might be valuable.

Limitations of Existing Research

Perhaps the greatest weakness of work–family research in Australia and New Zealand, is the limited coverage of gender. Given that studies of work–family conflict were largely motivated by the entry of women into the labor force in the last half-century, this lacuna is notable. Bardoel, De Cieri, and Santos (2008) found only eight of eighty-six articles addressing work–life in either Australia or New Zealand (or both) between 2004 and 2007 included gender as a theme, and this was after allowing for multiple themes. Further, they note that gender was often treated as one of many binary control variables.

In addition, there appears to be a significant neglect of ethnic diversity. Apart from a few studies in New Zealand (Haar et al., 2012, 2014) that focus on Māori employees, there is little attention given to indigenous populations – especially within Australia. Some cities within the region have large ethnic populations, which have not been explored specifically. For example, Pacific peoples account for 14.6% of the Auckland population, making it the world's largest Polynesian city (Mudd, Whitfield, & Harper, 2006). Despite this, no specific work–family research has been explored within this ethnic group. Similarly, the Aborigines of Australia provide potential streams of research to better understand the influences of work–family issues across population groups within the region.

One occupational group seldom researched in the work–family field – not just in Australia and New Zealand, but generally across the world – are blue-collar occupations. We understand little about the work–family issues for this occupational group. One barrier to this may be illiteracy rates. Although New Zealand and Australia both have overall high literacy rates, some pockets have poor levels of literacy. Within New Zealand, Walker et al. (1997) state, "[t]he majority of Māori, Pacific Islands people and those from other ethnic minority groups are functioning below the level of competence in literacy required to effectively meet the demands of everyday life" (p. 1). As such, there may be fundamental issues around data collection using survey instruments requiring a solid level of literacy. This provides a challenge for work–family researchers going forward, and these effects appear to be similar within the Australian aborigine population (Australian Curriculum, Assessment and Reporting Authority, 2015). A related factor is that Australia is highly urbanized, with 68% of the population concentrated in major cities (ABS, 2008), and many aborigines live in rural areas for which few studies are available.

Summary and Directions for Future Research

It is somewhat surprising that the strong linkage between concerns with gender equity and developing work–family private sector policies and government legislation, which is explicit in both nations, is only weakly echoed in academic research in the region (Bardoel, De Cieri, & Santos, 2008). However, this deficiency may have been remedied in part in recent years, particularly due to the HILDA, AWALI, WGEA, and Diversity Works NZ surveys. Specifically, articles using the HILDA data discussed above explicitly address gender in a solid majority of cases (i.e., Baker, 2011; Booth & Van Ours, 2009; Cai, Law, & Bathgate, 2014; Craig & Sawrikar, 2008; Drago, Wooden, & Black, 2009a, 2009b; Drago et al., 2011; Fok, Jeon, & Wilkins, 2013; Guest & Parr, 2013; Hosking & Western, 2008; Rammohan & Whelan, 2007; Reynolds & Aletraris, 2007; Risse, 2010), as do analyses of the AWALI data (e.g., Skinner & Pocock, 2007, 2014). That list bodes well for bringing research into line with the gender equity and diversity concerns driving public discussion and policies in the region.

Existing research could be usefully expanded in many directions. From an Australian and New Zealand public policy perspective, research regarding the relatively recent introduction of paid parental leave could ascertain how these policies have altered women's labor supply, fertility, and the division of household labor. Similarly, for Australia, while the AWALI data suggest that right-to-request flexibility legislation has had a minimal impact (Skinner & Pocock, 2014), a longitudinal analysis using the HILDA data might yield different results in both practice and gender equity.

Research addressing cross-cultural work and family issues would also be valuable. Although some research has explored differences between New Zealand Europeans and Māoris (Haar et al., 2014), little is known about Pacific Islanders in that nation, Aborigines in Australia, or individuals of Asian heritage in both nations. Such research could not only help us to understand how model parameters vary with culture, but also improve the ability of institutions in the two nations to successfully address diversity, including in the workplace.

In general, it is reasonable to conclude that the overall state of work and family research in Australia and New Zealand is healthy. The research has developed substantially in recent decades, and it is likely that the 86 articles on work–life for the 2004–2007 period identified by Bardoel, De Cieri, and Santos (2008) has continued to grow. Further, the disciplinary diversity of scholars in the region suggests that a valuable mix of disciplines and approaches is involved in the research.

References

ABS. Australian Bureau of Statistics. (2008). Australian Social Trends, 2008. No. 4102.0. Canberra ACT: ABS. www.abs.gov.au/AUSSTATS/abs@.nsf/Lookup/4102 .0Chapter3002008

ABS. Australian Bureau of Statistics. (2011). Australian Social Trends, December 2011. No. 4102.0. Canberra ACT: ABS. www.abs.gov.au/AUSSTATS/abs@.nsf /Lookup/4102.0Main+Features30Dec+2011

ABS. Australian Bureau of Statistics. (2013). Births, Australia, 2013. No. 3301.0 (downloads), Canberra ACT: ABS. www.abs.gov.au/AUSSTATS/abs@.nsf/DetailsPage/ 3301.02013?OpenDocument

ABS. Australian Bureau of Statistics. (2016). Labour Force, Australia, August 2016. No. 6202.0 (downloads), Canberra ACT: ABS. www.abs.gov.au/AUSSTATS/abs@ .nsf/DetailsPage/6202.0Aug%202016?OpenDocument

ACTU. Australian Council of Trade Unions. (2017). Casual workers fact sheet. Accessed Februar 2, 2017 www.australianunions.org.au/casual_workers_factsheet

Australian Curriculum, Assessment and Reporting Authority (2015). National Assessment Program: Literacy and Numeracy: Achievement in reading, persuasive writing, language conventions and numeracy. National Report for 2015. Australian Curriculum, Assessment and Reporting Authority: Sydney, Australia.

Australian Government. (2011). Australian Women in Politics. Canberra ACT: Australian Government. www.australia.gov.au/about-australia/australian-story/austn-women-in-politics

Australian Government. (2015). Australian Suffragettes. Canberra ACT: Australian Government. www.australia.gov.au/about-australia/australian-story/austn-suffragettes

Baker, D. (2011). Maternity leave and reduced future earning capacity. *Family Matters, 89,* 82–89.

Bardoel, E.A., & De Cieri, H.L. (2014). A framework for work–life instruments: A cross-national review. *Human Resource Management, 54,* 635–659.

Bardoel, E.A., De Cieri, H.L., & Santos, C. (2008). A review of work–life research in Australia and New Zealand. *Asia Pacific Journal of Human Resources, 46,* 316–333.

Bardoel, E.A., Drago, R., Cooper, B., & Colbeck, C. (2009). Bias avoidance: Cross-cultural differences in the US and Australian academies. *Gender, Work and Organization, 18,* e157–e179.

Bardoel, E.A., Moss, S.A., Smyrnios, K., & Tharenou, P. (1999). Employee characteristics associated with the provision of work–family policies and programs. *International Journal of Manpower, 20,* 563–577.

Bardoel, E.A., Pettit, T.M., De Cieri, H., & McMillan, L. (2014). Employee resilience: An emerging challenge for HRM. *Asia Pacific Journal of Human Resources, 52,* 279–297.

Barnett, R., & Barnett, P. (2004). Primary health care in New Zealand: Problems and policy approaches. *Social Policy Journal of New Zealand, 21,* 49–66.

Baxter, J. (2001). Marital status and the division of household labour: Cohabitation vs. marriage. *Family Matters, 58,* 16–21.

Baxter, J. (2013). Parents working out work. *Australian Family Trends, No. 1.* Melbourne, VIC: Australian Institute of Family Studies. https://aifs.gov.au/publications/parents-working-out-work

Biggs, A. (2004). Medicare—Background brief. E-Brief. Canberra ACT: Parliament of Australia. www.aph.gov.au/About_Parliament/Parliamentary_Departments/Parliamentary_Library/Publications_Archive/archive/medicare

Billing, T. K., Bhagat, R., Babakus, E., Srivastava, B. N., Shin, M., & Brew, F. (2013). Work-family conflict in four national contexts: A closer look at the role of individualism–collectivism. *International Journal of Cross Cultural Management, 14,* 139–159.

Bittman, M. (1999). Parenthood without penalty: Time use and public policy in Australia and Finland. *Feminist Economics, 5,* 27–42.

Boden Jr., R.J. (1999). Flexible working hours, family responsibilities, and female self-employment: Gender differences in self-employment selection. *American Journal of Economics and Sociology, 58,* 71–83.

Booth, A., & Van Ours, J. (2009). Hours of work and gender identity: Does part-time work make the family happier? *Economica, 76,* 176–196.

Buckmaster, L. (n.d.). Comparing the paid parental leave schemes. Canberra ACT: Parliament of Australia. www.aph.gov.au/About_Parliament/Parliamentary_Departments/Parliamentary_Library/pubs/BriefingBook44p/PaidParentalLeave

Cai, L., Law, V., & Bathgate, M. (2014). Is part-time employment a stepping stone to full-time employment? *Economic Record, 90,* 462–485.

Campbell, I., & Brosnan, P. (2005). Relative advantages: Casual employment and casualisation in Australia and New Zealand, *New Zealand Journal of Employment Relations, 30,* 33–45.

Carlson, D. S., Kacmar, K. M., Wayne, J. H., & Grzywacz, J. G. (2006). Measuring the positive side of the work–family interface: Development and validation of a work–family enrichment scale. *Journal of Vocational Behavior, 68*(1), 131–164.

Carlson, D. S., Kacmar, K. M., & Williams, L. J. (2000). Construction and initial validation of a multidimensional measure of work–family conflict. *Journal of Vocational Behavior, 56*, 249–276.

Craig, L., & Bittman, M. (2008). The incremental time costs of children: An analysis of children's impact on adult time use in Australia. *Feminist Economics, 14*, 59–88.

Craig, L., & Mullan, K. (2010). Parenthood, gender and work–family time in the United States, Australia, Italy, France, and Denmark. *Journal of Marriage and Family, 72*, 1344–1361.

Craig, L., Mullan, K., & Blaxland, M. (2010). Parenthood, policy and work–family time in Australia 1992–2006. *Work, Employment & Society, 24*, 27–45.

Craig, L., & Sawrikar, P. (2008). Satisfaction with work–family balance for parents of early adolescents compared to parents of younger children. *Journal of Family Studies, 14*, 91–106.

Drago, R., Pirretti, A., & Scutella, R. (2007). Work and family directions in the USA and Australia: A policy research agenda. *Journal of Industrial Relations, 49*, 49–66.

Drago, R., Sawyer, K., Shreffler, K.M., Warren, D., & Wooden, M. (2011). Did Australia's baby bonus increase fertility intentions and births? *Population Research and Policy Review, 30*, 381–397.

Drago, R., Wooden, M., & Black, D. (2009a). Long work hours: Volunteers and conscripts. *British Journal of Industrial Relations, 47*, 571–600.

Drago, R., Wooden, M., & Black, D. (2009b). Who wants and gets flexibility? Changing work hours preferences and life events. *Industrial and Labor Relations Review, 62*, 394–414.

Fok, Y., Jeon, S., & Wilkins, R. (2013). Does part-time employment help or hinder Australian lone mothers' movements into full-time employment? *Oxford Economic Papers, 65*, 523–547.

Flynn, S., & Harris, M. (2015). Mothers in the New Zealand workforce. Paper at the LEW16 conference, Wellington, 27–28 November 2014. Available from www.stats.govt.nz

Frone, M.R., Russell, M. & Cooper, M.L . (1992). Antecedents and outcomes of work–family conflict: Testing a model of the work-family interface. *Journal of Applied Psychology 77*, 65–78.

Gornick, J.C., & Meyers, M.K. (2003). *Families that Work: Policies for Reconciling Parenthood and Employment.* New York, NY: Russell Sage Foundation Press.

Goward, P., Mihailuk, T., Moyle, S., O'Connell, K. de Silva, N., Squire, S., & Tilly, J. (2005). Striking the balance: Women, men, work and family. Discussion paper 2005, Sydney NSW: Sex Discrimination Unit, Human Rights and Equal Opportunity Commission.

Gray, M., & Tudball, J. (2003). Family-friendly work practices: Differences within and between workplaces. *Journal of Industrial Relations, 45*, 269–291.

Guest, R., & Parr, N. (2013). Family policy and couples' labour supply: An empirical assessment. *Journal of Population Economics, 26*, 1631–1660.

Haar, J. (2008). Work–family conflict and job outcomes: The moderating effects of flexitime use in a New Zealand organization. *New Zealand Journal of Employment Relations, 33*(1), 38–51.

Haar, J. (2013). Testing a new measure of work–life balance: A study of parent and non-parent employees from New Zealand. *International Journal of Human Resource Management*, *24*(17/18), 3305–3324.

Haar, J., & Brougham, D. (2013). An indigenous model of career satisfaction: Exploring the role of workplace cultural wellbeing. *Social Indicators Research*, *110*(3), 873–890.

Haar, J., Roche, M., & Taylor, D. (2012). Work–family conflict and turnover intentions amongst indigenous employees: The importance of the whanau/family for Maori. *International Journal of Human Resource Management*, *23*(12), 2546–2560.

Haar, J., Russo, M., Sune, A., & Ollier-Malaterre, A. (2014). Outcomes of work–life balance on job satisfaction, life satisfaction and mental health: A study across seven cultures. *Journal of Vocational Behavior*, *85*(3), 361–373.

Haar, J., & Spell, C. (2003). The influence of media attention towards family-friendly practices: Was New Zealand's paid parental leave a family-friendly fashion whose time had come? *New Zealand Journal of Human Resources Management*, *3*, 1–23.

Health Funds Association (2010). Health Insurance Statistics July 2010. From www.actuaries .org.nz/Papers%202012/McLeod.pdf

Hofstede, G. (2001). *Culture's Consequences: Comparing Values, Behaviors, Institutions, and Organizations Across Nations*. Second Edition. Thousand Oaks, CA: Sage Publications.

Hofstede, G., Hofstede, G.J., & Minkov, M. (2010). *Cultures and Organizations: Software of the Mind*. Revised and Expanded Third Edition. New York, NY: McGraw-Hill USA.

Hosking, A., & Western, M. (2008). The effects of non-standard employment on work–family conflict. *Journal of Sociology*, *44*, 5–27.

Ironmonger, D. (Ed.) (1989). *Households Work: Productive Activities, Women and Income in the Household Economy*. Sydney, NSW: Allen and Unwin.

Kessler, R.C., Andrews, G., Colpe, L.J., Hiripi, E., Mroczek, D.K., Normand, S.-L. T., Walters, E.E., & Zaslavsky, A.M. (2002). Short screening scales to monitor population prevalences and trends in non-specific psychological distress. *Psychological Medicine*, *32*, 959–976.

Lapierre, L.M., Spector, P.E., Allen, T.D., Poelmans, S., Cooper, C.L., O'Driscoll, M.P., Sanchez, J.I., Brough, P., & Kinnunen, U. (2008). Family-supportive organization perceptions, multiple dimensions of work–family conflict, and employee satisfaction: A test of model across five samples. *Journal of Vocational Behavior*, *73*, 92–106.

Lingard, H., & Francis, V. (2004). The work–life experiences of office and site-based employees in the Australian construction industry. *Construction Management and Economics*, *22*, 991–1002.

Lingard, H., & Francis, V. (2006). Does a supportive work environment moderate the relationship between work–family conflict and burnout among construction professionals? *Construction Management and Economics*, *24*, 185–196.

Lingard, H., & Francis, V. (2007). Negative interference between Australian construction professionals' work and family role: Evidence of an asymmetrical relationship. *Engineering, Construction and Architectural Management*, *14*, 79–93.

Lu, L., Gilmour, R., Kao, S.F., & Huang, M.T. (2006). A cross-cultural study of work/family demands, work/family conflict and wellbeing: The Taiwanese vs British. *Career Development International*, *11*, 9–27.

McDonald, P. (2000). Gender equity, social institutions and the future of fertility. *Journal of Population Research*, *17*, 1–16.

McDonald, P. (2006). Low fertility and the state: The efficacy of policy. *Population and Development Review, 32*, 485–510.

McDonald, P. (2009). Explanations of low fertility in East Asia. In Jones, G., Staughan, P., & Chan, A. (Eds.). *Ultra-low Fertility in Pacific Asia: Trends, Causes and Policy Issues*. Oxford, UK: Routledge.

McDonald, P. (2013). Societal foundations for explaining low fertility: Gender equity. *Demographic Research, 28*, 981–994.

McDonald, P., & Moyle, H. (2010). Why English-speaking countries have relatively high fertility? *Journal of Population Research, 27*, 247–273.

Ministry for Culture and Heritage. (2014). Parliament's People: Women MPs. www.nzhistory.net.nz/politics/parliaments-people/women-mps

Ministry of Business, Innovations and Employment (2016). Good news for families with babies due or born after 1 April 2016. Ministry of Business, Innovations and Employment: Wellington, New Zealand. www.employment.govt.nz/assets/Uploads/tools-and-resources/employment-law/Parental-leave-changes-factsheet.pdf

Morrison, E., & Thurnell, D. (2012). Employee preferences for work–life benefits in a large New Zealand construction company. *Australasian Journal of Construction Economics and Building, 12*, 12–25.

Mudd, T., Whitfield, P., & Harper, L. (2006). *The Rough Guide to New Zealand*. Fifth Edition. UK: Rough Guides.

Pillay, S., Kluvers, R., Abhayawansa, S., & Vranic, V. (2013). An exploratory study into work/family balance within the Australian higher education sector. *Higher Educations Research and Development, 32*, 228–243.

Pocock, B. (2003). *The Work/Life Collision: What Work is Doing to Australians and What to Do about It*. Annandale, NSW: Federation Press.

Pocock, B., Skinner, N., & Williams, P. (2007). Work–life in Australia: Outcomes from the Australian work and life index (AWALI) 2007. Adelaide SA: University of South Australia.

Rammohan, A., & Whelan, S. (2007). The impact of childcare cost on the full-time/part-time employment decisions of Australian mothers. *Australian Economic Papers, 46*, 152–169.

Reynolds, J., & Aletraris, L. (2007). Work–family conflict, children, and hour mismatches in Australia. *Journal of Family Issues, 28*, 749–772.

Risse, L. (2010). '. . . And one for the country'—The effect of the baby bonus on Australian women's fertility intentions. *Journal of Population Research, 27*, 213–240.

Russell, G., James, D., & Watson, J. (1988). Work/family policies, the changing role of fathers and the presumption of shared responsibility for parenting. *Australian Journal of Social Issues, 23*, 249–

Russell, G., & Bourke, J. (1999). Where does Australia fit in internationally with work and family issues? *Australian Bulletin of Labour, 25*, 229–250.

Russell, G., & Bowman, L. (2000). Work and family, current thinking, research and practice. Canberra ACT: Department of Family and Community Services. www.dss.gov.au/sites/default/files/documents/work_family.pdf

Sawer, M., Bittman, M., & Smith, J. (2013). Counting for nothing: Cancellation of time-use survey. Editorial. Canberra ACT: Gender Institution, Australian National University. http://genderinstitute.anu.edu.au/news/counting-nothing-cancellation-time-use-survey

Siahpush, M., Spittal, M., & Singh, G.K. (2008). Happiness and life satisfaction prospectively predict self-rated health, physical health and presence of limiting long-term health conditions. *American Journal of Health Promotion, 23*, 18–26.

Skinner, N., & Ichii, R. (2015). Exploring a family, work, and community model of work–family gains and strains. *Community, Work and Family, 18*, 79–99.

Skinner, N., & Pocock, B. (2011). Flexibility and work–life interference in Australia. *Journal of Industrial Relations, 53*, 65–82.

Skinner, N., & Pocock, B. (2014). *The Persistent Challenge: Living, Working and Caring in Australia in 2014.* The Australian work and life index. Adelaide, SA: Centre for Work and Life, University of South Australia.

Smyrnios, K.X., Romano, C.A., Tanewski, G.A., Karofsky, R., & Yilmaz, M.R. (2003). Work–family conflict: A study of American and Australian family businesses. *Family Business Review, 16*, 35–52.

Spector, P.E., Cooper, C.I., Poelmans, S., Allen, D., et al. (2004). A cross-national comparative study of work–family stressors, working hours, and well-being: China and Latin America versus the Anglo world. *Personnel Psychology, 57*, 119–142.

Spector, P. E., Allen, T. D., Poelmans, S. A. Y., Lapierre, L. M., Cooper, C. L., O'Driscoll, M . . . Widerszal-Bazyl, M. (2007). Cross-national differences in relationships of work demands, job satisfaction, and turnover intentions with work–family conflict. *Personnel Psychology, 60*(4), 805–835.

Statistics New Zealand. (2001). Gender and unpaid work: Findings from the time use survey. Wellington NZ: Statistics New Zealand. www.stats.govt.nz/browse_for_stats/people_ and_communities/time_use/gender-and-unpaid-work.aspx

Statistics New Zealand. (2013). Introducing new measures of underemployment. Wellington NZ: Statistics New Zealand. www.stats.govt.nz/browse_for_stats/income-and-work/employment_and_unemployment/introducing-new-measures-underemployment.aspx#title4

Statistics New Zealand. (2015). 2013 Census quickstats about work and unpaid activities. Wellington NZ: Statistics New Zealand. www.stats.govt.nz/Census/2013-census/pro file-and-summary-reports/quickstats-work-unpaid/work_and_labour_force_status.aspx

Statistics New Zealand. (2016). Labour Force Status by Sex by Age Group. Infoshare database. Wellington NZ: Statistics New Zealand. www.stats.govt.nz

Statistics New Zealand. (n.d.). Population Indicators: Downloadable Excel File, Wellington NZ: Statistics New Zealand. www.stats.govt.nz/browse_for_stats/population/esti mates_and_projections/pop-indicators.aspx

Thanacoody, P.R., Bartram, T., & Casimir, G. (2009). The effects of burnout and supervisory social support on the relationship between work–family conflict and intention to leave: A study of Australian cancer workers. *Journal of Health Organization and Management, 23*, 53–69.

Walker, M. C., Udy, K., Pole, N., May, S., Chamberlain, G. S., & Sturrock, F. M. (1997). *Adult Literacy in New Zealand: Results from the International Adult Literacy Survey.* Ministry of Education: Wellington, New Zealand.

Ware, J.E., Snow, K.K., Kosinski, M., & Gandek, B. (2000), *SF-36 Health Survey: Manual and Interpretation Guide.* Lincoln, RI: QualityMetric Inc.

Workplace Gender Equity Agency. (n.d.) About the Workplace Gender Equality Act. www .wgea.gov.au/about-wgea/our-role-0

Wooden, M., Freidin, S., & Watson, N. (2002). The household, income and labour dynamics in Australia (HILDA) survey: Wave 1. *Australian Economic Review, 35*, 339–348.

PART V

Cultures within Cultures

22 A Cultures within Culture Perspective on Work and Family among United States Employees

Lillian T. Eby, Olivia Vande Griek, Cynthia K. Maupin, Tammy D. Allen, Emily Gilreath, and Valerie Martinez

Scholarly interest in the intersection of work and family life continues to flourish. One recent advance is greater attention to how macro-level influences such as national and cultural factors shape the intersection of work and family life. For example, research has increasingly focused on examining how national policies relate to work–family experiences (see den Dulk & Peper, 2016) and comparing work–nonwork experiences based on country of residence (see Ollier-Malaterre, 2016). Considering macro-level influences such as national family leave policies and cultural dimensions of gender egalitarianism, individualism–collectivism, and power distance, complements and extends the field's longstanding interest in how individual, supervisory, and organizational factors affect individual work–family experiences.

Although the investigation of macro-level factors has added significantly to our understanding of the work–family interface, this approach has not considered the heterogeneity that may exist within a particular cultural context. For example, within the United States there are likely distinct sub-cultures that, if examined systematically, could further enhance our understanding of the work–family interface. In this chapter we introduce this notion of "cultures within culture" to the work–family literature and delineate how within-culture differences are likely to influence men and women's work–family experiences in the United States. As we outline in the sections that follow, taking a cultures within culture approach is particularly important in a country such as the United States, which is characterized by a massive landmass and a rich cultural history of diversity.

We open the chapter by providing an overview of ecological systems theory (Bronfenbrenner, 1977), which posits that individuals and families are strongly influenced by the various systems in which they are embedded, which exist at various levels of abstraction. This provides a theoretical point of departure for the argument that considering sub-cultures within a larger cultural system is important to advance work–family scholarship. Next, we discuss the tradition of examining regional differences in attitudes, behaviors, and values within the United States, as a way to ground our cultures within culture approach in the extant literature. Given our interest in work–family issues, we focus on multidisciplinary research that has identified systematic differences in

(1) gender-related attitudes and expectations, (2) beliefs about self-protection, violence, and loyalty, (3) religiosity, and (4) political ideology and voting patterns within various areas of the United States. We conclude by offering an agenda for future research using a cultures within culture approach, proposing new ways of thinking about the intersection of culture, work, and family to advance work–family scholarship.

Overview of Ecological Systems Theory

Bronfenbrenner's (1977) ecological systems theory proposes that human development is a dynamic and progressive process that is influenced by the multiple environments in which individuals are embedded. These systems are nested within one another and influence individuals in complex ways. *Microsystems* refer to the relationship between an individual and his or her immediate setting where particular roles are enacted (e.g., the employee role is enacted in the workplace; the parent role is enacted at home). Specific microsystems are thought to exert individual-level effects on human development and behavior. Due to the fact that individuals have multiple roles, the theory also recognizes the *mesosystem*, which represents a system of microsystems. The mesosystem captures the interrelations between an individual's primary microsystems. For example, for a working parent, the mesosystem may include interactions among the workplace, family, and friendship microsystems. These mesosystems are further embedded in an *exosystem*, which includes other formal and informal social structures that influence or place boundaries on what occurs within the various settings that an individual resides in. The exosystem includes major social institutions in society, such as the neighborhoods and communities in which individuals live, the world of work, informal social networks, government agencies, and the mass media. At the highest level of analysis, and encompassing all of the systems just discussed is the *macrosystem*. The macrosystem is unique in that it reflects the overall cultural or subcultural customs, practices, norms, and expectations that overlay these other systems. The macrosystem manifests both informally (e.g., social values) and formally (e.g., laws and regulation) and provides normative information that both influences and guides individual behavior.

Scholars have applied Bronfenbrenner's (1977) theory to the work–family interface. This includes an examination of work–family crossover effects between husbands and wives (e.g., Desrochers, Sargent, & Hostetler, 2012), work–family facilitation (e.g., Wayne, Grzywacz, Carlson, & Kacmar, 2007), and community-level factors as predictors of work–family outcomes (e.g., Voydanoff, 2005). Additionally, conceptual work by Voydanoff (2002) discusses how work–family mesosystems are likely influenced by the larger systems in which they are embedded. However, empirical research focusing on exosystem influences on work–family, such as cultural differences *within the United States* in values, attitudes, behaviors, or other social phenomena, is notably absent.

Existing Research on Cultures within Culture in the United States

Although the work–family literature is silent with regard to cultural differences *within* the United States, there is a longstanding history of dividing the United States into distinct regions. These geographic areas are characterized by unique features, reflected in common characteristics of individuals who reside in them. The premise anchoring this line of research is that individual-level behaviors and attitudes eventually become expressed as higher-level social, political, economic, and health indicators (Rentfrow et al., 2013).

In political geography, research has focused on historical migration patterns and the consequent effects on political subcultures (Elazar, 1994) as well as how ethnic diversity relates to regional political values (Heppen, 2003). Geographic sociological research has examined regional differences in the pervasiveness of social capital (i.e., the extent to which Americans are connected to their families, neighbors, and communities), finding that people in the West, North Central, and Mountain states report higher levels of social capital than those living in the Mid-Atlantic and Southeast states, presumably due to differences in religiosity, ethnic diversity, and exposure to mass media (Putnam, 2000). Spatial epidemiologists have found regional differences in disease prevalence and mortality. This includes documented differences in stroke mortality in the United States, with higher rates in the South and lower rates in the Northeast and Mountain census regions of the West (Lanska, 1993). These differences presumably relate to socioeconomic, demographic, and lifestyle differences (e.g., social norms for health and nutrition) in different areas of the United States (Glymour, Avendano, & Berkman, 2007).

Of particular relevance to the study of work and family is the well-developed body of scholarship on regional differences in gender role attitudes (e.g., Powers et al., 2003; Twenge, 1997), beliefs about self-protection, violence, and loyalty (e.g., Cohen & Nisbett, 1994; Vandello, Cohen, Grandon, & Franiuk, 2009), religiosity (e.g., Furman, Benson, & Canda, 2004, 2011), and political ideologies and voting patterns (e.g., Lieske, 2010). Although researchers use somewhat different regional conceptualizations, findings consistently demonstrate more traditional attitudes and conservative ideologies in the Southern regions of the United States.

A Cultures within Culture Approach to Work–Family Scholarship

Research examining differences in attitudes, behaviors, and values within different areas of the United States has focused almost exclusively on examining regional differences. There are several distinct streams of research examining regional differences, yet they share a common emphasis on ideals for family life and/or societal expectations for women and/or men. It is these literatures that we review next. Before doing so, it is important to acknowledge that this literature is restricted in scope to a focus on geographically based regional differences. Nonetheless, it provides a useful starting point for thinking about how within-country differences in attitudes, behaviors, and values may relate to work and family, and how taking a cultures within culture approach captures a potentially important source of variability that has been largely ignored in industrial-organizational and organizational behavior work–family research. Although existing empirical research on regional differences provide an important starting point in thinking about cultures within culture, we will extend this thinking beyond regional differences in the future research section to consider other characteristic features such as urbanization, more discrete voting patterns within states, and community differences in access to high-quality childcare in an attempt to broaden our thinking about cultures within culture.

Regional differences in gender-related attitudes and expectations. Differences persist in the traits ascribed to men and women. Specifically, women continue to be perceived by others as more communal relative to men (i.e., warm, caring, sensitive) whereas men are perceived as more agentic relative to women (i.e., assertive, competitive, forceful) (Abele, 2003; Brosi, Spörrle, Welpe, & Heilman, 2016). Social role theory (Eagly & Steffen, 1984) posits that social perceivers derive their expectations of gender roles based on their experiences with individuals in "typical" social roles (i.e., where a specific gender is overrepresented compared to the rest of the population). Because women have been traditionally overrepresented in lower-status, communal roles such as nursing and childcare, and men have been overrepresented in higher-status, agentic roles such as management and politics, societal expectations and stereotypes have emerged in which women are expected to be more caring and nurturing and men more assertive and dominant. Even as women have become increasingly represented in non-traditional, agentic roles, research has demonstrated the persistence of gender-based expectations (Brosi et al., 2016).

Attitudes toward women and gender role expectations are closely intertwined with family, employment, and women's participation in social structures, such as political and religious institutions (Powers et al., 2003; Twenge, 1997). Social role theory and the emergence of stereotypes for people in their "typical roles" has led to the stereotype of the male breadwinner and the female homemaker (Eagly, Wood & Dieckman, 2000), reflecting differences in expectations regarding men and women's dedication to work and family. Moreover, there is some evidence that female college students still expect their future work and family lives to adhere to these gender expectations, anticipating that they will spend more time doing housework and caring for children than men, and earn lower salaries than their husbands (Fetterolf & Eagly, 2011). There is also evidence that, although men and women value work–life balance equally, men are less inclined to seek out flexibility to be with their children than women, partially due to gendered expectations regarding femininity and masculinity (Vandello, Hettinger, Bosson & Siddiqi, 2013).

Although gender role attitudes have become more egalitarian over time, numerous studies document that both men and women in the Southern United States (which includes states such as Alabama, Georgia, Louisiana, and South Carolina) hold more conservative beliefs about women's roles relative to people in other regions. For example, although the gap has reduced over time, longitudinal data from the General Social Science Survey indicates that Southerners still tend to have less favorable views about women in politics than non-Southerners (Campbell & Marsden, 2012). Moreover, Twenge's (1997) meta-analysis of changes in attitudes toward women found that for a twenty-five-year period (1979–1995), Southern men's attitudes toward women lagged behind other regions in the United States by five to ten years. Powers and colleagues (2003) likewise found more egalitarian gender role attitudes among both men and women in the non-South when compared to the South, although the differences were not large. There is also some evidence that gender role expectations are more clearly prescribed and culturally mandated for Southern women than for Southern men. As an illustration, Suitor and Carter (1999) found regional differences in college students' view of adolescent gender norms. Consistent with more conservative and traditional gender roles, students viewed adolescent girls in the South as more likely to report gaining prestige by having a good reputation/virginity than adolescent girls in the North. By contrast, college students perceived adolescent girls in the North to gain prestige with behaviors that countered traditional gender stereotypes, such as using drugs and alcohol and sexual activity. The ways that adolescent boys are perceived to gain status (e.g., sports, grades) did not vary by region.

Regional differences in beliefs about self-protection, violence, and loyalty. A more specific aspect of gender role attitudes and expectations involves normative prescriptions about violence, self-protection, and honor, which is referred to by Cohen and Nisbett (1994) as a "culture of honor" (p. 552). They argue that a strong culture of honor develops in social systems where law enforcement is absent and/or inadequate, and because of this, it is necessary for the preservation of oneself, one's family, and one's home. Building on this work, Vandello et al. (2009) argue that a culture of honor is tied to notions of *both* femininity and masculinity. In regions with a strong culture of honor, femininity is associated with loyalty, sacrifice, and altruism. These beliefs pervade romantic relationships and influence attitudes about male violence against women. By contrast, toughness and the belief in justifiable violence are key features of masculinity in cultures of honor (Cohen & Vandello, 2001). This manifests in men's need to control women and in their reactions to betrayal. In support of this idea, Vandello and colleagues (2009) found that men from a strong culture of honor were more likely to endorse a woman staying in an abusive relationship and a man's use of violence against a woman in situations involving infidelity compared to those not residing in a strong culture of honor.

Of particular interest to the present chapter is the finding that the culture of honor phenomenon is associated with the American South.[1] For example, Cohen and Nisbett (1994) found that white Southern males in particular hold much more favorable attitudes about the use of violence for self-protection, in response to insult, and for socializing children than do non-Southerners. Southern white men are also more likely to respond aggressively, have greater physiological stress responses, and

---

[1] Some studies also find evidence of a stronger culture of honor in the American West (see Cohen, 1998) and also among Latinos (Vandello et al., 2009).

are more likely to perceive a threat to their masculine reputation in response to an unprovoked insult (e.g., being called an "asshole" by a stranger) compared to Northern white men (Cohen, Nisbett, Bowdle, & Schwarz, 1996). Interestingly, Southern males are also more likely to believe that their peers endorse aggressive norms and to perceive that others encourage aggression when witnessing interpersonal conflicts (Vandello, Cohen, & Ransom, 2008). Collectively, this suggests that strong normative beliefs may help perpetuate a culture of honor in the South. In line with the notion of regional differences in culture of honor, 2010 data from the American Bar Association ("What are the State Laws that Mandate Arrest for DV Assault?," 2011) identifies 21 states that mandate arrest for domestic violence assault (Alaska, Arizona, Colorado, Connecticut, District of Columbia, Iowa, Kansas, Louisiana, Maine, Mississippi, Nevada, New Jersey, New York, Ohio, Oregon, Rhode Island, South Carolina, South Dakota, Utah, Virginia, Washington). Notably, only four of these states are those that are typically characterized as "Southern" (Louisiana, Mississippi, South Carolina, Virginia).

Regional differences in religiosity. Conservative religious beliefs can exert powerful influences on attitudes and behaviors regarding divorce, gender equality, and sexual activity (Adamczyk, 2013), among other issues. In the United States, Christian fundamentalism (also referred to as evangelicalism) exemplifies religious conservatism and is associated with patriarchy, female submissiveness, and traditional gender roles in the family (Bendroth, 1999; Hall, Anderson, & Willingham, 2004; Korb, 2010; Scanzoni, 1983). Conservative Christian subcultures also strongly encourage mothers to stay at home (Hall et al., 2004) and espouse the sacredness of life, which influences views on abortion and divorce (D'Antonio, 1983). The more literal interpretation of the Bible, which is associated with Christian fundamentalism, further reinforces traditional ideals about women. This includes passages in the Bible that discuss women's lesser status than men and the importance of obedience to one's husband (e.g., see Ephesians 5:22–23), as well as the role of motherhood as a central feature of women's religious identity (e.g., 1 Timothy 2:11-15a) (Brinkerhoff & MacKie, 1988).

There is also considerable research on the association between various aspects of religiosity and attitudes related to the work–family interface. Both religious behaviors (e.g., attending church) and religious attitudes (e.g., self-report religious beliefs, fundamentalism) are positively associated with more traditional gender role attitudes (Brinkerhoff & MacKie, 1988). Religious conservatism is also related to greater religious ethnocentrism (i.e., beliefs in the superiority of one's own religion; Altemeyer, 2003), opposition to women's right to abortion (Hoffman & Johnson, 2005), discriminatory attitudes toward others (e.g., blacks, women, homosexuals; Kirkpatrick, 1993), and the number of hours women spend on housework (Ellison & Bartowski, 2002). There is also some evidence that more conservative Christian women have children earlier in life, have more children, earn less income, place greater emphasis on the importance of mothering versus working, and attain lower levels of education than women raised in mainline churches (Gonsoulin, 2010). Finally, Colander and Giles (2008) found that Evangelical women are more likely to view work and motherhood as separate roles that should not be entered into simultaneously.

Regional differences in religiosity, and in particular Christian fundamentalism, are well documented. The American Bible Society's 2016 survey of Bible reading practices reports that the top five Bible-minded cities, an index that reflects Bible reading practices and beliefs about the accuracy of the Bible, in the United States are Chattanooga, Birmingham, Roanoke/Lynchburg, Shreveport, and the Tri-Cities in Tennessee (Kingsport, Bristol, Johnson City), all of which are in the South ("America's Most Bible-Minded Cities," 2016). Consistent with this survey, a 2011 Gallup poll (Newport, 2012) found that nine of the ten "most religious" states were in the South (e.g., Mississippi, Alabama, Georgia). The one exception was Utah, which ranked second in "most religious" due to the large concentration of Mormons. However, interestingly for Utah in particular, is the fact that this state has the largest percentage of non-religious Americans (28%) among these top ten states, indicating a rather polarized population regarding religion. It is also notable that none of the "least religious" states were in the South (e.g., Vermont, Maine, Alaska). The South also leads other regions in terms of both the percentage of Americans who have had a "born again" experience and church attendance (Dillon & Savage, 2006).

Regional differences in religiosity permeate many facets of life. For example, social workers in the South and Midwest were more likely to openly endorse the use of religion and spirituality in their work with clients (Furman et al., 2004). Individuals in the South also tend to have more discriminatory attitudes toward homosexuality (Herek, 2002; Sullivan, 2003), and native Southerners tend to be less willing to extend civil liberties to groups that hold beliefs that run counter to fundamentalist Christianity, such as atheists and homosexuals (Ellison & Musick, 1993). Likewise, corporal punishment of children is more strongly endorsed in the South compared to other regions of the United States (Flynn, 1994). This has been attributed to more literal interpretation of the Bible by those residing in the Bible Belt, a region that includes much of the American South, where fundamentalism is widely practiced.

Regional differences in political ideology and voting patterns. In the United States, the political structure is typically described as a two-party system, with the Republican Party espousing more conservative views on issues such as the importance of military strength, social welfare, LGBT issues, and government regulation, than the Democratic Party (Pew Research Center, 2014). In fact, sociological scholars argue that right-wing politically conservative think tanks have had a substantial impact on cultural values regarding sexual abstinence and virginity, as part of a larger social agenda to protect the sanctity of the American family (Deerman, 2012; Rose, 2005).

In terms of regional differences in political ideology, voting patterns indicate that the Southern states (with the exception of North Carolina and Florida) as well as some regions of the Midwest and Mountain states, in recent past history (i.e., past two decades) tend to vote Republican. By contrast the Western states have historically endorsed the Democratic Party in this same time period ("Election Polls—

Presidential Vote by Groups," 2016). As noted previously, individuals in Southern states also tend to hold the most conservative political attitudes on a wide range of topics of potential relevance to work–family (e.g., divorce law, abortion; Weakliem & Biggert, 1999). It has also been noted that by the late twentieth century, Southerners shared a conservative political agenda distinct from other regions of the United States (Markusen, 1989).

A discussion of political ideology must recognize its complex interplay with religious beliefs. The Pew Research Center's report on political preferences among religious groups in the United States found that Evangelical religions (e.g., Church of the Nazarene, Southern Baptist Convention) strongly lean toward or identify with the Republican Party whereas Jewish, Unitarian, and several historically black religious groups (e.g., African Methodist Episcopal Church, National Baptist Convention) endorse or lean toward the Democratic Party (Lipka, 2016). Some conservative religious leaders have also made strong public alliances with the Republican Party. A striking example of this is the Moral Majority, a prominent American political organization founded in 1970 by Baptist Minister, Jerry Falwell and associates, which openly supported Ronald Reagan's election in 1980 and mobilized millions of voters (Bendroth, 1999). A major platform of the Republican Party at this time was a focus on "family values" – efforts to protect the moral future of the American family by promoting traditional gender role norms, pro-life values, and a strong focus on traditional two-parent heterosexual households (Alphonso, 2016; Bendroth, 1999).

Another illustration of how politics and religion are closely intertwined is the National Right to Life movement ("National Right to Life," 2016), which is deeply rooted in Christian fundamentalist beliefs and endorsed by the Republican Party (Castle, 2011). In fact, the 2016 Republican Party Platform ("The 2016 Republican Party Platform," 2016) explicitly "opposes the use of public funds to perform or promote abortion or to fund organizations, like Planned Parenthood . . . (and) . . . will not fund or subsidize healthcare that includes abortion coverage" (p. 13). The platform goes on to note that they will support the appointment of judges that respect "traditional family values" (p. 13) and support states' rights to exclude abortion providers from Medicaid and other federal healthcare programs. In fact, recently enacted federal and state laws and policies aimed at restricting women's access to abortions have been put forward by conservative state legislators. Many of the states with the most restrictive provisions are in the South (i.e., Mississippi, South Carolina, West Virginia, Kentucky; Castle, 2011).

In addition to political ideology and voting patterns, conservative political beliefs relate in predictable ways to traditional gender roles and traditional family structures. Women scoring higher on measures of right-wing authoritarianism, which is strongly associated with conservative political beliefs and traditional gender roles (McAdams et al., 2008; Rubinstein, 1995), prefer more masculine and conventional partners. These women are also less likely to have an advanced degree, more likely to be married only once, more likely to have children, and are more likely to be under-employed than their less conservative counterparts (Duncan, Peterson, & Ax, 2003). There is also evidence that political views relate to family ideals and moral beliefs. In a two-part study, McAdams and colleagues (2008) found that political conservatives more often described their family ideals in terms of rules-reinforcement (i.e., the importance of authority, such as parents, government, church, God) and self-discipline (i.e., the ability to control one's emotions and urges to lead a more disciplined life) when compared to liberals. In the second study, they examined political conservatism and moral beliefs, finding that conservatives emphasized respect for authority, loyalty to family and country, and working hard to stay pure and good. By contrast, liberals emphasized commitment to reducing the suffering of others, as well as concerns for fairness, justice, and equality.

In summary, considerable research from psychology, sociology, political science, women's studies, and religion point to the importance of taking a cultures within culture approach to better understand the work–family experience of workers in the United States. When considered collectively, this research illustrates considerable within-country diversity on phenomena of high relevance to work and family and provides a foundation for other ways to think about systematic differences in attitudes, behaviors, and values within the United States.

An Agenda for Future Research

Given the dearth of work–family research taking a cultures within culture approach, there are many avenues for future research. We first discuss conceptual issues regarding how we might operationalize different cultural characteristics of the United States. This includes a discussion of the strategies used in the research described above, as well as a consideration of alternative operationalizations that may have utility for both widening and sharpening the lens by which we examine cultures within culture. Following this discussion, we outline three broad substantive topics to guide future research on the topic.

Existing and alternative approaches to study cultures within culture. A consideration of cultures within culture requires a categorization system that identifies discrete and relatively homogeneous within-country groupings of some sort. The traditional approach has been to classify states into various regions for comparison, although the theoretical and conceptual rationale for particular groupings is often given short shrift. Most frequently the South is compared to other regions of the United States. This might consist of South versus North comparisons (e.g., Vandello et al., 2008), Deep South (e.g., Alabama, Georgia, Louisiana), Border South (e.g., Kentucky, Oklahoma, Tennessee) and Non-South (e.g., Michigan, Arizona, New York) comparisons (e.g., Cohen & Nisbett, 1994), or comparisons between the South and the Non-South (e.g., Twenge, 1997). In other studies, United States Census classifications of states into regions (e.g., South, Midwest, West, Northeast; Cohen, 1996) were used for comparison.

Although this manner of examining cultural differences within the United States likely has utility for some work–family research questions, we encourage researchers to consider alternative approaches as well. One strategy is to create within-country groupings based on family-friendly legislation that expands upon federal laws (e.g., Pregnancy Discrimination Act of 1978, Family Medical Leave Act of 1993, breastfeeding provisions in the 2010 health reform law). For example, according to the National Partnership for Women and Families (2016a), thirty-five states have implemented (or are in the process of passing) at least one piece of family-friendly legislation expanding upon the current federal policies. For example, California, Rhode Island, Washington, New Jersey, and New York have each passed their own paid parental leave policies, with New York proposing the most generous policy to date of up to twelve weeks of paid parental leave for men and women (National Partnership for Women and Families, 2016b); notably, none of these are Southern states. Additionally, many states have passed domestic violence leave statutes (e.g., Oregon's safe leave act), expanded rights for nursing mothers (e.g., time and place to pump statutes), provided additional accommodations for pregnant workers (e.g., reasonable accommodations for pregnant workers statutes), and implemented requirements for employers to provide paid sick days (e.g., paid sick days statutes). As such, legislative differences in various areas of the United States may provide a unique vantage point by which to explore cultures within culture differences in work–family experiences without relying solely on geographic proximity to classify regions of the United States.

Another strategy is to create a cultures within culture metric that captures the number of women in key political positions (e.g., mayor, governor, House of Representatives, state senate), with the argument being that this in part reflects prevailing attitudes and normative expectations for women. Another approach would be to index the proportion of women business owners or CEOs in a community, zip code region, or state. Other family-related categorization systems to identify cultures within culture might involve examining divorce rates, ease of filing for divorce, and processing time for divorces to be finalized (The Huffington Post, September 5, 2013) or "baby friendliness," an index that considers parental leave policies, number of per capita mom groups, number of per capita childcare centers, and the percentage of nationally accredited childcare centers (Bernardo, 2016). The examination of community, state, and regional voting patterns, as well as church membership, may also be used to capture cultures within culture. Such measures may be used to reflect social norms and attitudes that have bearing on individuals' choices regarding work and family, as well as others' expectations for the integration of work and family roles. Finally, creating a classification system based on urbanization (e.g., comparisons of urban, suburban, and rural areas) may provide a unique vantage point to explore how cultures within culture relates to the work–family interface, given some evidence of nuanced differences in attitudes toward same-sex relationships, abortion, and religiosity as a function of the rurality (Dillon & Savage, 2006). Likewise, comparing areas of the United States based on the level of poverty ("Poverty USA Full Screen County Map," 2016) may shed light on a wide range of work–family experiences due to the constraints that poverty places on access to healthcare, childcare, education, and employment.

An agenda for future research. In this section we focus on three areas that we believe could benefit from a cultures within culture focus. This includes (1) individual perceptions of work–family experiences, (2) work and family decision-making, and (3) work–family experiences among individuals in non-traditional marriages and families. We recognize that there are many other areas of work–family inquiry that could also benefit from this approach. As such, the ideas presented below are selective and should be viewed as a starting point for work–family scholars, rather than an exhaustive list of research priorities.

One area that holds promise is an examination of *individual perceptions of work– family experiences*. An important starting point seems to be the investigation of systematic differences in the average reported level of work–family conflict for working women and men as a function of various features of one's place of residence in the United States. It may be that work–family conflict tends to be lower for both genders in areas with more family-friendly legislation, whereas women in particular may report more work–family conflict in areas of the country characterized by more traditional gender-related attitudes or religiosity. It would also be interesting to examine differences in the direction (work-to-family versus family-to-work) and/ or type (time-based, strain-based, behavior-based) of conflict using a cultures within culture approach (e.g., comparing areas in the United States based on the percentage of women in elected political positions or divorce rate), and again, exploring what role gender may play here. For example, in areas marked by more egalitarian gender role attitudes, working women may experience lower work-to-family and family-to-work conflict because social expectations for the caregiving role are more relaxed and there is greater acceptance of women working outside the home. By contrast, for women living in areas where gender role attitudes are more traditional, working women (but not men) may be in a double-bind such that both directions of work– family conflict are higher (due to stronger pressure for women to fulfill family obligations, which exacerbates both types of conflict). Somewhat consistent with this idea, a recent study by Clair and colleagues found that working moms (but not women without children or men) who lived in zip codes characterized by a greater proportion of women working outside the home (which may signal greater acceptance of working mothers) reported less negative work–life spillover (Clair, King, Anderson, Jones, & Hebl, 2015).

In terms of the type of work–family conflict, we may find that time-based conflict is higher in areas of the country with longer commute times ("WNYC Average Commute Times," 2013) or more "fast-paced" lifestyles, such as large metropolitan areas. By contrast, strain-based conflict may be greater in cultural niches characterized by greater environmental stressors (e.g., noise, population density), based on research linking allostatic load to the neighborhood characteristics of poverty, even after controlling for household poverty, self-reported neighborhood environment stress, stressful acute life events, and alcohol use (Schutz et al., 2012). The notion of "riskscapes" (Morello-Frosh & Shenassa, 2006, p. 1150) – characteristics of the social and physical environmental that contribute to poor health outcomes – may also be useful in framing a discussion of how community or regional differences in factors such as land use/zoning, housing quality, poverty, access to services, and neighborhood quality relate to the experience of strain-based work–family conflict in particular.

Another area where an examination of systematic within-United States differences may be informative involves *work and family decision-making*. For example, in areas of the country with more polarized views on appropriate behavior for men and women, we might expect differences in the division of paid and household labor among partnered men and women, which has been linked to a wide range of work–family outcomes (for a review, see Shockley & Shen, 2016). Although we are not aware of any research examining such differences within regions of the United States, this premise is consistent with socialization and gender role attitude theories which posit that early childhood experiences affect the way that women (and men) perceive themselves and form beliefs about what is expected of them by others (Shockley & Shen, 2016). Moreover, previous research examining the macro-level effects of nation-level factors (e.g., country of origin) on gender differences in both paid work hours and hours spent in childcare (Craig & Mullan, 2010) suggests that a cultures within culture focus may yield unique insight into work–family outcomes among American workers. It may also be that characteristic features of different areas of the United States are associated with different expectations for family life and anticipated work–family conflict, which in turn may influence decisions about both work and parenthood, particularly among young women.

Areas of the United States also differ in various aspects of childcare (Schute & Durana, 2016), family-friendly legislation (National Partnership, 2016a), and residential mobility (United States Census Bureau, 2012), all of which may affect decisions related to caregiving as well as where to work and live. With regard to caregiving, differences in cost, quality, and availability of childcare (Schute & Durana, 2016) undoubtedly affects parents' decision-making regarding care for their children. It is also likely that due to greater population density, more urban areas have greater formal childcare options, enhancing availability and perhaps quality as well, due to greater competition. However, informal care from family members, neighbors, and friends may be more common in less urbanized areas, regardless of regional or state differences in legislation, due to tighter-knit communities and strong kinship ties in more rural areas (Beggs, Haines, & Hulbert, 1996). We also know that there are differences in the "family friendliness" of various states, based on the presence or absence of family-friendly legislation. This may affect decision-making about where to live and work. It may also influence decisions regarding whether one or both parents take parental leave as well as the length of leave taken.

A final area that may benefit from a cultures within culture approach involves the study of *work–family experiences among individuals in non-traditional marriages and families*. Although there is evidence of increasing social acceptance of sexual minorities, there is considerable variability within the United States on a variety of indicators of social tolerance, such as the incidents of hate crimes ("Hate Crimes by State," 2016) and social acceptance of same-sex marriages. Prior to the 2015 landmark United States Supreme Court ruling allowing same-sex couples to marry, only 37 states and the District of Columbia had legalized gay marriage ("State Same-Sex Marriage State Laws Map," 2015). This may provide a unique vantage point to examine within the United States differences in the work–family experiences of sexual minorities. This might include examining the amount of work–family conflict experienced by LGBT employees and differences in actual and perceived organizational support for work–family among employees as a function of hate crimes committed in the area or the number of LGBT residents in one's community. A comparison of the family-friendly benefits available to LGBT employees as a function of where individuals live and work is also important, both in terms of cataloging the availability and use of particular benefits, and relating variation in benefits across communities, states, and regions to work–family outcomes.

Other non-traditional family structures may also be important to examine using a cultures within culture approach. This might involve examining regional or urban–rural differences in the effects of single parenthood, pregnancy, divorce status, and stay-at-home fatherhood on women's job and career experiences. A related line of research might focus on the acceptance of men's decisions to take paternal leave and stay at home to care for children, and the downstream effects of these decisions when men re-enter the workforce. We know that career interruptions are negatively related to pay for both genders (e.g., Evers & Sieverding, 2014), but we know nothing about how regional differences may attenuate or exacerbate such effects. Finally, there may be characteristic differences in extended family support systems across areas of the United States that are important to consider. For example, due to less geographic mobility in some areas of the country and stronger family ties, intergenerational caregiving may vary by region or urbanity. Although some research has documented the negative effects of eldercare responsibilities on employees (e.g., Barrah, Schultz, Baltes, & Stolz, 2004), in intergenerational families there may be care *benefits* as well. Although largely unexplored in industrial-organizational psychology and organizational behavior, grandparents may provide an important source of childcare support, as well as emotional support, to working parents.

In conclusion, we draw on ecological systems theory (Bronfenbrenner, 1977) to advocate for a cultures within culture approach when studying the intersection between work and family in the United States. Individuals are embedded in larger social systems, and these systems have the potential to impact how individuals experience and perceive work–family phenomena. We provide compelling evidence from complementary literatures that suggest systematic differences within the United States may affect how men and women perceive their roles and others' roles in society, which in turn may carry over to their expectations for both work and family, as well as their behaviors in each role. Extending research paradigms to include a cultures within culture perspective has the potential to provide novel insights and propel work–family scholarship in new and exciting directions.

References

Abele, A. E. (2003). The dynamics of masculine-agentic and feminine-communal traits: Findings from a prospective study. *Journal of Personality and Social Psychology*, *85*, 768–776. doi: 10.1037/0022–3514.85.4.768

Adamczyk, A. (2013). The effect of personal religiosity on attitudes toward abortion, divorce, and gender equality—does cultural context make a difference? *EurAmerica*, *43*, 213–253. Retrieved from www.ea.sinica.edu.tw/eu_file/13663433284.pdf

Alphonso, G. M. (2016). Resurgent Parenthood: Organic Domestic Ideals and the Southern Family Roots of Conservative Ascendancy, 1980–2005. Polity, 48(2), 205–223.

Altemeyer, B. (2003). Why do religious fundamentalists tend to be prejudiced? *The International Journal for the Psychology of Religion*, *13*, 17–28. doi: 10.1207/s15327582ijpr1301_03

America's most Bible-minded cities (2016, January 26). Retrieved from www.americanbible.org/features/americas-most-bible-minded-cities

Barrah, J. L., Schultz, K. S., Baltes, B., & Stolz, H. E. (2004). Men's and women's eldercare-based work–family conflict: Antecedents and work-related outcomes. *Fathering: A Journal of Theory, Research and Practice about Men as Fathers*, *2*, 305–330. doi: 10.3149/fth.0203.305

Beggs, J. J., Haines, V. A., & Hulbert, J. S. (1996). Revisiting the rural-urban contrast: Personal networks in nonmetropolitan and metropolitan settings. *Rural Sociology*, *61*, 306–325. doi: 10.1111/j.1549–0831.1996.tb00622.x

Bendroth, M. L. (1999). Fundamentalism and the family: Gender, culture, and the American pro-family movement. *Journal of Women's History*, *10*, 35–54. doi: 10.1353/jowh.2010.0537

Bernardo, R. (August 8, 2016). 2016's best & worst states to have a baby. Retrieved from www.babycenter.com/0_surprising-facts-about-birth-in-the-united-states_1372273.bc

Brinkerhoff, M. B., & MacKie, M. (1988). Religious sources of gender traditionalism. In D. L. Thomas (Ed.), *The Religion and Family Connection: Social Science Perspectives* (pp. 232–237). Provo, UT: Religious Studies Center, Brigham Young University. doi: 10.2307/3711579

Bronfenbrenner, U. (1977). Toward an experimental ecology of human development. *American Psychologist*, *32*, 513–531. doi: 10.1037//0003-066x.32.7.513

Brosi, P., Spörrle, M., Welpe, I. M., & Heilman, M. E. (2016). Expressing pride: Effects on perceived agency, communality, and stereotype-based gender disparities. *Journal of Applied Psychology*, *101*, 1319–1328. doi: 10.1037/apl0000122

Campbell, K. E., & Marsden, P. V. (2012). Gender role attitudes since 1972: Are Southerners distinctive? In P. V. Marsden (Ed.), *Social Trends in American Life: Findings from the General Social Survey Since 1972* (pp. 84–116). Princeton University Press: Princeton, NJ.

Castle, M. A. (2011). Abortion in the United States' Bible Belt: Organizing for power and empowerment. *Reproductive Health*, *8*, 1–11. doi: 10.1186/1742–4755-8–1

Clair, J., King. E. B., Anderson, A. J., Jones, K. P., & Hebl, M. (2015, April). 90210 revisited: Where you live matters in shaping work–life conflict. Paper presented at the annual meeting of the Society for Industrial and Organizational Psychology, Philadelphia, PA.

Cohen, D., & Nisbett, R. E. (1994). Self-protection and the culture of honor: Explaining Southern violence. *Personality and Social Psychology Bulletin*, *20*, 551–567. doi: 10.1177/0146167294205012

Cohen, D., Nisbett, R. E., Bowdle, B. F., & Schwarz, N. (1996). Insult, aggression, and the Southern culture of honor: An "experimental ethnography." *Journal of Personality and Social Psychology*, *70*, 945–960. doi: 10.1037//0022–3514.70.5.945

Cohen, D. (1996). Law, social policy, and violence: The impact of regional culture. *Journal of Personality and Social Psychology, 70*, 961–978. doi: 10.1037//0022–3514.70.5.961

Cohen, D. (1998). Culture, social organization, and patterns of violence. *Journal of Personality and Social Psychology, 75*, 408–419. doi: 10.1037//0022–3514.75.2.408

Cohen, D., & Vandello, J. A. (2001). Honor and "faking" honorability. In R. Nesse (Ed.), *Evolution and the Capacity for Commitment* (pp. 163–185). New York, NY: Russell Sage. doi: 10.1086/374522

Colander, C., & Giles, S. (2008). The baby blanket or the briefcase: The impact of evangelical gender role ideologies on career and mother aspirations of female evangelical college students. *Sex Roles, 58*, 526–534. doi: 10.1007/s11199-007-9352-8

Craig, L. & Mullan, K. (2010). Parenthood, gender and work–family time in the United States, Australia, Italy, France, and Denmark. *Journal of Marriage and the Family, 72*, 1344–1361. doi: 10.1111/j.1741–3737.2010.00769.x

D'Antonio, W. V. (1983). Family life, religion and societal values and structures. In W. V. D'Antonio & J. Aldous (Eds.), *Families and Religions: Conflict and Change in Modern Society.* Beverly Hills, CA: Sage. doi: 10.2307/3710907

Deerman, M. E. (2012). Transporting movement ideology into popular culture: Right-wing think tanks and the case of "virgin chic." *Sociological Spectrum, 32*, 95–113. doi: 10.1080/02732173.2012.646151

den Dulk, L., & Peper, B. (2016). The impact of national policy on work–family experiences. In T. D. Allen & L. T. Eby (Eds.), *The Oxford Handbook of Work and Family* (pp. 300–314). New York, NY: Oxford University Press. doi: 10.1093/oxfordhb/9780199337538.013.17

Desrochers, S., Sargent, L. D., & Hostetler, A. J. (2012). Boundary-spanning demands, personal mastery, and family satisfaction: Individual and crossover effects among dual-earner parents. *Marriage & Family Review, 48*, 443–464. doi: 10.1080/01494929.2012.677377

Dillon, M., & Savage, S. (2006, Fall). Values and religion in rural America: Attitudes toward abortion and same-sex relations. Carsey Institute Issue Brief No. 1. University of New Hampshire. Retrieved from http://scholars.unh.edu/carsey/12

Duncan, L. E., Peterson, B. E., & Ax, E. E. (2003). Authoritarianism as an agent of status quo maintenance: Implications for women's careers and family lives. *Sex Roles, 49*, 619–630. doi: 10.1023/b:sers.0000003132.74897.f3

Eagly, A. H., & Steffen, V. J. (1984). Gender stereotypes stem from the distribution of women and men into social roles. *Journal of Personality and Social Psychology, 46*, 735–754. doi: 10.1037//0022–3514.46.4.735

Eagly, A. H., Wood, W., & Dieckman, A. B. (2000). Social role theory of sex differences and similarities: A current appraisal. In T. Eckes (Ed.), *The Developmental Social Psychology of Gender*, (pp. 123–174). Mahwah, NJ: Lawrence Erlbaum. doi: 10.4324/9781410605245

Elazar, D. J. (1994). *The American Mosaic: The Impact of Space, Time, and Culture on American Politics.* Boulder, CO: Westview Press. doi: 10.1016/s0962-6298(97)86505–5

Election polls—Presidential vote by groups (2016, October 31). Retrieved from www.gallup.com/poll/139880/election-polls-presidential-vote-groups.aspx

Ellison, C. G., & Bartowski, J. P. (2002). Conservative Protestantism and the division of household labor among married couples. *Journal of Family Issues, 23*, 950–985. doi: 10.1177/019251302237299

Ellison, C. G., & Musick, M. A. (1993). Southern intolerance: A fundamentalist effect? *Social Forces*, *72*, 379–398. doi: 10.2307/2579853

Evers, A., & Sieverding, M. (2014). Why do highly qualified women (still) earn less? Gender differences in long-term predictors of career success. *Psychology of Women Quarterly*, *38*, 93–106. doi: 10.1177/0361684313498071

Fetterolf, J. C., & Eagly, A. H. (2011). Do young women expect gender equality in their future lives? An answer from a possible selves experiment. *Sex Roles*, *65*, 83–93. doi:10.1007/s11199-011-9981-9

Flynn, C. P. (1994). Regional differences in attitudes toward corporal punishment. *Journal of Marriage and the Family*, *56*, 314–324. doi: 10.2307/353102

Furman, L. D., Benson, P. W., & Canda, E. R. (2004). Religion, spirituality, and geographic region in the USA: An examination of regional similarities and differences among social workers in direct practice. *Social Work & Christianity*, *31*, 267–294.

Furman, L. D., Benson, P. W., & Canda, E. R. (2011). Christian social workers' attitudes on the role of religion and spirituality in U.S. social work practice and education: 1997–2008. *Social Work & Christianity*, *38*, 175–200.

Glymour, M. M., Avendano, M., & Berkman. L. F. (2007). Is the "stroke belt" worn from childhood? Risk of first stroke and state of residence in childhood and adulthood. *Stroke*, *38*, 2415–2421. doi: 10.1037/1040-3590.4.1.26

Gonsoulin, M. E. (2010). Gender ideology and status attainment of conservative Christian women in the 21st century. *Sociological Spectrum*, *30*, 220–240. doi: 10.1080/02732170903496141

Hall, M. E., Anderson, T. L., & Willingham, M. M. (2004). Diapers, dissertations, and other holy things: The experiences of mothers working in Christian colleges and universities. *Christian Higher Education*, *3*, 41–60. doi: 10.1080/15363760490264889

Hate crimes by state (2016, November 3). Retrieved from http://hate-crime-state.findthedata.com

Heppen, J. (2003). Racial and social diversity and U.S. presidential election regions. *Professional Geographer*, *55*, 191–205. doi: 10.1111/0033-0124.5502007

Herek, G. M. (2002). Heterosexuals' attitudes toward bisexual men in the United States. *The Journal of Sex Research*, *39*, 264–274. doi: 10.1080/00224490209552150

Hoffman, J. P., & Johnson, S. M. (2005). Attitudes toward abortion among religious traditions in the United States: Change or continuity? *Sociology of Religion*, *66*, 161–182. doi: 10.2307/4153084

Kirkpatrick, L. A. (1993). Fundamentalism, Christian orthodoxy, and intrinsic religious orientation as predictors of discriminatory attitudes. *Journal for the Scientific Study of Religion*, *32*, 256–268. doi: 10.2307/1386664

Korb, S. (2010). Mothering Fundamentalism: The transformation of modern women into Fundamentalists. *International Journal of Transpersonal Studies*, *29*, 68–86. Retrieved from http://digitalcommons.ciis.edu/ijts-transpersonalstudies/vol29/iss2/8

Lanska, D. J. (1993). Geographic distribution of stroke mortality in the United States: 1939–1941 to 1979–1981. *Neurology*, *43*, 1839–1851. doi: 10.1161/01.str.28.1.53

Lieske, J. (2010). The changing regional subcultures of the American states and the utility of a new cultural measure. *Political Research Quarterly*, *63*, 538–552. doi: 10.1177/1065912909331425

Lipka, M. (February 23, 2016). U.S. religious groups and their political leanings. Pew Research Center. Retrieved from www.pewresearch.org/fact-tank/2016/02/23/u-s-religious-groups-and-their-political-leanings

Markusen, A. (1989). *Regions: The Economics and Politics of Territory.* Landam, MD: Rowmand & Littlefield.

McAdams, D. P., Albaugh, M., Farber, E., Daniels, J., Logan, R. L., & Olson, B. (2008). Family metaphors and moral institutions: How conservatives and liberals narrate their lives. *Journal of Personality and Social Psychology, 95,* 978–990. doi: 10.1037/a0012650

Morello-Frosh & Shenassa, E. D. (2006). The environmental "riskscape" and social inequality: Implications for explaining maternal and child health disparities. *Environmental Health Perspectives, 114,* 1150–1153. doi: 10.1289/ehp.8930

National Partnership for Women and Families (2016a). Advancing a family-friendly America: How friendly is your state? Retrieved from www.nationalpartnership.org/issues/work–family/family-friendly-america/family-friendly-america-map.html

National Partnership for Women and Families (2016b). State paid family leave insurance laws. Retrieved from www.nationalpartnership.org/research-library/work–family/paid-leave/state-paid-family-leave-laws.pdf

National Right to Life (2016, October 15). Retrieved from www.nrlc.org

Newport, F. (March 27, 2012). Mississippi is most religious state. Retrieved from www.gallup.com/poll/153479/Mississippi-Religious-State.aspx

Ollier-Malaterre, A. (2016). Cross-national work–life research: A review at the individual level of analysis. In T. D. Allen & L. T. Eby (Eds.), *The Oxford Handbook of Work and Family* (pp. 315–330). New York, NY: Oxford University Press. doi: 10.1093/oxfordhb/9780199337538.013.18

Poverty USA. Full screen county map (2016, November 3). Retrieved from www.povertyusa.org/wp-content/themes/poverty2012/full-screen-county-map.php

Powers, R. S., Suitor, J. J., Guerra, S., Shackelford, M., Mecom, D., & Gusman, K. (2003). Regional differences in gender-role attitudes: Variations by gender and race. *Gender Issues. 21,* 41–54. doi:10.1007/s12147-003–0015-y

Putnam, R. D. (2000). *Bowling Alone: The Collapse and Revival of American Community.* New York, NY: Simon & Schuster. doi:10.1145/358916.361990

Rentfrow, P. J., Gosling, S. D., Jokela, M., Stillwell, D. J., Kosinski, M., & Potter, J. (2013). Divided we stand: Three psychological regions of the United States and their political, economic, social and health correlates. *Journal of Personality and Social Psychology, 105,* 996–1012. doi:10.1037/a0034434

Rose, S. (2005). Going too far? Sex, sin and social policy. *Social Forces, 84,* 1207–1232. doi: 10.1353/sof.2006.0032

Rubinstein, G. (1995). Right-wing authoritarianism, political affiliation, religiosity, and their relation to psychological androgyny. *Sex Roles, 33,* 569–586. doi: 10.1007/bf01544681

Scanzoni, J. (1983). *Shaping Tomorrow's Family: Theory and Policy for the 21st Century.* Beverly Hills, CA: Sage.

Schute, B., & Durana, A. (2016, September). The New America care report. Retrieved from www.newamerica.org/in-depth/care-report

Schutz, A. J., Mentz, G., Lachance, Johnson, J., Gaines, C., & Israel, B. A. (2012). Associations between socioeconomic status and allostatic load: Effects of neighborhood poverty and tests of mediating pathways. *American Journal of Public Health, 102,* 1706–1714. doi: 10.2105/ajph.2011.300412

Shockley, K. M., & Shen, W. (2016). Couple dynamics: Division of labor. In T. D. Allen & L. T. Eby (Eds.), *The Oxford Handbook of Work and Family* (pp. 125–139). New York, NY: Oxford University Press. doi: 10.1093/oxfordhb/9780199337538.001.0001

State same-sex marriage state laws map (2015, June 26). Retrieved from www.governing .com/gov-data/same-sex-marriage-civil-unions-doma-laws-by-state.html

Suitor, J. J., & Carter, R. S. (1999). Jocks, nerds, babes and thugs: A research note on regional differences in adolescent gender norms. *Gender Issues, 17*, 87–101. doi: 10.1007/ s12147-999-0005-9

Sullivan, M. K. (2003). Homophobia, history, and homosexuality: Trends for sexual minorities. *Journal of Human Behavior in the Social Environment, 8*, 1–13. doi:10.1300/ 1137v8n02_01

The Huffington Post (September 5, 2013). Divorce rates by state: How does your state stack up? Retrieved from www.huffingtonpost.com/2013/09/05/divorce-rate_n_3869 624.html

The Pew Research Center (June 12, 2014). Political polarization in the American public. Retrieved from www.people-press.org/2014/06/12/political-polarization-in-the-american-public

The 2016 Republican Party platform (2016, July 18). Retrieved from www.gop.com/the-2016-republican-party-platform

Twenge, J. M. (1997a). Attitudes toward women, 1970–1995: A meta-analysis. *Psychology of Women Quarterly, 21*, 35–51. doi: 10.1111/j.1471–6402.1997.tb00099.x

United States Census Bureau (2012). *Statistical Abstract of the United States*. Washington, DC: US Government Printing Office. Retrieved from www.census.gov/library/pub lications/2011/compendia/statab/131ed/population.html

Vandello, J. A., Cohen, D., Grandon, R., & Franiuk, R. (2009). Stand by your man: Indirect prescriptions for honorable violence and feminine loyalty in Canada, Chile, and the United States. *Journal of Cross-Cultural Psychology, 40*, 81–104. doi: 10.1177/ 0022022108326194

Vandello, J. A., Cohen, D., & Ransom, S. (2008). U.S. Southern and Northern differences in perceptions of norms about aggression: Mechanisms for the perpetuation of a culture of honor. *Journal of Cross-Cultural Psychology, 39*, 162–177. doi. 10.1177/0022022107313862

Vandello, J. A., Hettinger, V. E., Bosson, J. K., & Siddiqi, J. (2013). When equal isn't really equal: The masculine dilemma of seeking work flexibility. *Journal of Social Issues, 69*, 303–321. doi: 10.1111/josi.12016

Voydanoff, P. (2002). Linkages between the work–family interface and work, family, and individual outcomes: An integrative model. *Journal of Family Issues, 23*, 138–164. doi: 10.1177/0192513x02023001007

Voydanoff, P. (2005). Social integration, work–family conflict and facilitation, and job and marital quality. *Journal of Marriage and the Family, 67*, 666–679. doi: 10.1111/ j.1741–3737.2005.00161.x

Wayne, J. H., Grzywacz, J. G., Carlson, K. S., & Kacmar, K. M. (2007). Work–family facilitation: Theoretical explanation and model of primary antecedents and consequences. *Human Resource Management Review, 17*, 63–76. doi: 10.1016/j. hrmr.2007.01.002

Weakliem, D. L., & Biggert, R. (1999). Region and political opinion in the contemporary United States. *Social Forces, 77*, 863–886. doi: 10.1093/sf/77.3.863

What are the state laws that mandate arrest for DV assault? (2011, August 1). Retrieved from www.saveservices.org/dvlp/policy-briefings/what-are-the-state-laws-that-mandate-arrest-for-dv-assault

WNYC average commute times (2013, March 5). Retrieved from https://project.wnyc.org/commute-times-us/embed.html#5.00/42.000/-89.500

23 Cultures within Cultures in Israel: Jewish and Arab Cultures and the Work–Family Interface

Aaron Cohen

As evidenced by the current *Handbook*, issues of culture are increasingly recognized as having a significant impact on the work–family interface. This trend is likely due in part to the increase in dual-career and single-parent households relative to the number of traditional single-income households (i.e., consisting of a male breadwinner and a female caretaker) globally. Thus, responsibilities for housework, children, and bread-winning are no longer simply confined by traditional gender roles (Nordenmark, 2013). As a result, many employees find themselves struggling to juggle the competing demands of work and family (Cohen & Kirchmeyer, 2005).

Although there is evidence that the work–family interface is attracting increased international attention (e.g., Allen, French, Dumani, & Shockley, 2015), most cross-cultural studies tend to focus on nations as the delineating boundary. However, in any given nation, several different cultures can co-exist, each with its own norms, religion, language, and/or lifestyle. In fact, differences between ethnic or cultural groups within a nation may, at times, be larger than differences between countries (Clugston, Howell, & Dorfman, 2000; Cohen & Kirchmeyer, 2005). Thus, research combining different groups or cultures within a nation may not accurately represent the culture of a given country or, at the very least, fail to capture the meaningful variation found within the nation.

It is, therefore, important to examine cultural differences not only between nations, but also between cultural groups living within the same national borders (i.e., cultures within a culture approach). With this in mind, the purpose of this chapter is to explore the possibility that the members of different subgroups or cultures in Israel may differ in their experiences of the work–family interface. To this end, I review the relatively limited number of studies that have examined the work–family interface among the different cultures in Israel.

The Israeli Context

Israel, as a multicultural society, provides an interesting case for demonstrating significant cultural differences within one nation and fertile ground for considering the impact of such differences on the work–family interface. Israeli society is characterized by its various cultures, being composed of several ethnic and national groups

(Cohen, 2007b; Heilbrunn & Davidovitch, 2011). The deepest division is national, between Israeli Jews and Israeli Arabs. This division also overlaps with the division between Israeli Jews and Arabs in terms of religion. Below, I provide some background and context, but note that additional cultural variations exist within each group that cannot be fully captured in these brief summaries or generalizations.

The Israeli Arab culture has been described as communal (Glazer, Daniel, & Short, 2004), whereas Israeli Jews are associated with more individualistic values (Pines & Zaidman, 2003). Israeli Arabs, representing about one-sixth of Israel's population, are a permanent, non-assimilating minority. They are clearly distinguished from Israeli Jews by place of residence and culture, speak their own language, and adhere to their own traditions (Cohen, 2007b). Additionally, strong group affiliation has been found to characterize Israeli Arabs, and members of the group expect and are expected to share responsibilities and rewards (Nadler, 2002). This collectivistic orientation is expressed in ideals (e.g., solidarity, cooperation, commitment, mutual trust, support, and sense of belonging) that are believed to be present in the Arab nuclear and extended family and the community (Haj Yahia, 1997).

Israeli Arabs can be further distinguished by their religious affiliation as Muslims, Christians, and Druze. The Muslims represent a relatively traditional society that follows the dictates of the Koran. The Christians are considerably more Western-oriented and demonstrate a closer integration with Israeli Jewish values and culture. The Druze community in Israel, characterized by the Arab-Muslim culture and speaking Arabic, is officially recognized as a separate religious entity with its own courts and spiritual leadership.

The Israeli Jewish population encompasses a variety of family patterns and lifestyles. The mainstream Israeli Jewish family is most often described as Western, with its family patterns resembling those in other industrialized countries. Israeli Jews believe that life's trials and tribulations help form one's personality, and personal strength stemming from a solid inner core is crucial for a mature identity. These values encourage Israeli Jews to face challenges, confront problems, and favor proactive and direct coping strategies (Pines & Zaidman, 2003).

Similar to the Arab population, the Jewish population in Israel can also be further divided into subcultures based on religion. The secular Jews form the majority in Israel and can be characterized as a society that shares much in common with Western culture (and the paragraph above is most descriptive of this group). In contrast, the ultra-Orthodox and some communities of Orthodox Jews are concentrated in specific areas in various cities in Israel. These groups adhere strictly to Jewish law and in many cases are in conflict with secular Jews regarding the role Jewish law should play in Israel (Kulik, 2016).

The Work–Family Interface in Israel from a Demographic Perspective

The demographic composition of Israel provides an opportunity to compare the work–family interface among employees belonging to well-established, diverse cultures located in the same geographic part of the world. Specifically, such a setting enables an interesting comparison between the dominant westernized culture represented by the Israeli secular Jews and the Arab traditional minority culture as well as the ultra-Orthodox Jews, all of whom live within the same national boundaries. Additionally, such an approach may provide insights into and serve as an example of the cultures within a culture approach to understanding the work–family interface.

Israeli Jews and Israeli Arabs Comparisons. Demographic data of employed Arabs and Jews in Israel show important differences between these two ethnic groups. While Arabs over 15 years of age (i.e., the minimum working age) represent 17% of the population, only 12.5% of the Israeli workforce is Arab (Yashiv, 2012). This is probably because the proportion of Arabs who participate in the employment market is lower than that of Jews (i.e., $\approx$ 41% vs. 60%). On average, Arabs enter the workforce at a younger age and are less educated than their Jewish counterparts. Additionally, the unemployment rate is higher for the Arab compared to the Jewish subgroup (i.e., 8.5% vs. 7.4%; Yashiv, 2012).

Substantial differences can also be found by sex. In 2014, the participation of Arab women (27.6%) in the Israeli workforce was considerably lower than that of both Jewish women (65.5%) and Arab men (64.3%; Israel Bureau of Statistics, 2014). In terms of occupations, 43% of employed Arab men work in construction, agriculture, and industry (typically considered lower income trades), and 60% of employed Arab women work in education and healthcare. In terms of hourly rate, the income of Arab men is 60% of that of Jewish men, and Arab women earn 30% less than Jewish women. Data provided by Yashiv (2012) about the Arab population indicate that differences in workforce participation also exist among the different religious groups. Among Arab men, 58.6% of Muslims, 49.9% of Druze, and 67.2% of Christians participate in the labor market. Among Arab women, the participation rates are 16.8% for Muslims, 24% for Druze, and 34.4% for Christians.

The lower participation rate of Arab women in the Israeli workforce relative to other groups can be partially explained by the results of a recent survey conducted by the Israel Bureau of Statistics (2015). This survey found that more than half of unemployed Arab women who want to work reported that their main reason for not doing so is that they need to take care of family members or the household, and this percentage was substantially higher than for the other groups surveyed. These findings indicate that a high percentage of Arab women may have felt the need to or were compelled to choose family over career.

Additional data comparing employed Arab and Jewish women in Israel demonstrate consistent disadvantages for Arab women. A higher percentage of Arab women work part-time (43.9% vs. 32.4%) and do so unwillingly (61% vs. 22.4%) compared with Jewish women. It also takes Arab women considerably longer to find a job compared to Jewish women (63.2 vs. 25 weeks; The Israeli Ministry of Economy, 2012). Such large disparities reflect the disadvantages suffered by Israeli Arabs in general and Arab women in particular.

The above data lead me to draw several conclusions, the most important of which is that Arabs, belonging to a culture within the dominant Jewish culture, are a disadvantaged minority in almost every possible way concerning their participation in the workforce. Although Arab men are disadvantaged, Arab women are not only disadvantaged but also demonstrate a very low participation rate in the Israeli workforce. The results of the survey conducted by the Israel Bureau of Statistics (2015) regarding why Arab women who desire to work do not highlights the type of work–family conflict that Arab women face. Belonging to a more traditional society, Arab women may be expected to fulfill their roles as wife, mother, and household caretaker first. Thus, for many, building a career may not be an expected role.

The case of ultra-Orthodox Jews. An additional group that adds to the cultural complexity of Israel and may have unique work–family concerns is the ultra-Orthodox Jewish subgroup. The ultra-Orthodox Jewish population in Israel is a closed community; members live in insular, homogeneous regions, strive to maintain a traditional lifestyle, and seek to separate themselves from the general population. This subgroup is estimated to constitute 8–11.5% of the general population of Israel (Israel Central Bureau of Statistics, 2012). Life in this community is characterized by strict rules, and rabbis (i.e., Jewish religious leaders) are the sole source of authority. In the public arena, women adhere to codes of modest dress and there is complete separation between the genders. Men study the Torah and other holy texts throughout their lives, whereas women are tasked with providing material sustenance for the family and tending to their often numerous children (Kulik, 2016).

Given this division of labor, ultra-Orthodox women have always worked outside the home. Many are employed as teachers in their communities and serve as the family's main breadwinner to allow their husbands to dedicate their days to religious studies in the Kollel (i.e., rabbinic seminary). However, as processes of modernization have penetrated the traditional isolation of the ultra-Orthodox community in recent years, its members have become exposed to external influences. One manifestation of these trends is that ultra-Orthodox women now pursue training for and can be found in a variety of professional fields, including entrepreneurship, computer technology, and media. Thus, they are now more likely to seek jobs beyond the confines of their community, and many have integrated into the general Israeli labor market. In this process, ultra-Orthodox women face many obstacles when starting a job. For example, employer stereotypes that ultra-Orthodox women have low and inadequate work skills and do not dedicate themselves to work (Kulik, 2016).

Another difficulty in the integration of ultra-Orthodox women in the Israeli workforce is that they remain responsible for the majority of household tasks to a far greater extent than secular Jewish women (Ringel, 2007). Thus, they are often in the very difficult situation where they work outside the home (part- or full-time) and are still expected to be responsible for all the childcare, cooking, cleaning, and other household tasks and responsibilities. Here, I wish to highlight that the difficulties faced in the work–family interface for Jewish ultra-Orthodox and Arab Muslim women may demonstrate some similarities given that both cultures endorse relatively traditional ideologies regarding women's roles. In fact, Arab and ultra-Orthodox Jewish women are more similar in their values and how they cope with the work–family interface than are ultra-Orthodox and secular Jewish women (Lavee & Katz, 2003). Therefore, it is likely that the Arab women and Orthodox and ultra-Orthodox women participating in the Israeli workforce will experience greater work–family conflict than secular Jewish women as well as Arab and Jewish men.

The Work–Family Interface in Israel from a Cultural Perspective

In this section, I review extant research that sheds light on the work–family interface among the different ethnic and cultural groups in Israel. It should be noted that not many studies conducted in Israel have included Israeli Arabs. The position of Arabs as a minority group within the dominant Israeli culture and their sensitive situation in light of the Israeli Arab/Palestinian conflict make them very suspicious of any activity initiated by the Jewish majority group. Therefore, it is not easy for an Israeli Jewish researcher to collect data from any of the Arab groups. In addition, a secular Israeli Jewish researcher will also find it very difficult to collect data from the ultra-Orthodox Jews, who treat secular Jews with suspicion. Most of the data presented here were collected by Arab students who received cooperation from participants that a Jewish researcher would likely never have achieved.

Differences in cultural values. As described above, the culture of Israeli Arabs has been called more traditional and collectivistic, whereas Israeli Jews represent a more westernized and individualistic culture. Direct evidence of cultural differences between different Israeli groups were found in two studies. Cohen (2006) compared teachers from secular Jewish schools with teachers from Arab schools and found that the Arab teachers scored significantly higher than the Jewish teachers on collectivism (*Mean* = 3.83 vs 3.30; $F = 132.16$; $p \le .001$) and power distance (*Mean* = 2.85 vs 2.17; $F = 150.59$, $p \le .001$). Also, the Arab teachers scored higher than the Jewish teachers on masculinity (*Mean* = 2.82 vs 1.93; $F = 145.75$, $p \le .001$), while the Jewish teachers scored higher than the Arab teachers on uncertainty avoidance (*Mean* = 4.27 vs 4.05; $F = 31.63$, $p \le .001$).

In a second study, Cohen (2007b) compared teachers in Israel belonging to five cultural groups, four of which are relevant for this chapter: secular Jewish, Orthodox Jewish, Druze, and Arab teachers. (Note that the study did not include ultra-Orthodox Jews.) As expected, the Arab and Druze teachers, who represent more traditional cultures, scored highest on collectivism, power distance, and masculinity. The Orthodox teachers scored more moderately on all three cultural dimensions. Finally, the secular Jewish teachers scored the lowest on all three dimensions.

Implications for the work–family interface. In this section, I discuss empirical findings regarding differences in the work–family interface among the different cultural groups in Israel. Many of these investigations and findings are predicated on or explained by the authors using the group differences in cultural dimensions and values described above.

Comparative studies. In a study of Jewish, Muslim, and Christian nurses in Israel, Cohen and Kirchmeyer (2005) predicted that family demands would affect Arab women, especially those from the Muslim subgroup, more adversely based on the assumption that the family role is more salient for women in more traditional societies. In support of these arguments, they found that having more children was more strongly related to turnover intentions among Arab women compared to Jewish women and being married was more strongly related to frequent absences among Muslim women compared to Jewish women. Unexpectedly, having more children was positively related to absences for Christian women, but the relationship was negative for Muslim women. Overall, this study supports the general notion that family demands have a stronger effect on working women in more traditional cultures than on those in less traditional cultures – even within the same national context.

In the same study, Cohen and Kirchmeyer (2005) also examined the effects of full-time employment and supervisory responsibilities on work/nonwork conflict. They predicted that women in more egalitarian cultures may suffer more adverse effects from higher work demands due to their higher work salience. In support of their argument, they found that these work demands were related to greater conflict for Jewish women, but not for Arab women. Additionally, they also cite evidence that the negative relationship between job tension and work–family conflict was stronger for Christian compared to Muslim women as further support for their prediction. Overall, their main proposition, that the negative impact of job demands on women increases as a culture's ideologies about the appropriate division of labor between men and women become more egalitarian, was supported.

Cohen and Kirchmeyer (2005) also examined whether the use of personal coping strategies and availability of organizational support affected work outcomes differently for nurses with different cultural group membership. They found that personal coping had a favorable effect (i.e., negative relationship) on employment turnover only for Arab women. Additionally, the relationship between personal coping and absence frequency was stronger among Arab compared to Jewish nurses. Furthermore, the effect of personal coping more adversely affected absence duration for Christians compared to Muslim nurses. It seems that for Arab nurses, whose family demands may be especially strong, taking absences from work may be largely proactive in nature and represent another coping practice to manage the work–family interface. In contrast, for Jewish women, whose work demands may be especially strong, taking absences from work may be largely reactive in nature. Additionally, the relationship between organizational support and absence frequency was only significant for Arab women. In sum, there is evidence that women from different cultural groups in Israel cope with the work–family interface differently.

Cinamon (2009) also examined the way individuals from the different cultural groups experience the work–family interface in Israel. She compared married female teachers who worked in two different high school education sectors (Arab and

Jewish) in central Israel. Interestingly, she found that the Arab teachers (*Mean* = 2.74, *SD* =.79) reported significantly lower levels of work-to-family conflict than the Jewish teachers (*Mean* = 3.42, *SD* =.80, *F* = 43.12, *p* ≤.01), but found no differences between the two groups in family-to-work conflict (*Mean* for Arab teachers = 2.09, *SD* =.66; *Mean* for Jewish teachers = 2.10, *SD* =.68; *F* = 2.88, *ns*). This significant finding is particularly noteworthy considering that both groups of women worked in the same occupation and under similar work conditions, and the Arab teachers had, on average, more children at home.

Cinamon (2009) also examined the relationship between support systems and work–family conflict and whether they differed by culture. She found that support provided by the work organization and the family system was negatively related to both work-to-family and family-to-work conflict for Jewish, but not Arab teachers. Interestingly, this appears to differ from Cohen and Kirchmeyer's (2005) finding that support was negatively related to frequency and duration absence only for Arab rather than Jewish nurses. Generally, these findings highlight that both the antecedents of and experiences at the work–family interface appear to differ systematically for different ethnic and cultural groups within Israel.

In another comparative study, Feldman, Masalha, and Nadam (2001) examined and compared Israeli Jewish and Arab dual-earner families at the transition to parenthood using both interviews and observations (in dyadic and triadic interactions). Their findings showed that Arab parents, both mothers and fathers, reported better adaptation to work following the birth of the first child than Jewish parents. The explanation offered by Feldman et al. was that at the transition to parenthood the availability of trustworthy, affordable, and flexible childcare is a key factor in the lives of dual-earner families. In their study, approximately two-thirds of Arab infants were cared for by family members, which may reflect inter-generational support and serve to create a sense of historical continuity.

Feldman et al. (2001) also found that Arab mothers were more satisfied with the quality of childcare, and Arab parents reported adequate childcare as being more affordable. Additionally, as is customary in traditional societies, Arab parents also had more previous experience in caring for infant siblings than their Jewish counterparts. This experience possibly reduced parental stress related to the practicalities of childcare and the novelty of the caring situation to facilitate better adaptation. Generally, these findings indicate an interesting pattern in the Israeli–Arab culture. Specifically, Arab females may deal better with the work–family interface because of the benefits of being a member of an extended family that provides assistance in many household functions, including childcare, while Arab males may cope better with the work–family interface because their traditional role in the family prioritizes their needs.

Finally, Heilbrunn and Davidovitch's (2011) study found similar results to those obtained by Cinamon (2009) and Feldmen et al. (2001). Using a sample of Arab and Jewish female entrepreneurs in Israel, they found that Arab women experienced lower levels of work–family conflict compared to Jewish women. Heilbrunn and Davidovitch suggested that this finding could be explained by the greater family support enjoyed by the Arab women; nearly half of the businesses run by Arab women are home-based, and Arab women reported the higher levels of family support, particularly from immediate family members.

Studies focused on a single subculture. Above, I review comparative studies that contrast the experiences of different ethnic or cultural groups within Israel related to the work–family interface. However, another body of work, which focuses on particular cultures or groups, also provides insights about cultural effects on the work–family interface because one can still compare findings obtained from each of the specific groups.

Cohen and Abedalla (2013) examined the relationship between work–family variables and organizational commitment among female Arab teachers in Arab elementary schools in the north of Israel (note that 44% of Israeli Arabs live in this region). The results show a strong positive effect of organizational support for nonwork life on organizational commitment, but that general spousal support was not related to organizational commitment. Cohen and Abedalla concluded that for Arab female teachers, personal perceptions and experiences of support may be especially critical for building commitment because they increase perceptions of fair exchange with the organization. In contrast, the latter finding regarding the null effects of spousal support may be because in Arab traditional society women are expected to take care of all household responsibilities; whether or not they pursue a career does not change this expectation.

This final set of studies focuses solely on the Jewish Israeli setting (Cohen, 2009; Cohen & Liani, 2009; Cohen, Granot-Shilovsky, & Yishai, 2007). Generally, these studies indirectly demonstrate that Israeli secular Jews represent a more westernized culture compared to the more traditional cultures in Israel represented by the other Israeli groups (e.g., Orthodox Jews or Israeli Arabs). Cohen (2009) examined how individual values (i.e., power, achievement, hedonism, stimulation, self-direction, universalism, benevolence, tradition, conformity, and security; Schwartz, 2005) are related to variables that reflect the work–family interface (i.e., work-to-family conflict, family-to-work conflict, and coping strategies). The findings show that among secular Jewish employees working in the high-tech sector, the only value related to work–family variables was power. Power is a value that represents self-enhancement, a less common value in more traditional societies.

In a separate study, Cohen and Liani (2009) studied Jewish female nurses and found a strong and consistent relationship between working full-time and the work-to-family conflict as well as and a significant relationship between number of children and the family-to-work conflict. Additionally, organizational support variables were not related to either direction of conflict. Thus, Israeli secular women may have more difficulty managing the work–family interface. Perhaps this is because they do not receive the same assistance that women in more traditional cultures receive from their extended family. Further, given that organizational support does not appear to be effective for mitigating work–family conflict for this group, this may indicate that other sources of support (e.g., family) may be more critical for this group.

Finally, Cohen, Granot-Shilovsky, and Yishai (2007) examined promotion (measured as a dichotomous variable) among Jewish teachers and principals working in Jewish secular schools. They found that teachers' actual coping with work/nonwork conflicting demands had very little effect on whether or not they were promoted. Instead, those who were likely to be promoted were those who were more committed to the organization, had a mentor to guide their career, and perceived the organization to assist them in managing these conflicts (rather than their spouse or their own use of coping strategies). Overall, the three studies above indicate that secular Jewish employees may face different constraints in the work–family interface than more traditional Israeli groups (though these latter groups were not included or directly assessed in these studies), and as a result, their coping strategies may be different from individuals from the more traditional Israeli cultures. In addition, the secular Jews will look for support from work rather than expecting support from their family.

Discussion

The Israeli setting provides a unique opportunity to examine how different cultures living within the same national borders experience and cope with the work–family interface. In this ethnically and religiously diverse setting, it is meaningful to subdivide and examine the potential effects of being a member of these sub-cultures. The research above, which reveals that group membership does appear to moderate many of the relationships at the work–family interface, suggests that it may behoove researchers to consider more carefully the cultural and/or racial/ethnic characteristics of their samples. This practice has not been typical of research on this topic, and differently composed samples could account for some of the inconsistencies across studies (Allen et al., 2015; Lavee & Katz, 2003).

One would argue that Arabs face more difficulty in dealing with the work–family interface because they live in a more traditional culture and should therefore hold more traditional values (e.g., be more likely to endorse collectivism, masculinity, and power distance). Thus, work demands should increase the work–family conflict of Arabs, particularly women. On the other hand, the same theories would argue that in comparison to the Arab group, the Jewish population holding more westernized values should cope better with the work–family interface because sharing responsibilities for family demands is a common expectation in westernized cultures. However, the studies reviewed here show a considerably more complex reality. The findings to date indicate that the family structure of the Arab traditional cultures assists their members in coping with conflicting demands of work and family (Feldman et al., 2001), particularly for women, as the extended family is an important source of support (Aycan, 2008). I speculate that this may also be true for the ultra-Orthodox Jews because in collectivistic cultures extended family support is more expected by and available to working parents. For example, grandparents or aunts of working couples are often involved in childcare or care of household responsibilities (e.g., cooking). In contrast, in individualistic cultures, privacy is a pivotal value and the involvement of third parties in family matters is not desirable and, therefore, may result in lower levels of available support. An important caveat here is that the proportion of women who work in Arabs (particularly Muslims) and ultra-Orthodox Jews in the Israeli workforce is still much lower than that among the secular Jews. This indicates that many women from these cultures are still expected to fill their traditional roles of being responsible for the household first. In contrast, men from more traditional cultures may experience better outcomes at the work–family interface because their traditional sex role makes them less ambivalent about sharing home and childcare labor. The complementary nature of work and family roles may enable these fathers to invest more in the work role (Feldman et al., 2001).

It is interesting to note that the relationship between work–family interface and culture was examined in a cross-national meta-analysis of mean differences in work–family conflict that included more than forty countries (Allen et al., 2015). Allen et al. originally predicted that individuals from more (vs. less) collectivistic countries will report fewer conflicts in the work–family interface because in collectivist societies there tends to be a large network of family support and individuals are encouraged to seek help from family members. Allen et al. did not find support for this hypothesis. However, I advance two possible reasons for the contradiction in the conclusions of this chapter and the meta-analytic findings. First, Allen et al. examined and compared nations and ignored one of the main contentions advanced here that within one nation there may be several different cultures with different attitudes and behaviors relevant to the work–family interface. Second, no Arab country was included in Allen et al.'s meta-analysis. I argue that their hypothesis is much more relevant to the collectivist Arab society that encourages and values the extended family, perhaps even more so than other collectivistic societies (e.g., Confucian Asian cultures).

In addition to contributing to an understanding of the relationship between work and nonwork domains across different cultures within one national setting, the findings and ideas summarized in this chapter have practical implications for managing diverse workforces. The common strategies of work–family programs in North American organizations, such as helping workers develop life management skills and providing direct support for their nonwork life in the forms of flexible work hours and alternative work arrangements (Kirchmeyer & Cohen, 1999), may also benefit female employees from more traditional cultures. As mentioned above, more than half of unemployed Arab women who want to work reported that they do not join the workforce because they need to take care of family members or the household (Israel Bureau of Statistics, 2015). For these individuals, organizational work–family programs may be very relevant.

Finally, I see this chapter as a general call for more research comparing experiences at the work–family interface among different cultural groups living within the same country. Such research would greatly enrich and expand our understanding of this important topic. For future research conducted in the Israeli context, I note that the majority of research to date has focused on female-dominated occupations (e.g., teachers, nurses) and advocate for future work to extend to examining a broader range of occupational and professional groups, including male-dominated occupations.

References

Allen, T. D., French, K. A., Dumani, S., & Shockley, K. M. (2015). Meta-analysis of work–family conflict mean differences: Does national context matter? *Journal of Vocational Behavior, 90*, 90–100.

Aycan, Z. (2008). Cross-cultural perspectives to work–family conflict. In K. Korabik & D. Lero (Eds.), *Handbook of Work–Family Conflict* (pp. 359–371). London: Cambridge University Press.

Cinamon, R. G. (2009). Role salience, social support, and work–family conflict among Jewish and Arab female teachers in Israel. *Journal of Career Development, 36*(2), 139–158.

Clugston, M., Howell, J. P., & Dorfman, P. W. (2000). Does cultural socialization predict multiple bases and foci of commitment? *Journal of Management, 26*, 5–30.

Cohen, A. (2006). The relationship between multiple commitments and organizational citizenship behavior in Arab and Jewish culture. *Journal of Vocational Behavior, 69*(1), 105–118.

Cohen, A. (2007b). An examination of the relationship between commitments and culture among five cultural groups of Israeli teachers. *Journal of Cross-Cultural Psychology, 38*(1), 34–49.

Cohen, A. (2009). Individual values and the work/family interface: An examination of high tech employees in Israel. *Journal of Managerial Psychology, 24*(8), 814–832.

Cohen, A., & Abedallah, A. (2013). Work and nonwork determinants of organizational commitment: A study of Arab teachers in Israel. *International Journal of Management, 30*(4), 224–234.

Cohen, A., Granot-Shilovsky, L., & Yishai, Y. (2007). The relationship between personal, role, and organizational variables and promotion to managerial positions in the Israeli educational system. *Personnel Review, 36*(1), 6–22.

Cohen, A., & Kirchmeyer, C. (1995). A multidimensional approach to the relation between organizational commitment and nonwork participation. *Journal of Vocational Behavior, 46*, 189–202.

Cohen, A., & Kirchmeyer, C. (2005). A cross-cultural study of the work/nonwork interface among Israeli nurses. *Applied Psychology, 54*(4), 537–567.

Cohen, A., & Liani, E. (2009). Work–family conflict among female employees in Israeli hospitals. *Personnel Review, 38*(2), 124–141.

Feldman, R., Masalha, S., & Nadam, R. (2001). Cultural perspective on work and family: Dual-earner Israeli Jewish and Arab families at the transition to parenthood. *Journal of Family Psychology, 15*(3), 492–509.

Glazer, S., Daniel, S. C., & Short, K. M. (2004). A study of the relationship between organizational commitment and human values in four countries. *Human Relations, 57*(3), 323–345.

Haj Yahia, M. (1997). Toward culturally sensitive intervention with Arab families in Israel. *Contemporary Family Therapy, 17*, 429–447.

Heilbrunn, S., & Davidovitch, L. (2011). Juggling family and business work–family conflict of women entrepreneurs in Israel. *Journal of Entrepreneurship, 20*(1), 127–141.

Israel Central Bureau of Statistics. (2012). *Statistical abstract of Israel 2012, no. 63*. Jerusalem, Israel: Author.

Israel Bureau of Statistics (2014). Data from the workforce survey for December, the fourth quarter and for 2014; 29 January, 2015.

Israel Bureau of Statistics (2015). Data collection from the social survey 2013 on employment; 14 January, 2015.

The Israeli Ministry of Economy and Industry (2012). Profile of the working Arab woman, *Research & economy Administration*. Israel

Kirchmeyer, C., & Cohen, A. (1999). Different strategies for managing the work nonwork interface: A test for unique pathways to work outcomes. *Work & Stress, 13*(1), 59–73.

Kulik, L. (2016). Explaining employment hardiness among women in Israel's ultraorthodox community facilitators and inhibitors. *Journal of Career Assessment, 24*(1), 67–85.

Lavee, Y., & Katz, R. (2003). The family in Israel: Between tradition and modernity. *Marriage & Family Review, 35*(1–2), 193–217.

Nadler, A. (2002). Inter–group helping relations as power relations: Maintaining or challenging social dominance between groups through helping. *Journal of Social Issues, 58*(3), 487–502.

Nordenmark, M. (2013). Disagreement about division of household labour and experiences of work–family conflict in different gender regimes. *Multidisciplinary Journal of Gender Studies, 2*(3), 205–232.

Pines, A. M., & Zaidman, N. (2003). Israeli Jews and Arabs: Similarities and differences in the utilization of social support. *Journal of Cross-Cultural Psychology, 34*, 465–480.

Ringel, S. (2007). Identity and gender roles of Orthodox Jewish women: Implications for social work practice. *Smith College Studies in Social Work, 77*(2–3), 25–44.

Schwartz, S. H. (2005). Robustness and fruitfulness of a theory on universals in individual human values. In Tamayo, A. & Porto, J.B. (Eds.), *Valores e Trabalho* (Values and Work), Editora Universidade de Brasilia, Brasilia, pp. 56–95.

Yashiv, E. (2012). The Arabs in the Israeli labor market. In *Disputes in Economics*, second series. The Van Leer Jerusalem Institute, Jerusalem, pp. 1–30 (in Hebrew).

24 Modernity Meets Tradition: Managing the Work–Family Interface in South Africa

Nicole Dodd and Justin van der Merwe

South Africa is traditionally viewed as a deeply racially divided country. The people of South Africa are commonly dichotomized as Black or White. However, closer inspection reveals that this is too simplistic a treatment of a complex reality. For instance, the definition of "Black people" in South Africa encompasses three distinct racial groups: Africans (i.e., those of African descent), Coloureds (i.e., those of mixed-race descent), and Indians (i.e., those of Indian descent) (South Africa, 2003). Additionally, multiple linguistic and ethnic groups who share common historical and geographic heritages exist within the country and within the four predominant racial groups (i.e., Black African, Coloured, Indian, and White). The array of languages spoken in South Africa bear testament to the country's diversity. For example, Black Africans might speak one of nine indigenous languages, such as Ndebele, Sotho, Venda, Zulu, Xhosa, Tswana, Pedi, Swati, or Tsonga (Conner, 2004). These linguistic groups also reflect tribal and ethnic affiliations. On the other hand, members of the White, Coloured, and Indian racial groups typically speak English as their home language. Although Afrikaans speakers can be found in all racial groups in South Africa it is mostly the home language of many White and Coloured people.

There is also substantial diversity within these linguistic groups. Specifically, significant economic inequality and a large rural–urban divide add additional dimensions to cultural identity in South Africa. South Africa, therefore, represents a uniquely diverse and challenging cultural environment. Culture is a dynamic phenomenon where multiple levels interact to shape it (Erez & Gati, 2004). Both bottom-up and top-down factors inform culture. In South Africa, one key area where these factors intersect is in the workplace; specifically, there are ongoing negotiations and interactions between Western influences and traditional role expectations for work and family. This tension means that the work–family interface is of particular interest in South Africa. South Africa's long history of discrimination, including gender discrimination (Seekings, 2008), makes the work–family interface an even more complex terrain to negotiate. Superimposing globalized, westernized, work practices in traditional African environments may result in incompatibility between work and family demands, particularly when it comes to the often highly involved family demands related to birth, caregiving, bereavement, and marriage. Thus, we sought to understand and explore these tensions in the South African context in this chapter.

Our chapter is organized as follows. First, we provide some historical background and focus on defining family, care, and dependents in the South African context. Next, our discussion turns to family role obligations in birth, death, coming of age, and marriage across the African (e.g., Zulu, Xhosa, Tswana, Swati, Sotho, Venda, Tsonga and Ndebele), Coloured, and White cultural groups in South Africa – highlighting a cultures within culture perspective. Specifically, we focus on the following five questions regarding the work–family interface: (1) How are the obligations surrounding birth, death, coming of age, illness, and marriage dealt with in various South African cultures? (2) Do cultural obligations surrounding these events create demands that affect work? (3) How do various South African cultures define who are dependents, and are these definitions and responsibilities accepted and accommodated by South African employers? (4) Does having a partner help or hinder career satisfaction and/or success, and are benefits and challenges evenly distributed amongst men and women in different cultural groups? (5) Are traditional South African, culture-bound gender roles in conflict with role expectations in a modern, westernized work environment? Finally, the chapter concludes with a discussion of the implications of these cultural differences for the work–family interface.

South Africa's Post-Apartheid Reality

South Africans from different racial, ethnic, and social backgrounds experience varied social and economic opportunities because of the persistent structural inequality that is a legacy of apartheid (Seekings, 2003). This creates challenges for many individuals both at work and at home as well as in the interaction between these two spheres of life. The inequalities stem from the country's colonial history. Colonialism was predicated on the exploitation of South Africa's natural resources and peoples. South Africa's strategic geopolitical position as a halfway stop between West and East and the later discovery of gold and diamonds resulted in the country being firmly entrenched within global capitalism. Colonialism disenfranchised South Africa's indigenous peoples and dispossessed them of their land and resources (Butler, 2004).

The British founded a unitary state in 1910 in order to support their interests in mineral resources. This consolidated colonial power throughout modern-day South Africa enabled these powers to subject South Africa's indigenous people to cultural imperialism involving proselytizing (e.g., conversion to Christianity), hegemonic influences (e.g., eradication of indigenous knowledge systems), and legal influences (e.g., the introduction of laws that encouraged Western practices). These Western influences had profound social and cultural implications for the people of South Africa (Comaroff & Comaroff, 1997).

Colonialism gave way to apartheid, a policy officially instituted in 1948. Apartheid further entrenched White privilege in South Africa and formalized a policy of racial division and segregation within the economy, workplace, and more generally within living spaces. This policy had political, economic, and social implications, including the distribution of resources within the nation. In short, apartheid affected almost every aspect of South African life (Macdonald, 2006). Notably this includes work and family life and, by extension, the work–family interface.

"Family" is typically conceptualized differently in Western and African settings, adding to the complexity of the work–family interface in South Africa. Western sociologists traditionally define a family unit as "a social group characterized by common residence, economic cooperation, and reproduction. It includes adults of both sexes, at least two of whom maintain a socially approved sexual relationship, and one or more children, own or adopted, of the sexually cohabiting adults" (Murdock, 1949, cited in Haralambos & Holborn, 1995, p. 317). However, this Western model of the "family" does not apply in many South African cultures, which are often patrifocal (i.e., the father or a male relative serves as head of the family) and polygynous (i.e., involving polygamous marriages where there are multiple wives) societies arranged based on kinship with clearly defined gender- and age-related roles, customs, and traditions.

The apartheid system had a particularly pernicious effect on the South African family unit. Specifically, apartheid led to many male heads of households working long distances away from their families. This often reduced family units to a woman caring for children or grandchildren while relying on remittance income. As a result, many South African households have become matrifocal (i.e., a female relative as head of the family). Matrifocal families come into being when there are polygynous relationships and the male figure plays a relatively marginal role in the family. Father figures may hold marginal roles in the family unit because of migrant work patterns or desertion (Haralambos & Holborn, 1995). A multitude of psychological, social, and economic consequences could arise from this and manifest in work–family conflict. For example, single parents may lack spousal support and this could result in time- and strain-based conflict.

The extreme inequality caused by colonialism and apartheid have distinctively shaped individual experiences in the workplace and the home, and have affected the intersection between these two domains. Following the attainment of democracy in 1994, South Africa promulgated a liberal constitution (Act 108 of 1996). This law enshrined political and civil rights that redefined working and living conditions for the South African citizen. Under the democratic dispensation, the South African government set out to transform the country. In the workplace, legislation such as the Employment Equity Act (55 of 1998) was enacted to ensure greater representation of Black Africans, women, and those with disabilities. Home life also began to improve as the state provided universal access to basic services such as education, healthcare, electricity, water, and sanitation. Yet, South Africa continues to be a profoundly unequal society, and four inter-related dimensions, described in detail below, continue to exert great influence on contemporary South Africans' experiences of privilege and oppression concerning the work–family interface: culture, urbanization, class, and gender.

First, South Africa's population is composed of different cultural groups primarily centered on racial, ethnic, and linguistic identities. The majority of South Africans are Black African (79.2%), followed by Coloured (8.9%), White (8.9%), and Indian or Asian (2.5%) (Statistics South Africa, 2012). Within the Black African communities, the Zulu group is the largest, followed by the Xhosa, Pedi, Tswana, Sotho, Tsonga, Swati, Venda, and Ndebele groups. The majority of White and Coloured people in South Africa speak Afrikaans. However, English is the first language of approximately 9.6% of South Africans, who are mostly White, Asian, and Coloured (Statistics South Africa, 2012), and English is the most commonly used language in government, the formal economy, and mainstream media.

Second, there is an urban–rural divide in South Africa, attributable to apartheid's impact on land ownership and movement as it attempted to force the Black African population into one-seventh of the country's area (UNESCO, 1967). The Group Areas Act (41 of 1950), defined separate territories for White and Black peoples in South Africa, and Black Africans needed permission to move, visit, and seek work in urban and "White" areas that were often the center of commerce and employment opportunities (UNESCO, 1967). Black Africans residing in urban areas were considered migratory citizens who did not have political or social rights. These Black Africans could only live in locations (i.e., townships), native villages, and hostels within these urban areas, but these areas were often on the periphery of the cities or strategically located close to industrial areas or mines, which led to long daily commutes often without access to reliable public transport. Alternatively, Black Africans could live in "bantustans" or "homelands," which were even further from sites of employment and meant that migrant workers had to travel sometimes for days, and at great expense, to spend time with their families. This resulted in long absences from the home and created stress for working family members who could not provide sufficient care because of a lack of time. These spatial divides, although no longer formalized in policy and law, are still visible in the geographic distribution of racial groups in South Africa.

Third, the class system in South Africa was, and still is, stratified primarily along racial lines. Whites make up the majority of the upper and middle classes, although there is a burgeoning Black middle class (Southall, 2016). Again, this is part of apartheid's legacy as it affected employment and living conditions. A series of laws enforced divisions within the workplace, from mines to white-collar environments, as well as dictating land ownership rights (Van der Merwe, 2016). Apartheid also affected employment through racially based job opportunities and remuneration (Macdonald, 2006). Access to education also differed by race, with Black Africans being subjected to the Bantu education system (Gerhart, 1979). Apartheid systematically disempowered Black Africans by affording them limited access to economic and educational opportunities. Ultimately, colonialism, apartheid, and neoliberal reforms in the post-apartheid era, have created a highly unequal class structure in South Africa.

Fourth, most cultural groups in South Africa believe that women are subordinate to men (Hutson, 2007). Yet, women carry the burden of care, responsible for the care of children and the elderly, while also being expected to participate in the economy (Mokomane, 2009). Black women still withstand the worst socioeconomic hardship in South Africa and are more likely to live in poverty (Shisana, Rice, Zungu, & Zuma, 2010). This is because they have limited access to resources, education, and opportunities for meaningful participation in the economy. Black women in the rural areas are most disadvantaged by a lack of access to social and economic opportunities and are, therefore, more likely to be trapped in poverty (Kehler, 2013).

Another important point is that these four dimensions (i.e., culture, urbanization, class, and gender) interact to influence one's experiences. Thus, the experiences of an urbanized, middle-class, Xhosa male may differ quite markedly from those of a rural, poor, Xhosa woman and may, in fact, bear more similarities with a White, English male counterpart with the same spatial, economic, and gender advantages. As such, intersectional theory, which emphasizes that social and power structures give rise to privilege and oppression (Hankivsky, 2014), is highly instructive when considering South Africans' experiences. Given these vectors of difference, which are still prominent in contemporary South Africa, the country emerges as a particularly rich case study for analyzing the clash between Western influences and traditional African values and needs, including how these tensions influence the work–family interface. There is a need for research of this nature in South Africa as much of the work–family research in this area has focused on Western environments and contexts (Koekemoer & Mostert, 2010).

Work in South Africa

South Africa's work environment is shaped by the class structures engineered during the apartheid era. The working environment itself is still largely westernized (Mangaliso, 2001). This is because of South Africa's colonial history and the fact that the country remained under westernized influence until 1994. The westernized minority guided policy and legislation and held the majority of managerial and leadership posts in the workplace, thereby shaping this domain. For example, apartheid's architects sought to limit Black Africans' role in the workplace to mostly providing cheap labor, achieving this through legislative means. At the time, mining and agriculture had high demand for unskilled labor (Van der Merwe, 2016). Race determined the quality of education as well as the sort of work one could do. During apartheid, it was almost impossible to become an artisan if one was Black, owing to job reservation – a discriminatory employment system that only White males could work in certain professions (Wilson, 2011). Skilled managerial positions were typically reserved for White South Africans, while most Black Africans were assigned to unskilled or semi-skilled roles in the industrial, commercial, and domestic spheres. Some Black Africans joined the police or became teachers or members of the clergy. The result is that class and race are strongly conflated in South Africa.

Aided by employment equity legislation and Black economic empowerment, the labor market opened after the fall of apartheid. However, many Black Africans lack the skills to actively participate in the formal economy in skilled and managerial roles and continue to perform manual labor (Kraak, 2005). Thus, White South Africans continue to dominate managerial and professional roles, though Coloured and Black Africans are beginning to make some advances into these positions. Yet, the pace of transformation remains slow.

Family in South Africa

Two sources of tension between African culture and the Western organizational culture adopted by many firms in South Africa arise from Western cultures' tendencies towards individualism and femininity. In contrast, African cultures tend to be more collectivistic and masculine (Hofstede, 2001). We explore these tensions in relation to the understanding of different South African cultures concerning dependents and kinship as well as gender and the division of labor, drawing on Hofstede's (2001) dimensions of national culture.

Dependents and Kinship

Understanding African conceptualization of family is necessary if one is to understand the full complexity of the work–family interface in South Africa. Although Coloured and White families may resemble the typical Western nuclear family structure, South Africa's cultural, socioeconomic, and political history has resulted in greater networks of kinship and dependency for Black African families. Black African cultures are characterized by collectivism, in contrast with the more individualistic orientation typically seen in White families. In the latter families, the Protestant work ethic is evident and there are, arguably, stricter boundaries between work and family, with the former being prioritized (Bendix, 1996). White families primarily focus on meeting the needs of their immediate families, but will accommodate their extended families if there is a serious need or when the familial bonds are particularly strong (Nzimande, 2016). Burch (1976) highlights two types of family relationships: residential and interactional relationships. Applying this taxonomy, one could argue that White families perceive that their obligations are restricted to their residential families. This differs from Black African cultures in South Africa who favor more extended or interactional family relations.

A somewhat paradoxical situation exists in South Africa when it comes to marriage and family as employers fail to recognize conventions despite the fact that lawmakers have ratified them. In fact, South African legislation recognizes a number of different marital arrangements. Socially, patriarchal, family-based social systems abound and the notion of family extends to include the entire clan or tribe. Family comprises all those with the same surname or who are from the same clan (Mogaladi, 2016). African families embrace monogamous, polygamous, and extended family arrangements (Amoateng & Heaton, 2007). This extended understanding of family generally creates potential spillover or conflict from the family to the work domain.

Black African family members maintain their relationships with one another because of their interdependence. Black African cultures expect that those with resources, be they financial or time-based, take care of dependents (Cox, 2013). This interdependence translates to members of African families accepting responsibility for the welfare of not only their own children, but also their extended family (e. g., parents, siblings, nieces, and nephews), with those who earn more carrying more responsibility for their extended family members (Mogaladi, 2016; Makhathini,

2016). Family support provides the elderly, ill, unemployed, disabled, and orphaned with an extended social "safety net" and potentially increases both time- and strain-based work–family conflict as family members must care for their extended families. They may need to take time off work or may feel exhausted and unproductive at work because of their added responsibility. The extended family also jointly raises children, who may spend long periods living with their grandparents or aunts and uncles. This additional burden of care can create time-based conflict for working family members. These extended familial networks protect vulnerable family members, but also place pressure on those who are working and who are often held to the strictures of human resources policies that are based on nuclear family structures and do not always recognize extended family members as bona fide family members.

Caring for one's extended family increases the number of roles that each working family member holds and can have benefits. This is because fulfilling multiple roles including family roles outside the workplace, such as caring for dependents, can contribute to satisfaction and esteem needs. In fact, this may also serve as a motivating force, driving employees to work harder in order to support their extended family. However, the high burden of financial responsibility can contribute to dissatisfaction with pay, and may even be the source of labor unrest and strike action.

Gender and Division of Labor

Although already discussed as a dimension of difference, gender and division of labor warrant special emphasis in an African setting. Women in South Africa contend with economic pressures that compel them to be economically active, whilst cultural norms and expectations simultaneously compel them to retain the majority of family and household responsibilities (Sibiya, 2016). The pattern of fatherless households created by apartheid and migratory work further increases pressure on women in South Africa. The stronger the traditionalist normative pressures, the greater the difficulties faced by working women.

Gendered division of labor is deeply entrenched within the domestic sphere in South Africa in both White and Black communities. As an example, in the past, Swati women were groomed to perform duties associated with womanhood (i.e., childrearing and domestic duties) and discouraged from working or studying (Ndwandwe, 2016). Another notable example is the Zulu culture, where men contribute minimally in the home (Makhathini, 2016), and gender socialization favors masculinity and patriarchy (Uchendu, 2008). The perception also remains that men are the heads of their households and women are discouraged from showing assertiveness, as this is a masculine trait (Mogaladi, 2016; Uchendu, 2008).

However, some may argue that women are, to some extent, complicit in perpetuating this patriarchal system. Women make a conscious effort to compartmentalize their work and private identities thereby preventing the two domains from affecting each other (Makhathini, 2016). For example, even though secretly believing such gender roles are repressive, some Tsonga women still carry out traditional roles when with their extended family in order to keep up appearances (Bvuma, 2016). Further segmentation occurs at the family level. African families may live "double lives," living westernized lives in urban areas, then returning to their rural family homes for holidays, family events, and performing traditional gender roles while there.

The unequal relations demonstrated in the private sphere extend into the community. In many traditional African cultures, women are not extensively consulted during decision-making. In some instances, patriarchal traditional customs and customary law may even deny women basic rights such as property ownership (Thipe, 2013). Such unequal power relations create a disjuncture when integrating into Western-oriented organizational cultures that encourage egalitarianism.

An important distinction in terms of gendered division of labor in South Africa, and its impact on work–family interface, is the disproportionate "burden of care" carried by women (Foley & Powell, 1997 cited in Mashatola, 2016). Women are responsible for childcare, and are expected to look after an array of dependents (resulting from disability, age, and illness) as well as male family members at the expense of their work. Women may report late for work, leave early, or not go to work at all because of their family responsibilities (Nzimande, 2016).

On the other hand, there are also benefits that arise from collectivism that may bring relief to working family members. Support in the form of care and assistance from extended family members may create positive spillover from family-to-work and free up working women to focus on their careers. South Africa is slowly transitioning away from traditional gender role expectations. Urbanization, globalization, and education are systematically eroding and replacing some of these values and giving rise to new norms.

Rites of Passage in South Africa

Unique conflicts between African values and customs and westernized work environments arise out of the demands placed on families during rites of passage, which mark the transition from one point in life to another. These rites may involve separation (e.g., funerals), transition (e.g., coming of age) or incorporation (e.g., marriage) (Mhlahlo, 2009). In South Africa, these rites frequently involve extended family members and rituals that are time-consuming and costly. This has consequences for working family members who must reconcile the demands of their work and family roles. The cultural expectations surrounding birth, death, illness, marriage, and coming of age in South Africa are varied. Notably, the African cultures in South Africa tend to have more drawn-out activities and intricate rituals, involving more family members, compared to Coloured and White communities in South Africa, which tend to follow Judeo-Christian customs and engage in more westernized customs such as religious confirmation (Nzimande, 2016; Winster, 2016). These latter practices tend to be less involved and less time-intensive and, therefore, may interfere less with work obligations. Below, we briefly assess the potential impact of each rite of passage in turn on the work–family interface.

Birth

The Basic Conditions of Employment Act (75 of 1997) grants four months of paid maternity leave to pregnant women. When a child is born, within Coloured and White communities in South Africa, women tend only to take the legally prescribed maternity leave, and do not extend the maternity leave beyond this period (Sibiya, 2016). Conflict may arise as there is a widely held belief in the Tsonga and Venda cultures that women should stay at home for at least a year after birth, whereas many women believe they should return to work immediately if childcare is available (Bvuma, 2016; Chauke, 2016). Thus, Black African women may experience conflict as they struggle to reconcile the need to meet societal expectations of them as mothers and the expectations their employers may have of them as employees.

As legislation does not offer fathers paternity leave, men are not given adequate time to take care of their families post-birth, and this can create work–family conflict. In fact, South African labor legislation provides men with only three paid days of family responsibility leave per year. These days are supposed to provide paid time off for births, bereavement, and illnesses in the family. There is a marked cultural contrast between White and Coloured South Africans when compared with African cultures concerning the role of the father during childbirth and infancy. Generally, there is an expectation that White and Coloured fathers will provide some care during childbirth and their children's infancy (Sibiya, 2016). For Black African fathers, childbirth does not significantly affect the work–family interface or create much conflict because female family members provide support to the new mother, as is the case within the Venda culture (Chauke, 2016; Rapolai, 2016). An even more extreme instance of this is evident in traditional Swati culture, where men are not allowed to see their children until they are at least six months old (Ndwandwe, 2016). In the Venda, Ndebele, Zulu, and Tswana cultures, female members of the family, including the grandmother and elder sisters assist the new mother until she has regained her strength. This means that there is minimal pressure on fathers to provide care, allowing them to continue to focus on their work (Chauke, 2016; Gumede & Mthimkulu, 2006 cited in Mogaladi, 2016; Mokhuane, 2016; Mothoa, 2016).

Death

Regarding death, a similar divide occurs between African cultures on the one hand and White and Coloured cultures on the other within South Africa. White and Coloured families tend to have no prescriptive time for mourning. More urbanized families will typically attend the funerals of their immediate family members and have limited customs before, during, and after the funeral. These customs are typically not as time-consuming as those in African cultures. As a result, White and Coloured workers may not experience as much time-based conflict created by family responsibilities related to bereavement in comparison with Black Africans. In many Black African cultures, family members must be present from shortly after the time of death until after the burial and are expected to perform traditional ceremonies before, during, and after the burial (Mogaladi, 2016). These ceremonies and customs include slaughtering livestock, wearing specific mourning dress, adhering to a mourning period, and participating in cleansing ceremonies (Setsiba, 2016).

The family responsibility leave offered by South African employers fails to cover the time needed to participate in these ceremonies. Because South Africans are responsible for extended family members, they may even have multiple bereavements in one year. When this occurs, family members may experience increased work–family conflict. Resolving role conflict during bereavement is important because incompatible demands between work and family roles during bereavement may cause significant distress for the bereaved. This is pertinent in Africa as family members maintain a relationship with their deceased loved ones and ancestors, and many of the rituals associated with death are aimed at maintaining these relationships. As a result, violation of customs is viewed as disrespectful and an invitation for bad luck (Setsiba, 2016). Participation will, most likely, be prioritized over work responsibilities as a result.

The Zulu, Xhosa, Venda, and Swati cultures have rich and unique traditions and rituals surrounding death and mourning involving the extended family that require time away from work. Members of these groups perform rituals, typically dealing with ancestors and facilitating the transition to the afterlife. These rituals have deep symbolic and spiritual meaning; however, such rituals are time-consuming and employers are often unsympathetic to the nuances of such practices (Shange, 2009). Northern Sotho families view death as a "dark cloud" hanging over the family, particularly when the death was accidental or violent (Maloka, 1998). The family must perform death rituals overseen by a traditional healer in order to lift this cloud. The partner of the deceased may be expected to carry out customary rituals for two to three weeks (Mashatola, 2016). These rituals, often also involving the broader community, provide comfort during the grieving process and are an important means of coping with bereavement (Setsiba, 2016). However, employers may feel that providing paid time off for these activities is excessive. Conversely, given the broader family structure and number of dependents relying on them, employees may not be able to afford to take unpaid leave and this could cause further stress and work–family conflict.

There are often gender differences in terms of cultural practices surrounding death and mourning. Swati women are expected to mourn the loss of their husbands for as much as one year after their deaths. They are expected to wear a black mourning dress, may not look men in the eye, and cannot join gatherings where men are present. This may result in behavior-based work–family conflict at work as their work roles may not afford them the opportunity to fully observe mourning customs. On the other hand, Swati men have no such restrictions placed upon them after the death of their wives (Ndwandwe, 2016). As another example, Shangaan spouses also perform additional cleansing rituals before returning to work, sometimes taking as long as a month and these may also create work–family conflict (Rapolai, 2016). Clearly, such extended mourning periods are at odds with the modern work environment. In the Venda culture, the whole family must mourn for seven days preceding the burial of a family member in order to grieve and comfort each other and to use this time to make funeral arrangements (Chauke, 2016). Xhosa, Ndebele, and

Shangaan family members are also buried after a minimum period of seven days. This gives family members a chance to travel and congregate (Rapolai, 2016; Luzipo, 2016; Mothoa, 2016). Ndebele family members must further remain at home for one week following the burial. Work–family conflict emerges as family members must fulfill the family roles expected during bereavement, but are restricted by short family responsibility leave at work.

A notable distinction in the gendered division of labor seen between westernized and African cultures in South Africa is that in African cultures, the male head of the household is responsible for making all funeral arrangements and ensuring that the funeral runs smoothly (Mothoa, 2016), whereas women typically assume this responsibility in more westernized families. During this time, male family members may experience greater role conflict and may need more support in the workplace than their female counterparts. They may need more time off work, may experience more stress that has a negative spillover effect on their work, and may feel that their work role is interfering with their role as the male head of the family.

Coming of Age

Coming-of-age rituals signify the transition to adulthood and are gendered in African cultures. Boys are socialized into enduring hardship and girls are socialized into obedience and the role of caregiver (Mhlahlo, 2009). As an example, family members play a significant role in socializing children into gender roles in the Swati culture. Fathers groom sons to become men, teaching them "manly duties," while girls are socialized by older women (Ndwandwe, 2016). Entering the workplace may create behavior-based work–family conflict between these gendered roles and the typically more egalitarian Western work environment. Strain-based conflict could also occur if women experience guilt and stress based on the perception that they are taking on a role that is not socially sanctioned.

One notable coming-of-age ceremony in South Africa is the ulwaluko initiation rite undertaken by the Xhosa. This involves a period of isolation during which boys are circumcised, after which boys become men and are given the right to start their own families and greater rights within the community (Bidwell, Winschiers-Theophilus, & Dourish, 2015). This single rite involves separation (i.e., taking boys from their villages), transition (i.e., initiation and circumcision), and incorporation (i.e., reintroduction to the village as men) (Mhlahlo, 2009). For parts of ulwaluko, an older male family member accompanies the initiate to the initiation school. Male family members may experience work–family conflict, as they may need to take leave from work during this time. The initiation process also has financial implications as there is a cost for attendance of the initiation school, a celebration, and an outfit is purchased for the initiate at the end of the rite of passage. This may create strain-based conflict as the financial pressure may create stress that spills over negatively into the workplace.

In the Venda culture, girls are initiated in a three-phase process involving vusha, tshikanda, and domba at the onset of puberty, while boys are initiated prior to puberty (Mhlahlo, 2009). The Tsonga also have different rituals for men and women (Khosa,

2009, in Bvuma, 2016). Their initiation schools teach the responsibilities of being an adult. However, formal, westernized education has made it more difficult to strictly adhere to the coming-of-age rituals and many ceremonies are being discarded. Many families are shifting to the same, brief twenty-first birthday celebrations commonly found in White and Coloured families (Machaba, 2009 cited in Bvuma, 2016). This suggests that the process of westernization has lessened the impacts of coming-of-age rituals on the work–family interface in South Africa.

Illness

As mentioned, in African cultures individuals assume responsibility for the well-being of their extended families, with African women carrying a disproportionate portion of the "burden of care." This is particularly true in respect to childcare, but is not limited to this domain. For example, when a family member gets ill, it is the responsibility of those within the extended family to care for that person. The caregiver is usually a woman, and these responsibilities increase absenteeism from work (Mothoa, 2016; Rapolai, 2016). Public hospitals in South Africa are under-staffed and under-resourced. As a result, in South Africa, family members must often accompany ill family members to hospitals and perform many of the duties tradi-tionally performed by nurses. Disability benefits are minimal and there is the dual burden of financial responsibility as well as the need to provide care for disabled family members. Extended family members may help avoid conflict when they step in to look after the ill so that primary caregivers do not have to miss work.

Alternative healing is preferred over Western medicine amongst more traditional Black Africans (Ross, 2007). This sometimes delays the healing process because there is a preference for care by traditional healers instead of modern medicine, such as in the Zulu and Tswana culture (Mogaladi, 2016; Mokhuane, 2016). The Tsonga believe that ancestors cause some illnesses and misfortunes. In response, they too consult traditional healers (Bvuma, 2016). The reliance on traditional, instead of modern medicine, may translate to longer absences from work due to a slower (and possibly less effective) recovery rate, and organizations do not usually recognize diagnoses or medical certificates from traditional healers.

Marriage and Partnerships

South African law recognizes three types of marriages. The first and most common type of marriage is the civil marriage. The second type is the customary marriage. Customary marriages can be polygamous and are sometimes solemnized through traditional African marriage ceremonies. The third form, namely civil unions, afford same-sex couples the opportunity to marry (Grant, 2015).

Marriage ceremonies in South Africa are evidence of the confluence of Western and traditional African values. Traditional customs have not disappeared. Instead, these practices may live side by side. Many Black African couples are choosing to hold two sets of ceremonies. One is a traditional ceremony where they observe Black African customs, often at their family homes in the rural areas, and the other is a

Western, urban ceremony. Once again, working couples may experience time-based strain, as they need to take time away from work in order to participate in each ceremony. This is a further testament to the dual identities and roles played across urban and rural as well as public and private spaces in South Africa.

Swati culture retains the custom of arranged marriages (Das, 1993; Ndwandwe, 2016), but perhaps the most enduring traditional custom associated with marriage in South Africa is the payment of a dowry, lobola, or magadi (Tswana) to the bride's family (Luzipo, 2016; Ndwandwe, 2016). The price of the dowry is determined by the bride's level of education, number of children, birth order, and age, to mention a few of the criteria. Issues like arranged marriage and dowry perpetuate gender inequality. Those holding these beliefs may expect female coworkers to behave in a certain way or may treat them differently because of the values they hold and the practices they perform in their family roles.

Another area where work–family, or more broadly work–nonwork conflict, may arise is with one's role as a daughter-in-law. Once married, Black African women are expected to perform specific subservient and demanding functions in the family into which they marry, regardless of their employment status (S. Nyathi, personal communication, 12 August, 2016). They must reconcile the demands of their work and family roles and often do so at the expense of their leisure time, forgoing opportunities for personal development.

The contrast between the Western and traditional African family structure is perhaps most marked when dealing with the issue of polygamy. In the Zulu culture, women are absorbed into the husband's family upon marriage. The first, senior wife is the matriarch whose permission is required before additional wives can be incorporated into the family. Although the law recognizes polygamous customary marriages, many employers do not extend benefits such as medical care to multiple spouses. Lack of recognition and support may result in a perceived breach of the psychological contract and cause work–family conflict. These practices are changing as more families become urbanized (Mogaladi, 2016).

It is not surprising that marriage is a source of strength for male employees in South Africa as female spouses provide a great deal of psychosocial and domestic support. Many men in South Africa across all racial groups also believe that they are motivated to work harder because they subscribe to the traditionalist view that they should be the breadwinners in their families (Ndwandwe, 2016; Nzimande, 2016). Men also value the opportunity to provide financial support to their extended families. This is in keeping with the burden and obligation to care for the extended family. However, the trend towards dual-income families is beginning to challenge the notion that men should be the sole providers (Mashatola, 2016). Despite the rise in dual-income families and encouragement of greater gender equality in the workplace, women may be discouraged from pursuing careers because their success may cause jealousy and the disruption of the balance of power in the home, particularly when faced with traditional patriarchal values or when women earn more than their spouses (Bvuma, 2016). Choosing to have children also disrupts women's careers, as society expects mothers to provide childcare for at least the early years of their children's lives. Nevertheless, the benefits of greater financial security, increased well-being, and stronger role models provided by dual-income or dual-career families remain (Nzimande, 2016).

Organizational Implications and Recommendations

South African organizations often fail to provide adequate or appropriate support because they do not understand the demands of cultural and family-related roles placed upon a large portion of their employees, particularly those from Black African cultures, during rites of passage (Setsiba, 2009). South African legislation, and by extension employment conditions, potentially fail to recognize the demands that responsibilities linked to family membership place upon employees. There is a strong case for taking intersectionality into account in the formulation of human resources policies, as this may contribute to enhanced satisfaction, engagement, and commitment of all workers, and this is especially true for African workers. Managers must create inclusive work environments where diversity is valued. Ethnocentric employment practices exacerbate work–family conflict and could partially account for a lack of Black women in leadership positions in South Africa (Erasmus, 2007; Hearne, 2014).

Legislation and policy are not the only sources of barriers to advancement in the South African workplace. For instance, culture-bound gender roles restrict women within the workplace and affect how their colleagues treat them. This has implications for interactions both within and between cultures. For example, men and women raised in patriarchal environments, such as in rural Zulu or Swati communities, may treat women differently in the workplace than those raised in other environments. Similarly, Black African women from these communities may themselves act in a deferential way, being reluctant to assume leadership positions because of their cultural backgrounds and domestic responsibilities (Hearne, 2014).

The multitude of dimensions of diversity in South Africa places an array of demands on working families. As a result, there is no uniform solution. Instead, workplaces may prefer to encourage open communication of needs so that policies might be adapted to meet workers' needs. To facilitate this, training and development initiatives should make employees aware of their rights and responsibilities as well as equipping them with the skills needed for improved role management. These factors transcend cultural differences and are universal requirements in the workplace that could help employees to better meet the unique demands placed on them (Rantanen, Kinnunen, Mauno, & Tilleman, 2011). Role management skills encompass workplace behaviors such as time management, but also family interactions such as adopting proactive coping strategies and encouraging communication in the home. Employees could also benefit from training that exposes them to other cultures in South Africa so that they can develop empathy as well as to communicate and accommodate each other better.

Most of the work–family tension specific to South Africa seems to stem from the fact that the Western notion of the family, upon which most human resources management policies are based, does not extend beyond the nuclear family. One instance of mismatch between culture and policy is the absence of recognition, in both policy and legislation, of the time-consuming nature of African customs associated with rites of passage (i.e., death, illness, birth, marriage, and coming of age). Family responsibility leave also fails to take into account the burden of care specifically carried by women, which may lead to greater work–family conflict and absenteeism at work. As mentioned, both men and women experience pressure when it comes to taking time off to participate in family activities. Apartheid aggravated the situation by separating urban work environments and many family homes. Therefore, travelling to family events is time-consuming and costly, particularly when there is a need to use public transport. One solution would be to allow employees to save overtime hours to use as paid leave when needed.

As discussed, the notion of the family in Africa is broad and incorporates the extended family. The major challenge then is to extend benefits to acknowledge the African conceptualization of dependents, spouses, and family responsibilities in general. The number of cultural variations, evident across different regions within South African society, further complicates the process of providing equitable benefits. The abovementioned mismatch between culture and policy is further borne out by the fact that human resources policies do not recognize dependents such as the children of siblings or extended family members. Employers do not provide benefits for these family members, despite their importance in the African family structure. Flexible remuneration practices and the provision of subsidized benefits for extended family members may serve to address this concern.

Conclusion

The contrast between the demands of African family life and westernized work benefits lies at the core of many of the work–family conflicts described in this chapter. Many of the cultural practices discussed may seem at odds with a Western corporate structure, where work plays a central role in an individual's life and is potentially the person's strongest source of identity, with less emphasis on the importance of family. African loyalties and identities are bound more strongly to the family. Because of the multitude of variations in the urban–rural, modern–traditional, male–female, and professional–private roles that society expects of employees in South Africa, there is no uniform solution. Employers who wish to motivate, develop, and retain employees from diverse backgrounds within South Africa will need to establish authentic, consultative relationships with their staff and become responsive to their individual needs and realities.

References

Amoateng, A., & Heaton, T. (2007). *Families and Households in Post-Apartheid South Africa*. Cape Town, South Africa: HSRC Press.

Bendix, S. (1996). *Industrial Relations in South Africa*. Cape Town, South Africa: Juta.

Bidwell, N., Winschiers-Theophilus, H., & Dourish, P. (Eds.) (2015). *At the Intersection of Indigenous and Traditional Knowledge and Technology Design.* Santa Rosa, CA: Informing Science Press.

Burch, T. K. (1976). The size and structure of families: A comparative analysis of census data. *American Sociological Review, 32,* 347–363.

Butler, A. (2004). *Contemporary South Africa.* Basingstoke, UK: Palgrave Macmillan.

Bvuma, S. R. (2016). Work–family interface amongst the Tsonga. (Unpublished manuscript). Stellenbosch, South Africa: University of Stellenbosch.

Chauke, K. (2016). Work–family conflict in the Venda cultural group. (Unpublished manuscript). Stellenbosch, South Africa: University of Stellenbosch.

Comaroff, J. L., & Comaroff, J. (1997). *Of Revelation and Revolution: The Dialectics of Modernity on a South African Frontier.* Chicago, IL: Chicago University Press.

Conner, T. (2004). South Africa Seminar: Language systems in South Africa and their parallels to the linguistic struggle of blacks in the U.S. Retrieved November 10, 2016, from http://web.stanford.edu/~jbaugh/saw/Tracy_Language_&_Ebonics.html.

Cox, P. (2013, January 22). Employed South Africans have high number of dependents. Voice of America. Retrieved January 25, 2017, from www.voanews.com/a/employed-south-africans-have-high-number-of-dependents/1588436.html

Das, M. (1993). *The Family in Africa.* New Delhi, India: MD Publications.

Erasmus, L. J. (2007). The management of workforce diversity and the implications for leadership at financial asset services. (Unpublished master's dissertation). Johannesburg, South Africa: University of Johannesburg.

Erez, M., & Gati, E. (2004). A dynamic, multi-level model of culture: from the micro level of the individual to the macro level of a global culture. *Applied Psychology, 53*(4), 583–598.

Gerhart, G. (1979). *Black Power in South Africa.* Berkeley, CA: UCLA Press

Grant, L. (2015, May 19). 10 things about marriage in South Africa. *The Mail and Guardian.* Retrieved from http://mg.co.za/data/2015–05-19–10-things-about-marriage-in-south-africa-1

Hankivsky, O. (2014). *Intersectionality 101.* Vancouver, Canada: Institute for Intersectionality Research and Policy.

Haralambos, M., & Holborn, M. (1995). *Sociology.* London, UK: Collins Educational.

Hearne, M. (2014, September 9). Women still face discrimination in the South African workplace. *HR Pulse.* Retrieved from www.hrpulse.co.za/legal/employment-equity-act/231424-gender-inequality-persists-in-the-south-african-workplace.

Hofstede, G. (2001). *Culture's Consequences: Comparing Values, Behaviors, Institutions, and Organizations across Nations.* Second Edition. Thousand Oaks CA: Sage Publications.

Hutson, S. (2007). Gender oppression and discrimination in South Africa. *ESSAI Journal, 5* (26), 82–86.

Kehler, J. (2013). Women and poverty: the South African experience. *Journal of International Women's Studies, 3*(1), 41–53.

Koekemoer, E., & Mostert, K. (2010). An exploratory study of the interaction between work and personal life: Experiences of South African employees. *SA Journal of Industrial Psychology, 36*(1), 1–15.

Kraak, A. (2005). Human resources development and the skills crisis in South Africa: The need for a multi-pronged strategy. *Journal of Education and Work, 18*(1), 57–83.

Luzipo, P. (2016). Work–family interface in South African within the Xhosa culture. (Unpublished manuscript). Stellenbosch, South Africa: University of Stellenbosch.

MacDonald, M. (2006). *Why Race Matters in South Africa*. Cambridge, MA: Harvard University Press.

Makhathini, T. N. (2016). Work–family interface within the Zulu culture. (Unpublished manuscript). Stellenbosch, South Africa: University of Stellenbosch.

Maloka, T. (1998). Basotho and the experience of death, dying, and mourning in the South African mine compounds, 1890–1940 (Les Basotho et l'expérience de la mort, du deuil et des rites funéraires dans les concessions minières sud-africaines, 1890–1940).*Cahiers D'Études Africaines*, *38*(149), 17–40.

Mangaliso, M. P. (2001). Building competitive advantage from Ubuntu: Management lessons from South Africa. *The Academy of Management Executive*, *15*(3), 23–33.

Mashatola, N. J. (2016). Work and family interface of the Northern Sotho group in South Africa. (Unpublished manuscript). Stellenbosch, South Africa: University of Stellenbosch.

Mhlahlo, A. P. (2009). What is manhood? The significance of circumcision in the traditional Xhosa initiation ritual. (Unpublished MPhil thesis). Stellenbosch, South Africa: University of Stellenbosch.

Mogaladi, E. (2016). Work–family interface in Zulu families in South Africa. (Unpublished manuscript). Stellenbosch, South Africa: University of Stellenbosch.

Mokhuane, O. (2016). Work–family interface amongst the Tswana. (Unpublished manuscript). Stellenbosch, South Africa: University of Stellenbosch.

Mokomane, Z. (2009, September). Work–family conflict and gender equality in South Africa. In 26th IUSSP International Population Conference, Marrakech, Morocco, September 27–October 2.

Mothoa, D. A. (2016). Work–family interface within the Ndebele culture. (Unpublished manuscript). Stellenbosch, South Africa: University of Stellenbosch.

Ndwandwe, M. N. (2016). Work–family interface within the Swati population group. (Unpublished manuscript). Stellenbosch, South Africa: University of Stellenbosch.

Nzimande, Z. L. (2016). Work–family interaction: The experiences of Afrikaans-speaking working couples at the Military Academy. (Unpublished manuscript). Stellenbosch, South Africa: University of Stellenbosch.

Rantanen, J., Kinnunen, U., Mauno, S., & Tilleman, K. (2011). Introducing theoretical approaches to work-life balance and testing a new typology among professionals. In S. Kaiser, M. J. Ringsletter, D. R. Eikhof, & M. Pina e Cunha (Eds.), *Creating Balance? International Perspectives on the Work–Life Integration of Professionals* (First Edition, pp. 27–46). Berlin, Germany: Springer-Verlag.

Rapolai, J. K. (2016). Work–family interface in South Africa: Venda cultural variations. (Unpublished manuscript). Stellenbosch, South Africa: University of Stellenbosch.

Ross, E. (2007). Traditional healing in South Africa: ethical implications for social work. *Social Work in Health Care*, *46*(2), 15–33.

Seekings, J. (2003). Social stratification and inequality in South Africa at the end of apartheid. (CSSR Working paper no. 31). Cape Town, South Africa: Centre for Social Science Research, University of Cape Town.

Seekings, J. (2008). The continuing salience of race: Discrimination and diversity in South Africa. *Journal of Contemporary African Studies*, *26*(1), 1–25.

Setsiba, T. (2016). Mourning rituals and practices in contemporary South African townships: A phenomenological study. (Unpublished thesis). KwaDlangezwa, South Africa: University of Zululand.

Shange, L. O. (2009). Bereaved employees in organisations: Managers and workers co-responsibility. (Unpublished thesis). KwaDlangezwa, South Africa: University of Zululand.

Shisana, O., Rice, K., Zungu, N., & Zuma, K. (2010). Gender and poverty in South Africa in the era of HIV/AIDS: A quantitative study. *Journal of Women's Health*, *19*(1), 39–46.

Sibiya, G. (2016). The work–family interface of Coloured couples in South Africa. (Unpublished manuscript). Stellenbosch, South Africa: University of Stellenbosch.

Southall, R. (2016). *The New Black Middle Class in South Africa. Auckland Park*, Johannesburg, South Africa: Jacana.

South Africa (2003). Broad-based black economic empowerment Act no 53 of 2003. *Government Gazette*, (25899).

Statistics South Africa (2012). *Census 2011: Census in Brief*. Pretoria, South Africa: Statistics South Africa.

Thipe, T. (2013). Defining boundaries: Gender and property rights in South Africa's traditional courts bill. *Laws*, *2*, 483–511.

Uchendu, E. (2008). *Masculinities in Contemporary Africa*. Dakar, Senegal: Council for the Development of Social Science Research in Africa.

UNESCO. (1967). *Apartheid: Its Effects on Education, Science, Culture and Information*. Paris, France: UNESCO.

Van der Merwe, J. (2016). An historical geographical analysis of South Africa's system of accumulation: 1652–1994. *Review of African Political Economy*, *43*(147), 58–72.

Wilson, F. (2011). *Labour in the South African Gold Mines 1911–1969* (Vol. 6). Cambridge, UK: Cambridge University Press.

Winster, J. (2016). Work–family interface in South African coloured culture. (Unpublished manuscript). Stellenbosch, South Africa: University of Stellenbosch.

25 Work and Family among Immigrants

Joseph G. Grzywacz, Neena Gopalan,
and Fiorella L. Carlos Chavez

Immigration is fundamentally a work–family issue in many, if not most, instances. Regardless of whether the immigrant is a poorly educated individual from rural Mexico who crosses the border to perform farm work, a highly trained information-technology expert from eastern Asia working in the Silicon Valley, or a student from Africa earning a college degree in the United States, all three have left home and some vestige of "family" for a job or the promise of career growth. This basic reality illustrates a raw and salient phenomenon that remains virtually unstudied in the work and family literature. That is, although immigration may reflect a fundamental work–family issue, there is likely both substantial variability in work–family experiences among immigrants from similar countries and substantial variability across immigrants from different countries. The absence of research leaves a fundamental gap for employers and host communities in supporting the needs of the approximately 244 million immigrants globally (United Nations, 2016).

The overall goal of this chapter is to motivate systematic research on the work and family experiences of immigrants, as well as the structural, interpersonal, and individual consequences of those experiences. Despite the global experience of immigration, the literature on the work and family experiences of immigrants is, at best, nascent. Further, the limited research is scattered across diverse disciplines under different terms or conceptual circumstances. As examples, the management literature has studied individuals from one country sent to work in another country under the label of "expatriates" (Shaffer, Harrison, Gilley, & Luk, 2001), and occupational psychologists have studied the stress-related hardships of low wage workers forced to leave family in their country of origin because of the requirements of an H2a or H2b visa (Grzywacz et al., 2006, 2013). These realities highlight the stark contrast between the current literature and the goal of this chapter. Indeed, we contend that, in light of the virtual oversight of immigrants in the work–family literature, there is substantial need for work and family research among distinct immigrant groups, as well as comparative research across discrete groups of immigrants and between immigrants and non-immigrants.

Nevertheless, this chapter proceeds toward its goal by accomplishing five primary aims. First, we characterize the global experience of international immigration, including variability in the size, scope, and nature of immigrants across different regions of the world. Second, we illustrate the potential variation in the work and family experiences that are built into immigrants' experiences by virtue of laws and policies surrounding immigration and issuance of visas dictating parameters for international migration. Third, we summarize what is known about the work and family experiences of immigrants, including expatriates. Next, we articulate a theoretically informed conceptual framework for studying work and family experiences among immigrants. Finally, we outline a high-priority research agenda for systematically advancing basic and contextual understanding of immigrants' work and family experiences, and how to use this understanding to advance solutions that benefit workers, their families, and employers.

Meaning and Global Patterns of International Migration

Definitions and Key Concepts

Understanding the work and family experiences of immigrants requires acknowledging the complexity of the term "immigrant," a term that is commonly used but poorly understood. Migrate is a verb; it is the action of moving from one place to another, as in the "migration" of birds in season. An immigrant is a person (or group of people) that moves from one place to another. Indeed, the United Nations (UN) defines an international immigrant as "a person who moves to a country other than that of his or her usual residence."

The UN's definition of "immigrant" provides the backbone for measuring international migration around the world; nevertheless, it has several points of ambiguity. First, what does "... who moves to a country ..." mean? Does "move" have a temporal dimension? Toward that end, the UN does differentiate between long-term and short-term immigrants, defining the former as those whose move lasted twelve months or more and the latter as a move that lasted fewer than twelve months. Second and similarly, it is not clear whether the definition implies some expectation of permanency. Is an individual who takes a one-year assignment abroad considered an immigrant? Is a stereotypical migrant farmworker considered an immigrant from another country, a migrant because of the nature of the work, or both? Third, does the "move" need to be legitimized in some way for it to be considered immigration? If so, then how? Is an individual lacking legal authorization to reside in a country, such as that provided by a visa, an immigrant? Is a student from abroad pursuing an advanced degree in another country an immigrant? Finally, does the motivational force behind the "move" matter to the meaning or conception of immigrant? Is there a difference between a person who moves internationally for work or higher education and the person who seeks political asylum or is fleeing violence?

This chapter does not attempt to resolve the ambiguities inherent in the complexity of the term "immigrant." Indeed, there are entire disciplines committed to understanding immigration replete with theories, researchers, and empirical journals that are better equipped to address these issues. Rather, our purpose in highlighting these ambiguities is to simply illustrate the reality that, at the broadest level, immigrants comprise a diverse set of individuals.

The Global Picture

International migration is common. Approximately 244 million individuals, comparable to three-quarters of the population of the United States, engaged in international migration in 2015 (United Nations, 2016). Europe is the primary destination for international immigrants (76 million), followed by Asia (75 million) and North America (54 million). The United States has the largest number of international immigrants of any individual country in the world: essentially, one in five international immigrants arrived to the United States. Globally, most immigrants originated in middle-income countries in Asia (43%), Europe (25%), and Latin America or the Caribbean (15%). In 2015, nearly 20 million more individuals, largely women and children, left their home country as refugees seeking asylum in another country.

International migration is increasing rapidly. Estimates from the United Nations (2016) suggest that international migration increased by 28% between 2000 and 2010, and by another 10% between 2010 and 2015. There is substantial variability in the growth of international migration. Whereas immigrants to Europe increased by 35% from 2000 to 2015, the rate of change in Asia and North America during the same period was 53% and 35%, respectively.

The United States Picture

The United States is a country of immigrants. The Migration Policy Institute estimates approximately 42 million immigrants reside in the United States based on data from the American Community Survey (www.migrationpolicy.org). The number of immigrants and their share in the United States population has steadily increased since the lowest point in 1970 wherein 9.6 million immigrants represented 4.7% of the population. Depending on the estimation procedure used, between 12 and 14 million individuals immigrated to the United States between 2000 and 2010 (Jensen, Bhaskar, & Scopilliti, 2015). In 2015, about 26.3 million foreign-born persons were in the United States labor force, 48.8% of whom were Latino (Bureau of Labor Statistics, 2016). The overall description of immigrants in the US labor force indicates that about one in six workers in the United States is an immigrant, immigrants are under-represented in professional and managerial jobs, and about half of employed foreign-born women and nearly all employed foreign-born men have at least one dependent child at home. When combined with the law of large numbers, these realities highlight the glaring oversight of immigrants in the work–family literature.

"Immigrants" and visas. Entering a country legally requires some type of visa, either temporary or permanent. The US Secretary of State's Office reports that over 530,000 permanent visas or "green cards" were issued from Foreign Service posts in 2015, and an additional 11 million temporary visas were issued. These visas are issued for a wide variety of purposes and under various circumstances; however, only a fraction allow the holder to work. The number of permanent work-related visas increased by 43% between 2011 and 2015. The growth reflects substantial

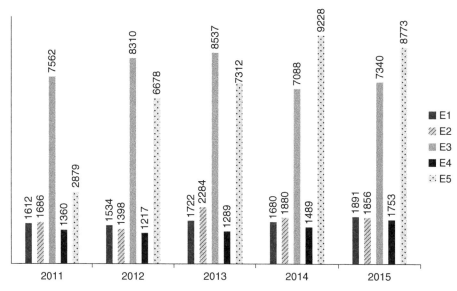

Figure 25.1 *Number of green cards issued by EB type (2011–2015).*

increases in E5 visas (Figure 25.1) which are issued to non-citizens who are making capital investments in new commercial enterprises that result in job creation.

The roughly 22,000 work-related permanent visas are dwarfed by the nearly 9 million temporary work-related visas issued by the Secretary of State's Office in 2015. Just over 7 million of these temporary visas are issued through the Business Visitor classification, singly (B-1) or in combined business-pleasure (B-1/B-2). Although the dominant temporary work-related visa, they are intended for short-term stays in the country for business-related reasons (e.g., attend a business convention, negotiate a contract, buy or sell an estate). Visas for entrance into the country for purposes of education (F-1) or other forms of training (e.g., M-1) are the second-largest type of temporary work-related visas issued: in 2015 over 650,000 education- or training-related visas were issued. The remaining 1.4 million temporary work-related visas issued are spread across approximately eighteen distinct types, but only four categories account for 10% or more (Figure 25.2). The largest percentage (28%) of temporary work-related visas are issued to crewmembers such as flight or cruise personnel and workers on cargo ships (C-1, D Visas) (Figure 25.2). The second largest (17%) temporary work visa is the H1b visa, which is designed for individuals in specialty occupations, frequently with advanced educational degrees or professional certifications. Finally, a comparable percentage of visas (11% in each) are issued to diplomats or government officials residing in the United States because of their work assignment (A-1, A-2, A-3 visas) and temporary agricultural workers (H-2A visa).

Of course, there are a substantial but unknown number of immigrants without legal authorization to live and/or work in the United States. The Pew Research

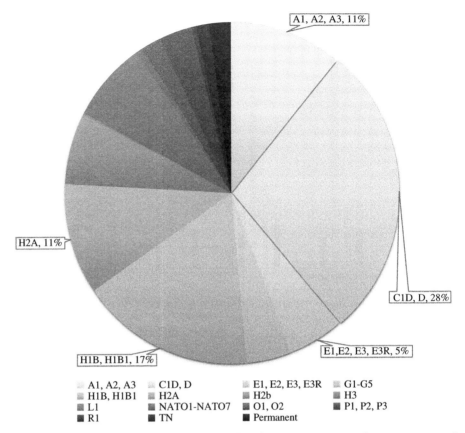

Figure 25.2 *Percentage of work-related visas, temporary and permanent, issued in 2015 (not inclusive of business visitor and study visas).*

Center estimates approximately 11.2 million unauthorized immigrants in the United States in 2012 (Passel & Cohn, 2014). An estimated 8.1 million unauthorized immigrants are in the United States Labor Force (Passel & Cohn, 2014). Although over half of the unauthorized immigrant population in the United States is Mexican, a sizeable minority of individuals from Europe and Canada exists, and the number of unauthorized immigrants from Asia, the Caribbean, and Central America is believed to be growing.

Visa requirements and constraints: Potential implications for work and family. The work and family experiences of immigrants are fundamentally shaped by how they entered the country. The work and family experiences of undocumented immigrants are likely shaped by their legal liminality. The absence of legal authorization to live and work in the country frequently places immigrants on the employment margins of society, frequently performing dirty, dangerous, and demeaning (3-D) jobs (Quandt et al., 2013) or other physically demanding and risky jobs not desired by native-born workers (Smith, Chen, & Mustard, 2009). Families of undocumented immigrants live in perennial fear of family fragmentation because of one or more members' forced deportation. Indeed, one poignant essay comments how undocumented immigrants with children will avoid going to children's school out of fear that police officers working at schools (largely in a traffic control context) will stop and potentially hold a parent for deportation, and that running errands occurs at odd hours to avoid potential confrontation with law enforcement officers (Zapata Roblyer & Grzywacz, 2015).

The clear majority of immigrants to the United States, and presumably other high-immigration destination countries, arrive under the auspices of a temporary work permit. Two major features of temporary work visas shape everyday work and family experiences of immigrants. First, many temporary work visas are issued to an employer for workers, not to workers for employment. Exemplified by the H-2A and H-2B visa programs that collectively account for 17% of temporary visas (Figure 25.2), the employer holds the worker visa and the visa is nontransferable from one employer to another. This means the worker is unable to change employers: the worker either works for the sponsoring employer or is sent home. Similarly, individuals working under the more professional H1B temporary work visa have disincentives to leave their primary employer. Upon loss or separation of employment from the primary employer, an H-1B visa holder must obtain another visa status, find alternative employment if a change status is authorized, or leave the country. These examples illustrate that, although more extreme for nonprofessional workers, immigrants entering the country under temporary work visas face threats and real constraints in securing and maintaining satisfying employment.

Temporary work visas also shape immigrants' family lives. When a temporary work visa is issued to an individual, it typically does not allow entrance permission to the country for the individual's spouse or any dependent children. Instead, family members of individuals with a temporary work visa must apply for their own visas (with a corresponding fee), and one condition for issuing the family member visas is the temporary worker's ability to financially support the family. Moreover, family members of temporary work visa holders are often unable to hold employment themselves. Indeed, there are many cases of spouses entering the country under a type of visa that does not allow employment who remain unemployed for five to ten years because they are unable to change their visa to one that allows employment. Collectively this suggests that many temporary workers make the decision of whether the family will accompany the individual with the temporary work visa, and if so, accompanying family members may generate financial burden because of both the costs of securing visas and travel and employment restrictions on family members.

The situation for permanent workers or those with "green cards" (i.e., EB-1, EB-2, EB-3, EB4, and EB-5 visas) is very different. Immigrants with green cards can change employers without restriction or the necessity to seek diplomatic approvals. This reality empowers the immigrant to seek and secure the most satisfying work arrangement available. In terms of family, the spouse and children of immigrants with a green card are admitted to the United States, and they can obtain permanent residency immigration status themselves. The process of applying for permanent residence for spouses and children takes time, and in the interim, they typically cannot obtain employment. Nevertheless, spouses of green card holders are frequently able to pursue employment and their children are able to attend school. Families of green card holders are the least encumbered by restrictions while also having the maximum liberty.

Visa mandates have real work and family implications. Much of the previous content in this section was generated from logical inferences made from visa eligibility and application requirements. In the absence of previous research on the topic of how the parameters of the visa shape work and family experiences of immigrants, we conducted an unofficial qualitative study on the topic. Specifically, we reached out to friends and colleagues ($N = 8$) currently in the United States on some form of work-related visa, including student visas. We asked our friends and colleagues to comment on the benefits and disadvantages of holding a temporary visa for self and for the family. When considering their families, we encouraged consideration of both those family members who may be in the United States as well as family members remaining in their country of origin.

Nearly all our interviewees commented that one of the benefits of an H1b visa is the legal right to work and live in the United States. These individuals commented that American employers are more likely to recognize and reward workers' contributions compared to firms in their country of origin. A few individuals commented that being on an H1b had direct benefits for their families; yet, this position seemed to be country-specific. H1b holders from Southeast Asian countries commented that H1b had no positive impact for family, while those from South Asian countries referenced economic gains from being on H1b that extended to their family as well.

All the individuals in our "study," regardless of region, commented on the work-related restrictions of the H1b visa. Restrictions in employment mobility, the pressure to maintain H1b status (by ensuring no gap in employment or being laid off), and the limited number of years an individual can hold an H1b were all problems spontaneously articulated by individuals. Additionally, several individuals commented on the inability of their spouse to work, although recent changes to immigration laws may now start to allow spouses on an H4 dependent visa to pursue an Employment Authorization Document (EAD) to enable employment.

A small fraction of individuals commented about a sense of isolation from family. The cost of airfare can range for $900 to $2,000 per ticket, and flights are often fifteen to nineteen hours in duration. These realities on top of visa restrictions that, in most cases, may allow a maximum of twenty-one days of total leave impede these workers' ability to be with family. Further, family members who want to visit the H1b visa-holder in the United States must complete an interview with the United States embassy, which can be "failed" for a variety of reasons. One individual in our study reported that she postponed her wedding in the United States because her parents did not get a visitor visa for her wedding. She reported that her parents were declined a visa because of their poor English skills and a wedding was not sufficient justification for a visa.

The individuals in our "study" on a student visa (F1) discussed the burden immigrating had on their family. It is not uncommon for families to pledge their property to take bank loans to financially support their children to acquire an American education. Although the financial burden borne by families may be elevated among student visa holders because of the added costs of living expenses (individuals on student visas are only allowed to work up to twenty hours at his/her higher education institution), families frequently leverage themselves to cover the costs of securing any type of visa and associated travel costs. Some universities have fewer restrictions on GPA or Test of English as a Foreign Language (TOEFL) requirements and open doors to many students from abroad. While many international students are able to come to the United States and avail themselves of superior higher education in this country, not all stories have a *happy* ending. There are foreign individuals who came to the United States to study, gained admission to "accredited" universities only to later discover the United States Customs and Immigration Service had revoked their visas. In 2016 over one thousand students, primarily from China and India, who thought they were registered students at the University of Northern New Jersey had their visas revoked because the University has neither faculty nor classes. Although the actual number of fraudulent visas issued to institutions on behalf of individuals globally is unknown, the fact that it has been uncovered highlights the precarious position individuals seeking international migration confront.

Work and Family among Immigrants: Existing Evidence

The diverse array of immigrant groups in the United States is studied by a wide range of researchers from diverse disciplines approaching the topic from diverse perspectives. Indeed, the work and family experiences of corporate executives who take a two-year international assignment abroad (i.e., corporate expatriates; please see chapter 26 of this volume (Dimitrova)) are likely to be very different from the undocumented day-laborer, which is also likely to be distinct from the highly educated professional drawn to Silicon Valley through an H1b visa. The body of evidence covered in this review cannot fully capture this diverse group of immigrants, in part because the research evidence is not evenly distributed across different immigrant groups. Moreover, it is not possible to approach the review with a well-developed a priori conceptual framework because the research spans different bodies of science.

Our literature review is therefore organized at two levels to accommodate the diverse array of studies across the body of evidence, and the substantial unevenness of coverage in any cognate area. First, we organize the review in three sections reflecting the dominant focus of the published research; those sections are "Work Experiences of Immigrants," "Family Experiences of Immigrants," and the "Work–family Experiences of Immigrants." Then, within each section, we organize covered material using three concepts intended to capture the broadest meaning of the diverse topics of study. Specifically, "demands" reflect those topics representing an environmental attribute at the cultural, social, or interpersonal level that poses a threat or challenge to immigrants. "Resources" reflect topics representing an environmental attribute, again at the any level, that is generative or enabling. Finally, "individual characteristics" represent between-person differences under study. Whenever possible we use the language of the original author(s) to clarify the type of immigrant under study (e.g., expatriate, international student, H1b visa holder, undocumented worker).

Work Experiences of Immigrants

Immigrants without legal authorization to reside in the United States have limited access to formal employment and frequently find themselves engaged in paid labor on the economic margins of society. Some authors suggest that undocumented immigrants from Mexico and Central America are disproportionately placed in jobs that are dirty, dangerous, and demeaning (3-D jobs) (Quandt et al., 2013). Investigators from other North American and European countries point out that immigrants (with unknown documentation) are over-represented in jobs that are physically demanding (Smith, Chen, & Mustard, 2009), psychosocially stressful (Hoppe, 2011), and may result in greater likelihood of job injury (Ahonen & Benavides, 2006). Immigrants with legal authorization to work, including those with a visa or green card, confront unique demands that impair or threaten performance and productivity on the job.

Regardless of documentation, cultural shifts in how work is performed impose a myriad of demands, oftentimes subtle, on immigrants and their work experience. Many immigrants are from collectivistic-oriented cultures (e.g., China, India) where individuals maintain strong power distance, engage in less indulgent behavior, provide hegemonic advantage to men, and elevate the well-being of groups over that of individuals (Hofstede, 1984). By contrast, the culture of destination countries for many immigrants, like the United States, are more individualistic such that power distance is attenuated, and the preferences of individuals supplant those of the group, including family. Beyond relatively obvious issues of language and verbal communication, immigrants may confront unfamiliar or conflicting religious practices (e.g., time off for Christmas but not Ramadan), they may be less aware of "taken for granted" expectations of workers (e.g., show up on time to meetings, workers have rights), and subtle yet powerful rules governing means of communication (e.g., how to handle the exchange of business cards).

Getting adjusted to a new culture will likely influenced immigrants' experiences of work. A study of corporate expatriates (Suárez-Orozco & Suárez-Orozco, 2001) reported that immigrants may begin to acquire some of the dominant practices of the host culture as they live and work in the host culture. Immigrant employees tend to internalize workplace behaviors that can lead to acculturation and identity change (Olson, Huffman, Leiva, & Culbertson, 2013), which may, in turn, contribute to enhanced workplace performance and development. Even when things do not go well in the work domain, expatriates often do not return to their native country prematurely (Kim & Slocum, 2008), which may negatively impact workplace effectiveness.

Researchers have considered a wide variety of workplace demands, beyond acculturation, as potential predictors of valued work outcomes for immigrants.

There is some evidence that expatriates experience frustration resulting from poor understanding of how the work in their role in their new country of residence is completed (Harris, 2002). Role ambiguity, not knowing the mode of operation or what is expected in the new role, can be a source of stress leading to poorer job satisfaction and hinder work adjustment (Kawai & Mohr, 2015). Decision-making authority has also been linked to work experiences of expatriates, such that lower authority is associated with higher experienced psychological demand (Harris, 2002). Expatriates who experienced marginalization at work had higher depressive symptoms (E. Kim, 2009), and some report feeling unsupported at work or not part of the "in-group" (Chen, Brockner, & Katz, 1998).

For those with international sponsors, such as expatriates, company-sponsored benefits contribute to the success of immigrants in their work assignment. Career and repatriation planning, rest and relaxation leave, and child education allowances seem to promote successful work assignments (Konopaske & Werner, 2005). Material, financial, or social supports from the organization can also assist international employees in adjusting to a new culture and performing better (Lee & Kartika, 2014). Support offered by the organization in the form of pre-departure training, counseling when needed, and other psycho-social support can result in expatriates accepting an international assignment (Konopaske & Werner, 2005) and feeling committed to their organization after assignment (Liu & Ipe, 2010).

Continuous cross-cultural training after the expatriate arrives on foreign soil is widely viewed as beneficial to expatriates' international assignment success (Bolino & Feldman, 2000; Bozionelos, 2009; Gudykunst, Guzley, & Hammer, 1996; Hogan & Goodson, 1990). When organizational policies are unclear to immigrant workers, a leader's flexibility and support is likely important for immigrants' success (Yang, 2007). Mentoring programs for expatriates have been found to contribute to success in the new work domain (Liu & Shaffer, 2005).

Research has considered how distinct individual characteristics shape the work experiences of immigrants, particularly expatriates. Kim and Slocum (2008) reported that greater English fluency was associated with better cross-cultural adjustment and performance, and more frequent behavioral self-monitoring was associated with enhanced workplace performance. Immigrant workers with an internal locus of control and an adaptable character were better able to adjust to their new work environment (Tucker, Bonial, & Lahti, 2004). Lee and Karthika (2014) studied the role of emotional intelligence and cultural intelligence and argued that those international immigrants who scored higher on these two types of intelligence adjusted better in their new working environment.

Family Experiences of Immigrants

Immigrants face difficult family decisions, regardless of the legalities underlying the transition or the anticipated duration of stay in the new country. A fundamental question confronting every immigrant is whether one or more family members will also migrate. In the case of some immigrants, like those on H2A or H2B visas, spouses and family members cannot accompany the worker unless they acquire a dependent visa, which is typically out of reach for these low-skilled workers. Evidence suggests that these types of workers who leave family behind may experience elevated anxiety and depressive symptoms while separated, although regular telephone communication dampens these effects (Grzywacz et al., 2006). Others have reported that immigrants feel guilty for not being physically able to take care of aging parents who are living in the country of origin (Khokher & Beauregard, 2014).

Spouses and family members play a critical role in the decision to immigrate (Richardson, 2006; Tharenou, 2008). Career-oriented spouses may have to forsake their job to join the immigrating spouse on an international assignment (Linehan, Scullion, & Walsh, 2001). Further, visa-mandated work restrictions for accompanying spouses could mean that spouses are unable to pursue or continue their career while on international assignment, which has career-long implications (Mehrotra & Calasanti, 2010). Indeed, for individuals coming to the United States as a spouse, the wait for work authorization can be substantial. Citizens of India and China who apply for an employment-related "green card" face wait times of five to ten years.

Family members who accompany immigrants invariably confront values, customs, and expectations that are culturally distant from their own (Hovey & Magaña, 2000). Acculturation, the process of adapting to the new culture (Ward, 1996), can create tensions within families (Olson et al., 2013). Evidence suggests that acculturation stressors, such as communication difficulties, direct threats to culturally embraced values, or experienced discrimination by anyone in the family, compromises within-family interactions and functioning (Gil & Vega, 1996; Rodriguez & Mearns, 2012).

Further, there is substantial literature highlighting how parents and children may experience the acculturation process differently and apply different acculturation strategies while navigating a new culture. These differences in acculturation are widely believed to create conflict between immigrant parents and their children (Birman & Trickett, 2001; Costigan & Dokis, 2006), regardless of whether the child accompanied the working parent or was born in the host country. Immigrant children tend to learn the language of the host country and assimilate to the local culture quicker than parents, primarily because of their interactions in the school system. Differential acculturation can pose challenges for immigrant parents in terms of discussing complex issues related to family expectations and obligations (Birman, 2006).

Documentation status, referring to whether one or more family members lacks legal authorization to reside in the country, undoubtedly shapes the family experiences of immigrants. Evidence from data obtained from presumably undocumented Latino immigrants suggests that direct threats to cultural values, such as women staying home rather than working, may contribute to partner conflict that escalates to violence (Grzywacz et al., 2007). Other research suggests that women accompanying immigrants face the risk of being "trapped" in potentially harmful relationships (Ingram, 2007) because individuals in undocumented families are hesitant to report problems out of fear of possible deportation. Immigrant women, particularly those from cultures that give hegemonic advantage to men, tend to believe that US laws on domestic violence do not apply to them (Orloff, Jang, & Klein, 1995). Likewise, family activities are often carefully circumscribed to eliminate the possibility of being "found out" and subsequent forced deportation of one or more family members leading to "family fragmentation" (Zapata Roblyer & Grzywacz, 2015). However, there is also fragmentation and separation of family and friends ties in the country of origin which may result in feelings of loss and a severe decrease in available coping resources (Hovey & Magaña, 2002).

Like work experiences, resources or factors that enable a seamless and potentially positive experience for immigrants' families have been studied. Family support can be a resource that helps an international worker adjust to foreign culture (Yang, 2007). A supportive family may buffer against potential difficulties related to adjusting to a new culture as well as provide the necessary emotional support and understanding to meet the demands of the new culture.

Family experiences of immigrants undoubtedly differ by gender. The vast majority of immigrants in the labor force are male (Bureau of Labor Statistics, 2016), although the representation of women in the international work force is increasing (Tharenou, 2008). Female employees accepting an international assignment are more likely than men to be single, married with no children, or married with few children (Hearn, Jyrkinen, Piekkari, & Oinonen, 2008). Gender differences are found in immigration decisions, including the decision to immigrate or not (e.g., Konopaske & Werner, 2005), due to the different roles men and women have traditionally played in their family.

Work–Family Experiences of Immigrants

Relatively few studies have focused on work–family concepts common in the literature, such as work–family conflict or work–family enrichment. Some data from rural-dwelling immigrant Latinos, most of whom were believed to be undocumented, suggest that work–family strains exceeded work–family "gains" – a variable similar to work–family enrichment – and these experiences were correlated with mental health outcomes (Grzywacz et al., 2005). However, data from a similar sample suggested that few immigrant Latinos reported experiencing work–family conflict, despite qualitative data suggesting otherwise (Grzywacz et al., 2007). This later finding began to raise questions about the cross-cultural equivalence of standard measures of work–family conflict (Grzywacz et al., 2007), and more research is still needed on this topic (French & Agars, 2016). Analyses of the 2002 National Study of the Changing Workforce indicated that immigrants do not experience more time- or strain-based work–family conflict than native workers (Ojha, 2011).

Few published studies could be located wherein researchers considered work–family experiences as explicit outcomes. Grzywacz and colleagues' (2007) study of immigrant Latino workers found that greater pressure to work fast and use of a large variety of skills were associated with more work-to-family conflict, while a safety-oriented culture was associated with less work-to-family conflict. Ojha (2011) found several differences in the correlates of time- and strain-based work–family between native and immigrant workers. Whereas greater coworker social support, less psychological demand, and fewer hours predicted time-based work–family conflict among immigrants, a different set of correlates predicted this outcome among native workers. Further, Ojha's models explained 24% of time-based work–family conflict among immigrants while 30% was explained for native workers. By contrast, models of strain-based work–family conflict were highly similar for immigrant and native workers. However, despite similarity in the amount of variance explained, the correlates of strained-based work–family conflict differed for the two groups, such that work-role ambiguity and work schedule were associated with greater strain-based conflict for native workers but not immigrant workers. Other research has found that perceived organizational support and spousal support were associated with better work–family experiences among expatriates (Kraimer, Wayne, & Jaworski, 2001).

Most work–family research among immigrants considers inter-relations among work and family experiences among expatriates. Chapter 26 in this volume (Dimitrova) provides a thorough review of the literature on work–family experiences of expatriates, but we highlight a few pieces here to help juxtapose the work and family experiences of expatriates with the broader array of immigrant workers. Family members' ability to adapt to a foreign culture has been linked with greater success in the workplace among expatriates and lower likelihood of premature resignation (Tung, 1981). Spousal support for the international assignment appears to be instrumental to expatriate success in their assignment; importantly, this support is needed across all phases of moving, settling, and reintegration (Mäkelä, Känsälä, & Suutari, 2011). Similarly, others have found that support from family members is associated with better adjustment to the new work culture (Lee & Kartika, 2014). Social support can provide safeguard against work pressure experienced by expatriates (Finch & Vega, 2003), while emotional support provided by one's family and friends can buffer against work demands (Vega, Kolody, Valle, & Weir, 1991).

However, there is also evidence that family life changes following international relocation. Some data suggests that immigrants work activities take on greater intensity (e.g., spending more time at work, being more preoccupied about work) leaving less time, energy, and resources for family (Olson et al., 2013). Consistent with this observation, other researchers have pointed out that expatriates' spouses report needing to take on additional family responsibilities that had previous been met by the expatriate before overseas assignment (Suutari & Mäkelä, 2007). Although most corporation-sponsored expatriates may hold well-paying jobs, undocumented immigrants often find work on the margins of the economy which can lead to financial constraints and decrements to family life satisfaction (Hatton, 1997).

Nevertheless, families also sometimes benefit from the decision to immigrate. For example, Khokher and Beauregard's (2014) study of Pakistani expatriates living in the United Kingdom reported the physical distance from their native culture aided some women, who reported having more freedom to make decisions related to childbearing. Others have reported that some corporate expatriates remain in the

United States, even when the assignment is not going well, because they believe an American-based education for their children and the pecuniary benefits of living in the United States is better than what is available in their home country (Kim & Slocum, 2008).

Gender is the primary individual characteristic discussed in the work and family literature, and evidence suggests that gender identities experienced in one's home country tend to be retained after immigration. Sometimes role-reversals may occur, particularly if the wife holds a student or temporary (e.g., H1b) visa. Nevertheless, Mehrotra et al. (2010) contend that family is one domain where gender-based responsibilities held in one country persist in the new country, a contention supported by evidence indicating that male and female immigrants report different kinds of work–family conflict and facilitation while on international assignments (Schütter & Boerner, 2013). Others, such as Mäkelä and colleagues (2011), view the interface between work and family as being more salient to women than men; while female expatriates do experience work–family enrichment, their experiences of conflict and enrichment seems to be more salient than for male expatriates (Mäkelä, et al., 2011).

Toward a Theoretically Informed Conceptual Framework

Based on this body of evidence we propose a framework for understanding the work and family experiences of immigrants. The proposed framework is informed by ecological theory (Bronfenbrenner, 1979), which argues that any form of human development or change must consider both the attributes of the individual and the social contexts the individual is embedded within. From this basic foundation we apply three distinct ideas. First, we borrow the heuristic device of multiple nested systems. This idea is visually represented (see Figure 25.3) in the symbolic representation of the individual immigrant (i.e., Individual), and the individual's embeddedness in at least two microsystems (i.e., "Work" and "Family"). Further, the work and family micro-systems overlap to create a mesosystem (i.e., Global Work–Family), and that these systems are embedded in an exosystem (Community) and a macrosystem (Society). Next, we borrow from bioecological theory (Bronfenbrenner & Ceci, 1994), an extension of ecological theory, the idea that individuals are active agents in creating the circumstances of life, a reality visually illustrated by the use of broad categories of individual characteristics commonly studied in the work and family literature (e.g., individual knowledge, skills, and abilities).

Third, and perhaps most importantly, the proposed framework borrows the core ideas inherent in the Person-Process-Context (P-P-C) model of ecological theory (Bronfenbrenner & Morris (2007). Specifically, the model proposes that outcomes of interest in each domain, such as those exemplified in the model, are a function of (minimally) the combination of individual or personal attributes along with specific processes within a given context (i.e., work or family microsystem or work–family mesosystem). Processes are conceptually defined as interactions of the individual with the persons, objects, and symbols within the environment or context that are increasingly complex (Bronfenbrenner & Ceci, 1994).

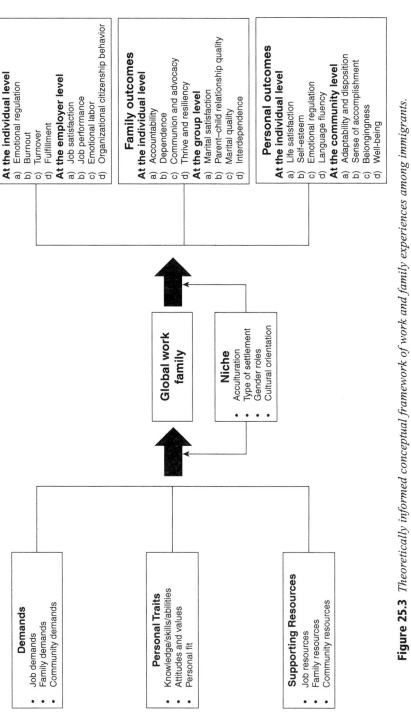

Figure 25.3 *Theoretically informed conceptual framework of work and family experiences among immigrants.*

Of course, the processes resulting from individuals interacting with demands and resources within distinct work and family contexts are numerous and likely multi-faceted. Our conceptual framework depicted in Figure 25.3 attempts to capture this complexity using four concepts.

The first concept is that of "inputs." "Inputs" are elements introduced into a system for one of two purposes: (1) system self-maintenance or (2) to support the production required of the system, such as goods and services (on the part of workplaces) and healthy individuals (on the part of families). Our conceptual framework identifies two broad inputs: "demands" and "resources." As used in our literature review, demands refer to external (vis-à-vis the self) attributes that pose a threat or challenge to an individual's role-related responsibilities within a social group or collective of individuals (e.g., work-team, family, community). In contrast, resources refer to external (vis-à-vis the self) or environmental attributes that enable or support an individual's role-related responsibilities within a social group. Just as a functional biological or mechanical system needs sufficient resources relative to demands to maintain itself and produce, our models posits that demands and resources contribute to maintenance and production of individual, workplace, and family (dys)function.

The second and third abstract concepts are "work–family experiences" and "out-comes." The former is intended to capture distinct experiences at the work–family interface (e.g., work–family conflict, work–family enrichment, or work–family balance) and associated processes (e.g., compensation, spillover, enhancement) (Edwards & Rothbard, 2000). The latter concept refers to the experience that is causally affected by, or dependent upon, other features of the model.

The fourth and last abstract concept is that of "niche," which are patterns or relatively stable sets of activities that link different domains together (Klein & White, 1992). Niche is perhaps the distinguishing concept of our model because it brings to light the inherent "mixing" of factors highly salient to immigrants' daily lives. For example, although all Pakistani immigrants arriving to the United States may contend with issues of discrimination, that potential is likely to be notably different in established gateway cities like New York, Los Angeles, or Chicago compared to new or emerging settlements in smaller metro or rural areas communities. Likewise, an "undocumented" Mexican arriving to Central Florida will face very different housing and employment options than a seemingly identical Puerto Rican who, although also "Latino," is a US citizen. Similarly, a corporate expatriate traveling from the United States to East Asia will confront an expanding focus on (and perhaps respect for) power distance, whereas an East Asian expatriate traveling to the United States will confront a contracted power distance. Niche is intended to capture these and myriads of others distinctive "mixes" of culture, person, and location as key indicators of context. Thus, this concept of niche may help to explain variation in immigrants' experiences, even among immigrants from the same home country migrating to the same new country of residence.

The preceding theoretical and conceptual content leads to several formal state-ments, and possible operational constructions for studying and understanding immi-grants' work and family experiences. Following from the implicit P-P-C formation of ecological theory, our model would posit that any outcome of interest to

Table 25.1 *Illustrative hypotheses derived from the P-P-C model and the proposed conceptual framework*

H1. Job satisfaction (job outcome) of American expatriates in China is higher when expatriates have written and verbal language fluency (personal skill), family members have specific goals for the experience (family resource), and the organization has human resources programs that anticipate her/his family needs (job resource). However, the strength and power of the personal skill and the family and job resources are dependent on the expatriate's respect for Chinese customs or variability in broader United States–Sino trade relations (niche characteristics).

H2. Risk of workplace injury (job outcome/individual outcome) among immigrant construction workers is lower when regular safety training occurs (job resource) and workers are familiar with the equipment and procedures used (individual knowledge). But, the efficacy of the safety training and the personal knowledge in reducing injury risk depends on the ability of the leadership to create a safety climate that overcomes cultural beliefs of fatalism (niche characteristic).

H3. Parent–child relationship quality (family outcome) among immigrants is poorer when the employer maintains rigid work schedules (job demand), the individual has not yet mastered the dominant language spoken in the workplace, and the immigrant uses a different acculturative strategy than her/his children (family demand). Moreover, the threats posed by job and family demands and the lack of language fluency are exaggerated when immigrants reside in communities with little racial or ethnic heterogeneity or when immigrants lack legal authorization to reside in the country (niche characteristics).

---

researchers is a function of: (1) person's knowledge, skills and abilities, (2) acting with and upon the processes resulting from the negotiation of demands or resources at work, in the family, and in the community to achieve all role-related responsibilities across life domains, which may become explicitly manifest in (3) work–family experiences. The interactions of person characteristics with demands and resources and the milieu of work–family experiences are shaped by (4) the characteristics of the niche (context) occupied by individual immigrants. These general propositions are made concrete using illustrative hypotheses informed by our conceptual framework and its underlying theory (see Table 25.1).

The generalized proposition derived from the model is clearly evident in the personal narratives described earlier in this chapter as part of our informal "study." That is, those personal narratives highlight the interplay of personal/individual characteristics, demands and resources as well as niche characteristics operating on immigrants' work and family experiences. Consider, for example, the narrative of those on an H1B visa who described limited freedom in the type of work that could be pursued or the limited ability to travel to the visa-holders' home country to visit family. Or even the indirect sanctions made on personal decisions like where and when to schedule a wedding in light of uncertainties about family members' ability to secure a visa to attend a wedding in the United States. Those individuals described work and personal restrictions [demands] that are built into the regulations governing the freedoms of H1B visa holders, as well as the ongoing pressure to maintain the H1B and move it toward "green card" status, a niche characteristic imbued with legal imperatives for realizing personal and oftentimes familial investments for long-term individual and family well-being. Many of these personal narratives highlighted personal hardships (e.g., uncertainty over how to care for aging parents) as well as sources of personal dissatisfaction (an individual or domain-specific outcome). Further, the narratives highlighted the vulnerability of immigrants, another niche characteristic clearly evident in the case of the students with whose F1 visa were revoked because their "hosting institution" violated United States Customs and Immigrant Services regulations.

High-Priority Next Steps

Research and theory surrounding the work and family experiences of immigrants is sorely underdeveloped given their sheer presence in the global labor force. In this last section we introduce several domains of inquiry that are needed. To be clear, these are not the only domains of inquiry needed, rather we view these as high-impact and necessary first steps to redress the substantial shortcomings in the literature.

The first high-priority area for research is the testing and validation of instruments to ensure cross-cultural equivalence of concepts and measurement. Although several of the standard tools for measuring work–family conflict or work–family enrichment have been translated and applied to other cultural groups (Spector et al., 2004), we could locate no published evidence establishing the cultural relevance of these concepts outside of Western and industrialized economies. This oversight is concerning given evidence indicating low frequency of work–family conflict on quantitative measures despite clear expressions that work–family conflict exists amongst some immigrant groups (Grzywacz et al., 2007).

Determining the cultural meaning and cross-cultural equivalence of "work" and "family" concepts should be the essential focus of much-needed measurement research. Despite early work to the contrary by a pioneer of the field (Kanter, 1977), the dominant paradigm of "work–family" in Western society is that work and family are separate spheres that are brought together by a hyphen or slash. By contrast, in more holistic cultures, from which many immigrants originate, work and family are much more integrated; work is essential for family and family gives work meaning and purpose. These divergent cultural views of work and family likely seep into the basic meaning of concepts like "work–family balance" or "work–family conflict," thereby requiring attentiveness to the basic meaning and cross-cultural equivalence of these concepts. Moreover, the ultimate meaning of concepts such as "work–family conflict" and "work–family balance" may differ based on the meaning of "family" (e.g., nuclear, extended), where "family" is located (e.g., those who accompanied the immigrant, those left in the country of origin), and the circumstances dictating daily life (e.g., visa-related allowances).

Further, beyond the cultural meaning of core concepts, measurement research needs to consider the often-intertwined nature of culture and class. For example, apparent contradiction between the qualitative and quantitative data reported by Grzywacz and colleagues' (2007) study of immigrant (presumably undocumented) Latinos could be attributed to at least two sources. First, it is possible that the survey items were worded in a way that did not capture experiences familiar to Latinos predominantly from rural Mexico. However, it is also possible that the contradiction reflects a more fundamental issue; that is, lack of familiarity in completing structured survey or research instruments. Whereas individuals in the United States (and perhaps other "developed" countries) become socialized to giving thoughtful responses to instruments used in research through years of taking standardized tests in school, many immigrants may be less familiar with these methods. Moreover, within immigrant groups there can be substantial variation in potential exposure to standardized testing with individuals from higher socioeconomic strata being accustomed to completing assessments, while the experience is relatively uncommon among individuals in lower strata. From this perspective, Grzywacz and colleagues' findings could reflect poor understanding of the questions (even though they were translated), inability to place personal answers into forced response categories, or some combination thereof among this lower socioeconomic status immigrant group. The cross-classification of culture and class (perhaps assessed through educational attainment) highlights the need for researchers to undertake measurement studies, perhaps using cognitive interviewing or "think aloud" techniques among major ethnic groups represented in the immigrant population.

There is substantial need for focused substantive work and family research among immigrants. Comparative research of immigrants and non-immigrants or native workers is sorely needed. The clear majority of research completed to date has been with specific samples of immigrants, either valuable workers on international assignments or undocumented workers without legal authorization to live and work in their current country. Researchers are encouraged to exploit existing data sources, including the most recent panels of the National Study of the Changing Workforce, the National Survey of Midlife Development, and perhaps the General Social Survey with appended Work Life Module to compare work–family experiences among immigrants and non-immigrants. Given that immigrants are a heterogeneous group, these results should be scrutinized closely to also examine within-group variation. However, even descriptive and exploratory results from these sources would move the field forward. Similarly, research with these same data sources that compares the putative antecedents and consequences of work–family experiences among immigrants and non-immigrants is needed. Ideally, these comparisons would be informed by culturally informed theories to promote clear interpretation of observed findings and appropriate generalization.

Substantive research that considers the structural influence of visa-related requirements is needed. Expatriate researchers have clear opportunity to undertake comparative research based on type of visa, as these "immigrants" often operate under very discrete visa programs. Are the challenges of combining work and family minimized or exacerbated by visa-related restrictions related to spouse or dependent employment? The answer to a question like this has substantial theoretical value given the extensive impact and reach of what visas allow or impede. Indeed, it is difficult to imagine how any meaningful understanding of work–family experiences of immigrants could be reached without considering the legal parameters underlying the migration. Practically, modifications to immigration laws, if warranted by sound research, could have positive and beneficial effects for many immigrants and their families.

Furthermore, researchers are encouraged to design studies of the psychological and social processes shaping work and family experiences among immigrants. Although there is evidence of some overlap in predictors of work and family experiences among immigrants and native workers, there also seems to be clear evidence of more difference than similarity (e.g., Ojha, 2011). While pursuing these questions, researchers are encouraged to cautiously consider potential cultural biases or implicit values. For example, although many Western, industrialized countries value gender neutrality when assigning or carrying out roles and responsibilities, such values cannot be assumed for other cultures. In the United States, having a spouse engage in childcare responsibilities or household management may be an essential ingredient of "work–family balance," but this ingredient may be less salient in cultures less sensitive to gender equality in the work and family domains. Likewise, the meaning of "family" is quite different in the United States and other developed countries (where nuclear family holds advantage) compared to cultures where many immigrants originate who have broader conceptions of family.

If we consider attending school to be a form of "work," an essential area for research is the work and family experiences of international students, particularly given their sheer numbers. Very little is known about the experiences of family members who accompany an international student or how the experiences of the international student compare to that of an international migrant performing work through a corporation. Are their experiences and those of their family members (both those that accompany the focal individual and those left in the country of origin) similar? What factors would ease the often long-term stay many of these students and their families live through?

Conclusion

Immigrants are a common feature in the world and in the workforce of most developed economies. Yet despite this reality, there is very little coherent research on this population. In this chapter we have highlighted the complexities of the term "immigrant" and we have indicated the central role that visas and other aspects of legal authorization to live and work in a country hold for shaping immigrants' work and family experiences. The small body of research suggests that immigrants may have more work and family challenges than native workers, but measurement challenges impede our ability to draw strong conclusions. The factors contributing to work and family experiences likely differ for immigrants than native workers because of the types of employment held, characteristics of culture and acculturation, and the inherent strains of leaving some family to pursue another life elsewhere in the world. Finally, we offered a theoretically based model of work and family experiences of immigrants and a set of high-priority research activities. For the sake of the over 2.6 million immigrant workers in the United States and the many more around the world, we hope this chapter enables and equips readers to engage in this important area of research.

References

Ahonen, E. Q., & Benavides, F. G. (2006). Risk of fatal and non-fatal occupational injury in foreign workers in Spain. *Journal of Epidemiology and Community Health, 60*(5), 424–426. https://doi.org/10.1136/jech.2005.044099

Birman, D. (2006). Acculturation gap and family adjustment—Findings with Soviet Jewish refugees in the United States and implications for measurement. *Journal of Cross-Cultural Psychology, 37*(5), 568–589. https://doi.org/10.1177/0022022106290479

Birman, D., & Trickett, E. J. (2001). Cultural transitions in first-generation immigrants—Acculturation of Soviet Jewish refugee adolescents and parents. *Journal of Cross-Cultural Psychology, 32*(4), 456–477. https://doi.org/10.1177/0022022101032004006

Bolino, M. C., & Feldman, D. C. (2000). Increasing the skill utilization of expatriates. *Human Resource Management, 39*(4), 367–379.

Bozionelos, N. (2009). Expatriation outside the boundaries of the multinational corporation: A study with expatriate nurses in Saudi Arabia. *Human Resource Management, 48* (1), 111–134. https://doi.org/10.1002/hrm.20269

Bronfenbrenner, U. (1979). *The Ecology of Human Development*. Harvard University Press.

Bronfenbrenner, U., & Ceci, S. J. (1994). Nature–nurture reconceptualized in developmental perspective: A bioecological model. *Psychological Review, 101*(4), 568–586. https://doi.org/10.1037/0033-295X.101.4.568

Bronfenbrenner, U., & Morris, P. A. (2007). The bioecological model of human development. In *Handbook of Child Psychology*. John Wiley & Sons, Inc. Retrieved from http://onlinelibrary.wiley.com/doi/10.1002/9780470147658.chpsy0114/abstract

Bureau of Labor Statistics. (2016). Foreign-born workers: Labor force characteristics: 2015. Accessed October 20, 2016 from www.bls.gov/news.release/forbrn.nr0.htm

Chen, Y.-R., Brockner, J., & Katz, T. (1998). Toward an explanation of cultural differences in in-group favoritism: The role of individual versus collective primacy. *Journal of Personality and Social Psychology, 75*(6), 1490–1502. https://doi.org/10.1037/0022-3514.75.6.1490

Costigan, C. L., & Dokis, D. P. (2006). Relations between parent–child acculturation differences and adjustment within immigrant Chinese families. *Child Development, 77* (5), 1252–1267. https://doi.org/10.1111/j.1467-8624.2006.00932.x

Edwards, J. R., & Rothbard, N. P. (2000). Mechanisms linking work and family: Clarifying the relationship between work and family constructs. *Academy of Management. The Academy of Management Review, 25*(1), 178–199.

Finch, B. K., & Vega, W. A. (2003). Acculturation stress, social support, and self-rated health among Latinos in California. *Journal of Immigrant Health, 5*(3), 109–117.

French, K. A., & Agars, M. D. (2016). Work–family culture in low-income environments: Can we generalize? *Journal of Career Development*. https://doi.org/10.1177/0894845316664178

Gil, A. G., & Vega, W. A. (1996). Two different worlds: Acculturation stress and adaptation among Cuban and Nicaraguan families. *Journal of Social and Personal Relationships*, *13*(3), 435–456. https://doi.org/10.1177/0265407596133008

Grzywacz, J. G., Arcury, T. A., Márin, A., Carrillo, L., Burke, B., Coates, M. L., & Quandt, S. A. (2007). Work–family conflict: experiences and health implications among immigrant Latinos. *The Journal of Applied Psychology*, *92*(4), 1119–1130. https://doi.org/10.1037/0021-9010.92.4.1119

Grzywacz, J.G., Quandt, S. A., Arcury, T. A., & Marín, A. (2005). The work–family challenge and mental health: Experiences of Mexican immigrants. *Community, Work & Family*, *8*, 271–279.

Grzywacz, J. G., Quandt, S. A., Early, J., Tapia, J., Graham, C. N., & Arcury, T. A. (2006). Leaving family for work: Ambivalence and mental health among Mexican migrant farmworker men. *Journal of Immigrant and Minority Health*, *8*(1), 85–97. https://doi.org/http://dx.doi.org.proxy.lib.fsu.edu/10.1007/s10903-006-6344-7

Gudykunst, W. B., Guzley, R. M., & Hammer, M. R. (1996). Designing intercultural training. In D. Landis & R. S. Bhagat (Eds.), *Handbook of Intercultural Training*. Second Edition (pp. 61–80). Thousand Oaks, CA: Sage Publications, Inc.

Harris, H. (2002). Think international manager, think male: Why are women not selected for international management assignments? *Thunderbird International Business Review*, *44*(2), 175–203. https://doi.org/10.1002/tie.10010

Hatton, T. J. (1997). The immigrant assimilation puzzle in late nineteenth-century America. *The Journal of Economic History*, *57*(1), 34–62.

Hearn, J., Jyrkinen, M., Piekkari, R., & Oinonen, E. (2008). "Women home and away": Transnational managerial work and gender relations. *Journal of Business Ethics*, *83* (1), 41–54. https://doi.org/10.1007/s10551-007-9655-2

Hofstede, G. (1984). Hofstede's culture dimensions: An independent validation using Rokeach's value survey. *Journal of Cross-Cultural Psychology*, *15*(4), 417–433. https://doi.org/10.1177/0022002184015004003

Hogan, G., & Goodson, J. (1990). The key to expatriate success. *Training and Development Journal*, *44*(1), 50–52.

Hoppe, A. (2011). Psychosocial working conditions and well-being among immigrant and German low-wage workers. *Journal of Occupational Health Psychology*, *16*(2), 187–201. https://doi.org/10.1037/a0021728

Hovey, J. D., & Magaña, C. (2000). Acculturative stress, anxiety, and depression among Mexican immigrant farmworkers in the Midwest United States. *Journal of Immigrant Health*, *2*(3), 119–131.

Hovey, J. D., & Magaña, C. G. (2002). Psychosocial predictors of anxiety among immigrant Mexican migrant farmworkers: Implications for prevention and treatment. *Cultural Diversity & Ethnic Minority Psychology*, *8*(3), 274–289. https://doi.org/10.1037//1099-9809.8.3.274

Ingram, E. M. (2007). A comparison of help seeking between Latino and non-Latino victims of intimate partner violence. *Violence Against Women*, *13*(2), 159–171. https://doi.org/10.1177/1077801206296981

Jensen, E. B., Bhaskar, R., & Scopilliti, M. (2015). Demographic analysis 2010: Estimates of coverage of the foreign-born population in the American Community Survey. *Population Division, US Census Bureau, Working Paper*, (103). Retrieved from https://census.gov/content/dam/Census/library/working-papers/2015/demo/POP-twps0103.pdf

Kanter, R. M. (1977). *Work and Family in the United States: A Critical Review and Agenda for Research and Policy.* Russell Sage Foundation.

Kawai, N., & Mohr, A. (2015). The contingent effects of role ambiguity and role novelty on expatriates' work-related outcomes. *British Journal of Management, 26*(2), 163–181. https://doi.org/10.1111/1467-8551.12089

Khokher, S. Y., & Beauregard, T. A. (2014). Work–family attitudes and behaviours among newly immigrant Pakistani expatriates: the role of organizational family-friendly policies. *Community, Work & Family, 17*(2), 142–162. https://doi.org/10.1080/13668803.2013.847060

Kim, E. (2009). Multidimensional acculturation attitudes and depressive symptoms in Korean Americans. *Issues in Mental Health Nursing, 30*(2), 98–103. https://doi.org/10.1080/01612840802597663

Kim, K., & Slocum, J. W. (2008). Individual differences and expatriate assignment effectiveness: The case of United States-based Korean expatriates. *Journal of World Business, 43*(1), 109–126. https://doi.org/10.1016/j.jwb.2007.10.005

Konopaske, R., & Werner, S. (2005). US managers' willingness to accept a global assignment: do expatriate benefits and assignment length make a difference? *The International Journal of Human Resource Management, 16*(7), 1159–1175. https://doi.org/10.1080/09585190500143998

Kraimer, M. L., Wayne, S. J., & Jaworski, R. A. A. (2001). Sources of support and expatriate performance: The mediating role of expatriate adjustment. *Personnel Psychology, 54*(1), 71–99. https://doi.org/10.1111/j.1744-6570.2001.tb00086.x

Lee, L.-Y., & Kartika, N. (2014). The influence of individual, family, and social capital factors on expatriate adjustment and performance: The moderating effect of psychology contract and organizational support. *Expert Systems with Applications, 41*(11), 5483–5494. https://doi.org/10.1016/j.eswa.2014.02.030

Linehan, M., Scullion, H., & Walsh, J. (2001). Barriers to women's participation in international management. *European Business Review, 13*(1), 10–19. https://doi.org/10.1108/09555340110366444

Liu, X., & Shaffer, M. A. (2005). An investigation of expatriate adjustment and performance: A social capital perspective. *International Journal of Cross Cultural Management, 5*(3), 235–254. https://doi.org/http://dx.doi.org.proxy.lib.fsu.edu/10.1177/1470595805058411

Liu, Y., & Ipe, M. (2010). The impact of organizational and leader–member support on expatriate commitment. *The International Journal of Human Resource Management, 21*(7), 1035–1048. https://doi.org/10.1080/09585191003783496

Mäkelä, L., Känsälä, M., & Suutari, V. (2011). The roles of expatriates' spouses among dual career couples. *Cross Cultural Management: An International Journal, 18*(2), 185–197. https://doi.org/10.1108/13527601111126012

Mehrotra, M., & Calasanti, T. M. (2010). The family as a site for gendered ethnic identity work among Asian Indian immigrants. *Journal of Family Issues, 31*(6), 778–807. https://doi.org/10.1177/0192513X09357557

Ojha, M. U. (2011). Job demands, social support, and work–family conflict: a comparative study of immigrant and native workers in the United States. Retrieved from http://uknowledge.uky.edu/gradschool_diss/198/

Olson, K. J., Huffman, A. H., Leiva, P. I., & Culbertson, S. S. (2013). Acculturation and individualism as predictors of work–family conflict in a diverse workforce: Cultural values and work–family conflict. *Human Resource Management, 52*(5), 741–769. https://doi.org/10.1002/hrm.21559

Orloff, L. E., Jang, D., & Klein, C. F. (1995). With no place to turn: Improving legal advocacy for battered immigrant women. *Family Law Quarterly, 29*(2), 313–329.

Passell, J. S., & Cohn, D. (2014). Unauthorized immigrant totals rise in 7 states, fall in 12. Accessed October 20, 2016 from www.pewhispanic.org/2014/11/18/unauthorized-immigrant-totals-rise-in-7-states-fall-in-14

Quandt, S. A., Arcury-Quandt, A. E., Lawlor, E. J., Carrillo, L., Marín, A. J., Grzywacz, J. G., & Arcury, T. A. (2013). 3-D jobs and health disparities: The health implications of Latino chicken catchers' working conditions. *American Journal of Industrial Medicine, 56*(2), 206–215. https://doi.org/10.1002/ajim.22072

Richardson, J. (2006). Self-directed expatriation: family matters. *Personnel Review, 35*(4), 469–486. https://doi.org/10.1108/00483480610670616

Rodriguez, J. K., & Mearns, L. (2012). Problematising the interplay between employment relations, migration and mobility. *Employee Relations, 34*(6), 580–593. https://doi.org/http://dx.doi.org.proxy.lib.fsu.edu/10.1108/01425451211267946

Schütter, H., & Boerner, S. (2013). Illuminating the work-family interface on international assignments: An exploratory approach. *Journal of Global Mobility: The Home of Expatriate Management Research, 1*(1), 46–71. https://doi.org/10.1108/JGM-09-2012-0012

Shaffer, M. A., Harrison, D. A., Gilley, K. M., & Luk, D. M. (2001). Struggling for balance amid turbulence on international assignments: work–family conflict, support and commitment. *Journal of Management, 27*(1), 99–121. https://doi.org/10.1177/014920630102700106

Smith, P. M., Chen, C., & Mustard, C. (2009). Differential risk of employment in more physically demanding jobs among a recent cohort of immigrants to Canada. *Injury Prevention: Journal of the International Society for Child and Adolescent Injury Prevention, 15*(4), 252–258. https://doi.org/10.1136/ip.2008.021451

Spector, P. E., Cooper, C. L., Poelmans, S., Allen, T. D., et al. (2004). A cross-national comparative study of work–family stressors, working hours, and well-being: China and Latin America versus the Anglo world. *Personnel Psychology, 57*(1), 119–142.

Suárez-Orozco, C., & Suárez-Orozco, M. M. (2001). *Children of Immigration* (Vol. x). Cambridge, MA: Harvard University Press.

Suutari, V., & Mäkelä, K. (2007). The career capital of managers with global careers. *Journal of Managerial Psychology, 22*(7), 628–648. https://doi.org/10.1108/0268394 0710820073

Tharenou, P. (2008). Disruptive decisions to leave home: Gender and family differences in expatriation choices. *Organizational Behavior and Human Decision Processes, 105* (2), 183–200. https://doi.org/10.1016/j.obhdp.2007.08.004

Tucker, M. F., Bonial, R., & Lahti, K. (2004). The definition, measurement and prediction of intercultural adjustment and job performance among corporate expatriates. *International Journal of Intercultural Relations, 28*(3–4), 221–251. https://doi.org/10.1016/j.ijintrel.2004.06.004

Tung, R. L. (1981). Selection and training of personnel for overseas assignments. *Columbia Journal of World Business, 16*(1), 68.

United Nations. (2016). *International Migration Report 2015: Highlights*. Accessed October 20, 2016 from www.un.org/en/development/desa/population/migration/publica tions/migrationreport/docs/MigrationReport2015_Highlights.pdf

Vega, W., Kolody, B., Valle, R., & Weir, J. (1991). Social networks, social support, and their relationship to depression among immigrant Mexican women. *Human Organization*, *50*(2), 154–162. https://doi.org/10.17730/humo.50.2.p34026639721 4724

Ward, C. (1996). Acculturation. In D. Landis & R. S. Bhagat (Eds.), *Handbook of Intercultural Training*. Second Edition (pp. 124–147). Thousand Oaks, CA: Sage Publications, Inc.

Yang, N. (2007). A cross-cultural contextual model of work–family interfaces in managing international assignments. *Journal of International Business Research*, *6*(1), 1.

Zapata Roblyer, M.I., & Grzywacz, J.G. (2015). "We thought we had a future." Adversity and resilience in mixed-status families (pp. 70–84). In A. Schueths & J. Lawston (Eds.), *In Between the Shadows of Citizenship: Mixed Status Families*. Seattle, WA: University of Washington Press.

26 Expatriation and the Work–Family Interface

Mihaela Dimitrova

As more and more companies expand their international presence and countries aim to attract needed international talent, global mobility is on the rise all over the world. Thus, numerous individuals and their trailing families relocate to foreign countries and often have to face rather difficult challenges, such as adjusting to the new culture and successfully navigating the new workplace environment. The successful adjustment and the positive overall experience of expatriates is an important goal for the organizations that have sent them abroad, but also for the host country governments that can benefit from this influx of needed talent. Although the focus has generally been on the expatriate, the expatriate's family has also become an important part of the scholarly conversation in the area of expatriation. In fact, the number one reason for failure of the expatriate assignment is family-related issues (e.g., Hays, 1971, 1974), and this is still true today (Brookfield Global Relocation Services, 2016). This has prompted researchers to also look beyond the expatriate to consider the experiences of their families (e.g., Caligiuri, Hyland, Joshi, & Bross, 1998; Shaffer & Harrison, 1998).

Although the literature is growing, we still know only fragments about the effects that expatriation has on the work–family interface. Thus, the aim of this chapter is to synthesize extant studies on the work–family interface in the context of global assignments and identify potential areas for future research. Adapting a lens from the domestic literature, this review will organize studies based on their contribution to work–family spillover, work–family conflict, work–family enrichment, and crossover between family members. In addition, there is evidence that experiences as part of the work–family interface depend to an extent on cultural and institutional differences between expatriate family members' home cultures and the host environment (e.g., Canhilal, Gabel Shemueli, & Dolan, 2015; Davies, Kraeh, & Froese, 2015; Waxin, 2004). Therefore, this review will also focus on the interplay between the host and home locations in regard to the work–family interface, which has not yet been systematically discussed.

This review examines the experiences of global employees and families who relocate abroad for an extended period of time, namely corporate and self-initiated expatriates. Corporate expatriates are assigned by their home company to a particular foreign location, while self-initiated expatriates relocate based on their own volition. Thus, this review will not discuss literature on the work–family interface in the context of other types of global employment (e.g., international business travel, short-term expatriates). Please see Shaffer, Kraimer, Chen, and Bolino (2012) for an in-depth look at the different challenges faced by the various types of global employees. Finally, the focus of this review is on the work–family interface and studies that more broadly examine spillover to and from the general life domain are not included. However, in relation to crossover between family members, moods and attitudes originating from or affecting all three domains are considered (i.e., work, family, and life).

Studies Examining Crossover and Spillover Effects

The process of crossover occurs when the experiences of one partner (e.g., the expatriate) affect the experiences of other family members (e.g., spouse, children) or vice versa (Westman, 2001). Crossover can happen between individuals across life domains (e.g., transfer of work-related strain from the expatriate to his or her spouse), as well as within the same domain (e.g., spouse family-related satisfaction increases expatriate family-related satisfaction). The experiences that are transferred between partners through crossover can be both positive and negative (Westman, 2001). On the other hand, spillover denotes the process through which attitudes, affect, and behaviors transfer from one life role to another (e.g., from work to family) for the same individual (e.g., the expatriate) (see Edwards & Rothbard, 2000, for a review).

Crossover

Spouse → expatriate in the work domain. Adjustment has been, and still is, a key construct in the expatriation literature (Takeuchi, 2010). Originally developed by Black (1988), adjustment refers to the level of comfort an individual feels in their new role and environment. It consists of three components: adjustment to the work environment in the host country (i.e., work adjustment), adjustment to the interaction with host-country nationals (i.e., interaction adjustment), and adjustment to the cultural and general nonwork environment (i.e., general adjustment). These three adjustment dimensions generally apply only to expatriates, as spouse adjustment is typically compromised solely of interaction and general adjustment (Black & Stephens, 1989), mainly based on the historical assumption that spouses do not work while on the international assignment.

Crossover of spouse adjustment to expatriate work adjustment has been proposed (Black, Mendenhall, & Oddou, 1991) and extensively researched. In examining primary studies, results vary, with some finding a positive association of one or both components of spouse adjustment with expatriate work adjustment (Black & Stephens, 1989; Nicholson & Imaizumi, 1993; Takeuchi, Yun, & Tesluk, 2002) and others do not (Black & Gregersen, 1991; Shaffer & Harrison, 1998; Shaffer, Harrison, & Gilley, 1999). However, more recently, the existence of this particular type of crossover has been supported in meta-analyses conducted by Bhaskar-Shrinivas, Harrison, Shaffer, and Luk (2005) and Hechanova, Beehr, and Christiansen (2003). On the other hand, there has been little support for the crossover of spouse adjustment to other work-related variables for the expatriate (e.g., work well-being, Nicholson & Imaizumi, 1993; job satisfaction, Shaffer & Harrison, 1998; work performance, Abdul Malek, Budhwar, & Reiche, 2015). Limited data exists on the crossover of other attitudes and experiences. However, Shaffer and Harrison (1998) provide some initial support that crossover of other variables beside adjustment is possible; they found that spouse satisfaction (i.e., overall satisfaction with living in the foreign location) positively influenced expatriate job satisfaction.

Spouse → expatriate in the family domain. Research involving the spouse's experiences crossing over and affecting the expatriate's experiences within the family domain is scarce. This is partially due to past research being almost exclusively focused on work-related outcomes or adjustment and satisfaction with the foreign environment. However, Lazarova, Westman, and Shaffer (2010) proposed a more comprehensive model of the work–family interface on international assignments by integrating the Job Demands-Resources (JD-R) model (Demerouti, Bakker, Nachreiner, & Schaufeli, 2001) with crossover and spillover processes. Among other propositions, the authors stress the importance of understanding crossover processes within the family domain, since these can ultimately affect expatriate performance. They also suggest that spouse family role adjustment may crossover and affect the degree to which expatriates are adjusted and engaged within their own family role. Thus, we need further empirical research to elucidate this particular type of crossover as well as other experiences that transfer from the spouse to the expatriate within the boundaries of the family domain.

Spouse → expatriate in the life domain. Studies have considered the role of the spouse not only on expatriates' experiences in the work domain, but also on their overall adjustment to living abroad and intention to complete the assignment. Similar to the effect of spouse adjustment on expatriate work adjustment, the crossover of spouse adjustment to expatriate interaction and general adjustment has been well supported in the literature (e.g., Black, 1988; Black & Gregersen, 1991; Black & Stephens, 1989; Nicholson & Imaizumi, 1993; Palthe, 2004, 2008; Shaffer & Harrison, 1998; Shaffer et al., 1999; Takeuchi et al., 2002). Furthermore, in meta-analytic syntheses, Bhaskar-Shrinivas et al. (2005) and Hechanova et al. (2003) confirmed that spouse adjustment is positively related to expatriate interaction and general adjustment. Besides the effect on expatriate adjustment, studies have shown that spouse adjustment is negatively related to expatriate withdrawal cognitions (Black & Stephens, 1989; Shaffer & Harrison, 1998) and positively related to expatriate nonwork satisfaction and nonwork well-being (Nicholson & Imaizumi, 1993).

The above research demonstrates that there is strong evidence for crossover of spouse adjustment to expatriate adjustment to life in the foreign country and other nonwork outcomes that are important for assignment success. However, more research is needed on other possible moods and attitudes that can cross over from the spouse and affect expatriates' experiences in the general life domain during the stay abroad. For example, Shaffer and Harrison (1998) show that spouse satisfaction can also cross over and affect the expatriate's nonwork satisfaction.

Expatriate → spouse. Although in the domestic work–family literature it has been proposed and empirically supported that crossover can occur bidirectionally between the two partners in the couple, there is only limited research that examines crossover from the expatriate to the spouse in the context of expatriation. Shaffer and Harrison (2001) provided initial support that expatriate adjustment was positively related to spouse adjustment. Similarly, Mohr and Klein (2004) found that expatriate adjustment is significantly related to their spouse's adjustment to the general living conditions and to their new role tasks and responsibilities. In their study of spillover and crossover effects, Takeuchi et al. (2002) observed that crossover occurred not only from the spouse to the expatriate, but also in the other direction. In particular, expatriate work and general adjustment crossed over and affected spouse general adjustment. In regard to crossover of other psychological states and attitudes, Van der Zee, Ali, and Salomé (2005) found a significant and positive relationship between expatriate general well-being and spouse well-being. Ali, Van der Zee, and Sanders (2003) also observed a positive crossover between expatriate work satisfaction and spouse intercultural adaptation (i.e., life satisfaction, intercultural interaction, and sociocultural adjustment). Although these studies provide some evidence for crossover from the expatriate to the spouse, this is largely limited to crossover that affects spouses' adaptation to the general cultural and living conditions while on the assignment.

In contrast, no crossover has been examined from the expatriate to their spouse's experiences within the family domain. However, in their conceptual paper, Lazarova et al. (2010) proposed that expatriate cultural and family role adjustment will cross over and influence spouse family role adjustment, thus emphasizing that spouses not only undergo a process of adjustment to their host environment but also to their redefined role within the family domain. Further empirical work is needed to examine this particular type of crossover.

Future directions. Although researchers make a distinction with regard to whether they hypothesize crossover from spouse to expatriate or vice versa, directionality cannot be clearly established. This is primarily due to the lack of longitudinal studies of crossover processes during expatriation. Measuring crossover between the partners at multiple time points can be beneficial in order to assess whether the bidirectional nature holds in the context of expatriation. Even though longitudinal research designs are still lacking, many studies do collect multi-source data from both spouses and expatriates (e.g., Black & Gregersen, 1991; Shaffer & Harrison, 1998, 2001; Takeuchi et al., 2002).

The literature has also focused primarily on the crossover of adjustment, but it would be beneficial to consider the transfer of other moods and attitudes, such as satisfaction or well-being, so that we can get a more comprehensive picture of the expatriate experience. In addition, we still lack studies that examine how the experiences of the spouse affect the experiences of the expatriate and vice versa within the family domain. For example, it is possible that spouse family-related strain would cross over and increase the strain that the expatriate experiences while at home. Finally, the studies discussed only consider crossover between spouse and expatriate, and there is only limited research on crossover to and from expatriate children. In one of the rare studies involving children of expatriates, Van der Zee, Ali, and Haaksma (2007) found that expatriate work satisfaction had a positive crossover effect on children's intercultural adaptation (i.e., quality of life and sociocultural adjustment).

Spillover

As discussed, work–family spillover represents the transfer of attitudes, affect, and behaviors within the same individual from the family to the work role and vice versa (Edwards & Rothbard, 2000). For example, expatriates experiencing high levels of family satisfaction might also feel satisfied with their job. In the context of expatriation, studies that examine spillover in this more pure form, without also implicitly or explicitly incorporating the constructs of work–family conflict and enrichment, are rare. In this section of the review, only such studies are discussed, while a review of literature on work–family conflict and enrichment is provided next.

The common direction is to examine transfer from family to work and only in regard to the experiences of expatriates. Caligiuri, Hyland, and Joshi (1998) proposed that a family that is adjusted (i.e., representing the perception that the whole family is adjusted, including the expatriate), creates a positive home environment where the expatriate feels comfortable, and this would in turn spill over and positively affect the expatriate's work adjustment. Caligiuri, Hyland, Joshi, and Bross (1998) did in fact find that family adjustment spills over and positively affects expatriates' work adjustment. However, in their theoretical model, Lazarova et al. (2010) considered the relationship between expatriate work and family role adjustment, as well as between work and family engagement, to be reciprocal. Later, Shaffer et al. (2016) provided some initial empirical support that there is a positive correlation between expatriates' work role adjustment and their family role adjustment, but further empirical work is needed in order to establish the reciprocal effect.

On the other hand, the spillover between the family and work roles for the spouse is not considered at all. One reason for this might be the fact that still only about 20% of expatriate spouses work while on the assignment (Brookfield Relocation Survey, 2016). However, without studies on this type of spillover, we fail to fully understand the work–family experiences of dual-career couples. Traditionally, the problems of dual-career couples have been discussed in terms of the challenges associated with spouses losing their employment after relocation (e.g., Harvey, 1997, 1998). However, more research is needed in regard to couples, where both spouses work while abroad. This can perhaps better be observed by studying self-initiated expatriates, instead of corporate expatriates. It may be more likely that both partners will work in the host country if they have expatriated due to their own initiative (Mäkelä & Suutari, 2013).

Work–Family Conflict in the Context of Expatriation

The concept of work–family conflict (WFC) is defined by Greenhaus and Beutell (1985) as "a form of interrole conflict in which the role pressures from the work and family domains are mutually incompatible in some respect. That is, participation in the work (family) role is made more difficult by virtue of participation in the family (work) role" (p. 77). Although specifically measuring or examining work–family conflict has become a common practice in domestic work–family literature, this is still a rare occurrence as part of expatriation research. In addition, not many studies examine the more narrow focus on the work and family domains; instead some focus on conflict between work and the broader life domain (e.g., Kempen, Pangert, Hattrup, Mueller, & Joens, 2015; Mäkelä, Suutari, & Mayerhofer, 2011).

Work-to-Family Conflict

Researchers have started to work towards remedying this gap through both theoretical and empirical work. Several studies exist that examine the antecedents to work-to-family conflict among expatriates. Harris (2004) proposed that expatriates' perceptions of lack of organizational support would increase their experience of work-to-family conflict. Further discussing the role of organization practices, Shih, Chiang, and Hsu (2010) looked at the impact of high-involvement work systems (i.e., HR systems that attempt to increase employee performance through encouraging employee involvement and commitment at work) and found that although the existence of such systems was beneficial in terms of increasing job satisfaction and performance, they also increased expatriates' experience of work-to-family conflict.

In qualitative studies, expatriates' long work hours and excessive work demands often lead to tensions at home and thus to work-to-family conflict (Lazarova, McNulty, & Semeniuk, 2015; Mäkelä & Suutari, 2011). Mäkelä and Suutari (2013) interviewed expatriates and found that a host country culture that emphasizes work can contribute to work-to-family conflict by not allowing expatriates the ability to spend enough time with their families. Family-related variables were also found to contribute to work-to-family conflict. Specifically, Van der Zee et al. (2005) observed a positive association between home demands and expatriates' work-to-family conflict.

Researchers have also looked at the outcomes of work-to-family conflict for expatriates. Shaffer, Harrison, Gilley, and Luk (2001) found that work-to-family conflict was, at least to an extent, responsible for expatriate withdrawal cognitions in terms of planning for premature departure. However, research on the consequences of work-to-family conflict for expatriates and their families is sparse.

Family-to-Work Conflict

In terms of the antecedents to family-to-work conflict, Harris (2004) suggested that women expatriates who receive adequate organizational support for their spouse and children will experience less family-to-work conflict. On the other hand, adjustment problems of the spouse might lead to an increase in family-to-work conflict. In a qualitative study, Schütter and Boerner (2013) observed that family-to-work conflict was occurring due to the necessity to spend time and energy on home-related activities. Similarly, Van der Zee et al. (2005) found a significant and positive effect of home demands on expatriates' family-to-work conflict. Furthermore, they also observed that adequate social support at work from supervisors and colleagues and the support received from family members are both negatively related to family-to-work conflict.

In terms of outcomes, Shaffer et al. (2001) found a positive association between family-to-work interference and expatriate withdrawal cognitions. Additionally, Van der Zee et al. (2005) observed a negative association of family-to-work conflict, experienced by the expatriate, with both the expatriate's general health and their spouse's psychological well-being. However, more work is needed that examines the consequences of family-to-work conflict for expatriates and their families.

Work–Family Enrichment in the Context of Expatriation

Although there are only few studies on the experience of expatriates and their families in regard to work–family conflict, there are even fewer instances where work–family enrichment is examined. Work–family enrichment (WFE) represents the degree to which positive experiences in one life domain (e.g., work) spill over and have beneficial effects on an individual's functioning in another life domain (e.g., family) or vice versa (Greenhaus & Powell, 2006).

The expatriation literature has mainly focused on how the family can enrich the work role. Harris (2004) proposed that female expatriates who are accompanied by their family and receive emotional support from them will experience family-to-work enrichment. Similarly, in their qualitative study, Mäkelä and Suutari (2013) observed that expatriates recognized the positive influence of their family on their work life. Expatriates specifically talked about how much being with their family abroad has provided them with the needed support to succeed in their work role. In an ethnographic study of Dutch expatriate families living in an expatriate housing compound in Saudi Arabia, Lauring and Selmer (2010) found that spouses were actively involved in facilitating the expatriate's career by organizing social gatherings and dinner parties that served as a networking platform among the expatriates and provided them with work-related opportunities.

Future directions. Overall, besides the generally few studies on work–family conflict and enrichment, another considerable limitation can provide an avenue for future research. Namely, many of the studies on both WFC and WFE use only qualitative methods (e.g., Lauring & Selmer, 2010; Mäkelä & Suutari, 2013; Schütter & Boerner, 2013). Such research design prevents scholars from incorporating the typical quantitative measures used to assess WFC and WFE. This makes it difficult to establish whether these qualitative studies are conceptualizing and referring to conflict and enrichment in the same way as the existing body of quantitative research. Thus, more research is needed that directly measures these constructs.

The Role of the Host and Home Culture on the Work–Family Interface

Many of the studies described above aim to generalize across expatriates and do not focus on the influence of the particular culture of origin or the foreign host location. However, expatriates and their families may experience greater challenges in some host countries and relatively few challenges in others (Brookfield Relocation Services, 2016). Furthermore, the degree of cultural differences between their home and host country can also influence the experiences of both expatriates and their families while abroad. The latter issue has been the most frequently examined in terms of attempting to incorporate the influence of the host–home country mix on the work–family interface during expatriation. In particular, studies have mainly focused on the role of cultural novelty, the degree of perceived cultural distance between the host and the home country. It is suggested that the greater the cultural novelty, the harder it is for the expatriate and their family to navigate the host country environment, which can lead to various negative consequences (Black et al., 1991; Mendenhall & Oddou, 1985).

In regard to the effect on the expatriate, Black et al. (1991) proposed that cultural novelty would be detrimental mostly for expatriate interaction and general adjustment, but not for their work adjustment. As expected, cultural novelty was found to have a negative influence on expatriate general and interaction adjustment (e.g., Black & Stephens, 1989; Kraimer, Wayne, & Jaworski, 2001; Palthe, 2004; Shaffer et al., 1999), but not on work adjustment (Black & Gregersen, 1991; Black & Stephens, 1989). However, although Parker and McEvoy (1993) further provided support that cultural novelty negatively affected interaction adjustment and had no effect on work adjustment, they found a counterintuitive significant and positive relationship between cultural novelty and general adjustment. Inconsistent results prompted Takeuchi, Lepak, Marinova, and Yun (2007) to propose that perhaps the effect of cultural novelty on adjustment is nonlinear, specifically a slanted S-shape. However, they did not find a significant nonlinear or linear effect on expatriate general adjustment. In contrast, in their meta-analysis Bhaskar-Shrinivas et al. (2005) provide support for a linear and negative association between cultural novelty and all aspects of expatriate adjustment, including work adjustment.

Cultural novelty has also been found to have a direct influence on expatriates' spouses. Shaffer and Harrison (2001) found evidence through both qualitative and quantitative data that cultural novelty had a negative influence in regard to most dimensions of spouse adjustment. However, others have found that cultural novelty has a nonlinear (i.e., slanted S-shape) effect on spouse general adjustment (Takeuchi et al., 2007). Specifically, Takeuchi and colleagues (2007) proposed that although people do not need to spend too much cognitive energy and resources when living in a very similar environment as the one at home, the greater the cultural novelty becomes, the more cognitive resources will need to be utilized for successful functioning in such an environment. However, as long as cultural novelty levels are low to moderate, individuals still may not employ the needed cognitive resources, essentially hindering their ability to successfully cope with the stressors caused by such relatively small, but frustrating, cultural dissimilarities. Thus, the relationship follows a slanted S-shape, where at very low levels of cultural novelty, spouse general adjustment is high and dramatically decreases as cultural novelty increases. Following a stabilization at medium levels of cultural novelty, when spouses would generally begin to use their cognitive resources to cope with the cultural stressors, further dramatic decrease in spouse general adjustment occurs if they perceive the novelty of the host culture to be too high. At this stage their cognitive coping processes are not able to offset the negative effects of very high cultural novelty.

The experience of cultural novelty was also found to cross over between the family partners and thus to affect adjustment. Black and Stephens (1989) observed that cultural novelty, as assessed by the expatriate, negatively related to spouse general adjustment. In addition, similarly to the nonlinear effect of cultural novelty perceived by the spouse on the spouse's own general adjustment, Takeuchi et al. (2007) observed a similar slanted S-shape effect of cultural novelty, as assessed by the spouse, on expatriate general adjustment.

Although the importance of the cultural distance between the host and home location for the experience of the expatriates and their families has been recognized, there are very few studies that look at the different combinations of host and home countries, beyond just measuring for the degree of cultural novelty. Even fewer studies consider the whole family, and not just the expatriate. Many of the studies collect their data from various sources without a dominant host or home location (e.g., expatriates are from a variety of countries and are placed in a variety of countries; Caligiuri et al., 1998; Shaffer & Harrison, 1998), while others focus on one home country (e.g., the United States) and a single host location (e.g., Germany), but do not incorporate this in their theorizing beyond acknowledging that there are perhaps some relevant cultural differences at play (e.g., Black, 1988; Takeuchi et al., 2002).

As an example, Takeuchi et al. (2007) suggested that a possible reason for not finding the hypothesized influence of parental demands on expatriate adjustment in their sample of Japanese expatriate families might be due to the strong distinction between gender roles in the Japanese culture, where the female spouse, who is often the trailing spouse, is solely responsible for care of the children. In his review on the expatriate adjustment literature, Takeuchi (2010) proposed that scholars need to consider the person–situation interaction perspective and take into account both person and situational factors in order to comprehensively understand the expatriation experience. Thus, for example, a relevant person factor can be the home culture of the spouse, which, if very culturally distant from the host location (situational factor), might then have negative consequences for the adjustment of the spouse, which can cross over and negatively affect expatriate adjustment.

One of the few studies examining the role of the host–home country mix is by Davies et al. (2015) who look at the effects of partner nationality. The authors found that an expatriate with a spouse who is originally from the host location, in time, would experience the highest level of adjustment. Expatriates with spouses who are third-country nationals also experienced a significant rise in adjustment over time. The least adjusted were expatriates with spouses from the home country. This provides some initial evidence that spouses who are natives of the host location can help expatriates navigate the challenges of the foreign environment. On the other hand, it is also possible that spouses from third countries are more accustomed to international relocation and may be more open to new experiences. Another article by Waxin (2004) specifically examined the role of the home culture on expatriates in India. In particular, they found that partner support significantly increased expatriate interaction adjustment for all expatriates (i.e., France, Germany, and Scandinavia) except for those from South Korea.

Due to the scarcity of research on the influence of the host–home country mix on the work–family interface, more research is needed in order for us to be able to understand the role of culture beyond simply assessing cultural novelty. One possible direction is to consider cultural differences. Some studies do either explicitly base their theorizing on Hofstede's (1980) cultural value dimensions (e.g., Suutari & Brewster, 1998; Waxin, 2004) or attribute certain findings post hoc to the possibility that cultural values might have played a role (e.g., Takeuchi et al., 2007). However, caution needs to be exercised to not assume that just because the host and home countries are culturally similar, the lives of expatriates and their families will be free of frustrations. For example, expatriate families who come from a culture that is similar in terms of language and historical roots may assume that they will have no adaptation problems, but in fact may experience vast differences in terms of living standards and institutional and organizational cultures (Canhilal et al., 2015).

Another avenue for future research is to further examine the role of spouse nationality. Davies et al. (2015) provided some initial insights, but this research can be expanded to assess the influence of spouse nationality on other aspects of the work–family interface, such as the spillover to the work role, in terms of effects on expatriate performance and satisfaction. It might also be fruitful to further assess the mix of nationalities of the partners within the couple. Are partners who are both third-country nationals better adjusted than couples where only one is a third-country national? If a spouse is from a country with high cultural distance from the host location but the expatriate is from a more culturally similar location, would this affect the dynamics between the spouses as they navigate the expatriation experience? One of the main reasons why research in the past has not often examined the host–home country mix is that it is hard to find data from couples from a variety of host and home locations. However, even conducting small-scale or qualitative studies can shed some light on the issue and further elucidate the experiences of expatriates and their families (e.g., Jackson & Manderscheid, 2015; Lauring & Selmer, 2010).

Such smaller-scale studies can also help provide more insight into the experiences of expatriate children and how these experiences transfer to other family members. For example, in their qualitative study, Fukuda and Chu (1994) discuss a unique aspect of Japanese expatriate families. Specifically, ensuring that children receive a Japanese-style education is very important for Japanese expatriates. However, since such type of education is often not available abroad, children are sent back to

Japan with the spouse, which creates additional problems for the family and the expatriate due to the prolonged physical separation.

Conclusion

Although significant advances have been made to elucidate the work–family interface during expatriation, there are issues that still need to be resolved. Specifically, we need to ensure that processes within the work–family interface are clearly defined and delineated, examine the whole family unit (not only the spouse–expatriate relationship), and assess the role of the host–home country mix. Figure 26.1 presents a summary of the aspects of the work–family interface discussed in this review and how these forces may interact with each other to shape experiences.

It can be especially helpful if future research focuses on developing more comprehensive and theoretically derived models. Theories from the domestic work–family literature are often borrowed and used in studies on expatriates and their families, but they are rarely utilized to their full potential by systemically examining the proposed mechanisms (Takeuchi, 2010). Although theoretical models specific to the context of expatriation have been proposed (see Caligiuri et al., 1998; Haslberger & Brewster, 2008; Haslberger, Hippler, &

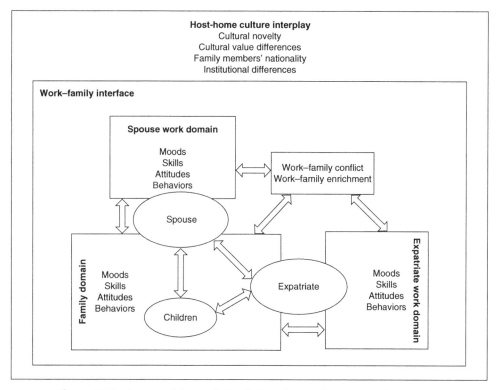

Figure 26.1 *Aspects of the work–family interface in the context of expatriation.*

Brewster, 2015; Lazarova et al., 2010), there are only a few empirical studies that test these or other similarly comprehensive models (e.g., see Caligiuri et al., 1998; Rosenbusch, Cerny, & Earnest, 2015; Shaffer et al., 2016; Takeuchi et al., 2002; Van der Zee et al., 2005).

Such integrative models should also consider different types of expatriates and situations. For example, women expatriates may have greater work and family pressures put on them, compared to male expatriates, and thus they could experience more work–family conflict (Linehan & Walsh, 2000). The situation for self-initiated expatriates may also be more challenging. Unlike corporate expatriates, they are more embedded within the host country and may thus be affected to a greater extent by local culture and regulations, which can lead to additional challenges, as well as benefits for the expatriate family (Mäkelä & Suutari, 2013). Generally, future work is needed that expands and deepens our understanding of the work–family experiences of the full range of different types of expatriates and their families.

References

Abdul Malek, M., Budhwar, P., & Reiche, B. S. (2015). Sources of support and expatriation: A multiple stakeholder perspective of expatriate adjustment and performance in Malaysia. *The International Journal of Human Resource Management, 26(2)*, 258–276.

Ali, A., Van der Zee, K., & Sanders, G. (2003). Determinants of intercultural adjustment among expatriate spouses. *International Journal of Intercultural Relations, 27(5)*, 563–580.

Bhaskar-Shrinivas, P., Harrison, D. A., Shaffer, M. A., & Luk, D. M. (2005). Input-based and time-based models of international adjustment: Meta-analytic evidence and theoretical extensions. *Academy of Management Journal, 48*, 257–281.

Black J.S. (1988). Work role transitions: A study of American expatriate managers in Japan. *Journal of International Business Studies, 19*, 217–294.

Black, J.S., & Gregersen, H.B. (1991). Antecedents to cross-cultural adjustment for expatriates in Pacific Rim assignments. *Human Relations, 44*, 497–515.

Black, J. S., Mendenhall, M., & Oddou, G. (1991). Toward a comprehensive model of international adjustment: An integration of multiple theoretical perspectives. *Academy of Management Review, 16*, 291–317.

Black, J. S., & Stephens, G. K. (1989). The influence of the spouse on American expatriate adjustment and intent to stay in Pacific Rim overseas assignments. *Journal of Management, 15*, 529–544.

Brookfield Global Relocation Services. (2016). Global mobility trend report. http://globalmo bilitytrends.brookfieldgrs.com. Accessed on September 9, 2016.

Caligiuri, P. M., Hyland, M. A. M., Joshi, A., & Bross, A. S. (1998). Testing a theoretical model for examining the relationship between family adjustment and expatriates' work adjustment. *Journal of Applied Psychology, 83*, 598–614.

Caligiuri, P.M., Hyland, M.M., & Joshi, A. (1998). Families on global assignments: Applying work/family theories abroad, In M. A. Rahim, R.T. Golembiewski, & C.C. Lundberg (Eds.), *Current Topics in Management (Vol. 3)* (pp. 313–328). USA: Elsevier Science/JAI Press.

Canhilal, S. K., Gabel Shemueli, R., & Dolan, S. (2015). Antecedent factors for success in international assignments: The case of expatriates in Peru. *Journal of Global Mobility, 3(4)*, 378–396.

Davies, S., Kraeh, A., & Froese, F. (2015). Burden or support? The influence of partner nationality on expatriate cross-cultural adjustment. *Journal of Global Mobility, 3(2)*, 169–182.

Demerouti, E., Bakker, A. B., Nachreiner, F., & Schaufeli, W. B. (2001). The job demands-resources model of burnout. *Journal of Applied psychology, 86(3)*, 499.

Edwards, J. R., & Rothbard, N. P. (2000). Mechanisms linking work and family: Clarifying the relationship between work and family constructs. *Academy of Management Review, 25(1)*, 178–199.

Fukuda, K. J., & Chu, P. (1994). Wrestling with expatriate family problems. Japanese experiences in East Asia. *International Studies of Management and Organizations, 24*, 36–47.

Greenhaus, J. H., & Beutell, N. J. (1985). Sources of conflict between work and family roles. *Academy of Management Review, 10(1)*, 76–88.

Greenhaus, J. H., & Powell, G. N. (2006). When work and family are allies: A theory of work–family enrichment. *Academy of Management Review, 31(1)*, 72–92.

Harris, H. (2004). Global careers: Work–life issues and the adjustment of women international managers. *The Journal of Management Development, 23*, 818–832.

Harvey, M. (1997). Dual-career expatriates: Expectations, adjustment and satisfaction with international relocation. *Journal of International Business Studies, 28(3)*, 627–658.

Harvey, M. (1998). Dual-career couples during international relocation: The trailing spouse. *International Journal of Human Resource Management, 9(2)*, 309–331.

Haslberger, A., & Brewster, C. (2008). The expatriate family: An international perspective. *Journal of Managerial Psychology, 23(3)*, 324–346.

Haslberger, A., Hippler, T., & Brewster, C. (2015). Another look at family adjustment. In L. Mäkelä & V. Suutari (Eds.), *Work and Family Interface in the International Career Context* (pp. 53–70). Switzerland: Springer International Publishing.

Hays, R. D. (1971). Ascribed behavioral determinants of success–failure among U.S. expatriate managers. *Journal of International Business Studies, 2*, 40–46.

Hays, R. D. (1974). Expatriate selection: Insuring success and avoiding failure. *Journal of International Business Studies, 5*, 25–37.

Hechanova, R., Beehr, T. A., & Christiansen, N. D. (2003). Antecedents and consequences of employees' adjustment to overseas assignment: A meta-analytic review. *Applied Psychology: An International Review, 52*, 213–236.

Hofstede, G. (1980). *Culture's Consequences: International Differences in Work-Related Values*. Newbury Park, CA: Sage.

Jackson, D., & Manderscheid, S. V. (2015). A phenomenological study of Western expatriates' adjustment to Saudi Arabia. *Human Resource Development International, 18 (2)*, 131–152.

Kempen, R., Pangert, B., Hattrup, K., Mueller, K., & Joens, I. (2015). Beyond conflict: The role of life-domain enrichment for expatriates. *The International Journal of Human Resource Management, 26(1)*, 1–22.

Kraimer, M. L., Wayne, S. J., & Jaworski, R. A. (2001). Sources of support and expatriate performance: The mediating role of expatriate adjustment. *Personnel Psychology, 54*, 71–100.

Lauring, J., & Selmer, J. (2010). The supportive expatriate spouse: An ethnographic study of spouse involvement in expatriate careers. *International Business Review, 19(1),* 59–69.

Lazarova, M., McNulty, Y., & Semeniuk, M. (2015). Expatriate family narratives on international mobility: Key characteristics of the successful moveable family. In L. Mäkelä & V. Suutari (Eds.), *Work and Family Interface in the International Career Context* (pp. 29–51). Switzerland: Springer International Publishing.

Lazarova, M., Westman, M., & Shaffer, M. A. (2010). Elucidating the positive side of the work–family interface on international assignments: A model of expatriate work and family performance. *Academy of Management Review, 35(1),* 93–117.

Linehan, M., & Walsh, J. S. (2000). Work–family conflict and the senior female international manager. *British Journal of Management, 11s,* 49–58.

Mäkelä, L., & Suutari, V. (2011). Coping with work–family conflicts in the global career context. *Thunderbird International Business Review, 53(3),* 365–375.

Mäkelä, L., & Suutari, V. (2013). The work–life balance interface of self-initiated expatriates: Conflicts and enrichment. In V. Vaiman & A. Haslberger (Eds.), *Talent Management of Self-Initiated Expatriates* (pp. 278–303). Basingstoke, UK: Palgrave MacMillan.

Mäkelä, L., Suutari, V., & Mayerhofer, H. (2011). Lives of female expatriates: Work-life balance concerns. *Gender in Management: An International Journal, 26(4),* 256–274.

Mendenhall, M., & Oddou, G. (1985). The dimensions of expatriate acculturation: A review. *Academy of Management Review, 10(1),* 39–47.

Mohr, A. T., & Klein, S. (2004). Exploring the adjustment of American expatriate spouses in Germany. *The International Journal of Human Resource Management, 15(7),* 1189–1206.

Nicholson N., & Imaizumi A. (1993). The adjustment of Japanese expatriates to living and working in Britain. *British Journal of Management, 4,* 119–134.

Palthe, J. (2004). The relative importance of antecedents to cross-cultural adjustment: Implications for managing a global workforce. *International Journal of Intercultural Relations, 28,* 37–59.

Palthe, J. (2008). The role of interaction and general adjustment in expatriate attitudes: Evidence from a field study of global executives on assignment in South Korea, Japan and the Netherlands. *Journal of Asia Business Studies, 3(1),* 42–53.

Parker, B., & McEvoy, G. M. (1993). Initial examination of a model of intercultural adjustment. *International Journal of Intercultural Relations, 17(3),* 355–379.

Rosenbusch, K., Cerny II, L. J., & Earnest, D. R. (2015). The impact of stressors during international assignments. *Cross Cultural Management, 22(3),* 405–430.

Schütter, H., & Boerner, S. (2013). Illuminating the work–family interface on international assignments: An exploratory approach. *Journal of Global Mobility, 1,* 46–71.

Shaffer, M. A., & Harrison, D.A. (1998). Expatriates' psychological withdrawal from international assignments: Work, nonwork, and family influences. *Personnel Psychology, 51(1),* 87–118.

Shaffer, M. A., & Harrison, D.A. (2001). Forgotten partners of international assignments: Development and test of a model of spouse adjustment. *Journal of Applied Psychology, 86,* 238–254.

Shaffer, M. A., Harrison, D. A., & Gilley, K. M. (1999). Dimensions, determinants, and differences in the expatriate adjustment process. *Journal of International Business Studies, 30,* 557–581.

Shaffer, M. A., Harrison, D. A., Gilley, K. M., & Luk, D. M. (2001). Struggling for balance amid turbulence on international assignments: Work–family conflict, support and commitment. *Journal of Management, 27(1)*, 99–121.

Shaffer, M. A., Kraimer, M. L., Chen, Y. P., & Bolino, M. C. (2012). Choices, challenges, and career consequences of global work experiences: A review and future agenda. *Journal of Management, 38(4)*, 1282–1327.

Shaffer, M. A., Reiche, B. S., Dimitrova, M., Lazarova, M., Chen, S., Westman, M., & Wurtz, O. (2016). Work-and family-role adjustment of different types of global professionals: Scale development and validation. *Journal of International Business Studies, 47(2)*, 113–139.

Shih, H. A., Chiang, Y. H., & Hsu, C. C. (2010). High involvement work system, work–family conflict, and expatriate performance—examining Taiwanese expatriates in China. *The International Journal of Human Resource Management, 21(11)*, 2013–2030.

Suutari, V., & Brewster, C. (1998). The adaptation of expatriates in Europe: Evidence from Finnish companies. *Personnel Review, 27(2)*, 89–103.

Takeuchi, R. (2010). A critical review of expatriate adjustment research through a multiple stakeholder view: Progress, emerging trends, and prospects. *Journal of Management, 36*, 1040–1064.

Takeuchi, R., Lepak, D. P., Marinova, S. V., & Yun, S. (2007). Nonlinear influences of stressors on general adjustment: The case of Japanese expatriates and their spouses. *Journal of International Business Studies, 38(6)*, 928–943.

Takeuchi, R., Yun, S., & Tesluk, P.E. (2002). An examination of crossover and spillover effects of spousal and expatriate cross-cultural adjustment on expatriate outcomes. *Journal of Applied Psychology, 87*, 655–666.

Van der Zee, K. I., Ali, A. J., & Haaksma, I. (2007). Determinants of effective coping with cultural transition among expatriate children and adolescents. *Anxiety, stress, and coping, 20(1)*, 25–45.

Van der Zee, K. I., Ali, A. J., & Salomé, E. (2005). Role interference and subjective well-being among expatriate families. *European Journal of Work and Organizational Psychology, 14(3)*, 239–262.

Waxin, M. F. (2004). Expatriates' interaction adjustment: The direct and moderator effects of culture of origin. *International Journal of Intercultural Relations, 28*, 61–79.

Westman, M. (2001). Stress and strain crossover. *Human Relations, 54(6)*, 717–751.

PART VI

Organizational Perspectives

27 The Work–Family Interface and Careers in the Global Workplace: Insights from Cross-National Research

Karen S. Lyness, Michael K. Judiesch, and Hilal E. Erkovan

Work–family scholars have long been concerned with the interface between employees' work and family roles. In keeping with this tradition, this chapter focuses on relationships among various aspects of the work–family (WF) interface and career-related outcomes for employees. Specifically, we provide an overview of the interdisciplinary literature about variations across countries and the theoretical explanations that have been offered to explain the variations. For example, childbirth may affect women's careers in different ways depending on aspects of the country context, such as WF-related cultural beliefs about whether mothers should personally care for their children or the availability of government-provided WF supports (e.g., paid maternity leaves and public childcare). Thus, mothers' career decisions and options often differ across countries, and characteristics of the country context, such as WF-related cultural values and legal policies, may help to explain why.

Despite the potential value of understanding cross-national variation, much of the relevant research has been conducted within specific countries, such as the United States, and less is known about whether this research holds across countries. Yet, these issues are timely and important due to the globalization of business, and have practical implications for multinational corporations (MNCs) and their employees. For example, insights about salient aspects of national context, such as cross-national differences in WF-related cultural values or governmental policies that might affect employees' WF interface and careers, could be helpful to MNCs in determining how to tailor their WF-related policies and programs to fit country characteristics. Also, there are important implications for country policy makers. Moreover, gaining a better understanding of these issues can potentially extend WF and career scholarship by informing the development of relevant theories and identifying various types of boundary conditions that might limit generalizability of theories and research findings across countries.

Accordingly, the objective of this chapter is to review examples of the extant cross-national literature about various aspects of the WF interface and employees' careers. Our review is based on cross-national studies with data from two or more

497

countries. In this chapter, we define the term "career" as referring to an individual's sequence of jobs and work experiences that occur throughout his or her life, in line with the broader career development literature (e.g., Arthur, Hall, & Lawrence, 1989; Lent & Brown, 2013).

We organized the chapter according to whether theoretical explanations for cross-national variation are based on cultural or structural characteristics of countries, with a few studies that incorporate both cultural and structural explanations. Our use of these theoretical explanations is consistent with the approach used in Ollier-Malaterre and Foucreault's (2017) interdisciplinary review of cross-national work–life (WL) research. Ollier-Malaterre and Foucreault defined culture as "a set of beliefs, values, and norms about what is good, right, and desirable in life that are shared by individuals who have a common historical experience" (p. 113). In addition, Ollier-Malaterre and Foucreault proposed that cross-national variation in individual or organizational WL-related constructs may be explained by various types of structures, defined as "institutions or systems that produce rules and norms that organize and constrain human interactions" (p.113). Examples of country structures that are relevant to the WF interface include legal structures (e.g., public policies regarding paid maternity leaves or childcare), economic structures (e.g., the wealth or industrialization of a country), and social structures (e.g., the degree of gender equality). We apply Ollier-Malaterre and Foucreault's ideas to organize our literature review and also extend them to explain the cross-national variation in related macro-level employment outcomes, such as labor force participation rates and compensation, that often vary according to gender and parental status. We include several examples of studies that draw on both types of explanations.

Although a comprehensive review of this multidisciplinary literature is beyond the scope of this chapter, we provide examples of cross-national research to illustrate the variety of approaches and findings. Our review begins with examples of how work and family roles may vary across countries, and the implications for careers. Then we review studies that illustrate the use of cultural values and structural characteristics to explain cross-national variation in careers, followed by research that incorporates both cultural and structural explanations. We also review studies at different levels of analysis, ranging from micro-level studies about individual-level variables (e.g., how women combine motherhood with work) to macro-level studies about relationships of country-level policies (e.g., length of paid maternity leaves) to aggregated employment measures (e.g., mothers' labor force participation rates). We also review studies that include organizational-level constructs which may be related to either individual-level or country-level variables, or to both. We conclude the chapter with a future research agenda grounded in the research and findings.

Cross-National Variation in Work and Family Roles

A key question that is important in cross-national comparative studies is the extent to which work or family roles differ across countries. For example, a study of five European countries found cross-national differences in beliefs about how parents should divide household responsibilities for breadwinning (i.e., financial support of the family) relative to responsibility for homemaking and caregiving, with greater adherence to the traditional male breadwinner/female homemaker household division of labor in Poland, more support for equal sharing of both work and family roles in Sweden, and Denmark, Finland, and Germany falling in between the two extremes with regard to preferred household arrangements (Edlund & Oun, 2016). Edlund and Oun explained that these differing attitudes about work and family roles were consistent with the countries' WF-related policies and argued that policies "may influence people's ideas about proper and desirable behavior of men and women in the realms of paid work and childcare" (p. 152). For example, the Nordic countries' policies, such as provision of public childcare and lengthy paid parental leaves, are available to both mothers and fathers, and support the "dual-earner family model." This contrasts with policies in continental Europe that provide generous child support and encourage mothers with young children to give up their paid work to care for their children, thus supporting the "traditional male breadwinner family model" (Edlund & Oun, 2016, pp. 153–154).

In addition, Corrigall and Konrad (2006) found that country cultural values about the division of household labor were related to the types of jobs women preferred, and interpreted their findings as reflecting differences in women's views of their work roles across the fourteen countries in this study. The authors reasoned that women's attitudes about the household division of labor would be consistent with the extent that their country culture reflected gender egalitarianism, based on the Project Globe research. The Project Globe research identified nine dimensions of culture, and developed measures of both cultural practices, that capture "how things are" and cultural values, that capture "how things should be" (Hanges & Dickson, 2004, p. 125).

Corrigall and Konrad's study used the Project Globe gender egalitarianism dimension of country culture, defined as "the degree to which . . . a society minimizes gender role differences while promoting gender equality," (House & Javidan, 2004, p. 12), and measured this cultural dimension with country gender egalitarian practice (GEP) scores (House, Hanges, Javidan, Dorfman, & Gupta, 2004). The authors predicted that GEP scores would be related to mothers' preferences for various job characteristics (Corrigall & Konrad, 2006). There was some support for these predictions as women who were thought to have primary household/caregiving responsibility (based on low country GEP scores) valued jobs that offered security and flexibility, suggesting that they wanted work that would accommodate their family responsibilities, whereas women who were thought to share work and family roles with their partners (based on high GEP scores) valued jobs that offered high income, reflecting their shared responsibility for providing family income (Corrigall & Konrad, 2006).

These two studies illustrate how both cultural and structural factors may be relevant to understanding cross-national differences in normative beliefs about women's and men's WF roles. Moreover, cross-national variations in beliefs about WF roles have implications for women's and men's careers and employment patterns, all of which are important themes for this chapter.

WF and Gender-Related Cultural Values

In this section, we will review research that illustrates how country WF-related cultural values can be used to explain cross-national variation in the WF interface and careers, beginning with relationships of country culture to individual-level WF and career variables. We first review qualitative research in which the authors use cultural values, such as collectivism, to interpret cross-national differences in WF and career variables, but these studies do not include direct measures of culture. We also provide examples of research using quantitative measures of culture, such as country scores representing various cultural dimensions taken from Project GLOBE (House et al., 2004), and tests of multi-level relationships between these country culture measures and various individual-level WF and career-related variables. In addition, we include two studies that measure gender egalitarianism with objective measures of country gender equality, which prior research has shown to be positively related to similar measures based on cultural values (Emrich, Denmark, & Den Hartog, 2004).

WF conflict. Much of the cross-national literature about WF roles focuses on strain resulting from the inability to meet the demands of work and family responsibilities (Goode, 1960), and various types of WF conflict, such as time-based, strain-based, and behavioral conflicts (Greenhaus & Beutell, 1985), with a frequent focus on women's careers. Cultural values related to WF issues or gender are often used to explain cross-national differences in work and family roles and conflict. For example, Peus and Traut-Mattausch (2008) compared perspectives of women in upper middle-level managerial positions in Germany and the United States and found that a majority of the German women viewed their work responsibilities as incompatible with motherhood and some had even decided to remain childless to focus on their careers, whereas the American women generally did not view their careers as incompatible with motherhood. These cross-national differences were attributed to West German cultural beliefs that children are harmed when non-family members care for them. In contrast, the American managers were less likely to share these concerns. Also, the American managers were more successful at combining their managerial and motherhood roles in part because they had access to a variety of supports from employers and other people, including non-family members. However, women from both countries mentioned prejudice against mothers as a barrier to career advancement for female managers.

Peus and Traut-Mattausch's (2008) research also suggested that there was some alignment between country cultural values regarding whether women should combine motherhood and managerial work roles and employers' provision of WF supports for working mothers. For example, the female managers from the United States described several types of organizational WF supports, including flexible career paths and supportive supervisors, which helped them combine their managerial careers with the responsibilities of motherhood, but these types of employer supports were generally not available in West Germany (Peus & Traut-Mattausch, 2008).

In a related study, Yang, Chen, Choi, and Zou (2000), tested predictions that collectivistic cultural values influence employees' perspectives on their work and family roles and whether they perceive WF conflict. Their results showed that the Chinese employees were willing to sacrifice time with their families for work because they viewed this personal sacrifice as benefiting their families, which is consistent with the Chinese collectivistic cultural values that prioritize what is best for the family and other collectives above personal concerns. Yang et al. contrasted this perspective with the individualistic cultural values in the United States, where priority is given to an individual's personal concerns, which can include his or her family, and sacrificing family time for work is viewed as a failure to care for their families. Similarly, a study of professional women in Hong Kong and Singapore found that in these cultures young women were expected to work in order to earn money to help support their families (Thein, Austen, Currie, & Lewin, 2010). Thus, these studies suggest that how work and family roles are viewed can affect perceptions of WF conflict as well as prioritization of work and family roles.

Although there are some differences in specific research questions and details, the findings from these studies generally support the idea that country cultural values and norms are useful for understanding variations in how work and family roles are perceived as well as whether these roles conflict. The specific findings about perceptions of work roles and family roles offer insights about reasons for WF conflicts, with important implications for careers, and especially women's careers after they become mothers.

WF facilitation. In contrast to the focus of these studies on negative outcomes, such as WF conflict, other WF role theories, such as WF enrichment, expansionist, and facilitation theories, suggest that engagement in multiple roles can have positive outcomes (e.g., Barnett & Hyde, 2001; Greenhaus & Powell, 2006). These theories posit that engagement in both family and work roles may result in enhanced energy, mental health, and other resources that can facilitate rather than interfere with performance within and across different types of roles (e.g., Barnett & Hyde, 2001; Greenhaus & Powell, 2006). For example, research in the Netherlands found evidence that women reported higher levels of WF facilitation than their male counterparts, which was attributed to men's requirement to work whereas women were more likely to be working because they chose to do so rather than due to financial necessity (van Steenbergen, Ellemers, & Mooijaart, 2007). Similarly, research in Great Britain found that many women valued their work because it provided stimulation, self-esteem, financial independence, and "a much-needed break from childcare and the isolation of the domestic sphere" (Wattis, Standing, & Yerkes, 2013, p. 12).

Lyness and Judiesch (2008) carried out a multilevel study to investigate the relationship between WL balance and potential for career advancement, based on multisource ratings of close to 10,000 managers working in 33 countries. WL balance was defined as "achieving satisfying experiences in all life domains (which requires that) personal resources such as energy, time, and commitment be well distributed across domains" (Kirchmeyer, 2000, p. 81). Specifically, the authors tested competing theory-based predictions about whether WL balance, measured with managers' self-ratings, would have a positive, negative, or no relationship to career advancement potential, based on supervisors' ratings. They also tested whether these relationships were similar in magnitude for men and women, and examined country gender egalitarianism (measured with Project Globe GEP scores) as a potential moderating variable.

The results revealed a significant three-way interaction showing that the relationship between WL balance and career advancement potential differed depending on whether the manager was a man or woman, with country gender egalitarian culture as an additional moderator. In high GEP countries, such as the Nordic region (represented by Denmark, Finland, and Sweden), there was a positive relationship between managers' self-rated WL balance and their supervisors' ratings of career advancement potential for women and a non-significant relationship for men. This pattern was reversed in low GEP countries, such as the Confucian Asian region (i.e., Hong Kong, Japan, People's Republic of China, Singapore, and South Korea), where there was a positive relationship for men and no relationship for women (Lyness & Judiesch, 2008). The authors used single-country research from these regions to interpret the three-way interaction. In the Netherlands (a relatively high GEP country), prior research found that women who worked voluntarily reported higher levels of WF facilitation than men (van Steenbergen et al., 2007), which may help to explain why WL balance had a positive relationship to career advancement potential ratings for women but not men. Also, studies in India (a low GEP country with traditional gender norms) found that men have more discretion about participation in family roles than women; the authors suggested that men's family involvement may help to restore them and result in more WF facilitation than was the case for their female counterparts who had to handle traditional family responsibilities in addition to their work roles (Aryee, Srinivas, & Tan, 2005; Larson, Verma, & Dworkin, 2001), which may help to explain why WL balance had a positive relationship to career advancement potential ratings for men but not women.

Moreover, Lyness and Judiesch (2008) found a positive relationship between WL balance and career advancement potential when both ratings were made by supervisors, which raises questions about the basis for supervisors' perceptions of their subordinates' WL balance as well as whether these perceptions influenced overall perceptions of their subordinates' career advancement potential. These questions led to Lyness and Judiesch's (2014) follow-up study, based on self-ratings and supervisors' ratings of WL balance for 40,000 managers working in 36 countries. In this study, the authors examined ratee gender differences in both sets of ratings, and also tested country gender egalitarianism as a potential moderator of gender differences in WL balance ratings.

Lyness and Judiesch (2014) applied ideas from Eagly and colleagues' cross-cultural extensions of social role theory (Eagly & Wood, 2012; Wood & Eagly, 2002) and hypothesized that country gender egalitarian cultural context would influence the extent that women and men conform to traditional gender-specific breadwinner/caretaker norms, and that other people's perceptions of women and men engaging in these normative behaviors would in turn influence beliefs about women's and men's attributes. These theoretical ideas are the basis for the authors' predictions that country gender egalitarian cultural context would influence supervisors' perceptions about gender differences in their managerial subordinates' WL balance. However, because self-ratings were assumed to reflect individual circumstances, it was less clear whether there would also be gender differences in self-ratings of WL balance, or whether gender differences would be related to the country context.

Lyness and Judiesch (2014) measured country gender egalitarianism with two types of measures: cultural value measures and egalitarian practices measures, intended to reflect actual gender equality. Cultural values were measured with Project GLOBE gender egalitarian values (GEV; i.e., "should be" scores; House et al., 2004) and a composite measure based on World Values Survey items (WVS v.20090901, 2009) that have been used to measure patriarchal norms and values in prior research (Seguino, 2007). Cultural practices were measured with Project Globe GEP scores and the Gender Inequality Index (GII), which is a broad, composite measure of gender disparities in important areas of life, such as women's (compared to men's) access to higher education and jobs, and women's representation in parliamentary institutions (United Nations Development Programme, 2010).

The ratee gender difference in overall self-ratings of WL balance (fixed effects across all countries) did not differ significantly by gender, and the variation in gender differences across countries (random effects) was also non-significant. In contrast, there was significant cross-national variation in ratee gender differences based on the supervisors' ratings. Notably, the magnitude of the gender gaps in the supervisors' ratings was moderated by country-level gender egalitarianism, with larger gender gaps in less egalitarian cultures, as measured by both of the cultural value measures and the objective GII measure of actual gender disparities. Specific findings showed that in low egalitarian countries, supervisors gave female managers lower ratings of WL balance than their male counterparts, whereas supervisors' ratings of female and male subordinates were similar in more egalitarian countries. It is also notable that only WL balance ratings of female subordinates differed depending on country culture; ratings of male subordinates were uniformly high regardless of country context.

The pattern of findings suggested that supervisors' perceptions reflected societal gender stereotypes and norms. A possible interpretation of supervisors' lower ratings of women in low egalitarian countries is that they reflect doubts about women's ability to balance work with traditional caretaker responsibilities, or less acceptance of female managers in the workplace, as compared with greater workplace acceptance and support of female managers in more egalitarian cultures. These results, combined with Lyness and Judiesch's (2008) findings that supervisors' ratings of their subordinates' WL balance were positively related to ratings of career advancement potential, raise concerns about the negative implications for female managers' career opportunities in low egalitarian countries.

Additional insight into the effects of country gender disparities is provided by Lyness and Kropf's (2005) study that examined relationships of the United Nations' GII measure to two types of organizational WF supports (i.e., supportive WF cultures and flexible work arrangements; FWA), which in turn were predicted to relate to managers' self-reported WF balance, based on surveys of managers in twenty European countries. Their specific results differed depending on whether managers worked in domestic organizations or multinational corporations. For managers who worked in domestic organizations, country GII was negatively related to supportive organizational WF cultures, which in turn had a positive relationship to managers' WF balance. For managers who worked in multinational corporations, GII in the headquarters' country was negatively related to organizational FWA, and the local country GII was negatively related to supportive WF culture and WF balance, and organizational FWA was positively related to managers' WF balance.

These findings linking country GII, organizational WF supports, and employees' WF balance offer a possible explanation about why cultural values are useful for explaining the employee WF interface and career outcomes in some of the other studies we reviewed. Organizational WF supports are generally thought to facilitate employees' ability to manage their work and family roles, with implications for their careers. Lyness and Kropf's (2005) research showed that GII was negatively related to organizational WF support (FWA and supportive cultures), and organizational WF supports sometimes mediated the relationships between GII and WF balance. These findings also suggest that managers who work in less egalitarian countries are thus less likely to have access to organizational WF supports, which is a possible explanation for why they might have lower WF balance, as was found in this study. Also, Lyness and Kropf's (2005) study did not find gender differences in managers' self-reported WF balance, which is consistent with the overall non-significant gender differences in managers' self-ratings of WL balance reported in Lyness and Judiesch (2014), which was based on a broader sample of thirty-six countries and included non-European countries.

In addition, Lyness and Kropf's (2005) results showing a negative relationship between country GII and organizational WF support may help to explain why supervisors rated women in low egalitarian countries lower in WL balance than their male counterparts. Because of the more traditional household division of labor in low egalitarian countries, women may have greater need than men for organizational WF supports, but Lyness and Kropf's (2005) results showed that organizational WF supports were less likely to be provided in low gender egalitarian countries than in higher gender egalitarian countries, which is consistent with supervisors' lower ratings of women's (vs. men's) WL balance in low egalitarian countries (Lyness & Judiesch, 2014).

Taken together, the studies in this section suggest that there are cross-national differences in employees' relative involvement in work and family roles that have implications for their careers, and that country-level contextual variables reflecting WF-related cultural values and related objective measures of gender disparities can help to explain these differences. Although not directly measured in the qualitative research, collectivistic versus individualistic cultural values were also used to explain cross-national differences in mothers' relative involvement in work and family roles. In addition, there is quantitative evidence, based on multisource ratings in thirty-three countries, that GEP scores moderated the relationship of WL balance to career advancement potential (Lyness & Judiesch, 2008); and that gender egalitarian cultural values and objective gender disparities (GII) help to explain supervisors' ratings of their female managerial subordinates' WL balance (Lyness & Judiesch, 2014). Also, Lyness and Kopf's (2005) study found that organizational WF supports may mediate and help to explain the relationships between country cultural values and workers' WF and career outcomes.

WF and Gender-Related Structural Factors

In this section we review research that draws on cross-national differences in WF-related structural variables, including economic, social, and public policy (legal) structures, to explain WF and career-related outcomes. Country structural characteristics have been used to explain organizational-level outcomes, such as organizations' provision of WF supports, as well as individual-level WF and career outcomes. However, much of the research that investigates country-level structural variables examines relationships to macro-level outcomes, such as employment patterns of mothers.

Lyness, Gornick, Stone, and Grotto's (2012) quantitative research illustrates the important role of country-level structural variables. Based on nationally representative samples of over ten thousand employees from twenty-one countries, they tested a model linking country-level structural variables to organizational WF supports, which in turn were related to employees' WF conflict and work attitudes. Specifically, Lyness and colleagues investigated several country-level structural variables, including economic structures (i.e., GDP per capita), legal structures (i.e., social welfare expenditure as a proportion of GDP and union coverage), and social structures (i.e., women's labor force participation rate), all of which were predicted to have positive relationships to organizational WF support, operationalized as workers' control over their work time and schedules. Thus, this study extended prior research based on the well-known welfare state regime taxonomy developed by Esping-Andersen (1990) by specifying and testing quantitative measures of specific country characteristics in order to clarify the basis for differences across countries rather than relying on country clusters. Lyness and colleagues' study also investigated the contention that employees' control over their working time is a critical WF support (Berg, Appelbaum, Bailey, & Kalleberg, 2004; Kelly, Moen, & Tranby, 2011) by testing predictions that workers' control would relate negatively to strain-based WF conflict and positively to work attitudes (i.e., job satisfaction and organizational commitment).

Most of the micro-level individual characteristics (e.g., gender, age, living with a partner, and education) and job characteristics (e.g., working full-time, being self-employed, high earnings, and promotion opportunities) had the predicted relationships to control over schedule and work hours, based on prior research, most of which was conducted in the United States. Notably, gender was significantly related to control over schedules and work hours, and the results showed that women had less control than men over both their work schedules and hours; also, the relationship of gender to work schedules was invariant across countries.

In addition, controlling for the micro-level variables, each of the macro-level structural variables was related to one or more type of control, but some relationships were not in the predicted directions. For example, country GDP per capita was associated with more schedule control, but less control over work hours, as reflected in working more hours than desired (Lyness et al., 2012). Also, women's labor force participation had a positive relationship to working more hours than desired, such that countries with higher female labor force participation rates were also more likely to be characterized by a general desire (i.e., across female and male workers) for fewer working hours, indicating that workers in these countries had less control over work hours than workers in countries with lower female participation rates. The authors interpreted this finding as suggesting that in these countries the general desire for fewer work hours may reflect an attempt to balance work with family by both women and men (Lyness et al., 2012). Also, Lyness and colleagues (2012) found that giving workers' control over their schedules and work hours generally had positive outcomes, as measured by workers' reduced WF conflict and better work attitudes.

However, there were several critical gender gaps, all of which disadvantaged women with implications for their WF interface and careers. Specifically, women had less control over their work schedules than their male colleagues, and they were more likely to report overwork (i.e., working more hours than desired, indicating a lack of control over their work hours). Thus, women had less control over their hours and schedules even though they may have greater need for control, as women are juggling work with a larger share of family and household responsibilities. Women's unmet need for control helps to explain why gender also moderated relationships of overwork to all three individual outcomes, with women reporting more negative outcomes than their male counterparts at comparable levels of control. These results suggest that lack of control over their work schedules and hours was more difficult for women than men. Moreover, the study found that lack of schedule control had a positive relationship to strain-based WF conflict for female workers, but this relationship was not significant for men (Lyness et al., 2012).

Thus, Lyness et al. (2012) found that women were less likely than men to experience the positive work outcomes associated with control over work schedules and hours, and the authors pointed out that these findings help to explain why women are more likely than men to work part-time in order to gain flexibility and hours that fit their family responsibilities, even though they may have to settle for less desirable jobs. These findings and implications are thus consistent with macro-level studies showing that motherhood is often associated with reduced hours as well as career penalties in compensation and occupational stature, and examples of these macro-level studies will be discussed in the following section.

Public policy structures. As mentioned earlier, there are country-level legal structures that provide various types of WF-related public policies intended to support workers with family responsibilities. Although the generosity and specific provisions show considerable variation across countries, most industrialized countries have implemented three types of WF policies: (1) job-protected dependent-care leaves,

(2) policies that increase FWA, such as mandated provisions for reduced hours or flexible schedules, and (3) publicly financed childcare (Hegewisch & Gornick, 2011). Other supportive WF policies include centralized collective bargaining agreements that protect workers' earnings and work conditions, and policies regarding taxation of dual-earning couples that can affect couples' career decisions. These policies are associated with gender egalitarian cultures and represent societal efforts to aid families and support women's labor market participation (Mandel & Semyonov, 2005). Also, as described above, country policies may influence organizational policies, which in turn can influence employees' individual-level WF and career outcomes (Lyness et al., 2012; Lyness & Kropf, 2005).

For example, a study by den Dulk, Groeneveld, Ollier-Malaterre, and Valcour (2013) tested relationships of both country WF-related policies and cultural values to organizational WF supports, based on data from over nineteen thousand organizations in nineteen European countries. They found evidence that both country cultural values, reflecting the centrality of work, and government WF policies, measured as public spending or regulations supporting childcare, parental leave, and employee rights to change their work hours for WF reasons, were related to organizational WF supports, measured as provision of three types of WF supports beyond statutory requirements. Their specific findings indicated that country-level WF supports were positively related to employer-provided FWA, parental leaves, and childcare, whereas cultural centrality of work was negatively related to FWA (den Dulk et al., 2013). Thus, these findings, showing that country WF policies influenced employers to provide additional WF supports, would amplify access to WF benefits for employees in these supportive countries as compared to employees living in countries where WF supports were not provided (den Dulk et al., 2013).

In contrast, Gregory and Milner (2011) studied WF supports from the perspective of fathers in France and the United Kingdom. The study examined country-level WL policies, organizational WL policies, and cultural norms relating to fatherhood, and used this information to explain differences in how fathers managed WL and career issues in the two countries. The authors highlighted the fact that WL issues are challenging for fathers due to organizational norms that still reflect the traditional household division of labor, with assumptions that women are caretakers and men are breadwinners. Although both France and the United Kingdom had implemented the European Union WL policies, such as parental leaves, the countries differed in their working time regulations; France limited the work week to thirty-five hours, whereas the United Kingdom gave employees the right to request a reduction in work hours to accommodate WF responsibilities. However, the study found that in the United Kingdom most requests for reduced hours were made by mothers rather than fathers, which is consistent with the traditional organizational assumptions that women's careers were viewed as secondary, whereas men's careers were thought to be the primary source of family income.

Notably, the findings showed that the shorter thirty-five-hour work weeks in France gave fathers, particularly those in non-management positions, more time with their families. However, in the United Kingdom, fathers often had to work long hours to make up for their wives' reduced income because these mothers had taken advantage of the United Kingdom's policies allowing them to reduce their work hours for WF reasons (Gregory & Milner, 2011).

Organizational implementation of WF policies also differed by country and exacerbated the differences in fathers' WF support. In France the WF and working time regulations tended to be formally regulated by organizational human resource departments, whereas the implementation was more informal in the United Kingdom where supervisors were given discretion about granting requests, which tended to limit fathers' access to WF supports.

Thus, the research suggests that organizations play an important mediating role in the relationships between well-intentioned country-level WF policies and individual fathers' WL balance. Also, Gregory and Milner (2011) noted that fathers in the United Kingdom would like more flexibility and balance, as shown by their use of paternity leaves, and programs that were offered universally, as when FWA was offered to a work team. Thus, the findings illustrate unintended consequences of organizational processes that undermined fathers' family involvement despite well-intentioned WF policies in the United Kingdom. These results also suggest that it is important to ensure that organizational WF-related assumptions and implementation of WF policies do not undermine employees' access to WF supports, and that access to these critical benefits does not vary by employee gender.

Macro-level relationships between public policies and labor force outcomes. In this section, we review related research that examines relationships of country-level public policies to macro-level career outcomes, such as labor force participation rates, wages, promotions, and career opportunities. These studies are relevant to the findings reviewed above as the results illustrate how women's labor force participation and outcomes differ depending on whether or not they are mothers. As discussed above, working mothers may have difficulty managing their work and family roles when they do not have access to national- and organizational-level WF-related supports.

However, the macro-level research discussed below indicates that there are often both positive and negative career tradeoffs for women when they do have access to various types of WF public policy supports. Country-level WF supports, such as paid leaves and publicly funded childcare, have been shown to increase women's labor force participation (Gornick & Meyers, 2003; Mandel and Semyonov, 2006). However, gender segregation is higher in welfare state countries that provide these benefits (i.e., Nordic and Continental Europe) than in liberal market countries (i.e., the United States, Canada, and Australia). Also, in countries offering WF supports, women with young children are more likely to work in lower-paying, female-typed (i.e., held mostly by women), service sectors jobs, and to work part-time (Mandel & Semyonov, 2006).

Mandel and Semyonov (2006) used data from twenty-two industrialized countries to examine the relationship between national WF policy supports, women's employment patterns, and gender inequality in occupational status. The authors measured country-level WF supports with a "Welfare State Intervention Index," a composite index that was developed by Mandel and Semyonov (2005) based on each country's number of fully paid weeks of maternity leave, the percentage of preschool children attending publicly funded daycare, and the percentage of the workforce employed in the public welfare sector. The results showed that women's labor force participation was positively related to generous maternity leave policies and the availability of publicly funded childcare facilities. However, Mandel and Semyonov (2006) found that country provision of these WF benefits was negatively related to the odds that women would advance to highly paid managerial positions.

Among the three components in their index, the length of maternity leaves had the strongest negative impact on women's odds of attaining managerial positions, which the authors noted was consistent with their argument that public policies that allow long absences from work may unintentionally encourage employers to engage in statistical discrimination, referring to discrimination against women or mothers as a group, based on assumptions that they will be less productive or more costly employees (Mandel & Semyonov, 2006). Thus, the study suggests that an unintended consequence of some country-provided WF supports is that women who use them may experience negative career consequences, as measured by reduced chances of advancing to managerial positions, compared with women whose countries did not provide these types of supports.

In addition, Blau and Kahn (2013) reached similar conclusions in their investigation of country rankings in 2010 showing that the labor force participation rate of women in the United States had fallen to seventeenth among the twenty-two countries included in the Organisation for Economic Co-operation and Development (OECD), as compared to 1990 when the United States had the sixth-highest labor force participation rate of women among OECD countries. Blau and Kahn concluded that the change was due to many countries' implementation of state-sponsored WF benefits, such as paid parental leaves, the job-protected right to change from working full-time to working part-time, provision of public childcare, and equal treatment of part-time workers, whereas the United States did not offer these types of WF policies. However, the authors' analyses indicated that women in the United States were more likely to hold managerial or professional jobs than women in countries that offered more generous WF supports (Blau & Kahn, 2013). This may be attributable to the fact that more generous WF supports are also associated with larger proportions of women working part-time, and that part-time work is not typically available in high-level positions. Thus, women wanting to work part-time may have to settle for lower-level positions that offer more flexibility in work hours. Consistent with the Mandel and Semyonov's (2006) findings, the authors also suggested that in countries that offer these WF supports, employers may be more likely to engage in statistical discrimination against promoting women to higher-level positions due to concerns that women may take advantage of WF options, such as changing from full-time to part-time work or taking long parental leaves (Blau & Kahn, 2013). Thus, both studies suggest that in countries that provide WF benefits, women's opportunities for career advancement may be more limited, and employers may stereotype women and engage in statistical discrimination against all women, including women who never used these WF policies in the past and do not intend to use them in the future.

There is also evidence from macro-level studies, such as the research discussed above, of "motherhood wage penalties," referring to findings that women who are mothers tend to receive lower wages than women without children. In contrast, there is evidence that in the United States and many other countries, fathers receive a "fatherhood bonus" referring to higher wages for fathers in comparison to men who are not fathers (Misra & Murray-Close, 2014).

A more in-depth, longitudinal study of the motherhood wage penalty per child in Great Britain, Germany, and the United States found that these penalties differed in size, ranging from 10% (in the United States) to 18% (in Germany) (Gangl & Ziefle, 2009), and also the reasons for the penalties differed by country. In the United States and Great Britain, mothers' wage penalties could be explained by mothers' career gaps and moves to lower-paying, "mother-friendly" (i.e., flexible) jobs that tended to be held by women. In contrast, because the wage penalties associated with motherhood were larger in Germany than the other countries, and could not be fully explained by mothers' career paths, the authors attributed the unexplained portion of the wage gaps to statistical discrimination against mothers by German employers (Gangl & Ziefle, 2009).

Notably, Gangl and Ziefle (2009) found that motherhood wage penalties were smaller in the United States than either Great Britain or Germany. This was somewhat surprising because the authors explained that the labor market in the United States was considered to be the least "mother-friendly" of the three countries due to greater wage penalties for moving into female-dominated jobs or part-time work. However, women in the United States were less likely than women in the other countries to move into low-status or part-time jobs after childbirth, which was thought to offer an explanation for why women in the United States had smaller motherhood wage gaps than mothers in the other two countries (Gangl & Ziefle, 2009).

There have been a number of other studies showing relationships between motherhood and wage penalties. In fact, Boeckmann, Misra, and Budig (2015) concluded that gender differences in compensation are actually due to wage penalties for mothers, as compensation for childless women is more similar to men's compensation. Based on an eighteen-country study, they identified several reasons for the motherhood wage penalty, including use of WF policies, the length of maternity leaves, and country cultural attitudes about working mothers, all of which appeared to operate as determinants of mothers' career patterns (Boeckmann, Misra, & Budig, 2015). The specific findings showed that in countries with generous WF supports, including very long, job-protected parental leaves, mothers are more likely to reduce their hours after childbirth than in countries without generous WF supports. On the other hand, in cultures where there is greater acceptance of mothers working full-time, there are smaller gender gaps in labor force participation rates and work hours than in countries with less cultural acceptance of mothers working full-time (Boeckmann et al., 2015).

Also, an eight-year longitudinal study in thirteen European countries found that in addition to the motherhood wage penalty, there was an occupational status penalty associated with motherhood (Abendroth, Huffman, & Treas, 2014). Births of a first and second child were each associated with a significant decrease in occupational status, and mothers typically did not recover their lost occupational status as their children grew older. However, in countries with public childcare, occupational status penalties for mothers were smaller, suggesting that when mothers have access to childcare, there is less need for them to switch to more flexible, but lower-status occupations after childbirth (Abendroth, Huffman, & Treas, 2014).

Thus, there is evidence that both structural characteristics, such as national WF policies allowing mothers to reduce their working hours, and cultural beliefs about whether mothers should be employed full-time were related to mothers' careers (Abendroth et al., 2014). Also, several studies have shown that supportive WF policies are associated with (unintentional) career penalties, such as reduced compensation, for mothers who utilize the WF supports. Boeckmann et al.'s (2015) study also suggests that the effects of WF policies on mothers' compensation were mediated by differences between mothers' careers, such as working fewer hours than other employees.

Thus, the studies that we reviewed suggest that country provision of generous WF supports and policies are often associated with reduced work hours for mothers as well as the related tendency for employers to statistically discriminate against women and limit their career advancement due to concerns that women will take advantage of these WF benefits. There have also been studies showing that WF policies are associated with increased occupational segregation of jobs by gender, with more lucrative jobs held by men rather than women, which offers an additional explanation for the pay gap between men and women (Hegewisch & Gornick, 2011).

Hegewisch and Gornick (2011) explained that the literature about the unintended negative career consequences, such as the motherhood wage penalty associated with country WF provisions, raises important questions about causality. Research that focuses on what the authors term the "demand side" argument suggests that in countries where women have access to WF supports, such as long leaves and flexibility to work part-time, employers are more likely to engage in statistical discrimination that reduces women's career advancement opportunities, especially for highly skilled women who might otherwise qualify for managerial or other highly paid jobs (Hegewisch & Gornick, 2011). In contrast, the "supply side" argument suggests that the women who take advantage of these WF supports self-select into less competitive, lower-compensated jobs because either they prefer these types of jobs due to their compatibility with motherhood, or mothers may not qualify for better jobs, in part because extended leave-taking reduces their qualifications, such as human capital accumulation (Hegewisch & Gornick, 2011). The authors also noted that both arguments are consistent with the empirical findings that WF policies are associated with more occupational segregation by gender as well as a larger gender earnings gap.

Conclusions and Future Research Ideas

Our review of this literature provides ample evidence that there are indeed many cross-national variations in employees' WF and career outcomes. Moreover, comparative cross-national research is critical for investigating and understanding the effects of WF-related country-level contextual variables, including both cultural values and structural factors. For example, we found research showing that country cultural values reflecting gender egalitarianism and objective measures of gender equality were related to both organizational WF supports and employees' WF/WL and career outcomes. There was also some evidence that country structural factors are related to organizational WF supports, but fewer structural studies examined relationships to individual outcomes.

Certainly, the most troubling findings that we reviewed are the unintended negative associations between well-intentioned country WF policies and mothers' wage and occupational status penalties. These findings also raise pressing questions for countries that want to strengthen their WF policies about how to do so without negative consequences. In our opinion, both the demand-side and supply-side arguments are relevant.

According to these two perspectives, there is general agreement that motherhood penalties can occur, but disagreement as to why they occur. For example, the demand-side argument suggests that in countries with generous WF benefits, such as long paid leaves, employers may engage in statistical discrimination against hiring and promoting mothers to avoid costs or lower productivity associated with the state-mandated WF policies (e.g., Gangl & Ziefle, 2009). On the other hand, the supply-side argument attributes motherhood wage penalties to choices that women make, such as moves to lower-paying but more flexible jobs or part-time work.

The macro-level research has been valuable for identifying linkages between specific public policies and motherhood penalties. However, in order to further address these issues, it is critical to first gain a more complete understanding of why this is occurring. Results of macro-level studies are limited as they do not provide insights about either the organizational processes or perspectives of individual mothers. Thus, based on our review, it appears that more comprehensive and different research approaches are needed, and we offer three specific recommendations.

First, the best way to find out about mothers' reasons for their career decisions is to ask them. In other words, rather than speculating about why mothers make career choices associated with motherhood wage gaps, we recommend that future research should incorporate direct measures of mothers' own perspectives regarding the reasons for their career decisions. These could include their cultural norms, needs, WF supports, organizational barriers, perceived options, and personal views about their WF roles and careers (e.g., Peus & Traut-Mattausch, 2008). Ideally, this research would be designed and carried out by interdisciplinary research teams with expertise about psychological career processes in addition to expertise about the extant research and policy issues involved.

Second, future research should investigate the critical mediating role that organizations play in relationships between country-level policies and individual-level employee career outcomes. Although this aspect of the cross-national literature is not well-developed, we found studies suggesting that countries' WF policies are sometimes undermined by organizations either intentionally (e.g., statistical discrimination) or unintentionally (e.g., unsupportive supervisors, rigid WF gender role assumptions, or unequal access to WF supports by employee gender). Thus, future research is needed to gain a better understanding of the critical organizational role in supporting employees' WF needs without career penalties.

Our third recommendation is that future research should take a more comprehensive approach. By organizing this review according to levels of analysis, it became clear that there are many gaps in the literature. We illustrated the value of research that incorporates country context, organizational WF supports, and individual outcomes by applying findings from Lyness and Kropf's (2005) study to interpret results of other studies that did not include all three levels of analysis. However, this patchwork approach is far from ideal.

Thus, we recommend that future research should take a more comprehensive approach by including both cultural and structural aspects of country context, as well as organizational WF supports, and individual-level employee WF and career outcomes. Also, more representative samples of countries, organizations, occupations, and employees will enhance the generalizability of the findings. Based on our review, there appeared to be unique insights from both qualitative and quantitative research, again suggesting that multiple approaches and multiple stakeholder perspectives would be beneficial, as well as interdisciplinary expertise, which is essential.

In conclusion, we hope that our review of this rich literature will motivate further cross-national research about these issues. Moreover, our review suggests that there is considerable value to be gained, with unique opportunities for addressing pragmatic questions as well as developing more comprehensive theories.

References

Abendroth, A.-K., Huffman, M. L., & Treas, J. (2014). The parity penalty in life course perspective: Motherhood and occupational status in 13 European countries. *American Sociological Review, 79*(5), 993–1014.

Arthur, M. B., Hall, D. T., & Lawrence, B. S. (Eds.). (1989). *Handbook of Career Theory*. Cambridge University Press.

Aryee, S., Srinivas, E. S., & Tan, H. H. (2005). Rhythms of life: Antecedents and outcomes of work–family balance in employed parents. *Journal of Applied Psychology, 90*, 132–146.

Barnett, R. C., & Hyde, J. S. (2001). Women, men, work, and family: An expansionist theory. *American Psychologist, 56*, 781–796.

Berg, P., Appelbaum, E., Bailey, T., & Kalleberg, A. L. (2004). Contesting time: International comparisons of employee control of working time. *Industrial and Labor Relations Review, 57*, 331–349.

Blau, F. D., & Kahn, L. M. (2013). Female labor supply: Why is the United States falling behind? *American Economic Review, 103*(3), 251–256.

Boeckmann, I., Misra, J., & Budig, M. J. (2015). Cultural and institutional factors shaping mothers' employment and working hours in postindustrial countries. *Social Forces, 93*(4), 1301–1333.

Corrigall, E. A., & Konrad, A. M. (2006). The relationship of job attribute preferences to employment, hours of paid work, and family responsibilities: An analysis comparing women and men. *Sex Roles*, *54*(1–2), 95–111.

Den Dulk, L., Groeneveld, S., Ollier-Malaterre, A., & Valcour, M. (2013). National context in work–life research: A multi-level cross-national analysis of the adoption of workplace work–life arrangements in Europe. *European Management Journal*, *31*(5), 478–494.

Eagly, A. H., & Wood, W. (2012). Social role theory. In P. A. M. Van Lange, A. W. Kruglanski, & E. T. Higgins (Eds.), *Handbook of Theories of Social Psychology*. (Vol. 2, pp. 458–476). Thousand Oaks, CA: Sage.

Edlund, J., & Oun, I. (2016). Who should work and who should care? Attitudes towards the desirable division of labour between mothers and fathers in five European countries. *Acta Sociologica*, *59*, 151–169.

Emrich, C. G., Denmark, F. L., & Den Hartog, D. N. (2004). Cross-cultural differences in gender egalitarianism: Implications for societies, organizations, and leaders. In R. J. House, P. J. Hanges, M. Javidan, P. W. Dorfman, & V. Gupta (Eds.), *Culture, Leadership, and Organizations: The GLOBE Study of 62 Societies* (pp. 343–394). Thousand Oaks, CA: Sage.

Esping-Andersen, G. (1990). *The Three Worlds of Welfare Capitalism* Princeton, NJ: Princeton University Press.

Gangl, M., & Ziefle, A. (2009). Motherhood, labor force behavior, and women's careers: an empirical assessment of the wage penalty for motherhood in Britain, Germany, and the United States. *Demography*, *46*(2), 341–369.

Goode, W. J. (1960). A theory of role strain. *American Sociological Review*, *25*, 483–496.

Gornick, J. C., & Meyers, M. K (2003). *Families that Work: Policies for Reconciling Parenthood and Employment*. New York, NY: Russell Sage Foundation.

Greenhaus, J. H., & Beutell, N. J. (1985). Sources of conflict between work and family roles. *Academy of Management Review*, *10*, 76–88.

Greenhaus, J. H., & Powell, G. N. (2006). When work and family are allies: A theory of work–family enrichment. *Academy of Management Review*, *31*, 72–92.

Gregory, A., & Milner, S. (2011). Fathers and work–life balance in France and the UK: Policy and practice. *International Journal of Sociology & Social Policy*, *31*(1/2), 34–52.

Hanges, P. J., & Dickson, M. W. (2004). The development and validation of the GLOBE culture and leadership scales. In R. J. House, P. J. Hanges, M. Javidan, P. W. Dorfman, & V. Gupta (Eds.), *Culture, Leadership, and Organizations: The GLOBE Study of 62 Societies* (pp. 122–151). Thousand Oaks, CA: Sage.

Hegewisch, A., & Gornick, J. C. (2011). The impact of work–family policies on women's employment: A review of research from OECD countries. *Community, Work & Family*, *14*(2), 119–138. doi:10.1080/13668803.2011.571395.

House, R. J., & Javidan, M. (2004). Overview of GLOBE. In R. J. House, P. J. Hanges, M. Javidan, P. W. Dorfman, & V. Gupta (Eds.), *Culture, Leadership, and Organizations: The GLOBE Study of 62 societies*. Thousand Oaks, CA: Sage.

House, R. J., Hanges, P. J., Javidan, M., Dorfman, P. W., & Gupta, V. (Eds.). (2004). *Culture, Leadership, and Organizations: The GLOBE Study of 62 Societies*. Thousand Oaks, CA: Sage.

Kelly, E. L., Moen, P., & Tranby, E. (2011). Changing workplaces to reduce work–family conflict: Schedule control in a white-collar organization. *American Sociological Review*, *76*(2), 265–290.

Kirchmeyer, C. (2000). Work–life initiatives: Greed or benevolence regarding workers' time? In C. L. Cooper & D. M. Rousseau (Eds.), *Trends in Organizational Behavior: Time in Organizational Behavior* (Vol. 7, pp. 79–93). Chichester, UK: John Wiley & Sons, Ltd.

Larson, R., Verma, S., & Dworkin, J. (2001). Men's work and family lives in India: The daily organization of time and emotion. *Journal of Family Psychology, 15*, 206–224.

Lent, R. W., & Brown, S. D. (2013). Social cognitive model of career self-management: Toward a unifying view of adaptive career behavior across the life span. *Journal of Counseling Psychology, 60*(4), 557.

Lyness, K. S., Gornick, J. C., Stone, P., & Grotto, A. R. (2012). It's all about control: Worker control over schedule and hours in cross-national context. *American Sociological Review, 77*, 1023–1049.

Lyness, K. S., & Judiesch, M. K. (2008). Can a manager have a life and a career? International and multisource perspectives on work–life balance and career advancement potential. *Journal of Applied Psychology, 93*, 789–805.

Lyness, K. S., & Judiesch, M. K. (2014). Gender egalitarianism and work–life balance for managers: Multisource perspectives in 36 countries. *Applied Psychology: An International Review, 63*(1), 96–129.

Lyness, K. S., & Kropf, M. B. (2005). The relationships of national gender equality and organizational support with work–family balance: A study of European managers. *Human Relations, 58*, 33–60.

Mandel, H., & Semyonov, M. (2005). Family policies, wage structures, and gender gaps: Sources of earnings inequality in 20 countries. *American Sociological Review, 70*(6), 949–967.

Mandel, H., & Semyonov, M. (2006). A welfare state paradox: State interventions and women's employment opportunities in 22 countries. *American Journal of Sociology, 111*(6), 1910–1949.

Misra, J., & Murray-Close, M. (2014). The gender wage gap in the United States and cross nationally. *Sociology Compass, 8*(11), 1281–1295.

Ollier-Malaterre, A., & Foucreault, A. (2017). Cross-national work–life research. *Journal of Management, 43*(1), 111–136.

Peus, C., & Traut-Mattausch, E. (2008). Manager and mommy? A cross-cultural comparison. *Journal of Managerial Psychology, 23*(5), 558–575.

Seguino, S. (2007). Plus ça change? Evidence on global trends in gender norms and stereotypes. *Feminist Economics, 13*(2), 1–28.

Thein, H. H., Austen, S., Currie, J., & Lewin, E. (2010). The impact of cultural context on the perception of work/family balance by professional women in Singapore and Hong Kong. *International Journal of Cross Cultural Management, 10*(3), 303–320.

United Nations Development Programme. (2010). *Human Development Report 2010: The Real Wealth of Nations: Pathways to Human Development*. Retrieved from New York, NY.

van Steenbergen, E. F., Ellemers, N., & Mooijaart, A. (2007). How work and family can facilitate each other: Distinct types of work–family facilitation outcomes for women and men. *Journal of Occupational Health Psychology, 12*, 279–300.

Wattis, L., Standing, K., & Yerkes, M. A. (2013). Mothers and work–life balance: exploring the contradictions and complexities involved in work–family negotiation. *Community, Work & Family, 16*(1), 1–19.

Wood, W., & Eagly, A. H. (2002). A cross-cultural analysis of the behavior of women and men: Implications for the origins of sex differences. *Psychological Bulletin, 128*, 699–727.

World Values Survey Association. (2009). World Values Survey 1981–2008 official aggregate v. 20090901. ASEP/JDS, Madrid.

Yang, N., Chen, C. C., Choi, J., & Zou, Y. (2000). Sources of work–family conflict: A Sino–U. S. comparison of the effects of work and family demands. *Academy of Management Journal, 43*, 113–123.

28 Managing Work–Life Effectiveness in a Multinational Firm: An Organizational Case Study

Angela K. Pratt, Kaitlin M. Kiburz, and Sarah L. Wallace

Managing work and family issues has become a popular topic; both the academic literature and the popular press have highlighted the importance of companies paying attention to their culture and the importance of employees balancing their work and life outside of work. Employees take notice of the efforts organizations are making to enable their work–life effectiveness, but millennials – those born between 1982 and 2000 who by 2020 will make up 75% of the workforce (Wilkie, 2015) – are paying especially close attention. Organizations have responded by offering programs to help employees balance their work and nonwork lives; for example, 79% of companies across thirteen countries offer remote work to employees (Robert Half Singapore, 2012). Offering work–life programs, such as flexible work hours, child and eldercare provisions, paid maternity leave, adoption assistance, leave/time off, education assistance, health assistance, and remote work, is growing as a technique to attract employees, expand the available talent pool, and enhance retention (Martin & MacDonnell, 2012; Spilker, 2014).

Although many multinational organizations see the importance of offering work–life programs, it is often difficult to find solutions that will work well across countries and cultures. For example, what is standard or legally mandated in one country, such as paid maternity leave and ample paid time off, is considered a luxury and even out of the ordinary in another. In fact, managing work and nonwork life of employees in a multinational organization brings several challenges, including different cultural norms, employment law, and requirements to work outside standard work hours in order to accommodate different time zones. In this chapter, we first detail how work–life issues are defined and measured before turning to descriptions of why organizations value such endeavors and a sampling of several multinational initiatives. We conclude by presenting a case study of how one multinational firm, the Kellogg Company, addresses work–life effectiveness.

Definitions and Semantics

Academic researchers often use Greenhaus and Beutell's (1985) definition of *work–family conflict*, "a form of interrole conflict in which the role pressures from the work and family domains are mutually incompatible in some respect" (p.77). In this literature, there are three types of work–family conflict: time-based, strain-based and behavior-based. In recent years, other constructs such as work–family enrichment and work–family balance have emerged. The term "balance" suggests that there is an equal ratio between one's work and one's nonwork life. For this reason, the term "balance" is not well regarded in organizations because many leaders think equal ratios between work and home are not feasible while simultaneously meeting the organization's goals.

Additionally, "work–family" suggests that an individual's spouse and children are the only part of an employee's life outside of work, or at least the only thing outside of work that comes with demands that may compete with work demands. For many employees, maintaining friendships, exercising, volunteering, attending school, or participating in hobbies are as important as their family demands (Sydell, 2014). Across a person's lifespan, the demands and importance that an employee places on work, family, and other aspects of life are likely to change. For these reasons, we view the term "work–family" as limiting and instead focus on employees' broader nonwork lives.

In an effort to get past the words and into action, some organizations use the term " work–life effectiveness" (e.g., Procter & Gamble) or simply "work–life" (e.g., Kellogg Company), but still measure time-based, strain-based, and behavior-based conflict to understand stressors on their employees. Following this lead, we use the general term "work–life effectiveness" throughout the chapter.

Measuring Work–Life Effectiveness in Organizations

Readers deeply ingrained in research at the intersection of work and nonwork life are familiar with popular peer-reviewed measures of work–life constructs, such as Netemeyer, Boles and McMurrian's (1996) and Carlson, Kacmar, and Williams' (2000) work–family conflict scales. In many organizations, including multinational firms, work–life effectiveness is measured both internally and externally. Internally, many companies conduct surveys of employees to understand their work–life situation, engagement, and intent to stay with the company among other topics. Survey items intended to understand the employee's work–life situation may ask employees about time-based, behavior-based, and strain-based conflict, as well as use of work–life policies. Example survey questions are, "I have sufficient flexibility to balance my work and nonwork life" and "I have energy to do the things I enjoy after leaving work." Human resources teams may also track the use of flexible work arrangements, such as telecommuting, compressed work weeks, and job shares, and other family-friendly policies, such as dependent care support. These data can then be analyzed in conjunction with other internal metrics (e.g., retention, performance) to elucidate connections.

Companies' work–life effectiveness is also observed, measured, and shared externally. Websites such as Glassdoor and Indeed informally collect data from current and past employees of many large organizations, asking employees to report on their employers' work–life programs as well as the employees' own work–life experiences. These aggregated data are then made available to the public, and are commonly used by applicants to explore the various work–life experiences of their potential employers. As with any public forum, the comments for most companies represent employees who are both very pleased and very unhappy with the work–life environment at that company. For example, Kellogg has "work–life balance" listed in both the pros and cons sections of Glassdoor and comments range from "The company provides everything you need for your work–life balance" and "great work–life balance for you and your family" to "work–life balance [is] almost nonexistent."

More formal external evaluations of organizations' work–life environments also shed light on which companies prioritize their employees' well-being through programs and support of having a life outside of work. *Fortune* produces an annual list of 100 Best Companies to Work For and 50 Best Workplaces for Flexibility. Similarly, *Working Mother* magazine publishes a list of the 100 Best Companies. The lists are based on criteria including flexible work arrangements, availability and usage of paid family leave, programs for parents, health and wellness programs (for weight-loss, smoking cessation, nap rooms, etc.), and other benefits offerings. Metrics included in these evaluations are produced through cooperation between the magazines and companies and also include formal confidential employee surveys. Status on such well-respected lists is an important goal for many organizations, as described in the next section, as jobseekers and customers are likely to use this information in deciding to apply for employment or do business with a company.

Value of Work–Life Effectiveness to Organizations

We suggest that there are three main reasons why organizations care about work–life effectiveness: (1) attraction/retention of key talent, (2) increased performance/engagement, and (3) healthier/happier employees. First, work–life programs can have a positive impact on organizations through employee attraction. Younger generations expect to have a more equitable balance between time spent working and time dedicated to personal interests (Shellenbarger, 1991; Thompson & Gregory, 2012) and they consider a company's work–life environment when job hunting. Not surprisingly, offering these policies to bolster work–life effectiveness is a technique to attract employees, expand the available talent pool, and enhance retention (Martin & MacDonnell, 2012; Spilker, 2014). In today's world, prospective employees often search social media sites, like Glassdoor.com, to find the job that fits their life. Glassdoor, like several other social media sites, includes a rating for work–life balance. In addition, some well-regarded "top company" awards take into account what companies are doing to increase work–life effectiveness. For example, *Working Mother* magazine looks at how much fully paid maternity leave is offered and how many employees make use of flextime policies. In addition, the *Sunday Times* in the United Kingdom measures employee well-being for their "Best Companies" list, which takes into account how staff feel about the pressure and balance between work and home duties. It is relatively easy and common for job candidates to view these awards and research current and past employees' impressions of work–life effectiveness at a given organization.

Many candidates consider what work–life programs are offered when deciding between employers (Thompson, Payne, & Taylor, 2014). Therefore, organizations often publish what they are doing to increase work–life effectiveness on their career sites to attract diverse talent. Then, once talent joins an organization, it is important to measure work–life effectiveness and ensure they are happy with the support they are receiving from the organization so that they remain with the organization. Research shows that employees who are satisfied with their work–life effectiveness tend to have lower turnover (Beauregard & Henry, 2009). The authors' global research at Kellogg also shows that higher work–life effectiveness (lower time-based and strain-based work–family conflict) is related to increased retention. Given the cost of replacing professional talent is estimated to be at least 1.5 to 2.5 times annual salary (see the Saratoga Institute or http://irle.berkeley.edu/files/2010/Employee-Replacement-Costs .pdf), organizations are very interested in reducing voluntary turnover.

In addition to being connected to attraction and retention, research also shows a link between work–life effectiveness and employee performance and engagement. There is evidence to show that employees who are satisfied with their work–life effectiveness tend to be more productive (Konrad & Mangel, 2000). From our own research at three large multinational organizations, we have seen that across many countries, higher work–life effectiveness is related to higher employee engagement (e.g., I would recommend Company X as a place to work; I am proud to work for Company X; I understand what I need to do to help Company X meet its goals and objectives).

However, some work–life arrangements that companies may offer do not always produce favorable results. Using remote work (also referred to as flexplace or telecommuting) as an example because it is one of the most popular work–life arrangements, many studies have found evidence that remote employees have higher job performance and are more productive than their counterparts working from a shared office location (e.g., Gajendran, Harrison, & Delaney-Klinger, 2014; Mekonnen, 2013). However, some studies did not find support for a relationship between remote work and job performance (Neufeld, 1997; Ramsower, 1983). The relationship between remote work and job performance also tends to vary depending on the measurement of remote work. For example, Gajendran and Harrison's (2007) meta-analysis found that remote work is related to employee performance as rated by supervisors and objective measures, but not with self-rated performance (Gajendran & Harrison, 2007). Therefore, although there is substantial support that those who report more work–life effectiveness also report more engagement, work–life policies do not necessarily equate to higher performance. This is probably because there is not a "one size fits all" solution that works across people, organizations, and cultures.

Finally, there is substantial research that shows when employees are able to successfully manage their work and nonwork life, they can avoid several stress-related consequences, which can relate to absenteeism and healthcare costs for organizations. For example, research shows that stress resulting from work–family conflict can have serious health consequences, including increased depression, anxiety, and substance abuse (Allen et al., 2000; Greenhaus et al., 2006). In addition, employees with more work–family conflict are more likely to have heightened blood pressure, higher body mass index, more physical symptoms, and lower overall health (Allen et al., 2000; Allen & Armstrong, 2006; Greenhaus et al. 2006). Absenteeism has a negative effect on organizations in several ways, and multiple research studies have demonstrated that work–life initiatives like flexible work arrangements (Baltes et al., 1999; Pierce & Newstrom, 1983) and health initiatives (Woo, Yap, Oh, & Long, 1999) mitigate absenteeism.

Work–Life Challenges for Today's Multinational Firms

Multinational organizations have additional unique concerns when it comes to managing work–life issues. Companies operating across multiple countries, continents, and time zones generally run their operations twenty-four hours a day, necessitating employees being available at nontraditional work hours to collaborate with coworkers or negotiate with customers around the globe. An employee in the United States, for example, may have a virtual meeting with Asian coworkers at 9:00 p.m. or European customers at 7:00 a.m. Flexible work arrangements including flexible hours or summer Fridays may enable employees to better manage their work and life demands, but could impact business results for multinational companies.

Additionally, the numerous national cultures present in a multinational organization may impact the concept of work–life effectiveness. Cultural norms shape how employees experience the work and family roles as well as their expectations and needs when it comes to managing these domains (Ollier-Malaterre, 2016). More specifically, aspects of culture such as collectivism/individualism and gender egalitarianism may impact the meaning of work and family, expectations of the organization, as well as the relationship between the two domains (Powell, Francesco, & Ling, 2009). For example, research has found that work demands are more strongly related to work–family conflict for individualistic countries (e.g., Australia, the Netherlands, the United States) than for collectivist countries (e.g., China, Korea, Japan; Lu, Gilmour, Kao, & Huang, 2006; Spector et al., 2007). That is, when work demands increase, such as workload or deadlines, employees from individualist countries are more likely to experience more work–family conflict than those from collectivist countries. Therefore, a one size fits all approach to work–life effectiveness may not be appropriate or sustainable within multinational organizations. As an example, time management skills training to deal with workload may have an impact on employees from individualist cultures, but not impact work–life outcomes for employees from collectivist cultures. Instead, work–life solutions need to be tailored to match the experiences, expectations, and needs of employees within different regions and cultures.

Employment law also impacts how multinational organizations are able to manage work and life. For example, several European countries (e.g., Denmark, Ireland) require that employees do not exceed thirty-seven work hours in a week. A new labor law in France provides employees with the right to disconnect from email, phones, and other work-related technology outside of working hours. On the other hand, works councils in some countries may limit the availability of flexible work arrangements to employees in particular countries (e.g., Germany, France). While work–life programs need to be tailored across countries, it is also important to maintain the appearance of fairness in program availability within a single employing multinational organization. Employees in any country can generally access policies and support information for their colleagues across the world. Even if the employee does not have access, collaboration with partners across the company will ensure that the knowledge is shared outside of a particular country. It is important that multinational firms do not have grossly different offerings, especially when employees develop their careers across country boundaries.

Work–Life Initiatives: Triumphs and Setbacks

Given the importance of work–life effectiveness to employees working at multinational organizations, many global companies have tried to address work–life through various programs, initiatives, and policies. One in particular, global financial services firm, J.P. Morgan's "Pencils Down" Initiative, recognizes the stressful work culture that exists in many organizations. It joins a number of other financial firms that have decided to enact programs to lessen the workload in order to keep new recruits on board (Kasperkevic, 2016). Previously, their investment bankers were only permitted one weekend off per month, and one-hundred-hour work weeks were not uncommon. J.P. Morgan's new initiative encourages taking weekends off, and involves tracking bankers' hours weekly. When a certain threshold is passed, a manager contacts the banker to discuss the necessity for excessive hours, and what may be done to fix the problem (Glazer & Huang, 2016). However, even with this initiative in place, some still decide to continue working very high-hour work weeks in order to handle the workload.

In 2015, Netflix implemented an impressive parental leave plan for its salaried workers – unlimited parental leave for up to a year following a child's birth or adoption. The company modified this plan in 2016, increasing the number of eligible employees. Now, both mothers and fathers get paid leave, but the amount varies by company division. For instance, those working in its customer service division are allowed fourteen weeks of paid leave (Alba, 2015). It is now much more common for technology companies to offer generous paid parental leave, even though some countries in which the firms operate do not require companies to provide these benefits (Adamczyk, 2015).

Additionally, as companies attempt to increase the diversity of their workforces by hiring more women and keeping them in the workforce longer, some companies are offering to pay to help extend fertility. For example, Facebook and Apple were among the first known companies to pay for egg-freezing for female employees. This is an option for women who choose to delay childbearing. The Facebook benefit plan covers up to $20,000 worth of procedures, typically two rounds of egg retrieval. The procedure is still only in its early phases of success, as it was only two years ago that the American Society of Reproductive Medicine lifted the experimental label from egg-freezing (Sydell, 2014).

Despite the many successful work–life initiatives, many organizations continue to struggle with striking the perfect balance – being a high-performing organization while keeping employees engaged and satisfied with their work–life effectiveness. Often there is not a one-size-fits-all answer that will increase performance, keep a company competitive, and keep employees satisfied with their work–life effectiveness across cultures. Additionally, if the existing organizational culture of a firm or national culture doesn't align with efforts toward managing work–life effectiveness, even best-in-class initiatives may not yield positive results. Many organizations that have made great efforts in the work–life arena have ended up rescinding their programs. For example, Yahoo! CEO Marissa Mayer eliminated her company's work from home program in June 2013 in order to strengthen the collaboration and culture of the company (Goudreau, 2013; Lavey-Heaton, 2014). Best Buy also ended their results-only work environment (ROWE) policy (Lee, 2013) and Hewlett-Packard has reduced the number of employees allowed to work away from the office (Hesseldahl, 2013; Lavey-Heaton, 2014). Most recently, Charter Communications acquired Time Warner Cable and quickly reduced work–life options like working from home and early departure on summer Fridays (Pressman, 2016). Despite the recent examples of organizations taking steps backward in the journey to ensure all employees have the flexibility to live a balanced life, companies continue to search for the right policies and perspective to encourage work–life effectiveness.

We now turn to a case study describing how one large multinational organization, the Kellog Company, approaches and addresses work–life effectiveness in their diverse global workforce.

Case Study: The Kellogg Company

The Kellogg Company was founded in 1906 by William Keith Kellogg, who created the first ever breakfast cereal, Kellogg's Corn Flakes. Motivated by his passion for people, quality, and nutrition, this simple corn flake led to many other innovations and ultimately started an entirely new industry. The Kellogg name soon became a trusted household brand in the United States, and by 2016 has grown to be ranked number four on a world brands value reputation list (https://medium.com/enso/brand-world-value-a-new-way-to-measure-how-valuable-brands-are-to-the-world-38b87e0acef1#.m3r108t4a). W.K. Kellogg's legacy continues to inspire Kellogg Company's more than thirty thousand employees as they develop and produce foods and brands that enrich and delight the world's consumers. The purpose of the company is very similar today as it was one hundred years ago: to nourish families so they can flourish and thrive. In addition to being a large manufacturer of food, steadfast in making foods people love, Kellogg is also committed to helping the communities in which they operate through charitable giving and environmental sustainability efforts. For example, Kellogg has provided more than 1.4 billion servings of cereal and snacks to children and families in need through their Breakfast for Better Days global hunger initiative, and partners with farmers around the world to improve the health of their soil and grow the highest-quality grains. Kellogg also plans to significantly reduce greenhouse gases in their facilities over the coming years.

Through a values-based culture that includes respect, integrity, and hunger to learn, Kellogg enriches communities and nurtures careers by putting people first in everything they do. These values, combined with best practices in diversity and inclusion, have enabled Kellogg Company to be recognized recently as one of *Fortune*'s World's Most Admired Companies, DiversityInc's Top 50 Companies for Diversity, *Working Mother*'s 100 Best Companies, National Association of Female Executives' Top Companies for Executive Women, and *Forbes*' World's Most Innovative Companies. Kellogg leaders maintain a commitment to grow and develop diverse employees. Part of this commitment includes work–life programs, helping employees define how they accomplish their work and live a fulfilling life inside and outside of work.

Today, Kellogg products are sold in over 180 countries worldwide; some of the leading brands include Special K, Kellogg's Frosted Flakes, Rice Krispies, Pringles, Eggo, Keebler, Kashi, and Cheez-It. With 2015 sales of $13.5 billion and more than 1,600 foods, Kellogg is currently the world's leading cereal company, the second-largest producer of cookies, crackers, and savory snacks, and a leading North America frozen foods company. In order to ensure the company is meeting the unique consumer needs around the world, it organizes itself in four primary regions: North America (the United States and Canada), Latin America (including Mexico and South America), Europe (including Russia and the Middle East), and Asia Pacific.

Kellogg's Global Opinion Survey

Like many large multinational companies, Kellogg conducts a regular employee opinion survey administered to all of its employees worldwide. The full survey, which takes approximately twenty minutes to complete, has fifty multiple-choice and two open-ended questions, all measuring critical areas important to performance, retention, and engagement at Kellogg. One such area is work–life effectiveness, composed of four items assessing workload (e.g., "The amount of work I'm expected to do is reasonable"), flexibility (e.g., "I have sufficient flexibility to effectively balance my work and personal life"), use of flexible work arrangements (e.g., "Which of the following flexible work arrangements do you use?"), and energy (e.g., "When I leave work, I have energy for things I enjoy"). Typically, over 75% of employees (20,000+) respond to the survey with strong representation from each region in the world. At the close of the survey cycle, top executives at Kellogg review the survey results and decide on the top two-to-three priorities for the company and for each region. In 2011, the CEO and his team decided that one of the top global priorities would be work–life effectiveness. Compared to benchmark results provided by Kellogg's survey provider of all other companies they work with, the 2011 scores on work–life effectiveness showed that Kellogg had significant room for improvement in this area.

To address the opportunity, a team was formed to begin to understand the results in more detail and recommend a plan to address work–life effectiveness at Kellogg. To start, the team conducted focus groups representing each of the four primary regions, different business areas (e.g., cereal, snacks, and frozen foods), and job level in the organization. The team also leveraged Kellogg's existing employee resource groups (ERGs), such as the "Women of Kellogg" and "Young Professionals," in order to understand what work–life effectiveness meant to employees and what they thought the company should do to address work–life effectiveness. The findings from the focus groups showed that work–life meant different things depending on an individual's personal and work situation. For example, one parent defined work–life effectiveness as being able to attend her children's sports or school events and spend valuable time with her children in the evenings and on weekends. Another employee, without children, defined work–life effectiveness as being able to play dodgeball after work and travel on the weekends. In order to focus on improvement rather than get stuck in the definition, Kellogg began using the term "work–life" instead of " work–life balance" or "work–life conflict." Several unique themes surrounding work–life effectiveness emerged from the focus groups: manager effectiveness, wellness, and the impact of technology on workload.

Manager effectiveness. Employees in the focus groups often referenced their manager when describing whether or not they felt they had the necessary flexibility to balance their work and nonwork lives. Findings showed that some managers were familiar with and used the company's existing policies around flexible hours and remote work, whereas others were not familiar with the policies. In addition, employees reported some managers were very supportive of their work and nonwork lives, while other employees reported that they didn't have choices when it came to managing their work–life effectiveness. For example, in the United States, a few employees reported that they lived in Chicago and commuted to Kellogg's headquarters in Battle Creek, MI (2.5+ hours) only when needed so they could live fulfilling lives outside of work. Other employees reported that their managers required them to be at their desks for forty hours per week regardless of nonwork demands.

Focus group and qualitative analysis from open-ended responses on the annual survey also suggested that managers modeled flexibility very differently. Employees described that some managers took advantage of company policies on flexible work arrangements, such as leaving at noon on Fridays during the summer, whereas others spent long hours at a desk every day. Focus group respondents explained that when their managers modeled flexibility, they felt more comfortable using flexible work arrangements themselves.

Employees also mentioned that they did not mind putting in extra hours in the evenings or on weekends when it was needed; however, they became frustrated when managers were not clear on objectives and/or priorities, resulting in wasted time and effort off-hours. Some employees reported being unclear about the importance of a project, where to focus their effort, and, often, what work could be taken off the priority list. Because of this, employees often worked extra hours on projects that ended up being deprioritized and not needed. Interestingly, this finding was mainly in Anglo countries (i.e., Australia, Canada, the United Kingdom, and the United States) – employees did not mention this as an issue in Asia or Latin America.

Wellness. In 2011 and 2012, one of the lowest-scoring items on the Global Opinion Survey was "When I leave work, I have energy for things I enjoy." Although respondents focused more on managers and workload in their open-ended responses on the annual survey, focus group respondents reported that they were uncertain how to increase their energy at work and at home. In some regions of the world, there were already health and wellness programs, such as "Feeling Great" in the United States to help employees stay fit and healthy (e.g., Fitbit step competitions, biometric testing, nutrition counseling); however, we found that not all locations offered something similar. Many employees did not understand the connection between health/nutrition/activity and energy levels.

Technology. Technology can be both an enabler and hindrance for work–life flexibility. Having a smartphone, and other mobile tools, connects employees to their work day and night. Research examining the association between technology use and employee stress has shown that frequent technology use, such as smartphones, is related to work-related strain (Brown, Duck, & Jimmieson, 2014). Increased connectivity has been associated with higher levels of strain, stress, and burnout, even after controlling for demographics, job variables, and job demands (Day, Paquet, Scott, & Hambley, 2012).

At Kellogg, employees discussed the ability of their managers to reach them at any time and the pressure they felt to respond immediately when their managers or other upper management asked a question. The perceptions of the need for immediate responsiveness were mostly employee-created due to a lack of clarification on communication expectations. Although many managers said they did not intend for employees to respond after 6 p.m. or on weekends, employees still felt obligated to do so. Many respondents to the Global Opinion Survey and focus groups requested clear boundaries to be established through technology cut-offs. For example, several requested no emails after 5 p.m. or on weekends. Although common, this request was not seen as practical by many executives given the global scale of the company. When the business is run in several time zones, it is considered important to respond during off-hours so that work can continue in another time zone. For example, work hours in Singapore and Eastern Standard Time in the United States do not overlap. Therefore, if a colleague in the United States has a question for a colleague in Singapore at the beginning of their work day, they will not be able to get the answer until the next work day unless one or both work off-hours.

The Work–Life Program

Based on the findings from the Global Opinion Survey and follow-up focus groups, Kellogg leaders executed a multiyear initiative to improve employees' work–life effectiveness through three main levers: (1) manager, (2) health and wellness, and (3) technology.

Manager. In the first year, the focus was on opening up communication between managers and their direct reports. In a relatively simple initiative, each manager around the globe was asked to have a fifteen-minute conversation with their direct reports during their mid-year performance review. Each manager was given a discussion guide where they were instructed to ask, "What is the one thing we can do together in the next year to improve your work–life?" This approach allowed for cultural and individual differences because the conversation was personalized. For example, the solutions discussed in China could be very different than the solutions discussed in Mexico. Although we did not collect feedback on what was discussed, we were told this solution worked in each country.

In order to support each manager and employee to have a thoughtful and effective conversation, Kellogg's work–life team created a work–life portal on the company's intranet that contains (1) links to global and local policies, (2) a resource center for employees, managers, and HR professionals, (3) success stories of employees who have found ways to reduce work and life stress, (4) a work–life personal inventory so employees can gain self-awareness of their current situation, and (5) links to global and local trainings for easy access and best practice sharing across regions. The initiative was rolled out by the chief HR officer and the chief technology officer, who partnered to explain the importance of the "One Thing" conversation and roll out the supporting work–life online portal. Each member of the global leadership team (top executives in the company) were asked to fully support the program and role-model the behaviors.

The portal gained much internal attention and the work–life success stories were especially big hits. A success story that stands out involves an employee in the finance division who explained to her manager that she was struggling to balance her home demands with the late evenings at work during times in the year when budgeting takes place. When her manager probed, she found out that the employee had to often rely on friends and family members to pick up her child from daycare because she couldn't get there before they closed. Often, she did not return home until after her child went to bed, creating tension in her marriage. The manager went to the work–life portal to look at policies and tools that may help. After reviewing stories from other employees and current policies, the manager and employee decided to make a commitment that the employee would leave work every day by 5:30 p.m. If additional work was needed after hours, the employee would do it from home after her child went to bed. They also agreed that if a late night was needed, the employee could take some additional time for her family on Friday afternoons.

The "manager" phase of improving work–life effectiveness at Kellogg had a positive impact. The "One Thing" discussion helped to drive policy awareness for both managers and employees and helped open the dialogue so that perceived barriers could be removed. Two months after launch, over 60% of managers reported that they had the conversation with their employees and there were thousands of downloads and engagements with the tools on the work–life portal.

Health and wellness. While the North America region of Kellogg already had a robust health and wellness program, this was not the case in other regions. With the push to improve work–life for Kellogg employees around the globe, best practices were shared and innovative programs were started around the world. For example, in Europe, they started a "Fit for Life" week, which was a week each year dedicated to health and wellness. Some locations began competitions (such as "Walk from Dublin to Geneva") during the Fit for Life week that lasted several months with check-ins and prizes throughout the competition. Each location in Europe could customize their Fit for Life week to meet the needs of the local environment, but many included yoga and/or meditation courses, nutrition education, walk and stretch breaks, and fitness competitions. In the Walk from Dublin to Geneva competition, employees at the Cereal headquarters location in Dublin were invited to track their steps to figuratively "walk" across Europe, stopping at each Kellogg location along the way, to the Snacks headquarters in Geneva. There were prizes for reaching each location, and recognition for the team that made it to Geneva first.

Although weight management is a major topic and concern in the United States, other countries decided to focus more on their local concerns. Most European countries emphasized energy and overall wellness, and others (e.g., Asia) focused on air quality and reducing pollution. The flexibility of the program allowed for different countries to discuss and act on what was most important to them. Health and wellness tips were also shared on the work–life portal, along with personal stories of staying fit and healthy and maintaining energy throughout the day. During this portion of the work–life initiative, the work–life portal continued to feature articles about employees who improved their work–life effectiveness by focusing on their health, tips on how to maintain energy throughout the day, and exercises employees could do at their desks.

Technology. Kellogg started a multiyear journey to improve its technologies not long after the first Global Opinion Survey in 2011. Part of this effort made working remotely much easier, by investing in Skype for Business which allows employees to speak and/or video conference with others through their computers or smartphones. Kellogg's IT team also started an initiative called "Work Anywhere." Through this, the IT team worked to enhance technology so that employees could get their work done whenever and wherever they wanted. In the past, Kellogg had a strong facetime culture where employees were expected to be in the office environment five days a week and be seen by leaders. The Work Anywhere initiative encouraged managers and employees to think differently about where work could get done. Part of this initiative included a questionnaire to help employees figure out the right technology solutions (e.g., type of computer, applications) depending on their personal situation. The work–life team also invested in training to help employees with email effectiveness, managing Outlook and the "delay send" button so employees can work at any hour without interrupting their team.

The largest step taken in 2016 was the decision that not all Kellogg employees should need to be accessible and available 24/7. Now, employees are not required to carry a mobile device unless their job necessitates extensive travel or international connection. With the new policy, most employees are no longer required to be accessible after regular business hours and management cannot expect responses outside the normal work day. It is too early to tell the impact of this recent change; however, some have already mentioned the improvement in their work–life effectiveness on Kellogg's intranet.

Results

As mentioned earlier, Kellogg began their multiyear journey to improve work–life effectiveness in 2011 and has been measuring progress ever since. Although employees did not report significantly better work–life effectiveness in 2012 or 2013, there has been significant improvement in the most recent 2015 survey results (please note that the survey went from annual to biennial in 2013, so no survey was administered in 2014). Although there is still room for improvement, in 2015, more employees around the world reported that they have more flexibility to use alternative work arrangements, and sufficient flexibility to effectively balance their work and home lives. While each region adjusted the corporate work–life strategy to fit local needs, each region has seen improvement. For example, in North America, where they heavily focused on manager-employee relationships, percent favorable scores increased by seven points overall on the work–life effectiveness dimension and ten points on flexibility to balance work and home life. Other regions saw improvement in the survey (energy or workload) based on where leaders focused their work–life initiatives. Kellogg will continue to work to improve employees' lives through building better manager-employee relationships, improving health and wellness, and focusing on the role of technology in their ongoing work–life programs. The company's leaders believe that people are the company's strongest competitive advantage and they are devoted to enriching and delighting not only their consumers, but also their employees.

Conclusion

In summary, there is a strong case for organizations to work on improving the work–life effectiveness of their employees. For multinational organizations, it can be difficult to come up with solutions that will work across cultures, countries, and individuals. At Kellogg, they found that a flexible approach that concentrated on improving manager–employee dialogue, health and wellness, and technology was well received and effective in improving work–life effectiveness, and thus engagement and retention. While this may not be right for every organization, similar approaches should allow for flexibility and differences across countries to improve overall results in work–life effectiveness.

References

Adamczyk, A. (2015, November 4). These are the companies with the best parental leave policies. Retrieved August 9, 2016, from http://time.com/money/4098469/paid-parental-leave-google-amazon-apple-facebook

Alba, D. (2015, December 9). Netflix adds hourly workers to its generous parental leave plan. Retrieved August 9, 2016, from www.wired.com/2015/12/netflix-adds-hourly-workers-to-its-generous-parental-leave-plan

Allen T. D., & Armstrong J. (2006). Further examination of the link between work–family conflict and physical health. *American Behavioral Scientist*, *49*, 1204–1221.

Allen T. D., Herst, D. E. L., Bruck, C. S., & Sutton M. (2000). Consequences associated with work-to-family conflict: A review and agenda for future research. *Journal of Occupational Health Psychology*, *5*, 278–308.

Baltes, B. B., Briggs, T. E., Huff, J. W., Wright, J. A., & Neuman, G. A. (1999). Flexible and compressed workweek schedules: A meta-analysis of their effects on work-related criteria. *Journal of Applied Psychology*, *84*, 496.

Beauregard, T. A., & Henry, L. C. (2009). Making the link between work–life balance practices and organizational performance. *Human Resource Management Review*, *19*, 9–22.

Brown R., Duck, J., & Jimmieson, N. (2014). E-mail in the workplace: The role of stress appraisals and normative response pressure in the relationship between e-mail stressors and employee strain. *International Journal of Stress Management*, *21*(4), 325–347.

Carlson, D. S., Kacmar, K. M., & Williams, L. J. (2000). Construction and initial validation of a multidimensional measure of work–family conflict. *Journal of Vocational Behavior*, *56*, 249–276.

Day A., Paquet, S., Scott, N., & Hambley, L. (2012). Perceived information and communication technology (ICT) demands on employee outcomes: the moderating effect of organizational ICT support. *Journal of Occupational Health Psychology*, *17*(4), 473–91. doi:10.1037/a0029837.

Gajendran, R. S., & Harrison, D. A (2007). The good, the bad, and the unknown about telecommuting: Meta-analysis of psychological mediators and individual consequences. *Journal of Applied Psychology*, *92*, 1524–1541.

Gajendran, R. S., Harrison, D. A., & Delaney-Klinger, K. (2014). Are telecommuters remotely good citizens? Unpacking telecommuting's effects on performance via i-deals and job resources. *Personnel Psychology*, *68*(2), 353–393.

Glazer, E., & Huang, D. (2016, January 21). J.P. Morgan to workaholics: Knock it off. Retrieved August 9, 2016, from www.wsj.com/articles/j-p-morgan-chase-tells-investment-bankers-to-take-weekends-off-1453384738

Goudreau, J. (2013, February). Back to the Stone Age? New Yahoo CEO Marissa Mayer bans working from home. *Forbes*. Retrieved from www.forbes.com/sites/jennagoudreau/2013/02/25/back-to-the-stone-age-new-yahoo-ceo-marissa-mayer-bans-working-from-home

Greenhaus, J. H., & Beutell, N. J. (1985). Sources of conflict between work and family roles. *Academy of Management Review*, *10*, 76–88.

Greenhaus, J. H., & Powell, G. N. (2006). When work and family are allies: A theory of work–family enrichment. *Academy of Management Review*, *31*, 72–92.

Hesseldahl, A. (2013, October). Yahoo redux: HP says "all hands on deck" needed, requiring most employees to work at the office (memo). *Wall Street Journal [All Things Digital]*. Retrieved from http://allthingsd.com/20131008/yahoo-redux-hp-says-all-hands-on-deck-needed-requiring-most-employees-to-work-at-the-office-memo

Kasperkevic, J. (2016, January 21). JPMorgan Chase wants employees to improve their work–life balance. *The Guardian*. Retrieved August 9, 2016, from www.theguardian.com/business/2016/jan/21/jpmorgan-chase-bankers-work–life-balance-weekends

Konrad, A. M., & Mangel, R. (2000). Research notes and commentaries the impact of work–life programs on firm productivity. *Strategic Management Journal, 21*, 1225–1237.

Lavey-Heaton, M. (2014, March). Working from home: How Yahoo, Best Buy and HP are making moves. *The Guardian*. Retrieved from www.theguardian.com/sustainable-business/working-from-home-yahoo-best-buy-hp-moves

Lee, T. (2013, March). Best Buy ends flexible work program for its corporate employees. *Star Tribune*. Retrieved from www.startribune.com/business/195156871.html

Lu, L., Gilmour, R., Kao, S. F., & Huang, M. T. (2006). A cross-cultural study of work–family demands, work/family conflict and well-being: The Taiwanese vs. British. *Career Development International, 11*, 9–27.

Martin, B. H., & MacDonnell, M. R. (2012). Is telework effective for organizations? *Management Research Review, 35*(7), 602–616.

Mekonnen, T. (2013). Examining the effect of teleworking on employees' job performance. (Unpublished doctoral dissertation). Walden University, Minneapolis, MN.

Netemeyer, R. G., Boles, J. S., & McMurrian, R. (1996). Development and validation of work–family conflict and family-work conflict scales. *Journal of Applied Psychology, 81(4),* 400–410.

Neufeld, D. J. (1997). Individual consequences of telecommuting. (Unpublished doctoral dissertation). The University of Western Ontario: London, ON.

Ollier-Malaterre, A (2016). Cross-national work–family research. In T. Allen & L. Eby (Eds.), *Oxford Handbook of Work and Family*. Oxford University Press.

Pierce, J. L., & Newstrom, J. W. (1983). The design of flexible work schedules and employee responses: Relationships and process. *Journal of Occupational Behaviour, 4*, 247–262.

Powell, G. N., Francesco, A. M., & Ling, Y. (2009). Toward culture-sensitive theories of the work–family interface. *Journal of Organizational Behavior, 30*, 597–616.

Pressman, A. (2016, July 5). No more working from home for former Time Warner Cable employees. *Fortune*, July 5, 2016, available at http://fortune.com/2016/07/05/time-warner-charter-employees/

Ramsower, R. M. (1983). Telecommuting: An investigation of some organizational and behavioral effects of working at home. (Unpublished doctoral dissertation). University of Minnesota, Minneapolis, MN.

Robert Half Singapore. (2012). Singapore employers embrace flexible work arrangements. Retrieved from www.roberthalf.com.sg/id/PR-03447/singapore-employers-embrace-flexible-work

Shellenbarger, S. (1991). More job seekers put family needs first. *Wall Street Journal*, 15(1).

Spector, P. E., Allen, T. D., Poelmans, S. A. Y., et al. (2007). Cross-national differences in relationships of work demands, job satisfaction, and turnover intentions with work–family conflict. *Personnel Psychology, 60,* 805–835.

Spilker, M. (2014). Making telework work: The effect of telecommuting intensity on employee work outcomes. (Unpublished doctoral dissertation). University of Missouri, St. Louis, MO.

Sydell, L. (2014, October 17). Silicon Valley companies add new benefit for women: Egg-freezing. NPR. Retrieved August 9, 2016, from www.npr.org/sections/alltechcon sidered/2014/10/17/356765423/silicon-valleycompanies-add-new-benefit-for -women-egg-freezing

Thompson, C., & Gregory, J. B. (2012). Managing millennials: A framework for improving attraction, motivation, and retention. *The Psychologist-Manager Journal, 15,* 237–246.

Thompson, R. J., Payne, S. C., & Taylor, A. B. (2014). Applicant attraction to flexible work arrangements: Separating the influence of flextime and flexplace. *Journal of Occupational and Organizational Psychology, 88*(4), 726–749.

Wilkie, D. (2015, September 29). The rush toward paid parental leave: Why now? Society for Human Resource Management. Retrieved from www.shrm.org/resourcesandtools/ hr-topics/employee-relations/pages/paid-parental-leave-.aspx

Woo, M., Yap, A. K., Oh, T. G., & Long, F. Y. (1999). The relationship between stress and absenteeism. *Singapore Medical Journal, 40,* 590–595.

29 Workplace Flexibility: Strategies to Help Organizations Navigate Global Expansion

Rebecca J. Thompson and Ellen Ernst Kossek

Workplace flexibility is a continually expanding practice that enables employees to improve work and nonwork objectives while facilitating the strategic expansion of organizational goals and initiatives. Researchers have defined workplace flexibility as an arrangement between employees and employers in which both parties mutually agree upon when, where, and how employees will conduct their work (Kossek, Hammer, Thompson, & Burke, 2014). More frequently than ever before, employers around the world are implementing some form of workplace flexibility, either as informal practices or formal policies (Chandra, 2012; Raghuram, London, & Larsen, 2001; Stavrou, Casper, & Ierodiakonou, 2015).

Despite the trends of increased availability of flexibility in the workforce, there are still theoretical and practical issues surrounding the implementation and ongoing use of flexible work arrangements for multinational organizations. In particular, there is considerable variability in the extent to which employers, both within Western countries as well as across the globe, offer distinct types of policies and practices. In addition, there are many country-level and cultural variations in interpretations of what workplace flexibility means, differing values surrounding the use of flexibility and the management of work–family boundaries, as well as contextual and legal constraints that pose unique challenges to workplace flexibility. Consequently, the purpose of this chapter is to explore the nuances of global trends in workplace flexibility and examine relevant concerns for multinational organizations.

We begin by defining workplace flexibility and reviewing broad patterns and trends of workplace flexibility, including a discussion of the central types of workplace flexibility studied in the research literature. This is followed by a summary of information on the use of flexibility across major geographic regions. Additionally, we review and discuss research that highlights cultural comparisons and differences that suggest patterns of effects across cultures. Next, the chapter will discuss important strategic outcomes of implementing workplace flexibility as well as key challenges for multiple stakeholders. Finally, the chapter will conclude with strategies for successful implementation of global flexibility and future considerations for research.

What Is Workplace Flexibility?

The literature surrounding workplace flexibility is quite expansive. Consequently, there are numerous definitions, ranging in scope from individual or task levels to broader, more organizational or procedural level perspectives (Kossek & Thompson, 2016). Some researchers have focused on the extent to which employees have control over some aspect of their work arrangement, such as when work is conducted or career breaks (Allen, Johnson, Kiburz, & Shockley, 2013; Berg, Kossek, Misra, & Belman, 2014; Hill, Grzywacz, Allen, Blanchard, Matz-Costa, Shulkin, & Pitt-Catsouphes, 2008). Alternatively, other scholars have examined how organizations implement policies at a process level, utilizing flexibility to maintain standing in a competitive market (Kossek & Thompson, 2016). Accordingly, workplace flexibility has been defined relative to the research questions and outcomes of interest for researchers.

Consistent with other definitions, the current chapter defines workplace flexibility as a mutually agreed upon arrangement between an employee and employer whereby both parties approve of when, where, or how the employee will conduct his/her work (Kossek et al., 2014). An important component within this definition is the ability of employees to control some aspect of their work, thereby increasing the likelihood of policies leading to positive outcomes for employees (Kossek et al., 2006; Kossek & Thompson, 2016). Similarly, the definition incorporates an agreement between both stakeholders. In other words, we acknowledge that some arrangements have led to implementation gaps, or disparities between the stated goals and objectives of flexibility policies (in theory or practice) and the experiences of those involved in the arrangement (Kossek & Thompson, 2016). Flexible policies and practices must meet organizational needs and goals (e.g., maintaining productivity and scheduling demands). Therefore, considering multiple perspectives when conceptualizing workplace flexibility allows for operationalizations that most benefit each of the various stakeholder groups.

It is important to begin the discussion of types of workplace flexibility by acknowledging that the United States is not the only country with workplace flexibility practices nor is it the most progressive. However, the preponderance of the top-tier research literature, at least in the areas of industrial-organizational psychology and organizational behavior, examines samples from the United States (Myers, 2016). Additionally, many researchers have pointed out that the majority of studies examining work–life issues conducted outside of the United States have been in Western European and Anglo countries (Chandra, 2012; Spector, Cooper, Poelmans, Allen, O'Driscoll, Sanchez, et al., 2004). However, researchers have identified cultural differences in the availability, use, and outcomes associated with flex policies and practices across the world (Raghuram et al., 2001; Stavrou & Kilaniotis, 2010), a discussion of which follows in a subsequent section of this chapter.

Types of Workplace Flexibility

Before diving into cultural differences regarding flexibility, it is important to first discuss the four primary conceptualizations of workplace flexibility: (1) flexibility in time or when work is conducted; (2) flexibility in place or where work is conducted; (3) flexibility in the amount of work or workload; and (4) flexibility in leave periods and career continuity (Kossek & Thompson, 2016).

Flexibility in time. Flexibility in time of work affords employees discretion over how their total work hours are distributed (Kossek et al., 2014; Thompson et al., 2015). Several formal work policies and informal practices offer flexibility in time, including flextime, compressed workweeks, flexible shifts, and part-year or seasonal work. These arrangements vary in both the degree to which they offer employee control as well as the span of time over which the flexibility occurs. For instance, flextime arrangements typically require a daily core time around which all employees are expected to work, but allow employees to choose the start/stop times of their individual workday as they see fit (Baltes, Briggs, & Huffcutt, 1999). Compressed workweeks allow employees to condense a typical workweek into fewer than five days each week or fewer than ten days in two weeks, thus affording them an additional day off compared to a standard work schedule (Kossek & Michel, 2011; Kossek et al., 2014). On the other hand, arrangements such as part-year and seasonal work offer employees the option to work during specific times of year, rather than having choice over parts of the day (Kossek & Thompson, 2016). Flexible shiftwork refers to arrangements that differ from traditional work schedules, often by extending organizational hours using work teams. There are many types of shiftwork arrangements, which vary along several dimensions including the length of shifts, continuity of coverage, inclusion of night work, and the nature of shift rotations (Smith, Folkard, Tucker, & Macdonald, 1998).

Time-based flexibility is thought to be desirable to employees because the increased control over work scheduling provides employees with a greater ability to manage their work demands around nonwork demands, therefore increasing resources to meet demands in both roles (Hobfoll, 2001; Voyandoff, 2005). In other words, by allowing some degree of discretion over when employees work, organizations enable employees to expand the times they are available for nonwork demands while still meeting their work demands (Thompson et al., 2015). Research has found that compared to flexibility in place, or where work is done, flexibility in the timing of work has stronger relationships with beneficial employee and employer outcomes (Allen et al., 2013; Thompson et al., 2015). In addition, employers benefit from time-based flexibility through the increased availability to clients (i.e., expanded business hours; Kossek, Thompson, & Lautsch, 2015).

Flexibility in place. Flexibility in place or the location of work, also known as flexplace, allows employees some degree of choice over where their work is conducted, relative to the central worksite (Kossek et al., 2014). The most frequently studied organizational practice of flexibility in place is telework or telecommuting (Gajendran & Harrison, 2007). Telework and other flexplace arrangements, such as remote work and hoteling, vary in the frequency with which employees work away from the central worksite.

While many employees choose to work from home, employees may also work from other locations such as a remote work center or satellite offices. Hoteling refers to when employers allocate temporary or as-needed office space for employees who typically work offsite (Kossek & Thompson, 2016). However, it is important to note that although many employees have the ability to *choose* to work somewhere other than the central worksite, not all flexplace arrangements are discretionary. In other words, organizations often utilize flexplace policies in order to maximize productivity and/or client outcomes. Gajendran and Harrison (2007) argue that control is an essential part of workplace flexibility, including telework, as it enhances employee perceptions of autonomy by presenting employees some degree of choice over the work demands. Thompson et al. (2015) argue that policies and practices that require employees to work offsite or travel to meet clients and are not under the control of the employee are not, in fact, flexible. For example, employers may require employees to work remotely at a client site or at home (in addition to work done at the office) to complete an ongoing project. Therefore, these uses of flexplace arrangements do not offer employees control over where they conduct their work, but rather are designed solely to enhance organizational goals.

Policies and practices involving flexibility in location are considered beneficial to employees as they allow employees to avoid going to the central work site with some predictability. This reduces work and nonwork boundary-spanning obstacles (e.g., commute time, task-appropriate clothing) and therefore enables employees to transition between work and nonwork roles more quickly and easily (Thompson et al., 2015). In addition, by having some amount of predictability over when they will have discretion over their work location, these practices may facilitate employees' ability to take advantage of nonwork opportunities that traditional work arrangements would not permit. For example, employees may prefer to live in locations that are far away from the central worksite while working remotely or apply unused commute time to attend a child's sports event (Kossek et al., 2015).

An additional consideration of flexplace arrangements is that many policies and practices that allow flexibility in location may also offer flexibility in time (e.g., telework); however, these types of flexibility are not necessarily concomitant. Some researchers even suggest that simply offering flexibility in location without also offering flexibility in time provides employees little more flexibility than working from the central worksite (Shockley & Allen, 2007).

Flexibility in the amount of work or workload. Flexibility in amount of work reflects arrangements that alter an employee's workload relative to a traditional assignment in order for the employee to maintain employment while managing nonwork demands. This facilitates employees' abilities to avoid recurring work and nonwork conflicts by changing the workload in a manner that meets the needs of both the employee and organization (Kossek et al., 2014). One type of arrangement is reduced-load work, which refers to working diminished duties relative to a full-time workload including a proportionate decrease in pay (Kossek, & Lee,

2008; Lee, MacDermid, & Buck, 2000). This reflects both the amount of time as well as the number of tasks an employee is expected to complete (Kossek & Lee, 2008). Another type of arrangement is job sharing, which is when two employees working on a part-time basis split the duties of a full-time job (Kossek et al., 2014).

Employees are likely to seek these arrangements when they have ongoing life demands (e.g., school, community, family) that prevent them from taking on or continuing to work a full workload. By working at a reduced or part-time load, employees are able to maintain benefits associated with employment while attending to their outside obligations. In other words, flexibility in workload allows employees to restructure their work around nonwork in a manner that maximizes resources to meet demands in both domains (Hobfoll, 2001). Employers benefit from these arrangements through the ability to hire and/or retain talented employees who may not be able to work on a traditional full workload. Correspondingly, not only can employers hire employees to work a reduced-load arrangement, but they may also allow current full-time employees to transition to a reduced load, thus enabling the employees to maintain employment and the organization to retain valuable organizational members (as well as reduce overall hiring and selection expenses).

Flexibility in leave periods and career continuity. Policies and practices focused on flexibility in continuity provide employees the opportunity to alter their work arrangement and even, at times, the trajectory of their career, in order to attend to temporary challenges or demands outside of work. These can include policies such as sabbaticals, implementation of leave policies, and career flexibility (Kossek et al., 2014). Sabbaticals refer to extended periods of absence taken by employees from employment for reasons varying from family demands, education, to military duties (Kossek et al., 2014). In the United States, the Family and Medical Leave Act (FMLA) entitles many employees to take unpaid, job-protected leave due to family or medical reasons while continuing health insurance coverage (US Department of Labor, 1993).

The benefit of continuity flexibility is that it allows employees to maintain long-term employment or even their career despite temporary or relatively short-term life demands (e.g., illness, death in the family, fluctuating dependent care demands) that have caused them to take advantage of continuity or break policies. In other words, employees who might otherwise have to quit their jobs or find alternative ways to support these important nonwork demands are able to meet their obligations with the assurance that they will be able to return to their workplace once they are able to do so, thus reducing the likelihood of burnout and conflict associated with having to manage multiple roles (Kossek et al., 2014). These policies may be particularly impactful for employees who experience multiple or ongoing life demands. For example, women often face career penalties when they take multiple breaks from work due to pregnancy/childbirth. In a study of US mid-level information technology careers, Simard and colleagues identified that nearly one-third of women reported delaying their career goals in order to have children as well as that women were more likely than their male counterparts to sacrifice traditional family (e.g., marriage/partnership, having children) to achieve career goals (Simard,

Henderson, Gilmartan, Schiebinger, & Whitney, 2008). Thus, flexibility in continuity may provide employees the opportunity to continue their career paths without forgoing or compromising on nonwork roles.

These policies also allow employers to retain employees who might otherwise be forced to leave their positions due to unexpected life events or relatively predictable periods of demand fluctuation due to life changes. This enables employers to preserve the institutional knowledge, relationships between employees and clients, as well as investment in talent.

Formal policies and informal practices. Another important distinction in the workplace flexibility literature is between formal policies, or those officially sanctioned through an organization's human resources area, and informal practices implemented on an ad hoc basis at the discretion of supervisors (Eaton, 2003; Kossek et al., 2014). As such, informal flexibility can be permitted by supervisors on a case-by-case basis and therefore may not be available to all employees. Consequently, not all employees may have equal access to use flexibility and therefore are not eligible for the associated advantages (Eaton, 2003). Additionally, the ability to choose when and who has access to flexibility makes supervisors de facto gatekeepers to these policies. Supervisors may not allow employees to use flexible policies for all types of nonwork commitments (e.g., family obligations, home or car repair, continuing education). This can foster perceptions of unfairness and potential conflict surrounding who is or is not most deserving of the ability to use flexible policies (Kossek et al., 2016).

However, simply offering policies is not sufficient to facilitate employees' control over their work arrangement. Researchers have found evidence that informal mechanisms of work–family support explain greater variance in employee outcomes than do formal mechanisms alone, suggesting that family-supportive workplace cultures are important components of the effectiveness of work–family initiatives (Behson, 2005; Kossek, Pichler, Bodner, & Hammer, 2011; Thompson, Beauvais, & Lyness, 1999).

Global Trends in Policies and Practices

The desire to balance work and nonwork demands is practically universal. However, individual responses to conflicting work and nonwork demands vary across countries and cultures (Chandra, 2012). Given the vast differences in the types of workplace flexibility, it is not surprising that there are wide-ranging global differences in the availability and use of the various policies and practices. In addition to individual-level factors, multinational organizations have faced a variety of challenges impacting the implementation of workplace flexibility on an international scale. The globalization of business interests, increasing technological advances, and societal changes in family dynamics across the world have all influenced how individuals experience the relationship between work and family, thus affecting the perceptions and utilization of workplace flexibility for today's employees (Chandra, 2012). Similarly, as corporations continue to expand and compete on international levels, implementing work–family policies such as workplace flexibility in their workforces across the world has become a nuanced challenge.

As researchers have pointed out, the terms surrounding "flexibility" and related policies and practices often refer to a variety of different behaviors and/or theories (Brewster, Mayne, & Tregaskis, 1997). Additionally, the availability and use of workplace flexibility varies across cultures as well as expectations regarding appropriate methods for resolving work–life conflict. Similarly, the meaning of specific flexibility policies and practices differs across countries and geographic regions, as a function of societal norms, laws, and cultural values. Consequently, multinational organizations can face a wide variety of challenges when implementing flexibility practices on a global scale. Therefore, it is critical to have an understanding of these issues when developing policies and practices that transcend geographic regions. Below, we discuss patterns researchers have identified regarding trends in workplace flexibility within and across major geographic regions as well as examples of cultural, legal, and socioeconomic factors that play a role in the these trends.

The United States. In a study of organizations in the United States, the 2014 National Study of Employers reported that 81% of employers allow at least some employees to periodically use flextime (Matos & Galinsky, 2014). Similarly, 67% of employers reported allowing employees to work some paid hours from home on an occasional basis. Thirty-six percent of employers reported allowing at least some employees to move from full-time to part-time load while remaining in the same position and 29% allowed at least some employees to share jobs (Matos & Galinsky, 2014). The report points out that employers of fifty or more employees most frequently allowed employees to have some control over when they take breaks (92%) and take time off for important family/personal needs without loss of pay (82%). The authors also note that employers were most likely to allow at least some groups of employees (74%) to return to work gradually after leave due to childbirth or adoption (Matos & Galinsky, 2014). In contrast, job sharing was one of the least frequently implemented workplace flexibility options in the United States, with only 29% of employers offering at least some employees the ability to job share (Matos & Galinsky, 2014).

Supporting ongoing efforts to implement workplace flexibility in the federal government, in 2010 the United States Congress signed the Telework Enhancement Act promoting the use of telework in government agencies (US Office of Personnel Management, 2011). In line with these trends, during the course of the 2012 fiscal year the United States Office of Personnel Management reported that 14% of Federal employees teleworked, a 2% increase from the previous year (US Office of Personnel Management, 2011).

Workplace flexibility has been and continues to be an issue of national interest in the United States. Employees of varying demographic backgrounds in the United States value and are interested in workplace flexibility (Matos & Galinsky, 2012), suggesting there is no specific person that is seeking or is the target of flexibility policies and practices. Kossek and colleagues (2014) stated that flexibility "is soon expected to become the 'new normal' for conducting business" in the United States (p. 2).

The European Union. Findings from recent studies and reports suggest somewhat similar trends in the European Union (EU) to those in the United States regarding the availability and use of workplace flexibility. The Third European Company Survey (ECS; Eurofound, 2015) was conducted in 2013 assessing organizations in all twenty-eight member-states of the EU. In line with the findings from the National Study of Employers in the United States, the ECS found that 66% of employers offered what was described as "flexitime" to at least some employees and 69% allowed at least one employee to utilize part-time work (Eurofound, 2015). Research trends indicate an increase in some forms of workplace flexibility across European countries, with part-time work being the most common, seeing major growth in recent years, in part, as a way for employees to manage work and nonwork demands (Beham, Präg, & Drobnič, 2012; Eurofound, 2011). In a study assessing the timing of work in the twenty-eight EU countries during 2015, the Sixth European Working Conditions Survey (EWCS; Eurofound, 2016) examined several common types of workplace flexibility policies and practices. The report identified that the majority of workers in the EU engaged in working time arrangements set by their organization with no possibility for change (56%). However, 18% of employees reported they had the ability to adapt their working hours within certain limits and 16% of employees reported they had complete control over the ability to determine the start and stop time of their workdays (Eurofound, 2016).

Despite the similarity to the United States regarding types of available policies, there were noticeable differences across EU regions (Eurofound, 2015; Giannikis, & Mihail, 2011). For instance, mostly western and northern EU countries (e.g., France, the United Kingdom, Denmark) indicated that 50% or more of organizations offered flexitime, with 90% of Denmark's organizations offering at least some employees some degree of choice over the start and/or stop times of their work days. In contrast, several eastern EU countries (e.g., Croatia, Poland, Greece) had less than 50% of organizations offer at least some employees flexitime in 2013, which was a decrease from previous years' surveys for some countries such as Bulgaria (Eurofound, 2015). The ECS report also points out that industry plays a large role in the extent to which organizations offer flexitime; as an example, 70% of organizations described as "financial" and 76% described as "other" offering flexitime to at least some employees compared to 56% of "construction" organizations. Despite reports of the rise of part-time work across Europe (Raghuram et al., 2001), the ECS (Eurofound, 2015) found there was stark variability across EU countries in the proportions of organizations offering at least one employee the ability to work part-time. The countries with the highest percentages of organizations offering part-time work in 2013 were again western and northern EU countries. Specifically, 93%, 90%, and 87% of organizations allowed at least one employee to work part-time in the Netherlands, Austria, and Belgium, respectively. However, only 14%, 22%, and 33% of organizations in Croatia, Portugal, and Cypress offered part-time work to at least one employee, respectively (Eurofound, 2015). Interestingly, while 66% of employees in the EU reported that it was "fairly easy" or "very easy" to take an hour or two off during working time to attend to nonwork demands in 2015, similar to the findings from the ECS, the 2015 EWCS found that there was striking variability across countries. Only 42% of employees in the Czech Republic reported having this flexibility option compared to 85% of employees in the Netherlands (Eurofound, 2016).

In a study examining the factor analytic structure of what the researchers labeled "working time arrangement bundles" across twenty-one European countries, Chung and Tijdens (2013) identified differences in usage of policies based on regional cluster. Specifically, southern European countries (e.g., Spain, Hungary) indicated low average scores of usage of both employee- and employer-centered work time arrangements. However, the northern European cluster (e.g., Sweden, Denmark, Poland) frequently utilized arrangements that benefitted both employers and employees, such as flexible working hours and part-time work. Finally, continental and Anglo European countries (where weekly working hours are longer; e.g., the United Kingdom, France, Belgium) utilized more employer-centered work time arrangements such as overtime and shift work (Chung & Tijdens, 2013).

In comparison to other types of workplace flexibility, telework has been a relatively new arrangement for employees working in Europe (Raghuram et al., 2001) in comparison to organizations in the United States which have been utilizing telework for several decades (Gajendran & Harrison, 2007). However, the results of the 2015 EWCS indicate the gap is closing, with similar patterns in telework usage in the EU to the United States. Specifically the report states that while 70% of employees in EU countries work in a central, regular work location, 30% conduct their work in multiple locations. Although there is at least some degree of work conducted away from the main work site by employees across all EU countries, the largest proportions reported were in the Nordic countries (40%) whereas the lowest were in Turkey (17%; Eurofound, 2016).

It is worth noting that the ECWS definition of employees who work in multiple work locations includes those who are self-employed, work at client sites, work from home, and work from public spaces. Further, the study defines telework as the practice of mainly working from home, excluding individuals who are self-employed who always work from home (Eurofound, 2016). In other words, it is unclear the extent to which the employees in the ECWS have control over their arrangement. As researchers have argued, telework policies that do not include employee control over the arrangement are not truly flexible (Gajendran & Harrison, 2007; Thompson et al., 2015). This may explain, in part, why the ECWS identified that individuals working from multiple locations were less likely to report that their working hours were a good fit with their family and social commitments (77%) than those who worked at a single main workplace (83%; Eurofound, 2016).

Researchers have identified trends regarding the cultural and regional differences in the availability, use, and outcomes associated with the various types of flex policies and practices across Europe (Raghuram et al., 2001; Stavrou & Kilaniotis, 2010). Raghuram and colleagues (2001) explain that shiftwork use has been associated with specific cultural values, such as high collectivism, low uncertainty avoidance, and high power distance. Similarly, the authors found associations between part-time work and low power distance as well as individualistic value systems.

Similarly, attitudes toward the amount of weekly work hours may also partially explain the frequency of use of various types of flexibility practices. Countries such as the United Kingdom view longer workweeks as socially acceptable, whereas France, the Netherlands, and Sweden have established more welfare models that have led to shorter workweeks (Eurofound, 2011). These trends have led to the expansion of part-time work as a means of managing work and nonwork demands. A particularly noteworthy reform occurred in France in 2016 when Law no. 2016–1088 was adopted by the French parliament and signed into law, in an effort to define what working time means (Eurofound, 2017). One of the most controversial provisions to the law was the "right to disconnect," enacted in January 2017. The goal of this amendment was to encourage organizations to respect employees' nonwork hours by enacting a fine of up to 1% of the employees' total remuneration for organizations who fail to comply with the requirements surrounding the use of electronic communication after work hours (Boring, 2017).

In addition to cultural distinctions, economic differences throughout the last few decades across European countries have impacted family development patterns, influencing the uptake of various family-related flexibility policies (Robila, 2012). While policies such as maternity leave are very common and often even longer in organizations in Eastern Europe than Western countries (Robila, 2012), other forms of workplace flexibility are less frequently observed. In addition, lack of access to quality and affordable childcare in some countries incentivizes some parents to utilize part-time work arrangements (Eurofound, 2011). Therefore, there seem to be a number of motives underlying the frequency of availability and usage of various policies and practices across the European Union.

Asia Pacific region. In contrast to findings in the United States and the EU, results from reports and studies examining countries in the Asia Pacific region suggest that employees working in these countries are less likely to have access to workplace flexibility policies and practices. In a study of representatives of multinational corporations operating in eleven countries in the Asia Pacific region, the Boston College Center for Work and Family (2007) found that 57% of respondents indicated their company has some sort of formal workplace flexibility policy in their operating country (but not necessarily all countries in which the company is located). Forty-eight percent of the respondents indicated that the workplace flexibility policies were available to all employees while 48% also said that these policies were only available to full-time employees.

The 2016 Hays Asia Salary guide assessed over three thousand employers across Asia on their hiring and salary practices, representing six million employees (Hays Recruitment, 2016). In line with the findings from the Boston College Center for Work and Family, the report found that 57% of employers indicated they allow flexible work practices. Of the employers offering flexible work practices, the most frequently offered policy was flexible working hours (70%) with the next most common practices being flexplace (49%) and part-time employment (29%). Only 10% of the employers indicated they offer job sharing (Hays Recruitment, 2016).

Although the availability of flexibility policies and practices has been notably lower in organizations operating in Asia Pacific region countries, some notable cultural trends have emerged across reports and research. For example, China's collectivist and paternalistic culture influences specific policy availability and therefore the unique work–life obstacles facing Chinese employees. Specifically, the "one-child policy" has seemingly led to a decrease in childcare demands for married couples, suggesting a potential decrease in need for policies and practices providing employees with greater ability to manage work and life demands. However, both child and elder care duties are still disproportionately placed upon women who also predominately work full-time (Cooke & Jing, 2009). This imbalance in work and nonwork demands may mean that women in China and countries with similar cultures could benefit from increased access to flexibility policies and practices.

In a study of the experiences of 1,834 high-potential employees working in nine Asian countries, Sabattini and Carter (2012) identified that while 67% of men and 62% of women agreed that their organization provided enough flexibility to manage work and personal life demands (gender differences were driven by China, Malaysia, and Thailand), an implementation gap or "mismatch" existed between what employees felt they needed and what was offered by their organizations. Specifically, the authors identified a discrepancy for more than 80% of participants between the workplace flexibility available and their stated work–life needs. Similarly, the researchers found that women were less likely (46%) to aspire to achieve a senior executive role as their ultimate career position compared to men (64%). Both groups cited job pressures, long hours, stress on relationships, and other life priorities as the primary reasons for their decision not to pursue senior leadership (Sabattini & Carter, 2012). These findings may be due in part to expectations for women to perform caregiving roles outside of the workplace. In other words, women in some Asian countries may be less likely to pursue their preferred career trajectories due to gendered cultural expectations as well as a lack of options to help them manage work and life demands. When asked about ways employers could help employees better manage work and life demands, participants indicated concerns of facetime and long hours, suggesting interest in flexible work arrangements, such as telecommuting and flextime (Sabattini & Carter, 2012).

Some researchers have pointed out the importance of monetary and material rewards in alleviating work–life conflict issues for Chinese employees (Cooke & Jing, 2009). Employees with higher incomes are able to utilize their resources to offset nonwork demands (e.g., via childcare); conversely employees without the same resources are compelled to work more hours to supplement wages, thus contributing to a culture valuing long working hours (Chandra, 2012). This shift of focus on utilizing monetary resources as a method of work–life boundary management may contribute to a perceived lack of need for workplace policies that support employees' ability to manage work and life demands. In other words, organizations may not clearly see a need for flexibility policies and practices because many employees are able to address work–life concerns by utilizing monetary resources earned through increased work hours, despite preferences for reduced work hours and increased work–life balance (Sabattini & Carter, 2012).

In response to growing employee work–life conflict, some employers in China offer collective employee bonding opportunities as well as financial mechanisms for relieving these strains, rather than employee control-based work arrangements that are more commonly utilized in Western cultures. Specifically, some employers offer opportunities among and between employees to provide emotional support for one another as well as monetary donations to colleagues undergoing challenging life demands (e.g., sick child or parent; Cooke & Jing, 2009). Willingness and dedication to work in the face of family demands and conflict reflect the Chinese work ethic as well as the strong collectivist culture (Cooke & Jing, 2009). There is a general mindset across many Asian countries that employees should be present in the office (Boston College Center for Work and Family, 2007), which may translate to the infrequent availability and use of certain types of flexibility policies, such as telework arrangements.

Similar trends have developed in other Asian countries, where long work hours are the norm and gender inequality may be the driving mechanism underlying work–life conflict. In contrast to efforts made in Western countries, socialization in Asian countries still primarily reinforces gender-based division of labor (Chandra, 2012). In Japan, 60% of men work forty-three or more hours each week compared to only 30% of women who work the same long hours (Boston College Center for Work & Family, 2000). Organizations and human resource programs view work–life balance as an individual-level issue to be handled by employees, rather than through employer provided policies. Rather than offer policies that support flexibility in managing life demands around long working hours, employers attempt to reduce the negative effects experienced by employees from the long work hours (Chandra, 2012). Although many of the policies do not specifically target work–life balance, some organizations in Asian countries offer more formalized support for women's roles as caregivers. For instance, in Bangladesh mothers (but not fathers) are eligible for three months of paid leave following childbirth (Jesmin & Seward, 2011), a policy that is still not nationally prescribed in the United States. This suggests that providing policies and practices that reinforce stereotypical gender roles is an accepted aspect of work in some Asian countries.

Conceptualizations of "flexible" employment practices may differ cross-culturally such that some organizations focus on flexibility that meets organizational goals, rather than employees' attempts to manage or gain control over their competing work and life demands. For example, MacVaugh and Evans (2012) recently concluded that Japanese organizations have what the authors call "historically flexible employment practices" in comparison to Western organizations, utilizing part-time work, job-sharing, and short-term contracts. However, providing these types of policies may suggest an emphasis on employer-focused needs (e.g., client availability, overtime requirements) rather than a desire to identify a mutually beneficial arrangement to support both the employees and employer. In a multinational study of the impact of workplace flexibility on employees, Japanese employees reported they only somewhat agreed that flexible work options have a positive impact on work/family balance and job success, the lowest of any country surveyed (Bhate, 2013). Thus, it may be the case that flexibility policies in some organizations have not been viewed as particularly beneficial as they may not have been developed or implemented with the recognition that employee control over work demands is an important component of successful flexibility policies.

Flexibility in Africa. The prevalence of and access to policies offering employee control over when, where, or how work is conducted appear to be much less frequent for employees in African countries compared to Western countries. There has been very little research conducted examining organizational policies and practices in African countries, particularly those designed to facilitate the management of work and life demands. Clear estimates of the frequency of availability and use do not seem to be readily available at a comparable level to the other geographic regions discussed in this chapter. However, some research has been conducted that examines work–life issues in this area and the emerging trends are discussed below.

Managing work and nonwork demands has been conceptualized quite differently in the developing countries in Africa. One potential explanation for this is that the socioeconomic conditions of the labor force as well as ongoing health crises have motivated different policy concerns for working adults in these countries compared to employees working in Western, more industrialized countries (Smit, 2011). As Dancaster and Baird (2016) explain, "not only has HIV/AIDS exacerbated care concerns, but also conditions of poverty, an increase in female labour force participation and minimal state infrastructure for those in need of care have contributed to what has been referred to as a 'care crisis' in South Africa" (p. 456). Due to these and other issues, little research has examined the prevalence of human resources policies and practices specifically aimed at improving work–family conflict in African countries. Instead, research has primarily focused on other types of healthcare policies and infrastructure support that organizations may offer.

While policies explicitly targeting work–family conflict are infrequent, formal attempts to support parenthood are prominent. Van der Meulen-Rodgers (1999), states that "maternity leave provisions are just as prevalent among developing countries" as in developed and Western countries (p. 18). Similarly, many of the South African Development Community (SADC) countries provide forms of maternal health protection policies, such as policies in Madagascar and Tanzania that protect women from strenuous work and dangerous working conditions during pregnancy and up to three months following their recovery period (Smit, 2011). Additionally, many SADC countries have legislation protecting pregnant women from working at night as well as the rights of women to breastfeed while at work (Smit, 2011).

Despite the lack of research examining traditionally defined flexibility policies, some researchers have examined these issues by broadening the scope of inquiry. In a study examining the frequency and patterns of what the researchers labeled "work–care arrangements" available in organizations listed on the Johannesburg Stock Exchange, Dancaster and Baird (2016) found that the overall adoption of arrangements across all categories was low. Interestingly, the study identified that the most frequently adopted practice was organizationally provided information about HIV/AIDS facilities and programs (81%). The authors suggest this is not surprising given the legal recommendations for organizations in South Africa (Dancaster & Baird, 2016). In addition, the authors also note that nearly 67% of the employers surveyed reported allowing employees to occasionally have flexible starting and finishing work times as well as nearly 45% of organizations reported allowing employees to work from home on an occasional basis. The authors found that both the proportion of females in senior management and the organizational size were characteristics that were associated with the adoption of flexible work arrangements in the surveyed African organizations (Dancaster & Baird, 2016).

Implementing Workplace Flexibility in Organizations to Manage a Multinational Workforce

Having discussed how workplace flexibility practices vary in a number of regions in the previous sections of this chapter, we turn now to issues in implementing workplace flexibility in a multinational work force. In this section, we consider the benefits, challenges, and strategies related to implementing workplace flexibility in global organizations.

Benefits of implementing workplace flexibility in global firms. Workplace flexibility affects global business success by enabling operations to run on a 24/7 basis, from service operations to manufacturing. By expanding the available times employees can work, employers also expand the number of days and hours they are able to meet organizational goals. Specifically, this enhances an organization's ability to produce work around the clock, which fosters efficient use of the workforce. Managing work 24/7 also helps foster the organizational ability to adjust hours to match customer availability. Specifically, companies can have operations running at different times around the world to match global customers' needs. For example, employees in Slovenia can work a second shift to match hours of customers in the United States in addition to providing labor cost savings compared to hiring a similar workforce in the United States (Kossek & Thompson, 2016). Creating shift schedules that provide employees with some degree of choice and control over their schedules may have the added benefit of increasing employee job control.

Workplace flexibility can also be used as part of a global supply chain to locate talent in the country where the skills and markets best match the organizational needs. This may foster the ability to adopt a customized menu of workplace flexibility practices linked to labor market solutions as part of a global workforce strategy. For example, in some countries, research and development (R&D) institutions may be located where particular universities and a highly skilled scientific workforce are available. However, in other countries, expertise may be provided on a cost-effective basis, rather than determined by the location of workers. For example, in order to maximize policy effectiveness, global firms might offer summer hours or telework in order to attract and retain exclusive R&D talent for their professional workforce on an infrequent basis, rather than relocate an entire facility to a remote location. In contrast, offering policies such as flextime and reduced work hours to support a large group of employees' nonwork demands (e.g., time for family, classes to complete degrees) might be an effective strategy for maximizing workforce productivity of a service workforce located in a less developed country. Consequently, workplace flexibility policies should not only be used to facilitate employee management of work–life demands, but also to enable a firm to match the hours and schedules of employees in various regional labor markets to organizational needs in order to maximize productivity.

Another benefit of leveraging workplace flexibility in a global firm is that it can enhance attraction and retention by offering opportunities for a global career. Expatriates may be more likely to want to work for firms that allow employees to experience different work–life cultures from their home society. For example, the United States and the United Kingdom are known for being more work-centric and having less access to long-term paid family leave with shared care between a father and mother. In these countries, work is seen as the primary duty of a responsible citizen – more so than spending time with raising a family or caring for elders (Patrick, 2012). Thus, offering an expatriate opportunity to work in a country with a more balanced life-centric approach, such as in a Scandinavian subsidiary, may be a way to attract and retain talent as well as cultivate a flexible global workforce.

Challenges of global flexibility. One noteworthy challenge that scholars have identified for multinational organizations seeking to implement flexibility policies is that the link between uses of flexible working arrangements and beneficial outcomes may vary by culture and type of practice. For example, one comparative study found that as flexibility related to what the authors called "unsocial hours" increased (e.g., overtime, shift work, weekend work) in Anglo countries, turnover increased correspondingly (Stavrou & Kilaniotis, 2010). In other words, the practices that may be effective in one country or industry may not be effective in another. Therefore, being able to adopt and manage different scheduling practices across cultures may add to organizational and management complexity and scheduling demands. This and other studies have raised questions about the comparative effectiveness of using similar flexible working arrangements internationally in global firms.

Further, the use of flexible practices may be beneficial for attracting a talented workforce, but organizational support for such policies as a means for managing work–life demands may depend on cultural factors. When used predominantly by women in countries lower in gender equality, flexibility practices may serve as barriers to women's labor force participation rather than facilitators. For example, one study of organizations across eight European countries found that organizations in countries high in gender empowerment were supportive of part-time work options, which corresponded to higher proportions of women employees. However, for organizations in countries that were lower in gender empowerment, the adoption of part-time work only corresponded to a greater proportion of women when there were labor shortages (Stavrou, Casper, & Ierodiakonou, 2015). The authors contend that some organizations may offer workplace flexibility as a mechanism to support work–life balance, or in contrast, others may simply offer these policies to meet organizational recruitment goals or needs (Stavrou et al., 2015). Although these practices can be successful in attracting women to the labor market, they are likely to simultaneously serve as a barrier to women's advancement to higher-level leadership positions, as few men use these practices, particularly in cultures that have rigidly prescribed gender roles. Thus, flexible work practices can serve to reinforce gender segregation as well as gendered working-time regimes in occupational groups and therefore limit women's long-term ability to advance their careers (Kossek, Su, & Wu, 2016).

Another important challenge in managing workplace flexibility globally, compared to the United States, is that there are varying legal restrictions in the implementation of flexibility policies. For example, workplace flexibility is collectively bargained for in some countries, such as Australia. One study (Berg, Kossek, Baird, & Block, 2013) found that unpaid or family and health leave and paid annual vacation leave were much more likely to be in the collective bargaining contract in Australian universities unlike their US counterparts. Employers in global firms headquartered in countries where union contracts do not cover workplace flexibility will need to develop their knowledge in how to implement workplace flexibility as a collective workforce benefit.

A third important challenge for multinational flexibility is the perceived lack of facetime, or reduced benefits from face-to-face interaction (Van Dyne, Kossek, & Lobel, 2007). Managers and colleagues of employees working in other geographic locations may have trouble communicating at a distance through technology. This may lead to perceptions of poor performance due to miscommunication or failure to set expectations and goals. Colleagues may find working cooperatively in a new format using unfamiliar equipment to be an added challenge to the already present communication barriers. Further, additional obstacles may surface for employees working in virtual teams or in remote locations, such as lack of cross-cultural awareness and stigmas surrounding cultural differences.

Strategies for successful global flexibility. Organizations seeking to successfully implement workplace flexibility with a global strategic view should first recognize and understand variation in regional and cultural values. However, an important consideration for global firms is that while there are many comparative studies on workplace flexibility at the country level assessing the availability of different types of flexibility across nations, there is very little international work on workplace flexibility using organizational-level data (Chung & Tijdens, 2013). One useful tool for employers seeking to develop nuanced strategies across the EU is the European Establishment Survey on Working Time and Work–Life Balance (ESWT), which examines the different types of workplace flexibility practices used within a firm to foster functional skill, job, or headcount flexibility while simultaneously considering employees' work preferences for managing work and personal life demands. Another important consideration is Chung and Tijdens' (2013) three clusters of flexibility regimes: 1) a southern European cluster with Hungary and Slovenia where most employers do not commonly offer workplace flexibility policies to serve either employer or employee interests; 2) a northern European country cluster that includes the Czech Republic and Poland, where workplace flexibility practices are frequently used by both employees and employers; and 3) a third cluster involving the main European continent countries as well as Anglo-Saxon countries, where flexibility is used mainly to meet employer needs with some moderate attention to employee preferences. Organizations in the third cluster typically offer more flexibility options than the first (the southern European countries) but less than the highly employee-centric, labor market-responsive Northern countries of the second cluster. Multinational organizations seeking to implement global workplace flexibility policies should identify how regional differences in preferences for and availability of workplace flexibility can influence the success of specific policies across sites. Utilizing knowledge of regional differences can help in the successful design and implementation of cross-national policies and practices within a single organization.

A second strategy organizations may consider is to design global flexibility policies that allow for customization across geographic locations (as laws, customs, and cultural values differ quite a bit depending on area). This approach may vary by level and nature of the global workforce. For example, large multinationals (e.g., IBM, Facebook) might adopt a global calendar with commonly utilized workdays and similar telework policies for the professional and manager workforce. However, for workers at the middle and lower levels, organizations might adopt the holiday calendar of the local country as the hours and working time may vary greatly across nations.

A third useful strategy might be to adopt employee training for employees on how to work with other employees across global time zones. Here, employees and managers might be trained in how to work and communicate with employees working at a distance via technology as well as how to overcome barriers that can cause remote employees to be viewed as less effective than face-to-face colleagues due to lack of facetime and communication issues. Training in cultural intelligence to show patience and understanding of accents and learning to speak slowly when on a conference call may be useful for enabling a virtual global workforce. Additionally, training in managing boundaries when working across time zones to allow employees to feel more in control of their working time (Kossek & Thomson, 2016) may be useful for global teams to be able to respect the flexible working hours of colleagues in another time zone. Here the teams might also engage in role play to discuss how to respect the national holidays, leisure time, and sleep hours of remote colleagues as well as agree to core global working hours so that some employees in one country are not always expected to take 2 a.m. calls when working with colleagues or customers across time zones. Finally, setting clear expectations among team members about communication patterns and task deadlines can facilitate positive work experiences.

Areas for Future Research

Given the vast differences in the amount of research assessing workplace flexibility across geographic regions, there is a clear need for additional research assessing both availability and use of common forms of flexibility in areas where little research has been conducted. For example, little research to date has adequately examined the frequency of availability and use of major types of flexible policies and practices in African countries, South American countries, or Australia. Similarly, little research has compared policies usage and effectiveness within multinational organizations located in meaningfully different geographic regions.

Additionally, future research is needed to understand how specific and unique cultural differences relate to flexibility availability and use, particularly in regards to relatively understudied or geographically specific cultural values. For example, Ashforth and colleagues (2000) maintain that the need for segmentation of work and life roles may differ as a function of cultures. Therefore, organizations in countries whose cultures value separation between work and life demands may be less likely to offer flexibility policies such as telework.

Finally, an important avenue for future research is the relationship between policies and societal and labor force outcomes. Specifically, many organizations offer workplace flexibility policies so that employees can more easily manage work and nonwork demands. However, as previously discussed, some organizations (and cultures) do not view this as the goal of these policies, but rather flexibility is a means to meet organizational goals (e.g., attracting a sufficient labor force). Differences in gender roles and expectations of the demographics of the workforce across countries may reveal interesting patterns relative to the prevalence of flexibility policies as societal values shift. Relatedly, as multinational organizations continue to grow in number, their expansion may correspond with cultural shifts in expectations of the workforce.

Conclusions

Implementing successful global workplace flexibility initiatives requires considerable theoretical knowledge and cultural awareness as the meaning and application of flexibility differs vastly both within and across countries. It is critical for multinational organizations wishing to utilize flexibility to meet their own needs and expand practices to take time to become familiar with the interests of the various stakeholder groups when designing and executing new approaches to flexibility.

Research suggests that flexibility is increasing in availability and use across the world. As cultural values and norms shift, so too will organizational practices designed to meet the demands of the workforce. As a part of a new, results-driven work culture, many organizations have begun to embrace the benefits that flexible options can provide to meet client, employee, and organizational goals. However, in order to remain competitive in a global marketplace, companies must also recognize the nuanced nature of implementing international business strategies.

References

Allen, T. D., Johnson, R. C., Kiburz, K. M., & Shockley, K. M. (2013). Work–family conflict and flexible work arrangements: Deconstructing flexibility. *Personnel Psychology*, *66*, 345–376

Ashforth, B. E., Kreiner, G. E., & Fugate, M. (2000). All in a day's work: Boundaries and micro role transitions. *Academy of Management review*, *25*(3), 472–491.

Baltes, B. B., Briggs, T. E., Huff, J. W., Wright, J. A., & Neuman, G. A. (1999). Flexible and compressed workweek schedules: A meta-analysis of their effects on work-related criteria.

Beham, B., Präg, P., & Drobnič, S. (2012). Who's got the balance? A study of satisfaction with the work–family balance among part-time service sector employees in five western European countries. *International Journal of Human Resource Management*, *23*(18), 3725–3741. doi:10.1080/09585192.2012.654808

Behson, S. J. (2005). The relative contribution of formal and informal organizational work–family support. *Journal of Vocational Behavior*, *66*(3), 487–500.

Berg, P., Kossek, E. E., Baird, M., & Block, R. N. (2013). Collective bargaining and public policy: Pathways to work-family policy adoption in Australia and the United States. *European Management Journal*, *31*(5), 495–504.

Berg, P., Kossek, E., Misra, K., & Belman, D. (2014). Do unions matter for work- life flexibility policy access and use? *Industrial and Labor Relations Review*, *67*(1), 111–136.

Boston College Center for Work and Families. (2007). *What companies are doing, why they are doing it and what lies ahead*. A report prepared for the members of the global workforce roundtable.

Boston College Center for Work and Families (2010). *Work and family issues in Japan and the Republic of Korea: Expanding our understanding of work and family experiences in North Asia*. Wallace E. Carroll School of Management.

Bhate, R. (2013). Flexibility at work: Employee perceptions. The Sloan Center on Aging & Work at Boston College.

Boring, N. (2017, Jan). France: Right to disconnect takes effect. *Global Legal Monitor*. The Library of Congress: United States. Retrieved from: www.loc.gov/law/foreign-news/article/france-right-to-disconnect-takes-effect

Brewster, C., Mayne, L., & Tregaskis, O. (1997). Flexible working in Europe. *Journal of World Business*, *32*(2), 133–151. doi:10.1016/S1090-9516(97)90004-3

Chandra, V. (2012). Work–life balance: Eastern and Western perspectives. *International Journal of Human Resource Management*, *23*(5), 1040–1056. doi:10.1080/09585192.2012.651339

Chung, H., & Tijdens, K. (2013). Working time flexibility components and working time regimes in Europe: using company-level data across 21 countries. The International Journal of Human Resource Management, 24(7), 1418–1434.

Cooke, F. L., & Jing, X. (2009). Work–life balance in China: Sources of conflicts and coping strategies. *NHRD Network Journal*, *2*(3), 18–28.

Dancaster, L., & Baird, M. (2016). Predictors of the adoption of work–care arrangements: a study of South African firms. *The International Journal of Human Resource Management*, *27*(4), 456–475.

Eaton, S. C. (2003). If you can use them: Flexibility policies, organizational commitment, and perceived performance. *Industrial Relations: A Journal of Economy and Society*, *42*(2), 145–167.

Eurofound. (2011). *Part-Time Work in Europe*. Dublin: European Foundation for the Improvement of Living and Working Conditions. Retrieved from: www.eurofound .europa.eu/sites/default/files/ef_files/pubdocs/2010/86/en/3/EF1086EN.pdf

Eurofound. (2015). Workplace practices: Patterns, performance and well-being. European Foundation for the Improvement of Living and Working Conditions. Retrieved: http://digitalcommons.ilr.cornell.edu/cgi/viewcontent.cgi?article=1448&context=intl

Eurofound. (2016). *Sixth European Working Conditions Survey – Overview report*. Publications Office of the European Union, Luxembourg. Retrieved from: www .eurofound.europa.eu/publications/report/2016/working-conditions/sixth-european -working-conditions-survey-overview-report

Eurofound. (2017). *France: New rules on working time enter into force*. Publications Office of the European Union, Luxembourg. Retrieved from: www.eurofound.europa.eu/ observatories/eurwork/articles/france-new-rules-on-working-time-enter-into-force

Gajendran, R. S., & Harrison, D. A. (2007). The good, the bad, and the unknown about telecommuting: meta-analysis of psychological mediators and individual consequences. *Journal of Applied Psychology, 92*(6), 1524.

Giannikis, S. K., & Mihail, D. M. (2011). Flexible work arrangements in Greece: A study of employee perceptions. *International Journal of Human Resource Management, 22* (2), 417–432. doi:10.1080/09585192.2011.540163

Hays Recruitment. (2016). *2016 Hays Salary Guide – Asia*. Retrieved from: www.hays.cn/cs/ groups/hays_common/@cn/@content/documents/digitalasset/hays_314891.pdf

Hill, J., Grzywacz, J., Allen, S., Blanchard, V., Matz-Costa, C., Shulkin, S., & Pitt-Catsouphes , M. (2008). Defining and conceptualizing workplace flexibility. *Community, Work and Family, 11*, 149–163.

Hobfoll, S. E. (2001). The influence of culture, community, and the nested-self in the stress process: advancing conservation of resources theory. *Applied psychology, 50*(3), 337–421.

Jesmin, S. S., & Seward, R. R. (2011). Parental leave and fathers' involvement with children in Bangladesh: A comparison with United States. *Journal of Comparative Family Studies, 42*(1), 95–112.

Kossek, E. E., Hammer, L. B., Thompson, R. J., & Burke, L. B. (2014). Leveraging workplace flexibility: Fostering engagement and productivity. *SHRM Foundation's Effective Practice Guidelines Series*. Alexandra, VA: SHRM Foundation.

Kossek, E. E., Lautsch, B. A., & Eaton, S. C. (2006). Telecommuting, control, and boundary management: Correlates of policy use and practice, job control, and work–family effectiveness. *Journal of Vocational Behavior, 68*(2), 347–367.

Kossek, E. E., Thompson, R. J., & Lautsch, B. A. (2015). Balanced Workplace Flexibility. *California Management Review, 57*(4), 5–25.

Kossek, E. E., & Lee, M. (2008). Implementing a reduced-workload arrangement to retain high talent: A case study. *Journal of Managerial Psychology, 11*, 49–64.

Kossek, E. E., & Michel, J. (2011). Flexible work scheduling. In S. Zedeck (Ed.), *Handbook of Industrial-Organizational Psychology* (Vol. 1, pp. 535–572). Washington, DC: American Psychological Association.

Kossek, E. E., Pichler, S., Bodner, T., & Hammer, L. B. (2011). Workplace social support and work–family conflict: A meta-analysis clarifying the influence of general and work–family-specific supervisor and organizational support. *Personnel Psychology, 64*(2), 289–313.

Kossek, E. E., & Thompson, R. J. (2016). Workplace flexibility: Integrating employer and employee perspectives to close the research–practice implementation gap. In T. Allen & L. Eby (Eds.), *The Oxford Handbook of Work and Family*, 255.

Kossek, E. E., Su, R., & Wu, L (2016). "Opting out" or "pushed out"? Integrating perspectives on women's career equality for gender inclusion and interventions. *Journal of Management*, 43, 228–254.

Lee, M. D., MacDermid, S. M., & Buck, M. L. (2000). Organizational paradigms of reduced-load work: Accommodation, elaboration, and transformation. *Academy of Management Journal*, *43*(6), 1211–1226.

MacVaugh, J., & Evans, J. (2012). A re-examination of flexible employment practices in Japan. *International Journal of Human Resource Management*, *23*(6), 1245–1258. doi: 10.1080/09585192.2011.561237

Matos, K., & Galinsky, E. (2014). *2014 National Study of Employers*. Families and Work Institute.

Myers, C. G. (2016). Where in the world are the workers? Cultural underrepresentation in IO research. *Industrial and Organizational Psychology*, *9*(01), 144–152.

Patrick, R. (2012). Work as the primary 'duty' of the responsible citizen: a critique of this work-centric approach. *People, Place & Policy Online*, *6*(1).

Raghuram, S., London, M., & Larsen, H. H. (2001). Flexible employment practices in Europe: Country versus culture. *International Journal of Human Resource Management*, *12*(5), 738–753. doi:10.1080/09585190110047811

Robila, M. (2012). Family policies in Eastern Europe: A focus on parental leave. *Journal of Child and Family Studies*, *21*(1), 32–41. doi:10.1007/s10826-010-9421-4

Sabattini, L., & Carter, N. M. (2012). Expanding work–life perspectives: Talent management in Asia. New York, NY: Catalyst.

Shockley, K. M., & Allen, T. D. (2007). When flexibility helps: Another look at the availability of flexible work arrangements and work–family conflict. *Journal of Vocational Behavior*, *71*, 479–493. doi:10.1016/j.jvb.2007.08.006

Simard, C., Henderson, A. D., Gilmartin, S. K., Schiebinger, L., & Whitney, T. (2008). *Climbing the technical ladder: Obstacles and solutions for mid-level women in technology*. Michelle R. Clayman Institute for Gender Research, Stanford University, Anita Borg Institute for Women and Technology.

Smit, R. (2011). Family-related policies in Southern African countries: Are working parents reaping any benefits? *Journal of Comparative Family Studies*, *42*(1), 15–36.

Smith, L., Folkard, S., Tucker, P., & Macdonald, I. (1998). Work shift duration: a review comparing eight hour and 12 hour shift systems. *Occupational and Environmental Medicine*, *55*(4), 217–229.

Spector, P. E., Cooper, C. L., Poelmans, S., Allen, T. D., O'Driscoll, M., Sanchez, J. I., ... & Lu, L. (2004). A cross-national comparative study of work-family stressors, working hours, and well-being: China and Latin America versus the Anglo world. *Personnel Psychology*, *57*(1), 119–142.

Stavrou, E. T., Casper, W. J., & Ierodiakonou, C. (2015). Support for part-time work as a channel to female employment: the moderating effects of national gender empowerment and labour market conditions. *International Journal of Human Resource Management*, *26*(6), 688–706.

Stavrou, E., & Kilaniotis, C. (2010). Flexible work and turnover: An empirical investigation across cultures. *British Journal of Management*, *21*(2), 541–554.

Thompson, C. A., Beauvais, L. L., & Lyness, K. S. (1999). When work–family benefits are not enough: The influence of work–family culture on benefit utilization, organizational attachment, and work–family conflict. *Journal of Vocational Behavior*, *54*(3), 392–415.

Thompson, R. J., Payne, S. C., & Taylor, A. B. (2015). Applicant attraction to flexible work arrangements: Separating the influence of flextime and flexplace. *Journal of Occupational and Organizational Psychology*, *88*(4), 726–749

US Department of Labor (1993). Wage and Hour Division. Family and Medical Leave Act. Retrieved from www.dol.gov/whd/fmla

US Office of Personnel Management (2011). *Guide to telework in the federal government*. Retrieved from: www.telework.gov/guidance-legislation/telework-guidance/telework-guide/guide-to-telework-in-the-federal-government.pdf

Van der Meulen Rodgers, Y. (1999). *Protecting women and promoting equality in the labor market: Theory and evidence*. World Bank, Development Research Group, Poverty Reduction and Economic Management Network.

Van Dyne, L., Kossek, E., & Lobel, S. (2007). Less need to be there: Cross-level effects of work practices that support work–life flexibility and enhance group processes and group-level OCB. *Human Relations*, *60*(8), 1123–1154.

Voyandoff, P. (2005). Consequences of boundary-spanning demands and resources for work-to-family conflict and perceived stress. *Journal of Occupational Health Psychology*, *10*, 491–503. DOI: 10.1037/1076-8998.10.4.491

30 Organizational Culture in the Context of National Culture

T. Alexandra Beauregard, Kelly A. Basile, and Cynthia A. Thompson

An organization's culture can have a profound impact on how its employees with caregiving responsibilities experience their work and family roles (Shockley, in press; Thompson, Beauvais, & Lyness, 1999). At the same time, national culture also influences individuals' preferences for how they manage those roles. For instance, workaholism among men is more common in cultures centered on achievement and material success than in cultures that emphasize quality of life; women are less likely to work outside the home in cultures featuring a strong breadwinner/ homemaker gender role ideology (Lewis, 2009; Snir & Harpaz, 2009). Given that globalization has increased international mobility for workers as well as the likelihood that home country workers are interacting with colleagues from or in other countries (Tams & Arthur, 2007), it has become paramount for work–family scholarship to recognize that multiple layers of culture are increasingly influencing employees' experiences in integrating work and family, as well as their perceptions of appropriate organizational work–family practices. It is important for work–family scholars to determine the efficacy of organizational work–family practices and policies, as these practices continue to expand beyond their Western points of origin and become implemented all over the world (e.g., Allen, 2013; Ollier-Malaterre, Valcour, Den Dulk, & Kossek, 2013).

In this chapter, we first outline the importance of organizational culture from a work–family perspective by reviewing extant research on how an employer's work–family culture influences individual outcomes, such as employees' job-related attitudes, contextual performance, experience of work–family conflict, and utilization of work–family benefits. Next, we examine the role of national culture in shaping work–family perceptions via culture frameworks and work–family role preferences. We go on to discuss the relationship between national culture and organizational work–family culture, before discussing the consequences of cultural alignment or misalignment – the match or mismatch between an employee's work–family role preferences and the role demands of an organization set forth by their work–family culture and policies. We posit that when there is no shared national culture framework influencing both individual preferences and organizational role demands, the propensity for mismatch will be higher. Finally, we present a new model of global work–family culture and briefly introduce its implications for theory and practice.

The Importance of Organizational Culture from a Work–Family Perspective

Organizational culture can be broadly defined as a shared set of assumptions, values, and beliefs (Schein, 2010). These are implicit notions, which are expressed and communicated partly in symbolic form; they are taught to organizational newcomers as the correct way to think and feel, via stories and myths about the organization's history (Alvesson, 2013; Schein, 2010). Employees use the information inferred during this process of socialization to guide their behavior; they also observe the behavior of other organizational members, particularly leaders, to gauge which actions are likely to be useful and promote success (Schneider, Ehrhart, & Macey, 2013). In this way, organizational culture serves as a means of signaling to employees how they are expected to manage their work and family roles. For example, do leaders endorse the value of nonwork interests and activities and role-model behaviors, such as leaving the workplace before dinnertime? Or do promotions and status come only to those who enact the role of the "ideal worker" by visibly working long hours and prioritizing job-related tasks over family time?

Assumptions, beliefs, and values among organizational members regarding the extent to which the organization exhibits support for its employees' efforts to balance work and family responsibilities is referred to as work–family culture (Thompson et al., 1999). Work–family culture can be viewed as a type of organizational support, and is generally held to incorporate such factors as supervisory support (both instrumental and emotional), organizational time demands on employees, and perceived career consequences of using work–family benefits or flexible work practices (Jahn, Thompson, & Kopelman, 2003; Thompson et al., 1999). Organizational cultures supportive of work–family issues have been shown to impact a number of employee outcomes – perceptions of work–family support have been linked to greater life satisfaction, job satisfaction, and organizational commitment, and decreased turnover intentions and absenteeism (see Andreassi & Thompson, 2008, and Shockley, Thompson, & Andreassi, 2013, for a review). In addition, perceptions of a supportive work–family culture have been related to lower levels of work stress and general psychological strain (Beauregard, 2011a; Thompson & Prottas, 2006).

Organizational cultures that demonstrate support for employees' efforts to manage work and family responsibilities are also associated with employee outcomes directly related to the combination of work and family roles. This support has been shown to reduce time- and strain-based conflict between domains, and increase positive spillover of emotions, knowledge, and skills. Individuals who perceive a supportive work–family culture within their organizations report lower levels of both work-to-family conflict and family-to-work conflict, and those whose supervisors exhibit family-supportive behaviors report higher levels of both work-to-family enrichment and family-to-work enrichment (Beauregard, 2011a; Greenhaus, Ziegert, & Allen, 2012; Odle-Dusseau, Britt, & Greene-Shortridge, 2012; Shockley et al., 2013).

Work–family culture also directly influences employees' choices regarding how to manage their work and family roles, by operating as either an incentive or an impediment to the utilization of work–family or flexible working initiatives. The extent to which employees perceive that the culture of their organization encourages or discourages the use of these initiatives has a considerable impact on the use of these practices. Prevailing organizational cultures often inhibit the use of work–family practices, with employees feeling unable to utilize available policies due to organizational values emphasizing the importance of working long hours and being visibly present in the workplace (Beauregard, 2008; Shockley & Allen, 2010). When working from home or a reduced hours load results in being perceived as less committed and less ambitious by managers and colleagues, the career risks of policy utilization can be viewed as too high.

When organizations are seen as providing a supportive environment for the reconciliation of work and family demands, employees are more likely to make use of the family-friendly initiatives offered (Andreassi & Thompson, 2008). The social context plays an important role here, signaling what is considered acceptable practice in an organization (Beauregard, 2011b). For instance, research has found that managers whose colleagues use flexible work arrangements are more likely to make use of these practices themselves (Kossek, Barber, & Winters, 1999; Lambert, Marler, & Gueutal, 2008). Seeing this tangible evidence that work–family initiatives are valued by other organizational members provides reassurance to employees that they will not be disadvantaged if they decide to take up these arrangements themselves. When senior managers in particular make use of work–family initiatives, they are helping to create an organizational culture in which family commitments are compatible with career advancement or high-level performance (Thompson, 2008).

The Impact of National Culture on Organizational Work–Life Perspectives

Organizational work–family culture is influenced to a considerable extent by national culture. National culture may impact the organization's expectations of how individuals will manage work and family roles, which in turn may affect the organization's demands upon employees' time and energy, the types of policies it offers that are aimed at promoting work–life balance, and the culture of support for employees' work–life balance. At the individual-level, national culture may influence an individual's preferences for managing multiple life roles; individuals may be more likely to prioritize roles that are most consistent with their own core values, which are, in part, shaped by their national culture. The concept of national culture builds on the idea that when groups of individuals engage in a shared experience, a shared perception of culture is established (House & Javidan, 2004). Donley, Cannon, and Mullen (1998) describe how this shared culture is developed at the national-level: "national culture as we view it is not a characteristic of individuals or nation states but of a large number of people conditioned by similar background, education, and life experience" (p. 607). The literature on national culture has identified specific dimensions of culture that differ across national boundaries, such as individualist versus collectivist beliefs; long-term versus short-term orientations; high levels of power inequality versus low levels; masculinity versus femininity; and achievement versus ascription (Hofstede, 1980; Trompenaars & Hampden-Turner, 1998). Although the impact of national culture has long been ignored in work–family research, recent literature has sought to better understand how dimensions of national culture influence organizational work–family culture (Powell, Francesco, & Ling, 2009).

Powell et al. (2009) identified four dimensions of national culture that influence perceptions of the work–family interface from both conflict and enrichment perspectives: individualism versus collectivism, gender egalitarianism, humane orientation, and specificity versus diffusion. These dimensions influence organizational culture and policies and, in turn, the work–family role demands placed on employees. For example, cross-cultural research on human resource management (HRM) practices demonstrates links between national-level collectivism and organizational provision of employee programs such as maternity leave, career break schemes, flexible benefit plans, housing assistance, and contributions toward children's education (Huo & von Glinow, 1995; Quinn & Rivoli, 1991; Sparrow & Budhwar, 1997). This body of research demonstrates that in collectivistic national cultures, organizational work–family cultures may place greater emphasis upon supporting employees' families directly. In more individualistic national cultures, organizational work–family cultures may be more likely to reflect the values of independent choice and action, and provide support in the form of greater individual control over work schedule flexibility so that employees can combine paid work and family life as they see fit.

These national cultural values may also transmit themselves to individual work–family role preferences. For example, individuals in collectivist cultures tend to identify themselves in relationship to the larger social group (or "collective"), whereas in individualist cultures, the self is more likely to be perceived as a unique and independent entity (Markus & Kitayama, 1991). While employees working in collectivist cultures may perceive working long hours to be a necessary sacrifice for the good of the family, employees from individualist cultures may interpret long hours of work as sacrificing one's family role for the pursuit of individual achievement (Powell et al., 2009). For example, Yang et al. (2012) found that despite working the same number of hours, individuals from individualistic countries perceived higher workloads and the relationship between these workload perceptions and greater job dissatisfaction and turnover intentions was stronger than for their collectivist counterparts. In addition, the more tightly coupled social roles found in collectivist cultures may also influence perceptions of the work–family interface (Hofstede, 1980; Powell et al., 2009). While employees in individualistic cultures may care for and be supported by their individual family unit, employees in more collectivist cultures may work to benefit the larger society and in turn receive support from a larger community in managing work and family needs.

National differences in gender egalitarianism may also influence experiences of the work–family interface (Powell et al., 2009). For example, in societies with pronounced differences in social roles for men and women, women may have greater domestic responsibilities that increase their levels of work–family conflict (Karimi, 2008). In national cultures where gender roles are less differentiated, unpaid work related to caregiving and household maintenance may be more equally shared. Workplace cultures may therefore be more attuned to the need for supporting employees' non-work commitments, because a more equal division of household labor means that both male and female employees will require work–family support. In support of this notion, Lyness and Kropf's (2005) study of twenty European countries found that national gender egalitarianism was positively related to a supportive work–family culture and flexible work arrangements within organizations.

Humane cultures are characterized by investment in the well-being of others, supportive and kind relationships, an interest in belonging or association with the larger group, and low levels of discrimination (House & Javidan, 2004). Similar to collectivist cultures, these values are likely to foster organizational cultures that are more supportive of employees in general. Employees in humane cultures may experience greater levels of support in managing their home and work roles (Powell et al., 2009), via the provision of family-friendly HRM practices and/or encouragement, understanding, and flexibility offered by sympathetic supervisors.

National cultures also differ according to the level of specificity, in which public and private roles are held separate, versus levels of diffusion, in which public and private roles are more likely to blend together (Powell et al., 2009). For example, China represents a diffuse culture in the sense that personal relationships are an important component to business relationships (Powell et al., 2009). This is reflected in organizational cultures that expect people to spend time socializing with work clients and colleagues outside of the traditional working hours; in a sense, individuals blend work and personal roles. Specificity is similar to Nippert-Eng's (1996) construct of work–life role segmentation and suggests that individuals have strong boundaries between work and family roles. In more diffuse cultures, there is likely to be greater integration (Nippert-Eng, 1996) of work and family roles. These differences across national cultures are likely to influence not only the segmenting or integrating nature of the work environment that organizations offer, but also the preferences of the employees native to those cultures. For example, a more diffuse national culture may manifest itself in an organizational culture that permits or encourages employees to work from home, to bring children in to the office after school or during school holidays, and to attend organization-sponsored events with their families. This environment, which allows for greater integration of work and family roles, may also promote individual preferences for integration. A national culture characterized by greater specificity is more likely to give rise to organizational cultures that expect employees to keep their work and family lives separate, as well as individuals who prefer work–family segmentation. In these environments, organizational cultures may provide employees with the tools to do so, such as family-related leaves of absence or access to childcare services that enable parents to work full-time hours.

National culture differences are inextricably linked to structural differences across national work systems and societies (Ollier-Malaterre & Foucreault, 2016). At the national level, culture plays a role in shaping institutional or regulatory frameworks, as the elected officials who initiate and maintain such frameworks and structures do so in a way that reflects the culture in which they operate. These culture-infused national institutional or regulatory frameworks are then likely to influence organizational policy on work–family relationships, as well as how individual workers organize these roles in their lives (Piszczek & Berg, 2014). For example, Sweden's recent move to a six-hour workday will likely influence both organizational and individual approaches to work and family roles. Organizations may need to restructure work schedules and activities to match the reduced schedules of their workers, and individuals may be able to scale back paid care for dependents and invest more time in the home environment (Matharu, 2015). Ollier-Malaterre and Foucreault (2016) describe the combined influence of culture and national structure as setting the premise for "social practices" for the work–family interface, which they define as "the ways in which the coexistence of multiple domains is experienced by individuals and by organizations and the behaviors and decisions that they enact to address this coexistence" (p. 4).

The Consequences of Alignment and Misalignment between National and Organizational Cultures

Above, we have described how national culture and institutions may influence organizational culture such that the two levels of culture are in alignment. However, this may not always be the case. Organizations with a diverse, cross-cultural workforce may face particular challenges in finding ways to align national and organizational cultural considerations. The organizational culture of multinational firms is often strongly shaped by the national culture of their country of origin, the characteristics of which may or may not match those of the national cultures of their global employees. For example, American firms operating in Japan may find that their shorter-term, profit-oriented, individualistic operating cultures struggle to motivate Japan-based employees who may possess more collectivist and long-term perspectives on the goals of work. Person–environment fit (P–E fit) occurs when an organization supplies an environment that aligns or is congruent with employee goals and values (Edwards, 1996). P–E fit research focuses primarily on organizational culture and the characteristics of individual employees, but we propose that this theoretical approach can be extended to incorporate the influence of national-level culture on fit or lack thereof. Employees whose expectations and preferences for managing work and family roles have been shaped by a particular national culture may find these expectations challenged when they enter an organization whose work–family culture is influenced by a very different national culture. For instance, an individual from a highly humane national culture may join an organization with the expectation of finding assistance with combining work and family responsibilities. This individual may perceive a lack of fit if the employer has a less humane organizational culture and expects employees to be self-reliant in managing the work–family interface. In contrast, an employee from a national culture low in gender egalitarianism who enters an organization with an individualistic culture may perceive a good degree of fit, because both cultural environments are character-ized by low levels of work–family supports and the expectation that family commit-ments are outside of the employer's remit.

Person–environment fit across the work–family interface is associated with posi-tive outcomes for both individuals and organizations, including well-being and work satisfaction (Edwards & Rothbard, 1999), increased productivity (Goodman & Svyantek, 1999), reduced turnover intentions (Verquer, Beehr & Wagner, 2003), and greater levels of organization citizenship behavior (Hoffman & Woehr, 2006). However, when there is misalignment between an individual's work–family role preferences and the organizational environment, negative consequences may result. From an individual perspective, research has demonstrated that lack of fit may generate work–family conflict and stress (Cable & Judge, 1997; Edwards & Rothbard, 1999). From an organizational perspective, lack of fit may result in reduced productivity and increased turnover intentions (Goodman & Svyantek, 1999; Verquer, Beehr & Wagner, 2003). This P–E fit research cited above does not take national culture into account, but we argue that national culture has a substantial role to play in determining the fit between employees' preferences for managing work and family roles, and their organizations' demands for how the work–family interface should be dealt with.

Misalignment between national and organizational culture can also negatively impact the effectiveness of organizational programs designed to help employees meet work and family demands. For example, global pharmaceutical leader Merck and Company, Inc. is familiar with the challenges associated with balancing global organizational culture with the individual national cultures present in their sub-sidiaries in over seventy countries worldwide (Muse, 2011). Known in the United States as a leader in offering workplace flexibility and family-supportive benefits, Merck witnessed uneven adoption and implementation of their flexible working initiative abroad (Muse, 2011; *Working Mother*, 2015). In order to ensure that a revised flexible working policy addressed the needs of employees across cultures, the organization launched a research initiative to identify the needs, values, and perspectives of employees from all seventy-seven countries, followed by a process of country-by-country review and implementation in order to ensure alignment with specific cultural and institutional frameworks (Muse, 2011). The results of the program have demonstrated strong cross-national acceptance and satisfaction with levels of workplace flexibility offered, demonstrating the importance of aligning organizational and national expectations (Muse, 2011). Building on the findings reviewed in this chapter, we argue for the importance of alignment between national and organizational work–family culture, and propose future research on this topic based on P–E fit. To guide this research, we develop a new theoretical model of global work–family culture that addresses the contributors to and con-sequences of alignment and misalignment between national culture and organiza-tional work–family culture. This model is presented in Figure 30.1.

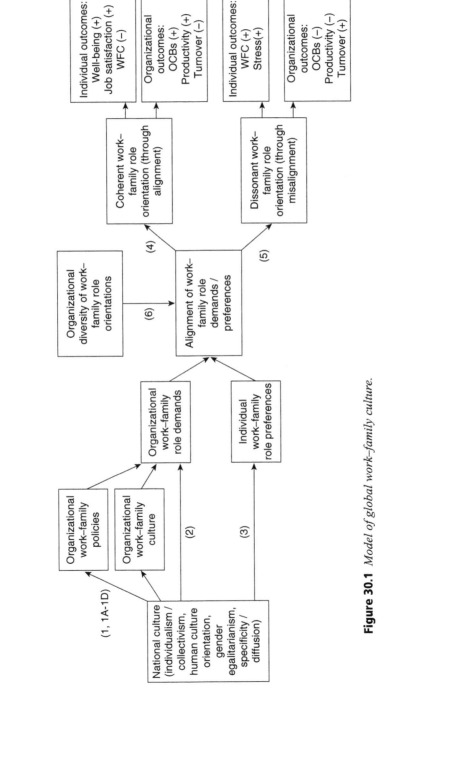

Figure 30.1 *Model of global work–family culture.*

Model of Global Work–Family Culture

As reviewed thus far, national culture influences both work–family policies offered by organizations as well as work–family culture within organizations. Therefore, the first set of propositions for this model are as follows:

Proposition 1: *National culture will be associated with the extent to which organizations offer supportive work–family policies and a supportive work–family culture.*

Proposition 1a: *National cultures higher in individualism will be associated with a) fewer organizational work–family policies and b) individual perceptions of a less supportive organizational work–family culture, compared to more collectivistic national cultures.*

Proposition 1b: *National cultures higher in humane orientation will be associated with a) more organizational work–family policies and b) individual perceptions of a more supportive organizational work–family culture, compared to national cultures lower in humane orientation.*

Proposition 1c: *National cultures higher in gender egalitarianism will be associated with a) more organizational work–family policies and b) individual perceptions of a more supportive work–family culture, compared to national cultures that are lower in gender egalitarianism.*

Proposition 1d: *National cultures higher in specificity will be associated with more organizational work–family policies oriented toward segmentation of work and family roles, and national cultures higher in diffusion will be associated with more organizational work–family policies oriented toward integration of work and family roles.*

Further, we argue that national cultures, through their relationship with organizational work–family policies and work–family culture, will be associated with organizational role demands.

Proposition 2: *National culture will influence organizational work–family role demands both directly and indirectly via mediation by organizational work–family policies and work–family culture.*

In addition, we argue that national culture will be associated with individual work–family role preferences. Individuals' beliefs and values are shaped in large part by national culture, and these in turn are likely to influence role enactment. For example, women in less gender-egalitarian national cultures may be more likely to prioritize a traditionally feminine role like caregiving over a traditionally male pursuit such as career advancement, either because they believe women should be the primary caregivers for family members, and/or because they believe that they will be socially penalized for doing otherwise.

Proposition 3: National culture will influence individual work–family role preferences.

Proposition 3a: *National cultures higher in individualism will be associated with a) less individual demand for organizational work–family policies and b) individual expectations of a less supportive organizational work–family culture, compared to more collectivistic national cultures.*

Proposition 3b: *National cultures higher in humane orientation will be associated with a) greater individual demand for organizational work–family policies and b) greater individual expectation for a supportive work–family culture, compared to national cultures lower in humane orientation.*

Proposition 3c: *National cultures higher in gender egalitarianism will be associated with a) greater individual demand for organizational work–family policies and b) greater individual expectation for a supportive work–family culture, compared to national cultures that are lower in gender egalitarianism.*

Proposition 3d: *National cultures higher in specificity will be associated with stronger individual preferences for the segmentation of work and family roles, and national cultures higher in diffusion will be associated with stronger individual preferences for the integration of work and family roles.*

For the global employee, a key element of the work–family interface is the alignment of one's individual work–family role preferences with organizational work–family role demands. We posit that when alignment exists, individuals experience a *coherent* work–family role orientation: their values and preferences for managing work and family roles, influenced by their national culture, match the expectations of their organization, and their overall approach to the work–family interface is therefore consistent. A coherent work–family role orientation will result in both organizational benefits (e.g., organizational citizenship behaviors) and individual benefits (e.g., well-being and satisfaction with work–life balance). However, when individual work–family role preferences do not align with organizational work–family role demands, individuals experience a *dissonant* role orientation: their preferred approach to managing work and family roles does not match what their employer encourages or permits them to do, and their management of the work–life interface is therefore characterized more by conflict and compromise. With a dissonant work–family role orientation, individuals and organizations may be affected by work–family conflict, stress, reduced productivity, and turnover intentions. The following propositions reflect these outcomes of alignment:

Proposition 4:
Alignment between organizational work–family role demands and individual work–family role preferences (a coherent work–family role orientation) will be associated with positive individual (well-being, job satisfaction, low work–family conflict) and organizational (organizational citizenship behaviors, productivity, low turnover intentions) outcomes.

Proposition 5:
Misalignment between organizational work–family role demands and individual work–family role preferences (a dissonant work–family role orientation) will be

associated with negative individual (work–family conflict, stress) and organizational (reduced productivity and turnover intentions) outcomes.

An important consideration regarding the alignment of individual work–family role preferences and organizational work–family role demands is the diversity of cultural perspectives that are represented in a particular organizational environment. Similar to the challenge faced by Merck in the example cited earlier in this chapter, when there is a high degree of *national culture* diversity within the work environment, it is more difficult for organizations to develop a work–family culture that aligns with the diversity of employees' work–family role preferences. Although Merck was able to counter these negative effects by adopting a more flexible approach to work–family supports, we argue that in the absence of a concentrated examination of both national and organizational work–family role culture, greater diversity of national cultures within an organization will be associated with less alignment overall between organizational role demands and individual work–family role preferences. As diversity increases, the more difficult it will be for a single contextual environment to meet the individual preferences of any single employee.

Proposition 6: *Greater intra-organizational diversity of individual work–family role preferences will be associated with more dissonant work–family role orientations.*

In sum, this model provides a new framework to enhance understanding of the interplay between national and organizational cultures and the influence of this interplay on individual and organizational outcomes.

Implications for Theory and Practice

This model seeks to contribute to theory on the work–family interface and person–environment fit by clearly defining the role of national culture in the alignment of organizational work–family culture and individual work–family role preferences. The incorporation of national culture as a confounding influence on values alignment broadens the scope of prior research on fit relating to the work–family interface (e.g. Cable & Judge, 1997; Edwards & Rothbard, 1999). For example, it has been well established that individuals have preferences for the integration or segmentation of work and family roles and that organizations can offer integrated or segmented experiences, leading to person–environment fit or misfit for the individual worker (Kossek, Noe, & DeMarr, 1999; Kreiner, 2006). This new model broadens the lens used to examine individual preferences and organizational offerings to better understand the cultural nature of their origins. Rather than attributing preferences to the individual alone or offerings to the whim of the organization, this model centers these positions in the context of national culture. By understanding the influence of national culture, both individuals and organizations may better assess personal preferences and environmental offerings (Hofstede, 1980). In addition, the consideration of culture as driving preferences and offerings may help to reduce potential misattribution when conflict occurs; through misattribution there is a tendency to blame conflict on the individual or organization, rather than on the broader contextual environment (Ross, 1977).

Several implications for practitioners can be derived from this framework. First, organizations need to consider the national cultural backgrounds of their employees as well as the diversity of cultures represented within the organization when considering their work–family policies. A starting point may be to conduct a strong analysis of the type of culture offered by the organization, as well as the preferred culture of current and prospective employees, in order to identify potential misalignment that could be harmful to both the organization and its employees. O'Reilly, Chatman, and Caldwell (1991) developed an organizational culture profile specifically aimed at assessing this cultural fit. Organizations may benefit from implementing assessment tools such as this in order to identify areas for concern.

In addition, as organizations expand globally and open offices in new geographical locations, national culture norms in terms of work and family roles must be taken into consideration when local work practices are established. Global organizations may find that they need to adhere to both emic (universally accepted) as well as etic (context-specific) work policies (Pearson & Entrekin, 2001). For example, a universally accepted policy may be that workers are offered a period of paid leave after having a child; however, a more context-specific policy might require local teams to specify the level of schedule flexibility or work-at-home options offered by the organization. In addition, organizations may find that different employees require different solutions even when co-located, due to their individual preferences and cultural background. Offering choice and giving employees greater control over the management of work and family roles may therefore reduce the likelihood of misalignment (Kelly, Moen, & Tranby, 2011).

This chapter has reviewed the influence of national culture on organizational work–family culture, and assessed how the relationship between these two levels of culture impacts employee experiences of the work–family interface. Drawing on the construct of P–E fit, this chapter introduces the idea that national culture needs to be a more frequent consideration in the examination of factors that influence the alignment of organizational and employee needs and preferences with regard to the work–family interface. Particularly in the context of multinational organizations, a more nuanced consideration of the influence of national culture on P–E fit leads to important implications for practitioners with regard to the development of HR policies and practices. Greater understanding and recognition of the impact of national culture on both organizational work–family culture and individual work–family role preferences and demands will allow organizations to develop more flexible and supportive practices, which can engender more positive individual and organizational outcomes.

References

Allen, T. (2013). Some future directions for work–family research in a global world. In S. Poelmans, J. Greenhaus, & M. Las Heras Maestro (Eds.), *Expanding the Boundaries of Work–Family Research: A Vision for the Future* (pp. 333–347). Basingstoke, UK: Palgrave Macmillan.

Alvesson, M. (2013). *Understanding Organizational Culture.* London, UK: Sage.

Andreassi, J. K., & Thompson, C. A. (2008). Work–family culture: Current research and future directions. In K. Korabik, D. S. Lero, & D. L. Whitehead (Eds.), *Handbook of Work–Family Integration: Research, Theories and Best Practices* (pp. 331–351). London, UK: Elsevier Academic Press.

Beauregard, T. A. (2011a). Direct and indirect links between organizational work–home culture and employee well-being. *British Journal of Management, 22*(2), 218–237.

Beauregard, T. A. (2011b). Corporate work–life balance initiatives: Use and effectiveness. In S. Kaiser, M. Ringlstetter, M. Pina e Cunha, & D. R. Eikhof (Eds.), *Creating Balance? International Perspectives on the Work–Life Integration of Professionals* (pp. 193–208). Berlin, Germany: Springer.

Beauregard, T. A. (2008). Managing diversity in organisations: Practitioner and academic perspectives. Report from a Gender in Management Special Interest Group research event. *Equal Opportunities International, 27*(4), 392–395.

Cable, D. M., & Judge, T. A. (1997). Interviewers' perceptions of person–organization fit and organizational selection decisions. *Journal of Applied Psychology, 82*(4), 546.

Donley, P. M., Cannon, J. P., & Mullen, M. R. (1998). Understanding the influence of national culture on the development of trust. *Academy of Management Review, 23*(3), 601–620.

Edwards, J. R. (1996). An examination of competing versions of the person–environment fit approach to stress. *Academy of Management Journal, 39*(2), 292–339.

Edwards, J. R., & Rothbard, N. P. (1999). Work and family stress and well-being: An examination of person–environment fit in the work and family domains. *Organizational Behavior and Human Decision Processes, 77*(2), 85–129.

Goodman, S. A., & Svyantek, D. J. (1999). Person–organization fit and contextual performance: Do shared values matter. *Journal of Vocational Behavior, 55*(2), 254–275.

Greenhaus, J. H., Ziegert, J. C., & Allen, T. D. (2012). When family-supportive supervision matters: Relations between multiple sources of support and work–family balance. *Journal of Vocational Behavior, 80*(2), 266–275.

Hoffman, B. J., & Woehr, D. J. (2006). A quantitative review of the relationship between person–organization fit and behavioral outcomes. *Journal of Vocational Behavior, 68*(3), 389–399.

Hofstede, G. (1980). Culture and organizations. *International Studies of Management & Organization, 10*(4), 15–41.

House, R. J., Hanges, P. J., Javidan, M., Dorfman, P. W., & Gupta, V. (Eds.). (2004). *Culture, Leadership, and Organizations: The GLOBE Study of 62 Societies.* Thousand Oaks, CA: Sage.

Huo, Y. P., & von Glinow, M. A. (1995). On transplanting human resource practices to China: A culture-driven approach. *International Journal of Manpower, 16*(9), 3–11.

Jahn, E. W., Thompson, C. A., & Kopelman, R. E. (2003). Rationale and construct validity evidence for a measure of perceived organizational family support (POFS): Because purported practices may not reflect reality. *Community, Work and Family, 6*, 23–140.

Karimi, L. (2008). Do female and male employees in Iran experience similar work–family interference, job and life satisfaction? *Journal of Family Issues*, *30*(1), 124–142.

Kelly, E. L., Moen, P., & Tranby, E. (2011). Changing workplaces to reduce work–family conflict schedule control in a white-collar organization. *American Sociological Review*, *76*(2), 265–290.

Kossek, E. E., Barber, A. E., & Winters D. (1999). Using flexible schedules in the management world: The power of peers. *Human Resource Management*, *38*, 33–49.

Kossek, E. E., Noe, R. A., & DeMarr, B. J. (1999). Work–family role synthesis: Individual and organizational determinants. *International Journal of Conflict Management*, *10*(2), 102–129.

Kreiner, G. E. (2006). Consequences of work–home segmentation or integration: A person–environment fit perspective. *Journal of Organizational Behavior*, *27*(4), 485–507.

Lambert, A. D., Marler, J. H., & Gueutal, H. G. (2008). Individual differences: Factors affecting employee utilization of flexible work arrangements. *Journal of Vocational Behavior*, *73*, 107–117.

Lewis, J. (2009). *Work–Family Balance, Gender and Policy*. Cheltenham, UK: Edward Elgar.

Lyness, K. S., & Kropf, M. B. (2005). The relationships of national gender equality and organizational support with work–family balance: A study of European managers. *Human Relations*, *58*(1), 33–60.

Markus, H., & Kitayama, S. (1991). Culture and the self: Implications for cognition, emotion, and motivation. *Psychological Review*, *98*(2), 224–253.

Matharu, H. (2015, October 1). Sweden introduces six-hour work day. *Independent*. Retrieved from www.independent.co.uk/news/world/europe/sweden-introduces-six-hour-work-day-a6674646.html.

Muse, L.A. (2011). Flexibility implementation to a global workforce: a case study of Merck and Company, Inc. *Community, Work and Family*, *14*(2), 249–256.

Nippert-Eng C (1996). *Home and Work: Negotiating Boundaries through Everyday Life*. Chicago, IL: University of Chicago.

Odle-Dusseau, H. N., Britt, T. W., & Greene-Shortridge, T. M. (2012). Organizational work–family resources as predictors of job performance and attitudes: The process of work–family conflict and enrichment. *Journal of Occupational Health Psychology*, *17*(1), 28.

Ollier-Malaterre, A., & Foucreault, A. (2016). Cross-national work–life research: Cultural and structural impacts for individuals and organizations. *Journal of Management*, doi: 10.1177/0149206316655873.

Ollier-Malaterre, A., Valcour, M., Den Dulk, L., & Kossek, E. E. (2013). Theorizing national context to develop comparative work–life research: A review and research agenda. *European Management Journal*, *31*(5), 433–447.

O'Reilly, C. A., Chatman, J., & Caldwell, D. F. (1991). People and organizational culture: A profile comparison approach to assessing person-organization fit, *Academy of Management Journal*, *34*(3), 487–516.

Piszczek, M. M., & Berg, P. (2014). Expanding the boundaries of boundary theory: Regulative institutions and work–family role management. *Human Relations*, *67*(12), 1491–1512.

Pearson, C., & Entrekin, L. (2001). Cross-cultural value sets of Asian managers: the comparative cases of Hong Kong, Malaysia and Singapore. *Asia Pacific Journal of Human Resources*, *39*(1), 79–92.

Powell, G. N., Francesco, A. M., & Ling, Y. (2009). Toward culture-sensitive theories of the work–family interface. *Journal of Organizational Behavior, 30*(5), 597–616.

Quinn, D. P., & Rivoli, P. (1991). The effect of American and Japanese-style employment and compensation practices on innovation. *Organization Science, 2*(4), 323–341.

Ross, L. (1977). The intuitive psychologist and his shortcomings: Distortions in the attribution process. *Advances in Experimental Social Psychology, 10*, 173–220.

Schein, E. H. (2010). *Organizational Culture and Leadership.* Fourth Edition. San Francisco, CA: Jossey-Bass.

Schneider, B., Ehrhart, M. G., & Macey, W. H. (2013). Organizational climate and culture. *Annual Review of Psychology, 64*, 361–388.

Shockley, K.M. (in press). Managing the work–family interface. In N. Anderson, C. Viswesvaran, H.K. Sinangil, & D. Ones (Eds.), *Handbook of Industrial, Work, and Organizational Psychology*, Sage.

Shockley, K. M., & Allen, T. D. (2010). Investigating the missing link in flexible work arrangement utilization: An individual difference perspective. *Journal of Vocational Behavior, 76*(1), 131–142.

Shockley, K.M., Thompson, C.A., & Andreassi, J.K. (2013). Workplace culture and work–life integration. In D. Major & R. Burke (Eds.), *Handbook of Work–Life Integration among Professionals: Challenges and Opportunities* (pp. 310–333). Cheltenham, UK: Edward Elgar.

Snir, R., & Harpaz, I. (2009). Cross-cultural differences concerning heavy work investment. *Cross-Cultural Research, 43*, 309–319.

Sparrow, P. R., & Budhwar, P. S. (1997). Competition and change: Mapping the Indian HRM recipe against world-wide patterns. *Journal of World Business, 32*(3), 224–243.

Tams, S., & Arthur, M. B. (2007). Studying careers across cultures: Distinguishing international, cross-cultural, and globalization perspectives. *Career Development International, 12*(1), 86–98.

Thompson, C. A. (2008). Barriers to the implementation and usage of work–life policies. In S. P. Poelmans & P. Caliguiri (Eds.), *Harmonizing Work, Family, and Personal Life: From Policy to Practice.* Cambridge, UK: Cambridge University Press.

Thompson, C. A., Beauvais, L. L., & Lyness, K. S. (1999). When work–family benefits are not enough: The influence of work–family culture on benefit utilization, organizational attachment, and work–family conflict. *Journal of Vocational Behaviour, 54*(3), 392–415.

Thompson, C. A., & Prottas, D. J. (2006). The mediating role of perceived control on the relationship between organizational family support, job autonomy, and employee wellbeing. *Journal of Occupational Health Psychology, 11*, 100–118.

Trompenaars, F., & Hampden-Turner, C. (1998). *Riding the Waves of Culture: Understanding Diversity in Global Business.* New York, NY: McGraw Hill.

Verquer, M. L., Beehr, T. A., & Wagner, S. H. (2003). A meta-analysis of relations between person–organization fit and work attitudes. *Journal of Vocational Behavior, 63*(3), 473–489.

Working Mother (2015). 2015 Working Mother 100 Best Companies. Retrieved from www.workingmother.com/2015-working-mother-100-best-companies-hub?page=2.

Yang, L. Q., Spector, P. E., Sanchez, J. I., Allen, T. D., Poelmans, S., Cooper, C. L., . . . & Antoniou, A. S. (2012). Individualism–collectivism as a moderator of the work demands–strains relationship: A cross-level and cross-national examination. *Journal of International Business Studies, 43*(4), 424–443.

31 Family-Supportive Supervision around the Globe

Ellen Ernst Kossek, Heather N. Odle-Dusseau, and Leslie B. Hammer

Family-supportive supervision (FSS) refers to the degree to which employees perceive their immediate supervisors as exhibiting attitudes and behaviors that are supportive of their family role demands (Hammer, Kossek, Zimmerman, & Daniels, 2007; Kossek, Pichler, Bodner & Hammer, 2011: Thomas & Ganster, 1995). A growing body of research suggests that leaders' and supervisors' social support of employees' needs to jointly carry out work and family demands is important for general health and job attitudes, such as satisfaction, work–family conflict, commitment, and intention to turn over (Hammer, Kossek, Anger, Bodner, & Zimmerman, 2009; Kossek et al., 2011). Thus, employee perceptions of FSS are critical to individual well-being and productivity (Hammer, Kossek, Yragui, Bodner, & Hansen, 2009).

Given the mounting theoretical and empirical importance of FSS in work–family research across many disciplines (e.g., psychology, management, occupational health, social work, and family development), the goal of this chapter is to provide an overview and updated examination of this construct and discuss future trends, including consideration of its emerging cross-cultural development. Family-supportive supervision has its origins in industrialized Western countries, but as our review will show, this construct is increasingly being studied in many other cultural contexts. We begin with a brief overview of the concept of FSS *perceptions*, and its evolution to more recent work that has evolved to assess *behaviors*, or FSSB (family-supportive supervisory behaviors; Hammer et al., 2009), the latter of which is increasingly being used in organizational intervention research. We then move to international research, and conclude with an agenda for future research.

What is Family-Supportive Supervision?

The concept of family-supportive supervision originated from the general psychological social support literature (Cohen & Willis, 1985). Social support is generally defined as interpersonal interactions related to communication of emotional caring, tangible or instrumental help with problems, and sharing of information to help others make decisions to solve problems (House, 1981). All of these forms of social support are resources employees can use to manage work–family conflicts and reduce or buffer work–life stressors. Explanations for why FSS might help reduce work–family conflict often draw on conservation of resources theory (Hobfoll, 1989). The theory suggests that employees strive to seek a world in which they minimize stress, and resources, such as support from supervisors, are used to buffer role demands from the family that interfere with work roles and vice versa.

Much of the seminal work on FSS emanated from the United States and focused on construct development, measurement, and validation. Taking a cross-national view, having FSS origins in the United States is not surprising, given that supervisors reflect the daily frontline delivery of work–family support to workers in the country's employment settings. The United States takes a market-minimalist approach to intervening in employers' support of work–family management (Kossek, 2006), and there are relatively few national or state government policies regarding workplace support of employees' needs to manage work–family roles. This is in stark comparison to other industrialized nations where, for example, the right to request a flexible schedule or take a paid leave of absence for family care (e.g., after the birth or adoption of a child, or self or eldercare needs) may be facilitated by public laws (Kossek & Ollier-Malaterre, 2013). In fact, the United States is one of only a handful of industrialized nations that does not federally mandate paid family leave after the birth of a child (ibid.). Instead, employees' access to work–family supportive practices in the United States is organizationally driven, with supervisors often serving as gatekeepers to work–family support policies (Kossek, 2005). The ability to use formal policies, which can often go under-utilized due to organizational cultural stigma (Thompson, Beauvais, & Lyness, 1999), unsupportive climates and cross-domain relationships (Kossek, Noe & Colquitt, 2001), and is supervisor-driven and influenced by supervisors' interpretation of norms regarding flexibility and work hours (Kossek, Barber, & Winters, 1999).

Supervisors make many decisions that informally affect employees' abilities to manage family demands. For example, they establish work deadlines and help implement staffing and cross-training policies that may facilitate or deter employees' abilities to have flexibility in when, where, or how long they work. They also conduct assessments regarding the quality and quantity of employees' productivity. Such attitudes and behaviors shape the degree to which supervisors are seen as demonstrating attitudes or behaviors that are seen by employees as socially helpful for managing their family role demands. When work–family policies are involved, direct supervisors often enable access, as well as make attributions about work–family impacts on employee behaviors (e.g., job performance) that have linkages to other employment decisions influencing pay, performance evaluation, and promotion, and even possible stigma following their use (Kossek, 2005).

Early Construct Development and Measurement

The early perceptions of supervisor support scales, such as that used by Thomas and Ganster (1995), were adapted from a scale published in a community psychology journal by Shin, Wong, Simko, and Ortiz-Torres (1989) assessing the importance of supervisor support for flexibility for working parents. This perceptual measure of family-supportive supervision (Thomas & Ganster, 1995) is still widely used and helps signify early work that identified supervisors as being especially important workplace sources of support for work–family roles. Thomas and Ganster (1995) identified four resource-related aspects of a family-supportive workplace of which supervisor support was one facet (the others being family information and referral services, dependent care service, and flexible schedules). Given these are resources that might be available as part of either the workplace or the local community, it is not surprising that some of the early measures and studies of family-supportive supervision appeared in community psychology journals as opposed to management journals (cf. Shin, Wong, Simko, & Ortiz-Torres, 1989).

That same decade, John Fernandez (1986), a renowned corporate consultant on supervisor support for family roles, published a book based on his work conducting needs assessments with major US employers to help them adapt workplaces to meet employees' increased work–family demands. Kossek (1990) brought this work into the academic personnel psychology journals by validating Fernandez's measure of FSS, and publishing some of the earliest papers linking supervisor support of family to important outcomes, such as employee work–family conflict. Kossek and Nichol (1992) and Goff, Mount, and Jamison (1990) extended this work and found that informal FSS was even more strongly related to work–family conflict than was the use of an employer-sponsored childcare center.

Later that the same decade, other important work developed in the area. Thompson, Beauvais, and Lyness (1999) introduced the idea of a supportive work–family organizational culture, defined as the "shared assumptions, beliefs, and values regarding the extent to which an organization supports and values the integration of employees' work and family lives" (p. 394). A challenge in using many of the measures that stemmed from the aforementioned studies was that supervisor support was often combined with other forms of support (e.g., flexibility, overall supportive organization, general supervisor support), making it difficult to disentangle the precise effects of the supervisor. Allen's (2001) conceptual and empirical work attempted to address this issue, arguing that it was important to measure perceptions of organizational-level support for family and general supervisor support separately as these are related but distinct constructs. Allen's (2001) work viewed general supervisor support and family-supportive organizational perceptions as being critical for positive employee attitudes and organizational effectiveness, beyond the number of formal work–family benefits offered. Recent reviews clearly suggest that FSS is a unique construct, which should be theoretically construed and measured separately from general supervisor support or organizational support (Kossek et al., 2011). As a body of work began to accumulate highlighting the importance of family-specific supervisor actions, the construct of family-supportive supervisor behaviors (FSSB) emerged (Hammer et al., 2009).

FSS Perceptions and Behaviors: Development of FSSB Training Intervention and Initial Empirical Findings

Arguing that work–family researchers needed to improve upon clarifying and measuring actual FSS *behaviors*, rather than simply assessing perceptions of the support, seminal work by Hammer, Kossek, and colleagues identified and subsequently developed the measure for FSSB (Hammer et al., 2009). This initial work was expanded into experimental field intervention studies wherein supervisor training for FSSB was developed as part of the NIH-funded Work, Family, and Health Network (WFHN, 2016) (www.WorkFamily HealthNetwork.org). The WFHN studies are unique in that they used a national interdisciplinary research team to develop highly rigorous randomized control methods to measure, develop, and implement interventions designed to reduce work–family conflict and improve employee health by altering the way work is culturally and practically enacted. The researchers sought to change supervisors' attitudes and behaviors regarding their role and how work should be carried out in ways that support employees' work and family demands while meeting business needs. Most previous supervisor family-specific support research focused on assessing support, rather than developing customizable interventions to increase support and assess proximal and distal changes across diverse organizational contexts to better understand the role support plays in relationships between work and family life (Kossek, Wipfli, Thompson, & Brockwood, 2017). Previous studies tended to use researchers from only one or two disciplines which likely provides an incomplete narrow view on work–family change, as work family issues are a problem drawing on many content areas (Kossek, Hammer, Kelly & Moen, 2014)

The first of two phases in the WFHN conceptually identified (Hammer, Kossek, Zimmerman, & Daniels, 2007) and validated (Hammer, Kossek, Yragui, Bodner, & Hansen, 2009) a measure assessing four types of family-supportive supervisory behaviors (i.e., FSSB): emotional support, instrumental support, role modeling, and creative work–family management. Emotional support refers to the degree to which a supervisor provides caring attitudes and behaviors related to challenges in managing work and family roles. An example would be providing sympathetic listening for employees' challenges in managing caregiving demands. Instrumental support refers to providing employees with tangible resources to solve work–family conflicts, such as informally allowing an individual to leave work early or attend to a sick child or parent, or helping them get access to work–family policies, such as the ability to work a flexible schedule. Role modeling refers to supervisor actions that exhibit attitudes and behaviors that suggest identification with devoting time and energy to the family role. Finally, creative work–family management refers to win-win behaviors that jointly facilitate employees' family role involvement yet also ensure the work gets done. For example, by allowing an employee to telework one day per week, the time saved from reduced commuting can facilitate increased productivity. During this early validation work, Hammer and Kossek identified a *perceptual gap* where nearly 100% of supervisors rated themselves as family supportive, yet only half of employees rated their supervisors as family supportive). This was an important advancement for the field as up until this time, much of the work–family literature assessed support from the employees' views but rarely was data collected from supervisors on their supportive behaviors. Later research validated a four-item short-form version of the scale (Hammer Kossek, Bodner, & Crain,

2013), ensuring that FSSB can be easily assessed by researchers as a specific form of supervisor support.

Following this early construct development work in Phase 1 of the WFHN (2005–2008), the Hammer and Kossek team developed a web-based training intervention specifically designed to increase supervisors' FSSB. This intervention was administered to grocery store supervisors and included an online training component, face-to-face role playing, and utilized cognitive self-monitoring to track supportive behaviors and increase transfer of training (see Hammer et al., 2011, and Kossek et al., 2014; Kossek, Wipfli, Thompson & Brickwood, 2017 for a full description). The previously validated measure of FSSB was used to assess the effectiveness of the training intervention. Not only did the intervention increase supervisors' quantity of work–family supportive behaviors, it also reduced work–family conflict and turnover for employees who reported higher work–family conflict prior to the training (Kossek & Hammer, 2008; Hammer et al., 2011).

A second phase of studies (2008–2013) by the WFHN focused on customizing FSSB training intervention materials for different work contexts, moving from retail grocery workers to healthcare workers and information technology professionals juggling global work (Kossek et al., 2014; Kossek, 2016; Kossek, Thompson, Wiplfi, & Brockwood, 2017). In addition to FSSB, these studies also examined performance-supportive supervision, defined as supervisors' supportive behaviors which facilitate performance in the work role, including providing measurement and direction, giving feedback and coaching, providing resources for the work role, and supporting organizational and job change. Focusing on broader support for not only family but also work role performance, the next wave of supervisor support research is linked to what has been referred to as a "dual agenda." Fletcher and Bailyn (2005) developed the term "dual agenda" to refer to the idea that family responsiveness is not adversarial to organizational functioning and certain initiatives can accomplish both work and family effectiveness. Dual-agenda organizational change also can be proactive by challenging basic assumptions of how work is designed, and supporting employees as whole people with responsibilities at both work and home, thus enhancing gender equity and family well-being. The rationale for teaching managers to increase work role-supportive behaviors is based on the assumption that support at work for the work role can have positive spillover to support for the family role and vice versa. Although much of the work focused on the dual agenda has been conducted via qualitative field studies, ongoing empirical work and replication are needed to further support these assumptions. We now turn to a review of the empirical literature linking FSS and outcomes at the work–family interface.

Empirical Linkages between FSS and Key Work and Family Outcomes

As the studies on FSS perceptions began to accumulate, a meta-analytic review was conducted which compared general social support at the supervisor level (i.e., supervisor support) and perceived organizational support with employee perceptions of supervisor support specifically targeting the family role (FSS) and employee perceptions of organizational support specifically targeting the family role (Kossek et al., 2011). Such analyses, along with Allen's (2001) earlier work, helped link FSS to the body of work on general and family-specific organizational support. Kossek et al.'s comprehensive study found that family-supportive supervisor perceptions are more strongly related to work–family conflict than is general supervisor support (Kossek et al., 2011). Results also showed that if employees perceive their supervisors as supportive of the family role, then they are also more likely to view their organizations as family supportive. Thus, supervisors' attitudes and actions may be viewed by employees as symbolic of the degree to which the workplace in general is supportive of family demands. Construct validation work suggests that FSS has multi-level implications, and that interventions should focus on supervisors as one aspect of workplace change (Allen, 2001; Kossek et al., 2011).

Beyond work–family conflict, other studies have found that FSS relates positively to job satisfaction (Hammer et al., 2009, 2011), work–family positive spillover (Hammer et al., 2009), organizational citizenship behavior (Hammer et al., 2016), and supervisor-rated subordinate performance (Odle-Dusseau, Britt, & Greene-Shortridge, 2012). It was also positively related to actual performance ratings collected by the organization's human resources department (Kossek et al., under review), sleep quality and safety performance (Kossek, Petty, Michel, Bodner, Yragui, Perrigino, & Hammer, 2017), health outcomes (Hammer & Sauter, 2013; Yragui, Demsky, Hammer, Van Dyck, & Neradilek, 2016) and mental health such as stress and psychological distress (Kossek, Thompson, Lawson, Perrigino, ... Bray, 2017).

Global Family-Supportive Supervision Research

In line with the goal of assessing the literature on FSS across cultures, we turn now to a qualitative review of the research *conducted* outside of the United States. We present the literature with a focus first on relationships of FSS with work–family outcomes, followed by the work on organizational outcomes. Finally, we consider contextual models and conclude with some ideas for moving forward with global research.

Relationships between FSS and key work–family constructs. The majority of cross-national studies on FSS outside of the United States have been conducted in Europe, with studies in Asia and South America also being prevalent. Only one study was found in the Middle East and no known studies have been conducted in Africa. Similar to many studies in the United States, research from other countries (see Table 31.1 for a summary) has further substantiated the relationship between FSS and key work–family variables, including work–family conflict, enrichment, and balance. For instance, consistent negative correlations of FSS with work–family conflict have been found in European countries, including Spain (Agarwala, Arizkuren-Eleta, Del Castillo, Muñiz-Ferrer, & Gartzia, 2014), Sweden (Allard, Haas, & Hwang, 2011), and the United Kingdom (Beauregard, 2011). One study on five western European countries (i.e., Sweden, the United Kingdom, the Netherlands, Germany, and Portugal) found that family-supportive

Table 31.1 *Summary of non-US studies using family supportive supervision measures across country and organization*

Author(s)	Country/ Countries Included in Analysis	Description of Sample Type of Employees	Measure of Family-Supportive Supervision	Independent Variables	Dependent Variables	Results
Agarwala, Arizkuren-Eleta, Del Castillo, Muñiz-Ferrer, & Gartzia (2014)	India Peru Spain	• Managers and executives • Recruited from multiple business organizations from manufacturing and service sectors	Thompson, Beauvais, & Lyness (1999) "managerial support" dimension	1. Work–life conflict (WLC) 2. Managerial support of family responsibilities 3. Gender 4. Care responsibilities	1. Affective organizational commitment	1. Managerial support correlated with lower WLC in Peru and Spain (but not India) 2. Managerial support correlated with affective commitment in all three countries 3. Effects of country went away when controlling for gender and care responsibilities
Allard, Haas, & Hwang (2011)	Sweden	• Married/ cohabitating fathers; from multiple levels in the organization • Recruited from a male-dominated	Developed for the study	1. Family-supportive culture 2. Top managers' work–family support	1. Work–family conflict (WFC) 2. Family–work conflict (FWC)	1. WFC and FWC were significantly related to perceived work–family support from top managers, but not direct supervisors

Study	Country/Sample	Measure	Variables	Findings
	private sector: manufacturing and service industries		3. Supervisor work–family support 4. Coworkers/work group work–family support 5. Work group flexibility 6. Time norms for advancement 7. Time norms for productivity	2. Both top manager support and direct supervisor support were significantly related to work-group support
Allen et al. (2014)	Australia Canada Finland Greece Japan Netherlands New Zealand Slovenia South Korea Spain United Kingdom United States • Managers in developed, industrialized countries who were married with children ages four and under, working 20+ hours/week, from various organizations and industries	Clark (2001) measure of family-supportive supervision	1. Paid leave policies 2. Family-supportive organizational perceptions (FSOP) tested as moderator 3. Family-supportive supervision (FSS) tested as moderator	1. Time-based work–family conflict (WFC) 2. Strain-based work–family conflict 3. Time-based family–work conflict (FWC) 4. Strain-based family–work conflict 1. FSS negatively related to time-based and strain-based WFC, as well as strain-based FWC across nations 2. FSS interacted with leave (parental and annual) policies to predict time-based FWC; longer leave predicted more strain-based FWC when FSS was low.
Aryee, Chu, Kim, & Ryu (2013)	South Korea • Employees and their supervisors at twelve firms • Four manufacturing firms, two financial firms	Thomas and Ganster (1995) measure of family-supportive supervision	1. Family-supportive organizational perceptions (FSOP) 2. Family-supportive supervision (FSS)	1. Contextual performance (supervisor rated) 2. Work withdrawal Mediators: 1. FSS related to performance and withdrawal, as well as control over work time and OBSE

Table 31.1 (cont.)

Author(s)	Country/ Countries Included in Analysis	Description of Sample Type of Employees	Measure of Family- Supportive Supervision	Independent Variables	Dependent Variables	Results
		service firms, four public firms, two other service			1. Control over work time 2. Org-based self-esteem (OBSE)	2. OBSE mediated effects of FSS on both outcomes 3. Control over work time mediated effects of FSS on performance
Beham, Drobnič, & Präg (2014)	Sweden UK Netherlands Germany Portugal	• Professional and non-professional employees across twenty organizations • Recruited from financial services, information and communication, technology, health-care, and retail	Dikkers, Geurts, Den Dulk, Peper, & Kompier (2004) measure of family-supportive supervision	1. Job autonomy 2. Family-supportive organizational culture 3. Family-supportive supervision (FSS) 4. Work–family support from coworkers (Dikkers, et al., 2004) 5. Use of flexible work arrangements Moderator: professional status	1. Work–home interference (WHI) 2. Subjective work–family balance (SWFB)	1. Job autonomy, family-supportive culture, and FSS were related to WHI 2. Family-supportive culture decreased WHI more for professional employees than non-professional 3. FSS decreased WHI more for non-professional employees than professional 4. Swedish participants reported highest perceptions of FSS; Dutch reported the second-highest

Author (Year)	Country	Sample	Measure	Independent variables	Dependent variables	Findings
Beauregard (2011)	UK	• Sample from government employees in the UK	Thompson et al. (1999) "managerial support" dimension	1. Organizational time demands 2. Negative career consequences 3. Managerial support Moderator: gender	1. Psychosomatic strain 2. Work–home interference (WHI) 3. Home–work interference (HWI)	1. WHI mediated effects of org time demands on strain for women (partially mediated for men) 2. Relationship between WHI and strain was weaker when managerial support was high 3. The positive relationship between WHI and strain was weaker with high managerial support, more so for women than men 4. The relationship between WHI and strain was stronger when org time demands were high, more so for men than women
Den Dulk, Peper, Mrčela, & Ignjatović (2016)	Netherlands, Slovenia	• Recruited from 1) Slovenian hospital, 2) Slovenian university, 3)	Hammer, Kossek, Bodner, & Crain, (2013) measure of family-supportive	1. General supervisor support	1. Work–family conflict (WFC)	1. FSSB (and LMX) negatively related to WFC in Slovenian hospital

Table 31.1 (*cont.*)

Author(s)	Country/ Countries Included in Analysis	Description of Sample Type of Employees	Measure of Family-Supportive Supervision	Independent Variables	Dependent Variables	Results
		consultancy firm in the Netherlands, and 4) university in the Netherlands	supervisor behaviors – short form	2. Family-supportive supervisor behaviors (FSSB) 3. Leader-member exchange; quality of relationship (LMX)	2. Work–family enrichment (WFE) 3. Work–life balance satisfaction (WLB)	2. FSSB (and LMX) positively related to WFE in Dutch university and Slovenian hospital 3. FSSB positively related to WLB satisfaction at Slovenian hospital and Dutch consultancy firm
Farhadi, Sharifian, Feili, & Shokrpour (2013)	Fars province (south Iran)	• Nurse and nurse assistants at eleven hospitals	Anderson, Coffey, & Byerly (2002) measure of family-supportive supervision (FSS)	1. Family-supportive supervision (FSS) 2. Work–family conflict (WFC) 3. Family–work conflict (FWC) 4. Job stress	1. WFC 2. FWC 3. Job stress 4. Family satisfaction 5. Life satisfaction 6. Turnover intentions	1. FSS negatively predicted WFC and job stress.
Las Heras, Bosch, & Raes (2015)	Brazil Chile Ecuador	• Recruited students from business schools, who also were asked to	Hammer, Kossek, Yrugui, Bodner, & Hansen (2009) measure of family-	1. FSSB 2. National context 3. Work–family positive spillover;	1. Job performance 2. Turnover intentions	1. FSSB predicted WFPS, job performance, and turnover intentions

Author	Country	Sample	Measure		Findings
		obtain additional respondents they knew (snowball); managerial and non-managerial • Multiple sectors: profit, non-profit, and government	supportive supervisor behaviors (FSSB); seven items	WFPS (tested as mediator) 4. Family–work positive spillover; WFPS (tested as mediator)	2. Both FWPS and WFPS mediated the relationship between FSSB and job performance. 3. With high unemployment, stronger effect of FSSB on turnover intentions 4. With high unemployment, stronger effect of FSSB on performance mediated by WF positive spillover 5. With high social expenditures, weaker relationship between FSSB and performance (via WF positive spillover)
O'Driscoll, Poelmans, Spector, Kalliath, Allen,	New Zealand	• Managerial personnel recruited through membership list of	Clark (2001) measure of family-supportive supervision	1. Availability and use of family-responsive org policies 1. Work–family interference (WFI)	1. Supervisor support correlated with WFI, FWI, and strain

Table 31.1 (cont.)

Author(s)	Country/ Countries Included in Analysis	Description of Sample Type of Employees	Measure of Family-Supportive Supervision	Independent Variables	Dependent Variables	Results
Cooper, & Sanchez (2003)		NZ Institute of Management. • Multiple industries: service and hospitality biggest proportion (44%)		2. Family-supportive organizational perceptions FSOP (tested as mediator) Moderator: supervisor support	2. Family–work interference (FWI) 3. Psychological strain	2. When WFI was high, those with high supervisor support had less strain than those with low supervisor support
Rofcanin, Las Heras, & Bakker (2016)	Mexico	• Recruited from a financial credit company, chosen randomly across occupations, locations, and hierarchical levels	Hammer et al. (2009) measure of family-supportive supervisor behaviors	1. Family-supportive supervisor behaviors (FSSB) Moderator: family-supportive org culture	1. Work engagement 2. Job performance (supervisor-rated)	1. FSSB positively related to work engagement and job performance 2. Culture moderated relationship between FSSB and engagement, where relationship is positive when culture is high, and negative when culture is low
Sivatte & Guadamillas (2012)	Spain	• Company managers, branch	Thompson et al. (1999) "managerial support" dimension	1. Use of flexible work arrangements (FWA)	1. Work–family conflict (WFC)	1. Supervisor support related to WFC, commitment,

Study	Country	Sample	Measure	Constructs / Variables	Findings
		directors, personal contacts • Multiple industries: information technologies, insurance, urban services, automobile components manufacture and wholesale, financial services, insurance		2. Family responsibilities 3. Supervisor support 4. Coworker FWA use 5. Work–family culture (managerial support, career consequences, org time demands, supervisor support) 6. Supervisory responsibilities 2. Employee commitment 3. Turnover intentions 4. Job satisfaction	turnover intentions, and job satisfaction 2. In regression with control variables and all work–family resources, supervisor support negatively predicted WFC
Wang, Walumbawa, Wang, & Aryee (2013)	China	• Employees and their direct supervisors recruited from a pharmaceutical company	Clark (2001) measure of family-supportive supervision	1. Family-friendly supervision (FSS) Mediators: 2. Job satisfaction 3. Relational identification with supervisor Moderator: 4. Work–family conflict (WFC) 1. Organizational citizenship behavior; (OCB; supervisor-rated) 2. Task performance (supervisor-rated)	1. FSS correlated with relational identification, job satisfaction, and OCB 2. Relational identification with supervisor mediated relationship between FSS and task performance 3. Job satisfaction mediated relationship between FSS and citizenship behaviors

Table 31.1 (*cont.*)

Author(s)	Country/ Countries Included in Analysis	Description of Sample Type of Employees	Measure of Family-Supportive Supervision	Independent Variables	Dependent Variables	Results
						4. Relationship between FSS and job satisfaction was stronger for those with more WFC than those with low WFC
Zhang & Tu (2016)	China	• Employees recruited from high-tech enterprise	Hammer et al. (2013) measure of family-supportive supervisor behaviors – short scale	1. Family-supportive supervisor behaviors (FSSB) 2. Work–family enrichment (WFE) 3. Ethical leadership	1. Family satisfaction (self- and supervisor-rated) 2. Life satisfaction (self- and supervisor-rated)	1. WFE mediated relationship between ethical leadership with family and life satisfaction; FSSB moderated these mediations, making indirect effects stronger 2. FSSB moderated relationship between ethical leadership and WFE, strengthening the relationship * all were self-ratings; supervisor ratings were not related to FSSB

culture and family-supportive supervision were both related to work–home interference in all countries (Beham, Drobnič, & Präg, 2014). FSS has also shown to be negatively related to work–family conflict and positively related to both work–family enrichment and satisfaction with work–family balance in a Slovenian hospital, as well as positively related to work–family enrichment in a Dutch university and work–family balance satisfaction at a Dutch consultancy firm (Den Dulk, Peper, Mrčela, & Ignjatović, 2016). The negative relationship between FSS and work–family conflict has also been demonstrated in samples in Iran (Farhadi, Sharifian, Feili, & Shokrpour, 2013), New Zealand (O'Driscoll, Poelmans, Spector, Kalliath, Allen, Cooper, & Sanchez, 2003), as well as South American countries like Peru (Agarwala et al., 2014). Beyond correlations, regression analysis has also found FSS to predict work–family conflict when controlling for satisfaction with job, gender, age, family responsibilities, and hours worked in a Spanish sample of employees from private organizations across multiple industries (Sivatte & Guidamillas, 2012). Thus, there is strong evidence that the link between FSS and work–family constructs is one that transcends national borders.

Global research linking FSS and organizational effectiveness. In addition to having positive relationships with work–family variables, FSS has also been associated with organizationally based work outcomes. In Spain, FSS has been significantly correlated with organizational commitment, turnover intentions, and job satisfaction (Sivatte & Guidamillas, 2012), and the effect of FSS on organizational commitment was found when controlling for job satisfaction, gender, age, family responsibility, and hours worked. In South Korea, employees from twelve firms (across several industries) were rated higher on performance by their supervisors and had less work withdrawal behavior when they perceived high levels of FSS; this pattern appeared to be explained by increases in organizational-based self-esteem, which was found to result from FSS perceptions (Aryee, Chu, Kim, & Ryu, 2013). In Latin America, across three countries (i.e., Brazil, Chile, and Ecuador), FSS predicted self-ratings of job performance through increases in both family-to-work and work-to-family positive spillover (Las Heras, Trefalt, & Escribano, 2015). As noted by the authors, this is consistent with research in the United States showing this positive spillover as the explanatory variable mediating the relationship between FSS and job performance (Odle-Dusseau, Britt, & Greene-Shortridge, 2012). Additional research from a study conducted with employees in Mexico found FSS to be positively related to work engagement and supervisor ratings of job performance (Rofcanin, Las Heras, & Bakke, 2016). Furthermore, perceptions of a family-supportive culture moderated the relationship between FSS and engagement, in that the relationship was positive when family-supportive culture was high, and negative when family-supportive culture was low (Rofcanin et al., 2016). In sum, there is considerable evidence of the global impact of FSS on organizational outcomes, including job performance.

FSS as a Positive contextual mechanism across cultural settings. As evidenced in the previously mentioned studies in South Korea and Latin America, researchers have attempted to uncover both underlying mechanisms of the positive effects of FSS (i.e., *why* does FSS have a positive impact), as well as contextual factors (i.e., *when* does FSS have a positive impact). In a sample of pharmaceutical workers in China, employees' relational identification with their supervisor mediated the relationship between FSS and supervisor ratings of task performance, and job satisfaction mediated the relationship between FSS and supervisor ratings of citizenship behaviors (Wang, Walumbaw, Wang, & Aryee, 2013). Moreover, work–family conflict moderated this relationship in that FSS and job satisfaction were more strongly related for those reporting high levels of work–family conflict (Wang et al., 2013). In another Chinese sample that reported perceptions of ethical leadership, results revealed that work–family enrichment mediated the effect of ethical leadership on family and life satisfaction, and that FSS moderated these mediations, making the indirect effects stronger (Zhang & Tu, 2016). Contextual considerations of FSS were also specifically assessed in a sample of government workers in the United Kingdom, where FSS was examined as the moderator of experiences of psychological strain (Beauregard, 2011). Results revealed that when FSS was high, the relationship between WFC and psychological strain was weakened; notably, this effect was even stronger for women than men (Beauregard, 2011).

Although discussing cross-cultural research that can be helpful for understanding the global consistency with which FSS shows positive impacts on employees, it is insightful to be able to observe direct comparisons across countries within the same study. Several large-scale studies have accomplished this. Allen et al. (2014) tested how country leave policies (i.e., annual/vacation leaves and maternity/paternity leaves) created a national context within which FSS predicted family-to-work conflict. Predicting that FSS would be negatively related to work–family conflict, and would moderate the relationship between paid leave and work–family conflict, they found in their study of thirteen developed, industrialized countries (see Table 31.1) that not only did FSS relate to WFC, but that individuals from countries with longer leaves available had more family-to-work conflict when FSS was low. Allen et al. (2014) concluded that for country leave policies to have an impact on WFC, these policies should be paired with family-supportive supervision. Additionally, in another study comparing three Latin American countries, national context was found to play a role in the positive relationship among FSS and job performance, in that countries with high unemployment saw a stronger effect of FSS on turnover intentions, and in countries with high social expenditures, there was a weaker relationship between FSS and job performance (Las Heras et al., 2015). Overall, through various empirical designs, FSS appears to interact with or create the context that produces positive effects on employees, in addition to working through a myriad of mechanisms.

Key Future Directions for Global and Cross-Cultural FSS

We see the expansion of FSS research globally and cross-culturally to be a key direction for future work–family research as the impact of national policies and cross-cultural contexts have a significant impact on work–family research across the globe (Korabik, Aycan, & Ayman, forthcoming). Below we conclude with several themes for future research. These include the need to attend to cultural issues shaping construct development and measurement, giving greater attention to intervention work that takes into account multi-level country and institutional influences, and the need for more cross-national samples to attend to moderators of job level, gender, and organizational size related to globalization and stage of economic development.

Enhancing Measurement and Construct Development across Cultures

Regarding methodological differences, very little research conducted outside of the United States has incorporated complex approaches to the study of FSS. Below we discuss the need for more research globally on interventions, multi-level influences, and construct development of measures that considers cultural values for support.

Global longitudinal intervention work. In general, regardless of the country in which the sample was collected, the preponderance of the research on FSS conducted outside of the United States tends to be cross-sectional, self-report employee data. Thus, future FSS research within a global context will be most beneficial if longitudinal, multi-source data are collected. Although research on interventions to increase FSS is gaining momentum in the United States, we could not find any studies outside of the United States that incorporated interventions, nor longitudinal, quasi-experimental, or experimental designs. Yet results from these rigorous designs would benefit the theoretical and practical understanding of how FSS creates positive effects on employees across cultural contexts. When utilizing an experimental or quasi-experimental design, researchers have opportunities to delineate organizational, industry, and national contextual variables that moderate the effects of FSS. Similarly, moving beyond cross-sectional designs allows for testing of underlying mechanisms or processes that explain how FSS affects employees, which need to be replicated across cultural contexts. Thus, global cross-cultural research should also consider more rigorous designs that incorporate interventions. We argue that cultural differences may influence how FSS is perceived, construed, measured; hence, future research on FSS should incorporate these more sophisticated designs to advance our understanding of cross-cultural work–family issues and linkages to organizational change in transforming societal contexts.

Cross-cultural considerations in examining FSS multi-level influences. Additionally, as multi-level research grows, it is important when comparing cultures to measure which country institutional level and agent of social support for family (e.g., from one's spouse, from one's supervisor, or from the employer or the government) is more important for reducing work–family conflict or other related outcomes, such as stress. For example, supervisor–employee dyads are very important to the enactment of work–life support in the United States. Perhaps this is because the United States is a very individualistic culture where work–life issues are often perceived as private and something the individual should manage on their own or work out arrangements with their individual manager on a case-by-case basis. As an illustration, an employee may ask their supervisor to work at home one day a week so they can coach their child's soccer team after work instead of facing a long commute. We suspect that one consequence of the United States' individualistic cultural proclivity is that there may be more customized variation in the way in which FSS is enacted in the United States as an idiosyncratic deal with one's supervisor compared to more collectivistic cultures.

Relevant to this view is Rousseau, Ho, and Greenberg's (2006) discussion of the concept of idiosyncratic deals (or i-deals) in the employment relationship, where access to and use of flexible arrangements is part of a social exchange between supervisors and employees as a way to motivate them (Kossek & Ruderman, 2012). Most of the research on work–family i-deals has been conducted within the United States or other Western contexts (e.g., Germany), and research is needed across cultures to look at how these informal supervisory negotiations play out around the globe. For example, in more collectivistic cultures than the United States, such as the Middle East, South America, and Asia, involvement in work may be perceived as a way of meeting family needs and thus, could lead to *reduced* work-to-family conflict. In other words, family responsibilities are seen as being met by engaging in work (Mortazavi, Pedhiwala, Shafiro, & Hammer, 2009). Thus, it is important to understand these multi-level employee–supervisor relationships on a global level and how FSS varies as a function of culture and supervisor–employee dyadic relationships.

Cultural variation in expectations and types of support. Relatedly, research is needed on cultural variation (e.g., cultural values, institutional, or legal) in the types of support expected and needed from a supervisor. Fundamental differences in these beliefs may impact the way that FSS is conceptualized and ultimately measured. Our review was unable to uncover any studies that focused on this issue, but other cross-cultural work on leadership styles suggest there is a theoretical reason to expect differences. For example, in terms of leadership style values across cultures, employees in non-US cultures may be more willing to accept more strict hierarchical and authoritarian communication styles that are less participatory, which may have ramifications for what is perceived as a family-supportive behavior (House, Hanges, Javidan, Dorfman, & Gupta, 2004; Mortazavi, Pedhiwala, Shafiro, & Hammer, 2009; Thomas, 2008). Similarly, institutional differences in laws, such as the right to request a flexible schedule, as in the case with Australia or the United Kingdom, may set up a national context where employees work with supervisors to develop a work agreement that is viewed as family supportive (Kossek & Ollier-Malaterre, 2013). An example of legal differences is the issue that in some countries the ability for women to work outside the home requires the husband's permission (e.g., Saudi Arabia). In such cases, supervisor beliefs regarding traditionalism in gender roles, such as whether it is appropriate for women to work outside the home, may influence their level of family-supportive supervision.

In terms of values, there is also cross-cultural variation related to masculinity and femininity that shape expectations related to patriarchy and supporting men working outside the home as the primary provider. What is considered "family supportive" may have some linkages to beliefs about the culturally acceptable roles of men and women in society as workers and caregivers. For example, in some countries women face more cultural stigma for returning to work quickly after the birth of a child. In such nations, having a supervisor support a woman returning from work after having a child in a country where cultural expectations are for women to stop working once a child is born may be empathic and relevant to FSS item development or interview protocols. Data supports this idea; qualitative interviews with employed Bahraini women attending a management development workshop revealed that maternity leave was not a common option (Metcalfe, 2007). Instead, women described being expected to leave the organization when a child was born, and that flexible work arrangements and part-time work were not available. In fact, 70% of the women reported there was a lack of family-oriented HR policies. Similarly, across nations, having a supervisor support a woman being able to leave work periodically to go to school while working full-time in a country such as Afghanistan where girls historically were not encouraged to be formally educated may create inherently different FSSB items for a scale. Additionally, people in some countries value strong separation between work and personal life (e.g., Germany or France) and employees in such cultures may not feel comfortable sharing personal problems with the direct supervisor but rather prefer the family to provide more support.

Although there is no known research on this topic, anecdotes also illustrate its applicability. The vice president of a major semiconductor firm told the first author of this chapter that referral to employee assistance plans (EAPs) run by the company can be quite effective in the United States, as people are very individualistic and accept workplace support. However, in this same company, EAPs are less utilized in Asian collectivist countries as in these countries the family is seen as the preferred provider of support to manage family issues that involve the need for mental health counseling. In summary, the construct of FSS clearly may vary across societies, and may reflect gender norms and practices in a specific culture. Researchers should be careful to not simply assume US developed measures have the same meaning in other cultures.

Future Cross-National Research on Often Overlooked Moderators in Non-US Samples

Future research taking a global view needs to broaden the types of jobs studied, examine gender in cross-national and organizational contexts, and consider stage of organizational size.

Broadening the job and income populations studied. There is a need for more non-US research based on samples of lower-level nonprofessional employees. In attempting to replicate the positive effects of FSS across countries, it becomes important to also show the effects across different levels of employees, relative to their status within the organization. In the United States, effects of FSS have been found for both managerial and professional-level employees (e.g., Kelly et al., 2014), as well as low-wage workers (e.g., Griggs, Casper, & Eby, 2013; Hammer et al., 2011; Muse & Pichler, 2011). A global review of family-supportive supervision research, however, reveals that studies appear to largely be conducted on managerial and professional-level employees outside of the United States (e.g., Agarwala et al., 2014; Den Dulk, Peper, Mrčela, & Ignjatović, 2016; O'Driscoll, Poelmans, Spector, Kalliath, Allen, Cooper, & Sanchez, 2003), while some have a mix of employee levels (e.g., Beham, Drobnič, & Präg, 2014), or where job level is not noted (e.g., Allen et al., 2014). An exception would be a sample of nurses and nurse assistants in Iran where family-supportive supervision was found to negatively predict work–family conflict and job stress (Farhadi et al., 2013). Another study across five countries in Western Europe did compare professional to non-professional employees, finding family-supportive culture as well as family-supportive supervision (FSS) decreased work–home interference more for professional employees than non-professionals (Beham et al., 2014). Nonetheless, given the lack of instrumental resources available to these populations (Griggs et al., 2013), more research on low-wage workers is important to show places where FSS is perhaps even more beneficial, as has been found in studies conducted in the United States (Muse & Pichler, 2011). In general, it is imperative that cross-cultural research provide information about the job context. Otherwise, it is difficult to isolate whether findings that vary across countries are attributable to differences in samples or other more macro variables.

Gender as a moderator of FSS in cross-national context. One particular variable that is often controlled for, although not explicitly examined in studies within and outside of the United States as a direct predictor of FSS, is gender. In our search, we found one study that compared male and female governmental employees in the United Kingdom, which revealed that the positive relationship between work-to-home interference and strain was weaker with high managerial support, more so for women than men, and that the relationship between work-to-home interference and strain was stronger when organizational time demands were high, more so for men than women (Beauregard, 2011). Another study was conducted only on fathers; work–family conflict and family–work conflict among a Swedish sample were significantly related to perceived work–family support from top managers, but not direct supervisors, while both top manager support and direct supervisor support were significantly related to work-group support (Allard, Haas, & Hwang, 2011). Given the varying mix of males and females across industries, not to mention the role that national context has on the availability of gender-based parental leaves, we were surprised to not find more non-US research where gender was explicitly used as a predictor or moderator, suggesting an area ripe for future research.

Organizational characteristics. Size and extent of globalization of the firm may also matter. Size is often linked to policy adoption rates and the number of policies available. For instance, larger firms simply have more human-resource and work–life policies available (Kossek, 2005), and this may relate to the extent of industrialization of the nation and the number of global firms operating in the country. In global firms, size may correlate with extent of cross-cultural complexity and multiculturalism in ways that shape the ways in which work–life issues are implemented. A multinational organization in one country may follow the work–life norms of the global parent county culture, while the local small employer in that same country might strictly follow national cultural work–life norms. For large global firms with US origins, there may be some convergence of what FSS means. In such contexts, researchers might find it useful to take two levels into account in intervention design – such as national cultural level and organizational level (Kossek & Ollier-Malaterre, 2013). Or alternatively, some firms may follow two-tiered supportive supervision across the hierarchy. Here the parent company's policies and norms may be available to the executive and professional levels, while local work–life norms and supports may be enacted for employees at the lower level.

Conclusions

This chapter has examined family-supportive supervision (FSS) origins and its expansion cross-nationally. We have discussed how the construct has evolved from measurement of perceptions to also include assessments of behaviors; and studies around the globe are demonstrating linkages between FSS and work–family conflict and organizational effectiveness. The movement to focus on measuring supervisor behaviors has fostered a new field of research on leadership development and training and interventions that needs increased attention in the design and implementation of studies outside of the United States. Given the increasingly global nature of work, it is important for research on supportive supervision for families and personal lives to evolve to capture cultural diversity within and across national borders.

References

Agarwala, T., Arizkuren-Eleta, A., Del Castillo, E., Muñiz-Ferrer, M., & Gartzia, L. (2014). Influence of managerial support on work–life conflict and organizational commitment: An international comparison for India, Peru and Spain. *International Journal of Human Resource Management, 25*(10), 1460–1483. doi:10.1080/09585192.2013.870315

Allard, K., Haas, L., & Hwang, C. P. (2011). Family-supportive organizational culture and fathers' experiences of work–family conflict in Sweden. *Gender, Work and Organization, 18*(2), 141–157. doi:10.1111/j.1468-0432.2010.00540.x

Allen, T. D. (2001). Family-supportive work environments: The role of organizational perceptions. *Journal of Vocational Behavior, 58*, 414–435.

Allen, T. D., Lapierre, L. M., Spector, P. E., Poelmans, S. Y., O'Driscoll, M., Sanchez, J. I., & . . . Woo, J. (2014). The link between national paid leave policy and work–family conflict among married working parents. *Applied Psychology: An International Review, 63*(1), 5–28. doi:10.1111/apps.12004

Anderson, S. E., Coffey, B. S., & Byerly, R. T. (2002). Formal organizational initiatives and informal workplace practices: Links to work–family conflict and job-related outcomes. *Journal Oo Management, 28*(6), 787–810. doi:10.1177/014920630202800605

Aryee, S., Chu, C. L., Kim, T., & Ryu, S. (2013). Family-supportive work environment and employee work behaviors: An investigation of mediating mechanisms. *Journal of Management, 39*(3), 792–813. doi:10.1177/0149206311435103

Beauregard, T. A. (2011). Direct and indirect links between organizational work–home culture and employee well-being. *British Journal of Management, 22*(2), 218–237. doi:10.1111/j.1467-8551.2010.00723.x

Beham, B., Drobnič, S., & Präg, P. (2014). The work–family interface of service sector workers: A comparison of work resources and professional status across five European countries. *Applied Psychology: An International Review, 63*(1), 29–61. doi:10.1111/apps.12012

Clark, S. C. (2001). Work cultures and work/family balance. *Journal of Vocational Behavior, 58*(3), 348–365. doi:10.1006/jvbe.2000.1759

Cohen, S., & Wills, T. A. (1985). Stress, social support, and the buffering hypothesis. *Psychological Bulletin, 98*, 310–357. doi:10.1037/0033-2909.98.2.310

Den Dulk, L., Peper, B., Mrčela, A. K., & Ignjatović, M. (2016). Supervisory support in Slovenian and Dutch organizations: A contextualizing approach. *Community, Work & Family, 19*(2), 193–212. doi:10.1080/13668803.2015.1134127

Dikkers, J., Geurts, S., Den Dulk, L., Peper, B., & Kompier, M.A. (2004). Relations among work–home culture, the utilization of work–home arrangements, and work–home interference. *International Journal of Stress Management, 11*, 323–345. doi: 10.1037/1072-5245.11.4.323

Farhadi, P., Sharifian, R., Feili, A., & Shokrpour, N. (2013). The effects of supervisors' supportive role, job stress, and work–family conflicts on the nurses' attitudes. *The Health Care Manager, 32*(2), 107–122. doi:10.1097/HCM.0b013e31828ef5e7

Fernandez, J. P. 1986. *Child Care and Corporate Productivity: Resolving Family/Work Conflicts*. Lexington, MA: Lexington Books.

Fletcher, J. K., & Bailyn, L. (2005). The equity imperative: Redesigning work for work–family integration. In E. Kossek & S. Lambert (Eds.), *Work and Life Integration: Cultural and Individual Perspectives*. Mahwah, NJ: Erlbaum.

Goff, S., Mount, M., & Jamison, R. 1990. Employer supported child care: Work–family conflict and absenteeism, a field study. *Personnel Psychology*, 43: pp. 793–809.

Griggs, T. L., Casper, W. J., & Eby, L. T. (2013). Work, family and community support as predictors of work–family conflict: A study of low-income workers. *Journal of Vocational Behavior, 82*(1), 59–68. doi:10.1016/j.jvb.2012.11.006

Hammer, L.B., Johnson, R.C., Crain, T.L., Bodner T., Kossek E.E., Davis, K.D., Kelly, E.L., Buxton, O.M., Karuntzos, G., Chosewood, C., Berkman, L., (2016). Intervention effects on safety compliance and citizenship behaviors: Evidence from the Work, Family, And Health study. *Journal of Applied Psychology*. 101: 2, 190–208.

Hammer, L. B., Kossek, E. E., Anger, W. K., Bodner, T., & Zimmerman, K. L. (2011). Clarifying work–family intervention processes: The roles of work–family conflict and family-supportive supervisor behaviors. *Journal of Applied Psychology, 96*(1), 134–150. doi:10.1037/a0020927

Hammer, L. B., Kossek, E. E., Bodner, T., & Crain, T. (2013). Measurement development and validation of the family supportive supervision behavior short-form (FSSB-SF).

Journal of Occupational Health Psychology. Online First Publication, June 3, 2013. doi: 10.1037/a0032612

Hammer, L., Kossek, E., Yragui, N, Bodner, T., & Hansen, G. (2009). Development and validation of a multi-dimensional scale of family supportive supervisor behaviors, (FSSB), *Journal of Management*, 35: 837–856.

Hammer, L. B., Kossek, E. E., Zimmerman, K., & Daniels, R. (2007). Clarifying the construct of family supportive supervisory behaviors (FSSB): A multilevel perspective. In P. L. Perrewe and D. C. Ganster (Eds.), *Research in Occupational Stress and Well-Being*. Volume Six. 171–211. Amsterdam, The Netherlands: Elsevier Ltd.

Hammer, L. B., & Sauter, S. L. (2013). Total worker health and work–life stress. *Journal of Environmental and Occupational Medicine*, 55(12), S25–S29.

Hobfoll, S. E. (1989). Conservation of resources: A new attempt at conceptualizing stress. *American Psychologist*, 44(3), 513–524.

House, J. S. (1981). *Work Stress and Social Support*. Reading, MA: Addison Wesley.

House, R.J., Hanges, P.J., Javidan, M., Dorfman, P.W., & Gupta, V. (Eds.). (2004). *Culture, Leadership, and Organizations: The GLOBE Study of 62 Societies*. Thousand Oaks, CA: Sage

Kelly, E., Moen, P., Oakes, M., Okechukwu, C., Hammer, L., Kossek, E., King, R., Hansen, G., Mierzwa, F., & Casper, L. (2014). Changing work and work–family conflict: Evidence from the Work, Family, and Health Network, *American Journal of Sociology*, 1–32, DOI: 10.1177/00031224145314

Korabik, K., Aycan, Z., & Ayman, R. (forthcoming). *The Work–Family Interface in Global Context*. New York, NY: Routledge.

Kossek, E. E., (1990). Diversity in child care assistance needs: Problems, preferences, and work-related outcomes. *Personnel Psychology*, 43(4): 769–791.

Kossek, E. E., (2005). Workplace policies and practices to support work and families. In S. Bianchi, L. Casper, & R. King (Eds.), *Work, Family, Health, and Well-Being* . (pp. 97–116). Mahwah, NJ: Erlbaum Press,.

Kossek, E. E. (2006). Work and family in America: Growing tensions between employment policy and a changing workforce. A thirty year perspective. Commissioned chapter by SHRM Foundation and University of California Center for Organizational Effectiveness for the 30th anniversary of the State of Work in America. In E. Lawler & J. O'Toole (Eds.), *America at Work: Choices and Challenges*. (pp. 53–72). New York, NY: Palgrave MacMillan.

Kossek, E. E. (2016). Implementing organizational work–life interventions: Toward a triple bottom line. *Community Work and Family*, (19: 2, 242–256, http://dx.doi.org/10 .1080/13668803.2016.1135540

Kossek, E. E. et al. (2017). Blinded under review.

Kossek, E.E., Barber, A. E., & Winters, D. (1999). Using flexible schedules in the managerial world: The power of peers. *Human Resource Management Journal*, 38: 36–46.

Kossek, E. & Hammer, L. (2008, November). Supervisor work/life training gets big results, *Harvard Business Review*, p. 36.

Kossek, E., Hammer, L., Kelly, E., & Moen, P. (2014). Designing organizational work, family & health change initiatives. *Organizational Dynamics*, 43, 53–63.

Kossek, E.E., & Ollier-Malaterre, A. 2013. Work–family policies: Linking national contexts, organizational practice and people for multi-level change. In S.A.Y. Poelmans, J. Greenhaus, & M. Las Heras Maestro (Eds.), *Expanding the Boundaries of Work–Family Research: A Vision for the Future*. (pp. 3–30). Basingstoke, UK: Palgrave.

Kossek, E. E., Nichol, V. (1992). The effects of employer-sponsored child care on employee attitudes and performance. *Personnel Psychology*, 45:485–509.

Kossek, E., Petty, R., Michel, J., Bodner, T., Yragui, N., Perrigino, M., & Hammer, L. 2017 Work–family subcultures: Workgroup multi-level influences on family supportive behaviors (FSSB) affecting individual sleep quality and safety performance. In Las Heras, M., Chinchilla, N., & Grau Grau, M. (Eds.), *The Work–Family Balance in Light of Globalization and Technology* (pp. 62–85). Cambridge, UK: Cambridge Scholars Publishing.

Kossek, E., Thompson R., Lawson, K., Bodner, K., Perrigino, M. Hammer, L., Buxton, O., Almeida, D., Moen, P., Hurtado, D., Wipfli, B. Berkman, L., Bray, J. 2017. Caring for the elderly on and off the job: *Journal of Occupational Health Psychology*, http://dx.doi.org/10.1037/ocp0000104

Kossek, E. E., Wipfli, B., Thompson, R., & Brockwood, K. (2017). The Work, Family and Health Network intervention: Core elements and customization for diverseoccupational health contexts. In F. Leon, D. *Occupational health disparities amongracial and ethnic minorities: Formulating research needs and directions* (pp. 181–215). Washington, DC: American Psychological Association.

Kossek, E., Pichler, S., Bodner, T., & Hammer, L. 2011. Workplace social support and work–family conflict: A meta-analysis clarifying the influence of general and work–family specific supervisor and organizational support, *Personnel Psychology*, 64: 289–313.

Kossek, E., & Ruderman, M. 2012. Work –family flexibility and the employment relationship. In, L. M. Shore, J. Coyle-Shapiro, & L. E. Tetrick (Eds.), *Understanding the Employee-Organization Relationship: Advances in Theory and Practice*. (pp. 223–253). New York, NY: Taylor and Francis.

Las Heras, M., Bosch, M. J., & Raes, A. L. (2015). Sequential mediation among family friendly culture and outcomes. *Journal of Business Research*, *68*(11), 2366–2373. doi:10.1016/j.jbusres.2015.03.042

Las Heras, M., Trefalt, S., & Escribano, P.I. (2015). How national culture moderates the impact of family-supportive supervisory behavior on job performance and turnover intentions. *Management Research: The Journal of the Iberoamerican Academy of Management*, *13*, 55–82. doi 10.1108/mrjiam-06-2014-0556

Metcalf, B.D. (2007). Gender and human resource management in the Middle East. *International Journal of Human Resource Management*, 18, 54–74. DOI: 10.1080/09585190601068292

Mortazavi, S., Pedhiwala, N., Shafiro, M., & Hammer, L. B. (2009). Work–family conflict related to culture and gender. *Community, Work, and Family*. 12, 251–273.

Muse, L. A., & Pichler, S. (2011). A comparison of types of support for lower-skill workers: Evidence for the importance of family supportive supervisors. *Journal of Vocational Behavior*, *79*(3), 653–666. doi:10.1016/j.jvb.2011.04.005

O'Driscoll, M. P., Poelmans, S., Spector, P. E., Kalliath, T., Allen, T. D., Cooper, C. L., & Sanchez, J. I. (2003). Family-responsive interventions, perceived organizational and supervisor support, work–family conflict, and psychological strain. *International Journal of Stress Management*, *10*(4), 326–344. doi:10.1037/1072-5245.10.4.326

Odle-Dusseau, H. N., Britt, T. W., & Greene-Shortridge, T. M. (2012). Organizational work–family resources as predictors of job performance and attitudes: The process of work–family conflict and enrichment. *Journal of Occupational Health Psychology*, *17*(1), 28–40. doi:10.1037/a0026428

Rofcanin, Y., Las Heras, M., & Bakker, A. B. (2016). Family supportive supervisor behaviors and organizational culture: Effects on work engagement and performance. *Journal of Occupational Health Psychology*, doi:10.1037/ocp0000036

Rousseau, D. M., Ho, V. T., & Greenberg, J. (2006). I-deals: Idiosyncratic terms in employment relationships. *Academy of Management Review, 31*(4), 977–994.

Shin, M., Wong, N. W., Simko, P. A., & Ortiz-Torres, B. (1989). Promoting the well-being of working parents: Coping, social support, and flexible job schedules. *American Journal of Community Psychology*, 17, 31–5.

Sivatte, I., & Guadamillas, F. (2012). The measurement of work–family culture in Spain and some applications to other economies. *The International Journal of Human Resource Management, 23*(9), 1930–1949. doi:10.1080/09585192.2011.602021

Thomas, D. (2008). Comparing cultures. *Essentials of International Management: A Cross-Cultural Perspective*. (pp 47–69). Thousand Oaks, CA: Sage.

Thomas, L. T., & Ganster, D. C. (1995). Impact of family-supportive work variables on work–family conflict and strain: A control perspective. *Journal of Applied Psychology, 80*, 6–15. doi: 10.1037/0021-9010.80.1.6

Thompson, C. A., Beauvais, L. L., & Lyness, K. S. (1999). When work–family benefits are not enough: The influence of work–family culture on benefit utilization, organizational attachment, and work–family conflict. *Journal of Vocational Behavior, 54*, 392–415.

Wang, P., Walumbwa, F. O., Wang, H., & Aryee, S. (2013). Unraveling the relationship between family-supportive supervisor and employee performance. *Group & Organization Management, 38*(2), 258–287. doi:10.1177/1059601112472726

Work Family Health Network (2016). www.WorkFamilyHealthNetwork.org

Yragui, N. L., Demsky, C. A., Hammer, L. B., Van Dyck, S., & Neradilek, M. B. (2016). Linking workplace aggression to employee work and well-being: The moderating role of family-supportive supervisory behaviors (FSSB). *Journal of Business and Psychology*, 1–18. doi:10.1007/s10869-016-9443-z

Zhang, S., & Tu, Y. (2016). Cross-domain effects of ethical leadership on employee family and life satisfaction: The moderating role of family-supportive supervisor behaviors. *Journal of Business Ethics*. doi:10.1007/s10551-016-3306-4

PART VII

Family Perspectives

32 Gender, Gender Norms, and National Culture: Global Work–Family at Multiple Levels of Analysis

Beth A. Livingston

In a world in which work spans ever-growing expanses of geography and time, we are rightfully interested in the ways in which nonwork intersects with work across countries, people, and organizations. Since the inception of work–life, or work–family, conceptualizations, gender has been at its forefront. Indeed, gendered norms, differences, and expectations emerge theoretically and conceptually in the earliest writings on the topic (Beutell & Greenhaus, 1983; Greenhaus & Beutell, 1985) and have continued to be thematically and empirically important (Clark et al., 2015; Pedulla & Thébaud, 2015). A discussion of work–life in a global context would thus be incomplete without an understanding of the role of gender.

With that said, a significant portion of research in the work–family interface has demonstrated the incompleteness of "gender" as an influence, inasmuch as gender is operationalized and conceptualized as biological sex (i.e., "male" and "female"). Research on gender differences in the work–family interface provides mixed results as to its influence (e.g., Byron, 2005; Duxbury & Higgins, 1991; Frone, Russell, & Cooper, 1992). This chapter argues that a global, forward-thinking perspective on the work–family interface requires complexity beyond the dichotomy of male/female, and even beyond biological sex in general. I provide a description of gender roles as normative and wide-ranging, grounding their known and potential impact on work–family in geographical and historical context.

To organize this chapter, I use Figure 32.1, which demonstrates some of the complexity involved in understanding the effect of gender and gender roles on the global work–life interface. It is not merely "sex" or "gender," whether defined simply or complexly, that affect work and family processes and outcomes. Instead, it is the interaction among constructs of gender and gender roles that create the unique, idiosyncratic work–life experiences of individuals, nested within families or organizations, nested within cultures. First I describe the constructs presented below and the interactions therein. Then I explain how these constructs are central to understanding work and family in a global context as we move into the future.

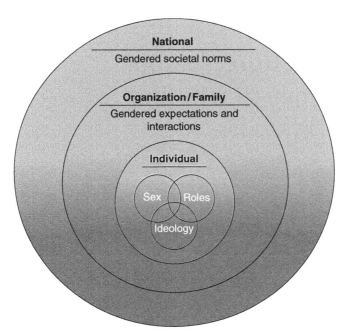

Figure 32.1 *Systems involved in the impact of gender and gender roles on the global work–life interface.*

Sex vs. Gender: An Age-Old Debate

When feminist studies and women's psychology courses and fields were in their infancy, sex was characterized as biology, and gender as "status" (West & Zimmerman, 1987). In other words, you were born with a sex and then, based on outward appearances, you achieved status via your gender, which encompasses cultural, psychological, and social mores. Indeed, commonly, sex is seen as the biologically based categories of "male" and "female" (Deaux, 1985) and gender as the psychological features associated with those biological categories (whether assigned by the individuals themselves or those external to them). Sex is biology; gender is socialization.

These psychological components of sex were among the first to be measured by psychologists who sought to understand the ways in which gender was distinct from sex. Bem (1981) was a pioneer in this space, designing her Sex Role Inventory (BSRI) based on the conception of the traditionally sex-typed person as a person who deeply understands the cultural definition of sex-appropriate behavior and who uses them as the ideal standard. Thus, femininity – a warm, nurturing conception of sex roles – and masculinity – an assertive, dominant conception of sex roles – emerged as a standard by which gender was assessed. This raised additional questions: were women (i.e., biological sex) more likely to be feminine (i.e., psychological gender)? What did it mean when a person was both masculine and feminine? Regardless of the specific questions being asked, however, "gender" was conceptualized as a trait-like construct held, and personified, by men and women via expected patterns. Although the BSRI is somewhat outdated (Colley, Mulhern, Maltby, & Wood, 2009; Wilcox & Francis, 1997), the general conceptualization of trait-like gender roles is still employed (Spence, 1993) in ways that assess narrower self-perceptions of socially desirable traits labeled not as masculine or feminine, but rather as agency or communion.

I expect that there remains some truth to this idea of "trait-like" gender or sex roles. Decades of research have used these scales, demonstrating mean differences in these traits by sex (e.g., Donnelly & Twenge, 2016; Spence, 1991; Wood & Eagly, 2015). Thus, it is important to account for the commonality of assessing "gender differences" (a) merely through the use of male vs. female (sex) and (b) via psychological trait-based conceptualizations of gender (femininity/communion vs. masculinity/agency) in the field of work and family (e.g., Livingston, Burley, & Springer, 1996).

Ideologies of Gender: Attitudes toward Traditional Women

With that said, our theoretical sophistication in the intersection of gender and work–family is growing. Biological sex and trait-like gender roles are both related to traditional gender ideologies. As Eagly and Wood (2011) describe in their social role theory, there are societal stereotypes about gender which form as people observe men and women. Observers then make assumptions about underlying gendered traits of communion and caring (for women) and agency or dominance (for men). These observations then lead others to enact roles similarly and societal socialization compounds the effect by supporting both the existence of and appropriateness of such norms. These observations – of women as nurturer and men as breadwinners – serve as self-fulfilling cycles, and also influence attitudes toward "traditional" views of gender, in which they are not merely descriptive, but prescriptive. Gender, sex roles, and gender role ideologies are thus closely related constructs in many ways. We know, for instance, that women are more likely to report more egalitarian gender role ideologies than men (Judge & Livingston, 2008). We also know that individuals who adhere to more traditional sex-types (read: "masculinity" and "femininity") tend to adhere to more traditional gender role ideologies as well (McCreary, Saucier, & Courtenay, 2005), and are more willing to justify the current gender "status quo" (Jost & Kay, 2005).

Traditional (and egalitarian) gender role ideologies have been shown to be increasingly important in the study of work and family. In the earliest conceptualization, Beutell and Greenhaus (1983) examined the gender role ideologies of women and their spouses, and examined how these women coped with work–family related conflict. Duxbury and Higgins (1991) implied the importance of traditional gender role ideologies by assuming greater role salience of home for women and work for men, as would be supported by traditional gender ideologies, in their hypothesizing. Bielby and Bielby (1992) linked gender role ideologies to the degree to which wives are willing to relocate for their husbands' careers, such that wives with more traditional ideologies were more likely to be willing to follow their husbands' careers, forgoing their own. In addition, Livingston and Judge (2008) found that gender role ideologies moderated the link between work–family conflict and guilt, more traditional-minded men felt more guilt when family interfered with work than did egalitarian men or traditional women, and Kaufman (2000) found that egalitarian and traditional attitudes affected fertility desires, such that egalitarian women were less likely to intend to have children than their more traditional counterparts. Finally, Judge and Livingston (2008) found that gender role ideologies helped to predict the gender wage gap, such that the gap was largest between traditional men and women. What is important to note about these examples, however, is that the adherence to a traditional gender role ideology really only matters inasmuch as sex is also considered. A man with a traditional gender role ideology will likely manage his work and family worlds differently than a woman with a traditional gender role ideology, as these ideologies are linked to prescriptions of appropriate gendered behaviors and roles.

Doing Gender: Gender as Interaction and Expectation

The expectations of one's family members or organizational colleagues are directly affected by the traditional gender ideologies described above, such that the ideologies one holds can affect how one expects a man, or a woman, to act, particularly regarding the work–family interface. However, the impact of these expectations on how individuals are perceived and treated indicates the critical importance of gender not only as ideology, role, or biological sex, but also as an interaction with other people. In their landmark article, West and Zimmerman (1987) lay out the argument that gender is not merely individual role enactment as described with trait-like sex roles or gender ideologies, but rather that "gender" is really something that is performed and enacted in the presence of others, particularly one's spouse. When one "does gender," he or she enacts activities and behaviors that reflect and convey expressions of a masculine or a feminine "nature." It is an emergent feature of social situations – often both an outcome of them and the impetus for them. When gender is performed, what is important is not that one has a particular biological sex, or possesses certain traits or ideologies, but rather whether they situate their conduct in light of conceptions of normative "maleness" or "femaleness."

The symbolic interactionism (Blumer, 1986) foundation of "doing gender" situates it in the sociological literature more firmly than the management literature writ large, but its implications are important for management and work–family scholars. As Coltrane (2000) notes in his review of household labor allocation, "doing gender" approaches argue that people are not automatically socialized into rigid roles; rather, there exists a give-and-take and adaptation to each situation and to each interaction partner. For example, the performance of gender may be most clearly observed between marital partners, as both partners exhibit strong relational goals (Gelfand et al., 2006) and presumably communicate often, and willingly, with their partner. As Coltrane (1989, 2000) suggests, the construction of gender between partners leads to individuals reacting to what they believe their partner expects of them regarding gendered behavior, particularly regarding household labor. As Bittman and colleagues (2003) find, women who make more money than their husbands do more household labor in order to assuage the ego damage they imagine their husbands to be suffering due to the "unconventional" household income segmentation.

This desire to act according to a spouse's genderd expectation in order to keep the peace, maintain a relationship, and assuage an ego can parallel other relationships a person has. Although this theory primarily has been applied to the relationship between husbands and wives, its theoretical conceptualization clearly suggests its relevance to any and all circumstances where individuals interact, particularly when ambiguity exists and one desires to continue the relationship with one's counterpart. In an organization, men and women regularly work together as business partners, colleagues, and also in subordinate/supervisor relationships. How these men and women interact with one another is dyad-specific, and stories of "work wives" (e.g., Rosenbury, 2013) and of the perils of "queen bees" (e.g., Derks et al., 2011) demonstrate the ways in which gender is constructed and performed at work, between pairs of employees or subordinate/supervisor pairs. It follows that these gendered interactions might be parallels of those we see among partners in families.

Global Gender: National Gender Norms and Culture

Finally, I include national gender norms in my expansive model of gender and work–family. The national level of analysis is one often ignored in work–family research and is more commonly explored in broader cross-national research, particularly when one considers conceptions of gender at a national level. We know that the individual gender role ideologies held by individuals can reflect shifting norms in countries (Sjöberg, 2010) and that managers' traditional gender role ideologies are affected by national culture, such as uncertainty avoidance and power distance (Parboteeah, Hoegl, & Cullen, 2008). And similar to what Judge and Livingston (2008) revealed regarding the relationship between more education and egalitarian gender ideologies, the average country-level education is related to more egalitarian attitudes.

But what, exactly, do societal gender role norms entail? Examining gender at the national culture level of analysis can tell us what the broader culture supports regarding the ways that family and work roles do and should differ based on sex (Harris & Firestone, 1998). The Hofstede (e.g., Hofstede, 1983) and GLOBE (House, Hanges, Javidan, Dorfman, & Gupta, 2004) studies both note the importance of assessing a society's view of gender as well as family and work, including the former's "masculinity" ratings and the latter's "gender egalitarian values and practices." These national-level evaluations are related to how individuals interact with men and women within those countries and to how people adapt to changing norms as they travel and relocate. They are, in some ways, aggregations of individuals' ideologies of gender and of trait-based sex roles. In other ways, individual attitudes and behaviors are affected by national norms. The endogeneity of this variable does not render it non-useful or ineffective; rather it demonstrates its complex, central role in understanding gender on a global scale.

Hofstede's (1983) analysis, for instance, defines masculine cultures as those that value assertiveness and competition (as opposed to feminine cultures premised on cooperation and consensus). He finds that countries like Japan, the United Kingdom, and the United States are higher in masculinity than countries like Brazil and Turkey. The GLOBE project (Grove, 2005), which built and expanded upon Hofstede's ground-breaking work, expands this notion into two separate analyses: gender egalitarianism and assertiveness. In egalitarian countries, women are more equal to men in terms of positions of power, education, etc. (e.g., the Nordic Europe cluster of countries). In less egalitarian countries, there are greater differences between men and women (e.g., Middle East cluster of countries). In assertive cultures, competition is valued over warmth (e.g., the Germanic Europe cluster vs. the Southern Asia cluster). Although distinct, both of these studies suggest that national culture greatly impacts perceptions of gender norms and equality. I expect that these norms both trickle down to affect individuals and their work–family outcomes and are they, themselves, affected by the gendered norms and actions of individuals within those countries, resulting in national-level work–family outcomes. For instance, arguments have been made that different types of national-level gender equity can affect national levels of fertility, such that having gender equity in the family increases fertility, while gender equity in the workplace and in education might decrease fertility rates (McDonald, 2000). Women's share of the labor force participation is higher in countries with more egalitarian cultures and their human capital attainment is greater (Clark, Ramsbey, & Adler, 1991). Additionally, wage differentials are narrowed in more egalitarian cultures when these human capital attainments are more equal (Fortin, 2005; Weichselbaumer & Winter-Ebmer, 2005).

Country-level gender egalitarianism has also been studied in relation to work–family conflict specifically; Allen, French, Dumani, and Shockley (2015) found no significant differences in work-to-family conflict by country-level egalitarianism; however, in countries with higher economic gender gaps (a signal of lower levels of gender egalitarianism), family-to-work conflict was higher. Further, in-depth research on work–family conflict and gender egalitarianism suggests that it does not moderate the effect of gender on work–family conflict (Shockley, Shen, Denunzio, Arvan, & Knudsen, 2014). In other words, women in more traditional cultures do not experience more (or less) conflict than men do.

As shown in the review of the above literature, country-level gender egalitarianism is measured in multiple ways. In some ways, aside from the Hofstede and GLOBE measures described above, many other measures almost approach the tautological, particularly in studies that rely on proxy measures (e.g., an egalitarian culture is one in which men and women are educated equally, which leads to greater gender equity; Fortin, 2005). There are, however, other measures of importance. The World Economic Forum's (WEF, 2013) Global Gender GAP Index includes multiple indicators of economic, educational, health, and political equality. The United Nations' Development Programme's Gender Inequality Index from 2012 approaches gender egalitarianism from the inequity side, measuring country-level inequality in human development, empowerment, and economic status.

Which measure one uses may matter, or may not (e.g., Shockley et al., 2014), in predicting work–family outcomes or when moderating the effect of other gender indicators on these outcomes. Researchers should, as a rule, adopt theoretical reasons for the measures they use; this advice is particularly important when the construct is constructed in so varied a way. For example, theories and hypotheses regarding attitudes toward women may be best served by GLOBE or Hofstede measures; those that concern themselves with household structure or income inequality may find the WEF or United Nations measures to be more suited to their purpose.

Theoretical and Practical Implications

Understanding the complex, multilevel nature of gender is critical to understanding the work–family interface on a global scale. Ecological systems theory (Bronfenbrenner, 1979, 1995) suggests that the work–family experience is a joint functioning of process, person, context, and time, and that each characteristic exerts a specific effect on the work–family experience (Grzywacz & Marks, 2000; Greenhaus & Parasuraman, 1986; Voydanoff, 1988). Systems theory thus can elucidate the ways in which a person's sex, interacting with their gender ideology (person), intersects with the actions of gender (process) within a national culture of gender (context) to predict specific work and family outcomes such as conflict, strain, balance, and crossover, or more general work and family outcomes such as satisfaction, commitment, and turnover. Figure 32.2 is a broad demonstration of how each level of gender and gender roles might affect outcomes at the national, family or organizational, and individual levels (bold arrows). There might also be interactive effects among the gender conceptualizations to predict these outcomes (dashed arrows).

The nested model in Figure 32.1 and the cross-level model of relationships in Figure 32.2 have many theoretical and practical implications for work–family researchers. The outcomes described at each level of analysis represent a cross-section of work–family-related outcomes of interest to academics and practitioners, but are not comprehensive; many additional processes and outcomes could be imagined at each level and many more may emerge in the future as the field grows and advances. Figure 32.2 provides an important starting point for researchers in this area and can invigorate research on gender in the global work–family interface. Below I describe a few ways in which the figure can inspire and ground future research.

For instance, though gender theory (i.e., "doing gender"; Ferree, 1991; West & Zimmerman, 1987) is commonplace throughout research on families, it is less widespread in research on relationships within workplaces. However, because of the likely widespread nature of gender-as-interaction, "doing gender" might affect

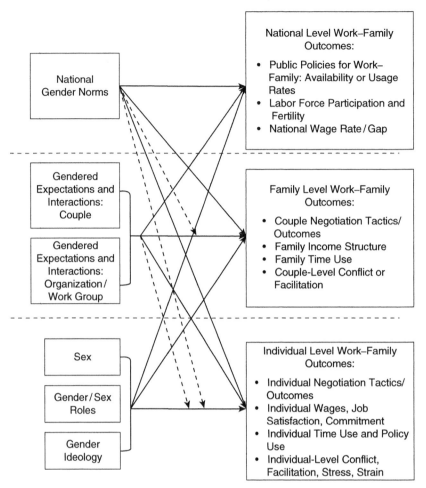

Figure 32.2 *Exemplars of how gender and gender roles affect outcomes at different levels of analysis.*

whether a person feels they are able to take advantage of work–family policies or not (e.g., via "idiosyncratic deals" [Rousseau et al., 2006] or otherwise), or whether they receive backlash in the workplace for taking advantage of them. For instance, does a manager's differential expectations of new fathers vs. new mothers in the workplace affect the idiosyncratic work–family deals (Rousseau, Ho & Greenberg, 2006) they are willing to grant their employees? Gender theory can help us to understand these possibilities.

Likewise, we know that gendered national cultures can affect nation-level impacts of public policy. There is an oft-discussed "motherhood penalty" in earnings which can be alleviated by public policies, such as paid maternity and paternity leave (particularly when part of the leave is reserved only for the father), but only when the national culture is more egalitarian toward gender (Budig, Misra, & Boeckmann, 2012). These attitudes also affect the relationship between employment rates for women and the gender wage gap within countries (Fortin, 2005). But how can the effects of gendered national cultures cross levels to predict other work–family-related outcomes? Some evidence has emerged demonstrating that supervisors expect their female employees to have lower work–family balance in countries with less egalitarian attitudes (Lyness & Judiesch, 2014), suggesting that national norms affect individual behaviors within organizations. We might also expect that national norms will interact with gender variables at different levels, such that women and men might react differently to societal norms, or that national gender norms might affect the ways in which couples recreate gender within their relationships. For example, Ruppanner and Huffman (2013) find that national culture cuts across levels to interact with gender to predict work–family interference, such that cultures that espouse gender empowerment show few gender or parent/non-parent differences in work-to-family conflict. The intersections between conceptualizations of gender at different levels provide ripe opportunities for future research in the areas of work and family.

Future Research Tips

Gender, and what it means in today's more global understanding of work–family, is complex. The models presented in Figures 32.1 and 32.2 cross multiple levels of analysis, but at each level a researcher could claim he or she was studying the "role of gender" on work–family outcomes. Thus, in order to provide a consolidating perspective of gender norms as they affect global work–family, there are a few tips that scholars might consider.

1. Be careful with language: sex, gender, ideology, roles, norms, etc.

Early American Psychological Association (APA) style guides made recommendations on the use of "sex" versus "gender" in manuscripts, although the sixth edition now states that sex is biological and gender is cultural (American Psychological Association, 2010) and focuses on the removal of biased language in general and less on this specific distinction. This does not dilute the importance of the distinction. It may seem trivial to some, but for researchers interested in construct clarity and communicating with others who may seek to replicate or extend their work, these distinctions are paramount.

This is particularly important given the cultural nature of gender. Genders other than "male" and "female" are recognized within many countries. For example, in Australia, one can select "X" as one's official gender (Dow, 2010) if one's sex is indeterminate (an option offered, and legally contested, in some other countries as well). In India, the Supreme Court has officially pronounced a third gender for *Hijra* (transgender women in South Asia, particularly India and Pakistan; Ghosh, 2014). Many other countries acknowledge the existence (and importance) of these "third genders" culturally and/or legally. One makes declarative statements about gender in a global context at their own peril; thus, the careful defining of gender, even concerning biological sex, in one's own research context is paramount.

2. Take an interactionist approach whenever possible, acknowledging or measuring the ways in which gender is created and recreated in the specific work–family context being researched

Whether work–family is conceptualized via systems theory (Brofenbrenner, 1979, 1995), role theory (Greenhaus & Beutell, 1985; Mead, 1934), or via newer theories such as border theory (Clark, 2000), gender theory (Ferree, 1991; West & Zimmerman, 1989) seems to be the one theory of gender that easily cuts across levels of analysis. The ways in which individuals interact with one another under the auspices of gendered norms and expectations cuts across contexts – across families, organizations, work groups, nations – and can predict work–family outcomes for individuals, families, companies, and cultures. Even if the specific theories chosen by a researcher do not encompass "doing gender" per se, filtering hypotheses, methods, analyses and results through an interactionist lens can be a useful tool when considering the implications and robustness of research combining gender and work–family.

Interactions are often affected by cultural norms of communication. Individuals from different cultures enact different cultural scripts when communicating with others (Wierzbicka, 1994). People speak differently, and in systematic ways, which reflect different values and priorities within those cultures. They may often align with the Hofstede (1980) and GLOBE (Grove, 2005) cultural values, beyond that of gender egalitarianism. For example, collectivistic cultures may favor forms of communication that preserve relationships and save face; those comfortable with high power distance may prefer forms of communication that preserve rank and hierarchy. Regardless, the ways in which gender is created, and recreated, between communication partners might vary based on the communication norms that are expected in the context of the study. Though the theoretical expectations regarding gender interactions and "doing gender" may be consistent across cultures, the ways in which this occurs may vary by communication styles and cultures. Acknowledging, and studying, this phenomenon can help advance our knowledge of gender at different levels of analysis.

3. As best as possible, match level of gender theory to level of work–family process or outcome measured

Choosing appropriate construct language is necessary, but insufficient. And, as shown above, the levels of analysis in which one is interested can vary. Thus, it is crucial to specify the level of analysis that is pertinent to the model one is testing. Relatedly, researchers should carefully consider the theories used to make their gender-role-related arguments. In this chapter, I extended "doing gender" or gender theory (Ferree, 1991; West & Zimmerman, 1989) to the organization, noting how gender can be created and recreated in organizational contexts as well as familial ones. Those extensions, however, require an interactionist level of analysis at the dyadic or group level to be appropriately tested. Extensions of social role theory (Eagly & Wood, 2011) have implications at the national level, for instance, but the theory as stated is typically employed at an individual level of analysis. As mentioned in the section on gender role ideologies, social role theory suggests that observations of men and women in society contribute to the development of ideologies of women-as-nurturers and men-as-breadwinners. This may serve as a very circular, slow-changing process when considering national-level gender norms: if a culture is not very egalitarian, women will be less likely to work in powerful jobs, which prevents women from being observed in powerful jobs (which would serve to shift norms toward egalitarianism). Alternatively, a global, multilevel perspective might note how social role theory might be affected when observations of men and women performing work and family roles (and "doing gender" along with them) can be made via media and technology more readily. Thus, scholars examining gender and work–family should make it clear how each theory aggregates, or disaggregates, at the level of analysis of interest. This is true even if the national level is not being expressly measured in one's current research.

4. Directly address national context and its relevance to gender-related effects on work–family outcomes at every level of analysis being assessed

Finally, there is a common United States and Western-centric perspective that runs through much of the work–family field (exceptions such as Spector et al., 2004; Yang et al., 2000 notwithstanding). This is particularly true when theorizing and testing the effects of gender within the field of work–family. It is critical, then, that scholars investigating both gender and work–family clarify the national context from which their theoretical perspectives stem and from which their data is collected. The ecological validity of research, particularly in the dynamic areas of gender norms and work–family, will vary based on these decisions, and should be addressed when proposing theory and when analyzing implications.

Above, I argued the importance of national gender egalitarianism as an important conceptualization of gender in its own right. But one does not need to measure gendered national culture or theorize about it to understand and discuss its implications. Though in this chapter I specifically discuss gender egalitarianism as a variable, national context in general affects how we interpret the effects of gender on the work–life interface. Even, or perhaps particularly, when one is not collecting data or measuring variables at the country level, contextual issues at the country level still can affect one's conclusions.

Imagine, for example, a simple main-effect story: an individual's gender (assessed as biological sex) will affect the perceived work–family conflict they experience. Many authors could theorize, test, and analyze such a story without considering the role of national context, but any finding must be contextualized by the location from which the data were collected. If our goal is to generate theoretical and practical implications that can move the literature forward and that can help organizations and individuals, it seems reckless to generalize research regarding gender, particularly those gender conceptualizations that rely on normative behaviors and expectations, to any and all countries – or metropolitan areas – of the world. Although Shockley et al. (2014) find no moderating effect of gender egalitarianism (measured four ways) on the main effect of gender on work–family conflict, the question remains relevant for researchers to consider.

Beyond actually measuring national context, or running multilevel analyses to control for country-level variance (which may, or may not, be feasible given one's research design), which ways can researchers address national context in their research? The most basic option is to spend time describing and addressing the culture in which the research is embedded in the description of the sample. But, if one is studying gender in the work–family interface, one should also consider the impact of national culture in the measures section by explicitly considering and describing how the assessments of gender and/or work–family may be culturally dependent or idiosyncratic to the location in which the data were collected. One might also consider discussing the ways in which implications for the research findings may vary by national culture in the same way we expect researchers to address the ecological validity and broad generalizability of one's research in the discussion section. Regardless of how one chooses to address national culture, it should become a habit. We, as scholars, should begin to expect discussion of national culture in the research we create and consume – though it may be particularly important when researching gender in the global work–family interface, it is surely a norm we should cultivate throughout academia.

Conclusion

Context, in general, is critical to work and family – and critically under-valued. Understanding how gender affects work–family at a global level requires an understanding of culture, and as demonstrated in this chapter, a nation's gender norms are part and parcel of that analysis. Conceptualizing gender and its effects across a global work–family interface may be complex, but it also inspires new examinations of old and simple questions regarding the role of "gender" on work and family. The models presented in this chapter suggest that this simple question is not quite so simplistic after all.

References

American Psychological Association. (2010). *APA manual (publication manual of the American Psychological Association)*. Washington, DC: American Psychological Association.

Bem, S. L. (1981). Gender schema theory: A cognitive account of sex typing. *Psychological Review, 88*(4), 354.

Beutell, N. J., & Greenhaus, J. H. (1983). Integration of home and nonhome roles: Women's conflict and coping behavior. *Journal of Applied Psychology, 68*(1), 43.

Bielby, W. T., & Bielby, D. D. (1992). I will follow him: Family ties, gender-role beliefs, and reluctance to relocate for a better job. *American Journal of Sociology*, 1241–1267.

Bittman, M., England, P., Sayer, L., Folbre, N., & Matheson, G. (2003). When does gender trump money? Bargaining and time in household work. *American Journal of Sociology, 109*(1), 186–214.

Blumer, H. (1986). *Symbolic Interactionism: Perspective and Method.* University of California Press.

Bronfenbrenner, U. (1979). *Ecology of Human Development: Experiments by Nature and Design.* Harvard University Press.

Bronfenbrenner, U. (1995). Developmental ecology through space and time: A future perspective. *Examining Lives in Context: Perspectives on the Ecology of Human Development, 619*, 647.

Budig, M. J., Misra, J., & Boeckmann, I. (2012). The motherhood penalty in cross-national perspective: The importance of work–family policies and cultural attitudes. *Social Politics: International Studies in Gender, State & Society, 19*(2), 163–193.

Byron, K. (2005). A meta-analytic review of work–family conflict and its antecedents. *Journal of Vocational Behavior, 67*(2), 169–198.

Clark, S. C. (2000). Work/family border theory: A new theory of work/family balance. *Human Relations, 53*(6), 747–770.

Clark, R., Ramsbey, T. W., & Adler, E. S. (1991). Culture, gender, and labor force participation: A cross-national study. *Gender and Society*, 47–66.

Clark, M. A., Rudolph, C. W., Zhdanova, L., Michel, J. S., & Baltes, B. B. (2015). Organizational support factors and work–family outcomes exploring gender differences. *Journal of Family Issues*, 0192513X15585809.

Colley, A., Mulhern, G., Maltby, J., & Wood, A. M. (2009). The short form BSRI: Instrumentality, expressiveness and gender associations among a United Kingdom sample. *Personality and Individual Differences, 46*(3), 384–387.

Coltrane, S. R. (1989). Household labor and the routine production of gender. *Social Problems, 36*(5), 473–490.

Coltrane, S. (2000). Research on household labor: Modeling and measuring the social embeddedness of routine family work. *Journal of Marriage and Family, 62*(4), 1208–1233.

Deaux, K. (1985). Sex and gender. *Annual Review of Psychology, 36*(1), 49–81.

Derks, B., Van Laar, C., Ellemers, N., & De Groot, K. (2011). Gender-bias primes elicit queen-bee responses among senior policewomen. *Psychological Science, 22*(10), 1243–1249.

Donnelly, K., & Twenge, J. M. (2016). Masculine and feminine traits on the Bem Sex-Role Inventory, 1993–2012: a cross-temporal meta-analysis. *Sex Roles*, 1–10.

Dow, S. (2010). Neither man nor woman. June 27, 2010. *Sydney Morning Herald.* Retrieved January 6, 2017.

Duxbury, L. E., & Higgins, C. A. (1991). Gender differences in work–family conflict. *Journal of Applied Psychology, 76*(1), 60.

Eagly, A. H., & Wood, W. (2011). Social role theory. *Handbook of Theories of Social Psychology, 2*, 458–478.

Ferree, M. M. (1991). The gender division of labor in two-earner marriages: Dimensions of variability and change. *Journal of Family Issues, 12*(2), 158–180.

Fortin, N. M. (2005). Gender role attitudes and the labour-market outcomes of women across OECD countries. *Oxford Review of Economic Policy, 21*(3), 416–438.

Frone, M. R., Russell, M., & Cooper, M. L. (1992). Antecedents and outcomes of work–family conflict: testing a model of the work–family interface. *Journal of Applied Psychology, 77*(1), 65.

Gelfand, M. J., Major, V. S., Raver, J. L., Nishii, L. H., & O'Brien, K. (2006). Negotiating relationally: The dynamics of the relational self in negotiations. *Academy of Management Review, 31*(2), 427–451.

Ghosh, D. (2014). Transgenders are the 'third gender', rules Supreme Court. *NDTV.* April 15, 2014. Retrieved January 6, 2017.

Greenhaus, J. H., & Beutell, N. J. (1985). Sources of conflict between work and family roles. *Academy of Management Review, 10*(1), 76–88.

Greenhaus, J. H., & Parasuraman, S. (1986). Vocational and organizational behavior, 1985: A review. *Journal of Vocational Behavior, 29*(2), 115–176.

Grove, C. N. (2005). Worldwide differences in business values and practices: Overview of GLOBE research findings. *Grovewell LLC. Global leadership solutions.*

Grzywacz, J. G., & Marks, N. F. (2000). Reconceptualizing the work–family interface: An ecological perspective on the correlates of positive and negative spillover between work and family. *Journal of Occupational Health Psychology, 5*(1), 111.

Harris, R. J., & Firestone, J. M. (1998). Changes in predictors of gender role ideologies among women: A multivariate analysis. *Sex Roles, 38*(3–4), 239–252.

Hofstede, G. (1983). The cultural relativity of organizational practices and theories. *Journal of International Business Studies, 14*(2), 75–89.

House, R. J., Hanges, P. J., Javidan, M., Dorfman, P. W., & Gupta, V. (Eds.). (2004). *Culture, Leadership, and Organizations: The GLOBE Study of 62 Societies*. Thousand Oaks, CA: Sage.

Jost, J. T., & Kay, A. C. (2005). Exposure to benevolent sexism and complementary gender stereotypes: consequences for specific and diffuse forms of system justification. *Journal of Personality and Social Psychology, 88*(3), 498.

Judge, T. A., & Livingston, B. A. (2008). Is the gap more than gender? A longitudinal analysis of gender, gender role orientation, and earnings. *Journal of Applied Psychology, 93* (5), 994.

Kaufman, G. (2000). Do gender role attitudes matter? Family formation and dissolution among traditional and egalitarian men and women. *Journal of Family Issues, 21* (1), 128–144.

Livingston, B. A., & Judge, T. A. (2008). Emotional responses to work–family conflict: An examination of gender role orientation among working men and women. *Journal of Applied Psychology, 93*, 207–216.

Livingston, M. M., Burley, K., & Springer, T. P. (1996). The importance of being feminine: Gender, sex role, occupational and marital role commitment, and their relationship to anticipated work–family conflict. *Journal of Social Behavior and Personality, 11* (5), 179.

Lyness, K. S., & Judiesch, M. K. (2014). Gender egalitarianism and work–life balance for managers: Multisource perspectives in 36 countries. *Applied Psychology, 63*(1), 96–129.

Mead, G. H. (1934). *Mind, Self, and Society.* Chicago, IL: University of Chicago Press.

McCreary, D. R., Saucier, D. M., & Courtenay, W. H. (2005). The drive for muscularity and masculinity: Testing the associations among gender-role traits, behaviors, attitudes, and conflict. *Psychology of Men & Masculinity, 6*(2), 83.

McDonald, P. (2000). Gender equity, social institutions and the future of fertility. *Journal of the Australian Population Association, 17*(1), 1–16.

Parboteeah, K. P., Hoegl, M., & Cullen, J. B. (2008). Managers' gender role attitudes: a country institutional profile approach. *Journal of International Business Studies, 39* (5), 795–813.

Pedulla, D. S., & Thébaud, S. (2015). Can we finish the revolution? Gender, work–family ideals, and institutional constraint. *American Sociological Review, 80*(1), 116–139.

Rosenbury, L. A. (2013). Work wives. *Harvard Journal of Law and Gender, 36*, 345.

Rousseau, D. M., Ho, V. T., & Greenberg, J. (2006). I-deals: Idiosyncratic terms in employment relationships. *Academy of Management Review, 31*(4), 977–994.

Ruppanner, L., & Huffman, M. L. (2013). Blurred boundaries: Gender and work–family interference in cross-national context. *Work and Occupations, 41*(2), 210–236.

Shockley, K.M., Shen, W., Denunzio, M., Arvan, M., & Knudsen, E. (2014). Clarifying gender and work–family conflict: A meta-analytic approach. In M.J. Mills (Chair) Work–Life Interface Meets Employee Gender: Challenge and Opportunity. Symposium presented at the Work Family Researchers Network conference. New York, NY.

Sjöberg, O. (2010). Ambivalent attitudes, contradictory institutions ambivalence in gender-role attitudes in comparative perspective. *International Journal of Comparative Sociology, 51*(1–2), 33–57.

Spector, P. E., Cooper, C. L., Poelmans, S., Allen, T. D., O'DRISCOLL, M., Sanchez, J. I., Siu, O. L., Dewe, P., Hart, P. & Lu, L. (2004). A cross-national comparative study of work-family stressors, working hours, and well-being: China and Latin America versus the Anglo world. *Personnel Psychology, 57*(1), 119–142.

Spence, J. T. (1991). Do the BSRI and PAQ measure the same or different concepts? *Psychology of Women Quarterly, 15*(1), 141–165.

Spence, J. T. (1993). Gender-related traits and gender ideology: evidence for a multifactorial theory. *Journal of Personality and Social Psychology, 64*(4), 624.

Voydanoff, P. (1988). Work role characteristics, family structure demands, and work/family conflict. *Journal of Marriage and the Family*, 749–761.

Weichselbaumer, D., & Winter-Ebmer, R. (2005). A meta-analysis of the international gender wage gap. *Journal of Economic Surveys, 19*(3), 479–511.

West, C., & Zimmerman, D. H. (1987). Doing gender. *Gender & Society, 1*(2), 125–151.

Wierzbicka, A. (1994). "Cultural scripts": A new approach to the study of cross-cultural communication. In M. Pütz (Ed.), *Language Contact and Language Conflict* (pp. 69–87). John Benjamins Publishing.

Wilcox, C., & Francis, L. J. (1997). Beyond gender stereotyping: Examining the validity of the Bem Sex-Role Inventory among 16-to 19-year old females in England. *Personality and Individual Differences, 23*(1), 9–13.

Wood, W., & Eagly, A. H. (2015). Two traditions of research on gender identity. *Sex Roles, 73* (11–12), 461–473.

World Economic Forum. (2013). *The Global Gender Gap Report*. Geneva, Switzerland: World Economic Forum.

Yang, N., Chen, C. C., Choi, J., & Zou, Y. (2000). Sources of work-family conflict: a Sino-US comparison of the effects of work and family demands. *Academy of Management Journal, 43*(1), 113–123.

33 Fatherhood, Work, and Family across the Globe: A Review and Research Agenda

Scott Behson, Erin Kramer Holmes, E. Jeffrey Hill, and Nathan L. Robbins

Although fatherhood is an under-researched and under-publicized topic, empirical evidence is clear that involved and caring fathers are important for the optimal development of children (Lamb, 2004; Raeburn, 2015). Whether biological, adoptive, or stepfathers, fathers can influence their children at every stage of development. Alternatively, their absence may have long-lasting repercussions. However, simply knowing that fathers are instrumental in their children's lives is not sufficient to guarantee involvement; research has also documented many barriers to parenting that men experience, as well as key areas in which fathers need encouragement to be the type of involved and caring parent their children need.

The purpose of this chapter is to focus on global and cross-cultural research establishing the benefits of increased father family involvement to children, women, men, and society. We further discuss the barriers to involvement that exist, focusing specifically on the work–family interface. We then explore ways in which men can be encouraged to be more involved fathers, including via public policy and workplace practice.

The Influence of Father Involvement on Children

Research shows that fathers can positively influence all four key aspects of child development: behavioral, emotional/psychological, social, and cognitive/academic. Involved fathers influence the emotional/psychological development of their children for good. Children with warm and emotionally responsive fathers are less emotionally reactive (Byrd-Craven, Auer, Granger, & Massey, 2012), have higher levels of overall well-being (Amato, 1994), and experience less depression (Culpin, Heron, Araya, Melotti, & Joinson, 2013) and mood and anxiety disorders (Goodwin & Styron, 2012). Father involvement with children at age seven reduces risk of psychological maladjustment and involvement at age sixteen predicts lower psychological distress in adulthood (Flouri & Buchanan, 2003).

Likewise, greater father involvement benefits children socially, behaviorally, and cognitively. Children with warm fathers tend to relate better with other children (Baker, Fenning, & Crnic, 2011) and to exhibit more prosocial behaviors towards others (Flouri, 2005). Behaviorally, father involvement is associated with decreased levels of externalizing behavior (Day & Padilla-Walker, 2009), less hyperactivity and dysregulation (Flouri, 2008), and greater behavioral self-regulation (Owen et al., 2013) in children. Finally, on average, children with more involved fathers have higher IQs (Yogman, Kindlon, & Earls, 1995), increased executive function (Meuwissen & Carlson, 2015), improved school conduct (Forehand & Nousiainen, 1993), and increased scholastic self-concept (DuBois, Eitel, & Felner, 1994).

The Influence of Father Involvement on Women

Involved fathers' influence on children has been a major area of focus in the last three decades of fathering research (Lamb, 2004), but its influence on women has only recently begun to be studied. These recent findings suggest that father involvement is associated with many positive outcomes for the mothers involved. Women whose partners are involved prenatally use more health services, experience lighter workloads, and have a lower risk of post-partum depression (Levtov, van der Gaag, Green, Kaufman, & Barker, 2015). The wage gap between genders has been well established, with women earning significantly less than men in the majority of developed nations (Levtov et al., 2015). The wage gap becomes larger when men and women have children, with men's wages increasing after they have children and women's wages decreasing (Kmec, 2011). However, in countries where fathers hold more egalitarian views towards childrearing and non-paid care, the wage gap is smaller (Andringa, Nieuwenhuis, & van Gerven, 2015). Fathers who are more involved in the home also promote future generations of involvement and gender equality; their daughters are more likely to have higher career aspirations (Croft, Schmader, Block, & Baron, 2014), and their sons are more likely to engage in more egalitarian behaviors in their own relationships (Levtov et al., 2015).

The Influence of Father Involvement on Men

One overlooked beneficiary of father involvement is the father himself. In fact, research shows that involved fathers tend to be happier and healthier than less involved fathers (Levtov et al., 2015; Palkovitz, 2002). Meaningful involvement with their children is reported by fathers to be among their most important sources of well-being and happiness (Eggebeen & Knoester, 2001). Health benefits are also associated with father involvement. Studies find that fathers who report close, non-violent connections with their children live longer, have fewer mental and physical health problems, are less likely to abuse drugs, are more productive at work, and report being happier than men who do not have this strong connection (e.g., Burgess, 2006). Most fathers aspire to success not just in their careers but also as involved, loving fathers (Behson, 2015a; Harrington, Van Deusen, & Humberd, 2011).

The Influence of Father Involvement on Society

In light of the positive influence of father involvement on children, women, and men, it is not surprising that involved fathers also benefit their communities and nations. Involved fathers are more likely to be involved in their neighborhoods, regularly attend religious service, and engage in community service (Eggebeen, Knoester, & McDaniel, 2013). In addition, considering the aforementioned influence of father involvement on gender equity at work and on women's paid work participation rates, support for fathers has brought economic benefits to a country. It is estimated that if women participated in the labor force at the same rate as men, it could lead to substantial increases in gross domestic product (GDP), ranging from 5% in the United States to 9% in Japan and 34% in Egypt (OECD, 2012). Finally, both men and women who report higher satisfaction with their work–family balance tend to be absent less and quit less often, as well as become more engaged and productive at work (Ladge, Humberd, Watkins, & Harrington, 2015). Employer support for working fathers, such as leave and flexibility, leads to better balance for both men and their working spouses (e.g., Harrington, Van Deusen, Fraone, Eddy, & Haas, 2014). Further, leave and flexibility have been linked to improved business results (Bond, Galinsky, & Hill, 2004).

Predictors and Barriers of Father Involvement

As a whole, men's involvement in parenting activities is susceptible to a wide amount of variation due to a number of factors. The largest and most consistent predictors of involvement can be broken into two categories: employment and the relationship with the mother, both of which are highly related with gender roles and norms. Despite overall increasing gender equality, a survey of twenty countries found that a majority of both men and women named financial provision as the primary responsibility of fathers (Munoz Boudet, Petesch, Turk, & Thumala, 2013). This belief makes employment the minimum requirement for father involvement, which is particularly problematic for low-income men (see Nelson, 2004). In more traditional settings, it makes financial provision the only requirement.

Several other predictors of a father's involvement stem from the relationship he has with the child's mother. These include maternal gatekeeping, or mothers acting in ways to discourage or promote father-child interactions (Allen & Hawkins, 1999; Schoppe-Sullivan, Brown, Cannon, Mangelsdorf, & Sokolowski, 2008), relationship satisfaction (Erel & Burman, 1995), co-parenting quality (Hohmann-Marriott, 2009), and family structure (Hofferth, Pleck, Goldscheider, Curtin, & Hrapczynski, 2013). Further, fathers who are not married to their child's mother as well as divorced non-custodial fathers are often prevented from being as involved with their children as they would like to be. This can be partially attributed to pervasive post-divorce preference for awarding primary custody to mothers, and by policies that make paternal access to children dependent upon financial provision (Heilman, Cole,

Matos, Hassink, Mincy, & Barker, 2016). For men with lower income potential or with barriers to employment, such as a past criminal record, these barriers may be insurmountable. Such obstacles are often at odds with the purported standard of the "best interest of the child" when adjudicating post-divorce arrangements (Raub, Carson, Cook, Wyshak, & Hauser, 2013).

Both categories of predictors (i.e., employment and the maternal relationship) are highly related to societal norms regarding gender roles held by both men and women. Men with more traditional views of the provisional father role tend to work longer hours and experience greater amounts of work–family conflict (Huffman, Olson, O'Gara, & King, 2014), and mothers' work hours are more predictive of father involvement than fathers' work hours (Norman, Elliot, & Fagan, 2014), indicating that a woman's decision to work or stay home has a large influence on a man's involvement as well. Parents' views on gender roles play a large part in how the maternal relationship impacts father involvement. Maternal gatekeeping might be viewed as, at least in part, a result of the belief that the woman is the primary caregiver and men have a more auxiliary role. Indeed, both the mother's (Maurer, Pleck, & Rane, 2001) and father's (Bonney, Kelley, & Levant, 1999) perceptions of the father's ability to parent have a large impact on whether he gets involved or not. Because role norms are often reinforced ubiquitously, and because of their inherent effect on men's involvement with their children, a multifaceted approach – both in the workplace and in the home – is required to encourage greater participation from men with their children and families.

Data indicates that gender norms vary by culture and across time. Throughout the world, gender norms range from relatively egalitarian societies to societies that exhibit high gender differentiation, hierarchy, and masculine orientation. In the latter cultures, the roles of men and women are particularly separate, leading to wider division of household labor, lower female labor force participation, and lower father involvement in day-to-day parenting and household management (e.g., Fuwa, 2004). Additionally, research focusing on generational differences in attitudes towards masculinity and parenting indicate that successively younger generations of fathers see themselves as both providers and caretakers, more commonly aspire to more egalitarian shared-care family arrangements, and are more likely to be married to women who work outside the home (e.g., Beutell & Behson, 2015; Samuel, 2016). Further, millennial men are more likely to seek out family-supportive employers even before they become fathers, and are more likely to demand workplace accommodations. Millennial dads also aspire to closer, more intimate relationships with their children, as opposed to models of fatherhood as distant authority figures (Harrington, Fraone, Lee, & Levey, 2016).

Paternal Leave and Encouragement of Involvement in the Home

Recent research on the effects of paternal leave has depicted experiences unfolding similarly among young couples awaiting their first child. Even after establishing equal divisions of domestic work and intending for these patterns of behavior to continue after the baby is born, parents slowly end up taking on more traditional roles of parenting (Miller, 2011). In the United States, this is due to the fact that mothers typically have at least three weeks of unpaid maternity leave while the father may take a day or two off work (Behson, 2015a). The mother begins to establish new patterns of primary care for the child, while the father's attempts at care slowly wane when his performance is seen as not on par with the mother's (Fagan & Barnett, 2003; Holmes, Duncan, Bair, & White, 2007).

Granting paternity leave has been proven to prevent this slide into gendered parenting patterns and promote more equality in childrearing. Fathers who take any paternity leave at all are much more likely to change diapers, feed the baby, and get up in the night with the child than fathers who do not (Tanaka & Waldfogel, 2007). Conversely, Tanaka and Waldfogel also found that fathers who work longer hours report a decrease in these activities. Rehel (2014) summed it up rather succinctly in her report on paternal leave, stating that "when the transition to parenthood is structured for fathers in ways comparable to mothers, fathers come to think about and enact parenting in ways that are similar to mothers" (p. 111). In other words, fathers are not simply engaging in more caretaking activities, they are embracing the attitudes and behaviors that come with being an equal partner in parenting.

It should be noted that making paternity leave available to men is not in and of itself sufficient. Although men who are offered paternity leave are five times more likely to take leave after childbirth than men to whom it is not available (Tanaka & Waldfogel, 2007), there are often larger factors at play. Even in households with equitable parenting and work attitudes between mothers and fathers, there are stigmas surrounding extended leave that may influence men differently than women. One study found that for women, the main consideration for the length of leave was her level of family orientation and the centrality of her role as a mother. For men, however, the primary influence on leave duration was the economic impact it would have (Duvander, 2014). Put differently, the financial costs involved in parental leave may be much higher for men than women.

In a more global context, while there are only two OECD countries that do not provide for some amount of maternity leave, only 67 of the 167 countries studied by the International Labour Office (Addati, Cassirer, & Gilchrist, 2014) provide for some form of paternity leave, and only 16 provide for leaves greater than 16 days. However, there has been considerable progress in many countries in extending parental leave to fathers, either by including wage replacement, setting aside "use it or lose it" leave designated for fathers (as in Portugal), or by allocating a certain amount of leave for a couple to divide between themselves for an arrangement that works best for them (as in Scandinavia). For example, the rates at which fathers utilized available paternity leave rose dramatically in Quebec, Canada and California, USA once there was a provision of partial wage replacement (Rehel, 2014). In California, the first American state to implement paid parental leave, the percentage of leaves taken by men has increased steadily to 31%, indicating that, over time, cultural norms can change (Milkman & Appelbaum, 2013). As mentioned earlier, paternity leave can increase father family involvement, and this involvement is associated with benefits for children, mothers, fathers, businesses, economies, and societies (Behson, 2015b; Heilman et al., 2016).

The Father-Friendly Work Environment

In a global study of working parents from seventy-four countries, Hill et al. (2012) found that fathers reported longer work hours and more overnight travel than mothers, but reported less organizational and supervisory work–family support. Compared with mothers, fathers were less aware of work–family programs, less likely to have used work–family programs in the past, and less likely to be planning to use work–family programs in the future. Fathers who used work–family programs evaluated them less favorably than mothers did. In addition, fathers were much more likely to use work–family programs that did not reduce their compensation (e.g., work at home) than programs that did (e.g., part-time employment, leaves). These results support the notion that fathers experience the workplace differently than women and may face additional hurdles to work–family balance and involved parenthood.

Evidence is growing, however, that workplaces that enact policies to encourage father involvement provide mutually beneficial results to both parties involved. Companies benefit because involved fathers work harder (Astone, Dariotis, Sonenstein, Pleck, & Hynes, 2010), show more loyalty (Leschyshyn & Minnotte, 2014), and have higher job satisfaction and less work–family conflict (Ladge, Humberd, Watkins, & Harrington, 2015). Other benefits include advantages in recruiting talented employees and even a short-term increase in stock prices when leave policies are announced (Behson, 2015b). Fathers and their families benefit because they live more healthily (Astone & Peters, 2014), engage in less risky behaviors (Weitoft, Burström, & Rosén, 2004), behave more altruistically in social relationships (Eggebeen, Dew, & Knoester, 2010), and attain higher incomes (Keizer, Dykstra, & Poortman, 2010). Men with flexible schedules report higher levels of involvement with their children, which is true even for low-income and nonresident fathers (Castillo, Welch, & Sarver, 2012). Australian fathers with lower levels of work–family conflict displayed warmer, less irritable, and more consistent parenting behaviors than men with higher levels of conflict (Cooklin, Westrupp, Strazdins, Giallo, Martin, & Nicholson, 2014). Fathers with rigid schedules and low levels of work–family balance report higher amounts of stress, which negatively impacts the work–family balance of working mothers (Fagan & Press, 2008), further disrupting family well-being.

In addition to research substantiating the benefits of supportive workplaces to both businesses and families, the results of some studies are less clear-cut and show that usage and acceptability may vary by gender. Research comparing the acceptability of different types of workplace flexibility showed that overall, using flextime was much more acceptable than using flexplace. If flexplace opportunities were requested, respondents viewed fathers' requests most favorably, followed by mothers and then men with no children (Singley & Hynes, 2005). These social norms are perpetuated outside of organizational settings as well; self-employed fathers were much more likely than self-employed mothers to work outside of the home (Craig, Powell, & Cortis, 2012). Additionally, both fathers and mothers alike are viewed as less agentic and less committed to employment than non-parents, though fathers are held to less strict standards than mothers and childless men (Fuegen, Biernat, Haines, & Deaux, 2004).

Recent research demonstrates that when it is offered, American men are increasingly taking two paid weeks of paternity leave (Harrington et al., 2014). It is further reported that 89% of American men consider paid paternity leave at least somewhat important when evaluating employers and potential employers. Despite these encouraging statistics, other research has found that American men who use paternity leave or other workplace accommodations for family face considerable stigma from their employers (Behson, 2013). Many are reluctant to use paternity leave for fear of being seen as uncommitted and unmanly, perceptions which are linked to lower performance evaluations, increased risks of being demoted or downsized, and reduced pay and rewards (Rudman & Mescher, 2013). Men also fear potential career consequences (Vandello, Hettinger, Bosson, & Siddiqi, 2013); specifically, fathers who are seen by bosses and coworkers as engaging in higher-than-average levels of childcare are subject to more workplace harassment and more general mistreatment as compared to their low-caregiving or childless counterparts (Berdahl & Moon, 2013). Finally, men who interrupt their employment for family reasons earn significantly less after returning to work (Coltrane, Miller, DeHaan, & Stewart, 2013).

Many men internalize this pressure themselves, in that they are attuned to societal norms regarding masculinity. Where they see other men using family policies and increasing family involvement, they are more likely to do so (Thebaud & Pedulla, 2016). This research indicates that cultural pressure comes not only from employers but also from peers and societal signals, such as media depictions of fathers. Thus, even American employees who can take paternity leave often feel social pressure at work that dissuades them. Furthermore, in the United States, the lack of federal policy on this matter means only about 44% of private-sector employees are offered paid paternity leave. As discussed earlier, the real and felt need for men to provide for their families makes unpaid leave more difficult for fathers to take.

In some countries, workplace environments have made significant progress. In Germany, for example, men who took parental leave were rated as more likeable and suffered no decrease in respect or competence, independent of whether they took two-, four-, or twelve-month leaves (Fleischmann & Sieverding, 2015). Other countries have made significant progress in some areas while lagging in others. For instance, in Sweden, flexible work arrangements and support of leave are much more acceptable in white-collar jobs than in working-class jobs (Haas & Hwang, 2009). There have been repeated calls by advocates, experts, government agencies, human resources professionals and some leading executives for companies to move beyond policy and accelerate cultural change to truly support working fathers.

Several media outlets, such as *Fortune* magazine, *Working Mother* magazine, and Fatherly.com have also compiled excellent comparative information on family-friendly and father-friendly employers. Business press also often describe best practices in this area. For example, Ryan, LLC implemented widespread flexibility and a new performance evaluation system that tracks performance instead of tracking where, when, and how people accomplished their goals. Volkswagen restricts the use of employee emails after-hours. State Street encourages managers to initiate conversations with employees regarding relevant flexibility options. EY and the other "Big Four" accounting firms have implemented long (eight-to-twelve-week) paid paternity leaves and encourage employee teams to support each other's need for time off and flexibility. IKEA offers a slate of work–family polices for workers. Other companies have initiated policies that reduce expectations for overwork, encourage full use of vacation and other paid time off, and provide childcare and other concierge services to make home life easier. Further, based on their survey of working fathers, Boston College's Center for Work and Family asked men what they look for in an employer and found that in addition to pay and job security, men equally valued time for life, flexibility, and the ability to do meaningful work (Harrington et al., 2011). Taken together, there is mounting evidence on how to better support working fathers and also how doing so is good for financial performance.

Cross-Cultural Fatherhood and Work–Family Research

In the introduction to his thesis in which he studies fatherhood and work–life in the Catalan region of Spain, Grau-Grau (2016) observes, "most of the research on WFB has been conducted in an Anglophone context (mainly the United States and the United Kingdom) and more recently in Europe, especially in Nordic countries and the Netherlands. Obviously, there are exceptions around the world, but the literature has been dominated by studies in post-industrial societies" (p. 7). In conducting the literature review for this chapter, we also made the same observation. However, we are encouraged by new work extending the reach of fatherhood research to a broader range of countries and cultures.

Some of this promising cross-cultural work includes research on dual-earner couples and fathers in Asia as well as research exploring the work–family interface in Africa. Much of the work conducted in Asia is chronicled in the *Handbook on Research on Work–Life in Asia* (2015), edited by Lu and Cooper. In addition, the research of Ishii-Kuntz 2013, 2015) has explored fatherhood and work in Japan. As an example of research conducted in the African context, Bagraim, Jaga and Gelb (2016) explore gender role centrality and work–family conflict among South African fathers. Additionally, we are most encouraged by the agenda for work–family issues in Africa set forth by Mokomane, van der Merwe, Khan, Jaga, and Dancaster (2017). These authors properly note that their work "has the potential to make a substantial contribution to strengthening and amplifying African voices in the global work–family discourse, which is currently dominated by research findings and literature from the Global North" (p. 1). Despite this progress, we call for more academic research on fatherhood and work–family issues in currently under-represented countries, cultures, and contexts.

Recommendations for Research, Policy, and Practice

In summary, we offer some final recommendations for public policy, business practice, and academic research. The current literature suggests that as we support fathers, we will not only benefit the men themselves but also children, mothers, families, employers, and societies.

Public Policy Recommendations

- Increased provision of parental leave geared specifically to men which includes partial wage replacement
- Greater parity between the amounts of parental leave provided to women and men
- Laws and precedent for equally shared custody of children as the default position for divorcing couples
- Efforts to promote the role of fathers throughout pregnancy and early parenthood by including them in pre-natal medical visits, classes, and education
- Federal programs and initiatives for encouraging gender equality at home and in the workplace
- Greater inclusion of men in advocacy and policy for work–family initiatives

Business Practice Recommendations

- Greater parity between the amounts of employer-based parental leave provided to women and men
- Expanded use of workplace flexibility, alternate scheduling, and other family-supportive practices for both female and male employees
- Changing workplace cultures and supervisory attitudes to reduce the flexibility stigma associated with men who prioritize family
- Increased communication between employees and expectant/new fathers to better understand their unique needs and challenges, and to shape policy
- Promotion of women and men who have faced work–family challenges to positions of leadership in order to provide more diverse and empathetic policy-making when it comes to matters of work–life balance
- Increased use of academic research to inform decision-making on work–family policies

Academic Research Recommendations

- Study focused on understanding the factors that influence father attitudes and role centrality
- Evaluation of the effectiveness of father education in changing men's attitudes toward gender roles
- Case studies of employers who have begun offering leave and the effects it is having
- Reports of economic impact and feasibility studies of the implementation of federally mandated leave policies in the United States and various countries
- Better understanding of the men and families who benefit most from paternal leave
- Examination of the effects of father-specific organizational work–family policies on employee well-being and business outcomes

- Increased partnership between academic researchers and practitioners in the field of public policy, management and human resources
- More research on fatherhood, work–family and their intersection in countries and cultures other than North America, Western Europe, and similar post-industrial societies
- More research on fatherhood, work–family and their intersection using samples other than professional and white-collar workers
- More partnerships between researchers from different parts of the world, which would spur new connections and cross-cultural insights

In conclusion, the amount and quality of research on fatherhood and work–family has increased greatly over the past decade. This work has helped establish that (a) involved fatherhood is beneficial to children, women, families, societies, and even fathers themselves; (b) there remain many legal, societal, cultural and workplace-based barriers to increased levels of father involvement; and (c) in many places, workplace and public policy have begun to address the concerns of working fathers striving for more family involvement. However, there is still much to be learned. More research is needed in a wider set of societies and cultures. There is a need for more cross-cultural research, and research in communities of differing socio economic levels. There is still significant disconnect between research and practice.

We are confident that the next decade will bring increased attention to how fathers around the world can be better supported at work, at home, and in their communities. We hope that, by compiling the extant research and proposing areas for future inquiry, our chapter contributes to this effort.

References

Addati, L., Cassirer, N., & Gilchrist, K. (2014). *Maternity and Paternity at Work : Law and Practice across the World*. Geneva, CHE: ILO.

Allen, S. M., & Hawkins, A. J. (1999). Maternal gatekeeping: Mothers' beliefs and behaviors that inhibit greater father involvement in family work. *Journal of Marriage and the Family, 61*(1), 199–212. http://doi.org/10.2307/353894

Amato, P. R. (1994). Father–child relations, mother–child relations, and offspring psychological well-being in early adulthood. *Journal of Marriage and the Family, 56*(4), 1031–1042. http://doi.org/10.2307/353611

Andringa, W., Nieuwenhuis, R., & van Gerven, M. (2015). Women's working hours: The interplay between gender role attitudes, motherhood, and public childcare support in 23 European countries. *International Journal of Sociology and Social Policy, 35*, 11–12.

Astone, N. M., Dariotis, J. K., Sonenstein, F. L., Pleck, J. H., & Hynes, K. (2010). Men's work efforts and the transition to fatherhood. *Journal of Family and Economic Issues, 31* (1), 3–13. http://doi.org/10.1007/s10834-009-9174-7

Astone, N. M., & Peters, H. E. (2014). Longitudinal influences on men's lives: Research from the transition to fatherhood project and beyond. *Fathering: A Journal of Theory, Research, and Practice about Men as Fathers, 12*(2), 161–173.

Bagraim, J. J., Jaga, A., & Gelb, J. (2016). Role centrality, gender role ideology and work–family conflict among working fathers in South Africa. *International Journal of Psychology*, *51*, 788–789.

Baker, J. K., Fenning, R. M., & Crnic, K. A. (2011). Emotion socialization by mothers and fathers: Coherence among behaviors and associations with parent attitudes and children's social competence. *Social Development*, *20*(2), 412–430. http://doi.org/10.1111/j.1467–9507.2010.00585.x

Behson, S.J. (2013). What's a working dad to do? *Harvard Business Review*. Digital Edition. Retrieved from https://hbr.org/2013/08/whats-a-working-dad-to-do

Behson, S. J. (2015a). *The Working Dad's Survival Guide: How to Succeed at Work and at Home*. Motivational Press.

Behson, S. J. (2015b). Give dads a gift they can really use this Father's Day: Paternity leave. *Quartz*. Retrieved from www.quartz.com

Berdahl, J. L., & Moon, S. H. (2013). Workplace mistreatment of middle class workers based on sex, parenthood, and caregiving. *Journal of Social Issues*, *69*(2), 341–366. http://doi.org/10.1111/josi.12018

Beutell, N., & Behson, S.J. (2015). Generations of working fathers: Career, family and life. Paper presented at conference of the Eastern Academy of Management Conference, Philadelphia, PA.

Bond, J. T., Galinsky, E., & Hill, E. J. (2004). When work works. New York, NY: Families and Work Institute.

Bonney, J. F., Kelley, M. L., & Levant, R. F. (1999). A model of fathers' behavioral involvement in child care in dual-earner families. *Journal of Family Psychology*, *13*(3), 401–415. http://doi.org/10.1037/0893–3200.13.3.401

Burgess, A. (2006). The costs and benefits of active fatherhood: Evidence and insights to inform the development of policy and practice. Retrieved from http://www.fatherhoodinstitute.org/index.php?id=0&cID=586

Byrd-Craven, J., Auer, B. J., Granger, D. A., & Massey, A. R. (2012). The father–daughter dance: The relationship between father–daughter relationship quality and daughters' stress response. *Journal of Family Psychology*, *26*(1), 87–94. http://doi.org/10.1037/a0026588

Castillo, J. T., Welch, G. W., & Sarver, C. M. (2012). Walking a high beam: The balance between employment stability, workplace flexibility, and nonresident father involvement. *American Journal of Men's Health*, *6*(2), 120–131. http://doi.org/10.1177/1557988311417612

Coltrane, S., Miller, E. C., DeHaan, T., & Stewart, L. (2013). Fathers and the flexibility stigma. *Journal of Social Issues*, *69*(2), 279–302. http://doi.org/10.1111/josi.12015

Cooklin, A.R., Westrupp, E.M., Strazdins, L., Giallo, R.R., Martin, A., & Nicholson, J.M. (2014). Fathers at work: Work–family conflict, work–family enrichment and parenting in an Australian cohort. *Journal of Family Issues*, *37*(11), pp. 1611–1635.

Craig, L., Powell, A., & Cortis, N. (2012). Self-employment, work–family time and the gender division of labour. *Work, Employment & Society*, *26*(5), 716–734. http://doi.org/10.1177/0950017012451642

Croft, A., Schmader, T., Block, K., & Baron, A. S. (2014). The second shift reflected in the second generation: Do parents' gender roles at home predict children's aspirations? *Psychological Science*, *25*(7), 1418–1428. http://doi.org/10.1177/0956797614533968

Culpin, I., Heron, J., Araya, R., Melotti, R., & Joinson, C. (2013). Father absence and depressive symptoms in adolescence: Findings from a UK cohort. *Psychological Medicine*, *43*(12), 2615–2626.

Day, R. D., & Padilla-Walker, L. M. (2009). Mother and father connectedness and involvement during early adolescence. *Journal of Family Psychology*, *23*(6), 900–904. http://doi.org/10.1037/a0016438

DuBois, D. L., Eitel, S. K., & Felner, R. D. (1994). Effects of family environment and parent-child relationships on school adjustment during the transition to early adolescence. *Journal of Marriage and the Family*, *56*(2), 405–414. http://doi.org/10.2307/353108

Duvander, A. (2014). How long should parental leave be? Attitudes to gender equality, family, and work as determinants of women's and men's parental leave in Sweden. *Journal of Family Issues*, *35*(7), 909–926. http://doi.org/10.1177/0192513X14522242

Eggebeen, D. J., Dew, J., & Knoester, C. (2010). Fatherhood and men's lives at middle age. *Journal of Family Issues*, *31*(1), 113–130. http://doi.org/10.1177/0192513X09341446

Eggebeen, D. J., & Knoester, C. (2001), Does fatherhood matter for men?. *Journal of Marriage and Family*, 63: 381–393. doi:10.1111/j.1741-3737.2001.00381.x

Eggebeen, D. J., Knoester, C., & McDaniel, B. (2013). The implications of fatherhood for men. In N. J. Cabrera & C. S. Tamis-LeMonda (Eds.), *Handbook of Father Involvement: Multidisciplinary Perspectives*. Second Edition (pp. 338–357). New York, NY: Routledge/Taylor & Francis Group.

Erel, O., & Burman, B. (1995). Interrelatedness of marital relations and parent-child relations: A meta-analytic review. *Psychological Bulletin*, *118*(1), 108–132. http://doi.org/10.1037/0033–2909.118.1.108

Fagan, J., & Barnett, M. (2003). The relationship between maternal gatekeeping, paternal competence, mothers' attitudes about the father role, and father involvement. *Journal of Family Issues*, *24*(8), 1020–1043. http://doi.org/10.1177/0192513X03256397

Fagan, J., & Press, J. (2008). Father influences on employed mothers' work–family balance. *Journal of Family Issues*, *29*(9), 1136–1160. http://doi.org/10.1177/0192513X07311954

Fleischmann, A., & Sieverding, M. (2015). Reactions toward men who have taken parental leave: Does the length of parental leave matter? *Sex Roles*, *72*(9–10), 462–476. http://doi.org/10.1007/s11199-015–0469-x

Flouri, E. (2005). *Fathering and Child Outcomes*. New York, NY: John Wiley & Sons Ltd.

Flouri, E. (2008). Fathering and adolescents' psychological adjustment: The role of fathers' involvement, residence and biology status. *Child: Care, Health and Development*, *34*(2), 152–161. http://doi.org/10.1111/j.1365–2214.2007.00752.x

Flouri, E., & Buchanan, A. (2003). The role of father involvement in children's later mental health. *Journal of Adolescence*, *26*(1), 63–78. http://doi.org/10.1016/S0140-1971(02)00116-1

Forehand, R., & Nousiainen, S. (1993). Maternal and paternal parenting: Critical dimensions in adolescent functioning. *Journal of Family Psychology*, *7*(2), 213–221. http://doi.org/10.1037/0893–3200.7.2.213

Fuegen, K., Biernat, M., Haines, E., & Deaux, K. (2004). Mothers and fathers in the workplace: How gender and parental status influence judgments of job-related competence. *Journal of Social Issues*, *60*(4), 737–754. http://doi.org/10.1111/j.0022–4537.2004.00383.x

Fuwa, M. (2004). Macro-level gender inequality and the division of household labor in 22 countries. *American Sociological Review, 69*(6), 751–767. http://doi.org/10.1177/000312240406900601

Goodwin, R. D., & Styron, T. H. (2012). Perceived quality of early paternal relationships and mental health in adulthood. *Journal of Nervous and Mental Disease, 200*(9), 791–795. http://doi.org/10.1097/NMD.0b013e318266f87c

Grau-Grau, M. (2016). Work–family enrichment experiences among working fathers: Evidence from Catalonia. (Unpublished doctoral dissertation). The University of Edinburgh, Scotland, UK.

Haas, L., & Hwang, C. P. (2009). Is fatherhood becoming more visible at work? Trends in corporate support for fathers taking parental leave in Sweden. *Fathering, 7*(3), 303–321. http://doi.org/10.3149/fth.0703.303

Harrington, B., Fraone, J.S., Lee, J., & Levey, L. (2016). The millennial new dad: Understanding the paradox of today's father. Research report published by the Boston College Center for Work & Family. Retrieved from: www.bc.edu/content/dam/files/centers/cwf/pdf/BCCWF%20The%20New%20Dad%202016%20FINAL.pdf

Harrington, B., Van Deusen, F., Fraone, J.S., Eddy, S., & Haas, L. (2014). The new dad: Take your leave. Perspectives on paternity leave from fathers, leading organizations, and global policies. Research report published by the Boston College Center for Work & Family. Retrieved from: www.bc.edu/content/dam/files/centers/cwf/news/pdf/BCCWF%20The%20New%20Dad%202014%20FINAL.pdf

Harrington, B., Van Deusen, F., & Humberd, B. (2011). The new dad: Caring, committed, and conflicted. Research report published by the Boston College Center for Work & Family. Retrieved from: www.bc.edu/content/dam/files/centers/cwf/pdf/FH-Study-Web-2.pdf

Heilman, B., Cole, G., Matos, K, Hassink, A., Mincy, R. & Barker, G. (2016). *State of America's Fathers: A MenCare Advocacy Publication.* Washington, DC: Promundo-US.

Hill, E. J., Aumann, K., Galinsky, E., Fellows, K. J. Carroll, S. J., & O'Sullivan, J. (2012, June). The new male mystique: How male professionals integrate work and family during transition to parenthood. Paper presented at the annual conference of the Work and Family Researchers Network, New York, NY.

Hofferth, S. L., Pleck, J. H., Goldscheider, F., Curtin, S., & Hrapczynski, K. (2013). Family structure and men's motivation for parenthood in the United States. In N. J. Cabrera & C. S. Tamis-LeMonda (Eds.), *Handbook of Father Involvement: Multidisciplinary Perspectives.* Second Edition (pp. 57–80). New York, NY: Routledge/Taylor & Francis Group.

Hohmann-Marriott, B. E. (2009). Father Involvement ideals and the union transitions of unmarried parents. *Journal of Family Issues, 30*(7), 898–920. http://doi.org/10.1177/0192513X08327885

Holmes, E. K., Duncan, T., Bair, S., & White, A. (2007). How mothers and fathers help each other count. In S. E. Brotherson & J. M. White (Eds.), *Why Fathers Count,* (pp. 43–58). Harriman, TN: Men's Studies Press.

Huffman, A. H., Olson, K. J., O'Gara, T. C. J., & King, E. B. (2014). Gender role beliefs and fathers' work–family conflict. *Journal of Managerial Psychology, 29*(7), 774–793. http://doi.org/10.1108/JMP-11-2012-0372

Ishii-Kuntz, M. (2013). Work environment and Japanese fathers' involvement in child care. *Journal of Family Issues, 34(2),* 250–269. doi: 10.1177/0192513X12462363

Izhii-Kuntz, M. (2015). Fatherhood in Asian Contexts. In Quah, S.R. (Ed.), *Routledge Handbook of Families in Asia*. Chapter 11, pp. 161–174. Routledge: London.

Keizer, R., Dykstra, P. A., & Poortman, A.-R. (2010). Life outcomes of childless men and fathers. *European Sociological Review, 26*(1), 1–15. http://doi.org/10.1093/esr/jcn080

Kmec, J. A. (2011). Are motherhood penalties and fatherhood bonuses warranted? Comparing pro-work behaviors and conditions of mothers, fathers, and non-parents. *Social Science Research, 40*(2), 444–459. http://doi.org/10.1016/j.ssresearch.2010.11.006

Ladge, J. J., Humberd, B. K., Watkins, M. B., & Harrington, B. (2015). Updating the organization man: An examination of involved fathering in the workplace. *Academy of Management Perspectives, 29*(1), 152–171.

Lamb, M.E. (2004). *The Role of the Father in Child Development*, 4th edition. Wiley: Hoboken, NJ.

Leschyshyn, A., & Minnotte, K. L. (2014). Professional parents' loyalty to employer: The role of workplace social support. *Social Science Journal, 51*(3), 438–446. http://doi.org/10.1016/j.soscij.2014.04.003

Levtov, R., van der Gaag, N., Green, M., Kaufman, M., & Barker, G. (2015). *State of the World's Fathers: A MenCare Advocacy Publication*. Washington, DC: Promundo, Rutgers, Save the Children, Sonke Gender Justice, and the MenEngage Alliance.

Maurer, T. W., Pleck, J. H., & Rane, T. R. (2001). Parental identity and reflected-appraisals: Measurement and gender dynamics. *Journal of Marriage and Family, 63*(2), 309–321. http://doi.org/10.1111/j.1741–3737.2001.00309.x

Meuwissen, A. S., & Carlson, S. M. (2015). Fathers matter: The role of father parenting in preschoolers' executive function development. *Journal of Experimental Child Psychology, 140*, 1–15. http://doi.org/10.1016/j.jecp.2015.06.010

Milkman, R., & Appelbaum, E. (2013). *Unfinished Business: Paid Family Leave in California and the Future of U.S. Work–Family Policy*. Ithaca: NY: Cornell University Press.

Miller, T. (2011). Falling back into gender? Men's narratives and practices around first-time fatherhood. *Sociology, 45*(6), 1094–1109. http://doi.org/10.1177/0038038511419180

Mokomane, Z., van der Merwe, S., Khan, M.S., Jaga, A.& Dancaster, L. (2017). Developing an African research network and research agenda on work–family interface. *Community, Work and Family*. Published online: January 22, 2017, pp. 1–11.

Munoz Boudet, A. M., Petesch, P., Turk, C., & Thumala, A. (2013). On norms and agency: Conversations about gender equality with women and men in 20 countries. The World Bank.

Nelson, T. J. (2004). Low-income fathers. *Annual Review of Sociology, 30*, 427–451. http://doi.org/10.1146/annurev.soc.29.010202.095947

Norman, H., Elliot, M., & Fagan, C. (2014). Which fathers are the most involved in taking care of their toddlers in the UK? An investigation of the predictors of paternal involvement. *Community, Work & Family, 17*(2), 163–180. http://doi.org/10.1080/13668803.2013.862361

OECD (2012). *OECD Employment Outlook 2012*. OECD Publishing. Retrieved from http://dx.doi.org/10.1787/emp_outlook-2012-en

Owen, M. T., Caughy, M. O., Hurst, J. R., Amos, M., Hasanizadeh, N., & Mata-Otero, A.-M. (2013). Unique contributions of fathering to emerging self-regulation in low-income ethnic minority preschoolers. *Early Child Development and Care, 183*(3–4), 464–482. http://doi.org/10.1080/03004430.2012.711594

Palkovitz, R. (2002). *Involved Fathering and Men's Adult Development: Provisional Balances*. Mahwah, New Jersey: Lawrence Erlbaum Associates.

Raeburn, P. (2015). *Do Fathers Matter?: What Science Is Telling Us About the Parent We've Overlooked*. New York, NY: Scientific American / Farrar, Straus and Giroux.

Raub, J. M., Carson, N. J., Cook, B. L., Wyshak, G., & Hauser, B. B. (2013). Predictors of custody and visitation decisions by a family court clinic. *Journal of the American Academy of Psychiatry and the Law, 41*(2), 206–218.

Rehel, E. M. (2014). When dad stays home too: paternity leave, gender, and parenting. *Gender & Society, 28*(1), 110–132. http://doi.org/10.1177/0891243213503900

Rudman, L. A., & Mescher, K. (2013). Penalizing men who request a family leave: Is flexibility stigma a femininity stigma? *Journal of Social Issues, 69*(2), 322–340. http://doi.org/10.1111/josi.12017

Samuel, L. (2016). *American Fatherhood: A Cultural History*. Lanham, MD: Rowman & Littlefield.

Schoppe-Sullivan, S. J., Brown, G. L., Cannon, E. A., Mangelsdorf, S. C., & Sokolowski, M. S. (2008). Maternal gatekeeping, coparenting quality, and fathering behavior in families with infants. *Journal of Family Psychology, 22*(3), 389–398. http://doi.org/10.1037/0893–3200.22.3.389

Singley, S., & Hynes, K. (2005). Transitions to parenthood work–family policies, gender, and the couple context. *Gender & Society, 19*(3), 376–397. http://doi.org/10.1177/0891243204271515

Tanaka, S., & Waldfogel, J. (2007). Effects of parental leave and work hours on fathers' involvement with their babies: Evidence from the millennium cohort study. *Community, Work & Family, 10*(4), 409–426. http://doi.org/10.1080/13668800701575069

Thebaud, S & Pedulla, D. (2016). Masculinity and the stalled revolution: How gender ideologies and norms shape young men's responses to work–family policies. *Gender & Society, 30*(4). 590–617.

Vandello, J. A., Hettinger, V. E., Bosson, J. K., & Siddiqi, J. (2013). When equal isn't really equal: The masculine dilemma of seeking work flexibility. *Journal of Social Issues, 69*(2), 303–321. http://doi.org/10.1111/josi.12016

Weitoft, G. R., Burström, B., & Rosén, M. (2004). Premature mortality among lone fathers and childless men. *Social Science & Medicine, 59*(7), 1449–1459. http://doi.org/10.1016/j.socscimed.2004.01.026

Yogman, M. W., Kindlon, D., & Earls, F. (1995). Father involvement and cognitive/behavioral outcomes of preterm infants. *Journal of the American Academy of Child & Adolescent Psychiatry, 34*(1), 58–66. http://doi.org/10.1097/00004583–199501000-00015

34 Crossover, Culture, and Dual-Earner Couples

Paula Brough and Mina Westman

In this chapter we assess the international scope of research conducted on *crossover*, the contagion of positive and negative emotions and experiences between individuals. We take a specific interest in how crossover is experienced within *dual-earner* or *dual-career* couples, when both partners of a couple are formally employed. Our focus on dual-earner couples recognizes changing employment practices across the globe; couples with children where both partners work full-time now represent the most common employment pattern within the Organization for Economic Co-operation and Development (OECD) countries. Figures indicate that between 50% (e.g., Denmark, Finland, Israel, Poland, and Portugal) and 66% (e.g., Slovenia) of working families are dual-earner couples (OECD, 2015). Dual-earner couples are also recognized as the most common employment demographic in other countries (e.g., China; Ho, Chen, Cheung, Liu, & Worthington, 2013). In addition, the "one-and-a-half earner" arrangement (i.e., couples consisting of one full-time and one part-time worker), reflective of approximately 35% of working families, is common in countries such as Austria, Germany, the United Kingdom, Australia, and the Netherlands (OECD, 2015).

Given these patterns, the crossover of dual work and family demands and benefits between both partners is a common occurrence across the globe. Specifically, crossover involves the transference of emotions and experiences from work to home (and vice versa) and between spouses. This chapter discusses recent developments in crossover research with a focus on international comparisons and dual-earner couples. We begin by defining the core constructs and mechanisms of crossover and discuss recent advancements in the crossover of *positive* emotions and experiences. We review the key theoretical explanations of crossover, including Westman's (2001) crossover model, the spillover-crossover model (Bakker & Demerouti, 2013), and the conservation of resources model (Hobfoll, 2002). Our international focus compares differences and similarities in crossover research between countries, but also considers more in-depth comparisons between national *cultures*. This includes a discussion of how *gender* impacts crossover and the extent to which gender differences can be attributed to national cultures. Finally, we provide recommendations for future crossover research.

The Crossover Process

Crossover and spillover are two processes in which stress, strain, or other emotions (including positive constructs) are carried over within and across individuals and domains. Spillover is the *within-person* transmission of experiences and/or emotions, from work to home or from home to work, for the same individual. Crossover is an *interpersonal* process that occurs when job stress, psychological strain, or other emotions experienced by one person affects the level of strain or outcomes experienced by another person in the same social environment (Bolger, DeLongis, Kessler, & Wethington, 1989).

Westman (2001) developed a conceptual crossover model which extended previous approaches by adding and focusing on the inter-individual level of analysis (i.e., the dyad) and describes three specific mechanisms by which experiences and emotions are transferred between partners. The model identifies specific experiences (e.g., stress and strain) as antecedents of the crossover process as well as interpersonal and individual variables as possible mediators and moderators of the process. The core assumption of the model is that one person's experienced stress or strain has an impact on close others in different settings.

Westman (2001) proposed three mechanisms delineating how these crossover processes occur. First, *direct crossover* describes when experiences and emotions between the partners are transmitted via empathy. The basis for this view is the fact that crossover effects appear between closely related partners who care for each other and share the greater part of their lives together. Accordingly, an individual's experience (e.g., strain) produces an empathic reaction in the partner that in turn increases the partner's level of strain (i.e., *empathic identification*). Second, *indirect crossover* posits that crossover occurs through moderating mechanisms displayed by the focal person, such as coping, social support, and undermining, which result in a partner's strain. Finally, crossover may occur because partners share some *common stressors* (e.g., parenting demands, economic stress), which then lead to shared, common affective states (e.g., dissatisfaction) in both partners. In this case the relationship between partners' dissatisfaction is a spurious form of crossover because what appears to be a crossover effect is actually the result of common experiences. Several researchers have tested and supported the tenets of this crossover model and its three mechanisms (e.g., Howe, Levy, & Caplan, 2004; ten Brummelhuis, Bakker, & Euwema, 2010).

In terms of exactly *what* is transferred via this crossover process, much of the early crossover research focused on the transmission of psychological stress and strain. This was primarily in response to the definition of crossover as a mechanism of stress contagion between individuals who worked or lived together (e.g., Westman, 2001; Westman & Etzion, 2005). The transmission of other negative experiences and emotions via crossover has also been demonstrated, including the transference of anxiety (Westman, Etzion, & Horovitz, 2004), burnout (Bakker & Schaufeli, 2000), distress (ten Brummelhuis, Haar, & van der Lippe, 2010), depression (Howe, Levy, & Caplan, 2004), work–family conflict (Westman & Etzion, 2005), health complaints (Westman, Keinan, Roziner, & Benyamini, 2008), and marital dissatisfaction (Westman, Vinokur, Hamilton, & Roziner, 2004). An important development in this field is evidence that crossover can also include the transmission of *positive* experiences and emotions between individuals, and this is described below.

Positive Crossover

Westman (2001) also suggested broadening the definition of crossover to include the transmission of *positive* experiences and states. Accordingly, just as stressful job demands have a negative impact on a partner's well-being, positive feelings following positive job events may also be transferred to partners and can have a beneficial impact on their well-being. Westman (2001) proposed that the three previously described crossover mechanisms are applicable to both negative and positive crossover. Thus, for example, work engagement expressed by one partner may fuel their partner's levels of engagement. The crossover of positive emotions may also occur indirectly, following a positive interaction between the partners (e.g., via social support).

The crossover of positive emotions reflects Fredrickson's (2001) broaden-and-build theory, which predicts that positive emotions broaden an individual's sense of self to enhance their identification with others, consequently producing greater feelings of self–other overlap and "oneness" (Waugh & Fredrickson, 2006). Most studies that have demonstrated positive crossover have focused on the crossover of engagement (Demerouti, Bakker, & Schaufeli, 2005; Westman, Etzion, & Chen, 2009), mood (Song, Foo, & Uy, 2008), and marital satisfaction (Liu, Ngo, & Cheung, 2016). One recent study conducted by Liu and Cheung (2015a) investigated the crossover of work–family enrichment (WFE) and found that a wife's level of WFE was linked to lower psychological strain as well as greater life, marital, and job satisfaction for her husband. In addition, the husband's level of WFE was positively associated with his wife's marital satisfaction. These results are encouraging because they indicate that WFE contributes not only to individual well-being, but also enhances a partner's well-being. According to the broaden-and-build theory (Fredrickson, 2001), positive emotions arising from an individual's perception of WFE should promote outwardly oriented thoughts and actions, stimulating the person to respond favorably to the needs of their partner through performing more generative activities, such as showing sympathy or concern about family issues or providing help and support. Accordingly, the partner should perceive improved relationship quality, which then translates to the partner's enhanced subjective well-being.

International Crossover Research

Despite the relative "youth" of the field of crossover research, it is reassuring to note the uptake of its application and use within a multitude of national contexts. Our review of this literature revealed a total of 101 published empirical crossover articles based on samples originating from seventeen different countries (illustrated in Figure 34.1). We note that this set of articles includes a study assessing burnout contagion for nurses employed in twelve European countries (Bakker, Le Blanc, & Schaufeli, 2005), and we categorized this study as "cross-national." It can be seen from Figure 34.1 that crossover research is primarily conducted with American and European, including Israeli, samples. However, crossover research

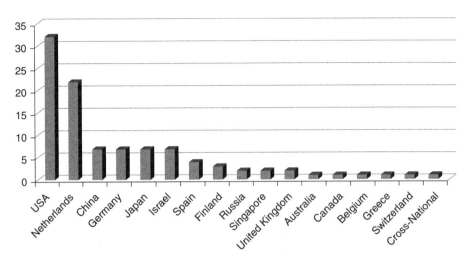

Figure 34.1 *Frequency of crossover studies from sixteen countries (N = 101).*

based on samples from Canada, Russia, and the Asia-Pacific region (e.g., Australia, China, Japan, and Singapore) are also represented, indicative of the wide international interest regarding the crossover phenomenon.

Whilst the country of inquiry is important to consider when comparing international findings, the application of crossover within different national *cultures* is of greater relevance. Increasingly prominent calls have been made for psychological theories derived within Western contexts to be validated within non-Western cultures. This is an essential practice for thorough theory-testing and knowledge advancement (e.g., Brough et al., 2013). Informed by the countries producing crossover research (see Figure 34.1), the pertinent question we focus on here is: *To what extent is the crossover process both similar and different between Western cultures (e.g., Western Europe, Canada, and the United States) and non-Western cultures (e.g., Asia-Pacific and Eastern Europe)?*

The sole cross-national crossover article which we identified in our review is a good starting point to assess this research question. In a study assessing samples of intensive care unit nurses employed in twelve different Western European countries, Bakker et al. (2005) demonstrated the existence of burnout contagion between nurses and their colleagues. Interestingly, the authors found that nurses who reported the highest prevalence of burnout experienced by their *colleagues* were also most likely to experience high levels of burnout *themselves*. Thus, perceptions of their colleagues' negative experiences had a greater impact upon nurses' perceptions of their own burnout compared to their own ratings of their work environment (i.e., akin to feeling that "I feel stressed because everyone around me is stressed"). This is also indicative of a "stress culture" which is commonly considered to be inherent to some work units or entire occupations. Bakker et al. noted that the country of origin had only a small impact upon these results (accounting in total for no more than 5% of the variance in burnout), implying that these results were generally consistent across these twelve European countries. One implication of this work is that the general individualistic "Western European culture" appears to account for the similar experiences of these nurses within each of the twelve countries sampled. Of course, this point requires testing in a markedly different national culture (e.g., a collectivist culture common to some Asian countries, such as China or Indonesia) to be fully supported.

Based on our review of the one hundred remaining published empirical crossover articles using samples originating from seventeen different countries and illustrated in Figure 34.1, several key findings are apparent and are briefly summarized here. First, it is evident that crossover occurs via a similar basic process between employees, their colleagues, and/or family members in *both Western national contexts*, including Canada (Haines, Marchand, & Harvey, 2006), Australia (Cowlishaw, Evans, & McLennan, 2010; Muller & Brough, 2017), Switzerland (Schaer, Bodenmann, & Klink, 2008), Finland (Schaer et al., 2008), the United Kingdom (Jones & Fletcher, 1993; Totterdell, 2000), and the United States (Beehr, Johnson, & Nieva, 1995; Bolger, DeLongis, Kessler, & Wethington, 1989; Carlson, Kacmar, Zivnuska, & Ferguson, 2015; Lawson, Davis, McHale, Hammer, & Buxton, 2014; Park & Fritz, 2015), *and within non-Western contexts*, including China (Ho et al., 2013; Li, Wang, Yang, & Liu, 2016; Lu, Lu, Du, & Brough, 2016), Japan (Bakker, Shimazu, Demerouti, Shimada, & Kawakami, 2014; Takeuchi, Yun, & Tesluk, 2002), Singapore (Lim & Sng, 2006; Song, Foo, & Uy, 2008), and Russia (Westman, Keinan, Roziner, & Benyamini, 2008; Westman, Vinokur, Hamilton, & Roziner, 2004). Thus, at face value, the processes of crossover do not appear to differ for couples living in Western or non-Western cultures.

Second, we note the increased focus on dual-earner workers and the transmission of emotions originating in both male and female workers, within this global research. Importantly, this focus occurs across a variety of national contexts, including Germany (Unger, Sonnentag, Niessen, & Kuonath, 2015), China (Lu et al., 2016), the United Kingdom (Crossfield, Kinman, & Jones, 2005), Japan (Shimazu, 2015), and the United States (Ferguson, Carlson, Kacmar, & Halbesleben, 2016; Neal & Hammer, 2009). The impact of dependent children within the crossover process for both male and female employees is also of increasing interest, aptly illustrating the influence of crossover research within the work–life balance field. Again, it is refreshing to observe that this assessment of the impact of dependent children occurs across national cultures, including for example, Germany (Hahn, Binnewies, & Dormann, 2014), Singapore (Song et al., 2008), and the United States (Barnett, Gareis, & Brennan, 2010; Bass, Butler, Grzywacz, & Linney, 2009; Lawson et al., 2014).

Third, it is also encouraging to note that advances in assessing the crossover of positive states and emotions, such as work engagement and self-esteem, are also clearly not restricted by national cultures. These recent scholarly discussions are informed by research conducted with, as examples, Belgium employees and their spouses demonstrating the crossover of social support (Schooreel & Verbruggen, 2016), a sample of dual-earner Australian couples (including same-sex couples) demonstrating the crossover of positive affect (Muller & Brough, 2017), a sample of Israeli business travelers and their spouses demonstrating crossover of the vigor component of engagement (Westman, Etzion, & Chen, 2009), studies of crossover of engagement among dual-earner couples in the Netherlands (Bakker & Xanthopoulou, 2009; Demerouti, 2012), American supervisors and employees demonstrating the crossover of work–family enrichment (Carlson, Ferguson, Kacmar, Grzywacz, & Whitten, 2011), and the crossover of positive mood between American employees and their spouses (Munyon, Breaux, Rogers, Perrewé, & Hochwarter, 2009).

It is, therefore, clearly apparent that more similarities than differences are evident within the international crossover research to date and this is enormously helpful to enable a focus on direct advancements of this field. It is pertinent to note that crossover research conducted within countries with a traditional gender ideology (discussed in more detail below) such as China, Japan, and Singapore, do include dual-earner samples, rather than adopting a "traditional" focus on male employees and their (non-employed) spouses. This is a pertinent observation because in similar research fields, such as work–life balance, the dominance of the male employee and the inequities experienced by female employees (especially working mothers) within these Asian countries have been observed (Brough, Timms, Siu, Kalliath, O'Driscoll, et al., 2013; Kawaguchi, 2013; Nemoto, 2013; Timms, Brough, Siu, O'Driscoll, & Kalliath, 2015). We note that one interesting avenue for future crossover research is to assess this impact of gender ideology within different national contexts in greater detail, and we discuss this point in more detail later in this chapter.

In the next section, we review three key components of crossover which have received recent attention and which have an impact for either theoretical and/or methodological advances in this field. We illustrate these discussions by reference to international comparisons of crossover research and, where available, investigations which include samples of dual-earner couples.

The Spillover–Crossover Model

One useful contribution to recent crossover discussions is the integration of the crossover and spillover literatures, producing improved insight into the processes that link the work and family domains. Bakker and Demerouti (2013) described a spillover–crossover model (SCM) where experiences built up at work first spill over to the home domain, influencing behavior at home, and then cross over to the partner's well-being. For example, Bakker, Demerouti, and Dollard (2008) found that job demands were positively related to the employee's own work–family conflict (i.e., negative spillover), which also impacted their partner's exhaustion (i.e., crossover). Shimazu, Bakker, and Demerouti (2009) also produced support for the SCM in a sample of Japanese employees. They found that job demands were related to work–family conflict and poor relationship quality (i.e., negative spillover) and to partners' depressive symptoms and physical complaints (i.e., crossover).

Focusing on positive outcomes, Rodríguez-Muñoz, Sanz-Vergel, Demerouti, and Bakker (2014) found in a daily diary study that work engagement had a direct effect on happiness (i.e., positive spillover) and also directly influenced partners' happiness (i.e., crossover) in a Spanish sample. Similarly, Bakker et al. (2014) noted that work engagement was positively related to work–family facilitation (i.e., positive spillover), which in turn, also predicted own and partner's life satisfaction one year later (i.e., crossover) in a Japanese sample. Finally, Liu et al. (2016) reported evidence for the spillover of work–family enrichment and crossover of marital satisfaction between Chinese partners. These findings demonstrate the bidirectional crossover of daily happiness between both partners and highlights that the positive effects of work engagement extend beyond the work setting and beyond the individual employee. Overall, evidence for cross-cultural similarities rather than differences is found in support of the SCM for both positive and negative experiences.

Crossover of Resources

A recent topic of research is the crossover of resources. According to the conservation of resources theory (COR; Hobfoll, 2002), resources are defined as "those entities that either are centrally valued in their own right (e.g., self-esteem, close attachments, health, and inner peace), or act as means to obtain centrally valued ends (e.g., money, social support)" (p. 307). Resources are not only necessary to deal with job demands, but also are instrumental in people's efforts "to protect against resource loss, recover from losses and gain resources" (Hobfoll, 2002, p. 349).

Using a German and Austrian sample, Neff, Sonnentag, Niessen, and Unger (2012) demonstrated how the two resources of performance self-esteem and job-related self-efficacy are transferred via crossover from one person to another, suggesting that one's partner can act as a source of these two positive work-related resources by transmitting these resources to the other partner. They based this research on self-expansion theory (Aron et al., 2005) and on the assumption that in the course of an intimate relationship, individuals increasingly incorporate their partners' resources, perspectives, and identities into their own self. More specifically, Neff, Sonnentag, Niessen, and Unger (2015) found, using a diary study design with a German sample, that levels of both job-related self-efficacy and self-esteem experienced by one partner during the day crossed over to the other partner in the evening, and also had an impact on the partner over six months. They argued that due to the intimacy of couples, witnessing a partner's self-esteem in the evening can cause similar self-evaluations. Theoretically, it may be that speaking about one's own accomplishments, which comes with high self-esteem, can enhance the partner's job-related self-efficacy beliefs. Thus, for intimate couples, partners' levels of self-esteem converge over time to a shared higher level. This point reflects the accumulation of resources described as *gain spirals* within the COR framework (Hobfoll, 2002). Gain spirals occur by a process of accumulation; the presence or an excess of resources leads to additional resources becoming available. It is suggested that this accumulation of resources protects individuals against the experiences of stress because they have a "bank" of resources they can use to resist or quickly recover from stressful experiences (Hobfoll, 2002). Individuals with a limited accumulation of resources, or resource depletion (*resource loss spirals*), have limited protection against adverse experiences and therefore experience high levels of stress (Hobfoll, 2002).

The accumulation of resources is also likely to result in positive emotional states and attitudes. Social support is one such resource; as it accumulates, it can broaden an individual's resource pool and replace or reinforce other resources that are lacking (Hobfoll, 1985). For example, Ferguson et al. (2016) found that work-related spousal social support has implications for both the employee and their spouse in an American sample. Consistent with the crossover model, spousal support provided for a partner's work problems positively impacted the partner's levels of family satisfaction and reduced tension (stress) through work–family balance. Social support resources lead individuals to feel more confident about their ability to successfully accomplish their role-related goals in both the work and family domains. It therefore appears that those who possess resources are not only more capable of resource gain for themselves, but also help generate gain spirals for the dyad overall. Although research to date supports the crossover of resources occurs between partners in dual-earner couples, this work has primarily been conducted with Western samples and its generalizability to non-Western samples is more limited.

Impact of Gender within the Crossover Process

Gender has been described as a key moderating variable within the crossover process, with findings suggesting that the crossover process is different for males and females. However, one pertinent issue which is commonly overlooked within these discussions is the *social culture or context* in which any gender differences occur. Several researchers have claimed that this moderating role of gender is actually a product of this social context (i.e., gender ideology) rather than a clearly delineated different experience of crossover between the sexes. Greenstein (1996a) defined gender ideology as "how a person identifies herself or himself with regard to marital and family roles that are traditionally linked to gender" (p. 586). Scholars have proposed that gender ideology provides a lens through which marital dynamics, such as the allocation of housework (Greenstein 1996b), women's economic independence (Sayer & Bianchi, 2000), and spousal support (Mickelson et al., 2006), are viewed.

As an example, Westman et al. (2004) studied a sample of officers in the Russian army and found strong unidirectional crossover of marital dissatisfaction from husbands to wives, but no such crossover from wives to husbands. A closer assessment of the results indicated that what appeared to be a gender difference was actually a result of cultural gender ideology. Although both spouses were dual-career workers and shared the role of breadwinners, they both held traditional gender attitudes regarding the key roles of husbands and wives – even when the wives were employed in more prestigious professions and earned more than their husbands. These attitudes included viewing the husband as the main breadwinner and head of the family, while the wife managed the housework and children. The women were, therefore, breadwinners from the income point of view, but had a traditional, supportive role from the cultural gender ideology perspective.

This perspective of cultural gender ideology explains why for couples (including dual-earners) who perceive that the breadwinner role is the primary role for men, work stress experienced by the husband has a greater impact upon their wives' levels of marital dissatisfaction, while the reverse (i.e., female work stress impacting husband's satisfaction) does not commonly occur. This is also referred to as *asymmetrical boundary theory* and is an important consideration in assessments of levels of family satisfaction and work–life balance (for further discussions see Ashforth, Kreiner, & Fugate, 2000; Hare-Mustin, 1987).

In another assessment of gender differences, and similar to the results reported by Westman et al. (2004) described above, Liu and Cheung (2015a) with a sample of Chinese dual-earner couples demonstrated gender differences in the crossover process stemming from the nature of the predictors and outcomes. Although a woman's negative work–family experiences (assessed as work–family conflict) were not associated with her husband's outcomes, the husband's level of work–family conflict significantly impacted his wife's marital dissatisfaction. The authors suggested that a husband's high levels of work–family conflict may result in his exhaustion and an inability to nurture his relationship with his wife. A second explanation is that work–family conflict may influence husbands to have a negative interaction pattern with their spouse, decreasing wives' marital satisfaction (i.e., indirect crossover).

Similarly, Liu and Cheung (2015b) examined the moderating role of empathy in the relationship between an employee's work–family conflict and work–family enrichment and their partner's outcomes (i.e., psychological strain and marital satisfaction) in a sample of Chinese dual-earner couples. They found that only wives' empathy moderated the crossover from husbands' work–family interface to wives' outcome variables. They suggested that the prominent role of women's empathy in the crossover process may be attributed to the traditional gender ideology of East Asian societies (e.g., China and Japan). Similar findings were found in Bakker et al. (2011) among Japanese dual-career couples. In Japan, women play a central role in the family domain, such as being responsible for childcare and housework, even in dual-earner couples (Japanese Cabinet Office, 2007). This means that women usually have to invest more effort in managing their family, which leads to less attention to issues such as their partners' work. It therefore appears that investigations of crossover in Japan, China, and other East Asian societies are likely to be influenced by traditional gender role beliefs.

Slightly different conclusions were reported by Ho et al. (2013) in their assessment of how gender influenced the crossover process. They measured work–life balance, personality, and social support experienced by dual-earner couples in China and reported significant gender differences in the associations between these variables. Importantly, they also reported that both genders had *similar* experiences of "family orientation" (defined as "an individual's relationship-oriented personality trait," p. 54). Regardless of gender, individuals with a strong sense of family orientation (i.e., who considered maintaining a harmonious atmosphere within the family to be important) had higher levels of family–work enhancement (i.e., spillover of positive family experiences impacting upon work outcomes) and lower levels of work–family conflict.

Although gender ideology is usually rooted in national culture, we also have to be careful about oversimplifying this issue. By which we mean it cannot simply be assumed that countries with more of an individualistic national culture (i.e., Western countries) *necessarily* have a significantly different gender ideology compared to countries with more of a collectivistic national culture (i.e., Asian countries). For example, there are discussions that a couple's social class, rather than national gender ideology per se, has a greater impact upon the structure of gender role patterns. Williams and Best (1990), for example, claimed that marital role egalitarianism is more likely to exist among middle-class professional families than working-class families. It was suggested that working-class families generally adopt more conservative (i.e., less egalitarian) gender roles which more strongly reflect national gender ideologies. However, the blurring of these class boundaries in relation to gender ideology has been more recently acknowledged (e.g., Brough, Timms, O'Driscoll, Kalliath, Siu, Sit, & Lo, 2014; Drummond, O'Driscoll, Brough, Siu, Kalliath, Riley, Timms, Sit, & Lo, 2017). For example, in the crossover study of dual-earner couples in China cited above, Ho et al. (2013) noted that individual (or dyadic) levels of interpersonal relationships, especially in terms of family orientation, have a greater impact upon work–family experiences (for working couples in China) than either national culture or social class.

Several studies have demonstrated similar crossover effects for both men and women, but have found a gender difference in the actual crossover mechanisms. For example, Lu, Lu, Du, and Brough (2016) found bidirectional crossover effects between husbands and wives in a sample of dual-earners employed in China. However, when introducing family identity salience to the model, they found that the wives' family identity salience mitigated the crossover effects of the husbands' work–family conflict, but the husbands' family identity salience did not moderate the crossover effect of the wives' work–family conflict. Similarly, Liu et al. (2016) reported similar crossover effects for work–family enrichment and marital satisfaction for both men and women in another assessment of dual-earners employed in China. However, the patterns of social interaction leading to the crossover process were different for each gender. Specifically, husbands' work–family enrichment related to wives' marital satisfaction indirectly through wives' perceptions of increased social support, whereas wives' work–family enrichment related to husbands' marital satisfaction through husbands' perceptions of decreased social undermining.

In sum, considering the underlying gender ideologies, including the importance each individual places on interpersonal relationships and family values, of a dyad enhances our understanding of how conflicts between work and family impact marital agendas and behavior, including crossover experiences between the spouses. It is critical, for example, to take into account both spouses' perspectives when examining the experiences of dual-earner couples, as each spouse often has his or her own experience that may differ from that of the partner (Bernard, 1971). This dual-perspective approach was frequently missing from early crossover research, where only the experiences and values of one individual (commonly the male) within the dyad were collected (see Westman, Brough, & Kalliath, 2009).

The traditional attitudes toward gender roles in the family may account for the unique unidirectional crossover effects from husbands to wives which were produced by some crossover investigations. These traditional attitudes shape the expectations of the husband and wife of each other, their interactions, and their emotional responses to these interactions. Given that gender roles are largely shaped by one's national culture as well as other factors such as social class, breadwinning roles, occupation, and the work status of both spouses, it seems critical to assess the broader context in which couples are operating. The heterogeneity of study samples, the differences in research methodologies, and the variety of outcome variables examined appears to contribute to the mixed and inconsistent findings within the existing crossover literature. We, therefore, suggest that crossover research should consider not only the culture, behaviors, and experiences of individuals and their spouses, but also the gendered beliefs, attitudes, and perceptions that shape how people interpret their lived experiences. Importantly, including assessments of the actual mechanisms of crossover in future research would also help to advance discussions concerning the impact of gender.

Conclusions and Future Research Recommendations

In this chapter we have reviewed the international crossover research with a focus on cultural contexts, gender, and dual-earner couples. The number of different countries conducting crossover research is reassuring, especially the quantity of recent investigations assessing cultural factors being produced by colleagues in China and Japan, as an example. It is apparent that recent investigations have expanded upon a number of original crossover components, noticeably the crossover of positive states and emotions and the impact of gender, ensuring that this field remains receptive to broader contexts including the emphasis upon positive psychology more generally (e.g., Seligman, 2002) and the changing roles of working men and women (e.g., Brough & O'Driscoll, 2015).

Our discussions in this chapter have identified a number of areas where further research is anticipated to further inform our understandings of the crossover process, especially in terms of the specific functioning of the mechanisms of crossover. For example, we do not yet know how *long-lasting* crossover effects are because longitudinal studies remain rare. Although a handful of studies demonstrate crossover effects occurring within a one-year time timeframe, research designs based on longer time lags are clearly required. It is also currently not clear which of the three key mechanisms of crossover (i.e., direct crossover, indirect crossover, and common stressors) have the greatest impact upon the transfer of positive and negative emotions, and which of these mechanisms most influence their duration over time. We anticipate that recent technological developments enabling increased opportunities to adopt innovative approaches to theory-testing and development, easier administrations to large research samples, inclusion of longitudinal data collection techniques, and the availability of statistical software enabling the testing of both multinational samples and complex research models, will ensure that this issue of time is increasingly considered by future investigations.

It is also feasible that the long-term impacts of negative and positive crossover may differ, and the extent to which this difference is impacted by gender, family size (i.e., dependent children and relatives), type of work, and social cultures are anticipated to be of considerable interest, but have yet to be considered by empirical research. Again we anticipate that recent advancements in statistical software especially will enable these potential moderating and/or mediating variables to be assessed in more detail. For example, statistical analysis allowing for the *simultaneous* testing of multiple moderators and mediators enables more complex, but also more realistic, theoretical explanations to be assessed (e.g., Drummond et al., 2017).

Finally, as this field gains more traction, we anticipate that alterative explanations of the crossover process will be introduced. We have observed the testing of new theoretical models occurring in related fields, such as occupational stress and work–life balance, and note the advancements to knowledge such assessments have produced. For example, the refinement of Westman's (2001) original conceptual crossover model into the crossover–spillover model (Bakker & Demerouti, 2013) generated a flurry of testing, resulting in an increased volume of recent crossover research. Other refinements to Westman's (2001) model are also emerging, including for example, a five-stage crossover process model described by Muller and Brough (2017). An important development described by Muller and Brough's model is that partners are not passive recipients within the crossover process, but instead *actively influence* their receipt (or not) of positive and negative emotions and states from their spouses. Thus research assessing how exactly this active influence occurs and under what specific circumstances, is anticipated to be produced over the next few years.

This chapter has provided a review of international crossover research. It is apparent that our changing work practices are producing new challenges and opportunities common in most countries for many employees. Perpetual economic pressures are also commonly experienced; ensuring that the factors impacting levels of employee well-being and work performance remain key research topics for organizational behavior researchers. In this chapter, we discussed the associations between crossover and levels of employee well-being and work performance, with a focus on performance for both partners of dual-career couples. It is apparent that the "contagion" of both positive and negative emotions and experiences has a significant impact between work colleagues (especially formal team members) and also between spouses. We discussed the impact of work experiences shared between spouses and the consequences for their own individual levels of health, satisfaction and subsequent work performance. Finally, we also discussed the issue of gender differences in crossover research. We noted that this area, in particular, has many fruitful avenues for researchers, especially with the advent of new research methodologies to complement traditional data collection experiences. We, therefore, look forward with keen interest as crossover research continues to expand its international breadth and applies a more detailed focus to inform working couples on how best to manage their dual work demands, personal health, and family lives.

References

Aron, A., Mashek, D., McLaughline-Volpe, T., Wright, S., Lewandowski, G., & Aron, E. N. (2005). Including close others in the cognitive structure of the self. In M. W. Baldwin (Ed.), *Interpersonal Cognition* (pp. 206–232). New York, NY: The Guildford Press.

Ashforth, B. E., Kreiner, G. E., & Fugate, M. (2000). All in a day's work: Boundaries and micro role transitions. *Academy of Management Review, 25*(3), 472–491.

Bakker, A. B., & Demerouti, E. (2013). The spillover-crossover model. In J. G. Grzywacz & E. Demerouti (Eds.), *New Frontiers in Work and Family Research*. Hove, UK: Psychology Press.

Bakker, A. B., Demerouti, E., & Dollard, M. F. (2008). How job demands affect partners' experience of exhaustion: integrating work–family conflict and crossover theory. *Journal of Applied Psychology, 93*(4), 901–911. doi:10.1037/0021-9010.93.4.901

Bakker, A. B., Le Blanc, P. M., & Schaufeli, W. B. (2005). Burnout contagion among intensive care nurses. *Journal Advanced Nursing, 51*(3), 276–287. doi:10.1111/j.1365-2648.2005.03494.x

Bakker, A. B., & Schaufeli, W. B. (2000). Burnout contagion processes among teachers. *Journal of Applied Social Psychology, 30*(11), 2289–2308. doi:10.1111/j.1559-1816.2000.tb02437.x

Bakker, A. B., Shimazu, A., Demerouti, E., Shimada, K., & Kawakami, N. (2011). Crossover of work engagement among Japanese couples: Perspective taking by both partners. *Journal of Occupational Health Psychology, 16*(1), 112–125. doi:10.1037/a0021297

Bakker, A. B., Shimazu, A., Demerouti, E., Shimada, K., & Kawakami, N. (2014). Work engagement versus workaholism: A test of the spillover-crossover model. *Journal of Managerial Psychology, 29*(1), 63–80. doi:10.1108/JMP-05-2013-0148

Bakker, A. B., & Xanthopoulou, D. (2009). The crossover of daily work engagement: Test of an actor-partner interdependence model. *Journal of Applied Psychology, 94*(6), 1562–1571. doi:10.1037/a0017525

Barnett, R. C., Gareis, K. C., & Brennan, R. T. (2010). School and school activity schedules affect the quality of family relations: A within-couple analysis. *Community, Work & Family, 13*(1), 35–41. doi:10.1080/13668800902753853

Bass, B. L., Butler, A. B., Grzywacz, J. G., & Linney, K. D. (2009). Do job demands undermine parenting? A daily analysis of spillover and crossover effects. *Family Relations, 58*(2), 201–215.

Beehr, T. A., Johnson, L. B., & Nieva, R. (1995). Occupational stress: Coping of police and their spouses. *Journal of Organizational Behavior, 16*(1), 3–25. doi:10.1002/job.4030160104

Bernard, J. (1971). *Women and the Public Interest*. London, UK: Transaction Publishers.

Bolger, N., DeLongis, A., Kessler, R. C., & Wethington, E. (1989). The contagion of stress across multiple roles. *Journal of Marriage and Family, 51*(1), 175–183. doi:10.2307/352378

Brough, P., & O'Driscoll, M.P. (2015). Integrating work and personal life. In Burke, R.J., Page, K.M., & Cooper, C.L. (Eds.), *Flourishing in Life, Work, and Careers: Individual Wellbeing and Career Experiences* (pp. 377–394). Cheltenham, UK: Edward Elgar Publishing.

Brough, P., Timms, C., O'Driscoll, M., Kalliath, T., Siu, O.L, Sit, C., & Lo, D. (2014). Work–life balance: A longitudinal evaluation of a new measure across Australia and New Zealand workers. *International Journal of Human Resource Management, 25*(19), 2724–2744. doi: 10.1080/09585192.2014.899262

Brough, P., Timms, C., Siu, O-l., Kalliath, T., O'Driscoll, M., Sit, C., Lo, D., & Lu, C-q. (2013). Validation of the job demands–resources model in cross-national samples: Cross-sectional and longitudinal predictions of psychological strain and work engagement. *Human Relations, 66*(10), 1311–1335. doi:10.1177/0018726712472915

Carlson, D. S., Ferguson, M., Kacmar, K., Grzywacz, J. G., & Whitten, D. (2011). Pay it forward: The positive crossover effects of supervisor work–family enrichment. *Journal of Management, 37*(3), 770–789. doi:10.1177/0149206310363613

Carlson, D. S., Kacmar, K., Zivnuska, S., & Ferguson, M. (2015). Do the benefits of family-to-work transitions come at too great a cost? *Journal of Occupational Health Psychology, 20*(2), 161–171. doi:10.1037/a0038279

Cowlishaw, S., Evans, L., & McLennan, J. (2010). Work–family conflict and crossover in volunteer emergency service workers. *Work & Stress, 24*(4), 342–358. doi:10.1080/02678373.2010.532947

Crossfield, S., Kinman, G., & Jones, F. (2005). Crossover of occupational stress in dual-career couples: The role of work demands and supports, job commitment and marital communication. *Community, Work & Family, 8*(2), 211–232. doi:10.1080/13668800500049779

Demerouti, E. (2012). The spillover and crossover of resources among partners: the role of work-self and family-self facilitation. *Journal of Occupational Health Psychology, 17*(2), 184–195. doi: 10.1037/a0026877

Demerouti, E., Bakker, A. B., & Schaufeli, W. B. (2005). Spillover and crossover of exhaustion and life satisfaction among dual-earner parents. *Journal of Vocational Behavior, 67*(2), 266–289. doi:10.1016/j.jvb.2004.07.001

Drummond, S., O'Driscoll, M., Brough, P., Siu, O.-L., Kalliath, T., Riley, D., Timms, C., Sit, C., & Lo, D. (2017). The relationship of social support with well-being via work–family conflict: Moderating effects of gender, dependants and nationality. *Human Relations, 70*(5), 544–565.

Ferguson, M., Carlson, D., Kacmar, K. M., & Halbesleben, J. R. (2016). The supportive spouse at work: Does being work-linked help? *Journal of Occupational Health Psychology, 21*(1), 37–50. doi:10.1037/a0039538

Fredrickson, B. L. (2001). The role of positive emotions in positive psychology: The broaden-and-build theory of positive emotions. *American Psychologist, 56*(3), 218. doi:10.1037/0003-066X.56.3.218

Gender Equality Bureau Cabinet Office. (2007). White Paper on Gender Equality. Tokyo, Japan. Retrieved from www.gender.go.jp/english_contents/about_danjo/whitepaper/pdf/ewp2007.pdf

Greenstein, T. N. (1996a). Gender ideology and perceptions of the fairness of the division of household labor: Effects on marital quality. *Social Forces, 74*(3), 1029–1042. doi:10.1093/sf/74.3.1029

Greenstein, T. N. (1996b). Husbands' participation in domestic labor: Interactive effects of wives' and husbands' gender ideologies. *Journal of Marriage and the Family, 58*(3), 585–595. doi:10.2307/353719

Hahn, V. C., Binnewies, C., & Dormann, C. (2014). The role of partners and children for employees' daily recovery. *Journal of Vocational Behavior*, *85*(1), 39–48. doi:10.1016/j.jvb.2014.03.005

Haines, V. Y., III, Marchand, A., & Harvey, S. (2006). Crossover of workplace aggression experiences in dual-earner couples. *Journal of Occupational Health Psychology*, *11*(4), 305–314. doi:10.1037/1076-8998.11.4.305

Hare-Mustin, R. T. (1987). The problem of gender in family therapy theory. *Family Process*, *26*(1), 15–27.

Ho, M. Y., Chen, X., Cheung, F. M., Liu, H., & Worthington, E. L., Jr. (2013). A dyadic model of the work–family interface: A study of dual-earner couples in China. *Journal of Occupational Health Psychology*, *18*(1), 53–63. doi:10.1037/a0030885

Hobfoll, S. E. (1985). Personal and social resources and the ecology of stress resistance. *Review of Personality and Social Psychology*, *6*, 265–290.

Hobfoll, S. E. (2002). Social and psychological resources and adaptation. *Review of General Psychology*, *6*(4), 307–324. doi:10.1037/1089-2680.6.4.307

Howe, G. W., Levy, M. L., & Caplan, R. D. (2004). Job loss and depressive symptoms in couples: common stressors, stress transmission, or relationship disruption? *Journal of Family Psychology*, *18*(4), 639–650. doi:10.1037/0893-3200.18.4.639

Jones, F., & Fletcher, B. (1993). An empirical study of occupational stress transmission in working couples. *Human Relations*, *46*(7), 881–903. doi:10.1177/001872679304600705

Kawaguchi, A. (2013). Equal Employment Opportunity Act and work–life balance: Do work–family balance policies contribute to achieving gender equality? *Japan Labor Review*, *10*(2), 35–56.

Lawson, K. M., Davis, K. D., McHale, S. M., Hammer, L. B., & Buxton, O. M. (2014). Daily positive spillover and crossover from mothers' work to youth health. *Journal of Family Psychology*, *28*(6), 897–907. doi:10.1037/fam0000028

Li, Y., Wang, Z., Yang, L. Q., & Liu, S. (2016). The crossover of psychological distress from leaders to subordinates in teams: The role of abusive supervision, psychological capital, and team performance. *Journal of Occupational Health Psychology*, *21*(2), 142–153. doi:10.1037/a0039960

Lim, V. K., & Sng, Q. S. (2006). Does parental job insecurity matter? Money anxiety, money motives, and work motivation. *Journal of Applied Psychology*, *91*(5), 1078–1087. doi:10.1037/0021-9010.91.5.1078

Liu, H., & Cheung, F. M. (2015a). The moderating role of empathy in the work–family crossover process between Chinese dual-earner couples. *Journal of Career Assessment*, *23*(3), 442–458. doi:10.1177/1069072714547612

Liu, H., & Cheung, F. M. (2015b). Testing crossover effects in an actor–partner interdependence model among Chinese dual-earner couples. *International Journal of Psychology*, *50*(2), 106–114. doi:10.1002/ijop.12070

Liu, H., Ngo, H. Y., & Cheung, F. M. (2016). Work–family enrichment and marital satisfaction among Chinese couples: A crossover-spillover perspective. *International Journal of Stress Management*, *23*(2), 209–231. doi:10.1037/a0039753

Lu, C.-q., Lu, J-J., Du, D.-y., & Brough, P. (2016). Crossover effects of work–family conflict among Chinese couples. *Journal of Managerial Psychology*, *31*(1), 235–250. doi:10.1108/jmp-09-2012-0283

Mickelson, K. D., Claffey, S. T., & Williams, S. L. (2006). The moderating role of gender and gender role attitudes on the link between spousal support and marital quality. *Sex Roles*, *55*(1–2), 73–82. doi:10.1007/s11199-006-9061-8

Muller, W., & Brough, P. (2017). Work, stress, and love: Investigating crossover through couples' lived experiences. In J. Fitzgerald (Ed.), *Foundations for Couples Therapy: Research for the Real World* (pp.464–474). New York, NY: Routledge.

Munyon, T. P., Breaux, D. M., Rogers, L. M., Perrewe, P. L., & Hochwarter, W. A. (2009). Mood crossover and relational reciprocity. *Career Development International, 14*(4–5), 408–427. doi:10.1108/13620430910989825

Neal, M. B., & Hammer, L. B. (2009). Dual-earner couples in the sandwiched generation: Effects of coping strategies over time. *The Psychologist-Manager Journal, 12*, 205–234. doi:10.1080/10887150903316230

Neff, A., Sonnentag, S., Niessen, C., & Unger, D. (2012). What's mine is yours: The crossover of day-specific self-esteem. *Journal of Vocational Behavior, 81*(3), 385–394. doi:10.1016/j.jvb.2012.10.002

Neff, A., Sonnentag, S., Niessen, C., & Unger, D. (2015). The crossover of self-esteem: A longitudinal perspective. *European Journal of Work and Organizational Psychology, 24*(2), 197–210. doi:10.1080/1359432x.2013.856298

Nemoto, K. (2013). Long working hours and the corporate gender divide in Japan. *Gender, Work & Organization, 20*(5), 512–527. doi:10.1111/j.1468-0432.2012.00599.x

OECD (2015). OECD Family database: The labour market position of families. Accessed December, 2016 from www.oecd.org/els/family/database.htm

Park, Y., & Fritz, C. (2015). Spousal recovery support, recovery experiences, and life satisfaction crossover among dual-earner couples. *Journal of Applied Psychology, 100*(2), 557–566. doi:10.1037/a0037894

Rodríguez-Muñoz, A., Sanz-Vergel, A. I., Demerouti, E., & Bakker, A. B. (2014). Engaged at work and happy at home: A spillover-crossover model. *Journal of Happiness Studies, 15*(2), 271–283. doi:10.1007/s10902-013-9421-3

Sayer, L. C., & Bianchi, S. M. (2000). Women's economic independence and the probability of divorce: A review and reexamination. *Journal of Family Issues, 21*(7), 906–943. doi:10.1177/019251300021007005

Schaer, M., Bodenmann, G., & Klink, T. (2008). Balancing work and relationship: Couples Coping Enhancement Training (CCET) in the workplace. *Applied Psychology: An International Review, 57*(s1), 71–89. doi:10.1111/j.1464-0597.2008.00355.x

Schooreel, T., & Verbruggen, M. (2016). Use of family-friendly work arrangements and work–family conflict: Crossover effects in dual-earner couples. *Journal of Occupational Health Psychology, 21*(1), 119–132. doi:10.1037/a0039669

Seligman, M. E. (2002). Positive psychology, positive prevention, and positive therapy. *Handbook of Positive Psychology, 2*, 3–12.

Shimazu, A. (2015). Heavy work investment and work–family balance among Japanese dual-earner couples. In L. Lu & C. L. Cooper (Eds.), *Handbook of Research on Work–Life Balance in Asia* (p. 61). Cheltenham, UK: Edward Elgar Publishing.

Shimazu, A., Bakker, A. B., & Demerouti, E. (2009). How job demands affect an intimate partner: A test of the spillover-crossover model in Japan. *Journal of Occupational Health Psychology, 51*(3), 239–248. doi:10.1539/joh.L8160

Song, Z., Foo, M. D., & Uy, M. A. (2008). Mood spillover and crossover among dual-earner couples: A cell phone event sampling study. *Journal of Applied Psychology, 93*(2), 443–452. doi:10.1037/0021-9010.93.2.443

Takeuchi, R., Yun, S., & Tesluk, P. E. (2002). An examination of crossover and spillover effects of spousal and expatriate cross-cultural adjustment on expatriate outcomes. *Journal of Applied Psychology, 87*(4), 655–666. doi:10.1037/0021-9010.87.4.655

ten Brummelhuis, L. L., Bakker, A. B., & Euwema, M. C. (2010). Is family-to-work interference related to co-workers' work outcomes? *Journal of Vocational Behavior*, *77*(3), 461–469. doi:10.1016/j.jvb.2010.06.001

ten Brummelhuis, L. L., Haar, J. M., & van der Lippe, T. (2010). Crossover of distress due to work and family demands in dual-earner couples: A dyadic analysis. *Work & Stress*, *24*(4), 324–341. doi:10.1080/02678373.2010.533553

Timms, C., Brough, P., Siu, O.-L., O'Driscoll, M., & Kalliath, T. (2015). Cross-cultural impact of work–life balance on health and work outcomes. In L. Lu & C. L. Cooper (Eds.), *Handbook of Research on Work–Life Balance in Asia* (pp. 295–314). Cheltenham, UK: Edward Elgar.

Totterdell, P. (2000). Catching moods and hitting runs: Mood linkage and subjective performance in professional sport teams. *Journal of Applied Psychology*, *85*(6), 848–859. doi:10.1037/0021-9010.85.6.848

Unger, D., Sonnentag, S., Niessen, C., & Kuonath, A. (2015). The longer your work hours, the worse your relationship? The role of selective optimization with compensation in the associations of working time with relationship satisfaction and self-disclosure in dual-career couples. *Human Relations*, *68*(12), 1889–1912. doi:10.1177/0018726715571188

Waugh, C. E., & Fredrickson, B. L. (2006). Nice to know you: Positive emotions, self-other overlap, and complex understanding in the formation of a new relationship. *Journal of Positive Psychology*, *1*(2), 93–106. doi:10.1080/17439760500510569

Westman, M. (2001). Stress and strain crossover. *Human Relations*, *54*(6), 717–751. doi:10.1177/0018726701546002

Westman, M., Brough, P., & Kalliath, T. (2009). Expert commentary on work–life balance and crossover of emotions and experiences: Theoretical and practice advancements. *Journal of Organizational Behavior*, *30*, 587–595. doi: 10.1002/job.616

Westman, M., & Etzion, D. (2005). The crossover of work–family conflict from one spouse to the other. *Journal of Applied Social Psychology*, *35*(9), 1936–1957. doi:10.1111/j.1559-1816.2005.tb02203.x

Westman, M., Etzion, D., & Chen, S. (2009). Crossover of positive experiences from business travelers to their spouses. *Journal of Managerial Psychology*, *24*(3), 269–284. doi:10.1108/02683940910939340

Westman, M., Etzion, D., & Horovitz, S. (2004). The toll of unemployment does not stop with the unemployed. *Human Relations*, *57*(7), 823–844. doi:10.1177/0018726704045767

Westman, M., Keinan, G., Roziner, I., & Benyamini, Y. (2008). The crossover of perceived health between spouses. *Journal of Occupational Health Psychology*, *13*(2), 168–180. doi:10.1037/1076-8998.13.2.168

Westman, M., Vinokur, A. D., Hamilton, V., & Roziner, I. (2004). Crossover of marital dissatisfaction during military downsizing among Russian army officers and their spouses. *Journal of Applied Psychology*, *89*(5), 769–779. doi:10.1037/0021-9010.89.5.769

Williams, J. E., & Best, D. L. (1990). *Sex and Psyche: Gender and Self Viewed Cross-Culturally*. London, UK: Sage.

35 Cultural Considerations in the Division of Labor

Lyn Craig and Ruth Habgood

When we think about work and labor, the spotlight is usually on paid employment. But also essential is non-market, or unpaid, work: housework, home maintenance, and looking after children and elders as well as family members who are sick or are living with a disability. These latter activities are not rest or leisure. They are not hobbies. They are work; specifically, what economists call household production (Kalenkoski & Foster, 2015). They require time and effort, and they have productive outcomes. How market and non-market work is divided by gender is a critical social issue. This chapter examines what we have discovered about the gender division of paid and unpaid work over the past few decades and how individual characteristics, family and workplace arrangements, and national contexts influence these patterns.

Paid Work and Unpaid Work Are Both Essential

Societies and economies rely on both market and non-market work. Both require time and effort and both are productive. That is to say, they have economically valuable outcomes. Following industrialization, paid and unpaid labor became gendered and spatially differentiated. Men worked for money outside the home; women's domestic production and mothering roles largely remained in the home. A consequence of this shift was that "work" came to be seen as only those activities which resulted in the production of goods and services that have monetary value. As non-market work was not exchanged for money, it was no longer conceptualized as economically productive and no longer widely recognized as being "real" work (Folbre, 2001).

As a consequence, over time, the value of domestic and caring work to household and to national well-being has become obscured. This is despite the crucial role that non-market work plays in underpinning the economy and perpetuating the society. Domestic labor and family care are not simply family or personal matters. They have benefits that extend to the whole of society because to function successfully, societies depend not only on the market economy but also on an adequate supply of unpaid work and family care (Fineman, 2004). This work is essential if children are to be

This chapter is a distillation of the first author's papers on aspects of the work–family interface and the gender division of labor written over the period 2006–2016.

born and reared into independent adults, daily family needs met, and disabled, infirm, or elderly relatives cared for. Consequently, both governments and the market are profoundly dependent on the unpaid domestic labor, care, and human capital inputs that individuals and families provide.

Although overlooked in conventional economic accounting, the unpaid economy is very large. Cross-national estimates of what it would cost to pay replacement wages for unpaid work range between 40% and 70% of GDP (OECD, 2016). Depending on the wage attributed, the replacement value of family care in the United States has been estimated at $140 billion, $257 billion, or $389 billion a year, and in the United Kingdom estimates have been put at £87 billion a year (Buckner & Yeandle, 2007).

Although costing unpaid work and care in monetary terms is very important, this approach on its own does not go far enough to understand the division of labor and its consequences. The social, economic, and personal significance of domestic work and care responsibilities is not only what they are worth in financial terms, but also the time they involve and the impacts that undertaking this work has on other activities and outcomes. Knowing how much time is spent in domestic work and caring activities is crucially important in understanding contemporary equality and barriers to it. In modern money-based economies, there are strong financial incentives to avoid doing unpaid domestic or care work, or to have others perform it on your behalf. Growing rewards in the labor market raises the opportunity cost of withdrawing from the workforce to care for family members; fewer people are able to do it, and as a result, both the supply of unpaid care and the well-being and financial security of those who still provide it are in jeopardy.

Raising children, for example, can be viewed as public-goods provision which, if not compensated, allows citizens who do not provide it to free-ride on the efforts of those who do (Folbre, 1994a). Public goods are those that cannot be supplied to any one person without benefiting others, and the use of which by any one person does not preclude their use by others (Caporaso & Levinde, 1992). An example is light-houses, which protect all ships from harm, including those that do not contribute to their cost (Bittman & Pixley, 1997). Children similarly generate diffuse benefits. Child-raising involves very substantial private investment in human capital and the cumulative cost to parents in terms of time, money, and energy from birth to adulthood is huge (Folbre, 1994b). The long-term economic return on this investment is also substantial, but it largely flows not to the parents who rear them, but to others, including the government, employers, and the whole community in the form of productive citizens, workers, and community members (Chesnais, 1998; Folbre, 1994a, 1994b).

The care penalty is reinforced in many modern economies by public policy shifts based on the expectation that all adults will be workers regardless of gender and notwithstanding care responsibilities (Lewis, 2006). For example, people who withdraw from paid work to care for children or others may not only lose income in the short term but also suffer cumulative material disadvantage over the lifetime through lost access to promotion opportunities, retirement income, and health funds (Sigle-Rushton & Waldfogel, 2007). This means that the costs of care over the lifetime include being at risk of poverty in old age. In such circumstances, providing care is a major life-course risk (Lewis, 2006). Conversely, if carers do not withdraw from the workforce, they may be subject to overwork and time strain, which can adversely affect their health and well-being (Strazdins & Loughrey, 2007). Time scarcity is at the center of significant concern about the quality of contemporary life. The feeling of being rushed, harried, and having too much to do is widely attributed to the ongoing challenge of balancing work and family demands and the division of paid and unpaid labor (Edwards & Wajcman, 2005). It is, therefore, important to make time spent in unpaid work and care visible alongside paid work and to show how much is done, who does it, and the consequences for those who do it.

The Division of Labor: What Do We Know?

To remedy the invisibility of unpaid work, to inform policy, and to calculate its worth to national economies, the United Nations advocates using time use surveys to calculate the quantum of non-market work and compile satellite accounts to supplement calculations of GDP. Time diaries involve data on the time people spend in all activities throughout the day, including sometimes data from multiple household members. This information can be used to identify the distribution of paid and unpaid work within households. Time use surveys have supported the emergence of a much clearer and more nuanced understanding of the family–paid work division of labor, its variability, its gendered nature, and its social and economic consequences (for more information on time use surveys in the work–family interface, see Chapter 12 of this handbook, Garcia Roman & Flood). Satellite accounts refer to measures of the size of economic sectors that are not defined as industries in national accounts (e.g., unpaid household work, the environment), which enables attention to be focused on these aspects of economic and social life that are often not included in national accounts of GDP.

Cross-national time use studies show that time spent in unpaid work and care amount to many hours per day and also that gender differences in time allocated to paid and unpaid work is universal (Hook, 2006). For example, a six-country study compared average minutes per day spent in domestic work (i.e., cooking, cleaning, clothes care, shopping, and childcare) by women and men in Canada (275 vs. 140), the United Kingdom (287 vs. 146), the United States (281 vs. 146), Denmark (232 vs. 132), Finland (239 vs. 137), and Sweden (288 vs. 172) (Gershuny & Sullivan, 2003). The study also compared women's and men's average minutes per day in paid work time in Canada (331 vs. 374), the United Kingdom (316 vs. 373), the United States (312 vs. 393), Denmark (283 vs. 364), Finland (271 vs. 343), and Sweden (274 vs. 354) (Gershuny & Sullivan, 2003). Thus, although national averages varied, in all cases men's average paid work time was higher than women's, and women's average unpaid work time was higher than men's. Recent data from the Organization for Economic Co-operation and Development (OECD) shows this pattern is still ubiquitous and occurs in countries as diverse as Turkey, Japan, and Korea (where men do about a fifth of the unpaid work that women do) and New Zealand and Poland (where men do about half the unpaid work that women do) (OECD, 2016).

As women entered the workforce in increasing numbers and gained income and bargaining power, it was expected that the gender division of both paid and unpaid work would become more equal (Bergmann, 1986). There has indeed been some gender convergence in market and family work over time, although the pace is slow in many countries (Altintas & Sullivan, 2016). Moreover, although men have increased their domestic participation over recent years, it has not been at the same rate as women have taken up market work. The convergence was largely because as more women entered the paid labor force they did less housework than in times past, lowering the overall quantum rather than directly trading-off with men (Bianchi, Milkie, Sayer, & Robinson, 2000). Even when both male and female household partners have full-time jobs, the woman still does significantly more housework than the man (Bianchi & Milkie, 2010). Indeed a recent comprehensive review of the research suggests that no matter what factors are taken into account, gender emerges as the strongest predictor of how labor is divided (Shockley & Shen, 2016).

Gender differences do vary by family structure, education, workforce participation status, and over the life course. However, generally speaking, at each life stage, more of men's labor is paid than women's. Men continue to specialize in paid work while women's labor includes a higher proportion of productive work, specifically housework, childcare, and elder care, that is unpaid (Lewis, 2009). This is true to an even greater extent when women are partnered compared to single and to the greatest extent of all when they are parents of young children. The transition to parenthood is the life course event that most clearly impacts the gender division of labor within families (Baxter, Hewitt, & Haynes, 2008). This is mainly because, on becoming fathers, men do not reduce their paid work time, but on becoming mothers, women are much more likely to cut back on paid work and to do more care (Craig & Bittman, 2008). It is still rare that fathers have the primary responsibility for childcare and women are still much more likely than men to move in and out of the workforce, or limit their paid work hours to care for young children or for other dependents (Baxter & Gray, 2008). However, there are exceptions, and some have argued that it is not "gender per se but gendered divisions of care giving labor, especially mothers' withdrawals and reductions in employment, that are the primary cause of continued male–female disparities in wages and occupational attainment" (Gornick & Meyers, 2007, p. 11). If men have the primary responsibility for care, they too suffer disadvantage in the workplace, and conversely, if women avoid it, they can compete more equally with men in the workplace (Folbre, 2007).

At the same time there is evidence that both mothers and fathers are spending more time with children than in times past, despite families becoming smaller. This is also despite mothers doing more paid work, and on average fathers not limiting theirs, which suggests that more overall time is being committed both to work and to family. The increase in childcare time is true for both genders and in most industrialized countries (Cooke & Baxter, 2010). It has been suggested that the trend is driven by burgeoning social expectations regarding what constitutes adequate parenting (Coltrane, 2007). Some argue this is a middle-class phenomenon (Lareau, 2003).

Educated fathers spend more time with children than less educated fathers, and more highly educated women seem reluctant to trade off time caring for their children either with their partners, or with paid employment despite their improved market opportunities (England & Srivastava, 2013). However, single mothers also prioritize childcare, despite arguably facing a starker choice between earning income and providing care for their children (Craig & Mullan, 2012). Over the life course other forms of care, including for sick or disabled relatives or for elder family members, are also more likely to be done by women than by men (Lewis, 2009).

Influences on the Division of Labor

Although broad patterns confirm the persistence of unequal gender division of care and other unpaid work, some factors have been identified as mitigating it. The bulk of the literature has focused on three possible levers: time availability, relative resources, and gender ideology (see Bianchi & Milkie, 2010 for an overview). These factors generate predictions about the gender division of labor within couples. For example, it is expected that the spouse with higher earning capacity (captured through education or earnings) will do the most market work, and the spouse who does the most market work will do the least non-market work. Those who work longer market hours will have less time for unpaid work than those who work short market hours. Couples with more conservative gender ideology are expected to adopt more traditional divisions of paid and unpaid work than those with more progressive ideology. Empirical research suggests that these explanations are partial at best, and none are sufficient to wholly explain the gender division of labor (see Lachance-Grzela & Bouchard, 2010 for an overview). This may be because they are inextricably linked, and gender is fundamental to all. Labor markets yield unequal earnings for men and women, which reflects and influences couples' decisions on who should commit more time to market work, affect mothers' and fathers' relative resources and household bargaining power, and reinforce attitudes about appropriate gender roles.

In the pursuit of factors that might support work–family reconciliation, a series of Australian studies considered the effects of work conditions and arrangements on the gender division of labor and subjective time pressure in two-parent family households. Predictors examined included part-time work, nonstandard work schedules, working at home and flexible hours, self-employment, non-parental childcare, and domestic outsourcing. The series of studies asked, in essence, what difference do family work sharing choices, outsourcing, and personal working conditions make to 1) household total work, 2) the gender division of labor, and 3) time stress? These questions are addressed in the sections below.

Non-parental childcare. When non-parental childcare was utilized, the gender division of labor was slightly more equal. Non-parental childcare can include formal day care, nannies, non-formal arrangements with family or friends, or some mixture of these. Mothers who used formal non-parental care did more paid work than mothers who did not. They did less domestic work than other mothers, but the reduction in the amount of childcare was much lower. This is probably because activities like bathing, feeding, and supervising homework are shifted to the evening after parents and children get home. Also, with formal care arrangements, mothers' time stress was higher, likely due to the added pressure of meeting deadlines, particularly for delivering children to day care before work and for picking them up at the end of the day (Craig & Powell, 2013).

Informal non-parental care was not associated with longer parental work hours or higher time pressure, perhaps because it is more flexible and usually provided by family. Increasing numbers of grandparents now provide regular care while parents work. Incidence echoes the patterns found among parents, namely that it is disproportionately done by women. Results suggest that as more young women are in paid work, some care is transferring from younger to older women, thus spreading care across the life course rather than being distributed more equally with men. Many grandmothers are giving up or cutting back on paid work to allow their own daughters to work. Regular care provision is associated with less leisure for grandparents of both genders and doubles the likelihood of grandmothers reporting high subjective time pressure (Craig & Jenkins, 2015).

Domestic outsourcing. Studies into whether domestic outsourcing (i.e., paid household help) improves the gender division of labor have found mixed results, with some suggesting that it reduces domestic time as much for men as for women (see Craig & Baxter, 2016 for an overview). Recent research using longitudinal data suggests, however, that for those women who can afford domestic help it can somewhat reduce housework time, narrow gender gaps, and lower women's subjective time pressure (Craig, Perales, Vidal Torre, & Baxter, 2016).

Work conditions/arrangements. Parents who work nonstandard hours (i.e., evenings, nights, or weekends) spend significantly longer in paid work and less time on housework and childcare than those who work standard hours. Nonstandard hours had mixed effects on the gender division of labor. Mothers' nonstandard hours have minor positive effects on the gender division of labor because fathers perform more childcare while the mother is absent. Conversely, when fathers work nonstandard hours, mothers do more housework and routine childcare, so the gendered division of labor intensifies (Craig & Powell, 2011). Fathers' nonstandard hours are also associated with working longer hours and doing less housework and care than fathers who work standard hours. These fathers also report more time stress, as do their partners (Craig & Brown, 2016).

Self-employment and working from home potentially offer parents the kind of flexibility they need to better manage work and family demands. Although these arrangements seem to facilitate some rescheduling, research suggests that they do not appear to involve gender redistribution of paid and unpaid work. They are associated with more variation in women's time than in men's, particularly in relation to the length of market work hours. As such, these arrangements are more likely to reinforce, rather than challenge, household gender divisions because they are associated with women doing more housework and care or result in men doing more paid and less unpaid work (Craig, Powell, & Cortis, 2012; Powell & Craig, 2015).

Despite the potential of the aforementioned arrangements to facilitate more equal sharing of paid and unpaid work, results suggest that they do so only marginally or not at all. Also, although some of the strategies studied had slightly positive effects on the gender division of labor, none reduced women's subjective time stress or overall workload when both paid and unpaid work are taken into account. This was because they facilitated rescheduling their paid work and family responsibilities around each other, allowing one type of work to take over from another. This was particularly apparent with part-time female work hours, the strategy most commonly adopted by Australian parents trying to balance work and family demands. Women's part-time work was associated with longer male paid work and less unpaid work, and the converse for women. Whether mothers worked full- or part-time, their total workloads were much the same. When they did less paid work, unpaid work took its place – although full-time work brought more subjective time stress (Craig & Powell, 2012).

Taken as a whole, the answer this series of Australian studies gave to the question of what difference various work strategies or family-level arrangements make to the gender division of labor was "not much." The results suggest that family-level variation in work/care strategies and arrangements have little overall effect on workloads, and only slightly alleviate or actually reinforce the gender division of labor. However, Australia is a country in which collective measures (e.g., national paid parental leave and accessible, affordable childcare) to assist work–family balance are relatively sparse, and the outcomes noted above may be related to the absence of broader policy support.

Cross-National Variation in the Division of Labor

Most research on the gender division of labor highlights the role of individual beliefs, family resources, and household circumstances. It is recognized, however, that beyond individual and household micro-level factors, the demands of work and family and the options for meeting them are strongly influenced by macro-level factors, including working-time systems and social policies (Gornick & Meyers, 2009).

Cross-nationally, social policies can facilitate or hinder combining work and family, including exacerbating or ameliorating gender differences in workforce participation. National context can also affect intra-household decisions by "influencing the terms of bargaining, the benefits of specialization, and the ease or difficulty of adhering to gender norms" (Hook, 2006, p. 642). Importantly, national contexts affect how much care families directly carry out and how it is divided between men and women. Norms and attitudes matter too. For example, there are cultural differences in ideas about what children need and who should best provide it and related variation in both the accessibility of substitute care and whether parents wish to use it (Duncan & Edwards, 2003). Although some countries provide extensive social supports, others regard family care as primarily a private responsibility. The institutional framework affects the gender division of labor, as the responsibility for non-market work usually reverts to women if no supports are provided (Lewis, 2009). Although the primary effect is on women's employment, cross-national differences in policies have also been found to predict men's family involvement (Hook, 2006).

The strength and importance of macro-level factors in shaping the division of labor is revealed in variety across different national contexts and in the different pace of change that has occurred over time (Altintas & Sullivan, 2016). Comparing time use surveys cross-nationally across different policy environments can tell us not only what is happening, but also what change is possible. In other words, it can help to identify *how* to make changes. For example, one cross-national study of how paid and unpaid work time allocation varies with parenthood, found that the gender division of labor is more likely to be more equal in countries where there is a suite of policies assisting work–family reconciliation (e.g., paid parental leave, available and affordable childcare, and state-subsidized elder care), as is often the case in Nordic social democracies (Lewis, 2009). These measures make it easier to divide paid and unpaid labor more equally by gender than in countries in which there is little public institutional support to balance work and family, such as Southern Europe, Asia, or liberal Anglo countries. For example, in the United States and Australia, solutions to the gender division of labor are more individual and must be implemented in the face of higher overall workloads (Craig & Mullan, 2010).

The interplay between policies and attitudes is iterative, complex, and multi-directional (Lewis, 2009). The normative ideal that young children need constant and sustained parental attention seems particularly strong in Anglo countries (Duncan & Edwards, 2003). In Northern European countries (e.g., Finland, Sweden, Denmark), there is more public acknowledgment of the important contribution that care makes to society, and this is reflected in the greater public provision of elderly and childcare services, as examples. It is important to note, however, that such policies mean that a more gender-equal division of labor results from the state relieving households of much direct responsibility for care. Thus women can do less, but it is not necessarily the case that men do more (Craig & Mullan, 2010). Also importantly, in these countries paid working hours are short by international standards, giving people more opportunity to do unpaid work with less career penalty than elsewhere. Reduced average full-time working hours for both men and women may be the most effective route to mitigating the gender division of labor.

Long working hours make it harder to divide paid and unpaid labor equally, and much more likely that both individuals and their families will feel time pressured. Levels of time stress are important measures of family welfare and of men and women's comparative well-being, which also vary with national context. Although long working hours are stressful for most people, including for single and coupled individuals, full-time work combined with care responsibilities is particularly demanding. Research suggests that mothers become time stressed at lower working hours than fathers, reflecting their greater non-market work burden. It is also the case that men's longer work hours are associated with higher time stress not only for the men themselves, but also for their partners (Craig & Brown, 2016). Time stress is particularly high when children are young. In Australia, over 90% of mothers and 70% of fathers working full-time with children under five report being "always" time stressed (Craig & Mullan, 2009). Although stress levels reduce as children age, they remain high. This is in contrast with Finland, where the level of time stress for both mothers and fathers is much lower, likely because lower average full-time work hours for both genders gives everyone more flexibility to balance work and family (Craig, Brown, Strazdins, & Jun, forthcoming).

However, time quality also impacts subjective time stress. For example, compared to inadequate good-quality leisure, adequate-quality leisure predicts better physical and mental health (Strazdins & Loughrey, 2007). Gender differences in leisure are related to the gendered division of labor and also affect the relative welfare of men and women. Leisure equality is an important supplementary indicator to economic equality. It offers a perspective on men and women's comparative well-being additional to that shown by gender gaps in market and non-market work (Shaw, 2008). As conventionally measured, average leisure time is higher in some countries than in others, but within most countries men and women have similar amounts. However, when the *quality* of leisure is considered, and specific demographic groups investigated, there is considerable gender divergence. Studies in the United States, for example, find that mothers have less leisure time than fathers, especially when both parents work or when children are young (Sayer, England, Bittman, & Bianchi, 2009). Mothers' personal leisure quality is lower than fathers' because it is less often child-free (Mattingly & Bianchi, 2003). As a result, mothers' free time does not reduce subjective time stress to the same extent as does fathers' (Craig & Brown, 2016). Overall leisure time is higher for parents in European countries than parents in non-European countries, but even in Europe the quantity and quality of leisure time, particularly the proportion that is child-free, still favors fathers more than mothers (Craig & Mullan, 2013).

Across a variety of areas and contexts, the studies above demonstrate the variability in the gender division of labor on a national rather than an individual scale and show the impact of policies supporting states sharing responsibility for care relative to contexts where this does not occur. National context and policy settings clearly make a difference.

National Policy Effects within Countries

Although comparative time use studies demonstrate that an unequal gender division of labor is ubiquitous, they also demonstrate its malleability. This work has uncovered considerable variation in how families manage paid and unpaid work in their lives, with varying household characteristics and employment conditions. These studies demonstrate the powerful role that government policies play in producing the gendered work and family care patterns that we observe. This is not only apparent in cross-national comparisons, but also over time within countries.

As an example, Australian research has demonstrated that substantial changes to work–family balance are possible within relatively short time frames. In the period from 1997 to 2006, Australia experienced booming economic conditions and increasing higher education levels, especially for women. These conditions could be expected to promote greater female workforce participation. However, a series of policy decisions were made by a socially conservative government that resulted in more gendered work–family arrangements over the time period (Craig, Mullan, & Blaxland, 2010). Specifically, there were tax disincentives for part-nered mothers to work, limited paid parental leave, and insufficient affordable childcare places, measures underpinned by high rhetorical support from the government for families with a full-time employed father and a part-time employed mother. The rhetorical support took the form of frequent policy and political speeches and media discussion of the topic. As a result, by 2006 there was lower average maternal market work and a higher proportion of families with young children conformed to the one-and-a-half-earner family form than in 1997 (Craig & Mullan, 2009). There was increased total household work, increased gender specialization in paid work and caring labor, and much higher subjective time pressure, especially for fathers and the relatively few mothers who were employed full-time (Craig et al., 2010).

Although the Australian case involved turning back the clock for gender parity, it does suggest that policies and government backing can influence changes in the gender division of labor relatively quickly. Research investigating the impacts of policy change in the Netherlands, for example, investigated the effects on mothers' workforce participation of three related policy developments: the introduction of part-time parental leave, strong growth in part-time jobs, and improvements in the labor market position of part-time workers (Begall & Grunow, 2015). The study found that first-time Dutch mothers were significantly less likely to exit the labor force or reduce their hours when they had access to these measures than when they did not. The effect of family policies on *men's* labor market outcomes were examined in a large study of twenty-eight European countries (Bünning & Pollmann-Schult, 2015). This study found that fathers do less paid work than childless men if they live in countries that offer generous family allowances or well-paid, non-transferable parental leave for fathers and short parental leave for mothers. However, there were educational differences in these results; specifically, for highly educated fathers, short maternal leaves were associated with shorter working hours, but for less educated fathers, reduced working hours were associated with generous family allowances and father-friendly parental leave schemes (Bünning & Pollmann-Schult, 2015).

Implications and Future Directions

Linking policies and outcomes in the ways described above is highly dependent on good-quality data being available (Lohmann & Zagel, 2015). Time use studies are particularly useful because they capture non-market work on the same metric as paid work. They can give more accurate and comprehensive measures of national productivity and its division by gender than economic data alone. On a micro-level they can show links between partners. They thus not only put the spotlight on undervalued and unnoticed activities, but can show how market and non-market work is divided within and across nations and within and across families.

In the future, the important contribution time use studies make to understanding the gender division of labor can be maintained and extended if national statistical agencies conduct them. This is an ongoing challenge, as high-quality data collection is expensive. As more countries (e.g., Inner Mongolia, China) collect time use data for the first time, others (e.g., Australia) have cancelled planned collections due to budgetary reasons. It is also necessary to ensure survey design is similar enough to be harmonized for international comparison, through projects such as the Harmonized European Time Use Study (HETUS) and the Multinational Time Use Study (MTUS). Also important to future knowledge is to examine time patterns over the life course. In the absence of panel studies collecting time use data, high-quality repeated cross-sectional collection from multiple countries can allow time-series analyses investigating cross-national trends over time for different age cohorts.

This work is necessary because the consequences of ignoring or devaluing socially necessary unpaid work and care are substantial both for those who do this work and for societies as a whole. Appropriately valuing and including unpaid work and care in political and policy decision-making is crucial to avoid inequity. Being disproportionately responsible for non-market work in a monetized economy that values little else has negative outcomes. This can only be avoided if it is shared more equally. To ensure this, unpaid work must be systematically measured and counted alongside other decision-making metrics. National time use collections need to be institutionalized and compulsory as for other social and economic data. But collecting information, although necessary, is not sufficient. We also need politicians and policy makers to want the evidence and to want to use it, not only to inform policy but to also systematically evaluate its effectiveness over time. Ongoing cross-national studies are needed to show how things can be done differently and to support effective change.

Systematic assessment of gender impact is required. In its absence, gender-neutral policy-making becomes male worker centric, a source of gender inequality and disadvantage and family-unfriendly outcomes. For example, in many countries contributory retirement incomes assume traditional male employment patterns (i.e., full-time over the working lifetime) that do not include caring responsibilities. Women avoiding care responsibilities could work to achieve individual gender equality, but this is not a socially sustainable solution. Asia and Southern Europe, for example, have very low fertility rates and rapidly aging populations. They also have particularly wide gender divisions of labor. Many scholars connect the two, effectively arguing that gender inequity in paid and unpaid work has caused a baby strike (de Laat & Sevilla-Sanz, 2011; Hobson, Olah, & Morrissens, 2006; McDonald, 2006).

Conclusion

Comprehensive work–family supports are needed as part of the basic social infrastructure to support the provision of socially necessary non-market work. The need to be available to care or be the recipient of care is lifelong and a fundamental social requirement. Lack of formal supports devalue non-market work and mean women remain the default providers. It also denies care to higher-need and less well-connected individuals. Care and unpaid work, and how it is divided by gender, needs to be as central to public debate as it is central to our lives. Unpaid work and care undergird the economy. It is vital and productive activity. It should count. Those who do it should count. If the future is to involve employment on equal terms for both men and women, then the division of unpaid work and care also has to be fair and sustainable.

References

Altintas, E., & Sullivan, O. (2016). Fifty years of change updated: Cross-national gender convergence in housework. *Demographic Research, 35*(16), 455–470.

Baxter, J., & Gray, M. (2008). Work and family responsibilities through life. Melbourne: Australian Institute of Family Studies.

Baxter, J., Hewitt, B., & Haynes, M. (2008). Life course transitions and housework: Marriage, parenthood, and time on housework. *Journal of Marriage and Family, 70*(2), 259–272.

Begall, K., & Grunow, D. (2015). Labour force transitions around first childbirth in the Netherlands. *European Sociological Review, 31*(6), 697–712.

Bergmann, B. (1986). *The Economic Emergence of Women*. New York, NY: Basic Books, Inc.

Bianchi, S., & Milkie, M. (2010). Work and family research in the first decade of the 21st century. *Journal of Marriage and Family, 72*(3), 705–725. doi: 10.1111/j .1741-3737.2010.00726.x

Bianchi, S., Milkie, M., Sayer, L., & Robinson, J. (2000). Is anyone doing the housework? Trends in the gender division of household labor. *Social Forces, 79*(1), 191–228. doi: 10.1093/sf/79.1.191

Bittman, M., & Pixley, J. (1997). *The Double Life of the Family*. St. Leonards, Australia: Allen and Unwin.

Buckner, L., & Yeandle, S. (2007). Valuing Carers – calculating the value of unpaid care. Carers UK, University of Leeds.

Bünning, M., & Pollmann-Schult, M. (2015). Family policies and fathers' working hours: cross-national differences in the paternal labour supply. *Work, Employment & Society, 30*(2), 256–274.

Caporaso, J. A., & Levinde, D. P. (1992). *Theories of Political Economy*. Cambridge, UK: Cambridge University Press.

Chesnais, J.-C. (1998). Below-replacement fertility in the European Union (EU-15): Facts and policies, 1960–1997. *Review of Population and Social Policy, 7*, 83–101.

Coltrane, S. (2007). *Fatherhood, Gender and Work–Family Policies*. Paper presented at the Real Utopias, The Havens Center, University of Wisconsin-Madison.

Cooke, L. P., & Baxter, J. (2010). 'Families' in international context: Comparing institutional effects across Western societies. *Journal of Marriage and Family, 72*, 516–536.

Craig, L., & Baxter, J. (2016). Domestic outsourcing, housework shares and subjective time pressure: gender differences in the correlates of hiring help. *Social Indicators Research*, *125*(1), 271–288. doi: 10.1007/s11205-014-083-1

Craig, L., & Bittman, M. (2008). The effect of children on adults' time-use: An analysis of the incremental time costs of children in Australia. *Feminist Economics*, *14*(2), 57–85. doi: 10.1080/13545700701880999

Craig, L., & Brown, J. (2016). Feeling rushed: gendered time quality, work hours, work schedules and spousal crossover. *Journal of Marriage and Family*, *79*(1), 225–242. doi: online first 10.1111/jomf.12320

Craig, L., Brown, J., Strazdins, L., & Jun, J. (forthcoming). Gendered time symmetry and subjective time pressure in Australia, Finland and Korea. In R. Connelly & E. Kongar (Eds.), *Gender and Time Use in a Global Context*. New York, NY: Palgrave MacMillan.

Craig, L., & Jenkins, B. (2015). Grandparents' childcare in Australia: Gender differences in the correlates and outcomes of providing regular grandparent care while parents work. *Community, Work & Family*, *19*(3), 281–301. doi: 10.1080/13668803.2015.1027176

Craig, L., & Mullan, K. (2009). The Policeman and the part-time sales assistant: Household labour supply, family time and subjective time pressure in Australia 1997–2006. *Journal of Comparative Family Studies*, *40*(4), 545–560.

Craig, L., & Mullan, K. (2010). Parenthood, gender and work–family time in USA, Australia, Italy, France and Denmark *Journal of Marriage and Family*, *72*(5), 1344–1361.

Craig, L., & Mullan, K. (2012). Lone and couple mothers' childcare time within context in four countries. *European Sociological Review*, *28* (4), 512–526. doi: 10.1093/esr/jcr013

Craig, L., & Mullan, K. (2013). Parental leisure time: a gender comparison in five countries. *Social Politics: International Studies in Gender, State and Society*, *20*(3), 329–357. doi: 10.1093/sp/jxt002

Craig, L., Mullan, K., & Blaxland, M. (2010). Parenthood, policy and work–family time in Australia 1992–2006. *Work, Employment and Society*, *24*(1), 1–19. doi: 10.1177/0950017012437006

Craig, L., Perales, P., Vidal Torre, S., & Baxter, J. (2016). Domestic outsourcing, housework and subjective time pressure: New insights from longitudinal data. *Journal of Marriage and Family*, *78*(5), 1224–1236. doi: online first 10.1111/jomf.12321

Craig, L., & Powell, A. (2011). Nonstandard work schedules, work–family balance and the gendered division of childcare. *Work, Employment and Society*, *25*(2), 274–291. doi: 10.1177/0950017011398894

Craig, L., & Powell, A. (2012). Dual-earner parents' work–family time: the effects of atypical work patterns and formal non-parental care. *Journal of Population Research*, *29* (3), 229–247. doi: 10.1007/s12546-012-9086-5

Craig, L., & Powell, A. (2013). Non-parental childcare, time pressure and the gendered division of paid work, domestic work and parental childcare. *Community, Work and Family*, *16*(1), 100–119. doi: 10.1080/13668803.2012.722013

Craig, L., Powell, A., & Cortis, N. (2012). Self-employment, work–family time and the gender division of labour *Work, Employment and Society*, *26*(5), 716. doi: 10.1177/0950017012451642

de Laat, J., & Sevilla-Sanz, A. (2011). The fertility and women's labor force participation puzzle in OECD countries: The role of men's home production. *Feminist Economics*, *7*(2), 87–119.

Duncan, S., & Edwards, R. (2003). State welfare regimes, mothers' agencies and gendered moral rationalities. In K. Kollind & A. Peterson (Eds.), *Thoughts on Family, Gender, Generation and Class. A Festschrift to Ulla Bjornberg* (pp. 22–40). Gothenburg, Sweden: Sociology Institute, Gothenburg University.

Edwards, P., & Wajcman, J. (2005). *The Politics of Working Life*: Oxford University Press.

England, P., & Srivastava, A. (2013). Educational differences in U.S. parents' time spent in child care: the role of culture and cross-spouse influence. *Social Science Research*, *42*(4), 971–988.

Fineman, M. (2004). *The Autonomy Myth: A Theory of Dependency*. New York, NY: The New Press.

Folbre, N. (1994a). Children as public goods. *The American Economic Review*, *84*(1552), 86–90.

Folbre, N. (1994b). *Who Pays for the Kids? Gender and the Structures of Constraint*. London, UK, and New York, NY: Routledge.

Folbre, N. (2001). *The Invisible Heart: Economics and Family Values*. New York, NY: The New Press.

Gershuny, J., & Sullivan, O. (2003). Time use, gender and public policy regimes. *Social Politics*, *10*(2), 205–228.

Gornick, J., & Meyers, M. (2007). Further thoughts. In E. O. Wright (Ed.), *Real Utopias: Institutions for Gender Egalitarianism: Creating the Conditions for Egalitarian Dual Earner / Dual Caregiver Families*. Madison, WI: University of Wisconsin-Madison.

Gornick, J., & Meyers, M. (Eds.). (2009). *Gender Equality: Transforming Family Divisions of Labor (Vol. IV Real Utopias Project)* London, UK: Verso.

Hobson, B., Olah, L., & Morrissens, A. (2006). The positive turn or birth-strikes? Sites of resistance to residual male breadwinner societies and to welfare state restructuring. Paper presented at the RC19 Meetings of the ISA Sept 2–5, Paris.

Hook, J. (2006). Care in context: Men's unpaid work in 20 countries, 1965–2003. *American Sociological Review*, *71*(4), 639–660.

Kalenkoski, C., & Foster, G. (2015). *The Economics of Multitasking*. New York, NY: Palgrave MacMillan.

Lachance-Grzela, M., & Bouchard, G. (2010). Why do women do the lion's share of housework? A decade of research. *Sex Roles*, *63*, 767–780.

Lareau, A. (2003). *Unequal Childhoods: Class, Race, and Family Life*. Berkeley, CA: University of California Press.

Lewis, J. (2006). Employment and care: The policy problem, gender equality and the issue of choice. *Journal of Comparative Policy Analysis: Research and Practice*, *8*(2), 103–114.

Lewis, J. (2009). *Work–Family Balance, Gender and Policy*. Cheltenham, UK, and Northhampton, MA: Edward Elgar.

Lohmann, H., & Zagel, H. (2015). Family policy in comparative perspective: The concepts and measurement of familization and defamilization. *Journal of European Social Policy*, *28*(1), 48–65.

Mattingly, M., & Bianchi, S. (2003). Gender differences in the quantity and quality of free time: The U.S. experience. *Social Forces*, *81*, 999–1030. doi: 10.1353/sof.2003.0036

McDonald, P. (2006). Low fertility and the state: The efficacy of policy. *Population and Development Review*, *32*(3), 485–510.

OECD. (2016). Paid and unpaid work. Organisation for Economic Co-operation and Development. www.oecd.org/gender/data/timespentinunpaidpaidandtotalworkby sex.htm.

Powell, A., & Craig, L. (2015). Gender differences in working at home and time use patterns: evidence from Australia. *Work, Employment and Society, 29*(4), 571–589. doi: 10.1177/0950017014568140

Sayer, L., England, P., Bittman, M., & Bianchi, S. (2009). How long is the second (plus first) shift? Gender differences in paid, unpaid, and total work time in Australia and the United States. *Journal of Comparative Family Studies, 40*, 523–544.

Shaw, S. (2008). Family leisure and changing ideologies of parenthood. *Sociology Compass, 2* (2), 688–703.

Shockley, K., & Shen, W. (2016). Couple dynamics: Division of labor. In T. Allen & L. Eby (Eds.), *Oxford Handbook of Work and Family*. Oxford, UK: Oxford University Press.

Sigle-Rushton, W., & Waldfogel, J. (2007). Motherhood and women's earnings in Anglo-American, Continental European, and Nordic countries. *Feminist Economics, 13*(2), 55–91.

Strazdins, L., & Loughrey, B. (2007). Too busy: Why time is a health and environmental problem. *NSW Public Health Bulletin, 18*(11–12), 219–221.

36 Affective Processes in the Work–Family Interface: Global Considerations

Xinxin Li and Remus Ilies

Work and family are two focal spheres in adult life, which are not isolated, but rather mutually influence each other. The work–family interface can generally be classified along three dimensions: (i) the direction of influence (i.e., work-to-family or family-to-work), (ii) the valence of effect (i.e., positive, such as enrichment or facilitation between domains, or negative, such as conflict or interference between domains), and (iii) the target of influence (i.e., spillover, whereby one's work or family spills over to the other domain, or crossover, whereby one's work or family experiences impact another's family or work experiences). Interest in understanding and managing the work–family interface has grown considerably in the past three decades.

Given that work, family, and their intersection are important sources of affective experiences, the role of affect in the work–family interface is worthy of research. Specifically, not only can work–family interface experiences elicit affective reactions, but one role may also influence another (i.e., work-to-family or family-to-work) through affective transference. Following Eby, Maher, and Butts (2010), we consider affect as an umbrella term involving feeling traits (i.e., relatively stable tendencies to experience positive and negative affect; Watson & Clark, 1984) and feeling states, including moods (i.e., generalized affective states not triggered by a specific stimulus), emotions (i.e., more intense discrete states elicited by specific events or targets), and general affective reactions to life domains (e.g., job satisfaction, family satisfaction, and life satisfaction). We include the latter category as feeling states because of their affective components, but do not deny that satisfaction also includes cognitive and evaluative components (e.g., Brief & Weiss, 2002).

In this chapter, we aim to review the literature linking affect and the work–family interface. First, we review research on affective processes underlying work–family spillover and crossover effects. Second, we review research on affective outcomes associated with the work–family interface. Finally, we propose avenues for future research on affective processes in the work–family interface, with a specific focus on the role of culture. This cultural perspective is particularly important in the light of the growing desire of multinational and domestic organizations with diverse employees to understand cultural influences on work–family dynamics and to develop culturally appropriate policies.

Affective Processes in Work–Family Spillover

Affective Spillover

Affective spillover, which reflects continuity of affective experiences across life domains, is one of the primary mechanisms underlying work–family spillover (Edwards & Rothbard, 2000). Two major reasons for affective spillover have been proposed in the literature. The first is that mood in one domain influences performance and rewards in the other domain (Edwards & Rothbard, 2000). Specifically, positive moods promote role performance through facilitating cognitive functioning, persistence, and positive social interactions. Effective role performance results in rewards, and thus enhances mood. This mechanism is also consistent with the affective path to work–family enrichment articulated by Greenhaus and Powell (2006). Similarly, negative moods in one role hamper role performance and rewards in the other role, eliciting negative moods in the latter role. The second explanation for affective spillover emphasizes the role of affect reinforcement processes via mood-congruent cognitions (see Judge & Ilies, 2004). This latter view reflects a perceptual pathway consistent with the mood congruency hypothesis, which postulates that positive moods activate positive stimulus processing and event interpretation that then elicit pleasant thoughts and feelings, whereas negative moods result in the opposite reactions (Rusting & DeHart, 2000). According to this view, employees who feel positive at work are more likely to have positive retrospective evaluations about work and interpret events at home in an optimistic way so as to maintain and reinforce their initial positive affect.

Increasing evidence about affective work–family spillover and its boundary conditions has emerged in the past two decades. The majority of the existing studies on affective spillover have adopted experience-sampling or daily diary designs. For example, Williams and Alliger's (1994) study of American working couples confirmed the bidirectional work–family spillover of distress and fatigue, with women displaying stronger effects in each direction than men. However, Williams and Alliger found weaker support for the spillover of pleasant moods. Specifically, no evidence for calmness spillover was found, and elation could spill over from family to work, but not vice versa.

Inconsistent with Williams and Alliger's (1994) findings, other studies examining spillover within the same day have found spillover effects for both positive and negative mood. For example, Song, Foo, and Uy's (2008) study of Chinese employees supported bidirectional work–family spillover of both positive and negative mood. Further, work orientation (i.e., the extent to which work is critical to one's self-identity) strengthened negative mood spillover from work to home. With a sample of American employees, Ilies, Schwind, Wagner, Johnson, DeRue, and Ilgen (2007) found that within individuals, both positive affect and negative affect experienced at work could spill over to affect experienced at home. Ilies et al. also found that negative affect at work partially mediated the within-individual effect of workload on negative affect at home. Furthermore, satisfaction can also spill over across domains. For example, Ilies, Wilson, and Wagner (2009) found that on days when job satisfaction was higher, employees had higher marital satisfaction as well as greater levels of positive affect and lower levels of negative affect at home.

Some studies have also tested lagged affective spillover effects. For example, using an American sample, Heller and Watson (2005) found evidence for both a concurrent association between job satisfaction in the afternoon and marital satisfaction at night, mediated by positive and negative mood, and a lagged association between marital satisfaction at night and job satisfaction the following afternoon. Similarly, Sonnentag and Binnewies (2013) not only examined affective spillover from work to family within days, but also tested whether the spillover effects persist until the next morning. With a sample of German and Swiss employees, they found that negative affect at work influenced affect at home, measured both at night and the next morning, whereas the work-to-family spillover of positive affect only occurred within a given day, but did not last till the next morning. These results suggest that negative spillover is more long-lasting than positive spillover. It is also worthwhile to note that Sonnentag and Binnewies examined factors accounting for within-individual variations in affective spillover. They found that psychological detachment from work in the evening attenuated positive and negative affective spillover within days. Further, psychological detachment from work and sleep quality attenuated the relation between negative affect at work and negative affect the next morning.

Despite the evidence for affective spillover and the increased focus on the antecedents of workplace affect, little research unpacks what determines affect at home. One exception is a study of German and Swiss employees by Sonnentag, Binnewies, and Mojza (2008), which found that low psychological detachment from work in the evening was associated with fatigue and negative activation the next morning, whereas relaxation and mastery experiences during the evening positively predicted morning serenity and positive activation, respectively. Additionally, sleep quality was related to all these aforementioned morning affect variables.

Emotional Exhaustion Linking Work and Family

In addition to the mechanism of affective spillover, experiences in one role may affect another role through emotional exhaustion, a state of energy shortage and emotional depletion (Maslach & Jackson, 1981). Because emotional exhaustion (or fatigue) after a demanding day at work indicates that (emotional-affective) resources have been depleted and thus are not readily available to facilitate effective performance in the family role, emotional exhaustion is thought to explain, at least in part, how demanding work influences family role performance.

Ilies, Huth, Ryan, and Dimotakis (2015) have showed such an effect in an experience-sampling study of American teachers. These authors further found that even though high workload influenced physical, cognitive, and emotional fatigue (i.e., emotional exhaustion), only emotional fatigue translated into work–family conflict perceptions at home. A longitudinal study conducted in Australia also suggested that job demands resulted in work–family conflict through emotional exhaustion (Hall, Dollard, Tuckey, Winefield, & Thompson, 2010). Another study conducted in Australia (Thompson, Kirk, & Brown, 2005) showed that supervisor support (but not coworker support) improved family functioning (i.e., more cohesion and less conflict) through the serial mediation of role stressors (i.e., role overload and role ambiguity) and emotional exhaustion. With an American sample, Carlson, Ferguson, Hunter, and Whitten (2012) found that abusive supervision positively predicted both directions of work–family conflict through the serial mediation of surface acting and burnout (of which emotional exhaustion is a dimension). These studies provide evidence that emotional exhaustion is one mechanism underlying the spillover of job stressors into family- or home-related outcomes.

Affective Processes in Work–Family Crossover

Crossover reflects "a bi-directional transmission of positive and negative emotions, mood, and dispositions between intimately connected individuals" (Westman, Brough, & Kalliath, 2009, p. 589). Westman (2001) proposed that crossover effects occur through direct empathic processes or indirect processes. Direct crossover occurs between closely related partners because they care for each other and one imagines his or her feelings in the position of another and thus has an empathic reaction (i.e., experiences and shares the feelings of the partner). Crossover can also be an indirect process whereby one's experiences or moods transmit to another person via coping mechanisms or social interaction processes. First, one's affective experiences influence one's own coping strategies and the coping strategies of the partner, and consequently, the partner's affective experiences. Second, in response to the partner's stress and strain, one may provide social support, which depletes resources and thus increases the support provider's stress and strain. Third, one's affective experiences will influence his or her undermining behaviors toward the partner (e.g., negative affect increases undermining), which further influences the partner's affect.

Affective crossover has been demonstrated in work–family research. The study described above by Song et al. (2008) found the crossover effects of positive and negative mood within couples when partners were physically together, using short time intervals between spouses' reports. Moreover, the presence of children at home weakened negative mood crossover within couples. Song and colleagues proposed three reasons for such a buffering effect. First, couples with children at home tend to shift some attention from the spouse to the children. Second, the presence of children may reduce a couple's physical proximity because the partners are more likely to work on different domestic tasks. Third, with children at home, couples may intentionally reduce negative exchanges (e.g., talking about negative work events) to avoid potential harm to their children's well-being.

Another study by Rodríguez-Muñoz, Sanz-Vergel, Demerouti, and Bakker (2014) found that Spanish employees' daily work engagement had crossover effects on partners' happiness through employees' own happiness. Additionally, supporting indirect crossover effects, Bakker, Demerouti, and Dollard's (2008) study of Dutch employees showed that employees who experienced work-to-family conflict (WFC) engaged in social undermining toward their spouses, which in turn raised spouses' home demands and emotional exhaustion.

Work–Family Interpersonal Capitalization

A social mechanism that mediates both work–family spillover and cross-over is work–family interpersonal capitalization, which refers to "an active response to positive work events that involves sharing or discussing such events with one's spouse or partner at home" (Ilies, Keeney, & Scott, 2011, p. 118). Such capitalization can be a mechanism underlying both work–family spillover and crossover processes because sharing work events may influence the family experiences of both employees and their families. For example, Ilies et al. (2011) demonstrated that capitalization on positive work events added to employees' daily job satisfaction over and above the effects of the event pleasantness and the number of positive work events. Additionally, capitalization has been shown to boost employees' positive affect and life satisfaction (Ilies, Keeney, & Goh, 2015).

Given that both of the studies described above were conducted in the United States, the generality of the effects of capitalization across cultures warrants more attention. Addressing this gap in the literature, Ilies, Liu, Liu, and Zheng (in press) conducted an experience-sampling study in China. Ilies et al. showed that work–family interpersonal capitalization mediated the effects of work engagement on the family domain (i.e., on family satisfaction and work–family balance), which confirms "the idea that work–family interpersonal capitalization is a potential mechanism through which work–family enrichment occurs" (Ilies et al., 2011, p. 124). This study also demonstrated that employees' daily family satisfaction mediated the relationship between their daily work–family interpersonal capitalization and their spouses' family satisfaction, providing insights as to the crossover mechanism underlying capitalization effects.

Affective Outcomes of the Work–Family Interface

Specific Affective Outcomes

As an unpleasant experience, work–family conflict induces negative emotions. For example, a meta-analysis indicates that both directions of work–family conflict are related to anxiety (Amstad, Meier, Fasel, Elfering, & Semmer, 2011). In their study, Williams and Alliger (1994) found that work–family juggling, or "unplanned intrusion of one role into the other" (p. 842), increased distress and decreased calmness, but did not influence elation or fatigue.

People who experience work–family conflict may also feel guilty for their failure to fulfill prescribed roles. Indeed, with an American sample, Livingston and Judge (2008) found that family-to-work conflict (FWC), but not WFC, was positively associated with guilt. These relationships were also found to be moderated by gender role orientation; specifically, the relationship between FWC and guilt was stronger for employees who held a more traditional gender role orientation, whereas the relationship between WFC and guilt was stronger for employees who held a more egalitarian gender role orientation. Additionally, the relationship between FWC and guilt was stronger for traditional men than egalitarian men or women regardless of gender role orientation. Similarly, Aycan and Eskin (2005) found that Turkish women felt more employment-related guilt than Turkish men. Finally, Judge, Ilies, and Scott's (2006) study of American employees found that within individuals, FWC and WFC positively predicted guilt and hostility at work and at home, respectively.

Although research on specific emotional reactions to work–family conflict is emerging, we know little about what determines such reactions and whether different emotions will result in different behaviors on and off the job. Given that individuals' attributions about the causes of events and outcomes may influence their emotional and behavioral reactions (e.g., Weiner, 1985), Ilies, De Pater, Lim, and Binnewies (2012) proposed a theoretical model that articulates the role of causal attributions in inducing specific emotions in response to work–family conflict. They proposed that sadness, dissatisfaction, and unhappiness are attribution-independent emotional reactions to work–family conflict. In contrast, guilt, shame, anger, frustration, and hopelessness depend on causal attributions related to the stability, locus, and controllability of work–family conflict. For example, when employees make internal, controllable, and unstable attributions, they will experience guilt. Further, specific emotions may drive employees to engage in adaptive or maladaptive coping behaviors. For example, employees who feel anger may engage in maladaptive coping, such as workplace aggression, while those feeling frustration may engage in adaptive behaviors, such as job crafting, or maladaptive behaviors, such as work withdrawal. Although evidence for specific emotional reactions to work–family conflict is accumulating, the role of attributions in determining emotions awaits future empirical testing.

Global Affective Outcomes

In addition to triggering specific affective reactions, the work–family interface also arouses global affective reactions. This includes both domain-specific (work- or family-related) and domain-unspecific, overall affective evaluations (e.g., depression and life satisfaction). Below, we review research linking the work–family interface to each type of outcome in turn.

Domain-specific outcomes. A sizable number of studies show that work–family conflict negatively relates to job satisfaction and family/home/marital satisfaction (for meta-analytic results, see Amstad et al., 2011). The generality of such findings across cultures has been tested in some cross-cultural studies. For example, based on a study of four cultural groups (i.e., Eastern, West-Developing, West-Affluent, and West-US) of IBM employees from forty-eight countries, Hill, Yang, Hawkins, and Ferris (2004) found that WFC and FWC negatively affected job satisfaction via work–family fit and that these relationships were similar across cultures. Similarly, Spector and colleagues' (2004) study of managers in fifteen countries from three regions (i.e., Anglo, China, and Latin America) revealed that work–family pressure was negatively associated with job satisfaction across cultures.

In contrast to these prior studies showing cultural similarity in the relationship between work–family conflict and job satisfaction, Janssen, Peeters, de Jonge, Houkes, and Tummers (2004) found that WFC was negatively related to job satisfaction among Dutch, but not American nurses. In another cross-sectional study, Galovan, Fackrell, Buswell, Jones, Hill, and Carroll (2010) found that WFC was negatively associated with job satisfaction in the United States, but not Singapore. The authors explained that because individualist cultures tend to value discretionary, individual time more so than collectivist cultures (Hofstede, 2001), such that WFC is a threat to autonomy, which results in lower satisfaction, in the United States, but not in Singapore. Additionally, Galovan et al. found that FWC was negatively related to marital satisfaction in both countries, whereas WFC was unrelated to marital satisfaction in both countries. Given the small body of cross-cultural research to date on these questions, we call for more research to clarify these inconsistent findings.

A limited number of work–family conflict studies have investigated career satisfaction as the outcome. Both Aryee and Luk's (1996) study of Hong Kong employees and Lyness and Thompson's (1997) study of American employees found null effects of WFC on career satisfaction. However, Martins, Eddleston, and Veiga (2002) found that WFC negatively affected women's and older men's, but not younger men's career satisfaction in an American sample. In contrast with inconsistent WFC findings, FWC appears to have a consistent negative effect on career satisfaction for American employees (Beutell & Wittig-Berman, 1999; Parasuraman, Purohit, Godshalk, & Beutell, 1996). We encourage scholars to pay more attention to the relation between work–family conflict and career satisfaction across diverse cultures.

Relative to work–family conflict, less attention has been paid to affective outcomes of work–family enrichment. McNall, Nicklin, and Masuda's (2010) meta-analysis indicates that both directions of work–family enrichment positively predict job and family satisfaction. Although researchers often use the affect perspective to explain the effects of work–family enrichment, the underlying mechanisms have seldom been empirically tested. One exception is Carlson, Hunter, Ferguson, and Whitten (2014) who examined the mechanisms linking work–family enrichment and satisfaction outcomes, drawing upon the broaden-and-build theory (Fredrickson, 2001) to argue that positive moods induced by enrichment broaden thought–action repertoires and thus allow individuals to build more resources, which further boost satisfaction. Carlson et al. also suggested that enrichment stimulates satisfaction by reducing psychological distress, a psychological state that narrows thought–action repertoires and further limits individuals' ability to build resources. Indeed, Carlson and colleagues found that psychological distress mediated the effects of both directions of work–family enrichment on job satisfaction and family satisfaction, while positive mood mediated the effects of the two kinds of work–family enrichment on job satisfaction, but not family satisfaction in a sample of American workers.

Similarly, very few studies have examined the affective outcomes of work–family balance. Scholars have not reached consensus on the definition of work–family balance (see Carlson, Grzywacz, & Zivnuska, 2009). However, we adopt the following definition for the purpose of this chapter: work–family balance refers to "accomplishment of role-related expectations that are negotiated and shared between an individual and his/her role-related partners in the work and family domains" (Grzywacz & Carlson, 2007, p. 458).

Carlson and colleagues (2009) found that work–family balance explained variance in job and family satisfaction above and beyond work–family enrichment and conflict, in a study of American employees. Wayne, Butts, Casper, and Allen (2017) differentiate balance satisfaction (an attitude) and balance effectiveness (a self-evaluation). With a sample of American employees, they found that both balance satisfaction and balance effectiveness were uniquely associated with job satisfaction and family satisfaction beyond additive spillover (i.e., main effects of conflict and enrichment) and multiplicative spillover (i.e., interaction of conflict and enrichment). However, when balance satisfaction and balance effectiveness were simultaneously added as predictors, both accounted for incremental variance in family satisfaction, but only balance satisfaction accounted for incremental variance in job satisfaction.

In terms of the domain-specific outcomes, there are two competing perspectives on whether the work–family interface has stronger effects on the originating or the receiving domain. The cross-domain perspective suggests that the costs of role conflict and the benefits of role enrichment mainly occur in the receiving domain (e.g., Ford, Heinen, & Langkamer, 2007; Greenhaus & Powell, 2006). The rationale for this perspective is that role conflict or enrichment, although originating in one domain, is harming or helping the other domain. Therefore, well-being in this other life domain is suppressed or enhanced. In contrast, the matching perspective argues that the work–family interface primarily affects the originating domain (Shockley & Singla, 2011). The rationale for the latter perspective is based on attributional processes (Amstad et al., 2011); people tend to attribute the causes of work–family conflict or enrichment to the originating domain, which shapes affective tones about this domain.

Although individual empirical studies offer mixed results regarding the above competing perspectives, meta-analytic evidence supports the matching hypothesis for both directions of work–family conflict (Amstad et al., 2011; Shockley & Singla, 2011) and work–family enrichment (Shockley & Singla, 2011). In other words, work-to-family enrichment (WFE) and WFC are more strongly related to job satisfaction than family/marital satisfaction, and family-to-work enrichment (FWE) and FWC are more strongly related to family/marital satisfaction than job satisfaction. Furthermore, Shockley and Singla also found that when the shared variance between WFE and FWE was accounted for, both WFE and FWE were only weakly related to satisfaction in the receiving domain, indicating small cross-domain effects of work–family enrichment on satisfaction outcomes.

Domain-general outcomes. As domain-specific affective reactions can generalize to domain-unspecific outcomes (Diener & Diener, 1995), the work–family interface also influences general affective evaluations in life. Consistent with this view, empirical studies indicate that work–family conflict is positively related to psychological strain and negatively associated with life satisfaction (Amstad et al., 2011). Additionally, many studies offer evidence that both WFC and FWC are related to depression (for a meta-analytic review, see Amstad et al., 2011).

However, we note that extant studies linking work–family conflict and domain-general outcomes have some limitations. First, most studies are cross-sectional. Longitudinal studies have yielded less consistent results. Specifically, Hammer, Cullen, Neal, Sinclair, and Shafiro (2005) found no association between work–family conflict and depression one year later. In contrast, using a four-year time lag, Frone, Russell, and Cooper (1997) found that FWC, but not WFC, was related to depression. Second, the research has been primarily conducted using Western samples. Thus, whether these findings generalize across cultures is worth testing. Providing some initial data on this question, Aryee, Fields, and Luk (1999) found that FWC did not affect life satisfaction, while WFC influenced life satisfaction directly and indirectly through family satisfaction in a Hong Kong sample. The cross-cultural study by Galovan et al. (2010) found that WFC and FWC were positively related to depression in both Singapore and the United States. However, FWC was more strongly related to depression than was WFC in Singapore, whereas the opposite pattern was found in the United States.

Some research has examined the relation between positive aspects of the work–family interface and depression. Using cross-sectional data, Hammer and colleagues (2005) found that for wives, FWE was negatively related to depression. However, for husbands, although FWE was also negatively related to depression, WFE was unexpectedly positively related to depression. Hammer and colleagues also found longitudinal crossover effects such that employees' WFE negatively predicted their spouses' depression one year later.

Emotional Exhaustion

As mentioned earlier, emotional exhaustion can induce work–family conflict. However, longitudinal evidence indicates that the relationships between emotional exhaustion and work–family conflict are bidirectional (Hall et al., 2010). Work–family conflict results in emotional exhaustion because negative affect caused by inter-role conflict may create emotional regulation demands, which consume limited self-regulatory resources. These resource depletion processes further lead to emotional exhaustion. Empirical research supports both between-individual (e.g., Bakker et al., 2008; Demerouti, Bakker, & Bulters, 2004) and within-individual effects (Liu, Wang, Chang, Shi, Zhou, & Shao, 2015) of inter-role conflict on emotional exhaustion. For example, based on a diary study of Chinese employees, Liu et al. (2015) found that morning FWC (but not WFC) was positively related to emotional exhaustion in the afternoon, which then predicted aggression towards coworkers, supervisors, and family members. They argued that a possible reason for the insignificant relationship between WFC and emotional exhaustion might be that on a daily basis, WFC is less salient in affecting self-regulation at work because employees tend to pay more attention to work issues instead of family issues when they are in the workplace. Future research on emotional exhaustion and work–family conflict should adopt longitudinal designs and consider these reciprocal relationships.

Directions for Future Research

With the lens of culture, researchers can discover both etic (i.e., culturally universal) and emic (i.e., culturally specific) phenomena in work–family experiences. However, although Greenhaus and Parasuraman (1999) called for investigations of cross-cultural influences in the work–family interface nearly two decades ago, cross-cultural work–family research is still lacking, and especially work that considers the role of affect. Although there has been cross-cultural research on constructs with an affective component, such as job satisfaction and depression (e.g., Galovan et al., 2010), and the work–family interface, research that specifically considers the role of affect and affective processes (e.g., spillover or crossover) has not yet followed. We speculate that this may be because of the added complexity of conducting research designed to capture such processes (e.g., experience-sampling studies) in two or more cultures; however, we hope that with the advent of new technologies for examining affective processes (see Ilies, Aw, & Lim, 2016), such studies will soon follow. Below, we propose avenues for future research examining affective processes in the work–family interface, with a special focus on the need for cross-cultural research. We start with two general suggestions for cross-cultural work–family research and then turn to provide a more detailed research agenda.

First, samples in the previous work–family research have been mainly based on Western managers or white-collar employees, leading to a lack of representation of the full range of ethnicities and occupations present in the working population (Grzywacz, Arcury, Marín, Carrillo, Burke, Coates, & Quandt, 2007). More attention should be paid to the work–family experiences of the "forgotten" employees (e.g., racial/ethnic minorities and low-wage, non-professional workers) because compared to their counterparts, these groups of workers may attach different meanings to work and family because of their unique culture or economic status.

Another important direction for cross-cultural studies pertains to the influences of a wide spectrum of cultural values on work–family experiences. Several cultural values have been proposed to be relevant to work–family issues, including individualism–collectivism, gender role ideology, power distance, uncertainty avoidance, monochronic–polychronic time orientation, tolerance for contradictions, and specificity (e.g., Aycan, 2008; Joplin, Shaffer, Francesco, & Lau, 2003; Korabik, Lero, & Ayman, 2003). These values affect the importance of work and family, assumptions about the work–family interface (e.g., whether work and family are integrated or segmented), and normative behaviors (e.g., what is expected at work and home). We suggest that scholars directly measure cultural values and test how they moderate affective processes in the work–family interface.

Affective Processes in Work–Family Spillover

Current research examining the role of affect in work–family spillover has mainly examined the spillover of positive and/or negative affect and some specific emotions. Little research has investigated specific emotions as mechanisms linking experiences in one domain and behaviors in the other domain. For instance, are leaders more authoritative to gain power on days when they are angry because of marital conflict? Will employees' happiness at home spill over to work and affect their risk-taking behaviors? Conversely, the behavioral outcomes of affective spillover in the family domain, such as the social behaviors studied by Ilies et al. (2007), warrant more research.

Another direction for affective work–family spillover pertains to sharing work and family events. Current research has only focused on one form of work–family sharing (i.e., work–family interpersonal capitalization, or sharing positive work events with families). Based on the direction (i.e., work-to-family or family-to-work) and event valence (i.e., positive or negative), conceptually there could be up to four kinds of work–family sharing. More research is needed to examine the effects of other forms of sharing. For example, will sharing negative work events at home increase (because of recall of and rumination about negative information) or decrease (because of buffering from social support) negative affect? Will sharing family events at work have similar effects on employees as sharing work events at home does?

The role of culture. There are cultural differences in work and family centrality (i.e., how important work or family is to one's life, respectively; Harpaz, Honig, & Coetsier, 2002; Snir, Harpaz, & Ben-Baruch, 2009) and these differences are likely to influence affective spillover processes and their outcomes. Future research could test whether work-to-family spillover effects are stronger in cultures with higher work centrality whereas family-to-work spillover effects are stronger in cultures with higher family centrality. Additionally, Ilies et al. (2009) found that work–family role integration (i.e., the extent to which work and family roles have overlap in terms of time, artifacts, and activities) influenced the strength of the spillover effects of job satisfaction to the family domain. Work–family role integration may be influenced by cultural factors. Therefore, cultural values should be integrated into the study of spillover processes as antecedents of work–family role integration.

Another avenue for future cross-cultural research on affective work–family spillover concerns the aforementioned work–family sharing. Because there might be cultural differences in the likelihood of discussing work (family) issues at home (work), we recommend that future research examine the role of cultural values in explaining the extent to which employees engage in different forms of work–family sharing. Additionally, it may also be the case that cultural values moderate the downstream effects of work–family sharing on affect and satisfaction.

Affective Processes in Work–Family Crossover

We begin with three future research directions pertaining to affective work–family crossover and then elaborate on the role of culture in such processes. First, we suggest the examination of diverse targets of work–family crossover. Previous research mainly focused on work-to-family crossover and studied partners as targets. Future research could examine family members other than spouses (e.g., children) as targets of work-to-family crossover and pay more attention to family-to-work cross-over (i.e., employees' family experiences influence colleagues' or customers' experiences). Another avenue for family-to-work crossover research would be to examine how leaders' affect at home transmits to followers. Leaders' daily behaviors at work may vary based on their affect before work. For example, on days when leaders are frustrated by family demands, they may displace aggression towards followers and, in turn, increase followers' negative affect. Researchers can adopt experience-sampling studies to test such possibilities. This approach not only adds to crossover research, but also contributes to leadership research by examining the within-individual variations in leadership behaviors.

Second, the mechanisms and the boundary conditions for affective crossover warrant additional examination. This would allow us to understand who are more susceptible to affective crossover and develop strategies to leverage the benefits and minimize the harm of affective crossover. For instance, if crossover occurs through emotional contagion, then recipients' traits such as susceptibility to emotional contagion (Hatfield, Cacioppo, & Rapson, 1992) may strengthen crossover effects. If crossover is a function of social behaviors, we can examine social support, social undermining, and withdrawal as mediating mechanisms as well as whether char-acteristics of the senders, recipients, and their relationship moderate the crossover effects. As an example, employees with low agreeableness or high hostility may be more likely to bring negative affect from work to home and undermine their families. In addition, neurotic family members' affect may fluctuate more in reaction to the focal employees' social behaviors at home.

Third, similar to spillover research, crossover research can also benefit from examining all the four types of work–family sharing. We provide some sample research questions that could be pursued: (1) Will sharing positive (negative) work events at home increase family members' positive (negative) affect? (2) How will sharing family events at work influence colleagues' affect? Will colleagues always feel an empathic emotional response to the focal employees? It is likely that when an employee shares positive family events, some colleagues may feel envy if upward social comparisons are triggered. Colleagues may also feel schadenfreude at the focal employees' negative family experiences. These crossover dynamics await future research.

The role of culture. There may be cultural differences in the direction and intensity of affective work–family crossover. First, culture may determine whether work-to-family crossover is stronger than family-to-work crossover or vice versa. People from cultures with high work centrality may be more likely to bring work experi-ences or demands home and thus their family members may be more likely to be influenced by their work affect. In contrast, people from cultures with high family centrality may be more likely to bring family issues to work and elicit affective crossover from family to the workplace.

Moreover, culture values may play a role in gender differences in work-to-family crossover within couples. For example, it is likely that in cultures with more egalitarian gender role ideologies, both husbands' and wives' affect at work may cross over to their partners. In contrast, in more gender-traditional cultures, husbands' affect at work is more likely to have crossover effects on their wives than vice versa.

Furthermore, culture may influence the intensity of direct crossover (i.e., emotional contagion). The first reason is that culture prescribes emotional display rules and determines what emotions are admired or despised (Mesquita & Ellsworth, 2001). Thus, when at home or work, employees' tendency to express affect elicited in the other domain may be regulated by culture. For example, it is less appropriate for Japanese to express anger, contempt, and disgust than Americans and Canadians, and Japanese endorse the expression of happiness less than Canadians (Safdar et al., 2009). Therefore, Japanese employees may suppress such feelings to follow display norms, which makes it more difficult for others to discern their true feelings. This may, in turn, inhibit affective crossover. The second reason is that culture values affect people's interdependence on others and interpersonal norms. Thus, people from different cultures have different sensitivity to others' affect (Westman, 2005). Given that both collectivistic and feminine cultures emphasize interdependence, sociability, and concern for people (Hofstede, 2001), we expect that direct affective crossover is stronger in cultures with high collectivism (vs. individualism) or femininity (vs. masculinity).

Finally, cultural values can influence indirect crossover processes (Westman, 2005). Affective crossover effects via undermining may be stronger in cultures characterized by individualism (vs. collectivism) or masculinity (vs. femininity) because such cultures highlight assertiveness and attach less importance to social goals (Hofstede, 2001). Moreover, power distance may influence leader-to-follower affective crossover because in high power distance cultures, leaders may legitimize aggression toward followers as a way to maintain control (Hofstede, Hofstede, & Minkov, 2010). Thus, frustrated leaders in such cultures are more likely to undermine followers and, in turn, trigger followers' negative affect. Given the above roles that culture may play, we suggest that future research empirically test cultural variations in the direction of crossover, gender differences in crossover, and the likelihood of direct and indirect crossover.

Affective Reactions to Work–Family Interface

There is a dearth of research examining how specific emotions influence behavioral coping with work–family conflict. We encourage scholars to enrich our understanding of this question, given that different emotions tend to engender different behavioral reactions. As an example, employees who feel guilty for WFC may attempt to improve their time management skills and engage in compensatory behaviors with their family members, whereas employees who feel shame may engage in maladaptive behaviors, such as family withdrawal.

It would also be worthwhile to examine the longitudinal effects of the work–family interface and employees' affective changes. Research shows that work–family conflict is related to poor concurrent well-being, but better well-being over time (Matthews, Wayne, & Ford, 2014). This finding supports adaptation theories (i.e., people adapt to stressful situations and experience increased well-being over time; Diener, Lucas, & Scollon, 2006) rather than the loss spiral hypothesis (i.e., stressors lead to greater stress and sensitivity to other stressors and further harm well-being over time; Hobfoll, 2001). Thus, it is possible that over time, employees who experience work–family conflict will exhibit lower levels of emotional exhaustion/negative affect and higher levels of job, family, and life satisfaction. We suggest that researchers adopt longitudinal designs to test these propositions and examine the affective adaptation in reaction to work–family conflict (see Kelloway & Francis, 2013, for a discussion of longitudinal research).

The role of culture. Cultural values may influence employees' short-term affective reactions to work–family conflict or enrichment. In cultures with low tolerance for contradictions, work and family are seen as separate and work–family conflict is more threatening. In contrast, in cultures with high tolerance for contradictions, work and family are integrated and compatible, and conflict is perceived as an opportunity for development (Aycan, 2008). These assumptions may result in different affective reactions; for example, employees in the former cultures may experience greater negative affect and less job/family/life satisfaction in response to work–family conflict. We encourage scholars to test these potential cultural variations in affective reactions to the work–family interface.

Cultural values may also affect employees' long-term adaptation to work–family conflict. First, cultural values influence how much social support employees can get from organizations. For example, organizations in feminine cultures may be more likely to provide work–family support, which can help employees have quicker and better recovery from episodes of work–family conflict. Second, culture can shape people's cognitive appraisals of stressors, coping goals, and coping strategies (Chun, Moos, & Cronkite, 2006). Given these cultural differences, we suggest that researchers test the role that culture plays in determining longer-term affective reactions to work–family conflict.

Emotion Regulation and the Work–Family Interface

Another area in need of future investigations is the role that emotion regulation plays in the work–family interface. As a specific type of self-regulation, emotion regulation depletes mental resources (Muraven, Tice, & Baumeister, 1998). Thus, employees who regulate emotions in one domain may not have sufficient resources to regulate their emotions and fulfill their role in the other domain. Will employees be less effective in dealing with emotional demands at home on days when they engage in surface acting at work because of depleted self-control? Are leaders more likely to be abusive when they suppress negative emotions before work with family members? We encourage future research to address these questions.

The role of culture. The effectiveness and costs of emotion regulation differ across cultures. For example, prior research has found that emotional suppression is more effortful for European Americans than for Asian Americans (Mauss & Butler, 2010; Richards & Gross, 2000). Additionally, habitual suppression is more maladaptive for the well-being of European Americans than for that of Asian Americans or East Asians (Cheung & Park, 2010; Soto, Perez, Kim, Lee, & Minnick, 2011). These cultural differences result from the different meanings of emotion suppression across cultures (Mesquita & Delvaux, 2012). As European Americans tend to have independent self-construals, suppression of feelings is more threatening to their identity. In contrast, as Asian Americans or East Asians tend to have interdependent self-construals, they pay more attention to situational cues and emphasize situational adjustment. Future research could test how culture influences the effects of emotion regulation in the work–family interface.

Conclusion

In an era of increased participation of women in the labor force, growing dual-earner couples, and an exceptionally competitive market, the interplay of work and family becomes a more salient issue and thus deserves greater research attention. Further, with rapid globalization and the increasingly diverse workplace, a cross-cultural approach can provide a more complete understanding of the work–family interface and help managers design culturally appropriate work–family policies and practices. This chapter reviews the affective processes in the work–family interface and evidence for cross-cultural differences in such processes. We hope that this chapter will arouse scholars' interest in the affective side of the work–family interface and stimulate cross-cultural research in this field.

References

Amstad, F. T., Meier, L. L., Fasel, U., Elfering, A., & Semmer, N. K. (2011). A meta-analysis of work–family conflict and various outcomes with a special emphasis on cross-domain versus matching-domain relations. *Journal of Occupational Health Psychology, 16,* 151–169.

Aryee, S., Fields, D., & Luk, V. (1999). A cross-cultural test of a model of the work–family interface. *Journal of Management, 25,* 491–511.

Aryee, S., & Luk, V. (1996). Work and nonwork influences on the career satisfaction of dual-earner couples. *Journal of Vocational Behavior, 49,* 38–52.

Aycan, Z. (2008). Cross-cultural approaches to work–family conflict. In K. Korabik & D. Lero (Eds.), *Handbook of Work–Family Conflict* (pp. 359–371). London, UK: Cambridge University Press.

Aycan, Z., & Eskin, M. (2005). Relative contributions of childcare, spousal support, and organizational support in reducing work–family conflict for men and women: The case of Turkey. *Sex Roles, 53,* 453–471.

Bakker, A. B., Demerouti, E., & Dollard, M. F. (2008). How job demands affect partners' experience of exhaustion: Integrating work–family conflict and crossover theory. *Journal of Applied Psychology, 93,* 901–911.

Beutell, N. J. & Wittig-Berman, U. (1999). Predictors of work–family conflict and satisfaction with family, job, career, and life. *Psychological Reports, 85,* 893–903.

Brief, A. P., & Weiss, H. M. (2002). Organizational behavior: Affect in the workplace. *Annual Review of Psychology, 53,* 279–307.

Carlson, D. S., Ferguson, M., Hunter, E., & Whitten, D. (2012). Abusive supervision and work–family conflict: The path through emotional labor and burnout. *The Leadership Quarterly, 23,* 849–859.

Carlson, D. S., Grzywacz, J., & Zivnuska, S. (2009). Is work–family balance more than conflict and enrichment? *Human Relations, 62,* 1459–1486.

Carlson, D. S., Hunter, E. M., Ferguson, M., & Whitten, D. (2014). Work–family enrichment and satisfaction mediating processes and relative impact of originating and receiving domains. *Journal of Management, 40,* 845–865.

Cheung, R. Y., & Park, I. J. (2010). Anger suppression, interdependent self-construal, and depression among Asian American and European American college students. *Cultural Diversity and Ethnic Minority Psychology, 16,* 517–525.

Chun, C., Moos, R. H., & Cronkite, R. C. (2006). Culture: A fundamental context for the stress and coping paradigm. In P. T. P. Wong & L. C. J. Wong (Eds.), *Handbook of Multicultural Perspectives on Stress and Coping* (pp. 29–53). Dallas, TX: Spring.

Demerouti, E., Bakker, A. B., & Bulters, A. J. (2004). The loss spiral of work pressure, work–home interference and exhaustion: Reciprocal relations in a three-wave study. *Journal of Vocational Behavior, 64,* 131–149.

Diener, E., & Diener, M. (1995). Cross-cultural correlates of life satisfaction and self-esteem. *Journal of Personality and Social Psychology, 68,* 653–663.

Diener, E., Lucas, R. E., & Scollon, C. N. (2006). Beyond the hedonic treadmill: Revising the adaptation theory of well-being. *American Psychologist, 61,* 305–314.

Eby, L. T., Maher, C. P., & Butts, M. M. (2010). The intersection of work and family life: The role of affect. *Annual Review of Psychology, 61,* 599–622.

Edwards, J. R., & Rothbard, N. P. (2000). Mechanisms linking work and family: Clarifying the relationship between work and family constructs. *Academy of Management Review, 25,* 178–199.

Ford, M. T., Heinen, B. A., & Langkamer, K. L. (2007). Work and family satisfaction and conflict: A meta-analysis of cross-domain relations. *Journal of Applied Psychology, 92,* 57–80.

Fredrickson, B. L. (2001). The role of positive emotions in positive psychology: The broaden-and-build theory of positive emotions. *American Psychologist, 56,* 218–226.

Frone, M. R., Russell, M., & Cooper, M. L. (1997). Relation of work–family conflict to health outcomes: A four-year longitudinal study of employed parents. *Journal of Occupational and Organizational Psychology, 70,* 325–335.

Galovan, A. M., Fackrell, T., Buswell, L., Jones, B. L., Hill, E. J., & Carroll, S. J. (2010). The work–family interface in the United States and Singapore: Conflict across cultures. *Journal of Family Psychology, 24,* 646–656.

Greenhaus, J. H., & Parasuraman, S. (1999). Research on work, family, and gender: Current status and future directions. In G. N. Powell (Ed.), *Handbook of Gender and Work* (pp. 391–412). Thousand Oaks, CA: Sage.

Greenhaus, J. H., & Powell, G. N. (2006). When work and family are allies: A theory of work–family enrichment. *Academy of Management Review, 31,* 72–92.

Grzywacz, J. G., Arcury, T. A., Marín, A., Carrillo, L., Burke, B., Coates, M. L., & Quandt, S. A. (2007). Work–family conflict: Experiences and health implications among immigrant Latinos. *Journal of Applied Psychology, 92,* 1119–1130.

Grzywacz, J. G., & Carlson, D. S. (2007). Conceptualizing work–family balance: Implications for practice and research. *Advances in Developing Human Resources, 9*, 455–471.

Hall, G. B., Dollard, M. F., Tuckey, M. R., Winefield, A. H., & Thompson, B. M. (2010). Job demands, work–family conflict, and emotional exhaustion in police officers: A longitudinal test of competing theories. *Journal of Occupational and Organizational Psychology, 83*, 237–250.

Hammer, L. B., Cullen, J. C., Neal, M. B., Sinclair, R. R., & Shafiro, M. V. (2005). The longitudinal effects of work–family conflict and positive spillover on depressive symptoms among dual-earner couples. *Journal of Occupational Health Psychology, 10*, 138–154.

Harpaz, I., Honig, B., & Coetsier, P. (2002). A cross-cultural longitudinal analysis of the meaning of work and the socialization process of career starters. *Journal of World Business, 37*, 230–244.

Hatfield, E., Cacioppo, J. T., & Rapson, R. L. (1992). Primitive emotional contagion. In M. S. Clark (Ed.), *Review of Personality and Social Psychology,* (vol. 14, pp. 151–177). Newbury Park, CA: Sage.

Heller, D., & Watson, D. (2005). The dynamic spillover of satisfaction between work and marriage: The role of time and mood. *Journal of Applied Psychology, 90*, 1273–1279.

Hill, E. J., Yang, C., Hawkins, A. J., & Ferris, M. (2004). A cross-cultural test of the work–family interface in 48 countries. *Journal of Marriage and Family, 66*, 1300–1316.

Hobfoll, S. E. (2001). The influence of culture, community, and the nested self in the stress process: Advancing conservation of resources theory. *Applied Psychology: An International Review, 50*, 337–421.

Hofstede, G. (2001). *Culture's Consequences: Comparing Values, Behaviors, Institutions, and Organizations across Nations*. Second edition. Thousand Oaks, CA: Sage.

Hofstede, G. H., Hofstede, G. J., & Minkov, M. (2010). *Cultures and Organizations: Software for the Mind*. New York, NY: McGraw-Hill.

Ilies, R., Aw, S. S., & Lim, V. K. (2016). A naturalistic multilevel framework for studying transient and chronic effects of psychosocial work stressors on employee health and well-being. *Applied Psychology: An International Review, 65*, 223–258.

Ilies, R., De Pater, I. E., Lim, S., & Binnewies, C. (2012). Attributed causes for work–family conflict: Emotional and behavioral outcomes. *Organizational Psychology Review, 2*, 293–310.

Ilies, R., Huth, M., Ryan, A. M., & Dimotakis, N. (2015). Explaining the links between workload, distress, and work–family conflict among school employees: Physical, cognitive, and emotional fatigue. *Journal of Educational Psychology, 107*, 1136–1149.

Ilies, R., Keeney, J., & Goh, Z. W. (2015). Capitalising on positive work events by sharing them at home. *Applied Psychology: An International Review, 64*, 578–598.

Ilies, R., Keeney, J., & Scott, B. A. (2011). Work–family interpersonal capitalization: Sharing positive work events at home. *Organizational Behavior and Human Decision Processes, 114*, 115–126.

Ilies, R., Liu, X., Liu, Y., & Zheng, X. (in press). Why do employees have better family lives when they are highly engaged at work? *Journal of Applied Psychology*.

Ilies, R., Schwind, K. M., Wagner, D. T., Johnson, M. D., DeRue, D. S., & Ilgen, D. R. (2007). When can employees have a family life? The effects of daily workload and affect on work–family conflict and social behaviors at home. *Journal of Applied Psychology*, *92*, 1368–1379.

Ilies, R., Wilson, K. S., & Wagner, D. T. (2009). The spillover of daily job satisfaction onto employees' family lives: The facilitating role of work–family integration. *Academy of Management Journal*, *52*, 87–102.

Janssen, P. P. M., Peeters, M. C. W., de Jonge, J., Houkes, I., & Tummers, G. E. R. (2004). Specific relationships between job demands, job resources and psychological outcomes and the mediating role of negative work-home interference. *Journal of Vocational Behavior*, *65*, 411–429.

Joplin, J. R., Shaffer, M. A., Francesco, A. M., & Lau, T. (2003). The macro-environment and work–family conflict development of a cross cultural comparative framework. *International Journal of Cross Cultural Management*, *3*, 305–328.

Judge, T. A., & Ilies, R. (2004). Affect and job satisfaction: A study of their relationship at work and at home. *Journal of Applied Psychology*, *89*, 661–673.

Judge, T. A., Ilies, R., & Scott, B. A. (2006). Work–family conflict and emotions: Effects at work and at home. *Personnel Psychology*, *59*, 779–814.

Kelloway, E. K., & Francis, L. (2013). Longitudinal research and data analysis. In R. R. Sinclair, M. Wang, & L. E. Tetrick (Eds.), *Research Methods in Occupational Health Psychology: Measurement, Design, and Data Analysis* (pp. 374–394). New York, NY: Taylor & Francis.

Korabik, K., Lero, D. S., & Ayman, R. (2003). A multi-level approach to cross-cultural work–family research. *International Journal of Cross Cultural Management*, *3*, 289–303.

Liu, Y., Wang, M., Chang, C. H., Shi, J., Zhou, L., & Shao, R. (2015). Work–family conflict, emotional exhaustion, and displaced aggression toward others: The moderating roles of workplace interpersonal conflict and perceived managerial family support. *Journal of Applied Psychology*, *100*, 793–808.

Livingston, B. A., & Judge, T. A. (2008). Emotional responses to work–family conflict: An examination of gender role orientation among working men and women. *Journal of Applied Psychology*, *93*, 207–216.

Lyness, K. S., & Thompson, D. E. (1997). Above the glass ceiling? A comparison of matched samples of female and male executives. *Journal of Applied Psychology*, *82*, 359–375.

Martins, L. L., Eddleston, K. A., & Veiga, J. F. (2002). Moderators of the relationship between work–family conflict and career satisfaction. *Academy of Management Journal*, *45*, 399–409.

Maslach, C., & Jackson, S. E. (1981). The measurement of experienced burnout. *Journal of Organizational Behavior*, *2*, 99–113.

Matthews, R. A., Wayne, J. H., & Ford, M. T. (2014). A work–family conflict/subjective well-being process model: A test of competing theories of longitudinal effects. *Journal of Applied Psychology*, *99*, 1173–1187.

Mauss, I. B., & Butler, E. A. (2010). Cultural context moderates the relationship between emotion control values and cardiovascular challenge versus threat responses. *Biological Psychology*, *84*, 521–530.

McNall, L. A., & Nicklin, J. M., & Masuda, A. D. (2010). A meta-analytic review of the consequences associated with work–family enrichment. *Journal of Business and Psychology*, *25*, 381–396.

Mesquita, B., & Delvaux, E. (2012). A cultural perspective on emotion labor. In A. Grandey, J. Diefendorff, & D. Rupp (Eds.), *Emotional Labor in the 21st Century: Diverse Perspectives on Emotion Regulation at Work* (pp. 251–272). New York, NY: Psychology Press/Routledge.

Mesquita, B., & Ellsworth, P. C. (2001). The role of culture in appraisal. In K. R. Scherer & A. Schorr (Eds.), *Appraisal Processes in Emotion: Theory, Methods, Research* (pp. 233–248). New York, NY: Oxford University Press.

Muraven, M., Tice, D. M., & Baumeister, R. F. (1998). Self-control as a limited resource: Regulatory depletion patterns. *Journal of Personality and Social Psychology, 74,* 774–789.

Parasuraman, S., Purohit, Y. S., Godshalk, V. M., & Beutell, N. J. (1996). Work and family variables, entrepreneurial career success, and psychological well-being. *Journal of Vocational Behavior, 48,* 275–300.

Richards, J. M., & Gross, J. J. (2000). Emotion regulation and memory: The cognitive costs of keeping one's cool. *Journal of Personality and Social Psychology, 79,* 410–424.

Rodríguez-Muñoz, A., Sanz-Vergel, A. I., Demerouti, E., & Bakker, A. B. (2014). Engaged at work and happy at home: A spillover–crossover model. *Journal of Happiness Studies, 15,* 271–283.

Rusting, C. L., & DeHart, T. (2000). Retrieving positive memories to regulate negative mood: Consequences for mood-congruent memory. *Journal of Personality and Social Psychology, 78,* 737–752.

Safdar, S., Friedlmeier, W., Matsumoto, D., Yoo, S. H., Kwantes, C. T., Kakai, H., & Yoo, S. H. (2009). Variations of emotional display rules within and across cultures: A comparison between Canada, USA, and Japan. *Canadian Journal of Behavioural Science, 41,* 1–10.

Shockley, K. M., & Singla, N. (2011). Reconsidering work–family interactions and satisfaction: A meta-analysis. *Journal of Management, 37,* 861–886.

Snir, R., Harpaz, I., & Ben-Baruch, D. (2009). Centrality of and investment in work and family among Israeli high-tech workers a bicultural perspective. *Cross-Cultural Research, 43,* 366–385.

Song, Z. L., Foo, M. D., & Uy, M. A. (2008). Mood spillover and crossover among dual-earner couples: A cell phone event sampling study. *Journal of Applied Psychology, 93,* 443–452.

Sonnentag, S., & Binnewies, C. (2013). Daily affect spillover from work to home: Detachment from work and sleep as moderators. *Journal of Vocational Behavior, 83,* 198–208.

Sonnentag, S., Binnewies, C., & Mojza, E. J. (2008). "Did you have a nice evening?" A day-level study on recovery experiences, sleep, and affect. *Journal of Applied Psychology, 93,* 674–684.

Soto, J. A., Perez, C. R., Kim, Y. H., Lee, E. A., & Minnick, M. R. (2011). Is expressive suppression always associated with poorer psychological functioning? A cross-cultural comparison between European Americans and Hong Kong Chinese. *Emotion, 11,* 1450–1455.

Spector, P. E., Cooper, C. L., Poelmans, S., Allen, T. D., O'Driscoll, M., Sanchez, J. I., ... Yu, S. (2004). A cross-national comparative study of work–family stressors, working hours, and well-being: China and Latin America versus the Anglo world. *Personnel Psychology, 57,* 119–142.

Thompson, B. M., Kirk, A., & Brown, D. F. (2005). Work based support, emotional exhaustion, and spillover of work stress to the family environment: A study of policewomen. *Stress and Health, 21,* 199–207.

Watson, D., & Clark, L. A. (1984). Negative affectivity: The disposition to experience aversive emotional states. *Psychological Bulletin, 96*, 465–490.

Wayne, J. H., Butts, M. M., Casper, W. J., & Allen, T. D. (2017). In search of balance: A conceptual and empirical integration of multiple meanings of work–family balance. *Personnel Psychology, 70,* 167–210.

Weiner, B. (1985). An attributional theory of achievement motivation and emotion. *Psychological Review, 92*, 548–573.

Westman, M. (2001). Stress and strain crossover. *Human Relations, 54*, 717–751.

Westman, M. (2005). Cross-cultural differences in crossover research. In S. A. Y. Poelmans (Ed.), *Work and Family: An International Research Perspective. Series in Applied Psychology* (pp. 241–260). Mahwah, NJ: Erlbaum.

Westman, M., Brough, P., & Kalliath, T. (2009). Expert commentary on work–life balance and crossover of emotions and experiences: Theoretical and practice advancements. *Journal of Organizational Behavior, 30*, 587–595.

Williams, K. J., & Alliger, G. M. (1994). Role stressors, mood spillover, and perceptions of work–family conflict in employed parents. *Academy of Management Journal, 37*, 837–868.

37 Implications of Work–Family Connections for Children's Well-Being across the Globe

Lorey A. Wheeler, Bora Lee, and Elizabeth Svoboda

Many scholars argue that family and work are the two most influential contexts that shape human well-being. Research has found that parents' work, in particular, has far-reaching implications for children's well-being. For example, some aspects of parents' work foster parents' well-being, parent–child relationships, and children's psychosocial adjustment, whereas conditions deemed stressful in nature are linked to parents' feelings of overload and distress, poor parent–child relationships, and child adjustment problems. Understanding work–family linkages from the most proximal level (e.g., parents' work experiences) to the broadest level (e.g., societal changes in light of globalization and economic conditions) is an important step in informing programs and policy related to enhancing the lives of children.

The work–family literature considering how work factors influence workers and their families is an interdisciplinary area of scholarship including developmental and clinical psychology, family science, occupational health, organizational behavior, and sociology. This area of research is broadly guided by ecological systems frameworks (Bronfenbrenner & Morris, 2006) primarily concerned with how development across the life course is shaped by individual characteristics, close relationships, proximal and distal processes in key settings, such as family (microsystem), work (exosystem), and larger contextual conditions (macrosystem; e.g., social stratification, cultural context), and time. Family systems perspectives (Cox & Paley, 1997) further inform this literature by highlighting the interconnections among family members.

Grounded within these areas of scholarship and building upon prior excellent reviews of work and family research (Bianchi & Milkie, 2010; Cooke & Baxter, 2010; Perry-Jenkins & Wadsworth, 2013; Updegraff, Crouter, Umaña-Taylor, & Cansler, 2008), our aim is to provide insights from current theory and empirical research about the role of fathers' and mothers' work for children's well-being as embedded within varying cultural and societal contexts. In our first section, we focus specifically on the literature on parental employment and child well-being, and describe salient dimensions of parents' work and processes that link parents' work to child well-being. In our second section, we focus on literature on specific cultural

The first and third authors were supported by a Layman Faculty Seed Grant from the University of Nebraska-Lincoln. Correspondence should be addressed to Lorey A. Wheeler, Nebraska Center for Research on Children, Youth, Families and Schools, University of Nebraska–Lincoln, 160D Whittier Research Center, P.O. Box 830858, Lincoln, NE 68583–0858; lorey@unl.edu.

factors that might play a role in affecting the relationship between the work–family interface and child well-being. Our final section briefly highlights potential areas for future research and policy implications for work–family linkages to child well-being. Throughout the chapter, we highlight what we know about the unique influences of culture and the differential impact of work–family challenges on families across the globe. We focus on broad indicators of children's well-being, including psychosocial (e.g., relationships, problem behavior) and physical health, and educational/vocational outcomes (e.g., academic achievement, work ethic), as the specific nature of positive child well-being likely varies to some degree across cultural contexts (Kasser, 2011).

Parental Employment and Child Well-Being: What Do We Know?

Research on parental employment and child well-being has conceptualized parental work around four themes, which we use to organize the review: (a) work status, schedule, and hours; (b) work conditions and experiences; (c) work–family conflict; and (d) work-related beliefs. Of note, the bulk of the research on parental employment has historically focused on white (European American) families, typically middle-class couples in professional occupations (Perry-Jenkins & Wadsworth, 2013). However, recently the literature has expanded to include research on low-income families, examinations of race and ethnic variation (e.g., experiences of black and Latino American families), and families outside of the context of the United States (Bianchi & Milke, 2010). Thus, we describe the state of the literature highlighting studies from these underrepresented families, where possible.

Parental Work Status, Schedule and Hours

Parents' work status. A popular topic in earlier studies on work and family stemming from developmental psychology was the examination of child well-being in relation to maternal employment (i.e., work status; whether or not mothers work). Although some studies report a positive association of maternal employment on child outcomes, other studies report a negative association (Bianchi & Milkie, 2010). Furthermore, there is variation in the findings by ethnicity and country of origin that may contribute to discrepancies. For example, children whose mothers were employed by age one exhibited poorer cognitive outcomes, but only among European Americans and not among black Americans (Han, Waldfogel, & Brooks-Gunn, 2001). Similarly, a study conducted with Chinese families found no relations between maternal employment and childhood obesity (Nie & Sousa-Poza, 2014), whereas studies conducted in the context of the United States, primarily with families of higher socioeconomic status, found that mothers' work intensity (e.g., hours worked, cumulative time employed) is particularly deleterious for a child's overweight status (e.g., Morrissey, Dunifon, & Kalil, 2011). To understand these discrepancies better, there is a need for future research to (a) move beyond examining work status to mechanisms linking parents' work status to child well-being (e.g., work conditions, work–family conflict, family routines); and (b) examine indicators of family, cultural and national contexts that may explain variability in the links between work status and child well-being (e.g., socioeconomic status, traditional gender roles).

In light of the recent global economic and financial crisis, unemployment may have become salient for a larger proportion of families, though the nature of links with child well-being is not fully understood (Kalil, 2013). Prior research in Western cultures has found unemployment to have a negative relationship with children's physical, cognitive, and social health. For example, in the United States, job loss of a family member relates to an increased risk of adolescent cigarette use (Unger, Hamilton, & Sussman, 2004). Likewise, young adults in Denmark who had long-term unemployed parents were more likely to show a lack of self-esteem and increased psychological problems (Christoffersen, 1994). Similarly, in a study conducted with Slovak and Dutch adolescents, Slovak boys with unemployed fathers were more likely to show poorer self-rated health and long-term well-being when compared to those whose fathers were employed (Sleskova et al., 2006).

Parents' job losses can also shape children's work values. A study conducted with a US cohort during the economic recession showed that adolescents whose parents were unemployed were more likely to endorse stronger extrinsic (e.g., good pay, security) and intrinsic values (e.g., using one's skills and abilities, opportunities to learn) than those whose parents who did not experience unemployment during the recession, but only among those whose parents received high school or less education (Johnson & Mortimer, 2015). The authors explained this link as a *compensation* process that when adolescents observe their low-educated parents not being rewarded extrinsically and intrinsically due to unemployment they tend to compensate for such loss by endorsing stronger values in both extrinsic and intrinsic domains. More generally, however, the study found that a *reinforcement/accentuation* process is applicable in parent–child value transmission. That is, when parents reported having increased rewards at work (e.g., advancement opportunity) during the recession, their adolescent offspring were likely to endorse stronger work values, and when parents reported perceiving decreased level of rewards at work (e.g., less job security) their adolescent offspring were likely to endorse weaker work values. Therefore, the compensation process of value development as a result of parental unemployment was only evident among a subgroup of families. Generally, endorsing stronger extrinsic and intrinsic work values relates to positive career development, such as increased level of career planning and exploration (Hirschi, 2010), so such findings regarding children's experiences with their parents' job losses may not necessarily lead to negative outcomes. It is not clear, though, whether or not the relationship between unemployment and child well-being is direct or indirect (Ström, 2003). For example, it might not be unemployment per se, but rather economic hardship or poor parental well-being associated with job loss, that lead to negative child outcomes. Understanding the mechanisms linking parental unemployment or underemployment to child well-being is critical to inform programming and policy for minimizing risks in families.

Parents' work schedule and hours. A focus solely on parental work status as related to child well-being has declined with more attention turning to "when" and "how much" parents work. With the world of work in many industrialized countries changing into a 24/7 service-oriented economy, it is not uncommon for parents to work nonstandard hours. For example, a third of dual-earner families in the United States have at least one parent working such shifts (McMenamin, 2007). These trends for parents are purportedly due to childcare needs or wanting to maximize time with children (Presser, 2003). Nonstandard work hours have been referred to in the literature as work schedules including evenings, nights, and weekends (see Li et al., 2014); though, traditional definitions of nonstandard work hours have become inherently arbitrary and problematic given the multiplicity of work start times (Presser & Ward, 2011). Thus, research has moved toward defining nonstandard work hours as a schedule primarily other than a regular day shift (e.g., regular evening or night shifts, or varying hours; Presser & Ward, 2011). In the United States, a nonstandard work schedule is much more prevalent in service, part-time, and low-wage jobs, and minority groups and those of low education disproportionately hold such jobs (Presser & Ward, 2011). Beyond the United States, nonstandard work schedules are also prevalent in other developed economies (e.g., Canada, Europe, Australia), with variation from 10% to 43% of workers depending on the country (Li et al., 2014). It is purported that parents with nonstandard work schedules may have less time to spend with children, thereby relating to adverse child outcomes. Therefore, it is important to understand the processes regarding how parental work schedule and hours relates to family dynamics in specific cultural contexts.

There is some evidence of relationships between nonstandard work hours and adverse child well-being. Li and colleagues (2014) highlighted in a critical review of the literature that the bulk of studies between 1980 and 2012 suggest direct and indirect links between nonstandard work hours to adverse child outcomes for internalizing and externalizing problems, cognitive development, school engagement, extracurricular activities, sleep, and body mass index. Thus, this review supports the general hypothesis that a nonstandard work schedule as a distal context has negative consequences for child well-being outcomes. The most consistent associations were for pre-school children's cognitive, mental health and behavioral problems and for adolescents' risk behavior, suggesting the salience of parents' work schedules across development but also highlighting its differential effects on outcomes for childhood as compared to adolescence. The literature also supports other moderators. Based on theoretical notions of different developmental needs related to child gender, the literature suggests that nonstandard schedules are more detrimental for boys' development than girls' (Li et al., 2014). Li and colleagues (2014) also identified other important moderators, including parents' choice of nonstandard schedule and resulting family dynamics. For example, if parents choose a nonstandard schedule, the stress of working these hours may be offset by the satisfaction of being able to spend more time with children. Alternatively, for families with mothers working nonstandard schedules, fathers may take on more parenting and household tasks, thus improving relations with children.

There has also been some research on the mechanisms that underlie the associations between nonstandard work schedules and child outcomes. Some studies suggest that parents' work schedules can place difficulties on spending time with youth (Wight, Raley, & Bianchi, 2008), which can limit the opportunities for parent–child interactions (Bryant, Zvonkovic, & Reynolds, 2006). There is also evidence for parenting behavior as an intervening factor. For example, mothers' lack of knowledge of their children's whereabouts and less frequent mealtimes with their families partly explain the link between parents' nonstandard hours and worse child cognitive outcomes (Han & Fox, 2011). Conversely, within-family studies (i.e., data collected from multiple family members using family as unit of analysis) show different patterns of results. A cross-sectional study with a predominantly European American sample of dual-earner families found that mothers' nonstandard work hours did not directly link to how much time they spent with their children or how children rated mothers' parenting skills (Barnett & Gareis, 2007). However, this varied by family context. Fathers with partners working the evening shift, spent more time with children (aged eight to fourteen years) as compared to fathers with partners working the day shift, which in turn, was related to lower levels of child socioemotional problems. These results suggest that mothers compensate for the nonstandard schedules by finding other times to spend with their children, and that fathers in these families spend more time with children, in general. Furthermore, it suggests the importance of examining the family as the unit of analysis to capture complex processes occurring within families.

How much parents work can also matter, but support for whether it is better to work fewer hours or more for children varies by study. Crouter, Davis, Updegraff, Delgado, and Fortner (2006a) found that Mexican American adolescents in two-parent families whose mothers worked part-time showed more depressive symptoms than those whose mothers worked full-time, with no difference between adolescents whose mothers worked less than ten hours a week as compared to those who worked full-time. In this study, there was no link between fathers' work hours and adolescents' depressive symptoms. Conversely, a study with a nationally representative sample of adults employed in the civilian US labor force depicted that, when mothers worked short hours, their adolescents showed more internalizing problems, whereas their fathers' work hours were not associated with problem behaviors or grades (Voydanoff, 2004). Generally, long hours can limit parents' time with their children, especially when tied with feelings of overload, but can also provide the children with financial resources (Bianchi & Milkie, 2010), and these relations are apt to vary according to the gender role expectations in cultural groups.

There are a number of limitations that have been identified in the literature on work status, schedule, and hours. Some of these limitations are methodological in nature and may introduce bias, including the reliance on cross-sectional data and single-source self-report measures of key constructs. Only half of the studies in Li and colleagues' review (2014) included longitudinal data to understand causal mechanisms linking parents' work schedules to child outcomes. However, many of these longitudinal studies still only measure work schedules at one point in time, precluding the understanding of the impact of varied versus continual exposure to parents' nonstandard work hours on child outcomes. The reliance on single-source studies may introduce method bias related to the reporter. Much of the literature has relied primarily on parent reports of child outcomes, with few studies using observational or teacher reports (Li et al., 2014). It has been suggested that child outcomes may vary based on the context (e.g., home vs. school) and the accuracy of reports may vary depending on the outcome being reported (Karver, 2006). Thus, multiple informants, in addition to observational measures, are needed to gain a more comprehensive understanding of the nature of the relationship between nonstandard work hours and child outcomes.

Another set of limitations relates to research design and choice of constructs examined. For example, many studies omit examining fathers' work schedules, which precludes understanding gender differences that may relate to family gender roles shaping childcare and household responsibilities (Li et al., 2014). The field will benefit from examining the complexities of family dynamics by including both mothers *and* fathers (within-family designs), as well as family structure differences (e.g., two-parent families, divorced parents sharing custody, single parents). Relatedly, many studies lack information on whether parents have *chosen* a nontraditional schedule (Li et al., 2014). Across different types of family structures, this information could shed light on variability in the impact of nonstandard schedules on child outcomes by serving to strengthen or weaken the relationship.

Lastly, a key criticism is the lack of attention to specific work conditions and experiences and the mechanisms that link parents' work to child well-being. For those parents working a nonstandard schedule, beyond family time dynamics, there may be important differences in work conditions that may help to explain the impact of work status variables. For example, there may be aspects of the work context related to parents' role in the organization (e.g., professional versus service roles) that may explain some of the relationship of nonstandard schedules to child outcomes; under what conditions do children fair better or worse?

Parental Work Conditions and Experiences

In moving beyond examinations of work status variables to understand mechanisms linking parents' work to child well-being, scholars have investigated specific work conditions and experiences. In this literature, scholars have operationalized the terms "work conditions" and "occupational conditions" as a broad array of conditions, including work hours, prestige level, and discrimination. In this review, we use the term "work conditions" to refer to the objective characteristics of the work environment or features closely tied to the job itself (e.g., self-direction, hazardous conditions). We use the term "work experiences" to indicate parents' subjective evaluations of or psychological and emotional responses to work (e.g., discrimination, pressure, stress). Much of this literature is guided by the theoretical and conceptual models of work socialization (Kohn & Schooler, 1982), occupational stress (Bolger, DeLongis, Kessler, & Wethington, 1989), and spillover/crossover (Edwards & Rothbard, 2000) that focus on varying explanations of mechanisms that link parents' work to child well-being.

Parental work conditions. In support of work socialization notions, there is evidence that relatively favorable work conditions are linked with positive child outcomes. One such condition is parents' occupational self-direction (i.e., the extent to which work offers opportunities for autonomy and complexity in tasks with minimal supervision; Perry-Jenkins & Wadsworth, 2013). There is evidence that parents' occupational self-direction can alleviate their children's behavioral problems and facilitate cognitive functioning (in the United States context with primarily middle-class workers; Perry-Jenkins & Wadsworth, 2013). Extending this literature beyond middle-class professional workers, Perry-Jenkins and Gillman (2000) examined parents' positive work conditions (i.e., self-direction, relationships, control) in the context of working-class dual-earner and single-mother families. They found variation by single as compared to two-parent families and by parent gender. In dual-earner families, fathers' positive work conditions related to daughters' positive internalized well-being, whereas mothers' positive conditions related to daughters' reports of lower well-being. Conversely, for single-parent families, mothers' positive work conditions related to lower levels of sons' aggression. Recent studies with Mexican American two-parent families found a similar pattern to earlier work on self-direction. In particular, mothers', but not fathers', self-directedness was concurrently associated with positive parent–adolescent relationships indirectly through mothers' lower levels of depressive symptoms (Wheeler, Updegraff, & Crouter, 2011). In a longitudinal extension, Wheeler, Updegraff, and Crouter (2015) found that fathers', but not mothers', self-directedness was related to decreased father–adolescent conflict and increased adjustment two years later. These studies underscore the importance of understanding these connections in diverse contexts concurrently and longitudinally.

Another positive condition of parents' work linked to child well-being is intrinsic rewards (i.e., interesting, meaningful, and important work; offers opportunities for learning). A recent longitudinal study showed that parents who, during the recession, reported their work to be rewarding were more likely to have adolescent children who endorsed stronger extrinsic and intrinsic work values; that is, the adolescents rated various aspects of work to be highly important (Johnson & Mortimer, 2015; see also Parents' Work Status section about the reinforcement/accentuation process). This might have been a result of direct socialization. Parents who work in rewarding jobs may emphasize the importance of a highly rewarding job to their children. However, youth also learn from observation. Thus, youth who see their parents in rewarding jobs, especially during an economically challenging time, might find similar jobs to be attractive and start to endorse work values that they think are important in choosing a job.

The literature on negative work conditions finds links with less favorable child outcomes. One such negative work condition is hazardous conditions, which may function as a stressor to parents, which in turn, crosses over to child well-being. Among Mexican American two-parent families, fathers', but not mothers', objective hazardous work conditions were linked concurrently with low levels of parent–adolescent warmth via fathers' role overload (Wheeler et al., 2011). Jobs characterized by hazardous conditions may be relatively more prevalent in cultures that are developing, but international studies addressing this topic are lacking, which leaves us with many unanswered questions.

Although the majority of research has used variable-oriented methods, scholars have recently extended the literature by using person-oriented approaches to identify patterns of multiple work conditions related to child well-being. Wheeler, Updegraff, Umaña-Taylor, and Tein (2014) quantified parents' work conditions with objective measures of self-direction, hazardous conditions, and physical activity by coding parents' occupations based on the Occupational Information Network (O*Net; Peterson et al., 2001), which provides the degree of importance of particular occupational attributes as previously validated by Crouter, Lanza, Pirretti, Goodman, and Neebe (2006b). They found three types of parental occupational profiles among Mexican American two-parent families: *differentiated high physical-activity occupations* (both parents' work involved high level of physical activity and low self-direction; characterized by low family income, lowest levels of occupational prestige and paternal educational attainment), *incongruent occupations* (dissimilar work conditions between the mothers and the fathers; characterized by low paternal acculturation and educational attainment, low income), and *congruent highly self-directed occupations* (both parents' work involved high self-direction; characterized by high family income and occupational prestige). These dual-earner family profiles were associated with varying patterns of parent–youth relationships and youth educational and career aspirations five years later, suggesting that the *differentiated* context is the most detrimental for adolescent outcomes (i.e., high levels of parent–youth conflict, low levels of educational aspirations), whereas the *congruent highly self-directed* context provided the most benefit (i.e., high levels of father–youth warmth and educational aspirations, low levels of parent–youth conflict). The *incongruent* context was more mixed, as it provided some benefits to parent–youth relationships but not as much benefit for youth's future aspirations. These findings may, in part, be explained by differences in family socioeconomic and immigrant status, but also highlight the importance of conditions that characterize parents' work contexts. These findings highlight the importance of examining within-family patterns of parents' work as well as between-family differences.

Parental work experiences. Research grounded in the occupational stress (Bolger et al., 1989) and spillover/crossover (Edwards & Rothbard, 2000) perspectives has indicated that parents' stress is an important component of the work context that relates to child well-being (Perry-Jenkins & Wadsworth, 2013). Generally, parents' work stress indirectly relates to child well-being through their own psychological functioning (Perry-Jenkins & Wadsworth, 2013). Yet, much of this literature has not directly measured stress, but rather aspects of parents' work perceived as stressful. One such aspect is job insecurity (i.e., perceptions of instability in current job situation) that may be particularly salient in light of the current economic context. Studies conducted with Singaporean families found links between job insecurity and child work attitudes and general self-efficacy. Lim and

Loo (2003) found in a cross-sectional, within-family study of Singaporean management undergraduates and their parents that youth perceptions of higher levels of maternal and paternal job insecurity were related to lower general self-efficacy (i.e., expectations of personal mastery and success), which in turn, was related to lower levels of positive attitudes toward working (i.e., work involvement and motivation). Later, another group reported a direct negative link between paternal job insecurity and career self-efficacy among daughters, but not sons (Zhao, Lim, & Teo, 2012). However, among the sons, the link was indirect (i.e., through the fathers' parenting behaviors), suggesting that the links may vary according to the family dynamics. Recent studies conducted with Mexican American two-parent families on work pressure also support such indirect links. Fathers' and mothers' work pressure positively related to role overload and depressive symptoms, which in turn, related to lower quality of parent–adolescent relationships (Wheeler et al., 2011). Extending the study with longitudinal data, the authors found fathers', but not mothers', work pressure related to more role overload, which related to better parent–adolescent relationships and lower educational expectations among adolescents two years later (Wheeler et al., 2015).

As work–family scholarship extends beyond middle-class professional working populations, culturally specific stressors, such as perceived ethnic-based discrimination (i.e., actions and behavior toward an ethnic group based on negative beliefs, attitudes, and feelings toward that group) is a particularly critical aspect of the work experience to consider (Hughes & Dodge, 1997). There is some evidence that discrimination at parents' workplaces can have a negative relationship with child well-being, particularly among those in ethnic minority groups. Among Mexican American two-parent families, when fathers reported experiencing discrimination at work, their children were more likely to show depressive symptoms (Crouter et al., 2006a). Mothers', but not fathers', workplace discrimination has also been found to directly relate to parent–adolescent relationships and indirectly to adolescents' decreased adjustment two years later (Wheeler et al., 2015).

Methodological innovations in the area of measuring and analyzing daily diary data have contributed to a focus on daily fluctuations in work experiences related to family and child well-being. Much of this limited research has focused on stressors, with only one study, to our knowledge, examining fluctuations in positive experiences. The literature on daily fluctuations in stress has found that mothers and fathers withdraw from family interactions after an especially busy or stressful day (Repetti, 1989; Repetti & Wood, 1997). Using a dyadic, longitudinal design with nonprofessional dual-earner European American families, one study has examined within-family and within-person fluctuations in work demands and found greater maternal perceived demands related to fathers having more positive interactions with children (Bass, Butler, Grzywacz, & Linney, 2009). The alternate crossover effect was not found for fathers to mothers. The authors speculate this is consistent with literature suggesting that maternal work experiences have a greater impact on families as compared to paternal (Costigan, Cox, & Cauce, 2003). Fathers compensate for mothers under stress with high job demands (Bryant & Zick, 1996), both resulting from traditional divisions of household labor with mothers being primarily responsible for parenting and household tasks. The one study examining fluctuations in positive experiences among primarily European American mothers with children aged nine to seventeen found that mothers' positive mood after work was directly related to youth's positive affect, better sleep quality, and longer sleep duration (Lawson, Davis, McHale, Hammer, & Buxton, 2014). In addition, mothers with more positive work experiences displayed less negative mood after work, and in turn, adolescents reported better well-being (i.e., less negative affect and fewer physical health symptoms). Both of these studies support a family systems perspective highlighting the importance of one family member's experiences having implications for others' behavior and well-being. This research highlights the utility of using a systemic approach by examining within-person and within-family fluctuations of work experiences as related to child well-being and is an area ripe for future studies.

Work–Family Conflict

The work–family conflict literature has been informed by notions of managing multiple roles (e.g., worker, spouse, parent) as it relates to family members' well-being and quality of relationships (Marks & MacDermid, 1996). Perceptions of work–family conflict result from feeling pressure from either domain (i.e., family or work) that makes it more difficult to fully participate in the other domain (Greenhaus & Beutell, 1985). Greenhaus and Beutell identify three forms of work–family conflict: (a) time-based, time devoted to one role makes it difficult to fulfill another role; (b) strain-based, work or family stressors producing strain in one domain that spillovers to the other domain; and (c) behavior-based, patterns of behavior in one role may conflict with behavior expectations in another role. Yet, not many studies have examined child well-being as an outcome of work–family conflict.

A limited number of studies suggest that when parents experience greater levels of conflict between work and their family roles, it can influence their offspring's adjustment. One study with a nationally representative sample of US workers found that strain-based work–family conflict reported by both mothers and fathers was positively associated with child internalizing and externalizing problems, while only fathers' strain-based work–family conflict was negatively associated with youth's school grades (Voydanoff, 2004). A study of dual-earner middle-class Israeli families examining crossover found a negative relationship between time-based work–family conflict (both work-to-family and family-to-work) and parent–child interaction quality (Cinamon, Weisel, & Tzuk, 2007).

Parental Work Values and Beliefs

Stemming from theoretical models of work socialization (Kohn & Schooler, 1982) and spillover (Edwards & Rothbard, 2000), there is a literature examining how parents' work values or beliefs about work relate to youth's work-related beliefs and attitudes (Bryant et al., 2006). Work values refer to aspects of work that individuals regard as important (when choosing a job and also in one's current job), and researchers have generally used the distinction of extrinsic versus intrinsic values in their research. Extrinsic values are values related to external factors of work (e.g., pay, status, benefits) and intrinsic values are values related to the content of the work itself (e.g., interesting work, contact with people). In contrast, work-related beliefs and attitudes refer to generalized thoughts and emotions attached to work or working. In black American families, the fathers' work ethic (i.e., defined as the belief that hard work is important), but not the mothers' work ethic, was positively associated with youth's work ethic (Lee, Padilla, & McHale, 2016). An Israeli study that included only working mothers and their adolescent children showed that daughters exhibit greater similarity to their mothers' work values than do sons, with sons reporting lower levels than mothers (Mannheim & Seger, 1993). This is consistent with gender intensification perspectives that suggest that youth are more receptive to their same-gender parent during adolescence (Galambos, Almeida, & Petersen, 1990).

How parents perceive their own work can transfer to child work motivation, but this research is in an early stage. In a sample of families in the United States, parents' positive emotions and thoughts about their work experiences were likely to be transmitted to their children's emotions and thoughts about their future work (i.e., work valences), which in turn was linked with the children's work and school motivation (Porfeli, Wang, & Hartung, 2008). However, Porfeli and colleagues found no link between parents' and children's negative work valences. A similar study among Italian families, however, found no link between parents' own work valences and their children's perceived parents' work valences, although the children's perceptions of their parents' work was positively linked to their own work valences (Porfeli, Ferrari, & Nota, 2012). The authors speculated that parents might color their work experiences into ones that are somewhat different from reality for the sake of their children's development (Galinsky, 1999), which might be the reason parents' work experiences did not transfer to children's perceptions of work. Knowing that the Italian study included a sample of relatively high proportion of mothers (76.5%) and fathers (95.3%) working in medium- and low-skilled jobs and the United States study included a sample showing a higher median household income than the national median, the difference in findings might be due to difference in socioeconomic status within a society. Parents working in managerial or professional jobs might not necessarily hinder their positive attitudes toward work, which in turn transmits to their offspring, whereas parents who work in jobs that require medium to low skills might want to disguise their attitudes towards work, whether it be negative or positive, because they want their offspring to aspire to jobs that have greater amount of authority and responsibility. However, this is only a speculation and studies need to be replicated to test whether this explanation holds true.

Parental Employment and Child Well-Being: Relevant Cultural Factors

Ecological frameworks (Bronfenbrenner & Morris, 2006) emphasize the importance of the connection between persons and interrelated contexts or systems. As previously discussed in this chapter, parents' work is one important exosystem that exerts an indirect influence on child well-being. The macrosystem is the broader context that encompasses all of the other systems in which any group (e.g., cultural/ ethnic group) whose members share values and belief systems is situated. This cultural context, thus, extends an important influence on (and is influenced by) all of the other systems, including the work–family interface as it relates to child well-being. With this in mind, a large proportion of the work–family literature has been conducted within the context of the United States. Thus, these findings may not generalize to other national contexts.

More broadly, the operationalization and influence of cultural constructs that may shape individuals' experiences of the work–family interface has largely been ignored in most theories and research of work–family phenomena as well as when considering the relations with child well-being. A notable exception is recent theoretical work by Powell, Francesco, and Ling (2009) applying notions of culture to the work–family interface, without explicitly focusing on the relation to child outcomes. Powell and colleagues purport that aspects of culture may act to moderate the influence of work on family outcomes. They suggest four dimensions of culture that might be especially relevant to the work–family interface: individualism/collectivism, humane orientation, specificity/diffusion, and gender egalitarianism (alternatively called gender role attitudes). Additionally, in recent research with Mexican American families (Updegraff et al., 2008), cultural orientation has also been identified as a salient cultural dimension that could be said to encompass Powell and colleagues' (2009) cultural dimensions. We briefly review the theoretical notions and limited empirical work related to each of these constructs, starting broadly with cultural orientation and then explicating each specific cultural dimension.

Scholars interested in American ethnic minority families have highlighted the importance of parents' cultural orientations, which include identification with a particular cultural group's values (e.g., traditional gender roles, individualism), behaviors (e.g., language use), and customs (e.g., food preferences). To our knowledge, only one study has examined the moderating role of cultural orientations on the links between parental work and child well-being. Crouter and colleagues' (2006a) study with a sample of Mexican American two-parent families examined maternal and paternal behavioral orientations toward Anglo (American) and Mexican culture (e.g., English and Spanish language use, cooking Mexican or American food) as a moderator of the association between fathers' income and perceptions of workplace discrimination on adolescents' depressive symptoms. For income, mothers' Anglo cultural orientation moderated the association such that when mothers were more strongly oriented toward Anglo culture, fathers' income related to lower levels of adolescent depressive symptoms. The authors suggested that when mothers have strong ties to Anglo culture, the family may embrace more materialistic and individualistic values, making fathers' income particularly important for child well-being. In relation to discrimination, the authors found that when families were more involved in Mexican culture (relative to Anglo culture), fathers' perceptions of workplace discrimination were related to higher levels of adolescents' depressive symptoms. In this instance, the authors suggested that as discrimination targets the culture they strongly identify with, it makes the experience of discrimination especially detrimental for these families.

Many scholars have highlighted the importance of individualism and collectivism as cultural values that emphasize relationships between people (Powell et al., 2009; Triandis, 1995). Individualistic cultural groups typically value independence and have looser personal relationships, typically living only with immediate family. Conversely, collectivistic cultural groups typically value interdependence and have closer personal relationships, typically living with immediate and extended family. Collectivist cultural groups may put the needs of the group above the individual, whereas individualist groups may do the opposite. Thus, members of collectivist groups may have greater concern for the quality of their work–family interface than members of individualist groups. Alternatively, humane orientation and specificity/ diffusion relate to societal values that may relate to the work–family interface (Powell et al., 2009). A societal humane orientation is the degree to which societies encourage humane treatment of individuals. Such societies have high levels of social support and individuals are willing to contribute to others' well-being, and thus may provide more support for families in managing the work–family interface. Specificity/diffusion refers to how societies define different constructs (e.g., as components of the whole or as an integrated whole). In relation to the work–family interface, specific cultures place more division between work and home, whereas diffuse cultures may have less clear boundaries between the two. To our knowledge, there is no empirical work that has examined these cultural constructs in relation to work and child well-being.

Traditional gender role attitudes in relation to work and family typically refer to distinct social roles for men and women, including childrearing and household tasks designated to women and educational achievement and economic provision to men (Hoffman & Kloska, 1995). Few studies of the work–family linkages have directly examined gender role attitudes, but instead have examined gender and reference gender roles as a potential explanation for differences. For example, when white, black, and Latino American workers were compared, Latino workers showed the greatest disparity between men and women in terms of self-reported work–family conflict, which according to the authors, is because Latino women who work contradict the most with their expected gender roles among the three ethnic groups (Roehling, Jarvis, & Swope, 2005). However, the level of reported work–family conflict did not differ by sex in Finland, which is a society where gender roles are relatively equal (Kinnunen & Mauno, 1998). Such findings indicate that role expectations regarding work and family for men and women are culturally embedded. Noting that mothers' and fathers' experiences of work–family conflict have an impact on child outcomes, it is possible that such parent–child links may differ depending on sociocultural context as well. Future research is needed that moves beyond proxy measures of culture, such as gender or ethnic group or nationality, to direct measures of cultural values, practices, and behaviors to help us better understanding the impact of cultural milieus.

Conclusion

In this review, we have highlighted key aspects of parents' work context that may have implications for child well-being. This section discusses three major recommendations for future culturally relevant research including children, families, and work around the globe and general conclusions. First, there is a continued need for more rigorous designs (including longitudinal designs) and theory-driven tests of hypotheses, with greater attention to understanding causal mechanisms linking parental work to child well-being. For example, as noted earlier, study designs using daily diaries can inform us with how work–family spillover and parent–child crossover functions on a day-to-day basis. Further, parents' cultural orientations or cultural values within a society are discussed as important milieus for child development, but empirical research is lacking in this area. Conducting research based on theories with cutting-edge research methodology is essential for the design of effective programming that addresses the well-being in both the work and family contexts.

Second, much of the research on parental employment approaches work as fairly static and unchanging. A life-course perspective would challenge researchers to consider how fluctuations in work status and conditions relate to children's developmental trajectories. Taking into account changes in work status and situations would be especially important given that the global economy is changing quickly and dynamically. Companies merge with each other or shut down, which results in employee layoffs, and with the development of robots and machines that replace human labor, old jobs are disappearing. Such changes in the world of work have affected individuals' work lives. It is no longer a norm for adults to have one job in their lives, and career development is no longer linear. These changes in parents' work can have differing effects on their offspring's well-being. Therefore, it would be desirable to consider parents' changing work status and situations when examining the linkages between parental work and child well-being.

Third, future research will also be shaped by structural and demographic changes, such as increased diversity of families and continued income inequalities. There is a need to expand the examination of work–family linkages with attention to these changing demographics, as there is some evidence to suggest that parents' work experiences within these families vary from research with middle-class European American families. This might also include examining how specific cultural orientations or values relate to variations in the links between parental work and child well-being to potentially explain differences in findings across cultural and national groups. Attention to these complexities using sophisticated methodologies (e.g., person-centered, within-person, within-family approaches) will shed light on how variation within family and national contexts shape the links between work and child well-being.

Employers, mental health practitioners, interventionists, and researchers focused on the effects of parental work on child well-being will benefit from considering the contextual and social precursors that lead to family and youth adjustment as highlighted by this chapter. Overall, there is a need for services that focus on the unique cultural context and stressors that children and their families face. Reducing risk for child adjustment problems as related to parental work will require comprehensive, community-wide interventions that address not only well-being, but also the circumstances in which people live and work. In the realm of policy, there have been calls for family-friendly workplace policies (White House Press Secretary, 2014). Based on the literature in this review, this might include the promotion of flexibility and empowerment of workers, opportunities to exert autonomy, and experiences of job complexity. This would also include policy initiatives focused on workplace discrimination, which are critical for the improvement of well-being for ethnic minority parents. This should not only include fair hiring and promotion practices, but also attention to the training of leadership on the creation of work environments that support and value diversity in the workforce. These recommendations would not only improve the lives of working parents but could positively spillover to support child well-being.

In conclusion, this review of work–family linkages on child well-being demonstrates the diversity of scholarship in this interdisciplinary field. Because of the vast array of studies linking parental work with child well-being, this review was necessarily selective and some topics have no doubt been given less attention than others. However, it is hoped that this review is informative for scholars, policymakers, and other professionals, who support working parents, design workplace programs that help workers manage both work and family life, and researchers hoping to push the field forward.

References

Barnett, R. C., & Gareis, K. C. (2007). Shift work, parenting behaviors, and children's socio-emotional well-being: A within-family study. *Journal of Family Issues, 28,* 727–748.

Bass, B. L., Butler, A. B., Grzywacz, J. G., & Linney, K. D. (2009). Do job demands undermine parenting? A daily analysis of spillover and crossover effects. *Family Relations, 58,* 201–215.

Bianchi, S. M., & Milkie, M. A. (2010). Work and family research in the first decade of the 21st century. *Journal of Marriage and Family, 72,* 705–725.

Bolger, N., DeLongis, A., Kessler, R. C., & Wethington, E. (1989). The contagion of stress across multiple roles. *Journal of Marriage and the Family, 51,* 175–183.

Bronfenbrenner, U, & Morris, P. A. (2006). The bioecological model of human development. In R. M. Lerner (Ed.), *Handbook of Child psychology, Vol. I, Theoretical Models of Human Development.* Sixth edition, pp. 793–828. Hoboken, N.J.: Wiley.

Bryant, B. K., Zvonkovic, A. M., & Reynolds, P. (2006). Parenting in relation to child and adolescent vocational development. *Journal of Vocational Behavior, 69,* 149–175.

Bryant, W. K., & Zick, C. D. (1996). An examination of parent-child shared time. *Journal of Marriage and the Family, 58,* 227–237.

Christoffersen, M. N. (1994). A follow-up study of longterm effects of unemployment on children: loss of self-esteem and self-destructive behavior among adolescents. *Childhood, 2,* 212–220.

Cinamon, R. G., Weisel, A., & Tzuk, K. (2007). Work–family conflict within the family: Crossover effects, perceived parent-child interaction quality, parental self-efficacy, and life role attributions. *Journal of Career Development, 34*, 79–100.

Cooke, L. P., & Baxter, J. (2010). "Families" in international context: Comparing institutional effects across western societies. *Journal of Marriage and Family, 72*, 516–536.

Costigan, C. L., Cox, M. J., & Cauce, A. M. (2003). Work-parenting linkages among dual-earner couples at the transition to parenthood. *Journal of Family Psychology, 17*, 397–408.

Cox, M. J., & Paley, B. (1997). Families as systems. *Annual Review of Psychology, 48*, 243–267.

Crouter, A. C., Davis, K. D., Updegraff, K., Delgado, M., & Fortner, M. (2006a). Mexican American fathers' occupational conditions: Links to family members' psychological adjustment. *Journal of Marriage and Family, 68*, 843–858.

Crouter, A. C., Lanza, S. T., Pirretti, A., Goodman, W. B., Neebe, E., & The Family Life Project Key Investigators. (2006b). The O*Net jobs classification system: A primer for family researchers. *Family Relations, 55*, 461–472.

Edwards, J. R., & Rothbard, N. P. (2000). Mechanisms linking work and family: Clarifying the relationship between work and family constructs. *Academy of Management Review, 25*, 178–199.

Galambos, N. L., Almeida, D. M., & Petersen, A. C. (1990). Masculinity, femininity, and sex role attitudes in early adolescence: Exploring gender intensification. *Child Development, 61*, 1905–1914.

Galinsky, E. (1999). *Ask the Children: What America's Children Really Think about Working Parents*. New York, NY: William Morrow and Company.

Han, W. J., & Fox, L. E. (2011). Parental work schedules and children's cognitive trajectories. *Journal of Marriage and Family, 73*, 962–980.

Han, W. J., Waldfogel, J., & Brooks-Gunn, J. (2001). The effects of early maternal employment on later cognitive and behavioral outcomes. *Journal of Marriage and Family, 63*, 336–354.

Hirschi, A. (2010). Positive adolescent career development: The role of intrinsic and extrinsic work values. *Career Development Quarterly, 58*, 276–287.

Hoffman, L. W., & Kloska, D. D. (1995). Parents' gender-based attitudes toward marital roles and child rearing: Development and validation of new measures. *Sex Roles, 32*, 273–295.

Hughes, D., & Dodge, M. A. (1997). African American women in the workplace: Relationships between job conditions, racial bias at work, and perceived job quality. *American Journal of Community Psychology, 25*, 581–599.

Johnson, M. K., & Mortimer, J. T. (2015). Reinforcement or compensation? The effects of parents' work and financial conditions on adolescents' work values during the Great Recession. *Journal of vocational behavior, 87*, 89–100.

Kalil, A. (2013). Effects of the great recession on child development. *The ANNALS of the American Academy of Political and Social Science, 650*, 232–250.

Karver, S. M. (2006). Determinants of multiple informant agreement on child and adolescent behavior. *Journal of Abnormal Child Psychology, 34*, 251–262.

Kasser, T. (2011). Cultural values and the well-being of future generations: A cross-national study. *Journal of Cross-Cultural Psychology, 42*, 206–215.

Kinnunen, U., & Mauno, S. (1998). Antecedents and outcomes of work–family conflict among employed women and men in Finland. *Human Relations, 51*, 157–177.

Kohn, M. L., & Schooler, C. (1982). Job conditions and personality: A longitudinal assessment of their reciprocal effects. *American Journal of Sociology, 87*, 1257–1286.

Lawson, K. M., Davis, K. D., McHale, S. M., Hammer, L. B., & Buxton, O. M. (2014). Daily positive spillover and crossover from mothers' work to youth health. *Journal of Family Psychology, 28*, 897.

Lee, B., Padilla, J., & McHale, S. M. (2015). Transmission of work ethic in African-American families and its links with adolescent adjustment. *Journal of Youth and Adolescence, early view*. doi:10.1007/s10964-015-0391-0

Li, J., Johnson, S., Han, W., Andrews, S., Strazdins, L., Kendall, G, & Dockery, A. (2014), Parents' Non-standard Work Schedules and Child Wellbeing. A Critical Review of the Literature, *Journal of Primary Prevention, 35*, 53–73.

Lim, V. K., & Loo, G. L. (2003). Effects of parental job insecurity and parenting behaviors on youth's self-efficacy and work attitudes. *Journal of Vocational Behavior, 63*, 86–98.

Mannheim, B., & Seger, T. (1993). Mothers' occupational characteristics, family position, and sex role orientation as related to adolescents' work values. *Youth and Society, 24*, 276–298.

Marks, S. R., & MacDermid, S. M. (1996). Multiple roles and the self: A theory of role balance. *Journal of Marriage and the Family, 58*, 417–432.

McMenamin, T. M. (2007, December). A time to work: Recent trends in shift work and flexible schedules. *Monthly Labor Review*, 3–15.

Morrissey, T. W., Dunifon, R. E., & Kalil, A. (2011). Maternal employment, work schedules, and children's body mass index. *Child Development, 82*, 66–81.

Nie, P., & Sousa-Poza, A. (2014). Maternal employment and childhood obesity in China: Evidence from the China Health and Nutrition Survey. *Applied Economics, 46*, 2418–2428.

Perry-Jenkins, M., & Gillman, S. (2000). Parental job experiences and children's well-being: The case of two-parent and single-mother working-class families. *Journal of Family and Economic Issues, 21*, 123–147.

Perry-Jenkins, M., & Wadsworth, S. M. (2013). Work and family through time and space: Revisiting old themes and charting new directions. In G. W. Peterson & K. R. Bush (Eds.), *Handbook of Marriage and the Family* (pp. 549–572). New York, NY: Springer.

Peterson, N. G., Mumford, M. D., Borman, W. C., Jeanneret, P. R., Fleishman, E. A., Levin, K. Y., . . . Dye, D. M. (2001). Understanding work using the Occupational Information Network (O*Net): Implications for practice and research. *Personnel Psychology, 54*, 451–492.

Porfeli, E., Ferrari, L., & Nota, L. (2012). Work valence as a predictor of academic achievement in the family context. *Journal of Career Development, 13*, 371–389.

Porfeli, E. J., Wang, C., & Hartung, P. J. (2008). Family transmission of work affectivity and experiences to children. *Journal of Vocational Behavior, 73*, 278–286.

Powell, G. N., Francesco, A. M., & Ling, Y. (2009). Toward culture-sensitive theories of the work–family interface. *Journal of Organizational Behavior, 30*, 597–616.

Presser, H. B. (2003). *Working in a 24/7 Economy: Challenges for American Families*. New York, NY: Russ Sage Foundation.

Presser, H. B., & Ward, B. W. (2011, July) Nonstandard work schedules over the life course: a first look. *Monthly Labor Review*, 3–16.

Repetti, R. L. (1989). Effects of daily workload on subsequent behavior during marital interaction: The roles of social withdrawal and spouse support. *Journal of Personality and Social Psychology, 57*, 651–659.

Repetti, R.L., & Wood, J. (1997). The effects of daily stress at work on mothers' interactions with preschoolers. *Journal of Family Psychology, 11*, 90–108.

Roehling, P. V., Jarvis, L. H., & Swope, H. E. (2005). Variations in negative work–family spillover among white, black, and Hispanic American men and women: Does ethnicity matter? *Journal of Family Issues, 26*, 840–865.

Sleskova, M., Tuinstra, J., Geckova, A. M., van Dijk, J. P., Salonna, F., Groothoff, J. W., & Reijneveld, S. A. (2006). Influence of parental employment status on Dutch and Slovak adolescents' health. *BMC Public Health, 6*, 250.

Ström, S. (2003). Unemployment and families: A review of research. *Social Service Review, 77*, 399–430.

Triandis, H. C. (1995). *Individualism and Collectivism*. Boulder, CO: Westview.

Unger, J. B., Hamilton, J. E., & Sussman, S. (2004). A family member's job loss as a risk factor for smoking among adolescents. *Health Psychology, 23*, 308.

Updegraff, K. A., Crouter, A. C., Umaña-Taylor, A. J., & Cansler, E. (2008). Work–family linkages in the lives of families of Mexican origin. In J.E. Lansford, K. Deater-Deckard, & M. H. Bornstein (Eds.). *Immigrant Families in Contemporary Society* (pp. 250–267). New York, NY: Guilford.

Voydanoff, P. (2004). Work, community, and parenting resources and demands as predictors of adolescent problems and grades. *Journal of Adolescent Research, 19*, 155–173.

Wheeler, L. A., Updegraff, K. A., & Crouter, A. (2011). Work and Mexican American parent–adolescent relationships: The mediating role of parent well-being. *Journal of Family Psychology, 25*, 107–116.

Wheeler, L. A., Updegraff, K. A., & Crouter, A. (2015). Mexican-origin parents' work conditions and adolescents' adjustment. *Journal of Family Psychology, 29*, 447–457.

Wheeler, L. A., Updegraff, K. A., Umaña-Taylor, A., & Tein, J. Y. (2014). Mexican-origin parents' latent occupational profiles: Associations with parent–youth relationships and youth aspirations. *Developmental Psychology, 50*, 772–783.

White House Press Secretary. (June, 2014). Fact sheet: The White House summit on working families. Retrieved: www.whitehouse.gov/the-press-office/2014/06/23/fact-sheet-white-house-summit-workingfamilies

Wight, V. R., Raley, S. B., & Bianchi, S. M. (2008). Time for children, one's spouse and oneself among parents who work nonstandard hours. *Social Forces, 87*, 243–271.

Zhao, X., Lim, V. K., & Teo, T. S. (2012). The long arm of job insecurity: Its impact on career-specific parenting behaviors and youths' career self-efficacy. *Journal of Vocational Behavior, 80*, 619–628.

PART VIII

Individual Perspectives

38 Segmentation/Integration of Work and Nonwork Domains: Global Considerations

Carrie A. Bulger and Mark E. Hoffman

Researchers have studied the ways people manage the multiple roles in their lives for decades, particularly the management of work and family (sometimes "nonwork") roles (e.g., Sieber, 1974). Marks and MacDermid (1996) and Nippert-Eng (1996) suggested that people actively organize and maintain their roles in order to successfully juggle role demands and obligations. Nippert-Eng introduced the notion that people have preferences for keeping their work and family domains separated or not, and that they construct and maintain boundaries around their work and family lives in order to ensure that these domains remain segmented from one another or integrated with one another. She also introduced the idea of the *segmentation–integration continuum*, suggesting that people tend to fall closer to one end or the other as they construct boundaries around work and family.

Ashforth, Kreiner, and Fugate (2000), in their examination of boundary theory and role transitions, discussed the idea of segmentation–integration of work and family domains. Ashforth et al. argued that the transitions between domains are an indicator of the extent to which domains are segmented or integrated. Boundaries may be physical, temporal, and psychological. Physical boundaries stem in part from having a separate workplace and family dwelling, but physical boundaries also may be erected in other ways, such as putting away one's work laptop at the end of the workday. Temporal boundaries exist when individuals specify certain times for work and family activities. Psychological boundaries are related to maintaining different types of behaviors and affect in certain domains. For example, a manager may respond to anger-inducing situations differently at home versus at work.

Segmentation exists when the boundary around a given domain is low in flexibility (e.g., individual could and would leave one domain to attend to the other) and permeability (e.g., elements of one domain enter the other) as well as when people are unlikely to transition out of the domain or interrupt a domain activity, in order to attend to the other domain. In keeping with the types of boundaries, people may build segmented boundaries that are physical, temporal, and/or psychological. Further, segmentors may also actively avoid cognitively engaging with their family domain while they are at work and with work while they are on family time. On the other hand, integration exists when the boundary around a given domain is high in flexibility and permeability as well as when people would be highly likely to transition out of the domain or interrupt a domain activity, in order to attend to the other domain. For integrators, physical, temporal, and psychological boundaries are built such that they are easily crossed. Integrators will also cognitively engage with one domain while physically located in the other.

Clark (2000), in her work–family border theory, suggests that the strength of the boundary is affected by individual preference as well as by other factors, such as norms in the organization or family and family members or coworkers (i.e., border keepers). Ashforth et al. (2000) argue that segmentation and integration each have advantages and disadvantages. For instance, they suggest that transitioning between integrated domains would be much simpler and likely less stressful than for segmented domains. However, people who segment between domains would likely experience less role conflict than people who integrate domains.

This chapter explores the state of the research on segmentation and integration, particularly with an eye to how the construct is examined across the globe. We examine segmentation–integration as individual preferences and behaviors, as well as organizational and societal/cultural influences on the segmentation–integration of work and family. We also examine outcomes of segmentation and integration, including how these relationships may be influenced by cultural or societal factors. Finally, we raise some questions about the state of the literature and offer suggestions for further examination of segmentation–integration from a global work–family interface perspective.

Segmentation–Integration Preferences

Nippert-Eng (1996) clearly argued that preference for segmenting versus integrating life domains is an individual difference that varies among people. She developed the idea following an intensive case study of workers in a single organization. In an attempt to capture this via measurement, Kreiner (2006) developed a scale to assess segmentation–integration preference that distinguishes preference for segmenting work from nonwork and preference for segmenting nonwork from work. For example, some people may gladly allow family phone calls or texts during work hours, but strongly prefer to keep work matters at work and during work hours. Recently, Methot and LePine (2016) provided further evidence that there are two distinct dimensions of segmentation–integration preferences. That is, they showed that individuals have separate segmentation–integration preferences for work and home. They refer to these as preference to protect work and preference to protect home. Although they did not examine correlates of such preferences, they did find that people allow fewer non-domain intrusions into the protected domain. Other researchers have reported some similar findings that people establish different boundaries around different domains, often referring to this practice as asymmetric boundaries or differential permeability (e.g., Bulger, Matthews, & Hoffman, 2007).

There is growing evidence for the nomological network of segmentation–integration preference as an individual difference variable that can impact work and family outcomes. For instance, Olson-Buchanan and Boswell (2006) found that segmentation preference was related to role involvement or centrality. In particular, they found that role involvement was related to the integration of one role into the other. In another study, McNall, Scott, and Nicklin (2015) found that positive affectivity and preference for integration were independently related to higher work-to-family enrichment. Additionally, recent research has also investigated the interaction of segmentation–integration preference and personality traits on outcomes related to work and family. Michel and Clark (2013) found that preference for segmentation moderated the relationship between several personality traits and work–family conflict and facilitation. Specifically, preference for segmentation strengthened the effect of negative affect on work-to-family conflict, neuroticism on family-to-work conflict, positive affect on work-to-family facilitation, and core self-evaluations on family-to-work facilitation.

Although there is some evidence that segmentation–integration is an individual difference variable, there is also evidence that segmentation–integration preference is influenced by other life factors. Moen and her colleagues (Moen, Kelly, & Huang, 2008; Moen, 2011) have argued that work–family researchers should use a life-course perspective in understanding the ways people attempt to manage their multiple roles. They argue that roles are dynamic and change over the course of one's life, resulting in different needs and desires with regard to work and nonwork roles. This suggests that segmentation–integration preference may change within individuals as they advance in their careers or change jobs, as the makeup of their household changes due to relationship changes and/or children, among various other life events.

In an Australian qualitative study, Skinner, Elton, Auer, and Pocock (2014) found evidence for some of Moen and colleagues' arguments. Skinner et al. studied health professionals at various stages in the life course and found differences and some similarities in their perspectives on work and nonwork. Workers at all stages described a need for flexibility from their work, yet the reasons for flexibility were different. For instance, younger workers who were just entering the workforce described the significance of the change in lifestyle that accompanied entering the workforce full-time as impacting their ability to form and maintain important relationships, including romantic relationships, outside of work. Mid-career individuals expressed the most pressures from both work and nonwork as these individuals were the most likely to be advancing toward new positions in their career as well as to be juggling responsibilities that come with having children at home. Finally, older workers described a desire to continue to work as they approached retirement, yet also desired flexibility in the number of hours worked and in the way the hours were scheduled. Although this is a cross-sectional study, it is one attempt to identify potential life course influences on the way the work–family interface is viewed.

Other research suggests that in addition to life-course changes, there may also be generational effects or changes in segmentation-integration preferences. In a recent cross-sectional study, Haeger and Lingham (2014) found a trend toward increasing "fusion" of work and nonwork (an idea similar to integration), particularly for younger workers in the millennial generation. They suggest this trend is a result of increasingly available smart, mobile technologies allowing for access to both domains at any given moment, as well as to the changing needs and desires for segmentation–integration for younger workers.

Little research seems to have investigated segmentation–integration preference either as an individual difference or from a life-course or generational perspective at the cross-national or global level. One exception to this is a study that compared workers from Canada and the United States (Schieman & Young, 2015). Using national databases from both countries, Schieman and Young investigated what influences people to engage in "work–family multitasking," which they defined as being engaged in tasks related to one domain while physically located in the other. Schieman and Young used a single item to measure work–family multitasking, and found that many factors influence it, including characteristics of the individual (e.g., more educated), the type of job (e.g., owner of the business), working from home, and job demands (e.g., frequent contact with work outside regular hours). In addition, the authors note Canadian and US workers were quite similar in terms of the influences on work–family multitasking. It should be noted that work–family multitasking is very similar to the notion of inter-domain transitions introduced by Matthews and colleagues (Matthews & Barnes-Farrell, 2010; Matthews, Barnes-Farrell, & Bulger, 2010; Matthews, Winkel, & Wayne, 2014) in that both are intended to measure the connection between work and family domains. However, inter-domain transitions (Matthews et al., 2010) are intended to measure the frequency with which work and family come into contact both physically and *cognitively*.

Segmentation–Integration Behaviors, Norms, and Policies

Most researchers agree that although individuals may hold certain preferences for segmentation versus integration and strive to create and maintain boundaries to support that preference, they also must contend with demands from work and nonwork that may not conform to their preferences. As such, a great deal of research has focused on behaviors related to segmentation–integration not only at the level of the individual, but also the influence of organizations and cultural or societal norms.

Kreiner, Hollensbe, and Sheep (2009) introduced the notion of *boundary work tactics*. These are the actions people take to establish boundaries around work and home domains that are more or less flexible to promote more or less integration versus segmentation. In a qualitative study of Episcopal priests, Kreiner and colleagues identified four categories of boundary work tactics: behavioral, temporal, physical, and communicative. Behavioral tactics may include such actions as using other people (i.e., border keepers) to help maintain the boundary or focusing on urgent demands first. Temporal tactics involve taking advantage of time within each domain to the fullest as well as seeking a respite from demands. Physical tactics may include managing the physical boundaries around domains, for example by turning off notifications for a personal email account during work time. Finally, communicative tactics involve setting expectations with members of each domain about how demands will be handled, such as letting coworkers know that work email will not be answered during the weekend.

Kreiner et al. (2009) showed that people employ boundary work tactics to establish boundaries to match their individual segmentation–integration preferences, as well as to satisfy influences from the environment (e.g., job) and from other domain members (e.g., family, supervisors). This finding is in line with the propositions put forth by Clark (2000), suggesting that people contend with their own preferences, norms, and the "border keepers" in their domains. Similar findings were obtained by von Borell de Araujo, Tureta, and von Borell de Araujo (2015), who interviewed sixty-three Brazilian professional working mothers in dual-earner couples to explore segmentation–integration preferences and the boundary management tactics employed by these women. Their results confirmed the four categories of boundary work tactics described by Kreiner et al. (2009). However, their work was also suggestive of new directions for research on boundaries and segmentation–integration. One example is the notion of "setting expectations," which Kreiner et al. identified as a communicative tactic. The interviewees in von Burell de Araujo et al.'s study also discussed setting expectations for segmentation and integration, but noted that sometimes demands changed, resulting in the need for a new tactic: "renegotiating expectations." This is an interesting finding, particularly in line with the ideas discussed earlier about the dynamic nature of boundaries and changes in the life course.

Santos (2015) interviewed male and female Portuguese academics to understand their work and family segmentation–integration from a life-course perspective. She notes that the work environment for Portuguese academics has changed in that more is demanded of these employees with less offered in return (i.e., fewer tenure-track positions). Santos describes preferences first in terms of whether the respondents described work and family as being complementary domains or whether one domain was subordinate to the other. She notes that only a small number of her respondents described a subordination narrative; most described work and family as complementing the other domain. Santos did not directly study the kinds of boundary work tactics described by Kreiner et al. (2009) and von Burell de Araujo et al. (2015), rather she describes a set of what she calls "micro-narratives" about work and family. A full unpacking of her findings is not appropriate here, but the narratives she describes include crafting boundaries of variable strength around domains that vary according to several variables including individual preference for segmentation versus integration, identity and/or role centrality, gender, relationship status, career stage, and presence of children as well as ages of children. Thus, this study is in line with much of the research described earlier on the multiple influences on segmentation–integration preference and behavior.

Ba' (2011) examined segmentation and integration in dual-earner couples in the United Kingdom. His findings suggest that whether they are striving to segment or integrate work and family, the overarching goal for the individuals in his study is to "harmonise" (p. 321) the demands of work and family, thereby reducing conflict and stress. In addition, Ba' suggests that whether people aim to segment or integrate their work and family domains, one way in which they make sense of their domains is by attaching symbolic meaning to the cognitive and emotional experiences of work and family. For instance, Ba' asked participants about particularly gratifying activities they did with their children. One respondent described taking children to the theater as being an activity she felt was meaningful because her work was in a creative field. Ba' argues that this is an example of ascribing symbolism to "creativity" for this mother as she integrates her work and family life.

Despite many calls to investigate the nonwork domain beyond the family (e.g., Casper, Weltman, & Kwesiga, 2007; Fisher, Bulger, & Smith, 2009), few studies have taken up the call. One study has looked at the impact of segmentation–integration on friends and friendship (Pedersen & Lewis, 2012). This study was conducted using a Danish sample of employed individuals to try to determine how people managed to maintain friendships outside of work and family. Pedersen and Lewis found that participants managed to maintain friendships by integrating friends with both the work and family domains to some degree. For example, individuals often spend time with friends and family together or with friends and co workers together. Each study described here supports the tenets of early work on boundaries and segmentation–integration in that the process of boundary work is active and dynamic, based on individual needs and desires, and influenced by demands from the domains.

There have been some attempts to develop boundary management profiles related to segmentation–integration based on much of the research identified above. In one of the first studies, Bulger, Matthews, and Hoffman (2007) used cluster analysis to identify patterns of boundary profiles. The main finding in this study was that there is not a simple segmentation–integration continuum. Rather, the clusters identified included one that seemed mainly integration-oriented, two clusters that integrated one domain but protected the other, and one cluster that did not demonstrate high degrees of segmenting or integrating either domain. Based on these findings, the authors suggested that the segmentation–integration continuum was not necessarily simple and straightforward. Although this study is important for being one of the first to examine profiles, it did not directly assess segmentation–integration preferences. Rather, the clusters were identified based on boundary strength (e.g., the flexibility and permeability of the boundary) and behaviors associated with crossing boundaries.

Kossek, Ruderman, Braddy, and Hannum (2012) also investigated types of boundary management profiles in a study conducted in the United States. Their profiles were based on a combination of role centrality, perceived boundary control, and frequency of other domain interruptions. Thus, the profiles they developed were based on an individual difference variable, a behavior, and a perception of the ability to control the boundary. Their results suggested six boundary management profiles, ranging from high segmentation (i.e., Dividers) to high integration (i.e., Fusion Lovers) to other profiles that seem to segment and integrate (i.e., Family Guardians). What is not clear is the extent to which these profiles are stable over time, may be influenced by environmental factors, or whether similar studies conducted in other countries would result in the same profiles.

Ammons (2013) conducted a study of boundary management profiles in an organization before and after a large-scale cultural change aimed in part at work–life balance, changing the focus at work to results-oriented rather than physical presence-oriented.

In one way, her findings were similar to Bulger et al. (2007) and Kossek et al. (2012); there was a wide variety of strategies employed by participants. An important contribution of her study is the finding that despite the organization-wide effort to change work norms, most employees made only small (often no) changes to the way they managed their work and family boundaries. This lack of change in strategy was reported despite employees also reporting shifts in boundary preference toward somewhat more integration. Ammons suggested that perhaps the respondents in her study were satisfied with their boundary strategies and felt no need to change them despite changes in boundary preference. It may also be that more effort could be made to train people on boundary management strategies that best fit their desired segmentation–integration preference.

Ammons (2013) also called for researchers to focus on the fit between individual preferences and the types of segmentation–integration practices allowed by organizations. In this call, she echoes earlier work on the fit between preferences and organizational policies or actions. Rothbard, Phillips, and Dumas (2005) conducted one of the first studies on fit between segmentation–integration preference and organizational actions. They found that misfit in either direction was related to negative outcomes. Namely, when presented with organizational programs that promote integration (e.g., onsite childcare), people who had higher preference for segmentation reported lower satisfaction and organizational commitment. The reverse was also true: people with a preference for integration reacted to segmentation-promoting policies with lower satisfaction and organizational commitment.

Kreiner (2006) also explored the impact of the resources for segmentation–integration provided by the organization. In particular, he examined the fit or congruence between segmentation–integration preference and segmentation–integration supplies offered by the organization, and how congruence or incongruence was related to various outcomes. In general, his study showed that the impact of congruence was positive: when segmentation preferences and supplies matched, people reported less work–home conflict, less stress, and higher levels of job satisfaction. Incongruence in general was related to negative outcomes, with the exception of having an over-supply of segmenting resources. When resources exceed preferences for segmentation, people reported less work–home conflict. A more recent study in Germany by Koch and Binniewies (2015) found that supervisors model segmentation behaviors for their employees. That is, when supervisors engaged in segmentation tactics, their employees tended to do the same, and those employees who did so had positive outcomes related to well-being.

These findings certainly raise the question of the global work–family interface: do segmentation–integration behaviors look similar or different in different cultures? A few studies have attempted to shed some light on this question. Zhang, Li, and Foley (2014) suggest that understanding the context of social expectation and social change in China matters for understanding the work–family interface. First, Chinese employees may be more tolerant of integration and any resulting conflict because they expect long-term gains for their family. The authors introduce the concept of *prioritizing work for family*, meaning that Chinese employees are highly committed to the success of their families and will, therefore, focus on work over family for the longer-term gain this practice will bring to the family. Ryu (2014) suggests that in South Korea, Asian cultural norms influence segmentation of the work and family domains. In particular, the author suggests that Korean people are taught to leave family issues at home when they go to work, which may explain why family stressors were not associated with job satisfaction in this study, while job stressors were associated with life satisfaction. However, boundary strength was not directly measured in this study. Rather, these other measures of spillover and crossover were used as proxies for segmentation versus integration.

In another recent study, Bodolica, Spraggon, and Zaidi (2015) conducted a case study of one family firm in the United Arab Emirates. They found that the organization began with high integration, which may be expected when the family is running the business. However, over time, the firm made use of segmentation practices, including protecting work and/or family sometimes, but not always. The authors suggest that many factors contribute to successful boundary management strategies, including factors related to organizational culture, the cultural context related to the country/region, and individual/family preferences.

Clearly more research is needed to examine global issues related to segmentation–integration. To date, only one study has directly examined segmentation–integration behaviors and preferences using a cross-national sample. Sanséau and Smith (2012) examined the impact of changes in working time laws in France and in the United Kingdom. In France, the working time was reduced to thirty-five hours from forty hours, while in the United Kingdom working time laws changed to mandate a maximum of forty-eight hours per week (where there was no maximum prior). One result in France was a greater flexibility in the organization of work, but also increased work intensification and decreased work porosity: people worked less, worked more intensely during that time, and did not allow for interruptions. In the United Kingdom, however, long work hours persisted and increased for women. There were some less obvious changes in the flexibility of work hours. In terms of employee well-being, satisfaction with integration of work and nonwork decreased in France and increased in the United Kingdom. The authors suggest that there are many factors at play, including individual preferences as well as societal norms and expectations and slowly changing gender roles in both countries.

Outcomes of Segmentation and Integration

Much of the research on segmentation–integration preferences and behaviors has focused on outcomes related to either the preference or the behavior. These outcomes may be directly or indirectly related to segmentation–integration, and may be themselves attitudinal, behavioral, psychological, and even physiological.

Inter-domain transitions. Matthews and colleagues have demonstrated that the strength of the boundary around a domain is related to the frequency with which people tend to leave that domain to attend to another domain, a process they termed *inter-domain transitions* (Matthews & Barnes-Farrell, 2010; Matthews, Barnes-

Farrell, & Bulger, 2010; Matthews, Winkel, & Wayne, 2014). Inter-domain transitions may be seen as an integrating boundary management tactic, particularly because they are related to flexibility of the boundary (Matthews et al., 2010). In addition, inter-domain transitions are related to outcomes such as work–family conflict (Matthews et al., 2010, 2014). In a study of couples, Carlson, Kacmar, Zivnuska, and Ferguson (2014) showed that family-to-work transitions related to increased strain for the individual, and individual strain was related to boundary management for the spouse. This suggests that this integrating tactic has outcomes for the person engaging in transitions and for others in his or her domain. They also showed that more frequent family-to-work transitions were positively related to work–family enhancement, work–family conflict, and to relationship tension.

As noted earlier, Methot and LePine (2016) conducted three studies and found that the two dimensions of segmentation–integration preference function differently. In particular, they found that people reported or allowed fewer intrusions (i.e., inter-domain transitions) into the protected domain. In their second study, they found that segmentation–integration preference impacted the likelihood of taking a job in a firm where the significant other was employed and the likelihood of establishing a romantic relationship with a coworker. Finally, in their third study, preference to segment their work or nonwork was related to satisfaction with the preferred domain (e.g., preference to segment work from home was related to satisfaction with home).

Spouses, partners, and children. Clark (2000) asserted that certain members of the work and family domains are border keepers who influence the boundary and its outcomes. One recent study investigated a particular form of integration and potential border keepers: work-linked couples. Halbesleben, Zellars, Carlson, Perrewé, and Rotondo (2010) defined work-linked couples as those who work in the same organization, in the same occupation, or both. Perhaps not surprisingly, they found that spouses who are work-linked integrate domains more than spouses who are not work-linked. Further, they found that being work-linked moderates the relationship between spouse instrumental support and emotional exhaustion, such that the negative relationship between support and exhaustion was stronger for work-linked couples.

The impact of segmentation–integration on family members has also been studied by Danner-Vlaardingerbroek, Kluwer, van Steenbergen, and van der Lippe (2013) in a study in the Netherlands. These authors found that residual negatives from work, such as mood, exhaustion, and rumination, were linked with lower-quality interactions with children due to decreased psychological availability by the parents. Interestingly, this was shown to be the case for those who preferred integration, but not for those who preferred segmentation. In addition, positive residuals, namely positive mood and vigor, were linked with greater psychological availability and higher-quality interactions with children for those who preferred segmentation, but not for those who preferred integration. This study provides support for Clark's (2000) proposition regarding the importance of role of border keepers; in this case, children as border keepers.

Hahn and Dormann (2013) also found evidence for the role of border keepers. First, they found that employees' and their partners' segmentation preference was related to psychological detachment, or the act of disengaging both cognitively and physically from work, such that psychological detachment was higher when both the employee and his or her spouse had a preference for segmentation. Also, children in the house moderated the relationship between segmentation preference and detachment, such that even those with a low segmentation preference were more likely to detach when children lived in the home.

Mellner, Aronsson, and Kecklund (2014) studied Swedish telecom employees to explore the impact of working flexible hours and in flexible locations on segmentation–integration. Overall, they found that the employees showed a stronger preference for segmentation than integration as well as a perception of having low control over the boundary between work and home. But they also found that men with a preference for segmentation had higher perceived boundary control than anyone else, while women with a preference for segmentation living with a partner and children had the lowest perceived boundary control. Men with a preference for segmentation reported the highest work–life balance. The authors suggest that although most employees say they would prefer segmentation, there is a strong and perhaps increasing norm for integration in many workplaces. Thus, employees in general perceive lower boundary control as they attempt to meet integration demands. They further speculate that segmentation may be a more accepted traditional gender-based norm for men, whereas integration is a gender-based norm for women, and this may explain the gender differences related to preference for segmentation and boundary control.

Mellner et al. (2014) suggest that many psychosocial work factors were related to perceived boundary control, including working outside of normal work time and place, goal clarity, and work support. Interestingly, while those who preferred segmentation worked outside of time and place less than those who preferred integration, these psychosocial factors were related to low boundary control only for those who preferred segmentation. This was also true of goal clarity and work support. This study certainly has implications for the many influences *on* segmentation–integration as well as the influences *of* segmentation–integration. In fact, their findings underscore some of the earliest tenets suggested by Nippert-Eng (1996): 1) boundaries are idiosyncratic and 2) people construct boundaries both proactively and reactively.

The findings reported by Mellner et al. (2014) also provide some avenues for future research on these issues. For instance, to what extent do traditional gender norms for work and family impact segmentation–integration preferences, boundary management, and outcomes related to work and family? In addition, because their study was conducted in an organization where people have a great deal of flexibility in working time and place, it would be interesting to extend the study to other types of jobs and organizations in order to further examine the various influences on segmentation–integration and the outcomes of segmentation–integration.

Psychological detachment. Psychological detachment has become an important area of study in the work–family literature because it has been shown to influence outcomes in both the work and family domains (e.g., Sonnentag, Mojza, Binniewies, & Scholl, 2008). Thus, researchers have looked at the impact of segmentation–integration on psychological detachment. For instance, Michel, Bosch, and Rexroth (2014) trained a sample of German employees in mindfulness. They found that mindfulness was positively related to psychological detachment and satisfaction with work–life balance and negatively related to strain-based work–family conflict. The authors argue that mindfulness can be used as a strategy to maintain segmentation–integration preferences. Further, although not directly a study on psychological detachment, Dettmers, Vahle-Hinz, Bamberg, Friedrich, and Keller (2016) found in a sample of German employees that the requirement to be available after work hours, also known as "extended work availability," was linked with next-morning negative mood and higher cortisol level.

Work and nonwork conflict and enrichment. Certainly the most studied outcomes of segmentation–integration preferences and behaviors are work–family conflict and facilitation. Importantly, many of the most recent studies have looked at both phenomena, resulting in many of the researchers to note that segmentation–integration may be a "double-edged sword." For instance, Paustian-Underdahl, Halbesleben, Carlson, and Kacmar (2016) indicated that integration has both positive and negative impacts for employees. Namely, integration was related to increased family involvement and thus family-to-work enrichment, but also negatively impacted supervisors' perceptions of employee promotability. As noted earlier, Carlson et al. (2014) found that family-to-work transitions had both positive and negative outcomes, which suggests that using family-to-work transitions are a "double-edged sword."

In a study of Chinese bank employees and their spouses, Liao, Yang, Wang, and Kwan (2016) found that segmentation preferences moderated the relationship between leader–member exchange (LMX) and work–family enrichment, such that the relationship was stronger for those who preferred integration over segmentation. However, segmentation preferences also moderated the relationship between work–family enrichment and family performance, such that the relationship was stronger for those who preferred segmentation over integration. The authors actually use the "double-edged sword" (p. 680) language to describe this, in that there is positive family impact but a negative work impact for preferring integration.

Kubicek and Tement (2016) also found both positive and negative effects of segmentation–integration in an Austrian study. In particular, they found that work–home segmentation, measured as an organizational norm, reduced work–home conflict and was a moderator of the relationship between work intensification and the affective component of work–home enrichment, such that a work–home segmentation norm buffered the negative impact of work intensification on affective work–home enrichment. In addition, the effect of work intensification on time-based work–home conflict was stronger for employees who used integration strategies than for those who used segmentation strategies. Further, the effect of work intensification on work–home enrichment was complex. In terms of enrichment as the transfer of competencies, the effect of work intensification was negative for those who used integration strategies. Yet, in terms of enrichment as the transfer of positive mood, the effect was negative for those who used segmentation strategies.

One recent Chinese study also indicated that segmentation–integration preferences are related to various outcomes in complicated ways. Liu and Cheung (2015), in a study of Chinese teachers, showed that work–family role integration partially mediated the relationship between job demands and work–family conflict and the relationship between job resources and work–family enrichment. Here again we see evidence for the dual process, or double-edged sword, in that higher job demands were negatively related to work–family role integration, but higher job resources were positively related to work–family role integration. In addition, work–family role integration was negatively related to work–family conflict and positively related to work–family enrichment. The authors suggest that high job demands result in a perceived incompatibility between work and family, while high job resources stimulate "an integration mindset" (p. 9).

Taken together, the results of these studies on work–family conflict and enrichment underscore the complexity of the work–family interface. In particular, they signify the need to investigate the nature of the possible dual process of experiencing both work–family conflict and enrichment, and how this may be influenced by segmentation–integration preferences and behaviors. It is also clear, based on the notion that there may be cultural influences on segmentation–integration preferences and behaviors, that these studies should take a cross-national and/or global approach. To date, although studies have looked at work–family issues around the globe, none have specifically looked at similarities and differences that may be grounded in or influenced by culture nor have they specified what aspect of culture or which cultural dimensions may be important for understanding segmentation–integration.

Technology, Globalization, and Segmentation–Integration

Changing technologies and telework. Increasingly available smart, mobile technology is having a significant impact on both the work and nonwork domains (Hoffman & Bulger, 2009; Purcell & Rainie, 2014). There is an assumption, perhaps warranted, that technology is significantly blurring the boundaries between and around work and nonwork. Hoffman and Bulger argue that although technology certainly affords highly flexible, integrated boundaries, it does not dictate those boundaries. Rather, boundaries may still be actively constructed by individuals. Research indicates that this is the case. For instance, Park, Fritz, and Jex (2011) demonstrated that higher segmentation preferences and perceived segmentation norms were related to higher psychological detachment. They further showed that this relationship is partially mediated by technology use at home. Those who had higher segmentation preferences and perceived segmentation norms used less technology at home and were more likely to detach.

Sayah (2013) studied German independent contractors in the information technology and media sectors. She found information and communication technologies do allow for work and family to impact one another, but that the impact is not automatic. Rather, her respondents reported on various ways in which they manage the use of their information and communication technologies as they engage in boundary work tactics. She found that information and communication technology use can be deliberately designed to establish full segmentation or integration, as well as segmenting one domain and integrating the other. Organizational expectations and norms also influenced whether technology use had a positive or negative (or both) impact on work–family outcomes. In a study in Romania, Köffer, Junglas, Chiperi, and Niehaves (2014) found that people who reported organizational cultures that encouraged use of mobile technologies to do work also reported higher work-to-life conflict, and this relationship was stronger for those who prefer segmentation. Barber and Santuzzi (2015) recently coined the term *telepressure* to refer to when individuals feel a need to respond to communications coming in over information and communication technologies. They found that telepressure was influenced by organizational norms for segmentation versus integration. In addition, telepressure was linked with stress outcomes in their study.

Employers are increasingly offering flexible working arrangements to employees, including telework. Some organizations may also implement telework organization-wide, resulting in employees working in telework arrangements involuntarily. LaPierre, van Steenbergen, Peeters, and Kluwer (2016) found that employees working involuntarily in a telework situation had higher strain-based work–family conflict than those teleworking voluntarily. Contrary to the authors' expectations, using segmentation tactics as a boundary management strategy did not moderate this relationship, but self-efficacy in balancing work and family did attenuate the negative impact of involuntary telework on work–family conflict.

Global organizations and expatriates. There is very little research on how globalization of work impacts segmentation–integration, yet there is a great deal of speculation that global work will require more integration for employees as work crosses both time zones and cultural norms. Richardson, McKenna, Dickie, and Kelliher (2015) studied expatriate mining professionals representing fourteen different nationalities. They found that work and nonwork are "inextricably intertwined" for expatriates, mainly because expatriates rely heavily on coworkers and supervisors for support. See Chapter 26 (Dimitrova) in this handbook for further exploration of the work–family interface for expatriates.

Concluding Thoughts

Dumas and Sanchez-Burks (2015) review various theoretical perspectives on work and family. They suggest that there are dual pressures on employees to both integrate and segment work and family stemming from a need to navigate the demands from both domains, while maintaining a particular work identity as an ideal worker. Specifically, they conclude that the norm of the "ideal worker" as someone who is work-focused and always ready to contribute to the organization holds a place of primacy. The ideal worker would, thus, segment family out of work, but also integrate work into family. This is echoed by Williams, Berdahl, and Vandello (2016) in their review of literature on segmentation–integration and flexible work practices. They suggest that the notion of the ideal worker holds a great deal of sway in organizations and in the minds of individuals, possibly resulting in resistance to efforts to offer resources that would better enable people to manage their work–family boundaries. Williams et al. further suggest that there are also potential culturally and socially bound notions of the importance of being work-focused as a sign of masculinity for men as well as the clash of ideals for women workers who need to be both always available for work (e.g., ideal worker) and always available for family (e.g., ideal mother). Both sets of authors suggest that these norms are old-fashioned and that researchers and employers should rethink and revamp what is needed for work and workers.

Still it seems likely that the norms identified by Williams et al. (2016) and Dumas and Sanchez-Burks (2015) may inform what the research findings described here suggest. Research has borne out the proposition first made by Nippert-Eng (1996) that boundaries are idiosyncratic and actively constructed. Segmentation–integration preferences are at least partially an individual difference variable, but may also be related to the demands from the work and family domains as well as cultural norms. Boundary work behaviors, enacted to establish segmentation or integration, can be useful in meeting domain demands. However, a mismatch between the segmentation–integration preferences or behaviors on the part of an individual and the resources for segmentation–integration offered by the organization can lead to negative outcomes. In addition, there are both positive and negative outcomes associated with segmentation–integration preferences and behaviors. Technology may be integration-affording, but it can also be used to segment domains. Further, family members, coworkers, supervisors and other "border keepers" do impact work and nonwork boundaries and the effects of managing boundaries.

There remain many unanswered questions about segmentation–integration, particularly as related to the global work–family interface. Some of the literature described here asserts that there are cultural differences in norms for segmenting versus integrating work and family, yet there is little empirical evidence for such differences. As such, researchers should undertake carefully designed studies aimed at further understanding the similarities and differences in segmentation–integration norms at the cultural level and how these norms inform both individual and organizational norms and expectations for segmentation–integration. There seems to be at least a possibility that cultural norms have an impact on the practice of segmentation–integration and the outcomes of segmenting versus integrating work and family. For example, there may be differences in segmentation–integration norms based on whether the culture is more individualistic or collectivistic, resulting in systematic cultural differences in segmentation–integration preferences.

Alternately, it may be that cultural norms are related to the types of segmentation–integration behaviors employed to manage work and nonwork demands. Future studies could identify types of segmentation–integration behaviors that are more common in various cultures, and could explore whether cultural norms and values influence psychological, familial, and/or organizational outcomes of those behaviors. In countries where there are strong laws related to work time, family-friendly practices, and the like, what are the expectations for segmentation versus integration? On the other hand, in developing nations, how are segmentation–integration norms developing? Most of the studies cited here were conducted in the United States, Australia, Europe, and developed countries in Asia. Future research should investigate how work and nonwork issues are handled in developing economies in Asia, Africa, and South America.

Pertinent to all of these questions is the ever-changing role of technology. Smart, mobile technology has been available since IBM introduced a device called "Simon" in 1992 that was able to make calls and had features similar to a personal data assistant, such as the ability to send faxes (Reed, 2010). The ensuing years saw the introduction of other devices that were mobile and smart, such as the Palm Pilot in 1996 and the Blackberry in 2006. But the explosion in ownership of smart, mobile devices is generally traced to 2007 when both the iPhone and the Android operating systems were introduced (McCarty, 2011; Reed 2010). In the decade since then, we have seen a tremendous impact of that technology on both the work and family domain. The applications and capabilities associated with smartphones are improving rapidly, suggesting that there may be continued impact of these technologies on segmentation–integration. Ollier-Malaterre et al. (2013) suggest that boundary management now also includes social media, in that individuals and organizations must actively determine what kinds of information is shared on social media.

In addition, cultural norms may impact how smart, mobile technology influences segmentation preferences and practices, particularly as use of the internet and smart technology permeates developing economies. To date, there is little research on this question, but a recent survey by the Pew Research Center (Poushter & Stewart, 2016) indicated that smartphone ownership is rising fairly dramatically in developing nations, from a reported 21% (in twenty-one developing nations) in 2013 to 37% in 2015. Further, even in those nations, the majority of respondents reported owning some form of mobile technology even if it was not a smartphone. This study also points to some possible cultural impacts of technology on segmentation–integration of work and nonwork. One example is the gender gap in both internet use and smartphone ownership; in twenty of the nations studied, men were far more likely than women to be internet users and smartphone owners, particularly in some African nations. Whether and how this relates to cultural norms and practices related to work and nonwork issues should be examined in future research.

Given all of these remaining questions, we echo Allen, Cho, and Meier (2014) and call for continued research on segmentation–integration. Specifically, we believe that cross-cultural research on segmentation–integration preferences practices is sorely needed. Furthermore, we encourage additional theoretical and conceptual work that goes beyond simple comparisons to develop theory and an empirical research base regarding *why* culture and which aspects of culture may affect workers' boundaries, role transitions, and preferences.

References

Allen, T.D., Cho, E., & Meier, L.L. (2014). Work–family boundary dynamics. *Annual Review of Organizational Psychology and Organizational Behavior, 1*, 99–121.

Ammons, S.K. (2013). Work–family boundary strategies: Stability and alignment between preferred and enacted boundaries. *Journal of Vocational Behavior, 82*, 49–58.

Ashforth, B.E., Kreiner, G.E., & Fugate, M. (2000). All in a day's work: Boundaries and micro role transitions. *Academy of Management Review, 25*, 472–491.

Ba', S. (2011). Symbolic boundaries: Integration and separation of work and family life. *Community, Work & Family, 14*, 317–334.

Barber, L.K., & Santuzzi, A.M. (2015). Please respond ASAP: Workplace telepressure and employee recovery. *Journal of Occupational Health Psychology, 20*, 172–189.

Bodolica, V., Spraggon, M., & Zaidi, S. (2015). Boundary management strategies for governing family firms: A UAE-based case study. *Journal of Business Ethics, 68*, 684–693.

Bulger, C.A., Matthews, R.A., & Hoffman, M.E. (2007). Work and personal life boundary management: Boundary strength, work/personal life balance and the Segmentation–integration continuum. *Journal of Occupational Health Psychology, 12*, 365–375.

Carlson, D.S., Kacmar, K.M., Zivnuska, S., & Ferguson, M. (2014). Do the benefits of family-to-work transitions come at too great a cost? *Journal of Occupational Health Psychology, 20*, 161–171, http://dx.doi.org/10.1037/a0038279

Casper, W.J., Weltman, D., & Kwesiga, E. (2007). Beyond family-friendly: The construct and measurement of a singles-friendly work culture. *Journal of Vocational Behavior, 70*, 478–501.

Clark, S.C., (2000). Work/family border theory: A new theory of work/family balance. *Human Relations, 53*, 747–770.

Danner-Vlaardingerbroek, G., Kluwer, E.S., van Steenbergen, E.F., & van der Lippe, T. (2013). The psychological availability of dual-earner parents for their children after work. *Family Relations, 62*, 741–754.

Dettmers, J., Vahle-Hinz, T., Bamberg, E., Friedrich, N., & Keller, M. (2016). Extended work availability and its relation with start-of-day mood and cortisol. *Journal of Occupational Health Psychology, 21*, 105–118.

Dumas, T.L., & Sanchez-Burks, J. (2015). The professional, the personal, and the ideal worker: pressures and objectives shaping the boundary between life domains. *The Academy of Management Annals, 9*, 803–843.

Fisher, G.G., Bulger, C.A., & Smith, C.S. (2009). Beyond work and family: A measure of work/nonwork interference and enhancement. *Journal of Occupational Health Psychology, 14*, 441–456.

Haeger, D.L., & Lingham, T. (2014). A trend toward work–life fusion: A multi-generational shift in technology use at work. *Technological Forecasting and Social Change, 89*, 316–325.

Hahn, V.C., & Dormann, C. (2013). The role of partners and children for employees' psychological detachment from work and well-being. *Journal of Applied Psychology, 98*, 26–36.

Halbesleben, J.R., Zellars, K.L., Carlson, D.S., Perrewé, P.L., & Rotondo, D. (2010). The moderating effect of work-linked couple relationships and work–family integration on the spouse instrumental support-emotional exhaustion relationship. *Journal of Occupational Health Psychology, 15*, 371–387.

Hoffman, M.E., & Bulger, C.A. (2009). Whither boundaries? The internet and the blurring of work and personal life. In S. Kleinman (Ed.), *The Culture of Efficiency: Technology in Everyday Life* (pp. 322–328). New York, NY: Peter Lang.

Koch, A.R., & Binniewies, C. (2015). Setting a good example: Supervisors as work–life friendly role models within the context of boundary management. *Journal of Occupational Health Psychology, 20*, 82–92.

Köffer, S., Junglas, I., Chiperi, C., & Niehaves, B. (2014). Dual use of mobile IT and work-to-life conflict in the context of IT consumerization. *Proceedings of the Thirty Fifth International Conference on Information Systems* (pp. 1–19), Auckland, New Zealand: The University of Auckland Business School.

Kossek, E.E., Ruderman, M.N., Braddy, P.W., & Hannum, K.M. (2012). Work–nonwork boundary management profiles: A person-centered approach. *Journal of Vocational Behavior, 81*, 112–128.

Kreiner, G.E. (2006). Consequences of work–home segmentation or integration: A person–environment fit perspective. *Journal of Organizational Behaviour, 27*, 485–507.

Kreiner, G.E., Hollensbe, E.C., & Sheep, M.L. (2009). Balancing borders and bridges: Negotiating the work–home interface via boundary work tactics. *Academy of Management Journal, 52*, 704–730.

Kubicek, B., & Tement, S. (2016). Work intensification and the work–home interface: The moderating effect of individual work–home segmentation strategies and organizational segmentation supplies. *Journal of Personnel Psychology, 15*, 76–89.

LaPierre, L.M., van Steenbergen, E.F., Peeters, M.W., & Kluwer, E.S. (2016). Juggling work and family responsibilities when involuntarily working more from home: A multiwave study of financial sales professionals. *Journal of Organizational Behavior, 37*, 804–822.

Liang, Y., Yang, Z., Wang, M., & Kwan, H.K. (2016). Work–family effects of LMX: The moderating role of segmentation preferences. *The Leadership Quarterly, 27*, 671–683.

Liu, H., & Cheung, F.M. (2015). The role of work–family role integration in a job demands-resources model among Chinese secondary schools teachers. *Asian Journal of Social Psychology, 18*, 288–298.

Marks, S.R., & MacDermid, S.M. (1996). Multiple roles and the self: A theory of role balance. *Journal of Marriage and the Family, 58*, 417–432.

Matthews, R.A., & Barnes-Farrell, J.L. (2010). Development and initial evaluation of an enhanced measure of boundary flexibility for the work and family domains. *Journal of Occupational Health Psychology, 15*, 330–346.

Matthews, R.A., Barnes-Farrell, J.L., & Bulger, C.A. (2010). Advancing measurement of work and family domain boundary characteristics. *Journal of Vocational Behavior, 77*, 447–460.

Matthews, R.A., Winkel, D.E., & Wayne, J.H. (2014). A longitudinal examination of role overload and work–family conflict: The mediating role of interdomain transitions. *Journal of Organizational Behavior, 35*, 72–91.

McCarty, B. (2011, December 6). The History of Smartphones. *TheNextWeb*. Retrieved November 6, 2017 from https://thenextweb.com/mobile/2011/12/06/the-history-of-the-smartphone/ and work–life balance among full-time employed professionals in knowledge-intensive, flexible work. *Nordic Journal of Working Life Studies, 4*, 7–23.

Methot, J.R., & LePine, J.A. (2016). Too close for comfort? Investigating the nature and functioning of wok and nonwork role segmentation preferences. *Journal of Business Psychology*, *31*, 103–123.

Michel, A., Bosch, C., & Rexroth, M. (2014). Mindfulness as a cognitive-emotional segmentation strategy: An intervention promoting work–life balance. *Journal of Occupational and Organizational Psychology*, *87*, 733–754.

Michel, J.S., & Clark, M.A. (2013). Investigating the relative importance of individual differences on the work–family interface and the moderating role of boundary preference for segmentation. *Stress & Health*, *29*, 324–336.

Moen, P. (2011). From 'work–family' to the 'gendered life course' and 'fit': Five challenges to the field. *Community, Work, & Family*, *14*, 81–96.

Moen, P., Kelly, E., & Huang, Q. (2008). Work, family, and life-course fit: Does control over work time matter? *Journal of Vocational Behavior*, *73*, 414–425.

Nippert-Eng, C. E. (1996). *Home and Work*. Chicago, IL: The University of Chicago Press.

Ollier-Malaterre, A., Rothbard, N.P., & Berg, J.M. (2013). When worlds collide in cyberspace: How boundary work in online social networks impacts professional relationships. *Academy of Management Review*, *38*, 645–669.

Olson-Buchanan, J.B., & Boswell, W.R. (2006). Blurring boundaries: Correlates of integration and segmentation between work and nonwork. *Journal of Vocational Behavior*, *68*, 432–445.

Park, Y., Fritz, C., & Jex, S.M. (2011). Relationships between work–home segmentation and psychological detachment from work: The role of communication technology use at home. *Journal of Occupational Health Psychology*, *16*, 457–467.

Paustian-Underdahl, S.C., Halbesleben, J.R.B., Carlson, D.S., & Kacmar, K.M. (2016). The work–family interface and promotability: Boundary integration as a double-edged sword. *Journal of Management*, *42*, 960–981.

Pedersen, V.B., & Lewis, S. (2012). Flexible friends? Flexible working time arrangements, blurred work boundaries, and friendship. *Work, Employment, and Society*, *26*, 464–480.

Poushter, J., & Stewart, R. (2016, February). Smartphone ownership and internet usage continues to climb in emerging economies. Pew Research Center. Available at www.pewglobal.org/2016/02/22/smartphone-ownership-and-internet-usage-continues-to-climb-in-emerging-economies

Purcell, K., & Rainie, L. (2014, December). Technology's impact on workers. Pew Research Center. Available at www.pewInternet.org/2014/12/30/technologys-impact-on-workers

Reed, B. (2010, June 18). A Brief History of Smartphones. *PCWorld*. Retrieved November 6, 2017, from www.pcworld.com/article/199243/a_brief_history_of_smartphones.html#slide1.

Richardson, J., McKenna, S., Dickie, C., & Kelliher, C. (2015). Integrating the work–life interface during expatriation: A case study of expatriate mining professionals. In L. Mäkelä & V. Suutari (Eds.), *Work and Family Interface in the International Career Context.* (pp. 11–28). Cham, Switzerland: Springer International Publishing.

Rothbard, N.P., Phillips, K.W., & Dumas, T.L. (2005). Managing multiple roles: Work–family policies and individuals' desires for segmentation. *Organization Science*, *16*, 243–258.

Ryu, G. (2014). The cross-domain effects of work and family role stressors on public employees in South Korea. *Review of Public Personnel Administration*, *35*, 238–260.

Sanséau, P., & Smith, M. (2012). Regulatory change and work–life integration in France and the UK. *Personnel Review, 41*, 470–486.

Santos, G.G. (2015). Narratives about work and family life among Portuguese academics. *Gender, Work, and Organization, 22*, 1–15.

Sayah, S. (2013). Managing work–life boundaries with information and communication technologies: the case of independent contractors. *New Technology, Work and Employment, 28*, 179–196.

Schieman, S., & Young, M. (2015). Who engages in work–family multitasking? A study of Canadian and American workers. *Social Indicators Research, 120*, 741–767.

Sieber, S.D. (1974). Toward a theory of role accumulation. *American Sociological Review, 39*, 567–578.

Skinner, N., Elton, J., Auer, J., & Pocock, B. (2014). Understanding and managing work–life interaction across the life course: A qualitative study. *Asia Pacific Journal of Human Resources, 52*, 93–109.

Sonnentag, S., Mojza, E.J., Binniewies, C., & Scholl, A. (2008). Being engaged at work and detached at home: A week-level study on work engagement, psychological detachment and affect. *Work & Stress, 22*, 257–276.

Von Borell de Araujo, B.F., Tureta, C.A, & von Borell de Araujo, D. (2015). How do working mothers negotiate the work–home interface? *Journal of Managerial Psychology, 30*, 565–581.

Williams, J.C., Berdahl, J.L., & Vandello, J.A. (2016). Beyond work–life "integration." *Annual Review of Psychology, 67*, 515–539.

Zhang, M., Li, H., & Foley, S. (2014). Prioritizing work for family: A Chinese indigenous perspective. *Journal of Chinese Human Resource Management, 5*, 14–31.

39 The Meanings of Work–Life Balance: A Cultural Perspective

Suzan Lewis and T. Alexandra Beauregard

The popularity of the term "work–life balance" (WLB) belies its lack of an established definition in the research literature. WLB is both a social construct (i.e., a notion that is "constructed" through social practice and which may or may not represent objective reality) and a discourse. It tends to be either (a) defined as an individual experience or aspiration, with particular focus on time-squeezed white-collar workers, or (b) used as an adjective to describe workplace policies or practices (e.g., flexible work arrangements) or public policies (e.g., parental leave) that purport to enhance these individual experiences (i.e., WLB policies, practices, or supports).

Both these uses of the WLB term tend to underemphasize diverse understandings of the components of work, life, and balance. They also position WLB as a matter of individual choice and responsibility with regard to establishing priorities and organizing schedules. This neglects structural, cultural, and practical constraints on individuals' agency (Caproni, 2004; Lewis, Gambles, & Rapoport, 2007), which impact individuals' sense of entitlement and capability to achieve some form of "balance" in practice (Hobson, 2014). In this chapter, entitlement is defined not in the negative way in which it is used in the managerialist academic literature to refer to unreasonable expectations (see Chatrakul Na Ayudhya & Smithson, 2016), but rather as a set of beliefs and feelings about what supportive practices it is fair and reasonable to expect from employers (and governments) (Chatrakul Na Ayudhya & Smithson, 2016; Herman & Lewis, 2012; Lewis & Smithson, 2001). These expectations, which are influenced by perceptions of what is normative, feasible, and socially acceptable, are highly context dependent and may influence understandings of "balance" in relation to work and the rest of life.

Although WLB is increasingly used in research in diverse contexts, given that WLB is a social construct that originated in the industrialized West, the relevance of the WLB discourse within broader social and cultural contexts has been questioned (Lewis et al., 2007; Rajan-Rankin, 2016). It is not clear whether and how the interpretation of WLB and use of WLB practices vary across time and place, within and across countries, nor how this can be assessed in culture-sensitive ways. Thus, the purpose of this chapter is to reflect on the often-contested meanings and understandings of WLB in a range of contexts, drawing on and integrating two streams of literature: work–family interface research and critical management and organizational studies. First, we provide an overview of the term "work–life balance" and its contested definitions in the two literatures. We then theorize understandings of WLB as shaped by intersecting layers of context: global, national (noting diversity within as well as across national contexts), organizational, and temporal. Finally, we address gaps and limitations in extant research, and speak to questions about the future of work–life balance in an increasingly connected and globalized world.

What Is Work–Life Balance?

There is no single understanding or use of the term WLB. Rather, multiple and overlapping WLB discourses within organizations and among academic researchers are dynamic and shift across time and place (Lewis et al., 2007; Lewis, Anderson, Lyonette, Payne, & Wood, 2017a; Lewis, Anderson, Lyonette, Payne, & Wood, 2017b). Work–family interface scholars tend to define WLB at an individual level. Some explicitly focus on work–*family* balance. For example, Grzywacz and Carlson (2007) discuss the "accomplishment of role-related expectations that are negotiated and shared between an individual and his/her role-related partners in the work and family domains" (p. 458). Other scholars define the "life" domain more broadly (Lewis et al., 2017a; Lewis et al., 2017b). For instance, Haar, Russo, Suñe, and Ollier-Malaterre (2014) characterize WLB as an individual's assessment of how well multiple life roles are balanced. Nevertheless, the majority of the work–life literature treats, at least implicitly, the "life" domain as being interchangeable with that of "family," particularly as represented by caregiving responsibilities for dependent children (Özbilgin, Beauregard, Tatli, & Bell, 2011).

The concept of balance is itself problematic. The term was initially understood by researchers as signifying low levels of conflict between work and nonwork demands (see Wayne, Butts, Casper, & Allen, 2016, for a review). However, the word "balance" implies a goal of equal participation in work and nonwork activities and overlooks the diverse ways in which individuals manage occupancy of multiple roles, not all of which involve balance (Clark, 2000; Gambles et al., 2006; Hobson, 2014). For instance, Rajan-Rankin (2016) argues that the messy reality of family and community life and the blurring of boundaries she found in her research on Indian call centers cannot be accounted for by Western discourses of WLB idealized as tidy, segmented lives. A growing critical literature argues that these definitions imply a false dichotomy, as work (paid and unpaid) is part of life rather than a separate element to be balanced with life (Bloom, 2016; Fleetwood, 2007; Gambles et al., 2006; Lewis et al., 2007).

Given the difficulties in determining the meaning of WLB as an individual experience, the use of the term to describe workplace policies or practices is also highly problematic. Specifically, it is often unclear what such policies are designed to achieve. These WLB policies and practices are also often labelled as "family-friendly." However, this labelling within the WLB discourse has been criticized for implying gender neutrality when considerable research has established that women remain disproportionately responsible for caregiving in addition to the demands of paid work (Lewis et al., 2007; Smithson & Stokoe, 2005). Women are more likely than men to use WLB practices and to have a low sense of entitlement to advance in their careers if they do so (Herman & Lewis, 2012).

Critics also argue that labeling workplace policies as WLB policies implies an employee-led focus , or favors granted to employees, which can mask the employer benefits of such policies and practices (Fleetwood, 2007; Gatrell & Cooper, 2008; Lewis et al., 2007; Lewis et al., 2016a; Özbilgin et al., 2011; Smithson & Stokoe, 2005). The emphasis on individual choices and outcomes in understandings of WLB has also been criticized for camouflaging the general shift in responsibility for well-being from state to individual effected by neoliberalism, a form of capitalism in which state-provided services (e.g., state-funded childcare centers) are replaced with market-based alternatives (e.g., organizational voucher schemes through which parents are offered some financial support for their choice of privately operated daycare) (Fleetwood, 2007). While purporting to empower individual workers, neoliberalism is acknowledged by scholars as increasing the power of business and corporations to determine public policies and setting regulatory frameworks that are advantageous to themselves rather than to workers (Fleetwood, 2007; Harvey, 2005).

According to Fleetwood (2007), Western WLB discourses have increased in recent years because they help to legitimize employer-driven flexible working practices that are presented as offering employees greater choice and freedom, but which often manifest themselves in employee-unfriendly ways. For example, research has found that access to available practices can be inconsistent within organizations and fuel employee perceptions of unfairness (Beauregard, 2014). Additionally, managers and professionals using flexible working practices often experience work intensification in the form of longer hours and greater work effort, professional isolation and fewer networking opportunities, a reputation among peers and superiors for being less committed to the organization, increased work–family conflict, and reduced prospects for career advancement (Allen, Johnson, Kiburz, & Shockley, 2013; Beauregard, 2011; Leslie, Manchester, Park, & Mehng, 2012; Kelliher & Anderson, 2010). As such, so-called WLB policies can actually obstruct the achievement of individual experiences of work–life "balance" rather than facilitate it.

The reason why many WLB policies may fail to lead to actual experiences of WLB on the part of workers may be because these policies are rarely accompanied by changes to workplace structures, cultures, and practices, which continue to be based on outdated assumptions about ideal workers and the way that work should be carried out (Lewis et al., 2007). Specifically, employers continue to view those individuals who value work above all else and have fewer nonwork obligations as the ideal workers (Dumas & Sanchez-Burks, 2015). Thus, the attainment of WLB has been depicted by critical management scholars as "an eternally unfinished journey of self-discovery" (Bloom, 2016, p. 596), in which individuals' modern-day identity is structured by the simultaneous desire and inability to achieve equilibrium between work and nonwork roles.

Comparative Research on Work–Life Balance

These definitional problems may be one factor explaining why WLB is one of the least frequently studied concepts in the work–family interface literature (Greenhaus & Allen, 2011), and why there are fewer cross-cultural studies on work–life balance compared to those on conflict and enrichment (Ollier-Malaterre, 2016 Ollier-Malaterre & Foucreault, 2017). There is some evidence suggesting that WLB is valued by employees across many national contexts (Hill, Yang, Hawkins, & Ferris, 2004; Kossek, Valcour, & Lirio, 2014). However, the value of WLB may be moderated by national culture – highlighting the need to include cultural dimensions in research using cross-national designs (Haar et al., 2014).

Some limited comparative research has examined differences in the provision of so-called policies and practices to support WLB (Chandra, 2012). However, WLB is a Western construct and although it is increasingly emerging in a wider range of national contexts in employee and employer discourses as well as in organizational research (e.g., Abubaker & Bagley, 2016; Atsumi, 2007; Chandra, 2012), the majority of the WLB research literature remains focused on Western contexts and largely neglects the contested and culture-sensitive nature of the WLB concept. There are issues relating to both interpretation of WLB in diverse contexts and also how to take account of intersections between layers of contexts that shape these interpretations. Surveys assessing individual experiences of WLB include items such as, "I manage to balance the demands of my work and personal life/family well" (Haar et al., 2014). Interpretations of balance and judgments about doing this "well" are highly subjective, and we cannot rule out the possibility that these are related to contextual social expectations, norms, and comparisons that impact personal expectations and sense of entitlement to invest differently in work and family or personal life.

It is important for research to reflect on and take into account the possibilities of diverse interpretations of WLB and the layers of context in which they are rooted. Both quantitative and qualitative research have a role in providing more nuanced accounts of meanings and experiences of WLB. In relation to mostly quantitative research, Ollier-Malaterre and Foucreault (2017) argue that the inclusion of "more structural and cultural factors (is) a step towards capturing the polycontextuality (Von Glinow, Shapiro, & Brett, 2004) of country-level contexts – that is, the interactions of multiple layers of context" (p. 4). Qualitative researchers argue for more in-depth qualitative case studies to draw out intersections of multiple layers of context in comparative cross-national research (Nilsen, Brannen, & Lewis, 2013). Case studies are particularly useful for understanding processes whereby conceptual understandings of constructs such as WLB shift across time as well as place (Lewis et al., 2017a; Tatli, Vassilopoulou, Al Ariss, & Özbilgin, 2012). Below, we discuss some of the intersecting layers of context that can shape diverse understandings of the construct of WLB.

Contexts Shaping the Meanings of Work–Life Balance

Global Context

At the broadest layer of context, it has been argued that understandings of WLB are influenced by the spread of neoliberal values that prioritize profit over personal lives (Fleetwood, 2007; Gambles et al., 2006). These understandings are also influenced by directives, such as those set by the International Labour Organization (ILO) and European Union (EU), which increasingly use the WLB terminology to replace family-friendly discourses, and by the responses of for-profit organizations, especially multinational companies. This may contribute to or be a consequence of international recognition of the term WLB, but it assumes common understandings of its meanings.

Global processes intersect with national contexts, influencing the ways in which WLB is interpreted and used at different times (Lewis et al., 2017a). Taking India as an example, a qualitative study by Gambles et al. (2006) noted that the opening of the economy in India in 1991 brought more exposure to global competitiveness and opportunities for economic growth, coupled with increasingly demanding workloads and long working hours for "new economy" workers (Lewis et al., 2007, p. 363). The term WLB entered the Indian vocabulary when used by global corporations in their multinational staff surveys (Lewis et al., 2007). It resonated with their workers, but was not used by the majority of the Indian population whose work and family struggles were of a different nature; some just strove to earn a livelihood and others were concerned with the societal costs of the developing economy and the impact of Westernized work practices on cultural values (e.g., time spent with one's extended family and caring for one's parents in their old age).

More recent research from India highlights the complexity of the WLB discourse in global call centers, where global processes intersect with Indian culture. For example, male IT workers offered the opportunity to work from home abandoned this practice within two weeks, citing the mockery of neighbors and the shame of their wives in having a husband who did not spend his days in an office and was, therefore, assumed to be unemployed (Rajan-Rankin, 2016). In contrast, the WLB discourse became familiar much earlier in the United Kingdom. It was introduced in policy discourses in the 1990s and was widely discussed in the media, although this did not guarantee consensus or stability of interpretation (Gambles et al., 2006; Lewis et al., 2017a).

National context

Following calls over many years for more attention to context in the work and family literature (e.g., Lewis, Izraeli, & Hootsman, 1992), increasing attention has been paid to the national layer of context in work–family and work–life research, although exploration of layers of contextual influences and their intersections remains relatively limited (Lewis, Brannen, & Nilsen, 2009; Nilsen et al., 2013). National contexts are usually compared in terms of structural differences (e.g., public policy support and laws) or cultural factors (e.g., values and norms). The latter are usually examined in terms of dimensions such as individualism–collectivism or gender egalitarianism, based on those identified by Hofstede (1980), Trompenaars and Hampden-Turner (1998), and Project GLOBE (House, Javidan, & Dorfman, 2001). More rarely, both structural and cultural variables are examined (Ollier-Materre & Foucreault, 2017), which is important as these tend to be related. For example, countries higher in gender egalitarianism are more likely to introduce policies to support working families than those lower in gender egalitarianism (Brandth & Kvande, 2015; Haas & Hwang, 2008).

Cultural differences between and within national contexts can impact interpretations of WLB. For example, individuals in many Asian societies are defined by their relationship to family members, and extended families are strong institutions maintained by obligations such as regular visits, financial support, and caregiving (Joplin, Francesco, Shaffer, & Lau, 2003; Tingvold, Middelthon, Allen, & Hauff, 2012; Zhan & Montgomery, 2003). In collectivistic cultures such as these, work tends to be viewed as a way of supporting and advancing the family; conflict between these two domains is perceived as an unavoidable byproduct of promoting the family's financial stability, and is thus experienced by individuals as being less harmful (Lu et al., 2010; Spector et al., 2007). Hence the notion of WLB may be less meaningful, except perhaps for workers employed by multinational corporations (Hill et al., 2004) or in countries such as Japan, where the term is used in government policies aimed at increasing the low birthrate (Atsumi, 2007; Gambles et al., 2006; Lewis et al., 2007).

In contrast, studies of managers and professionals in the United States indicate that extended kin ties are relatively weak, and parents' jobs and children's activities are prioritized over contact with extended family members (Gerstel, 2011; Lareau, 2011). In the individualistic cultures present in many Western nations, work is more often viewed as an achievement by and for the individual that is irreconcilable with family responsibilities (Spector et al., 2007). Thus, although research has shown that individuals across the world express a desire for WLB (Hill et al., 2004) and WLB has significant implications for individuals' well-being and work productivity (Lyness & Judiesch, 2014), the experience of WLB differs among cultural contexts according to the way in which work and family are positioned relative to one another. As an example, a cross-cultural study by Haar et al. (2014) found that higher levels of WLB were more strongly and positively associated with job and life satisfaction for individuals in individualistic cultures, where engagement in work is more often viewed as being primarily for personal achievement and advancement, compared to those in collectivistic cultures, where the purpose of working is more frequently conceptualized as being for the promotion of the family.

Most of the extant cross-cultural research on the work–life interface can be more accurately termed cross-national; little of it takes into account the diversity of cultures, both geographic and ethnic, that exists within many countries. The experience or meaning of WLB may be different for ethnic minorities whose cultural values related to family are at odds with the mainstream cultural norms surrounding work. This mismatch may produce increased difficulties in combining work and family roles, and thereby in achieving "balance." For example, ethnic Pakistani and Bangladeshi women in the United Kingdom are expected to undertake considerable household duties and caregiving responsibilities for both immediate and extended family members, while simultaneously fulfilling work demands and career ambitions (Dale, 2005; Kamenou, 2008; Khoker & Beauregard, 2014). This tension between collectivistic family values and individualistic work expectations creates a sense of WLB as being unattainable, compared to individuals whose caregiving commitments do not extend beyond the nuclear family unit. Similarly, a comparative qualitative study of work and family in five European states found fundamental social class differences in experiences of and sense of entitlement to policies and practices that support WLB (Nilsen et al., 2013).

Organizational Context

Workplaces constitute another important context that intersects with other layers of context, contributing to within- and between-country differences in interpretations of WLB. Most research on WLB focuses on middle-class, relatively privileged, knowledge workers, who are mostly employed in large organizations and struggle to make time for nonwork activities in the face of demanding workloads. Research suggests that knowledge workers in the global economy or in the same multinational company understand and experience WLB in similar ways cross-nationally (Hill et al., 2004). This raises the possibility that the concept of WLB as a personal experience may be more similar cross-nationally for workers with similar backgrounds or life circumstances than it is across diverse workers within countries.

More research is needed to explore the ways in which WLB is interpreted by diverse groups in a wider range of workplace contexts, including self-employed (Annink, den Dulk, & Steijn, 2015), working-class, and blue-collar workers (Warren, 2017). We especially encourage research on those in precarious low-paid work (e.g., workers on the zero-hours contracts common in the accommodation and food service sectors, retail, and residential care). The assumption underpinning research on workers in high-status jobs is that experiences of WLB relate primarily to having too much work or work that spills over into personal time, creating the need to balance this with other activities. However, in many circumstances it is not just the time squeeze that is the problem, but genuine financial hardship because of too little work and/or inadequate pay (Warren, 2017). WLB may take on a very different meaning in such circumstances.

At the organizational layer, discourses of WLB can vary within and between organizations. Managers and workers may understand WLB differently. For instance, Mescher, Benschop, and Doorewaard's (2010) analyses of company websites showed that there is often a mismatch between explicit employer statements of support for WLB and more implicit messages framing WLB arrangements as a privilege.

Understandings of WLB as an adjective to describe policies or practices also vary across intersecting national and organizational contexts. For example, Chandra's (2012) comparison of Eastern and Western perspectives on WLB found that among multinational firms, American companies focused on flexible working practices, while Indian companies focused on employee assistance programs (EAPs) offering a range of cultural, recreational, health, and educational services (e.g., fitness centers, flower arrangement workshops, and yoga classes). In a more context-specific study of WLB in transnational call centers located in India, Rajan-Rankin (2016) argues that "while the language, discourses and messages of WLB are outsourced along with the work, their meanings and implications for call centre workers can be quite different from the flexible working messages being imparted in the Western outsourcing country" (p. 237). In this setting, WLB discourses and practices served as a symbol of modernity and neoliberalism, but were located in a context characterized by paternalistic leadership styles commonly attributed to collectivistic societies.

Qualitative case studies also demonstrate how different meanings of WLB can exist within workplaces in otherwise very similar contexts. For example, Herman and Lewis (2012) found that four-day work weeks were offered as a form of WLB support in the French headquarters of two multinational companies in the same sector, but in one organization WLB was constructed in terms of flexibility for employed mothers while in the other it was understood to be more gender neutral, with both men and women taking up this practice. The difference was explained by the fact that one company was unionized and had negotiated a collective agreement that included better conditions (including little income reduction) for the four-day week, which encouraged men as well as women to make use of this option. Employment relations thus emerge as a further layer of context in which the meaning of WLB may be rooted.

Temporal Context

Finally, context is not just about place but also time. Management discourses such as equal opportunities, diversity, and WLB are dynamic and change to reflect shifting contexts (Fleetwood, 2007; Lewis et al., 2016a; Tatli et al., 2012). Thus meanings of WLB can shift over time in response to specific events in specific places (Fleetwood, 2007; Gambles et al., 2006; Lewis et al., 2007, 2017a). This is illustrated by a recent study of HR professionals' accounts of WLB practices in the United Kingdom public sector at a time of stringent government cuts in public funding following the 2008 global recession. Evidence emerged of a shift in the understandings and use of the term WLB from an earlier focus on offering "choices" through flexible work arrangements of mutual benefit to employer and employees, toward a reconstruction of WLB as an organizational tool for saving money. New policies such as non-voluntary remote working were therefore branded as WLB polices, masking the cost-saving motivations to support cash-strapped organizations (Lewis et al., 2017a).

Building on the discursive processes literature that explains how the meanings of management constructs develop (Lombardo, Meier, & Verloo, 2009, 2010; Tatli et al., 2012), Lewis et al. (2017a) describe a process whereby the WLB discourse had first become fixed and embedded in organizations in terms of a mutual benefits argument following a high-profile UK government WLB campaign during the

1990s, but in a later context of financial challenges, the meaning of WLB became strategically stretched to include new practices, shrunk to exclude notions of employee choice once constructed as central to WLB policies (Eikhof, Warhurst, & Haunschild, 2007; Gregory & Milner, 2009; Smithson & Stokoe, 2005), and bent to incorporate the additional goal of explicit cost-savings. Thus WLB discourses were adapted and reconstructed by specific actors (i.e., HR professionals) in a specific time and place. HR professionals in this study acknowledged some employee resistance to changing practices (e.g., non-voluntary home-based work), but further research is needed to examine whether employees accept or resist new definitions of WLB within specific contexts.

The Future

This chapter has discussed the problematic nature of meanings of WLB. As the language used to describe a particular concept influences the ways in which individuals and organizational actors think about and respond to it (Lewis et al., 2007), this is not a trivial issue. The ways in which individual workers understand "balance" in relation to work and personal life in diverse contexts influence whether they see balance as feasible and attainable, the supports that they expect or would like, and the "choices" they can make.

Similarly, understandings of WLB vary within and across organizations. For example, if WLB is conceptualized as a health issue with implications for employee well-being and performance, then it may help to challenge practices that encourage work to spill over into nonwork time. In contrast, if WLB is conceptualized as a luxury and support for WLB as a favor, then WLB-supportive policies and practices will be vulnerable, especially in more difficult economic circumstances.

Evidence suggests that WLB may be regarded as a luxury or favor in contexts where there is a long-hours culture, particularly in professional and managerial work (e.g., Moen, Lam, Ammons, & Kelly, 2013). Interestingly, WLB is also likely to be regarded as a luxury in smaller businesses with limited resources, which may be struggling to compete for survival, and in developing country contexts and subsistence economies. As most WLB research takes place in large organizations and in industrialized countries, more research is needed to understand whether and how WLB is interpreted in other contexts. Moreover, most research focuses on high-status, middle-class workers. More needs to be known about the meanings and usefulness of the WLB concept to those working in low-paid and insecure work, for whom the main priority is simply earning enough to get by (Warren, 2017).

Moreover, the concept of WLB is not static. Evidence that meanings of WLB can change over time within a given context, as discussed in this chapter, suggests, that future scholarship in this vein is likely to be fruitful. To expand our knowledge of how individuals in a particular place and time understand WLB, more research is needed into how these meanings develop, and how they impact individuals' sense of entitlement to use WLB provisions, such as flexible or reduced working hours (Herman & Lewis, 2012; Lewis & Smithson, 2001), and their capability for accessing WLB supports (Hobson, Fahlén, & Takács, 2014) to achieve WLB according to their perception of this concept.

Theory-building in this regard would have practical benefits. For instance, HR practitioners could guide the processes of change in meaning of WLB in a more conscious manner, taking account of employee perspectives, and thereby ensure greater and more effective employee take-up of WLB practices. Individuals could examine their understanding of WLB more closely and perhaps challenge employers whose mixed messages regarding WLB contribute to the maintenance of standard ways of working and thereby generate little or no improvement in employee experiences of WLB.

More broadly, the dearth of research investigating the meanings attached to WLB in cultures outside the Western sphere means that it is reasonable to ask how and why these meanings might vary cross-culturally. Looking forward, we might also ask whether cultural differences in the meaning of work and life will gradually attenuate with increasing globalization and industrialization. With distinctions between "work" and "life" domains already perceived as artificial in some cultural contexts (Rajan-Rankin, 2016), an important question for both scholarship and practice is whether WLB remains a useful term or whether the WLB discourse that has helped to raise awareness about some paid-work and personal-life issues now constitutes a barrier to thinking more widely about the diversity of experiences and how these might change in the future.

References

Abubaker, M., & Bagley, C. (2016). Work–life balance and the needs of female employees in the telecommunications industry in a developing country: A critical realist approach to issues in industrial and organizational social psychology. *Comprehensive Psychology, 5*, 1–12.

Allen, T. D., Johnson, R. C., Kiburz, K. M., & Shockley, K. M. (2013). Work–family conflict and flexible work arrangements: Deconstructing flexibility. *Personnel Psychology, 66*(2), 345–376.

Annink, A., den Dulk, L., & Steijn, B. (2015). Work–family state support for the self-employed across Europe. *Journal of Entrepreneurship and Public Policy, 4*(2), 187–208.

Atsumi, N. (2007). Work–life balance strategies for advanced companies. *Japan Labor Review, 4*(4), 37–58.

Beauregard, T. A. (2011). Corporate work–life balance initiatives: Use and effectiveness. In S. Kaiser, M. Ringlstetter, M. Pina e Cunha, & D. R. Eikhof (Eds.), *Creating Balance? International Perspectives on the Work–Life Integration of Professionals* (pp. 193–208). Berlin, Germany: Springer.

Beauregard, T. A. (2014). Fairness perceptions of work–life balance initiatives: Effects on counterproductive work behaviour. *British Journal of Management, 25*(4), 772–789.

Bloom, P. (2016). Work as the contemporary limit of life: Capitalism, the death drive, and the lethal fantasy of 'work–life balance'. *Organization, 23*(4), 588–606.

Brandth, B., & Kvande, E. (2015). Parental leave and classed fathering practices in Norway. In Eydal, G. B., & Rostgaard, T. (Eds.), *Fatherhood in the Nordic Welfare States: Comparing Care Policies and Practices* (pp. 121–140). Bristol, UK: Policy Press.

Caproni, P. J. (2004). Work/life balance: You can't get there from here. *Journal of Applied Behavioral Science*, *40*(2), 208–218.

Chandra, V. (2012). Work–life balance: Eastern and western perspectives. *International Journal of Human Resource Management*, *23*(5), 1040–1056.

Chatrakul Na Ayudhya, U., & Smithson, J. (2016). Entitled or misunderstood? Towards the repositioning of the sense of entitlement concept in the generational difference debate. *Community, Work & Family*, *19*(2), 213–226.

Clark, S. C. (2000). Work/family border theory: A new theory of work/family balance. *Human Relations*, *53*(6), 747–770.

Dale, A. (2005). Combining family and employment: Evidence from Pakistani and Bangladeshi women. In D. M. Houston (Ed.), *Work–Life Balance in the 21st Century* (pp. 230–245). Basingstoke, UK: Palgrave Macmillan.

Dumas, T. L., & Sanchez-Burks, J. (2015). The professional, the personal, and the ideal worker: Pressures and objectives shaping the boundary between life domains. *Academy of Management Annals*, *9*(1), 803–843.

Eikhof, D. R., Warhurst, C., & Haunschild, A. (2007). Introduction: What work? What life? What balance? Critical reflections on the work–life balance debate. *Employee Relations*, *29*(4), 325–333.

Fleetwood, S. (2007). Why work–life balance now? *International Journal of Human Resource Management*, *18*(3), 387–400.

Gambles, R., Lewis, S., & Rapoport, R. (2006). *The Myth of Work–Life Balance: The Challenge of Our Time for Men, Women and Societies*. Chichester, UK: John Wiley & Sons.

Gatrell, C. J., & Cooper, C. L. (2008). Work–life balance: Working for whom? *European Journal of International Management*, *2*(1), 71–86.

Gerstel, N. (2011). Rethinking families and community: The color, class, and centrality of extended kin ties. *Sociological Forum*, *26*(1), 1–20.

Greenhaus, J., & Allen, T. D. (2011). Work–family balance: A review and extension of the literature. In J. C. Quick & L. E. Tetrick (Eds.), *Handbook of Occupational Health Psychology*. Second edition (pp. 165–183). Washington, DC: American Psychological Association.

Gregory, A., & Milner, S. (2009). Editorial: Work–life balance: A matter of choice? *Gender, Work & Organization*, *16*(1), 1–13.

Grzywacz, J. G., & Carlson, D. S. (2007). Conceptualizing work–family balance: Implications for practice and research. *Advances in Developing Human Resources*, *9*(4), 455–471.

Haar, J. M., Russo, M., Suñe, A., & Ollier-Malaterre, A. (2014). Outcomes of work–life balance on job satisfaction, life satisfaction and mental health: A study across seven cultures. *Journal of Vocational Behavior*, *85*(3), 361–373.

Haas, L., & Hwang, C. P. (2008). The impact of taking parental leave on fathers' participation in childcare and relationships with children: Lessons from Sweden. *Community, Work and Family*, *11*(1), 85–104.

Harvey, D. (2005). *A Brief History of Neoliberalism*. Oxford, UK: Oxford University Press.

Herman, C., & Lewis, S. (2012). Entitled to a sustainable career? Motherhood in science, engineering, and technology. *Journal of Social Issues*, *68*(4), 767–789.

Hill, E., Yang, C., Hawkins, A., & Ferris, M. (2004). A cross-cultural test of the work–family interface in 48 countries. *Journal of Marriage and the Family, 66*(5), 1300–1316.

Hobson, B. (Ed.). (2014). *Worklife Balance: The Agency and Capabilities Gap.* Oxford, UK: Oxford University Press.

Hobson, B., Fahlén, S., & Takács, J. (2014). A sense of entitlement? Agency and capabilities in Sweden and Hungary. *Worklife Balance: The Agency and Capabilities Gap,* (pp. 57–91). Oxford, UK: Oxford University Press.

Hofstede, G. (1980). Motivation, leadership, and organization: Do American theories apply abroad? *Organizational Dynamics, 9*(1), 42–63.

House, R., Javidan, M., & Dorfman, P. (2001). Project GLOBE: An introduction. *Applied Psychology, 50*(4), 489–505.

Joplin, J. R. W., Francesco, A. M., Shaffer, M., & Lau, T. (2003). The macro-environment and work–family conflict: Development of a cross-cultural comparative framework. *International Journal of Cross Cultural Management, 3*, 305–328.

Kamenou, N. (2008). Reconsidering work–life balance debates: Challenging limited understandings of the 'life' component in the context of ethnic minority women's experiences. *British Journal of Management, 19*, 99–109.

Kelliher, C., & Anderson, D. (2010). Doing more with less? Flexible working practices and the intensification of work. *Human Relations, 63*(1), 83–106.

Khokher, S. Y., & Beauregard, T. A. (2014). Work–family attitudes and behaviours among newly immigrant Pakistani expatriates: The role of organizational family-friendly policies. *Community, Work & Family, 17*(2), 142–162.

Kossek, E. E., Valcour, M., & Lirio, P. (2014). The sustainable workforce: Organizational strategies for promoting work–life balance and well-being. In C. Cooper & P. Chen (Eds.), *Work and Wellbeing* (pp. 295–318). Oxford, UK: Wiley-Blackwell.

Lareau, A. (2011). *Unequal Childhoods: Class, Race, and Family Life.* Oakland, CA: University of California Press.

Leslie, L. M., Manchester, C. F., Park, T. Y., & Mehng, S. A. (2012). Flexible work practices: A source of career premiums or penalties? *Academy of Management Journal, 55*(6), 1407–1428.

Lewis, S., Anderson, D., Lyonette, C., Payne, N., & Wood, S. (2017a). Public sector austerity cuts in the UK and the changing discourse of work–life balance. *Work, Employment and Society.* Vol. 31(4) 586–604.

Lewis, S., Anderson, D., Lyonette, C., Payne, N., & Wood, S. (2017b). *Work–Life Balance in Times of Recession, Austerity and Beyond.* New York, NY: Routledge.

Lewis, S., Brannen, J., & Nilsen, A. (2009). *Work, Families and Organisations in Transition: European Perspectives.* Bristol, UK: Policy Press.

Lewis, S., Gambles, R., & Rapoport, R. (2007). The constraints of a 'work–life balance' approach: An international perspective. *International Journal of Human Resource Management, 18*(3), 360–373.

Lewis, S., Izraeli, D. N., & Hootsman, H. (1992). Towards balanced lives and gender equality. *Dual Earner Families: International Perspectives.* Newbury Park, CA: Sage.

Lewis, S., & Smithson, J. (2001). Sense of entitlement to support for the reconciliation of employment and family life. *Human Relations* 55(11). 1455–1481.

Lombardo, E., Meier, P., & Verloo, M. (Eds.). (2009). *The Discursive Politics of Gender Equality: Stretching, Bending and Policy-Making.* London, UK: Routledge.

Lombardo, E., Meier, P., & Verloo, M. (2010). Discursive dynamics in gender equality politics: What about 'feminist taboos'? *European Journal of Women's Studies, 17*(2), 105–123.

Lu, L., Cooper, C. L., Kao, S.-F., Chang, T.-T., Allen, T. D., Lapierre, L. M., O'Driscoll, M. P., Poelmans, S. A. Y., Sanchez, J. I., & Spector, P. E. (2010). Cross-cultural differences on work-to-family conflict and role satisfaction: A Taiwanese–British comparison. *Human Resource Management, 49*(1), 67–85.

Lyness, K. S., & Judiesch, M. K. (2014). Gender egalitarianism and work–life balance for managers: Multisource perspectives in 36 countries. *Applied Psychology, 63*(1), 96–129.

Mescher, S., Benschop, Y., & Doorewaard, H. (2010). Representations of work–life balance support. *Human Relations, 63*(1), 21–39.

Moen, P., Lam, J., Ammons, S., & Kelly, E. L. (2013). Time work by overworked professionals: Strategies in response to the stress of higher status. *Work and Occupations, 40*(2), 79–114.

Nilsen, A., Brannen, J., & Lewis, S. (2013). *Transitions to Parenthood in Europe*. Bristol, UK: Policy Press.

Ollier-Malaterre, A. (2016). Cross-national work–life research: A review at the individual level. In T. D. Allen & L. E. Eby (Eds.), *Oxford Handbook of Work and Family* (Chapter 23). Oxford, UK: Oxford University Press.

Ollier-Malaterre, A., & Foucreault, A. (2017). Cross-national work–life research: Cultural and structural impacts for individuals and organizations. *Journal of Management. 43*(1), 111–136.

Özbilgin, M. F., Beauregard, T. A., Tatli, A., & Bell, M. P. (2011). Work–life, diversity and intersectionality: A critical review and research agenda. *International Journal of Management Reviews, 13*(2), 177–198.

Rajan-Rankin, S. (2016). Paternalism and the paradox of work–life balance: Discourse and practice. *Community, Work & Family, 19*(2), 227–241.

Smithson, J., & Stokoe, E. H. (2005). Discourses of work–life balance: Negotiating 'gender-blind' terms in organizations. *Gender, Work & Organization, 12*(2), 147–168.

Spector, P. E., Allen, T. D., Poelmans, S. A. Y., Lapierre, L. M., Cooper, C. L., O'Driscoll, M., et al. (2007). Cross-national differences in relationships of work demands, job satisfaction, and turnover intentions with work–family conflict. *Personnel Psychology, 60*(4), 805–835.

Tatli, A., Vassilopoulou, J., Al Ariss, A., & Özbilgin, M. F. (2012). The role of regulatory and temporal context in the construction of diversity discourses: The case of the UK, France and Germany. *European Journal of Industrial Relations, 18*(4), 293–308.

Tingvold, L., Middelthon, A. L., Allen, J., & Hauff, E. (2012). Parents and children only? Acculturation and the influence of extended family members among Vietnamese refugees. *International Journal of Intercultural Relations, 36*(2), 260–270.

Trompenaars, F., & Hampden-Turner, C. (1998). *Riding the Waves of Culture: Understanding Diversity in Global Business*. London, UK: Nicholas Brealey Publishing.

Warren, T. (2017). Work–life balance and class: In search of working-class work-lives. In Lewis, S., Anderson, D., Lyonette, C., Payne, N., & Wood, S., *Work–Life Balance in Times of Recession, Austerity and Beyond* (pp 112–131). New York, NY: Routledge.

Wayne, J. H., Butts, M. M., Casper, W. J., & Allen, T. D. (2016). In search of balance: An empirical integration of multiple meanings of work–family balance. *Personnel Psychology*. doi: 10.1111/peps.12132.

Zhan, H. J., & Montgomery, R. J. V. (2003). Gender and elder care in China: The influence of filial piety and structural constraints. *Gender & Society, 17*, 209–229.

40 A Cross-National View of Personal Responsibility for Work–Life Balance

Tammy D. Allen, Eunae Cho, Kristen M. Shockley, and Andrew Biga

Within the work–family literature, a great deal of research attention has centered on what organizations can and should do to aid employees in their efforts to balance their work and family responsibilities. This focus is driven by the point of view that individual experiences such as work–family conflict are largely determined by employees' work and/or family situations (e.g., Lewis, Gambles, & Rapoport, 2007). Accordingly, considerable knowledge has been amassed with regard to the association between work/family stressors and demands with constructs such as work–family conflict (e.g., Michel, Kotrba, Mitchelson, Clark, & Baltes, 2011). Moreover, solutions for managing work and family often focus on organizational policies, such as flexible work arrangements and dependent care support, and governmental level policy, such as paid leave (e.g., Butts, Casper, & Yang, 2013; Neal & Hammer, 2007).

There is also a growing body of research that acknowledges important individual differences associated with work–family experiences. For example, an increasing number of studies involve the examination of decisions individuals make when faced with a specific work–family dilemma or conflict (Greenhaus & Powell, 2003; Poelmans, 2005; Powell & Greenhaus, 2006; Shockley & Allen, 2015). Another body of research has examined dispositional variables (e.g., negative affect, conscientiousness) associated with work–family conflict and with enrichment (e.g., Bruck & Allen, 2003; Wayne, Musisca, & Fleeson, 2004). In concert, the results of these studies suggest that both individual and situational factors contribute to work–family experiences.

Building on individual differences research, we propose that a neglected, but potentially important line of research is needed that examines the extent individuals perceive *personal responsibility for their own work–life balance* (PRWLB). Similar to the way Greenhaus and Allen (2011) define work–family balance as "an overall appraisal of the extent to which individuals' effectiveness and satisfaction in work and family roles are consistent with their lives values at a point in time" (p. 174), we suggest that PRWLB also encompasses a consideration of priorities across the lifespan. Specifically, we define PRWLB as a self-directed attitude toward work–life balance that recognizes personal choice and priorities. Such a perspective is consistent with the protean career concept, which suggests that the person, not the organization, takes responsibility for his/her career management (Hall, 2004).

However, PRWLB is not based on pitting responsibility for balance on the organization versus the self, but rather reflects an individual's belief that s/he can achieve balance through personal efforts. This may even be accomplished through one's organization, such as by negotiating with a supervisor (e.g., requesting to work from home one day a week). As a preliminary investigation of the construct, we examine whether PRWLB varies across country, gender, and cultural context based on data from multiple countries that differ in terms of work–family-relevant cultural variables; specifically, institutional collectivism and gender egalitarianism. Of note, we also contribute to cross-national work–family research by including countries that have received relatively little attention in the work–family literature (e.g., Morocco, Nigeria).

To place our review and our study in context, we recognize that multiple constructs exist with regard to work–family experiences, including work–family conflict, work–family enrichment, and work–family balance. Moreover, there are variants of constructs that represent negative (e.g., work–family conflict, negative spillover) and positive (e.g., work–family enrichment, positive spillover) interdependencies between work and family. A review of definitions and differences is beyond the scope of this chapter (the interested reader may see Allen, 2012 for a review). PRWLB specifically references balance, but given known relationships between balance, conflict, and enrichment (e.g., Wayne, Butts, Casper, & Allen, 2016), research that pertains to work–family experiences such as conflict and enrichment is relevant and is included as such.

Existing Research on Individual Differences

The role of individual differences in the work–family interface has become of increasing interest within the work–family literature. To date, most of the existing research has focused on work–family conflict. Meta-analytic studies support relationships between personality and both directions of work–family conflict (Allen, Johnson, Saboe, Cho, Dumani, & Evans, 2012; Michel, Clark, & Jaramillo, 2011). In general, negative trait-based variables (e.g., negative affect, neuroticism) appear to make individuals more vulnerable to both directions of work–family conflict, while positive trait-based variables (e.g., positive affect, optimism) appear to protect individuals from work–family conflict. Moreover, there is evidence of a stable predisposition, distinct from Big Five personality traits, associated with both negative and positive work–family spillover (Cho, Tay, Allen, & Stark, 2013). These studies are an important contribution to the work–family literature in that the effect sizes associated with dispositional variables rival those associated with work and family demands and exceed those associated with work–family practice initiatives, such as flextime (Allen, Johnson, Kiburz, & Shockley, 2013).

In addition to personality, individual beliefs about one's own capabilities have been investigated as predictors of work–family conflict. Specifically, self-esteem, internal locus of control, and self-efficacy are each negatively associated with both directions of work–family conflict (Wayne, Michel, & Matthews, 2016). In addition,

Butler, Gasser, and Smart (2004) examined self-efficacy specific to the work–family interface, defined as beliefs about one's ability to competently manage conflicts between work and family. Sample items included, "Handling the conflicting demands of work and family is well within my abilities," and, "My past experiences increase my confidence that I will be able to handle conflicting demands of work and family." They found that work–family self-efficacy was negatively associated with both directions of work–family conflict. Personal preferences and strategies for managing work and family boundaries, such as segmenting versus integrating roles, have also become of interest to work–family researchers with mixed results concerning relationships with work–family conflict (Allen, Cho, & Meier, 2015). The focus of PRWLB is likely related to perceived ability and to strategic preferences, but unique in that it centers on personal responsibility and priorities, recognizing that priorities can shift across the life course. Moreover, PRWLB is specific to the work–life interface whereas constructs such as locus of control are part of a set of stable traits that reflect one's fundamental overall evaluation of the self (Judge, Locke, & Durham, 1997).

Cultural Values

It has long been recognized that context factors, such as country and culture, influence the work–life interface (Powell, Francesco, & Ling, 2009). However, the scope of inquiry has been somewhat limited. To date, most multinational work–family research has focused on differences in work–family conflict (e.g., Allen, French, Dumani, & Shockley, 2015). Moreover, from a cultural perspective, much of the focus has been on the examination of collectivism as the explanatory variable (e.g., Spector et al., 2007; Yang, Chen, Choi, & Zou, 2000). To provide a better understanding of cultural influences, it seems important to recognize other ways by which country and culture relate to the work–family interface. Societal culture can also shape the way individuals view the responsibility of the self with regard to work–family balance.

Beliefs with regard to PRWLB are likely to be influenced by the environment. Some research exists to support this point of view. Lewis and Smithson (2001) found cross-national differences with regard to the extent that European men and women under the age of thirty felt entitled to support from the state (e.g., childcare, parental leave) with regard to management of work and family. Variation corresponded with degree of existing support provided by the state. Specifically, those in Norway and Sweden, where greater supports exist, demonstrated a greater degree of entitlement than did those in Ireland, Portugal, and the United Kingdom, where fewer supports exist. Thus, there is evidence that existing societal norms may play a role in the extent that individuals view the self as responsible for work–family balance.

As an environmental characteristic, cultural values associated with one's own context may help determine the extent individuals believe they are responsible for work–family balance. We propose that two cultural values have implications for PRWLB: institutional collectivism (IC) and gender egalitarianism (GE). GE refers to the role that societies ascribe to men and women (House & Javidan, 2004). In more egalitarian societies, gender differences are minimized. Societies that hold more gender egalitarian values shun rigid social norms that dictate gender roles and behaviors based on biological sex (Emrich, Denmark, & Den Hartog, 2004). Instead, men and women are viewed as equal in ability. Gender roles tend to be more segregated in lower GE societies while in higher GE societies men and women are more likely to share equally in both work and family responsibilities. It seems likely that the expectation that work and family responsibilities are to be shared by men and women makes the challenge of attaining work–life balance more salient, increasing the likelihood that individuals espouse personal responsibility. In contrast, when gender roles are segregated, the primacy of a single role likely renders the notion of personal responsibility for work–family balance less salient.

IC refers to the degree that institutional practices at the society level encourage and reward collective action. Powell et al. (2009) suggest that members of more collectivistic cultures may express greater concern for the quality of the work–family interface than members of less collectivistic cultures because the greater sense of connectedness leads them to care more about the effect that their participation in the work role has on important others in their life. In contrast, individualists are primarily motivated by their own goals and preferences and balance may be less salient to them. Given the concern that collectivists tend to have with regard to the quality of life of others in their family sphere, they seem more likely than individualists to assume responsibility for work–life balance in an effort to minimize potential negative impact on others. Thus, it seems likely that greater IC (i.e., greater collectivism) will be associated with greater PRWLB.

Gender

Gender is inextricably intertwined with the work–life interface, owing at least in part, to a persistent gendered division of work and family labor (Leslie, Manchester, & Kim, 2016; Shockley & Shen, 2016). Although gender differences in work–family variables, such as work–family conflict, would be expected, meta-analytic evidence suggests few differences exist (Shockley, Shen, Denunzio, Arvan, & Knudsen, 2014). Some research has examined gender differences in general feelings of personal control, with mixed results as well, but among a sample of married parents Cassidy and Davies (2003) found women reported lower levels of general personal control than did men. Given differences in the social organization of work and family roles, we explore whether there are mean differences in PRWLB across gender and whether gender interacts with culture in relation to PRWLB.

Method

Participants

Participants were 3,446 employees from eight countries within a multinational organization. The countries were Egypt ($n = 373$), Hungary ($n = 379$), Kazakhstan

(n = 147), Morocco (n = 233), Nigeria (n = 145), Poland (n = 798), Russia (n = 857), and Turkey (n = 514). A total of 1,244 of the participants were female, 2,034 were male, and 159 did not report their gender. Data were collected via the organization's annual employee opinion survey.

Measures

Personal Responsibility for Work–Life Balance. PRWLB was assessed with a single item, "My work–life balance is a function of my personal choice and priorities according to the different stages of my life." Responses were based on a five-point scale (i.e., strongly disagree to strongly agree).

Gender. Gender was coded 1 = male, 2 = female.

Cultural values. Based on "as is" data from Project GLOBE (House et al., 2004), countries were clustered into different groups. GLOBE country scores have a possible range of 1 to 7, but actual scores tend to range between 2 and 6 and the range tends to vary across dimensions. Low GE was represented by Egypt, Morocco, Turkey, and Nigeria (mean GLOBE score = 2.89). High GE was represented by Kazakhstan, Poland, Russia, and Hungary (mean GLOBE score = 4.00). Low IC was represented by Hungary, Morocco, Turkey, and Nigeria (mean GLOBE score = 3.89). High IC was represented by Kazakhstan, Russia, Egypt, and Poland (mean GLOBE score = 4.46). To examine GE and IC in combination we also created four clusters: low IC-low GE (Morocco, Nigeria, and Turkey); low GE-high IC (Egypt); low IC-high GE (Hungary); high IC-high GE (Kazakhstan, Poland, and Russia). The GLOBE world average score for GE is 3.40 and for IC is 4.24.

Region. The eight countries represented in the data can also be clustered into three regions consistent with the clusters identified in the GLOBE study (Gupta, Hanges, & Dorfman, 2002). Egypt, Morocco, and Turkey were grouped into the Arabic cluster. Hungary, Kazakhstan, Poland, and Russia were grouped into the Eastern Europe cluster. Sub-Saharan Africa was represented by Nigeria.

Results

To examine mean differences in PRWLB at the country-level, we conducted a one-way analysis of variance. Results indicated significant mean differences across the eight countries (F = 24.28, p <.001). A Tukey honestly significant difference (HSD) post hoc test was conducted to determine which countries significantly differed from one another. Results are shown in Table 40.1. Hungary had the lowest mean at 3.09 while Russia had the highest mean at 3.79. We next examined mean differences across region clusters and found significant differences (F = 14.68, p <.001). The Arabic cluster (M = 3.38) significantly differed from the Sub-Saharan cluster (M = 3.56) and the Eastern European cluster (M = 3.58).

We next tested for differences in PRWLB as a function of cultural values. We first tested for mean differences in low versus high GE clusters and low versus high IC

Table 40.1 *PRWLB means by country*

Country	Subset 1	Subset 2	Subset 3	Subset 4
Hungary	3.09 (1.08)			
Egypt	3.29 (1.02)	3.29 (1.02)		
Morocco		3.37 (.97)	3.37 (.97)	
Turkey		3.45 (1.07)	3.45 (1.07)	
Kazakhstan		3.53 (1.13)	3.53 (1.13)	
Nigeria			3.56 (1.03)	3.56 (1.03)
Poland			3.59 (.94)	3.59 (.94)
Russia				3.79 (.87)

Note: Countries within the same subset do not significantly differ from one another. Standard deviations appear in parentheses.

Table 40.2 *PRWLB means by cultural cluster*

Cluster	Subset 1	Subset 2	Subset 3	Subset 4
Low IC-high GE	3.09 (1.04)			
Low GE-high IC		3.29 (1.02)		
Low IC-low GE			3.45 (1.04)	
High IC-high GE				3.68 (.93)

Note: Clusters within the same subset do not significantly differ from one another. Standard deviations appear in parentheses.

clusters. Results indicated that participants in the high GE cluster ($M = 3.58$, $SD = .98$) reported greater PRWLB than did participants in the low GE cluster ($M = 3.40$, $SD = 1.03$) ($t = 4.96$, $p < .001$). Results also indicated that participants in the high IC cluster ($M = 3.61$, $SD = .96$) reported greater PRWLB than did participants in the low IC cluster ($M = 3.34$, $SD = 1.06$) ($t = 7.56$, $p < .001$).

We tested for differences across the four clusters that varied in their combination of GE and IC. One-way analysis of variance supported a significant difference in the four clusters ($F = 47.96$, $p < .001$). A Tukey HSD post hoc test was conducted to determine which clusters significantly differed from one another. As shown in Table 40.2 each cluster significantly differed from the other. Those in the high IC-high GE cluster reported the greatest PRWLB ($M = 3.68$) while those in the low IC-high GE cluster reported the lowest PRWLB ($M = 3.09$).

To further probe the interaction between GE and IC, we conducted a hierarchical regression analysis in which imputed GLOBE values were used to represent GE and IC and the interaction between the two was computed. The interaction was significant (R^2 change $= .01$, $F = 40.70$, $p < .001$). The interaction was plotted based on levels of the variables one standard deviation above and below the mean (see Figure 40.1). As shown in Figure 40.1, the relationship between GE and PRWLB is

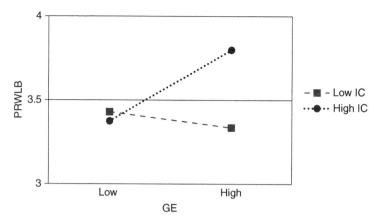

Figure 40.1 *Gender egalitarian (GE) by institutional collectivism (IC) interaction.*

positive when coupled with high IC, but the sign of the relationship switches to negative when coupled with low IC.

Lastly, we examined gender. First, an independent samples t-test was conducted to test whether PRWLB differed by gender. Results indicated women reported greater PRWLB ($M = 3.58$, $SD = .99$) than did men ($M = 3.49$, $SD = 1.00$) ($t = 2.53$, $p = .01$). However, it should be noted that this difference was small in magnitude (Cohen's $d = .09$). Next we examined whether gender interacted with IC or GE. Analysis of variance based on the low-high clusters of GE revealed no interaction with gender ($F = 2.02$, $p = .15$). Similarly, no interaction between gender and low-high IC clusters was detected ($F = 1.05$, $p = .31$). Gender in conjunction with the four-group culture cluster was examined next. A significant interaction emerged ($F = 2.72$, $p = .04$) (see Figure 40.2). Results based on t-tests revealed significant differences in the low IC-low GE group ($t = -2.79$, $p = .01$) such that women reported greater PRWLB ($M = 3.58$, SD = 1.00) than did men ($M = 3.38$, SD = 1.04) (Cohen's $d = .20$). Gender differences were not significant within the other three clusters. Finally, we tested for an interaction between gender and regional cluster. The interaction was not significant ($F = 2.76$, $p = .06$).

Discussion

The most common approach to addressing the management of work and family has been to focus on environmental conditions, which tends to place the role of the individual as that of passive reactor (Kreiner, Hollensbe, & Sheep, 2009). We suggest that individuals are active agents who can shape their own work–family experiences. Considering work–life issues from an individual perspective has been likened to "blaming the victim" (Grzywacz & Carlson, 2007). However, we contend that allowing for agentic capacity in managing the work–family interface is not intended to imply that individuals fully control their work–family situations. As noted by Bandura (2006), "People do not operate as autonomous agents. Nor is their

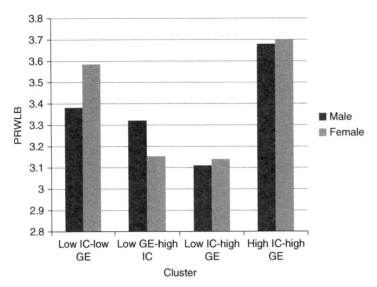

Figure 40.2 *Culture combination cluster by gender interaction.*

behavior wholly determined by situational influences. Rather human functioning is a product of a reciprocal interplay of intrapersonal, behavioral, and environmental determinants" (p. 165). We propose inclusion of personal responsibility beliefs as a supplement to existing research that has focused on situational factors widens the lens through which we are able to theorize and find solutions to work–family management.

Our descriptive research helps establish a baseline understanding of PRWLB and how it varies across different groups and contexts. Our findings suggest that there is meaningful variation in the extent that individuals agree with the notion that they are personally responsible for their own work–life balance. Our research shows that this variation is, at least in part, a function of country, region, culture, and gender.

Consistent with our expectations that PRWLB would be higher in high GE versus low GE and in high IC versus low IC cultures, we found that high IC coupled with high GE was associated with the highest level of PRWLB. Individuals are most likely to feel that they are personally responsible for their work–life balance when gender roles are egalitarian and when institutional practices encourage collective action.

In contrast to our expectations, low IC coupled with high GE resulted in the lowest level of PRWLB. This group was represented solely by Hungary, which reported the lowest country mean overall. As such it is difficult to discern if the result is due to unique aspects of Hungary versus the combination of low IC-high GE. To better understand what may be driving this finding, we specifically compared Hungary with Poland, which had one of the highest country scores on PRWLB. Poland and Hungary share many commonalities. Like Poland, Hungary is a Central European post-communist country. Moreover, both became members of the European Union in 2004 and have similar economic conditions (Bakacsi, Sandor, Andras, & Victor,

2002). In terms of social policy related to work–family, Hungary has 24 weeks of maternity leave paid at 70% while Poland has 16 weeks paid at 100% (Hausmann, Tyson, & Zahidi, 2012). One factor that differentiates the two is their standing in terms of gender equity. Although according to GLOBE both countries are high in GE, the gender equity gap in Hungary is consistently greater than is the gender equity gap in Poland (Hausmann et al., 2012). Furthermore, although the economic participation of men and women is similar across the two countries, disparities in the educational attainment and political empowerment of women versus men are considerably larger in Hungary than in Poland. The net result may be that societal practices in Hungary are more in line with that of lower GE countries, which could help explain the lower PRWLB findings. To test this speculation a wider array of countries that can be classified as high in GE and low in IC is needed (e.g., Colombia, Portugal).

With regard to regional differences, we found that individuals in the Arabic region reported lower PRWLB than did individuals in other regions. The countries in this cluster share a legacy of being under foreign control for many decades. They also are high-power-distance, low-future-orientation countries that ascribe low significance to planning and influencing the future (Kabasakal & Bodur, 2002). These factors may help explain the lower likelihood of espousing personal responsibility for work and family balance.

Finally, we found that women reported more PRWLB than did men in low IC-low GE contexts. The countries that represented this cluster are all countries where economic, political, educational, and health disparities between men and women are large (e.g., Hausmann et al., 2012). In such societies, work might be thought of as more of a choice for women and outside of the norm. Such conditions may increase the extent that women perceive that they must assume responsibility for balancing work and family demands.

There are several limitations to the current study. One limitation is that a single item, which prevented an assessment of reliability, represented PRWLB. As noted by Dierdorff and Ellington (2008), who used a single-item measure of work interference with family, the use of single-item measures is sometimes a trade-off for use of broad-reaching survey data. Given these initial findings regarding the PRWLB construct, we encourage researchers to develop multi-item measures that can be subjected to more rigorous psychometric assessments. Another limitation concerns the extent that our findings with regard to cultural values are generalizable beyond the specific countries included in our analyses. Although the set of countries included in our investigation include those not often found in work–family research and can be considered a strength, the lack of literature on these countries renders our explanations of findings particularly speculative. Moreover, the data come from employees of a single organization and as such there may be greater similarity among these workers than among workers in the general population due to attraction-selection-attrition processes. Additional research with a wider array of cultural and organizational contexts is needed. Finally, we note that the R^2 change associated with the IC-GE interaction was small, raising potential concerns with regard to practical importance. The extent that small effects may be of practical import is an issue for further consideration as findings with regard to PRWLB accumulate across different contexts.

The study has implications for the development of culture-sensitive theories of work–family phenomena. The desire to balance work–life may be universal, but the perspective that one takes in terms of personal responsibility meaningfully varies across cultural contexts. Future research is needed that expands the nomological network of the PRWLB construct. For example, research is needed to help determine whether PRWLB relates to less work–family conflict, more work–family enrichment, and/or greater work–family balance. Moreover, research that examines the impact of individual PRWLB on interactions with family members and coworkers would also be beneficial. For example, individuals high on PRWLB may be more likely to initiate negotiations with role partners to help achieve work–life balance. Additional research that examines interactions between PRWLB and other situational factors not included in the current study (e.g., family-supportive work practices, state support such as parental leave) would also lead to a richer understanding of the predictive power of PRWLB in explaining work–family experiences.

Conclusion

Our goal with the current research was to help spur conversation with regard to individual perspectives on responsibility for work–life balance and how it is viewed around the globe. Such a focus examines the abilities of the individual rather than making the individual dependent on the organization or the state for support. The role of the individual should be integrated with the situational approach to work–family management. It cannot be assumed that individuals will directly benefit or change as a result of situational benefits or policies. Ultimately, responsibility for work–life balance is one that is shared by the individual, the organization, and society.

References

Allen, T. D. (2012). The work–family interface. In S. W. J. Kozlowski (Ed.), *Oxford Handbook of Industrial and Organizational Psychology* (pp. 1163–1198). New York, NY: Oxford University Press.

Allen, T. D., Cho, E., & Meier, L. L. (2014). Work–family boundary dynamics. *Annual Review of Organizational Psychology and Organizational Behavior, 1*, 99–121.

Allen, T. D., French, K. A., Dumani, S., & Shockley, K. M. (2015). Meta-analysis of work–family conflict mean differences: Does national context matter? *Journal of Vocational Behavior, 90*, 90–100.

Allen, T. D., Johnson, R. C., Kiburz, K., & Shockley, K. M. (2013). Work–family conflict and flexible work arrangements: Deconstructing flexibility. *Personnel Psychology, 66*, 345–376

Allen, T. D., Johnson, R. C., Saboe, K. N., Cho, E., Dumani, S., & Evans, S. (2012). Dispositional variables and work–family conflict: A meta-analysis. *Journal of Vocational Behavior, 80*, 17–26.

Bakacsi, G., Sandor, T., Andras, K., & Viktor, I. (2002). Eastern European cluster: Tradition and transition. *Journal of World Business, 37*, 69–80.

Bandura, A. (2006). Toward a psychology of human agency. *Perspectives on Psychological Science, 1*, 164–180.

Bruck, C. S., & Allen, T. D. (2003). The relationship between big five traits, negative affectivity, type A behavior, and work–family conflict. *Journal of Vocational Behavior, 63*, 457–472.

Butler, A., Gasser, M., & Smart, L. (2004). A social-cognitive perspective on using family-friendly benefits. *Journal of Vocational Behavior, 65*, 57–70.

Butts, M. M., Casper, W. J., & Yang, T. S. (2013). How important are work–family support policies? A meta-analytic investigation of their effects on employee outcomes. *Journal of Applied Psychology, 98*, 1–25.

Cassidy, G. L., & Davies, L. (2003). Gender differences in mastery among married parents. *Social Psychology Quarterly, 66*, 48–61.

Cho, E., Tay, L., Allen, T. D., & Stark, S. (2013). Identification of a dispositional tendency to experience work–family spillover. *Journal of Vocational Behavior, 82*, 188–198.

Dierdorff, E. C., & Ellington, J. K (2008). It's the nature of the work: Examining behavior-based sources of work–family conflict across occupations. *Journal of Applied Psychology, 93*, 883–892.

Emrich, C. G., Denmark, F. L., & Den Hartog, D. N. (2004). Cross-cultural differences in gender egalitarianism: Implications for societies, organizations, and leaders. In R. J. House, P. J. Hanges, M. Javidan, P. W. Dorfman, & V. Gupta (Eds.), *Culture, Leadership, and Organizations: The GLOBE Study of 62 Societies* (pp. 343–394). Thousand Oaks, CA: Sage.

Greenhaus, G. H., & Allen, T. D. (2011). Work–family balance: A review and extension of the literature. In L. Tetrick & J. C. Quick (Eds.), *Handbook of Occupational Health Psychology*. Second edition (pp. 165–183). Washington, DC: American Psychological Association.

Greenhaus, J. H., & Powell, G. N. (2003). When work and family collide: Deciding between competing demands. *Organizational Behavior and Human Decision Processes, 90*, 291–303.

Grzywacz, J. G., & Carlson, D. S. (2007). Conceptualizing work–family balance: Implications for practice and research. *Advances in Developing Human Resources, 9*, 455–471.

Gupta, V., Hanges, P. J., & Dorfman, P. (2002). Cultural clusters: Methodology and findings. *Journal of World Business, 37*, 11–15.

Hall, D. T. (2004). The protean career: A quarter-century journey. *Journal of Vocational Behavior, 65*, 1–13.

Hausmann, R., Tyson, L. D., & Zahidi, S. (2012). *The Global Gender Gap Report*. Geneva, Switzerland: World Economic Forum.

House, R. J., & Javidan, M. (2004). Overview of GLOBE. In R. J. House, P. J. Hanges, M. Javidan, P. W. Dorfman, & V. Gupta (Eds.), *Culture, Leadership, and Organizations: The GLOBE Study of 62 Societies* (pp. 9–28). Thousand Oaks, CA: Sage.

Judge, T. A., Locke, E. A., Durham, C. C. (1997). The dispositional causes of job satisfaction: A core evaluations approach. *Research in Organizational Behavior. 19*, 151–188.

Kabasakal, H., & Bodur, M. (2002). Arabic cluster: A bridge between East and West. *Journal of World Business, 37*, 40–54.

Kreiner, G. E., Hollensbe, E. C., Sheep, M. L. (2009). Balancing borders and bridges: Negotiating the work–home interface via boundary work tactics. *Academy of Management Journal, 52*, 704–730.

Leslie, L. M., Manchester, C. F., & Kim, Y. (2016). Gender and the work–family domain: A social role-based perspective. In T. D. Allen & L. T. Eby (Eds.). *The Oxford Handbook of Work and Family*, (pp. 125–139). New York, NY: Oxford University Press.

Lewis, S., Gambles, & Rapoport, R. (2007). The constraints of a 'work–life balance' approach: An international perspective. *International Journal of Human Resource Management, 18*, 360–373.

Lewis, S., & Smithson, J. (2001). Sense of entitlement to support the reconciliation of employment and family life. *Human Relations, 54*, 1455–1481.

Michel, J. S., Clark, M. A., & Jaramillo, D. (2011). The role of the Five Factor Model of personality in the perceptions of negative and positive forms of work-nonwork spillover: A meta-analytic review. *Journal of Vocational Behavior, 79(1)*, 191–203.

Michel J. S., Kotrba, L. M., Mitchelson, J. K., Clark, M. A., & Baltes B. B. (2011). Antecedents of work–family conflict: A meta-analytic review. *Journal of Organizational Behavior, 32*, 689–725.

Neal, M. B., & Hammer, L. B. (2007). *Working Couples Caring for Children and Aging Parents: Effects on Work and Well-Being.* Mahwah, NJ: Lawrence Erlbaum Associates.

Poelmans, S. A. Y. (2005). The decision process theory of work and family. In E. E. Kossek & S. J. Lambert (Eds.), *Work and Life Integration* (pp. 263–286). Mahwah, NJ: Lawrence Erlbaum Associates.

Powell, G. N., Francesco, A. M., & Ling, Y. (2009). Towards culture-sensitive theories of the work–family interface. *Journal of Organizational Behavior, 30*, 597–616.

Powell, G. N., & Greenhaus, J. H. (2006). Managing incidents of work–family conflict: A decision-making perspective. *Human Relations, 59*, 1179–1212.

Shockley, K.M., & Allen, T.D. (2015). Deciding between work and family: An episodic approach. *Personnel Psychology, 68(2)*, 283–318.

Shockley, K.M., & Shen, W. (2016). Couple dynamics: Division of labor. In T. D. Allen & L. T. Eby (Eds.). *The Oxford Handbook of Work and Family*, (pp. 125–139). New York, NY: Oxford University Press.

Shockley, K.M., Shen, W., Denunzio, M., Arvan, M., & Knudsen, E. (2014). Clarifying gender and work–family conflict: A meta-analytic approach. In M.J. Mills (Chair) Work–Life Interface Meets Employee Gender: Challenge and Opportunity. Symposium presented at the Work and Family Researchers Network conference. New York, NY.

Spector, P. E., Allen, T. D., Poelmans, S., Lapierre, L. M., Cooper, C. L., O'Driscoll, M., Sanchez, J. I., Abarca, N., Alexandrova, M., Beham, B., Brough, P., Ferreiro, P., Fraile, G., Lu, C. Q., Lu, L. et al. (2007). Cross-national differences in relationships of work demands, job satisfaction and turnover intentions with work–family conflict. *Personnel Psychology, 60*, 805–835.

Wayne, J. H., Butts, M. M., Casper, W. J., & Allen, T. D. (2016). In search of balance: A conceptual and empirical integration of multiple meanings of work–family balance. *Personnel Psychology.* Online first, doi: 10.1111/peps.12132

Wayne, J. J., Michel, J. S., & Matthews, R. A. (2016). Is it who you are that counts? The importance of personality and values to the work–family experience. In T. D. Allen &

L. T. Eby (Eds.), *The Oxford Handbook of Work and Family* (pp. 81–94). New York, NY: Oxford University Press.

Wayne, J. H., Musisca N., & Fleeson, W. (2004). Considering the role of personality in the work–family experience: Relationships of the Big Five to work–family conflict and facilitation. *Journal of Vocational Behavior, 64*, 108–130.

Yang, N., Chen, C. C., Choi, J., & Zou, Y. (2000). Sources of work–family conflict: a Sino–US comparison of the effects of work and family demands. *Academy of Management Journal, 41*, 113–123.

PART IX

Conclusion

41 Charting a Path Forward

Winny Shen, Kristen M. Shockley, and Ryan C. Johnson

As evidenced by the wealth of research reviewed within this volume, as well as the myriad new ideas and insights generated by the chapter authors themselves, international and cross-cultural research on work–family dynamics and management is alive and thriving. In this concluding chapter, we take the opportunity to acknowledge and celebrate the achievements of the field thus far, while charting a path forward by highlighting as yet unanswered questions and persistent challenges and providing suggestions for fruitful avenues for future inquiry and how they may be tackled. Specifically, we organize our thoughts and recommendations around issues of who, what, when, where, why, and how.

Who?

There is no doubt that conducting a multi-national or cross-cultural work–family study is a challenging endeavor. One of the first issues to be addressed when attempting such a feat is who will be sampled or included in such a study across nations. To date, scholars have advocated minimizing differences across samples by constraining them to particular jobs or occupations in order to better isolate and observe the effects of culture (Lytle, Brett, Barsness, Tinsley, & Janssens, 1995; Spector, Liu, & Sanchez, 2015). Although doing so does allow for better isolation of cultural effects, it has also resulted in the side effect that much of the cross-cultural literature documents differences between a very specific segment of the workforce, namely managers or other professional workers, mimicking the sampling focus of the broader work–family literature (Casper, Eby, Bordeaux, Lockwood, & Lambert, 2007).

Given that managers may have greater experiences in interacting with individuals from other cultures within the organizational setting, focusing on managerial samples may contribute to *underestimating* cultural effects on work–family experiences. That is, managers' mere exposure to diverse cultural contexts may make the influence of their own culture less impactful. Alternatively, it could be argued that perhaps culture may exert larger effects on managerial employees, given that they have more autonomy in decision-making compared to lower-level employees, who may simply have to act in a given way that is embedded within their local cultural norms and rules. If this is the case, the focus on managers may be causing us to generally *overestimate* the impact of culture on work–family experiences.

Furthermore, multi-national organizations have been fruitful ground for the study of cross-national work–family experiences, yet by their global nature, these contexts may obscure or magnify cross-cultural variation. Thus, we generally caution researchers to more carefully consider to what extent our knowledge of cross-cultural differences in work–family experiences may generalize to all (or even most) workers within a given national or cultural setting and the trade-offs between specificity and generalizability when making sampling decisions.

Research on cultural or structural effects on work–family experiences to date have almost exclusively been focused on the national level-of-analysis. However, as evidenced by several chapters within this Handbook, this does not necessarily have to be the case; unique sub-cultures may exist or structures, such as laws and policies, may differ across geographic regions (e.g., states or provinces) within a national culture and this may reflect another opportunity to study the impact of the broader context on work–family dynamics. These variations within a culture have generally been ignored or treated as error in prior cross-cultural work–family research, but we encourage future work to capitalize on such variation to shed light on cultural influences on work–family processes. This approach also has the added benefit that a scholar interested in cultural effects may be able conduct a work–family study without having to connect with and organize efforts among a number of scholars in different countries. A spotlight on within-culture variation also highlights that scholars should consider whether such sub-cultures have typically been represented in existing cross-cultural work–family research (e.g., has existing research mainly sampled majority group members?) or the possibility that general patterns and trends regarding work–family variables may not hold for some portion of the population.

What?

Within the sphere of work–family experiences, cross-cultural research has most commonly focused on the construct of work–family conflict, in line with the broader literature. Thus, less is currently known regarding cross-cultural similarities and differences – either mean differences or moderating effects – for other work–family related variables, including work–family enrichment/facilitation, work–family balance, and segmentation-integration preferences. We encourage future research to pursue these questions, as the impact of culture or context on these variables and relationships may differ substantially from those uncovered for conflict and are important to understand in their own right.

In the literature and in several of the chapters in the current Handbook, there has been discussion that WFC – or other work–family variables – may have a different *meaning* across different cultural contexts. Several authors invoked a study by Grzywacz et al. (2007), who found that immigrant Latino workers who were employed in the poultry processing industry reported low levels of work–family conflict when completing quantitative survey measures, but qualitative interviews suggested that conflict *was* a significant concern for these workers. Thus, this mismatch between quantitative and qualitative measures of conflict may indicate that nuances or the full meaning regarding work–family experiences may be lost when only examining quantitative measures, at least for certain subgroups or sub-cultures. Nonetheless, the majority of cross-cultural research employs only quantitative measures and only a minority of studies have engaged in measurement invariance testing to demonstrate that scores can be interpreted equivalently across cultural contexts (Shockley, Douek, Smith, Yu, Dumani, & French, 2017). Unfortunately, Grzywacz et al.'s study suggests that even if quantitative scores are found to be statistically equivalent across cultural groups, they may not tell the whole picture regarding individuals' work–family experiences. Thus, we encourage future work–family research to further explore how workers interpret and understand these experiences and constructs across cultures, which may necessitate greater use of qualitative methods and attempts to directly assess and compare workers' response processes when completing quantitative measures rather than relying only on the resultant scores.

When?

Scholars have complained that work–family research has been "divorced from temporally sensitive theories" (Matthews, Wayne, & Ford, 2014, p. 1173). Although the authors were mainly speaking to relationships between work–family conflict and subjective well-being outcomes, we would argue that this statement applies broadly to work–family research, including work on cultural influences. We strongly encourage future cross-cultural work–family research to consider issues of timing, both as it refers to individuals' lifespan development and a culture's evolution. For example, although developmental approaches have been used to understand individuals' careers on the work side (e.g., Savickas, 2001) and both romantic relationships and parenting on the family side (e.g., Cassidy, 2000; Umberson & Gove, 1989), we argue that a developmental approach that takes into account issues such as age or life stage has been underutilized in the work–family literature (see Erickson, Martinengo, & Hill, 2010, and Allen & Finkelstein, 2014, for recent exceptions). Furthermore, to our knowledge, research has not explored how *culture* may alter relationships between age or life stage and work–family experiences, which may be a fruitful area for future research.

On the cultural side, although research capturing the influence of culture on work–family variables reflect a snapshot in time, little research acknowledges this fact. In other words, researchers appear to assume that culture is relatively immutable and that findings around the impact of culture on work–family variables or relationships within a given culture will remain stable and generalizable over time. However, macro-level factors such as global economic conditions may influence, through either amplifying or depressing, observed cultural differences in work–family experiences. Alternatively, although cultural change may generally and historically be slow, there are specific regions of the world currently undergoing rapid changes in diverse domains (e.g., climate, economic development) that may have important consequences for our understanding of both culture and work–family issues. One exemplary work that has taken this into consideration is a theoretical paper by Trefalt, Drnovsek, Svetina-Nabergoj, and Adlesic (2013) that focuses on the societal and economic transitions occurring in countries that shifted from socialist to capitalist after the fall of the Berlin Wall. The authors highlight the fact that these cultural shifts may not only affect patterns of relationships observed before and after the changes occurred, but the change variable in and of itself (i.e., living in a rapidly changing society) may function as a meaningful cultural variable. The fall of the Berlin Wall is admittedly a world event with cascading impacts, and such events are not commonplace. However, smaller events within single countries, such as the legalization of same-sex marriages in the United States by the Supreme Court in 2015, could also be important markers against which to study temporal work–family dynamics.

Where?

We echo calls by other scholars that cross-cultural research on work–family issues should more carefully consider the sampling of countries (Shockley et al., 2017; Spector et al., 2015). Given the difficulty of conducting multi-national or cross-cultural research, the inclusion of many countries in multi-country datasets appears to be due more to convenience and access than purposive sampling choices. We encourage future research to more carefully consider the sampling of countries in order to ensure variation on cultural dimensions or social structures (e.g., laws and policies) of interest as well as to minimize potential confounds. Moreover, as evidenced by the reviews in this volume, there is a general lack of research on work–family issues in Africa and the Middle East. Without gaining an understanding of how the work–family interface functions within these cultures, it is difficult to take the next step in making cross-cultural comparisons. Furthermore, existing research attention on cultural dimensions that influence work–family experiences has tended to focus heavily on individualism-collectivism; we encourage scholars to consider other relevant cultural factors (e.g., humane orientation, tightness-looseness) that may also have implications for work–family relations, particularly those outside of Hofstede and GLOBE's ground-breaking cultural models, which tend to dominate this area of inquiry.

Returning to a cultures-within-culture perspective, one key dimension of variation within cultures that may also serve to bridge research across cultures, is the urban-rural divide. Urban and rural communities can be found in many developed and developing nations worldwide (e.g., Africa, China, and United States) and thus represents an understudied but likely important contextual factor. The urban-rural divide is likely important to understand work–family dynamics as it likely affects the types of jobs available within the community, access to resources and public programs (e.g., childcare), prevalence of different family structures, and numerous other factors that shape one's work, family, and work–family interactions. Future research should thus examine how living within urban, suburban, or rural communities may affect individuals' and families' work–family experiences and management within and across cultures.

Why?

We view issues of "why" as amongst the most critical issues to tackle in order for cross-cultural work–family research to progress. Collecting or finding multi-country datasets is challenging; thus, it is not surprising that, at times, it seems that theorizing is outstripping empirical testing in cross-cultural work–family research. However, a recent review by Shockley et al. (2017) reveals that this complex network of theorizing has led to a literature with theoretical predictions that often contradict each other. As an example, some scholars have argued that cultural collectivism (vs. individualism) should be negatively related to work–family conflict because work is viewed as beneficial to family and thus the two roles are therefore complementary (e.g., Galovan et al., 2010), or because collectivistic cultures are less likely to encourage long work hours that tend to increase the likelihood of conflict given their lower emphasis on competition (e.g., Aycan, 2008). In contrast, other scholars have argued that cultural collectivism (vs. individualism) should be associated with *greater* work–family conflict as family demands should be greater in collectivistic cultures since one's view of family is broader (e.g., includes obligations to extended family), creating more opportunities for conflict to arise (Oishi et al., 2015).

In order to disentangle and sort out these theoretical and conceptual issues, cross-cultural work–family research will need to move beyond current practices. For example, rather than simply imputing cultural values and observing mean differences or moderating effects, researchers will need to directly measure and assess posited mediating mechanisms that underlie cultural differences (e.g., in the example above, measuring both work hours and family demands). Strong and direct tests of competing hypotheses in this literature are also needed. Furthermore, it appears that culture's effects are often complex, as some cultural dimensions may simultaneously influence factors that are protective and harmful to work–family experiences, requiring the assessment and consideration of multiple mediating pathways simultaneously. By tackling these challenges head on, these efforts should help to shed light on existing inconsistencies in the literature and clarify "why" culture affects work–family variables.

How?

How will we as a field accomplish these goals given the complexity and challenge inherent in conducting cross-cultural work–family research? The way forward almost certainly requires innovative thinking and new strategies and approaches. For example, one of the biggest barriers to cross-cultural work–family research is access to multi-country data. One way to address this issue might be the creation of a public database, where work–family researchers from around the world could upload anonymized data that identifies country (or other important contextual information) for their datasets to facilitate secondary data analysis. Of course, for such an approach to succeed, researchers will need to rethink "ownership" of data, and incentives would need to be put in place to encourage participation and use. However, we argue that there would be numerous benefits for such a data repository; it would greatly facilitate research in this domain, particularly research that requires access to primary data. For example, although meta-analytic methods can be used to accumulate means and correlational findings, such that the direct effect of culture (or cultural variables) and the moderating effect of culture can be relatively easily estimated from data reported in the literature, it would be difficult (if not impossible) to estimate and cumulate the effect of culture in more complex models (e.g., how culture moderates the interactive relationship between gender AND parental status on work–family conflict) without access to primary data.

A tension that exists within the work–family literature is the decision to use quantitative versus qualitative methods. Although quantitative or survey assessments of work–family variables are extremely common in the literature, particularly in cross-cultural work, these measures have been critiqued in that they may provide limited insight into individuals' rich and complex work and family lives and experiences *as lived* compared to qualitative methods. The latter, of course, suffers from other limitations, such as greater potential subjectivity and difficulties in making direct comparisons between participants and cultures. To reconcile and better capitalize on the strengths of each approach, we encourage future cross-cultural work–family research to more commonly employ mixed-methods designs. For reference, readers may turn to Yang, Chen, Choi, and Zou (2000) and Joplin, Shaffer, Francesco, and Lau (2003); both represent worthy examples of combining qualitative and quantitative methodologies within a single paper.

Generally, we strongly encourage the exploration of new potential sources of data and methodologies. For example, how can work–family researchers capitalize on the big data trend to examine cross-cultural questions? Might social media platforms, such as Facebook, Twitter, and Instagram be mined to generate insights regarding work–family dynamics? For example, to what extent do workers post about work issues during non-work time or family issues during work hours? Does this differ across cultures? Do these actions provide scholars with insight into the segmentation-integration practices of workers globally? Similarly, one difficulty often encountered with qualitative methods is that the unstructured data that results requires substantial amounts of effort and time in order to organize, code, and interpret. Thus, most qualitative studies, including those on work–family topics, are based on relatively small samples. Might new methodologies, such as machine learning algorithms that can learn to mimic human coders, be used to handle and code larger samples, including cross-cultural samples, of qualitative data? Technology has opened a brave new world; we believe that many opportunities lie ahead for cross-cultural work–family scholars who are able to identify and make use of these new data sources or creatively apply emerging data analytic techniques.

Final Thoughts

Serving as editors of this Handbook has been a great honor for us. We have greatly enjoyed and appreciated the opportunity to work with scholars from around the globe who have generously contributed their time and knowledge to this Handbook as well as dedicated their careers to generating critical knowledge regarding the work–family issues faced by workers, their families, and their organizations globally. This Handbook documents how far the field has come in a short time, and we hope that its contents may serve as a valuable source of both information and inspiration for both researchers and practitioners into the future as we each continue to tackle, both personally and professionally, the challenges of managing complex work and family lives within a constantly evolving, interconnected, and global context.

References

Allen, T. D., & Finkelstein, L. M. (2014). Work–family conflict among members of full-time dual-earner couples: An examination of family life stage, gender, and age. *Journal of Occupational Health Psychology, 19*, 376–384.

Aycan, Z. (2008). Cross-cultural perspectives to work–family conflict. In K. Korabik & D. Lero (Eds.), *Handbook of Work–Family Conflict* (pp. 359–271). London, UK: Cambridge University Press.

Casper, W. J., Eby, L. T., Bordeaux, C., Lockwood, A., & Lambert, D. (2007). A review of research methods in IO/OB work–family research. *Journal of Applied Psychology, 92*, 28–43.

Cassidy, J. (2000). Adult romantic attachments: A developmental perspective on individual differences. *Review of General Psychology, 4*, 111–131.

Erickson, J. J., Martinengo, G., & Hill, E. H. (2010). Putting work and family experiences in context: Differences by family life stage. *Human Relations, 63*, 955–979.

Galovan, A. M., Fackrell, T., Buswell, L., Jones, B. L., Hill, E. J., & Carroll, S. J. (2010). The work–family interface in the United States and Singapore: Conflict across cultures. *Journal of Family Psychology, 24*, 646–656.

Grzywacz, J. G., Arcury, T. A., Marin, A., Carrillo, L., Burke, B., Coates, M. L., & Quandt, S.A. (2007). Work–family conflict: Experiences and health implications among immigrant Latinos. *Journal of Applied Psychology, 92*, 1119–1130.

Joplin, J., Shaffer, M., Francesco, A., & Lau, T. (2003). The macro environment and work family conflict: development of a cross cultural comparative framework. *International Journal of Cross Cultural Management, 3*, 305–328.

Lytle, A. L., Brett, J. M., Barsness, Z. I., Tinsley, C. H., & Janssens, M. (1995). A paradigm for confirmatory cross-cultural research in organizational behavior. *Research in Organizational Behavior, 17*, 167–214.

Matthews, R. A., Wayne, J. H., & Ford, M. T. (2014). A work–family conflict/subjective well-being process model: A test of competing theories of longitudinal effects. *Journal of Applied Psychology, 99*, 1173–1187.

Oishi, A. S., Chan, R. K. H., Wang, L. L.-R., & Kim, J.-H. (2015). Do part-time jobs mitigate workers' work–family conflict and enhance wellbeing? New evidence from four East-Asian societies. *Social Indicators Research, 121*, 5–25.

Savickas, M. L. (2001). A developmental perspective on vocational behaviour: Career patterns, salience, and themes. *International Journal for Educational and Vocational Guidance*, *1*, 49–57.

Shockley, K. M., Douek, J., Smith, C. R., Yu, P. P., Dumani, S., & French, K. A. (2017). Cross-cultural work and family research: A review of the literature. *Journal of Vocational Behavior*, *101*, 1–20.

Spector, P. E., Liu, C., & Sanchez, J. I. (2015). Methodological and substantive issues in conducting multinational and cross-cultural research. *Annual Review of Organizational Psychology and Organizational Behavior*, *2*, 101–131.

Trefalt, S., Drnovsek, M., Svetina-Nabergoj, A., & Adlesic, R. (2013). Impact of changes in national context on work–life conflict, enrichment and balance. Structuration, social comparison and choice overload as explanatory mechanisms. *European Management Journal*, *31*, 448–463.

Umberson, D., & Gove, W. R. (1989). Parenthood and psychological well-being: Theory, measurement, and stage in family life course. *Journal of Family Issues*, *10*, 440–462.

Yang, N., Chen, C. C., Choi, J., & Zou, Y. (2000). Sources of work–family conflict: A Sino-U.S. Comparison of the effects of work and family demands. *Academy of Management Journal*, *43*, 113–123. doi:10.2307/1556390

Index

References to figures are in *italics*, and tables in **bold**.